THE
EXPOSITOR'S
BIBLE
COMMENTARY

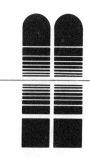

THE
EXPOSITOR'S
BIBLE
COMMENTARY

with

The New International Version

of

The Holy Bible

IN TWELVE VOLUMES

VOLUME 9

(JOHN - ACTS)

ZONDERVAN
PUBLISHING HOUSE

OF THE ZONDERVAN CORPORATION | GRAND RAPIDS, MICHIGAN 49506

THE EXPOSITOR'S BIBLE COMMENTARY
Copyright © 1981 by The Zondervan Corporation
Grand Rapids, Michigan

Library of Congress Cataloging in Publication Data (Revised)

Main entry under title:

THE EXPOSITOR'S BIBLE COMMENTARY.

 Includes bibliographies.
 CONTENTS: v. 1. Introductory articles.—[etc.] — v. 9.
John–Acts. — v. 10. Romans–Galatians. — v. 11.
Ephesians–Philemon.
 1. Bible—Commentaries. I. Gaebelein, Frank Ely, 1899-
II. Douglas, James Dixon. III. Bible. English.
New international. 1976.
BS491.2.E96 220.7′7 76-41334
ISBN 0-310-36510-4 (v. 9)

The translation used in THE EXPOSITOR'S BIBLE COMMENTARY is the New
International Version, New Testament, Copyright © 1973 by New York
Bible Society International, Copyright © 1974 by New York Interna-
tional Bible Society. Used by permission.

Printed in the United States of America

CONTENTS

CONTRIBUTORS TO VOLUME 9

The Gospel of John: Merrill C. Tenney

Th.B., Gordon College; A.M., Boston University; Ph.D. Harvard University

Professor of Bible and Theology, Emeritus, Wheaton College

The Acts of the Apostles: Richard N. Longenecker

A.B., Wheaton College; A.M., Wheaton Graduate School; Ph.D., University of Edinburgh (New College)

Professor of New Testament, Wycliffe College, University of Toronto

PREFACE

The title of this work defines its purpose. Written primarily by expositors for expositors, it aims to provide preachers, teachers, and students of the Bizle with a new and comprehensive commentary on the books of the Old and New Testaments. Its stance is that of a scholarly evangelicalism committed to the divine inspiration, complete trustworthiness, and full authority of the Bible. Its seventy-eight contributors come from the United States, Canada, England, Scotland, Australia, New Zealand, and Switzerland, and from various religious groups, including Anglican, Baptist, Brethren, Free, Independent, Methodist, Nazarene, Presbyterian, and Reformed churches. Most of them teach at colleges, universities, or theological seminaries.

No book has been more closely studied over a longer period of time than the Bible. From the Midrashic commentaries going back to the period of Ezra, through parts of the Dead Sea Scrolls and the Patristic literature, and on to the present, the Scriptures have been expounded. Indeed, there have been times when, as in the Reformation and on occasions since then, exposition has been at the cutting edge of Christian advance. Luther was a powerful exegete, and Calvin is still called "the prince of expositors."

Their successors have been many. And now, when the outburst of new translations and their unparalleled circulation have expanded the readership of the Bible, the need for exposition takes on fresh urgency.

Not that God's Word can ever become captive to its expositors. Among all other books, it stands first in its combination of perspicuity and profundity. Though a child can be made "wise for salvation" by believing its witness to Christ, the greatest mind cannot plumb the depths of its truth (2 Tim. 3:15; Rom. 11:33). As Gregory the Great said, "Holy Scripture is a stream of running water, where alike the elephant may swim, and the lamb walk." So, because of the inexhaustible nature of Scripture, the task of opening up its meaning is still a perennial obligation of biblical scholarship.

How that task is done inevitably reflects the outlook of those engaged in it. Every biblical scholar has presuppositions. To this neither the editors of these volumes nor the contributors to them are exceptions. They share a common commitment to the supernatural Christianity set forth in the inspired Word. Their purpose is not to supplant the many valuable commentaries that have preceded this work and from which both the editors and contributors have learned. It is rather to draw on the resources of contemporary evangelical scholarship in producing a new reference work for understanding the Scriptures.

A commentary that will continue to be useful through the years should handle contemporary trends in biblical studies in such a way as to avoid becoming outdated when critical fashions change. Biblical criticism is not in itself inadmissible, as some have mistakenly thought. When scholars investigate the authorship, date, literary characteristics, and purpose of a biblical document, they are practicing biblical criticism. So also when, in order to ascertain as nearly as possible the original form of the text, they deal with variant readings, scribal errors, emendations, and other phenomena in the manuscripts. To do these things is essential to responsible exegesis and exposition. And always there is the need to distinguish hypothesis from fact, conjecture from truth.

The chief principle of interpretation followed in this commentary is the grammatico-historical one—namely, that the primary aim of the exegete is to make clear the meaning of the text at the time and in the circumstances of its writing. This endeavor to understand what in the first instance the inspired writers actually said must not be confused with an inflexible literalism. Scripture makes lavish use of symbols and figures of speech; great portions of it are poetical. Yet when it speaks in this way, it speaks no less truly than it does in its historical and doctrinal portions. To understand its message requires attention to matters of grammar and syntax, word meanings, idioms, and literary forms—all in relation to the historical and cultural setting of the text.

The contributors to this work necessarily reflect varying convictions. In certain controversial matters the policy is that of clear statement of the contributors' own views followed by fair presentation of other ones. The treatment of eschatology, though it reflects differences of interpretation, is consistent with a general premillennial position. (Not all contributors, however, are premillennial.) But prophecy is more than prediction, and so this commentary gives due recognition to the major lode of godly social concern in the prophetic writings.

THE EXPOSITOR'S BIBLE COMMENTARY is presented as a scholarly work, though not primarily one of technical criticism. In its main portion, the Exposition, and in Volume 1 (General and Special Articles), all Semitic and Greek words are transliterated and the English equivalents given. As for the Notes, here Semitic and Greek characters are used but always with transliterations and English meanings, so that this portion of the commentary will be as accessible as possible to readers unacquainted with the original languages.

It is the conviction of the general editor, shared by his colleagues in the Zondervan editorial department, that in writing about the Bible, lucidity is not incompatible with scholarship. They are therefore endeavoring to make this a clear and understandable work.

The translation used in it is the New International Version. To the New York International Bible Society thanks are due for permission to use this most recent of the major Bible translations. The editors and publisher have chosen it because of the clarity and beauty of its style and its faithfulness to the original texts.

To the associate editor, Dr. J. D. Douglas, and to the contributing editors—Dr. Walter C. Kaiser, Jr. and Dr. Bruce K. Waltke for the Old Testament, and Dr. James Montgomery Boice and Dr. Merrill C. Tenney for the New Testament—the general editor expresses his gratitude for their unfailing cooperation and their generosity in advising him out of their expert scholarship. And to the many other contributors he is indebted for their invaluable part in this work. Finally, he owes a special debt of gratitude to Dr. Robert K. DeVries, executive vice-president of the Zondervan Publishing House; Rev. Gerard Terpstra, manuscript editor; and Miss Elizabeth Brown, secretary to Dr. DeVries, for their continual assistance and encouragement.

Whatever else it is—the greatest and most beautiful of books, the primary source of law and morality, the fountain of wisdom, and the infallible guide to life—the Bible is above all the inspired witness to Jesus Christ. May this work fulfill its function of expounding the Scriptures with grace and clarity, so that its users may find that both Old and New Testaments do indeed lead to our Lord Jesus Christ, who alone could say, "I have come that they may have life, and have it to the full" (John 10:10).

FRANK E. GAEBELEIN

ABBREVIATIONS

A. General Abbreviations

A	Codex Alexandrinus	mg.	margin
Akkad.	Akkadian	MS(S)	Manuscript(s)
א	Codex Sinaiticus	MT	Masoretic text
Ap. Lit.	Apocalyptic Literature	Mid	Midrash
Apoc.	Apocrypha	n.	note
Aq.	Aquila's Greek Translation	n.d.	no date
	of the Old Testament	Nestle	Nestle (ed.) *Novum*
Arab.	Arabic		*Testamentum Graece*
Aram.	Aramaic	no.	number
b	Babylonian Gemara	NT	New Testament
B	Codex Vaticanus	obs.	obsolete
C	Codex Ephraemi Syri	OL	Old Latin
c.	*circa*, about	OS	Old Syriac
cf.	*confer*, compare	OT	Old Testament
ch., chs.	chapter, chapters	p., pp.	page, pages
cod., codd.	codex, codices	par.	paragraph
contra	in contrast to	Pers.	Persian
D	Codex Bezae	Pesh.	Peshitta
DSS	Dead Sea Scrolls (see E.)	Phoen.	Phoenician
ed., edd.	edited, edition, editor; editions	pl.	plural
e.g.	*exempli gratia*, for example	Pseudep.	Pseudepigrapha
Egyp.	Egyptian	Q	Quelle ("Sayings" source
et. al.	*et alii*, and others		in the Gospels)
EV	English Versions of the Bible	qt.	quoted by
f., ff.	following (verse, verses, pages, etc.)	q.v.	*quod vide*, which see
fem.	feminine	R	Rabbah
fl.	flourished	rev.	revised, reviser, revision
ft.	foot, feet	Rom.	Roman
gen.	genitive	RVm	Revised Version margin
Gr.	Greek	Samar.	Samaritan recension
Heb.	Hebrew	SCM	Student Christian
Hitt.	Hittite		Movement Press
ibid.	*ibidem*, in the same place	Sem.	Semitic
id.	*idem*, the same	sing.	singular
i.e.	*id est*, that is	SPCK	Society for the Promotion
impf.	imperfect		of Christian Knowledge
infra.	below	Sumer.	Sumerian
in loc.	*in loco*, in the place cited	s.v.	*sub verbo*, under the word
j	Jerusalem or	Syr.	Syriac
	Palestinian Gemara	Symm.	Symmachus
Lat.	Latin	T	Talmud
LL.	Late Latin	Targ.	Targum
LXX	Septuagint	Theod.	Theodotion
M	Mishnah	TR	Textus Receptus
masc.	masculine	tr.	translation, translator,
			translated

UBS	The United Bible Societies' Greek Text	vol.	volume
Ugar.	Ugaritic	v., vv.	verse, verses
u.s.	*ut supra*, as above	vs.	versus
viz.	*videlicet*, namely	Vul.	Vulgate
		WH	Westcott and Hort, *The New Testament in Greek*

B. Abbreviations for Modern Translations and Paraphrases

AmT	Smith and Goodspeed, *The Complete Bible, An American Translation*	LB	The Living Bible
		Mof	J. Moffatt, *A New Translation of the Bible*
ASV	American Standard Version, American Revised Version (1901)	NAB	The New American Bible
		NASB	New American Standard Bible
		NEB	The New English Bible
Beck	Beck, *The New Testament in the Language of Today*	NIV	The New International Version
		Ph	J. B. Phillips *The New Testament in Modern English*
BV	Berkeley Version (The Modern Language Bible)	RSV	Revised Standard Version
JB	The Jerusalem Bible	RV	Revised Version — 1881–1885
JPS	*Jewish Publication Society Version of the Old Testament*	TCNT	Twentieth Century New Testament
KJV	King James Version	TEV	Today's English Version
Knox	R.G. Knox, *The Holy Bible: A Translation from the Latin Vulgate in the Light of the Hebrew and Greek Original*	Wey	*Weymouth's New Testament in Modern Speech*
		Wms	C. B. Williams, *The New Testament: A Translation in the Language of the People*

C. Abbreviations for Periodicals and Reference Works

AASOR	*Annual of the American Schools of Oriental Research*	AThR	*Anglican Theological Review*
		BA	*Biblical Archaeologist*
AB	*Anchor Bible*	BASOR	*Bulletin of the American Schools of Oriental Research*
AIs	de Vaux: *Ancient Israel*		
AJA	*American Journal of Archaeology*	BAG	Bauer, Arndt, and Gingrich: *Greek-English Lexicon of the New Testament*
AJSL	*American Journal of Semitic Languages and Literatures*	BC	Foakes-Jackson and Lake: *The Beginnings of Christianity*
AJT	*American Journal of Theology*	BDB	Brown, Driver, and Briggs: *Hebrew-English Lexicon of the Old Testament*
Alf	Alford: *Greek Testament Commentary*		
ANEA	*Ancient Near Eastern Archaeology*	BDF	Blass, Debrunner, and Funk: *A Greek Grammar of the New Testament and Other Early Christian Literature*
ANET	Pritchard: *Ancient Near Eastern Texts*		
ANF	Roberts and Donaldson: *The Ante-Nicene Fathers*	BDT	Harrison: *Baker's Dictionary of Theology*
ANT	M. R. James: *The Apocryphal New Testament*	Beng.	Bengel's *Gnomon*
		BETS	*Bulletin of the Evangelical Theological Society*
A-S	Abbot-Smith: *Manual Greek Lexicon of the New Testament*	BJRL	*Bulletin of the John Rylands Library*

BS	*Bibliotheca Sacra*	HJP	Schürer: *A History of the*
BT	*Babylonian Talmud*		*Jewish People in the*
BTh	*Biblical Theology*		*Time of Christ*
BW	*Biblical World*	HR	Hatch and Redpath:
CAH	*Cambridge Ancient History*		*Concordance to the*
CanJTh	*Canadian Journal of Theology*		*Septuagint*
CBQ	*Catholic Biblical Quarterly*	HTR	*Harvard Theological Review*
CBSC	*Cambridge Bible for Schools*	HUCA	*Hebrew Union College Annual*
	and Colleges	IB	*The Interpreter's Bible*
CE	*Catholic Encyclopedia*	ICC	*International Critical*
CGT	*Cambridge Greek Testament*		*Commentary*
CHS	Lange: *Commentary on the*	IDB	*The Interpreter's Dictionary*
	Holy Scriptures		*of the Bible*
ChT	*Christianity Today*	IEJ	*Israel Exploration Journal*
Crem	Cremer: *Biblico-Theological*	Int	*Interpretation*
	Lexicon of the New	INT	E. Harrison: *Introduction to*
	Testament Greek		*the New Testament*
DDB	*Davis' Dictionary of the Bible*	IOT	R. K. Harrison: *Introduction*
Deiss BS	Deissmann: *Bible Studies*		*to the Old Testament*
Deiss LAE	Deissmann: *Light From the*	ISBE	*The International Standard*
	Ancient East		*Bible Encyclopedia*
DNTT	*Dictionary of New Testament*	ITQ	*Irish Theological Quarterly*
	Theology	JAAR	*Journal of American*
EBC	*The Expositor's*		*Academy of Religion*
	Bible Commentary	JAOS	*Journal of American*
EBi	*Encyclopaedia Biblica*		*Oriental Society*
EBr	*Encyclopaedia Britannica*	JBL	*Journal of Biblical*
EDB	*Encyclopedic Dictionary*		*Literature*
	of the Bible	JE	*Jewish Encyclopedia*
EGT	Nicoll: *Expositor's Greek*	JETS	*Journal of Evangelical*
	Testament		*Theological Society*
EQ	*Evangelical Quarterly*	JFB	Jamieson, Fausset, and
ET	*Evangelische Theologie*		Brown: *Commentary on the*
ExB	*The Expositor's Bible*		*Old and New Testament*
Exp	*The Expositor*	JNES	*Journal of Near Eastern*
ExpT	*The Expository Times*		*Studies*
FLAP	Finegan: *Light From*	Jos. Antiq.	Josephus: *The Antiquities*
	the Ancient Past		*of the Jews*
GR	*Gordon Review*	Jos. War	Josephus: *The Jewish War*
HBD	*Harper's Bible Dictionary*	JQR	*Jewish Quarterly Review*
HDAC	Hastings: *Dictionary of*	JR	*Journal of Religion*
	the Apostolic Church	JSJ	*Journal for the Study of Judaism*
HDB	Hastings: *Dictionary of*		*in the Persian, Hellenistic and*
	the Bible		*Roman Periods*
HDBrev.	Hastings: *Dictionary of*	JSOR	*Journal of the Society*
	the Bible, one-vol. rev.		*of Oriental Research*
	by Grant and Rowley	JSS	*Journal of Semitic Studies*
HDCG	Hastings: *Dictionary of*	JT	*Jerusalem Talmud*
	Christ and the Gospels	JTS	*Journal of Theological Studies*
HERE	Hastings: *Encyclopedia of*	KAHL	Kenyon: *Archaeology*
	Religion and Ethics		*in the Holy Land*
HGEOTP	Heidel: *The Gilgamesh Epic*	KB	Koehler-Baumgartner: *Lexicon*
	and Old Testament Parallels		*in Veteris Testament Libros*

KD	Keil and Delitzsch: *Commentary on the Old Testament*	RTWB	Richardson: *A Theological Wordbook of the Bible*
LSJ	Liddell, Scott, Jones: *Greek-English Lexicon*	SBK	Strack and Billerbeck: *Kommentar zum Neuen Testament aus Talmud und Midrash*
LTJM	Edersheim: *The Life and Times of Jesus the Messiah*		
MM	Moulton and Milligan: *The Vocabulary of the Greek Testament*	SHERK	*The New Schaff-Herzog Encyclopedia of Religious Knowledge*
MNT	Moffatt: *New Testament Commentary*	SJT	*Scottish Journal of Theology*
MST	McClintock and Strong: *Cyclopedia of Biblical, Theological, and Ecclesiastical Literature*	SOT	Girdlestone: *Synonyms of Old Testament*
		SOTI	Archer: *A Survey of Old Testament Introduction*
NBC	Davidson, Kevan, and Stibbs: *The New Bible Commentary*, 1st ed.	ST	*Studia Theologica*
		TCERK	Loetscher: *The Twentieth Century Encyclopedia of Religious Knowledge*
NBCrev.	Guthrie and Motyer: *The New Bible Commentary*, rev. ed.		
		TDNT	Kittel: *Theological Dictionary of the New Testament*
NBD	J. D. Douglas: *The New Bible Dictionary*	TDOT	*Theological Dictionary of the Old Testament*
NCB	*New Century Bible*		
NCE	*New Catholic Encyclopedia*	Theol	*Theology*
NIC	*New International Commentary*	ThT	*Theology Today*
NIDCC	Douglas: *The New International Dictionary of the Christian Church*	TNTC	*Tyndale New Testament Commentaries*
		Trench	Trench: *Synonyms of the New Testament*
NovTest	*Novum Testamentum*	UBD	*Unger's Bible Dictionary*
NSI	Cooke: *Handbook of North Semitic Inscriptions*	UT	Gordon: *Ugaritic Textbook*
		VB	Allmen: *Vocabulary of the Bible*
NTS	*New Testament Studies*		
ODCC	*The Oxford Dictionary of the Christian Church*, rev. ed.	VetTest	*Vetus Testamentum*
		Vincent	Vincent: *Word-Pictures in the New Testament*
Peake	Black and Rowley: *Peake's Commentary on the Bible*	WBC	*Wycliffe Bible Commentary*
PEQ	*Palestine Exploration Quarterly*	WBE	*Wycliffe Bible Encyclopedia*
PNFl	P. Schaff: *The Nicene and Post-Nicene Fathers* (1st series)	WC	*Westminster Commentaries*
		WesBC	*Wesleyan Bible Commentaries*
		WTJ	*Westminster Theological Journal*
PNF2	P. Schaff and H. Wace: *The Nicene and Post-Nicene Fathers* (2nd series)	ZAW	*Zeitschrift für die alttestamentliche Wissenschaft*
PTR	*Princeton Theological Review*	ZNW	*Zeitschrift für die neutestamentliche Wissenschaft*
RB	*Revue Biblique*		
RHG	Robertson's *Grammar of the Greek New Testament in the Light of Historical Research*	ZPBD	*The Zondervan Pictorial Bible Dictionary*
		ZPEB	*The Zondervan Pictorial Encyclopedia of the Bible*
		ZWT	*Zeitschrift für wissenschaftliche Theologie*

D. Abbreviations for Books of the Bible, the Apocrypha, and the Pseudepigrapha

OLD TESTAMENT

Gen	2 Chron	Dan
Exod	Ezra	Hos
Lev	Neh	Joel
Num	Esth	Amos
Deut	Job	Obad
Josh	Ps(Pss)	Jonah
Judg	Prov	Mic
Ruth	Eccl	Nah
1 Sam	S of Sol	Hab
2 Sam	Isa	Zeph
1 Kings	Jer	Hag
2 Kings	Lam	Zech
1 Chron	Ezek	Mal

NEW TESTAMENT

Matt	1 Tim
Mark	2 Tim
Luke	Titus
John	Philem
Acts	Heb
Rom	James
1 Cor	1 Peter
2 Cor	2 Peter
Gal	1 John
Eph	2 John
Phil	3 John
Col	Jude
1 Thess	Rev
2 Thess	

APOCRYPHA

1 Esd	1 Esdras	Ep Jer	Epistle of Jeremy
2 Esd	2 Esdras	S Th Ch	Song of the Three Children
Tobit	Tobit		(or Young Men)
Jud	Judith	Sus	Susanna
Add Esth	Additions to Esther	Bel	Bel and the Dragon
Wisd Sol	Wisdom of Solomon	Pr Man	Prayer of Manasseh
Ecclus	Ecclesiasticus (Wisdom of	1 Macc	1 Maccabees
	Jesus the Son of Sirach)	2 Macc	2 Maccabees
Baruch	Baruch		

PSEUDEPIGRAPHA

As Moses	Assumption of Moses	Pirke Aboth	Pirke Aboth
2 Baruch	Syriac Apocalypse of Baruch	Ps 151	Psalm 151
3 Baruch	Greek Apocalypse of Baruch	Pss Sol	Psalms of Solomon
1 Enoch	Ethiopic Book of Enoch	Sib Oracles	Sibylline Oracles
2 Enoch	Slavonic Book of Enoch	Story Ah	Story of Ahikar
3 Enoch	Hebrew Book of Enoch	T Abram	Testament of Abraham
4 Ezra	4 Ezra	T Adam	Testament of Adam
JA	Joseph and Asenath	T Benjamin	Testament of Benjamin
Jub	Book of Jubilees	T Dan	Testament of Dan
L Aristeas	Letter of Aristeas	T Gad	Testament of Gad
Life AE	Life of Adam and Eve	T Job	Testament of Job
Liv Proph	Lives of the Prophets	T Jos	Testament of Joseph
MA Isa	Martyrdom and Ascension	T Levi	Testament of Levi
	of Isaiah	T Naph	Testament of Naphtali
3 Macc	3 Maccabees	T 12 Pat	Testaments of the Twelve
4 Macc	4 Maccabees		Patriarchs
Odes Sol	Odes of Solomon	Zad Frag	Zadokite Fragments
P Jer	Paralipomena of Jeremiah		

E. Abbreviations of Names of Dead Sea Scrolls and Related Texts

CD	Cairo (Genizah text of the) Damascus (Document)	1QSa	Appendix A (Rule of the Congregation) to 1Qs
DSS	Dead Sea Scrolls	1QSb	Appendix B (Blessings) to 1QS
Hev	Nahal Hever texts	3Q15	Copper Scroll from Qumran Cave 3
Mas	Masada Texts		
Mird	Khirbet mird texts	4QExod a	Exodus Scroll, exemplar "a" from Qumran Cave 4
Mur	Wadi Murabba'at texts		
P	Pesher (commentary)	4QFlor	Florilegium (or Eschatological Midrashim) from Qumran Cave 4
Q	Qumran		
1Q, 2Q, etc.	Numbered caves of Qumran, yielding written material; followed by abbreviation of biblical or apocryphal book.	4Qmess ar	Aramaic "Messianic" text from Qumran Cave 4
		4QpNah	Pesher on portions of Nahum from Qumran Cave 4
QL	Qumran Literature		
1QapGen	Genesis Apocryphon of Qumran Cave 1	4QPrNab	Prayer of Nabonidus from Qumran Cave 4
1QH	*Hodayot* (Thanksgiving Hymns) from Qumran Cave 1	4QpPs37	Pesher on portions of Psalm 37 from Qumran Cave 4
1QIsa a, b	First or second copy of Isaiah from Qumran Cave 1	4QTest	Testimonia text from Qumran Cave 4
1QpHab	Pesher on Habakkuk from Qumran Cave 1	4QTLevi	Testament of Levi from Qumran Cave 4
1QM	*Milhamah* (War Scroll)	4QPhyl	Phylacteries from Qumran Cave 4
1QpMic	Pesher on portions of Micah from Qumran Cave 1	11QMelch	Melchizedek text from Qumran Cave 11
1QS	*Serek Hayyahad* (Rule of the Community, Manual of Discipline)	11QtgJob	Targum of Job from Qumran Cave 11

TRANSLITERATIONS

Hebrew

א = ʾ		ד = $\underline{d}$		י = y		ס = s		ר = r
ב = b		ה = h		כ = k		ע = ʿ		שׂ = ś
ב = $\underline{b}$		ו = w		כ = $\underline{k}$		פ = p		שׁ = š
ג = g		ז = z		ל = l		פ = $\underline{p}$		ת = t
ג = $\underline{g}$		ח = ḥ		מ = m		צ = ṣ		ת = $\underline{t}$
ד = d		ט = ṭ		נ = n		ק = q		

(ה)ָ = â (h)	ָ = ā	ַ = a	ֲ = ^{a}
ֵי = ê	ֵ = ē	ֶ = e	ֱ = ^{e}
ִי = î		ִ = i	ְ = ^{e} (if vocal)
וֹ = ô	ֹ = ō	ֹ = o	ֳ = ^{o}
וּ = û		ֻ = u	

Aramaic

ʾ b g d h w z ḥ ṭ y k l m n s ʿ p ṣ q r ś š t

Arabic

ʾ b t ṯ ǧ ḥ ḫ d ḏ r z s š ṣ ḍ ṭ ẓ ʿ ġ f q k l m n h w y

Ugaritic

ʾ b g d ḏ h w z ḥ ḫ ṭ ẓ y k l m n s ṣ ʿ ġ ṗ ṣ q r š t ṱ

Greek

α	—	a	π	—	p	αι	—	ai
β	—	b	ρ	—	r	αὐ	—	au
γ	—	g	σ,ς	—	s	ει	—	ei
δ	—	d	τ	—	t	εὐ	—	eu
ε	—	e	υ	—	y	ηὐ	—	ēu
ζ	—	z	φ	—	ph	οι	—	oi
η	—	ē	χ	—	ch	οὐ	—	ou
θ	—	th	ψ	—	ps	υι	—	hui
ι	—	i	ω	—	ō			
κ	—	k				ῥ	—	rh
λ	—	l	γγ	—	ng	ʽ	—	h
μ	—	m	γκ	—	nk			
ν	—	n	γξ	—	nx	ᾳ	—	ā
ξ	—	x	γχ	—	nch	ῃ	—	ē
ο	—	o				ῳ	—	ō

THE GOSPEL OF JOHN
Merrill C. Tenney

THE GOSPEL OF JOHN

Introduction

1. Background

The Gospel of John was probably the last of the Gospels to be written and circulated; yet it is definitely a document belonging to the first century. Its action took place between A.D. 30 and 36, when Pontius Pilate was removed from office by the order of Tiberius Caesar. Although it contains fewer allusions to contemporary history than the Synoptics, John's Gospel depends on information that was parallel to theirs.

Much of Jerusalem was destroyed by the Roman suppression of the Jewish revolt of A.D. 66–70. Thus the detailed references in John to many of the ancient landmarks indicate that the author was acquainted with them and that he must have been in Jerusalem before A.D. 70. He mentions the five colonnades at the Pool of Bethesda (John 5:2), which recent excavation has revealed; the Colonnade of Solomon at the outer edge of the temple enclosure, where Jesus taught (10:23); the palace (praetorium) (18:28) and "The Stone Pavement" (19:13), where the hearing before Pilate was held; the place of execution called "Golgotha" (Heb. for "skull") (19:17); and the garden of Joseph where Jesus' body was buried (19:41).

Furthermore, the author was acquainted with Jewish religion. He mentions the Passover (2:13, 23: 4:45; 6:4; 11:55–56; 12:1, 12, 20; 13:1; 18:28, 39; 19:14), the Feast of Tabernacles (7:2, 8, 10–11, 14, 37), and the Feast of Dedication (10:22). He was familiar with Jewish customs such as weddings (2:1–10), Sabbath-keeping (5:9–10; 9:14–16; 19:31), methods of burial (11:44; 19:40), and the methods of observing the feasts (7:37; 13:1–11). Insofar as these allusions to places and customs are paralleled by reference to other literature, they corroborate the setting of the action presented in the Gospel.

The writer of this Gospel knew the topography of Palestine. He refers correctly to the divisions of the land into Judea, Samaria, and Galilee. Details about cities and towns such as Nazareth (1:45–46), Cana (2:1), Capernaum (2:12), and Sychar (4:5) are all accurate.

This Gospel was probably written at a time when the church was composed of second- and third-generation Christians who needed more detailed instruction about Jesus and new defenses for the apologetic problems raised by apostasy within the church and by growing opposition from without. The understanding of the person of Christ that had depended on the testimony of his contemporaries was becoming a philosophical and theological problem. Doctrinal variations had begun to appear, and some of the assertions of the basic Christian truths had been challenged. A new presentation was necessary to meet the questions of the changing times. As the Gospel states, "These things are written that you may maintain your belief that Jesus is the Christ, the Son of God" (20:31).[1]

The Gospel of John is, therefore, more theological and in some respects more cosmopolitan than the Synoptics. It is not necessarily less Jewish. It has, however, a wider appeal to growing Christian experience and to an enlarging Gentile constituency than the others.

The question has been raised whether John's Gospel is a theological treatise rather than a historical narrative. Does it represent Jesus as he really was, or does it clothe the human figure with an imaginative dress of deity? Theological it certainly is, but so are the Synoptics; and the difference between them largely reflects the respective intended readership, not the person described. In all four Gospels Jesus is unique in his character, authority, and message. The Synoptics present him for a generation in process of being evangelized; John presents him as the Lord of the maturing and questioning believer.

This Gospel contains little information about general historical events. It does refer to the ministry of John the Baptist (1:19–37; 3:22–36; 4:1); Herod's rebuilding of the temple (2:20); the high priesthood of Annas and Caiaphas (18:13–14); and the person of Pontius Pilate (18:28–19:16, 38), prefect of Judea. The Roman domination of Palestine is implied but not featured. There is almost no direct allusion to current political affairs and no mention of the church by name. While the Gospel must have been written for the use of believers, virtually nothing is said about their organization. The author seems to be concerned less with time than with eternity.

2. Unity

The combination of intricacy and simplicity in the structure of the Gospel of John conveys the unavoidable impression that it is the product of one mind. Its consistency of structure, distinctive vocabulary, uniformity of style, and directness of purpose can best be explained by ascribing it to a single author. It may be conceded that it has some chronological gaps and literary peculiarities hard to explain. For example, the opening words of ch. 6, "Some time after this, Jesus crossed to the far shore of the Sea of Galilee," abruptly begin a new topic after narrating Jesus' argument with the Jews in Jerusalem. Also, his statement at the end of ch. 14, "Come now; let us leave" (v. 31), is followed by an extended discourse before he finally leaves for Gethsemane. Some scholars have explained these anomalies by attributing them to "sources" that were incorporated into

---

[1]For a discussion of this rendering of v. 31, see Note on 20:31.

the Gospel without regard for their interrelationship by a series of editors, the last of whom produced the final work.

Others have suggested that the apparent irregularities come from a primitive disarrangement of the original MS, which was then reorganized by an editor who did not know how to restore the sequence.[2] There is, however, no existing MS evidence of such dislocations; and attempts to reconstruct the initial order have proved fruitless.

Without denying that the author may have had numerous sources of information about Jesus' activities and teaching apart from his own experience, there is no good reason to assume that he used a scissors-and-paste method of composing this Gospel. Nor is it necessary to assume that he needed sources other than his own participation in the events of Jesus' life and his personal contacts with other participants. Neither is the theory of accidental dislocation inevitable. Some of the sharp transitions in the Gospel may show that the author assumed a knowledge on the part of his readers that would not be possible today, or that he was less interested in chronological sequence than in the consecutive impact of his presentation. He says plainly that his method is selective, but the episodes he chose are united by the single purpose of promoting belief.

The criterion of unity does not lie in literary smoothness so much as in the purpose of the work. Lightfoot states, "From beginning to end this Gospel is a compact whole" (p. 19). After observing the method the author has used to present his picture of Christ, Lightfoot adds, "The unity of this Gospel is not only a unity of structure, it is also a unity of themes" (p. 21). The different topics it deals with—such as the "signs," the "I Am's," the debates and personal interviews, and the discourses to the disciples—may not all appear in uniform sequence; nevertheless, there is complete unity in their teaching. All of them focus on the purpose expressed in the author's final note (20:30–31) and give the impression that they are just the sort of thing a friend of Jesus would remember about him.

3. Authorship

a. External Evidence

The earliest tradition of the church ascribes the fourth Gospel to John the son of Zebedee, one of the first of Jesus' disciples, and one who was closest to him. Irenaeus bishop of Lyons (fl. c. 180) stated plainly that "John, the disciple of the Lord, who also had leaned upon his breast, had himself published a Gospel during his residence in Ephesus in Asia" (*Against Heresies* 3.1). Irenaeus's testimony has been corroborated by other writers. Theophilus of Antioch (fl. c. 165) alluded to the Gospel (*To Autolycus* 2.22). Clement of Alexandria (fl. c. 220) quoted at considerable length from almost every chapter of John. Tertullian of Carthage, Clement's contemporary, used it freely in his works. Tatian (fl. c. 150) included it in his *Diatessaron*, or Harmony of the Four Gospels,

---

[2]Hoare, Bernard, and Moffat hold this or a similar view. The only instance where a positive textual variant may be found to support this hypothesis occurs in John 18, where the Sinaitic Syriac text changes the order of the verses to 13, 24, 14–15, 19–23, 16–18, 25–27; a somewhat similar arrangement appears in 225 and in a quotation by Cyril of Alexandria (c. 444). By far the oldest MSS and the vast majority of the extant witnesses do not support the variant. It seems that in the latter case the variant is due to a late alteration and that the hypothesis of accidental confusion of order in the original text, while not impossible, cannot be proved. See further discussion in section on Displacement of Text, p. 21.

which he produced about the third quarter of the second century. Eusebius, the church historian of the fourth century, attributed the Gospel to "John, the companion of Peter, James, and the other apostles" (*Historia Ecclesiastica* 3.34.5). Although Eusebius seemed uncertain concerning the authorship of the Apocalypse, he agreed with the other witnesses concerning the Gospel. The early Fathers did not hesitate to acknowledge the Johannine authorship of the Gospel, and from the time of Irenaeus there was almost unanimous agreement about this.

b. *Internal Evidence*

Internal evidence also testifies to the unity of this Gospel. The epilogue closes by focusing on "the disciple whom Jesus loved" as the witness and writer of the content of the Gospel (21:20–24). He was among those Jesus appeared to at the Sea of Tiberias (Galilee) after their night of unsuccessful fishing (21:7). This disciple was a particular friend of Peter and was one of the sons of Zebedee (John 21:2; cf. Matt 4:21; 10:2). The preceding chapters couple him with Peter in the events on the morning of the Resurrection (20:2–8) and also identify him as the one Jesus committed his mother to at the Crucifixion (19:25–27). It is possible that he is the one who is called "another disciple," the one who led Peter into the court of the high priest's palace at the trial of Jesus (18:15–16). He was present at the Last Supper, where he reclined next to Jesus and was questioned by Peter (13:23–24). Undoubtedly he belonged to the Twelve and was probably a member of the inner circle. Obviously he was not Peter nor one of those mentioned in the third person in the main body of the Gospel. Presumably he was John, for he was Peter's close associate after the Resurrection (Acts 3:1–11; 4:13–20; Gal 2:9). He would have been able to hear both Jesus' public and private discourses and would have been actively engaged in the development of the church from its inception.

The characteristics of the Gospel confirm the credibility of apostolic authorship. Westcott demonstrated from internal testimony that it must have been written by a Jew who was acquainted with Jewish opinions and learning and with the details of Jewish customs (1:ix–lix). The author's vocabulary and general style are Semitic; though the Gospel was written in Greek. The OT is frequently quoted, and the necessity of prophetic fulfillment is emphasized (John 13:18; 15:25).

Second, the author was a Palestinian Jew, not a member of the Diaspora. His knowledge of Palestinian topography was accurate. He distinguished between Bethany, the suburb of Jerusalem where Mary and Martha lived (11:1), and "Bethany on the other side of the Jordan," where John the Baptist preached (1:28). Some of the sites he alluded to, such as Aenon (3:23) and Ephraim (11:54), are not described elsewhere; but, obviously, they were actual places well known to him. His description of the features of Jerusalem, such as the pool by the "Sheep Gate" (5:2), the "pool of Siloam" (9:7), the "Stone Pavement" (Gr. *lithostrōton*, 19:13), and the varied references to the temple (2:14–16; 8:20; 10:23), show that he was familiar with the city before its destruction. (The devastation was so complete by the middle of the second century that the face of the city had changed entirely. The buildings had been razed, and the surface of the land had been buried under their rubble. Following the Second Revolt of 133–135, Hadrian built a new town, Aelia Capitolina.) Archaeological investigations have confirmed the accuracy of many of the author's allusions, though complete data are presently unattainable.

The genuineness of the fourth Gospel has been challenged on the basis of its language, which differs from the synoptic record of Jesus' discourses and also from that of the early Fathers. For example, the contrast of light and darkness that appears in the first chapter has frequently been regarded as evidence of a Hellenistic influence in the Gospel. Yet the discovery at Qumran of the Jewish writing *The War of the Sons of Light and the Sons of Darkness* shows that this contrast was current in Judaism during the intertestamental period and was not necessarily an importation from Hellenism.

A further deduction from the internal evidence of the Gospel is that the author personally witnessed the events he described, or else he must have had contemporary informants who were themselves eyewitnesses. He spoke easily and familiarly of the disciples and associates of Jesus (6:5–7; 12:21; 13:36; 14:5, 8, 22) and knew the background of those Jesus had only casual contact with, such as Nicodemus (3:1) or Annas (18:13). Small details appear frequently, such as the barley bread used at the feeding of the five thousand (6:9), the fragrance of the ointment Mary poured on Jesus (12:3), or the time at which Judas left the Last Supper (13:30). These are not the creation of literary imagination, but they are the natural touches that come from personal memory. As Westcott said, "The age of minute historical romance had not yet come when the Fourth Gospel was written, even if such a record could possibly be brought within the category" (1:xliv).

Not only must the writer have been an eyewitness, but he also was closely acquainted with the personal career of Jesus from beginning to end. The author was aware of the thinking of the disciples, and apparently he shared their interests and hopes. He reports the private discourses of Jesus at some length; and even though the criticism has been raised that they are given in the Johannine style rather than in the epigrammatic style quoted in the Synoptics, some quotations in the Synoptics show that Jesus occasionally used the same language when alluding to himself (Matt 10:24–27; 26:64). Even if the author reported Jesus' words in his own style, he cannot justly be charged with inaccuracy. Also, he shows knowledge of Jesus' inner consciousness that would have been possible only to a close associate (6:6, 61, 64; 13:1–3, 11; 18:4).

Although the author never names himself, it seems that his identity was well known to his contemporaries. Just why he or his colleagues who wrote the final colophon should have left the Gospel anonymous is not clear; though, as a matter of fact, none of the Gospels mentions the name of its author. If it were written during a period of persecution, the writer possibly would have preferred to remain unidentified, though some of the recipients must have known who produced it.

By process of elimination, it seems reasonably certain that this anonymous disciple and author must have been John the son of Zebedee. Peter did not write the fourth Gospel, for it mentions him frequently in the third person. James the son of Zebedee did not write it, for he was executed by Herod Agrippa I prior to A.D. 44 (Acts 12:2). The remaining possibility is John, who fits the requirements of its authorship quite well. Although tradition is not always reliable, in this case it corroborates the implications of the internal evidence. It also confirms the conclusion that this Gospel was written by one who knew Jesus personally, who had followed him throughout his career, and who had become one of the leaders in the movement that grew out of Jesus' life and teaching. We accept it as a genuine document of the first-century witness.

Objections to the Johannine authorship have been raised from time to time. It has been suggested that a fisherman like John would have been incapable of composing a Gospel of such profound meaning. To be sure, the enemies of Peter and John characterized them as "unschooled, ordinary men" (Acts 4:13), but that does not mean they were illiterate or stupid. It does mean they had not received the formal education in the Law that was the prerogative of biblical scholars of their day. They were not lacking in knowledge of the content of the OT, nor were they devoid of the ability to apply their knowledge. If they can be judged by the fragmentary defense recorded in Acts, they made so good a case for themselves that their opponents had no resort left to them but violence. Furthermore, by the time he wrote this Gospel, John had possibly fifty or more years' experience after his early appearances before the Jewish council. In that time he could have gained greatly in knowledge, depth of insight, and facility of expression.

Another objection—that John died as a martyr in the early years of the church—is based on a statement of Philip of Side, a church historian of the fifth century. He remarked that Papias, a disciple of John the Theologian, wrote in vol. 2 of his *Exposition of Dominical Oracles*, a five volume work, that "John the Theologian" and James his brother were put to death by the Jews. Papias's *Oracles* were a collection of unwritten traditions from around the first century; but, unfortunately, none of them survived. For what it is worth, Philip of Side was regarded by his contemporaries as a conceited and untrustworthy author whose writings were unreliable (Smith and Wace, 4:356). Furthermore, James the brother of John was executed by Herod, not by the Jews. And the statement is not even self-consistent because it asserts the early martyrdom of John while affirming that Papias had been his disciple. The evidence for the early decease of John is negligible.

Still another objection to the Johannine authorship is grounded on Eusebius's interpretation of a statement of Papias:

> And I shall not hesitate to append to the interpretations all that I ever learned well from the presbyters and remember well, for of their truth I am confident. For unlike most I did not rejoice in those who say much, but in those who teach the truth, nor in those who recount the commandments of others, but in those who repeated those given to the faith by the Lord and derived from the truth itself; but if ever anyone comes who followed the presbyters, I inquire into the words of the presbyters, what Andrew or Peter or Philip or Thomas or James or John or Matthew or any other of the Lord's disciples had said, and what Aristion and the presbyter John, the Lord's disciples, were saying [*legousin*, present tense, "are saying"]. For I did not suppose that information from books would help so much as the word of a living and surviving voice (*Historia Ecclesiastica* 3.39).

From this statement Eusebius deduced that there were two Johns, the former being the son of Zebedee and the latter the "presbyter John," to whom Eusebius ascribed the Book of Revelation. A different interpretation is possible, however. The two verbs "had said" and "are saying" imply that the former group of men mentioned by Papias had preceded his time; but with the latter two, Aristion and John, he apparently had some personal contact. He may have meant that the two Johns were identical, especially since the term *elder* (*presbyteros*) could have been applied to any of them and particularly to John the son of Zebedee, if he were the last survivor of the apostolic band. The fact that his great age is implied in the epilogue to the Gospel (John 21:23) and that "elder" is applied to the writer of the Second and Third Epistles (2 John 1; 3 John 1) tends to strengthen this conclusion. The witness of Irenaeus, who long preceded Eusebius, should take precedence over a quotation of Papias that is given out of context and that may have been garbled or misunderstood.

In summation, it may be said that while there have been objections to the traditional authorship, the more recent trend is toward a partial if not complete acceptance of the Johannine origin. At least, the basic content of the Gospel in early annals goes back to apostolic teaching. Morris, in his exhaustive commentary, says, "I accept the view that John the Apostle was the author of the Gospel. . . . This one seems to account for the facts best" (p. 30). Brown concludes: "When all is said and done, the combination of external and internal evidence associating the Fourth Gospel with John, son of Zebedee, makes this the strongest hypothesis, if one is prepared to give credence to the Gospel's claim of an eyewitness source" (p. xcviii).

4. Date

The date of the Gospel has been variously estimated at almost any point between 45, shortly after the dispersion of Christians from Jerusalem following the persecution under Paul (Acts 8:1–4), and the middle of the second century. The latter point was advocated by the Tübingen school in the early nineteenth century on the supposition that John represented a type of theological thinking that arose late in the first century or early in the second century and was not put in written form until approximately 150. The discovery of the Rylands fragment of John 18:31–33, 37–38, by C.H. Roberts about 1935, shows that this Gospel had been incorporated in a papyrus MS produced not later than 135. It must, therefore, originally have been written at some time prior to the date of the MS into which it was copied. The Egerton papyrus, which was written about the same time as the Rylands fragment, confirms this conclusion, for its phraseology incorporates unmistakable allusions to John (see Bell and Skeat, pp. 17–19, 42–51).

On the other hand, C.C. Torrey maintained that John was originally written in Aramaic and was later translated into Greek (p. 264). He openly challenged his colleagues to produce any direct evidence to the contrary. Although Torrey's contention that John was translated from Aramaic may be disputed, he seems to have demonstrated effectively that it may well be a product of a Palestinian Jew who wrote with firsthand knowledge of the land and who could have composed the Gospel earlier than the end of the first century. Several critics hold this viewpoint. E.R. Goodenough (2:145–82) argued that it could have been composed well before the destruction of Jerusalem in A.D. 70.[3] Albright stated that "the advanced teachings of Jesus as transmitted by the Gospel of John contain nothing that can be reasonably adduced as evidence of a late origin" ("Scrolls"). He also added that "the Gospel of John is not a product of the early second century A.D., but dates substantially, though not in its present form, from before A.D. 70."[4]

The explanation in ch. 21 concerning Jesus' words "If I want him to remain alive until I return, what is that to you?" (v.22) seemingly implies that "the disciple whom Jesus loved" must have attained a great age and must have been a contemporary of the second-generation church. Possibly so, but that would not have precluded his writing the Gospel at an earlier date. Nor, on the other hand, would it allow for a composition date later than the end of the first century. Most conservative scholars suggest a date around 85 to 90, when the author had achieved advanced age but was still in full possession of his memory and active in ministry. It may be, however, that the Gospel was composed at a fairly early date but that its "publication" or wide circulation began later.

If the Gospel were written before the end of the first century, or even by 85, it would still have been read by men only one generation removed from the contemporaries of

---

[3]Goodenough holds that the writer of the fourth Gospel was unacquainted with the synoptic Gospels. Some of his arguments are quite radical, but he has at least made the option of an early date possible.

[4]See also his *Archaeology of Palestine* (Baltimore: Penguin, 1951), pp. 239–49.

Jesus. Thus it could have been verified or contested by those who had authentic information concerning him. Brown states that "the positive arguments seem to point to 100–110 as the latest plausible date for the writing of the Gospel, with strong probability favoring the earlier limit of 100" (p. lxxxiii). He has set the latest limit, including redaction, at this point and suggests that the "first edition" may have been written prior to A.D. 70. Robinson does not believe that there is anything in the language of John that demands a composition date later than the 60s (pp. 259–85).

5. Place of Origin

The place of origin is uncertain. Tradition, based largely on the statements of Irenaeus (*Against Heresies* 3.1) and Eusebius (*Historia Ecclesiastica* 4.14.3–8) holds that John wrote from Ephesus, where he had settled after leaving Palestine subsequent to the war of 66–70. Ephesus was a large cosmopolitan center of the ancient world, where the cultures of East and West mingled. The apostle Paul previously had founded an active church in Ephesus (Acts 19:1–20), having spent more than two years there, during which time he evangelized most of the province of Asia (v.10).

A final decision on the matter of place cannot be reached on the basis of available evidence. The best that can be said is that Ephesus is as good a probability as any. It was one of the largest Christian centers in the Gentile world of the first century. The use of *logos* in John would appeal to the Greeks, and the direct allusion to the Greek interest in Jesus mentioned in John 12:20–22 may indicate that the Gospel was written with an eye on the Gentile world, though it cannot be attributed to a Greek writer.

6. Destination

The intended recipients of John's Gospel are not clearly identified. From the writer's habit of explaining Jewish usages, translating Jewish names, and locating Palestinian sites, it would seem that he was probably writing for a Gentile church outside Palestine. If the reading "believe" in John 20:31 is the present tense, it would imply that the Gospel was written to Christians who needed encouragement and deepening of their faith. If "believe" is in the aorist tense, it would suggest that the Gospel was addressed, at least in part, to a pagan constituency to bring them to belief in Jesus as Christ and the Son of God. The content of the Gospel does not give overwhelming support to either possibility. Its presentation of Jesus deals largely with the questioning of the Jews. But the language of the Prologue and the introduction of the Greeks in ch. 12 reveal the author's interest in Gentiles.

Probably it will not be too wrong to suggest that the Gospel of John was written for Gentile Christians who had already acquired a basic knowledge of the life and works of Jesus but who needed further confirmation of their faith. By the use of personal reminiscences interpreted in the light of a long life of devotion to Christ and by numerous episodes that generally had not been used in the Gospel tradition, whether written or oral, John created a new and different approach to understanding Jesus' person. John's readers were primarily second-generation Christians he was familiar with and to whom he seemed patriarchal. If the Johannine Epistles are any guide, the writer must have been a highly respected elder within the structure of the church. John considered himself responsible for its welfare and did not hesitate to assert his authority (2 John 1,

4, 8; 3 John 9–10). The doctrinal digressions implied by the counsel given in these Epistles indicate that the church was being imperiled, if not actually deceived, by false teachers who came in the guise of itinerant preachers.

There is no clue concerning the geographical location of the intended audience. If the Gospel was written at Ephesus, it could have been directed to the Christians of the province of Asia. There is no implication that it was written to a local church. Whether the recipients were Jews or Gentiles is not stated. John 20:31 is, as already noted, somewhat ambiguous because of alternate readings.

7. Occasion

We cannot discern any specific occasion for the composition of this Gospel. It lacks the personal preface of Luke. Neither does it seem to have been written simply as a piece of informative news like Mark. There is no personal dedication. It is not a complete narrative, nor is it an essay. It is not strongly historical in the sense that it reflects any particular time or place. Because of the rather defensive doctrinal position it takes, it may well have been written to combat the rising tide of Cerinthianism, which threatened the theological foundation of the church.

According to Irenaeus, Cerinthus was a teacher who contended that Jesus was merely a human personality who was possessed by the Christ-spirit at his baptism and who relinquished this spirit on the cross (*Against Heresies* 1.26.2). Contrary to this teaching, the Gospel asserts that the Word became flesh (John 1:14) and that the descent of the Holy Spirit on Jesus at the baptism was the proof of his mission, not the origin of it (1:32–34). The Cross did not terminate his ministry; it simply marked the end of one stage of it. The Son returned to the Father in person; he did not cease to be the Son by death. The stress on sonship throughout the Gospel conveys the idea that it was a live issue in the church; and that impression is strengthened by the warning "Such a man is the antichrist—he denies the Father and the Son. No one who denies the Son has the Father; whoever acknowledges the Son has the Father also" (1 John 2:22–23).

8. Purpose

John wrote this Gospel to meet the spiritual need of a church that had little background in the OT and that may have been endangered by the plausible contention of Cerinthus or men like him. John's intention is stated with perfect clarity: "These [signs] are written that you may believe that Jesus is the Christ, the Son of God, and that by believing you may have life in his name" (John 20:31). The total thesis of the Gospel is belief in the Son who came from the Father.

The Gospel gives an initial impression of discontinuity. Many of its episodes have little direct chronological or logical connection with one another. Nevertheless, they show a remarkable unity built on the one purpose of convincing the reader that Jesus was supernatural in his origin, powers, and goal. He was the *Logos* who had come into the world from another sphere (1:14). He performed miracles, or "signs," that illustrated his many-faceted powers, especially applied to human need. He died an unusual death, but he rose from the dead to send his disciples out on a universal mission. The last sentences of the Gospel imply the promise of his return. An entirely new revelation of the plan and power of God is latent in this Gospel (1:18).

9. Literary Form and Structure

The Gospel of John is a narrative composed of various scenes from the career of Jesus. It does not pretend to be a complete biography. The chronological gaps leave an impression of incompleteness for those expecting a complete chronicle of Jesus' career. Because the Gospel has an apologetic or possibly polemic purpose, it utilizes only the episodes that will best illustrate its presentation of Jesus as the object of faith. Nothing is said of Jesus' youth; the baptism is not described as it is in the Synoptics; the Galilean ministries with their parables and numerous miracles are not recounted in detail; the eschatological discourses and parables are missing. Much attention is given to aspects of Jesus' visits to Jerusalem, of which the Synoptics say relatively little.

On the other hand, certain personal interviews between Jesus and others are given at length. Dialogue and discourse between Jesus and his disciples are emphasized. Miracles are few and are selected for individual illustrative purpose. The vocabulary is distinctive and is limited to major ideas such as those expressed by the words *believe, witness, love, abide, the Father, the Son, the Counselor* (*paraklētēs*, referring to the Holy Spirit), *light, life, darkness, Word, glorify, true* (*alēthēs*), *real* (*alēthinos*), and others. Most of these are used metaphorically and represent the leading ideas of the Gospel. The peculiarities of vocabulary, which are evident in all the Gospels, are more pronounced in the Gospel of John. It is almost impossible to read a single paragraph in the fourth Gospel that does not identify itself as Johannine by at least one word or phrase.

The structure of this Gospel may be analyzed from various viewpoints. The author uses at least five different approaches to his subject: (1) a central theme, which can be traced through the progress of the narrative from beginning to end; (2) the phases of the ministry of Jesus, which are marked by growing tension between him and his opponents; (3) a chronological sequence, which is not perfectly defined but follows a general scheme, organized loosely around the feasts of the Jewish year; (4) a geographic allocation of activity between Galilee, where the first sign was performed, and Jerusalem, where the final action took place; and (5) the personal interviews that delineate so plainly Jesus' interest in different types of personality and his method of dealing with them.

a. Theme

The first of these criteria concerns the central theme "belief." The varied episodes and teachings of the Gospel are all subordinate to the definition and development of this concept. The Prologue introduces the ministry of John the Baptist by stating that "he came as a witness . . . so that through him all men might believe" (John 1:7). The closing words of the main narrative that precedes the Epilogue (ch. 21) declare that "these [things] are written that you may believe that Jesus is the Christ, the Son of God" (20:31). The word "believe" (*pisteuō*) appears ninety-eight times in the Gospel, more often than any other key word, and is obviously the major theme.

All the signs, teachings, and events in the Gospel are used to stimulate faith in Christ and are so ordered that they mark growth in this faith on the part of his disciples. Growth was not always uniform, as Simon Peter's experience shows, and generally was countered by a growth of unbelief, as seen in the conduct of Jesus' enemies. The conflict between belief and unbelief, exemplified in the actions and utterances of the main characters, forms the plot.

The development of "belief " in John's work affords one key to its interpretation and marks its progressive evangelistic appeal. The following outline shows its general progress:

1. The Prologue: The Proposal for Belief
   1:1–18
2. The Presentation for Belief
   1:19–4:54
3. The Reactions of Belief and Unbelief
   5:1–6:71
4. The Crystallization of Belief and Unbelief
   7:1–11:53
5. The Crisis of Belief and Unbelief
   11:54–12:50
6. The Assurance for Belief
   13:1–17:26
7. The Rejection by Unbelief
   18:1–19:42
8. The Vindication of Belief
   20:1–31
9. Epilogue: The Dedication of Belief
   21:1–25

The Johannine presentation of belief describes the nature of the person on whom belief is fixed. Each of the interviews in section 2 describes a different personality with a different need and a different challenge to faith. Section 3 gives further illustrations of belief and unbelief, accompanied by explanatory discourses that define the claims of Christ more exactly and intensify his personal appeal to his hearers. The feeding of the five thousand (6:1–69) marks the watershed of Jesus' ministry. At this point the popular following began to diminish, and the band of loyal disciples declared their settled purpose of adhering to him. Section 4 marks the fixation of these attitudes: the rulers became set in their hatred of Jesus and in their consequent resolve to remove him; the disciples, though somewhat uncertain of themselves, still clung to him and maintained their loyalty. Section 5, the Crisis, is concerned largely with Jesus' own reaction. Realizing that his hour had come, he accepted the will of the Father and resolutely moved toward the ultimate conflict. The ensuing action is twofold. The episode of the foot washing and the following long discourse (chs. 14–16) contain Jesus' confrontation with unbelief in his dismissing of Judas and his encouragement of the hesitant belief of the others by his attempt to prepare them for his own removal. The prayer to the Father (ch. 17) expresses Jesus' confidence in the sovereignty and purpose of his Father as related to himself, his disciples, and the world.

Section 7, which deals with Jesus' death, reveals the final division that belief and unbelief made in all those who knew him. His enemies were implacable, and their hatred, scorn, and utter rejection of him illustrate the real meaning of unbelief. Conversely, the loyalty of those who remained with him, however feeble, shows an attitude of trust in him, even though these disciples may not have fully comprehended the significance of the events they were involved in.

Sections 8 and 9 provide the vindication of the disciples' faith. The Resurrection dissolved their perplexity, dried their tears, and dispelled their doubts. The Epilogue launched the disciples on a new career as they followed a risen Christ to a larger life and a fuller ministry.

b. *Phases of Ministry*

The first approach to the ministry of Jesus is topical rather than biographical, though it is built on biographical episodes. The author is not so much concerned with a regular sequence of events as with the creation of a relationship. His main purpose is to involve his reader in an active faith in Jesus as the Christ, the Son of God; and the selection of events and teachings are shaped to this end.

Notwithstanding this fact, the Gospel is still strongly biographical. The phases of the ministry of Jesus follow a definite progression from the initial questioning of his authority down to its ultimate repudiation by his enemies. In the outline that follows this introduction five major divisions are noted:

I. The Prologue states the basic preparation for understanding the ministry of Jesus. "The Word became flesh and lived for a while among us" (1:14).

II. As in the Synoptics, Jesus is publicly introduced through the ministry of John the Baptist. The gaining of disciples, the miracles, the assertion of his authority and defense of his claims, and his rise to the peak of his popularity are keyed to specific "signs" (*sēmeia*) and claims that resulted in controversy. The decline that led directly to the Cross began at the highest point in Jesus' ministry, which John, along with the Synoptics, locates at the feeding of the five thousand. As Jesus' popularity waned, he became increasingly concerned for his disciples. When the multitude finally turned from him, and the power of his enemies increased, he gave more time to the needs of his disciples, until in his last hour his attention was concentrated on their future.

III. Chapters 13 through 17, which contain Jesus' farewell discourses in the Upper Room and his final prayer, occupy about 20 percent of the text. This section contains the teaching by which Jesus sought to prepare the disciples for the shock of his death and the responsibility that would fall to them. He showed no sense of defeat, nor did he anticipate that the disciples would fail in their mission. The prayer (ch. 17) that followed his counsel implies that he would achieve his objective even in death and that he would be reunited with the Father. Likewise he expected that the disciples would be preserved by divine power and that they would discharge their mission in the world adequately.

IV. The story of Jesus' death and resurrection is brief. John does not give an exhaustive account of its details. He does not include many of the events recorded in the Synoptics, such as the prayer in Gethsemane, the trial before the Sanhedrin, the suicide of Judas, the hearing before Herod Antipas, the utterances of the two brigands executed with him, the earthquake and darkness, the rending of the veil of the temple, and the comment of the centurion who commanded the execution squad. If John was absent from the scene long enough to take Jesus' mother to his home in Jerusalem, it is quite likely that he missed some of the action at the cross.

Had the Gospel ended with the burial of Jesus, it would have been a disastrous tragedy. His life would have become the supreme example of injustice because holiness would have been eclipsed by evil, truth would have succumbed to expediency, love would have been shattered by hatred, and life would have been extinguished by death. The Resurrection reversed all these possibilities. It authenticated Jesus' teaching, broke the power of evil, and brought hope out of despair. Jesus' postresurrection presence brought a new dimension to belief.

V. The Epilogue, possibly added as a postscript to the main body of the Gospel, solidifies the power and appeal of Jesus. Not only has he risen, but he calls his disciples to follow him to new conquests.

c. The Chronological Framework

The chronological framework of the Gospel is loose. The segment from John 1:19 to 2:11 represents the consecutive events of a few days, which are well marked by the phrase "the next day" (1:29, 35, 43), or some related expression. The major divisions of action following the initial sign (ch. 2) are indicated by the occurrences of feasts (2:13; 5:1; 6:4; 7:2, 14; 10:22; 12:1), one of which is not identified (5:1). The chief reason for mentioning them seems to be social, not chronological. They provide the historical association for understanding the meaning of Jesus' teaching or action. His offering of the water from within parallels the ceremonial outpouring of water at the Feast of Tabernacles (Dodd, pp. 348–49). The demand of the Jews for a declaration of messiahship at the Feast of Dedication (Hanukkah) reflects the desire for a renewal of political liberation such as the Maccabees had achieved (Lightfoot, pp. 45, 49). The Last Supper at the Passover season recalls Paul's statement "Christ, our Passover lamb, has been sacrificed" (1 Cor 5:7). Notwithstanding the difficulty of placing the events of this Gospel in a fixed chronological order, it is still true that John seems to have had a knowledge of such an order and that he adhered to it, allowing for gaps at those places where he chose to be silent.

The order of the last week begins with John 12. The opening verse says that Jesus arrived at Bethany "six days before the Passover" (12:1). On that day Mary and Martha gave a dinner for him. The crowd that came to see him was so large that the chief priests were alarmed, and they began to plot the destruction of both Jesus and Lazarus, whose raising had attracted much attention (vv.10–11).

On the next day, Jesus, mounted on a donkey, formally entered Jerusalem. The acclaim of the crowd further exasperated his enemies, who felt helpless in the face of Jesus' widespread popularity (12:12–19). John does not provide a complete sequence for the next few days. He mentions the inquiry of the Greeks concerning Jesus and says that after this discourse Jesus hid himself (v.36).

John resumes the narrative with the evening meal in the Upper Room, which was "just before the Passover Feast" (13:1). According to the sequence of the narrative, this took place on the same evening as the betrayal and arrest, with the hearings before Pilate and the Crucifixion following on the next morning. If so, Jesus must have eaten the Last Supper with the disciples on Thursday evening, which by Jewish reckoning would be the beginning of Friday. Therefore, the Crucifixion and interment would have been concluded just prior to Friday evening, the beginning of the Sabbath. This conclusion accords well with the statement that the interview with Pilate occurred on the "day of Preparation (*paraskeuē*) of Passover Week" (19:14), which would be Friday. Jesus' body was removed from the cross before sunset, since the next day was a "special Sabbath" because of the Passover (19:31). The Sabbath followed immediately.

Lightfoot says that the Last Supper in John is not the normal paschal meal; for upon the dismissal of Judas, the disciples thought Jesus wanted Judas to purchase what might be needed for the feast (13:29) (pp. 352–55). The ritual Passover Feast was eaten on Friday afternoon (18:28), but Jesus died at that time. Perhaps in his mind he was celebrating the Passover early because he knew that he would be arrested prior to the stated feast. Such an interpretation gives a more vivid understanding of Luke's report of Jesus' words: "I have eagerly desired to eat this Passover with you before I suffer" (Luke 22:15).

The tomb was found to be empty on "the first day of the week" (20:1); and in the afternoon of the same day Jesus appeared to the disciples in the Upper Room (v.19). Another manifestation occurred a week later in the same place (v.26). The episode by the Sea of Galilee, which belongs to the Epilogue, is somewhat indefinitely located "afterward" (21:1). John does not attempt a closed chronological system. He locates events by groups, not always completely stating their relation to each other. It would be unfair to say that his chronology is erroneous, though it was not completely systematic.

d. *Geographical Structure*

The Gospel's structure by location does not seem to follow any particular design, except that it emphasizes Jesus' activity in Jerusalem. He began his work in the region where John was baptizing, either at "Bethany on the other side of the Jordan," near the southern end of the Jordan River, a little north of the Dead Sea (John 1:28), or at Aenon (4:23), which has generally been located either at springs near Mount Gerizim, or at a site 8 miles south of Scythopolis (Beth-shean), on the west side of the Jordan.

There are three allusions to Galilee in the main narrative: (1) an indefinite stay in Capernaum, no particulars of which are chronicled (2:12); (2) the healing of the nobleman's son in Capernaum (4:43–54); and (3) the feeding of the five thousand at Bethsaida on the Sea of Galilee (6:1–15), followed by the address in the synagogue at Capernaum (vv.25–70). Except for the brief visit in Samaria (4:1–42) and in Ephraim (11:54), a city on the border of the Judean wilderness, the narrative of Jesus' action was centered in Jerusalem.

The main purpose of the fourth Gospel is to show, against the background of his opposition, who Jesus was, not to supply a full chronicle of his deeds. Since opposition seemed to come largely from the leaders of the Jewish hierarchy whose headquarters were in Jerusalem, the main scene is laid where the sharpest theological debates occurred and where the closing scenes of Jesus' life took place.

The apparent neglect of the Galilean ministry, with its extensive teaching, does not mean that the author of this Gospel was ignorant of it. Opinion has differed widely as to whether John was familiar with the Synoptic Gospels. Lightfoot declares that his commentary was "written in the belief that the evangelist knew not only the synoptic tradition, but the three Synoptic Gospels themselves" (p. 29). Whether or not John knew the Synoptics cannot be determined with certainty, and there seems to be no indisputable quotation from any of them in the text of his Gospel. On the other hand, there is a sense in which the fourth Gospel complements the others; and often it seems to begin its narrative at a point where the others have stopped, or to assume a knowledge they would supply. An instance of the former appears in the account of the Last Supper. John tells how the disciples reclined for the meal without the customary footwashing as they entered the room and how Jesus himself felt obligated to supply the lack of service (John 13:2–14). Luke tells us how on that occasion the disciples were bickering with one another for the highest place in the coming kingdom (Luke 22:24). If their attitude toward one another was rivalry for the best position in the coming rule of Jesus, it explains why no one was ready to wash the feet of the others.

e. *Personal Interviews*

One marked feature of John's Gospel is the partiality to personal interviews. The Synoptics emphasize Jesus' public ministry as he talked to the crowds, though they do lay considerable emphasis on the training of the disciples. Although the Gospel does on several occasions say that many believed in him in response to his public actions or appeals (2:23; 4:39; 7:31; 8:30; 10:42; 11:45; 12:11, 42), it records fewer of his general discourses. The personal interviews are rather widely distributed through the earlier part of the Gospel: Nicodemus in Jerusalem (3:1–15), the woman of Samaria (4:1–26), the nobleman of Cana (4:43–53), the paralytic in Jerusalem (5:1–15), the blind man (9:1–38), and Mary and Martha in Bethany (11:17–40). These interviews represent different classes of society, occur at different times during Jesus' career, and have different occasions followed by varying appeals. All of them, however, whether implicitly or explicitly, illustrate the nature and consequences of belief. Some, like the interview with Nicodemus, were with people who became Jesus' lasting followers; others, like the one with the paralytic, seem to have been wholly casual. Each interview is included in some narrative of action and the person interviewed is not simply a wooden figure or puppet used to make an abstract point. All of the interviews depict Jesus' personal concern for people.

The general interviews with groups are similar in content and teaching. In time and place they approximately parallel the individual interviews. "Many" listened to him in Jerusalem (2:23); "many of the Samaritans" received him willingly after his conversation with the woman (4:39); a crowd gathered to hear him in Capernaum after the feeding of the five thousand (6:24–40). And on his last visit to Jerusalem the pilgrims from Galilee (12:12), the followers who had come with him to the Passover (v.17), and the crowd in Jerusalem (vv.29–36) all gave him audience to the last day of his life. In no way does John minimize Jesus' universal appeal, though he says less about Jesus' continual itinerant ministry.

John gives a great deal of attention to Jesus' personal ministry to the disciples. Andrew (1:40; 6:8), Peter (1:42; 6:68; 13:6–9; 18:11; 21:15–22), Philip (1:43–44; 6:5; 12:22; 14:8–10), Nathanael (1:47–51; 21:2), Thomas (11:16; 14:5; 20:26–29), Judas Iscariot (12:4–8; 13:26–30), the other Judas (14:22–24), and Mary of Magdala (20:10–18) received Jesus' compassionate counsel. Although these disciples are not always mentioned by name, they reappear in the narrative frequently enough to show that Jesus had a continuing concern for them.

In contrast, John records interviews with hostile persons. At least six conflicts with "the Jews" are mentioned (2:18–20; 5:16–47; 6:41–59; 7:15–44; 8:31–58; 10:22–39). The title "The Jews" apparently is not given solely for the purpose of distinguishing their nationality from Samaritans or Gentiles but to identify Jesus' opponents. The Pharisees are included under this title in 8:13–29 and in the text of 8:3–9 also. Each of these instances indicates the progress of unbelief that leads to the climax of the Cross. The interview with Pilate is the only instance of a hostile individual confrontation in this Gospel, and Pilate's hostility is due more to his political dilemma than to personal enmity.

These personal interviews, with their varying degrees of success and their wide range of character, demonstrate the breadth of appeal of this Gospel and Jesus' technique in dealing with people. While the interviews do not in themselves constitute a consistent basis for outlining the progressive development of the Gospel, they illustrate it. Thus they serve much the same purpose as pictures in a book. The interviews clearly relate to the main theme and forcibly convey the revelation given through Christ and the effects of the power he exercised. They form a distinct thematic approach to the total teaching of the Gospel.

10. Theological Values

The Gospel of John is predominantly theological. Although all four Gospels present the person of Jesus from a theological viewpoint, John emphasizes it most strongly. His initial assertion—"In the beginning was the Word, and the Word was with God, and the Word was God. . . . The Word became flesh and lived for a while among us" (John 1:1, 14)—declares that Jesus was no ordinary person. He was the incarnation of the eternal God, who chose that means of revealing himself perfectly to men. This declaration is amplified by the further statement of John 1:18; "No one has ever seen God, but God the only [Son], who is at the Father's side, has made him known." Throughout the Gospel the essential deity of the Lord Jesus Christ is stressed.

A second theological aspect is the concept of atonement. Jesus was introduced by John the Baptist as the sacrificial "Lamb of God, who takes away the sin of the world" (John 1:29). Jesus told Nicodemus that "just as Moses lifted up the snake in the desert, so the Son of Man must be lifted up, that everyone who believes in him may have eternal life" (3:14–15). He spoke of his flesh, which he would "give for the life of the world" (6:51), and called himself "the good shepherd [who] lays down his life for the sheep" (10:11). The doctrine of the Atonement is not stated so explicitly as in some of the Pauline writings, but it is unmistakably latent in John's Gospel.

Another prominent theme is eternal life. Life in the sum of its total expression is a major subject of the Prologue: "In him was life, and that life was the light of men" (John 1:4). His gift to believers is eternal life (3:15–16; 10:10; 20:31), bestowed on those who commit themselves to him (3:36; 4:13; 5:21, 24; 8:12).

A very important body of teaching on the person and functions of the Holy Spirit appears in Jesus' farewell discourse to the disciples (John 14:25–26; 15:26; 16:7–15). His intermediary relation between Christ and the believer and his functional relation to God, the believer, and the world are plainly defined.

Perhaps the greatest theological contribution of the Gospel is a full discussion and demonstration of the nature of belief. Both by definition and by example its essence is described. Belief is equated with receiving (1:12), following (1:40), drinking (fig., 4:13), responding (4:51), eating (fig., 6:57), accepting (6:60, lit. "hear"), worship (9:38), obeying (11:39–41), and commitment (12:10–11). The lives of those who "believed" show both the method and result of their faith.

Numerous other theological topics mentioned in John will be discussed in the body of the text. Those that have been cited here suffice to show the wealth of material this Gospel contributes to Christian theology.

11. Canonicity

From a very early date the Gospel of John has been part of the NT canon. The Rylands fragment shows that the Gospel was circulated by the first third of the second century, and the allusions in the Egerton papyrus 2 confirm that conclusion. The Muratorian Canon, an incomplete list of accepted works dating from the second century (c. 170), included John and elaborated on a tradition concerning its origin. Tatian, a pupil of Justin Martyr who alluded to the "Memoirs of the Apostles" (*First Apology* 67), incorporated sections from it in his *Diatessaron*, a combined narrative of the four Gospels, which was widely used in the Syrian church in the second, third, and fourth centuries. Heracleon, a Gnostic, wrote a commentary on the Gospel about 170. He would scarcely have written a commentary on what he did not consider to be an authoritative work, though his personal beliefs were unorthodox. The Bodmer papyri of the early third century contain parts of two copies of this Gospel. The Fathers of the late second century—Irenaeus, Clement of Alexandria, and Tertullian—all accept it as authoritative. By the middle of the third century its place in the canon was fixed. Origen (c. 250) wrote an extensive commentary on it, and the subsequent church councils that had anything to say about the canon all recognized its authority. Eusebius, the church historian of the fourth century, classified the canon by (1) the acknowledged books, (2) the disputed books, and (3) the spurious works. John was classed among the undisputed works. Its canonicity was above question.

12. Text

The text of John is fairly stable. Most of the variants in the MS tradition are not important. There are, however, a few that deserve special comment. See the Notes for a discussion of them in loc.: 1:13; 1:18; 5:4; 7:53–8:11.

Numerous other readings are scattered throughout the text of John, some of which will be noted in the pages of this commentary. Those just mentioned, however, are of greater than average importance. On the whole, the Johannine text has fewer variants than most other NT books.

13. Special Problems

a. The Relation of John to the Synoptics

Since both the Gospel of John and the three other Gospels deal with narratives of the life of Jesus, the question of interrelationship naturally occurs. Matthew, Mark, and Luke distinctly resemble one another, not only in general subject and order of narrative but also in many instances of extended discourse. In some of these it would be difficult for anyone but a scholar to identify a given quotation as belonging to any one of the Synoptics, whereas the text of John differs radically in its form and content from the other Gospels.

The Gospel of John parallels the others in general order. It begins with the ministry of John the Baptist, narrates the early contacts with disciples, contains accounts of Jesus' conflicts with the scribes and Pharisees, and places the feeding of the five thousand and the walking on the water at the turning point of his ministry. The story of the Passion Week begins with the entry into Jerusalem and terminates with the Crucifixion and the Resurrection.

On the other hand, John the Baptist's introduction of Jesus to his disciples is highlighted rather than his general preaching-of-repentance ministry. Jesus' initial contact with the disciples is quite different from the calling of the first four disciples as reported elsewhere. The discourses of Jesus in John are mainly apologetic and theological rather than ethical and practical, as in the Sermon on the Mount. Only seven miracles are recounted, and of these only two duplicate those of the Synoptic Gospels. Chronological order is different, for John places a cleansing of the temple early in Jesus' ministry, whereas the Synoptics locate it in Passion Week. The events of the Last Supper, the betrayal, the hearing before Pilate, and the Crucifixion are reported quite differently from the other three Gospels; and the Resurrection account has only slight resemblance to the others.

These phenomena have evoked many questions, and various theories have been advanced to account for them. The similarities are sufficient to establish the identity of the

Jesus of John with the figure of the Synoptics, but the dissimilarities show that John did not lean on the written accounts of Matthew, Mark, and Luke. Whatever interrelationship may have existed between them, there is no convincing evidence that they affected John directly. Reconciliation of the chronological differences and the disparity of content and style may be difficult but it is not impossible. The best conclusion to be drawn is that John was written independently of the others, not simply because he used different sources, but because he had a different purpose in organizing his material. He wrote as a first-hand witness making a special presentation of Jesus. John possessed knowledge of many facts of Jesus' life mentioned in the Synoptics, but he also knew much they did not record. He utilized this material in a different way and shaped it for a different purpose. Each of the Gospel writers presented Jesus in accord with the needs of his readers and out of his own understanding of the Lord. All of them were drawing on the same sources of knowledge and were moved by the same Spirit.

The Johannine style is so different from that of the Synoptics that some scholars have repudiated the historical validity of the Gospel. F.C. Burkitt remarked:

> It is quite inconceivable that the historical Jesus of the Synoptic Gospels could have argued and quibbled with opponents as he is represented to have done in the Fourth Gospel. The only possibility is that the work is not history, but something else in historical form. . . . It is a deliberate sacrifice of historical truth, and as the evangelist is a serious person in deadly earnest, we must conclude that he cared less for truth than for something else (pp. 225, 228).

The current opinion concerning the historicity of John is not quite so drastic as that of Burkitt, whose conclusion overlooks the fact that a writer may have different styles for different occasions. The bulk of the teaching recorded in the first three Gospels was delivered to crowds that gathered to hear his words of wisdom or to opponents who contended with him. The larger part of the teaching in the fourth Gospel (e.g., John 14:17) was intended for the ears of his disciples only. A short passage in Matthew and another in Luke (Matt 11:25–30; Luke 10:21–22) are in similar style. Although these passages are brief, they are sufficient to show that Jesus could, and undoubtedly did, use both approaches in dealing with his contemporaries. Luke indicates that these words were spoken to the seventy-two disciples (NIV) after they had returned from a preaching tour rather than to the multitude at large.

b. Historical and Theological Interpretation

The interpretation of this Gospel has varied from regarding it as a historical narrative containing the *ipsissima verba* (very words) of Jesus to a mythological creation of an anonymous writer who used the name of Jesus to support his approach to Christianity. It may be conceded that the author's interest was primarily theological rather than biographical; indeed, all four Gospels contain theological interpretations of Jesus. The conclusions of any commentator on this aspect of John will be influenced as much by his personal suppositions as by the text. If he regards Jesus as merely a wandering Galilean prophet who happened to possess a singularly devout nature coupled with profound psychological insight, he would almost inevitably treat the Gospel as an allegory or fiction or both. If, on the other hand, he begins with the conviction of the author that "the Word became flesh and lived for a while among us" (John 1:14), he will conclude that the theological nature of the career of Jesus was inescapable and that there could be no other way of interpreting him or the Gospel. If Jesus was the Son of God, any attempted account of him would inevitably be theological; otherwise, it would not do him justice.

The author himself took this viewpoint when he stated that "these [things] are written that you may believe that Jesus is the Christ, the Son of God" (John 20:31). He did not, however, attempt to implement this purpose either by emotional appeal to imaginary scenes or by purely syllogistic reasoning. Like the Synoptics, John used occurrences in the life of Jesus to illustrate his teaching and gave no hint that they were imaginary. The events themselves are actual; the principles they exemplify may be abstract.

Furthermore, if the writer of the fourth Gospel did emphasize theology more than the authors of the Synoptics, he must have had a reason for doing so. The claims and deeds of Jesus, which John professes to have known and not to have fully recorded (John 20:30), demanded an explanation beyond ordinary cause and effect. Even if the author granted that the "signs" were narrated to illustrate some theological principle, it is still logical to believe they were selected because they had that inherent significance and were not composed for the occasion. The significance of the "signs" is determined by what Jesus actually said and did, not by the author's imagination.

While the intent of the author was neither to produce a complete biography of Jesus nor to recount all the miracles he did, there is no need to assume that he fabricated stories. As a matter of fact, the authors of the Synoptics also recount miracles; and while they do not always make their conclusions as explicit theologically as John does, their procedure is much the same. The events recorded in John are historical, though their exact sequence is not always clear. The deductions drawn from them are the basis for Johannine theology.

c. Displacement of Text

The existence of seeming gaps in the order of the fourth Gospel has led some scholars to speculate that the text may have suffered from disarrangement. For instance, some have suggested that the narrative makes better sense if chs. 5 and 6 are inverted. Chapter 6 opens with Jesus crossing "to the far shore of the Sea of Galilee," which had not been mentioned in the preceding context, the scene of which is laid in Jerusalem. John 5 begins with an unnamed feast in Jerusalem that Jesus attended. Since ch. 4 concludes in Galilee, there is a much more natural connection to another event in the same territory if ch. 6 follows at this point. Yet the same abruptness would appear if ch. 7 were to follow ch. 5 immediately. There is no hint in the MS tradition that such a displacement ever occurred. An arbitrary rearrangement of the text only creates another problem in the place of the one that it attempts to solve. Hunter remarks that, while scribal displacements might have occurred, "all such rearranging implies that we know the order John intended—a pretty big assumption" (p. 2).

A further difficulty arises from the size of the so-called displaced segments. If they were all the same length or multiples of the same length, the theory of wrongly arranged codex pages would be plausible. The segments, however, are of odd lengths that cannot be reduced to multiples of the same unit. It is, therefore, unlikely that any accidental dislocation would occur; and there is no convincing reason for concluding that the theoretical displacements were intended. If the author's order does not coincide with our theories, it is better to admit that he has simply utilized episodes without holding strictly to chronological or topographical sequence.

14. Bibliography

Commentaries

Barrett, C.K. *The Gospel According to John.* London: SPCK, 1958.
Bernard, J.H. *The Gospel of John.* ICC. 2 vols. New York: Scribner, 1929.
Brown, Raymond E. *The Gospel According to John.* AB. Vols. 29, 29A. Garden City, N.Y.: Doubleday, 1966, 1970.
Hendriksen, William. *Exposition of the Gospel According to John.* New Testament Commentary. 2 vols. Grand Rapids: Baker, 1953–54.
Hunter, A.M. *The Gospel According to John.* Cambridge Bible Commentary. Edited by P.R. Ackroyd, C.R.C. Leaney, J.W. Packer. Cambridge: Cambridge University, 1965.
Lightfoot, R.H. *St. John's Gospel: A Commentary.* Edited by C.F. Evans. London: Oxford University, 1969.
Lindars, Barnabas. *The Gospel of John.* NCB. London: Oliphants, 1972.
Marsh, John. *The Gospel of St. John.* Pelican New Testament Commentaries. Edited by D.E. Nineham. Hammondsworth, Middlesex, England: Penguin Books, 1972.
Morgan, G. Campbell. *The Gospel of John.* Old Tappan, N.J.: Revell, n.d.
Morris, Leon. *The Gospel According to St. John.* NIC. Grand Rapids: Eerdmans, 1971.
Sanders, J.M., and Mastin, B.A. *The Gospel According to St. John.* Black's New Testament Commentaries. London: Adam & Charles Black, 1968.
Turner, George A., and Mantey, J.R. *The Gospel According to St. John.* Evangelical Commentary. Grand Rapids: Eerdmans, 1964.
Westcott, B.F. *The Gospel According to St. John.* 2 vols. London: John Murray, 1908.

Special Studies

Boice, James. *Witness and Revelation in the Gospel of John.* Grand Rapids: Zondervan, 1970.
Dodd, C.H. *The Interpretation of the Fourth Gospel.* Cambridge: Cambridge University, 1965.
Edwards, H.E. *The Disciple Who Wrote These Things.* London: James Clarke & Co., 1953.
Gardner-Smith, P. *St. John and the Synoptic Gospels.* Cambridge: Cambridge University, 1938.
Headlam, A.C. *The Fourth Gospel as History.* Oxford: Basil Blackwell, 1948.
Higgins, A.J.B. *Jesus and the Son of Man.* Philadelphia: Fortress, 1964.
Hoare, F.R. *Original Order and Chapters of St. John's Gospel.* London: Burns, Oates, & Washbourne, 1944.
Macgregor, G.H.C., and Morton, A.Q. *The Structure of the Fourth Gospel.* Grand Rapids: Eerdmans, 1948.
Morris, Leon. *Studies in the Fourth Gospel.* Grand Rapids: Eerdmans, 1969.
Tenney, Merrill C. *John: The Gospel of Belief.* Grand Rapids: Eerdmans, 1948.

Articles

Albright, W.F. "The Dead Sea Scrolls." *The American Scholar* 23 (1952–53): 77–85. Washington, D.C.: United Chapters of Phi Beta Kappa.
_____. "Recent Discoveries in Palestine and the Gospel of John" in *The Background of the New Testament and Its Eschatology,* edited by L.A. Davis and D. Daube. Cambridge: Cambridge University, 1956, pp. 153–71.
Goodenough, Erwin R. "John: A Primitive Gospel." JBL 64 (1945), Part II, 145–182.
Haas, N. "Anthropological Observations on the Skeletal Remains from Giv'at ha-Mivtar." IEJ 20 (1970): 49–59.
Hanhart, K. "The Structure of John 1:35–54." In *Studies in John: Presented to Dr. J.H. Sevenster on the Occasion of His Seventieth Birthday.* Leiden: Brill, 1970.

Hoehner, Harold. "The Significance of the Year of Our Lord's Crucifixion for NT Interpretation." In *New Dimensions in New Testament Study*, edited by R.N. Longenecker and M.C. Tenney. Grand Rapids: Zondervan, 1974, pp. 115–25.

Metzger, B.M. "On the Translation of John 1:1." ET 63 (1951–52): 125.

Tenney, Merrill C. "The Footnotes of John's Gospel." BS 117 (1960): 350–64.

General Works

Bell, H.I., and Skeat, T.C. *Fragments of an Unknown Gospel.* London: Trustees of the British Museum, 1935.

Burkitt, F.C. *The Gospel History and Its Transmission.* Edinburgh: T. & T. Clark, 1906.

Gaster, Theodor H., ed. *The Dead Sea Scriptures in English Translation.* Garden City, N.Y.: Doubleday, 1956.

Metzger, B.M. *A Textual Commentary on the Greek New Testament.* New York: UBS, 1971.

Roberts, C.H., ed. *An Unpublished Fragment of the Fourth Gospel.* Manchester: Manchester University, Press. 1935.

Robinson, J.A.T. *Redating the New Testament.* Philadelphia: Westminster, 1976.

Smith, William, and Wace, Henry. *A Dictionary of Biography.* 4 vols. London: John Murray, 1880.

Stauffer, Ethelbert. *Jesus and His Story.* New York: Alfred Knopf, 1959.

Torrey, C.C. *The Four Gospels.* New York: Harper, 1933.

Turner, C.H. *Historical Geography of the Holy Land.* Washington, D.C.: Canon Press. 1973.

15. Outline and Map

I. Prologue: Revelation of the Word (1:1–18)
    A. The Preincarnate Word (1:1–5)
    B. The Prophetic Announcement (1:6–8, 15)
    C. The Reception of the Word (1:9–13)
    D. The Incarnation of the Word (1:14, 16–18)
II. The Public Ministry of the Word (1:19–12:50)
    A. The Beginning Ministry (1:19–4:54)
        1. The witness of John the Baptist (1:19–34)
        2. The first disciples (1:35–51)
        3. The first sign (2:1–11)
        4. The interlude at Capernaum (2:12)
        5. The cleansing of the temple (2:13–22)
        6. The interview with Nicodemus (2:23–3:21)
            a. Nicodemus's visit (2:23–3:15)
            b. The author's comment (3:16–21)
        7. Further testimony of John the Baptist (3:22–36)
        8. The Samaritan ministry (4:1–42)
            a. The woman at the well (4:1–26)
            b. The return of the disciples (4:27–38)
            c. The faith of the Samaritans (4:39–42)
        9. The interview with the nobleman (4:43–54)
    B. The Rise of Controversy (5:1–47)
        1. The healing of the paralytic (5:1–15)
        2. Jesus' defense of his sonship (5:16–47)
            a. The prerogatives of sonship (5:16–30)
            b. The witnesses to his authority (5:31–47)
    C. The Beginning of Conflict (6:1–8:59)
        1. The feeding of the five thousand (6:1–15)
        2. The walking on the water (6:16–21)
        3. The address in the synagogue (6:22–59)
        4. The division among the disciples (6:60–71)
        5. The visit to Jerusalem (7:1–52)
            a. The journey (7:1–13)
            b. The popular debate (7:14–36)
            c. The climactic appeal (7:37–44)
            d. The rejection by the leaders (7:45–52)
        6. [The woman taken in adultery (7:53–8:11)]
    D. The Intensification of Controversy (8:12–59)
        1. Teaching in the temple area (8:12–30)
        2. The discourse to professed believers (8:31–47)
        3. The response of the unbelievers (8:48–59)
    E. The Manifestation of Opposition (9:1–11:57)
        1. The healing of the blind man (9:1–41)
            a. The healing (9:1–12)
            b. The consequences (9:13–41)
        2. The Good Shepherd discourse (10:1–21)
        3. The debate in Solomon's Colonnade (10:22–42)

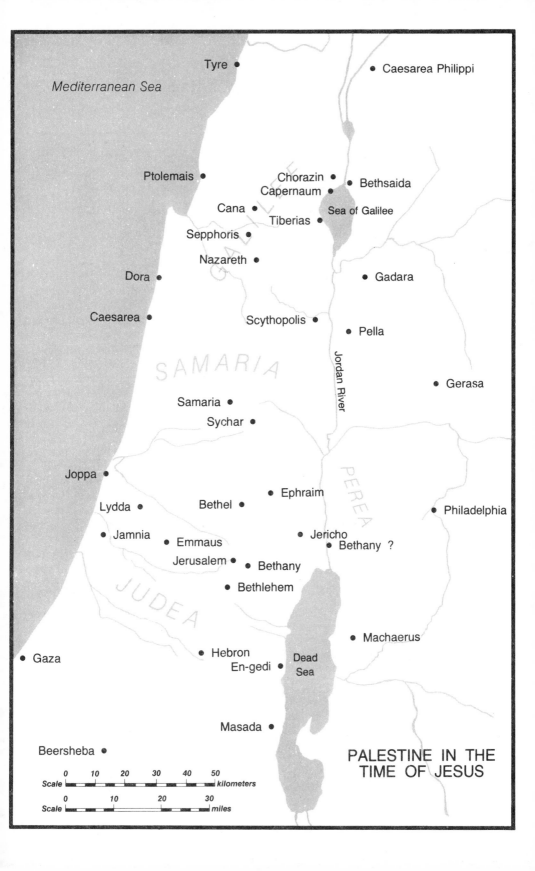

Tyre

Caesarea Philippi

Mediterranean Sea

Ptolemais

Chorazin
Capernaum
Bethsaida

Cana

GALILEE

Sea of Galilee

Sepphoris

Tiberias

Nazareth

Gadara

Dora

Caesarea

Scythopolis

Pella

SAMARIA

Jordan River

Gerasa

Samaria

Sychar

PEREA

Joppa

Ephraim

Lydda

Bethel

Philadelphia

Jamnia

Emmaus

Jericho

Bethany ?

Jerusalem

Bethany

Bethlehem

JUDEA

Machaerus

Gaza

Hebron
En-gedi

Dead
Sea

Masada

Beersheba

Scale 0 10 20 30 40 50 kilometers

Scale 0 10 20 30 miles

PALESTINE IN THE
TIME OF JESUS

Text and Exposition

I. Prologue: Revelation of the Word (1:1–18)

A. *The Preincarnate Word*

1:1–5

> [1]In the beginning was the Word, and the Word was with God, and the Word was God. [2]He was with God in the beginning.
> [3]Through him all things were made; without him nothing was made that has been made. [4]In him was life, and that life was the light of men. [5]The light shines in the darkness, but the darkness has not understood it.

1 "In the beginning" recalls the opening words of Genesis 1:1: "In the beginning God created the heavens and the earth." The expression does not refer to a particular moment of time but assumes a timeless eternity. "Word" is the Greek *logos,* which has several meanings. Ordinarily it refers to a spoken word, with emphasis on the meaning conveyed, not just the sound. *Logos,* therefore, is an expression of personality in communication. Scripture also tells us that it is creative in its power: "By the word [*logos,* LXX] of the Lord were the heavens made, their starry host by the breath of his mouth" (Ps 33:6). This verse clearly implies that the expression of God had creative power and called the universe into being. To the Hebrew "the word of God" was the self-assertion of the divine personality; to the Greek the formula denoted the rational mind that ruled the universe. John is asserting that the "Word" is the source of all that is visible and antedates the totality of the material world.

The use of *logos* implies that John was endeavoring to bring out the full significance of the Incarnation to the Gentile world as well as to the Jewish people. He does not adopt the Greek concept in its entirety, but he uses this term to indicate that Jesus had universal rather than local significance and that he spoke with ultimate authority. He was preexistent, involved in the act of creation, and therefore superior to all created beings. This presentation lifts Christ above the materialistic, pagan concept of deities just as the Incarnation brings the Hebrew concept of God into everyday life.

The preposition "with" in the phrase "the Word was with God" indicates both equality and distinction of identity along with association. The phrase can be rendered "face to face with." It may, therefore, imply personality, coexistence with the Creator, and yet be an expression of his creative being. The position of the noun *God* in the Greek text marks it as a predicate, stressing description rather than individualization. The "Word" was deity, one with God, rather than "a god" or another being of the same class. This is the real meaning of the phrase. Unity of nature rather than similarity or likeness is implied. The external coexistence and unity of the Word with God is unmistakably asserted.

2 This verse may seem to be repetitious, and it is just that, but with divine intent. John succinctly summarizes the great truths of v.1 by the effective means of restatement. The Word's preexistence, distinctiveness, and deity are brought out in the statement "he was with God in the beginning."

3 The word "made" (*egeneto*) has the meaning "became" rather than "constructed." The action refers to an event rather than a process. The visible universe with all its

complexity owes its origin to the creative mind and power of God. Apart from his Word, existence is impossible. The priority of Christ over creation is taught here and it also is mentioned in Colossians 1:16 and Hebrews 1:2.

4 The term "life" (*zōē*) is uniformly used throughout the Gospel. Wherever it appears, it refers either to the principle of physical life (vitality) or, most often, to spiritual life. Frequently it is coupled with the adjective "eternal" to denote the quality and power of the believer's life. It occurs thirty-six times in John. The life was embodied in Christ, who demonstrated perfectly what eternal life is by his career (cf. John 14:6; 17:3). Christ is the "life" that is the "light of men." In him God's purpose and power are made available to men. He is their ultimate hope.

5 The metaphorical contrast between light and darkness as representing the powers of good and evil was common in John's day. The same imagery appears in the Qumran Scrolls, one of which is *The War of the Sons of Light and the Sons of Darkness.* A better translation of v.5b is "The darkness did not overcome it," for the underlying verb (*katelaben*) can be translated both ways. John, however, uses it elsewhere only in the sense of "overtake" or "overcome" (John 6:17; [8:3–4]; 12:35).

Notes

1 The preexistence of the Word is strongly brought out by the phrase Ἐν ἀρχῇ ἦν ὁ λόγος (*en archē ēn ho logos*, "in the beginning was the word"). Ἀρχῇ (*archē*) according to H. Bietenhard "is an important term in Gk. philosophy," which means, among other things, "starting point, original beginning" (DNTT, 1:164). By itself, this may not seem too significant, for few would debate that we are dealing with the "original beginning." It is the presence of the verb ἦν (*ēn*, "was") that brings out the importance of this phrase. Literally, it could and should be rendered "When the beginning began, the Word was already there." This is the sense of *ēn*, which is in the imperfect tense and implies continuing existence in the past. So before the beginning began, the Word was already in existence. This is tantamount to saying that the Word predates time or Creation.

The three statements of v.1 bring out three different aspects of the nature of the Word. The first speaks of his preexistence (see above). The second statement, "The Word was with God," is an assertion of the Word's distinctiveness. The preposition πρός (*pros*) indicates both equality and distinction of identity. Robertson says, "The literal idea comes out well, 'face to face with God'" (RHG, p. 623). Thus this implies personality and coexistence with God. Robertson says it bespeaks of "the fellowship between the Logos and God."

The third statement, "The Word was God," is especially significant. This is a clear statement of deity inasmuch as the noun θεός (*theos*, "God") is anarthrous; that is, it lacks the article. Much confusion has spawned over this point of Gr. grammar. Robertson et al. have aptly demonstrated that the lack of the article in the predicate is intentional so that the subject can be distinguished. In other words, in the phrase θεός ἦν ὁ λόγος (*theos ēn ho logos*, "God was the Word"), were it not for the article ὁ (*ho*) before the word λόγος (*logos*), the subject of the phrase would be indeterminate. But the presence of the article shows that it is the "Word" that is the subject. The fact that *theos* is a predicate shows that it is describing the nature of the Word; he is of the same nature and essence as the noun in the predicate; that is, the Word is divine (RHG, p. 767).

E.C. Colwell says that "a predicate nominative which precedes the verb cannot be translated as an indefinite or 'qualitative' noun solely because of the absence of the article; if the context suggests that the predicate is definite, it should be translated as a definite noun in spite of the absence of the article. In the case of a predicate noun which follows the verb the reverse is true; the absence of the article in this position is a much more reliable indication that the noun is indefinite" ("A Definite Rule for the Use of the Article in the Greek New Testament," JBL 52 [1933]: 20–21).

To say that the absence of the article bespeaks of the nonabsolute deity of the Word is sheer folly. There are many places in this Gospel where the anarthrous *theos* appears (e.g., 1:6, 12, 13, 18), and not once is the implication that this is referring to just "a god."

3 It is significant that the verb used three times in this v. is different from that used in the previous two vv. In vv.1–2 the verb is the imperfect of εἰμί (*eimi*, "to be"), ἦν (*ēn*, "was"), which is a verb describing a state of being. In v.3, however, the verb γίνομαι (*ginomai*, "to become") is used, which has the force of "coming into being." This, then, is another assertion of the deity of the Word. Through him all things "came into being," ἐγένετο (*egeneto*), but he always was (*ēn*). This latter truth is emphasized by the "I am's" of Christ mentioned throughout this Gospel.

5 Καταλαμβάνω (*katalambanō*, "overcome," which is the mg. reading in NIV) is a very forceful word. B. Siede says it "is used in the NT to designate the attack of evil powers.... The lad with epilepsy was attacked by a dumb spirit and dashed to the ground (Mark 9:18)" (TDNT, 3:750). Considering John's underlying concept of the battle between good and evil, perhaps "understood" is too mild a rendering. Metaphorically we have a preview of the triumph of light over darkness, which is later personified in Christ's work on the Cross.

B. *The Prophetic Announcement*

1:6–8, 15

> 6There came a man who was sent from God; his name was John. 7He came as a witness to testify concerning that light, so that through him all men might believe. 8He himself was not the light; he came only as a witness to the light.
>
> 15John testifies concerning him. He cries out, saying, "This was he of whom I said, 'He who comes after me has surpassed me because he was before me.'"

6 In vv.6–8 the human agent for introducing the Word to men is presented. This Gospel stresses the function of John the Baptist rather than his origin or character, as Luke does (Luke 1:5–24, 57–80). John takes for granted that the Baptist's identity was known by the reader. He states his importance as the forerunner of Christ but emphasizes his subordinate role (cf. John 3:22–30). Possibly this was directed toward the sect that survived John and perpetuated his teaching but had no knowledge of the completion of the work of Christ (Acts 18:24–25; 19:1–7). The important thing about John the Baptist was that he was "sent." The use of this word refers to the authority that commissioned him; the identification by name is incidental. John's function is defined in v.7.

7–8 "Witness" is distinctly a Johannine word. It is especially pertinent in this Gospel, which is an attempt to establish by adequate testimony the claims of Jesus as the Son of God. The preaching of John the Baptist, which must have been known to the readers of the fourth Gospel, was preparatory to the coming of the Christ. The Synoptics agree with John on this point (Matt 3:11–12; Mark 1:1–8; Luke 1:17; 3:15–17). John the Baptist told the crowds listening to him that he was only the forerunner of another who would confer on them the Holy Spirit and that they must repent, or change their attitude, in anticipation of meeting him. The author was careful to specify that John the Baptist was not the genuine light but that he came to attest it.

Although vv.6–8 seem alien to the general content of the text, they are not irrelevant. As the Word came to bring the heavenly light to humanity, so John came to speak from a human level and to awaken people to their need of God's revelation.

15 The author reverts to the witness of John the Baptist to explain further the Baptist's position as to Christ. The manifestation of Jesus came after John's appearance, but in importance Jesus took precedence over him. "Surpassed" (*emprosthen*) is the translation of an adverb that denotes positional precedence, whereas "before" (*prōtos*, lit. "first") refers to rank of importance. Jesus surpassed John because he was intrinsically greater.

Notes

6 Ἐγένετο (*egeneto*, "came") is the aorist of γίνομαι (*ginomai*), which was identified as a verb signifying "coming into being" (see Note on v.3). In the Gr. the contrast between the Word's state of always "being" and that of John the Baptist's "coming into being" is unmistakable. Morris says, "Jesus 'was' in the beginning. John 'came into existence' " (NIC, p. 88).

C. The Reception of the Word

1:9–13

> [9]The true light that gives light to every man was coming into the world. [10]He was in the world, and though the world was made through him, the world did not recognize him. [11]He came to that which was his own, but his own did not receive him. [12]Yet to all who received him, to those who believed in his name, he gave the right to become children of God—[13]children born not of natural descent, nor of human decision or a husband's will, but born of God.

9 "True" (*alēthinon*) means "real" or "genuine" as opposed to "facsimile" or "secondary" rather than "false." Christ is the real light of humanity who was about to enter the world. The text should be understood to mean, not that he had already illumined everyone, but that his function would be to give the light of truth to all whom his ministry would affect, whether in greater or lesser degree. The translation is somewhat ambiguous because the participle "coming" used with the verb "was" may refer either to "light" or to "man." An alternate translation is "he was the real light that illuminates every man as he comes into the world." In this context the action of coming better fits the advent of the light than the arrival of every man.

10 "World" (*kosmos*) refers to the current organization or culture in which people live, whether applied to the natural environment (John 16:21) or to the present order as contrasted with the spiritual order (6:14; 9:39; 11:27; 16:28; 18:37). Here it plainly refers to the total environment that the Word created (1:3). The second part of the verse places the emphasis on the ancient world of men and women who did not recognize him. The aorist tense of the verb "know" (*egnō*) implies that there was no flash of awareness concerning his real person. Compare the statement of his opponents on a later occasion: "Isn't this the carpenter's son?" (Matt 13:55).

11 In the phrase "he came to that which was his own, but his own did not receive him," the former "own" refers to things; and the phrase may mean "his own property" or "his home" as in John 19:27. The latter "own" refers to "his own people," the nation he belonged to. Jesus came to the place he had created and had a right to possess. Those who inhabited it turned him away in rejection.

12–13 Just as there is a sharp antithesis in vv.4–5 between darkness and light, so here is an equally direct contrast between rejection and reception. In spite of the many who rejected the Word, there were some who received him. This provides the initial definition of "believe" by equating it with "receive." When we accept a gift, whether tangible or intangible, we thereby demonstrate our confidence in its reality and trustworthiness. We make it part of our own possessions. By being so received, Jesus gives to those who receive him a right to membership in the family of God.

"Become" indicates clearly that people are not the spiritual children of God by natural birth, for we cannot become what we already are. This verb implies a change of nature. The word *children* (*tekna*) is parallel to the Scottish *bairns*—"born ones." It emphasizes vital origin and is used as a term of endearment (cf. Luke 15:31). Believers are God's "little ones," related to him by birth. "Not of natural descent" excludes a purely physical process; "nor of human decision" rules out the result of any biological urge; "or a husband's will" shows that this kind of birth is not merely the outcome of a legal marriage. The relation is spiritual, not biological. NEB translates: ". . . not born of human stock, or by the fleshly desire of a human father." There is a connection with the concept of the new birth, elaborated in Jesus' conversation with Nicodemus (John 3:3–8). There also the writer lays the emphasis on believing, though his approach is different.

Notes

13 In a very few MSS the relative pronoun οἱ (*hoi*, which is rendered "children" in the NIV) and its following verb ἐγεννήθησαν (*egennēthēsan*) are singular ὃς ἐγεννήθη (*hos egennēthē*), not plural. In this case the passage should be translated: "Who was born not of natural descent, nor of human decision or of a husband's will, but born of God." The MS evidence is so slight and so late that it would probably never have been considered had not Tertullian, one of the Latin church fathers at the end of the second century, insisted that it was the correct reading (Tertullian *De Carne Christi* 19). A few quotations from the Latin fathers support his contention, but the reading does not occur in any Greek MSS and is, therefore, regarded as unauthentic.

D. *The Incarnation of the Word*

   1:14, 16–18

   14The Word became flesh and lived for a while among us. We have seen his glory, the glory of the one and only ⌞Son⌟, who came from the Father, full of grace and truth.
   16From the fullness of his grace we have all received one blessing after another. 17For the law was given through Moses; grace and truth came through Jesus Christ. 18No one has ever seen God, but God the only ⌞Son⌟, who is at the Father's side, has made him known.

14 Verse 14 marks the fourth statement about the Word in this introduction to the presentation of Jesus. Note the contrast between vv.1 and 14. Verse 1 states that the Word "was," referring to its permanent condition or state, while v.14 states that the Word "became" flesh, involving a change in state. This is the basic statement of the Incarnation, for Christ entered into a new dimension of existence through the gateway of human birth and took up his residence among men. The verb translated "lived" means "to pitch a tent, to dwell temporarily" (BAG, p. 762). He left his usual place and accepted the conditions of human life and environment, with the attendant temporal limitations that all humans experience. Allusions to this appear elsewhere in various sections of the Gospel (3:17; 6:38–42, 51; 7:29; 8:23; 9:5; 10:36; 16:28).

John's presentation of Christ as the Word is not primarily metaphysical but practical (cf. comment in v.1). The term *Logos* was used by the philosophers of the day, particularly the Stoics, to express the central principle of the universe, the spirit that pervaded the world, or the ultimate Reason that controlled all things. John did not superimpose the philosophical concept on the person of Christ, but he adopted the Greek term as the best medium of expressing the nature of Christ. As the preexistent Son of God, he was the Creator of the world and the Executor of the will of the Father. As the incarnate Son of God, he exercised in his human existence these same powers and revealed effectively the person of the Father.

The writer indicates that he is not speculating on a philosophical concept but is bearing witness to an experiential reality. "We have seen his glory" implies a personal observation of a new reality. Probably there is an allusion to the Transfiguration (Matt 17:2–8; Mark 9:2–8; Luke 9:28–36), when Jesus appeared with a divine radiance and the voice of God acknowledged him as his beloved Son. His incarnation was the full manifestation of grace and truth because it was the greatest possible expression of God's compassion for people and the most perfect way of conveying the truth to their understanding.

The "one and only Son" represents the Greek *monogenēs*, which is derived from *genos*, which means "kind" or "species." It means "literally 'one of a kind,' 'only,' 'unique' (*unicus*), not 'only-begotten.' . . . The emphasis is on the thought that, as the 'only' Son of God, He has no equal and is able fully to reveal the Father" (MM, pp. 416–17). God's personal revelation of himself in Christ has no parallel elsewhere, nor has it ever been repeated.

16 Verse 15 has already been discussed as part of the section concerning John the Baptist. Verse 16 connects directly with v.14, which says that the Son was full of the grace and truth of the Father. The writer reminds his readers that they have already experienced that grace in increasing measure. "One blessing after another" is an attempt to express in modern English the Greek phrase "grace in exchange for [*anti*] grace." When one supply of grace is exhausted, another is available.

17 The contrast between law and grace as methods of God's dealing with men is expressed here as plainly as in the Pauline writings (see Rom 5:20–21; Eph 2:8). The law represented God's standard of righteousness; grace exhibited his attitude to human beings who found that they could not keep the law. This attitude was depicted in the person and life of Jesus. This contrast has a parallel in the argument of Hebrews 3:5–6: "Moses was faithful as a servant in all God's house, testifying to what would be said in the future. But Christ is faithful as a son over God's house." Hebrews stresses the superiority of the Son to a servant. The servant can by his commission administer the law of the house correctly. The Son, who is the ruler of the house, can act with ultimate authority that surpasses the authority of the servant. Compare the words of Jesus in the Sermon on the Mount: "You have heard that it was said. . . . But I tell you" (Matt 5:21–22, 27–28, 33–34, 38–39, 43–44).

18 The noun *God* (*theon*) has no article in the Greek text, which indicates that the author is presenting God in his nature of being rather than as a person. "Deity" might be a more accurate rendering. The meaning is that no human has ever seen the essence of deity. God is invisible, not because he is unreal, but because physical eyes are incapable of detecting him. The infrared and ultraviolet rays of the light spectrum are invisible because the human eye is not sensitive enough to register them. However, photographic plates or a spectroscope can make them visible to us. Deity as a being is consequently known only through spiritual means that are able to receive its (his) communications.

"At the Father's side" is substantially the same expression as that used in John 13:23 concerning "the disciple whom Jesus loved," who "was reclining next to him." It shows intimate association, which presupposes close fellowship. As the confidant of the Father, Jesus is peculiarly qualified to act as the intermediary who can carry the knowledge of God to men. The word translated "is" is more accurately rendered "being," since it is a present participle. This implies constant relationship and presupposes preincarnate existence.

The phrase "has made him known" (*exēgēsato*) comes from the verb from which "exegesis" is derived, which means to "explain" or "interpret." The being and nature of God, which cannot be perceived directly by ordinary senses, has been adequately presented to us by the Incarnation. Obviously the author implies that his writing gives an adequate record of this revelation. The life and words of Jesus are more than an announcement; they are an explanation of God's attitude toward men and of his purpose for them.

Notes

14 Ὡς μονογενοῦς (*hōs monogenous*, "as an only begotten") is another controversial term. The critics of Christ's deity stress the "begotten" aspect, thus asserting that Christ was a "created" being, and this notwithstanding the strong statements to the contrary in vv.1–3. Marcus Dods decries the emphasis on the absoluteness of the phrase by saying, "Ὡς introduces an illustrative comparison, as is indicated by the anarthrous μονογενοῦς. Holtzmann expands thus: 'The impression which the glory made was so specific a character that it could be taken for nothing less than such a glory as an only son has from a father, that is, as the only one of its kind; for besides the μονογενής a father has no other sons' " (EGT, 1:690). Westcott says, "The thought in the original is centered in the personal Being of the Son and not in His generation. Christ is the One only Son, the One to whom the title belongs in a sense completely unique and singular" (p. 12).

18 The phrase "one and only Son" follows the majority of Gr. MSS, which read ὁ μονογενὴς υἱός (*ho monogenēs huios*). A number of MSS, including the two oldest papyri, read "only God" (μονογενὴς θεὸς, *monogenēs theos*). This is supported by a large number of quotations from the Fathers and several other MSS that also include the article ὁ (*ho*). If the rule is accepted that the more difficult reading is preferred—the latter reading in this case—there can be no doubt that this text also asserts the deity of Christ.

II. The Public Ministry of the Word (1:19–12:50)

Having introduced the figure of the incarnate Word by the Prologue, and having identified the forerunner by his name and by his mission, the author proceeds to present the ministry of the Word in some detail. Broadly, the book can be divided into two sections: the public and the private ministries of Christ. The former occupies the larger chronological section; the latter is brief and is closely related to the Passion, which concludes the narrative.

A. The Beginning Ministry (1:19–4:54)

1. The witness of John the Baptist

1:19–34

> [19]Now this was John's testimony when the Jews of Jerusalem sent priests and Levites to ask him who he was. [20]He did not fail to confess, but confessed freely, "I am not the Christ."
>
> [21]They asked him, "Then who are you? Are you Elijah?"
>
> He said, "I am not."
>
> "Are you the Prophet?"
>
> He answered, "No."
>
> [22]Finally they said, "Who are you? Give us an answer to take back to those who sent us. What do you say about yourself?"
>
> [23]John replied in the words of Isaiah the prophet, "I am the voice of one calling in the desert, 'Make straight the way for the Lord.' "
>
> [24]Now some Pharisees who had been sent [25]questioned him, "Why then do you baptize if you are not the Christ, nor Elijah, nor the Prophet?"
>
> [26]"I baptize with water," John replied, "but among you stands one you do not know. [27]He is the one who comes after me, the thongs of whose sandals I am not worthy to untie."
>
> [28]This all happened at Bethany on the other side of the Jordan, where John was baptizing.
>
> [29]The next day John saw Jesus coming toward him and said, "Look, the Lamb of God, who takes away the sin of the world! [30]This is the one I meant when I said, 'A man who comes after me has surpassed me because he was before me.' [31]I myself did not know him, but the reason I came baptizing with water was that he might be revealed to Israel."
>
> [32]Then John gave this testimony: "I saw the Spirit come down from heaven as a dove and remain on him. [33]I would not have known him, except that the one who sent me to baptize with water told me, 'The man on whom you see the Spirit come down and remain is he who will baptize with the Holy Spirit.' [34]I have seen and I testify that this is the Son of God."

19 The miracle of the Incarnation called for witnesses to substantiate its reality. First in order is that of John the Baptist. His preaching attracted such large crowds that the Jewish hierarchy in Jerusalem decided to investigate him. The priests represented the theological authorities of the nation; the Levites were concerned with the ritual and service of the temple. John did not seem to fit into any ecclesiastical category familiar to the Jewish authorities, and his unusual success demanded an explanation.

20 "Christ" is the Greek equivalent of the Hebrew "Messiah," meaning "Anointed." It was the title of the prophesied deliverer, who would bring renewal and political freedom to Israel (cf. John 4:25). John the Baptist disclaimed the title because it had political implications that would have made him appear to the Romans as a potential insurrectionist.

21-22 The suggestion that John the Baptist might be identified with Elijah reflected the Jewish expectation that the return of Elijah would precede the advent of the Messiah. Malachi had prophesied: "See, I will send you the prophet Elijah before that great and dreadful day of the Lord comes. He will turn the hearts of the fathers to their children, and the hearts of the children to their fathers; or else I will come and strike the land with a curse" (Mal 4:5-6). Because John's rough exterior and ascetic tendencies corresponded to Elijah's type of personality (cf. Mark 6:14), some identified him with the stormy prophet who had challenged Ahab (1 Kings 17-19). John rejected the suggestion and denied that he was Elijah raised from the dead. Again they asked, "Are you the Prophet?" referring probably to God's word to Moses: "The Lord your God will raise up for you a prophet like me from among your own brothers. You must listen to him" (Deut 18:15). The identity of "the Prophet" is not clear; and numerous speculations have been offered. Obviously the investigating committee was still uncertain of it. The populace of Jerusalem later ventured the same guess (John 7:40). Since the prophecy said that he would be like Moses, the Jews were inquiring whether Jesus would lead them in a new Exodus and overcome their enemies. When John disclaimed identity with all these persons, the delegation demanded in exasperation, "Who are you?"

23 The reference to Isaiah is taken from the opening words of the second section of the prophet's writing, which deals with the long-range prophecies of the future. It uses the figure of preparing a road for the king through open and uneven territory so that he may travel over a smooth highway. John the Baptist called himself the "roadbuilder" for one greater than he who would follow him with a fuller revelation. Isaiah said that "the glory of the Lord will be revealed, and all mankind together will see it" (Isa 40:5). This "glory" was revealed in the person of Jesus, of whom the writer of the Gospel said, "We have seen his glory" (1:14).

24-25 The Pharisees represented the strict interpreters of the Law and were particularly interested in examining the credentials of any new religious teacher in Judaism. John does not show unvarying hostility toward them. Nicodemus was a Pharisee and was apparently a sincere if unenlightened person. As a class, however, they were hostile toward Jesus because he did not observe traditional rules and because he openly rebuked their superficial and often hypocritical religiosity. When the delegates from the religious leaders in Jerusalem challenged John concerning his right to baptize, he stated that he did not profess to speak with ultimate authority. He was preaching repentance (Luke 3:3) and was calling for baptism as a confession of repentance in expectation of the greater person who was yet to appear.

26-27 It is not unlikely that John's baptism followed the pattern of proselyte baptism, which required a renunciation of all evil, complete immersion in water, and then reclothing as a member of the holy community of law-keepers.

John drew his reference to untying the sandals of his successor from the practice of using the lowest slave of a household to remove the sandals and wash the feet of guests. John's witness, therefore, reflected the exalted nature of Jesus and placed the latter far above himself.

28 "Bethany on the other side of Jordan" was so named to distinguish it from the Bethany near Jerusalem (see John 12:1). Its exact site is unknown. That it was located "on the other side" shows that the author must have been accustomed to thinking of the west side of the Jordan as his home territory.

29 The chronological scheme of this section is indicated by the reference to successive days: the first day, when the delegation from Jerusalem questioned John (1:19–28); the "next" (second) day, when John saw Jesus approaching (1:29–34); the "next" (third) day, when John pointed out Jesus to his disciples and when they visited him (1:35–42); and the "next" (fourth) day, when Jesus "decided to leave for Galilee" (1:43–50). A reference to the "third day" appears in John 2:1, suggesting a continuing sequence, but it seems ambiguous. If each of these "days" is regarded as one of a series, the "third day" will not fit the scheme since four days have already been mentioned. If the uses of "next" are all references to the same day, meaning "next after the first," they do not explain satisfactorily the differences in action. Perhaps the best solution is to interpret "the third day" as the third day after the departure to Cana. If Jesus were encountered first by the disciples on the east bank of the Jordan River somewhere opposite Jericho, the journey to Cana would have taken at least two days, if not a little longer.

The witness of John the Baptist was positive as well as negative and focused on Jesus rather than on himself. Verses 29–34 contain his presentation of the person of Jesus. Two aspects stand out in the titles by which he introduced Jesus. "The Lamb of God" reflects the sacrificial character of Christ's mission. The word here translated "Lamb" (*amnos*) appears in only four places in the NT: twice in this chapter (1:29, 36), once in Acts 8:32, and again in 1 Peter 1:19. The passage in 1 Peter is an allusion to Isaiah 53:7: "He was led like a lamb to the slaughter, and as a sheep before her shearers is silent, so he did not open his mouth." In the NT the quotations from Isaiah 53 apply directly to Christ (Matt 8:17; Luke 22:37; John 12:38; Acts 8:32–35; 1 Peter 2:22–24). These references assert the atoning work of Christ, who by one final sacrifice of himself removed the guilt of our sins and opened the way to God. John the Baptist limited his own function to introducing Jesus and declared that the latter could take away sin.

The sacrifice of a lamb to take away sin appears frequently in the OT. Offerings by Abel and Noah are mentioned (Gen 4:4; 8:20), but the first specific mention of a lamb is the offering of Isaac by Abraham (Gen 22:2–8). A lamb was prescribed as a guilt-offering (Lev 14:10–25) and as an accompaniment of taking the Nazirite vow (Num 6:1, 12). These have no direct messianic connection. But obviously the title used by John relates Jesus directly to an atoning ministry and death. In Revelation the same concept appears (Rev 5:6–13; 6:1–3, 5, 7; 7:9–10, 14, 17; 13:8; 14:1, 4, 9–10; 15:2–3; 19:7, 9; 21:9, 14, 22, 23; 22:1, 3), though the term for "Lamb" is different (*arnion*). Revelation employs this as a triumphal title, memorializing the completion of Christ's sacrificial work. It combines in one descriptive term the concepts of innocence, voluntary sacrifice, substitutionary atonement, effective obedience, and redemptive power like that of the Passover lamb (Exod 12:21–27). The theology of atonement is developed more fully in the First Epistle of John than in the Gospel (1 John 1:7; 2:2; 4:9–14), but the allusions to the atonement in the Gospel are unmistakable (1:29; 3:14; 6:51; 10:11; 11:49–52; 12:24; 18:11).

30 This verse is essentially a restatement of v.15. There is one significant addition, however. John says, "A man who comes after me." The Greek term *anēr* is introduced here; it means "man" with emphasis on maleness—an emphasis that is lost in the more generic *anthrōpos*. This use of *anēr* intimates the headship of Christ over his followers in the sense of the man-woman relationship in marriage (TDNT, 2:563).

31 The identity of the Messiah was unknown to John the Baptist. This does not mean, necessarily, that John did not know Jesus, for, after all, they were relatives (Luke 1:36). John's ministry was twofold: he sought to lead his hearers to repentance (Mark 1:4) and he was to reveal Messiah to Israel. Somehow John understood that the revelation of Messiah would take place in conjunction with his baptizing ministry; therefore, he remained faithful to his calling. However, even after Messiah had been revealed to Israel at the baptism of Jesus, John continued the other aspect of his ministry.

32–33 Another aspect of John's witness related to the work of the Holy Spirit, who both authenticated the mission of Jesus and was the seal of his work in individual lives. John did not pretend to impart the Spirit to his followers; he could only announce that Jesus would do so. To "baptize with the Holy Spirit" means that just as the common experience of baptism in water signified repentance and confession of sin, so the indwelling of the Holy Spirit is the seal and dynamic of the new life. Repentance and confession are the conditions on which the believer receives the gift of the Spirit (cf. Acts 2:38; Gal 3:2; 5:16–25).

The manifestation of the presence of the Spirit in Jesus' case was visible. The Gospel records the Baptist's subsequent reflection on the event. Luke's Gospel preserves the testimony of eyewitnesses who reproduced the actual scene. The phenomena of the descent of the Spirit and the voice from heaven identified Jesus unmistakably as the predicted Messiah and prompted another aspect of John's witness.

34 John the Baptist's solemn avowal that he had seen the descent of the Spirit on Jesus and that he is the Son of God is the climax of his testimony. The significance of the title can be best understood in the light of 1:18, which emphasized the revelatory function of sonship. Since Jesus shared the nature of the Father, he was able to reveal him understandably. Jesus is the final word from God, for nobody else has such a close relationship to deity, nor is there any other who has been similarly commissioned. The prophets spoke for God, but none of them could say that he came "from the bosom of the Father" (1:18, lit. Gr.). John's emphatic declaration was the reason why the disciples left him to follow Jesus.

Notes

1 The sequence of the "days" in John 1:19–2:1 is paralleled to some degree by the last week of Jesus' life introduced in John 12:1. The "days" of the first series begin with 1:19 and of the second series with 12:1.

Series 1	Series 2
1. Self-identification of John (1:19–28)	1. Presentation of Jesus at Bethany (12:1–11)
2. Announcement of the Son of God (1:29–34)	2. Entry into Jerusalem (12:12–50)
3. Introduction of first disciples (1:35–42)	3. Last Supper with disciples (chs. 13–17)

4. Nathanael: "The King of Israel" (1:43–51)

4. Crucifixion: "The King of the Jews" (18–19:37)

5. A day of silence

5. Burial and silence (19:38–42)

6. "The third day"—the wedding (2:1-5)

6. "The third day"—resurrection (ch. 20)

7. The first miracle (2:6–11)

7. The last miracle (ch. 21)

---

2. The first disciples

1:35–51

35The next day John was there again with two of his disciples. 36When he saw Jesus passing by, he said, "Look, the Lamb of God!"

37When the two disciples heard him say this, they followed Jesus. 38Turning around, Jesus saw them following and asked, "What do you want?"

They said, "Rabbi" (which means Teacher), "where are you staying?"

39"Come," he replied, "and you will see."

So they went and saw where he was staying, and spent that day with him. It was about the tenth hour.

40Andrew, Simon Peter's brother, was one of the two who heard what John had said and who had followed Jesus. 41The first thing Andrew did was to find his brother Simon and tell him, "We have found the Messiah" (that is, the Christ).

42Then he brought Simon to Jesus, who looked at him and said, "You are Simon son of John. You will be called Cephas" (which, when translated, is Peter).

43The next day Jesus decided to leave for Galilee. Finding Philip, he said to him, "Follow me."

44Philip, like Andrew and Peter, was from the town of Bethsaida. 45Philip found Nathanael and told him, "We have found the one Moses wrote about in the Law, and about whom the prophets also wrote—Jesus of Nazareth, the son of Joseph."

46"Nazareth! Can anything good come from there?" Nathanael asked.

"Come and see," said Philip.

47When Jesus saw Nathanael approaching, he said of him, "Here is a true Israelite, in whom there is nothing false."

48"How do you know me?" Nathanael asked.

Jesus answered, "I saw you while you were still under the fig tree before Philip called you."

49Then Nathanael declared, "Rabbi, you are the Son of God; you are the King of Israel."

50Jesus said, "You believe because I told you I saw you under the fig tree. You shall see greater things than that." 51He then added, "I tell you the truth, you shall see heaven open, and the angels of God ascending and descending on the Son of Man."

35–36 The section immediately following John's testimony gives the response of Jesus' first disciples, who came to him largely because of John's influence. The whole section is tied together by a chronological framework that begins in v.29 of the preceding section and continues in the following section with a reference to "the third day" (John 2:1). The entire episode of John's introduction of Jesus and the opening of his public ministry is treated as a unit in the recollection of the writer. The first section deals with John's preparatory statement; the second, with the initial meeting between Jesus and his potential disciples; and the third, with the sign that demonstrated his power and confirmed their faith. The repeated allusion to the Lamb (*amnos*) of God focused the attention of John's disciples on Jesus as the basis for the divine forgiveness of sin and for the assurance that their repentance would be accepted. It stirred their interest and prompted them to investigate who Jesus was.

37–39 As John's disciples followed him, Jesus turned to challenge their motives by asking, "What do you want?" He probed them to find out whether they were motivated by idle curiosity or by a real desire to know him. Their reply was not merely an inquiry for his address but a courteous request for an interview. "Rabbi" was a term of respect accorded Jewish teachers (1:49). Literally, it means "Master." It was applied to John the Baptist (3:26), and in a longer form Mary Magdalene used it in addressing Jesus (20:16). Jesus encouraged the two disciples to become acquainted with him and to spend time with him. "The tenth hour" probably means about four o'clock in the afternoon, since Jewish time was ordinarily reckoned from sunrise. If "that day" implies any great length of time, the two disciples must have remained with Jesus overnight. "That day" would have to be interpreted loosely as including the next day, which by Jewish practice would begin at sunset.

40 Of the two disciples who heard John, only Andrew is named. The identity of the other is uncertain, though it may well have been the author himself. Throughout the Gospel it is obvious that he had an interest in Simon Peter. On this occasion the author wished to explain the origin of Simon's association with Jesus.

41 Andrew's testimony shows that the interview of the preceding hours must have been related to Jewish hopes and to Jesus' character. The statement "We have found the Messiah" does not necessarily imply an explicit claim by Jesus, but it does indicate a settled conclusion on the part of Andrew. Andrew's declaration does not imply that he had a correct concept of Jesus' messiahship. It only shows that he regarded Jesus as the candidate for that title. The expectation of a national deliverer was widespread in Judaism in the first third of the first century. Probably all the disciples expected that Jesus would fulfill their hopes for an independent kingdom and consequent political power for those who joined him (cf. Mark 10:28, 35–45).

42 The introduction of Peter to Jesus was brief but direct. The simple pronouncement " 'You are Simon son of John. You will be called Cephas' (which, when translated, is Peter)" was really a diagnosis of Peter's personality. Simon, or Simeon (cf. Acts 15:14), was the name of Jacob's second oldest son (Gen 29:33), who, with his brother Levi (29:34), had ruthlessly avenged the violation of their sister by one of the Canaanite princes (Gen 34:25–31). The rash and impulsive character of Simeon was mirrored in Simon, whose conduct as reported by all the Gospels reflects the same recklessness and tendency to violence (cf. John 18:10). Jesus accepted Simon as he was but promised that he should become Cephas, an Aramaic name, which, like the Greek "Peter," means "a rock." The development of Peter as recorded in this Gospel demonstrates the progress of that change.

43–45 Whereas the first disciples were introduced to Jesus by John the Baptist or by one of the other disciples, Jesus took the initiative in calling Philip. He, like Andrew and Peter, was a Galilean and quite likely a fisherman. The name Bethsaida, his hometown, means "house of fishing." Like Andrew, Philip found another, Nathanael, and by his witness brought him to Jesus. The identity of Nathanael is uncertain. Some have equated him with Bartholomew, others with Matthew. Since Bartholomew equals Bar-Tolmai, "son of Tolmai," it is not a proper name but merely indicates ancestry; and Nathanael Bar-Tolmai would be parallel to Simon Bar-Jona. The name Nathanael means "Gift of God." Since Matthew means "Gift of Jahweh," some have equated Nathanael and Matthew, but without convincing proof. Hanhart suggests that Nathanael represents Matthew and represents the first Gospel, with which John was familiar (pp. 22–24). Hanhart's argument is circuitous and seems fanciful.

Nathanael seems to have been a student of the Torah, or Pentateuch. Philip appealed to him on the basis of the prediction in the Law and the Prophets. Jesus' phrase "under the fig tree" (v.48) was used in rabbinic literature to describe meditation on the Law.

46 The response of Nathanael indicates that Nazareth did not enjoy a good reputation in Galilee. Perhaps Nathanael, who came from Bethsaida, looked down on Nazareth as a rival village, either poorer or morally worse than his own.

47–51 Jesus' comment on Nathanael suggests that the latter had been reading of Jacob's experience at Bethel (Gen 28:10–17). Jacob was filled with guile and had been forced to leave home because he had lied to his father and had swindled his brother. If under these circumstances Jacob was eligible for a revelation from God, would not Nathanael be even more worthy of such a blessing? Jesus said that Nathanael was free from guile (KJV) and used the imagery of Jacob's dream to describe the greater revelation he would give to Nathanael. Jesus implied that he himself would be the medium of that revelation, and his order of the angels' procedure implies that they rose from earth to heaven with their inquiries and then returned to earth with the answers. His mission is to answer human need and to make sure that the answers are proclaimed. The term "Son of Man" is used here for the first time in John's Gospel. According to all the Gospels, Jesus used it concerning himself to represent his relation with human affairs. For a fuller treatment of this title, see the comment on John 13:31.

3. The first sign

2:1-11

> [1]On the third day a wedding took place at Cana in Galilee. Jesus' mother was there, [2]and Jesus and his disciples had also been invited to the wedding. [3]When the wine was gone, Jesus' mother said to him, "They have no more wine."
>
> [4]"Dear woman, why do you involve me?" Jesus replied, "My time has not yet come."
>
> [5]His mother said to the servants, "Do whatever he tells you."
>
> [6]Nearby stood six stone water jars, the kind used by the Jews for ceremonial washing, each holding from twenty to thirty gallons.
>
> [7]Jesus said to the servants, "Fill the jars with water"; so they filled them to the brim.
>
> [8]Then he told them, "Now draw some out and take it to the master of the banquet."
>
> They did so, [9]and the master of the banquet tasted the water that had been turned into wine. He did not realize where it had come from, though the servants who had drawn the water knew. Then he called the bridegroom aside [10]and said, "Everyone brings out the choice wine first and then the cheaper wine after the guests have had too much to drink; but you have saved the best till now."
>
> [11]This, the first of his miraculous signs, Jesus performed in Cana of Galilee. He thus revealed his glory, and his disciples put their faith in him.

1 The wedding at Cana is linked to the preceding text by a chronological tie: "on the third day." Whether this means that "the next day" of vv.29, 35, and 43 refers to three events on the same day, or whether the "third day" means three days after Jesus' departure from the place of baptism, is not clear. The latter alternative seems more probable, for some time would be necessary for traveling; and Jesus with his new disciples could hardly have journeyed back to Cana in less than two days' time. The entire span between John's initial introduction of Jesus and the appearance at Cana can hardly have been less than a week.

Cana was a village in the hills of Galilee. Its exact location is disputed, but the best site seems to be that of Khirbet Qana, about nine miles north of Nazareth. It lay on a road that ran from Ptolemais on the Mediterranean coast southeastward to Sepphoris, the center of Roman administration in Galilee, and thence southward through Nazareth to Samaria and Jerusalem.

2–3 A wedding is always a gala occasion, and in a village like Cana it would be a community celebration. "Refreshments" were provided for all guests. Of these, wine was very important. To fail in providing adequately for the guests would involve social disgrace. In the closely knit communities of Jesus' day, such an error would never be forgotten and would haunt the newly married couple all their lives. The situation prompted Mary's urgency when she informed Jesus of the emergency.

4–5 Jesus' reply to Mary was not so abrupt as it seems. "Woman" (*gynai*) was a polite form of address. Jesus used it when he spoke to his mother from the cross (19:26) and also when he spoke to Mary Magdalene after the Resurrection (20:15). Two translations of Jesus' rejoinder to his mother are possible: (1) "What business is that of ours?" or (2) "What authority do you have over me?" The second alternative is based on the analogy of the question of the demoniac, "What do you want with us, Son of God?" (Matt 8:29), which employs exactly the same phraseology. Since Jesus' mother expressed neither surprise nor resentment, the former translation is probably more acceptable in this instance. She acknowledged that he should act independently, and she confidently told the servants to follow his orders. She fully expected that he would take appropriate action. He did indicate that he was no longer under her authority but that he was living by a new pattern timed by the purpose of God. Jesus had begun his miracles, not at the request of earthly parents whom he still respected, but according to the purpose of his heavenly Father. The "time" refers to the first hour when he manifested the real reason for which he came: "Father, the hour has come. Glorify your Son, that your Son may glorify you" (John 17:1).

6–7 The stone jars were large, containing about twenty gallons apiece. By the social rules of the day each guest was expected to wash his hands before eating, and a considerable amount of water would be needed for this. At the lowest estimate, 120 gallons of water would be available. If made into wine, it would supply approximately two thousand four-ounce glasses; and if, as was frequently customary, the wine was further diluted by three parts of water to one of wine, there would have been enough to last for several days.

8–10 The "master of the banquet" was not the host; he was the headwaiter or toastmaster. Usually he was called in to take care of the distribution of food and drink at a large social occasion. He was astounded by the high quality of the wine since generally a poorer quality was served once the taste of the guests became dulled.

11 The purpose of Jesus' first miracle after entering Galilee is not stated. In fact, for the most part its occurrence was unknown. The specific details of place and time emphasize the historicity of the miracle and lessen the likelihood that it should be interpreted allegorically. The nature of the miracle is very plain. Jesus had come to bring about conversion: water to wine, sinners to saints. And this latter miracle of transformation occurred in almost complete obscurity. Few know when or how it happened, but they know that it did happen.

The effect of this miracle is noteworthy. It marked the beginning of a ministry accompanied by supernatural power; and it proved so convincing to the new disciples that they "put their faith in him." The deed helped confirm the conclusion they had drawn from their previous interviews with him: Jesus must be the Messiah.

4. The interlude at Capernaum

2:12

> [12]After this he went down to Capernaum with his mother and brothers and his disciples. There they stayed for a few days.

12 This verse covers an unspecified period of time. It is introduced by the indefinite phrase "after this" and it says that Jesus' family and disciples stayed at Capernaum "for a few days." There is no clear indication that Jesus traveled in Galilee for some time between this sojourn and his trip to Jerusalem. Since the synoptic Gospels seem to imply that he had an early ministry in Galilee, it may fit at this point.

The allusion to Jesus' brothers recurs also in the synoptic Gospels. According to Mark 6:3, Jesus had four brothers and some sisters. Little is said about them in the Gospels; and only James appears later in the Book of Acts, as the moderator of the church in Jerusalem. Another allusion to them occurs in John 7:2–10. Several interpretations have been offered concerning Jesus' siblings: (1) they were children of Joseph by a previous marriage, (2) they were really Jesus' cousins, or (3) they were younger children of Joseph and Mary. The second view is probably incorrect since the word for cousin (*anepsios*) existed in the Greek language and could have been used if needed. The theory that they may have been stepbrothers of Jesus might be possible and might explain why Jesus did not bequeath the care of his mother to them at the time of his death. The most logical solution is to conclude that they were younger children of Joseph and Mary, born subsequent to Jesus. It accords with the implication of Matthew 1:24–25. The first or second view is supported by those who contend for the perpetual virginity of Mary.

5. The cleansing of the temple

2:13–22

> [13]When it was almost time for the Jewish Passover, Jesus went up to Jerusalem. [14]In the temple courts he found men selling cattle, sheep and doves, and others sitting at tables exchanging money. [15]So he made a whip out of cords, and drove all from the temple area, both sheep and cattle; he scattered the coins of the money changers and overturned their tables. [16]To those who sold doves he said, "Get these out of here! How dare you turn my Father's house into a market!"

¹⁷His disciples remembered that it is written: "Zeal for your house will consume me."

¹⁸Then the Jews demanded of him, "What miraculous sign can you show us to prove your authority to do all this?"

¹⁹Jesus answered them, "Destroy this temple, and I will raise it again in three days."

²⁰The Jews replied, "It has taken forty-six years to build this temple, and you are going to raise it in three days?" ²¹But the temple he had spoken of was his body. ²²After he was raised from the dead, his disciples recalled what he had said. Then they believed the Scripture and the words that Jesus had spoken.

13-14 About the time of the Passover, Jesus went up to Jerusalem from Galilee for the annual feast. The narrative poses a chronological puzzle, for the synoptic Gospels unitedly attach this event to Jesus' last visit to Jerusalem at the time of his death (see Matt 21:10-17; Mark 11:15-19; Luke 19:45-46). Either John is right and the Synoptics mistaken, or the Synoptics are right and John mistaken, or John has transplanted the account for topical or theological purposes, or there were *two* such occasions, only one of which was recorded by John and the other by the Synoptics. While each of these theories has been argued with some degree of logic, the last seems the best. The language of John and that of the Synoptics differ strongly. Sheep and oxen are not mentioned in the Synoptics; John does not allude to Jesus' command not to carry merchandise through the temple (Mark 11:16); the Synoptics do not mention Jesus' challenge, "Destroy this temple, and I will raise it again in three days" (John 2:19). Matthew and Mark, however, mention these words in connection with the trial before the Sanhedrin. Two witnesses appeared to testify that he had threatened to destroy the temple and to rebuild it in three days (Matt 26:61; Mark 14:57-58). Both mention that the accusation was repeated by the mob at the Crucifixion (Matt 27:39-40; Mark 15:29-30). Jesus' words must have impressed the crowd sufficiently so that they were remembered. It is not at all improbable that he may have cleansed the temple twice, two Passovers apart, and that the second so enraged the hierarchy that their animosity toward him exploded into drastic action. Interfering with their privileges once was impudent, twice would be inexcusable.

The sale of cattle and doves and the privilege of exchanging money were permitted in the temple court as a convenience for pilgrims who would need animals for sacrifice and temple shekels for their dues. Under the chief priests, however, the concessions had become merely a means of making money and had debased the temple into a commercial venture.

15-16 Jesus' action precipitated wild confusion. The animals would be bawling and running about aimlessly; the money changers would be scrambling for their coins in the dust and debris on the floor of the court; the officials would be arguing with Jesus about the rights of the case. Jesus' expression "my Father's house" reveals his feeling toward God. The merchandising of privilege was an insult to God and a desecration of the Father's house.

17 Jesus' vehemence revealed his inward passion for the Father and his jealous guardianship of the Father's interests. The Scripture brought to the disciples' minds is Psalm 69:9, from which other passages have been applied to Christ, dealing with his anguish of soul (vv.1-4), the gall and vinegar of the Cross (v.21), and his estrangement from his people (v.8).

18–21 The Jews' demand for a sign is quite in agreement with their general attitude toward Jesus during his lifetime. He commented on it at a later occasion when the Pharisees said, "Teacher, we want to see a miraculous sign from you" (Matt 12:38). He replied, "A wicked and adulterous generation asks for a miraculous sign! But none will be given it except the sign of the prophet Jonah" (v.39). Both Matthew and Mark cite a later instance that practically duplicates this one (Matt 16:1; Mark 8:11), and Luke adds one that may be still another (Luke 11:16). On this particular occasion, however, Jesus answered enigmatically, "Destroy this temple, and I will raise it in three days" (John 2:19). His critics assumed that he was speaking of Herod's temple, which had been in process of construction for forty-six years and was still incomplete. Jesus, says the author, really meant the temple of his body, which he would raise up in three days' time.

22 The author's comment indicates that from the first of his ministry Jesus had the end of it in view. One can hardly escape the conviction that the fourth Gospel depicts the career of Jesus as a voluntary progress toward a predetermined goal. The allusions to the destruction of the temple of his body (2:22), to the elevation on a cross (3:14; 12:32–33), to the giving of his flesh for the life of the world (6:51), to his burial (12:7), and the announcement of his betrayal and death to his disciples (13:19, 21) attest to his consciousness of the fate that awaited him in Jerusalem. Though the disciples did not comprehend the situation during Jesus' career, the Resurrection placed the memory of his sayings in a new perspective. The author's note illustrates the principle that the Gospel presents the life of Jesus in the light of the Resurrection and of the apostolic experience based on the results of that event.

Notes

---

19 The distinction in the words translated "temple" in vv.14 and 19–21 is worth noting. In v.14 the word is ἱερόν (*hieron*), which refers to a "shrine" or "holy building." This usage is consistent throughout the NT. The word ναός (*naos*) appears in vv.19–21 and signifies the "dwelling place" of deity. In the NT it is used metaphorically of the bodies of believers (1 Cor 3:16–17; 6:19). So whereas the Jews were thinking in terms of a physical building, Jesus was referring to his body. The apparent threat to destroy the temple was long remembered by Jesus' enemies. Not only did the false witnesses quote him at the time of his appearance before the Sanhedrin (Matt 26:60–61; Mark 14:57–58), but the same accusation was repeated at the arraignment of Stephen: "For we have heard him say that this Jesus of Nazareth will destroy this place [the temple] and change the customs Moses handed down to us" (Acts 6:14).

21–22 Jesus' technique of using a paradoxical statement to bewilder his enemies, which he subsequently explained for his disciples, frequently appears in John's Gospel. In this instance the disciples understood the enigma after the Resurrection and by their realization came to a fuller knowledge of the truth.

---

6. *The interview with Nicodemus (2:23–3:21)*

a. *Nicodemus's visit*

2:23–3:15

   ²³Now while he was in Jerusalem at the Passover Feast, many people saw the miraculous signs he was doing and believed in his name. ²⁴But Jesus would not

entrust himself to them, for he knew all men. [25]He did not need man's testimony about man, for he knew what was in a man.

[1]Now there was a man of the Pharisees named Nicodemus, a member of the Jewish ruling council. [2]He came to Jesus at night and said, "Rabbi, we know you are a teacher who has come from God. For no one could perform the miraculous signs you are doing if God were not with him."

[3]In reply Jesus declared, "I tell you the truth, unless a man is born again, he cannot see the kingdom of God."

[4]"How can a man be born when he is old?" Nicodemus asked. "Surely he cannot enter a second time into his mother's womb to be born!"

[5]Jesus answered, "I tell you the truth, unless a man is born of water and the Spirit, he cannot enter the kingdom of God. [6]Flesh gives birth to flesh, but the Spirit gives birth to spirit. [7]You should not be surprised at my saying, 'You must be born again.' [8]The wind blows wherever it pleases. You hear its sound, but you cannot tell where it comes from or where it is going. So it is with everyone born of the Spirit."

[9]"How can this be?" Nicodemus asked.

[10]"You are Israel's teacher," said Jesus, "and do you not understand these things? [11]I tell you the truth, we speak of what we know, and we testify to what we have seen, but still you people do not accept our testimony. [12]I have spoken to you of earthly things and you do not believe; how then will you believe if I speak of heavenly things? [13]No one has ever gone into heaven except the one who came from heaven—the Son of Man. [14]Just as Moses lifted up the snake in the desert, so the Son of Man must be lifted up, [15]that everyone who believes in him may have eternal life.

23–24 The interview with Nicodemus is connected with the first trip to Jerusalem. Jesus had already begun performing miraculous works. These signs attracted the attention of the crowd and brought many to a stage of belief parallel to that of the disciples (2:11). They reasoned that since Jesus possessed such power, he must have the favor of God—a line of reasoning followed later by the blind man (9:30–33). Jesus, however, was not satisfied with a superficial faith, even though it was genuine as far as it went. He did not trust himself to those who had professed belief only on the basis of his miracles.

25 Jesus had a thorough understanding of human nature. The principle stated here is basic to his dealing with all the personalities mentioned in the Gospel. He could read people more accurately than a doctor can read physical symptoms in diagnosing an illness. The prelude of these verses (23–25) is introductory to the three typical interviews in chs. 3 and 4: Nicodemus the Pharisee, the Samaritan woman, and the royal official at Cana.

3:1 Nicodemus was introduced as a man of the upper class, conservative in his beliefs, and definitely interested in Jesus' teaching. As a Pharisee he belonged to the strict religious sect of Judaism in contrast to the Sadducees, who were less rigid in their beliefs and were more politically minded. As a member of the ruling council or Sanhedrin, he would have been sensitive to the prevailing doctrinal trends of the time. His interest in Jesus had been prompted by the miracles he had witnessed, and he came for an interview to obtain more information. His approach shows that he was cautious, open-minded, and ready to receive a new revelation from God if he was sure of its genuineness.

2 The fact that Nicodemus came by night does not necessarily mean that he was timid, though in the light of the later references to him in this Gospel he does not seem to have been aggressive in his discipleship (7:45–52; 19:38–42). His salutation was courteous, and he showed no sign of hostility.

3 Jesus' reply was cryptic and abrupt. He informed Nicodemus that no man could even see the kingdom of God without a spiritual rebirth. Birth is our mode of entrance into the world and brings with it the potential equipment for adjustment to the world. To be born again, or "born from above," means a transformation of a person so that he is able to enter another world and adapt to its conditions. *Anōthen,* which NIV and many others translate as "again," in the Johannine writings normally means "from above," and it should be rendered thus here. To belong to the heavenly kingdom, one must be born into it.

4 Nicodemus's reply may be interpreted in two ways. At first sight he appears to be quite materialistic in his attitude, thinking that Jesus was advocating the impossibility of a second physical birth. On the other hand, he may not have so understood Jesus' statement. Perhaps he meant, "How can a man whose habits and ways of thinking have been fixed by age expect to change radically?" Physical rebirth is impossible, but is spiritual change any more feasible?

5 In response, Jesus repeated his solemn assertion, "I tell you the truth [KJV, 'verily, verily'], unless a man is born of water and the Spirit, he cannot enter the kingdom of God." Various interpretations have been suggested for the water. Does it refer to natural birth, which is accompanied by watery fluid? Or is it a symbol of the Spirit (John 7:37–39) so that "water" and "Spirit" are merely a hendiadys, two words referring to the same thing? Or is it a symbol of baptism? The best answer seems to be that if Jesus was attempting to clarify his teaching for Nicodemus, he would answer in familiar terms; and the author would want his readers to understand his phraseology. Since Jesus' ministry came shortly after that of John the Baptist, Jesus may have been referring to John's preaching, which dealt with the baptism of water, signifying repentance, and with the coming messenger of God who would endow men with the Holy Spirit (John 1:31–33). The new birth is conditioned on the repentance and confession of the individual in response to the appeal of God and by the transformation of life by the gift of the Holy Spirit.

6–8 Jesus asserted that the entrance into the kingdom of God that Nicodemus desired could not be achieved by legalism or outward conformity. It requires an inner change. Membership in the kingdom of God is not a prerogative of any particular race or culture, nor is it hereditary. It is given only by the direct act of God. The origin and the destination of the wind are unknown to the one who feels it and acknowledges its reality. Just so, the new life of one born of the Spirit is unexplainable by ordinary reasoning; and its outcome is unpredictable, though its actuality is undeniable.

9 Nicodemus's question "How can this be?" should not be interpreted as an exclamation expressing incredulity. Rather, it is a plea for direction. He wanted to know how this experience could become his. Nothing in the Judaism he knew offered anything like this. It is true that Jesus' words are paralleled by a promise in Ezekiel: "I will sprinkle clean water on you, and you will be clean; I will cleanse you from all your impurities and from all your idols. I will give you a new heart and put a new spirit in you; I will remove from

you your heart of stone and give you a heart of flesh. And I will put my Spirit in you and move you to follow my decrees and be careful to keep my laws" (Ezek 36:25–28). The spiritual principle of these verses accords with that of the new birth that Jesus enunciated.

Proselytes to Judaism were washed completely, issued new clothing, and then received into the commonwealth of the people of God; but Israelites were regarded as sons of Abraham and children of God by covenant from birth. In effect, Jesus was telling Nicodemus that his descent from Abraham was not adequate ground for salvation. He would have to repent and begin a new life in the Spirit if he expected to enter the kingdom of God (cf. John 8:37–44).

Jesus illustrated his point by a play on words applicable both in Hebrew and Greek. The word for "spirit" (Heb., *rûah;* Gr., *pneuma*) is the word for "wind" in both languages and can be translated either way, depending on the context. Verse 8 could be rendered, "The Spirit breathes where he wills." NIV and other translations are undoubtedly correct, for the allusion to sound in the second sentence would not make much sense in sequence with "spirit." Possibly Nicodemus called on Jesus at the time when the evening wind was blowing through the city so that it was a ready illustration.

10 The Greek text uses the definite article with "teacher": "Are you *the* teacher of Israel?" (lit. tr.). Nicodemus's exact position in the theological circles of Israel is not defined, but the language suggests that he was a very important person. Jesus implies that as the outstanding teacher of the nation, Nicodemus should have been familiar with the teaching of the new birth. Evidently Jesus felt that since the OT contained this teaching in principle, those who read the Scriptures were responsible for knowing and believing the truth.

11 No doubt Nicodemus thought Jesus to be presumptuous when he said, "We speak of what we know." Jesus spoke with an air of authority. However, though the Pharisees spoke with a humanly imposed authority, Jesus spoke with an inherent authority. The use of "we" by Jesus is unusual. Perhaps his disciples were present and he was including them. Or Jesus may have been speaking as the earthly representative of the godhead. Throughout the years the "people" had rejected God's instruction as ministered through the prophets and the Scriptures. And things were no different now.

12–13 The "earthly things" Jesus alluded to were probably the phenomena he used for illustrations, such as the wind. If Nicodemus couldn't grasp the meaning of spiritual truth as conveyed by concrete analogy, how would he do so if it were couched in an abstract statement? No one had ever entered into heaven to experience its realities directly except Jesus himself, the Son of Man, who had come from heaven. Revelation, not discovery, is the basis for faith.

14–15 The reference to the Pentateuch (Num 21:4–9) would have been familiar to Nicodemus, for the Jewish scholars spent the larger part of each day in the study of Scripture and often memorized not only the Pentateuch but the entire OT. Although Jesus did not elaborate the details of this allusion, it has several applicable aspects:
  1. The ancient Israelites were guilty of disobedience and a grumbling and unthankful spirit.
  2. They were under the condemnation of God and were being punished for their sin.
  3. The object elevated before them was the emblem of their judgment.

4. They were unable to rescue themselves.
5. The poison of the serpents was deadly, and there was no antidote for it.
6. They were urged to *look* at the serpent in order to receive life.

Jesus insisted that he would be "lifted up," a word used elsewhere for crucifixion (8:28; 12:32–34). There is a possibility that the Greek word *hypsoō* was used to translate the Aramaic term *z*ᵉ*qap*, which could mean either "to elevate" or "to execute on a gibbet." It was a summons to receive Jesus as God's provision for the cure of sin and to place complete confidence in him for the future. Such confidence or belief would ensure partaking in the life of the age to come.

Notes

2:23–24 There is an interesting contrast here that is lost in the English translation. The same verb πιστεύω (*pisteuō*, "believe") is applied to the "many people" and to Jesus, but its first use is intransitive and the second use is transitive: literally, they "trusted in his name" (v. 23); and he did not "entrust himself to them" (v.24). Jesus would not believe in them unless they fully believed in him.

3:3 Should ἄνωθεν (*anōthen*) be rendered "again" or "from above"? It is used both ways in the NT. Luke at least once uses it to indicate "from time past" (Acts 26:5) and probably with the same meaning in Luke 1:3. James invariably has the meaning "from above" (James 1:17; 3:15, 17). Paul's use in Gal 4:9 accords more nearly with Luke's. The other instances in John unmistakably mean "from above" (3:31; 19:11, 23).

The infinitive ἰδεῖν (*idein*), translated "see," implies discernment or perception of meaning rather than simply registering a visual image, whereas βλέπω (*blepō*) means "to have the power of sight." The implication in John 3:3 is that without spiritual rebirth one cannot even perceive the reality of the kingdom of God.

9 The rabbis connected the concept of baptism with the ceremonial purification of complete immersion, basing it on the instructions for washing in Exod 19:10. The sprinkling of blood, immersion, and the submission to the Law (Exod 24:8) were the rites performed on proselytes "to bring them under the wings of the Shekinah." Baptism was not merely for the purpose of expiating special transgressions, as was the case chiefly in the violation of the so-called heretical laws of purity, but was the first step in a practice of holy living and a preparation for the attainment of a closer communion with God (cf. Jos. Antiq. 18. 5. 82). The Essenes followed the same practice. The purpose of baptizing the proselyte was for cleansing from the impurity of idolatry. The bathing in water constituted a rebirth and made him a "new creature" (cf. S. Kraus, "Baptism," JE I, pp. 499, 509; LTJM, 2:745–47).

14 Kittel, commenting on ὑψόω (*hypsoō*, "lift up") remarks: "In Jn. ὑψόω has intentionally a double sense in all the passages in which it occurs.... It means both exaltation on the cross and also exaltation to heaven" (TDNT, 8:610).

b. *The author's comment*

3:16–21

> [16]"For God so loved the world that he gave his one and only Son, that whoever believes in him shall not perish but have eternal life. [17]For God did not send his Son into the world to condemn the world, but to save the world through him. [18]Whoever believes in him is not condemned, but whoever does not believe stands condemned already because he has not believed in the name of God's one and

only Son. [19]This is the verdict: Light has come into the world, but men loved darkness instead of light because their deeds were evil. [20]Everyone who does evil hates the light, and will not come into the light for fear that his deeds will be exposed. [21]But whoever lives by the truth comes into the light, so that it may be seen plainly that what he has done has been done through God."

16 Commentators are divided as to whether vv.16-21 are a direct continuation of the conversation between Jesus and Nicodemus or whether they represent only the author's comment on Jesus' words. In either case, they express the most important message of the Gospel (emphasized elsewhere in many ways)—that salvation is a gift received only by believing God for it. The nature of belief is implied in the illustration of Moses lifting up the serpent in the wilderness (v.14). Belief consists of accepting something, not doing something. The result of belief is that one receives eternal life. He is freed from condemnation and lives in a relation of total honesty with God, for he does not fear having his real self exposed.

"Eternal," the new life God gives, refers not solely to the duration of existence but also to the quality of life as contrasted with futility. It is a deepening and growing experience. It can never be exhausted in any measurable span of time, but it introduces a totally new quality of life. The believer becomes imperishable; he is free from all condemnation; he is approved by God.

The verb "perish" depicts the opposite of salvation. It is used of death as opposed to life (Mark 3:6, transitive), "destroy" as opposed to preserve (1 Cor 1:19), "loss" as opposed to win or gain (2 John 8). It may be used of sheep that have gone astray (Matt 10:6) or a son who has wandered from his father's house (Luke 15:24). Its use here clearly implies that those without God are hopelessly confused in purpose, alienated from him in their affections, and futile in their efforts. Positive belief in Christ is necessary; all that one has to do to perish is nothing. To perish is to fail completely of fulfilling God's purpose and consequently to be excluded forever from his fellowship.

The presentation of the good news of God's love offers only two options: to believe or to perish. Eternal life, which is accepted by believing, is a gift of God and brings with it the fullest blessings God can bestow. To perish does not mean to cease to exist; it means to experience utter failure, futility, and loss of all that makes existence worthwhile. Its use with reference to Judas in John 17:12 is a vivid illustration.

17-18 Notwithstanding this gloomy picture of "lost" or "perish," God's purpose toward man is positive. God's attitude is not that of suspicion or hatred but of love. He is not seeking an excuse to condemn men but is rather endeavoring to save them. His purpose in sending Jesus into the world was to show his love and to draw men to himself. If they are lost, it is because they have not committed themselves to God, the only source of life. Beginning at this point, the contrast between belief and unbelief is increasingly exemplified. John has here defined the crux of belief and unbelief and has indicated the effects of each. The progress of both in the characters of those associated with Jesus becomes increasingly evident as the drama of this Gospel unfolds.

19-21 The difference between the believer and the unbeliever does not lie in the guilt or innocence of either; it lies in the different attitudes they take toward the "light." The unbeliever shrinks from the light because it exposes his sin; the believer willingly comes to the light so that his real motives may be revealed. This verse is paralleled by 1 John 1:8-9: "If we claim to be without sin, we deceive ourselves and the truth is not in us.

If we confess our sins, he is faithful and just and will forgive us our sins and purify us from all unrighteousness."

In John 1:5 we're told of the natural antipathy that exists between light and darkness. Verses 19–21 of ch. 3 lift this battle from the realm of the abstract to the concrete by showing that it is the love of evil deeds that keep men from responding to the light. There's no missing the fact that men are held accountable for their actions, and the choice is theirs: evil deeds or truth.

Notes

---

16 Morris says: "In the first century there were no devices such as inverted commas to show the precise limits of quoted speech.... Perhaps the dividing point comes at the end of v.15.... But in v.16 the death on the cross appears to be spoken of as past, and there are stylistic indications that John is speaking for himself" (NIC, p. 228).

---

7. Further testimony of John the Baptist

3:22–36

22After this, Jesus and his disciples went out into the Judean countryside, where he spent some time with them, and baptized. 23Now John also was baptizing at Aenon near Salim, because there was plenty of water, and people were constantly coming to be baptized. 24(This was before John was put in prison.) 25An argument developed between some of John's disciples and a certain Jew over the matter of ceremonial washing. 26They came to John and said to him, "Rabbi, that man who was with you on the other side of the Jordan—the one you testified about— well, he is baptizing, and everyone is going to him."

27To this John replied, "A man can receive only what is given him from heaven. 28You yourselves can testify that I said, 'I am not the Christ but am sent ahead of him.' 29The bride belongs to the bridegroom. The friend who attends the bridegroom waits and listens for him, and is full of joy when he hears the bridegroom's voice. That joy is mine, and it is now complete. 30He must become greater; I must become less.

31"The one who comes from above is above all; the one who is from the earth belongs to the earth, and speaks as one from the earth. The one who comes from heaven is above all. 32He testifies to what he has seen and heard, but no one accepts his testimony. 33The man who has accepted it has certified that God is truthful. 34For the one whom God has sent speaks the words of God; to him God gives the Spirit without limit. 35The Father loves the Son and has placed everything in his hands. 36Whoever believes in the Son has eternal life, but whoever rejects the Son will not see life, for God's wrath remains on him."

22–24 This period of Jesus' ministry in Judea is not paralleled by any account in the synoptic Gospels. It occurred before the arrest and imprisonment of John the Baptist, for he and Jesus were preaching and baptizing simultaneously. Mark begins the active ministry of Jesus after John's imprisonment (Mark 1:14) and states that Jesus summoned the disciples to follow him at that time. Matthew's account agrees with Mark's in substance (Matt 4:12–21). Luke does not specify that John's arrest preceded Jesus' ministry, though he mentions the imprisonment at the outset of his narrative (Luke 3:19). Both exercised a rural rather than urban ministry at this time. Jesus and his disciples remained in the Judean country; John was preaching farther north.

23 The exact location of Aenon is uncertain. Two sites are possible: one south of Beth-shan, where there were numerous springs; another a short distance from Shechem. Of the two, the former seems to be the better possibility. Eusebius and Jerome both mention it; and the ancient mosaic Madaba map of sacred sites depicts an "Aenon near to Salim" near the Jordan south of Scythopolis, the later name of Beth-shan. C.H. Turner observes that in this region John would have been in the territory of the Greek city of Scythopolis, outside the domain of Herod Antipas (p. 202).

25–26 The argument between a Jewish inquirer and the disciples of John indicates that there must have been confusion over the respective merits of Jesus and John. If both were baptizing, whose baptism was valid? By popular acclaim Jesus' influence was growing and John's was waning. John's interrogators felt that their friend and teacher had been eclipsed by Jesus' sudden popularity, and they wanted an explanation.

27–30 John showed no jealousy whatever; on the contrary, he reaffirmed his subordinate position. He would not claim for himself final authority but avowed that he had been sent in preparation for the Messiah. As the bridegroom is more important than the best man, or "friend" of the bridegroom who acted as the bridegroom's assistant, so he would be content to act as an assistant to Jesus.

Just how far the simile of bride and bridegroom should be pressed is questionable. Should the bride represent Israel, to whom the Messiah came, or the church? The imagery is applied to both (cf. Hos 2:19–20; Eph 5:32), but the focus of this passage is on the bridegroom, not the bride. The emphasis is on the relation of Jesus and John rather than on the relation of Jesus to Israel or to the church. To what extent this explanation of the relation of John the Baptist to Jesus was prompted by later conditions in the church is not stated. Adherents to John's preaching and baptism certainly existed in the middle of the first century and were widespread. Apollos of Alexandria, who ministered at Ephesus, was one of this company. Aquila and Priscilla later instructed him in the ministry of Christ (Acts 18:24–26). When Paul arrived at Ephesus, he found others who held the same belief. Paul himself brought them into a full understanding of the work of Christ (Acts 19:1–7). It is likely that this halfway understanding persisted among John's converts.

31–36 This paragraph, like vv.16–21, may be the author's reflection on what he had just written. Its phraseology accords better with the style of vv.16–21 than with that of John the Baptist. It is valuable as a testimony to the person of Christ in the light of what the author has just written. It declares in no uncertain terms that (1) Jesus came from heaven and spoke with a higher authority than that of earth; (2) that he spoke from observation, not from theory; (3) that he spoke the words of God; (4) that the Father's love had caused him to endow the Son with complete authority to execute his purpose. These qualities made Jesus superior in every way to John the Baptist, though the latter had an important and divinely authorized message. John spoke as one "from the earth." The Son, however, was not merely the messenger of God; he was the revealed object of faith. Once again the dividing line is affirmed. The believer in the Son has eternal life; the unbeliever will never possess that life, for he is already under condemnation. The wrath of God remains on him.

This is the only passage in the Johannine Gospel and Epistles in which "wrath" is mentioned. The word does not mean a sudden gust of passion or a burst of temper. Rather, it is the settled displeasure of God against sin. It is the divine allergy to moral evil, the reaction of righteousness to unrighteousness. God is neither easily angered nor vindictive. But by his very nature he is unalterably committed to opposing and judging all disobedience. The moral laws of the universe are as unvarying and unchangeable as its physical laws, and God cannot set aside either without violating his own nature. The rejection of his Son can be followed only by retribution. Acceptance of Christ is the personal appropriation of God's truth—an appropriation that might be compared to the practice of endorsing a check to cash it.

8. *The Samaritan ministry* (4:1–42)

a. *The woman at the well*

4:1–26

> [1]The Pharisees heard that Jesus was gaining and baptizing more disciples than John, [2]although in fact it was not Jesus who baptized, but his disciples. [3]When the Lord learned of this, he left Judea and went back once more to Galilee.
>
> [4]Now he had to go through Samaria. [5]So he came to a town in Samaria called Sychar, near the plot of ground Jacob had given to his son Joseph. [6]Jacob's well was there, and Jesus, tired as he was from the journey, sat down by the well. It was about the sixth hour.
>
> [7]When a Samaritan woman came to draw water, Jesus said to her, "Will you give me a drink?" [8](His disciples had gone into the town to buy food.)
>
> [9]The Samaritan woman said to him, "You are a Jew and I am a Samaritan woman. How can you ask me for a drink?" (For Jews do not associate with Samaritans.)
>
> [10]Jesus answered her, "If you knew the gift of God and who it is that asks you for a drink, you would have asked him and he would have given you living water."
>
> [11]"Sir," the woman said, "you have nothing to draw with and the well is deep. Where can you get this living water? [12]Are you greater than our father Jacob, who gave us the well and drank from it himself, as did also his sons and his flocks and herds?"
>
> [13]Jesus answered, "Everyone who drinks this water will be thirsty again, [14]but whoever drinks the water I give him will never thirst. Indeed, the water I give him will become in him a spring of water welling up to eternal life."
>
> [15]The woman said to him, "Sir, give me this water so that I won't get thirsty and have to keep coming here to draw water."
>
> [16]He told her, "Go, call your husband and come back."
>
> [17]"I have no husband," she replied.
>
> Jesus said to her, "You are right when you say you have no husband. [18]The fact is, you have had five husbands, and the man you now have is not your husband. What you have just said is quite true."
>
> [19]"Sir," the woman said, "I can see that you are a prophet. [20]Our fathers worshiped on this mountain, but you Jews claim that the place where we must worship is in Jerusalem."
>
> [21]Jesus declared, "Believe me, woman, a time is coming when you will worship the Father neither on this mountain nor in Jerusalem. [22]You Samaritans worship what you do not know; we worship what we do know, for salvation is from the Jews. [23]Yet a time is coming and has now come when the true worshipers will worship the Father in spirit and truth, for they are the kind of worshipers the Father seeks. [24]God is spirit, and his worshipers must worship in spirit and in truth."
>
> [25]The woman said, "I know that Messiah" (called Christ) "is coming. When he comes, he will explain everything to us."
>
> [26]Then Jesus declared, "I who speak to you am he."

1–3 Jesus' early ministry in the region of Judea was gaining increasing attention. The growing number of his disciples excited the curiosity of the Pharisees, who constituted the ruling religious class. The growth of any messianic movement could easily be interpreted as having political overtones, and Jesus did not want to become involved in any outward conflict with the state, whether Jewish or Roman. In order to avoid a direct clash, he left Judea and journeyed northward to Galilee.

4 The shortest route from Jerusalem to Galilee lay on the high road straight through Samaritan territory. Many Jews would not travel by that road, for they regarded any contact with Samaritans as defiling. Immediately after the fall of the northern kingdom in 722 B.C., the Assyrians had deported the Israelites from their land and had resettled it with captives from other countries. These had brought with them their own gods, whose worship they had combined with remnants of the worship of Jehovah and Baal in a mongrel type of religion. When the descendants of the southern captivity returned from Babylon in 539 B.C. to renew their worship under the Law, they found a complete rift between themselves and the inhabitants of Samaria, both religiously and politically. In the time of Nehemiah, the Samaritans opposed the rebuilding of the walls of Jerusalem (Neh 4:1–2); and later, in Maccabean times, they accepted the Hellenization of their religion when they dedicated their temple on Mount Gerizim to Zeus Xenios. By the time of Jesus a strong rivalry and hatred prevailed.

The words "had to" translate an expression of necessity. While the term speaks of general necessity rather than of personal obligation, in this instance it must refer to some compulsion other than mere convenience. As the Savior of all men, Jesus had to confront the smoldering suspicion and enmity between Jew and Samaritan by ministering to his enemies.

5 Sychar was a small village near Shechem, about half a mile from Jacob's well, which is located in the modern Shechem or Nablus. Opinion differs as to whether Sychar was the modern Askar or the Tell Balatah, where the old city of Shechem was found. El Askar is farther from the well than ancient Shechem and had a spring of its own. Although the old city had been largely destroyed by John Hyrcanus in 107 B.C., it is probable that some inhabitants remained in the vicinity and used this well for their water supply.

6 The well of Jacob lies at the foot of Mount Gerizim, the center of Samaritan worship. It is one of the historic sites in Palestine that we are reasonably certain of. The "sixth hour" would probably have been about noon, reckoning from daybreak. It was an unusual time for women to come to a village well for water. Perhaps the Samaritan woman had a sudden need, or perhaps she did not care to meet the other women of the community. In consideration of her general character, the other women may have shunned her.

7–8 Undoubtedly the woman was surprised to find a man sitting by the well and doubly surprised to be addressed by a Jew. Jesus' initial approach was by a simple request for water, which would presuppose a favorable response. One would hardly refuse a drink of cold water to a thirsty traveler in the heat of the day. The request did have a surprising element, however, for no Jewish rabbi would have volunteered to carry on a public conversation with a woman, nor would he have deigned to drink from a Samaritan's cup, as she implied by her answer.

9–10 There was a trace of sarcasm in the woman's reply, as if she meant, "We Samaritans are the dirt under your feet until you want something; then we are good enough!" Jesus paid no attention to her flippancy or to her bitterness. He was more interested in winning the woman than in winning an argument. He appealed to her curiosity by the phrase "If you knew." He implied that because of the nature of his person he could bestow on her a gift of God that would be greater than any ordinary water. His allusion was intended to lift her level of thinking from that of material need to spiritual realities.

11 The woman heard his words but missed his meaning. "Living water" meant to her fresh spring water such as the well supplied. She could not understand how he could provide this water without having any means of drawing it from the well. Her comment was appropriate to one whose comprehension was tied to the earthy and material, for the well even today is over seventy-five feet deep; and "it has prob. been filled with much debris over the years since it was dug" (ZPEB, 3:388).

12 The woman's reference to "our father Jacob" was perhaps designed to bolster the importance of the Samaritans in the eyes of a Jewish rabbi. She was well aware of the low esteem the Jews had of her people. Josephus tells us that the Samaritans claimed their ancestry through Joseph and Ephraim and Manasseh (Antiq. 11.341).

13–15 Jesus' second reply emphasized the contrast between the water in the well and what he intended to give. The material water would allay thirst only temporarily; the spiritual water would quench the inner thirst forever. The water in the well had to be drawn up with hard labor; the spiritual water would bubble up from within. Because of her nonspiritual perspective, the woman's interests were very selfish. All she wanted was something to save the effort of the long, hot trip from the village.

16–17 Jesus' request to call her husband was both proper and strategic—proper because it was not regarded as good etiquette for a woman to talk with a man unless her husband were present; strategic because it placed her in a dilemma from which she could not free herself without admitting her need. She had no husband she could call, and she would not want to confess her sexual irregularities to a stranger. The abruptness of her reply shows that she was at last emotionally touched.

18 Jesus shocked the woman when he lifted the curtain on her past life. The conversation had passed from the small-talk stage to the personal. Her evil deeds were being exposed by the light, but was she willing to acknowledge the truth?

19–20 Realizing his superhuman knowledge, the woman called him a prophet; but then she tried to divert him. Since his probing was becoming uncomfortably personal, she began to argue a religious issue. She raised the old controversy between Jews and Samaritans, whether worship should be offered on Mount Gerizim, at the foot of which they stood, or at Jerusalem, where Solomon's temple had been built.

The Samaritans founded their claim on the historic fact that when Moses instructed the people concerning the entrance into the Promised Land, he commanded that they set up an altar on Mount Ebal and that the tribes should be divided, half on Ebal and half on Gerizim. As the Levites read the Law, the people responded antiphonally. Those on Gerizim pronounced the blessings of God and those on Ebal, the curses of God on sin (Deut 27:1–28:68). The Jews held that since Solomon had been commissioned to build the temple in Jerusalem, the center of worship would be located there. The controversy was endless, and Jesus did not intend to allow himself to be drawn into a futile discussion.

21-23 Jesus avoided the argument by elevating the issue above mere location. He made no concessions and intimated that the Samaritans' worship was confused: "You Samaritans worship what you do not know." Probably he was alluding to the error of the woman's ancestors, who had accepted a syncretism of foreign deities with the ancestral God of the Jewish faith. True worship is that of the spirit, which means that the worshiper must deal honestly and openly with God. She, on the contrary, had been furtive and unwilling to open her heart to God.

24 "God is spirit, and his worshipers must worship in spirit and in truth" carries one of the four descriptions of God found in the New Testament. The other three are "God is light" (1 John 1:5), "God is love" (1 John 4:8, 16), and "God is a consuming fire" (Heb 12:29). Jesus was endeavoring to convey to the woman that God cannot be confined to one place nor conceived of as a material being. He cannot be represented adequately by an abstract concept, which is intrinsically impersonal, nor can any idol depict his likeness since he is not material. Only "the Word become flesh" could represent him adequately.

25 Mystified by Jesus' words, the woman finally confessed her ignorance and at the same time expressed her longing: "I know that Messiah is coming. When he comes, he will explain everything to us." It was the one nebulous hope that she had of finding God, for she expected that the coming Messiah would explain the mysteries of life. There was a Samaritan tradition that the prophet predicted by Moses in Deuteronomy 18:15 would come to teach God's people all things. On this sincere though vague hope Jesus founded his appeal to her spiritual consciousness.

26 This is the one occasion when Jesus voluntarily declared his messiahship. The synoptic Gospels show that normally he did not make such a public claim; on the contrary, he urged his disciples to say nothing about it (Matt 16:20; Mark 8:29-30; Luke 9:20-21). In Galilee, where there were many would-be Messiahs and a constant unrest based on the messianic hope, such a claim would have been dangerous. In Samaria the concept would probably have been regarded more as religious than political and would have elicited a ready hearing for his teaching rather than a subversive revolt. Furthermore, this episode presumably occurred early in his ministry when he was not so well known.

Notes

6, 11-12 Two different words are translated "well" in this incident. The first, in v.6, is πηγή (*pēgē*), which refers to the source or spring discovered by Jacob. The second word, φρέαρ (*phrear*), used in vv.11-12, denotes the shaft dug into the ground to reach the water. The well tapped a subterranean spring that never ran dry. God supplied the water, but access to it was gained through a man. Now a greater than Jacob was offering through himself access to water that would satisfy throughout eternity.

24 The KJV rendering of πνεῦμα ὁ θεός (*pneuma ho theos*) as "God is a spirit" is misleading. Greek grammar has no indefinite article; its inclusion or exclusion is at the translators' discretion, whose decision, hopefully, is based on context and other Scripture. The point Jesus was trying to make here is not that God is one spirit among many. Rather, Jesus was seeking to lift the conversation into the sphere of the spiritual and heavenly since the woman kept referring to human ancestry, Mount Gerizim, and traditional worship practices. The anarthrous construction and Gr. word order place the emphasis on the essential character of God; thus the essence of true worship must be on God's terms and in accord with his nature.

---

b. *The return of the disciples*

4:27–38

> 27Just then his disciples returned and were surprised to find him talking with a woman. But no one asked, "What do you want?" or "Why are you talking with her?"
>
> 28Then, leaving her water jar, the woman went back to the town and said to the people, 29"Come, see a man who told me everything I ever did. Could this be the Christ?" 30They came out of the town and made their way toward him.
>
> 31Meanwhile his disciples urged him, "Rabbi, eat something."
>
> 32But he said to them, "I have food to eat that you know nothing about."
>
> 33Then his disciples said to each other, "Could someone have brought him food?"
>
> 34"My food," said Jesus, "is to do the will of him who sent me and to finish his work. 35Do you not say, 'Four months more and then the harvest'? I tell you, open your eyes and look at the fields! They are ripe for harvest. 36Even now the reaper draws his wages, even now he harvests the crop for eternal life, so that the sower and the reaper may be glad together. 37Thus the saying, 'One sows and another reaps' is true. 38I sent you to reap what you have not worked for. Others have done the hard work, and you have reaped the benefits of their labor."

27 The disciples had left Jesus at the well. He was tired, and there would have been no need for him to have accompanied them into the town to buy food. They were surprised to find him talking with a woman—an apparent violation of custom—but they respected him too highly to question his behavior.

28–29 As the disciples approached, the woman made her way back to Sychar to report the interview to her fellow villagers. She was so excited that she forgot her water pot. At the village she was bold enough to suggest that perhaps the new person she had met might be the Messiah. "You don't suppose this could be the Messiah, do you?" would be a fair translation of her words.

30 It would be unlikely that the elders of Sychar would accept theological information from a woman of her reputation, and she did not venture to make a dogmatic pronouncement. Nevertheless, her manner was so sincere and her invitation so urgent that they immediately proceeded to the well to investigate.

31–34 The disciples were mainly interested in Jesus' physical welfare. He must have been exhausted by the travel of the morning. They were amazed that he was not hungry and wondered whether somebody else had given him food. He tried to tell them that the satisfaction of completing the work the Father had entrusted to him was greater than any food he might have been given. If the "had to" in v.4 reflects the plan of the Father for this trip, Jesus was telling the disciples that he did not live on bread alone but on every word that comes from the mouth of God (cf. Matt 4:4).

35 "Four months more and then the harvest" is probably a quotation of a current proverb. Having once sowed the grain, all the farmer needed to do was wait for it to ripen. Jesus was pointing out that the spiritual harvest is always ready and must be reaped before it spoils. As he was speaking, the Samaritans were leaving the town and coming across the fields toward him (v.30). The eagerness of the people the Jews regarded as alien and rejected showed that they were like grain ready for harvesting.

36–38 The disciples would not have to wait indefinitely for the result of their mission; the sowing and reaping could go on together. Jesus implied that they had already received a commission to reap for him and that they could benefit from the preparation he and the prophets had made. The reaping of people for the granary of God is not the task of any one group, nor is it confined to one era. Each reaps the benefit of its forerunners, and succeeding generations in turn gain from the accomplishments of their predecessors. As Paul said, "I planted the seed, Apollos watered it, but God made it grow" (1 Cor 3:6). Perhaps v.38 is an allusion to the preaching of John the Baptist, whose message of repentance had prepared the way for the disciples' preaching about Jesus.

c. *The faith of the Samaritans*

4:39–42

> 39Many of the Samaritans from that town believed in him because of the woman's testimony, "He told me everything I ever did." 40So when the Samaritans came to him they urged him to stay with them, and he stayed two days. 41And because of his words many more became believers.
> 42They said to the woman, "We no longer believe just because of what you said; now we have heard for ourselves, and we know that this man really is the Savior of the world."

39–42 These few verses indicate two necessary and interrelated bases for belief: (1) the testimony of others and (2) personal contact with Jesus. This woman's witness opened the way to him for the villagers. If he could penetrate the shell of her materialism and present a message that would transform her, the Samaritans also could believe that he might be the Messiah. That stage of belief was only introductory, however. The second stage was hearing him for themselves, and it brought them to the settled conviction expressed in "we know" (v.42). "No longer" implies that they maintained their belief in him, but not solely on the basis of the woman's testimony. They had progressed from a faith built on the witness of another to a faith built on their own experience.

Notes

42 Two verbs may be translated "know": γινώσκω (*ginōskō*) and οἶδα (*oida*). The former usually implies knowledge by contact or experience; the second more generally denotes knowledge of facts or knowledge by intellectual process. While it would be precarious to contend that John always draws a sharp line between the two, the use of the latter in v.42 seems to fit the distinction, because it states a knowledge of fact that results in a settled conviction. The Samaritans are expressing assurance of a truth, not merely a progressive acquaintance with a person or situation.

9. *The interview with the nobleman*

4:43–54

> ⁴³After the two days he left for Galilee. ⁴⁴(Now Jesus himself had pointed out that a prophet has no honor in his own country.) ⁴⁵When he arrived in Galilee, the Galileans welcomed him. They had seen all that he had done in Jerusalem at the Passover Feast, for they also had been there.
>
> ⁴⁶Once more he visited Cana in Galilee, where he had turned the water into wine. And there was a certain royal official whose son lay sick at Capernaum. ⁴⁷When this man heard that Jesus had arrived in Galilee from Judea, he went to him and begged him to come and heal his son, who was close to death.
>
> ⁴⁸"Unless you people see miraculous signs and wonders," Jesus told him, "you will never believe."
>
> ⁴⁹The royal official said, "Sir, come down before my child dies."
>
> ⁵⁰Jesus replied, "You may go. Your son will live."
>
> The man took Jesus at his word and departed. ⁵¹While he was still on the way, his servants met him with the news that his boy was living. ⁵²When he inquired as to the time when his son got better, they said to him, "The fever left him yesterday at the seventh hour."
>
> ⁵³Then the father realized that this was the exact time at which Jesus had said to him, "Your son will live." So he and all his household believed.
>
> ⁵⁴This was the second miraculous sign that Jesus performed, having come from Judea to Galilee.

43 The progress to Galilee is closely connected with the episode at Samaria. John seems to focus his Gospel on clusters of events. Compare 1:19, 29, 35, 43, and 2:1, as well as those chronological groupings that appear later.

44 The Johannine footnote "Now Jesus himself had pointed out that a prophet has no honor in his own country" is recorded also in Matthew 13:57 and Mark 6:4. Both of these express Jesus' reaction to the negative attitude the inhabitants of Nazareth in Galilee took toward him. Chronologically that episode occurred later than the visit to Galilee recorded in this chapter. The author was applying to the immediate situation a principle that Jesus stated on two other occasions. Did he intend to apply it to Judea or to Galilee? While the immediate context might be taken to relate to some previous experience in Judea, there is no indication that Jesus had at this time been the object of a wholesale rejection there, though some hostility may have been manifested by the Pharisees (4:1). In the light of Jesus' comment to the nobleman in v.48, it seems more likely that John was simply stating that Jesus had already been rebuffed in Galilee (cf. Luke 4:24–29) and that he was questioning the motives of the nobleman in the light of past experience. At this time the Galileans were somewhat more receptive because of the miracles they had witnessed at the Passover in Jerusalem. John says little in this Gospel about Jesus' Galilean activities, though he shows knowledge of them (2:1–11; 4:43–54; 6:1–7:13).

45 The Galileans hoped Jesus would duplicate the signs they had witnessed in Jerusalem while they were attending the Passover Feast. They were disappointed to discover that Jesus had no intention of exhibiting his powers to satisfy their curiosity. In Nazareth he performed few miracles, and it was probably the attitude of these people that caused him to rebuff the nobleman (v.48).

46 The reason for revisiting Cana is not given. It may be that Jesus expected to find some disciples who had believed on him after the miracle at the wedding. The royal official (*basilikos*) may have been a member of Herod's court. His son had been ill for some time and was not recovering from his sickness. Therefore, the father felt compelled to seek some further aid. It is possible that the official was a Gentile. If so, the three persons Jesus interviewed in this early ministry represented the Jews, the Samaritans, and the Gentiles —in short, the world he came to save. John's Gospel, though it chronicles chiefly the ministry of Jesus in Jerusalem, has a much wider horizon than the area of his residence.

47 The report that Jesus had healed people in Jerusalem must have reached this man's ears. Learning that Jesus had returned to Galilee, the man immediately sought Jesus out and urged him to heal his son, who was dangerously ill. The imperfect tense of the verb "begged" (*ērōta*, from *erōtaō*, to "ask" or "request") implies repeated or persistent action. The request was not casual but insistent.

48 The reply of Jesus seems like a heartless rejection. He seemed to insinuate that the official, like the rest of the Galileans, was only giving an excuse for eliciting a miracle from him. On the other hand, Jesus' words may express his hope more than his exasperation. He desired a belief characterized by dedication rather than amazement, and the second half of the episode shows that his aim was to inculcate a genuine commitment rather than merely to perform a cure.

49 The genuine distress of the father is demonstrated by his words: "Sir, come down at once before my little boy dies!" (lit. tr.). The use of the aorist tense of "die" (*apothanein*) to describe the impending crisis is in contrast with the present tense in v.47 (*apothnēskein*), which describes the progress of the illness. This indicates that the case was desperate.

50 Jesus' response still seems somewhat impersonal and casual. By dismissing the official with the statement that his son was alive, Jesus created a dilemma of faith. If the father refused to return to Capernaum without taking Jesus with him, he would show that he did not believe Jesus' word and would consequently receive no benefit because of his distrust. On the other hand, if he followed Jesus' order, he would be returning to the dying boy with no outward assurance that the lad would recover. He was forced to make the difficult choice between insisting on evidence and thus showing disbelief and of exercising faith without any tangible proof to encourage him. The official chose the second horn of the dilemma; he "took Jesus at his word" (ASV "believed the word") and set out on his return journey. He learned faith by the compulsion of necessity.

51–52 People are amazed by coincidences, but generally they do not attribute them to the direct activity of God. The official took a "chance" and went home as Jesus had commanded him to, and a miraculous report greeted him "while he was still on the way." There is an interesting progression in the description of the boy's condition. First the news came that "his boy was living." But more than that, the man was curious to know "the time when his son got better." Finally, he was told, "The fever left him yesterday at the seventh hour."

53–54 When the father considered the details of his meeting with Jesus and the good news concerning his son's recovery, he was convinced that it was more than coincidence at work. The timing was miraculous, and the boy's recovery was more than even circumstances could have brought about. "So he and his household believed."

The notation of succession in signs mentioned in v.54 is not repeated in the remainder of the Gospel. Though John says little about Jesus' Galilean ministry in general, he regarded it as important. If, as his footnote (v.44) implies, the Galileans were unlikely to believe on Jesus because he was well known to them, the convincing character of the two signs recorded here and the forceful demonstration of God's response to faith afforded by the second provided cogent illustrations for the main theme of belief.

Notes

---

49 "Little boy" is the translation of παιδίον (*paidion*), a diminutive that expresses the father's feelings more vividly than the more formal υἱός (*huios*, "son") of vv.46–47.

B. *The Rise of Controversy* (5:1–47)

1. *The healing of the paralytic*

5:1–15

> ¹Some time later, Jesus went up to Jerusalem for a feast of the Jews. ²Now there is in Jerusalem near the Sheep Gate a pool, which in Aramaic is called Bethesda and which is surrounded by five covered colonnades. ³Here a great number of disabled people used to lie—the blind, the lame, the paralyzed. ⁵One who was there had been an invalid for thirty-eight years. ⁶When Jesus saw him lying there and learned that he had been in this condition for a long time, he asked him, "Do you want to get well?"
>
> ⁷"Sir," the invalid replied, "I have no one to help me into the pool when the water is stirred. While I am trying to get in, someone else goes down ahead of me."
>
> ⁸Then Jesus said to him, "Get up! Pick up your mat and walk." ⁹At once the man was cured; he picked up his mat and walked.
>
> The day on which this took place was a Sabbath, ¹⁰and so the Jews said to the man who had been healed, "It is the Sabbath; the law forbids you to carry your mat."
>
> ¹¹But he replied, "The man who made me well said to me, 'Pick up your mat and walk.'"
>
> ¹²So they asked him, "Who is this fellow who told you to pick it up and walk?"
>
> ¹³The man who was healed had no idea who it was, for Jesus had slipped away into the crowd that was there.
>
> ¹⁴Later Jesus found him at the temple and said to him, "See, you are well again. Stop sinning or something worse may happen to you." ¹⁵The man went away and told the Jews that it was Jesus who had made him well.

1 The words "some time later" mark a break in chronological sequence. Comparison with the Synoptic accounts shows that a measurable amount of time may have elapsed between the healing of the son of the royal official at Capernaum and the episode of the paralytic at the Pool of Bethesda. The reference to the feast does not define the time since the feast is unnamed. Some MSS employ the definite article, calling it "the feast." If this were the Passover, the time would be almost a year later than Jesus' arrival in Galilee as described in John 4:46. Apparently John was less interested in chronology than in following the trend of Jesus' conflict with unbelief.

2 The traditional location of the pool is beneath the present site of the Church of Saint Anne, on the northwest corner of Jerusalem and near the gate by the sheep market. Excavations have shown that it was surrounded by a colonnade on all four sides and down the middle of the pool, making five "porches" (ASV) in all.

The name of the section of the city where the pool was located is variously given in the MS tradition as Bethzatha, Bethesda, and Bethsaida. The various readings may arise from differing attempts to transliterate the Hebrew or Aramaic original. Bethesda (house of mercy) has the support of the majority of MSS and corresponds to the section of the city best suited to the description given by John.

3–4 Another problem arises from the absence of v.4 from the best MS texts. It is omitted by all MSS dated prior to the fourth century, though the rest generally include it with numerous variations. It is generally regarded as a gloss that was introduced to explain the intermittent agitation of the water, which the populace considered to be a potential source of healing. There is no question that they congregated at the pool, hoping to be cured of their ailments. The explanation of the moving of the water was probably added later.

5–6 Confinement to a bed for thirty-eight years would leave the sufferer so weak he would be unable to walk or even stand for any length of time. His case would be hopeless. Jesus selected for his attention the person who seemed most needy. Since he had been afflicted for thirty-eight years, he must have been well on in years. Jesus' question must have seemed rather naive to him. Who would not want to be healed from utter helplessness? Yet the question also implies an appeal to the will, which the long years of discouragement may have paralyzed. Jesus thus challenged the man's will to be cured.

7 The invalid's reply shows that he had lost his independent determination. He was waiting for somebody to assist him. Such efforts as he had been able to make had proved futile, and he was despairing of success.

8 The healing was not a response to a request, nor did it presuppose an expression of faith on the part of the man. Jesus asked him to do the impossible, to stand on his feet, pick up his bedroll, and go his way. Renewed by the miraculous influx of new power, the man responded at once and did so. Jesus supplied even the will to be cured!

9–10 The outcome of the miracle was twofold: the paralytic was healed and a controversy was precipitated. Since the healing took place on the Sabbath, it brought Jesus directly into conflict with the religious authorities. The rabbinic application of the fourth commandment involved all kinds of casuistic interpretation, much of which was overdrawn. The Synoptics record other occasions on which Jesus' activities on the Sabbath excited the criticism of his opponents (Matt 12:1–14; Mark 2:23–3:6; Luke 6:1–11). Jesus' healing on the Sabbath was one of the factors that brought him into disfavor with the religious leaders in Jerusalem.

11–12 The paralytic seems to have felt no particular gratitude to Jesus for his healing. He took no responsibility for the action on the Sabbath; and after Jesus had dealt with him the second time, he immediately informed the Jewish leaders who it was that had transgressed the Sabbath law. It seems quite unlikely that he would have been ignorant of the reason for their inquiry.

13 John indicates that on at least four occasions Jesus quietly withdrew from a scene of controversy. Each of these occurred after an argument with the Jews over his claims (8:59; 10:39; 12:36). All these reinforce the concept of the fourth Gospel that Jesus was immune to danger until the hour of his passion arrived (7:30; 8:20).

14–15 Jesus' interest in the man is implied in the word "find." Apparently Jesus searched for him because he was prompted by concern for his spiritual state as well as for his physical illness. The command "Stop sinning" presupposes the possibility that the man's affliction may have been caused by his own sin. There is no indication that this encounter strengthened the man's faith and attachment to Jesus; in fact, the contrary could easily be inferred. But he did confess Jesus as his healer.

Notes

1 External evidence favors the anarthrous use of ἐορτή (*heortē*, "feast") in "a feast of the Jews." The two oldest papyri texts, P⁶⁶, ⁷⁵, and a number of other important MSS support this reading, though some add the definite article ἡ (*hē*). There may have been many speculations concerning which feast it might have been; and even with the article the conclusion would still be uncertain, though probably that would refer to the Passover. If it is the Passover, it affords a chronological basis for concluding that Jesus' ministry occupied three and a half years, on the assumption that each reference to the Passover represents a different year (2:13; 6:4; 11:55).

2 There seems to be no agreement among commentators on the proper transliteration of "Bethesda." Morris favors "Bethesda" (NIC, pp. 300–301); Hendriksen accepts "Bethzatha" (1:190); R. Brown agrees on "Bethesda" (29:206–7). J.T. Milik cites from 3Q15 (11.12–13, #57) an allusion to treasure buried on the eastern hill of Jerusalem "in Bet Esdatayin, in the pool at the entrance to its smaller basin" (*Discoveries in the Judean Desert* [Oxford: Oxford University, 1962], 3:271). "Bethsaida" is attested by P⁶⁶, but it is probably an assimilation to the name of the Galilean town mentioned earlier in John 1:44. Despite the ambiguity of the name as given in the MSS, the location seems now to be fairly well settled.

Turner and Mantey follow the older suggestion of Robinson, Schaff, and G.A. Smith that the pool should be identified with Gihon, which has intermittent action that would cause the water to be "stirred" (v.7) (pp. 129–31). However, current archaeological evidence has left this view with few advocates.

4 Verse 4 is omitted in the important, early MSS and by representatives of the versions. It is generally understood to be an explanatory gloss, dating probably from the late second century.

2. Jesus' defense of his sonship (5:16–47)

a. The prerogatives of sonship

5:16–30

¹⁶So, because Jesus was doing these things on the Sabbath, the Jews persecuted him. ¹⁷Jesus said to them, "My Father is always at his work to this very day, and I, too, am working." ¹⁸For this reason the Jews tried all the harder to kill him; not only was he breaking the Sabbath, but he was even calling God his own Father, making himself equal with God.

¹⁹Jesus gave them this answer: "I tell you the truth, the Son can do nothing by himself; he can do only what he sees his Father doing, because whatever the

Father does the Son also does. ²⁰For the Father loves the Son and shows him all he does. Yes, to your amazement he will show him even greater things than these. ²¹For just as the Father raises the dead and gives them life, even so the Son gives life to whom he is pleased to give it. ²²Moreover, the Father judges no one, but has entrusted all judgment to the Son, ²³that all may honor the Son just as they honor the Father. He who does not honor the Son does not honor the Father, who sent him.

²⁴"I tell you the truth, whoever hears my word and believes him who sent me has eternal life and will not be condemned; he has crossed over from death to life. ²⁵I tell you the truth, a time is coming and has now come when the dead will hear the voice of the Son of God and those who hear will live. ²⁶For as the Father has life in himself, so he has granted the Son to have life in himself. ²⁷And he has given him authority to judge because he is the Son of Man.

²⁸"Do not be amazed at this, for a time is coming when all who are in their graves will hear his voice ²⁹and come out—those who have done good will rise to live, and those who have done evil will rise to be condemned. ³⁰By myself I can do nothing; I judge only as I hear, and my judgment is just, for I seek not to please myself but him who sent me.

16 This verse introduces the element of controversy between Jesus and his opponents. The immediate cause was the healing on the Sabbath, which they interpreted as a violation of the fourth commandment: "Remember the Sabbath day by keeping it holy.... On it you shall not do any work" (Exod 20:8, 10). John records one other occasion when a healing was performed on the Sabbath for the same reason and with the same reaction. The synoptic Gospels also add other instances (Mark 2:23–28; 3:1–6; Luke 13:10–16; 14:1–6). The underlying provocation for the controversy was Jesus' attitude toward the Jewish traditions, which had grown up as interpretation of the Law and were often more rigid than the Law itself. Jesus contended that allaying human need was no violation of the Divine Law. He reminded his critics that if the Law allowed a man to rescue an animal from danger on a Sabbath day, the restoration of a man to health should certainly be permitted (Luke 14:5).

17 Jesus' argument for healing on the Sabbath was that God does not suspend his activities on the Sabbath. The laws of nature take no holiday. If a man cuts himself on the Sabbath, the healing process begins immediately. But more important than pointing out the unceasing laws of nature, Jesus identified his activities with those of the Father. Jesus claimed to be continuing the creative work of God.

18 The Jews were angry because of Jesus' violation of the Sabbath, but they were furious when he was so presumptuous as to claim equality with the Father. This claim of Jesus widened the breach between his critics and himself, for they understood that by it he was asserting his deity. His explanation shows that he did not claim identity with the Father as one person, but he asserted his unity with the Father in a relationship that could be described as sonship. This sonship has many facets, as shown in vv.19–24.

19 The Son is dependent on the Father. He does not act independently apart from the Father's will and purpose. Throughout this Gospel Jesus continually asserted that his work was to do the will of the Father (4:34; 5:30; 8:28; 12:50; 15:10). Equality of nature, identity of objective, and subordination of will are interrelated in Christ. John presents him as the Son, not as the slave, of God, yet as the perfect agent of the divine purpose and the complete revelation of the divine nature.

20 The Son is loved by the Father. The relationship is not that of master and slave, nor of employer and employee, but of a Father and a Son who are united by love. The Father has revealed to the Son the purpose and plan of his activity, much as the head of a family discusses with the others the plan he wishes to follow.

21 The Son is empowered by the Father. God is the source of life. He alone has power to reverse the processes of the material world and to bring life out of death. This supreme power the Father has conferred on the Son. The demonstration of this power appears in the later sign of the raising of Lazarus (John 11:41–44).

22–23 The Son is entrusted with the power of judgment. He possesses equal dignity with the Father and shares with him judicial as well as executive authority. Conversely, since the Son is equal in authority, he can rightly claim equal honor with God.

24 The Son is the arbiter of destiny. The determination of this destiny is immediate: "Whoever hears my word and believes him who sent me has eternal life and will not be condemned." Eternal life becomes the possession of the believer at the moment of acceptance; the future judgment will only confirm what has already taken place. The assurance of salvation does not begin at death or at a future judgment. "He has crossed over" is in the perfect tense, which indicates an accomplished transit and a settled state.

25 The phrase "and has now come" may refer to the present era that will terminate in the return of Christ and the resurrection of the dead, or it may refer to the power Jesus had to raise the dead during his lifetime, as in the case of Lazarus. There is another sense in which our Lord's words are true. As the source of life, he was promising to those who were spiritually dead, like the woman at the well, a new and eternal life if they would listen to his voice.

26 We do not have inherent life within us. Our life is derived from others. In the physical sense, our life is given to us by our parents. However, even that transaction is shrouded in deep mystery. Again Jesus claimed deity by saying he was not dependent on another for life just as the Father derived his life from no one. Jesus possesses inherent life, the power to create and the power to renew life that has been extinguished.

27 The title "Son of Man" has appeared twice previously in this Gospel: once in describing Jesus' function as a revelator of divine truth (1:51) and once in connection with his function as a Redeemer (3:14). Generally it is used only by Jesus concerning himself. As the Son of Man he is qualified to judge humanity because he belongs to it and can understand the needs and viewpoints of men. As the Epistle to the Hebrews states, "He had to be made like his brothers in every way, in order that he might become a merciful and faithful high priest in service to God, and that he might make atonement for the sins of the people" (Heb 2:17). Hebrews emphasizes Jesus' priestly function rather than his judicial position, but the underlying concept is the same.

28–29 This passage contains one of the few references to eschatology in John's Gospel. No chronological distinction is drawn here between the resurrection of the righteous and that of the wicked, neither is any such distinction excluded. John says little about a program, but he does emphasize the fact that Jesus will be the door to the eternal world.

The double resurrection assumes that both the righteous and the wicked will receive bodies in the future life and that presumably each body will express the character of the person who is resurrected. Some commentators claim that the resurrection of v.25 is wholly spiritual while that of vv.29 and 30 is physical and future. There seems to be an unnecessary distinction here, even though Jesus said that the time had already come when the dead would hear the voice of the Son of God, thus referring it to the present as he experienced it. The raising of Lazarus (ch. 11) can be taken as a demonstration of his meaning. Verses 29-30 are simply more explicit and completely future. Obviously spiritual resurrection from being dead in transgressions and sins (Eph 2:1) must precede physical resurrection.

30 Verse 30 marks a transition from self-affirmation to testimony. Jesus spoke with the confidence of being commissioned by the Father, not with the arrogance of self-assertion. Twenty-five times in this Gospel he asserts that he was sent by the Father. Two different words are used: *pempō*, which means to "send" in a broad or general sense, and *apostellō*, which has the additional connotation of "equip," "commission," or "delegate." In many of the occurrences in John these words seem to be used interchangeably since both are applied to the person of Christ. The former, however, is generally used descriptively in a participial form, "he who sent"; the latter is used as a finite verb in making an assertion of action. *Apostellō* is used exclusively in Jesus' prayer of John 17, where he speaks directly to the Father. Both appear in the last instance in John 20:21: "As the Father has sent (*apestalken*) me, I am sending (*pempō*) you." If any real difference can be detected, Jesus is saying, "In the same way that the Father commissioned me, so am I dispatching you on my errand." Perhaps it is better not to strain a point but merely to say that wherever either of these verbs is used concerning Jesus, it refers to his commission for the ministry, which distinguishes him as the Son of God.

b. *The witnesses to his authority*

5:31-47

31"If I testify about myself, my testimony is not valid. 32There is another who testifies in my favor, and I know that his testimony about me is valid.

33"You have sent to John and he has testified to the truth. 34Not that I accept human testimony; but I mention it that you may be saved. 35John was a lamp that burned and gave light, and you chose for a time to enjoy his light.

36"I have testimony weightier than that of John. For the very work that the Father has given me to finish, and which I am doing, testifies that the Father has sent me. 37And the Father who sent me has himself testified concerning me. You have never heard his voice nor seen his form, 38nor does his word dwell in you, for you do not believe the one he sent. 39You diligently study the Scriptures because you think that by them you possess eternal life. These are Scriptures that testify about me, 40yet you refuse to come to me to have life.

41"I do not accept praise from men, 42but I know you. I know that you do not have the love of God in your hearts. 43I have come in my Father's name, and you do not accept me; but if someone else comes in his own name, you will accept him. 44How can you believe if you accept praise from one another, yet make no effort to obtain the praise that comes from the only God?

45"But do not think I will accuse you before the Father. Your accuser is Moses, on whom your hopes are set. 46If you believed Moses, you would believe me, for he wrote about me. 47But since you do not believe what he wrote, how are you going to believe what I say?"

31 Because the authority of Jesus was questioned by his critics, he summoned witnesses to vouch for him. "Witness" or "testimony," whether verb or noun, is a common word in this Gospel. The verb *martyreō* occurs thirty-three times. This term is used to describe the attestation of Jesus' character and power. Jesus gives five specific sources of testimony about himself.

Although Jesus discounts his own witness, "If I testify about myself," he still implies that it is valid. He said that it is "not valid" because under Jewish law the self-testimony of any man was not accepted in court. On another occasion he had said, "Even if I testify on my own behalf, my testimony is valid, for I know where I came from and where I am going" (John 8:14). The apparent contradiction can be resolved because the statement in John 5 is based on legal grounds whereas that in ch. 8 is based on personal knowledge. In consideration of Jesus' essential truthfulness, his witness concerning himself is sound, though in legal process it would not be admitted.

32 "There is another who testifies in my favor" could refer either to the Father or to John the Baptist, both of whom are mentioned in the context. The present tense of "testifies" (*martyrōn*), which implies continuing action in contrast to the perfect tense "has testified" (*memartyrēken*) applied to John the Baptist (v.33), favors the former view. Jesus was constantly conscious of the Father's confidence and support. On the other hand, the witness of John the Baptist follows immediately with v.33 and seems likely to be the elaboration of the statement in v.32.

33–34 "You have sent to John" is obviously a reference to the delegation sent from the Jewish rulers to John the Baptist when he was preaching in the Judean wilderness (1:19). The fact that they had already asked him for an explanation bound them to give proper consideration to his testimony. John had refused the title of Messiah but had predicted the coming of Jesus and had identified him at his appearance in such a way that his own disciples accepted Jesus as the Messiah (1:40). The testimony of John was effective; his preaching reached a wide audience of people and prepared the way for a further revelation of truth in the person of Jesus. Jesus appealed to the popular response that John elicited by pointing out that his audience had accepted John's message, which gave Jesus a place of ultimate authority. They could not consistently accept John's preaching and reject Jesus.

35 The content of the witness of John the Baptist has already been discussed in the comments on 1:19–34. He introduced Jesus to the public and to his disciples in particular as the Lamb of God and as the Son of God. John had burned himself out in his ministry. Possibly by this time he had been imprisoned; the past tense of the verb may imply that his ministry had closed. Jesus reminds his hearers that they had enjoyed John's preaching and had responded to it, but their response had been short lived and superficial. Now that Jesus had come with the fulfillment of John's message, they were paying scant attention to him.

36 Another witness is that of the works Jesus was doing. The Johannine use of this term "works" (*erga*) refers to those deeds that revealed Jesus' divine nature. As the quality of a man's deeds show his moral standards, skill, and personal competence, so Jesus' works marked him as superhuman in both his compassion and his power (cf. 3:19–21). He said later to those who questioned him, "The miracles I do in my Father's name speak for me" (10:25). In his final discourse to the disciples he asked them to believe him "on the evidence of the miracles [works] themselves" (14:11). Although he never performed miracles for the purpose of drawing attention to himself, he regarded them as valid proofs of his claims.

The Gospel lists seven of these works:
1. The turning of water into wine   (2:1–11)
2. The healing of the official's son   (4:43–54)
3. The healing of a paralytic   (5:1–15)
4. The feeding of the multitude   (6:1–14)
5. The walking on the water   (6:16–21)
6. The cure of the blind man   (9:1–41)
7. The raising of Lazarus   (11:1–44).

Each of these miracles demonstrated Jesus' power in a different area of human experience. They are called "signs" (*sēmeia*) because they point to something beyond themselves. Their significance does not lie in their extraordinary character but in the fact that Jesus was able to meet the emergencies of life directly and satisfactorily. It is noteworthy that they were generally followed by a confession of belief on the part of many of the spectators (2:11; 4:53; 6:66, 69; 9:38; 11:45).

37–38 The witness of the Father is distinguished from the works that the Father gave Jesus to perform. The allusion seems somewhat obscure, especially since Jesus disclaimed any visible or audible communication from God to the crowd in general. Nevertheless there were occasions on which a voice from heaven spoke, expressing approval of Jesus and affirming his sonship. The voice at the baptism and the utterance at the Transfiguration are recorded only by the Synoptics (see Matt 3:17; Mark 1:11; Luke 3:22; and Matt 17:5; Mark 9:7; Luke 9:35); the third appears in John 12:28. The first and third witnesses of the Father, though public, seem not to have been understood by the mixed crowd; the second was private. To a Jew, the voice from heaven would have meant the approval of God; yet this seems to have had little effect on the multitude. Jesus implies that his hearers had not apprehended the revelation of God because they had not believed him whom the Father had sent. Openness of belief must precede the reception of truth.

39–40 The verb "study" could be either an imperative, as KJV translates it, or an indicative, as in NIV. Probably the latter is the correct translation, for Jesus was stating a fact, not giving a command. After the destruction of the temple of Solomon in 586 B.C., the Jewish scholars of the Exile substituted the study of the Law for the observance of the temple ritual and sacrifices. They pored over the OT, endeavoring to extract the fullest possible meaning from its words, because they believed that the very study itself would bring them life. By so doing they missed the chief subject of the OT revelation. Jesus claimed the Law, the Prophets, and the Psalms (Writings) as witnesses to his person and claims (Luke 24:44). He rebuked his hearers for their inconsistency in studying the Scriptures so diligently while rejecting his claims, which were founded on those same Scriptures.

Jesus' statement reveals his attitude toward the OT. He accepted its divine authority and averred that its prophecies spoke of him (cf. Luke 24:27, 44). Not only did he affirm its predictive accuracy, but he also took both the principles and the predictions written in the Scriptures as a guide for his attitude and career. They prefigured his sacrifice (John 3:14–15), marked some of the events of the Passion (12:14–15; 18:9; 19:24, 28, 36), and seemed to be in the forefront of his thinking as the end approached.

41–42 The Scriptures are so designed that when people read them, they are to recognize and acknowledge God's glory. Even the Jews would agree to that. But Jesus said the people were incapable of both interpreting and applying the Scriptures, for as students of the Scriptures they should have known that they spoke of him. Because the Jews did not give "praise" (actually, the word is "glory" [*doxa*]) to Jesus, it was evident that they were spiritually unable to make the connection between the Scriptures and the Savior. But this came as no surprise to Jesus. The expression "I know you" is singularly forceful, for the perfect tense of the verb "know" (*egnōka*) implies a settled state of knowledge based on past experience (cf. John 2:24). Jesus would not entrust himself to those who responded solely on the basis of external circumstances, such as miracles. Outward adulation is of short duration.

43–44 Jesus expressed disappointment because the people would not accept his credentials though they would accept the personal claims of another who acted solely on his own authority. Jesus was not there as a representative of Caesar, or Zeus, or even himself. Men are more apt to receive other men than they are to receive one who comes in the name of God. Compare the choice of Barabbas over Jesus at the final trial (Luke 23:18–23). Verse 44 rebukes those students of the Scriptures who are more interested in establishing their competitive reputations for scholarship than in obeying the revelation of God so as to bring his approval.

45–47 Moses, the writer of the Law, was highly revered by the Jewish nation. The people would not knowingly do anything that would be contrary to the teaching of Moses and the Law. Their obedience to him was a source of pride. In fact, their very hope in securing God's favor and blessing lay in their relationship to Moses. Jesus' statement that their rejection of him would make them guilty before God even according to Moses was startling. Jesus told the people that the law of Moses would condemn them in their rejection of him because their failure to believe in him was essentially a rejection of Moses since Moses had prefigured him. Jesus said that a real belief in the revelation of the Law through Moses would lead to a belief in himself (cf. Luke 16:29–31).

Notes

36 Ἔργον (*ergon*, "work") appears twenty-seven times in the Gospel of John. In each instance the term implies the characteristic activity of the person it is ascribed to, whether men (3:19, 20, 21; 7:7; 8:39), God (4:34; 5:20; 6:28, 29; 9:3, 4; 10:37; 14:10), Satan (8:41), or Jesus (5:36; 7:3, 21; 10:25, 32–33, 38; 14:11, 12; 15:24; 17:4). Jesus referred several times to the work God had committed to him (4:34; 5:36; 9:3; 10:37; 17:4) and remarked that the Father was in him, doing his work (14:11). On a few occasions NIV translates ἔργον by "miracle" (7:3, 21; 10:25, 32, 38; 14:11; 15:24). While this is not a mistranslation since the "works" were in many instances miraculous, the stress lies more on the characteristic manifestations of Jesus' personality and commission than on the miraculous quality of his deeds. Not all were miracles, though the miracles should be included in the "works."

The application of the term ἔργον ("work") to Satan appears in the contrast Jesus drew between the works of Abraham and the works of his opponents' father. As a servant of God, Abraham set a standard for spiritual life his descendants had forgotten. Jesus reminded them that they were no longer walking in the steps of their forefather.

Jesus considered the "works" he performed to be one of the strongest witnesses to his claims (5:36; 14:10–11). They were not abnormal activities or special occasional miracles but were rather the usual mode of Jesus' activity when confronting a challenging situation. Because of this, the witness is doubly strong, for the "works" revealed the normal powers he exercised when they were needed.

42 The phrase τὴν ἀγάπην τοῦ θεοῦ (tēn agapēn tou theou, "the love of God") can denote either the "love from God" or the "love for God," depending on whether τοῦ θεοῦ (tou theou) is a subjective or objective genitive. In the former case it is God who supplies the love (cf. 1 John 4:7, 10, 19). Men do not respond to the person of Christ because they have not been the recipients of God's love. In the latter, the love is that which is directed towards God. Men do not love the Lord Jesus because they have no real love for God within them.

This is the first use of the noun ἀγάπη (agapē, "love") in the Gospel. John uses it seven times (13:35; 15:9, 10 bis, 13; 17:26), in addition to the copious use of the verb. As it is used in John, it speaks of a self-sacrificing, giving love (3:16). It is a love of action more than emotion and has in view the loved one's need.

C. *The Beginning of Conflict* (6:1–8:59)

Chapter 6 of John marks the watershed of Jesus' career. Up to this point his popularity had been increasing, in spite of the opposition of the leaders and the occasional grumbling of disaffected hearers or disciples. The interview with the disciples at Caesarea Philippi and the Transfiguration, which occurred shortly afterward, called for a new commitment on the part of the disciples and was followed by a new program on the part of Jesus. He openly declared to them that he would proceed to Jerusalem where he would be delivered up to death (Matt 16:13–17:13; Mark 8:27–32; Luke 9:18–36). John does not narrate these incidents, but his account parallels them to some degree. The feeding of the multitude is identical; there is an allusion to his impending death (John 6:51); and from that point the number of his disciples diminished (6:66), and the controversy with the Pharisees grew increasingly bitter.

1. *The feeding of the five thousand*

6:1–15

[1]Some time after this, Jesus crossed to the far shore of the Sea of Galilee (that is, the Sea of Tiberias), [2]and a great crowd of people followed him because they saw the miraculous signs he had performed on the sick. [3]Then Jesus went up on the hillside and sat down with his disciples. [4]The Jewish Passover Feast was near.

[5]When Jesus looked up and saw a great crowd coming toward him, he said to Philip, "Where shall we buy bread for these people to eat?" [6]He asked this only to test him, for he already had in mind what he was going to do.

[7]Philip answered him, "Eight months' wages would not buy enough bread for each one to have a bite!"

[8]Another of his disciples, Andrew, Simon Peter's brother, spoke up, [9]"Here is a boy with five small barley loaves and two small fish, but how far will they go among so many?"

[10]Jesus said, "Have the people sit down." There was plenty of grass in that place, and the men sat down, about five thousand of them. [11]Jesus then took the loaves, gave thanks, and distributed to those who were seated as much as they wanted. He did the same with the fish.

[12]When they had all had enough to eat, he said to his disciples, "Gather the pieces that are left over. Let nothing be wasted." [13]So they gathered them and filled twelve baskets with the pieces of the five barley loaves left over by those who had eaten.

[14]After the people saw the miraculous sign that Jesus did, they began to say, "Surely this is the Prophet who is to come into the world." [15]Jesus, knowing that

they intended to come and make him king by force, withdrew again into the hills
by himself.

1–4 This miracle is the only one that is mentioned in all the Gospels. This fact alone
should alert us to its significance. The phrase "some time after this" shows that John does
not specify the exact lapse of time between this event and the one previously recorded.
The fact that Jesus was in Galilee may indicate that a segment of the Galilean ministry
is presupposed as having already occurred. The feeding of the multitude took place in
the spring shortly before the Passover (v.4). Perhaps some of the people belonged to a
crowd of pilgrims who had come together from different parts of northern Galilee, in
preparation for the annual pilgrimage to Jerusalem. Jesus was well known because of the
miracles he had performed on sick people. John uses the word "signs" (*sēmeia*), though
he gives no details of their character. His usage confirms his statement that Jesus performed "many other miraculous signs" during his ministry (20:30). The very fact that this
one was selected enhances its importance.

The Synoptics indicate that Jesus had several motives in retreating to the north shore
of the Sea of Galilee. The time had come to prepare the disciples for his death and to
sort out those who would be loyal from those who would not. The determination of Jesus'
enemies to remove him became known to him and to his disciples, and they had to
confront this rapidly growing hostility. Furthermore, as the account shows, Jesus refused
to take the part of a political Messiah or king. He was willing to meet basic needs but
he would not assume the responsibility of leading a revolt or of creating a new nation.
Knowing these things, he called the disciples together so that they could report on their
recent ministries (Mark 6:30; Luke 9:10). Matthew adds that Jesus had just learned of
the execution of John the Baptist (Matt 14:12–13) and that he withdrew to the wilderness
with his disciples for consultation.

5–6 John's interest concentrates mainly on the relation of this occasion to the disciples.
The crowd had come unbidden, prompted by curiosity and eagerness to share in Jesus'
teaching and healing power. As the day declined, Jesus recognized that they were
hungry. Desirous of involving the disciples in the responsibility for ministry, Jesus turned
to Philip, asking, "Where shall we buy bread for these people to eat?" Jesus was not at
a loss for a solution to the problem; he wished to educate the disciples by calling their
attention to their responsibilities and by leading them to propose some plan of action.

7 Philip's reply shows that while he had a practical turn of mind, he was rather un-
imaginative. His calculations, however accurate, were futile, for he could only produce
statistics to show what could not be done. The text translates "eight months' wages"
rather than the literal "two hundred denarii" (*diakosiōn dēnariōn*). A denarius, which
was worth approximately seventeen cents, was a day's wage for an unskilled laborer or
soldier. If a man worked for six days a week, two hundred denarii would represent the
pay for thirty-three weeks, which would be just about eight months. It would take a long
time to save the equivalent of such a sum. No doubt none of the disciples would have
enough money to subsidize the purchase of food for a crowd of approximately ten
thousand persons, including women and children (Matt 14:21).

8–9 In contrast to Philip's pessimism, Andrew was more hopeful. He made the positive presentation of a boy's lunch: five small, flat barley cakes, made of the cheapest grain available, and the two fish, which probably were small pickled fish which served as hors d'oeuvres. Andrew doubted the value of his own suggestion, for he commented, "How far will they go among so many?"

10 The action of Jesus reveals both natural wisdom and supernatural power. His order to have the people sit down was necessary to stabilize the crowd so that there would not be a rush for the food. It also served to organize them in groups to facilitate serving. John mentions only the men, who numbered about five thousand; Matthew remarks that there were women and children also (Matt 14:21).

11 The multiplication of the food was obviously not done with great fanfare. As the disciples distributed it, Jesus seems to have increased it by breaking it indefinitely until all were satisfied.

12-13 In spite of the miraculous power that effectively produced the ample supply, Jesus permitted no waste of the surplus. Twelve baskets full of remnants were salvaged—possibly one for each of the disciples—and carried back to Capernaum. The term for "basket" (*kophinos*) usually denotes a large basket, such as might be used for fish or bulky objects. The detail of collecting the remaining fragments of bread and fish may have been introduced to emphasize the ample sufficiency that Jesus provided, or it may indicate that he combined generosity with economy.

14 The miracle excited the wonder of the people and compelled them to recognize that Jesus was an unusual person. The allusion to "the Prophet" is probably a reflection of Deuteronomy 18:15, Moses' prediction of a prophet like himself who would command their hearing. It gives an indication of the undercurrent of popular expectation that earlier appeared in the question of the Pharisees to John the Baptist (John 1:21) and also later in the discussion at the Feast of Tabernacles (7:40, 52 mg.). Since Moses had provided food and water in the desert (Exod 16:11–36; 17:1–6; Num 11:1–33; 20:2–11), the people expected that the Prophet like Moses would do likewise.

15 The desire of the multitude to make Jesus king marks both the height of his popularity and the moment of decision for him. They wanted someone to rule them who would feed them and guarantee their security; they had no comprehension of his spiritual mission or purpose. He, on the other hand, refused to become a political opportunist or demagogue. His kingdom could not be promoted by organizing a revolt against the existing political powers or by promising a dole to all who would join his banner.

2. The walking on the water

6:16–21

> [16]When evening came, his disciples went down to the lake, [17]where they got into a boat and set off across the lake for Capernaum. By now it was dark, and Jesus had not yet joined them. [18]A strong wind was blowing and the waters grew rough. [19]When they had rowed three or three and a half miles, they saw Jesus approaching the boat, walking on the water; and they were terrified. [20]But he said to them, "It is I; don't be afraid." [21]Then they were willing to take him into the boat, and immediately the boat reached the shore where they were heading.

16–17 "Evening" could be any time in the afternoon shortly before sunset. The disciples probably planned to cover the short distance between Bethsaida and Capernaum while daylight lasted. Twilight is brief in the Palestinian springtime, and they would naturally wish to reach home before dark. They actually "went down to the lake," for the terrain around the lake is hilly. For the feeding of the five thousand, the group had journeyed some distance inland. John states that darkness had already fallen before they actually began to cross the lake. The statement that "Jesus had not yet joined them" may imply that they half-expected him to do so and waited until the last minute, hoping that he would come.

18 The Sea of Galilee is six hundred feet below sea level, in a cuplike depression among the hills. When the sun sets, the air cools; and as the cooler air from the west rushes down over the hillside, the resultant wind churns the lake. Since the disciples were rowing toward Capernaum, they were heading into the wind; consequently, they made little progress.

19 "Three or three and a half miles" shows that the disciples were still a considerable distance from the shore at Capernaum. Mark says that "the boat was in the middle of the lake" (6:47). As the disciples looked back, they were terrified to see a human form coming toward them across the water. The hypothesis that Jesus was walking on the lake shore and only appeared to be walking on the water is scarcely adequate. The fishermen who were well acquainted with the Sea of Galilee would certainly be able to discern the difference between a person's walking on the shore and his walking on the surface of the water. Mark states that "they thought he was a ghost" (Mark 6:49), adding that "all saw him and were terrified."

20–21 Jesus calmed their fears by speaking to them. When they recognized his voice, they were willing to take him into the boat. The miracle was designed to demonstrate that Jesus could be with them under all circumstances. As the multiplication of the loaves and fishes showed his power over matter, so the walking on the water revealed his power over the forces of nature. It was one more step in the education of the disciples' faith.

3. *The address in the synagogue*

6:22–59

22The next day the crowd that had stayed on the opposite shore of the lake realized that only one boat had been there, and that Jesus had not entered it with his disciples, but that they had gone away alone. 23Then some boats from Tiberias landed near the place where the people had eaten the bread after the Lord had given thanks. 24Once the crowd realized that neither Jesus nor his disciples were there, they got into the boats and went to Capernaum in search of Jesus.

25When they found him on the other side of the lake, they asked him, "Rabbi, when did you get here?"

26Jesus answered, "I tell you the truth, you are looking for me, not because you saw miraculous signs but because you ate the loaves and had your fill. 27Do not work for food that spoils, but for food that endures to eternal life, which the Son of Man will give you. On him God the Father has placed his seal of approval."

28Then they asked him, "What must we do to do the works God requires?"

29Jesus answered, "The work of God is this: to believe in the one he has sent."

30So they asked him, "What miraculous sign then will you give that we may see it and believe you? What will you do? [31]Our forefathers ate the manna in the desert; as it is written: 'He gave them bread from heaven to eat.' "

[32]Jesus said to them, "I tell you the truth, it is not Moses who has given you the bread from heaven, but it is my Father who gives you the true bread from heaven. [33]For the bread of God is he who comes down from heaven and gives life to the world."

[34]"Sir," they said, "from now on give us this bread."

[35]Then Jesus declared, "I am the bread of life. He who comes to me will never go hungry, and he who believes in me will never be thirsty. [36]But as I told you, you have seen me and still you do not believe. [37]All that the Father gives me will come to me, and whoever comes to me I will never drive away. [38]For I have come down from heaven not to do my will but to do the will of him who sent me. [39]And this is the will of him who sent me, that I shall lose none of all that he has given me, but raise them up at the last day. [40]For my Father's will is that everyone who looks to the Son and believes in him shall have eternal life, and I will raise him up at the last day."

[41]At this the Jews began to grumble about him because he said, "I am the bread that came down from heaven." [42]They said, "Is this not Jesus, the son of Joseph, whose father and mother we know? How can he now say, 'I came down from heaven'?"

[43]"Stop grumbling among yourselves," Jesus answered. [44]"No one can come to me unless the Father who sent me draws him, and I will raise him up at the last day. [45]It is written in the Prophets: 'They will all be taught by God.' Everyone who listens to the Father and learns from him comes to me. [46]No one has seen the Father except the one who is from God; only he has seen the Father. [47]I tell you the truth, he who believes has everlasting life. [48]I am the bread of life. [49]Your forefathers ate the manna in the desert, yet they died. [50]But here is the bread that comes down from heaven, which a man may eat and not die. [51]I am the living bread that came down from heaven. If a man eats of this bread, he will live forever. This bread is my flesh, which I will give for the life of the world."

[52]Then the Jews began to argue sharply among themselves, "How can this man give us his flesh to eat?"

[53]Jesus said to them, "I tell you the truth, unless you eat the flesh of the Son of Man and drink his blood, you have no life in you. [54]Whoever eats my flesh and drinks my blood has eternal life, and I will raise him up at the last day. [55]For my flesh is real food and my blood is real drink. [56]Whoever eats my flesh and drinks my blood remains in me, and I in him. [57]Just as the living Father sent me and I live because of the Father, so the one who feeds on me will live because of me. [58]This is the bread that came down from heaven. Our forefathers ate ˌmannaˌ and died, but he who feeds on this bread will live forever." [59]He said this while teaching in the synagogue in Capernaum.

22–25 Although the people were unaware of Jesus' miracle of walking on the water, they knew that something had transpired. They knew that the disciples had used the lone boat and that Jesus had not departed with the disciples. The people were interested in seeing Jesus again, but they did not know where to find him. When boats became available (v.23) and the people came to the realization that Jesus and his disciples had departed, they "went to Capernaum in search of Jesus" (v.24). The crowd's surprise at finding Jesus with the disciples once again is evidenced by the statement, "When did you get here?" (v.25). Apparently Jesus' miracle of walking on the water was only for his disciples, for he did not tell the people how he had arrived at Capernaum.

26–27 Jesus was not flattered by the attention of the crowds, but immediately he began his instruction. The several answers he gave to their questions are mostly corrections of their opinions. The first is a reply to materialism: "You are looking for me, not because you saw miraculous signs but because you ate the loaves and had your fill" (v.26). His reply was "Do not work for food that spoils, but for food that endures to eternal life, which the Son of Man will give you" (v.27). This parallels his words to the Samaritan woman concerning the "living water" that did not come from the well. Like the Samaritan woman, the people could not lift their minds above the physical necessities of life. Jesus was not commanding them to stop working for a living, but he was saying that their main quest should not be for food that readily perishes. The "food that endures to eternal life" is himself, as the later mystical utterance in v.54 states.

28–29 The second question, "What must we do to do the works God requires?" implies both desire and a sense of self-sufficiency. The people seemed sure that if they wished to do so, they were capable of doing the works of God. As used in John, "works" (*erga*) refers to those acts that distinguish the peculiar abilities of some person (see Note on 5:36). In this setting it refers to the works God requires of those who please him. To Jewish questioners, obtaining eternal life consisted in finding the right formula for performing works to please God. Jesus directed them to the gift of God that could be obtained by faith in him. Again there is a similarity to his conversation with the Samaritan woman: "If you knew the gift of God" (John 4:10). Jesus contradicted directly the presuppositions of his interrogators.

30 The third question was "What miraculous sign then will you give that we may see it and believe you?" In consideration of the spectacular miracle he had performed on the preceding day, it seems incredible that they would have asked this question. The sequence of the text seems to indicate that those who looked for Jesus and then questioned him were part of the crowd who had eaten of the bread and fish he had multiplied. They were either forgetful or naive.

31 The best solution for this literary puzzle is that the crowd was, as usual, demanding a sign and had forgotten that the Lord had just provided one. They were attempting to evaluate him by the ministry of Moses, who had provided manna for their forefathers in the wilderness.

32–33 Jesus informed the people that Moses did not give them the real spiritual bread. The Greek word for "true" (*alēthinos*) means "genuine" or "original." Jesus did not mean that the manna had no food value; he meant it was not the means of sustaining spiritual life. He claimed to be the genuine and only source of spiritual nourishment. This may be an oblique reference to Deuteronomy 8:3: "Man does not live on bread alone but on every word that comes from the mouth of the LORD." As physical food is necessary for physical life, so spiritual food is necessary for spiritual life.

34–36 The request that Jesus should give the people the bread of life parallels the request of the Samaritan woman for the water of life (4:15). In both cases the petition indicates that the speaker did not understand Jesus' real meaning and reveals a materialistic frame of mind. Jesus had already startled the people by saying that Moses did not give them real bread from heaven. Now he shocked them a second time by announcing that he was the bread the Father had given. Jesus claimed to be the only permanent satisfaction for the human desire for life. The attainment of this satisfaction hinges on belief. The definition of this term varies between the people's use of it (v.30) and Jesus' (v.35). To them "belief" meant acceptance of his competence on the basis of miracles;

to him it meant commitment, not finally on the basis of the miracles, but on trust in his person. The assertion "I am the bread of life" is the first in a series of such declarations that are peculiar to this Gospel (8:12; 10:7, 11; 11:25; 14:6; 15:1). Each represents a particular relationship of Jesus to the spiritual needs of men: their light in darkness, their entrance into security and fellowship, their guide and protector in life, their hope in death, their certainty in perplexity, and their source of vitality for productiveness. He desired that men should receive him, not simply for what he might give them, but for what he might be to them. The use of the definite article "the" in "the life" (*tēs zōēs*) is definitive and restrictive. Jesus was talking about "the" bread that gives eternal life; but this was beyond their comprehension, just as the miracles Jesus had performed in their sight did not lead them to believe in him.

37 "All" (*pan*) is a neuter singular rather than a masculine plural and refers to everything the Father has put under Jesus' control (cf. John 5:19–27). It includes the people who are his. The paradox latent in this text has puzzled many. How can one be sure that the Father has really given him to Christ? Will he come only to be rebuffed? Jesus made plain that human salvation is no surprise to God. He summons men to himself by his Word and by his Spirit. They can come only at his invitation. The invitation, however, is not restricted to any particular time or place, nor is it exclusively for any one nation, race, or culture. No man needs to fear that he will come in vain, for Jesus said emphatically that he would not refuse anyone. Man does not make his opportunity for salvation; he accepts its free offer. A superficial attachment to God is not enough, for if the desire for salvation is not inspired by God, true salvation will not result.

38–40 Six times in this immediate context Jesus says that he "came down from heaven" (6:33, 38, 41, 50, 51, 58). His claim to heavenly origin is unmistakable. Jesus also repeatedly affirmed that he had come to do his Father's will. That will is made clear here: Jesus will "lose none of all that he has given" him (v.39). Not only does Jesus' keeping ministry apply to this life, but he will "raise them up at the last day." Jesus' constant allusion to the Father who gave him the believers, who sent him to give eternal life, and who draws believers to him indicates his close relationship with the Father. This relationship is not merely that of a prophet who speaks God's message; it is that of a Son who fulfills the Father's purpose (v.40). His prerogative of resurrection is the final proof of his authority.

41–42 "The Jews" in John usually represent those who are opposed to Jesus, not simply a group of Jewish origin (cf. 2:18, 20; 5:16). They might be called "the opposition party." In this instance they seem to be local persons, for they show some acquaintance with Jesus' family. They took for granted that he was the son of Joseph and Mary, whom they had known for several years. To them his claim of heavenly origin was incredible.

43–45 Jesus rebuked the people for their grumbling and told them that they would never come to him unless the Father initiated the action. Again Jesus spoke of the promise of resurrection for those who belonged to him (v.44; cf. v.39). Verse 45 indicates that God would do his drawing through the Scriptures and that those who were obedient to God's will as revealed in the Scriptures would come to Jesus. He had been delegated by the Father to have life, give life, secure life, and restore life.

46 Jesus' statement is the foundation for the assertion in John 1:18: "No one has ever seen God, but God the only Son, who is at the Father's side, has made him known." Jesus claimed authoritative knowledge of God such as a son could claim concerning his own father.

47 "I tell you the truth" is the NIV translation for the double *amēn* that prefaces Jesus' solemn assertions in this Gospel. As emphatically as he could, Jesus was saying that the one who believes in him has "everlasting life." The particular construction used here to describe the believer is a participle, which indicates that the person's life is characterized by belief in Jesus and does not just begin in faith.

48–50 Again Jesus says, "I am the bread of life" (cf. v.35). Before, he linked this statement with the supplying of man's basic needs; hunger and thirst would be permanently alleviated. This time Jesus links the statement to life itself. When the Jews ate the heavenly bread ("manna") in the wilderness, their physical needs were met. However, they still died (v.49). But Jesus said that he "is the bread that comes down from heaven, which a man may eat and not die" (v.50).

51 The key to a genuine experience with God lies in the sequence of statements in this verse. It is vested in the person of Christ, who descended from heaven to provide for man what his nature requires. To eat of this bread means to appropriate Christ as one's life. It is a figure of belief, for no one will eat what he cannot trust to be edible. To eat a meal implies that it is wholesome, nourishing, and real. This verse introduces the concept of Jesus' vicarious death, the sacrifice of his body for the sins of the world. (For a full discussion of the bread from heaven, see Morris, NIC, pp. 373–81.)

52 The last reaction of Jesus' opponents was prompted by the apparent impossibility of his statement. They took literally the figure of eating his flesh. Unless one has spiritual perception, spiritual truth makes no sense whatsoever. Nicodemus could not comprehend the new birth; so, too, now the Jews considered the Lord's words to be utter nonsense. It hardly seems possible that they misunderstood what he said, for they responded, "How can this man give us his flesh to eat?"

53–54 Jesus made himself perfectly clear. He repeated the statement with this added emphasis: "I tell you the truth." And with that, he added another aspect that was even more repulsive to the Jews: "Unless you eat the flesh of the Son of Man and *drink his blood*" (italics mine). If what Jesus said before was nonsense, this latter statement bordered on gross sin. The law of Moses expressly forbade any drinking of blood on penalty of being cut off from the people (Lev 17:10–14). Three times in this context Jesus refers to the importance of eating his flesh and drinking his blood. There could be no mistaking what he said now.

The progression in thought in vv.51–54 is significant. First, Christ said he gives his flesh "for the life of the world" (v.51). Then he says whoever has not partaken of his flesh and blood has "no life" in him (v.53). But then whoever eats his flesh and drinks his blood "has eternal life, and I will raise him up at the last day" (v.54). The Lord again gives the promise of resurrection to those who are associated with him (cf. vv.39–40, 44). If there were any Sadducees among the "Jews," they really would have been infuriated. They did not believe in resurrection, and Jesus was offering them something their theology denied.

55–57 Jesus explains what he means by his flesh and blood in these two verses. First of all, what he is talking about is as real to him as are the physical counterparts that his opponents had in mind. It is a real food and a real drink that produces a real life. To partake of the elements that Christ offers brings one into an abiding relationship with him. The reality of the Christ-imparted life has been attested to by the myriads of Christians throughout the age who have partaken of Christ's body and blood, in sweet communion with him. Jesus likened the relationship that believers would sustain with him to that existing between the Father and himself. The intimacy that the Son shared with the Father would be parallel to the intimacy between the Lord Jesus and his disciples.

58–59 Jesus climaxed his discourse by once more referring to the "bread that came down from heaven," the forefathers who ate it in the wilderness and died, and the promise of everlasting life to those who received him. Moses was great. It was through him that the people were sustained in the wilderness. But Jesus is far greater, for what he provides satisfies throughout all eternity. Ironically, this conversation took place at "the synogogue in Capernaum." What better place to promise eternal life than where people gather to seek that very thing through their religion!

Whether or not this text is sacramental in the sense that it is a Johannine substitute for the Synoptic account of the Lord's Supper has been argued at length. There are at least two factors that argue against the sacramental interpretation: (1) the equation of "eating" and "drinking" with belief, which is not a physical action, and (2) Jesus' own explanation to the disciples that his words "are spirit and life" (v.63). Undoubtedly the Lord's Supper as later established was intended to perpetuate the concept implied here, namely, that a constant renewal of faith and the outward confession of renewal should be expressed by participation in the bread and wine. There is no hint that Jesus was at this point instituting a sacrament or that the celebration of the Eucharist carried with it intrinsic saving power. Justin Martyr (c. 140) stated that no one was allowed to partake of it except (1) those who believed that the things Christians teach are true and (2) those who had already confessed their faith in baptism (*Apology* 1.66).

Notes

---

37 The Gr. construction employs the emphatic double negative: οὐ μὴ ἐκβάλω (*ou mē ekbalō*, "I will never drive away").

51, 53, 54, 56 The use of the aorist tense of ἐσθίω (*esthiō*, "to consume") in vv.51 and 53 implies a decisive action at the outset, an acceptance. The present tense of τρώγω (*trōgō*, "to gnaw" or "chew") refers to a progressive action that applies to the maintenance of a continuing state.

---

4. *The division among the disciples*

6:60–71

⁶⁰On hearing it, many of his disciples said, "This is a hard teaching. Who can accept it?"

⁶¹Aware that his disciples were grumbling about this, Jesus said to them, "Does this offend you? ⁶²What if you see the Son of Man ascend to where he was before! ⁶³The Spirit gives life; the flesh counts for nothing. The words I have spoken to you are spirit and they are life. ⁶⁴Yet there are some of you who do not believe." For Jesus had known from the beginning which of them did not believe and who would

betray him. 65He went on to say, "This is why I told you that no one can come to me unless the Father has enabled him."

66From this time many of his disciples turned back and no longer followed him.

67"You do not want to leave too, do you?" Jesus asked the Twelve.

68Simon Peter answered him, "Lord, to whom shall we go? You have the words of eternal life. 69We believe and know that you are the Holy One of God."

70Then Jesus replied, "Have I not chosen you, the Twelve? Yet one of you is a devil!" 71(He meant Judas, the son of Simon Iscariot, who, though one of the Twelve, was later to betray him.)

60 The enigmatic words of Jesus puzzled some of the disciples just as much as they did the mixed crowd. "Disciples" refers to the total group of adherents who had attached themselves to Jesus, however loosely, not solely to the Twelve. Those who could not understand him, or who were unwilling to trust him completely, withdrew. It was a turning point in their experience. They lacked the spiritual perception to grasp his meaning.

61 Jesus' inward knowledge of the disciples enabled him to detect their attitude. The language reemphasizes the principle stated in John 2:25: "He knew what was in a man." His questions reveal surprise that they were mystified. If they could not understand the meaning of eating his flesh and drinking his blood, how would they be able to interpret his resurrection (implied) and his ascension? If they were bewildered by his language, how much more difficult would they find the final event that would lead to his return to God?

62 This reference to the Ascension is one of several in the Gospel, though the act itself is not recorded (3:13; 8:21; 16:10; 17:11; 20:17). The disciples had complained that the concept of Jesus' being the true bread that comes down from heaven was incomprehensible. He intimated that if they witnessed his ascension, as he apparently expected, they would be even more astonished. They had difficulty in believing that he could belong to two different realms. When on the morning of his resurrection Mary grasped him in order to keep him in her existing world lest he should vanish again, he reassured her that he had not yet departed permanently to the Father (20:17). His intention of ultimate departure is clearly stated in John 14:3 and 17:11.

63 Jesus undoubtedly was referring to the Holy Spirit. The Spirit imparts life to the believer; it is not transmitted by the process of physical eating. Jesus was saddened by the dullness of some of his disciples that prevented their believing in the sense that they did not appropriate him.

64 Jesus' reference to those who did not believe is explained by his later allusion to Judas (v.70). Jesus had given ample opportunity for faith to all those who followed him; yet from the beginning his spiritual discernment made him aware of those whose faith was genuine and those whose attachment was only superficial.

65 Jesus strongly implied that faith is the result of God's enabling. Unbelief is natural to those who are selfish and alienated from God and who cannot accept the idea that he can do the impossible. Complete commitment to God is impossible for a selfish heart; the Holy Spirit must awaken and empower it to believe. This does not destroy the

voluntary character of faith; it is rather in accord with the cry of the man who said to Jesus, "I do believe; help me overcome my unbelief " (Mark 9:24). Unbelief is part of the fabric of human mentality; the intervention of divine grace is necessary to transform it to faith.

66 "From this time" is a possible translation of *ek toutou*. It could also mean "Because of this [utterance]." The latter makes good sense because it was not simply the chronology that changed the disciples' attitude. It was the difficulty of comprehending Jesus' saying or the offense it gave to their self-sufficiency.

67 The desired response to a question can often be prompted by the way the question is framed. Our Lord ever wishes to encourage faith that is weak, and he had a great deal of concern and love for his disciples. That's why he asked, "You do not want to leave too, do you?"

68 The words of Simon Peter parallel those in the Great Confession given in the Synoptics (Matt 16:16; Mark 8:29; Luke 9:20). Peter spoke as the representative of the Twelve. He declared that nobody else had the life-giving message of Jesus and that there was no other source that would satisfy them. The statement reveals that, in spite of all his usual awkwardness, Simon's faith in Jesus was genuine; and he evidenced true spiritual sensitivity.

"Words of eternal life" refers to the nature of Jesus' teaching rather than to any specific formula he might have used. The Greek article, which marks definiteness, is lacking here. Simon Peter recognized the difference between the authoritative declaration of Jesus and the speculations of the religious teachers of his day. Peter's statement represents the spiritual discernment the disciples had developed during their association with Jesus.

69 The emphatic use of the first personal plural pronoun implies a contrast between the Twelve and those who had deserted Jesus: "*We* believe" (italics mine). Actually, the use of the perfect tense with the verbs "believe" and "know" indicates the verse should be translated "We have believed and have known." This shows a fixed and settled decision, which is expressed here by the English present tense. Peter is affirming that they have reached a final conviction that Jesus is indeed "the Holy One of God." This term is rare in the NT as a title of Jesus. It appears again in Peter's sermon at Pentecost, where he quotes Psalm 16:10 as a prophecy of Jesus' resurrection: "Nor will you let your Holy One see decay" (Acts 2:27), and also in his speech on Solomon's Colonnade: "You disowned the Holy and Righteous One" (Acts 3:14). It bears a strong resemblance to the expression "the Holy One of Israel," which occurs frequently in the prophecy of Isaiah (41:14; 43:3; 47:4; 48:17; and elsewhere).

70 Jesus indicated that his choice of the Twelve was conscious and deliberate; yet he included one he knew would be a traitor. Judas had no less opportunity than any of the others to know and serve Jesus; nor was he a victim of discrimination, for he was given a prominent place among them as treasurer of the group (John 12:6). He was dishonest in his financial administration and selfish in his attitude. In contrast with Simon Peter, who denied Jesus, it can be said that Judas acted by choice, Peter by impulse. Whereas Judas regarded Jesus as a means of attaining his ambition, Peter thought of Jesus as a friend. Judas was motivated by selfishness; Peter, by fear. The word "devil" (*diabolos*) means literally "slanderer." Generally it refers to Satan; only three times in the NT is it applied to human beings, twice in the Pastoral Epistles (2 Tim 3:3; Titus 2:3), where it is translated "slanderous" or "slanderer," and in this one instance in John. The two other instances in this Gospel unmistakably refer to Satan.

71 This verse reads like a footnote or side comment. Although the Gospels never indulge in lengthy denunciation of Judas, almost invariably his name is followed by the phrase "who betrayed him (Jesus)" (Matt 10:4; Mark 3:19; Luke 6:16; John 12:4; 18:2). "Iscariot" is derived from the transliteration *'îš q^erîyôt̤*, which means "man of Kerioth." Kerioth was a city in the southern part of Judah (Josh 15:25), south of Hebron in the dry Negeb. There was another city with the same name located in Moab, but the former seems more likely to have been the home of Judas.

5. The visit to Jerusalem (7:1–52)

a. The journey

7:1–13

> ¹After this, Jesus went around in Galilee, purposely staying away from Judea because the Jews there were waiting to take his life. ²But when the Jewish Feast of Tabernacles was near, ³Jesus' brothers said to him, "You ought to leave here and go to Judea, so that your disciples may see the miracles you do. ⁴No one who wants to become a public figure acts in secret. Since you are doing these things, show yourself to the world." ⁵For even his own brothers did not believe in him.
> ⁶Therefore Jesus told them, "The right time for me has not yet come; for you any time is right. ⁷The world cannot hate you, but it hates me because I testify that what it does is evil. ⁸You go to the Feast. I am not yet going up to this Feast, because for me the right time has not yet come." ⁹Having said this, he stayed in Galilee.
> ¹⁰However, after his brothers had left for the Feast, he went also, not publicly, but in secret. ¹¹Now at the Feast the Jews were watching for him and asking, "Where is that man?"
> ¹²Among the crowds there was widespread whispering about him. Some said, "He is a good man."
> Others replied, "No, he deceives the people." ¹³But no one would say anything publicly about him for fear of the Jews.

1 The chronological sequence is indicated by the indefinite reference "After this." The writer evidently knew of Jesus' later Galilean ministry but chose not to record it. He shows that Jesus did not return to Judea at once after the feeding of the multitude because his life would be in danger. Ever since the healing of the paralytic in Jerusalem, his opponents had been attempting to kill him (5:18); and as time progressed, their hatred increased (7:19, 30, 32, 44; 8:59; 10:39; 11:8, 53) until they finally accomplished his death. From this point the opposition to Jesus becomes increasingly prominent in this Gospel.

2 The Feast of Tabernacles was celebrated in the autumn "on the fifteenth day of the seventh month" (Lev 23:34), which would compare roughly to the second week of October in our calendar. It began five days after the Day of Atonement (Yom Kippur) and lasted eight days (Lev 23:33–36; Deut 16:13–17). Each family constructed its own temporary shelter of branches to live in for the period of the feast. This typified the years of wandering in the desert before the people entered the Promised Land. The feast was joyful in character and was a time of thanksgiving for the harvest that marked the transition from nomadic poverty to stable affluence in their own land. It was one of the three annual feasts at which attendance was required of all Jewish men (Deut 16:16).

3-5 Because the gathering in Jerusalem brought together pilgrims from every section of Palestine, Jesus' brothers saw an excellent opportunity for him to acquire some publicity. Their advice to him was to join the crowds in Jerusalem so that he might enhance his reputation and gain more followers. Their suggestion may have been more sarcastic than serious, since they did not believe in him (v.5). To "believe in him" may carry with it a recognition of his purpose and sympathy with it, which his brothers did not have. Consequently their counsel may have been for him to abandon the idealism of teaching multitudes in obscurity and of risking death. If he possessed the powers his miracles seemed to imply, he should display them to the best advantage and capitalize on them.

6 Jesus' reply strongly resembles the one he gave his mother's request at the wedding in Cana of Galilee (2:4). He asserted that he was not living by the chance of casual opportunity but by a divine calendar predetermined by the Father. For this reason the world did not understand his action, and the difference in standards created both misunderstanding and hostility.

7 Again Jesus asserted that he did not belong to this world. The world regarded him as an alien and an antagonist because he condemned its evil works. The same idea is reiterated in the discourse to the disciples in John 15:18-21 and in the prayer to the Father in 17:14, 16. Jesus and the world at large lived in two different dimensions.

8-9 The word "yet" does not occur in many of the MSS, but it is included in the older papyri and in some of the older uncial MSS. The more difficult reading makes Jesus say, "I am not going up to this Feast." But v.10 tells us that afterwards "he went up also." Of course, Jesus' reference to "the right time" shows that the latter sense could be tenable. Morris (NIC, p. 401) notes that "not publicly" is the exact opposite to the brothers' suggestion (v.4). Jesus avoided all publicity and fanfare. He did not organize a delegation of disciples nor travel with a company of pilgrims.

10-11 The secret departure for Jerusalem was not an act of deception. It was an attempt to avoid unwelcome publicity. Jesus' enemies were watching for him, obviously for the purpose of arresting him (cf. v.1).

12-13 Public opinion was divided. The people who favored him were intimidated by the religious hierarchy, which was hostile toward Jesus. The atmosphere was tense, and Jesus did not wish to precipitate a crisis at this time.

Notes

8 The UBS text has οὐκ (ouk, "not") rather than οὔπω (oupō, "not yet"). The main support for the former is ℵ. The latter's main support is P66, 75. B. Metzger states that "the reading οὔπω was

introduced at an early date ... in order to alleviate the inconsistency between ver. 8 and ver. 10" (*Textual Commentary*, p. 216). It might be harder to explain the substitution of *ouk* for *oupō* on textual grounds than the opposite; but it is still true that the older MSS contain the easier reading.

---

b. *The popular debate*

7:14–36

¹⁴Not until halfway through the Feast did Jesus go up to the temple courts and begin to teach. ¹⁵The Jews were amazed and asked, "How did this man get such learning without having studied?"

¹⁶Jesus answered, "My teaching is not my own. It comes from him who sent me. ¹⁷If any one chooses to do God's will, he will find out whether my teaching comes from God or whether I speak on my own. ¹⁸He who speaks on his own does so to gain honor for himself, but he who works for the honor of the one who sent him is a man of truth; there is nothing false about him. ¹⁹Has not Moses given you the law? Yet not one of you keeps the law. Why are you trying to kill me?"

²⁰"You are demon-possessed," the crowd answered. "Who is trying to kill you?"

²¹Jesus said to them, "I did one miracle, and you are all astonished. ²²Yet, because Moses gave you circumcision (though actually it did not come from Moses, but from the patriarchs), you circumcise a child on the Sabbath. ²³Now if a child can be circumcised on the Sabbath so that the law of Moses may not be broken, why are you angry with me for healing the whole man on the Sabbath? ²⁴Stop judging by mere appearances, and make a right judgment."

²⁵At that point some of the people of Jerusalem began to ask, "Isn't this the man they are trying to kill? ²⁶Here he is, speaking publicly, and they are not saying a word to him. Have the authorities really concluded that he is the Christ? ²⁷But we know where this man is from; when the Christ comes, no one will know where he is from."

²⁸Then Jesus, still teaching in the temple courts, cried out, "Yes, you know me, and you know where I am from. I am not here on my own, but he who sent me is true. You do not know him, ²⁹but I know him because I am from him and he sent me."

³⁰At this they tried to seize him, but no one laid a hand on him, because his time had not yet come. ³¹Still, many in the crowd put their faith in him. They said, "When the Christ comes, will he do more miraculous signs than this man?"

³²The Pharisees heard the crowd whispering such things about him. Then the chief priests and the Pharisees sent temple guards to arrest him.

³³Jesus said, "I am with you for only a short time, and then I go to the one who sent me. ³⁴You will look for me, but you will not find me; and where I am, you cannot come."

³⁵The Jews said to one another, "Where does this man intend to go that we cannot find him? Will he go where our people live scattered among the Greeks, and teach the Greeks? ³⁶What did he mean when he said, 'You will look for me, but you will not find me,' and 'Where I am, you cannot come'?"

---

14 Jesus remained in seclusion until the feast was half completed and then appeared in the temple court to teach. His absence during the first half of the week had aroused the curiosity of the pilgrims who had expected that he would come in order to take advantage of the eager crowds. From the following text one might suppose that the crowd at the feast was either critical or hostile. The atmosphere reflected the turn of events after the feeding of the five thousand, when many of Jesus' disciples turned from him. Although the final crisis had not come, he had passed the apex of his popular ministry.

15 Even Jesus' critics admitted his acumen and learning. They could not comprehend how he could have acquired such knowledge without engaging in formal rabbinical study. Their comment recalls that of Mark: "The people were amazed at his teaching, because he taught them as one who had authority, not as the teachers of the law" (Mark 1:22).

16 Jesus insisted that his teaching did not originate with himself but that the message and the power came from God. As the perfect man and messenger of God, he gave all credit to the Father who had "sent" him (see comment on 5:30).

17–18 "If any man chooses to do God's will" does not simply mean that if one happens to do God's will in the future he will know the origin of Jesus' teaching. Rather, it means there must be a definite act of the human will to do God's will, a settled, determined purpose to fulfill it. Spiritual understanding is not produced solely by learning facts or procedures, but rather it depends on obedience to known truth. Obedience to God's known will develops discernment between falsehood and truth.

19 Jesus accepted the fact that Moses transmitted the Law to Israel and acknowledged the authority of that Law. He accused his opponents, who claimed to be champions of the Law, with failing to keep it. His charge that they were plotting to kill him was amply substantiated by their action at the end of the feast (7:44–45). His charge should be interpreted in the light of his own teaching on the sixth commandment (Matt 5:21–22), in which he declared that the act of murder results from contempt and hatred of another personality.

20 The response of the crowd to Jesus' accusation shows that the decision of the rulers had not been widely publicized. The people were bewildered by Jesus' statement. Curiously the only allusions in John to demonic activity are accusations made against Jesus (8:48–52; 10:20). Miracles of healing demoniacs are not mentioned in this Gospel. The synoptic Gospels also record a similar accusation (Matt 9:34; 12:24; Mark 3:22; Luke 11:15), though they ascribe Jesus' powers to demonic influence rather than discounting his words as those of a disordered mind.

21–22 Jesus is not saying that he did only "one miracle." By this time he had performed several; but these were of little interest to the "Jews," even if they were aware of them. The reference to circumcision on the Sabbath shows that the issue of healing on the Sabbath was central to Jesus' controversy with the Jewish rulers. So, no doubt, the "one miracle" refers to the healing of the paralytic at the Pool of Bethesda (John 5:1–18), which initiated the hostile criticism of "the Jews."

23–24 Circumcision was initiated by Abraham (Gen 17:9–14) and explicitly commanded in the law of Moses (Lev 12:3). Because it had to be observed on the eighth day after birth, it was allowable on the Sabbath. Circumcision was emblematic of separation from all other peoples, who were consequently called "the uncircumcision" (Eph 2:11). Jesus argued that if a rite were permitted that marked purification by affecting only one member of the body, why should he not be allowed to make the entire man whole on the Sabbath? The translation "stop judging" correctly implies that his enemies should cease making superficial pronouncements on his work and that they should evaluate it objectively.

25–27 Generally, the people were confused about the conflict between Jesus and the religious authorities. They wondered why he wasn't censored if he was such a threat to the nation. The reason the authorities did not promptly have him arrested was that they were uncertain of the sentiments of the people. If they acted hastily, they feared an uprising among the people that would most assuredly bring disciplinary action from the Romans.

The people were uncertain of Jesus' real identity. They knew the authorities sought to kill him, but their reluctance to act led the people to conclude that perhaps there was some validity to Jesus' messianic claim. What further confused them, however, was that they believed the Messiah would rise up out of total obscurity, that no one would "know where he is from." But this attitude reflected an ignorance of the prophetic Scriptures. The priests were familiar with the prophecy that he would be born in Bethlehem (Matt 2:5). It may be, however, that popular legend asserted that the Messiah would suddenly appear out of obscurity.

28–29 In the midst of all this confusion, Jesus replied positively. His first statement may be ironic. It can be translated, "So you know me and where I am from, do you?" The people must have been aware of his boyhood in Nazareth and no doubt considered him to be the son of Joseph and Mary (6:42). Jesus' reply was a renewed affirmation of his origin in God and his divine commission. He had not undertaken his mission by his own volition, but he had been "sent." His assertion evoked the dual response of belief and unbelief. The popular misunderstanding prevailed through his contacts at the feast, for it reappeared in vv.41–44.

30 Jesus' enemies attempted to seize him, but they failed because the hour of crisis had not come. Not only did "the hour" restrain him from sudden independent action (2:4), but it assured him of divine protection until the moment for action came (cf. Luke 22:53).

31 The response of many was belief, though it was hesitant. They did not affirm that he was the Messiah but cautiously suggested that the Messiah would perform no more miracles than Jesus did. Consequently they tended to believe that he might be the promised leader they anticipated. An incidental implication of this statement is that Jesus had been performing miracles during his ministry in Jerusalem. No particulars are given, however.

32 The favorable reaction of those who believed prompted the chief priests and Pharisees to action. To delay longer might result in more people turning to Jesus. The arrest was made official since the temple guards constituted the arresting party.

33–35 Jesus' reply to the action gave an intimation of his coming death. The declaration that he would go where he could neither be followed nor found excited the curiosity of the crowd. They surmised that he expected to leave Palestine and minister among the Dispersion and the Gentiles.

At the time this Gospel was written, the message of Jesus had already been taken to the Gentiles by those who preached among the Jewish Diaspora and the Gentiles. An ironic touch is thus given to the speculation of the crowd, who had spoken of Jesus' going to the Gentiles as an improbability. The episode illustrates the exclusiveness of Judaism and implies the universality of the Gospel as the author saw it.

36 The perplexity of the crowd over Jesus' answer was echoed later by Simon Peter, who, upon hearing him speak similar words, said, "Lord, why can't I follow you now? I will lay down my life for you" (13:37). The crowd could not follow Jesus because of their ignorance of his identity and purpose; Simon was incapable because he lacked courage.

c. *The climactic appeal*

7:37–44

37On the last and greatest day of the Feast, Jesus stood and said in a loud voice, "If a man is thirsty, let him come to me and drink. 38Whoever believes in me, as the Scripture has said, streams of living water will flow from within him." 39By this he meant the Spirit, whom those who believed in him were later to receive. Up to that time the Spirit had not been given, since Jesus had not yet been glorified.

40On hearing his words, some of the people said, "Surely this man is the Prophet."

41Others said, "He is the Christ."

Still others asked, "How can the Christ come from Galilee? 42Does not the Scripture say that the Christ will come from David's family and from Bethlehem, the town where David lived?" 43Thus the people were divided because of Jesus. 44Some wanted to seize him, but no one laid a hand on him.

37 The climax of the controversy came "on the last and greatest day of the Feast" of Tabernacles. According to the provision of the law, the feast was held for seven days, followed by an eighth day of spiritual observance, including an offering to God. The feast was established as a memorial to the wandering in the wilderness, where water and food were scarce. When the people emerged from the desert into the land of Canaan, they enjoyed regular rainfall and plentiful crops. The celebration of the Feast of Tabernacles included a daily procession of priests from the temple to the Pool of Siloam, from which they drew water that was poured out as a libation at the altar. This was accompanied by the recital of Isaiah 12:3: "With joy you will draw water from the wells of salvation."

Whether the "last day" of the feast was the seventh or the eighth day is not clear. Deuteronomy 16:13 calls for seven days; Leviticus 23:36 prescribes an eighth day, which follows the routine of the first seven. Josephus (Antiq. 3. 10. 4) says that on the eighth day there should be a sacrifice of a calf, a ram, seven lambs, and a kid in propitiation of sins. If "the last and greatest day of the Feast" refers to the eighth day, it makes the appeal of Jesus all the more meaningful. On that day Jesus took the opportunity to make a public announcement concerning himself. "Said in a loud voice" is the same verb translated "cried out" in v.28. He wanted to make himself and his claims known to the entire multitude present.

38 The offering of water memorialized God's provision for the thirsty people in the wilderness, but the water had been poured out and had left them unsatisfied. Now Jesus appeals to the individual: "Whoever believes in me." He was requiring an individual response of faith rather than a collective observance of a ritual. The marginal translation of this verse given in NIV, "If a man is thirsty, let him come to me. And let him drink, who believes in me," makes better poetic parallelism than the usual rendering; but it does not really solve the problem as to whether "from within him" refers to the believer or to Christ. The resultant punctuation would make the words beginning with "as the Scripture has said" an independent sentence. Verse 39 connects the manifestation of the Spirit with the believer rather than with Christ.

If "as the Scripture has said" refers to some particular passage, it is impossible to locate it. There are numerous allusions to water in the OT, but none accords exactly with this utterance. In the celebration of the feast, the words of Isaiah 12:3, quoted above, were employed as part of the ritual. Similar imagery with reference to "the pouring out" of the Holy Spirit occurs in Isaiah 32:15; 44:3; Ezekiel 39:29; Joel 2:28–32. Jesus took the symbolism of the OT and applied it to the gift he intended to bestow on the disciples after his passion was completed. He enlarged this teaching for them in his farewell discourse (14:16–17, 25–26; 15:26; 16:12–15).

39 John's statement shows that the passion of Christ was the important aspect of Jesus' revelation about the Holy Spirit, for it divided the era of law from that of the Spirit (John 1:17). The prophecy of Ezekiel concurs with this: "I will give you a new heart and put a new spirit in you; I will remove from you your heart of stone and give you a heart of flesh. And I will put my Spirit in you and move you to follow my decrees and be careful to keep my laws" (Ezek 36:26–27).

"Glorified" is the first use of this distinctly Johannine verb. It has varied meanings in this Gospel. It may refer to establishing status or to enhancing a reputation (8:54; 12:28; 13:32; 14:13; 15:8; 16:14; 17:1, 4, 5, 10; 21:19). In this particular context it refers to Jesus' death, which, despite all appearances, would be the entrance to glory for him (7:39; 11:4; 12:16, 23; 13:31). The death and resurrection of Jesus would demonstrate the perfection of God's love and power through humiliation. Compare the Pauline statement in Philippians 2:8–9: "He humbled himself and became obedient to death—even death on a cross! Therefore God exalted him to the highest place and gave him the name that is above every name, that at the name of Jesus every knee should bow, in heaven and on earth and under the earth."

40–41 "The Prophet" is presumably an allusion to the prediction of Moses that after him another prophet would appear who would command the attention of the people and who would bring them a further revelation from God (Deut 18:15). Moses explained that the prophet would not be accompanied by the frightening manifestations of Sinai, the great voice and the fire. He would rather be a fellow countryman, familiar to them, and one of their own level. Some so regarded Jesus; others suggested that he might be the Messiah.

42–44 The ignorance of the crowd in Jerusalem concerning Jesus is revealed by their uncertainty about his origin. On the basis of Scripture (Micah 5:2), they decided that Jesus could not be the Messiah since Micah's prophecy said the Messiah would come from Bethlehem and Jesus came from Nazareth. The confusion was such that no decision was made concerning his person and no action was taken to arrest him. Perhaps this is another illustration of Johannine irony, for Jesus *was* born in Bethlehem. The very passage that convinced his critics that he could not be the Messiah was one of the strongest to prove that he was.

d. *The rejection by the leaders*

7:45–52

> [45]Finally the temple guards went back to the chief priests and Pharisees, who asked them, "Why didn't you bring him in?"
> [46]"No one ever spoke the way this man does," the guards declared.

47"You mean he has deceived you also?" the Pharisees retorted. 48"Has any of the rulers or of the Pharisees believed in him? 49No! But this mob that knows nothing of the law—there is a curse on them."

50Nicodemus, who had gone to Jesus earlier and who was one of their own number, asked, 51"Does our law condemn a man without first hearing him to find out what he is doing?"

52They replied, "Are you from Galilee, too? Look into it, and you will find that a prophet does not come out of Galilee."

45 Although the previous context states that there was no attempt to seize Jesus, it did not state that there was no official action. The phrase "the temple guards" shows that the chief priests and Pharisees had sent an arresting party, who failed in their mission. Since the high priest belonged to the Sadducean party, the coalition of the Pharisees and Sadducees was significant. The two groups were strongly opposed to each other in doctrine (Acts 23:7). In spite of their differences, their common animosity toward Jesus induced them to combine for action against him.

46 The report of the guards showed that Jesus had a strong influence on all who listened to him. Although they had been officially commissioned to arrest him, his teaching had so overawed them that they could not carry out their orders. "No one ever spoke the way this man does" could be translated stronger; for instead of a negative pronoun the text literally reads, "Never did any *man* talk in this fashion." In the Greek the word "man" (*anthrōpos*) occurs in the emphatic position at the end of the sentence and implies by contrast that he must be more than an ordinary human being.

47-49 The Pharisees were irate when the guards returned without Jesus. Their question, "Has any of the rulers or of the Pharisees believed in him?" opens with a particular construction that calls for a negative answer. It might be translated: "No one of the Pharisees has believed in him, has he?" The religious snobbishness of the rulers was revealed in their contemptuous dismissal of the guards' testimony. They assumed that nobody could be right except themselves. If they did not believe in Jesus, he must be unreliable and his claims must be fraudulent. They regarded the mass of the people as ignorant of the law and consequently incapable of any intelligent faith.

50-51 Nicodemus reappears in the Gospel at this point. John again explains that Nicodemus was a ruler of the Jews, "one of their own number." His tentative question, "Does our law condemn a man without first hearing him to find out what he is doing?" was not an open declaration that he had faith in Jesus. Rather, it was a protest raised on a legal technicality. Nicodemus may have felt that if he championed Jesus' cause unequivocally, he would lose his case; but if he raised a legitimate legal objection, he might prevent drastic action. This does imply that he was willing to defend Jesus' rights.

52 The scornful reply "Are you from Galilee, too?" intimates that Nicodemus was taking the stand of the crude and ignorant Galileans who were gullible enough to trust in the wandering prophet, Jesus. The rulers in Jerusalem had a dim view of the intellectual status of the Galileans. The statement "a prophet does not come out of Galilee" seems inconsistent with the fact that some of the OT prophets, like Jonah, did originate from northern Israel.

Notes

52 One of the oldest papyrus texts of John, P[66], which antedates the majority of the texts, reads "the prophet" (ὁ προφήτης, *ho prophētēs*). If that reading is correct, the statement of the Pharisees is probably a direct reference to "the prophet" mentioned in v.40 and would obviate the inconsistency mentioned above. The reading, however, is not otherwise attested; and there seems to be no particular reason in the OT for saying that "the prophet" could not come from Galilee. More probably the statement is simply the arbitrary rejection of all possibility that Jesus could be the Messiah or even a prophet.

6. *The woman taken in adultery*

7:53–8:11

> [53]Then each went to his own home.
> [1]But Jesus went to the Mount of Olives. [2]At dawn he appeared again in the temple courts, where all the people gathered around him, and he sat down to teach them. [3]The teachers of the law and the Pharisees brought in a woman caught in adultery. They made her stand before the group [4]and said to Jesus, "Teacher, this woman was caught in the act of adultery. [5]In the Law Moses commanded us to stone such women. Now what do you say?" [6]They were using this question as a trap, in order to have a basis for accusing him.
> But Jesus bent down and started to write on the ground with his finger. [7]When they kept on questioning him, he straightened up and said to them, "If any one of you is without sin, let him be the first to throw a stone at her." [8]Again he stooped down and wrote on the ground.
> [9]At this, those who heard began to go away one at a time, the older ones first, until only Jesus was left, with the woman still standing there. [10]Jesus straightened up and asked her, "Woman, where are they? Has no one condemned you?"
> [11]"No one, sir," she said.
> "Then neither do I condemn you," Jesus declared. "Go now and leave your life of sin."

Although this narrative is included in the sequence of the outline, it can hardly have belonged to the original text of this Gospel. It is absent from most of the oldest copies of the Gospel that precede the sixth century and from the works of the earliest commentators. To say that it does not belong in the Gospel is not identical with rejecting it as unhistorical. Its coherence and spirit show that it was preserved from a very early time, and it accords well with the known character of Jesus. It may be accepted as historical truth; but based on the information we now have, it was probably not a part of the original text.

7:53–8:1 The words "Then each went to his own home" show that the following account must have been related to some longer narrative of which it was a part. The subjects of this verse must be people at a gathering in the city of Jerusalem at which Jesus was present, for the next verse says, "But Jesus went to the Mount of Olives." "But" implies continuity with a mild contrast: the members of the group, whatever it was, went to their homes while Jesus made his way to the Mount of Olives, where he spent the night. This does not fit well with the preceding text because Jesus was not present at the meeting of the Sanhedrin to which the guards had reported. Furthermore, the withdrawal to the Mount of Olives would fit better the Passover season, when Jesus slept more than once under the shadow of the trees there. The reference to the temple courts (8:2) fits with his teaching described in 7:14, but this does not make convincing evidence. Since he used the Court of the Gentiles on numerous occasions, the event more probably occurred during one of his visits to Jerusalem during the last year of his life, either at the Feast of Dedication (10:22) or at the Final Passover (12:12).

2–3 The episode took place in the temple court at dawn. The entire affair had the appearance of trickery, a trap specially prepared to catch Jesus. The Sanhedrin would probably not have arisen early in the morning unless there was a special reason for doing so. They forced their way into the center of the group and interrupted Jesus' teaching by posing a question that created an apparently impossible dilemma for him.

4 The guilt of the woman was indisputable; she had been "caught in the act." There is no indication here that Jesus challenged the charge. He accepted the alternatives that it entailed.

5 The dilemma that the scribes and Pharisees posed was this: The woman was guilty, and under Mosaic law she would be condemned to death. The law's requirement was this: "If a man commits adultery with another man's wife—with the wife of his neighbor —both the adulterer and the adulteress must be put to death" (Lev 20:10). The nature of the penalty—stoning—was defined by the Deuteronomic law: "If a man is found sleeping with another man's wife . . . you shall take both of them to the gate of that town and stone them to death" (Deut 22:22–24). If, then, Jesus refused to confirm the death penalty, he could be charged with contradicting the law of God and would himself be liable to condemnation. If, on the other hand, he confirmed the verdict of the Pharisees, he would lose his reputation for compassion; and, as Morris suggests, he could have been reported to the Romans as inciting the Sanhedrin to independent exercise of the death penalty (NIC, p. 887).

6–8 The Pharisees' question was emphatic: "You, there! What do you say?" Jesus made no reply but "bent down and started to write on the ground with his finger." There have been several conjectures as to what he wrote. Some say he may have simply made marks in the dust to cover his embarrassment; or, as has also been suggested, he may have started to make a list of the sins of those who stood in front of him. It was, incidentally, the only occasion on record that refers to his writing. When his questioners kept pressing him for an answer, Jesus finally stood erect and replied, "If any one of you is without sin, let him be the first to throw a stone at her." Then he resumed his writing.

His reply put the dilemma back on his questioners. In this particular offense there would normally be no witnesses, since its nature would demand privacy. Either the witnesses became such by accident, which would be unusual; or they were present purposely to create the trap for Jesus, in which case they themselves were guilty; or they condoned the deed, and this would make them partners in it. According to Jewish law, in any case of capital punishment the witnesses must begin the stoning. Whether Jesus by his statement implied that they were guilty of condoning or of committing adultery with this woman, or whether he was speaking about past personal guilt is uncertain. In either case, each one of the accusers would either have to admit that he was guilty or else refrain from demanding the woman's death.

9 The accusers "began to go away one at a time, the older ones first." The older ones either had more sins for which they were answerable or else had more sense than to make an impossible profession of righteousness. Finally the woman was left alone.

10 Jesus straightened up and addressed the woman: "Woman, where are they? Has no one condemned you?" His address was respectful (cf. 2:4; 20:13). Her accusers had made her the bait for a trap. They were more interested in destroying Jesus than in saving her. Their vicious hatred of him was as bad as her immorality. His rebuke had prevented their pronouncing sentence on her. Jesus did not pronounce sentence either. But neither did he proclaim her to be innocent.

11 Jesus dismissed the woman by saying, "Go now and leave your life of sin." Meeting a man who was interested in saving rather than exploiting and in forgiving rather than condemning must have been a new experience for her. Jesus' attitude provided both the motivation and the assurance she needed. Forgiveness demands a clean break with sin. That Jesus refrained from condemning her was a guarantee that he would support her.

Notes

The textual status of this passage is uncertain. It is lacking in the major papyri MSS of the early third century (P[66] and P[75]), in the great uncials that precede the sixth century (א B probably A and C T W), in some of the later uncials (N X Θ Ψ), and in a considerable number of the best cursive MSS (33 157 565 and others). The oldest Syriac and Egyptian versions omit it, as do also the Georgian, Gothic, and some of the MSS of Old Latin. It is included by some of the representatives of the "Western" text (D G) and by a number of the later uncials and cursives (28 700 et al.). One MS (225) places it after John 7:36; a few, after 7:44; some uncials append it to the end of the Gospel; and one family of MSS, the Ferrar Group, place it after Luke 21:38. No early commentator contains it, nor is it quoted in any of the church fathers before Irenaeus, and then only in the Latin version, which was translated possibly as late as the fourth century. The multiplicity of small variants within this pericope indicate that it may have had a checkered literary history.

D. The Intensification of Controversy (8:12–59)

1. Teaching in the temple area

8:12–30

12When Jesus spoke again to the people, he said, "I am the light of the world. Whoever follows me will never walk in darkness, but will have the light of life."
13The Pharisees challenged him, "Here you are, appearing as your own witness; your testimony is not valid."
14Jesus answered, "Even if I testify on my own behalf, my testimony is valid, for I know where I came from and where I am going. But you have no idea where I come from or where I am going. 15You judge by human standards; I pass judgment on no one. 16But if I do judge, my decisions are right, because I am not alone. I stand with the Father who sent me. 17In your own Law it is written that the testimony of two men is valid. 18I am one who testifies for myself; my other witness is the one who sent me—the Father."
19Then they asked him, "Where is your father?"

"You do not know me or my Father," Jesus replied. "If you knew me, you would know my Father also." [20]He spoke these words while teaching in the temple area near the place where the offerings were put. Yet no one seized him, because his time had not yet come.

[21]Once more Jesus said to them, "I am going away, and you will look for me, and you will die in your sin. Where I go, you cannot come."

[22]This made the Jews ask, "Will he kill himself? Is that why he says, 'Where I go, you cannot come'?"

[23]But he continued, "You are from below; I am from above. You are of this world; I am not of this world. [24]I told you that you would die in your sins; if you do not believe that I am ˌthe one I claim to beˌ, you will indeed die in your sins."

[25]"Who are you?" they asked.

"Just what I have been claiming all along," Jesus replied. [26]"I have much to say in judgment of you. But he who sent me is reliable, and what I have heard from him I tell the world."

[27]They did not understand that he was telling them about his Father. [28]So Jesus said, "When you have lifted up the Son of Man, then you will know who I am and that I do nothing on my own but speak just what the Father has taught me. [29]The one who sent me is with me; he has not left me alone, for I always do what pleases him." [30]Even as he spoke, many put their faith in him.

12 The segment that follows at this point is long and constitutes a chronological unit, though we have divided it for convenience in explaining the content. Precisely at what time during Jesus' visit to Jerusalem this took place, John does not say. It may have been shortly after the close of the Feast of Tabernacles, while Jesus was still in the city. This incident introduces the second of the great "I am's," "I am the light of the world." This recalls the statement of the Prologue: "In him was life, and that life was the light of men. The light shines in the darkness, but the darkness has not understood [overcome] it" (John 1:4–5). Jesus professed to be not only the inexhaustible source of spiritual nourishment, but he also was the genuine light by which truth and falsehood could be distinguished and by which direction could be established. Perhaps Jesus drew his illustration from the great candlestick or Menorah that was lighted during the Feast of Tabernacles and cast its light over the Court of the Women where Jesus was teaching. The Menorah was to be extinguished after the feast, but his light would remain.

13–14 As usual, the Pharisees challenged Jesus' claims. Legally his testimony concerning himself would be unacceptable because it would presumably be biased. Jesus had on a previous occasion admitted as much, for he had said, "If I testify about myself, my testimony is not valid" (5:31). Here he protested vigorously: "Even if I testify on my own behalf, my testimony is valid, for I know where I came from and where I am going." While a person's testimony about himself may be biased by self-interest, it is equally true that no one knows more about his own nature and experience than the person himself. No individual can be sure of his own origin apart from external testimony, nor can he be sure of his future circumstances. Jesus, however, possessed that knowledge concerning himself. When the final crisis of his life came, John says that Jesus knew "that he had come from God and was returning to God" (13:3). His testimony about himself was therefore more accurate than that of his opponents, for they had no idea of his origin or his destiny, as the confusion reported in ch. 7 shows (vv.25–44).

15–18 Jesus argued further that the Pharisees were not qualified to render a verdict on the validity of his witness because they used the wrong criterion: "You judge by human standards." To form a correct estimate of him, they must have the proper standard, and Christ is not measurable by "human standards." The actual word used here for "human standards" is "flesh" (*sarx*), which is used metaphorically to refer to the human nature. The ordinary categories for measuring personality would not apply to Jesus. He appealed to the rule of the law that prescribed two witnesses for an acceptable proposition (Deut 17:6). He would be qualified as one of the witnesses and his Father as the other. Jesus referred, of course, to God and emphasized again that the Father had "sent" him (cf. John 5:23-24, 37). Morris notes that "no human witness can authenticate a divine relationship. Jesus therefore appeals to the Father and Himself, and there is no other to whom He can appeal" (NIC, p. 443).

19 Whether the Pharisees' question is a bewildered inquiry or an intentional insult is hard to determine. In Western culture it would more likely be the former. In the East, to question a man's paternity is a definite slur on his legitimacy. It may be unwise to read into this question more hostility than is necessary; yet in the ensuing discussion the same idea recurs (v.41). Jesus was referring to God, and the Pharisees were unwilling to admit that he had so intimate a relation with God. Jesus asserted that the knowledge of the Father depended on knowing him. As the one whom the Father had sent (v.18), Jesus claimed to be an adequate and authoritative representative.

20 "Yet no one seized him, because his time had not yet come" is a footnote John adds that relates to the program of Jesus' life (see 2:4; 7:6, 30; 12:23, 27; 17:1). Jesus lived a protected life until his work was completed.

21-24 The following discourse marks the dual destiny of Jesus and his opponents: he would return to the Father, and they would die in their sins. Jesus claimed that he belonged to a totally different world from that of his questioners. To him the difference was natural; to them it was unnatural—something they could explain only by assuming that he belonged to the realm of the dead. He had come from the presence of God, and he asserted that only by faith could they attain his level. An insurmountable barrier separated them—unbelief (v.23). The attitude of unbelief is not simply unwillingness to accept a statement of fact; it is resistance to the revelation of God in Christ. Not only did they repudiate his claims, they completely rejected his person.

25 The question "Who are you, anyway?" shows the Pharisees' exasperation with Jesus' hints and seemingly extravagant claims. The crowd had ventured many guesses about his identity: "the Prophet" (7:40), "the Christ" (7:41), and others. The longer his explanation, the less satisfying it seemed to be. Jesus avoided making a direct claim to deity, but he relied on his works and character to speak for themselves. They witness to the fact that he had come from another world, that he was different from humanity in general, and that he had a unique mission to fulfill.

The translation of the second half of v.25 is difficult. The construction is unique to the Gospel of John. KJV renders it "Even the same that I said unto you from the beginning"; the Amplified Bible, "I am exactly what I have been telling you from the first"; NASB, "What have I been saying to you from the beginning?"; RSV, "Even what I have told you from the beginning"; NEB, "Why should I speak to you at all?"; Beck, "What should I tell you first?" The problem lies in the translation of the word *archēn*, which means literally "beginning." Its construction does not seem to fit the general sense of the passage, and there is no good analogy that can be used to explain it. The NIV rendering

—"Just what I have been claiming all along"—seems to be as satisfactory as any of the others.

26 Jesus certainly had enough accusations that he could have mustered forth to bring judgment on his accusers. The remainder of the verse implies that this judgment is tied to their unwillingness to acknowledge Jesus' relationship to the Father. Because he was speaking what the Father told him, the Father's judgment would come on them, too.

27-28 Jesus' questioners did not understand that he was speaking to them of God; so they missed the point of his peculiar relationship to the Father. Jesus asserted that when they had lifted him up, they would recognize him for what he was.

Two words in this context deserve special emphasis. "Lift up" (*hypsoō*) is used in John 3:14 to refer to the cross, which Jesus compared to the "banner-staff" on which the bronze serpent was elevated in the wilderness (Num 21:9). Usually the verb means "to set in a place of prominence," "to exalt." It may carry an additional meaning: that Jesus would be glorified by the cross. Such a concept goes well with his own statement in 12:23: "The hour has come for the Son of Man to be glorified," and its equal in 12:32: "But I, when I am lifted up from the earth, will draw all men to myself." The second word is "I am" in "then you will know that *I am*" (lit. trans.). "I am" (*egō eimi*) occurs three times in this discourse, in vv.24, 28, 58. It may be translated as in v.24, "I am [the one I claim to be]," that is, the Son of Man. Stauffer states that it may be the translation of "I AM," the title of God manifested (pp. 186–94). This title was revealed to Moses at the time of his commission to lead the people of Israel out of Egypt (Exod 3:14). The term predicates self-existence, eternal being. Along with this claim to divine nature, Jesus reaffirmed his subordination to the Father as the bearer of his message. Both his nature and his message come from God.

29 Four times in this discourse Jesus affirmed that he had been sent by the Father (vv.16, 18, 26, 29). He disclaimed originality for his message; he was simply conveying the truth of the one who had sent him and was carrying out his orders. His whole purpose was to please the Father. His utter devotion produced a life of complete holiness. This revelation forms a contrasting background to the slavery of sin that follows in the next paragraph.

30 The validity of the belief referred to here seems questionable. The people's lack of perception and shallowness of commitment are reflected in their response to Jesus' initial counsel. The following paragraphs begin with proud resentment on the part of the Jews and conclude with an attempted stoning.

2. *The discourse to professed believers*

8:31–47

[31]To the Jews who had believed him, Jesus said, "If you hold to my teaching, you are really my disciples. [32]Then you will know the truth, and the truth will set you free."

[33]They answered him, "We are Abraham's descendants and have never been slaves of anyone. How can you say that we shall be set free?"

[34]Jesus replied, "I tell you the truth, everyone who sins is a slave to sin. [35]Now a slave has no permanent place in the family, but a son belongs to it forever. [36]So if the Son sets you free, you will be free indeed. [37]I know you are Abraham's descendants. Yet you are ready to kill me, because you have no room for my word.

³⁸I am telling you what I have seen in the Father's presence, and you do what you have heard from your father."

³⁹"Abraham is our father," they answered.

"If you were Abraham's children," said Jesus, "then you would do the things Abraham did. ⁴⁰As it is, you are determined to kill me, a man who has told you the truth that I heard from God. Abraham did not do such things. ⁴¹You are doing the things your own father does."

"We are not illegitimate children," they protested. "The only Father we have is God himself."

⁴²Jesus said to them, "If God were your Father, you would love me, for I came from God and now am here. I have not come on my own; but he sent me. ⁴³Why is my language not clear to you? Because you are unable to hear what I say. ⁴⁴You belong to your father, the devil, and you want to carry out your father's desire. He was a murderer from the beginning, not holding to the truth, for there is no truth in him. When he lies, he speaks his native language, for he is a liar and the father of lies. ⁴⁵Yet because I tell the truth, you do not believe me! ⁴⁶Can any of you prove me guilty of sin? If I am telling the truth, why don't you believe me? ⁴⁷He who belongs to God hears what God says. The reason you do not hear is that you do not belong to God."

31 There must have been some sort of avowal of faith by the Jews that evoked the author's comment, "to the Jews who had believed him." Jesus evidently began his discourse with the assumption that they, having declared an initial faith, would proceed to a further commitment on the basis of his teaching. Receiving his teaching would mark them as genuine disciples and would lead them into a deeper experience of truth. The truth thus learned would liberate them from legalism and superstition, which had developed over the years. Jesus did not wish to break a bruised reed nor extinguish a smoldering wick of faith (cf. Matt 12:20), but he felt the necessity of making perfectly clear the conditions of discipleship.

32–33 The freedom Jesus spoke of was spiritual freedom from sin and its effects, as the following context shows. The Jews' response indicates that they were thinking of political freedom, since they spoke of being enslaved to persons (v.33). Their protest was ill-founded, for they forgot the slavery of Egypt, the numerous oppressions of the time of the Judges, the Exile in Babylon, and the current Roman domination of their land. Because they were descendants of Abraham, with whom God had established a permanent covenant (Gen 12:1–3; 15:1–21; 17:1–14, 19; 22:15–18), they considered themselves exempt from any spiritual danger.

34 Jesus' reply dealt with the spiritual aspect of freedom. Sin enslaves because every act of disobedience to God creates an atmosphere of alienation and a trend to further disobedience that inevitably makes escape impossible. Sin can possibly be overcome, but the attitude and habit of sin are inescapable. The participial construction "everyone who sins" is in the present tense, which implies a continual habit of sinning rather than an occasional lapse.

35–36 A slave has no security, for he can claim no family ties that entail an obligation toward him. The son of a family has permanent status within it. Jesus enlarged this analogy by stating that while *a* son is rightfully a partaker of family privileges, *the* Son can confer them. The hope for real freedom does not lie in the ancestry of Abraham but in the action of Christ.

37–38 The contrast between the attitude of Abraham and that of his self-styled descendants was proof that they were falsely claiming him as their spiritual ancestor. They were murderous in intent and impervious to revelation. Jesus had brought a message from the Father, and, unlike Abraham, they would not receive it. John the Baptist had made a similar observation in his preaching (Luke 3:8). Jesus' contrast of what he had "seen" and what they had "heard" reinforces the concept of authority implicit in his repeated claim to have been "sent" by the Father (John 8:29). He spoke from firsthand knowledge; they were acting on misinformation. They had been misled by Satan himself.

39 Contrary to the Jews' claim, Jesus insisted that they were not the true children of Abraham. Their hatred of Jesus, refusal to listen to truth, and lack of simple faith belied their profession.

40–41 The Jews' insistence that they were children of Abraham implied that they regarded their relationship to God as secure because of their lineal descent from the man with whom God had confirmed his covenant. While the covenant had not been abrogated, Jesus made it plain that his hearers needed to exercise individual faith to participate in it. His words give substance to his teaching on the new birth and are paralleled by Paul's explanation of Abraham's faith in Galatians 3:16–29. The heirs of Abraham are not merely those who are descended from him by blood but those who exercise his faith. The Jews' insistence that they were true descendants of Abraham brought Jesus' flat denial of their spiritual claims, and he attributed their attitude to another source. Their protest, "We are not illegitimate children," may carry the implication of a sneer: "*We* are not illegitimate children"—but you are! While John does not speak directly of the virgin birth, there may be hints that he knew of it and that some of the people knew that there was a mystery surrounding Jesus' origin. In any case, the Jews were unwilling to listen to Jesus' claims; yet, at the same time, they were insisting that they came from God.

42 Jesus gave another evidence of the Jews' hypocrisy. If they truly loved God, they would evidence that love by showing love to his Son. Love for God is a family affair; it involves loving all whom the Father has sent. This love should especially be manifested toward the Father's most beloved representative, his Son.

43–44 The people might have been confused as to why they did not love Jesus if he was indeed sent from the Father. Jesus spoke to that point with a rhetorical question: "Why is my language not clear to you?" The word "clear" really means "know" (*ginōskō*). In essence, Jesus was asking, "Why don't you know what I am saying?" Then he gave the answer: "You are unable to hear what I say." The word "unable" (*ou dynasthe*) speaks of an inherent inability. The reason the people didn't respond to Jesus' teaching was that they belonged to another. Their family association was wrong. Jesus said, "You belong to your father, the devil." And because of this family tie, they were inclined to carry out their father's desire, just as Jesus carried out his Father's desire. The devil is a murderer and a liar. He seeks to deprive life and distort truth. The Jews were merely demonstrating the truth of the adage "Like father, like son."

45 "Truth" is an abstract that is difficult for people to know and appreciate. Pilate had become so enmeshed in politics that he no longer knew what truth was (18:38). Jesus told the Jews that because they were children of their father, they didn't know what truth was. They lived in a world of lies, distortion, and falseness. In a sense, truth was a foreign language to them; their native language was lies.

46 Jesus' challenge "Can any of you prove me guilty of sin?" would have been impossible for anyone else to utter. No human being could risk making that challenge without many flaws in his character being made known. The verb "prove" (*elenchei*) implies more than an accusation; it is a conviction on the basis of evidence. Had Jesus not been sinless, someone in the hostile crowd would eagerly have charged him with at least one sin.

47 Jesus closed the argument by repeating that the Jews refused to hear him because they did not belong to God. Their bitterness toward him and their obtuseness toward his teaching contradicted their spiritual claims.

3. *The response of the unbelievers*

8:48–59

48The Jews answered him, "Aren't we right in saying that you are a Samaritan and demon-possessed?"

49"I am not possessed by a demon," said Jesus, "but I honor my Father and you dishonor me. 50I am not seeking glory for myself; but there is one who seeks it, and he is the judge. 51I tell you the truth, if a man keeps my word, he will never see death.

52At this the Jews exclaimed, "Now we know that you are demon-possessed! Abraham died and so did the prophets, yet you say that if a man keeps your word he will never taste death. 53Are you greater than our father Abraham? He died, and so did the prophets. Who do you think you are?"

54Jesus replied, "If I glorify myself, my glory means nothing. My Father, whom you claim as your God, is the one who glorifies me. 55Though you do not know him, I know him. If I said I did not, I would be a liar like you, but I do know him and keep his word. 56Your father Abraham rejoiced at the thought of seeing my day; he saw it and was glad."

57"You are not yet fifty years old," the Jews said to him, "and you have seen Abraham!"

58"I tell you the truth," Jesus answered, "before Abraham was born, I am!" 59At this, they picked up stones to stone him, but Jesus hid himself, slipping away from the temple grounds.

48 The hardened opposition to Jesus' claims appears in the accusation that he was "a Samaritan and demon-possessed." "Aren't we right in saying" may imply that this was an accusation frequently leveled at him. The Samaritans held many beliefs in common with the Jews, for they also relied on the Pentateuch as the supreme authority for their faith. They differed, however, in their interpretation of it and were much more lax in their attitude toward other religious influences. Since Jesus did not agree with all the traditional interpretations of the Law, the Jews may have classed him with the Samaritans as a heretic. According to John, demon-possession was attributed to Jesus on three occasions (7:20; 8:52; 10:20). In this context it is the equivalent of calling a man crazy, though the Gospels as a whole deal with demon-possession as an actual phenomenon. Demon-possession is characterized by both a disordered mind and definite control by evil.

49–50 Jesus denied the allegation and placed the burden of proof back on his adversaries. His aim was to honor the Father; theirs, to bring Jesus into disgrace. He disclaimed all selfish desire for prestige and relegated the final evaluation of his works to the judgment of God.

51 With the solemn affirmation "I tell you the truth," Jesus declared that any man who received his message would not experience death. It is a negative statement of a positive principle later declared by Jesus: "I have come that they may have life, and have it to the full" (John 10:10). It is the summary of his mission, for he came "to destroy the devil's work" (1 John 3:8) and to undo the penalty for sin pronounced in Eden: "You must not eat from the tree of the knowledge of good and evil, for when you eat of it you will surely die" (Gen 2:17). A fuller statement of this principle appears later in Jesus' promise to Martha: "I am the resurrection and the life. . . . whoever lives and believes in me will never die" (John 11:25).

52 To receive eternal life by keeping Jesus' word seemed to be the height of absurdity. The Jews felt that their charge of demon-possession was confirmed. If Abraham, the father of the nation, and the prophets, the accredited messengers of God, died, how could this obscure Galilean claim to have the power of life and death?

53 A better translation of this question would be "You are not greater than our father Abraham, are you?" A negative answer is assumed. Morris points out that Jesus' opponents frequently charged him with " 'making' Himself divine (5:18; 10:33; 19:7)" (NIC, p. 470). On the contrary, Jesus seldom asserted his deity, but he preferred so to live and act that men would observe his divine nature and confess it spontaneously (cf. Matt 16:13–17). He did not refuse such confessions, but he did not advertise himself.

54 Again Jesus referred his defense to the Father. God was responsible for Jesus' message and vindication. He reminded them that the God they claimed to be theirs was his Father. Their relation to God was formal; his was familial.

55 In this verse two different Greek words are used for "know." The word *ginōskō* is used in the phrase "you do not know him." The other word, *oida*, is used elsewhere in this verse. It may be that they do not really differ in meaning, since they appear in the same context and since the Johannine use of synonyms seems at times to observe no distinctions. But *ginōskō* implies a knowledge of experience whereas *oida* implies an instinctive perception of a fact. Jesus may have been saying, "You have not really attained an experience of God; I have a full consciousness of him." Jesus could not deny his knowledge without making himself a liar.

56 Jesus claimed that Abraham had a preview of his ministry and had rejoiced in it. This may refer to the promise God gave Abraham that his seed should become the channel of divine blessing to all the nations (Gen 12:3). By "my day" Jesus may have been referring to his redemptive work, which would summarize his career. Perhaps Isaac represented to Abraham the "seed" through which God would fulfill his promise: the miraculous birth of the son, his unquestioning trust in his father, his willingness to become a sacrifice to fulfill the command of God, and his deliverance from certain death. These may have spoken of the later Seed who cooperated in obedience to his Father, surrendered himself to the Father's will, and emerged victorious from death. Although this interpretation is not founded on any specific statement of Scripture, it would mean that Abraham's personal experience at the sacrifice of Isaac could have been an object lesson to him of the coming incarnation, death, and resurrection of the promised Seed (see Gen 22:1–18; Heb 11:17–19).

57 The Jews' retort that Jesus was "not yet fifty years old" affords an interesting sidelight on Jesus' age. Fifty years was the limit observers would assign to him on the basis of appearance. If he were born between 6 and 4 B.C., and if the Crucifixion took place in A.D. 33, as Hoehner suggests (see note), Jesus would not have been older than his late thirties. Perhaps the tensions of his life had aged him prematurely, yet he was obviously less than fifty years of age. Luke says Jesus "was about thirty years old when he began his ministry" (Luke 3:23).

58 The rejoinder of Jesus, "Before Abraham was born, I am (*egō eimi*)" could only mean a claim to deity. "Was born" could be better translated "came into being" or "became," since the aorist tense of *ginomai* ("to become") is used. The same verb is used in John 1:14 to denote the Incarnation: "The Word became flesh." It implies the event of entering into a new state or condition of existence. "I am" implies continuous existence, including existence when Abraham appeared. Jesus was, therefore, asserting that at the time of Abraham's birth, he existed. Furthermore, I AM was recognized by the Jews as a title of deity. When God commissioned Moses to demand from Pharaoh the release of the Israelites, he said, "This is what you are to say to the Israelites: I AM has sent me to you" (Exod 3:14). Stauffer states that "the phrase harbors within itself the most authentic, the most audacious, and the most profound affirmation by Jesus of who he was" (p. 174). The same use of "I am" appears also in the theistic proclamations of the second half of Isaiah: "I, the Lord—with the first of them and with the last—I am he" (Isa 41:4; cf. 43:11–13; 44:6; 45:6, 18, 21; 48:17). The title became part of the liturgy of the Feast of Tabernacles, the time when this controversy recorded in John occurred. The phrase occurs in Jesus' response to the challenge of the high priest at his final hearing. When asked, "Are you the Christ, the Son of the Blessed One?" Jesus replied, "I am . . . and you will see the Son of Man sitting at the right hand of the Mighty One and coming on the clouds of heaven" (Mark 14:61–62). The violent reaction of the high priest in Mark 14:63 indicates that he regarded the use of the title as a blasphemous claim on Jesus' part to possess the quality of deity.

59 The crowd unmistakably understood Jesus' words as a blasphemous claim and immediately prepared to stone him. He did not protest their action as a mistake of judgment; he simply withdrew. How he managed to escape their wrath is not explained. He had done so on previous occasions, for "his time had not yet come" (John 7:30; cf. Luke 4:30).

Notes

57 Hoehner contends that the later date for the Crucifixion accords better with the known astronomical data and with the historical situation involving Pilate. The unwillingness of Pilate to risk the wrath of Tiberius may have been due to his appointment by Sejanus, prefect of the Praetorian Guard, who had fallen out of favor with the emperor. Sejanus had been executed, and Pilate did not wish to endanger his head and his career by a political misstep (pp. 115–26).

E. *The Manifestation of Opposition* (9:1–11:57)

The widening rift between belief and unbelief, which had become clearly apparent at the time of the feeding of the five thousand and was accentuated at the Feast of Tabernacles, at this point became an open breach. Not only had many of Jesus' disciples abandoned his cause (John 6:66), but the religious authorities also were becoming actively hostile (7:32). The last five or six months of Jesus' life were filled with controversy and with attempts on the part of the priests and scribes to trap him by his words or his actions. Jesus, however, being fully aware of their designs, maintained his usual ministry and became bolder in his resistance. John's Gospel deals with this period largely from the viewpoint of Jerusalem.

1. *The healing of the blind man* (9:1–41)

a. *The healing*

9:1–12

¹As he went along, he saw a man blind from birth. ²His disciples asked him, "Rabbi, who sinned, this man or his parents, that he was born blind?"

³"Neither this man nor his parents sinned," said Jesus, "but this happened so that the work of God might be displayed in his life. ⁴As long as it is day, we must do the work of him who sent me. Night is coming, when no one can work. ⁵While I am in the world, I am the light of the world."

⁶Having said this, he spit on the ground, made some mud with the saliva, and put it on the man's eyes. ⁷"Go," he told him, "wash in the pool of Siloam" (this word means Sent). So the man went and washed, and came home seeing.

⁸His neighbors and those who had formerly seen him begging asked, "Isn't this the same man who used to sit and beg?" ⁹Some claimed that he was.

Others said, "No, he only looks like him."

But he himself insisted, "I am the man."

¹⁰"How then were your eyes opened?" they demanded.

¹¹He replied, "The man they call Jesus made some mud and put it on my eyes. He told me to go to Siloam and wash. So I went and washed, and then I could see."

¹²"Where is this man?" they asked him.

"I don't know," he said.

The cure of the blind man probably occurred shortly after the Feast of Tabernacles, while Jesus was still in Jerusalem. The episode is a unit by itself; it could easily be regarded as a story independent of its context. It is used as an illustration of Jesus' utterance recorded in 8:12: "I am the light of the world. Whoever follows me will never walk in darkness, but will have the light of life." The healing was not only a sample of Jesus' ability to restore sight to a man who was congenitally blind; but it also represented, figuratively, and for the blind man, experientially, the dawning of spiritual light. Furthermore, the healing brought new light to the disciples on one of the mysteries of life that had bewildered them.

1 Although Jesus had healed blind persons on other occasions (Matt 9:27–31; 12:22; 15:30; 21:14; Mark 8:22–26; 10:46–52), this "sign" was an outstanding case because the man had been born blind. Also, the sign was related to the issue of fate, which the disciples raised; and it illustrates the origination and development of faith, which is the theme of this Gospel. The encounter of Jesus and the blind man seems to have been

a casual one. Since blind beggars had little opportunity for employment, they were dependent on charity for their sustenance; and in a depressed economy, they usually fared rather badly.

2 The interest of the disciples was prompted by theological curiosity rather than compassion. For them the blind man was an unsolved riddle rather than a sufferer to be relieved. Their query, "Rabbi, who sinned, this man or his parents, that he was born blind?" was based on a principle stated in the law: "He [God] does not leave the guilty unpunished; he punishes the children and their children for the sin of the fathers to the third and fourth generation" (Exod 34:7). They construed this to mean that if a person suffered from any ailment, it must have been because his parents or grandparents had committed some sin against God (cf. Exod 20:5). To this they added the thought that perhaps he might have sinned before birth, whether as an embryo or in a preexistent state. Such a concept appears in the rabbinical writings.

3 Jesus refused to accept either alternative suggested by the disciples' question. He looked on the man's plight, not as retribution for some offense committed either by his parents or by himself, but as an opportunity to do God's work. Jesus did not consider the blindness as punishment or as a matter of irrational chance; it was a challenge to manifest God's healing power in the man's life.

4–5 The growing pressure of hostility rising from unbelief warned Jesus that his time was short. The twilight of his career was beginning and the darkness would soon fall. As all the Gospels show, Jesus was working under the shadow of the coming cross (Matt 16:21; Mark 8:31; Luke 9:22). While he had the opportunity, he must let his light shine on the darkness around him by healing both bodies and minds. The use of "we" shows that he included his disciples in his ministry. They also would pass through perils and opposition, but they would have the support of the Father who had sent him. "I am the light of the world" is a repetition of 8:12, but it is not superfluous. The healing of the blind man illustrates the positive and practical application of the principle. Jesus dealt not only in ideas but also in the application of them.

6 To make known his intention to the blind man, Jesus made clay from dust and spittle and placed it on the sightless eyes. Lindars suggests that the use of clay parallels the creative act of God in Genesis 2:7 (p. 343). Since the blindness was congenital, the healing would be creative rather than remedial. However, the emphasis of John seems to be on compassion rather than creation. The touch of a friendly hand would be reassuring. The weight of the clay would serve as an indicator to the blind man that something had been done to him, and it would be an inducement to obey Jesus' command.

7 The Pool of Siloam was located at the southern end of the city, probably a considerable distance from the place where the blind man was. The walk would call for some exertion. Certainly the man would not want to continue sitting by the roadside with mud smeared over his eyes. If his lifelong affliction had tended to make him apathetic, he now had at least one motive for obeying what must have seemed a foolish command. How could washing in a public pool restore the sight he never had? The trip the man made must have been a venture of faith. Jesus had not even told him that he would be healed but had merely commanded him to wash. If the man had overheard Jesus' conversation with

the disciples, he would have expected something to happen. Yet so extraordinary a miracle as giving sight to a man born blind would have seemed impossible.

8–9 The man's recovery of his sight created a genuine sensation. The effects of the miracle are described vividly by the responses of four groups or individuals: (1) the neighbors, (2) the Pharisees, (3) the parents, and (4) the man himself. The neighbors and acquaintances knew very well the man they had supported by their charity. To see him walking with normal sight was so incredible that they thought it must be a case of mistaken identity. He quickly settled the dispute by avowing that he was the man they had known.

10–12 The curiosity of the neighbors demanded an explanation. The man replied in matter-of-fact fashion, narrating the event just as it happened. His reply, however, indicates the first stage of faith: he accepted the fact. He made no attempt to evaluate Jesus' person but spoke of him simply as "the man they call Jesus." He showed no previous knowledge of him, nor had he bothered to investigate his person. In fact, the man was even unaware of Jesus' current whereabouts.

Notes

2 The Pharisees, Sadducees, and Essenes differed from one another on the concept of fate. The Pharisees held that all events are predestined but that some are conditioned by the human will. The Sadducees rejected any intervention of God in human affairs. The Essenes attributed all occurrences to divine predestination (see A. Broyde, "Fatalism," JE, 5:356). The debate must have been carried on in Jesus' day and must have provided a background for the disciples' query. R.H. Lightfoot states that "Jewish thought regarding even congenital defect as a punishment for sin, was inclined in such a case to explain it as having been committed in the womb, or in a previous existence, or by the parents" (p. 202).

3 The absence of a definite verb in the Greek text immediately before the "so that" (ἵνα, hina) clause raises a question of interpretation. Normally this type of clause expresses purpose. Should it therefore be interpreted to mean that the affliction of blindness was not a penalty for some sin of the past but was allowed that God might be glorified in the healing of the man? Such an explanation implies that years of misery were inflicted on him for the express purpose of demonstrating Jesus' power. Some expositors (e.g., G. Campbell Morgan, pp. 164–65) have suggested that the hina clause is dependent on the following verb rather than on the one preceding. The translation would then read: "But that the work of God might be displayed in his life, as long as it is day, we must do the work of him who sent me." In that case the purpose clause would express the intent of the definite verb "sent" in v.4 rather than the intent of the indefinite idea "this happened." Such a construction would be out of keeping with the general usage of this Gospel. Hina can express result as well as purpose and is so used elsewhere in John's writings (1 John 1:9). If it can be so interpreted here, it would mean that the blindness was not the divine purpose but that it was rather the accident of birth. The purpose was the healing, not the malady.

b. *The consequences*

9:13–41

¹³They brought to the Pharisees the man who had been blind. ¹⁴Now the day on which Jesus had made the mud and opened the man's eyes was a Sabbath.

¹⁵Therefore the Pharisees also asked him how he had received his sight. "He put mud on my eyes," the man replied, "and I washed, and now I see."

¹⁶Some of the Pharisees said, "This man is not from God, for he does not keep the Sabbath."

But others asked, "How can a sinner do such miraculous signs?" So they were divided.

¹⁷Finally they turned again to the blind man, "What have you to say about him? It was your eyes he opened."

The man replied, "He is a prophet."

¹⁸The Jews still did not believe that he had been blind and had received his sight until they sent for the man's parents. ¹⁹"Is this your son?" they asked. "Is this the one you say was born blind? How is it that now he can see?"

²⁰"We know he is our son," the parents answered, "and we know he was born blind. ²¹But how he can see now, or who opened his eyes, we don't know. Ask him. He is of age; he will speak for himself." ²²His parents said this because they were afraid of the Jews, for already the Jews had decided that anyone who acknowledged that Jesus was the Christ would be put out of the synagogue. ²³That was why his parents said, "He is of age; ask him."

²⁴A second time they summoned the man who had been blind. "Give glory to God," they said. "We know this man is a sinner."

²⁵He replied, "Whether he is a sinner or not, I don't know. One thing I do know. I was blind but now I see!"

²⁶Then they asked him, "What did he do to you? How did he open your eyes?"

²⁷He answered, "I have told you already and you did not listen. Why do you want to hear it again? Do you want to become his disciples, too?"

²⁸Then they hurled insults at him and said, "You are this fellow's disciple! We are disciples of Moses! ²⁹We know that God spoke to Moses, but as for this fellow, we don't even know where he comes from."

³⁰The man answered, "Now that is remarkable! You don't know where he comes from, yet he opened my eyes. ³¹We know that God does not listen to sinners. He listens to the godly man who does his will. ³²Nobody has ever heard of opening the eyes of a man born blind. ³³If this man were not from God, he could do nothing."

³⁴To this they replied, "You were steeped in sin at birth; how dare you lecture us!" And they threw him out.

³⁵Jesus heard that they had thrown him out, and when he found him, he said, "Do you believe in the Son of Man?"

³⁶"Who is he, sir?" the man asked. "Tell me so that I may believe in him."

³⁷Jesus said, "You have now seen him; in fact, he is the one speaking with you."

³⁸Then the man said, "Lord, I believe," and he worshiped him.

³⁹Jesus said, "For judgment I have come into this world, so that the blind will see and those who see will become blind."

⁴⁰Some Pharisees who were with him heard him say this and asked, "What? Are we blind too?"

⁴¹Jesus said, "If you were blind, you would not be guilty of sin; but now that you claim you can see, your guilt remains."

13-15 The case was so mysterious that the neighbors took the man to the religious authorities, the Pharisees, who supposedly would be able to offer an explanation. Since the day on which the miracle was performed was a Sabbath, the Sabbath law was involved. The Pharisees inquired how the man received his sight, and he repeated the story he had given first to the neighbors.

There are both parallels and contrasts between the healing in ch. 9 and that in ch. 5. Both occurred at a public pool; both concerned apparently incurable cases; and both occurred on the Sabbath, which precipitated the question of the Sabbath law. In the previous instance, however, the man healed reported voluntarily to the Pharisees and identified Jesus afterward. In this instance the man had no knowledge of Jesus' where-abouts, nor did he report the matter to the authorities. Furthermore, Jesus implied that the former man had sinned and adjured him to cease doing so (5:14); of this he stated that his condition was not the result of sin (9:3). There is no evidence that the former man became a believer whereas the man born blind demonstrated a growing faith.

16 The response of the Pharisees revealed reasoning from prejudice: "This man is not from God, for he does not keep the Sabbath." For the Pharisees there could be no other conclusion. Others, however, were hesitant and asked how a sinner could have the power to perform such miracles. The use of the plural "miraculous signs" (*sēmeia*) suggests that they knew other miracles of Jesus comparable to this one. The people took into consideration the source of the miracle, not simply this single instance. The contrast of these responses brings into focus an important principle of interpretation: Should Jesus be judged by an a priori application of the law or by an a posteriori consideration of his works?

The division among the Pharisees shows that there must have been at least a small minority who were not inflexibly hostile to Jesus. Perhaps Nicodemus and Joseph of Arimathea were among the number. The minority's question, "How can a sinner do such miraculous signs?" sounds much like Nicodemus's opening words to Jesus: "No one could perform the miraculous signs you are doing if God were not with him" (3:2).

17 Again the man himself was questioned to help bring a decision in the dispute. His verdict was more definite than the preceding one: "He is a prophet," the man said. The prophets were the agents of God, and in some instances they performed miracles; for example, Elisha (2 Kings 2:19–22; 4:18–44; 5:1–14). If, then, Jesus had performed an indisputable miracle, it was prima facie evidence that he must have a divine commission. As an emissary of God, he could be empowered to heal on the Sabbath, if necessary; and he would be above the jurisdiction of any human tribunal.

18–23 The evidence was still insufficient to remove the objections of "the Jews." In this context it seems that "the Jews" was synonymous with "the Pharisees." Unconvinced of the genuineness of the cure, they proceeded to query whether the man really had been born blind; for if he had not been blind from birth, the miracle could be disputed. They interrogated his parents, who, fearing excommunication from the synagogue, evad-ed the issue by stating that their son was an adult capable of answering for himself.

24 To the Jews there was only one solution. The Law forbade working on the Sabbath. Jesus had healed on the Sabbath; therefore, Jesus was a sinner. So the man was com-manded to "give glory to God" for his healing.

25–27 The ensuing argument between the blind man and the Pharisees was a duel between an obvious fact and a legal syllogism. The fact of the healing was undeniable and was admitted by the blind man's opponents. Their incessant questioning exhausted his patience, and he indulged in some sarcasm by insinuating that their repeated inquir-ies showed an interest in becoming disciples of Jesus.

28–29 Such a response to learned rabbis on the part of an illiterate man was surely considered insulting. The Jews quickly retorted that they were abiding by the authority of Moses, whose law for centuries had been the standard of Israel's religion. Jesus they rejected as a nobody, a vagrant prophet who did not keep the law.

30–33 Again the blind man pressed the pragmatic argument, and he also employed an argument of his own. Since, according to the assumption of the Jews, "God does not listen to sinners" (cf. Ps 66:18; Prov 28:9; Isa 1:15), how could Jesus have performed this miracle if he were under divine condemnation? Rather, the man reasoned, the healing should be ample evidence that Jesus came from God.

34 To this argument the Jews had no real answer. So they attacked the man by character assassination and made him feel unworthy to answer on his behalf or Jesus'. Then they excommunicated him, thus isolating him from his family and friends and debarring him from employment.

35–36 In contrast to the negative result of rejection is the positive result of Jesus' response. "Found" implies that Jesus looked for the man so that he might confirm his faith by discipleship. The question "Do you believe in the Son of Man?" is a summons to commitment. The Greek pronoun *su* ("you") used with the verb makes the inquiry doubly emphatic. It demanded a personal decision in the face of opposition or rejection. Since the healing of the man occurred after Jesus' first interview, he would not have recognized Jesus by sight; and the question, couched in the third person, would not instantly identify the questioner as the object of faith. The change in reading from "Son of God" (KJV) to "Son of Man" is common to all modern versions. It seems less likely that "Son of God" should have been supplanted by "Son of Man" in the thinking of the early church than that the opposite should have occurred. Both terms were used of Christ to express his deity (see John 3:13; 5:27; 6:27; cf. Matt 26:63–64).

37–38 When Jesus said that the "Son of Man" was the person speaking, the man instantly responded by worshiping Jesus. He was ready to believe on the one who had healed him. His attitude was already positive. Probably he recognized Jesus as his healer by his voice. He needed only the identification to take the final step of faith. The progress in spiritual understanding of the person of Christ is marked by progressive descriptions: "The man they called Jesus" (v.11); "he is a prophet" (v.17); "from God" (v.33); "Son of Man" (v.35); and, lastly, "Lord" (v.38). This progression illustrates the man's movement from darkness to light, both physically and spiritually.

39–41 The negative result is illustrated by the Pharisees' response. Jesus' remark, "For judgment I have come into this world, so that the blind will see and those who see will become blind," makes him the pivot on which human destiny turns. The Pharisees, assuming that they could "see" without his intervention, asked in resentment, "Are we blind too?" Jesus' reply indicated that if they had acknowledged blindness, they could be freed from sin; but if they asserted that they could see when they were really blind, there would be no remedy for them. If they acted in ignorance of the light, they could not be held responsible for not knowing it; but if they claimed to understand it and still rejected it, they would be liable for judgment. Deliberate rejection of light means that "the light within . . . is darkness" (Matt 6:23).

Notes

34 Excommunication in this passage is not a late reflection of an ecclesiastical practice. Expulsion from the community of Israel was prescribed in the Mosaic law for a number of offenses, some ceremonial and some moral: eating leavened bread during the Feast of Unleavened Bread (Exod 12:15), misuse of holy oil (Exod 30:33), neglect of the Passover (Num 9:13), defilement by touching a corpse or neglect of purification afterwards (Num 19:3–20), eating flesh sacrificed in a peace offering (Lev 7:20), eating of blood (Lev 7:27; 17:10), slaughtering sacrifices outside the tabernacle (Lev 19:8), sexual abuses and perversions (Lev 18:29; 20:18), idolatry (20:3), and occult practices (20:6). There is a second allusion to the punishment in John 16:2, where it is mentioned as a possible danger for the disciples of Jesus.

The exact method of excommunication followed is not explained, and there seems to be little evidence concerning its usage either in the OT or in rabbinic teaching. It implied exclusion from all the fraternal benefits that the Jewish community could provide. Since the Jewish concept of salvation was built on membership in the covenant people, excommunication probably implied the loss of salvation as well. The Johannine usages (9:22; 12:42; 16:2) may relate to "The Heretical Blessings," the curse pronounced on "heretics," i.e., Jewish Christians, which would be relevant to Christians only after the destruction of the temple in A.D. 70 (Barrett, pp. 299–300). This view assumes that the Johannine narrative is interpreting the story of the blind man in the setting of the late first century, when the Gospel was presumably written. Since there is no explicit evidence concerning the practices of Judaism prior to A.D. 70, it may perhaps be assumed that the action against the blind man was taken on the basis of OT law: "Anyone who desecrates it [the Sabbath] must be put to death; whoever does any work on that day must be cut off from his people" (Exod 31:14).

35 Ἀνθρώπου (anthrōpou, "man") is the reading of the oldest MSS, some of the versions, and Chrysostom. The other sources read θεοῦ (theou, "God"). Both "Son of Man" and "Son of God" are used as titles of Jesus elsewhere in John; so the argument from style is indeterminate. Metzger remarks that "the external support for ἀνθρώπου . . . is so weighty, and the improbability of θεοῦ being altered to ἀνθρώπου is so great that the Committee regarded the reading adopted for the text as virtually certain" (*Textual Commentary*, pp. 228–29).

2. *The Good Shepherd discourse*

10:1–21

1"I tell you the truth, the man who does not enter the sheep pen by the gate, but climbs in by some other way, is a thief and a robber. 2The man who enters by the gate is the shepherd of his sheep. 3The watchman opens the gate for him, and the sheep listen to his voice. He calls his own sheep by name and leads them out. 4When he has brought out all his own, he goes on ahead of them, and his sheep follow him because they know his voice. 5But they will never follow a stranger; in fact, they will run away from him because they do not recognize a stranger's voice." 6Jesus used this figure of speech, but they did not understand what he was telling them.

7Therefore Jesus said again, "I tell you the truth, I am the gate for the sheep. 8All who ever came before me were thieves and robbers, but the sheep did not listen to them. 9I am the gate; whoever enters through me will be saved. He will come in and go out, and find pasture. 10The thief comes only to steal and kill and destroy; I have come that they may have life, and have it to the full.

11"I am the good shepherd. The good shepherd lays down his life for the sheep. 12The hired hand is not the shepherd who owns the sheep. So when he sees the wolf coming, he abandons the sheep and runs away. Then the wolf attacks the flock and scatters it. 13The man runs away because he is a hired hand and cares nothing for the sheep.

¹⁴"I am the good shepherd; I know my sheep and my sheep know me—¹⁵just as the Father knows me and I know the Father—and I lay down my life for the sheep. ¹⁶I have other sheep that are not of this sheep pen. I must bring them also. They too will listen to my voice, and there shall be one flock and one shepherd. ¹⁷The reason my Father loves me is that I lay down my life—only to take it up again. ¹⁸No one takes it from me, but I lay it down of my own accord. I have authority to lay it down and authority to take it up again. This command I received from my Father."

¹⁹At these words the Jews were again divided. ²⁰Many of them said, "He is demon-possessed and raving mad. Why listen to him?"

²¹But others said, "These are not the sayings of a man possessed by a demon. Can a demon open the eyes of the blind?"

Chapter 10 opens a new topic, the discourse on the Good Shepherd. It is seemingly unrelated to the previous narrative, though the reference in v.21 to opening the eyes of the blind shows that the author connected it with the preceding text. Whether the discourse was given at the Feast of Tabernacles (7:2, 14, 37), or whether it introduced the Feast of Dedication (10:22) is not made perfectly clear. The language of 10:22, "Then came the Feast of Dedication," would seemingly indicate a break in chronology at this point. The writer was drawing events from memory as they suited his purpose and recounting them in general chronological order, without supplying all the details of a continuing story.

The Good Shepherd discourse in some respects resembles the parables of the Synoptics. Matthew (18:12–14) and Luke (15:3–7) both cite a parable of a shepherd and his sheep; and all three Gospels (Matt, Luke, John) emphasize the aspect of careful concern that the shepherd feels for them. The Johannine presentation, however, is not concentrated on one point but utilizes the allegory with a wider meaning than do the Synoptics. The teaching is based on the practice of sheep herding, and several aspects are utilized to create a picture of the relation of Christ to his people.

1 "I tell you the truth" is a translation of the double use of the adverb "truly, truly" (*amēn, amēn*), or as in the KJV, "verily, verily." This is a phrase peculiar to the fourth Gospel, and it generally introduces a solemn asseveration about Jesus or his mission (cf. 1:51; 5:19, 24, 25; 6:26, 32, 47, 53; 8:34, 51, 58; 10:1, 7; 12:24; 13:16, 20, 21, 38; 14:12; 16:20, 23). In a few instances it refers either to a general principle of salvation or to the future action of a person (3:3, 5, 11; 21:18). Its use in this immediate context emphasizes the importance of the teaching the allegory contains, particularly as it represents the ministry of Jesus himself.

The imagery of the first two paragraphs is based on the concept of the "sheep pen." It was usually a rough stone or mud-brick structure, only partially roofed, if covered at all, or very often a cave in the hills. It had only one opening through which the sheep could pass when they came in for the night. The pen served for the protection of the sheep against thieves and wild beasts. The thief, who would not have any right of access by the gate, used other means of entrance. He would not follow the lawful method of approach.

"Thief " and "robber" are different in meaning. "Thief " (*kleptēs*) implies subtlety and trickery; "robber" (*lēstēs*) connotes violence and plundering. The latter term was sometimes used of bandits or guerrillas. The purpose of both was exploitation; neither was concerned for the welfare of the sheep.

2 The shepherd enters by the gate, which is the lawful method of entry. Jesus was contrasting himself with the false messiahs who by pretence or violence attempted to gain control of the people. He came as the legitimate heir of the chosen seed and claimed to be the fulfillment of the promises of the OT revelation.

3 The "watchman" cannot be identified with any particular person, but, rather, the word illustrates Jesus' coming at the right time and in the right way. He alone has the right to spiritual leadership of his people. This leadership of the sheep is self-authenticating. They "listen to his voice." The Oriental shepherd usually named his sheep and he could summon them by calling them.

4 A pen frequently held several flocks; and when the time came to go out to morning pasture, each shepherd separated his sheep from the others by his peculiar call. Instead of driving them, he led them so that they followed him as a unit. Wherever they went, the shepherd preceded them to provide guidance to the most advantageous pasturage and guardianship against possible danger.

5–6 The sheep refused to follow a stranger because his voice was unfamiliar. In fact, if a stranger should use the shepherd's call and imitate his tone, the flock would instantly detect the difference and would scatter in panic. Jesus used this figure to depict the relation between the disciples and himself.

In view of the fact that shepherds and sheep were so common in Palestine, it seems incredible that Jesus' metaphor should not be understood. His hearers, however, failed to comprehend his meaning because of their spiritual deadness. If they would not recognize his claims, they would not accept him as a shepherd; and their assumption that they were God's flock because they were descendants of Abraham (8:39) would eliminate the necessity of personal faith in Jesus for salvation.

7 The sudden shift of metaphor from shepherd to gate seems rather strange to us, but in reality it is not. When the sheep returned to the fold at night after a day of grazing, the shepherd stood in the doorway of the pen and inspected each one as it entered. If a sheep were scratched or wounded by thorns, the shepherd anointed it with oil to facilitate healing; if the sheep were thirsty, he gave them water. As Psalm 23:5–6 says, "You anoint my head with oil; my cup overflows." After all the sheep had been counted and brought into the pen, the shepherd lay down across the doorway so that no intruder —man or beast—could enter without his knowledge. The shepherd became the door. The emphatic singular pronoun "I" (*egō*) emphasizes that the shepherd is the sole determiner of who enters the fold and who is excluded. It parallels the later statement: "I am the way and the truth and the life. No one comes to the Father except through me" (John 14:16).

8 "All who ever came before me were thieves and robbers" cannot refer to the prophets who preceded Jesus. It must refer to the false messiahs and supposed deliverers of the people who had appeared in the period following the restoration from the Exile and especially in the century before Jesus' advent. After the death of Herod the Great in 4 B.C., there were many factions that contended for the leadership of the nation and attempted by violence to throw off the Roman yoke. Jesus' purpose was not political, as the emphasis of the discourse shows.

Hendriksen suggests that Jesus was referring to the religious leaders of the Jews as the "thieves and robbers" (2:308). They were attempting to gain the allegiance of the people and were not above using violence if it would serve their purpose (cf. John 8:59).

9–10 Jesus' main purpose was the salvation (health) of the sheep, which he defined as free access to pasture and fullness of life. Under his protection and by his gift they can experience the best life can offer. In the context of John's emphasis on eternal life, this statement takes on new significance. Jesus can give a whole new meaning to living because he provides full satisfaction and perfect guidance (cf. Ezek 34:15).

11 The concept of a divine shepherd goes back to the OT. Psalm 23 opens with the statement "The LORD is my shepherd" (v.1); Jeremiah speaks of gathering the nation as a flock of sheep that has been scattered (23:1–3); and Ezekiel prophesied: "As a shepherd looks after his scattered flock when he is with them, so will I look after my sheep. I will rescue them ... I myself will tend my sheep and have them lie down" (34:12, 15). To the disciples the figure would have been specially apt since sheep herding was one of the major occupations in Palestine. It involved both protective concern and a sacrificial attitude. This latter is expressed in the words "the good shepherd lays down his life for the sheep." The phrase "lays down his life" is unique to the Johannine writings and means a voluntary sacrificial death (10:11, 17, 18; 13:37–38; 15:13; 1 John 3:16). The verb is used elsewhere in John to mean "lay aside, strip off " (13:4). In addition, the preposition *hyper*, translated "for," is generally used with a connotation of sacrifice (John 13:37; 15:13; cf. Luke 22:19; Rom 5:6–8; 1 Cor 15:3). "Life" (*psyche*) implies more than physical existence; it involves personality and is more frequently translated "soul." The good shepherd stands ready to sacrifice his total self for the sake of the sheep.

12 Jesus' statement "the hired hand is not the shepherd" indicates the difference between himself and the religious leaders of the day. The hireling, though not a brigand bent on the destruction of the sheep, is concerned more for his own safety than for that of the sheep. When the flock is attacked by a wolf, the hireling deserts them. The difference is not so much that of activity as of attitude. The hireling may guide the sheep to pasture, but he will not endanger himself for them. Without proper and courageous leadership, the sheep will be dispersed and easily made the victims of their enemies.

13 The hireling's main concern is his pay. This discourse anticipates Peter's words: "Be shepherds of God's flock that is under your care, serving as overseers—not because you must, but because you are willing, as God wants you to be; not greedy for money, but eager to serve; not lording it over those entrusted to you, but being examples to the flock" (1 Peter 5:2–3).

14–15 The reaffirmation "I am the good shepherd" is based on knowledge of the sheep. "Know" (*ginosko*) in this Gospel connotes more than the cognizance of mere facts; it implies a relationship of trust and intimacy. The definitive analogy given here is drawn from Jesus' relation to the Father. The Shepherd is concerned for the sheep because they are his property and because he loves them individually.

16 The sheep "not of this sheep pen" probably refers to the Gentiles whom Jesus sent his disciples to (Matt 28:19) and whom he wished to include in his salvation. He stresses this idea of unity later in his farewell prayer (17:20).

17 The thrice-repeated allusion to laying down his life (10:11, 15, 17) gives the basis for Jesus' sacrifice as the means of our reconciliation both to God and to one another. See 1 John 3:16: "This is how we know what love is: Jesus Christ laid down his life for us. And we ought to lay down our lives for our brothers."

18 Two important aspects of Jesus' death are clarified by his authority. The first is that his death was wholly voluntary. His power was such that no human hand could have touched him had he not permitted it. The Gospel has already made clear that Jesus had avoided capture or execution (5:18; 7:44-45; 8:20, 59; 10:39; 11:53-54). Only when he declared that "the hour has come" (12:23) was it possible for his enemies to arrest him. The second aspect is his authority to lay down his life and take it up again. The death of Jesus, though voluntary, was not merely assent to being killed, a sort of indirect suicide; it was part of a plan to submit to death and then emerge from it victoriously alive. Anyone can lay down his life, if that means simply the termination of physical existence; but only the Son of the Father could at will resume his existence. He was acting in accord with a divine plan that involved a supreme sacrifice and a manifestation of divine power. The entire plan was motivated by his love for the Father and his readiness to carry out his Father's purpose. "Authority" means that he was not the helpless victim of his enemies' violence but that he had both the right and the power to become the instrument of reconciliation between man and God and between Jew and Gentile.

19-21 The reaction of the populace was divided. His enemies accused him of insanity for making a claim that seemed both unreasonable and impossible. The accusation of demon-possession had been leveled against him on other occasions (7:20; 8:48). His claims seemed so exaggerated and so contradictory to the popular understanding of the unity of God that they could be attributed only to the irrational and blasphemous utterance of a demoniac. Curiously, Johannine writings never mention any miracle of exorcism on Jesus' part but employ this language only to report the way his opponents described his utterances and behavior. On the contrary, many of the crowd regarded Jesus as sane. His words did not correspond to the ravings of a demoniac, nor did demoniacs cure the blind. The reference to the miracle narrated in ch. 9 shows that it must have left a strong impression in Jerusalem.

Notes

8 Josephus (Antiq. 17.10.4-8) describes in detail a number of these revolts and adds: "And so Judea was filled with brigandage. Anyone might make himself king as the head of a band of rebels ... and then would press on to the destruction of the community." In this category the revolts mentioned in Acts 5:36-37 fell.

16 The word translated "pen" (αὐλή, aulē) means a courtyard or "fold" (KJV), an enclosure open to the sky where sheep can be kept at night. The word "flock" (ποίμνη, poimnē) means the group as a unit and does not refer to the place where sheep are kept. The sheepfold or pen is the artificial means by which unity is established; the flock is determined by the nature of the animals. To speak of a flock immediately raises the question as to kind: sheep, goats, geese, or doves. A "pen" connotes a place where the "flock" is kept. The "flock" refers to the nation of Israel in distinction from all other groups because of their heritage and location. Ultimately the

sheep from another flock would be united with them to make one flock of the redeemed. The concept of the flock gathered from all nations pervades the Gospels. Matthew quotes Jesus as telling his disciples to make disciples "of all nations" (Matt 28:19); Mark records his command to herald the gospel "to all creation" (Mark 16:15); and Luke stresses his command that repentance and forgiveness of sins should be proclaimed in his name "to all nations" (Luke 24:47). The word translated "nations" (ἔθνη, ethnē) is also rendered "Gentiles." Jesus intended that his message should reach both the house of Israel and all the peoples of the earth and that both should be drawn together in him.

---

3. The debate in Solomon's Colonnade

10:22–42

22Then came the Feast of Dedication at Jerusalem. It was winter, 23and Jesus was in the temple area walking in Solomon's Colonnade. 24The Jews gathered around him, saying, "How long will you keep us in suspense? If you are the Christ, tell us plainly."

25Jesus answered, "I did tell you, but you do not believe. The miracles I do in my Father's name speak for me, 26but you do not believe because you are not my sheep. 27My sheep listen to my voice; I know them, and they follow me. 28I give them eternal life, and they shall never perish; no one can snatch them out of my hand. 29My Father, who has given them to me, is greater than all; no one can snatch them out of my Father's hand. 30I and the Father are one."

31Again the Jews picked up stones to stone him, 32but Jesus said to them, "I have shown you many great miracles from the Father. For which of these do you stone me?"

33"We are not stoning you for any of these," replied the Jews, "but for blasphemy, because you, a mere man, claim to be God."

34"Jesus answered them, "Is it not written in your Law, 'I have said you are gods'? 35If he called them 'gods,' to whom the word of God came—and the Scripture cannot be broken—36what about the one whom the Father set apart as his very own and sent into the world? Why then do you accuse me of blasphemy because I said, 'I am God's Son'? 37Do not believe me unless I do what my Father does. 38But if I do it, even though you do not believe me, believe the miracles, that you may learn and understand that the Father is in me, and I in the Father." 39Again they tried to seize him, but he escaped their grasp.

40Then Jesus went back across the Jordan to the place where John had been baptizing in the early days. Here he stayed 41and many people came to him. They said, "Though John never performed a miraculous sign, all that John said about this man was true." 42And in that place many believed in Jesus.

22–23 The Feast of Dedication, now known as Hanukkah, was established as a memorial to the purification and rededication of the temple by Judas Maccabeus on Kislev (December) 25, 165 B.C., after its profanation three years earlier by Antiochus IV Epiphanes. Antiochus, the king of Syria, had captured Jerusalem, plundered the temple treasury, and sacrificed a sow to Jupiter on the temple altar. His attempt to Hellenize Judea resulted in the Maccabean revolt, which, after three years, was successful in defeating the Syrian armies and liberating the Jewish people. Solomon's Colonnade (or Porch) was a long walkway covered by a roof supported on pillars on the east side of the temple, overlooking the Kidron Valley. The Colonnade served as a shelter from the heat of the sun in summer and from the cold rain in winter. Jesus used it as a center for informal teaching and preaching since there would almost always be some people present for worship at the temple.

24 The verb translated "gathered around him" (*ekyklōsan*) means "encircled" and implies that the Jews wanted to compel Jesus to make a categorical statement of his identity. Their demand, "How long will you keep us in suspense? If you are the Christ, tell us plainly," reveals their impatience. If he was the Messiah, they wanted him to fulfill his calling by achieving independence for the nation; if he was not the Messiah, they would look elsewhere. They could not escape the fact that his miracles (*erga*, "works") exceeded the powers of any ordinary man and that his teachings carried an authority greater than that of the established religious leaders. On the other hand, he had not formally presented himself as the Messiah, nor had he evinced any political ambitions. The crowd was demanding a declaration that would either dispel an illusion or enlist their allegiance.

25–26 Jesus' reply placed the burden of proof on his questioners. He reminded them that his previous sayings and works (*erga*) should be sufficient to establish his messianic mission (cf. John 5:16–47; 6:32–59; 7:14–30). He charged them with unbelief because they refused the evidence he had so plainly given them. He said the reason they did not believe was that they were not his sheep. By telling them that they did not belong to his flock, he implied that it was not descent from the chosen line that was the criterion of salvation. His sheep manifested their nature by following him. They enjoyed the favor of God. His immediate hearers refused to believe and thus cut themselves off from further revelation.

27–28 The sheep that belong to the Lord's flock are characterized by obedience, recognition of the shepherd, and allegiance to him. They are guaranteed eternal life and permanent protection. All the resources of God are committed to their preservation. Eternal life is given to them, not earned by them, and they themselves are given to Christ by the Father. Christ promises his personal protection to the sheep that the Father has given him: "No one can snatch them out of my hand."

29 The marginal reading of this verse, "What my Father has given me is greater than all," is probably the correct reading, though the MS evidence seems rather evenly divided. If so, the gift of the Father is the "sheep" viewed collectively. The Father assures their destiny, for nobody can wrest them from his hand. Throughout the preceding discourse, Jesus stressed his relationship with the Father, his intimate knowledge of the Father (10:15), and the love of the Father for him (v.17). He said that his miracles (*erga*, "works") were performed "in my Father's name" (v.25), which means that they were done by the power of the Father and for his honor. The final claim was "I and the Father are one" (v.30).

30 "I and the Father" preserves the separate individuality of the two Persons in the Godhead; the neuter pronoun "one" (*hen*) asserts unity of nature or equality (cf. 1 Cor 3:8). The Jews were quick to apprehend this statement and reacted by preparing to stone Jesus for blasphemy because he, a man, had asserted that he was one with God. For them Jesus' language did not mean simply agreement of thought or purpose but carried a metaphysical implication of deity. The Father and the Son functioned as one.

31 The verb translated "picked up" literally means "to carry." It is doubtful whether there were any loose stones in the paved courtyard of Solomon's Colonnade that could have been picked up. But not far off was the temple that was in the process of being built, and certainly stones would have been readily available there. Stoning was the punishment prescribed for blasphemy according to the law of Moses (Lev 24:16), and the opponents of Jesus were preparing for just such an execution.

32 Jesus' question challenged the people's action on the ground that he had performed only helpful deeds. His question was designed to make them take stock of what he had done. Then they would see that stoning would be incongruous with his actions.

33 The Jews replied that the question was not the quality of his works but the nature of his claims, and they charged him with blasphemy. Had Jesus not meant to convey a claim to deity, he undoubtedly would have protested the action of the Jews by declaring that they had misunderstood him.

34–35 On the contrary, Jesus introduced an *a fortiori* argument from the Psalms to strengthen his statement. Psalm 82:6 represents God as addressing a group of beings whom he calls "gods" (Heb. *elōhîm*) and "sons of the Most High." If, then, these terms can be applied to ordinary mortals or even angels, how could Jesus be accused of blasphemy when he applied them to himself whom the Father set apart and sent into the world on a special mission? Jesus was not offering a false claim; he was merely asserting what he was by rights.

The parenthetic statement "and the Scripture cannot be broken" illustrates the high regard Jesus had for the OT. Throughout this Gospel the constant assumption is that the Scripture is the revelation of God, setting the timing, content, and character of Jesus' ministry. The Gospel quotes with approval Philip's words to Nathanael: "We have found the one Moses wrote about in the Law, and about whom the prophets wrote—Jesus of Nazareth, the son of Joseph" (1:45). The resurrection was explained for the disciples by Scripture and Jesus' words (2:22). Jesus used the episode of the bronze serpent (John 3:14–15; cf. Num 21:4–9) to illustrate for Nicodemus the meaning of his death and the power of faith. Jesus told his hearers plainly that the Scriptures bore witness to him (5:39). Scripture set the pattern Jesus followed in going to the Cross (12:14–16; 13:18; 19:18, 24, 28, 36). Whether all these other passages refer to Jesus' explicit statements or to the writer's explanation of his action, they presuppose a confidence in the authority and trustworthiness of Scripture that is in keeping with Jesus' attitude.

36 Jesus unmistakably referred to himself as the Son of God. To him it was not a strained assertion but a logical statement, for he was fully aware of his relation to the Father and to the responsibility the Father had committed to him. The accusation of blasphemy seems to be utterly unreasonable in the light of that relationship.

37–39 Jesus' appeal to his opponents summed up the attitude and method of his argument. He took his position, not on the basis of his personal authority, but on the attestation of his works. If they showed that he was demonstrating divine compassion and exercising divine authority over men and matter, he was divinely accredited. The word "miracles" (*erga,* "works") in John refers to those acts of Jesus that are peculiarly expressive of his nature and have evidential value. They especially reveal his personality and mission. For those who were predisposed not to believe in him, he offered pragmatic proof of his special relationship with God: "The Father is in me, and I in the Father." The appeal failed; and once again "they tried to seize him, but he escaped their grasp."

40–42 Having eluded their attempt to capture him, Jesus retreated to Perea, on the east side of the Jordan, where he would be comparatively safe from arrest. There he found a better reception, and again it is stated that "many believed on him." Perea was the domain of Herod Antipas, where the rulers in Jerusalem had no authority. Jesus thus would be safe from harassment there—at least temporarily.

The Jews' allusion to the testimony of John the Baptist indicates that his ministry had enduring influence, and they accepted Jesus on that basis. As in the case of the woman of Samaria, faith in Christ was preceded by the witness of another.

Notes

40 The place Jesus retired to may have been the "Bethany on the other side of the Jordan" (John 1:28), where John the Baptist was preaching when he first met Jesus. The exact location is unknown. It may have been just east of Jericho across the Jordan. Some, including Origen, identified it with Bethabara, about 10 miles south of the Sea of Galilee. The former option would be nearer to Jerusalem.

---

4. The miracle at Bethany (11:1–44)

a. The announcement of death

11:1–16

¹Now a man named Lazarus was sick. He was from Bethany, the village of Mary and her sister Martha. ²This Mary, whose brother Lazarus now lay sick, was the same one who poured perfume on the Lord and wiped his feet with her hair. ³So the sisters sent word to Jesus, "Lord, the one you love is sick."

⁴When he heard this, Jesus said, "This sickness will not end in death. No, it is for God's glory so that God's Son may be glorified through it." ⁵Jesus loved Martha and her sister and Lazarus. ⁶Yet when he heard that Lazarus was sick, he stayed where he was two more days.

⁷Then he said to his disciples, "Let us go back to Judea."

⁸"But Rabbi," they said, "a short while ago the Jews tried to stone you, and yet you are going back there?"

⁹Jesus answered, "Are there not twelve hours of daylight? A man who walks by day will not stumble, for he sees by this world's light. ¹⁰It is when he walks by night that he stumbles, for he has no light."

¹¹After he had said this, he went on to tell them, "Our friend Lazarus has fallen asleep; but I am going there to wake him up."

¹²His disciples replied, "Lord, if he sleeps, he will get better." ¹³Jesus had been speaking of his death, but his disciples thought he meant natural sleep.

¹⁴So then he told them plainly, "Lazarus is dead, ¹⁵and for your sake I am glad I was not there, so that you may believe. But let us go to him."

¹⁶Then Thomas (called Didymus) said to the rest of the disciples, "Let us also go, that we may die with him."

The account of the raising of Lazarus is the climactic sign in the Gospel of John. Each of the seven signs illustrates some particular aspect of Jesus' divine authority, but this one exemplifies his power over the last and most irresistible enemy of humanity—death.

For this reason it is given a prominent place in the Gospel. It is also extremely significant because it precipitated the decision of Jesus' enemies to do away with him. Furthermore, this episode contains a strong personal command to believe in Jesus in a crisis, when such belief would be most difficult. All that preceded is preparatory; all that follows it is the unfolding of a well-marked plot.

1–2 At this point Lazarus is introduced, though Mary and Martha are mentioned in Luke (10:38–42), with a possible allusion in Matthew (26:6–12) and Mark (14:3–9) that would correspond to the Johannine account. Apparently Jesus was frequently a guest in their home when he visited Jerusalem. Mark states that in the early days of the Passion Week Jesus "went out to Bethany with the Twelve" (11:11). Of Lazarus, however, nothing is known apart from the Johannine record. The identification of Mary by the action recorded later in this Gospel is unusual, unless the author presupposed some knowledge of her action on the reader's part. It seems probable that the story of Mary's anointing of Jesus may have been narrated in the church prior to the writing of this Gospel. John mentions it in order to identify Lazarus and to indicate Jesus' relations with the family.

3 Knowing Jesus' interest in them and the power of God to heal the sick, the sisters sent for him when Lazarus became ill. The malady must have been serious, for they were sufficiently alarmed to call Jesus back to the area where a price had been set on his head. The appeal was on the basis of love. The sisters' implication was that if Jesus loved Lazarus, he would return. They seemed quite confident that he would be prompt.

4–6 Jesus' reaction was optimistic and purposeful. He gave assurance to the disciples, and possibly a message to be sent back to the sisters, that Lazarus's illness would not terminate in death, and stated that Lazarus's illness would be an important aspect of his own glorification. Having said that, Jesus deliberately "stayed where he was two more days." His action may have appeared to the disciples, and almost certainly to the sisters, as unfeeling and selfish. Since he had the power to heal Lazarus, why should he not reply instantly? Perhaps the disciples were not particularly puzzled because their subsequent remarks indicated that they were well aware of the danger that threatened him in Jerusalem. His response, however, was quite different from that in the case of Jairus's daughter, when he acted promptly (Luke 8:41–42, 49–56), or in the case of the widow of Nain, whose son he raised when he met the funeral procession on the way to the burial ground (Luke 7:11–16).

7–8 His proposal to the disciples that they should return to Judea was not welcomed with enthusiasm. They remembered the previous conflicts with the rulers and feared for Jesus' life, and possibly for their own as well. The emphatic position of the adverb *there* at the end of the sentence gives the impression that they would be more willing to go with him if his destination were not Judea.

9–10 Jesus countered the disciples' objection with the following enigmatic statement: "Are there not twelve hours of daylight? A man who walks by day will not stumble, for he sees by the world's light. It is when he walks by night that he stumbles, for he has no light." The expression of Jesus may have been a current proverb like the one underlying the remark in John 9:4: "As long as it is day, we must do the work of him who sent me. Night is coming, when no one can work." In both instances, Jesus was thinking of his obligation to perform the work the Father had committed to him. Realizing that he was acting in accord with the purpose of the Father who had sent him and that he had clear illumination concerning his duty, Jesus resolutely decided to return to Jerusalem in spite of the peril. John in his First Epistle employed this same figure of speech: "If we claim to have fellowship with him yet walk in the darkness, we lie and do not live by the truth" (1 John 1:6). To digress from God's purpose is to walk in darkness; to remain in fellowship with God is to walk in the light. Jesus may have had the same concept in mind when he warned his disciples that the light would be with them only a little longer and that darkness would shortly overtake them (12:35). His presence was their illumination; when he was removed, they lost their sense of spiritual direction, as Peter's denial and Thomas's incredulity demonstrated.

11 In order to explain his action, Jesus informed his disciples that Lazarus was asleep and that he intended to wake him. The explanation was intended to be a part of the education of the disciples. Their interest and loyalty were plainly revealed by their willingness to listen to him and to move back into the area of danger if he so desired.

12-13 The disciples lacked imagination and took literally Jesus' announcement that Lazarus had fallen asleep. Assuming that "sleep" would mean that the fever had passed its crisis, they expressed their hope for Lazarus's recovery. Jesus, however, used the word *sleep* in a figurative sense, meaning "death." This does not mean that the dead are in a state of total unconsciousness, for Jesus' illustration of the rich man and the beggar predicates consciousness after death (Luke 16:19-31). It does show that Jesus looked on the death of Lazarus as a parenthesis after which there would be an awakening, not as a permanent removal from life.

14-15 Jesus' rejoinder to the disciples' comment made Lazarus's state unmistakable: "Lazarus is dead, and for your sake I am glad I was not there, so that you may believe. But let us go to him." Jesus' words seem strange. Why should he be glad that he was not present to save Lazarus from death, or to comfort the sisters, and why should Lazarus's death bring any benefit to the disciples? Jesus considered this an opportunity for a supreme demonstration of power that would certify the Father's accreditation of him as the Son and confirm the faith of the sisters and the disciples. He was certain of the outcome. He knew that positive belief and joy would be the result.

16 Thomas's comment marks his first appearance in this book. John's Gospel does not contain a complete list of the Twelve, though they are mentioned as a group on two occasions (6:67, 70-71; 20:24). Generally they are presented only as individuals and once in the Epilogue as a smaller group on the occasion of the fishing party in Galilee (21:1-2). Thomas appears four times: here, once in the discourse in the upper room (14:5), once after the Resurrection (20:24-29), and finally with the group described in the Epilogue (21:1). In the upper room incident, his attitude seems to be pessimistic and querulous. His comment in John 11:16 is paradoxical: "Let us also go, that we may die with him." "Him" no doubt refers to Jesus, not to Lazarus. Thomas expected that Jesus would be seized and executed and that his disciples would suffer with him. Notwithstanding this unhappy prospect, Thomas's loyalty is revealed by his readiness to share Jesus' peril. The skepticism that Thomas later evinced regarding the Resurrection was probably prompted by grief over Jesus' death rather than by disillusionment because of apparent failure.

Notes

11 Two words are used in the NT to express the idea of sleeping and/or death. Κοιμάω (koimaō), which appears in this passage in the perfect tense κεκοίμηται (kekoimētai), occurs eighteen times in the NT: in Matt, Luke, John, Acts, 1 Cor, 1 Thess, and 2 Peter. And except for three instances, it is uniformly a figurative description of death. The other word, καθεύδω (katheudō), appears in the Gospels sixteen times and in the Pauline Epistles four times and is invariably taken literally, with one possible exception (Eph 5:14), which is quoted in a fragment of Christian hymnody. Eph 5:14 appears to refer to death in terms of spiritual dullness rather than to physical disease.

There has been considerable controversy as to whether κοιμάω (koimaō) implies that the dead actually exist in a state of total unconsciousness until resurrection or whether it is merely a description of death based on the analogy of appearance. A person who is sleeping seems inert and unaffected by external stimuli. The use of this verb as a metaphor for death appears in the Greek classics, in the LXX, in the vernacular of the papyri, and in the patristic writings. In the light of such passages as Luke 23:43—the promise to the dying thief, "I tell you the truth, today you will be with me in paradise"— and Paul's declaration of his longing to "depart and be with Christ, which is better by far" (Phil 1:23), death for the child of God could hardly be an unconscious state. From Jesus' standpoint, Lazarus's death was comparable to a nap, which cut off consciousness of this world temporarily but did not mean a permanent severance.

b. *The conversation with Martha and Mary*

11:17–37

[17]On his arrival, Jesus found that Lazarus had already been in the tomb for four days. [18]Bethany was less than two miles from Jerusalem, [19]and many Jews had come to Martha and Mary to comfort them in the loss of their brother. [20]When Martha heard that Jesus was coming, she went out to meet him, but Mary stayed at home.

[21]"Lord," Martha said to Jesus, "if you had been here, my brother would not have died. [22]But I know that even now God will give you whatever you ask."

[23]Jesus said to her, "Your brother will rise again."

[24]Martha answered, "I know he will rise again in the resurrection at the last day."

[25]Jesus said to her, "I am the resurrection and the life. He who believes in me will live, even though he dies; [26]and whoever lives and believes in me will never die. Do you believe this?"

[27]"Yes, Lord," she told him, "I believe that you are the Christ, the Son of God, who was to come into the world."

[28]And after she had said this, she went back and called her sister Mary aside. "The Teacher is here," she said, "and is asking for you." [29]When Mary heard this, she got up quickly and went to him. [30]Now Jesus had not yet entered the village, but was still at the place where Martha had met him. [31]When the Jews who had been with Mary in the house, comforting her, noticed how quickly she got up and went out, they followed her, supposing she was going to the tomb to mourn there.

[32]When Mary reached the place where Jesus was and saw him, she fell at his feet and said, "Lord, if you had been here, my brother would not have died."

[33]When Jesus saw her weeping, and the Jews who had come along with her also weeping, he was deeply moved in spirit and troubled. [34]"Where have you laid him?" he asked.

"Come and see, Lord," they replied.

[35]Jesus wept.

[36]Then the Jews said, "See how he loved him!"

[37]But some of them said, "Could not he who opened the eyes of the blind man have kept this man from dying?"

17-18 The time between Lazarus's death and Jesus' arrival at Bethany was four days. Presumably the time required for the journey of the messengers and the time needed for Jesus' return to Bethany would be approximately the same. Also, two full days intervened between their arrival where Jesus was and his departure for Bethany (v.6). So the death of Lazarus must have occurred not long after Jesus was first informed of his illness. The trip each way would have taken not much less than a day's travel since Bethany was more than twenty miles distant from Jesus' refuge in Perea (10:40–42). After three days all hope of resuscitation from a coma would be abandoned; and in the hot Palestinian climate, decay would have begun.

19 The family at Bethany must have been well known in Jerusalem, with connections within the Jewish hierarchy, since many "Jews" came to comfort Martha and Mary over the loss of Lazarus. A procession composed of relatives, friends, and sometimes hired mourners accompanied a body to the grave; and mourning usually lasted for several days afterward.

20 Martha, being more aggressive, "went out to meet" Jesus. Mary was quiet and contemplative: she "stayed at home." This portrayal of the sisters by John agrees with that found in Luke 10:38–42.

21-22 The words Martha addressed to Jesus express both a repressed reproach and a persistent faith. She was disappointed that Jesus had not responded to her first news of Lazarus's illness, but that did not lead her to break her relationship with him. Despite her remorse, she was confident that God would grant Jesus' desire in this matter.

23-26 Martha interpreted Jesus' promise (v.23) that her brother would rise again in terms of the expectation of a general resurrection. She may have taken his words as a conventional expression of comfort; he intended them to describe what he would do. Martha's reply indicates that she shared the Pharisaic belief in an ultimate resurrection for the just (Acts 23:7). By his reply, Jesus turned Martha's acceptance of a dogma into faith in his person. In what is surely one of his most majestic and comforting utterances, Jesus said that he embodied the vital power to bring the dead to life: "I am the resurrection and the life. He who believes in me will live, even though he dies; and whoever lives and believes in me will never die" (vv.25–26). The one who believes in Christ has eternal life that transcends physical death. If he is living and believing, he will never die but will make an instant transition from the old life to the new life. Jesus' words are amplified by Paul's statement in 1 Thessalonians 4:16–17: "The dead in Christ will rise first. After that, we who are still alive and are left will be caught up with them in the clouds to meet the Lord in the air." There is, however, no specific reference in John 11:25 to the second advent of Christ. Whether Jesus had this event in mind and whether Martha would so have understood his words is uncertain. In any case, Jesus was saying that he embodied the resurrection life that could overcome death and that believers would be assured of an inheritance in the age to come. On this basis, he asked her directly whether she believed.

27 Martha's commitment reveals a firm belief that Jesus was the Messiah, the Son of God, as preached by John the Baptist (1:34) and accepted by the disciples (1:49; 6:68), and the deliverer foretold by the prophets. Her language is emphatic: "Yes, Lord, ... I believe."

28-30 The action of Mary, though less assertive, reveals a similar trust in Jesus. Martha told Mary that Jesus was asking for her. To Mary, this was equivalent to a command to come. Mary wasted no time in going to Jesus: "she got up quickly and went to him." Jesus had not entered the village. He was waiting for Mary to come to him. Perhaps he remained outside Bethany so as not to precipitate an argument in the event his enemies discovered him.

31 The Jews knew something was afoot when Mary left so hastily. Since they had come to mourn with the sisters, they thought it only fitting to follow her, supposing that she was going to the tomb.

32 Mary's greeting to Jesus was similar to Martha's; in fact, the words are identical except for their sequence. Martha's sentence, "Lord, if you had been here *my* brother would not have died" (italics added), puts the possessive pronoun at the end of the sentence in the Greek, while Mary's words, by their order, emphasize "my *brother*" (italics added). The difference is small and may simply be a result of rhetoric. But if the Greek order is taken to be significant, it may be that Martha was grieving because she had lost a precious possession while Mary was thinking of the life that had ended too soon. Morris says, "In view of John's habit of making slight alterations when statements are repeated these variations should not be regarded as significant" (NIC, p. 554, n. 62).

33-35 The response of Jesus to this calamity illustrates his human and divine natures. Up to this point he had been perfectly calm, assuring Martha that her brother would rise and asserting that he was the resurrection and the life. He was completely in command of the situation and challenged Martha's faith. But when Mary appeared, crushed with sorrow and accompanied by the waiting mourners, Jesus was moved with deep emotion. His feeling is expressed by three words: "deeply moved," "troubled" (v.33), and "wept" (v.35). The first of these (*enebrimēsato*) means literally "to snort like a horse" and generally connotes anger. It could not have indicated displeasure with the sisters whom he was trying to comfort and for whom he felt the strongest compassion. Perhaps it expressed his resentment against the ravages of death that had entered the human world because of sin.

The second word, "troubled" (*etaraxen*), expresses agitation, confusion, or disorganization. Here it implies agitation rather than complete confusion. Jesus was not apathetic or unnerved by the prevailing mood of sorrow. Lazarus had been a beloved friend, and Jesus shared in the common feeling of grief over his death. His human feelings were normal and are revealed by the crisis of the moment. Overcome by emotion, he gave way to weeping. Williams's translation reads: "Jesus burst into tears." His grief was spontaneous.

36-37 Jesus' true humanity was emphasized by the response of the people at Lazarus's tomb. Some were impressed by Jesus' open show of emotion and took it as an evident token of his love for Lazarus. Others, perhaps not so lovingly, wondered why Jesus had not prevented Lazarus's death by one of his miracles. The reference to the healing of the blind man shows that it must have created a sensation in Jerusalem since it was remembered several months after it had occurred.

Notes

---

27 The first person pronoun ἐγώ (*egō*, "I") used with the verb πεπίστευκα, (*pepisteuka*, "have believed") in the perfect tense gives added impact to Martha's personal conviction and implies not only a past decision but also a present state of mind. There could have hardly been a stronger expression of faith on her part.

33 Ἐνεβριμήσατο (*enebrimēsato*, "deeply moved") is used in Mark 14:5 to describe the attitude of the disciples toward Mary at the anointing in Bethany, and Matt 9:30, where it relates to Jesus' stern injunction to the blind men not to declare that he had healed them. The object of Jesus' anger is not stated.

The verb ταράσσω (*tarassō*, "troubled") is used to describe a sea in a storm (Isa 24:14 LXX) and the effect of fear or surprise on the human mind (Matt 2:3; 14:26; Luke 1:12; 24:38).

35 The third word, ἐδάκρυσεν (*edakrusen*, "wept"), means to shed tears quietly. It may be contrasted with the loud and ostentatious "weeping" (κλαίοντας, *klaiontas*) of the hired mourners (v.33), which was artificial.

36 The imperfect tense "were saying" (ἔλεγον, *elegon*) implies repeated or continued action. Jesus' sorrow impressed the onlookers with the depth of his concern.

---

c. The raising of Lazarus

11:38–44

> 38Jesus, once more deeply moved, came to the tomb. It was a cave with a stone laid across the entrance. 39"Take away the stone," he said.
>
> "But, Lord," said Martha, the sister of the dead man, "by this time there is a bad odor, for he has been there four days."
>
> 40Then Jesus said, "Did I not tell you that if you believed, you would see the glory of God?"
>
> 41So they took away the stone. Then Jesus looked up and said, "Father, I thank you that you have heard me. 42I knew that you always hear me, but I said this for the benefit of the people standing here, that they may believe that you sent me."
>
> 43When he had said this, Jesus called in a loud voice, "Lazarus, come out!" 44The dead man came out, his hands and feet wrapped with strips of linen, and a cloth around his face.
>
> Jesus said to them, "Take off the grave clothes and let him go."

38 The repetition of "deeply moved" (*embrimōmenos*), the present participle of the verb, shows that Jesus was still under the same emotional tension that his first contact with the mourners had aroused. He faced the necessity of fulfilling his prediction to the disciples that the outcome of Lazarus's death would be to the glory of God. He would also keep his promise to Martha that her brother should rise again. The burial place was a chamber cut in limestone rock and closed by a stone laid over the entrance.

39 Having challenged Martha's faith, Jesus now faced a challenge of his own. He ordered the covering stone to be removed. Martha's protest was natural. It would seem improper to expose a decaying corpse. She had to put faith in Jesus.

40 To Jesus the raising of Lazarus was no problem. The chief difficulty was to remove the uncertainty and hesitancy from Martha's attitude that the glory of God might be revealed to her and all present.

41–42 When Martha met his condition, which was the last step of faith she could take, Jesus took the next step. He did not ask God to raise Lazarus; he thanked him for having already answered. So great was Jesus' faith in the Father that he assumed this miracle that was necessary to his mission to be as good as done. Only raising Lazarus would complete the expectations Jesus had aroused in the disciples and in Mary and Martha. He said in his prayer that the transaction was already complete, but he asked for the raising of Lazarus as a convincing sign to the assembled people that he had been sent by the Father.

43–44 Having uttered this prayer, Jesus addressed the dead man. Jesus had said on a previous occasion that a time would come when all who were in their graves would hear his voice (John 5:28). This occasion was a single demonstration of that authority. The words spoken were brief, direct, and imperative and can be paraphrased, "Lazarus! This way out!" as if Jesus were directing someone lost in a gloomy dungeon. The creative power of God reversed the process of corruption and quickened the corpse into life. The effect was startling. The dead man appeared at the entrance to the tomb, still bound by the graveclothes that had been wound around him. Jesus then ordered that he be released from the wrappings and returned to normal life. It was a supreme demonstration of the power of eternal life that triumphed over death, corruption, and hopelessness.

5. The decision to kill Jesus

11:45–57

> ⁴⁵Therefore many of the Jews who had come to visit Mary, and had seen what Jesus did, put their faith in him. ⁴⁶But some of them went to the Pharisees and told them what Jesus had done. ⁴⁷Then the chief priests and the Pharisees called a meeting of the Sanhedrin.
>
> "What are we accomplishing?" they asked. "Here is this man performing many miraculous signs. ⁴⁸If we let him go on like this, everyone will believe in him, and then the Romans will come and take away both our place and our nation."
>
> ⁴⁹Then one of them, named Caiaphas, who was high priest that year, spoke up, "You know nothing at all! ⁵⁰You do not realize that it is better for you that one man die for the people than that the whole nation perish."
>
> ⁵¹He did not say this on his own, but as high priest that year he prophesied that Jesus would die for the Jewish nation, ⁵²and not only for that nation but also for the scattered children of God, to bring them together and make them one. ⁵³So from that day on they plotted to take his life.
>
> ⁵⁴Therefore Jesus no longer moved about publicly among the Jews. Instead he withdrew to a region near the desert, to a village called Ephraim, where he stayed with his disciples.
>
> ⁵⁵When it was almost time for the Jewish Passover, many went up from the country to Jerusalem for their ceremonial cleansing before the Passover. ⁵⁶They kept looking for Jesus, and as they stood in the temple area they asked one another, "What do you think? Isn't he coming to the Feast at all?" ⁵⁷But the chief priests and Pharisees had given orders that if anyone found out where Jesus was, he should report it so that they might arrest him.

45–46 The response to the sign was twofold. "Many" of the Jews believed on the basis of the evidence they had seen, for the fact of Lazarus's restoration was incontrovertible. In contrast, others went to inform the religious leaders of Jesus' action, apparently as a gesture of disapproval. It seems unlikely that any of the believing Jews made up the delegation that went to the Pharisees. Those who believed would no doubt want to stay with Jesus, whereas the skeptics would be desirous of letting the religious authorities know what had happened so that they could take the necessary action.

47–48 The impact of Jesus' miracle in Bethany resulted in the calling of a meeting of the Sanhedrin. The council expressed not only disapproval but also frustration. They anticipated that the miracles of Jesus would bring such a wave of popular support that the Romans, fearing a revolution, would intervene by seizing complete authority, thus displacing the Jewish government and destroying the national identity. Their fears revealed a complete misunderstanding of the motives of Jesus, who had no political ambitions whatever. He had already indicated by his refusal to be made king that he had no intention of organizing a revolt against Rome. Jesus' reply concerning the lawfulness of paying tribute to Caesar, "Give to Caesar what is Caesar's, and to God what is God's" (Matt 22:21), confirmed that decision.

49–50 Caiaphas, the high priest, was the son-in-law of Annas, who is mentioned later in the account of Jesus' trial. Annas had been high priest from A.D. 7 to 14 and was succeeded by three of his sons and finally by Caiaphas from A.D. 18 to 36. The phrase "that year" may be an indirect allusion to the fact that the Roman government had changed the high priest so often that it became almost an annual appointment. That would not be true of Caiaphas, however, for he held office uninterruptedly for eighteen years; but in the long memory of the writer that year would have been outstanding as the year of Jesus' death. The utterance of Caiaphas reveals his cynicism and duplicity. He was contemptuous of the indecisive attitude of the Pharisees and recommended the elimination of Jesus rather than risking the possibility of a long contest with Rome.

51–52 John takes Caiaphas's statement as a kind of double entendre, an unconscious and involuntary prophecy that Jesus would become the sacrifice for the nation that it might not perish. The prophetic quality is attributed to Caiaphas's high priestly office rather than his personal character. Assuredly Caiaphas would not be reckoned among the prophets. The irony of the statement, which indirectly affirms the sacrificial aspect of Jesus' death, is paralleled by the record of the rulers' mockery of Jesus at the Crucifixion: "He saved others, but he can't save himself!" (Mark 15:31). In both instances the sneering remark expressed an unintended truth. The entire statement of Caiaphas is thus interpreted by the author and applied, not only to the nation of Israel, but also to the children of God who had been scattered throughout the world. These words might apply to the Jews of the Dispersion. But in the light of the universalism of this Gospel, they probably refer proleptically to the ingathering of the Gentiles, who become the children of God when they acknowledge the saviorhood of Christ (John 1:12; 10:16).

53 The growing hostility of the Pharisaic party and of the Sadducean priesthood had developed into a settled decision to do away with Jesus. Although the hierarchy feared a popular uprising in his support, they were resolute that he should die. John indicates that their opposition had reached the point of no return.

54 For this reason Jesus left Bethany, where danger threatened him, and removed to Ephraim, a village north of Jerusalem. Ephraim has been identified with Et Taiyibeh, a few miles northeast of Bethel. Perhaps it may be the city called Aphairema, mentioned in the account of the Maccabean wars (1 Macc 11:34). The town was on the edge of the Judean desert, into which Jesus could flee if necessary.

55–56 Just before the Passover, pilgrims from distant parts of the country began to assemble in Jerusalem. Ceremonial cleansing would take considerable time when a large crowd was involved, and the people wanted to be ready to participate in the sacred feast. Jesus had been present in Jerusalem at the Feasts of Tabernacles and Dedication and had been regularly engaged in teaching. Since the Passover would bring an even larger crowd to Jerusalem, the populace expected that Jesus would be there also. His previous visits had been accompanied by much controversy, and there had been several futile attempts to arrest or stone him (cf. John 5:18; 7:30, 44; 8:20, 59; 10:38). On each occasion, however, he had eluded his enemies, for "his time had not come." His foes were powerless to take him till he was ready to fulfill the final sacrifice of death (7:8, 30; 8:20, 59).

57 The high council of Judaism had issued a warrant for Jesus' arrest and had ordered that anyone who knew of his whereabouts should declare it. Silence meant complicity and could be punishable. In the light of this situation, it might be concluded that Judas was a messianist loyal to his nation and that his loyalty to the ruling priesthood took precedence over his personal loyalty to Jesus.

Notes

45 The UBS text has ἃ ἐποίησεν (ha epoiēsen, "[things] he did") rather than ὃ ἐποίησεν (ho epoiēsen, "[thing] he did"). Although the MSS evidence slightly favors the former, to us the latter seems more logical, since the context is focused on the one great sign of the raising of Lazarus rather than on a summary of miracles in general. Metzger favors the opposing view (*Textual Commentary*, p.235).

48 Morris suggests that "our place" probably refers to the temple (NIC, p. 566). Τόπος (*topos*) can be interpreted as "position" or "office" and is so used by Ignatius (*Smyrneans* 6:1) and Clement of Rome (1 Clement 40:5; 44:5). In every other instance in John the meaning is geographical.

F. *The Crisis of the Ministry* (12:1–50)

Chapter 12 of John is devoted to the crisis of Jesus' ministry that preceded its conclusion. As previously noted, the hostility of the religious authorities had been increasing and had intensified because they had been unable to entangle Jesus in any compromising dilemma or defeat him in public debate. Despite the fact that there had been a decline in his popularity because he refused to become involved in a political coup (6:15) and because some of his teaching was obscure to his listeners (6:52–66), he nevertheless retained a loyal group of disciples; and a large segment of the populace still regarded him with awe. They expected that he might still decide to use his miraculous powers on their behalf and establish a new political and economic order that would make Israel dominant among the nations. The division of attitudes prevailed both among the disciples and among the people.

For Jesus himself, the period was critical because the forces for and against him were crystallizing, and he had to make a decision as to which way he should turn. He had been living by a program established by the Father and outlined progressively by Scripture and by experience. No doubt the temptation to deviate from it for considerations of power or safety was always with him (Luke 4:13). Now, as the moment for the fulfillment of the divine purpose approached, the tension increased; and the indications that the climax was near multiplied.

John presents a series of events, each of which foreshadow the coming end. The first of these was the feast at the house of Mary and Martha.

1. *The dinner at Bethany*

12:1-11

> [1]Six days before the Passover, Jesus arrived at Bethany, where Lazarus lived, whom Jesus had raised from the dead. [2]Here a dinner was given in Jesus' honor. Martha served, while Lazarus was among those reclining at the table with him. [3]Then Mary took about a pint of pure nard, an expensive perfume; she poured it on Jesus' feet and wiped his feet with her hair. And the house was filled with the fragrance of the perfume.
>
> [4]But one of his disciples, Judas Iscariot, who was later to betray him, objected, [5]"Why wasn't this perfume sold and the money given to the poor? It was worth a year's wages." [6]He did not say this because he cared about the poor but because he was a thief; as keeper of the money bag, he used to help himself to what was put into it.
>
> [7]"Leave her alone," Jesus replied. "It was meant that she should save this perfume for the day of my burial. [8]You will always have the poor among you, but you will not always have me."
>
> [9]Meanwhile a large crowd of Jews found out that Jesus was there and came, not only because of him but also to see Lazarus, whom he had raised from the dead. [10]So the chief priests made plans to kill Lazarus as well, [11]for on account of him many of the Jews were going over to Jesus and putting their faith in him.

1 At this point the time schedule becomes more definite than previously. Although there are chronological references in this Gospel, there are also general gaps introduced by such expressions as "after this," "after these things" (2:12; 3:22; 5:1; 6:1; 7:1; 9:1; 10:40). While several of the events introduced by these rather vague expressions are connected with definite times and places, the intervals between them are not precisely measured. In this final period, however, the sequence is more definite.

The explanation that Bethany was the home of Lazarus, whom Jesus had raised from the dead, seems rather strange since the previous chapter had explained Jesus' relation to the family. Brown suggests that if this episode were incorporated into the text of John at a late date, the explanation would have been necessary to identify Bethany (29:446). On the other hand, if the Gospel were transcribed by a disciple of John from discourses that he gave at different times, a link would have been needed to resume the flow of narration.

2 The dinner was given for Jesus by Martha and Mary. The notation that Lazarus was among the guests seems unnecessary at first reading. If the dinner was an expression of gratitude for the restoration of Lazarus, he would naturally be expected to attend it. Perhaps the writer is giving a hint that after Lazarus's restoration to life he retired from any public appearance since he would be an object of general curiosity, as v.9 indicates. On this occasion Lazarus may have come out of seclusion to honor Jesus.

3 The anointing of Jesus' feet by Mary was not difficult because of the custom of reclining to eat instead of sitting at a table. Guests usually reclined on divans with their heads near the table. They leaned on cushions with one arm and ate with the other. Their

feet would project at the end of the divan away from the table. Mary could easily have slipped from her couch, walked around the other couches, and reached down to pour the ointment on Jesus' feet.

Spices and ointments were quite costly because they had to be imported. Frequently they were used as an investment because they occupied a small space, were portable, and were easily negotiable in the open market. Mary's offering was valued at three hundred denarii (v.5 Gr.), approximately a year's wages for an ordinary workingman. Perhaps it represented her life savings. She presented it as an offering of love and gratitude, prompted by Jesus' restoration of her brother to the family circle. Wiping his feet with her hair was a gesture of utmost devotion and reverence. The penetrative fragrance of the ointment that filled the house told all present of her sacrificial gift.

4-6 Judas Iscariot reappears here. He had been mentioned previously in a parenthetical statement appended to Jesus' comment on Simon Peter's confession of faith: "Have I not chosen you, the Twelve? Yet one of you is a devil" (6:70). Jesus knew Judas's tendencies and was well aware of his coming defection. Whereas many of Jesus' disciples deserted him (6:66), Judas remained to betray him. The others merely lost interest or were bewildered by his teaching and were reluctant to meet his moral demands. Judas determined to make Jesus serve his purpose—by treachery if necessary.

Judas had been appointed treasurer of the band of disciples; and, according to John, Judas used his office for his own enrichment. His remonstrance over the gift of the ointment revealed that he had a sharp sense of financial values and no appreciation of human values. Pouring the ointment on Jesus seemed to him an economic waste. Mary, on the contrary, was the only one who was sensitive to the impending death of Jesus and who was willing to give a material expression of her esteem for him.

7-8 Jesus' reply revealed his appreciation of Mary's act of devotion and the understanding it denoted. His words disclose also the current of his thought, for he was anticipating death. His comment on the poor was not a justification for tolerating unnecessary poverty; but it was a hint to Judas that if he were really concerned about the poor, he would never lack opportunity to aid them. The contrast of the attitude of Mary with that of Judas is unmistakable. Mary offered her best to Jesus in sacrificial love; Judas was coldly utilitarian. Jesus interested him only as a ladder for his ambitions.

The dinner marked the crisis of friendship with Jesus. Martha, Mary, and Lazarus risked all they had to do him honor and to demonstrate their loyalty in the face of approaching danger and death. Jesus' comment on Mary's action may or may not imply a premonition on her part of his approaching peril. In any event, her gift was an expression of the highest gratitude and devotion.

9-11 Quite simultaneously, the response of the crowds to Jesus brought another crisis to his enemies. So many became his followers that the priestly party was sure that their fears as expressed by Caiaphas were justified. Their resolution to destroy Jesus was strengthened, and in their wild madness of unbelief they even contemplated the possibility of removing Lazarus also, since his restoration to life was an undeniable witness to Jesus' power.

Notes

8 The latter half of v.8, μεθ' ἑαυτῶν ... ἔχετε (meth' heautōn ... echete, "with you ... you have") is omitted by P[75], and the entire verse is omitted by the Western text. However, it is included by the majority of MSS. Brown states that "this verse in John is omitted by witnesses of the Western group, and the fact that it agrees with Matthew instead of with Mark suggests that it was a later scribal addition copied from the traditional Matthew" (29:449). Metzger, recognizing this problem, affirms that "the overwhelming manuscript support for the verse seemed to a majority of the Committee to justify retaining it in the text" (*Textual Commentary*, p. 237). While there are some problems in reconciling the Johannine account with those of Matt 26:6–13 and Mark 14:3–9, the placement of the accounts and the strong correspondence of most of the accompanying features reflect the same situation. Matthew and Mark say that the unnamed woman anointed Jesus' head; John says it was his feet. But this difference is scarcely sufficient to preclude identity. A similar episode mentioned in Luke 7:36–50 is probably not the same. The latter was located in Galilee; the woman involved was "a sinner"; and the discourse accompanying it was quite unlike that mentioned in John. Some commentaries, however, equate all these passages.

2. The entry into Jerusalem

12:12–19

¹²The next day the great crowd that had come for the Feast heard that Jesus was on his way to Jerusalem. ¹³They took palm branches and went out to meet him, shouting,

"Hosanna!"
"Blessed is he who comes in the name of the Lord!"
"Blessed is the King of Israel!"

¹⁴Jesus found a young donkey and sat upon it, as it is written,

¹⁵"Do not be afraid, O Daughter of Zion;
see, your king is coming,
seated on a donkey's colt."

¹⁶At first his disciples did not understand all this. Only after Jesus was glorified did they realize that these things had been written about him and that they had done these things to him.
¹⁷Now the crowd that was with him had continued to spread the word that he had called Lazarus from the tomb, raising him from the dead. ¹⁸Many people, because they had heard that he had given this miraculous sign, went out to meet him. ¹⁹So the Pharisees said to one another, "See, this is getting us nowhere. Look how the whole world has gone after him!"

12 Again John recounts a story that appears in all the synoptic Gospels (Matt 21:1–11; Mark 11:1–10; Luke 19:28–40). Although these accounts differ in details, they agree on the event itself and on the behavior of the crowds. John identifies two distinct multitudes: one composed of the "great crowd" of pilgrims who had come to Jerusalem for the Passover and were currently residing there (v.12) and the other composed of those who were traveling with Jesus and had witnessed the raising of Lazarus (v.17). The former multitude was probably larger, for John calls it "great."

13 If the former crowd came from Galilee, it would be well aware of Jesus' works there and would probably contain a number who had wished for a long time that he would declare himself as the expected Messiah. They applied to him the words of Psalm 118:25–26, one of the Songs of Degrees customarily sung by Passover pilgrims on their way to Jerusalem. These words ascribed to him a messianic title as the agent of the Lord, the coming king of Israel.

14 The entry into Jerusalem was Jesus' announcement that his hour had come and that he was ready for action, though not according to the expectation of the people. He did not come as a conqueror but as a messenger of peace. He rode on a donkey, not the steed of royalty, but that of a commoner on a business trip. John couples this entry with the prophecy of Zechariah (9:9), who announced that the king of Israel would appear in humility without pomp and ceremony. The pilgrims who had come to Jerusalem to attend the feast went out to greet Jesus; the other crowd gathered in his train. "Hosanna" is a Hebrew expression meaning literally "Save now!" It may be interpreted as a plea for immediate action on the part of the king. The blessing is the peoples' acclamation of him as the ruler of Israel (v.13).

15 The quotation from Zechariah 9:9 reads literally, "Cease from your fears, O daughter of Zion." "Daughter of Zion" is a personification of the city of Jerusalem; it occurs frequently in the OT, especially in the later prophets (Isa 1:8; 52:2; 62:11; Jer 4:31; 6:23; Lam 2:4, 8, 10, 13; Mic 4:8; Zeph 3:14; Zech 2:10).

16 This parenthetical statement by the author states that the disciples did not then understand the situation but that they later comprehended it. Similar parenthetical statements appear in John 2:17, 22. The author seems to be recalling the days of early discipleship and confessing how ignorant and obtuse he and his companions had been. His comments demonstrate that the Gospel must have been written when he and the others had attained a spiritual perception they did not possess in the years of their travels with Jesus. The Passion and the Resurrection were keys in unlocking the mystery of Jesus' person.

17–18 The second group in this account consists of those who were following Jesus, some of whom had witnessed the raising of Lazarus in Bethany. These people continued to publicize Jesus' miracle and aroused the curiosity of many in the city. These, in turn, joined the crowd that was on the way to meet Jesus as he neared Jerusalem.

19 The convergence of the pilgrims from a distance with Jesus' enthusiastic supporters from Jerusalem made a popular following that caused the rulers to become apprehensive. They felt that their attempts to stop Jesus were too few and too late.

Notes

17 The NIV follows the reading ὅτι (hoti, "that") rather than ὅτε (hote, "when"). Metzger observes that the reading ὅτε is preferable to ὅτι because it is supported by generally superior external testimony (*Textual Commentary*, p. 237). The Western reading, ὅτι, however, makes better sense of the passage and explains more adequately the pressure on the Pharisees.

3. *The response to the Greeks*

12:20–36

> ²⁰Now there were some Greeks among those who went up to worship at the Feast. ²¹They came to Philip, who was from Bethsaida in Galilee, with a request. "Sir," they said, "we would like to see Jesus." ²²Philip went to tell Andrew; Andrew and Philip in turn told Jesus.
>
> ²³Jesus replied, "The hour has come for the Son of Man to be glorified. ²⁴I tell you the truth, unless a kernel of wheat falls to the ground and dies, it remains only a single seed. But if it dies, it produces many seeds. ²⁵The man who loves his life will lose it, while the man who hates his life in this world will keep it for eternal life. ²⁶Whoever serves me must follow me; and where I am, my servant also will be. My Father will honor the one who serves me.
>
> ²⁷"Now my heart is troubled, and what shall I say? 'Father, save me from this hour'? No, it was for this very reason I came to this hour. ²⁸Father, glorify your name!"
>
> Then a voice came from heaven, "I have glorified it, and will glorify it again." ²⁹The crowd that was there and heard it said it had thundered; others said an angel had spoken to him.
>
> ³⁰Jesus said, "This voice was for your benefit, not mine. ³¹Now is the time for judgment on this world; now the prince of this world will be driven out. ³²But I, when I am lifted up from the earth, will draw all men to myself." ³³He said this to show the kind of death he was going to die.
>
> ³⁴The crowd spoke up, "We have heard from the Law that the Christ will remain forever, so how can you say, 'The Son of Man must be lifted up'? Who is this 'Son of Man'?"
>
> ³⁵Then Jesus told them, "You are going to have the light just a little while longer. Walk while you have the light, before darkness overtakes you. The man who walks in the dark does not know where he is going. ³⁶Put your trust in the light while you have it, so that you may become sons of light." When he had finished speaking, Jesus left and hid himself from them.

20 Another element that contributed to the crisis was the request of the Greeks to see Jesus. Their identity is uncertain, and they appear only briefly in the narrative. They were not Hellenistic Jews but Gentile Greeks who had joined the Jewish pilgrims to Jerusalem. Probably they were inquirers who had become interested in the Jewish faith but had not become full proselytes. They may have come from Galilee or the Decapolis, the ten Gentile cities generally east of Galilee and the Jordan, stretching from Damascus on the north to Philadelphia (Amman) on the south. Jesus had followers from these cities in his earlier ministry (Matt 4:25), and his reputation must have spread among their cities.

21–22 Just why these Greeks approached Philip rather than one of the other disciples is not stated. He had a Greek name, but this was not uncommon for Jews. Andrew's name also was of Greek origin. Philip in turn referred them to Andrew, and both of them carried the request to Jesus himself.

23 Curiously enough, there is no record that Jesus either gave these Greeks an audience or sent a reply back to them. The pronoun "them" in "Jesus answered them" (Gr.), which is omitted in NIV, could refer either to the Greeks themselves or to Andrew and Philip. In another sense, the action of Jesus is an answer to the Greeks' inquiry, because he announced openly that the great hour of his life had arrived. He felt the pressure of the Gentile world and realized that the time had come to open the way to God for the

Gentiles and to fuse Jewish and Gentile believers into one body. To accomplish this objective, he had to sacrifice himself (cf. John 10:16).

24 The likeness of the grain of wheat that is buried in the cold soil only to rise again multiplied for harvest is applicable to all believers in Christ. Until the seed is planted in the ground and dies, it bears no fruit; and if it is sacrificed, it produces a large crop.

25 The man who attempts to preserve his life will lose it, while the man who readily sacrifices his will keep it for eternal life. The two words translated "life" are different. The first, *psychē*, is generally rendered "soul" and denotes the individual personality, with all its related experiences and achievements. The second, *zōē*, in Johannine usage is usually coupled with the adjective *eternal* (*aiōnios*) and means the spiritual vitality that is the experience of God (John 17:3). Parallels to this statement appear in the synoptic Gospels (Matt 10:39; Mark 8:36; Luke 14:26). These were not all spoken on the same occasion. The statement in Matthew was part of a charge given to the disciples when Jesus sent them on a mission; that in Mark was given to them and a crowd that joined them (Mark 8:34); and the Lukan pronouncement was spoken to a mixed audience at an undefined point in Jesus' career, at some time within the last year of his life. Since this seems to have been a major principle of his teaching, its repetition at different times and under different circumstances is not at all unlikely.

The expression "who hates his life" need not be understood to mean a contempt for oneself or a suicidal impulse. Rather, it is a hyperbolic expression that means one is to base his priorities on that which is outside of himself. He is to place others or another above himself. In this instance, it is to make Christ the Master of one's life.

26 Jesus explained what it means to hate one's life by saying, "Whoever serves me must follow me; and where I am, my servant also will be." The impending Cross would involve the disciples in the same way it would involve Jesus, and he was informing them that he was the model for them to follow. He had already implied this in his discourse on the Good Shepherd, when he said, "When he has brought out all his own [out of the pen], he goes on ahead of them" (John 10:4). "Going ahead of them" implies that he does first what he asks them to do and that he confronts the dangers before they encounter them. Serving Christ implies the obligation of following him; conversely, he promised that wherever he might go, his servants would be privileged to accompany him and share his glory (cf. John 17:24).

27–28a Turning from the crisis as it would affect the disciples, Jesus revealed how it affected him. His dilemma corresponds to that in Gethsemane as recorded in the synoptic Gospels. There he shrank from a death that was imposed unjustly, executed cruelly, and could brand him as a rebel and a criminal. So he prayed, "My Father, if it is possible, may this cup be taken from me" (Matt 26:39; Mark 14:36; Luke 22:42). At the same time, he recognized that his death was necessary to carry out the divine program of redemption, for without the conflict there could be no conquest. Consequently he concluded his prayer by the resolute petition "Yet not as I will, but as you will" (Matt 26:39). John reveals that the prayer in Gethsemane, which he does not quote, was the culmination of a struggle that preceded it. In these words spoken publicly in the period of crisis, Jesus said, "Now my heart is troubled," or in a more literal rendering, "Now has my soul [*psychē*] been thrown into confusion." His language indicates that he is breaking under the strain of the crisis; its dangers and irrationality are overwhelming him. Should he ask the Father to spare him from the cataclysm that was so rapidly approaching? Had he done so, he might have averted seeming disaster at the price of failing to achieve his redemptive purpose. Nevertheless, he adhered boldly to his original purpose of completing the mission God had entrusted to him: "No, it was for this very reason that I came to this hour." The whole of his life's dedication is concentrated in this statement. The question was tentative; the resolution was final. He wanted the Father's name to be glorified, no matter what the cost!

28b–30 The voice from heaven is the third instance of its kind recorded in the Gospel narratives and the first such in John. On each occasion it was a public acknowledgment of the sonship and authority of Jesus and an endorsement of his work by the Father. John asserts unmistakably that the voice was a genuine, audible sound. It was not generally understood, however, for the crowd said that it had thundered. Others said that "an angel had spoken to him." The Father's audible commendation of Jesus appeared on three occasions: at his baptism, where Jesus commenced his career (Matt 3:17; Mark 1:11; Luke 3:21–22); at his transfiguration, which marked the turning point of his ministry (Matt 17:5; Mark 9:7; Luke 9:35); and at the conclusion of his ministry, as here. Jesus explained that the voice from heaven was intended to encourage the disciples and to inform the crowd, not to encourage him. If they did not understand it, the information would not benefit them greatly. Nevertheless, some did remember this occasion and found it helpful, as did John who recorded the event.

John does not tell his readers directly whether or not Jesus replied to the Greeks. The response, beginning in v.23, seems to have been directed to his disciples; and the words of vv.27–28 are more like a soliloquy.

31 Jesus recognized and announced unmistakably that the final crisis had arrived. Both the disciples and the more sympathetic segment of the crowd were uncertain of what his fate would be. For several months the prevailing attitude seems to have been uncertainty (John 6:60–66; 7:25–27, 40–44; 10:19–24; 11:55–56). Now he declared that a decisive action must follow. God's purpose is to glorify him. The hour for judgment has come, and the prince of the world must be exposed for what he is. "Judgment" does not imply that the final day of judgment has come or that only now is retribution for sin exercised. In the second commandment of the Mosaic law, God pronounced divine judgment by "punishing the children for the sin of the fathers to the third and fourth generation of those who hate me" (Exod 20:5). The moral and physical laws of God inevitably judge those who transgress them. Jesus conveyed the meaning that God, having now made his final revelation, must hold men responsible for their obedience or disobedience.

There is a parallel in Paul's address to the Athenians: "In the past God overlooked such ignorance, but now he commands all people everywhere to repent. For he has set a day when he will judge the world with justice by the man he has appointed" (Acts 17:30–31). Paul's outlook is more definitely eschatological than the Johannine presentation, but the essential idea is the same. The revelation of God in Christ is itself a disclosure of sin and a judgment on it.

"The prince of this world" can be none other than Satan. The same title is used in John 14:30 and 16:11. There are parallel expressions in the Pauline writings (2 Cor 4:4; Eph 2:2; 6:12). The Cross and the Resurrection spelled Satan's defeat. These events marked the glorification of all he renounced and the reversal of all he sought to attain. Satan was motivated by self-will; Jesus, by the will of the Father. Satan's power brought destruction and death; Jesus' power imparted renewal and life. Though Satan is still active, his action is only the desperation of futility (cf. Rev 12:12).

32-33 The preposition "from" (*ek*) in "lifted up from the earth" really means "out from" rather than "away from." It connotes not only being lifted or suspended above the earth, as on a cross, but being brought up out of the earth. Jesus had in mind not only the fact that he would be elevated on the cross but also that he would be exalted by the Resurrection. The verb *lifted up* (*hypsoō*) is used in John exclusively to refer to Jesus' death (John 3:14; 8:28; 12:32, 34), while elsewhere in the NT it means "exalt." It lends itself well to the double meaning of the method of death as specifically stated here (v.33) and the exaltation to spiritual sovereignty described in apostolic preaching (Acts 2:33; 5:31; Phil 2:9).

"All men" does not imply that all men will ultimately be saved; instead, it means that Christ draws men to himself indiscriminately, without regard to nationality, race, or status. Jesus' utterance was prompted by the presence of the Greek Gentiles and should be evaluated by the setting of the occasion. There is, however, a clear differentiation between believers and unbelievers, between the saved and the lost, in all the Johannine writings (John 1:11; 3:18, 36; 5:29; 6:40, 53, 64; 8:44; 1 John 3:10, 15; 5:12).

34 The crowd was puzzled by Jesus' prediction of his death. According to their understanding, the Messiah would be a supernatural person and would inaugurate his final and eternal reign as God's Anointed, the Son of David. In making the covenant with David, God promised him that his descendants would reign "forever" (2 Sam 7:12-13, 16). Psalm 89, a hymn in praise of God's favor to David, affirms the same thing (vv.26-29, 35-36). There is no specific passage in the Pentateuch that affirms the eternity of the Messiah, but if by "the Law" the people meant the OT in general, the Davidic Covenant may have been their source of information. The people were confused by Jesus' reference to the "Son of Man" and wanted to know who he was.

Although John 12:32 uses the first person pronoun "I" rather than "Son of Man," Jesus must have spoken of himself by this title. It appears frequently in the synoptic Gospels and also in John. If it was an apocalyptic title, the people did not understand that Jesus was so using the term. Their query, "Who is this 'Son of Man'?" implies that his concept of its meaning was different from theirs. The apocalyptic Son of Man would not die. Jesus enlarged the concept by applying it to the whole of his work: his true humanity, his suffering, his exaltation, and his judicial work. At this point he did not attempt a full answer to the questioning of the crowd. He adopted a pragmatic approach such as that given in John 7:17.

35-36 Jesus spoke with urgency. The light would not always be available, as he said to his disciples at the healing of the blind man: "Night is coming, when no one can work" (9:4). If his hearers wished to walk with certainty, they should act at once, for after his departure they might find themselves in the darkness. "Put your trust" (*pisteuete*) is continuative, similar to the command given later to the disciples in the upper room (John 14:1), and implies a persistent faith, not solely a momentary decision.

Notes

24 Blaiklock observes that the symbolism of the grain of wheat could have been especially significant to Greek Gentiles (E.M. Blaiklock, *Who Was Jesus?* Chicago: Moody, 1974, p. 56). The head
of wheat was a common symbol for life in the Eleusinian mysteries. According to the myth that
underlies the rites of this mystery religion, Demeter, the goddess of the earth, had lost her
daughter to Hades, the king of death, who had abducted her to the underworld. In her distress,
Demeter had been aided by Triptolemus, king of Eleusis. When Zeus intervened and compelled
Hades to return his bride to her mother for six months each year, Demeter presented Triptolemus with a grain of wheat which, like her daughter, had to descend into darkness and later
bear fruit. A dramatic representation of this event was part of the mystic ritual.

There is no indication that the Gospel of John was patterned after the myth or even paralleled
it; but the concept of life in a seed that was buried and rose into a new life was common to both
and is also developed in 1 Cor 15:37–38.

31 The word "world" is κόσμος (*kosmos*), which refers to the world system, not the created,
material world. Satan is the prince of the present world system, but it has been judged and
condemned; it will not lead to utopia. When Christ returns, he will set up the perfect world
system, which he will rule in perfect righteousness.

4. *The response to unbelief*

12:37–50

[37]Even after Jesus had done all these miraculous signs in their presence, they
still would not believe in him. [38]This was to fulfill the word of Isaiah the prophet:

"Lord, who has believed our message
and to whom has the arm of the Lord been revealed?"

[39]For this reason they could not believe, because, as Isaiah says elsewhere:

[40]"He has blinded their eyes
and deadened their hearts,
so they can neither see with their eyes,
nor understand with their hearts,
nor turn—and I would heal them."

[41]Isaiah said this because he saw Jesus' glory and spoke about him.
[42]Yet at the same time many even among the leaders believed in him. But
because of the Pharisees they would not confess their faith for fear they would
be put out of the synagogue; [43]for they loved praise from men more than praise
from God.
[44]Then Jesus cried out, "When a man believes in me, he does not believe in me
only, but in the one who sent me. [45]When he looks at me, he sees the one who
sent me. [46]I have come into the world as a light, so that no one who believes in
me should stay in darkness.
[47]"As for the person who hears my words but does not keep them, I do not judge
him. For I did not come to judge the world, but to save it. [48]There is a judge for
the one who rejects me and does not accept my words; that very word which I
spoke will condemn him at the last day. [49]For I did not speak of my own accord,
but the Father who sent me commanded me what to say and how to say it. [50]I know
that his command leads to eternal life. So whatever I say is just what the Father
has told me to say."

Verses 37–50 are the author's explanation of the significance of his narrative up to this point. They focus on the conflict of belief and unbelief and include Jesus' final appeal for decision. The historical crisis must be resolved by immediate action that reveals either the belief or unbelief of those involved. The spiritual crisis that occurs when one confronts Christ is resolved through personal decision.

37-38 The author expresses surprise and regret that in spite of Jesus' numerous "signs" the people still obstinately refused to believe in him. Unbelief was rapidly approaching the climax attained in the rejection and crucifixion of Jesus. John connected this with the prophecy of Isaiah, thus plainly affirming that Jesus was the subject of the passage on the Suffering Servant (Isa 52:13-53:12). The implication of this identification extends beyond the immediate application. John refers simply to Isaiah 53:1, which by its rhetorical question implies that the Servant was not believed and that the revelation of God's power through him was not apprehended. The entire prophecy is quoted repeatedly in the NT and is an important basis for the doctrine of the Atonement. Prophecy played a large part in apostolic preaching. Peter in his address to the people after the healing of the lame man repeatedly alluded to the prophets: "But this is how God fulfilled what he had foretold through all the prophets, saying that his Christ would suffer" (Acts 3:18); "He must remain in heaven until the time comes for God to restore everything, as he promised long ago through his holy prophets" (v.21); "Indeed, all the prophets from Samuel on, as many as have spoken, have foretold these days" (v.24). Prophecy was the general foundation for the doctrine of the early church.

39-40 Not only did prophecy describe unbelief, it also explained it. Why should not the hearers of Jesus believe in him when the signs so unmistakably accredited his claims? John quotes from Isaiah 6 to show that unbelief is the result of the rejection of light, which act, by the sovereign law of God, gradually makes belief impossible. The antecedent text is taken from the commission of Isaiah. God appointed the prophet to preach to the inhabitants of Judah but warned him in advance that his mission would not be successful. The verbs as given in Isaiah 6:9-10 are imperatives. Isaiah was told to announce his message even though it merely hardened the hearts of those who heard him. God offered the opportunity of faith, but the very offer made the recipients of it more obstinate. John interprets the prophecy by its effect rather than by its intention. It was not God's desire to alienate his people; but without the offer of faith and repentance, they would never turn to him anyway. The cumulative effect of unbelief is a hardened attitude that becomes more impenetrable as time progresses.

41 The implication in this verse is startling. Isaiah 6 opens by saying, "In the year that King Uzziah died, I saw the Lord seated on a throne, high and exalted, and the train of his robe filled the temple." The prophet was looking at a manifestation of Deity and said, "My eyes have seen the King, the LORD Almighty" (6:5). John says that Isaiah saw Jesus and spoke of him. He identified Jesus with the Jehovah (Yahweh) of the OT.

42-43 John notes that many of the leaders believed. Probably Joseph of Arimathea and Nicodemus were among that number (John 19:38-39; cf. Mark 15:43; Luke 23:50-51). Possibly John learned of this movement among the national leaders through his acquaintance with Nicodemus. Since the attitude of the council as a whole would call for the excommunication of any avowed believers in Jesus (John 9:22), these remained silent. Though they did not agree with the attitude or action of the majority of the Sanhedrin, they still sought its approval.

44-46 Jesus equated belief in him with belief in God (cf. John 14:1). As John stated it in his First Epistle, "No one who denies the Son has the Father; whoever acknowledges the Son has the Father also" (1 John 2:23). The Father and the Son are inseparable; though they are two personalities, they work as one being. Jesus spoke of the Father as the one who had sent him, and he claimed to be the light that illumines the darkness of those who are without God.

47-50 Judgment on unbelief is not arbitrary but inevitable. The message of Christ when refused will become the condemnation of man in the last days since nobody who refused it can plead ignorance. The emphasis, however, is positive. Jesus' mission was intended to evoke belief and to rescue men from darkness. The Father's sovereign purpose is to lift men out of helplessness and death and give them eternal life. Because Jesus speaks the message the Father commanded him to speak, he is the Word of God.

At this point John closes the account of Jesus' public ministry of teaching. His subsequent teaching concerns only the disciples and their preparation for the final act of his life. Jesus' words before the chief priests and Pilate were defensive rather than didactic. Insofar as Jesus appeared publicly, he manifested the message of God to the world by what he did as well as by what he said.

III. The Private Ministry of the Word (13:1-17:26)

A. The Last Supper (13:1-30)

1. The washing of feet

13:1-20

¹It was just before the Passover Feast. Jesus knew that the time had come for him to leave this world and go to the Father. Having loved his own who were in the world, he now showed them the full extent of his love.

²The evening meal was being served, and the devil had already prompted Judas Iscariot, son of Simon, to betray Jesus. ³Jesus knew that the Father had put all things under his power, and that he had come from God and was returning to God; ⁴so he got up from the meal, took off his outer clothing, and wrapped a towel around his waist. ⁵After that, he poured water into a basin and began to wash his disciples' feet, drying them with the towel that was wrapped around him.

⁶He came to Simon Peter, who said to him, "Lord, are you going to wash my feet?"

⁷Jesus replied, "You do not realize now what I am doing, but later you will understand."

⁸"No," said Peter, "you shall never wash my feet."

Jesus answered, "Unless I wash you, you have no part with me."

⁹"Then, Lord," Simon Peter replied, "not just my feet but my hands and my head as well!"

¹⁰Jesus answered, "A person who has had a bath needs only to wash his feet; his whole body is clean. And you are clean, though not every one of you." ¹¹For he knew who was going to betray him, and that was why he said not every one was clean.

¹²When he had finished washing their feet, he put on his clothes and returned to his place. "Do you understand what I have done for you?" he asked them. ¹³"You call me 'Teacher' and 'Lord,' and rightly so, for that is what I am. ¹⁴Now that I, your Lord and Teacher, have washed your feet, you also should wash one another's feet. ¹⁵I have set you an example that you should do as I have done for you. ¹⁶I tell you the truth, no servant is greater than his master, nor is a messenger greater than the one who sent him. ¹⁷Now that you know these things, you will be blessed if you do them.

18"I am not referring to all of you; I know those I have chosen. But this is to fulfill the scripture: 'He who shares my bread has lifted up his heel against me.'
19"I am telling you now before it happens, so that when it does happen you will believe that I am He. 20I tell you the truth, whoever accepts anyone I send accepts me; and whoever accepts me accepts the one who sent me."

1 The full Johannine account of the Passion begins at this point. The new stage of the conflict between belief and unbelief is marked by a chronological reference to the main feast of the year and by relation to the progress of the program of Jesus' life. John alludes to the nearness of the Passover as if to remind his reader that Jesus had been introduced by John the Baptist as the "Lamb of God, who takes away the sin of the world" (1:29). As the first Passover had been the turning point in the redemption of the people of God, so the Cross would be the opening of a new era for believers. John connects this with the manifestation of Jesus' love for his disciples. "To the fullest extent" is a better rendering of the original *eis telos* than KJV "unto the end." It does not mean that Jesus continued to love his disciples only up to the end of his career but that his love has no limits. "His own" refers to his disciples, of whom he had said that they were given him by the Father (10:29). Jesus had accepted the responsibility for them and was obliged to instruct and protect them (17:6–12).

2 Whether this meal was the actual Passover or not has been warmly debated. Yet it seems that it occurred on the same night as the arrest and betrayal. If so, it was presumably Thursday night; and the Crucifixion occurred on Friday, the day before the Passover, which would have begun on Friday evening. Luke states that when the day came on which the Passover lamb was to be sacrificed, Peter and John were sent to arrange the meal that the Lord and his disciples ate that evening (Luke 22:7–14). Matthew (26:17–20) and Mark (14:12–17) agree that the meal was on the day on which the Passover lamb was killed, which preceded the Passover itself. John stated later (18:28) that the Jewish delegates could not enter Pilate's hall on Friday morning because they would be defiled and unable to eat the Passover. In that case, the Last Supper must have preceded the Passover by twenty-four hours. If, then, the Passover began on Friday night, the meal could have taken place on Thursday night but would not have been the standard Passover Feast. The question is complicated by the fact that the Synoptics imply that Jesus did intend to eat the Passover with his disciples (Matt 26:18; Mark 14:14; Luke 22:11). No mention is made of the Passover lamb, however.

Several solutions for this impasse have been suggested, two of which may be plausible. One is that two calendars were in simultaneous use and one national group, using one calendar, ate the Passover on Thursday night whereas the other group, using the other calendar, ate the Passover on Friday night. There have been several variants of this theory: (1) one calendar was figured by the solar year, the other by the lunar year; (2) there was a difference between the time prescribed by the temple and that by the Qumran Essenes; or (3) Jesus, having been repudiated by the priesthood and consequently considered apostate, would not have been allowed to obtain a lamb for sacrifice and would have been compelled to celebrate the feast at a different time (see Stauffer, pp. 113–18). Whatever solution may be accepted, there seems to be no other conclusion than that Jesus did celebrate the meal with his disciples on Thursday night, that the hearing before Pilate and the Crucifixion took place on Friday, and that his body was placed in the tomb before sunset late that afternoon.

The focus of action lies in Jesus' washing the feet of the disciples. The circumstances are listed in detail. Judas had already determined to betray Jesus (13:2). His specific motive is not stated, and the impulse is attributed to satanic suggestion. The casual allusion to the devil at this point implies a deeper significance to the conflict than a mere political or theological squabble. The conflict was basically actuated by a rebellion against God, the absolute opposite of the attitude of Jesus. It is possible that Judas, realizing that Jesus' enemies were implacably hostile and that they were politically powerful, concluded that Jesus was foredoomed to lose in the struggle and so decided that he might as well gain immunity from sharing Jesus' fate. Judas could compensate himself by claiming the reward for betrayal. His act, however, was more serious than an incidental piece of treachery; he sold himself to the power of evil. As v.27 states, "Satan entered into him," and he came under the devil's control.

3-5 John emphasizes the fact that Jesus was not the innocent victim of a plot, unaware of what was transpiring around him. He knew "that the Father had put all things under his power, and that he had come from God and was returning to God." Jesus was fully aware of his authority, his divine origin, and his destiny. John says much more about the inner consciousness of Jesus than the Synoptics do, either because he was more observant or because Jesus confided in him. Furthermore, Jesus' inward awareness of his power and office did not deter his ministry to the men he had chosen and was trying to prepare for the final catastrophe.

The immediate situation was that they had come to the banquet room directly from the street. Ordinarily on such an occasion the host would have delegated a servant to the menial task of removing the sandals of the guests and washing their feet. Since the meeting was obviously intended to be secret, no servants were present. None of the disciples was ready to volunteer for such a task, for each would have considered it an admission of inferiority to all the others. John the Baptist had used the act of such a servant as his standard of the lowest and meanest kind of service that could be required of any man (John 1:27).

Sometime during the meal Jesus rose, removed his outer cloak, tied a towel around his waist, and began to perform the work of the servant who was not present. It was a voluntary humiliation that rebuked the pride of the disciples. Perhaps it accentuated the tension of the situation, because Luke notes that when the disciples entered the room, they had been arguing about who among them would be the greatest in the kingdom of heaven (Luke 22:24).

6-8a The response of Simon Peter may have been representative of the common feeling that Jesus ought not to demean himself by washing their feet. The emphatic use of pronouns in Peter's surprised question, "Lord! You [su] are washing my [mou] feet?" and his equally emphatic negative reply, "NEVER to all eternity shall you wash my feet!" (my trans.), reveal both the impetuousness of his disposition and the high regard he had for Jesus. Peter felt that Jesus should not degrade himself by assuming such a position.

8b Jesus' rejoinder, "Unless I wash you, you have no part with me," expresses the necessity, not only for the cleansing of Peter's feet to make him socially acceptable for the dinner, but also for the cleansing of his personality to make him fit for the kingdom of God. The external washing was intended to be a picture of spiritual cleansing from evil.

9–10 Peter, mistaking Jesus' veiled figure for the literal act, expressed his devotion by asking for a bath. Separation from Jesus was abhorrent to him. Jesus reminded him that a person once bathed needed to wash only his feet. "You are clean, though not every one of you" gives the clue to the interpretation of this action. One of the disciples had consistently refused Jesus' spiritual ministration. The others, who had been loyal though sometimes slow to understand, needed only occasional correction.

11 This Gospel emphasizes strongly the self-consciousness of Jesus concerning himself and his work. From the beginning of his ministry he had supernatural discernment of the potentialities of his disciples (1:42, 47–48, 51). He predicted his death and resurrection (2:19; 3:14; 6:51; 8:28; 10:18; 12:32). He claimed a peculiar relationship with God (5:19, 26; 10:38). Now, at the close of his ministry, the Gospel emphasizes even more strongly his supernatural awareness of the significance of what was occurring. Jesus realized that the time had come to leave his disciples (13:1), that the Father had committed all action to his authority (v.3), that the betrayer was already at hand (vv.10–11), that the identity of the chosen believers was settled (v.18), that the outcome of the existing situation was fixed (v.19; cf. 18:4), and, finally, that the moment of consummation had come (v.21; cf. 19:28). The progress of realization is reflected also in the synoptic Gospels, though not quite so definitely.

12–14 A second lesson Jesus wished to impart to the disciples by this act was one of love and humble service. His question, "Do you understand what I have done for you?" contrasts with his remonstrance of Peter: "You do not realize now what I am doing, but later you will understand" (v.7). The discernment of the disciples developed slowly. It took them a long time to begin to comprehend the intensity of Jesus' love for them and the nature of his humility in dealing with them. "Teacher" and "Lord" are both titles of respect that placed Jesus on a level above the disciples. Nicodemus, himself a teacher, had so greeted Jesus (John 3:2), and Jesus had returned the compliment (v.10). "Lord"—like the English "Mr.," an abbreviation of "Master"—was a common salutation, which could be both a greeting (John 4:11, 15, 19) or an acknowledgment of authority (13:6, 9). Jesus emphasized the fact that if he, whom they regarded as their leader, had stooped to serve their needs, they should do the same for one another. He made the action of necessity the pattern for dedicated living. For similar passages in the Synoptics, see Matthew 10:24, connected with the commission of the Twelve; Luke 6:40, a short discourse resembling the Sermon on the Mount; John 15:20, virtually a repetition of John 13:16. The concept of the servant-master relationship appeared frequently in Jesus' teaching.

15 The "example" does not necessarily imply the perpetuation of footwashing as an ordinance in the church. The only other allusion to footwashing in the NT occurs in 1 Timothy 5:10, where it does not refer to a regular custom but seems to allude to charitable ministrations to the poor. John calls this act an "example," which implies that the emphasis is on the inner attitude of humble and voluntary service for others. Perhaps it was the basis for the Pauline exhortation to the Philippians: "Your attitude should be the same as that of Christ Jesus, who, being in very nature God, did not consider equality with God something to be grasped, but made himself nothing, taking the very nature of a servant, ... and became obedient to death—even death on a cross!" (Phil 2:5–8).

16–17 The recurrence of "sent" (*pempsantos*) at this point is a reminder that Jesus was constantly conscious of being commissioned by the Father. Jesus included his disciples in the commission and also included them in the action of servanthood. Jesus portrayed for them the true nature of Christian living: serving one another. And for those who would be willing to take this role on themselves, Jesus said there would be blessings.

18 Jesus' reason for washing the disciples' feet was not solely good manners and sanitation. The imminence of the betrayal was pressing in on him, and the resultant anguish was tearing at his heart. He knew that the disciples would fail at the crucial moment, but he despaired of none except Judas. While the lesson applied to all of them, it was particularly an appeal to Judas. The psalm Jesus quoted was attributed to David, who lamented the defection of a trusted confidant (Ps 41:9). A parallel occurs in Psalm 55:12–14. Quite probably it referred originally to Ahithophel, who had been David's counselor and diplomatic advisor but deserted him in Absalom's rebellion (2 Sam 15:12; 16:15–23; 17:4, 14, 23). Again this is an example of prophecy by parallelism.

19–20 Jesus was not merely asking for personal loyalty but for belief that he was the One sent by God ("I am He"). The expression is identical with that which he used in controversy with his enemies at the Feast of Tabernacles (8:24, 28, 58). He wanted the disciples to commit themselves to his claims before the events would seemingly invalidate them and before the Resurrection would confirm them (cf. John 2:22). He said that accepting the messenger whom he sent was equivalent to receiving him and that receiving him involved also receiving God. The language implies a close connection between the disciple and the master and an equally close connection between Jesus and God. As the disciples could claim to speak with Jesus' authority, so Jesus claimed to speak for God.

Notes

2 The reading γινομένου (*ginomenou*, "being"), the present participle, rather than γενομένου (*genomenou*, "having been"), the aorist participle, which indicates a past action, not only has better MS support but also fits better with the expression "he got up from the meal" (v.4), which implies an interruption. So, apparently, the meal was still in progress when Jesus got up.

10 The meaning of Jesus is clear in the choice of the words meaning "wash." Νίπτω (*niptō*, vv.5, 6, 8, 10) means to wash a part of the body; "bath" (v.10) is derived from the verb λούω (*louō*), which involves a complete washing. The difference between λελουμένος (*leloumenos*, "having been bathed") and νίψασθαι (*nipsasthai*, "to be washed") in v.10 is not only in their meaning but also in the tenses of the verbs. *Leloumenos* is a perfect tense, which implies a settled state; *nipsasthai* is an aorist, which refers to a single act. A parallel to this idea may be found in Hebrews 10:10: "And by that will, we have been made holy [ἡγιασμένοι, *hēgiasmenoi*, a perfect tense] through the sacrifice of the body of Jesus Christ once for all," and v.14: "Because by one sacrifice he has made perfect [τετελείωκεν, *teteleiōken*, perfect tense] forever those who are being made holy" (ἁγιαζομένους, *hagiazomenous*, a present tense). The work of Christ draws a permanent line between those who have been cleansed and those who are not clean. There is need, however, for washing from incidental defilement and for the Christian's continuing growth in grace.

11 The verb οἶδα (*oida*, "know") is generally used in John to denote certain knowledge of a fact rather than experiential acquaintance with a situation or person (cf. 14:4). It is connected with Jesus' supernatural knowledge of his origin, destiny, or circumstances. He *knew* that the witness

of John the Baptist was valid (5:32), what his procedure would be for the feeding of the five thousand (6:6), that his disciples were grumbling about his enigmatic speech (6:61), who really believed in him and who did not (6:64). He was sure of his origin with the Father who had sent him (7:29; 8:14, 55). These instances are multiplied in the account of the private ministry and the Passion. Jesus was conscious that his time had come (13:1) and that the Father had conveyed to him full authority to complete the mission for which he had come (v.3). He also knew the identity of the traitor (v.11) and he knew those who were loyal (v.18). He was well aware of the outcome of the impending events (18:4) and the prophetic program outlined for him in the Scriptures (19:28). The total impression given by this use of *oida* is that Jesus was living by a program he completely understood and that it was not simply a series of accidents he had to meet fortuitously. The concept fits with John's general picture of him as the divine Son of God, who came to perform the Father's will.

---

2. The prediction of the betrayal

13:21–30

> 21After he had said this, Jesus was troubled in spirit and testified, "I tell you the truth, one of you is going to betray me."
>
> 22His disciples stared at one another, at a loss to know which of them he meant. 23One of them, the disciple whom Jesus loved, was reclining next to him. 24Simon Peter motioned to this disciple and said, "Ask him which one he means."
>
> 25Leaning back against Jesus, he asked him, "Lord, who is it?"
>
> 26Jesus answered, "It is the one to whom I will give this piece of bread when I have dipped it in the dish." Then, dipping the piece of bread, he gave it to Judas Iscariot, son of Simon. 27As soon as Judas took the bread, Satan entered into him.
>
> "What you are about to do, do quickly," Jesus told him, 28but no one at the meal understood why Jesus said this to him. 29Since Judas had charge of the money, some thought Jesus was telling him to buy what was needed for the Feast, or to give something to the poor. 30As soon as Judas had taken the bread, he went out. And it was night.

21 Jesus was not surprised that Judas would betray him. He had announced it to the disciples at least a year earlier (John 6:70). Nevertheless, it still weighed heavily on his mind (13:18). The writer of the Gospel repeatedly mentions the betrayal when he alludes to Judas (12:4; 13:2). "Troubled" is the same verb used of Jesus' agitation at the grave of Lazarus (11:33) and at the request of the Greeks to see him (12:27). As "the hour" approached, the bitterness of the betrayal Jesus anticipated became known. The desertion by many of his disciples evoked an expression of disappointment; here, the injury was felt more poignantly. The quotation in v.18, which the author cites as prophetic of Jesus' feeling, contains in its context an allusion to "my close friend, whom I trusted" (Ps 41:9). Among the sorrows contributing to the agony of the Cross was the voluntary and selfish defection of Judas.

22 The announcement startled the disciples. Although Jesus had previously announced the betrayal, they had not taken it to heart. Now, realizing the hostility of the authorities in Jerusalem and knowing that Jesus' death might be imminent, the act that had seemed remote became an immediate possibility.

23–25 Simon Peter signaled to his friend who occupied the place next to Jesus, asking him to inquire who the traitor might be. Simon's inquiry demonstrated not only his persistent trait of curiosity but also his loyalty. He may have contemplated preventive action; for if he could know in advance who the person might be, he could intervene. "The disciple whom Jesus loved," presumably the author of the Gospel, made the inquiry.

26 Jesus gave no specific identification. He simply indicated that the offender would be the one to whom he would give the special morsel he had dipped into the dish. "Bread" in this context does not mean the modern spongy loaf used in most Western nations. It was probably a piece of flat bread, somewhat leathery in consistency, which could be used to scoop bits of meat taken from the pot in which they were cooked. For the host to select such a tidbit from the main dish and give it to a guest would be a mark of courtesy and esteem. The disciples, seeing this, would conclude only that Jesus regarded Judas as a friend he had confidence in. Perhaps he so favored others in turn. Jesus' reply would answer the question for the beloved disciple; but he could scarcely have communicated his knowledge to Peter at that moment without disturbing the peace of the group and violating the confidence of Jesus.

27a "Satan entered into him." This moment was Judas's last opportunity to renounce his treachery. If the other disciples were ignorant of Judas's intentions, he could change the course of his action without explanation, and none but Jesus would be the wiser. Once Judas left the room to seal his bargain with the priests, he would pass the point of no return. His yielding to selfish impulse opened the way to satanic control.

27b–28 "Quickly" (*tacheion*) is the comparative form of the adverb that means "fast," or, in this construction, "as fast as possible." Conscious that the time had come for his sacrifice (13:1), Jesus wished Judas to get on with his plot and leave. Once Judas had departed, Jesus would be able to continue his intimate ministry with his disciples in the upper room.

29 The reference to making a purchase for the Passover may corroborate the view that the Last Supper was held on the night preceding the killing of the Passover lamb. It seems unlikely that Jesus would wait until this moment to obtain the lamb; and the text says that the disciples didn't know the reason for Jesus' statement to Judas, which would hardly be the case if the lamb was missing.

30 The repetition of the phrase "As soon as Judas had taken the bread" (cf. v.27) indicates that Satan's control of Judas and Judas's departure from the group must have been simultaneous. There are depths of tragedy in the terse comment "And it was night." Perhaps as Judas opened the door to leave, John saw the city veiled in darkness. His four words correspond to Jesus' statement when Judas betrayed him: "This is your hour—when darkness reigns" (Luke 22:53).

John's comment "And it was night" heightens the implication that Jesus' life was one of conflict. The opposition of darkness and light is announced in the Prologue (1:5) and is illustrated by the growing hostility between Jesus and his enemies. As the conflict becomes more marked, Jesus says it reflects the contrast between what he had seen with his Father and what they had heard from theirs. When they protested, he declared plainly that God was his Father and that the devil was their father (8:38, 42–44). John notes the progress of the spiritual conflict in 13:27; 14:30; 17:15.

B. *The Last Discourse* (13:31-16:33)

With the departure of Judas, Jesus commenced the long farewell discourse to his disciples. At its beginning there is a prime example of wrong chapter division, for the unity of the text is not broken at 14:1. The dialogue comprising the first section really begins with Jesus' statement that his "glorification" is about to take place.

1. *Questions and answers* (13:31-14:31)

a. *The new commandment*

13:31-35

> [31] When he was gone, Jesus said, "Now is the Son of Man glorified and God is glorified in him. [32] If God is glorified in him, then God will glorify the Son in himself, and will glorify him at once.
> [33] "My children, I will be with you only a little longer. You will look for me, and just as I told the Jews, so I tell you now: Where I am going, you cannot come.
> [34] "A new commandment I give you: Love one another. As I have loved you, so you must love one another. [35] All men will know that you are my disciples if you love one another."

31 The title "Son of Man" appears twelve times in the Gospel of John, of which this is the last occurrence. As the "Son of Man," Jesus reveals divine truth (1:51); he has a supernatural origin (3:13; 6:62); his death by being "lifted up" achieves salvation for men (3:14; 8:28; 12:34); he exercises the prerogative of final judgment (5:27); he provides spiritual nourishment (6:27). This title is also used of his being "glorified" (12:23; 13:31), which John applies specifically to death and resurrection (7:39; 12:16). John does not emphasize the apocalyptic aspect of the title that appears in Matthew (Matt 16:27; 25:31), though it appears once in such a context (John 5:27). The sacrificial aspect of the title appears in Jesus' announcement of the betrayal given in the synoptic accounts of the Last Supper (Matt 26:24; Mark 14:21; Luke 22:22). In its general usage it is the title of the incarnate Christ who is the representative of humanity before God and the representative of deity in human life. In the perfection of Christ's humanity, God finds the fullness of his expression to men.

32 The Johannine use of "glorify" (*doxazō*) is peculiar. The word occurs five times in vv.31-32 in what seems to be unnecessary repetition. Intrinsically *doxazō* means "exaltation." But as Jesus used it, it relates to his death. He connected it with the accomplishment of his work and the fulfillment of the hour for which he had been destined (12:23). The Cross would become the supreme glory of God because the Son would completely obey the will of the Father. The meaning of "exalt" or "magnify" seems to fit better the last two uses in this verse: "God will glorify the Son in himself, and will glorify him at once." This dual dimension of "glorify" appears also in the prayer of ch. 17, in which Jesus reports that he has glorified the Father by completing the task that had been assigned to him (v.4) and then asks that he be restored to the glory he enjoyed with the Father in his preincarnate state (v.5). In this concept the Cross and the Resurrection are united as phases of a single redemptive event by which the purpose of God is completed and his righteousness vindicated. A similar presentation, though in different language, is Paul's description of the humiliation of Christ and his subsequent exaltation given in Philippians 2:4-11.

33 "My children" (*teknia*) is expressive of Jesus' love and concern for the Eleven, who must have seemed to him to be weak and immature. John uses the same term seven times in his First Epistle (2:1, 12, 28; 3:7, 18; 4:4; 5:21), generally to introduce an admonition, as Jesus does here. Jesus recalled to their memory his words to the Jews: "Where I go, you cannot come" (8:21). To the disciples he was speaking of the fact that they were unprepared to follow him but would rejoin him later (14:3). To the Jews he made no such promise; instead, he predicted that they would die in their sins because of their unbelief.

34–35 The most important instruction that Jesus left for the Eleven was this "new commandment" to love one another. "New" (*kainēn*) implies freshness, or the opposite of "outworn" rather than simply "recent" or "different." If their motive in following him had been to obtain a high place in the messianic kingdom (John 1:40, 49), Jesus knew that the spirit of rivalry would disrupt their fellowship before they could accomplish his commission to them. The attitude of love would be the bond that would keep them united and would be the convincing demonstration that they had partaken of his own spirit and purpose. He had loved them without reservation and without limit (13:1–5) and expected them to do the same.

b. *The question of Peter*

13:36–14:4

> 36Simon Peter asked him, "Lord, where are you going?"
> Jesus replied, "Where I am going, you cannot follow now, but you will follow later."
> 37Peter asked, "Lord, why can't I follow you now? I will lay down my life for you."
> 38Then Jesus answered, "Will you really lay down your life for me? I tell you the truth, before the rooster crows, you will disown me three times!
> 1"Do not let your hearts be troubled. Trust in God; trust also in me. 2In my Father's house are many rooms; if it were not so, I would have told you. I am going there to prepare a place for you. 3And if I go and prepare a place for you, I will come back and take you to be with me that you also may be where I am. 4You know the way to the place where I am going."

The structure of this dialogue offers a contrast between the attempt of Jesus to present some consecutive teaching in preparation of his departure and the nervous unrest of the disciples who were disconcerted by the awareness of impending danger. As usual, Simon Peter was the first to speak.

36 Unfortunately the written text cannot convey the tone of Peter's question; but if he said, "Where *are* you going?" he would have expressed bewilderment and perhaps slight exasperation. Jesus had previously spoken publicly of going away (8:21). On that occasion his enemies were mystified and wondered whether he was contemplating suicide. Now, in the intimacy of his inner circle, the disciples are equally puzzled, though conceivably less critical. Jesus' answer reflects Peter's underlying meaning, for Jesus' promise, "You will follow later," implies that Peter had asked the question so that he might go with him. Peter's affection for Jesus, though often expressed clumsily, was undeniably genuine.

37–38 Peter was impatient and avowed that he was ready to lay down his life. Jesus, who understood the situation as Peter did not, and who knew Peter's inner weakness, was gently incredulous. His answer, "Before the rooster crows, you will disown me three times," reveals his estimate of Peter. Cock-crow was reckoned as the watch between twelve midnight and three o'clock in the morning, when the light of dawn began to glimmer on the eastern horizon. When Peter heard this word, he must have been completely baffled. He would not question Jesus' authority. Yet he was so sure of his own devotion that he could not imagine such a failure.

14:1 Furthermore, the other disciples must have been equally perturbed, for Jesus added, "Do not let your hearts be troubled." At this point he began to address the entire company of disciples, as the plural pronoun *hymōn* ("your") indicates. The form of the imperative *mē tarassesthō* implies that they should "stop being troubled." "Set your heart at ease" would be a good translation. He urged them to maintain both their trust in God and in himself. The verb "trust" (*pisteuete*) could be either indicative or imperative; i.e., a statement, "You trust in God and also trust in me," or a command, as translated by NIV. This double imperative seems to be the better choice. The first part of the verse is unquestionably an imperative, and Jesus was plainly endeavoring to encourage the disciples to persist in faith. Their uncertainty and discouragement had weakened them, and he wanted to strengthen them against complete collapse in the imminent tragedy.

2 In spite of the threatening circumstances, Jesus spoke with calm assurance of the divine provision for them and took for granted that they would have a place in the eternal world. Jesus never speculated about a future life; he spoke as one who was as familiar with eternity as one is with his hometown. The imagery of a dwelling place ("rooms") is taken from the oriental house in which the sons and daughters have apartments under the same roof as their parents. The purpose of his departure was to make ready the place where he could welcome them permanently. Certainly he would not go to prepare for friends unless he expected that they would finally arrive. Although he was well aware of their weakness and impending failure, he took the responsibility of bringing them to the Father's house.

3 "I will come back" is one of the few eschatological allusions in this Gospel. Jesus was not speaking of a general resurrection but of his personal concern for his own disciples. Though he did not elaborate on the promise, the guarantee is unmistakable. His return is as certain as his departure, and he would take them with him to his Father's house. This promise does not refer to death. Jesus left by the road of death; he will return by the road of life, as he said later in this discourse: "Because I live, you also will live" (v.19).

4 Verses 1–4 not only contain Jesus' answer to Peter's question but also indicate an attempt on Jesus' part to return to the theme of the discourse he had first begun. He assumed that they knew the way to their destination; all they would need to do would be to follow the road. His sheep would follow him and find "the house of the Lord" at the end of their journey (Ps 23:6; John 10:27–28).

c. *The question of Thomas*

14:5-7

> ⁵Thomas said to him, "Lord, we don't know where you are going, so how can we know the way?"
> ⁶Jesus answered, "I am the way and the truth and the life. No one comes to the

Father except through me. ⁷If you really knew me, you would know my Father as well. From now on, you do know him and have seen him."

5 Thomas's abrupt question was like Peter's questions (13:6, 36–37), characteristic of its proponent. Thomas was utterly honest, pessimistic, and uninhibited. He did not suppress his feelings but voiced his despair. He had already declared his willingness to follow Jesus and to die with him if necessary when he proposed the journey to Bethany (John 11:16). Thomas despaired of ever learning the way and was not ready to accept a state of permanent bewilderment. His question revealed a man who was confused by life and felt that its riddles were insolvable.

6 Jesus' reply is the ultimate foundation for a satisfactory philosophy of life. First, it is personal. He did not claim merely to know the way, the truth, and the life as a formula he could impart to the ignorant; but he actually claimed to *be* the answer to human problems. Jesus' solution to perplexity is not a recipe; it is a relationship with him. Second, he did not counter Thomas's skepticism with an argument or a quotation drawn from his memory. He responded with an authoritative assertion as the master of life. He *is* the way to the Father because only he has an intimate knowledge of God unmarred by sin. He *is* the truth because he has the perfect power of making life one coherent experience irrespective of its ups and downs. He *is* the life because he was not subject to death but made it subject to him. He did not live with death as the ultimate end of his life; he died to demonstrate the power and continuity of his life. Because he is the way, the truth, and the life, he is the only means of reaching the Father. Jesus was not exhibiting a narrow arrogance. Rather, he was making the only possible deduction from the fact that he, the unique Son, was the sole means of access to the Father. Jesus' claim parallels the author's pronouncement: "No one has ever seen God, but God the only Son, who is at the Father's side, has made him known" (John 1:18). Jesus is the only authorized revelation of God in human form and he is the only authorized representative of humanity to God.

7 "If you really knew me" could probably be better rendered "If you have attained a realization of who I am, you will know my Father also." Jesus declared that he had adequately presented the Father in his own person. The statement has its parallel in Paul's teaching: "He is the image of the invisible God" (Col 1:15). "Knew" implies experience rather than intuition or theoretical knowledge. To the extent that the disciples had come to a satisfactory understanding of Jesus, they had a comprehension of the being of God.

Notes

7 Textual evidence for "knew" or "had known" is divided between ἐγνώκατέ (egnōkate) and ἐγνώκειτέ (egnōkeite). The former reading favors a first-class condition; the second reading, a second-class condition. The former assumes that they knew Jesus but had not realized his representation of the Father; the second is a contrary-to-fact condition.

d. *The request of Philip*

14:8–15

> ⁸Philip said, "Lord, show us the Father and that will be enough for us."
> ⁹Jesus answered: "Don't you know me, Philip, even after I have been among you such a long time? Anyone who has seen me has seen the Father. How can you say, 'Show us the Father'? ¹⁰Don't you believe that I am in the Father, and that the Father is in me? The words I say to you are not just my own. Rather, it is the Father, living in me, who is doing his work. ¹¹Believe me when I say that I am in the Father and the Father is in me; or at least believe on the evidence of the miracles themselves. ¹²I tell you the truth, anyone who has faith in me will do what I have been doing. He will do even greater things than these, because I am going to the Father. ¹³And I will do whatever you ask in my name, so that the Son may bring glory to the Father. ¹⁴You may ask me for anything in my name, and I will do it.
> ¹⁵"If you love me, you will obey what I command."

8 If Thomas was a skeptic, Philip was a realist. Having determined in his thinking that the Father of whom Jesus spoke must be the Ultimate Absolute, Philip demanded that he and his associates might see him. Philip was materialistic; apparently abstractions meant little to him. Nevertheless he had a deep desire to experience God for himself. If he and the other disciples could only apprehend God with at least one of their senses, they would be satisfied. Perhaps he had in mind such a manifestation of God as "the angel of the Lord" who appeared to Jacob at Peniel (Gen 32:24, 30) and to the parents of Samson (Judg 13:3–22) or the experience of Moses on Mount Sinai (Exod 34:4–8).

9 Jesus was both pleased and saddened by Philip's request: pleased by his earnestness and saddened by his obtuseness. His union with the Father was so natural that he was astonished that Philip had not observed it. "I am in the Father, and . . . the Father is in me" (v.10) was his description of the relationship both in instructing the public and in his final prayer to the Father (cf. 10:38; 14:20; 17:21). For this reason he could say, "Anyone who has seen me has seen the Father." No material image or likeness can adequately depict God. Only a person can give knowledge of him since personality cannot be represented by an impersonal object.

10–11 Furthermore, if a personality must be employed to represent God, that personality cannot be less than God and do him justice, nor can it be so far above humanity that it cannot communicate God perfectly to men. For this reason John says that "the only Son, who is at the Father's side, has made him known" (John 1:18). The way Jesus made known the character and reality of the Father was by his words and works. The truth of God filled Jesus' words; the power of God produced his works.

12 Jesus again slowly resumed the main current of his teaching. He wanted to impress on the disciples that he was not disbanding them in anticipation of his departure but, rather, he was expecting them to continue his work and do even greater things than he had accomplished. Such an expectation seems impossible in the light of his character and power; yet, through the power of the Spirit whom Jesus sent after his ascension, there were more converts after the initial sermon of Peter at Pentecost than are recorded for Jesus during his entire career. The influence of the infant church covered the Roman world, whereas Jesus during his lifetime never traveled outside the boundaries of Palestine. Through the disciples he multiplied his ministry after his departure. The Book of Acts is a continuous record of deeds that followed the precedent Jesus had set. As the living Lord he continued in his church what he had himself begun. He expected that the church would become the instrument by which he could manifest his salvation to all people.

13-15 The power of the disciples originated in prayer. Jesus could hardly have made more emphatic the declaration that whatever they should ask in his name, he would do. The phrase "in my name," however, is not a talisman for the command of supernatural energy. He did not wish it to be used as a magical charm like an Aladdin's lamp. It was both a guarantee, like the endorsement on a check, and a limitation on the petition; for he would grant only such petitions as could be presented consistently with his character and purpose. In prayer we call on him to work out his purpose, not simply to gratify our whims. The answer is promised so that the Son may bring glory to the Father. The disciples' obedience to him will be the test of their love.

e. The promise of the Spirit

14:16-21

> 16And I will ask the Father, and he will give you another Counselor to be with you forever—17the Spirit of truth. The world cannot accept him, because it neither sees him nor knows him. But you know him, for he lives with you and will be in you. 18I will not leave you as orphans; I will come to you. 19Before long, the world will not see me anymore, but you will see me. Because I live, you also will live. 20On that day you will realize that I am in my Father, and you are in me, and I am in you. 21Whoever has my commands and obeys them, he is the one who loves me. He who loves me will be loved by my Father, and I too will love him and show myself to him."

16-17 With the preceding words, Jesus returend from the answer to Philip's question to the more general theme of preparation for his departure. His absence would make more difficult the realization of the person of the Father whom he represented. In his place he promised to send the Holy Spirit, the "Counselor." "Counselor" is an attempted translation of the Greek *paraklētos*, which means literally "a person summoned to one's aid." It may refer to an advisor, a legal advocate, a mediator or intercessor (BAG, p. 623). In the First Epistle of John it is applied to Jesus' present ministry as "the one who speaks to the Father in our defense" (1 John 2:1). The Spirit's function is to represent God to the believer as Jesus did in his incarnate state. "Another" (*allon*) means another of the same kind, not of a different kind. The concept of the Holy Spirit was not new, for the Spirit of God was the active agent in creation (Gen 1:2) and in remonstrating with men who were sinning against God (Gen 6:3). He called and empowered men to do unusual deeds (Judg 3:10; 13:24-25; 14:6, 19; 15:14) and to prophesy (Zech 7:12). John the Baptist had predicted that Jesus would baptize with the Holy Spirit (Matt 3:11; Mark 1:8; Luke 3:16; John 1:33). In his discussion of the new birth, Jesus had already spoken to Nicodemus of the work of the Holy Spirit (John 3:5). The ministry of the Spirit, however, would be directed primarily to the disciples. He would direct their decisions, counsel them continually, and remain with them forever. He would be invisible to all and unapprehended by the world at large since the world would not recognize him. To use a modern metaphor, he would not operate on the world's wavelength. His presence was already *with* the disciples insofar as they were under his influence. Later, he would indwell them, when Jesus himself had departed. This distinction marks the difference between the Old Testament experience of the Holy Spirit and the post-Pentecostal experience of the church. The individual indwelling of the Spirit is the specific privilege of the Christian believer (see John 7:39).

18–19 Jesus' allusion to a return may refer to his reappearance after the Resurrection. He did reveal himself to his disciples in order to impart final instructions and comfort, but he did not remain visible for long. There was no public manifestation, as he intimated, and the private manifestation of the postresurrection appearances would verify his acceptance by the Father and his union with the Father. He would appear only to those who loved and obeyed him. The motive for these appearances was the need for reassuring the disciples, whom his departure would leave as helpless orphans in an unfriendly world. Jesus looked upon them as spiritual children (13:33) who needed the strong protection and guidance of a parent in order to survive. The resurrection of Jesus would also be the guarantee of life for the disciples. The eternal life that he would demonstrate is the same eternal life he promised to them.

20 The coming of the Spirit to indwell believers would bring the realization that the Father, Son, and Holy Spirit are united in purpose and operation and that there would be a new intimate relationship between them and believers. Furthermore, the Spirit's coming would be a confirmation of Jesus' exaltation to the Father's right hand to begin his present ministry as Advocate and Intercessor (John 15:26; Acts 2:33; 5:31–32).

21 Jesus reiterated the statement of v.15 because of its importance. Love is the basis of relationship with God. His love has been manifested in the gift of Jesus (1 John 4:9–10). Our love for him is manifested in obedience (1 John 5:3). Jesus said that there are great benefits for those who obey his commands, thus showing their love for him. Jesus said that the Father would love the obedient disciple, Jesus himself would love him, and Jesus would make himself known to him. Loving Christ pays unmatched dividends.

f. *The question of Judas (not Iscariot)*

14:22–24

> ²²Then Judas (not Judas Iscariot) said, "But, Lord, why do you intend to show yourself to us and not to the world?"
> ²³Jesus replied, "If anyone loves me, he will obey my teaching. My Father will love him, and we will come to him and make our home with him. ²⁴He who does not love me will not obey my teaching. These words you hear are not my own; they belong to the Father who sent me.

22 The last question in this impromptu dialogue was posed by Judas (not Iscariot). Nothing is known of him beyond his name, unless he can be identified with Thaddaeus (Matt 10:3; Mark 3:18). Only Luke mentions a second disciple by this name (Luke 6:16; Acts 1:13). Judas could not understand how Jesus would appear to the disciples without being at the same time subject to public scrutiny. Either Jesus would be visible or he would not; for Judas there was no possibility of both.

23 Jesus in his reply did not discuss the question of postresurrection appearances. He focused the disciples' attention on the broader revelation that would come to them through obedience to his known teaching and through the work of the Holy Spirit. The reality of Jesus' and the Father's presence would be conditioned on obedience. The bond of love that would provide the atmosphere for the fellowship would be resultant rather than conditional, for obedience is the consequence of love. Obedience is not, however, the condition of God's love for men but the proof of their realization of his love and of their love for him.

24 Being obedient to Jesus' words extends beyond keeping the charges he personally delivered. Jesus equated his teaching with the Father's will. Thus, loving Jesus is demonstrated by one's obedience to the revealed will of God, the Bible.

g. *Parting comfort*

14:25–31

> [25]"All this I have spoken while still with you. [26]But the Counselor, the Holy Spirit, whom the Father will send in my name, will teach you all things and will remind you of everything I have said to you. [27]Peace I leave with you; my peace I give you. I do not give to you as the world gives. Do not let your hearts be troubled and do not be afraid.
>
> [28]"You heard me say, 'I am going away and I am coming back to you.' If you loved me, you would be glad that I am going to the Father, for the Father is greater than I. [29]I have told you now before it happens, so that when it does happen you will believe. [30]I will not speak with you much longer, for the prince of this world is coming. He has no hold on me, [31]but the world must learn that I love the Father and that I do exactly what my Father has commanded me. Come now; let us leave.

25–26 Jesus resumed his teaching on the Holy Spirit because Judas's question evoked it. Through the Spirit Jesus' presence would be perpetuated among them. The phrase "in my name" used previously in vv.13, 14, means that the Spirit would be Jesus' officially delegated representative to act in his behalf. Just as Jesus himself demonstrated the personality and character of God to men, so after his departure the Holy Spirit would make the living Christ real to his followers. The function of the Spirit is teaching. He instructs from within and recalls to the memory what Jesus taught. The Spirit will, therefore, impress the commandments of Jesus on the minds of his disciples and thus prompt them to obedience.

27 The peace Jesus spoke of could not be exemption from conflict and trial. Jesus himself was "troubled" (12:27) by the impending Crucifixion. The peace he spoke of is the calmness of confidence in God. Jesus had this peace because he was sure of the Father's love and approval. The world can give only false peace, which mostly comes from the ignorance of peril or self-reliance. Jesus, fully aware of the distressing suffering confronting him, had such confidence in the purpose and power of the Father that he moved forward unhesitatingly to meet the crisis without fear. His peace would be the source of courage for the disciples. With his promise of peace, he repeated the words of comfort he had spoken in reply to Peter's question: "Do not let your hearts be troubled and do not be afraid" (cf. v.1). The disciples must have continued to show their dismay as they contemplated Jesus' departure.

28 In concluding this discourse, Jesus reminded them that he was about to return to the Father and that he had forewarned them so that their faith might not be disrupted by his removal. The statement "the Father is greater than I" refers to position rather than essence. Jesus was speaking from the standpoint of his humanity, the incarnate state he assumed in order to fulfill the purposes of redemption. He had already acknowledged that "the Son can do nothing by himself; he can do only what he sees his Father doing" (John 5:19). The numerous statements that the Father had sent him confirm that Jesus was acting under authority and was obligated to fulfill the Father's commands.

29 In this instance "believe" is Jesus' own word, not the author's interpretation. Throughout the Gospel the necessity of believing is emphasized (1:50; 3:12, 15; 4:21, 41; 5:24, 44, 46; 6:29, 35, 47, 64; 7:38; 8:24, 45; 9:35; 10:38; 11:25, 41; 12:37, 44; 13:19; 14:1, 11; 16:31; 17:20; 20:27). Jesus insisted that acceptance of his person is pivotal to spiritual experience.

"Believe" (*pisteusēte*) is an aorist subjunctive, which normally indicates the beginning of an action. After the previous statements that the disciples had believed (1:50; 2:11; 6:69), such a construction seems inconsistent. Nevertheless the final arrest and death they witnessed would undoubtedly shake their faith to its foundations, and Jesus wished to prepare them for the strain this crisis would place on them.

30–31 "The prince of this world" refers to Satan. Jesus was constantly aware of Satan's hostile presence and was preparing for his last attack. This Gospel makes no mention of the temptation of Jesus that is recorded in the Synoptics (Matt 4:1–11; Mark 1:12; Luke 4:1–13). Luke, however, indicates that the temptation was not Jesus' sole conflict with the devil, for he says, "When the devil had finished all this tempting, he left him until an opportune time" (Luke 4:13). Luke does not define what that "opportune time" was, but there could scarcely have been a more favorable moment for pressure than when Jesus was confronted with the final issue of his life. The betrayal by Judas, the frustration of human hopes, the disappointment of apparent failure, the agony of death—these would make him especially susceptible to suggestion or temptation. Jesus did not fear Satan because Satan had no claim on him. There was nothing in Jesus' character or action that could be used against him. Satan had no valid accusation that could be used as leverage to divert Jesus from the will of his Father. His obedience had been perfect, and he intended to complete the Father's purpose irrespective of what it might cost him.

At this point Jesus proposed leaving the upper room. Whether chs. 15–17 were spoken en route to Gethsemane or whether he and the disciples lingered while he finished the discussion is not plain; but in either case the words conclude the open dialogue.

Notes

30 The NIV translation "has no hold on me" does not seem to carry the full meaning of the text. The KJV "hath nothing in me" is absolutely literal, but it does not express the sense in modern idiom. "Has nothing on me" might be colloquial, but it would probably be a closer approximation to the meaning.

2. *The discourse on relations* (15:1–27)

In this section of the Farewell Discourse, Jesus dealt with three relationships that involve the disciples: (1) their relationship with him, (2) their relationship with one another, and (3) their relationship with the world around them. Jesus knew his disciples would constitute a distinct body or community with a definite function, and he wished to prepare them for the change his departure would make in their manner of living. Viewed from the standpoint of the writer and his time, this section previews the church and its development in the postresurrection period, though the word "church" does not appear here.

a. *The relation of the disciples to Christ*

15:1-11

> [1] "I am the true vine and my Father is the gardener. [2] He cuts off every branch in me that bears no fruit, while every branch that does bear fruit he trims clean so that it will be even more fruitful. [3] You are already clean because of the word I have spoken to you. [4] Remain in me, and I will remain in you. No branch can bear fruit by itself; it must remain in the vine. Neither can you bear fruit unless you remain in me.
>
> [5] "I am the vine; you are the branches. If a man remains in me and I in him, he will bear much fruit; apart from me you can do nothing. [6] If anyone does not remain in me, he is like a branch that is thrown away and withers; such branches are picked up, thrown into the fire and burned. [7] If you remain in me and my words remain in you, ask whatever you wish, and it will be given you. [8] This is to my Father's glory, that you bear much fruit, showing yourselves to be my disciples.
>
> [9] "As the Father has loved me, so have I loved you. Now remain in my love. [10] If you obey my commands, you will remain in my love, just as I have obeyed my Father's commands and remain in his love. [11] I have told you this so that my joy may be in you and that your joy may be complete.

The first of these relationships is primary, for the very existence of the group depended on the union of each individual with Christ. To illustrate it, Jesus used the analogy (or parable) of the vine. Viticulture was one of the common features of Palestinian life and would have been familiar to the disciples. It is possible that if the text of this discourse was spoken as they walked from the upper room in Jerusalem down into the Kidron Valley and across to the Mount of Olives, they could have seen the great golden vine, the national emblem of Israel, on the front of the temple. This symbolism has its precedent in the OT. Psalm 80 refers to Israel as a vine: "You brought a vine out of Egypt; you drove out the nations and planted it. You cleared the ground for it, and it took root and filled the land" (vv.8–9). An even better example is found in Isaiah 5:1-2, 7:

> My loved one had a vineyard
> on a fertile hillside.
> He dug it up and cleared it of stones
> and planted it with the choicest vines.
> He built a watchtower in it
> and cut out a winepress as well.
> Then he looked for a crop of good grapes,
> but it yielded only bad fruit. . . .
> The vineyard of the Lord Almighty
> is the house of Israel,
> and the men of Judah
> are the garden of his delight.

1 Jesus, using the vine metaphor, expanded its scope to all believers and individualized its application. In adapting it to the immediate situation, he stressed certain features. The first was that there is a genuine stock. The major essential in horticulture is to plant

the right kind of vine or tree in order to assure the proper quality of fruit. No fruit can be better than the vine that produces it. Jesus said, "I am the true vine." Unless the believer is vitally connected with him, the quality of his fruitfulness will be unacceptable. There may be many branches, but if they are to bear the right kind of fruit, they must be a part of the real vine.

The second feature is that God the Father is the gardener (geōrgos). The noun is quite general and really means "farmer," though here it is applied to an expert in growing grapes. Success in raising any crop depends largely on the skill of the farmer or gardener. The relation of the believer to God is that of the vine to the owner of the vineyard. He tends it, waters it, and endeavors to protect it and cultivate it so that it will produce its maximum yield.

2 Another emphasis is on pruning. Two aspects are noted: the removal of dead wood and the trimming of live wood so that its potential for fruitbearing will be improved. The verb translated "cut off" (aireō) means literally "to lift up" or "to take away"; the second, "trims clean" (kathaireō), a compound of the first, means "to cleanse" or "to purify." Here the translation "cut off" and "trim" is accurate, though it represents a special application of a more general term. Pruning is necessary for any vine. Dead wood is worse than fruitlessness, for dead wood can harbor disease and decay. An untrimmed vine will develop long rambling branches that produce little fruit because most of the strength of the vine is given to growing wood. The vine-grower is concerned that the vine be healthy and productive. The caring process is a picture of the divine dealing with human life. God removes the dead wood from his church and disciplines the life of the believer so that it is directed into fruitful activity.

3 "Clean" recalls Jesus' statement to the disciples at the footwashing: "And you are clean, though not every one of you" (John 13:10). There he singled out Judas, who was consciously and deliberately planning to betray him. Jesus did not equate "clean" with "perfect" but rather with sincere devotion that unites others to him as branches are united to the vine. Judas was an example of a branch that was cut off.

The means by which pruning or cleaning is done is the Word of God. It condemns sin; it inspires holiness; it promotes growth. As Jesus applied the words God gave him to the lives of the disciples, they underwent a pruning process that removed evil from them and conditioned them for further service.

4 Continued production depends on constant union with the source of fruitfulness. Branches that are severed from the parent stock may produce leaves temporarily, but inevitably they will wither because there is no source of life to sustain them; and they will never bear fruit. The effectiveness of the believer depends on his receiving the constant flow of life from Christ.

5 Fruitbearing is not only possible but certain if the branch remains in union with the vine. Uniformity of quantity and quality are not promised. But if the life of Christ permeates a disciple, fruit will be inevitable.

6 Failure to maintain a vital connection brings its own penalty—rejection and uselessness. NIV translates this verse as most other versions do: "Like a branch that is thrown away." The Greek text contains the definite article: "Like *the* branch that is thrown away." Morris observes that the use of the definite article "the" (*to*) with "branch" (*klema*) may imply that it refers to the person who did not abide in the vine at the outset (NIC, p. 671, n. 17). Possibly it could be a reference to Judas Iscariot (cf. John 17:12). The indefiniteness of subject that characterizes the passive verb *exēranthē* ("withers" NIV) and the use of the plural "branches" in the second part of the sentence indicate Jesus' intent to show that fruitfulness is normal for believers. An absolutely fruitless life is prima facie evidence that one is not a believer. Jesus left no place among his followers for fruitless disciples. The aorist verbs translated "is thrown away" and "withers" refer to accomplished action in the past. They are used here to emphasize the immediacy and finality of action.

7 The connection is maintained by obedience and prayer. To remain in Christ and to allow his words to remain in oneself means a conscious acceptance of the authority of his word and a constant contact with him by prayer. The prayer request must be related to a definite need and must be for an object Jesus himself would desire. He was evidently referring back to the counsel in the preceding part of the discourse: "You may ask me for anything in my name, and I will do it" (John 14:14). He was not promising to gratify every chance whim. But so long as the believer was seeking the Lord's will in his life, Jesus would grant every request that would help accomplish this end.

8 The proof of discipleship is fruitbearing. This statement coincides with Jesus' teaching in the synoptic Gospels: "By their fruit you will recognize them" (Matt 7:20; cf. Luke 6:43–44). Just as Jesus glorified God by his life, so the disciples would glorify God by theirs.

9–11 Love is the relationship that unites the disciples to Christ as branches are united to a vine. Two results stem from this relationship: obedience and joy. Obedience marks the cause of their fruitfulness; joy is its result. Jesus intended that the disciples' lives should be both spontaneous and happy rather than burdensome and boring. Obedience in carrying out his purpose would be a guarantee of success, for Jesus never planned failure for his disciples. Joy logically follows when the disciples realize that the life of Christ in them is bringing fruit—something they could never produce in their own strength.

Notes

1 The adjective ἀληθινός (*alēthinos*) means "true" or "real" in the sense of original rather than derivative, or genuine rather than imitation. The related adjective ἀληθής (*alēthēs*) means "true" in opposition to that which is false or counterfeit. By this usage Jesus asserted that there may be other vines, but he is the only genuine and original stock.

b. *The relation of the disciples to one another*

15:12–17

12My command is this: Love each other as I have loved you. 13Greater love has no one than this, that one lay down his life for his friends. 14You are my friends if you do what I command. 15I no longer call you servants, because a servant does

not know his master's business. Instead, I have called you friends, for everything that I learned from my Father I have made known to you. [16]You did not choose me, but I chose you to go and bear fruit—fruit that will last. Then the Father will give you whatever you ask in my name. [17]This is my command: Love each other.

12–13 Jesus repeated his command to "love each other" (cf. 13:34) because he knew that the future of the work among men depended on the disciples' attitude toward one another. His stress on love had been underscored earlier in this discourse (14:15, 21, 23, 28). Unity instead of rivalry, trust instead of suspicion, obedience instead of self-assertion must rule the disciples' common labors. The measure of their love for one another is that of his love for them (cf. 13:34), which would be further demonstrated by his forthcoming sacrifice. John caught the meaning of the statement and repeated it in his First Epistle: "This is how we know what love is: Jesus Christ laid down his life for us. And we ought to lay down our lives for our brothers" (1 John 3:16).

14–15 Again Jesus defined friendship in terms of obedience. Christian friendship is more than a casual acquaintance; it is a partnership of mutual esteem and affection (14:21). Jesus elevated the disciples above mere tools and made them partners in his work. A slave is never given a reason for the work assigned to him; he must perform it because he has no other choice. The friend is a confidant who shares the knowledge of his superior's purpose and voluntarily adopts it as his own. Jesus declared that he had revealed to the disciples all that the Father had given to him. The disclosure of the mind of God concerning his career and theirs would give them assurance that they were engaged in the right task and that God would ultimately bring it to a successful conclusion.

16–17 The disciples had not followed Jesus by some chance impulse; they had been chosen. He had invited them to interview him (1:39), he had promised to reshape them to his requirements (v.42), and he had summoned them to follow him (v.43). His miracles had clinched their original faith (2:11), and he had solicitously pleaded with them not to forsake him when many had departed from him (6:66–67). At that time he said that he had chosen them (v.70). He claimed them as his peculiar flock (10:27) and asserted that they would never perish (v.28). He expected that they would fulfill his purpose for them and that their work would be enduring. For this reason he urged them to maintain the relationship of love for one another that would facilitate the fulfillment of his hopes. Again he emphasized the need of prayer for the continuation of their mission: "Then the Father will give you whatever you ask in my name" (15:16; cf. 14:26). The effectiveness of prayer is linked to fruitbearing, which, in turn, is linked to obedience (vv.10, 14). He repeated the command to love one another, for in seeking to be obedient to the Lord and to be fruitful, it is possible to forget the brethren.

c. *The relation of the disciples to the world*

15:18–27

[18]"If the world hates you, keep in mind that it hated me first. [19]If you belonged to the world, it would love you as its own. As it is, you do not belong to the world, but I have chosen you out of the world. That is why the world hates you. [20]Remember the words I spoke to you: 'No servant is greater than his master.' If they persecuted me, they will persecute you also. If they obeyed my teaching, they will obey yours also. [21]They will treat you this way because of my name, for they do

not know the One who sent me. [22]If I had not come and spoken to them, they would not be guilty of sin. Now, however, they have no excuse for their sin. [23]He who hates me hates my Father as well. [24]If I had not done among them what no one else did, they would not be guilty of sin. But now they have seen these miracles, and yet they have hated both me and my Father. [25]But this is to fulfill what is written in their Law: 'They hated me without reason.'

[26]"When the Counselor comes, whom I will send to you from the Father, the Spirit of truth who goes out from the Father, he will testify about me; [27]but you also must testify, for you have been with me from the beginning.

18 The term "world" (*kosmos*) has several uses in the Johannine writings. It may refer to the universe as the object of creation (1:10), the materialistic order that allures men from God (1 John 2:15–16), or mankind in general as the object of God's love (3:16). Here it refers to the mass of unbelievers who are indifferent or hostile to God and his people. Jesus reminded the disciples that in spite of the fact that he had come on an errand of love, the world at large hated him. The perfect tense of the verb "hate" (*memisēken*) implies that the world's hatred is a fixed attitude toward him—an attitude that carries over to his disciples as well. The world assumes this attitude because it rejects all who do not conform to its life style.

19–20 Jesus' choice of the disciples had set them apart for a different kind of life and for a different purpose. Therefore, the world would exclude them. Jesus' choice was also the guarantee that the lives of his disciples would have permanent value, but it did not guarantee immunity from attack. Jesus could promise them nothing more than what he himself had received.

21 There are two reasons for the obstinate attitude of the world. The first is ignorance: "They do not know the One who sent me." The world has no proper concept of (*ouk oidasin*, "they do not know") God. Consequently, the world cannot evaluate adequately the messenger whom he sent. Compare the statement of Paul: "Since they did not think it worthwhile to retain the knowledge of God, he gave them over to a depraved mind, to do what ought not to be done" (Rom 1:28). This ignorance is both intellectual and spiritual.

22 A second reason is resentment of Jesus' claims and standards. Both by his life and words he rebukes human sin and condemns it. He uncovers the inner corruption and hypocrisy of men, and they react violently to the disclosure. He strips away all excuses and exposes their selfishness and rebellion against God.

23 The connection between Jesus and the Father appears as strongly in this passage as it did in the argument of ch. 5. Jesus said that those who hated him would hate the Father, also. He and the Father belong in the same category; neither can be accepted or rejected without the other.

24 The sin of Jesus' enemies was both deliberate and inexcusable. Accredited by the miracles that he performed, he brought condemnation on them (cf. John 9:30–33, 39–41). His foes had heard his words and had witnessed his supporting miracles. Consequently, their reaction against him could not have been attributed to ignorance of his words or to lack of evidence substantiating them.

25 To explain his position and express his response, Jesus quoted from Psalm 69: "Those who hate me without reason outnumber the hairs of my head" (v.4). The quotation is partial. No doubt Jesus wished to emphasize only the phrase "without reason." The irony of his quotation is clear: the men who posed as the champions of the Law were fulfilling the prophecy concerning the enemies of God's servant.

26 In response to this attitude of hatred there must be a continuing witness to the love and grace of Christ. The last two verses of this chapter define the expected action of the disciples who will maintain the testimony of Jesus after he has left the earth. He completed the list of witnesses of ch. 5 (vv.31–40) by adding the witness of the Holy Spirit, whose ministry he had already partially described (14:16–17, 26), and also the witness of the disciples themselves.

27 The verb "testify" (*martureite*) could be indicative, as ASV translates it, or imperative, as NIV indicates by the insertion of "must." The latter translation is probably preferable since the whole discourse is instructional and preparatory to a new ministry for the disciples. "From the beginning" probably refers to the beginning of Jesus' public ministry.

Later, when the disciples felt that it was necessary to choose a successor for Judas Iscariot, one requirement was that of having belonged to the company of disciples "the whole time that the Lord Jesus went in and out among [them], beginning from John's baptism to the time when Jesus was taken up" (Acts 1:21–22). For the important task of witnessing to Jesus and his message, one must have complete experiential knowledge of his person. The apostles were committed to the transmission of sober facts; they were not creating a fictional legend. The coupling of the witness of the Spirit with that of the disciples defines their reciprocal relationship. Without the witness of the Spirit, the disciples' witness would be powerless; without the disciples' witness, the Spirit would be restricted in his means of expression.

3. *The discourse on revelation* (16:1–33)

a. *The revelation of rejection*

16:1–4

> 1"All this I have told you so that you will not go astray. 2They will put you out of the synagogue; in fact, a time is coming when anyone who kills you will think he is offering a service to God. 3They will do such things because they have not known the Father or me. 4I have told you this, so that when the time comes you will remember that I warned you. I did not tell you this at first because I was with you.

1–2 Chapter 16 is a discussion of the revelation Jesus intended to give his disciples preparatory to their coming mission. He linked it with the preceding section of his final discourse by sharpening the warning he had already given to them concerning the hatred of the world. He applied this revelation particularly to their local conditions and predicted that they would suffer excommunication from the synagogue and even death. The episode of the healing of the blind man furnishes a graphic analogy, for he was expelled from the synagogue because of his defense of Jesus (9:22, 34). The raising of Lazarus so disturbed the Jews that they tried to kill both Jesus and Lazarus (12:10). While

Jesus was with the disciples, he could shelter and direct them. They needed to realize, however, that even his resurrection would not be sufficiently convincing to his enemies to remove the hatred that existed between them and his followers.

3 Jesus attributed the action of his foes to ignorance, not the ignorance of intellectual knowledge, but the lack of a personal experience of God and Christ. Their attitude was determined by who they thought Jesus was, and consequently by who they thought God was, rather than by actual contact with either. So warped had that attitude become that their contact with Jesus had generated hate for both himself and the Father (John 15:24). The principle is well summarized by Jesus' own words: "If then the light within you is darkness, how great is that darkness!" (Matt 6:23).

4 It may well be that this particular utterance of Jesus was reported by John because of the pressing need for courage in the church of his day. The Apocalypse indicates that there was a wide break between the church and the synagogue at the end of the first century (Rev 2:9; 3:9) and that those who professed to believe in Jesus were completely disowned by their Jewish compatriots. John's use of the term "the Jews" seems to confirm this.

b. *The revelation of the Holy Spirit*

16:5-15

> 5"Now I am going to him who sent me, yet none of you asks me, 'Where are you going?' 6Because I have said these things, you are filled with grief. 7But I tell you the truth: It is for your good that I am going away. Unless I go away, the Counselor will not come to you; but if I go, I will send him to you. 8When he comes, he will convict the world of guilt in regard to sin and righteousness and judgment: 9in regard to sin, because men do not believe in me; 10in regard to righteousness, because I am going to the Father, where you can see me no longer; 11and in regard to judgment, because the prince of this world now stands condemned.
> 12"I have much more to say to you, more than you can now bear. 13But when he, the Spirit of truth, comes, he will guide you into all truth. He will not speak on his own; he will speak only what he hears, and he will tell you what is yet to come. 14He will bring glory to me by taking from what is mine and making it known to you. 15All that belongs to the Father is mine. That is why I said the Spirit will take from what is mine and make it known to you.

5-6 The time had come for a new revelation. Previously Jesus had been with the disciples to counsel them and answer their questions. Now, in view of his imminent removal, they needed someone to take his place. He revealed to them the coming of the Holy Spirit, whom he had already mentioned in the general discourse (14:16-17, 26; 15:26). The statement "none of you asks me, 'Where are you going?' " seems incongruous with Peter's question in the earlier part of the discourse (13:36). At that point Peter's question was casual, and neither he nor the other disciples pressed the issue to ascertain what Jesus' plans really were. There was little concern about his future; they were interested mainly in their own future. They were sorrowful because they would lose him. So they made no inquiry about the reasons for his departure nor about the objectives he might wish to attain.

7 Jesus told the disciples that his separation from them was in their best interest. As long as he was with them in person, his work was localized; and it would be impossible to

communicate with them equally at all times and in all places. The coming of the "Counselor" would equip them for a wider and more potent ministry.

8 Three major aspects of the ministry of the Holy Spirit are described in vv.8–15:

1. To the world—conviction of sin, righteousness, and judgment.
2. To the disciples—direction and truth.
3. To Jesus—revealing him more perfectly to and through those who represent him.

The key to this first aspect of the Spirit's ministry is the word "convict" (*elenchō*). KJV translates it "reprove," but that rendering is not strong enough. The word is a legal term that means to pronounce a judicial verdict by which the guilt of the culprit at the bar of justice is defined and fixed. The Spirit does not merely accuse men of sin, he brings to them an inescapable sense of guilt so that they realize their shame and helplessness before God. This conviction applies to three particular areas: sin, righteousness, and judgment. The Spirit is the prosecuting attorney who presents God's case against humanity. He creates an inescapable awareness of sin so that it cannot be dismissed with an excuse or evaded by taking refuge in the fact that "everybody is doing it." The Spirit's function is like that of Nathan the prophet, who said to David, "You are the man" (2 Sam 12:7), and compelled him to acknowledge his misdeeds. David was so convicted that he was reduced to a state of complete penitence: "Against you, you only, have I sinned and done what is evil in your sight" (Ps 51:4).

9 The essence of sin is unbelief, which is not simply a casual incredulity nor a difference of opinion; rather, it is a total rejection of God's messenger and message. A court can convict a man of murder, but only the Spirit can convict him of unbelief. Jesus insisted that sin was fundamentally repudiation of his message and his mission.

10 The second area in which the Spirit convicts people is righteousness. He enforces the absolute standard of God's character, to which all thought and action must be compared. Apart from a standard of righteousness, there can be no sin; and there must be an awareness of the holiness of God before a person will realize his own deficiency. There is an infinite gap between the righteousness of God and the sinful state of man that man himself cannot bridge. The first step toward salvation must be the awareness that a divine mediatorship is necessary.

The connection between righteousness and Jesus' return to the Father is not immediately clear. Probably it should be interpreted as meaning that his return to the right hand of God was a complete vindication of all he had done and consequently established him as the standard for all human righteousness. Apostolic preaching conveyed this concept. Peter's statement in Acts 3:14–15 conveys much the same idea: "You disowned the Holy and Righteous One and asked that a murderer be released to you. You killed the author of life, but God raised him from the dead." Whereas righteousness had previously been defined by precepts, it now has been revealed in the incarnate Son, who exemplified it perfectly in all his relationships. John crystallized this thought in his First Epistle: "In him is no sin" (1 John 3:5).

11 Judgment always occurs when an act or thought is evaluated by an absolute principle. Actions are judged by their accord with law or by their lack of conformity to it. When human sin is confronted by the righteousness of Christ, its condemnation is self-evident. In this context "judgment" refers to the condemnation of satanic self-will and rebellion by the obedience and love toward the Father exhibited by Jesus. The Cross was the utter condemnation and defeat of the "prince of this world." "Condemned" is in the perfect tense (*kekritai*), which expresses a settled state. Satan is already under judgment; the sentence is fixed and permanent. (For discussion of "the prince of this world," see comments on 14:30.)

12–13 Jesus told his disciples directly that the revelation to date was incomplete. They were not sufficiently mature to understand all he wished to impart. A second function of the Holy Spirit would be to lead them into the full comprehension of all he could give them. The Spirit would not present an independent message, differing from what they had already learned from him. They would be led further into the realization of his person and in the development of the principles he had already laid down. They would also be enlightened about coming events. He would unfold the truth as the disciples grew in spiritual capacity and understanding. In this promise lies the germinal authority of the apostolic writings, which transmit the revelation of Christ through his disciples by the work of the Holy Spirit. He would conduct them (*hodēgeō*) into the unknown future as a guide directs those who follow him into unfamiliar territory.

14–15 The third function of the Spirit is to glorify Christ. His chief purpose is not to make himself prominent but to magnify the person of Jesus. The Spirit interprets and applies the character and teaching of Jesus to the disciples and by so doing makes him central to their thinking. He makes God a reality to people.

c. *The revelation of Jesus' reappearance*

16:16–24

> [16]"In a little while you will see me no more, and then after a little while you will see me."
> [17]Some of his disciples said to one another, "What does he mean by saying, 'In a little while you will see me no more, and then after a little while you will see me,' and 'Because I am going to the Father'?" [18]They kept asking, "What does he mean by 'a little while'? We don't understand what he is saying."
> [19]Jesus saw that they wanted to ask him about this, so he said to them, "Are you asking one another what I meant when I said, 'In a little while you will see me no more, and then after a little while you will see me'? [20]I tell you the truth, you will weep and mourn while the world rejoices. You will grieve, but your grief will turn to joy. [21]A woman giving birth to a child has pain because her time has come; but when her baby is born she forgets the anguish because of her joy that a child is born into the world. [22]So with you: Now is your time of grief, but I will see you again and you will rejoice, and no one will take away your joy. [23]In that day you will no longer ask me anything. I tell you the truth, my Father will give you whatever you ask in my name. [24]Until now you have not asked for anything in my name. Ask and you will receive, and your joy will be complete.

16 Jesus' remark "In a little while you will see me no more, and then after a little while you will see me" was obscure to his disciples and is still enigmatic to the reader of this Gospel. His prediction of disappearance refers to his death, but to what does the second appearance refer? He did not have in mind a coming in the person of the Holy Spirit because he had emphasized the distinction between himself and the Spirit and between their respective ministries. The disciples were confused by his language, both by the concept of his going to the Father and by the time element involved. The best solution seems to be that he was referring to the Resurrection, which would take place "a little while" after he had left them.

17-18 The two problems that vexed the disciples were the prediction of disappearance and then reappearance after a short interval and the concept of "going to the Father." The second was an allusion to his words recorded in John 14:28. The disciples had not yet established the mental perspective Jesus wished them to have and were thinking only in terms of the present situation. The use of the imperfect tense in "kept asking" (*elegon*) shows that they must have held a consultation among themselves about it and that the discourse did not proceed as an uninterrupted lecture. Apparently it was a casual conversation with periods of silence on Jesus' part.

19-22 The subsequent narrative develops the postresurrection period as a time in which the disciples' fears were quelled, their doubts dispelled, and their commission confirmed. Jesus compared their parting to the painful birth of a child, which, when fully accomplished, brings joy. The disciples were disappointed because the kingdom had not come; and they were distressed because of the calamity that was about to overtake Jesus, in which they all would share. The "world" would rejoice that he had been removed and would pride itself in a victory, but the disciples would mourn the untimely loss of their leader. In his resurrection, however, the conditions would be reversed, and their lamentations would be transformed into joy because he would return to them.

On the words "ask" and "asking," see Notes, p. 161.

23-24 The verb "ask" (*erōtaō*) in the phrase "in that day you will no longer ask me anything" means "to ask a question" rather than "to request a favor." While the sense is somewhat obscure, since the verb came to mean "to request of an equal," Jesus may have meant that at his reappearance after the Resurrection the truth of his claims and the status of his person would be self-evident. At that time the disciples would no longer question him as one of their number but would present their petitions to the Father in his name (cf. 14:13). As his disciples they would be eligible for the Father's response to their needs.

d. *The revelation of the Father*

16:25-33

> [25]"Though I have been speaking figuratively, a time is coming when I will no longer use this kind of language but will tell you plainly about my Father. [26]In that day you will ask in my name. I am not saying that I will ask the Father on your behalf. [27]No, the Father himself loves you because you have loved me and have believed that I came from God. [28]I came from the Father and entered the world; now I am leaving the world and going back to the Father."
>
> [29]Then Jesus' disciples said, "Now you are speaking clearly and without figures of speech. [30]Now we can see that you know all things and that you do not even need to have anyone ask you questions. This makes us believe that you came from God."
>
> [31]"You believe at last!" Jesus answered. [32]"But a time is coming, and has come, when you will be scattered, each to his own home. You will leave me all alone. Yet I am not alone, for my Father is with me.
>
> [33]"I have told you these things, so that in me you may have peace. In this world you will have trouble. But take heart! I have overcome the world."

25 Jesus had used figurative or parabolic language to the disciples because of their spiritual immaturity. After the Resurrection, he would be at liberty to speak plainly about the Father. Little is said in the Gospels concerning the instruction Jesus imparted to the disciples during the forty days prior to his ascension. However, it is probable that during this period he gave them much of the teaching that was reflected in their later preaching and writing (Acts 1:3).

26–27 It would be unnecessary for Jesus to make requests on their behalf, for they would be able to present their own petitions. The phrase "in my name" recurs frequently in this farewell discourse (14:13–14, 26; 16:23–24, 26) and indicates Jesus' sponsorship of the disciples. Their standing with God will depend on his merits. Because of his work they will be able to approach the Father directly with their petitions. The relation Jesus had established with the disciples became the ground for their direct relationship with the Father. Because they had committed themselves to him and had "believed" (*pepisteukate*), the ground of this relationship was fixed.

28–30 Jesus' declaration that he had come from the Father and was about to return to the Father satisfied their inquiry. They felt that he was no longer talking in riddles. Their response to Jesus' straightforward declaration was a further confession of belief. They implied that their questions to him had been occasioned by their bewilderment over his figurative language. The direct statement he had just made clarified their understanding and eliminated the need for further questioning. In the light of that understanding they reaffirmed their belief that he had come from God.

31–32 Jesus was skeptical of the firmness of the disciples' avowed belief (NIV mg.). He was completely aware of their impending failure. Already he had expressed the same apprehension to Simon Peter, when the latter protested that he would be loyal regardless of whatever the other disciples did (John 13:37; cf. Matt 26:33–35; Mark 14:29–31; Luke 22:33–34). "You will leave me all alone" reveals Jesus' disappointment and emotional tension. The sympathy and support of these men, imperfect as they were, meant much to him. Nevertheless, his chief resource was the Father, whose purpose he came to fulfill and by whose power he was able to execute it.

33 Jesus imparted to his disciples the information concerning his death and his provision for them that they might be calm and confident in the face of disillusionment and apparent disaster. "Peace" reiterates the statement of John 14:27: "Peace I leave with you; my peace I give you." Even in the hour of his greatest suffering he had an unshakable confidence in the victorious purpose of God. Jesus did not overlook the trial that would affect them as well as himself, for that was inevitable in a world alienated from God. He did proclaim victory over it.

Notes

19–26 In this general passage the synonyms ἐρωτάω (*erōtaō*) and αἰτέω (*aiteō*) are used interchangeably.

16:19—"Jesus saw that they wanted to *ask* him about this" (ἐρωτᾶν, *erōtan*).

16:19—"Are you *asking* one another" (ζητεῖτε, *zēteite*).

16:23—"You will no longer *ask* me anything" (ἐρωτήσετε, *erōtēsete*).
16:23—"My Father will give you whatever you *ask*" (αἰτήσητε, *aitēsēte*).
16:24—"Until now you have not *asked* for anything" (ἠτήσατε, *ētēsate*).
16:24—"*Ask* and you will receive" (αἰτεῖτε, *aiteite*).
16:26—"In that day you will *ask* in my name" (αἰτήσεσθε, *aitēsesthe*).
16:26—"I am not saying that I will *ask* the Father" (ἐρωτήσω, *erōtēsō*).

Ζητεῖτε (*zēteite*, 16:19) means simply "to investigate" or "interrogate" and is often translated "seek." Sometimes it connotes an argument. Ἐρωτάω (*erōtaō*, 16:19, 23, 26) does not refer to making a petition but to simple questioning between those who stand on equal footing. It implies that Jesus, as a human being, was open to dialogue and inquiry with others. His use of the term concerning himself and the Father again implies equality since his removal from the world would elevate him to a new relationship with God. Αἰτέω (*aiteō*, 16:23-24, 26) refers to making a petition for a favor rather than for an answer to a question and implies that the request is addressed to a superior. (For a full discussion, see Trench, pp. 143-46.)

C. The Last Prayer (17:1–26)

The prayer of Jesus recorded in this chapter is not identical with the prayer in Gethsemane reported in the Passion narrative of the synoptic Gospels (Matt 26:36-45; Mark 14:32-41; Luke 22:39-46). Its content is closely linked to that of the preceding chapters, especially those reputedly spoken in the upper room. The vocabulary, which contains such Johannine terms as "glory," "glorify," "sent," "believe," "world," "love," connects its content with the same topics in preceding sections of the Gospel. And Jesus' concern for his disciples makes more lucid his attitude toward them on previous occasions. The prayer is intended to summarize in Jesus' own words his relationship with the Father and the relationship he wished his disciples to maintain with him and the Father.

The prayer is divisible into three parts: (1) Jesus' prayer concerning himself (1–5), (2) his prayer for the disciples (6–19), and (3) his prayer for all believers present and future (20–26). Apparently the prayer was spoken either just before the small company left the room where they had eaten together or as they made their way out of the city, across the Kidron Valley to Gethsemane.

1. The prayer concerning himself

17:1–5

> ¹After Jesus said this, he looked toward heaven and prayed:
> "Father, the time has come. Glorify your Son, that your Son may glorify you. ²For you granted him authority over all people that he might give eternal life to all those you have given him. ³Now this is eternal life: that they may know you, the only true God, and Jesus Christ, whom you have sent. ⁴I have brought you glory on earth by completing the work you gave me to do. ⁵And now, Father, glorify me in your presence with the glory I had with you before the world began.

1 John recorded even the gesture of Jesus: "He lifted up his eyes" (lit. Gr.). This was a typical Jewish gesture of prayer, whether offered to God or to idols (Ps 121:1; 123:1; Ezek 33:25; Dan 4:34; John 11:41). The general conversation ended as Jesus began to talk to the Father. The prayer began with the announcement "The time has come." Jesus' consciousness of living by a "calendar" was manifest from the beginning of the Gospel. When Mary spoke to him at the wedding of Cana, evidently suggesting that he should

intervene in the tense social situation by manifesting his power, he informed her that his time had not yet come, (2:4). He did not present himself as the Messiah, for though he did perform a miracle, few knew what had taken place or who was responsible for the new supply of wine. When his brothers urged him to go to Jerusalem to gain publicity for himself, he refused to do so because "the right time has not yet come" (7:8). Twice in the prolonged controversy with his enemies Jesus escaped death because "his time had not yet come" (7:30; 8:20); but now he acknowledged that the time of crisis had arrived (cf. 12:23; 13:1). This announcement enhances the significance of the prayer because it becomes Jesus' evaluation of the purpose of his life, death, resurrection, and ascension.

The word "glorify" should be applied to the total complex of these events as the climax of the Incarnation. The Son glorified the Father by revealing in this act the sovereignty of God over evil, the compassion of God for men, and the finality of redemption for believers. It is the Johannine parallel to what Paul called the "mind" of Christ (Phil 2:5 KJV, translated in NIV as "attitude"). Jesus focused his entire career on fulfilling the Father's purpose and on delivering the Father's message. He now petitioned the Father to glorify him by returning him to the place he had before the world was created (v.5). The words accord with the statement of John 1:18: "God the only Son, who is at the Father's side [lit. 'in the bosom of the Father'], has made him known."

2-3 The two sentences following the petition are parenthetical and explanatory. The first (v.2) indicates the scope of the authority Christ exercised in his incarnate state. He was empowered to impart eternal life to those who had been given to him. This Gospel is replete with assertions that life is in Christ: "In him was life, and that life was the light of men" (1:4). "The Son of Man must be lifted up, that everyone who believes in him may have eternal life" (3:15-16). "The water I give him will become in him [who drinks it] a spring of water welling up to eternal life" (4:14). See also 5:21, 26; 6:33, 54; 10:10; 11:25; 14:6. These words and others like them emphatically express the central purpose of Jesus: to glorify the Father by imparting life to men.

The second sentence (v.3) defines the nature of eternal life. It is not described in chronological terms but by a relationship. Life is active involvement with environment; death is the cessation of involvement with the environment, whether it be physical or personal. The highest kind of life is involvement with the highest kind of environment. A worm is content to live in soil; we need not only the wider environment of earth, sea, and sky but also contact with other human beings. For the complete fulfillment of our being, we must know God. This, said Jesus, constitutes eternal life. Not only is it endless, since the knowledge of God would require an eternity to develop fully, but qualitatively it must exist in an eternal dimension. As Jesus said farther on in this prayer, eternal life would ultimately bring his disciples to a lasting association with him in his divine glory (v.24).

4-5 Although the final act of his career remained to be performed, Jesus asserted that he had completed his task. He took for granted that the last step would be taken. A clue to the proleptic assertion may be found in John 12:27-28: "For this very reason I came to this hour. Father, glorify your name." Though he was aware that he had the option of refusing the Cross and so escaping death, he had resolved irrevocably to complete the work for which he had been sent. To all intents and purposes it was already done. Though the obstacles were many and though the prospect was terrifying, Jesus never once faltered from doing the Father's will. He had one main petition: that the Father would receive him back to the glory he had relinquished to accomplish his task. This petition for a return to his pristine glory implies unmistakably his preexistence and equality with the Father. It confirms his claim that he and the Father are one (John 10:30).

2. The prayer concerning the disciples

17:6–19

> 6"I have revealed you to those whom you gave me out of the world. They were yours, you gave them to me and they have obeyed your word. 7Now they know that everything you have given me comes from you. 8For I gave them the words you gave me and they accepted them. They knew with certainty that I came from you, and they believed that you sent me. 9I pray for them. I am not praying for the world, but for those you have given me, for they are yours. 10All I have is yours, and all you have is mine. And glory has come to me through them. 11I will remain in the world no longer, but they are still in the world, and I am coming to you. Holy Father, protect them by the power of your name—the name you gave me—so that they may be one as we are one. 12While I was with them, I protected them and kept them safe by that name you gave me. None has been lost except the one doomed to destruction so that Scripture would be fulfilled.
>
> 13"I am coming to you now, but I say these things while I am still in the world, so that they may have the full measure of my joy within them. 14I have given them your word and the world has hated them, for they are not of the world any more than I am of the world. 15My prayer is not that you take them out of the world but that you protect them from the evil one. 16They are not of the world, even as I am not of it. 17Sanctify them by the truth; your word is truth. 18As you sent me into the world, I have sent them into the world. 19For them I sanctify myself, that they too may be truly sanctified.

By far the largest part of Jesus' prayer relates to the disciples. He was much more concerned about them than about himself. He was sure of the suffering that was inevitable and the victory that was certain. The disciples, however, were a variable quantity; in themselves they were likely to fail. He had already predicted that they would desert him (Matt 26:31; John 16:32). Nevertheless, he prayed for them with confidence that they would be kept by the Father's power and presented for a future ministry. Jesus gives the reasons for his confidence in the next three verses.

6–8 The disciples had been given to Jesus by the Father. The gift was irrevocable and the Father was able to guarantee it. Jesus had no doubt of the final outcome. The disciples were obedient; they had accepted the message Jesus gave them. In spite of much misunderstanding on their part, there is no evidence that those who were with Jesus in the upper room had rejected or doubted the truth he imparted to them. They may not have comprehended it instantly, as the text of John shows (2:22; 20:9). They recognized that Jesus' message came from God; and they accepted him as a messenger of God, as their own confession declared (16:30). From the outset of his ministry, the disciples had received him as the Messiah, and their conviction of his messiahship had grown progressively during the period of association with him. Now that the supreme test of their faith was impending, Jesus prayed that they might be preserved against the persecution that could separate them from him and from one another.

9 At this point, Jesus' intercession was confined to the Eleven who were present with him. He reminded the Father that these men were under his peculiar care. As in his prayer at Lazarus's grave, Jesus took for granted the concern of the Father for the immediate need and the provision he had already made in order to meet it.

10 Jesus' statement "All I have is yours, and all you have is mine" assumes his equality with the Father. Each has full title to the possessions of the other; they share the same interests and responsibilities. Jesus' words are a sample of the continued intercession that constitutes his present ministry (Rom 8:34).

11 Jesus asked for the continuation of the Father's protection of the disciples in the period of danger that lay ahead of them. The title "Holy Father" is unusual and is comparable to the phrase "Righteous Father" that appears in v.25. The holiness of God contrasts with the selfishness and evil of the world that confronted the disciples. On the basis of the holiness of God's character, Jesus requested the Father to preserve the disciples. The verb "protect" (*tēreō*) is generally used in John to mean "obey" in the sense of keeping commandments (8:51–52, 55; 14:15) or to "observe" the Sabbath (9:16). Here (17:11–12, 15) it is applied to persons in the sense of "preserve," with an implication of defense. "Name" stands for the power of God manifested in his person (cf. 5:43; 10:25; 12:28; 17:6, 26), for a name represents authoritatively the person it describes.

The unity mentioned here is not simply a unity achieved by legislation. It is a unity of nature because it is comparable to that of the Son and the Father. The unity of the church must spring from the common life that is imparted to all believers by the new birth; and it is manifested in their common love for Christ and for one another as they face a hostile world. The unity of the Son and the Father was manifested in the deep love that each sustained for the other and by the perfect obedience of the Son to the Father and the perfect response of the Father to the Son.

12 Jesus' request for the protection of the disciples was occasioned by the prospect of his leaving the world. They would still be remaining in it, exposed to its temptations and hostility. In reviewing his care of them to date, he used two different words: "protected" and "kept them safe." The former (*tēreō*) has been defined in the comment on the preceding verse; the latter (*phylassō*) means "to guard," "protect," or "observe conventions." Like other Johannine synonyms, the two may at times be used interchangeably, but there is a slight difference between them. *Tēreō* has the sense of protection by conservation; *phylassō*, by defense against external attack. Jesus stated that he had kept safely all the disciples except Judas. "The one doomed to destruction" (lit. "son of perdition") is a phrase used in only one other passage in the NT. In 2 Thessalonians 2:3 it is applied to the Antichrist. Because of this singular coincidence, some have assumed that the Antichrist will be Judas resurrected! More likely this phrase was a common Semitism denoting an abandoned character, one utterly lost and given over to evil. The language does not imply that Judas was a helpless victim who was destined to perdition against his will. Rather, it implies that, having made his decision, he had passed the point of no return; and, by so doing, he carried out what the Scriptures had indicated would happen. John does not identify the specific passage Jesus had in mind. A comparison with Peter's statement in Acts 1:20, after Judas's death, suggests that it was probably Psalm 69:25 or Psalm 109:6–8.

13 Jesus prayed not only for the safety of the disciples but also that they might have joy in spite of the coming conflict. The same sentiment had been expressed in the dialogue with them (15:11; 16:22, 24). There would be nothing in the attitude of the world to promote their joy; but, as with Jesus, their awareness of the approval of the Father and the consciousness of a task accomplished and the expectancy of glory would create true joy for them.

14 The very fact that the disciples received the message of God from Jesus differentiated them from the world at large. They had a different nature and a different affiliation. Such a radical contrast drew the hatred of the world, which always demands conformity to its viewpoint and practices. They had taken their stand with Jesus and would therefore be susceptible to the same rejection he had experienced.

15–16 Jesus did not, however, ask that they be removed from a disagreeable and dangerous environment. Like him, they had a mission to discharge and must remain to fulfill it, however perilous it might be. He did ask for protection for them from the evil one.

The declaration that "they are not of the world" gives the negative aspect of the previous prayer that they may be one as Jesus and the Father are one. The disciples' unity binds them to Christ and at the same time separates them from the world. John stresses the separation that results from difference of nature. This principle appears in the separation of antichrists from believers: "They went out from us, but they did not really belong to us" (1 John 2:19). The separation is inherent, not artificial.

17 "Sanctify" (*hagiazō*) means "to separate" or "to set apart," usually for some specially good purpose or use. Its derivative meaning thus becomes "dedicate" or "consecrate" and then "to revere" or "to purify." The believer is so changed by the working of God's Word in his life that he is separated from evil and to God. This new devotion, which results in separation from evil, produces purification of life and consecration to God's service. Since the Word of God is truth, it provides the unchanging standard for the course and character of life. The form of the expression "your word" raises the possibility that Jesus may have been referring to himself when he spoke. He had said that he was "the truth" (14:6); so as the Logos of God he embodied truth in its totality.

18 "Sent" implies equipment for a definite mission. Jesus united the disciples with himself in the work he began and expected them to continue. Just as the Father sent him with authority, so he gave them authority (cf. Matt 28:18–20); as he had come with a message of God's love and forgiveness, so they should proclaim the same; as he had come into danger and peril of death, so they would encounter the same problems; and as the Father had sent him to the victory of the Resurrection, so they could expect the same. His words include warning, commission, and encouragement.

19 In keeping with his words in v.17, Jesus did not mean that he intended to make himself more holy than he already was, when he said, "For their sakes I sanctify myself." Rather, he was devoting himself to God in the interest of his work for the disciples. His example of dedication to the will of the Father, demonstrated in his unswerving acceptance of the Cross, would be the standard for their sanctification.

The petitions of Jesus' prayer for the disciples define certain aspects of eternal life. The first is the authentic revelation of the Father in contrast to erroneous information or delusive myth. Jesus reinforced his claim to be the authorized revealer of the true God (v.6; cf. 1:18; 14:9–11). As his revelation was accepted, the disciples progressed to a knowledge of the Father and to a solid faith (v.8; cf. 16:25). This faith united them with Jesus so that they came under his protection and experienced security that eternal life imparts (v.12; cf. 10:28–29). Eternal life also implies sanctification—being set apart for the service of God.

Notes

---

15 The substantival adjective πονηροῦ (ponērou, "evil") may be either masculine or neuter. If the former, it means "from the evil person"; if the latter, "from the evil thing," or from evil as a principle. The allusions in the general context to Satan (13:2, 27; 14:30; 16:11) make the former rendering seem more fitting to this occasion.

17 "Your word" (ὁ λόγος ὁ σός, ho logos ho sos) is an unusual construction. Instead of using the genitive of the personal pronoun to express the idea of "your," the personal possessive pronoun is used, which generally emphasizes quality rather than possession alone. It implies that the "word" is peculiarly God's; it originates from him and is qualified by his personality rather than being a message that might originate with anyone but which he happened to give. If "word" (λόγος, logos) in this phrase is applied to Christ, the expression would be singularly appropriate because Jesus was the full and original expression of the Father's nature and mind and could have come only from him.

17, 19 Only the verb "sanctify" (ἁγιάζω, hagiazō) is used in John, perhaps because this Gospel emphasizes the act of sanctification rather than the process or quality. The verb (ἁγίασον, hagiason) in v.17 is aorist imperative, which speaks of an initial, and presumably complete, separation. In v.19 ἡγιασμένοι (hēgiasmenoi, "have been sanctified") is a perfect passive participle, which implies a fixed and final state. As Jesus used the word concerning himself, he may have been referring to the settled determination he had from eternity past (Rev 13:8) to carry out the Father's will, even to death. This act of sanctification by Christ would set apart his followers for all eternity.

---

3. The prayer concerning future believers

17:20–26

20"My prayer is not for them alone. I pray also for those who will believe in me through their message, 21that all of them may be one, Father, just as you are in me and I am in you. May they also be in us so that the world may believe that you have sent me. 22I have given them the glory that you gave me, that they may be one as we are one: 23I in them and you in me. May they be brought to complete unity to let the world know that you sent me and have loved them even as you have loved me.

24"Father, I want those you have given me to be with me where I am, and to see my glory, the glory you have given me because you loved me before the creation of the world.

25"Righteous Father, though the world does not know you, I know you, and they know that you have sent me. 26I have made you known to them, and will continue to make you known in order that the love you have for me may be in them and that I myself may be in them."

20 The last section of Jesus' prayer shows that he expected the failure of the disciples to be only temporary. The entire tone of the farewell discourse is built on the assumption that after the Resurrection they would renew their faith and carry on a new ministry in the power of the Holy Spirit. The provisions and warnings of the upper room discourse presuppose the continuation of Jesus' work through these men. It illumines his declara-

tion recorded by Matthew: "I will build my church" (Matt 16:18). Jesus expected the ministry of the Spirit in the disciples to result in adding more believers to their number. So his prayer includes all believers in all ages.

21 At this point, the burden of the prayer is for unity. Jesus had already stressed the need for mutual love that would bind them together for their common task. Now, foreseeing the addition of many more who would increase the diversity of temperaments, backgrounds, and interests, he made a special plea that all might be one. The standard is not an institutional but a personal unity: "Just as you are in me and I am in you. . . . that they may be one as we are one" (vv.21–22). He was not calling for uniformity, since he and the Father are distinct from each other and have different functions; nor was he calling for agreement in external opinion. He predicated that the unity would be one of nature; for he and the Father, while distinguishable in person, are one being. As previously stated, the new birth brings believers into the family of God by spiritual generation (1:12–13). The concept parallels the Pauline teaching on the body of Christ, that all believers belong by a vital rather than merely a formal relationship (1 Cor 12:12–13). The Johannine symbol of the vine in ch. 15 contains the same idea of a vital unity in which every separate branch is still an integral part of the one vine. The purpose of this unity is the maintenance of a convincing testimony before the world to the revelation of God in Christ and to his love for the disciples. Through the common witness and experience of the disciples, Jesus wished to establish the fact of his divine origin and of the love of God for men. The unity is another aspect of eternal life because where there is a common source of life there must be a common likeness of expression. As the central life of the vine appears in all the branches and makes them fruitful, so genuine eternal life imparted by Christ will unify his people.

22–23 The "glory" the Father had given Jesus was the triumphant task of redeeming men to God. As Hebrews states, he was "crowned with glory and honor because he suffered death" in the process of "bringing many sons to glory" (Heb 2:9–10). By sharing in his calling, they participate in his glory and are united with him and with one another. God and man are together involved in bringing the new creation into being. The effect of this united testimony is a confirmation of the divine mission of Jesus and of God's love for believers.

24 The final aspect of eternal life relates to ultimate destiny. The final attainment would be to be with Christ (cf. 14:3) and to see his glory. "See" (*theōrōsin*) in this context means more than to recognize by form; "observe" would be a better translation. The disciples had witnessed his incarnate life, which was a humiliation, voluntarily accepted for their sakes. Its process was epitomized by Jesus' action at the Last Supper, when he took the place of a servant to wash the disciples' feet (13:1–15). Now, on the eve of being "glorified," he desired that the disciples might see him as he really was. Perhaps the writer had this in mind when he wrote in his First Epistle, "'We shall be like him, for we shall see him as he is" (1 John 3:2). "Before the creation of the world" is a further assertion of Christ's preexistence. This shows that the binding power of unity in the Triune God is love.

25–26 The title "Righteous Father" parallels the title "Holy Father" in v.11. Both are unique and appear only in this prayer. The entire prayer is based on the righteousness of God, who will vindicate the Son by glorifying him. Jesus' revelation of God was

167

founded on personal knowledge and personal communion. When he spoke of God, it was on the basis of intimate acquaintance and not philosophical speculation. The essence of the revelation lay in the love of God, which Jesus exhibited toward the disciples. His purpose was to perfect his union with them, that they in turn might know the Father. Jesus wanted to include them in the inner fellowship of the Triune God.

IV. The Passion of the Word (18:1–20:31)

A. *The Arrest in Gethsemane*

18:1–11

> ¹When he had finished praying, Jesus left with his disciples and crossed the Kidron Valley. On the other side there was an olive grove, and he and his disciples went into it.
> ²Now Judas, who betrayed him, knew the place, because Jesus had often met there with his disciples. ³So Judas came to the grove, guiding a detachment of soldiers and some officials from the chief priests and Pharisees. They were carrying torches, lanterns and weapons.
> ⁴Jesus, knowing all that was going to happen to him, went out and asked them, "Who is it you want?"
> ⁵"Jesus of Nazareth," they replied.
> "I am he," Jesus said. (And Judas the traitor was standing there with them.) ⁶When Jesus said, "I am he," they drew back and fell to the ground.
> ⁷Again he asked them, "Who is it you want?"
> And they said, "Jesus of Nazareth."
> ⁸"I told you that I am he," Jesus answered. "If you are looking for me, then let these men go." ⁹This happened so that the words he had spoken would be fulfilled: "I have not lost one of those you gave me."
> ¹⁰Then Simon Peter, who had a sword, drew it and struck the high priest's servant, cutting off his right ear. (The servant's name was Malchus.)
> ¹¹Jesus commanded Peter, "Put your sword away! Shall I not drink the cup the Father has given me?"

1 Jesus and the disciples left the room where they had convened, descended from the city, crossed the Kidron Valley, and made their way up the lower slope of the Mount of Olives, which lay to the east of Jerusalem. The Kidron River is a winter torrent, dry in the summer, but a flowing stream during the winter and spring rains. It runs southward along the east side of the city and joins the Valley of Hinnom and the Tyropoeon Valley south of Jerusalem. Gethsemane, the name assigned to the olive grove on the side of the mountain where Jesus and his disciples went, means "oil press." The city was filled with visitors at the Passover season and would have had little room for lodging within its walls. Neither Jesus nor the disciples were wealthy; so they probably camped outdoors during their visit to the temple for the Passover Week. The site of the garden is still marked by a small grove of ancient trees.

2 Jesus often used the Garden of Gethsemane as a meeting place with his disciples (cf. Luke 22:39). Judas, probably having attempted to find Jesus at the house where he and the others ate the Last Supper, went to Gethsemane, expecting to locate him there.

3 The Greek word for "detachment of soldiers" (*speira*) has been traditionally rendered "cohort," from the Latin *cohors*, which denotes a tenth of a legion, or about six hundred men. The noun is accompanied by the definite article, which refers to some particular

band of men, perhaps the detachment connected with the Castle of Antonia, the Roman barracks in Jerusalem. The synoptic Gospels agree that the arrest was effected by a "crowd" (*ochlos*), which connotes an armed mob rather than an organized military guard (Matt 26:47; Mark 14:43). Luke uses the phrase "officers of the temple guard" (Luke 22:52), which would refer to the temple police rather than to Roman legionnaires. It is not impossible that the hysterical alarm of the priests caused them to ask aid from Pilate in arresting Jesus, since the temple police had failed on a previous occasion (John 7:32, 45–47). Pilate, knowing the volatile character of the Passover pilgrims, would probably have been disposed to granting such a request, though a full complement of six hundred men would hardly seem necessary. The torches and the lanterns were needed, as the arrest took place at night and would require a search in the darkness of the olive grove.

4–6 The author lays great emphasis on Jesus' consciousness of surrounding circumstances and his own destiny (cf. John 6:64; 13:1, 3, 11, 18). He was not taken unwillingly or by surprise. For a long time he had been aware of the plot against his life and, had he wished, he could have escaped. On at least two previous occasions he had withdrawn from the danger zone: once when he retreated beyond the Jordan into Perea (John 10:40) and again after the raising of Lazarus, when he moved into the desert region (11:54). Now "the time" had come (cf. 17:1). He did not wait to be apprehended but voluntarily confronted his enemies.

In the darkness of the garden they were not sure which man they wanted. So in answer to his question they replied, "Jesus of Nazareth." John omits the signal of Judas and mentions only Jesus' own statement for the identification. Jesus' reply startled the arresting party by its openness and readiness and possibly because it was like the claim he had made previously: "I am" (8:24, 28, 58). If it were intended as an assertion of deity, his calm demeanor and commanding presence temporarily unnerved his captors.

7–9 Jesus' chief intent seems not to have been to advance a claim but rather to shield the disciples. In a sense, he sacrificed himself for their safety. He had promised the Father that he would protect them (17:12), and he fulfilled his guarantee in the voluntary surrender of his life. The utterance in v.8 is a graphic illustration of the principle of substitutionary atonement that pervades this Gospel (cf. 1:29; 3:14–16; 10:11, 15–18; 12:32; 17:19).

10 The action of Peter illustrates the curious combination of loyalty and obtuseness that characterized him. Realizing that Jesus was endangered, Peter was courageous enough to come to his defense and risk his own safety by doing so. To this extent he justified his boastful promise that if all others should forsake Jesus, he would not (John 13:37; cf. Mark 14:29–31). Evidently Peter was excited and missed his aim, for he cut off the right ear of Malchus, the high priest's servant. The use of the definite article "the" with "servant" may indicate that Malchus was the special deputy of the high priest in this action and that he was in the forefront of confrontation. Someone in the apostolic band, presumably the writer, remembered the man and his name. This incidental recollection is a hint that the Johannine account rests on eyewitness testimony.

11 Jesus' command to Peter declared his disapproval of Peter's sudden and violent intervention. Had Jesus desired defense, he could have summoned angelic aid, but he did not do so (cf. Matt 26:52–53). "Shall I not drink the cup the Father has given me?" expresses both the necessity of his suffering and his absolute commitment to the fulfillment of the Father's purpose. The word "cup" connects this statement with the prayer in Gethsemane, which only the Synoptics record (Matt 26:42; Mark 14:36; Luke 22:42). Though the writer must have known of Jesus' struggle, he recorded only the outcome. Jesus accepted the Father's will and calmly moved on to its fulfillment.

B. *The Hearing Before Annas*

18:12–14, 19–24

> [12]Then the detachment of soldiers with its commander and the Jewish officials arrested Jesus. They bound him [13]and brought him first to Annas, who was the father-in-law of Caiaphas, the high priest that year. [14]Caiaphas was the one who had advised the Jews that it would be good if one man died for the people.
>
> [19]Meanwhile, the high priest questioned Jesus about his disciples and his teaching.
>
> [20]"I have spoken openly to the world," Jesus replied. "I always taught in synagogues or at the temple, where all the Jews come together. I said nothing in secret. [21]Why question me? Ask those who heard me. Surely they know what I said."
>
> [22]When Jesus said this, one of the officials nearby struck him in the face. "Is that any way to answer the high priest?" he demanded.
>
> [23]"If I said something wrong," Jesus replied, "testify as to what is wrong. But if I spoke the truth, why did you strike me?" [24]Then Annas sent him, still bound, to Caiaphas the high priest.

12–14 With the willing surrender of Jesus, the arrest was complete. The "commander" (*chiliarchos*) was the officer in charge, possibly the executive of the Roman garrison in Jerusalem (cf. the use of the same term in Acts 22:24, 26, 27, 28; 23:17, 19, 22). The technical expression strengthens the impression that the Romans supported the action of the Jewish hierarchy. Jesus was taken at once to the residence of the high priest. Tradition places it on the south side of Jerusalem, just west of the Tyropoeon valley and not far from the city wall. Annas had served as high priest from A.D. 6 to 15, when he was deposed by the Roman procurator, Valerius Gratus. Four of Annas's sons were among those who succeeded him. His son-in-law, Caiaphas, held office from A.D. 18 until A.D. 36, within which period Jesus' active ministry occurred. Although others held the priestly office, Annas seems to have been the elder statesman and advisor, particularly for Caiaphas.

John's Gospel alone takes note of Christ's appearance before Annas. Luke suggests that some time may have elapsed between the interview with Annas and the confrontation with Caiaphas and the council because he locates the latter at "daybreak" (Luke 22:66). If Jesus were held in custody till the elders could be summoned to a meeting in the morning, it is quite possible that he was somewhere in the house of the high priest. The main hearing seems to have followed in the early hours of the morning, before the members of the Jewish tribunal. The hearing before Annas was probably a preliminary attempt to evaluate the case and enable them to formulate some sort of charge to lay before Pilate. As the elder statesman, Annas was regarded with great respect by his contemporaries and must have been considered an expert in religious matters. If it is assumed that the text is in its original order (see note), he is called "high priest" (as also is Caiaphas, 18:24). Since Luke speaks of "the high priesthood of Annas and Caiaphas" (Luke 3:2), it may be that while Caiaphas was the official priest recognized by the Roman government, Annas remained "the power behind the throne."

19 The questioning focused on Jesus' disciples and his teaching. The number and activity of the former would be important if subversion was suspected, and the teaching would be scrutinized for possible revolutionary elements.

20–21 Jesus had nothing to hide. He had so frequently and openly declared the principles of his kingdom that there would be many witnesses who could narrate in detail what he had taught. The interrogation by Annas was unnecessary because public testimony to Jesus' teaching and attitude would be easily available, especially in Jerusalem, where he had been speaking to crowds for several days.

22–24 Jesus' answer impressed one of the retainers as disrespectful to the high priest, and he struck Jesus in the face. The act was illegal. No sentence had been passed, and a prisoner was not subject to abuse, especially when uncondemned. In spite of Jesus' protest, nothing was done; and he was sent bound to Caiaphas. Just how far Jesus had to be transported from Annas to Caiaphas is not known. It is possible that they occupied rooms in the same building, in which case little time would be required for the transfer. John says nothing about the hearing before Caiaphas. The Synoptics indicate that it included an appearance before the council of the elders, who must have been specially summoned for the occasion (Matt 26:57–68; Mark 14:53–65: Luke 22:66–71).

Notes

12–27 The Sinaitic Syriac changes the order of these verses to vv.12–13, 24, 14–15, 19–23, 16–18, 25–27; a somewhat similar arrangement occurs in the Palestinian Syriac. Although this change of order would simplify the account and facilitate harmonization with the Synoptics, the textual evidence is not sufficient to support it. Morris comments that a general corruption of the original text into its present form is quite unlikely and that the change in the Sinaitic Syriac is probably a harmonizing expedient. The existing text does present a difficulty, but it is not insuperable (NIC, pp. 748–49).

C. *The Denial by Peter*

18:15–18, 25–27

15Simon Peter and another disciple were following Jesus. Because this disciple was known to the high priest, he went with Jesus into the high priest's courtyard, 16but Peter had to wait outside at the door. The other disciple, who was known to the high priest, came back, spoke to the girl on duty there and brought Peter in.

17"Surely you are not another of this man's disciples?" the girl at the door asked Peter.

He replied, "I am not."

18It was cold, and the servants and officials stood around a fire they had made to keep warm. Peter also was standing with them, warming himself.

25As Simon Peter stood warming himself, he was asked, "Surely you are not another of his disciples?"

He denied it, saying, "I am not."

26One of the high priest's servants, a relative of the man whose ear Peter had cut off, challenged him, "Didn't I see you with him in the olive grove?" 27Again Peter denied it, and at that moment a rooster began to crow.

15-16 The imperfect tense of the verb "to follow" (*ēkolouthei*) is descriptive. It implies that Peter and an unnamed disciple had traced Jesus and his captors back from Gethsemane over the Kidron Valley to the residence of the high priest in Jerusalem. The identity of the other disciple is not disclosed, nor does the account specify that it was "the disciple whom Jesus loved" (cf. 13:23; 19:26; 20:2–3; 21:20, 24). The association of the two, however, would favor that view since they appear together both at the Last Supper (13:23–24) and on the morning of the Resurrection (20:2–3). This anonymous disciple was known to the household of the high priest and readily obtained access for himself and Peter. The basis for this acquaintance is not explained. On the assumption that this disciple was John, it may be that the family had connections with the priesthood, either by business relationships or possibly by marital ties. Salome, the mother of John, was a sister of Mary, Jesus' mother (cf. John 19:25 with Mark 15:40), and would have been equally related to Elizabeth, whose husband, Zechariah, was a priest (Luke 1:36). The evidence is tenuous, but the author does exhibit a considerable knowledge of Jerusalem and the events that took place there. "Courtyard" is a translation of the Greek *aulē*, which could be rendered "palace" (cf. Note on 10:16). The former rendering (NIV) is preferable here in view of the fact that Peter was not in an inner assembly room but was standing with servants and retainers by a fire (v.18).

17 Apparently Peter's first statement of denial accompanied his admittance to the courtyard; the last occurred somewhat later, perhaps just as Jesus was about to be taken to the council chamber. There are minor differences in all four accounts of the denial, but there are broad general agreements. The first denial was a reply to a question asked by the girl who tended the gate and granted access to Peter and the other disciple. The wording of the Greek text, *me kai su* ("are you not?"), implies that the girl recognized both the unnamed disciple and Peter as followers of Jesus. Matthew and Mark agree that the first questioner was a servant girl (Matt 26:69; Mark 14:66), but they do not connect her with the disciples' entrance into the courtyard. Luke agrees that the first accuser was a servant girl who thought Peter was one of Jesus' disciples (Luke 22:56).

18 Jerusalem is twenty-six hundred feet above sea level, and on a spring night the air is chilly. The servants had lighted a charcoal fire (*anthrakian*), which would warm only those near it and would not give off a great deal of light. Peter must have edged toward it, hoping to absorb some warmth, yet not wishing to make himself visible. He certainly did not want to be recognized again!

25 The focus of attention on Peter is interrupted by the author's reversion to the interrogation of Jesus by the high priest (vv.19–24). Matthew and Mark agree that the second interrogator was a girl; Luke, however, does not state whether it was a man or a woman (Matt 26:71; Mark 14:69; Luke 22:58). The first two questions were introduced by the particle *mē*, which calls for a negative answer. Peter's answer to this suggested negative drew him into a position he could not escape from and caused him to make an emphatic denial: "I am not."

26-27 The third question, according to John, was raised by a relative of Malchus and was worded in such a way as to expect an affirmative answer. He was sure that he had seen Peter in the olive grove. Matthew and Mark agree that the questioner identified Peter as Galilean (Matt 26:73; Mark 14:70), and Luke agrees with them at this point (Luke 22:59). As the questioning proceeded from suspicion to reasonable certainty,

Peter became more nervous. With increasing vehemence he disavowed any connection with Jesus, and on the third occasion the rooster crowed. The shrill sound must have recalled Jesus' words spoken a few hours before: "Before the rooster crows, you will disown me three times" (John 13:38). The author adds no further comment at this point, but the fact that he recorded the denial implies that it was a turning point in Peter's experience. It was a revelation of his own weakness that he could not escape. It no doubt prompted self-examination, and Peter's response was exactly the opposite of that of Judas. Judas in his failure fell into despair; Peter returned to Christ.

D. *The Trial Before Pilate*

18:28–19:16

28Then the Jews led Jesus from Caiaphas to the palace of the Roman governor. By now it was early morning, and to avoid ceremonial uncleanness the Jews did not enter the palace; they wanted to be able to eat the Passover. 29So Pilate came out to them and asked, "What charges are you bringing against this man?"

30"If he were not a criminal," they replied, "we would not have handed him over to you."

31Pilate said, "Take him yourselves and judge him by your own law."

"But we have no right to execute anyone," the Jews objected. 32This happened so that the words Jesus had spoken indicating the kind of death he was going to die would be fulfilled.

33Pilate then went back inside the palace, summoned Jesus and asked him, "Are you the king of the Jews?"

34"Is that your own idea," Jesus asked, "or did others talk to you about me?"

35"Do you think I am a Jew?" Pilate replied. "It was your people and your chief priests who handed you over to me. What is it you have done?"

36Jesus said, "My kingdom is not of this world. If it were, my servants would fight to prevent my arrest by the Jews. But now my kingdom is from another place."

37"You are a king, then!" said Pilate.

Jesus answered, "You are right in saying I am a king. In fact, for this reason I was born, and for this I came into the world, to testify to the truth. Everyone on the side of truth listens to me."

38"What is truth?" Pilate asked. With this he went out again to the Jews and said, "I find no basis for a charge against him. 39But it is your custom for me to release to you one prisoner at the time of the Passover. Do you want me to release 'the king of the Jews'?"

40They shouted back, "No, not him! Give us Barabbas!" Now Barabbas had taken part in a rebellion.

19:1Then Pilate took Jesus and had him flogged. 2The soldiers twisted together a crown of thorns and put it on his head. They clothed him in a purple robe 3and went up to him again and again, saying, "Hail, O king of the Jews!" And they struck him in the face.

4Once more Pilate came out and said to the Jews, "Look, I am bringing him out to you to let you know that I find no basis for a charge against him." 5When Jesus came out wearing the crown of thorns and the purple robe, Pilate said to them, "Here is the man!"

6As soon as the chief priests and their officials saw him, they shouted, "Crucify! Crucify!"

But Pilate answered, "You take him and crucify him. As for me, I find no basis for a charge against him."

7The Jews insisted, "We have a law, and according to that law he must die, because he claimed to be the Son of God."

8When Pilate heard this, he was even more afraid, 9and he went back inside the palace. "Where do you come from?" he asked Jesus, but Jesus gave him no answer. 10"Do you refuse to speak to me?" Pilate said. "Don't you realize I have power either to free you or to crucify you?"

11Jesus answered, "You would have no power over me if it were not given to you from above. Therefore the one who handed me over to you is guilty of a greater sin."

12From then on, Pilate tried to set Jesus free, but the Jews kept shouting, "If you let this man go, you are no friend of Caesar. Anyone who claims to be a king opposes Caesar."

13When Pilate heard this, he brought Jesus out and sat down on the judge's seat at a place known as The Stone Pavement (which in Aramaic is Gabbatha). 14It was the day of Preparation of Passover Week, about the sixth hour.

"Here is your king," Pilate said to the Jews.

15But they shouted, "Take him away! Take him away! Crucify him!"

"Shall I crucify your king?" Pilate asked.

"We have no king but Caesar," the chief priests answered.

16Finally Pilate handed him over to them to be crucified. So the soldiers took charge of Jesus.

This account of Jesus' trial before Pilate is the longest in the four Gospels. Whereas the other three accounts deal largely with the legal charges, John's narrative places more importance on Jesus' concern with Pilate and on Pilate's shifting attitude. Its psychological portrait of Pilate is comparable to that of the Samaritan woman at the well of Sychar (ch. 4) or that of the blind man (ch. 9). The Johannine presentation makes it more of an interview than a trial, though some of the legal details are plainly described.

28 John does not describe the early morning session of the council. There Caiaphas put Jesus on oath to declare whether or not he was the Son of God; and on his assertion that he was, Jesus was condemned on a charge of blasphemy (Mark 14:60–64). The penalty under Jewish law was death. But because the high priest had no authority to execute a death sentence, it was necessary to transfer the case to the Roman prefect, Pontius Pilate. He was in Jerusalem at that time, for the Passover Week was always a period when Jewish nationalistic sentiment ran high and uprisings were likely to occur. In order to keep close control of the city, Pilate and his troops were there to handle any emergency that might arise.

After the verdict of the Sanhedrin, the prisoner was moved to Pilate's residence. The location is uncertain. It may have been the palace of Herod, on the west side of the city, near the present Jaffa gate; or it may have been the Tower of Antonia, on the north side of the temple enclosure, where the Roman barracks were located.

"Early morning" would probably mean about seven or eight o'clock. There may have been time for the last session of the Jewish council after sunrise since it was illegal to pronounce a death sentence at night. The Jewish delegation did not enter into the courtroom because entering a Gentile home or business room entailed seven days' defilement. Inasmuch as the Passover was imminent, they did not wish to be excluded from the feast for ceremonial uncleanness.

29–30 Pilate's initial question was the normal opening inquiry of a trial: "What charges are you bringing against this man?" Pilate was proceeding by the usual routine of Roman law and would not automatically pronounce a sentence without knowing the alleged crime. The answer was elusive. The high priest no doubt knew that Jesus was not guilty of any crime under Roman law and that there was no evidence to support a charge.

31 Pilate took much the same position Gallio did at Paul's arrest in Corinth (Acts 18:12–16). An argument about the ceremonial requirements of Jewish law had no standing in a Roman court, and Pilate was ready to dismiss the case. There is a possibility that

he had already been approached by the priest concerning the arrest of Jesus and was unconvinced of the justice of their case. He may have been suspicious of the legality of of their action and would not want to do anything that would place his rulership in jeopardy. The Jews' admission that they could not execute the prisoner was a confession of their intention. Pilate was shrewd enough to realize that their motive was not a sincere desire to remove a dangerous revolutionary. Matthew states that Pilate "knew that it was out of envy that they had handed Jesus over to him" (Matt 27:18).

32 The introduction of Roman action at this point insured death by crucifixion, if the Jews could persuade Pilate to render a verdict against Jesus. Jewish capital punishment was inflicted by stoning; but crucifixion would place Jesus under the curse of God (Deut 21:22–23; cf. Gal 3:13). His messianic claims would be discredited, and the rejection would be justified. The manner of death is explicitly connected with Jesus' own prophecy (John 3:14; 12:32–33). Ironically, the death that the Jewish hierarchy regarded as a final negation of Jesus' claims became the means of justification apart from the law (Gal 3:13).

33 Puzzled by the Jewish attitude, Pilate withdrew to the audience chamber within the building and summoned Jesus. His question to Jesus was emphatic: "Are *you* the king of the Jews?" (italics mine), as if he were asking for a straightforward answer because he did not trust the priests. The sentence could be translated as an exclamation: "So *you* are the king of the Jews, are you!" Pilate may also have been expressing his surprise that Jesus did not look like a pretender to the vacant throne of Judaism and seemed much less assertive than such persons usually are. Pilate had expected to meet a sullen or belligerent rebel and met instead the calm majesty of confident superiority. He could not reconcile the character of the prisoner with the charge brought against him.

34 Jesus' reply irritated Pilate, for he was accustomed to receiving answers to his questions, not challenges. Since he had shown sufficient interest in Jesus to confer with him personally, Jesus began to probe him to ascertain how sincere that interest might be. Was Pilate asking for information on his own initiative, or was he merely following a legal procedure at the instigation of the Jewish hierarchy?

35 Pilate's reply was a question that expressed his indignation. Literally, he asked, "I am not a Jew am I?" His question is introduced by the particle *mēti*, which calls for a negative answer. The response conveys the feeling that Pilate did not want to be classified as a Jew. He insisted that he was merely endeavoring to find the key to the puzzling case the Jewish leaders had brought before him. He had not originated the accusation, but he wanted to know what Jesus had done to arouse their hatred.

36 Jesus' answer to this question bewildered Pilate. Jesus asserted that his kingdom was not of this world because he had no military support and did not relate to any geographic locality. He did not, however, deny that "king" could be his proper title. He affirmed that his kingdom had a different origin and a different character from any Pilate knew. Those who served Jesus were not fighting men. Had he been an ordinary revolutionary, he would have offered armed resistance to those who took him captive.

37 Without attempting to argue about an abstraction that must have seemed irrational to him, Pilate came back to the central question: "So you are a king, then, aren't you?" (my translation). Jesus assented by confirming Pilate's conclusion. Then Jesus declared that his purpose was to bear testimony to truth, and he intimated that anyone who was devoted to truth would listen to him. The obvious inference from his words would be that he came into the world from another realm, that whoever did not listen to him would not be characterized by truth, and that if Pilate really wanted to know what truth was, he would give Jesus his earnest attention. Jesus was more interested in appealing to Pilate than in defending himself. This method appears in all of his other interviews in this Gospel. In each of them Jesus' focus was on reaching the heart of the person he addressed, not simply in magnifying himself. He made an appeal to Pilate, not for acquittal or mercy, but for recognition of truth.

The combined statement, "For this reason I was born, and for this I came into the world" can be linked with John 1. Morris points out that this expression is a peculiar combination (NIC, p. 771). It reinforces Jesus' statement in this Gospel that he was fully aware of both his origin and destiny (John 8:14). Jesus must have meant that he had existed in a preincarnate state. Instead of advertising his deity, Jesus simply took it for granted.

38 Pilate's reply, "What is truth?" is difficult to interpret. Was it facetious, scornful, impatient, despairing, or sincere? Even from the context it is not possible to be sure what he meant. Pilate's immediate response was to declare Jesus innocent of any crime. He may have regarded him as a harmless philosopher or as an impractical dreamer. Certainly he did not look on Jesus as a dangerous subversive. His language does not imply that he attributed moral perfection to Jesus but only that Jesus had not transgressed any law that would have made him liable to punishment.

39 Aware, however, that there were political overtones in the situation that called for some sort of action, Pilate groped for a solution that would be satisfactory to all concerned. Although no other record of it can be found, there must have been the custom of releasing one prisoner at every Passover as a means of placating the Jewish population. Pilate seized on the opportunity to appeal to the masses and suggested that he would release Jesus if they demanded it. His proposal assumed that Jesus was popular with the general crowd, who did not always favor the hierarchy. Pilate may also have been indulging in finely honed sarcasm when he referred to Jesus as "the king of the Jews." If Jesus were not released, the people would be guilty of the death of the one they called their king.

40 Pilate miscalculated the attitude of the crowd at this point. They had been instructed by the priests to ask for the death of Jesus; so instead of his release, they demanded that of a brigand named Barabbas. Quite likely Barabbas was a guerrilla "resistance fighter" who had been captured by the Romans and was being held for execution. In the eyes of the people, he was considered a champion of a free Israel and possibly something of a hero. The word applied to him (*lēstēs*) does not refer to a thief in the ordinary sense but to an outlaw or insurrectionist. The name Barabbas is Aramaic, meaning "son of the father." By a strange irony the pseudo-son of the father was released, but the real Son of the Father was crucified.

19:1 The scourging of Jesus was the usual accompaniment of crucifixion. The Roman scourge consisted of a wooden handle to which several rawhide thongs were fastened. Into each thong small butterfly shaped pieces of metal or bone were fixed. Wielded by a powerful arm, the scourge was a deadly weapon, which in a few strokes would strip the flesh from a man's back. Frequently death followed immediately so that the victim did not survive for crucifixion. Evidently Pilate intended to make an appeal to the sympathy of the mob, in hope that they would be satisfied with the scourging and would call for Jesus' release.

2–3 The legionnaires who had been detailed to administer the scourging amused themselves by a crude joke. Knowing that Jesus was called "king of the Jews," they threw a scarlet cloak about his shoulders, twisted a crown from a thorny vine that grew in the vicinity, and mocked him with the salutation "Hail, O king of the Jews!" as they slapped his face.

4–5 As the soldiers brought him out to the view of the crowd, Pilate, having once more declared Jesus' innocence, said, "Here is the man!" Pilate may have thought that the ironic spectacle of a king whose crown was thorns, his robe a cast-off cloak, and his status a prisoner would change their attitude. If so, he was speedily disillusioned.

6–7 The Jewish officials demanded crucifixion for no good reason Pilate could determine. In disgust he told them to crucify him themselves, for no charge could be brought against him. Pilate must have realized that the Sanhedrin could not execute the sentence. His apparent relegation of Jesus to them was an act of sarcasm. The Jews knew this and made a new approach to Pilate, claiming that by their law Jesus was worthy of death for blasphemy because he claimed to be the Son of God. Their charge corroborates the fact that he had claimed to be the Son of God (see comments on 10:34–38). So they invoked the law of blasphemy (Lev 24:16) as the ground for their insistence on Jesus' crucifixion.

8–9 To the Jews, Jesus' claim was the height of sacrilege. For Pilate, however, it had a different meaning. In pagan mythology the Olympian deities frequently consorted with men and women, and their semi-divine offspring, such as Hercules, had appeared on the earth and performed miraculous deeds. Hardened as he was, Pilate feared lest he should offend one of these visitors. His further questioning of Jesus was an attempt to ascertain who Jesus was. If Jesus really was a supernatural being, Pilate did not wish to be responsible for mistreating him. Divine judgment would certainly be the inevitable consequence. The silence of Jesus, like his silence in the presence of Herod (Luke 23:6–11), meant that he could accomplish nothing with a trifler. Pilate had already pronounced Jesus innocent; so the case resolved itself to the alternative of release or a gross perversion of justice.

10 Jesus' refusal to answer him angered Pilate, whose conceit and arrogance were shown by his question: "Don't you realize I have power either to free you or to crucify you?" He was insulted because Jesus had not shown him more deference. Pilate's assertion of authority seems almost ridiculous in contrast with the weakness and indecision he exhibited in this case. Jesus, who could view the situation in its true light, knew that though Pilate had the legal authority of which he boasted, he was really hampered by political pressures.

11 Jesus looked on Pilate as checked by the hand of God. Pilate was simply an instrument in the divine purpose. The real guilt lay with those who had delivered Jesus to Pilate in the first place. The reference is to Caiaphas and the Jewish hierarchy who had initiated the trial.

12 Jesus' penetrating analysis of the situation made Pilate more eager than ever to release him. But the popular pressure was too strong. The cry "If you let this man go, you are no friend of Caesar" carried the day. The phrase "a friend of Caesar" was more than a casual allusion to Roman patriotism. It usually denoted a supporter or associate of the emperor, a member of the important inner circle. The cry was a veiled threat: if Pilate exonerated Jesus, the high priest would report to Rome that Pilate had refused to bring a rival pretender to justice and was perhaps plotting to establish a new political alliance of his own. Tiberius, the reigning emperor, was notoriously bitter and suspicious of rivals. If such a report were sent to him, he would instantly end Pilate's political career and probably his life, too.

13 Jesus' analysis of Pilate's situation accentuated the dilemma he found himself entangled in. If he condemned Jesus to satisfy the Jewish hierarchy, he would be making a travesty of Roman justice. If he released Jesus, he would add to his contention with the hierarchy and would endanger his already shaky political future.

The decision could no longer be deferred. "The Stone Pavement" could have been in the Castle of Antonia, which housed the Roman garrison in Jerusalem. The castle stood on a rocky height of land, which accords with the Aramaic "Gabbatha," meaning "ridge" or "height."

14–15 The time in view here depends on the method of reckoning "the sixth hour." If it were reckoned from midnight, it would be about six o'clock in the morning; if from sunrise, which accords better with John's general procedure, it would be about noon. The problem is further complicated by the testimony of Mark, who states that the Crucifixion took place at "the third hour" (Mark 15:25). Perhaps the best solution is that Mark indicates that the trial came early and that the execution occurred on mid-morning, while John stresses the fact that it was accomplished before noon. The expressions of time are approximations rather than precise statements of hours; John qualified his expression by saying "about."

Pilate presented the bleeding, disheveled figure to the crowd with these words: "Here is your king." In their bitter irony, these words show Pilate's contempt for the Jews. As the people clamored for Jesus' crucifixion, Pilate scornfully asked, "Shall I crucify your king?" The reply of the chief priests is astonishing: "We have no king but Caesar." The official heads of the nation, who would gladly have welcomed independence, put themselves on record as subjects of the pagan emperor. Even allowing for the fact that the Sadducean priesthood was willing to compromise with the Romans for the sake of political advantage, nothing revealed their lack of spiritual principles so vividly as this act of betrayal. It was the final step in the process initially described in the Prologue: "He came to that which was his own, but his own [people] did not receive him" (John 1:11).

16 Realizing that the priests were implacable and that resisting them would only endanger his career. Pilate finally gave in and ordered the Crucifixion. Certain features of Pilate's examination of Jesus are significant. Pilate's behavior shows that he was apprehensive of trouble. From the outset he was uncertain of his position. He oscillated between public confrontation with the Jewish mob and private interrogation of Jesus. Seven times in this brief narrative the author says or implies that Pilate "went out" or "went in" (18:29, 33, 38; 19:1, 4, 9, 13). Beneath his arrogant manner, there was an uncertainty that came from the conflict between Pilate the Roman judge and Pilate the politician. He finally succumbed to expediency.

From the standpoint of Jesus, Pilate was a person in need; and Jesus gave him the opportunity of receiving truth if he would have it. Jesus made a greater effort to penetrate Pilate's mind than to defend himself. When Pilate asked, "What is truth?" (18:38), he was near to the kingdom of God because incarnate truth was standing before him. Pilate sacrificed truth for what he thought was security and lost both.

Notes

18:28 In the phrase "to the palace of the Roman governor" (εἰς τὸ πραιτώριον, eis to praitōrion), the words "of the Roman governor" are possibly a correct interpretation; but they are not found in the Greek text. The exact title of Pilate is uncertain. Matthew 20:8 and Luke 8:3 use the term ἐπίτροπος (epitropos), the Greek equivalent of the Latin "procurator," a title generally held by the governors of Judea in the reign of Claudius (A.D. 41–54) or afterwards. Josephus states that Pilate was sent by Tiberius as procurator to Judea (Wars 2. 9. 2). A fragmentary Latin inscription discovered in Caesarea in 1961 calls Pontius Pilate the prefect of Judea. Under Augustus (27 B.C.–A.D. 14) the prefect was an officer, sometimes chosen from the privileged class of the equites (the elite Roman calvary) and possibly even a freedman, appointed by the emperor to a position of authority. (See Jerry Vardaman, "A New Inscription Which Mentions Pilate as a Prefect," JBL 81 [1962]: 70–71, and also A.N. Sherwin-White, Roman Society and Roman Law in the New Testament [Oxford: Clarendon, 1963], pp. 6–7, 12.) Pilate was subordinate to Vitellius, the governor of Syria, who later dismissed him and sent him to Rome to be examined by the emperor for misconduct in office (Jos. Antiq. 18. 4. 2). Only the death of Tiberius saved him from disgrace.

The place Jesus was taken is identified in John 19:13 as "The Stone Pavement," or "'Gabbatha," the Aramaic name for "The Ridge." In the basement of the Convent of the Sisters of Zion an extensive pavement has been excavated, consisting of massive slabs of stone, laid over subterranean cisterns and grooved to allow for the entrance of horses. Carved rudely on some of these slabs are gameboards at which the Roman soldiers amused themselves while off duty. This site seems to fit John's description better than Herod's palace.

Technically, πρωΐ (prōi, "early morning") refers to the fourth watch of the night between 3 A.M. and sunrise (BAG, p. 732). It seems rather improbable that the meaning should be confined to the technical sense since it is unlikely that Pilate would have been available before dawn.

37 The Greek οὐκοῦν (oukoun, "so") calls for a positive answer. Jesus' reply, Σὺ λέγεις ὅτι βασιλεύς εἰμι (Su legeis hoti basileus eimi, "You say that I am a king"), is really an affirmative assent. A comparison of the same construction in Matthew 26:64 with the parallel passage in Mark 14:62 (ἐγώ εἰμι, egō eimi) demonstrates that it was equivalent to the personal statement "I am." It is similar to the English slang "You said it!"

19:2 The crown of thorns (στέφανος ἐξ ἀκανθῶν, stephanos ex akanthōn) was possibly an attempt to mock the radiate crown that appeared on the heads of the emperors in the Roman coinage of that time (see H. St. John Hart, JTS III, [1952], 66–75). The radiate crown was the symbol of the emperor's divinity and would thus express even more strongly the derision of the soldiers. Furthermore, if John intended this connotation, it showed another stroke of irony in which the guards' crude jest was truer than they realized.

3 In the phrase "they kept coming (ἤρχοντο, ērchonto) and saying (ἔλεγον, elegon)," the verbs are in the imperfect tense, which implies repeated action, as NIV shows.

6 The right of the Jewish council to inflict the death penalty was limited to the execution of Gentiles who intruded into the sacred enclosure of the temple. They had no right to execute criminals. Rome reserved that power (the *ius gladii*) for itself in order to strengthen the control over subject provinces or client kingdoms. It was, however, within the power of the Roman prefect to accept the sentence of the Sanhedrin, whether on the basis of a political or religious charge (see Sherwin-White, *Roman Law*, pp. 32–47).

E. *The Crucifixion*

19:17–27

[17]Carrying his own cross, he went out to The Place of the Skull (which in Aramaic is called Golgotha). [18]Here they crucified him, and with him two others—one on each side and Jesus in the middle.

[19]Pilate had a notice prepared and fastened to the cross. It read, Jesus of Nazareth, The King of the Jews. [20]Many of the Jews read this sign, for the place where Jesus was crucified was near the city, and the sign was written in Aramaic, Latin and Greek. [21]The chief priests of the Jews protested to Pilate, "Do not write 'The King of the Jews,' but that this man claimed to be king of the Jews."

[22]Pilate answered, "What I have written, I have written."

[23]When the soldiers crucified Jesus, they took his clothes, dividing them into four shares, one for each of them, with the undergarment remaining. This garment was seamless, woven in one piece from top to bottom.

[24]"Let's not tear it," they said to one another. "Let's decide by lot who will get it."

This happened that the Scripture might be fulfilled which said,

> "They divided my garments among them
> and cast lots for my clothing."

So this is what the soldiers did.

[25]Near the cross of Jesus stood his mother, his mother's sister, Mary the wife of Clopas, and Mary of Magdala. [26]When Jesus saw his mother there, and the disciple whom he loved standing nearby, he said to his mother, "Dear woman, here is your son," [27]and to the disciple, "Here is your mother." From that time on, this disciple took her into his home.

17 Under Pilate's orders, Jesus was turned over to the execution squad, which normally consisted of four legionnaires and a centurion. Whether more were involved as a precaution against violence because of the popular tumult is not stated. The division of Jesus' garments (v.23) seems to show that only four legionnaires were involved. It was customary for the condemned person to wear a placard (v.20) giving his name and the nature of his crime and to carry the transverse beam of his cross. The procession moved from Pilate's judgment seat to a place outside the city called "The Place of the Skull." Contrary to current hymnology, there is no evidence that it was a hill. The reason for its name is uncertain. It is unlikely that skulls were left on the ground, which would be an affront to Jewish custom, or that the topography resembled a skull. The exact location is unknown.

18 Apart from this simple statement, the writer makes no attempt to describe the process of crucifixion, probably because it was well known to the readers and he did not want to dwell on the physical horror of the Cross. The victim carried the crossbeam to the place of execution (cf. v.17), where he was affixed to the cross by nails driven through

the hands or wrists and through the feet. Generally, a rope was tied around the chest, knotted between the shoulders, and then tied to the wooden stake behind the body to prevent its falling forward as fatigue weakened the muscles. A peg was set in the upright stake to act as a supporting seat. The victim was stripped of his clothing and left shamefully naked, exposed to the mocking people, the heat of the sun by day, and the chill and dampness of night, which in the spring at the altitude of Jerusalem might drop to 40 or 50 degrees Fahrenheit.

An ossuary unearthed near Jerusalem in Giv'at ha-Mivtar revealed the only known instance of the skeleton of a man who had been crucified. It showed that the feet had been nailed sideways to the cross whereas the body had been facing forward. Such a position would create a twist of about ninety degrees at the waist. The unnatural position, growing thirst, exposure to the weather, some loss of blood, and impaired breathing contributed to bring about a lingering and painful death. The tension on the arms prevented normal breathing, which caused the lungs to slowly fill with moisture. The victim drowned slowly by internal accumulation of fluid. The action of the heart was seriously affected. Frequently a crucified man might live as long as thirty-six hours, or even longer in an increasing agony, unless by exhaustion or dementia he finally lapsed into unconsciousness. Crucifixion was probably the most diabolical form of death ever invented. Paul, in writing of the humiliation of Christ, says, "He humbled himself and became obedient to [the point of] death—*even death on a cross*" (Phil 2:8, italics mine). Paul's statement reveals the feeling toward death by this method. Death for Jesus was unbelievable, but crucifixion was unthinkable.

John gives no details concerning the two others crucified with Jesus. The synoptic accounts describe them as "robbers" or brigands (Matt 27:38; Mark 15:27; Luke 23:32–33, 39) like Barabbas (cf. comment on 18:40). It may be that these two and Barabbas were guerrilla fighters captured by the Romans in some skirmish in Galilee. Anti-Roman unrest was rife at this time, and the rebels often replenished their food supplies or treasury by robbery of wealthy landholders. Jesus was classed with subversives and criminals.

19-22 The placard on the cross was the conventional announcement of the offense the victim had committed. The languages were intended to make the inscription plain to all: Aramaic, for the local inhabitants; Latin, for the officials; Greek, the lingua franca of the eastern Mediterranean world. Its content was Pilate's psychological revenge on the Jewish hierarchy for forcing his decision. It proclaimed loudly to all passers-by that Rome had crucified the king of the Jews as a common criminal. Stung by the insult, the priests remonstrated, asking that Pilate make clear that it was Jesus' claim to be King of the Jews, not that it was in fact true. Having succeeded by his unjust compromise in removing any possible ground of accusation that he was derelict in his duty to the Roman state, Pilate resumed his haughty attitude and refused to change the wording. "What I have written, I have written" means essentially, "Take it and like it!"

23-24 Usually the clothing of a crucified man became the property of the executioners. Jesus' simple wardrobe was composed of five items: a turban or headdress; an outer robe; a sash or girdle, the folds of which would provide pockets; sandals; and a fairly long tunic, woven in one piece, that was an undergarment. The first four were easily divided among the four legionnaires, but the fifth would be of no value if cut into four parts. Gambling was as well known in the Roman army as it is among soldiers today. So the tunic was awarded to one of them at the cast of the dice. John's reason for mentioning this episode was its illustration or fulfillment of the prophecy of Psalm 22. Psalm 22 is a startling picture of the Crucifixion, which begins with Christ's fourth word from the cross: "My God, my God, why have you forsaken me?" (Matt 27:46; Mark 15:34). If Pilate's inscription shows that he exploited Jesus' crucifixion as a means of psychological vengeance, the gambling of the legionnaires shows their callous and mercenary attitude.

25-27 The harsh brutality of the scene is softened by the allusion to Jesus' care for his mother. Four women are mentioned here: Mary, the wife of Clopas; Mary Magdalene; Mary, the mother of Jesus; and his mother's sister, who was presumably Salome, the mother of James and John (cf. Matt 27:56; Mark 10:35; 15:40). The identity of Mary of Clopas is uncertain. She may have been the wife or daughter of Clopas. If she were the former, a question arises whether Clopas and Alphaeus, who was the father of James the younger (Mark 3:18), were identical. Most of these women were related in some way to the Twelve and were among Jesus' most loyal followers. Mary of Magdala appears in Luke's list of those who helped support Jesus by their contributions (Luke 8:2). There is nothing in the NT to imply that she was of loose moral character. "Magdalene" refers to her home in Magdala, a town on the western side of the Sea of Galilee, named probably from the Hebrew *migdol*, or "watchtower."

The anguish and terror of Jesus' mother at the Crucifixion must have been indescribable. His tender concern for her in the hour of his mortal agony illustrates his true humanity and compassion. On the assumption that John was "the disciple whom he loved," it could well be that Jesus consigned his mother to John's care because none of his brothers was present and because John was the nearest available relative. Apparently John removed Mary from the scene at once and took her to his home in Jerusalem. There could not have been time to go to Galilee, for the writer resumes his narrative at the close of the Crucifixion. His temporary absence may account for the omission of some of the details found in the Synoptics, including Jesus' dialogue with the criminals who were crucified with him. Mary must have remained in Jerusalem for a time since she was present at the session of prayer that preceded Pentecost.

Notes

17 Two places have been claimed as the site of the Crucifixion. One is at the present site of the Church of the Holy Sepulchre, which was built in honor of Helen, the mother of Constantine, in the fourth century, after an attempt to identify the original site. The devastation of the city after the first and second revolts destroyed all landmarks or buried them so deeply under rubble that they cannot now be identified. The second place is Gordon's Calvary, located outside the present wall, north of the Damascus Gate on the Nablus Road. It is now a Muslim cemetery on the brow of a ridge that encircles the northern wall. While the rocky eminence and the adjacent garden containing an ancient tomb seem to fit the description of the Gospels, it is doubtful whether either would have been used before A.D. 70. Until the location of the "Second Wall" that bounded the northwest side of the city in Jesus' time can be settled, the exact location of Calvary will be debatable. The data of the Gospels are not specific; all that can be known is that the Crucifixion took place outside the city walls, not far from one of the main roads.

18 The process of crucifixion has been vividly illustrated by the discovery of the remains of a man executed in this manner. In 1968 a number of ossuaries were found in burial caves during a building project at Giv'at ha-Mivtar in northeast Jerusalem, slightly to the northwest of Mount Scopus. A full report on "Anthropological Observations on the Skeletal Remains from Giv'at

ha-Mivtar" was published in IEJ, vol. 20, nos. 1, 2 (1970). The analysis of the remains of the crucified man is on pp. 49–59 of the report. The body had been affixed to a cross by nails through the wrists between the ulna and the radius; the feet had been transfixed by a single spike through a wooden cleat, the right side of the right heel and the right side of the left heel, and then into the upright stem of the cross. The latter was made of olive wood that was so hard that the tip of the spike was bent and could not be extracted from the bones through which it had been driven. The resultant position of the body was such that the knees were bent to the left while the torso was fixed at a ninety-degree angle to the thigh bones. The lower legs had been shattered by a single blow that had crushed the right leg and cracked the left leg against the edge of the upright of the cross. The body had been supported by a peg or cleat in the cross under the left hip. The identity of the victim is unknown. Apparently he died at the time of the Fall of Jerusalem in A.D. 70, or possibly earlier. This is the only known archaeological evidence of the practice of crucifixion.

27 The phrase "into his home" is the Greek εἰς τὰ ἴδια (*eis ta idia*), the same phrase that appears in John 1:11. It means "the things peculiarly one's own," hence, "one's home." The entire Gospel indicates that the "disciple whom he [Jesus] loved" was well acquainted with Jerusalem and that it was the center of action for much of his narrative. Even if he were Galilean by origin, he may well have been living in the city at times. It has been suggested that he may have been the Jerusalem agent for Zebedee & Sons, Fishmongers!

F. *The Death of Jesus*

19:28–37

> [28]Later, knowing that all was now completed, and so that the Scripture would be fulfilled, Jesus said, "I am thirsty." [29]A jar of wine vinegar was there, so they soaked a sponge in it, put the sponge on a stalk of the hyssop plant, and lifted it to Jesus' lips. [30]When he had received the drink, Jesus said, "It is finished." With that, he bowed his head and gave up his spirit.
> [31]Now it was the day of Preparation, and the next day was to be a special Sabbath. Because the Jews did not want the bodies left on the crosses during the Sabbath, they asked Pilate to have the legs broken and the bodies taken down. [32]The soldiers therefore came and broke the legs of the first man who had been crucified with Jesus, and then those of the other. [33]But when they came to Jesus and found that he was already dead, they did not break his legs. [34]Instead, one of the soldiers pierced Jesus' side with a spear, bringing a sudden flow of blood and water. [35]The man who saw it has given testimony, and his testimony is true. He knows that he tells the truth, and he testifies so that you also may believe. [36]These things happened so that the Scripture would be fulfilled: "Not one of his bones will be broken," [37]and, as another Scripture says, "They will look on the one they have pierced."

28 The phrases preceding Jesus' last request (his sixth word from the cross) show that he was consciously fulfilling the program the Father had set for him. "Knowing that all was now completed" accords with the declaration in his prayer: "I have brought you glory on earth by completing the work you gave me to do" (17:4). Unerringly and methodically Jesus carried out the commission the Father had assigned to him. To some extent this commission had been prescribed by OT prophecy. The phrase "I am thirsty" recalls Psalm 69:21: "They put gall in my food and gave me vinegar for my thirst." Jesus' loss of blood, his nervous tension, and his exposure to the weather had generated a raging thirst.

29 The "vinegar" was probably the cheap sour wine the legionnaires drank. Though it provided some refreshment, it was a strong astringent that could contract the throat muscles and prevent the condemned victim from crying out with pain. Just what is meant by "hyssop" is uncertain. The word may describe more than one plant. It could have been a brush used for sprinkling (Exod 12:22), which has been identified with sorghum grass. This, however, did not grow a stalk of sufficient rigidity to act as a rod for supporting a sponge. It has been suggested that there is a primitive error in the text. Instead of reading *hyssōpō* with the majority of the MSS, it should read *hyssō*, meaning "javelin." If so, one of the soldiers could easily have impaled a sponge filled with the vinegar on the end of his javelin and reached it up to moisten Jesus' lips. This reading, however, occurs in only one MS (1242) of late date. In four MSS of the Old Latin it is rendered *perticae*, meaning "a long pole." Although this is a tempting speculative emendation, the evidence is not sufficient to sustain it. The elevation of the body on the cross would not be at a very great height, and the stalk of a plant growing nearby would be sufficient to support a light sponge. W.E. Shewell-Cooper states that "it could easily be the *Capparis sicula*," which "is found in the Sinai desert, and grows on the walls of Jerusalem" (ZPEB, 3:235). The thirst consummated Jesus' physical suffering. Having passed that stage, he had completed his work and was ready to end his mission.

30 The use of the perfect tense in "It is finished" (*tetelestai*) signifies full completion of Jesus' work and the establishment of a basis for faith. Nothing further needed to be done. Jesus' act was voluntary and confident, for he had discharged perfectly the Father's purpose and was leaving the scene of his human struggle. The expression may be interpreted in various ways: as a cry of relief, because suffering is ending; as a cry of anguish, because his ministry has ended in failure; or as a shout of victory, because the purpose of God has triumphed in his death. The last of these seems to be the author's intent. He makes it the final report of Jesus to the Father, who will now exalt him to glory. The final word says that "he bowed his head and gave up his spirit." It could also be translated "he laid his head to rest and dismissed his spirit." Jesus retained consciousness and command of himself till the very end.

31–32 Mark (15:42) agrees with John that Jesus died on the day preceding the Sabbath, hence, on Friday, "the day of Preparation." The day began at sunset on Thursday and ended at sunset on Friday. The meal Jesus and his disciples ate must have been on Thursday night, which would actually fall on the Passover since the day began in the evening, not in the morning, as in the Western calendar. The removal of bodies from the cross was a concession to Jewish religious scruples. The Romans usually left the bodies of criminals on their crosses as a warning to potential offenders, much as pirates in the eighteenth century were hung in chains so that passing ships might see their fate. The Jewish law forbade leaving hanged bodies on a gallows overnight (Deut 21:22–23; Josh 8:29). The soldiers broke the legs of the living victims to hasten death. The only way a crucified man could obtain a full breath of air was to raise himself by means of his legs to ease the tension on his arms and chest muscles. If the legs were broken, he could not possibly do so; and death would follow shortly because of lack of oxygen.

33 The execution squad was well acquainted with the signs of death. Consequently, not fracturing Jesus' legs shows that the squad considered him to be already dead. Jesus' swift death marks either the climax of inner tension, the fatal results of the scourging, or, as the text seems to indicate, a voluntary ending of his life because his work was ended. He had said of himself that he could lay down his life that he might take it again (10:17).

34–37 One of the soldiers pierced Jesus' side with his spear, probably to see whether there would be any reaction. The flow of "blood and water" has been variously explained. Ordinarily dead bodies do not bleed because there is no action of the heart to produce arterial pressure. One suggestion is that since the body was erect, the flow was due to gravity and that the crassamentum (the heavy, red corpuscles) and the serum (the yellowish white aqueous part) of the blood had already begun to separate. Another is that either the stomach or the lungs contained water that flowed with the blood. The author places great importance on the fact, emphasizing that he had witnessed it for himself and that he was telling the truth. He connected it with OT prophecy. The bones of the Passover lamb were left unbroken (Exod 12:46), and the divine protection of a righteous man guarantees that God "protects all his bones, not one of them will be broken" (Ps 34:20). The prophetic significance of the pierced side is referred to in Zechariah 12:10, where it is related to the final manifestation of the Lord to Israel. Verses 35–37 are a footnote giving the author's viewpoint in the third person, a usage in keeping with his practice throughout the Gospel (cf. M.C. Tenney, "Footnotes," pp. 350–64).

Notes

30 The verb τελέω (*teleō*, "to finish") was used in the first and second centuries in the sense of "fulfilling" or "paying" a debt and often appeared in receipts. Jesus' statement "It is finished" (τετέλεσται, *tetelestai*) could be interpreted as "Paid in full," or, as the words of a gospel hymn read, "Jesus paid it all" (see MM, p. 630).

The verb κλίνω (*klinō*, "bow," "rest") used in the phrase κλίνας τὴν κεφαλὴν, (*klinas tēn kephalēn*, "bowed his head"), appears also in Matt 8:20 and Luke 9:58. The world afforded Jesus only a cross on which to lay his head.

G. *The Burial of Jesus*

19:38–42

[38]Later, Joseph of Arimathea asked Pilate for the body of Jesus. Now Joseph was a disciple of Jesus, but secretly because he feared the Jews. With Pilate's permission, he came and took the body. [39]He was accompanied by Nicodemus, the man who earlier had visited Jesus at night. Nicodemus brought a mixture of myrrh and aloes, about seventy-five pounds. [40]Taking Jesus' body, the two of them wrapped it, with the spices, in strips of linen. This was in accordance with Jewish burial customs. [41]At the place where Jesus was crucified, there was a garden, and in the garden a new tomb, in which no one had ever been laid. [42]Because it was the Jewish day of Preparation and since the tomb was nearby, they laid Jesus there.

38 Burial in the Middle East usually takes place within twenty-four hours after death. In this case, the body of Jesus would probably have been flung into a common pit with the bodies of the two other victims, had not his friends intervened. Jesus had no estate of his own from which to pay for his burial, and his relatives were either too poor or too

afraid of the authorities to assume responsibility for it. Joseph of Arimathea is mentioned in all four Gospels (Matt 27:57-60; Mark 15:42-46; Luke 23:50-56). Matthew says he was wealthy; Mark, that he was a member of the Sanhedrin ("Council") and was "waiting for the kingdom of God"; Luke, that he had not concurred in the vote of the council to condemn Jesus. Joseph's action was courageous, for his petition was a tacit admission that he was a friend of Jesus and consequently an associate in whatever supposed subversion Jesus might have advocated. Joseph took the initiative and petitioned Pilate for permission to remove the body. His request was an open confession of his faith, for up to this time he had been a secret believer.

39 Nicodemus, another distinguished member of the Jewish aristocracy, shared the responsibility for receiving Jesus' body with Joseph. This marks Nicodemus's third appearance in the Gospel: one at his initial interview with Jesus (ch. 3), the second at his defense of Jesus before the council (7:45-52), and finally at the burial. Like Joseph, Nicodemus was a secret disciple whose faith grew slowly. As a member of the Sanhedrin, he had more at stake than the Galilean fishermen who had become followers of Jesus early in his career. His cooperation with Joseph in the burial shows that his faith had finally matured. Neither of these men appears in the Jewish records or traditions of the time. For that reason some have regarded them as legendary; but were that so, there is no obvious reason for introducing them gratuitously into the narrative. If they had been regarded by their Sanhedrin contemporaries as traitors to Judaism, their names would have been erased from the records.

The mixture of spices that Nicodemus provided was a very large quantity. Spices were generally imported and were very expensive. Myrrh is a gum exuded by a tree that grows in Arabia and is prized for its perfume. It was one of the gifts of the wise men to Jesus (Matt 2:11). Aloes are derived from the pulp in the leaves of a plant that belongs to the lily family. The spice is fragrant and bitter to the taste. Used with myrrh, it acts as a drying agent; and the fragrance would counteract the odor of decaying flesh. The quantity of one hundred Roman pounds (75 lbs. avdp.) revealed both Nicodemus's wealth and his appreciation of Jesus.

40 The burial of the body was hasty and had to be completed before sundown. The process is uncertain. The spices, being of somewhat gummy character, may have been laid in the folds of the cloth to provide a rigid casing for the body, or they may have been ground and mixed with oil to form an ointment to rub on the body. The former procedure agrees better with the text. "Strips of linen" is a translation of *othoniois.* Later usage in the koine Greek made the term a generic equivalent of clothes (cf. MM, p. 439). In the case of Lazarus, the graveclothes were wrapped around him in such a way that he had to be released after he was raised. The entire process was really the preparation of the body for instant burial rather than final interment.

41 The place of burial was a private garden, not a public cemetery. The privacy of this garden allowed the women to visit the tomb. No doubt they would have been hesitant to enter a public cemetery at any time—especially before daylight. Matthew states that the burial place was Joseph's own rock-hewed tomb (Matt 27:60). The location was near the place of execution and was probably just outside the Second North Wall of the city. Brown states that the tombs of the Hasmonean high priests John Hyrcanus and Alexander Jannaeus were located in this general vicinity (29a: 941-43). Joseph, as a wealthy member of the Sanhedrin, apparently owned property in this area.

42 The allusion to the "day of Preparation," which was ending, creates the impression that the burial was hasty. The amount of spices used militates against an expected temporary burial; it is more likely that as far as Joseph and Nicodemus were concerned, it was final. On the other hand, they may not have completed all they wished to do. The women had observed the place of the entombment. Consequently they knew where to go in order to fulfill their desire for a part in the burial of Jesus.

Notes

---

40 Ἐνταφιάζειν (entaphiazein, "to prepare for burial") refers to laying out a body and anointing it rather than to the actual burial (cf. MM, p. 217).

H. *The Resurrection* (20:1–29)

If the narrative of John had ended with ch. 19, it would not have been exceptional; all human biographies end with death. The picture of Jesus would have been that of a man of exceptional character, who made extraordinary claims, and whose sincerity could not be reasonably doubted. Nevertheless, the main narrative would have been closed with a sense of frustration. His claims would have been negated, his aspirations would have been unrealized, and his teaching would have seemed too lofty to be true. The major difference between the life and teachings of Jesus and those of any other great religious leader lies in the fact that Jesus rose from the dead and the others did not, however persistent their influence may be.

In presenting the evidence for Jesus' resurrection, John deals more with its effect on human personality than with the material proofs the Western mind would prefer. He assumes the fact and then shows how it influenced certain disciples in such a way that its reality becomes indisputable.

1. *The witness of Peter and John*

20:1–9

> ¹Early on the first day of the week, while it was still dark, Mary of Magdala went to the tomb and saw that the stone had been removed from the entrance. ²So she came running to Simon Peter and the other disciple, the one Jesus loved, and said, "They have taken the Lord out of the tomb, and we don't know where they have put him!"
> ³So Peter and the other disciple started for the tomb. ⁴Both were running, but the other disciple outran Peter and reached the tomb first. ⁵He bent over and looked in at the strips of linen lying there but did not go in. ⁶Then Simon Peter, who was behind him, arrived and went into the tomb. He saw the strips of linen lying there, ⁷as well as the burial cloth that had been around Jesus' head. The cloth was folded up by itself, separate from the linen. ⁸Finally the other disciple, who had reached the tomb first, also went inside. He saw and believed. ⁹(They still did not understand from Scripture that Jesus had to rise from the dead.)

1 "The first day of the week" would be the day after the Sabbath. In the Jewish method of reckoning time, it would begin with sundown on Saturday and continue until sundown on Sunday. The text seems to indicate, however, that the visit of the women to the tomb occurred early on Sunday morning. Only Mary Magdalene is mentioned by name, but others are listed in the synoptic Gospels (Matt 28:1; Mark 16:1; Luke 24:10). Quite likely Mary Magdalene, noticing that the stone had been rolled away from the door of the tomb, ran to warn the disciples while the others investigated further.

2 Mary hastened to find Peter and John, the leaders of the Twelve, and announced that the body was missing from the tomb: "They have taken the Lord." No identification is given for "they." Either the word is an impersonal plural or else, as is more likely, it is an oblique reference to the Jewish hierarchy who had designed Jesus' death. Obviously Mary thought the body had been secretly removed by Jesus' enemies.

3 The quick response of Peter and the other disciple shows that the disciples were not responsible for removing the body. Had they been aware of an official removal, or had some of their own number been involved in a conspiracy, they would not have been so concerned.

4 Both Peter and the other disciple "ran" to the tomb. The only other passage in the NT that refers to running, apart from metaphorical use or to an athletic contest, is Matthew 28:8, which describes how the women "ran" to bring the disciples the news. The disciples' running shows they were activated by a powerful emotion, possibly either consternation, as in the case of Mary, or joy, as with the women. Peter, perhaps being the older and heavier of the two, was unable to maintain as swift a pace as his companion. The unnamed disciple arrived first but did not venture to enter the tomb.

5 Having seen that the graveclothes were still within, the other disciple probably concluded that the body was also there and so refrained from entering. Either he felt that he should not enter the tomb out of respect for the dead, or else he feared the ceremonial defilement of touching a corpse.

6–7 Peter, who by this time had overtaken his partner, had no such inhibitions. He entered directly into the tomb. He also saw the graveclothes and observed that the headcloth was not lying with the other pieces but was rolled up in a place by itself. This means the headcloth still retained the shape the contour of Jesus' head had given it and that it was still separated from the other wrappings by a space that suggested the distance between the neck of the deceased and the upper chest, where the wrappings of the body would have begun. Peter must have been wondering why the graveclothes were left in this position if the body had been stolen. A robber would not have left them in good order. He would have stripped the body completely, leaving the clothing in a disorderly heap; or he would have taken the body, graveclothes and all.

8 At this point, the "other disciple" summoned up courage to enter the tomb, perhaps wondering what had reduced Peter to silence. The disciple saw the meaning of the empty graveclothes and "believed." The unique phenomenon of the graveclothes looking as if the body were in them when no body was there undoubtedly recalled Jesus' previous words (cf. John 2:22; 11:25; 16:22).

9 The teaching of Scripture, however, was not yet clear to the disciples, and they required fuller explanation by Jesus (cf. Luke 24:25–27, 44–47). To what "Scripture"

does this passage refer? There is a parallel in John 2:21, which asserts that the disciples understood Jesus' statement about raising the temple of his body in connection with Scripture. The Gospel of John contains no specific text that might be interpreted as a prediction of the Resurrection. Perhaps Psalm 16:10, quoted by Peter in his address on the Day of Pentecost (Acts 2:24–31), is the best possibility for the "Scripture." For these two key disciples, the realization of the truth of the Resurrection began with material evidence, the significance of which dawned on them slowly. Their eagerness to visit the tomb showed their concern for Jesus. Had they dismissed him from their consciousness after his death, they would not have exerted themselves by running to Joseph's garden early in the morning. Their understanding, however, was slow in spite of Jesus' repeated predictions of his passion and resurrection.

Notes

5 Three words are used in this account to denote the visual perception of the disciples. In v.5, John "looked in at" (βλέπει, *blepei*) the linen clothes, implying that he had a clear picture of them and did not act on hearsay. In v.6, Peter "saw" (θεωρεῖ, *theōrei*), or "contemplated," "observed," the strips of linen, implying that he scrutinized them carefully but did not know how to interpret the phenomenon. In v.8, the "other disciple . . . saw" (εἶδεν, *eiden*), meaning that he perceived the significance of what registered on the retina of his eyes. The first two verbs are not always distinguishable in meaning, though in Johannine usage the second seems to denote studying a person or thing for its significance (cf. 2:23; 4:19; 7:3; 12:19).

7 The participle ἐντετυλιγμένον (*entetyligmenon*), translated "wrapped up by itself," comes from the word ἐντυλίσσω (*entylissō*), which means "to wrap up" or "to roll up." It is used in the papyri to refer to fettering prisoners, wrapping children in clothes, or entangling fish in a net (MM, p. 219). It implies that the cloth had been wound around the head into the shape of a sphere and not folded flat like a table napkin. In the NT this word is used only in the description of Jesus' entombment (cf. Matt 27:59; Luke 23:53).

---

2. *The appearance to Mary Magdalene*

20:10–18

[10]Then the disciples went back to their homes, [11]but Mary stood outside the tomb crying. As she wept, she bent over to look into the tomb [12]and saw two angels in white, seated where Jesus' body had been, one at the head and the other at the foot.

[13]They asked her, "Woman, why are you crying?"

"They have taken my Lord away," she said, "and I don't know where they have put him." [14]At this, she turned around and saw Jesus standing there, but she did not realize that it was Jesus.

[15]"Woman," he said, "why are you crying? Who is it you are looking for?"

Thinking he was the gardener, she said, "Sir, if you have carried him away, tell me where you have put him, and I will get him."

[16]Jesus said to her, "Mary."

She turned toward him and cried out in Aramaic, "Rabboni!" (which means Teacher).

[17]Jesus said, "Do not hold on to me, for I have not yet returned to the Father. Go instead to my brothers and tell them, 'I am returning to my Father and your Father, to my God and your God.' "

¹⁸Mary of Magdala went to the disciples with the news: "I have seen the Lord!" And she told them that he had said these things to her.

10 Puzzled but convinced that something unusual had occurred at the tomb, Peter and the other disciple returned to their lodgings in Jerusalem. The phraseology seems to indicate that they had a fixed place where they were staying, possibly the "upper room," or perhaps the same place the unnamed disciple took Mary at the time of the Crucifixion. No details are given in the Gospels.

11 Mary Magdalene had returned to the tomb and stood outside, wailing for the loss of Jesus. On looking into the tomb, she saw two figures in white seated on the shelf where the body of Jesus had been lying, one at the foot and the other at the head. Presumably the position of the graveclothes indicated which was the foot and which was the head of the burial position. The tomb was a horizontal chamber cut through the soft limestone rock that Jerusalem was built on. Usually such tombs had a small antechamber into which the low entrance opened and from which the burial chambers radiated. Some were cut to contain only one body; others were rooms in which a family might be buried. This tomb seems to have been large enough to accommodate several living persons in addition to the burial cells.

12 No description is given of the angels. When angels appear in the Bible, they are usually recognized by their powers rather than by any significant difference from human form. Mary did not respond to them in any unusual way, possibly because her eyes were clouded with tears, or because she was preoccupied with the loss of Jesus' body. The sole feature noted in the text is that the angels were clothed in white. This parallels Luke's description of the men who appeared at the ascension of Jesus (cf. Acts 1:10).

13 The question the angels asked Mary brought from her only an expression of grief and frustration. The death of Jesus, which she had witnessed, was in itself distressing and unnerving; the disappearance of the body from the place of burial would add apprehension and mystery to her grief. She had hoped for the sad consolation of completing the burial, and even that had been taken from her.

14 As Mary turned back toward the outside of the tomb, she saw a person standing there whom she took for the keeper of the garden. She was aware of his presence, but she did not recognize him. The same two words are used here that occur in the preceding section (cf. vv.5–6, 8): Peter "saw" or "observed" the content of the tomb, but John "perceived" its meaning. Mary likewise "observed" the figure standing before her, but at first she paid scant attention to him because of her overwhelming concern for the body of Jesus.

15 The person addressed her first as a stranger, using the polite salutation "Woman" and asking the reason for her grief. From her lamentations one would conclude that she had lost some possession or some person. Thinking that Jesus was the keeper of the garden, she assumed that he would know she was looking for a body. So she requested that if he had removed it, he would tell her where she might find it that she might take it for final burial. Her words reveal her devotion. She never paused to consider how she would carry the corpse of a full-grown man or how she would explain her possession of it.

16 Only one thing was necessary to establish Jesus' identity—his uttering her name. One of the strange commonplaces of life is that the most penetrating utterance one can understand, no matter by whom spoken, is his personal name. Furthermore, the way it is spoken often identifies the speaker. No gardener would ever know her name, and no one else would pronounce it the way Jesus did. Turning again for a second look, she addressed him in Aramaic as "Rabboni." Strictly it means "my dear lord," but John defines it in this instance as "Teacher." In this ecstatic moment of recognition, Mary must have prostrated herself before him and clasped his feet, as the other women did according to Matthew's report (Matt 28:9).

17 In reply to her action, Jesus said, "Do not hold onto me." He was not refusing to be touched but was making clear that she did not need to detain him, for he had not yet ascended to the Father. He planned to remain with the disciples for a little while; she need not fear that he would vanish immediately. Ultimately he would return to God, and he urged her to tell the disciples that he would do so. The use of the word "brothers" includes more than the members of his immediate family. It placed the disciples on a new plane of relationship with himself. Having passed through death and resurrection, Jesus had become the representative man, the Lord from heaven, who "is not ashamed to call them brothers" (Heb 2:11). During his early ministry, Jesus expressed the same feeling. When his mother and brothers came to summon him from his preaching, he replied, "Who are my mother and my brothers?" (Mark 3:33). Then he answered his own question, "Whoever does God's will is my brother and sister and mother" (v.34).

The way Jesus stated his destination is illuminating: "I am returning to my Father and your Father, to my God and your God." Nowhere in the Gospels did Jesus himself address God as "our Father" or "our God." One seeming exception is the prayer Jesus taught his disciples, which is commonly referred to as the Lord's Prayer (Matt 6:9–13; Luke 11:2–4). But in that prayer Jesus was teaching the disciples to address God and was not necessarily including himself in the petition. The reason for the distinction in his word to Mary was not, of course, that there were two gods but rather that her relationship with God was different from his. He is the eternal Son of the Father; she, as well as all the disciples, had become a member of the family by receiving him (cf. John 1:12). Both relationships concerned only one God.

18 Mary's announcement to the disciples that she had seen the Lord was an additional confirmation of the belief that rested on inference from material evidence. The beloved disciple had believed, but he had not yet personally seen the risen Lord Jesus. Mary brought the witness of her experience to corroborate his deduction.

Notes

11 The Greek word κλαίω, (klaiō, "to cry") is the same one used concerning the mourners at Lazarus's death (John 11:31, 33) and at the death of Jairus's daughter (Luke 8:52). It represents loud and uncontrollable wailing.

12 Apart from the disputed verse of John 5:4, angels are mentioned only three times in this Gospel: in John 1:51, in 12:29, and again in 20:12. The first is an allusion to Genesis 28:12; the second is a casual reference to angelic intervention to explain a mysterious phenomenon; the third speaks directly of an angelic appearance. According to Luke, angels appeared in connection

with the annunciation of the births of John the Baptist and Jesus (Luke 1:11-20, 26-38), the suffering of Jesus in Gethsemane (22:43), and the Resurrection (24:4, 23). The angels seem to have appeared and disappeared at will; they delivered information and provided protection. They excel mankind in intelligence, strength, and duration. Hebrews 1:14 describes their function: "Are not all angels ministering spirits sent to serve those who will inherit salvation?"

17 The NIV translation "Do not hold on to me" is accurate. The verb ἅπτω (haptō) does not mean to touch with the tip of a finger to test whether an object is real or not but to "clutch" or "grip." Jesus was not protesting that Mary should not touch him lest he be defiled, but he was admonishing her not to detain him because he would see her and the disciples again. The use of the particle μή (mē, "not") with the present imperative means to stop an action already begun rather than to avoid starting it.

"Returned" is the translation of ἀναβέβηκα (anabebēka), the perfect tense of ἀναβαίνω (anabainō), and implies a state rather than an action. In essence, Jesus was saying, "I have not yet entered into an ascended state." The Gospel of John makes several allusions to the Ascension. The use of ἀναβέβηκεν (anabebēken, "has . . . gone" NIV) in John 3:13 does not speak directly of Jesus' ascension. It merely asserts that no man has ever ascended directly into the presence of God. A more direct implication lies in the question Jesus addressed to his querulous disciples: "What if you see the Son of Man ascend to where he was before!" (6:62). They were complaining that his assertion about eating his flesh and drinking his blood was too difficult to understand. He countered by asking them what they would say if they saw him ascend. Luke uses plainer language concerning the Ascension (Luke 9:51; 24:51; Acts 1:9; 2:33-34), though he makes no attempt to explain its mystery. The concept seems to imply the entrance into a new dimension of living rather than a mechanical change of location.

---

3. The appearance to the disciples

20:19-23

> [19]On the evening of that first day of the week, when the disciples were together, with the doors locked for fear of the Jews, Jesus came and stood among them and said, "Peace be with you!" [20]After he said this, he showed them his hands and side. The disciples were overjoyed when they saw the Lord.
>
> [21]Again Jesus said, "Peace be with you! As the Father has sent me, I am sending you." [22]And with that he breathed on them and said, "Receive the Holy Spirit. [23]If you forgive anyone his sins, they are forgiven; if you do not forgive them, they are not forgiven."

19-20 The third episode came in the evening of the first day. John does not cite the appearances to Simon and to the travelers on the road to Emmaus that appear in the Lukan account (Luke 24:13-35). This appearance came to the collective group for the purpose of allaying their fears. They had narrowly escaped arrest with Jesus in Gethsemane; they realized that as the disciples of one who was regarded as a dangerous agitator they would be under suspicion; and they were probably holding a consultation on the best method of withdrawing from the city without attracting the notice of the temple police or the Roman authorities. The doors were locked for fear that the Jews would send an arresting detachment for them as they had for Jesus.

The appearance of Jesus in the room excited both amazement and fear. The implication is clear that Jesus was not impeded by locked doors. The resurrection body has properties different from the body of flesh; yet it is not ethereal. There was a definite continuity between the physical body of Jesus' earthly career and the new body since his hands and side still showed the scars that identified him. His greeting of "Peace" and the assurance of his identity calmed their fears and demonstrated by unmistakable proof that he was alive. They were overjoyed, not only to see him again, but also to realize that he was undefeated by death and that his claims were validated.

21 The repetition of the common greeting "Peace" (Gr. *eirēnē*; Heb. *šalôm*) reassured the disciples of his real presence. Not only did his appearance renew their devotion and their hopes, but it also renewed their commission as disciples. Had there been no Resurrection, there would have been little motive for them to undertake a mission in his name. But since he had risen, the old commitment was even more compelling. "As the Father has sent me," he said, "I am sending you." He had come into the world to fulfill the Father's purpose and had completed his task. Now he expected them to continue his work in his absence. As the Father had sent him to speak his words, to do his works, and to lay down his life for the salvation of men, so he expected them to deliver his message (15:27), to do greater works than he had done (14:12), and to give their lives in his service. They would have all the privileges, all the protection, and all the responsibilities that he had during his ministry.

22-23 For this ministry Jesus provided the Holy Spirit and the commission to proclaim the forgiveness of sins. These are linked together for a new ministry. This was the initial announcement of which Pentecost was the historic fulfillment. The descent of the Spirit on the church at Pentecost brought the proclamation by Peter to his hearers: "Repent and be baptized, every one of you, in the name of Jesus Christ so that your sins may be forgiven" (Acts 2:38). The words of Jesus emphasize that the Holy Spirit is not bestowed on the church as an ornament but to empower an effective application of the work of Christ to all men.

The commission to forgive sins is phrased in an unusual construction. Literally, it is: "Those whose sins you forgive have already been forgiven; those whose sins you do not forgive have not been forgiven." The first verbs in the two clauses are aorists, which imply the action of an instant; the second verbs are perfects, which imply an abiding state that began before the action of the first verbs. God does not forgive men's sins because we decide to do so nor withhold forgiveness because we will not grant it. We announce it; we do not create it. This is the essence of salvation. And all who proclaim the gospel are in effect forgiving or not forgiving sins, depending on whether the hearer accepts or rejects the Lord Jesus as the Sin-Bearer.

Notes

19 For a discussion of the meaning of κεκλεισμένων (*kekleismenōn*), translated "locked" in NIV, see LSJ, p. 957. KJV renders the word "shut," but the sense of the passage is clearer if Jesus entered when the doors were impassable by ordinary means of access.

22 There is no definite article with "Holy Spirit" (πνεῦμα ἅγιον, *pneuma hagion*) in the Greek text; but in the light of Jesus' instruction in the Upper Room Discourse, the disciples could not have mistaken his meaning. "Breathed on" (ἐνεφύσησεν, *enephysēsen*) appears in a similar construction elsewhere only in the LXX of Gen 2:7, with reference to the creation of man. God formed man from the dust of the earth and then "breathed into" him the breath of life so that

he became a living being. Jesus "breathed" into the disciples the breath of the new creation that gave them spiritual vitality. The first man was given responsibility for the material creation, but the disciples were to have responsibility for the new creation.

23 A similar expression occurs in Jesus' commission to Peter: "Whatever you bind on earth will be bound in heaven, and whatever you loose on earth will be loosed in heaven" (Matt 16:19). In both statements the Greek verb of the second clause is a periphrastic future perfect ($\check{\epsilon}\sigma\tau\alpha\iota$ $\delta\epsilon\delta\epsilon\mu\acute{\epsilon}\nu o\nu$, *estai dedemenon*, "will be bound"; $\check{\epsilon}\sigma\tau\alpha\iota$ $\lambda\epsilon\lambda\upsilon\mu\acute{\epsilon}\nu o\nu$, *estai lelumenon*, "will be loosed"), a rare form in koine Greek. Generally it is explained as an alternative for the simple future passive, having lost its original force. Apparently, however, in this instance it may retain the meaning of the future perfect, which implies that its action precedes that of the first verb of each sentence. As in English today, the future perfect was a dying tense that ultimately disappeared from common usage. The appearance of the form is therefore all the more significant. The delegation of power to the disciples to forgive or to retain the guilt of sin thus depends on the previous forgiveness by God. Perhaps this concept underlies Paul's verdict on the man in the church at Corinth who was guilty of gross immorality and seemed unrepentant (1 Cor 5:1–5). For a discussion of the grammatical problem involved, see J.R. Mantey, "The Mistranslation of the Perfect Tense in John 20:23, Matt 10:19, and Matt 18:18" in JBL 58 (1939): 243–49. Mantey points out that the Greek fathers never quoted this passage in support of absolution. In the Matthean passages the future perfect is translated as a simple future passive, but properly the distinction of completed action should have been retained. The distinction between the periphrastic and the nonperiphrastic use is that in the periphrastic the participles and auxiliary have nothing between them except postpositives: note, e.g., the nonperiphrastic instances in Gen 41:36 (LXX); Exod 12:6 (LXX); Luke 12:52; and the periphrastic instances in Matt 10:22; John 6:31; 16:24; 19:19; Eph 5:5; James 5:15.

---

4. *The confession of Thomas*

20:24–29

> [24]Now Thomas (called Didymus), one of the Twelve, was not with the disciples when Jesus came. [25]When the other disciples told him that they had seen the Lord, he declared, "Unless I see the nail marks in his hands and put my finger where the nails were, and put my hand into his side, I will not believe it."
>
> [26]A week later his disciples were in the house again, and Thomas was with them. Though the doors were locked, Jesus came and stood among them and said, "Peace be with you!" [27]Then he said to Thomas, "Put your finger here; see my hands. Reach out your hand and put it into my side. Stop doubting and believe."
>
> [28]Thomas said to him, "My Lord and my God!"
>
> [29]Then Jesus told him, "Because you have seen me, you have believed; blessed are those who have not seen and yet have believed."

24 Thomas is singled out for special treatment because his confession provides a climactic illustration of the triumph of belief. His name is the Aramaic term for "twin," of which Didymus is the Greek equivalent (cf. John 11:16; 21:2). In some of the Syrian MSS he is called Judas Thomas and identified with "Judas, not Iscariot" of John 14:22. It seems hardly credible that two names should be used for the same man in the same context. A Syrian tradition identified Thomas with the Judas of Mark 6:3 and made him the twin brother of Jesus, a conclusion which seems impossible in the light of the Gospel accounts of the birth of Jesus. In John 11:16 and 14:5 Thomas appears as a loyal, outspoken, and rather pessimistic person who was uncertain of the future but closely attached to Jesus. Much the same picture emerges from the episode presented here. He was absent from the gathering on the first day of the week, though he must have been in contact with the rest of the disciples afterwards.

25 In spite of the repeated assurances of his colleagues that Jesus had risen (*elegon*, "they kept saying," is the imperfect tense of repeated action), Thomas was obstinate. He was so certain of the death of Jesus that he would not credit the report of his reappearance and insisted that he would not believe unless he could actually touch Jesus' body. Thomas would be satisfied by nothing less than material evidence. His incredulity is testimony to the fact that the resurrection appearances were not illusions induced by wishful thinking.

26 "A week later" literally reads "after eight days" in the Greek text. In reckoning of a span of time, the days on both ends of the span were counted. The appearance to Thomas occurred on the evening of the Sunday one week after the Resurrection. The disciples had remained in Jerusalem during that time. On this occasion Thomas was present. He must have recovered somewhat from the original shock of Jesus' death and was willing to rejoin his old associates. It may well be that the depth of his grief and his inability to reconcile the death of Jesus with the raising of Lazarus hindered him from rejoining the others on the occasion of the previous week. The reappearance of Jesus took place under the same conditions as the previous appearance, which the disciples had described to Thomas. Therefore, he could not charge them with having fabricated their report when Jesus greeted them in the same manner as before.

27 Jesus' appeal to Thomas shows that he knew what Thomas had said to his colleagues when they told him of the first appearance. Since Jesus had not been visibly present to hear his reaction to their report, Thomas must have been startled to hear Jesus quote his very words. Jesus did not immediately upbraid him for his doubts, but he challenged him to make the test that he had suggested. Jesus' words can be translated "Stop becoming an unbeliever and become a believer." Jesus halted Thomas on the road to a despairing unbelief and offered him the positive evidence he could build an enduring faith on.

28 Thomas was disposed to believe in Jesus by his personal attachment to him, as he demonstrated previously by his resolute adherence in impending danger (11:16). Jesus may have felt that the faith of all the disciples was fragile, for he told them explicitly that the raising of Lazarus was designed to give them a solid basis for a continuing faith (11:15). Now, having been challenged to make a personal test of Jesus' reality, Thomas expressed fullest faith in him. For a Jew to call another human associate "my Lord and my God" would be almost incredible. The Jewish law was strictly monotheistic; so the deification of any man would be regarded as blasphemy (10:33). Thomas, in the light of the Resurrection, applied to Jesus the titles of Lord (*kyrios*) and God (*theos*), both of which were titles of deity.

29 Jesus' commendation of Thomas was extended to all others who, like Thomas, would place a final faith in him and who, unlike Thomas, would have no opportunity to see him in his postresurrection form. Thomas's declaration is the last assertion of personal faith recorded in this Gospel. It marks the climax of the book because it presents Christ as the risen Lord, victorious over sin, sorrow, doubt, and death. It also presents the faith that accepts not only the truth of what Jesus said but also the actuality of what he was—the Son of God. In the experience of Thomas, the writer has shown how belief comes to maturity and how it changes the entire direction of an individual life.

Notes

27 "Stop" is a translation of μὴ γίνου (*mē ginou*), the present middle imperative of γίνομαι (*ginomai*, "to become"). The construction parallels that of ἅπτου (*haptou*, "hold") in v.17 and means to discontinue what has already begun. Jesus wished to stop the already evident failure of Thomas's faith.

I. *Statement of Purpose*

20:30–31

> [30]Jesus did many other miraculous signs in the presence of his disciples, which are not recorded in this book. [31]But these are written that you may believe that Jesus is the Christ, the Son of God, and that by believing you may have life in his name.

30–31 The last two verses of this chapter are really the conclusion of the Gospel. They summarize its strategy, subject, and purpose. The strategy is to use selected works of Jesus as "signs" (*sēmeia*) that illustrate his character, demonstrate his power, and relate him to human need. Seven of these signs have been narrated, exclusive of the final sign, the Resurrection. Each one involved a human personality and showed how the power of Jesus can be applied to human emergencies. These signs were performed in the presence of the disciples so that they were attested by sympathetic and competent witnesses as well as by those who happened to be present at the time, whether friendly or hostile to Jesus. The criteria for selection seems to be magnitude, varied individual significance, and effect both on the disciples and the public.

The signs, however, are not of primary intrinsic importance. The chief subject of the Gospel is the Lord Jesus Christ, whom the author desires to present as the Christ (Messiah), the Son of God. Christ (Gr. *Christos;* Heb. *Māšîah*) means "Anointed One" and refers primarily to the deliverer appointed by God, who would come to free the nation from bondage and restore the Davidic kingdom. Jesus was given this title by the earliest disciples (1:41), but it appears seldom in the Gospel; and Jesus did not use it concerning himself because it had political implications he did not intend to fulfill at the time. He told Pilate that his kingdom was not of this world (18:36), and he made no attempt to inaugurate a revolutionary movement. "Messiah," however, did represent the deliverer from sin promised in the Old Testament as the fulfillment of the covenants with the patriarchs and David and who would consummate God's purpose for the nation and the world. At that time the Jewish nation was still looking for the Messiah; John asserts that he had already come.

The title "Son of God" appears at intervals in the text of this Gospel. John the Baptist introduced Jesus by this title (1:34); Nathanael applied it to him (1:49); and on several occasions Jesus applied it to himself (5:25; 9:35, a questionable reading; 10:36; 11:4). "Son of God" would appeal to the Gentile world rather than to the Jew, for the Gentiles did not have the same reservations about it as the Jews did. The title does not, of course, imply biological descent like that of the Greco-Roman demigods; but the metaphor of sonship expresses the unity of nature, close fellowship, and unique intimacy between Jesus and the Father. Human fatherhood and sonship are only a faint copy of the relation between God the Father and God the Son. To believe that Jesus is the Christ (Messiah) and the Son of God involves the total acceptance of the revelation of God that he offers, the acknowledgment of his divine authority, and the fulfillment of the commission he entrusted to his disciples. The total scope of this belief is illustrated in the narrative of this Gospel. Its result is eternal life, a new and enduring experience of God by the believer. This conclusion ties together the three persistent themes of the Gospel: the "signs" that demonstrate Christ's nature and power; the response of "belief" that is exemplified in the crises and growth in the lives of the disciples; and the new "life" that is found in the relationship with Christ.

Notes

31 The mg. rendering of NIV, "may continue to believe," rests on the present subjunctive $\pi\iota\sigma$-$\tau\epsilon\acute{u}\eta\tau\epsilon$ (*pisteuēte,* "believe"). The reading followed by the main text is the aorist subjunctive $\pi\iota\sigma\tau\epsilon\acute{u}\sigma\eta\tau\epsilon$ (*pisteusēte,* "may believe"), which refers to an initial or single act of belief, and which is supported by a wider range of MS evidence. While the latter affords a broader range of testimony dating from the fifth century, the former is older, beginning with the third century, if P[66] has been correctly interpreted. Metzger says that it is difficult to choose between the two readings (*Textual Commentary,* p. 256). If the author was exact in his usage, the former would refer to the maintenance of faith by Christians, the latter to the initial commitment of nonbelievers.

V. The Epilogue (21:1–25)

Chapter 21 of John is a postscript to the main development of the book. It is not irrelevant to the preceding text; in fact, it completes it by illustrating the result of belief. It reads like a reminiscence that the author might have added subsequent to the composition of the first part by dictation to an assistant or scribe who added his own comment in the last two verses. The language bears a strong likeness both to the Synoptics and to other sections of John. The miracle of the catch of fish resembles the initial episode related to the call of the disciples (Luke 5:1–11); the action of Simon Peter is completely in character with other representations of his tendency toward impulsive speech or action (Matt 16:21–23; 26:33–35; John 13:36–38; 18:10–11, 15–18, 25–27; 20:6); the allusion to "sheep" follows the figure of 10:1–18; and v.19 uses phraseology concerning Peter that is applied to Jesus in 12:33. Apart from its relation to the themes and language of the main body of this Gospel, it owes its origin to the need for dispelling a false legend that had become current concerning Jesus' supposed prediction that the author of John would not die before Jesus' return.

There is no textual evidence for considering John 21 as a late addition to the main body of the Gospel. Every complete MS of John contains it. Evidently it is integral to the Gospel as a whole, though it may have been written as a special section.

A. *The Appearance at the Sea*

21:1–14

¹Afterward Jesus appeared again to his disciples by the Sea of Tiberias. It happened this way: ²Simon Peter, Thomas (called Didymus), Nathanael from

Cana in Galilee, the sons of Zebedee, and two other disciples were together. ³"I'm going out to fish," Simon Peter told them, and they said, "We'll go with you." So they went out and got into the boat, but that night they caught nothing.

⁴Early in the morning, Jesus stood on the shore, but the disciples did not realize that it was Jesus.

⁵He called out to them, "Friends, haven't you any fish?"

"No," they answered.

⁶He said, "Throw your net on the right side of the boat and you will find some." When they did, they were unable to haul the net in because of the large number of fish.

⁷Then the disciple whom Jesus loved said to Peter, "It is the Lord!" As soon as Simon Peter heard him say, "It is the Lord," he wrapped his outer garment around him (for he had taken it off) and jumped into the water. ⁸The other disciples followed in the boat, towing the net full of fish, for they were not far from shore, about a hundred yards. ⁹When they landed, they saw a fire of burning coals there with fish on it, and some bread.

¹⁰Jesus said to them, "Bring some of the fish you have just caught."

¹¹Simon Peter climbed aboard and dragged the net ashore. It was full of large fish, 153, but even with so many the net was not torn. ¹²Jesus said to them, "Come and have breakfast." None of the disciples dared ask him, "Who are you?" They knew it was the Lord. ¹³Jesus came, took the bread and gave it to them, and did the same with the fish. ¹⁴This was now the third time Jesus appeared to his disciples after he was raised from the dead.

1 "Afterward" implies an indefinite lapse of time (cf. 2:12; 3:22; 5:1, 14; 6:1; 7:1; 11:7, 11; 13:7; 19:28, 38), but not always a long time. Since this event is categorized as Jesus' third appearance to the disciples after the Resurrection (v.14), it must have taken place between the beginning of the second week and the Ascension. According to Luke, the Ascension took place outside Jerusalem near Bethany (Luke 24:50–53; cf. Acts 1:1–12). The account in Mark 16:19 does not specify the place of the Ascension. Matthew states only that the Great Commission was given to the disciples in Galilee, but he does not mention the Ascension. Paul speaks of Jesus' meeting with five hundred brethren at once, which was probably in Galilee (cf. Matt 28:7, 10; 1 Cor 15:6). The record of Jesus' postresurrection ministry is as fragmentary as that of his career prior to the Resurrection, and the Gospel emphases on it differ. Matthew, Mark, and John 21 speak of a Galilean manifestation; Luke and John 20 deal only with Jerusalem.

John is the only NT writer to use the name "Sea of Tiberias" for the Sea of Galilee, as it is called in the other Gospels (Matt 4:18; 15:29; Mark 1:16; 7:31), or the Lake of Gennesaret (Luke 5:1). John speaks once of the "Sea of Galilee" but qualifies it: "that is, the Sea of Tiberias" (6:1).

"Appeared," translated as "happened" at its second occurrence in this verse, is a characteristic Johannine word. It was the most frequently used to denote the self-revelation of Christ (1:31; 2:11; 9:3). It occurs three times in the Epilogue (21:1 bis, 14) in preparation for the final revelation of Jesus regarding the commissioning of Peter for his coming ministry. The First Epistle of John uses the term in the same way concerning both the incarnate Christ (1:2; 3:5, 8; 4:9) and his return (2:28; 3:2). Not only was this occasion an appearance of Christ after his resurrection, but it was also a disclosure of his purpose for the disciples.

2 The seven disciples who were present include several previously named in this Gospel: Simon Peter (1:40–42, 44; 6:8, 68; 13:6–9, 24, 36–38; 18:10–11, 15–18, 25–27;

20:2-7); Thomas (11:16; 14:5-6; 20:24-29); Nathanael (1:45-50); the sons of Zebedee, who are not mentioned directly in this Gospel; and two others, who could have been Philip (1:43-46; 6:5-7; 12:21-22; 14:8-10) and Andrew (1:40-42, 44; 6:8; 12:22). The identity of the last two is uncertain, for no names are given. The reason for the disciples' return to Galilee may have been to escape scrutiny and criticism by the mob in Jerusalem or to obey the command of Jesus (Matt 28:7, 10; Mark 16:6). Or perhaps they were discouraged by Jesus' death and decided to return to their old occupation of fishing. The kingdom had not arrived, and they had to make a living.

3 The leadership of Simon Peter is apparent at this point. Whether he was actuated by the need of earning money for his family or whether he simply wanted some activity to relieve the mental tension after the preceding fortnight in Jerusalem is speculative. The others assented to Peter's proposal; so they embarked in a boat that was available for a night of fishing. The presence of the definite article "the" (*to*) with "boat" (*ploion*) suggests that the boat was Peter's. Their enthusiasm ended in frustration, for no fish were caught.

4 Jesus appeared in the early morning, just as day was breaking. The fishermen no doubt were cold, wet with the dampness and spray of the lake, and discouraged by their lack of success. They failed to recognize Jesus, perhaps because they were preoccupied with their failure, or because they could not see him clearly through the morning mist on the lake.

5 Literally, in the Greek, Jesus was asking the disciples whether they had anything to eat; but in this context it is clear that he was referring to fish, as NIV so renders. The construction of the question implies that he knew they had caught nothing. This was confirmed by their dispirited answer: "No."

6 The command to cast the net on the right side of the ship may be interpreted in two ways. Either Jesus was testing their faith by recommending a procedure the Galilean fishermen never used, or he could discern the presence of a school of fish from the more advantageous viewpoint of the shore. Concrete evidence for the former interpretation is lacking (for a discussion of this, see Morris, NIC, p. 863, n. 17). Whatever the reason for the suggestion, the disciples evidently felt that one more attempt at casting the net could be no more futile than their night-long efforts had been; and it might be worthwhile. The resultant catch was so great that they could not load it into the boat.

Although there are similarities between this episode and that recorded in Luke 5:1-11, there are also important differences; and there is no reason to try to equate the two. In this account the fishermen were still on the lake, not on land; Jesus was not recognized at once, whereas Luke states that Jesus had been talking with them previously and was certainly known; and this event occurred shortly after daybreak whereas Luke says that it was after Jesus had been teaching for a period of time, while the fishermen were mending their nets. A much better explanation is that the similarity of the occasion prompted the recognition of Jesus.

7 "The disciple whom Jesus loved" was the first of the disciples to recognize the mysterious stranger on the shore as none other than the Lord Jesus himself. The repetition of the miracle of the large catch of fish no doubt was a key to John's recognition of Jesus.

Peter's quick reaction revealed his real feeling toward Jesus. Grasping his outer cloak, which he had laid aside to give him more freedom in working, he wrapped it around himself and dived overboard. His eagerness to see Jesus was consistent with his former profession of loyalty, which he had intended to keep and had not. This was probably not the moment of reconciliation, for Luke states that Jesus had met him personally on the first day of the Resurrection (Luke 24:35) as well as at the locked-door episodes (John 20:19–29).

8 A net full of live fish swimming toward the depths rather than toward the shore would be difficult to manage. The disciples in the ship pulled the net into shallow water where they could disembark and then sort out the fish.

9–10 Jesus had breakfast ready for the disciples, but he suggested that they bring some of the fish they had caught. Earlier, in the miraculous feedings of the multitudes with the fish and the loaves (Matt 14:15–21; 15:32–39; Mark 6:30–44; 8:1–10; Luke 9:10–17; John 6:1–14), the Lord had taken what the disciples had provided and had multiplied it and used it to supply the needs of many. Here he showed that he would continue to multiply and bless their efforts. However, they were yet to be told what direction those efforts were to take.

11 Simon Peter returned to the boat and pulled the net to land. If he did this by himself, he must have possessed unusual strength. One hundred and fifty-three fish plus a wet net would probably weigh as much as three hundred pounds, or more. The observation of the exact number of the fish and the fact that the net did not break reflect both an eyewitness account and a fisherman's perspective. John was impressed by the numerical size of the catch and the preservation of the net under the stress. Numerous attempts have been made to establish a symbolic meaning for the number of the fish, but no solid results have been achieved. All attempts are too fanciful to be credible. The soundest conclusion is that the figure represents the count taken as the fish were sorted, perhaps for distribution among the disciples, and that the record is the remembrance of an eyewitness.

12–13 When the catch had been safely brought to land and presumably sorted, Jesus invited the men to eat with him. Their attitude was peculiar. They desired to ask his identity, but they dared not do so because somehow they "knew" he was the Lord. He had appeared in their beloved Galilee and had repeated the same kind of miracle by which they first had been called to him. In spite of an apparent change in his outward appearance, the disciples' spiritual instinct confirmed his identity. His action in serving them with the bread and fish must have recalled the Last Supper, when he offered them bread and wine. There was, however, no sacramental overtone to this occasion.

14 The text states that this was Jesus' "third" appearance to the disciples since his resurrection. However, a close count of the resurrection appearances will show that in actuality this was the seventh appearance. Apparently what John meant by "the third time" is linked to the word "disciples." This was the third time Jesus had appeared to the official group of disciples, who were often designated as the Twelve. The other "two" appearances to the disciples were in the locked room, with and without Thomas (John 20:19–29).

B. *The Reinstatement of Peter*

21:15-23

¹⁵When they had finished eating, Jesus said to Simon Peter, "Simon son of John, do you truly love me more than these?"

"Yes, Lord," he said, "you know that I love you."

Jesus said, "Feed my lambs."

¹⁶Again Jesus said, "Simon son of John, do you truly love me?"

He answered, "Yes, Lord, you know that I love you."

Jesus said, "Take care of my sheep."

¹⁷The third time he said to him, "Simon son of John, do you love me?"

Peter was hurt because Jesus asked him the third time, "Do you love me?" He said, "Lord, you know all things; you know that I love you."

Jesus said, "Feed my sheep. ¹⁸I tell you the truth, when you were younger you dressed yourself and went where you wanted; but when you are old you will stretch out your hands, and someone else will dress you and lead you where you do not want to go." ¹⁹Jesus said this to indicate the kind of death by which Peter would glorify God. Then he said to him, "Follow me!"

²⁰Peter turned and saw that the disciple whom Jesus loved was following them. (This was the one who had leaned back against Jesus at the supper and had said, "Lord, who is going to betray you?") ²¹When Peter saw him, he asked, "Lord, what about him?"

²²Jesus answered, "If I want him to remain alive until I return, what is that to you? You must follow me." ²³Because of this, the rumor spread among the brothers that this disciple would not die. But Jesus did not say that he would not die; he only said, "If I want him to remain alive until I return, what is that to you?"

15–17 The chief reason for the narration of this episode seems to be to let Peter know that the Lord still loved him and had not cast him out (cf. 15:6). The three questions Jesus addressed to Peter stand in contrast to Peter's three denials. The disciples were no doubt aware of Peter's denial of Jesus, and the commission that Jesus renewed with him in their presence would reassure them of Peter's place among them. The wording of the first question, "Do you truly love me more than these?" contains an ambiguity. There are three possible solutions:

1. Do you love me more than these other men do?
2. Do you love me more than you love these men?
3. Do you love me more than these things—the boats, the fish, etc.?

Grammatically, the comparative adverb "more" (*pleon*) is followed by the ablative of comparison "these" (*toutōn*). Whether the ablative represents the first or second alternative is not clear (see BDF, 185.1, p. 99). In view of Peter's boastful promise that whatever the others did he would not fail, the former alternative seems more likely. The third solution seems least probable.

The words translated "love" have also raised considerable debate. Two different terms are used: *agapaō* is used in Jesus' first two questions and *phileō* is used in Jesus' third question and in Peter's three replies. *Agapaō* is the same word "love" that appears in John 3:16. It is used of divine love and usually carries the connotation of will or purpose as well as that of affection. *Phileō* implies affinity, friendship, and fondness. Both words represent a high aspect of love. Since they are used of both God (3:16; 5:20) and men (14:21; 16:27) in this Gospel, they seem to be interchangeable with no great difference in meaning. Morris has a thorough discussion of the synonyms in this passage (NIC, pp. 870–75). He maintains that there is no essential difference in meaning between them. On the other hand, a good case can be made for a difference in Jesus' emphasis. There was less doubt concerning Peter's attachment to Jesus than there was concerning his will to love at all costs; and the change of term in Jesus' third question makes his probing of Peter even deeper. If the latter alternative is adopted, it explains better Peter's distress when questioned a third time, since Jesus would not only be challenging his love but would be implying that it was superficial. NIV brings out the nuance between *agapaō* and *phileō* by translating *agapaō* "truly love" and *phileō* "love."

Peter's affirmative answer to each question is substantially the same. The verb "know" (*oida*) implies the intellectual knowledge of a fact. In his third reply, however, Peter strengthened his statement by using *ginōskō* for "know." This word denotes knowledge gained through experience. While one cannot assert beyond contradiction that the distinctions between these two pairs of synonyms are always uniformly observed, in a context where a definite change is made the difference is worth considering. Peter's protestations are emphatic; and even if the conversation were carried on in Aramaic, which would not use separate words where the Greek employs these synonyms, they may represent accurately the meaning of the dialogue as the writer heard and remembered it.

Jesus' commands to Peter also contain fine distinctions:
1. "Feed (pasture) my lambs" (v.15).
2. "Take care of (shepherd) my sheep" (v.16).
3. "Feed (pasture) my sheep" (v.17).

The first and third imply only taking the sheep to pasture where they are fed; the second implies the total guardianship a shepherd exercises. This threefold injunction does not necessarily give Peter the sole responsibility for the oversight of Christ's followers; all of his spiritually mature disciples were called to be shepherds (cf. 1 Peter 5:2). This challenge to Peter demanded a total renewal of his loyalty and reaffirmed his responsibilities.

18-19 The introduction of v.18 by "I tell you the truth," rendered "verily, verily" in KJV, makes the statement of Jesus solemn and important. The author adds an explanation of Jesus' enigmatic words. They were a prediction of Peter's career: a new responsibility, a new danger, and violent death. Jesus placed Peter in a category with himself—a life spent for God and ultimately sacrificed to glorify God. Similar language was used concerning Jesus earlier in the Gospel (12:27-32; 13:31). The command "Follow me" is a present imperative, which literally means "Keep on following me." Jesus showed Peter that if he were to fulfill his promise of loyalty, he would have to follow him to his own cross.

20-21 Peter's question concerning John reflects curiosity and possibly uneasiness. Peter had been given an important commission, but what would his friend be expected to do? Would he share equally in both the responsibilities and the perils of the same task?

22-23 Jesus' reply indicated that even if he intended that "the disciple whom Jesus loved" should outlive Peter, Peter's main concern should not be a comparison of his lot with that of his friend; rather, Peter's concern was to be the fulfillment of Jesus' purpose. The use of the second person pronoun in Jesus' command makes the statement emphatic: "*You* must follow me" (italics mine). Jesus was urging Peter to take his attention off his colleague and focus it on Jesus himself.

Jesus' reference to his return is one of the few clear allusions to the Second Coming in this Gospel. The use here is hyperbolical, for it marks the utmost point to which the beloved disciple could survive and remain active. This utterance was remembered in the church and formed the basis of the rumor that Jesus had promised John that he would live until Jesus returned. As a matter of fact, Jesus had offered a supposition, not a promise. The author's explanation of Jesus' announcement may be taken as evidence that the disciple was still living at the time this Gospel was written and that he was the source of its content. Obviously, if he had died early, the rumor would have had no credence.

C. *The Colophon*

21:24–25

> ²⁴This is the disciple who testifies to these things and who wrote them down. We know that his testimony is true.
> ²⁵Jesus did many other things as well. If every one of them were written down, I suppose that even the whole world would not have room for the books that would be written.

24 The Epilogue contains a number of parenthetic statements that may have been the author's explanatory notes on the scene at the Sea of Galilee. Peter's removal of his cloak (v.7), the hesitancy of the disciples to ask Jesus to identify himself (v.12), the comment on Jesus' prediction of Peter's death (v.19), the identification of the beloved disciple (v.20), and the correction of the false rumor that the beloved disciple would not die mark the author as one of the participants. At the same time, these leave the impression that the account was written for a second generation of believers who were historically remote from the original events. This impression is corroborated by the last two verses, which are the endorsement of the narrative. Although v.24 is in the first person plural ("we know"), as if it were being certified by the testimony of a group, a different division on one word would make it a first person singular. In that case the author (or scribe) would be saying, "And I for my part know that his testimony is valid."

25 The tremendous content of Jesus' teaching and deeds is acknowledged again by the writer. This Gospel must have been written at a period when Christian literature was beginning to multiply and the church was becoming conscious of it. The letters of Paul were collected and circulated before the turn of the century, and the Gospels or writings like them were already known in the church (cf. Luke 1:1). Though John admits that what he recorded is only a fraction of what Jesus said and did, the content of this Gospel is one of the most valuable assets the church possesses.

Notes

24 The early Gr. uncial MSS of the NT were written in all caps. and without word divisions. Thus OIΔAMEN (*oidamen*, "we know") could be divided into OIΔA MEN (*oida men*, "I surely know"), and both renderings of the text are possible. The suggestion is purely speculative, but in its favor is the fact that a rendering of the verb as a first person singular would be in keeping with the second sentence of v.25. However, there are no MSS that make the division in this manner when divisions are recognized.

THE ACTS OF THE APOSTLES

Richard N. Longenecker

THE ACTS OF THE APOSTLES

Introduction

"The Acts of the Apostles" is the name given to the second part of a two-volume work traditionally identified as having been written by Luke, a companion of the apostle Paul. Originally the two volumes circulated together as two parts of one complete writing. But during the late first or early second century, the first volume became associated with the Gospels identified with Matthew, Mark, and John, thus forming the fourfold Gospel. Luke's second volume was left to go its own way. It was at this time, it seems, that the second volume received its present title, with the word "Acts" (*praxeis*) evidently meant to suggest both movement in the advance of the gospel and heroic exploits by the apostles. The reference to "the Apostles," however, is somewhat misleading, because the work deals almost exclusively with Peter and Paul and the persons and events associated with their ministries. Acts is the third longest of the NT writings, being about one-tenth shorter than its companion volume Luke (the longest NT book) and almost exactly the length of Matthew. Together Luke-Acts comprises almost 30 percent of the material in the NT, exceeding both the Pauline and the Johannine writings in size.

It is said that James Denney, on being asked by a student to recommend a good "Life of Christ," looked quizzically at the questioner and replied, "Have you read the one by Luke?"[1] The point is apt because too often we favor modern syntheses over primary sources. The issue is heightened when we ask about a "History of the Early Church." Luke, who in the preface to his Gospel acknowledges the existence of other Gospels, makes no allusion to anything like his Acts. Moreover, in the NT we have only his account of the early church. Indeed, if we did not have Acts, or if Acts were proved basically unreliable, we would know nothing of the earliest days of the Christian movement except for bits of data gathered from the letters of Paul or inferred by looking back from later developments. To attempt a study of early Christianity apart from Acts, therefore,

---

[1]Cf. A.M. Hunter, *Introducing the New Testament* (London: SCM, 1957), p. 48.

is to proceed mainly *ignotum per ignotius* ("the unknown [explained] by the still more unknown"), for information about the early church gained from Paul's letters often lacks an historical context. Cadbury has spoken of "the extraordinary darkness which comes over us as students of history when rather abruptly this guide leaves us with Paul a prisoner in Rome" (*Book of Acts*, p. 3). And, in fact, there is nothing to replace Acts. If one or two of the four Gospels had been lost, we should be much the poorer; but we should still have the others. Acts, however, stands alone.

It is of utmost importance, therefore, to ask some searching questions about Acts. But before asking specific questions, we must know something of how the issues have been treated in the past so that we may learn how to frame our questions in the light of our knowledge today. Therefore what follows first is a brief history of the criticism of Acts during the past 150 years in order to learn what questions ought to be asked and what steps others have taken toward answering them. From that we will move on to consider the nature of historical writing in antiquity and the relation of proclamation to the writing of history in Acts to learn how to frame the questions in a manner appropriate to the material at hand. Then from such a background, the more traditional issues having to do with the purpose or purposes of the writing, its sources, the formulation of its narrative, the composition of its speeches, the form and structure of the work, its date, and its author can be treated with greater precision.

1. The Criticism of Acts

Criticism of the Acts of the Apostles during the past century and a half has progressed through various phases, taken various forms, and focused on various issues. In the nineteenth century it was largely dominated by the Tübingen school of German critics and their so-called tendency criticism, based on an Hegelian understanding of the course of early Christian history. In 1831 F.C. Baur proposed that early Christianity developed from a conflict between Peter, who expressed the faith of the earliest believers and was in continuity with Jesus himself, and Paul, who epitomized a later Christian viewpoint, with Acts being a second-century endeavor to work out a synthesis between the original thesis of Peter and the antithesis of Paul.[2] For Baur, the conciliatory nature of Acts clearly indicates that the work is a later synthesis, perhaps written between A.D. 110 and 130, and that the Paul who wrote the *Hauptbriefe*—i.e., the authentic epistles (Rom, 1 and 2 Cor, Gal)—could not possibly be the same Paul of Acts. According to Baur, in his own letters Paul is the champion of Christian freedom whereas in Acts he is portrayed as compromising by repeatedly yielding to Jewish scruples. Furthermore, Baur argued that a close study of Acts shows that it abounds in the kind of historical errors to be expected of a second-century author trying to impose a fictitious uniformity and tranquillity upon an earlier more turbulent time and that it also contains such errors as an author would make who wrote well after the events occurred.

Baur himself wrote no commentary on Acts. But the suggestions in his five monographs and numerous articles about understanding the course of early Christian history were followed (though not uniformly) by such biblical and theological scholars as David

---

[2]F.C. Baur, "Die Christuspartei in der korinthischen Gemeinde, der Gegensatz des petrinischen und paulinischen Christentums in der ältesten Kirche," *Tübinger Zeitschrift für Theologie* (1831), 61–206; cf. also his *Paulus, der Apostel Jesu Christi* (Stuttgart: Becher & Müller, 1845), tr. by E. Zeller as *Paul, His Life and Works*, 2 vols. (London: Williams & Norgate, 1875).

Strauss, Bruno Bauer, and Albrecht Ritschl. In particular, Eduard Zeller, Baur's son-in-law and closest disciple, undertook a full-scale investigation of the narrative of Acts, arguing from its conciliatory purpose for the thoroughly tendentious, nonhistorical, and mythical character of the book.[3]

Not everyone, however, was enamored with the Tübingen treatment of the NT materials generally and of Acts in particular. W.C. van Manen of Leiden, the leading representative of the so-called Radical Dutch school, criticized Baur for not going far enough in applying his principles, which he believed ultimately negated the authenticity of the entire NT. And Bruno Bauer to some extent echoed this criticism. On the other hand, most scholars came to believe that it was not just F.C. Baur's application of his principles but his principles of criticism themselves which were ill-founded and ran roughshod over the evidence. By 1914, in fact, when the nineteenth-century world of thought finally came to an end, the vast majority of scholars had rejected his views.

Of great significance in bringing about a more positive attitude toward the reliability of Acts during the later part of the nineteenth century were the works of J.B. Lightfoot, Theodore Zahn, William M. Ramsay, and Adolf Harnack—four very different scholars whose work in concert tended to support the historicity of Acts. Lightfoot, in his 1865 commentary on Galatians, objected strongly to Baur's assertion that a conciliatory purpose in Acts reflects seriously upon the credibility of the account. Lightfoot declared, "Such a purpose is at least as likely to have been entertained by a writer, if the two Apostles were essentially united, as if they were not. The truth or falsehood of the account must be determined on other grounds."[4] Moreover, both Lightfoot and Zahn, in separate studies of the apostolic fathers, demonstrated that the evidence does not support Baur's tendency criticism at a point crucial to its reconstruction of early Christianity and one where it can be readily tested—viz., with regard to the origin of the Clementine and Ignatian writings.[5] Such a demonstration was a crushing blow to the Tübingen view of Acts: if an Hegelian understanding could not be supported regarding the Clementine and Ignatian writings, it could not be supported anywhere.

In addition, Ramsay's investigation of historical and geographical details in Acts,[6] coupled with various literary and source-critical studies that culminated in the work of Harnack,[7] tended to confirm in most minds at the turn of the century the basic reliability of Acts. What doubts remained centered around the portrayal of the character and activities of Paul in Acts, for where the Paul of Acts could be compared with the Paul of the Epistles, there seemed to be some serious discrepancies—though Harnack was able to quiet most of the doubts in his day by insisting that the apostle must be understood more broadly than usual. But though there remained this nagging suspicion about the presentation of Paul in Acts, it could not displace the general confidence in Acts engendered by the work of Lightfoot, Zahn, Ramsay, and Harnack.

The end of the nineteenth century witnessed a growing concern regarding the question of Luke's literary dependence. This erupted into a vigorous debate in the first

---

[3]Eduard Zeller, *Die Apostelgeschichte nach ihrem Inhalt und Ursprung kritisch Untersucht* (Stuttgart: Becher & Müller, 1854).

[4]J.B. Lightfoot, *Epistle to the Galatians* (London: Macmillan, 1865), p. 359.

[5]See esp. J.B. Lightfoot, *The Apostolic Fathers*, 5 vols. (London: Macmillan, 1869–85); idem, *Essays on "Supernatural Religion"* (London: Macmillan, 1889); Theodore Zahn, *Ignatius von Antiochien* (Gotha: Perthes, 1873).

[6]See esp. Ramsay, *Church in the Roman Empire; St. Paul the Traveller;* and *Trustworthiness of the New Testament.*

[7]See esp. Harnack, *Luke; Acts;* and *Date of the Acts.*

quarter of the twentieth century. Was Luke's work based on an earlier source or sources (whether written or oral) that can still be identified through various linguistic features and stylistic alterations in the text? Or are we to consider his book a free composition in the manner of certain ancient historians, with the recognizable Semitic flavor of chapters 1–15 being the result of the author's modeling of his language—either consciously or unconsciously—on the LXX?

This period of source criticism began with Weiss's survey in 1886 of the evidence for the use of sources in the composition of Acts.[8] And many believed that the next twenty years of source-critical discussion reached its apex in Harnack's argument for multiple written sources underlying the first half of Acts, with resultant doublets in the narrative, and primarily personal sources (chiefly verbal accounts and Luke's own travel journal) for the second half. But the debate veered to an extreme position in C.C. Torrey's argument that the Semitic flavor of chapters 1–15 is the result of Luke's use throughout these chapters of a single Aramaic source that he translated rather mechanically into Greek.

Attempting to correct Torrey's view, Henry Cadbury, F.J. Foakes Jackson, and Kirsopp Lake combined the linguistic arguments for an Aramaic substructure for Acts 1–15 with an acceptance of multiple underlying sources and the acknowledgment that some of the apparently Semitic features of the narrative may also be explained along the lines of Septuagintal influence (BC, 2:9–10,129–30,145). J. de Zwaan and W.K.L. Clarke departed further from Torrey in viewing so-called Semitisms more as Septuagintisms, though they did not entirely deny the possibility of some Semitic source material behind the narrative here and there (BC, 2:30–105). And in 1923, taking a stance diametrically opposed to that of Torrey, Dibelius argued that a Septuagintal styling on the part of the author of Acts is fully sufficient of itself to explain the Semitic flavor of the narrative that has led so many to postulate the presence of Aramaic sources (*Studies in Acts*, pp. 1–25).[9] Generally speaking, those scholars who argued for Semitic source material underlying the first half of Acts also stressed the author's faithfulness to his material and the basic reliability of the record, whereas those who explained the Semitic flavor as Septuagintal styling usually laid emphasis upon the creative ability of the writer in archaizing his presentation and viewed Acts as quite a free composition without any demonstrable historical authenticity.

Contemporary critical expositions of Acts are heavily influenced by the "new hermeneutic," "form criticism," and the embryonic "redaction criticism" of Bultmann, Schmidt, and Dibelius. While the basic approach of these men was detailed in 1919 in separate programmatic studies on the Gospels,[10] it was in a series of articles that appeared from 1923 till his death in 1947 that Dibelius applied the methodology to Acts.[11] In his earliest treatments of Acts, which drew on the analysis of literary structures made by Norden,[12] Dibelius focused his attention on the individual units of material in Acts (the form critical method); later on, however, he began to deal more with the

---

[8]Bernhard Weiss, *Lehrbuch der Einleitung in das Neue Testament* (Berlin: Reimer, 1886), pp. 569–84.

[9]This originally appeared in *Eucharisterion für H. Gunkel* (Göttingen: Vandenhoeck & Ruprecht, 1923), 2:27–49.

[10]Cf. Rudolf Bultmann, *Die Geschichte der synoptischen Tradition* (Göttingen: Vandenhoeck & Ruprecht, 1919) = *The History of the Synoptic Tradition*, tr. J. March (New York: Harper & Row, 1963); Karl L. Schmidt, *Der Rahmen der Geschichte Jesu* (Berlin: Reimer, 1919); Martin Dibelius, *Die Formgeschichte des Evangeliums* (Tübingen: Mohr, 1919) = *From Tradition to Gospel*, tr. B.L. Woolf (London: Nicholson and Watson, 1934).

[11]These articles are now incorporated in his *Studies in Acts*.

[12]Edward Norden, *Agnostos Theos* (Leipzig: Teubner, 1913).

personal contribution of the author in the presentation of his materials (the redaction critical method). This approach gained wide acceptance through the writings of Bultmann[13] and has been crystalized in the works of Hans Conzelmann and Ernst Haenchen.[14]

What the new hermeneutic is saying is that so-called historical writings tell us more about the authors who wrote them than they do about the events they purport to relate. What form criticism aims to do (at least as Bultmann and Dibelius used it) is to retrace the situation in the life of the writer and his church that gave rise to the fabrication of the units of material he incorporates. This it does by analyzing the literary forms and their development. And what redaction criticism aims at is to discover a profile of the author as he reveals himself in his editorial activity of fitting together the various units of material at his disposal in order to construct his portrayal. Thus redaction criticism is almost entirely occupied with the theological concerns of the author—concerns that spring from his own personal situation and can be detected primarily in the seams and structure of his composition. Accompanying this method there is often a disavowal of the relevancy of the historical facticity of the composition studied and a greatly diminished concern for the question of its sources.

When applied to Acts, such an approach usually works from two basic postulates: (1) Acts must be judged either as Christian proclamation or as an historical treatise and that if it is taken to be proclamation—which it obviously is—it cannot be taken seriously as history; (2) the futuristic hope of the earliest believers precluded any historical interest on their part, so that when the author of Acts begins to take himself seriously as an historian he only shows how far removed he is from the original faith and from the events he claims to present (Conzelmann, *Theology of Luke,* pp. 12–15, 210–11; Haenchen, *Acts of the Apostles,* pp. 90–110). The kerygmatic (declarative) nature of Acts, therefore, prohibits our asking whether the sermon illustrations in it are really authentic, and its attempt to be historical shows just how far removed from its actual situation the work really is.

Literary criticism, according to this view, has repeatedly shown that as a matter of fact Acts is historically quite inaccurate and preserves at best only a few names from the earliest Christian times.[15] And form criticism has shown that the work must be classed as a late first-century or early second-century production engaged in historicizing the primitive eschatology in an attempt to counter rising disillusionment because of the delay of the Parousia and the threat of Gnosticism. So in chapters 1–15 of Acts the author must be judged as producing an edifying piece of religious propaganda rather than anything that can be identified as history. Sources are at a minimum. The narrative and speeches reflect more the author's interests than those of the early church, and the pseudo-Semitized flavor he gives the composition shows something of the fabricated nature of the whole. Moreover, what is true for the first half of the work carries over into the rest because, if anything, the author is consistent in the way he writes.

This is not to say that modern critics of the type we have been describing have lost interest in Acts or have ceased to consider it important for the study of early Christianity. Certainly not! A great deal of scholarly research has been and is being done on Acts by

---

[13]Principally this is through Rudolf Bultmann's *Theology of the New Testament,* 2 vols., tr. K. Grobel (London: SCM, 1952), which first appeared in German in 1948 and 1951.

[14]See esp. Conzelmann, *Theology of Luke,* and Haenchen, *Acts of the Apostles.*

[15]Cf. E. Haenchen, "The Book of Acts as Source Material for the History of Early Christianity," in Keck and Martyn, pp. 258–78.

those most influenced by Bultmann and Dibelius. Nevertheless, there is a widespread confidence in contemporary scholarly circles that Acts provides us with historical information only for the postapostolic period of the church and cannot be used (except inferentially) for anything earlier. Haenchen, who is now the most important Bultmannian commentator on Acts, offers the following words: "To him who knows how to read between the lines and to hear what is left unsaid, the book of Acts gives rich information about what is commonly called 'the postapostolic age.' "[16]

Our survey of the criticism of Acts during the past 150 years has necessarily been brief. Much more could be said, for there have been many significant crosscurrents and eddies in the flow of critical thought.[17] We have only provided an overview of the course of the criticism of Acts and, in doing this, highlighted certain issues of continuing importance for any treatment of Acts today.

Chief among these issues is the question of the kerygmatic nature of the work and the significance of this for the author's treatment of history. This requires an understanding of both what Luke is attempting to do in his presentation and the nature of historical writing in antiquity. Equally important is the question of Luke's eschatology and how it varied from that of early Christianity and affected his portrayal of early Christianity. But though such queries stand at the forefront of every critical discussion of Acts, the more traditional matters having to do with sources, narrative, speeches, structure, date, and author continue to be important—as do also such common topics as the conciliatory nature of Acts and the relation of the Paul of Acts to the Paul of the Epistles. All these issues, together with a number of others, will be treated in what follows, both in the introductory sections and in the commentary itself.

2. Historical Writing in Antiquity

Ancient historiography reached its zenith shortly after the NT period in the works of the Greek biographer Plutarch and the Roman historians Tacitus and Suetonius. But these writers drew on traditional techniques reaching back to and developed from the fifth-century B.C. Greek historian Thucydides and his *History of the Peloponnesian War*.

Underlying all truly historical writing in antiquity, as opposed to the mere chronicling of events, was the conviction that the actions and words of distinctive people in their respective periods represent more adequately the situation than any comments by the historian; that is, that the "ethos" (*ēthos*) of the times is conveyed best through a portrayal of the "acts" (*praxeis*) of the participants (Stanton, p. 122). Xenophon (469–399 B.C.), for example, at the beginning of his *Memoirs of Socrates* (c. 380 B.C.), writes regarding his hero: "In order to support my opinion that he benefited his companions, alike by actions that revealed his own character and by his own conversations, I will set down what I recall of these" (1.3.1).[18]

The "acts" of the subjects, understood in terms of both their actions and their words, were the building blocks for the historians and biographers of antiquity. But while the Greek word *praxeis* ("acts") suggests movement and exploits, what these historians and

---

[16]Ibid., p. 261.

[17]For two important histories of the criticism of the Acts of the Apostles, see J. Dupont's *The Sources of Acts* and W.W. Gasque's *A History of the Criticism.*

[18]Cf. also *Agesilaus* 1.6, where Xenophon insists that the deeds of a man best disclose the nature of his character. This same emphasis is found in Isocrates *Evangoras* 76.

biographers were primarily interested in were illuminating vignettes that gave insight into the ethos of a period or of a person's character. Plutarch (c.A.D. 50–130), for example, in his *Vita Alexander* 1.2, states the following in commencing his portrayal of Alexander the Great:

> It is not always in the most illustrious deeds that men's virtues or vices may be best discerned, but often an action of small note, a short saying or a jest, will distinguish a person's real character more than the greatest sieges or the most important battles. Therefore, as painters in their portraits labor the likeness in the face, and particularly about the eyes, in which the peculiar turn of mind most appears, and run over the rest with a more careless hand, so we must be permitted to strike off the features of the soul in order to give a real likeness of these great men—leaving to others the circumstantial detail of their labors and achievements.

The historians and biographers of antiquity, therefore, were interested in what might be called indirect character portrayals by means of the actions and words of their subjects. And in the selection of those actions and words, they were more interested in setting out representative vignettes having to do with the ethos of the period than in merely chronicling exploits.

Furthermore, in writing their histories the ancients frequently grouped their material *per species*, without always specifying chronological relationships. The *Life of Euripides* by the third-century B.C. biographer Satyrus, which is the only extant work from the Peripatetic school of biographical writing, contains "only one section which can in any way be called chronological; yet there is a clear tendency towards an orderly grouping of material, at least under broad captions" (Stanton, p. 120). Likewise Plutarch, who is supposed to have followed Peripatetic practices, makes no endeavor in his *Parallel Lives* to be precise chronologically but repeatedly uses such vague expressions as "about this time" or "some time after this." He refers to military campaigns, of course, in succession, but his basic method is to group his material under various categories.

Of the Roman historians, only Tacitus employs a chronological framework throughout in marking off the various stages of Agricola's career. Suetonius in his *Lives of the Emperors* quite naturally works chronologically in treating first one emperor and then another. But he holds himself to a portrayal based on chronology only with regard to Julius Caesar, the first in his series. More commonly he groups his portrayals under such topics as conduct, business, family, attitude toward society, and friends. In fact, he explains his method in his portrayal of Augustus: "Having given as it were a summary of his life, I shall now take up its various phases one by one, not in chronological order, but by classes [*per species*], in order to make the account clearer and more intelligible" (*Augustus* 9).

There has been a great deal of discussion about the attitude of the ancient historians and biographers toward factual accuracy in their writings. For the past half century, Cadbury's dicta have reigned almost supreme in NT circles: "Instead of accuracy the purpose of ancient historians tended to make the form the chief point of emphasis" (BC, 2:11), and "from Thucydides downwards, speeches reported by the historians are confessedly pure imagination" (ibid., 2:13). But that Cadbury's views are extreme has been demonstrated by Mosley in a study of the intent and practice of such writers as Lucian, Dionysius, Polybius, Ephorus, Cicero, Josephus, and Tacitus.[19] The ancients, according

---

[19]A.W. Mosley, "Historical Reporting in the Ancient World," NTS, 12 (1965), 10–26.

to Mosley's analysis, did ask the question "Did it happen in this way?" and while some were slovenly and uninformed in their reporting, others "tried to be as accurate as possible and to get information from eyewitnesses."[20]

Furthermore, Glasson has pointed out that those who cite Thucydides's words "I have used language in accordance with what I thought the speakers in each case would have been most likely to say," as though that settles the matter in favor of the thoroughly imaginative character of the Thucydidean speeches, are distinctly unfair to what Thucydides was actually saying:

> With reference to the speeches in this history, some were delivered before the war began, others while it was going on; it was hard to record the exact words spoken, both in cases where I was myself present, and where I used the reports of others. But I have used language in accordance with what I thought the speakers in each case would have been most likely to say, adhering as closely as possible to the general sense of what was actually spoken (*History of the Peloponnesian War* 1.22).

From this Glasson has aptly observed: "He does not claim to reproduce the precise words like a stenographer but in writing the speeches he keeps as closely as possible to 'the general sense of *what was actually spoken.*' . . . This is a very different matter from the imaginative composing of speeches suitable to the occasion [italics his]."[21]

Contrary to many current statements about historical writing in antiquity, we must maintain, therefore, that the ancients were interested in what actually happened. Nevertheless, it must also be insisted that history, as opposed to the mere formulation of chronicles, was written by the ancients for moral, ethical, and polemical purposes and not just to inform or entertain. This was true for the Greek Plutarch and the whole tradition of biographical writing he represents. It was true for the Roman historians Tacitus and Suetonius in their portraits of the emperors and their times. And it was true for the Jewish historian Josephus in his presentations of Jewish history and thought before a Roman audience. It is true as well for Luke's Acts, wherein, like the historiography of the OT, there is the tracing of the activity of God in various historical events as viewed from a particular perspective.

3. Kerygma and History in Acts

While earlier generations fixed their attention first upon the Pauline letters and then upon the Johannine corpus, the focus of scholarly attention today is more on the Lukan materials—the third Gospel and the Book of Acts. And prominent among the issues being discussed today is that regarding the relation of kerygma and history in Acts: If Acts is truly of the nature of proclamation, can it also be considered history? and if Acts presents itself as history, can it really represent in fact the original proclamation of the earliest Christians?

Modern theology, in reaction to earlier historic treatments of a more positivistic persuasion, has laid great stress on the fact that Acts is really Christian proclamation and not just a simple reproduction of what happened apart from any interpretation or bias.

---

[20]Ibid., p. 26.
[21]T.F. Glasson, "The Speeches in Acts and Thucydides," ExpT, 76 (1965), 165.

And this understanding into the nature of Acts is important and helpful, as far as it goes. Certainly Luke did not write for money, literary recognition, or only to add to human knowledge. He wrote, rather, as he tells us in the Prologue to his two-volume work, to proclaim the certainty of what his audience had been taught (Luke 1:1-4).

Some, however, have taken the fact that Acts is Christian proclamation and not a simple, noninterpretative record of what happened to an unwarranted extreme. They have divorced the kerygmatic and the historical in Acts. As a result many feel constrained to choose between the subjectivism of a demythologizing approach or the sterility of a mere historicism. But interpretation and bias are inherent in every historical writing, for history, as distinct from chronicle, is the interplay between selected events and their interpretation. "All history at whatever level," as Turner reminds us, "involves construction on the part of the historian, but this does not imply that he is condemned to mere imaginative 'doodling' in the sands of time."[22] The question is not whether the historian has an interpretation of the data he is putting forward but whether, given the fact of a bias, he has exercised his craft with due exactness so as not to falsify his data or distort their significance in the interests of his thesis.

Indeed, the author of Acts has his own interests, theological viewpoint, and purposes in writing. And to a considerable extent these have affected his selection, arrangement, and shaping of the particular units of material that he incorporates. But to argue that therefore his narrative must be viewed as historically suspect is a non sequitur. The question as to whether the event or the kerygma is decisive for faith in Acts (and, for that matter, throughout the NT) may not be answered in the form of an alternative.[23] The record contains an intermeshing of events, for which facticity is asserted, and the significance of those events, for which inspiration is assumed. Both the events themselves and their significance are vital for an understanding of God's mighty acts by his Spirit through his church. "Acts, like the Gospels," as Dix has insisted, "is written throughout with a strong sense of the *sacredness* of the concrete facts it narrates, because the author believes that it is through what actually happened that the 'Counsel of God' was manifested and fulfilled [italics his]" (p. 39).

Furthermore, we must recognize that every history is to some extent refractive. The passage of time between an event and how it was originally understood, on the one hand, and the historian's record of that event in the light of his appreciation and interests, on the other, no matter how homogeneous the development of understanding between the two, modifies to some extent immediate perceptions and initial responses—if not in the content itself, at least in the ability to appreciate more fully significances and implications. And this is true for Acts, written as it is from the perspective of the resurrection faith and coming to birth in the context of the theology that resulted from that faith.

It is beyond doubt that Luke's theology was more developed at the time of writing than it could ever have been at the time of the events he relates. To this extent, the new hermeneutic, form criticism, and redaction criticism are certainly correct. But it does not necessarily follow that Luke had little interest in reproducing the details and nuances of an earlier situation. And even where events are reported from the perspective of a fuller theology and a broader understanding of how they fit together, it must be remembered that the NT authors, Luke included, were convinced that such a presentation of

---

[22]H.E.W. Turner, *Historicity and the Gospels* (London: Mowbray, 1963), p. 18.
[23]Cf. O. Cullmann, *Salvation in History*, tr. S.G. Sowers (New York: Harper & Row, 1967), pp. 89-90, passim.

the facts "was more empiric and historic, more adequate, correct and true than the immediate picture had been."[24]

As to the question whether Acts in purporting to be an historical treatise does not thereby show itself to be quite removed from early Christian convictions and thereby unable to represent in fact early Christian proclamation, we must consider the very large issue of the nature of early Christian eschatological thought. Those who ask the above question assume that the eschatology of the earliest believers was so entirely futuristic or "proleptic" that they gave no thought to formulating their convictions into some kind of basic system, to structuring their communal experiences, to extending their outreach through some kind of mission, or to writing down their history for others either geographically or chronologically removed from them. Those who hold this point of view also assume that the experiences of the earliest believers and their expectation of an imminent return of Jesus left them with no interest in and no time for the matters just mentioned. Moreover, all that Acts reflects as to Christology, ecclesiology, a theology of mission, and, particularly, writing the church's history only shows how far removed the author really was from the stance of the earliest believers. In fact, he was so far removed from it that the Parousia expectation was no longer primary or vital to him. Thus its delay caused him not only to restructure his own Christian faith into a form that can be identified as "Early Catholicism," but, in accordance with this "Early Catholicism," he tried to restructure the proclamation and convictions of the earliest Christians in an endeavor to gain support for his own views.

Futuristic hopes were certainly strong among the earliest believers in Jesus, and we must never deny this. But this fact does not mean that we must assert the impossibility of "realized eschatology" coexisting with a futuristic emphasis. Nor does it force us to believe that an understanding of eschatology as in some sense fulfilled could only have arisen from the abandonment of a futuristic orientation. Undoubtedly there was much uncertainty and perplexity in the early church because of the delay of the Parousia. But if we understand the faith of the earliest Christians to be best characterized as "inaugurated eschatology" (which I believe to be the case), then we must judge that their lives and thoughts were focused more on a person than a program. And while that person's return was delayed, his work for them and his presence with them provided the essential basis for their Christian experience. Or as van Unnik has aptly said:

> I cannot help confessing that the exegetical basis for many statements in the modern approach to Luke-Acts is often far from convincing, at least highly dubious in my judgment. . . . Has the delay of the *parousia* really wrought that havoc that it is sometimes supposed to have done, or did the early Christians react differently from the way modern scholars would have done? In the light of the history of early Christianity this effect of the *Parousieverzögerung* is highly overrated. The faith of the early Christians did not rest on a date but on the work of Christ.[25]

4. Luke's Purposes in Writing Acts

Basic to every evaluation of Acts is the question of the purpose or purposes of its author. Tendency criticism began here, arguing that the nature of Acts can be explained

---

[24]B. Reicke, "Incarnation and Exaltation. The Historic Jesus and the Kerygmatic Christ," Int, 16 (1962), 159.
[25]W.C. van Unnik, "Luke-Acts, a Storm Center in Contemporary Scholarship," in Keck and Martyn, p. 28.

entirely on the basis of a conciliatory purpose and its extent of treatment can be explained by the fact that its author was unwilling to say more. All forms of redaction criticism, whether ancient or modern, also begin with the insistence that to have a profile of an author from his writing is to possess the most important key to the nature of his work.

With the necessity of evaluating Acts as to the purpose(s) for which it was written, all seem to agree. But the question of the exact definition of that purpose remains. Under the spell of the Tübingen school, the conciliatory purpose of Acts was taken to be supreme. At the end of the nineteenth century, however, most were prepared to view the apologetic purpose as dominant. Influenced by Ramsay and Harnack, many during the first half of the twentieth century considered Luke's purposes to be primarily historical and didactic. And since the middle of the present century, Luke's kerygmatic purpose has been emphasized almost to the exclusion of all others. While at various times certain clusters of opinion as to why Acts was written have emerged, even within these there has existed a range of ideas as to exactly how Luke expressed his purpose and how he should be understood. Therefore, in what follows we must set forth more precisely what can be said about Luke's purposes and show something of the nature of the supporting evidence.

Luke himself states that his purpose in writing his two-volume work was "so that you may know the certainty of the things you have been taught" (Luke 1:4). The "most excellent Theophilus" (Luke 1:3; cf. Acts 1:1) to whom Luke addressed his work seems to have been a man who, though receptive to the gospel and perhaps even convinced by its claims, had many questions about Christianity as he knew it. From the way Luke writes to him, we may surmise that Theophilus was concerned about how the Christian faith related to Jesus' ministry, to Jews and the world of Judaism, to the lifestyle of certain scrupulous Jewish Christians, to the more universalistic outlook of Gentiles, and to the sanctions of Roman law. Also, he was undoubtedly interested in how the gospel had been received and what success it had met in the various centers of influence known to him in the eastern part of the empire, from Jerusalem to Rome.

Certainly when receiving his first instruction in the gospel, Theophilus had been told of Jesus' death and resurrection. But, judging from Luke's Gospel, apparently the meaning and implications of that death and resurrection were not quite clear to him; and a number of references to persons and events associated with the ministry of Jesus baffled him. Likewise, the subsequent experiences of the early Christians seem to have been somewhat vague to him. The advent and activity of the Holy Spirit, the early ministries of the disciples, the conversion of Paul and his relation to the Jerusalem apostles, the nature and extent of Paul's ministry—and probably more—were all things that Theophilus had questions about. So Luke writes to deal with his friend's uncertainties and the queries of others like him who will read his account.

Acts, therefore, like many another work, was probably written with multiple purposes in view. Primary among the reasons for its composition was undoubtedly a *kerygmatic purpose.* It proclaims the continued confrontation of men and women by the Word of God through the church and shows (1) how that gospel is related to the course of redemptive history, (2) its rootage in and interaction with secular history, (3) its universal character, (4) how it has been freed from the Jewish law, and (5) how that behind the proclamation of the Word of God stands the power and activity of the Holy Spirit.

In his first volume, Luke shows how men and women were confronted by the Word of God in the earthly ministry of Jesus (cf. Luke 5:1; 8:11, 21; 11:28). In Acts Luke seeks to show how men and women continue to be confronted by that same Word through the ministry of the church (cf. 4:29, 31; 6:2, 4, 7; 8:4, 14, 25; 10:36; 11:1, 19; 12:24; 13:7,

44, 46, 48–49; 14:25; 15:35–36; 16:6, 32; 17:11, 13; 18:5, 11; 19:10). The Word of God is for Luke, as Haenchen rightly observes, "the clamp which fastens the two eras together and justifies, indeed demands, the continuation of the first book (depicting the life of Jesus as a time of salvation) in a second; for the salvation which has appeared must be preached to all peoples, and the very portrayal of this mission will serve the awakening of belief, and hence the attainment of that salvation" (*Acts of the Apostles*, p. 98).

Haenchen, of course, along with Bultmannians in general and Conzelmann in particular (*Theology of Luke*, passim), thinks that Luke's stress on the Word of God as being the message of salvation in Jesus is a secondary and erroneous concept of salvation-history entirely of Luke's own creation and introduced to solve the embarrassing problem of the delay of the Parousia. Others, however (myself included), view it as primary and rooted inextricably in the confessions of the earliest believers and the consciousness of Jesus himself. Be that as it may, for Luke the message of salvation in Jesus proclaimed by the church is in direct continuity with the ministry and teaching of Jesus. That is why Luke wrote a sequel to his Gospel, thus making explicit what was presupposed in the earliest Christian preaching.

Furthermore, this Word of God is firmly fixed in the context of world history. It began with the miraculous births that took place "in the time of Herod king of Judea" (Luke 1:5) and during the reign of Caesar Augustus, "while Quirinius was governor of Syria" (Luke 2:1–2). It focuses on a ministry that commenced "in the fifteenth year of the reign of Tiberius Caesar—when Pontius Pilate was governor of Judea, Herod tetrarch of Galilee, his brother Philip tetrarch of Iturea and Trachonitis, and Lysanias tetrarch of Abilene—during the high priesthood of Annas and Caiaphas" (Luke 3:1–2) and that culminated under the judgment of Pilate and Herod Antipas (Luke 23:1–25). And it spread throughout the Roman world principally during the reign of the emperor Claudius (Acts 11:28; 18:2), when Gallio was proconsul of Achaia (Acts 18:12–17), when Felix and Festus ruled in Judea and Ananias was the high priest in Jerusalem (Acts 24–25), and between the times of the Jewish kings Herod Agrippa I (Acts 12:1–23) and Herod Agrippa II (Acts 25:13–26:32).

In addition, this Word regarding salvation in Jesus has permeated the Jewish homeland of Palestine-Syria and has been received with a measure of acceptance in the main centers of the eastern part of the Roman Empire, finally entering the capital city itself "without hindrance" (the adverb *akōlytōs* being the final word of Luke's two-volume work). It is a universal message. It began in Jerusalem among Jews and spread "to the ends of the earth" (as promised by Jesus himself, Acts 1:8) to include all kinds of people. It is a message that by means of a process under the Spirit's direction, a process that can be depicted in its various stages, finally and inevitably freed itself from the shackles of Jewish legalism and a Jewish lifestyle. It is a Word of God that affected the lives of many through the power and activity of the Holy Spirit, that selfsame Spirit who came upon Jesus at his baptism and through whom he accomplished his mission.

There is also inherent throughout the presentation of Acts an *apologetic purpose*. Its author seeks to demonstrate that Christianity is not a political threat to the empire, as its Jewish opponents asserted, but rather that it is the culmination of Israel's hope and the true daughter of Jewish religion—and, therefore, should be treated by Roman authorities as a *religio licita* along with Judaism.

Roman law, for entirely pragmatic reasons, identified certain religions as *licita*, or legal and permitted, and others as *illicita*, or illegal and forbidden. Those accepted as legal had been dominant in various areas or among certain ethnic groups and could serve to reinforce the Pax Romana. Those forbidden were the minority faiths that tended to

218

fracture loyalties and splinter peoples and therefore deserved harsh treatment. Judaism was considered a *religio licita*, both in Palestine and throughout the Diaspora, simply because of its refusal to be taken as anything else and because of the troubles it caused Rome when attempts were made to amalgamate it with other religions.

Christianity, however, had its problems in respect to legality as it moved out into the empire, even though it had been born within Judaism. Its founder had been crucified as a messianic pretender in Jerusalem, its separate identity as "Christian" had been asserted by others in its mission to Antioch of Syria (Acts 11:26), and Jews within the Diaspora were insisting that it had no right to imperial protection since it was sectarian.

Acts acknowledges the fact of such accusations. At Philippi the charge brought against Paul and Silas is given as disturbing the peace "by advocating customs unlawful for us Romans to accept or practice" (Acts 16:20–21). At Thessalonica the charge is one of "defying Caesar's decrees, saying that there is another king, one called Jesus" (Acts 17:7). And at Corinth it is that of "persuading the people to worship God in ways contrary to the law" (Acts 18:13). Furthermore, at Paul's later trials the Jews charged him with being a sectarian who stirred up riots within the Jewish communities and therefore deserved to be tried under Roman law (Acts 24:5–9).

Luke also takes pains to point out that despite differences between the Christian message and that of Judaism, the charge of *religio illicita* had never been accepted by any well-informed Roman official. In his Gospel he shows the Crucifixion to be a gross miscarriage of justice from the perspective of Roman law and reports that Pilate three times declared Jesus' innocence (Luke 23:4, 14, 22). And in Acts, Luke speaks of a number of Roman officials, both Gentile and Jewish, who acknowledge that there is no factual basis for the accusation of *religio illicita* brought against Paul and his coworkers. At Paphos, the proconsul of Cyprus, Sergius Paulus, "an intelligent man," was converted to Christianity (Acts 13:6–12). At Philippi the magistrates apologized to Paul and Silas for illegally beating and imprisoning them (Acts 16:35–39). At Corinth the proconsul of Achaia, Gallio, judged Paul and Silas guiltless of any offense against Roman law, viewing the Jews' dispute with them as an intramural matter (Acts 18:12–17). At Ephesus some of the officials of the province were Paul's friends, and the city clerk absolved him of the charge of sacrilege (Acts 19:31, 35–41). In Palestine the governors Felix and Festus found Paul innocent of the charges against him, with Herod Agrippa II agreeing upon examination that "this man is not doing anything that deserves death or imprisonment" and saying that "this man could have been set free, if he had not appealed to Caesar" (Acts 24:1–26:32). Perhaps the manner in which Luke closes his narrative (ch. 28) shows that he wants his readers to understand that even at Rome no formal accusation was made against Paul, either by a delegation from Jerusalem or by the leaders of the Jewish community there, and that therefore the apostle was set free. But that is not certain and must be discussed later.

It seems evident, therefore, that in writing Acts Luke also had an *apologetic purpose*. But to speak of this apologetic purpose entails asking to whom that apology was directed, and the answer to that is not clear. At the close of the last century, many viewed Acts as something of a trial document sent to a Roman magistrate named Theophilus and perhaps meant eventually for the eyes of the emperor. Barrett may have overreacted against this idea when he insisted:

> It was not addressed to the Emperor, with the intention of proving the political harmlessness of Christianity in general and of Paul in particular; a few passages might be construed to serve this purpose, but to suggest that the book as a whole should be

> taken in this way is absurd. No Roman official would ever have filtered out so much of what to him would be theological and ecclesiastical rubbish in order to reach so tiny a grain of relevant apology (*Luke the Historian,* p. 63).

But granted that no Roman official would have done so, that does not mean Luke could not have written with such an intent, much as the later apologists did—even though they seldom, if ever, received the hearing they desired. Still, the view of Acts as a trial document much overstates the case and ignores other emphases in the book.

On the other hand, we need not conclude that if the work is not a trial document its apologetic element was addressed only to those already in the church—either to Jewish Christians in Rome, urging them to be more conciliatory toward Gentiles since various Roman officials had a favorable attitude toward the early Christian mission (cf. Zeller), or to Christians with a Gnostic bent, arguing that an appreciation of the Christian faith cannot be restricted only to the initiated (cf. Barrett, *Luke the Historian*). Instead, it is better to conclude that while Acts as an apology had Theophilus primarily in view because of his concern regarding Christianity's legal status in the empire, it was also meant for other Gentiles, whether they were Christians or not.

A third purpose for writing Acts seems to have been, as Baur, Zeller, and others long ago asserted, a *conciliatory purpose*—though the Tübingen scholars much overstated this and drew illegitimate implications from it. Acts presents the careers of Peter (chs. 1–12) and Paul (chs. 13–28) in strikingly parallel fashion. (For a detailed presentation of this, see the introduction to Acts 2:42–12:24.) Likewise, Acts presents Paul as conceding primacy in the church to Peter and apostleship to the Twelve based on their earthly companionship with Jesus; whereas Peter and the Jerusalem apostles, in turn, concede to Paul another mode of apostolic authority as well as Peter's initiative in the law-free outreach to Gentiles.[26] Luke is a master at setting up his material in balanced form, as we shall see later in discussing the structure of Acts. Moreover, to again quote Lightfoot's famous dictum on the Tübingen formulation of the conciliatory purpose, "Such a purpose is at least as likely to have been entertained by a writer, if the two Apostles were essentially united, as if they were not. The truth or falsehood of the account must be determined on other grounds."[27]

Paul's own letters, in fact, indicate quite clearly that at Jerusalem some were pitting Peter and the Jerusalem apostles against him because they preferred Peter to him. And even in Paul's own churches, similar party factions arose, with some saying, "I follow Paul"; others, "I follow Apollos"; or, "I follow Cephas"; and still others, "I follow Christ" (1 Cor 1:12). Surely it is not too hard to imagine that when Acts was written, Luke well knew of continuing sentiment in the churches that would sharply divide the ministries of Peter and Paul. So while Luke necessarily had to portray their differences, he also needed to delineate the continuity and points of comparison between them, and do it through the structure of his presentation and, wherever possible, in its details.

Finally, Luke may well have written Acts with a *catechetical purpose* in mind. In antiquity, tractates and letters were often circulated widely even though addressed to only one person or group. Josephus, for example, in the work dubbed *Contra Apion,* addresses one he calls "most excellent Epaphroditus" in the prologue to volume 1 and "my most esteemed Epaphroditus" in the prologue to volume 2. Yet he did this fully

---

[26]Baur, *Paul,* 1:6, 88–89.
[27]Lightfoot, *Galatians,* p. 359.

expecting his defense of the Jewish religion against various forms of Greek speculation to be widely circulated and read—which it certainly was. Epaphroditus may have been a grammarian who wrote on Homer and possessed a large library and became Josephus's patron. But while he undoubtedly received *Contra Apion* from Josephus's own hand, the work was meant to instruct many more readers than Epaphroditus. In a much less formal way, Paul's letters also were meant to be read widely, as we see from his instruction to the Colossians: "After this letter has been read to you, see that it is also read in the church of the Laodiceans and that you in turn read the letter from Laodicea" (Col 4:16).

So, too, Luke probably wrote his treatise to Theophilus with the expectation that in addition to its kerygmatic, apologetic, and conciliatory purposes, it could also be used within various churches for instructional purposes, to show how Christianity moved out from its origins in Palestine to become a movement of God's Spirit in the Roman Empire. Thus Luke portrays in dramatic vignettes drawn from the early church's history the essence of early Christian preaching, the activity of the Holy Spirit in applying and spreading the message, the gospel's power, its transforming quality, its type of adherents, their sacrifices and triumphs, and the ultimate entrance of the Christian proclamation into the city of Rome itself. Undoubtedly, as its author surely intended, such a catechetical purpose met a vital need among scattered congregations only recently formed—a need for instruction about the nature of the faith and the church's early history. Also, this instructional material helped draw believers together spiritually. And while Luke could hardly have visualized anything beyond the needs of the churches of his day, his writing continues to do just that today.

5. The Sources of Acts

The question of the sources Luke used in writing Acts is more easily raised than answered. In fact, it has to be asked in two ways because the first part of Acts has a definite Semitic cast whereas the second half has more a Greek cast, like the Prologue to Luke-Acts (Luke 1:1–4). Most discussions of the sources of Acts, therefore, are concerned with source-critical issues for chapters 1–15 and form-critical issues for chapters 16–28. And this must be our procedure as well.

The identification of sources underlying the presentation of Acts 1–15 was viewed during the first decades of this century with great optimism. Of the various analyses of the text proposed, Harnack's may be taken as representative (*Acts*, pp. 162–202). Harnack discerned in Acts (1) a Jerusalem-Antiochean source behind 11:19–30 and 12:25–15:35, which has considerable historical value for at least the material from 13:4 on; (2) a Jerusalem-Caesarean source underlying 3:1–5:16; 8:5–40; 9:29–11:18; and 12:1–24, which was in written form for chapters 3–4 and 12 (though perhaps transmitted orally for the rest) and which in its "Recension A" provides "the more intelligible history of the outpouring of the Holy Spirit and its consequences" as now appears in 3:1–5:16; (3) a "Recension B" of the Jerusalem-Caesarean source that provides rather confused material as now found in 2:1–47 and 5:17–42, thereby setting up a number of doublets in the finished text; (4) a separate source in 6:1–8:4 having to do with the martyrdom of Stephen, though related to the Jerusalem-Antiochean source and with an interpolated reference to Paul at the end; (5) a separate source in 9:1–28 dealing with the conversion of Saul; and (6) legendary material in chapter 1. Harnack doubted that the usual literary clues of vocabulary, style, and historical blunders can be used to differentiate one source from another. He insisted that Luke has so reworked his sources as to impose his own personal stamp throughout the finished product. But he did believe that one can group the material according to the persons and places depicted, with the doublets furnishing particularly useful indicators of the presence of source material involved.

Most obvious and most important among the doublets of Acts 1–15 was the double arrest of the apostles and their two appearances before the Jewish Sanhedrin in 4:1ff. and 5:17ff., which Harnack claimed were simply two versions of the same event. In 1937, however, Jeremias showed that far from being repetitious and therefore artificial in their dual inclusion, the two narratives reflect with accuracy a significant point in Jewish jurisprudence and complement each other.[28] Jewish law, as Jeremias pointed out, held that a person must be aware of the consequences of his crime before being punished for it. This meant that in noncapital cases the common people had to be given a legal admonition before witnesses and could only be punished for an offense when they relapsed into the crime after due warning. Thus Acts 4:1ff. says that the Sanhedrin realized the apostles were "unschooled, ordinary men" (v.13) and they were given a legal warning not to speak anymore in the name of Jesus (v.17), while Acts 5:17ff. says the Sanhedrin reminded the apostles of its first warning (v.28) and turned them over to be flogged because they persisted in their sectarian ways (v.40).

With this demonstration of the correlation of these two accounts, which has been convincing to most scholars today,[29] Jeremias effectively set aside what Harnack had considered to be the clearest and surest instance of a doublet resulting from Luke's use of parallel source materials. And with Jeremias's demonstration, most attempts to support a thesis of parallel sources underlying the narrative of Acts 1–15 have come to an end—though, of course, doublets in Acts are still being proposed by literary critics on the basis of Luke's interpolations into his primary source material (e.g., 11:27–30 and 15:1–33, as Jeremias himself argues), but no longer on a thesis of parallel sources.

Although most scholars today no longer argue for parallel sources for Acts, the possibility remains that some basic source or sources, either written or oral, underlie the substructure of the first half of the book. The probability of this depends largely on how one evaluates the markedly Semitic cast and coloring of chapters 1–15. It also depends on the question of whether such Semitic features are to be credited mainly to translation, underlying sources, or an imitation of the language of the LXX—or, in some way, to a combination of these factors. But precise answers to such questions on a strictly linguistic basis are, as Black rightly warns, "only very rarely possible."[30] Nonetheless, there are some things that can be said to the issue and need to be pointed out here.

Through linguistic analysis, Black and Wilcox have concluded that while certain "Semitisms" may be explainable as merely Lukan "Septuagintisms," there are also in Acts 1–15 a number of "hard-core Semitisms" that cannot be explained except on some theory of Aramaic (perhaps also Heb.) sources underlying the composition.[31] And Martin, on the basis of a series of studies on such unconscious syntactical traits as the frequency and positioning of conjunctions, prepositions, and articles, has argued convincingly that while certain phrases and idioms in Acts reflect Septuagintal influence,

---

[28]Joachim Jeremias, "Untersuchungen zum Quellenproblem der Apostelgeschichte," ZNW, 36 (1937), 205–21, esp. 208–13.

[29]Reicke, however, in *Glaube und Leben* (pp. 108–10), continues to speak of one Sanhedrin trial presented in two parallel forms, based on the remarkable symmetry he discovers between 2:42–4:31 and 4:32–5:42.

[30]Matthew Black, "Second Thoughts—X. The Semitic Element in the New Testament," ExpT, 77 (1965), 20.

[31]Contra Wilcox, see J.A. Emerton's detailed review article in JSS, 13 (1968), 282–97.

there are, however, a number of Semitic syntactical features particularly which are more common in the first half of Acts, *indeed in certain subsections* of the first part of Acts. This phenomenon is difficult, if not impossible, to explain on the basis of conscious or unconscious influence of the Septuagint on the writer, and most naturally to be explained as the result of Semitic sources underlying these subsections [italics his].[32]

Indeed, in his 1974 monograph on the subject, Martin identifies these subsections as being "16 sections which clearly do go back to written Semitic sources (1:15–26; 2:1–4; 4:23–31; 5:17–26; 5:27–32; 5:33–42; 6:1–7; 6:8–15; 7:9–16; 7:17–22; 7:30–43; 9:10–19a; 11:1–18; 13:16b–25; 13:26–41; 14:8–20) and 6 others which probably go back to Semitic sources (2:29–36; 2:37–42; 7:1–8; 7:44–50; 9:19b–22; 9:32–35)" (*Semitic Sources*, pp. 2–3, passim).

This is not to suggest that such Semitic features in the text must be viewed as merely the result of translation, as Torrey asserted in proposing his "unified Aramaic source" theory and as Martin (along with Winter and Albright[33]) tends to think has resulted through the use of multiple complementary sources. Nor does the recognition of Semitic features imply our ability to identify the nature or extent of the sources. Black is undoubtedly right in speaking of Luke's use of sources as more literary than slavishly literal (*Aramaic Approach*, pp. 274–75);[34] and Turner should probably be heeded in his insistence that we consider Lukan source material in more an ultimate than an immediate sense.[35] But the presence, character, and distribution of such "hard-core Semitisms" have much to say against the view that Luke was merely attempting to archaize his presentation by using Septuagintal language. And though Sparks has eloquently tried to argue the Septuagintal and archaizing nature of Luke's material,[36] the fact "that such primitive elements have been preserved is 'a rather strong indication of the general authenticity' of the first fifteen chapters of the Acts of the Apostles."[37]

As for possible source materials underlying the writing of Acts 16–28, attention has always been directed first of all to four passages in the narrative where the writer uses the pronoun "we"—16:10–17 (travel to and evangelization of Philippi); 20:5–15 (ministry in Troas and travel to Miletus); 21:1–18 (journey from Miletus to Jerusalem); and 27:1–28:16 (journey from Caesarea to Rome).[38] The "we" of these passages has been explained in four ways:

1. The editor of Acts, working from an earlier "travel document" or "diary," either accidentally or carelessly left the pronoun stand without noting that he was quoting directly.

---

[32]Raymond A. Martin, "Syntactical Evidence of Aramaic Sources in Acts I–XV," NTS, 11 (1964), 38–39.

[33]Cf. Paul Winter, "Some Observations on the Language in the Birth and Infancy Stories of the Third Gospel," NTS, 1 (1955), 111–21; idem, "The Proto-Source of Luke 1," NovTest, 1 (1956), 184–99; W.F. Albright, *New Horizons in Biblical Research* (London: Oxford, 1966), p. 50.

[34]F.J. Foakes-Jackson and K. Lake have said, "The truth seems to be that although there is a *prima facie* probability for the use of written sources in Acts, and especially for Aramaic sources in the earlier chapters, the writer wrote too well to allow us to distinguish with certainty either the boundaries of his sources or the extent of his own editorial work" (BC, 2:133).

[35]Nigel Turner, "The Relation of Luke I and II to Hebraic Sources," NTS, 2 (1956), 102.

[36]H.F.D. Sparks, "The Semitisms of the Acts," JTS, ns., 1 (1950), 16–28; cf. his earlier "The Semitisms of St. Luke's Gospel," JTS, 44 (1943), 129–38. See also Haenchen, *Acts of the Apostles*, pp. 73–77.

[37]Black, "Second Thoughts," p. 22, quoting Wilcox, p. 181.

[38]Or three sections, if the Miletus discourse of 20:17–38 is understood as offering no opportunity for the first person plural and therefore 20:5–21:18 is viewed as a single unit.

2. The author of Acts designedly left the pronoun in his source materials stand in his finished product, thus attempting to gain greater acceptance for his work by passing himself off as one of Paul's companions.

3. The author of Acts used the "we" as a kind of "last-minute embellishment," or "stylistic device," apart from any necessary source materials, in order to give the narrative the appearance of a "a fellow-traveler's account."

4. The author of Acts had from time to time been a companion of Paul in his travels and discreetly indicated this by using "we" in those places in the narrative where he tells of events at which he had been present.[39]

Linguistically, as has often been observed, the "we" sections are inextricably bound up with the whole of Luke-Acts, which suggests that they cannot be explained simply on the basis of source criticism and that the use of "we" must be related more to the author of Acts than to his possible sources. Furthermore, there are striking similarities between these sections and the more readily identifiable editorial material in Luke-Acts in matters of vocabulary, syntax, style, manner of presentation, and even in what is neglected[40]—similarities that do not appear in Luke's Gospel when there is a dependence upon either Mark or Q and that do not appear in the first part of Acts where Semitic sources seem to have been used. In addition, it is in these "we" sections that a greater fullness of detail appears in the portrayal of Paul's ministry, whereas elsewhere the narrative is briefer. All the evidence of this kind seems to require the conclusion either that the author of Acts was exceedingly skillful in creating the impression of eyewitness reporting or that these sections must be judged to be based on firsthand observation. Of the two, the majority of critics have preferred the latter.

To hold that the "we" sections in Acts are firsthand accounts on the part of the author himself is supported by what his prologue to Luke-Acts reveals about him (Luke 1:1–4). "A careful study of the prologue shows," Dupont insists, "that the writer is presenting himself as a contemporary and eyewitness of a part of the facts he recounts and this statement indicates the importance that should be attributed to the passages he writes in the first person" (p. 102). On the other hand, the main argument against accepting the "we" sections as the result of firsthand observation is that no companion of Paul would so grossly misrepresent his character and ministry. Luke 1:1–4 and its testimony regarding authorship will be discussed later. As for the portrayal of Paul in Acts, this will be dealt with in what immediately follows. Here it is sufficient to say that on the basis of literary and form-critical considerations alone, the "we" sections of the second half of Acts give every indication of being the firsthand report of the author of Acts.

A great part of what remains in the presentation of chapters 16–28 is made up of three missionary sermons of Paul, one pastoral discourse, and five speeches in which he defends himself.[41] The missionary sermons—at Antioch of Pisidia (13:16–41), Lystra (14:15–17), and Athens (17:22–31)—each have their own form, manner of presentation, and type of argument. The first is very Jewish, the second more pedestrian, and the third philosophical. The pastoral discourse to the Ephesian elders at Miletus (20:17–38) also has its own form and content, being similar to the Pauline Epistles. As for Paul's speeches in his own defense—before a Jerusalem crowd (22:3–21), the Sanhedrin (23:1–6), the governor Felix (24:10–21), the governor Festus (25:8–11), and Herod Agrippa

---

[39]On numbers, 1, 2, and 4, see the summary of J.C. Hawkins, *Horae Synopticae* (Oxford: Clarendon, 1899), pp. 182–83. On number 3, see Haenchen, *Acts of the Apostles*, p. 85, whose descriptive phrases are quoted.

[40]Cf. esp. Harnack, *Luke*, pp. 26–120; idem, *Acts*, pp. 49–263.

[41]Also, of course, it contains Paul's preaching to Jewish leaders at Rome (28:25–28), though Luke gives only the final words and not a précis of the apostle's preaching.

(26:2–29)—these have their own distinctive style and mode of argument, dependent on the audience and situation he was addressing. One may, of course, insist that all this variety of presentation and fitting of sermonic material to the situation shows the creative genius of the author. But it is more probable that these things show that Luke was using various sources for his accounts of Paul's sermons and defenses, even though Luke's thorough reworking of these sources prevents us from identifying or recreating them.

Likewise, though there have been many attempts to reconstruct the sources underlying the "they" sections of the narrative in Acts 16–28—and though we may gain the impression from the narrative itself that its author must have had access to various documents—Luke's literary ability and his liberty in handling his materials was evidently too great to enable us to identify with any certainty the presence, extent, or nature of his sources. The writer of Acts was truly an author, not a compiler or an editor. The recognition of Semitic sources underlying the first half of Acts and of eyewitness reports embodied in the second half, with various other materials possibly used elsewhere, certainly increases our general level of confidence in the historical worth of the presentation. But ultimately Acts must be judged as a finished product and not just on the basis of its sources, even though these sources may be judged historically respectable.

6. The Narrative of Acts

Probably the most extensive attack ever mounted against the historical reliability of the narrative of Acts was that by Zeller in the mid-nineteenth century.[42] Beginning with the position of his father-in-law, F.C. Baur, on the conciliatory purpose of Acts, Zeller undertook an exhaustive examination of its details, disparaging its facticity because of its numerous historical blunders, inclusion of the miraculous, and portrayal of Paul. But the Hegelianism and tendency criticism of Baur and Zeller soon fell out of favor. Although the superstructure of Tübingen collapsed, the debris remains—in fact, many of its building blocks are being reused in the scholarly study of Acts today.

Modern critics continue to fault Acts for its historical blunders, inclusion of the miraculous, and portrayal of Paul. They also add such charges against it as that its kerygmatic purpose preempts any real interest in historical veracity, that it readjusts the earliest proclamation to meet the problem of eschatological disillusionment (also, perhaps, to meet the problem of rising Gnosticism, though that is more hotly debated), and that it is incomplete and fails to deal with the historically significant issues of the day. But though objections to the historical reliability of Acts appear formidable, much can be said to put matters in a fairer perspective.

We have already discussed Luke's purposes in writing Acts, arguing that the work does reflect a dominant kerygmatic purpose and also a conciliatory intent. But we have not drawn the same implications from such observations that others have drawn. Likewise we have argued that, though some early Christians may have been disillusioned by the delay of the Parousia, the faith of the earliest Christians was in a person, not in a program. Whatever "readjustments" are to be found in Luke-Acts must be seen as a recapturing of the essential convictions of the early church and not just the product of an author's

---

[42]Cf. Eduard Zeller, *Apostelgeschichte*, which incorporated in revised form a series of articles he originally wrote between 1848 and 1851 for the *Theologische Jahrbücher*.

creative genius. Moreover, while we recognize that many take the impossibility of the miraculous as an axiom of historical criticism, we regard that as a matter of philosophical outlook and personal skepticism rather than one of historical investigation and careful research. The issues, however, that need to be dealt with here have to do with the portrayal of Paul in Acts and Luke's manner of treating historical details.

The most weighty argument against the authenticity of Acts in the opinion of many is "that the Paul of the Acts is manifestly quite a different person from the Paul of the Epistles."[43] Adolf Hausrath, the nineteenth-century Heidelberg church historian, once insisted:

> One could as well believe that Luther, in his old age, made a pilgrimage to Einsiedeln, walking on peas, or that Calvin on his death bed vowed a golden robe to the Holy Mother of God, as that the author of Romans and Galatians stood for seven days in the outer court of the Temple, and subjected himself to all the manipulations with which rabbinic ingenuity had surrounded the vow, and allowed all the liturgical nonsense of that age to be transacted for him by unbelieving priests and Levites.[44]

Many today, without being quite so colorful, agree with this because they believe that the author of Acts has grossly misrepresented Paul in portraying his activities and presenting his theology. So they judge Luke's description of the relations between Paul and the Jerusalem church to be "a happier one than the facts warrant" (Barrett, *Luke the Historian*, p. 74).

Lightfoot and Harnack, however, were notable dissenters from this type of criticism and insisted that the split between the Paul of Acts and the Paul of the Epistles is more a scholar's construction than a fact of history.[45] In my book *Paul, Apostle of Liberty* (esp. pp. 211–63), I have argued for an understanding of Paul's background and teaching that will allow for a more adequate appreciation of his practices as portrayed in Acts; and in *The Christology of Early Jewish Christianity*, I have argued for a better understanding of the commitments of the earliest Jewish believers in Jesus.

Undoubtedly there are differences between the Paul of his own letters and the Paul of his "biographer," and undoubtedly Pauline Christianity and early Jewish Christianity were distinguishable entities. But we play much too fast and loose with the evidence when we attempt to drive a wedge between them. Paul writes as an evangelist and pastor to his converts, affirming the essentials of his message within a context of personal humility, whereas Luke writes as an historian and admirer of the apostle, with a sense for the historical unfolding of the gospel and a desire to highlight the heroic. While we must ask for a body of agreement in the respective portrayals, we cannot reasonably call for identity in details or uniformity in viewpoints.

The situation is somewhat comparable to Plutarch's treatment of the members of the Roman family Gracchus in his *Parallel Lives* and Appian's depiction of these same leaders in his *Civil Wars*. While both wrote in the second century A.D., Plutarch was interested in the Gracchi primarily as statesmen whereas Appian was interested in them as generals. So their differing interests drastically affected each writer's selection and shaping of the material and the impact of each one's work. Yet there is also a large body

---

[43]Baur, *Paul*, 1:11.

[44]Cf. W.M. MacGregor, *Christian Freedom* (London: Hodder & Stoughton, 1914), p. 71, quoting Hausrath, *Der Apostel Paulus*, p. 453.

[45]See esp. Lightfoot, *Galatians*, pp. 347–48, and Harnack, *Date of the Acts*, pp. 67–89.

of agreement between Plutarch's and Appian's treatment of the Gracchi. As Underhill observed:

> It is not wonderful therefore that, starting from such very different points of view, and with such arbitrary methods of selecting and arranging their materials, Plutarch and Appian should have written two very different accounts of the Gracchi and their doings. The wonder is rather that they should agree so well as they do. Thus to attempt to pronounce in general terms which is to be preferred before the other, is almost an idle task: the better course is to compare the two narratives in detail, and to discuss the value of each part separately.[46]

So "it is not wonderful" that Luke portrays Paul as a great miracle worker whereas Paul himself laid claim to "the things that mark an apostle—signs, wonders and miracles" (2 Cor 12:12) only when forced to assert his apostleship; or that Luke thought of his hero as an outstanding orator whereas Paul acknowledged that some were saying that "in person he is unimpressive and his speaking amounts to nothing" (2 Cor 10:10); or that Luke should depict Paul's apostleship as related to and in continuity with that of the Jerusalem Twelve whereas Paul himself insisted that his apostleship was in a real sense unique.[47] If we really believe in redaction criticism, we must allow various portrayals to be influenced by the respective purposes of authors at the time of writing. Real life is broader than the precision of mathematical equations, though those who fault Acts for its portrait of Paul often tend to forget that. (For further discussion of these matters, see the commentary in loc.)

As for Luke's treatment of historical details in Acts, almost all of Zeller's identifications of historical discrepancies have been effectively countered by the extensive research of Ramsay. Therefore we seldom hear of Zeller today. On the other hand, Ramsay became so impressed with the historical trustworthiness of Acts and the "true historic sense" of its author that at times his presentations suggest that Luke wrote only as an historian without any purpose but to inform.[48] Thus Ramsay is usually neglected because of the kerygmatic concerns of scholars and theologians today. Nevertheless, Ramsay's basic point that on matters having to do with Hellenistic geography and politics, as well as with Roman law and provincial administration, Acts is an extremely reliable guide to the situation of the mid-first century A.D. was well made and has been supported of late by the Roman historian Sherwin-White. Likewise, Ramsay's insistence that "a writer who proves to be exact and correct in one point will show the same qualities in other matters" is a legitimate inference from his more limited area of investigation and deserves general credence (*Trustworthiness of the NT,* p. 80).

There still remain, however, a number of historical problems in Acts that seem to go beyond any ready explanation and beyond what scholars believe to have been the

---

[46]G.E. Underhill, *Plutarch's Lives of the Gracchi* (Oxford: Clarendon, 1892), p. xix.

[47]I am interacting with Haenchen's three claimed "discrepancies" between "the 'Lucan' Paul and the Paul of the epistles" (*Acts of the Apostles,* pp. 113–15).

[48]E.g., "It is rare to find a narrative so simple and so little forced as that of 'Acts.' It is a mere uncoloured recital of the important facts in the briefest possible terms. The narrator's individuality and his personal feelings and preferences are almost wholly suppressed. He is entirely absorbed in his work; and he writes with the single aim to state the facts as he has learned them. It would be difficult in the whole range of literature to find a work where there is less attempt at pointing a moral or drawing a lesson from the facts. The narrator is persuaded that the facts themselves in their barest form are a perfect lesson and a complete instruction, and he feels that it would be an impertinence and even an impiety to intrude his individual views into the narrative" (*St. Paul the Traveller,* pp. 20–21).

situation in the first century. Most notorious of these is the reference to the Jewish revolutionaries Theudas and Judas the Galilean in Gamaliel's speech recorded in Acts 5:36–37:

> Some time ago Theudas appeared, claiming to be somebody, and about four hundred men rallied to him. He was killed, all his followers were dispersed, and it all came to nothing. After him, Judas the Galilean appeared in the days of the census and led a band of people in revolt. He too was killed, and all his followers were scattered.

The major historical blunders in the passage appear to be (1) its disagreement with Josephus as to the chronological order of these rebellions, for Josephus depicts that of Judas as having taken place first about A.D. 6 (Antiq. XVIII, 4–10 [i.1]), with that of Theudas coming later in about A.D. 44 (Antiq. XX, 97–98 [v.1]); and, more seriously, (2) its making Gamaliel in about A.D. 34 refer to an uprising of Theudas that did not occur until a decade or so later. Nineteenth-century critics were quick to highlight this problem, usually explaining it as a result of Luke's confused dependence upon Josephus. They argued that the writer of Acts had confused Josephus's later reminiscence (Antiq. XX, 102 [v.2]) of Judas's revolt with the earlier actual revolt and had forgotten some sixty years or more after the event (if indeed he ever knew) that Gamaliel's speech preceded Theudas's rebellion by a decade or so and did not follow it.

The arguments for Luke's dependence upon Josephus, however, have been pretty well demolished by the literary analyses of such scholars as Schürer and Thackeray.[49] It may well be that the Theudas of Gamaliel's reference was one of the many insurgent leaders who arose in Palestine at the time of Herod the Great's death in 4 B.C. and not the Theudas who led the Jewish uprising of A.D. 44 and that Gamaliel's examples of Jewish insurrectionists refer to a Theudas of about 4 B.C. and to Judas the Galilean of A.D. 6 whereas Josephus focused upon Judas of A.D. 6 and another Theudas of A.D. 44. The problem with Acts 5:36–37 may therefore result as much from our own ignorance as from what we believe we know as based upon Josephus.

Kümmel enumerates a number of factors relating to incomplete narration and selectivity of material that convince him that the author of Acts lacked historical interest. So he discredits the historical worth of what is presented on the ground that "we do not learn the historically significant things about [Paul]."[50] Such objections, however, tell us only that Kümmel's view of what was significant in apostolic history and Luke's own understanding are quite different—something of little importance as an argument against the facticity of Luke's account. Turner has pointed out the following respecting the historical NT materials:

> The fact that a number of questions which we should wish to put to the documents are unanswerable does not by itself cast doubt on their veracity as historical documents. It may merely imply that we are selecting the wrong criteria to get the best out of our subject-matter or framing the wrong questions to put to our sources. However legitimate its methods and aims, criticism can easily and imperceptibly turn into hypercriticism and become in the process as ham-fisted as literalism.[51]

---

[49]Emil Schürer concluded: "Either Luke had not read Josephus, or he had forgotten all about what he had read" ("Lucas und Josephus," ZWT, 19 [1876], 582); cf. Henry St.J. Thackeray, *Selections from Josephus* (New York: Doran, 1919), p. 194.

[50]Werner Kümmel, *Introduction to the New Testament,* tr. A.J. Mattill, Jr. (London: SCM, 1965), pp. 116–17.

[51]Turner, *Historicity and the Gospels,* pp. 1–2.

And van Unnik has observed:

> Would it not be wise to be somewhat more moderate in the questions we ask of Luke? Because he was not omniscient on all events of the apostolic age, it does not follow that he was unreliable in what he does tell us, or that he is a pious but untrustworthy preacher. We must grant him the liberty of not being interested in all matters that interest us.[52]

Luke, it is true, varies considerably from modern historians. He does not cite authorities and strive for completeness. Nor does he interact with competing viewpoints. He presents his material in dramatic vignettes, which "present not so much a single picture as a series of glimpses" (Foakes-Jackson and Lake, BC, 1:301). He is more interested in impressions than the establishment of causes and effects; he is more interested in portraying the advances of the gospel than in detailing resultant implications. And what he does tell us often leaves us baffled and searching for the thesis that will unify the whole. Because Luke has presented his material in a unique way, is uninterested in many of the issues that preoccupy modern historians, and uses his narrative to proclaim the continuing activity of the ascended Christ in the world through his Spirit in the church, we do not have to relegate his presentation to the historically unreliable. In Luke's view, which was that of most other historians and biographers of his day, this was the only way his narrative could achieve its aim and compel interest.

7. The Speeches in Acts

The tone for contemporary critical study of the speeches in Acts was set in 1922 by Cadbury in "The Greek and Jewish Traditions of Writing History":

> To suppose that the writers were trying to present the speeches as actually spoken, or that their readers thought so, is unfair to the morality of one and to the intelligence of the other. From Thucydides downwards, speeches reported by the historians are confessedly pure imagination. They belong to the final literary stage. If they have any nucleus of fact behind them it would be the merest outline in the *hupomnēmata* [i.e., remembrances] (BC, 2:13).

A number of studies have been written during the past half-century in support of Cadbury's claim, arguing (1) that Luke, indeed, as a Greek historian, followed the Thucydidean model; (2) that the speeches of Acts fit too neatly into their redactional contexts for the material to be drawn from the primitive church; and (3) that the theological content and vocabulary of the speeches are that of Luke himself (as determined by comparison with his editorial activity elsewhere in Luke-Acts) and therefore cannot be that of the earliest Christian preachers.[53] Yet critical opinion regarding the sermons and

---

[52]van Unnik, "Luke-Acts," p. 29. He goes on to say: "I am sure that if the same tests to which Luke has often been subjected were applied to historians of our times, e.g., about World War II, they would not stand the test. It would be very wholesome to many a N.T. scholar to read a good many sources of secular history—and not only theological books. Then it would appear that sometimes a single story may be really significant for a great development, and that summaries as such are not a sign of lack of information" (ibid.).

[53]See esp. Dibelius, *Studies in Acts*, pp. 138–85; P. Vielhauer, "On the 'Paulinism' of Acts," in Keck and Martyn, pp. 33–50; E. Schweizer, "Concerning the Speeches in Acts," in Keck and Martyn, pp. 208–16; U. Wilckens and P. Schubert, "The Final Cycle of Speeches in the Book of Acts," JBL, 87 (1968), 1–16.

addresses of Acts has not moved in only one direction, and many have come to feel that such judgments are extreme.

As has already been noted in the Historical Writing in Antiquity section, ancient historians did ask questions as to what really happened and sought to be as accurate as possible. We pointed out from the example of Thucydides that even though verbatim reporting was disclaimed, the attempt was to adhere "as closely as possible to the general sense of what was actually spoken" (*History of the Peloponnesian War* 1.22).

As for the similarity of structure between the speeches themselves and between the speeches and the narrative of Acts, this may be freely acknowledged without necessarily denigrating the content. To an extent, of course, all the speeches in Acts are necessarily paraphrastic, for certainly the original delivery contained more detail of argument and more illustrative material than Luke included—as poor Eutychus undoubtedly could testify (Acts 20:7-12)! Stenographic reports they are not, and probably few ever so considered them. They have been reworked, as is required in any précis, and reworked, moreover, in accord with the style of the narrative. But recognition of the kind of writing that produces speeches compatible with the narrative in which they are found should not be interpreted as inaccurate reporting or a lack of traditional source material. After all, a single author is responsible for the literary form of the whole.

Comparing Luke's Gospel with Matthew's, we can demonstrate that Luke did not invent sayings for Jesus. On the contrary, he seems to have been more literal in transmitting the words of Jesus than in recounting the events of his life. Evans believes that such a comparison is fallacious since the discourses of Jesus and the sermons of the apostolic men in Acts are two entirely different literary genres, the one composed of independent *logia* and the other of more rounded and carefully constructed units.[54] And Dibelius insisted that the comparison should not be taken as presumptive evidence for a similarity of treatment by Luke in Acts:

> When he wrote the Gospel, Luke had to fit in with a tradition which already had its own stamp upon it, so that he had not the same literary freedom as when he composed the Acts of the Apostles. On the other hand, unless we are completely deceived, he was the first to employ the material available for the Acts of the Apostles, and so was able to develop the book according to the point of view of an historian writing literature (*Studies in Acts*, p. 185).

Yet even though we have no comparable "Matthew" for Acts, and though the literary genre of the discourses in Luke and the speeches in Acts differ, there is no prima facie reason why Luke's handling of the material in the latter should be assumed to differ widely from his treatment in the former. And though his respect for the speakers behind the latter never rivaled his veneration for the person of the former, it is difficult to believe that such a difference would have appreciably affected the desire for accuracy of content, if not also of word, that he evidences in his Gospel. We must, therefore, continue to insist on a presumption in favor of a similarity of treatment in Luke's recording of the words of Jesus and his recording of the addresses of Peter, Stephen, Philip, James, and Paul that engenders confidence in the reliability of the content of the speeches in Acts, even though it has been reworked by Luke into its present précis form.

That Luke actually strove for accuracy of content in presenting the speeches, or at least did not impose his own theology on them and pervert their original character, has

---

[54]C.F. Evans, "The Kerygma," JTS, 7 (1956), 27.

been argued in significant articles by Ridderbos and Moule.[55] Ridderbos points to the lack of developed theology in the speeches of Peter as a mark of reliable historiography rather than of inventive genius. And Moule convincingly insists that in spite of frequent claims to the contrary the Christology of Acts is not uniform, either between the speakers themselves or between them and Luke—that there are a "number of seemingly undesigned coincidences and subtle nuances," which indicate a retention of the essential nature of the content.[56]

The problem as to why in Acts 1–15 the early Christian leaders are portrayed as quoting (in the main) from the LXX when their sermons and addresses had their origin (for the most part) in an Aramaic-speaking community is a difficulty without a ready solution. Many have asserted that this phenomenon of Greek biblical citations in material credited to Aramaic-speaking preachers lies heavily against the authenticity of the speeches. But both the observation and the conclusion drawn from it fail to take into account a number of pertinent factors.

In the first place, while the quotations of Acts are fairly representative of the LXX in general, the LXX alone is not sufficient to explain all their textual features. J. de Waard points out that the quotations of Acts 3:22–23 (Deut 18:15, 18–19), 7:43 (Amos 5:26–27), 13:41 (Hab 1:5), and 15:16 (Amos 9:11) are prime examples of where "certain New Testament writings show affinities to the DSS as regards the Old Testament text" (p. 78). Likewise, there is the possibility that in Acts Luke assimilated Aramaic or more Hebraic type text-forms to the text that was, to quote C.C. Torrey, "familiar to those for whom he wrote" (p. 58). In support of Torrey's thesis at this point, Max Wilcox has shown that while the biblical quotations in Acts 1–15 are strongly Septuagintal, the allusions, because they are less capable of exact identification and therefore less subject to special treatment, seem to have escaped a process of assimilation and retain more their original Semitic cast (pp. 20–55). Perhaps some credit for the Septuagintal features of the quotations should also be given to a Greek testimonia collection of OT passages circulating within the church about the time of Luke's composition (ibid., pp. 181–82).

It seems, therefore, that we are faced with at least two issues regarding the text-form of the quotations in the first fifteen chapters of Acts: (1) the variety of biblical versions in the first century and (2) assimilation for the sake of Greek-speaking readers. In addition, the possible presence of a Greek testimonia collection(s) adds a further complication. Until additional evidence is available, we may be well advised to leave questions as to textual sources and deviations in early Christian preaching somewhat open. We may suspect that the answer to our problem lies in one or more of the suggestions alluded to above, and we may be able to build a reasonable case in defense of a thesis. But all we really know is that the biblical quotations in Acts are dominantly Septuagintal, with a few parallels to the biblical texts at Qumran. None of this, however, necessarily impinges upon or supports authenticity.

8. The Structure of Acts

The Acts of the Apostles was originally written as the second part of a two-volume work, and its inseparable relation to Luke's Gospel must be kept in mind if we are to

---

[55]See C.F.D. Moule, "The Christology of Acts," in Keck and Martyn, pp. 159–85.
[56]Ibid., pp. 181–82.

understand the work. As Cadbury insisted over fifty years ago: "Their unity is a fundamental and illuminating axiom. . . . They are not merely two independent writings from the same pen; they are a single continuous work. Acts is neither an appendix nor an afterthought. It is probably an integral part of the author's original plan and purpose."[57] The Prologue to the two-volume work (Luke 1:1–4) suggests, in fact, that the author's intention was to write "an account of the things that have been fulfilled among us"—things that stretched from the birth of John the Baptist to the entrance of the Good News into Rome.[58] And his use of the emphatic verb "began" ($\bar{e}rxato$) as he commences his second volume (Acts 1:1) sets up the parallel between "all that Jesus *began* to do and to teach (italics mine)" as recorded in his Gospel and what he *continued* to do and to teach through his church as is shown in Acts.

Luke alone of the evangelists seems to have viewed the history of the advance of the gospel as of comparable importance to the life, death, and resurrection of Jesus—understanding, it seems, that Jesus' accomplishment of redemption and the extension of that redemption through the activity of the church as being part and parcel of the same climactic movement in the drama of salvation. On the one hand, therefore, Luke has taken pains to construct his second volume with an eye to the first; he sets up numerous parallels in the portrayal of events in the two volumes and repeatedly stresses features in the second that fulfill anticipations expressed in the first. The geographical movement of Jesus in the Gospel from Galilee to Jerusalem, for example, is paralleled in Acts by the geographical advance of the gospel from Jerusalem to Rome. The importance of the Holy Spirit in the birth narratives, in the Spirit's descent on Jesus at his baptism, and in the Spirit constantly undergirding his ministry (cf. Jesus' declaration of this fact found only in Luke 4:18–19) is paralleled in Acts by the Spirit's coming upon the disciples at Pentecost and the repeated emphasis upon the Spirit as the source of the church's power and progress.

Similarly, Luke's stress in Acts upon the special significance of the apostles, the centrality of Jesus Christ in the early apostolic preaching, and the universal dimensions of that preaching finds roots in his Gospel in such unique ways as calling the disciples "apostles" (Luke 6:13) and extending the quotation of Isaiah 40:3 to include the universalistic statements of vv.4–5 (Luke 3:5–6), as well as more inferentially at many other places. Further instances of such parallel phenomena are much too numerous to mention here; they will be dealt with in the commentary in loc. Often the parallelism is so subtly presented in the narratives that it is easily overlooked unless one studies Acts with Luke's Gospel constantly in mind. This structural parallelism and tying in of details between the two volumes runs throughout Luke's writings—not crudely or woodenly, but often very subtly and skillfully—and we do well to watch for it.[59] "St. Luke," as Ehrhardt said, "is far too good a writer and too honest an historian to labour this parallelism; but the structural similarity is close enough to deserve our careful attention" (*Ten Lectures on Acts*, p. 13).

On the other hand, Acts is not simply a parallel to the Gospel, ending at Rome as the Gospel ended at Jerusalem. If it were, it would be the less important part of Luke's two-volume work—something like a shadow of the original. But Acts is important in its

---

[57]Henry J. Cadbury, *The Making of Luke-Acts* (New York: Macmillan, 1927), pp. 8–9.

[58]Cf. Henry J. Cadbury, "The Knowledge Claimed in Luke's Preface," Exp, 24 (1922), 401–20; idem, BC, 2:489–510; idem, *Luke-Acts*, pp. 344–48, 358–59.

[59]For detailed lists of parallels between Luke's Gospel and Acts, see C.H. Talbert, *Literary Patterns, Theological Themes, and the Genre of Luke-Acts* (Missoula, Mont.: Scholars, 1974), pp. 15–23, 58–65.

own right as the logical and geographical completion of Jesus' journey to Jerusalem. Indeed, none of the apostolic figures of Acts is portrayed as paralleling the life, death, and resurrection of Jesus. Probably that is why Luke had no interest in closing Acts with an account of Paul's death. If he knew of it, he evidently did not consider it appropriate to include it; if it had not occurred when he was writing Acts, he felt no compulsion to wait for it before completing the book. Nevertheless, Luke presents the apostolic ministry as the necessary extension of the redemption effected by Christ. Luke views both the accomplishment of salvation and the spread of the Good News as inseparable units in the climactic activity of God's redemption of mankind—a truth probably picked up from Paul (cf. Rom 8:17; Phil 3:10–11; Col 1:24). So for Luke, as O'Neill points out, "the full significance of the central happenings at Jerusalem is not worked out in history until Paul has reached Rome" (p. 6).

Various proposals about Luke's construction of the second volume of his work have been made. Some scholars have divided it according to underlying sources and others according to topics. What is required in any structural analysis of Acts, however, is a thesis that takes into account both the parallel features in Luke's Gospel and the structural phenomena in Acts. In particular, four features need to be kept in mind in considering the structure of the Gospel:

1. It begins with an introductory section of distinctly Lukan cast, dealing with Jesus' birth and youth (1:1–2:52) before taking up the narrative held in common with Mark and Matthew.
2. The Nazareth pericope (4:14–30) serves as the topic paragraph for all that Luke presents in his two volumes; most of what follows this pericope is an explication of the themes it contains.[60]
3. In his presentation of Jesus' ministry, Luke follows an essentially geographical outline that moves from the Galilean ministry (4:14–9:50), through the ministry in Perea and Judea (9:51–19:28), and concludes in Jerusalem (19:29–24:53).
4. Luke deliberately sets up a number of parallels between our Lord's ministry in Galilee and his ministry in the regions of Perea and Judea.[61]

In addition, five phenomena relating to the structure of Acts need to be recognized:

1. It begins, like the Gospel, with an introductory section of distinctly Lukan cast dealing with the constitutive events of the Christian mission (1:1–2:41) before it sets forth the advances of the gospel "in Jerusalem, and in all Judea and Samaria, and to the ends of the earth" (1:7).
2. This introductory section is followed by what appears to be a thematic statement (2:42–47). This material, while often viewed as a summary of what precedes, most probably serves as the thesis paragraph for what follows.
3. In his presentation of the advance of the Christian mission, Luke follows an essentially geographical outline that moves from Jerusalem (2:42–6:7), through Judea and Samaria (6:8–9:31), on into Palestine-Syria (9:32–12:24), then to the Gentiles in the

---

[60]Some representative comments on the importance of the Nazareth pericope for Luke's structure are: "a frontispiece to the Ministry" (W. Manson, *The Gospel of Luke* [London: Hodder & Stoughton, 1930], p. 41); "a programmatic prologue" (D. Hill, "The Rejection of Jesus at Nazareth (Luke 4:16–30)," NovTest, 13 [1971], 170); "a main pillar of [Luke's] whole structure" (Conzelmann, *Theology of St. Luke*, p. 29, n.5); "the foundation stone of his gospel" (J. Sanders, "From Isaiah 61 to Luke 4," in J. Neusner, ed., *Christianity, Judaism, and Other Greco-Roman Cults*, Part I [Leiden: Brill, 1975], p. 104); "a prelude to the whole of Luke-Acts" (S. MacL. Gilmour, "The Gospel according to St. Luke," IB, 8:96); "the rest of the Gospel is simply the working out of this programme" (G.B. Caird, *The Gospel of St. Luke* [London: Black, 1968], p. 86).

[61]For detailed lists of parallels within Luke's Gospel, see Talbert, *Genre of Luke-Acts*, pp. 26–29, 39–56.

eastern part of the Roman Empire (12:25–19:20), and finally culminates in Paul's defenses and the entrance of the gospel into Rome (19:21–28:31).

4. In his presentation, Luke deliberately sets up a number of parallels between the ministry of Peter in the first half of Acts and that of Paul in the last half.[62]

5. Luke includes six summary statements or "progress reports" (6:7; 9:31; 12:24; 16:5; 19:20; and 28:31), each of which seems to conclude its own "panel" of material.[63]

Taking all these literary and structural features into account, we may conclude that Luke developed his material in Acts along the following lines:

Introduction: The Constitutive Events of the Christian Mission (1:1–2:41)
Part I: The Christian Mission to the Jewish World (2:42–12:24)
Panel 1—The Earliest Days of the Church at Jerusalem (2:42–6:7)
Summary Statement: "So the word of God spread. The number of disciples in Jerusalem increased rapidly, and a large number of priests became obedient to the faith" (6:7).
Panel 2—Critical Events in the Lives of Three Pivotal Figures (6:8–9:31)
Summary Statement: "Then the church throughout Judea, Galilee and Samaria enjoyed a time of peace. It was strengthened; and encouraged by the Holy Spirit, it grew in numbers, living in the fear of the Lord" (9:31).
Panel 3—Advances of the Gospel in Palestine-Syria (9:32–12:24)
Summary Statement: "But the word of God continued to increase and spread" (12:24).
Part II: The Christian Mission to the Gentile World (12:25–28:31)
Panel 4—The First Missionary Journey and the Jerusalem Council (12:25–16:5)
Summary Statement: "So the churches were strengthened in the faith and grew daily in numbers" (16:5).
Panel 5—Wide Outreach Through Two Missionary Journeys (16:6–19:20)
Summary Statement: "In this way the word of the Lord spread widely and grew in power" (19:20).
Panel 6—To Jerusalem and Thence to Rome (19:21–28:31)
Summary Statement: "Boldly and without hindrance he preached the kingdom of God and taught about the Lord Jesus Christ" (28:31).

Laying out the structure of Acts in this way highlights not only the parallelism that exists between Luke's second volume and his first but also the parallelism built into Acts in its portrayal of the ministry of Peter in chapters 1–12 and that of Paul in chapters 13–28. Likewise, accepting such a scheme for the construction of the book provides us with a cogent explanation for one of the most difficult questions about Acts: Why does it end as it does? The reader is left at 28:30–31 with Paul a prisoner for two years in his own rented quarters at Rome, where "boldly and without hindrance he preached the kingdom of God and taught about the Lord Jesus Christ." But it is very strange that we are told no more, and so various explanations have been proposed for this abrupt ending.

One common explanation is that Luke was prevented by his own death from writing more. Another is that he really intended to write a trilogy, with the third volume dedicated to the apostle's ministry in the western part of the empire (as his second volume had dealt with the apostle's ministry in the east) and with the inclusion of an

---

[62]Ibid.

[63]Cf. C.H. Turner, "The Chronology of the New Testament," HDB, 1:421; though, of course, Turner's first panel included 1:1–2:41.

account of Paul's martyrdom; but for some reason he never completed it. Those who propose this usually point to the classical distinction between the word *prōtos* used in Acts 1:1, which means the "first" of a series and could suggest the intention of more than two volumes, and the comparative *proteros*, which signifies the "former" of two. Furthermore, they often cite Paul's intention expressed in Romans 15:23–24, 28 of carrying on a ministry beyond Rome that would extend to Spain (cf. 1 Clement 5). But the classical distinction between "first" and "former" probably did not always hold in latter times among common people, and there are reasons to believe that Paul's hope for a ministry beyond Rome in the western part of the empire never materialized.

Another explanation for the abrupt ending of Acts has been advanced by many who see Acts as a trial document for presentation before the imperial authorities. They have suggested that Luke stopped where he did because there he rested his case and, with the condemnation of his client, had no desire to complete the book. Others have insisted that Acts ends where it does because, writing about A.D. 62, Luke knew nothing more about Paul. And still others have proposed that in saying that Paul resided for two whole years at Rome without any formal charge being laid against him, Luke was obliquely implying that Paul was not brought to trial but that his case was dismissed according to Roman law—actually an appropriate ending for the book and one that stresses the fact that all the accusations against Paul had come to nothing.

Each of these proposals has some merit and can be argued rather convincingly. Some of them can be joined with others in a common argument. But Luke was not writing a biography of Paul, even though he included many biographical details about him in Acts. Luke was showing how the Good News of man's redemption had swept out from Jerusalem, across Palestine, into Asia Minor, then on throughout Macedonia and Achaia, and how it finally entered Rome, the capital of the empire. And when Paul's goal was reached, his story was told. The structure of Acts as laid out above not only parallels the structure of Luke's Gospel and conforms most adequately to the text of Acts itself, it also implies that Luke ended where he did because his purpose in writing was completed. The gospel that Jesus effected in his ministry from Galilee to Jerusalem had reached its culmination in its extension from Jerusalem to Rome. And with that victory—as he visualized it—accomplished, Luke felt free to lay down his pen.

9. Date of Composition

We have held back discussion of the date of Acts till after dealing with the structure of the book, for the question of date has traditionally been connected with a particular explanation for the ending of Acts. Baur, like many today, saw no correlation. But at the turn of the century a majority explained the abrupt ending by the maxim "the narrative has caught up with the events." So they concluded that Acts was written shortly after the last event mentioned. Adolf Harnack led the way in establishing this position, and a number of commentators have since taken a similar stance (e.g., A. Wikenhauser, F.F. Bruce). Much that Harnack and his successors said about an early date for Acts is still valuable and important. But if we are unable to give the same explanation as Harnack and his successors for the ending of Acts, we cannot equate the issues of its ending and date in the same manner. We believe that to date Acts by the nature of its ending is a non sequitur because it fails to take into account Luke's main purpose in writing the book.

Broadly speaking, scholars today are divided into three camps respecting the dating of Acts: those who argue for the composition of the book somewhere around A.D. 115–30, those who hold to a date somewhere between A.D. 80 and 95, and those who hold to a date prior to A.D. 70. An early second-century date has often been argued on the basis of the work's apparent "Early Catholicism" (i.e., its recasting of the earliest futuristic eschatology and Spirit-controlled enthusiasm into such forms as Christology, ecclesiology, realized eschatology, and missionary outreach) and its "anti-Gnosticism." But these matters are hotly debated—and, even if true, could have existed earlier than the second century.

O'Neill has recently taken the lead in arguing for Acts as having been written between A.D. 115 and 130. He begins with the thesis that "the only way now left to solve the problem about the date of Acts is to decide where its theological affinities lie" (p. 1). O'Neill finds the closest parallels to the theology of Acts in the writings of Justin Martyr, particularly in his *First Apology,* and argues for an early second-century date on the basis of the arguments "that Luke and Justin Martyr held common theological positions without being dependent on each other, and that Luke-Acts was completed in time for Luke to be used by Marcion" (pp. 21–22). But as Barclay aptly observes about O'Neill's view: "Of the ingenuity and of the scholarship with which it is supported there is no question; but it has failed to gain general acceptance, if for no other reason, because an easier explanation of the facts is that Justin knew Acts."[64] Furthermore, to attribute to an early second-century writer the fabrication of the earlier part of Paul's story and then to view such a writer as hesitating to produce an account of Paul's experiences in Rome is hard to imagine. "It is certain," as Ehrhardt points out, "that the mind of the early second-century Church, which produced a great number of apocryphal Acts of various Apostles, did not work in this way" (*Ten Lectures on Acts,* p. 3).

Most scholars today date Acts somewhere between A.D. 80 and 95. They reason like this: Acts cannot have been written before the Fall of Jerusalem because the third Gospel cannot have been written before that date, and the third Gospel is earlier than Acts. On the other hand, Acts cannot have been written after A.D. 95 because the case for a member of Paul's missionary team having written the "we" sections is strong. Furthermore, it must have been written sometime after Paul's death, for Paul might have objected to certain things Acts describes him as having said and done. Yet Acts must have been written before Paul's letters were gathered into some kind of recognizable collection, for the book says nothing of its hero as a correspondent. The *terminus a quo,* therefore, is held to be set by the references to the Fall of Jerusalem in Luke 19:43–44 and 21:20–24, which require the Gospel to have been written after A.D. 70, and by the general sequence of synoptic relationships epitomized by the revision of Mark 13:14–20 in Luke 21:20–24, which also seems to point to a date after A.D. 70. As for the *terminus ad quem,* it is set sometime after Paul's death but before the collection of the Pauline letters—a collection that seems to have been known in at least elementary form by Clement of Rome, who wrote the work known as 1 Clement about A.D. 96.

Nevertheless, Acts contains a number of features that point to an earlier date than A.D. 70 for its composition. Chief among these is the portrayal of *the situation of the Jews.* They are represented as being both a spiritual and political power who had influence with the Roman courts and whose damaging testimony against the Christians must be countered. But how could the Jews act as Luke depicts them acting *after* their destruction as a nation in the war of A.D. 66–70? And why would Luke *after* that time want to

---

[64]William Barclay, *The Gospels and Acts,* 2 vols. (London: SCM, 1976), 2:256.

argue before a Gentile audience that Christianity should be accepted as a *religio licita* because of its relation to Judaism? True, Vespasian and Titus waged their war against the Jews of Palestine, and particularly against their Zealot leadership, without mounting a general persecution against Diaspora Jews or imposing official restrictions on them. Yet in the eyes of the Roman world Palestinian Judaism was largely defunct after A.D. 70, and Diaspora Judaism undoubtedly came under something of a cloud as a result. Luke's apologetic, however, is built upon the dual premises that (1) the Jewish leaders throughout the Diaspora and particularly the Jewish authorities at Jerusalem are at the time an important voice before Roman courts of law, even the imperial court at Rome; and (2) Judaism both in the Diaspora and at Jerusalem is accepted by Rome as a *religio licita.* Apart from such assumptions, Luke's apologetic makes no sense at all. Yet this was hardly the case at any time between A.D. 80 and 95, though it came to be the case to some extent through the efforts of Rabbi Akiba between A.D. 110 and 130.[65] But acceptance of Judaism by Rome as a *religio licita* was the situation prior to the outbreak of hostilities and the disastrous conflagration that followed in A.D. 66–70.

Likewise, *the estimation of Roman justice* implicit in Acts argues for its early composition. Acts expresses a generally hopeful outlook regarding Christianity's acceptance in the Gentile world and its recognition by Roman authorities. This could hardly have been the case after the Neronian persecution of Christians that began in A.D. 65. If Luke had known of the martyrdom of Paul and Peter under Nero at Rome (cf. 1 Clement 5), and along with them the martyrdom of many other Christians, "the last word of Acts [i.e., *akōlytōs*, 'without hindrance'], which," as Plooij long ago pointed out, "surely not without significance stands in its prominent place as the crown of the narrative, would be not only meaningless, but *in its tendency* nearly equal to a lie [italics his]."[66] The attitude of Acts toward Roman power and justice is more like that of Paul in Romans 13:1–7, written before Nero's persecutions, than that of John the Seer in Revelation 17:1–6, written during the last years of the first century.

In addition, *the archaic nature of the language* in Acts says something about its date, suggesting either that its author wrote before circumstances and expressions had changed or that he was extremely ingenious in historicizing. Ramsay has documented Luke's surprising accuracy in geographical, political, and territorial details. Regarding the regional boundary between Phrygian Iconium and the Lycaonian cities of Lystra and Derbe in 14:6, for example, he has shown that such "was accurate at no other time except between 37 and 72 A.D." (*St. Paul the Traveller,* pp. 110–13). And Harnack has shown that the language of Acts appears to be the language of the earlier days of the church, particularly in such matters as the titles ascribed to Jesus, the designations employed for Christians, and the manner of speaking about the church (*Date of the Acts,* pp. 103–14). It is possible, of course, to credit all these features to the ingenuity and genius of Luke. But they are best explained by the hypothesis of an early date for the writing of Acts.

Finally, there is the surprising fact that *Acts reflects no knowledge of Paul's letters,* either in what is said or what is assumed on the part of its readers. In support of this we cite but two examples drawn from letters that were undoubtedly written before Acts,

---

[65] Rabbi Akiba ben Joseph was the leading Jewish rabbi of A.D. 110–35. His Mishnah was a forerunner to that of Rabbi Judah the Prince (A.D. 150–85), and under his leadership relations with Rome were stabilized for almost two decades. Under pressure of the Zealots, however, he proclaimed Simeon ben Kosebah to be Messiah and sided with him against Rome, and in A.D. 135 he was one of ten prominent rabbis put to death by Rome.

[66] D. Plooij, "Again: The Work of St. Luke," Exp. 13 (1917), 121.

no matter how early we date it: There is no integration of Paul's statements in Galatians 1 and 2 regarding his personal contacts with the Jerusalem apostles and his visits described in Acts 9, 11, and 15. Nor is there any correlation between the many experiences referred to in 2 Corinthians (esp. ch. 1–2 and 11–12) and Paul's missionary journeys recorded in Acts. These phenomena may, of course, be interpreted as evidence for the personal aloofness and the chronological distance of the author of Acts from his hero. Thus it may be used to support a late date for the work. On the other hand, the phenomena just mentioned suggest a very early date for Acts—viz., that it was before the significance of the Pauline correspondence was appreciated and by a companion not actually with Paul (to judge by the distribution of the "we" sections in Acts) when he wrote the letters in question.

To sum up, there is much to be said in support of an early date for Acts. On our view, the *terminus a quo* would be the writing of Luke's Gospel (which, of course, precedes Acts, and which, in turn, rests on the publication of Mark's Gospel and at least the knowledge that Matthew wrote a Gospel) and Paul's two-year imprisonment at Rome (c.61–63), referred to in Acts 28:30. As for the *terminus ad quem*, it would be the outbreak of hostilities in Palestine between the Jewish Zealots and the Roman Tenth Legion in A.D. 66 and the start of the Neronian persecutions at Rome in A.D. 65—all of which points to about A.D. 64 for the composition of Acts.

The major objections to such a date are that it places the development of the synoptic tradition too early and treats the Olivet Discourse of Mark 13, Matthew 24–25, and Luke 21 (together with Luke 17:22–37 and 19:43–44) as predictive prophecy. But the nature of the development of the synoptic tradition and the dates to be assigned to that development continue to be matters of great dispute. We may, for instance, believe in the commonly accepted theory of synoptic relationships (Markan priority, a basic two-document hypothesis, et al.), as we do, and still question the validity of a set of dates for the synoptic Gospels that are later than the destruction of Jerusalem. After all, dating the Synoptics and Acts depends largely on one's view of the origin of the material making up the Olivet Discourse. And ultimately dating the Olivet Discourse comes down to the question of the possibility or impossibility of genuine predictive prophecy on the lips of our Lord during his earthly ministry—a possibility that this commentary affirms.

10. Authorship

The discussion of the authorship of Acts has been left to the last (though Luke has been repeatedly spoken of as having written the third Gospel and Acts) because the question of authorship depends largely on how one views other introductory matters. But now that these have been dealt with, the question of authorship arises naturally and logically.

Two observations from Acts itself must govern the discussion of its authorship. The first is that stylistically and structurally the Gospel of Luke and the Acts of the Apostles are so closely related that they have to be assigned to the same author. This has been so extensively demonstrated by linguistic studies that it need not be elaborated here. More important, however, are the structural parallels between the two books and the comprehensive plan that is maintained throughout them. All this necessitates that, for both critical and interpretative purposes, Luke-Acts be considered a single, unified work in two volumes. Hardly anyone today would dispute this basic observation.

The second observation regarding the question of authorship is that Luke-Acts claims to have been written by one who reports at firsthand some of the events he records. In the Prologue (Luke 1:1–4) to his two-volume work, the author's use of the expression "among us" (en hēmin) should probably be taken to imply his contemporary status with some of the events he purposes to narrate, though he disavows being an eyewitness "from the first." And his insistence that "I myself have carefully investigated everything [parēkolouthēkoti] from the beginning" suggests more than just historical knowledge of the events depicted. Dupont points out: "The verb parakoloutheō is in point of fact very appropriate for expressing the distinction between information received at second hand and that coming from the writer's personal presence at the events" (p. 106, cf. pp. 101–12). More particularly, however, the use of the first person plural in Acts 16:10–17; 20:5–15; 21:1–18; and 27:1–28:16 appears to be a deliberate endeavor to indicate that the writer was a traveling companion of Paul on certain of his missionary journeys. This leaves us with a plain choice: either to accept the suggestion made by the book itself as true or to reject it in favor of some other explanation.[67]

Having dated the composition of Acts about A.D. 64, there is little reason for us to dispute the implications of its "we" passages. In fact, accepting the author as a traveling companion of Paul during some of his missionary journeys explains quite adequately two rather peculiar features about the plan of Acts: on the one hand, the disproportion of the work, which devotes more than three-fifths of its space to Paul; and, on the other, the disproportion that appears in the portrayal of Paul, whose first mission is narrated with great brevity while certain parts of the second and third missionary journeys, Paul's five defenses, and the journey to Rome are described much more fully. No writer who was altogether a stranger to apostolic times or working entirely from sources would have devoted so much space to the latter part of Paul's ministry. His work would have been more symmetrically planned.

Traditionally, the author of the third Gospel has been identified as Luke, the companion of Paul mentioned in Colossians 4:14, Philemon 24, and 2 Timothy 4:11. Nor has tradition ever considered any author other than Luke. His authorship was accepted by Marcion (c.A.D. 135), is included in the Anti-Marcionite Prologue to the third Gospel (c.A.D. 170), and taken for granted by the compiler of the Muratorian Canon (c.A.D. 180–200). Likewise, in the MSS of the Gospels the heading "According to Luke" (kata Loukan) is always found for the third Gospel. The situation regarding Acts is not quite the same. Indications of the use of Acts in the early second century are very scarce (e.g., Marcion did not use it and seems not to have known of it, even though he knew and used Luke). And while the MSS of Acts bear the title "The Acts of the Apostles," they do not name its author. Nevertheless, with Luke-Acts being originally one work in two volumes, which sometime during the last part of the first century or very early in the second began to circulate as two separate works, what is said regarding the one as to authorship must apply equally well to the other. Of lesser unanimity within the early church was the tradition that Luke was an Antiochian of Syria, which is the claim made in the opening words of the Anti-Marcionite Prologue to the third Gospel and is repeated by Eusebius (Ecclesiastical History 3. 4) and Jerome (On Illustrious Men 7; Preface to the Commentary on Matthew).

In support of the traditional ascription, we need not insist that the author of Luke-Acts necessarily employed a vocabulary special to the medical profession of his day or expressed interests that were overtly those of a doctor, thereby confirming Paul's description of Luke in Colossians 4:14 as a physician. In 1882 Hobart proposed such a view

---

[67]Cf. A. Ehrhardt, "The Construction and Purpose of the Acts of the Apostles," ST, 12 (1958), 45–79.

based on a comparison of the language of Luke-Acts with that of such Greek medical writers as Hippocrates (c.460–357 B.C.) and Aretaeus, Galen, and Dioscorides, who lived during the first and second centuries A.D.[68] Many scholars at the turn of the century followed him, particularly Adolf Harnack who was so influential in propagating this thesis. But in 1919 Cadbury demonstrated in the publication of his Harvard doctoral thesis that the majority of the so-called medical words identified by Hobart in Luke-Acts can be found in about the same frequency in such ancient writers as Josephus and Lucian of Samosata, who were not physicians.[69] And he followed that with a series of studies arguing that the supposed medical terminology of Luke-Acts was employed very widely in the ancient world—even among, as he called them, "horse-doctors."[70] The gibe has frequently been made that Cadbury won his doctorate by taking Luke's away from him. All Cadbury did, however, was demonstrate by linguistic evidence that one cannot prove that the author of Acts was a physician and therefore "Luke, the beloved physician" (Col 4:14). Yet while the language of Luke-Acts does not require us to believe that "Luke, the beloved physician" wrote Acts, it puts no obstacle in the way of that belief.

What we can say positively is that the tradition that Luke wrote the third Gospel and Acts goes back at least to the early second century, that it was unanimously accepted within the church, and that it would be very strange were it not true. If an early ecclesiastical writer were attempting to pass off Luke-Acts as the work of someone close to an apostle in order to invest it with authority, why did he not attribute it to Paul himself—or at least to Timothy or Titus, both of whom were better known than Luke? Why, indeed, ascribe it to an individual who played no major part in the advance of the gospel and whose name appears only three times in the NT? To be sure, attempts have been made to set aside the tradition; but none of them is convincing. Consequently there are no compelling reasons to reject the tradition that Luke, Paul's physician friend, who appears to have been a Gentile (Col 4:10 –15), was the writer of Acts.

11. Bibliography

Note: Only selected commentaries and monographs are listed here. For a full listing of commentaries, monographs, and journal articles on Acts up through the mid-sixties, see A.J. and M.B. Mattill, *A Classified Bibliography of Literature on the Acts of the Apostles* (Leiden: Brill, 1966).

Barclay, William. *Turning to God. A Study of Conversion in the Book of Acts and Today.* London: Epworth, 1963.
Barrett, C.K. *Luke the Historian in Recent Study.* London: Epworth, 1961.
———. *The Signs of an Apostle.* Philadelphia: Fortress, 1972.
Black, Matthew. *An Aramaic Approach to the Gospels and Acts.* 3d. ed. Oxford: Clarendon, 1967.
Blaiklock, E.M. *The Acts of the Apostles: An Historical Commentary.* Grand Rapids: Eerdmans, 1959.
Blunt, A.W.F. *The Acts of the Apostles.* Oxford: Clarendon, 1922.
Bruce, F.F. *The Acts of the Apostles: The Greek Text with Introduction and Commentary.* Grand Rapids: Eerdmans, 1951.

---

[68]W. Hobart, *The Medical Language of St. Luke* (Dublin: Hodges, Figgis & Co., 1882).

[69]See *The Diction of Luke and Acts,* vol. 1 of *Method of Luke.*

[70]See esp. H. Cadbury, "Lexical Notes on Luke-Acts, II—Recent Arguments for Medical Language," JBL, 45 (1926), 190 –209; idem, "Lexical Notes on Luke-Acts, V—Luke and the Horse-Doctors," ibid., 52 (1933), 55–65.

_____. *The Book of the Acts: The English Text with Introduction, Exposition and Notes.* Grand Rapids: Eerdmans, 1954.

_____. *Paul: Apostle of the Free Spirit.* Exeter: Paternoster, 1977. (Also published by Eerdmans under the title *Paul: Apostle of the Heart Set Free.*)

Bultmann, Rudolf. *Primitive Christianity in its Contemporary Setting.* Translated by R.H. Fuller. London: Thames & Hudson, 1956.

Burkitt, F.C. *Christian Beginnings.* London: University of London, 1924.

Cadbury, Henry J. *The Style and Literary Method of Luke.* 2 vols. Cambridge: Harvard University, 1919–20.

_____. *The Book of Acts in History.* London: Black, 1955.

Caird, George B. *The Apostolic Age.* London: Duckworth, 1955.

Calvin, John. *Commentary Upon the Acts of the Apostles.* 2 vols. Edited by H. Beveridge. Grand Rapids: Eerdmans, 1949.

Chadwick, Henry. *The Circle and the Ellipse.* Oxford: Clarendon, 1959.

Chrysostom, John. *The Homilies of S. John Chrysostom, Archbishop of Constantinople, on the Acts of the Apostles.* London: F. & J. Rivington, 1851–52.

Conzelmann, Hans. *The Theology of St. Luke.* Translated by G. Buswell. New York: Harper & Row, 1961.

_____. *History of Primitive Christianity.* Translated by J.E. Steely. Nashville: Abingdon, 1973.

Davies, W.D. *Paul and Rabbinic Judaism.* London: SPCK, 1955.

_____. *The Gospel and the Land. Early Christianity and Jewish Territorial Doctrine.* Berkeley: University of California, 1974.

Dibelius, Martin. *Studies in the Acts of the Apostles.* Edited by H. Greeven. Translated by M. Ling. London: SCM, 1956.

Dix, Gregory. *Jew and Greek. A Study in the Primitive Church.* London: Dacre, 1953.

Dodd, C.H. *The Apostolic Preaching and Its Developments.* London: Hodder & Stoughton, 1936.

Dunn, James D.G. *Baptism in the Holy Spirit.* London: SCM, 1970.

_____. *Jesus and the Spirit.* London: SCM, 1975.

_____. *Unity and Diversity in the New Testament. An Inquiry into the Character of Earliest Christianity.* London: SCM, 1977.

Dupont, Jacques. *The Sources of Acts.* Translated by K. Pond. London: Darton, Longman & Todd, 1964.

Ehrhardt, Arnold. *The Acts of the Apostles. Ten Lectures.* Manchester: Manchester University, 1970.

Ellis, E. Earle. *Eschatology in Luke.* Philadelphia: Fortress, 1972.

Epp, Eldon J. *The Theological Tendency of Codex Bezae Cantabrigiensis in Acts.* Cambridge: Cambridge University, 1966.

Filson, Floyd V. *Three Crucial Decades.* New York: Abingdon, 1963.

Foakes-Jackson, F.J. *The Acts of the Apostles.* London: Hodder & Stoughton, 1931.

Gärtner, Bertil. *The Areopagus Speech and Natural Revelation.* Translated by C.H. King. Lund: Gleerup, 1955.

Gasque, W. Ward. *A History of the Criticism of the Acts of the Apostles.* Grand Rapids: Eerdmans, 1975.

Gasque, W.W., and Martin, R.P., edd. *Apostolic History and the Gospel.* Exeter: Paternoster, 1970.

Goppelt, Leonhard. *Apostolic and Post-Apostolic Times.* Translated by R.A. Guelich. New York: Harper & Row, 1970.

Green, E.M.B. *Evangelism in the Early Church.* Grand Rapids: Eerdmans, 1970.

Haenchen, Ernst. *The Acts of the Apostles.* Translated by R. McL. Wilson. Philadelphia: Westminster, 1971.

Harnack, Adolf. *Luke the Physician.* Translated by J.R. Wilkinson. London: Williams & Norgate, 1907.

_____. *The Acts of the Apostles.* Translated by J.R. Wilkinson. London: Williams & Norgate, 1909.

_____. *The Date of the Acts and of the Synoptic Gospels.* Translated by J.R. Wilkinson. London: Williams & Norgate, 1911.

Jeremias, Joachim. *Jerusalem in the Time of Jesus.* Translated by F.H. and C.H. Cave. Philadelphia: Fortress, 1969.

Jewett, Robert. *A Chronology of Paul's Life.* Philadelphia: Fortress, 1979.

Jones, A.H.M. *Cities of the Eastern Roman Provinces.* Oxford: Clarendon, 1937.

_____. *The Herods of Judaea.* Oxford: Clarendon, 1938.

Judge, E.A. *The Social Pattern of the Christian Groups in the First Century.* London: Tyndale, 1960.

Keck, L.E., and Martyn, J.L., edd. *Studies in Luke-Acts.* Nashville: Abingdon, 1966.

Knox, John. *Chapters in a Life of Paul.* New York: Abingdon, 1950.

Knox, Wilfred L. *St. Paul and the Church of Jerusalem.* Cambridge: Cambridge University, 1925.

_____. *St. Paul and the Church of the Gentiles.* Cambridge: Cambridge University, 1939.

_____. *Some Hellenistic Elements in Primitive Christianity.* London: Oxford, 1944.

_____. *The Acts of the Apostles.* Cambridge: Cambridge University, 1948.

Lietzmann, Hans. *The Beginnings of the Christian Church.* Translated by B.L. Woolf. London: Nicholson & Watson, 1937.

Lightfoot, J.B. *Biblical Essays.* London: Macmillan, 1893.

Longenecker, Richard N. *Paul, Apostle of Liberty.* New York: Harper & Row, 1964.

_____. *The Christology of Early Jewish Christianity.* London: SCM, 1970.

_____. *Biblical Exegesis in the Apostolic Period.* Grand Rapids: Eerdmans, 1975.

Marshall, I. Howard. *Luke: Historian and Theologian.* Grand Rapids: Zondervan, 1970.

Martin, Raymond A. *Syntactical Evidence of Semitic Sources in Greek Documents.* Missoula, Mont.: Scholars, 1974.

Moule, C.F.D. *Christ's Messengers: Studies in the Acts of the Apostles.* New York: Association, 1957.

_____. *The Origin of Christology.* Cambridge: Cambridge University, 1977.

Munck, Johannes. *Paul and the Salvation of Mankind.* Translated by F. Clarke. Richmond, Va.: John Knox, 1959.

_____. *The Acts of the Apostles.* Garden City, N.Y.: Doubleday, 1967.

O'Neill, J.C. *The Theology of Acts in Its Historical Setting.* Rev. ed. London: SPCK, 1970.

Ramsay, William M. *The Historical Geography of Asia Minor.* London: J. Murray, 1890.

_____. *The Church in the Roman Empire Before A.D. 170.* London: Hodder & Stoughton, 1893.

_____. *St. Paul the Traveller and the Roman Citizen.* London: Hodder & Stoughton, 1897.

_____. *The Cities of St. Paul: Their Influence on His Life and Thought.* London: Hodder & Stoughton, 1907.

_____. *The Bearing of Recent Discovery on the Trustworthiness of the New Testament.* London: Hodder & Stoughton, 1915.

Reicke, Bo. *Diakonie, Festfreude und Zelos.* Uppsala: Lundequistska, 1951.

_____. *Glaube und Leben der Urgemeinde.* Zürich: Zwingli, 1957.

Ridderbos, Herman N. *The Speeches of Peter in the Acts of the Apostles.* London: Tyndale, 1962.

Scharlemann, Martin H. *Stephen: A Singular Saint.* Rome: Pontifical Biblical Institute, 1968.

Schlatter, A. *The Church in the New Testament Period.* Translated by P.P. Levertoff. London: SPCK, 1955.

Schmithals, Walter. *Paul and James.* Translated by D.M. Barton. London: SCM, 1965.

Schoeps, Hans J. *Paul: The Theology of the Apostle in the Light of Jewish Religious History.* Translated by H. Knight. Philadelphia: Westminster, 1961.

_____. *Jewish Christianity. Factional Disputes in the Early Church.* Translated by D.R.A. Hare. Philadelphia: Fortress, 1969.

Sevenster, J.N. *The Roots of Pagan Anti-Semitism in the Ancient World.* Leiden: Brill, 1975.

Sherwin-White, A.N. *Roman Society and Roman Law in the New Testament.* London: Oxford, 1963.

Simon, Marcel. *St. Stephen and the Hellenists in the Primitive Church.* London: Longmans, Green, 1958.

Stanley, David M. *Structural Developments of Early Christianity: Acts of the Apostles.* Toronto: Jesuit Seminary, 1955.

_____. *The Apostolic Church in the New Testament.* Westminster, Md.: Newman, 1965.

Stanton, Graham N. *Jesus of Nazareth in New Testament Preaching.* Cambridge: Cambridge University, 1974.

Stauffer, Ethelbert. *Christ and the Caesars.* Philadelphia: Westminster, 1955.

Stonehouse, Ned B. *The Witness of Luke to Christ.* Grand Rapids: Eerdmans, 1951.

_____. *Paul before the Areopagus and Other New Testament Studies.* Grand Rapids: Eerdmans, 1957.

Talbert, Charles H. *Literary Patterns, Theological Themes, and the Genre of Luke-Acts.* Missoula, Mont.: Scholars, 1977.

Torrey, C.C. *The Composition and Date of Acts.* Cambridge: Harvard University, 1916.

Trites, Allison, A. *The New Testament Concept of Witness.* Cambridge: Cambridge University, 1977.

de Waard, J. *A Comparative Study of the Old Testament Text in the Dead Sea Scrolls and in the New Testament.* Leiden: Brill, 1965.

Wilckens, Ulrich. *Die Missionsreden der Apostelgeschichte. Form- und traditionsgeschichtliche Untersuchungen.* 3d ed. (Neukirchen: Kreis Moes, 1961).

Wilcox, Max. *The Semitisms of Acts.* Oxford: Clarendon, 1965.

Williams, C.S.C. *The Acts of the Apostles.* London: A. & C. Black, 1957.

Wilson, Stephen G. *The Gentiles and the Gentile Mission in Luke-Acts.* Cambridge: Cambridge University, 1973.

Zehnle, Richard F. *Peter's Pentecost Discourse. Tradition and Lukan Reinterpretation in Peter's Speeches of Acts 2 and 3.* Nashville: Abingdon, 1971.

12. Outline and Maps

G. A Summary Statement (16:5)

Panel 5—Wide Outreach Through Two Missionary Journeys (16:6–19:20)

A. Providential Direction for the Mission (16:6–10)

B. At Philippi (16:11–40)
  1. Arrival in the city (16:11–12)
  2. The conversion of Lydia (16:13–15)
  3. The demon-possessed girl (16:16–18)
  4. Paul and Silas in prison (16:19–34)
  5. Paul and Silas leave the city (16:35–40)

C. At Thessalonica (17:1–9)

D. At Berea (17:10–15)

E. At Athens (17:16–34)
  1. Inauguration of a ministry (17:16–21)
  2. Paul's address before the council of Ares (17:22–31)
  3. The response to Paul's address (17:32–34)

F. At Corinth (18:1–17)
  1. Arrival at Corinth (18:1–4)
  2. An eighteen-month ministry (18:5–11)
  3. Before the proconsul Gallio (18:12–17)

G. An Interlude (18:18–28)
  1. Paul's return to Palestine-Syria (18:18–23)
  2. Apollos at Ephesus and Corinth (18:24–28)

H. At Ephesus (19:1–19)
  1. Twelve men without the Spirit (19:1–7)
  2. A summary of the apostle's ministry (19:8–12)
  3. The seven sons of Sceva (19:13–19)

I. A Summary Statement (19:20)

Panel 6—To Jerusalem and Thence to Rome (19:21–28:31)

A. A Programmatic Statement (19:21–22)

B. The Journey to Jerusalem (19:23–21:16)
  1. The riot at Ephesus (19:23–41)
  2. A return visit to Macedonia and Achaia (20:1–6)
  3. The raising of Eutychus (20:7–12)
  4. From Troas to Miletus (20:13–16)
  5. Paul's farewell address to the Ephesian elders (20:17–38)
  6. On to Jerusalem (21:1–16)

C. Various Events and Paul's Defenses at Jerusalem (21:17–23:22)
  1. Arrival at Jerusalem (21:17–26)
  2. Arrest in the temple (21:27–36)
  3. Paul's defense before the people (21:37–22:22)
  4. Paul claims his Roman citizenship (22:23–29)
  5. Paul's defense before the Sanhedrin (22:30–23:11)
  6. A plot to kill Paul (23:12–22)

D. Imprisonment and Defenses at Caesarea (23:23–26:32)
  1. Imprisonment at Caesarea (23:23–35)
  2. Paul's defense before Felix (24:1–27)
  3. Paul's defense before Festus (25:1–12)
  4. Festus consults with Herod Agrippa II (25:13–22)
  5. Paul's defense before Herod Agrippa II (25:23–26:32)

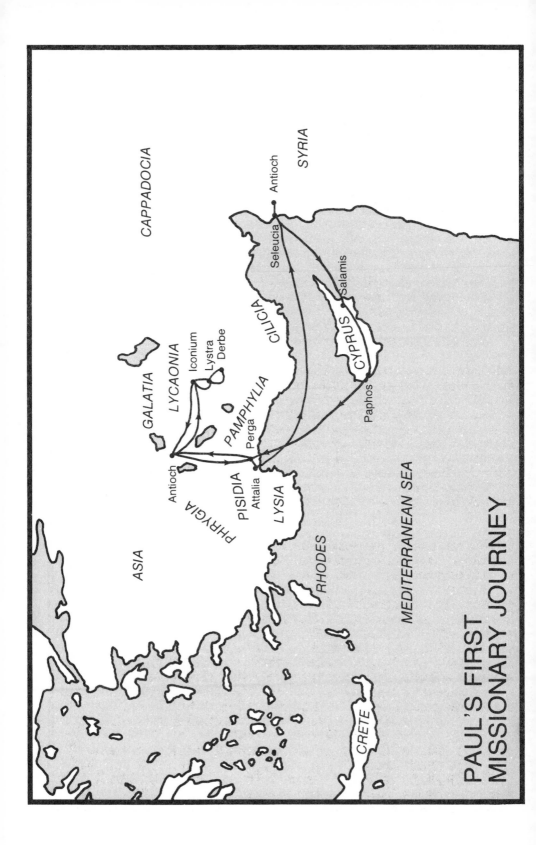

PAUL'S FIRST
MISSIONARY JOURNEY

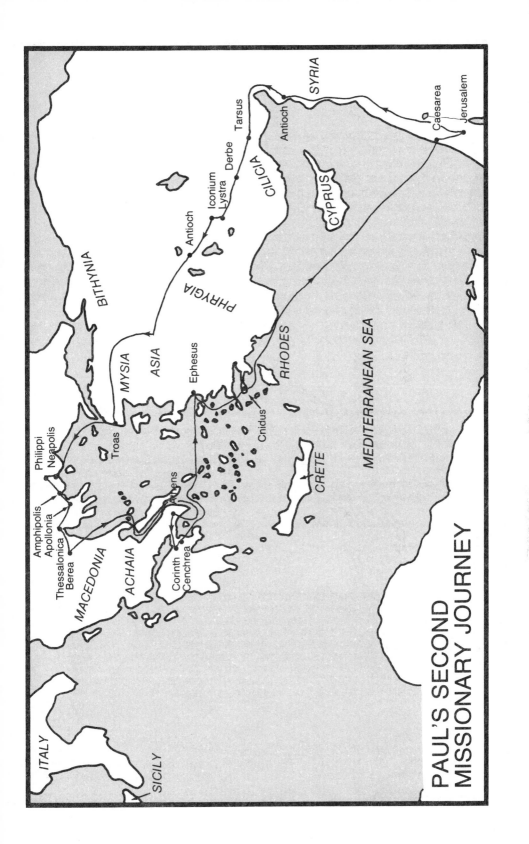

PAUL'S SECOND
MISSIONARY JOURNEY

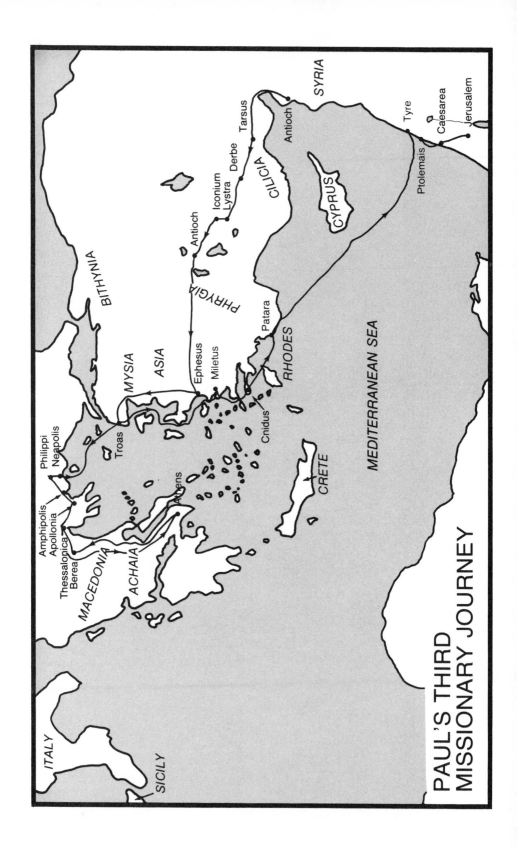

PAUL'S THIRD
MISSIONARY JOURNEY

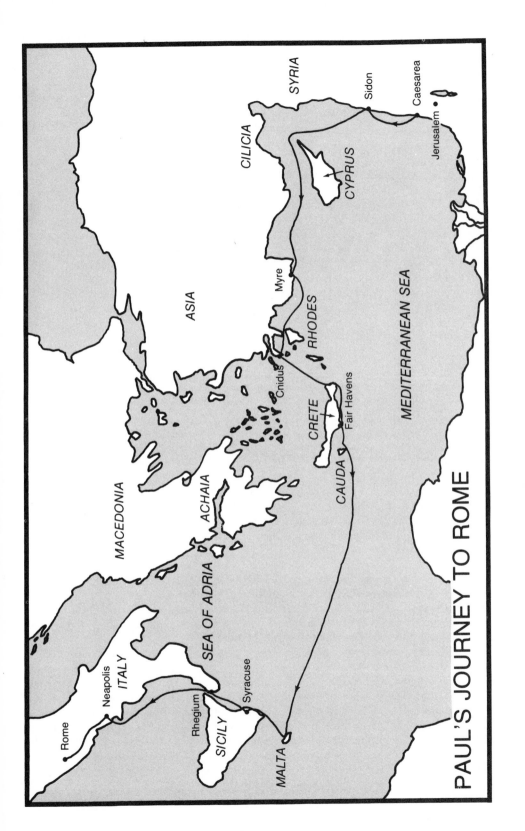

PAUL'S JOURNEY TO ROME

Text and Exposition

Introduction: The Constitutive Events of the Christian Mission (1:1–2:41)

The structural parallelism between Luke's Gospel and his Acts is immediately seen in the comparative size of the two books and the time spans they cover. Each would have filled an almost equal-sized papyrus roll; each covers approximately thirty-three years—though, of course, the Gospel is somewhat longer and more controlled in focus by existing traditions within the church. The parallelism is also evident in the plan and purpose of the opening chapters of each book. Luke 1:5–2:52 (after the Prologue of 1:1–4) is essentially a preparation for 3:1–4:13, and together these two sections constitute material introductory to the narrative of Jesus' ministry that begins with the pericope of 4:14–30. So, too, Acts 1:6–26 (after its Preface of 1:1–5) serves to prepare for 2:1–41, and together these two chapters comprise an introduction to the ministry of the church that commences with the thesis paragraph 2:42–47 and continues by means of a series of illustrative vignettes beginning at 3:1.

A. A Resumptive Preface

1:1–5

> ¹In my former book, Theophilus, I wrote about all that Jesus began to do and to teach ²until the day he was taken up to heaven, after giving instructions through the Holy Spirit to the apostles he had chosen. ³After his suffering, he showed himself to these men and gave many convincing proofs that he was alive. He appeared to them over a period of forty days and spoke about the kingdom of God. ⁴On one occasion, while he was eating with them, he gave them this command: "Do not leave Jerusalem, but wait for the gift my Father promised, which you have heard me speak about. ⁵For John baptized with water, but in a few days you will be baptized with the Holy Spirit."

The Prologue to Luke-Acts is really Luke 1:1–4. Here, however, Luke begins his second book with what may be called a "resumptive preface" which serves to link the two books and anticipates the features he wants to stress as being constitutive for the Christian mission.

1 Luke calls his Gospel "my former book" (*ton prōton logon*). The Greek article *ton* specifies an antecedent writing and the suffix of the verb translated "I wrote" (*epoiēsam-ēn*) calls for the possessive "my." Luke uses the word *logos* (usually translated "word" or "message" in the NT) in the technical sense of a section of a work that covers more than one papyrus roll. The occurrence of the adjective *prōtos* ("first"; NIV, "former") rather than its comparative *proteros* ("former") need not imply that Luke intended his Gospel to be the first in a series of three or more treatises, as Zahn and Ramsay have supposed. While the classical usage of *proteros* as "former" to be contrasted with "present" or "latter" is maintained by Josephus in the Preface to Book II of *Contra Apion* and also appears in the Pauline letters (cf. Gal 4:13; Eph 4:22; 1 Tim 1:13), Luke never uses *proteros*, which is rare in the nonliterary papyri of the day. Just as we today use "first" for "former" even when speaking about only two things, Luke should probably be understood as using *prōtos* as a comparative (cf. Acts 7:12) without any implication that his work was intended to go beyond the two volumes.

Luke says that the subject of his first volume is "all that Jesus began to do and teach" up to his ascension. Throughout his two volumes Luke uses the word "all" as a general expression that the context in each case must define. So we cannot assume he meant his Gospel to be any more exhaustive than Acts. In a number of places in the NT "many" (*polloi*) and "all" (*pantes*) are used interchangeably (e.g., Matt 20:28, Mark 10:45 [cf. 1 Tim 2:6]; Matt 12:15, Mark 3:10; Rom 5:12–21), with the context alone determining in each case the precise nuance. "To do" (*poiein*) and "to teach" (*didaskein*) describe the nature of the third Gospel, combining as it does Mark's stress on the activities of Jesus and the material from the "Sayings" source (Q) about what Jesus taught. "He began to" (*ērxato*), while used as something of a redundant auxiliary elsewhere in Acts (cf. 2:4; 11:4, 15; 18:26; 24:2; 27:35), probably appears here for emphasis, much as it does in 11:15. As such it serves to stress Luke's intent to show in Acts what Jesus *continued* to do and to teach through his church, just as Luke had previously presented "all that Jesus *began* to do and to teach" in his Gospel.

Acts, like the Gospel, is addressed to Theophilus, who is called "most excellent Theophilus" (*kratiste Theophile*) in Luke 1:3. *Kratistos* appears in Acts in addressing the Roman governors Felix and Festus (cf. 23:26; 24:3; 26:25). This suggests that the word should be taken here as an honorific title for a highly placed Roman official. But it was often employed as a form of polite address, and that is probably how Luke used it of Theophilus. It is precarious to suppose (cf. Origen and others after him) that "Theophilus" (etymologically, "Friend of God" or "Loved by God") is a symbolic name for either an anonymous person or a class of people. The name occurs as a proper name at least three centuries before Luke, and the practice of dedicating books to distinguished persons was common in his day.

2 The Greek of v.2 is awkward, chiefly because of the unnatural separation of "he was taken up" (*anelēmphthē*) at the end of the verse from "until the day" (*achri hēs hēmeras*) at its beginning and because it separates "[whom] he had chosen" (*hous exelexato*) from "the apostles" (*tois apostolois*). But the awkwardness was evidently intentional; through this awkward word order Luke highlights four important introductory matters in about the order in which he sets them out in his first two chapters and according to his priorities throughout Acts.

By the placing of the adverbial participle *enteilamenos* ("after giving instructions"), Luke gives first place to Jesus' mandate to witness. The instructions he has in mind are undoubtedly those already set out in Luke 24:48–49 as the climax of Jesus' earthly teaching: "You are witnesses of these things. I am going to send you what my Father has promised; but stay in the city until you have been clothed with power from on high." In slightly revised form, Luke quotes these instructions in Acts 1:4–5 and develops them in 1:6–8 as the theme of Acts. Apparently Luke also wanted to show through the word order of v.2 that Jesus' mandate to witness was given to the apostles, who acted through the power of the Holy Spirit, whose coming was a direct result of our Lord's ascension. Each of these four factors—the witness mandate, the apostles, the Holy Spirit, the ascended Lord—is a major emphasis that runs throughout Acts; each receives special attention in chapters 1 and 2.

3 Having stated the relation of his present book to its predecessor and shown his interest in the four factors named above, which comprise the constitutive elements of the Christian mission, Luke turns back to the time before the Ascension. He will recapitulate and expand upon certain features in Jesus' ministry crucial to the advance of the gospel as he will present it in Acts. In view of v.2, this is slightly redundant; but Luke wants to be very explicit. Like Paul in 1 Corinthians 15:5–7, Luke's emphasis is on the living Christ, who "after his suffering ... showed himself ... alive" and demonstrated his resurrection by "many convincing proofs." "Many convincing proofs" doubtless looks back to such things as the events in Luke 24:13ff. "Over a period of forty days" implies that during that time the risen Lord showed himself at intervals, not continuously. When he did so, he "spoke about the kingdom of God."

The theme of "the kingdom of God" (*hē basileia tou theou*) is a common one in the OT and NT. Primarily it refers to God's sovereign rule in human life and the affairs of history, and secondarily to the realm where that rule reigns. God's sovereignty is universal (cf. Ps 103:19). But it was specially manifested in the life of the nation Israel and among Jesus' disciples; it is expressed progressively in the church and through the lives of Christians; and it will be fully revealed throughout eternity. In the Gospels the kingdom is presented as having been inaugurated in time and space by Jesus' presence and ministry (cf. Mark 1:15, passim). ("The kingdom of heaven" is Matthew's reverential form of the same idea, adapted to Jewish sensibilities.) In Acts the phrase "the kingdom of God" usually appears as a convenient way of summarizing the early Christian proclamation (cf. 8:12; 19:8; 20:25; 28:23, 31). In this Jesus is explicitly identified as the subject (cf. 8:12; 28:23, 31).

We may infer that Jesus' teaching during the "forty days" dealt in essence with (1) the validation and nature of his messiahship, (2) the interpretation of the OT from the perspective of his resurrection, and (3) the responsibility of his disciples to bear witness to what had happened among them in fulfillment of Israel's hope. This is what Luke 24:25–27, 44–49 reveals as the content of Jesus' postresurrection teaching, and this is what Acts elaborates in what follows.

4 In vv.4–5 Luke parallels his emphasis on the living Christ by stressing the coming and baptism of the Holy Spirit as essential to the advance of the gospel. Luke gives us an individualized scene (so the inserted connective "on one occasion," NIV) of Jesus and his disciples eating together at the time when he commanded them not to leave Jerusalem but to wait for the coming of the Holy Spirit, who had been promised by God the Father and spoken of by Jesus. The command not to leave Jerusalem is a repetition of the one in Luke 24:49, with *Hierosolyma*, the Hellenized name for Jerusalem, being used. This breaks the usual pattern in Acts where *Ierousalēm* appears exclusively in chapters 1–7 and always on the lips of those whose native tongue was Aramaic. "The gift my Father promised" also repeats Luke 24:49 and is defined in v.5: "You will be baptized with the Holy Spirit." It is a promise that Jesus had made on behalf of the Father; its tradition has been incorporated in John's Gospel (cf. John 14:16–21, 26; 15:26–27; 16:7–15).

5 The statement appears to come from Mark 1:8, with parallels in Matthew 3:11 and Luke 3:16 (which add "and with fire"), where it is part of the message of John the Baptist. One might take v.5 as an explanatory comment on Luke's part, but its parallel in Acts 11:16, where it is given as the word of the Lord Jesus, suggests that here too it should be understood as being attributed to Jesus. It may be that the transferral of the *logion* ("saying") from the Baptist to the lips of Jesus occurred in the early church before Luke wrote Acts, though by the common attribution of the saying to the Baptist in the synoptic tradition (including Luke's Gospel) this seems doubtful. The ascription of the statement to Jesus is probably Luke's own doing. But this need not be considered strange, particularly for an author who can quote the same *logion* of Jesus in two such diverse forms and in two so closely connected passages as Luke 24:49 and Acts 1:4.

Notes

1 Cf. *Contra Apion* I, 1(1), where Josephus's patron Epaphroditus is addressed Κράτιστε ἀνδρῶν Ἐπαφρόδιτε (*kratiste andrōn Epaphrodite*, "most excellent of men Epaphroditus") and *Contra Apion* II, 1 (1), where he is addressed as τιμιώτατέ μοι Ἐπαφρόδιτε (*timiōtate moi Epaphrodite*, "my most esteemed Epaphroditus"), with the expressions evidently used interchangeably as terms of polite address.

3 For the idea of "continuously throughout the period," the accusative without a preposition would have been used rather than δι᾽ ἡμερῶν τεσσεράκοντα (*di' hēmerōn tesserakonta*, "over forty days"). This is the only place in the NT where the length of Jesus' postresurrection ministry is mentioned.

Acts 14:22 clearly has only a futuristic sense in view, but in all other passages in Acts beyond 1:3, while a future aspect may certainly be involved, Luke uses "the kingdom of God" in an evangelistic setting as a shorthand way of speaking about the entire Christian proclamation that centers in Jesus (cf. Stanton, pp. 17–18).

4 Συναλιζόμενος (*synalizomenos*) is taken as a temporal adverbial participle, built on the noun ἅλς (*hals*, "salt") and meaning "while eating [salt] together with someone"—or, more generally, "while eating with someone." The rendering "being assembled together" has often been conjectured but remains unproven. Luke speaks of Jesus' eating with his disciples during these forty days (Luke 24:42–43; Acts 10:41). The word is used for the evening meal in *Pseudo-Clementine Homilies* 13.4 and *Recognitions* 7.2.

In the NT Ἰερουσαλήμ (*Ierousalēm*, "Jerusalem"), the Hebraic name that has a sacred connotation, occurs seventy-six times, while Ἱεροσόλυμα (*Hierosolyma*, "Jerusalem"), the profane designation for the city (used more by non-Jewish writers and by Jews addressing a Greek-speaking audience), occurs sixty-three times. The authors of Heb and Rev always use *Ierousalēm*, for they are speaking of the heavenly and eschatological city. Mark and John, however, never use the more sacred form. Luke usually reworks Mark's *Hierosolyma* to *Ierousalēm* in his Gospel (using *Hierosolyma* only four times and *Ierousalēm* twenty-six times) and continues to use *Ierousalēm* in Acts 1–7. From Acts 8 onward he uses both forms without much distinction; *Ierousalēm* occurs thirty-nine times throughout Acts and *Hierosolyma* twenty-five times. Here, however, we have the exception to the usual pattern found in Acts 1–7.

B. *The Mandate to Witness*

1:6–8

⁶So when they met together, they asked him, "Lord, are you at this time going to restore the kingdom to Israel?"
⁷He said to them: "It is not for you to know the times or dates the Father has set by his own authority. ⁸But you will receive power when the Holy Spirit comes on you; and you will be my witnesses in Jerusalem, and in all Judea and Samaria, and to the ends of the earth."

Though 1:6–8 is usually treated either as the last part of the Preface (1:1–8) or as an introduction to the Ascension narrative (1:6–11), in reality it serves as the theme, setting the stage for all that follows in Acts: "You will be my witnesses in Jerusalem, and in all Judea and Samaria, and to the ends of the earth" (v.8). The concept of "witness" is so prominent in Acts (the word in its various forms appears some thirty-nine times) that everything else in the book should probably be seen as subsumed under it—even the primitive kerygma that, since Dodd's *Apostolic Preaching*, so many have taken as the leading theme of Acts. So as Luke begins his second book, he highlights this witness theme and insists it comes from the mandate of Jesus himself.

6 The expression *men oun* ("so," NIV) is a favorite connective of Luke's, used sometimes, as here, in beginning a new pericope (e.g., 8:4; 11:19; 12:5), at other times in conclusions (e.g., 2:41; 5:41; 8:25; 9:31; 16:5), and frequently within the narrative to tie its various parts together. The question the disciples asked reflects the embers of a once blazing hope for a political theocracy in which they would be leaders (cf. Mark 9:33–34; 10:35–41; Luke 22:24). Now the embers are fanned by Jesus' talk of the coming Holy Spirit. In Jewish expectations, the restoration of Israel's fortunes would be marked by the revived activity of God's Spirit, which had been withheld since the last of the prophets. But though his words about the Spirit's coming rekindled in the disciples their old nationalistic hopes, Jesus had something else in mind.

7 Jesus' answer to his disciples' misguided question is not a denial of any place for the nation of Israel in God's future purposes. Paul speaks in Romans 9–11 not only of a remnant within Israel responding to God but also of the nation of Israel still being involved in some way in God's redemptive program (Rom 11:15–16) and yet to be "saved" in the future (vv.25–29). Luke's presentation of Jesus' words here is not in opposition to that. Jesus' answer does, however, lay stress on the fact that the disciples were to revise their thinking about the divine program, leaving to God the matters that are his concern and taking up the things entrusted to them.

Jesus' insistence that "it is not for you to know" echoes his teaching in Matthew 24:36 and Mark 13:32, which Luke did not include in his Gospel either in 17:22–37 or 21:5–36 —evidently preferring to hold that aspect of Jesus' eschatological message for this place in Acts. The "times" (*chronoi*) and "dates" (*kairoi*) refer, it seems, to the character of the ages preceding the final consummation of God's redemptive program and to the particular critical stages of these ages as they draw to a climax (cf. 1 Thess 5:1). These "the Father has set by his own authority," and they are not to be the subject of speculation by believers—a teaching that, sadly, has been all too frequently disregarded.

8 Here the mandate to witness that stands as the theme for the whole of Acts is explicitly set out. It comes as a direct commission from Jesus himself—in fact, as Jesus' last word before his ascension and, therefore, as one that is final and conclusive. All that follows in Acts is shown to be the result of Jesus' own intent and the fulfillment of his express word. This commission lays an obligation on all Christians and comes to us as a gift with a promise. It concerns a person, a power, and a program—the person of Jesus, on whose authority the church acts and who is the object of its witness; the power of the Holy Spirit, which is the *sine qua non* for the mission; and a program that begins at Jerusalem, moves out to "all Judea and Samaria," and extends "to the ends of the earth." The Christian church, according to Acts, is a missionary church that responds obediently to Jesus' commission, acts on Jesus' behalf in the extension of his ministry, focuses its proclamation of the kingdom of God in its witness to Jesus, is guided and empowered by the self-same Spirit that directed and supported Jesus' ministry, and follows a program whose guidelines for outreach have been set by Jesus himself.

Whereas the geographical movement of Luke's Gospel was from Galilee through Perea to Jerusalem, in Acts the movement is from Jerusalem through "Judea and Samaria" and on to Rome. The joining of Judea and Samaria by one article (*tē*) in the Greek (*en pasē tē Ioudaia kai Samareia*, "in all Judea and Samaria") suggests a single geographical area that can be designated by its two ethnological divisions. And the fact that neither Galilee nor Perea is included in Acts 1:8 as a place to be evangelized (even though 9:31 speaks in summary fashion of a growing church in "Judea, Galilee and Samaria") probably reflects Luke's emphasis in his Gospel on Jesus' evangelization of those areas. So here Jesus' mandate to witness not only gives us the theme of Acts but also a basic table of contents by the threefold reference to "Jerusalem," "all Judea and Samaria," and "the ends of the earth." To be sure, Luke's development of this table of contents is fuller and more subtle than its succinct form here. Nevertheless, in what follows he shows through a series of vignettes how the mission of the church in its witness to Jesus fared at Jerusalem (2:42–8:3), throughout Judea and Samaria (8:4–12:24), and as it progressed until it finally reached the imperial capital city of Rome (12:25–28:31).

Notes

6 The other instances of μὲν οὖν (*men oun*, "then," "so") in Acts are 1:18; 12:5; 13:4; 14:3; 15:3, 30; 17:12, 17, 30; 19:32, 38; 23:18, 22, 31; 25:4, 11; 26:4, 9; 28:5. Where Luke worked more from written sources (the first half of Acts), he used, it seems, *men oun* in his redactional introductions and conclusions to tie the units of material together. Where he wrote more on the basis of verbal reports and personal reminiscences (the second half), he used the expression within his narrative to connect the various parts of the account.

7 The expression ἐν τῇ ἰδίᾳ ἐξουσίᾳ (*en tē idia exousia*, "by his own authority") is taken as an instrumental use of the dative, not a locative.

8 Luke's stress on the importance of the Spirit in the ministry of Jesus and in the mission of the church can readily (though somewhat mechanically) be seen by noting the comparative frequency of πνεῦμα (*pneuma*, "spirit") in the Gospels and Acts: nineteen times in Matt, twenty-three times in Mark, thirty-six times in Luke, twenty-four times in John, and seventy times in Acts—though, admittedly, a few of these occurrences refer to the human spirit (e.g., Acts 17:16) or even to unclean spirits (e.g., Luke 4:33; 6:18).

C. *The Ascension*

1:9–11

> [9]After he said this, he was taken up before their very eyes, and a cloud hid him from their sight.
> [10]They were looking intently up into the sky as he was going, when suddenly two men dressed in white stood beside them. [11]"Men of Galilee," they said, "why do you stand here looking into the sky? This same Jesus, who has been taken from you into heaven, will come back in the same way you have seen him go into heaven."

Luke next speaks of the second constitutive factor of the Christian mission, the church's ascended Lord. The Greek of v.2 includes this as a fourth element in its logical listing of constitutive factors, but here Luke is proceeding more chronologically. So he speaks of the Ascension before mentioning the full complement of apostles and the coming of the Holy Spirit. The Ascension, of course, has been referred to in Luke 24:50–51 and Acts 1:2, and many have questioned the appropriateness of three references to it. But each occurrence has its own purpose in Luke's writing.

Here the important thing is that attention is focused on (1) the fact of Jesus' ascension and entrance "into heaven" (*eis ton ouranon*)—an expression repeated four times in vv.10–11—and (2) on the angel's message that rebukes the disciples for their lack of understanding and assures them of their Lord's return. There is no explanation of how the Ascension occurred or of the psychological state of the disciples—features so common to legendary development. Nor are there any apocalyptic details like those in Luke 17:22–37 (also perhaps Luke 21) as to when that return might be expected. "The story," as Haenchen says, "is unsentimental, almost uncannily austere" (*Acts of the Apostles*, p. 151). Luke's point is that the missionary activity of the early church rested not only on Jesus' mandate but also on his living presence in heaven and the sure promise of his return.

Many modern scholars have asserted that looking for the Parousia paralyzes missionary activity and inhibits Christian social action by diverting attention away from present needs to the "sweet by and by" and that the early church only turned to missions when it had to renounce its futuristic eschatology. Nevertheless, in Acts 1:9–11 Luke insists that Christian mission must be based on the ascended and living Lord who directs his church from heaven and who will return to consummate what he has begun. Rather than the missionary enterprise being a stopgap measure substituted by some sub-apostolic Christian theologians for the unrealized hope of the kingdom of God, Luke's position is, as Oscar Cullmann says, "that 'missions' are an essential element in the eschatological divine plan of salvation. The missionary work of the Church is the eschatological foretaste of the Kingdom of God, and the Biblical hope of the 'end' constitutes the keenest incentive to action" ("Eschatology and Mission in the New Testament," *The Background of the New Testament and its Eschatology*, edd. W.D. Davies and D. Daube [Cambridge: Cambridge University, 1964], p. 409).

9 For Jesus' ascension Luke uses the single Greek verb *epērthē* ("he was taken up"). He tells us very little else about it except that it occurred after Jesus had given his mandate to witness and while the disciples were watching. Not even the place where the Ascension occurred is mentioned in v.9, though in v.12 Luke says it took place on the Mount of Olives. More important for Luke than the description of the Ascension is its significance, and this he gives us in saying that "a cloud hid him from their sight."

The cloud is undoubtedly meant to symbolize the shekinah, the visible manifestation of the divine presence and glory. Such a cloud hovered above the tabernacle in the wilderness as a visible token of the glory of God that dwelt within the tabernacle (cf. Exod 40:34). Such a cloud enveloped Jesus and three of his disciples on the Mount of Transfiguration as a visible sign of God's presence and his approval of his Son (cf. Mark 9:7, par.). Something very similar is presented here: Jesus as the ascended Lord is enveloped by the shekinah cloud, the visible manifestation of God's presence, glory, and approval.

10 Luke describes the disciples as "looking intently up into the sky as he was going." The word translated "to look intently" (*atenizein*) is a favorite of Luke, who uses it in twelve of its fourteen NT occurrences, mainly for dramatic effect. So it is probably illegitimate to read too much into *atenizein* regarding the psychological state of the disciples. Perhaps some of them expected the cloud to dissipate and leave their Lord standing with them alone, as on the Mount of Transfiguration. Or, perhaps, others thought he would return momentarily. Some might have been in an attitude of worship, though probably most were simply awestruck by the sight. But they were soon challenged by the message of the two angels "dressed in white."

11 The angels' message was twofold: (1) The Jesus the disciples had known now had a heavenly existence. This is stressed by the double use of the phrase "into heaven." (2) The Jesus they had known (the emphasis is on the intensive demonstrative pronoun *houtos*—i.e., "this same" Jesus) would return "in the same way you have seen him go into heaven." "In the same way" (*hon tropon*, which corresponds to the adverb *houtōs*) probably refers to Jesus' being enveloped in the cloud of the divine presence and glory. See Jesus' description of his Parousia in the Olivet Discourse (Matt 24:30; Mark 13:26; cf. Luke 21:27) and his reply to Caiaphas at his trial (Matt 26:64; Mark 14:62).

Notes

9 D and the Syraic sahidic version (sa) have the cloud envelop Jesus while he is still standing on the ground, thus making a more exact parallel with the Transfiguration narratives.
10 On the use of the verb ἀτενίζω (*atenizō*, "gaze upon"), see Luke 4:20; 22:56; Acts 3:4, 12; 6:15; 7:55; 10:4; 11:6; 13:9; 14:9; 23:1. Also cf. 2 Cor 3:7, 13; 3 Macc 2:26; Jos. War V, 517 [xii.3].
   On the garb of heavenly beings, see Matt 28:3; Mark 16:5; Luke 24:4; John 20:12; cf. 2 Macc 11:8 (also Jesus' transfigured appearance in Mark 9:2-3)—though, of course, others also wore white as a sign of holiness (cf. 1QpMic 8-10; CD 6:2-11; 7:9-20, where "Lebanon" stands for the communal council since *laban* means "white" and the council dressed in white).

D. *The Full Complement of Apostles* (1:12-26)

Luke's third factor underlying the rise and expansion of the early Christian mission is the centrality of the apostles and their ministry. His interest in the apostles was evident in chapter 6 of his Gospel, where in reporting Jesus' choosing his twelve disciples he alone among the evangelists adds "whom he also designated apostles" (Luke 6:13). Now he resumes that interest, telling how under God's direction the apostolic band regained its full number after the defection of Judas Iscariot.

Structurally, the passage appears to be the intermingling of early source material with Luke's editorial statements. Here the seams between the two are more obvious than in many other passages in Acts. They are the basic Christian tradition regarding the selection of Matthias (vv.15-17, 21-26), Luke's own introduction to the pericope (vv.12-14), his short comment at the end of v.15, and a longer and particularly obvious comment in vv.18-19. Luke's writing in Acts is usually so artistic as to make it almost impossible to separate his editorial comments from his source material. Here, however, different strands are apparent.

1. *In the upper room*

1:12-14

12Then they returned to Jerusalem from the hill called the Mount of Olives, a Sabbath day's walk from the city. 13When they arrived, they went upstairs to the room where they were staying. Those present were Peter, John, James and Andrew; Philip and Thomas, Bartholomew and Matthew; James son of Alphaeus and Simon the Zealot, and Judas son of James. [14]They all joined together constantly in prayer, along with the women and Mary the mother of Jesus, and his brothers.

12 The disciples had been instructed by Jesus to "stay in the city [of Jerusalem] until you have been clothed with power from on high" (Luke 24:49). They were "not [to] leave Jerusalem, but wait for the gift my Father promised" (Acts 1:4) and begin their witness "at Jerusalem" (Luke 24:47; Acts 1:8). So they returned to Jerusalem from the Mount of Olives, a distance Luke speaks of as being "a Sabbath day's walk from the city." The Mishnah tells us that travel on the Sabbath was limited to two thousand cubits (*Sotah* 5.3), which would be somewhere around eleven hundred meters (NIV mg.). Therefore we may estimate that the disciples' journey from the place of the Ascension on Olivet back to Jerusalem was about a kilometer, or about two-thirds of a mile.

13 Upper rooms in Palestinian cities were usually the choicest rooms because they were above the tumult of the crowded streets and beyond the prying eyes of passersby. For the wealthy, the upper room was the living room. Sometimes upper rooms were rented out. Often they served as places of assembly, study, and prayer (SBK, 2:594). On their return to Jerusalem, the disciples "went upstairs to the room where they were staying." The use of the definite article in speaking of "the room" (*to hyperōon*) and the emphatic place these words have at the beginning of the clause suggest that the room was well known to the early Christians—perhaps the room where Jesus and his disciples kept the Passover just before his crucifixion (Mark 14:12–16, par.). Perhaps it was the room where he appeared to some of them after he rose from the dead (Luke 24:33–43; cf. John 20:19, 26). Or, though this is more inferential, it may have been a room in the house of Mary, John Mark's mother, where the church later met (Acts 12:12).

Luke has already listed the names of the Twelve in his Gospel (6:14–16). Now he lists them again—though without Judas Iscariot. This is another instance of parallelism in Luke's writings. Here, however, the list points to the incompleteness of the apostolic band and sets the stage for the account of its rectification through the choosing of Matthias. All this prepares for the coming of the Holy Spirit and the beginning of the apostolic ministry. In obedience to their Lord and in anticipation of what is to follow, the apostles have returned to Jerusalem—only they lack the full complement needed for their witness within Jewry.

14 In addition to the Eleven, there were also present in the upper room "the women and Mary the mother of Jesus, and his brothers." They fill out the nucleus of the early church and in some way are to be included in the apostolic witness. The reference to "the women" undoubtedly has in mind those mentioned in Luke 8:2–3; 23:49; and 23:55–24:10, who followed Jesus throughout his ministry—even to his death—and contributed out of their personal incomes to support him and his followers. The Western text (D) has "the wives and children" (*syn gynaixin kai teknois,* paralleling Acts 21:5), presumably of the apostles, and thus minimizes the independent activity of women in the early church. But Luke's mention of "the women" fully accords with the attitude toward women as portrayed in his Gospel and the consciousness within the church of the implications of the gospel proclamation. So the Western text must be viewed as unnecessarily restrictive.

The reference here to "Mary the mother of Jesus" continues Luke's interest in Mary begun in chapter 1 of his Gospel, though this is the last occasion where she is recorded as being involved in the redemptive history of the NT. The reference to Jesus' "brothers" (*adelphoi*) is particularly interesting because Mark 3:21-35 shows that during his ministry they thought him to be "out of his mind," perhaps even demon possessed, and because John 7:2-10 presupposes their disbelief. Paul, however, recounts an appearance of the risen Christ to James (cf. 1 Cor 15:7), and we may infer that Joses (or Joseph), Judas (or Jude), and Simon (cf. Matt 13:55-56; Mark 6:3) likewise came to believe in Jesus and attached themselves to the congregation of early Christians. These all are depicted as being assiduous in prayer, with the article (*tē*) in *tē proseuchē* ("the prayer") suggesting an appointed service of prayer (cf. Acts 2:42; 6:4). There must also have been others who were at various times with the Eleven, the women, Mary, and Jesus' brothers in that upper room, for Acts 1:15 speaks of the total number of believers at the selection of Matthias as being "about a hundred and twenty."

Notes

13 The listing of disciples in Luke 6:14-16 is generally in line with Matt 10:2-4 and Mark 3:16-19, though with two notable exceptions: (1) Luke identifies the tenth in his listing as Σίμωνα τὸν καλούμενον Ζηλωτὴν (*Simōna ton kaloumenon Zēlōtēn*, "Simon who was called the Zealot"), whereas Matthew and Mark speak of the eleventh in their listings as Σίμωνα τὸν Καναναῖον (*Simōna ton Kananaion*, "Simon the Cananaean"); and (2) Luke lists Ἰούδαν Ἰακώβου (*Ioudan Iakōbou*, "Judas son of James") as the eleventh. Matthew and Mark do not mention a Judas other than Judas Iscariot and refer to a Thaddaeus (or, variously in other MS traditions, to a "Lebbaeus," or a "Lebbaeus called Thaddaeus," or a "Thaddaeus called Labbaeus") as the tenth disciple. But as H.-C. Hahn has pointed out, "*kananaios* may translate Aram. *qan'ān*, zealot" (DNTT, 3:1167), which Matthew and Mark transliterated and Luke translated into Gr. (ζηλωτής, *zēlōtēs*). And the words Θαδδαῖος (*Thaddaios*) and Λεββαῖος (*Lebbaios*) convey a nuance of "breast" or "heart" and may have been used as epithets or nicknames in the early Christian tradition. C.E.B. Cranfield may be right in commenting: "Possibly Judas is the correct name, and Thaddaeus or Lebbaeus an additional name or nickname" (*The Gospel According to St. Mark* [Cambridge: Cambridge University, 1963], p. 132).

The reference in John 14:22 to a disciple named "Judas (not Judas Iscariot)" tends to support Luke's reference to a "Judas son of James" (6:16). The variations in the synoptic ordering with respect to the placing of Andrew (fourth in Mark, second in Matt and Luke), of Matthew and Thomas (seventh and eighth respectively in Mark and Luke, eighth and seventh in Matt), and of Thaddaeus/James and Simon (tenth and eleventh respectively in Mark and Matt, eleventh and tenth in Luke) seem inconsequential and follow no discernible pattern. They probably result only from personal preference in passing on the traditions, as do also Luke's variations of order in Acts 1:13 from that already given in Luke 6:14-16 in the positioning of Andrew, John, James, and Thomas.

14 The reference to τοῖς ἀδελφοῖς αὐτοῦ (*tois adelphois autou*, "his brothers") is most naturally taken as referring to uterine brothers of Jesus. In defense of the doctrine of the perpetual virginity of Mary, it was early argued that "his brothers" were either half-brothers of Jesus (the sons of Joseph by an earlier marriage) or his first cousins (the sons of Alphaeus by Mary of Clopas, who was the sister of Mary the mother of Jesus, as inferred, erroneously it seems, from John 19:25).

On one occasion after his resurrection, Jesus appeared to over five hundred of his own at one time (1 Cor 15:6). This suggests a larger pre-Pentecost nucleus in the church than Acts 1:15

261

indicates. But this was probably in Galilee, with most of those referred to remaining in Galilee, whereas the number "about a hundred and twenty" (v.15) should probably be taken as referring only to the Jerusalem contingent of early believers.

---

2. Matthias chosen to replace Judas Iscariot

1:15–26

> ¹⁵In those days Peter stood up among the believers (a group numbering about a hundred and twenty) ¹⁶and said, "Brothers, the Scripture had to be fulfilled which the Holy Spirit spoke long ago through the mouth of David concerning Judas, who served as guide for those who arrested Jesus— ¹⁷he was one of our number and shared in this ministry."
>
> ¹⁸(With the reward he got for his wickedness, Judas bought a field; there he fell headlong, his body burst open and all his intestines spilled out. ¹⁹Everyone in Jerusalem heard about this, so they called that field in their language Akeldama, that is, Field of Blood.)
>
> ²⁰"For," said Peter, "it is written in the book of Psalms,
>
> " 'May his place be deserted;
> let there be no one to dwell in it,'
>
> and,
>
> " 'May another take his place of leadership.'
>
> ²¹Therefore it is necessary to choose one of the men who have been with us the whole time the Lord Jesus went in and out among us, ²²beginning from John's baptism to the time when Jesus was taken up from us. For one of these must become a witness with us of his resurrection."
>
> ²³So they proposed two men: Joseph called Barsabbas (also known as Justus) and Matthias. ²⁴Then they prayed, "Lord, you know everyone's heart. Show us which of these two you have chosen ²⁵to take over this apostolic ministry, which Judas left to go where he belongs." ²⁶Then they drew lots, and the lot fell to Matthias; so he was added to the eleven apostles.

---

15 "In those days" (*en tais hēmerais tautais*) marks the beginning of a self-contained unit of traditional material (cf. 6:1; 11:27), which Luke ties to his introduction in vv.12–14 by the conjunction *kai* ("and") in the Greek text. In keeping with his character portrayal of Peter throughout his Gospel, Luke here presents Peter as taking the lead among the apostles. The Western text and the TR have him standing among and speaking to "the disciples" (*tōn mathētōn*), and the probable reading of Bodmer P⁷⁴ has him here among "the apostles" (*tōn apostolōn*). Both readings seem to be later attempts to clarify the possible confusion between "the brothers" of v.14 and those of v.15. But the better-attested reading here is "among the brothers" (*en mesō tōn adelphōn*; cf. also the use of *adelphoi* ["brothers"] in the salutation of v.16), with "brothers" in Luke's source material used as a religious idiom and "brothers" in v.14 of his own introduction referring to a blood relationship. Though evidently Luke did not anticipate any possible confusion, NIV rightly translates "brothers" in v.15 as "believers" to bring out the religious nuance for much the same reason that later Greek texts read "disciples" and "apostles."

16–17 The Greek literally reads "Men, brothers" (*Andres, adelphoi;* NIV, "Brothers"), which corresponds to nothing we know in the rabbinic literature stemming from the Pharisaic schools or in the nonconformist writings of either the intertestamental apocalyptic texts or the DSS. Outside of Acts, it appears only in 4 Maccabees 8:19. On the ground of its use in Acts, where it is attributed to Peter (1:16; 2:29; 15:7), to the people of Jerusalem (2:37), to Stephen (7:2), to the synagogue rulers at Antioch of Pisidia (13:15), to James (15:13), and to Paul (13:26, 38; 22:1; 23:1, 6; 28:17)—and always in the context of a gathering of Jews—we may assume that it represents a type of formal address found within first-century synagogues (cf. 13:15, 26, 38) and among Jewish congregations generally.

Peter's words in v.16, and again later in v.21, speak of the "necessity" (*dei*) of Scripture being fulfilled in relation to Judas's defection and the choice of another to replace him. In Luke's writings *dei* stresses the compulsion inherent in the divine plan—a stress usually accompanied by an emphasis on man's inability to comprehend God's workings. At times that divine necessity is explained in terms of the fulfillment of Scripture (e.g., Luke 22:37; 24:26, 44). But more often that is not the case (e.g., Luke 2:49; 4:43; 9:22; 13:16, 33; 17:25; 19:5; 24:7). This suggests that the concept of "divine necessity" is broader than just "the fulfillment of Scripture" with its usual introductory formula "it is written," though it may contain the latter.

Here in vv.16 and 21 divine necessity is connected directly with the fulfillment of Scripture, "which the Holy Spirit spoke long ago through the mouth of David concerning Judas." But in neither case (and particularly not in v.21) should we say that the necessity concerns only a prophecy or certain prophecies of Scripture. The understanding expressed here is rather (1) that God is doing something necessarily involved in his divine plan; (2) that the disciples' lack of comprehension of God's plan is profound, especially with respect to Judas who "was one of our number and shared in this ministry" yet also "served as guide for those who arrested Jesus"; and (3) that an explicit way of understanding what has been going on under divine direction is through a Christian understanding of two psalms that speak of false companions and wicked men generally, and which by means of the then widely common exegetical rule *qal waḥomer* ("light to heavy," or *a minore ad majorem*) can also be applied to the false disciple and wicked man par excellence, Judas Iscariot.

18–19 Luke now adds a parenthesis concerning the awful fate of Judas. Luke's characteristic *men oun* (which is almost untranslatable here) shows that he is adding to the tradition he has received (cf. v.6), with the purpose of emphasizing the awfulness of Judas's fate and thus suggesting a basis for the disciples' perplexity in trying to comprehend the plan of God.

The difficulty of reconciling 1:18–19 with Matthew 27:3–10 is well known and often considered the most intractable contradiction in the NT. The problem chiefly concerns how Judas died. But it also involves such questions as Who bought the field? and Why was it called "Field of Blood"? These latter matters are perhaps not too difficult. Probably the common explanation suffices: The chief priests bought the potter's field in Judas's name with the thirty silver coins belonging to him, and the local Jerusalemites (particularly Christians) nicknamed it "Field of Blood" because they felt it had been purchased with "blood money."

The major question as to how Judas died, however, is not so easily answered. Had he "hanged himself" (Matt 27:5)? Or was it that "he fell headlong, his body burst open and all his intestines spilled out" (Acts 1:18)? We shall probably never know the exact answer. Augustine may have been right in saying that both were true. But though the precise solution seems imponderable, the problem is not very different from many another difference among the evangelists in presenting the words and activity of Jesus or, within the Acts itself, in Luke's presentation of the sermons and events in the outreach of the gospel (e.g., the three reports of the conversion of Paul in Acts 9, 22, and 26). If we really believe that each writer wrote from the standpoint of his own theological purposes to the specific interests and appreciation of his audience (as redaction criticism rightly holds), it is not too difficult to believe that in the context of Matthew's fulfillment theme it was sufficient for him and his readers to portray Judas's awful end with the terse expression "he hanged himself" *(apēnxato)*. After all, suicide of itself was heinous for Jews. But this would hardly suffice for Luke, Theophilus, and others in the Gentile world who would read Luke's account. Gentiles under Stoic influence generally looked on suicide as morally neutral. But Luke wanted to stress the awfulness of Judas's situation in a way that would grip his readers. So he evidently took the liberty of breaking into his received tradition in order to spell out the gory details of Judas's suicide—details he had gathered from some other source (either written or oral). He did this to emphasize Judas's terrible fate and to highlight its relation to the divine plan. There was, then, a divine necessity, Luke is telling us, in all that happened in regard to Judas. Just how incomprehensible that was to the earliest believers he shows through details of the awful death of the betrayer.

20 The OT passages Luke uses to support the divine necessity manifest in Judas's defection and replacement are Psalms 69:25 (MT=69:26) and 109:8. These psalms speak of false companions and wicked men who have become enemies of God's servant. They lament over his condition and give us his prayers for deliverance and his desire for retribution. Dodd has shown that Psalm 69 was one of the major blocks of OT material used variously within the early church on the topic of "The Servant of the Lord and the Righteous Sufferer" and applied to Jesus the Christ, the Servant and Righteous Sufferer par excellence (C.H. Dodd, *According to the Scriptures* [London: Nisbet, 1952], esp. pp. 61–108). Psalm 69:4 is quoted in John 15:25 ("hated me without reason") as a lament of Jesus applied to himself; the first half of v.9 is quoted in John 2:17 ("Zeal for your house will consume me") as recalled by the disciples at the cleansing of the temple; the last half of v.9 is quoted by Paul in Romans 15:3 ("The insults of those who insult you have fallen on me") as characterizing Jesus' ministry; and Psalm 69:22–23 is quoted in Romans 11:9–10 ("May their table become a snare and a trap, a stumbling block and a retribution for them; may their eyes be darkened so they cannot see, and their backs be bent forever") as describing Israel's present condition. Judging by frequency and variety of usage in the NT, therefore, the Christian use of Psalm 69 from the earliest days of the church is well established. So here in v.20 we have another example of the Christian use of this block of messianic material, to which, on the commonly accepted exegetical principle of analogous subject (Hillel's sixth exegetical rule: $k^e y \hat{o} \d{s} \bar{e}$' $b \hat{o}$ $b^e m \bar{a} g \hat{o} m$ '$a \d{h} \bar{e} r$, "as found in another place"), Peter added the ominous words of Psalm 109:8: "May another take his place of leadership."

We need not insist that the early Christians believed that the primary reference of these two psalms was to Judas, as if no one could have understood them prior to the betrayal. What they seem to be saying, however, is that just as the psalmist's portrayals of "The Servant of the Lord and the Righteous Sufferer" can on the basis of the Semitic concept of corporate solidarity be applied to God's Messiah, Jesus, the Servant and Righteous Sufferer, so the retribution spoken of as coming upon false companions and wicked men in general is especially applicable to Judas, who above all other men was false. So Peter quotes Psalm 69:25 in a Christian context and applies it to Judas's defection. In itself, of course, this verse gives no justification for replacing Judas—in fact, it even opposes it. Therefore Peter goes on to cite Psalm 109:8 on the Jewish exegetical principle of analogous subject in order to defend the legitimacy of replacing a member of the apostolic band.

21-22 The divine necessity for filling Judas's place was supported by Psalm 109:8, as understood in a Christian manner, according to the Semitic concept of corporate solidarity (cf. above on v.20). The twelvefold witness was required if early Jewish Christianity was to represent itself to the Jewish nation as the culmination of Israel's hope and the true people of Israel's Messiah. The "remnant theology" of Late Judaism made it mandatory that any group that presented itself as "the righteous remnant" of the nation, and had the responsibility of calling the nation to repentance and permeating it for God's glory, must represent itself as the true Israel, not only in its proclamation, but also in its symbolism. The Qumran convenanters thought it necessary to have twelve leaders heading up their community, with three either from within the group of twelve or in addition to it forming an inner circle of authority (cf. 1QS 8.1). This is an evident parallel to the twelve tribes of Israel, with a developing stress on final authority resting with a smaller body of two or three. Likewise, Jesus predicted that "at the renewal of all things," his disciples will "sit on twelve thrones, judging the twelve tribes of Israel" (Matt 19:28; Luke 22:30). And John the Seer pictures the consummation of God's redemption as a "Holy City, Jerusalem, coming down out of heaven from God," having twelve gates with "the names of the twelve tribes of Israel" written on them and twelve foundations with "the names of the twelve apostles of the Lamb" written on them (Rev 21:10, 12, 14). It was, then, for just such a reason that the early church found itself required to replace the defector Judas so as to have a full complement of twelve in its apostolic ranks.

For a candidate to succeed Judas among the apostles, the first qualification laid down by Peter is that the man must "have been with us the whole time the Lord Jesus went in and out among us, beginning from John's baptism to the time when Jesus was taken up from us." The expression "went in and out among us" is a Semitic idiom for familiar and unhindered association (cf. Deut 31:2; 2 Sam 3:25; Ps 121:8; Acts 9:28). The length of time designated for this association was from John's baptism to Jesus' ascension. Perhaps not all the Eleven themselves could claim association with Jesus from the days of John the Baptist (John 1:35-51 suggests that about half could). But they evidently wanted to make quite sure that there would be no deficiency on this first point.

The second qualification was that of having been a witness to Christ's resurrection. So the candidate must be both a guarantor of the gospel tradition because he had been a companion of the earthly Jesus and a witness to Christ's resurrection because he had been personally met by the risen Lord. It is from vv.21-22 that we may derive a strict definition of the term "apostle" and one that determines much of what Luke presents in the remainder of Acts (though, of course, Luke also uses the word "apostle" more broadly). An apostle, then, was not an ecclesiastical functionary, nor just any recipient of the apostolic faith, nor even a bearer of the apostolic message; he was a guarantor of the gospel tradition because he had been a companion of the earthly Jesus and a witness to the reality of his resurrection because the risen Lord had encountered him.

23 The fifth-century Western text in its reading *estēsen* (in line with a growing monarchial emphasis) understood that Peter "proposed" the two candidates to succeed Judas. But by far the better reading is *estēsan*, "they proposed," most likely meaning by "they" the eleven apostles together (note the three occurrences of the pronoun "us" with reference to the apostles in vv.21-22). The two men proposed were Joseph, who was called by Aramaic-speaking Jews "Barsabbas" (which means "Son of the Sabbath," presumably because he was born on the Sabbath) and who was also known by his Roman cognomen Justus, and Matthias (a shortened form of Mattathias). Perhaps more were considered, as v.21 seems to suggest ("one of the men who have been with us"). Only two, however, had the necessary qualifications.

24-25 But it was not enough to possess the qualifications other apostles had. Judas's successor must also be appointed by the same Lord who appointed the Eleven. Likewise, though the church could not represent itself as the righteous remnant of Israel with one apostle lacking, it could hardly symbolize its consciousness as being the true Israel of God with one apostle too many. Therefore, prayer was offered to the Lord for his selection from among the two candidates.

While it is not clear linguistically whether God the Father or Jesus is here being addressed in prayer by the vocative "Lord," contextually it is most natural to understand the same referent for the title here as in v.21: "the Lord Jesus." Furthermore, the parallel seems to be consciously drawn by Luke in his use of the same verb *eklegomai* ("to choose") for those selected by Jesus in Acts 1:2 and for this man who was to be selected by "the Lord" to replace Judas. And if it was important for them to have the qualifications given in vv.21–22, it was at least as important for them all to have been appointed by the same Lord.

Tēs diakonias tautēs kai apostolēs is probably a hendiadys (i.e., two connotative words connected by a conjunction that are used to express a single complex idea normally expressed by an adjective and a substantive noun), with the definite article *tēs* ("the") tying the two elements together, and is best translated as "this apostolic ministry." The phrase "to go where he belongs" (or, "to go to his own place") is likely a euphemism for "to go to hell" (SBK, 4.2:1097–98), which shows spiritually the awfulness of Judas's fate (cf. on vv.18–19).

26 After determining qualifications and praying, they "drew lots, and the lot fell to Matthias." The Greek literally reads, "They gave lots to them" (*edōkan klērous autois*), which is a Hebrew idiom for "casting" or "throwing" down various kinds of marked objects in order to determine God's will. The practice was common within Israel and the ancient world, generally, and is probably best illustrated by Proverbs 16:33: "The lot is cast into the lap, but its every decision is from the Lord." So by the appointment of Christ himself, the full complement of apostles was restored and the church was ready for the coming of the Holy Spirit and the beginning of its mission.

This pericope on the selection of Matthias has a number of significant implications. In the first place, it shows the necessity of a hermeneutical methodology that is able to distinguish between normative principles and culturally restricted practices in the progressive revelation of the Bible. We are exhorted as Christians to "search the Scriptures" and to "know what is the will of the Lord"—exhortations that are normative. But the early church's midrashic exegesis and the practice of casting lots were methods for interpreting the OT and determining God's will used at that time, and we need not be bound by them today. Second, the pericope suggests that a Christian decision regarding vocation entails (1) evaluating personal qualifications, (2) earnest prayer, and (3) appointment by Christ himself—an appointment that may come in some culturally related fashion, but in a way clear to those who seek guidance.

In addition, it should be noted that it was Judas's defection and not simply the fact of his death that required his replacement. While the NT lays great stress on the apostolic message and faith and Luke stresses the importance of the apostles themselves, the pericope gives no justification for the theological necessity of an apostolic succession of office, as is sometimes claimed for it. According to vv.21–22, the task of the twelve apostles was unique: to be guarantors of the gospel tradition because of their companionship with Jesus in his earthly ministry and to be witnesses to the reality of his resurrection because they had seen the risen Christ. Such criteria cannot be transmitted from generation to generation. Thus when James the son of Zebedee was executed by Herod Agrippa I in A.D. 44 (cf. 12:1–2), the church took no action to replace him. He had faithfully functioned as a guarantor of the gospel tradition and as a witness to the reality of Jesus' resurrection for some fifteen years; and now, as the church was growing, that ministry was not to be repeated.

Finally, and contrary to an oft-heard claim that the apostles were wrong in selecting Matthias and should have awaited God's choice of Paul to fill the vacancy, it should be pointed out (1) that Paul had not been with Jesus during his earthly ministry—in fact, he acknowledges his dependence upon others with respect to the gospel tradition (e.g., 1 Cor 15:3–5); (2) that the necessity of having exactly twelve apostles in the early church sprang largely from the need for Jewish Christians ministering within the Jewish nation to maintain this symbolic number, and, while Paul could appreciate this, he did not feel its necessity for his primarily Gentile ministry; and (3) that Paul himself recognized the special nature of his apostleship—viz., it was in line with that of the Twelve, but it also rested on a somewhat different base (cf. his reference to himself as an apostle "abnormally born" in 1 Cor 15:7–8). Paul's background, ministry, and call were in many ways different from those of the Twelve. Yet he insisted on the equality of his apostleship with that of the other apostles—an equality he never interpreted in terms of either opposition or identity.

Notes

---

15 Luke's habit is to qualify his numerical data by the particles ὡς (*hōs*) and ὡσεί (*hōsei*), both meaning "about"; cf. Acts 2:41; 4:4; 5:7, 36; 10:3; 13:18, 20; 19:7, 34.

16 Δεῖ (*dei*, "it is necessary") in the Lukan writings always requires consideration of the context of the statement or the predicate of the sentence or both in order to provide the specification. Here, of course, that specification is provided by the predicates πληρωθῆναι τὴν γραφὴν (*plērōthēnai tēn graphēn*, "the Scripture had to be fulfilled") of v.16 and γέγραπται (*gegraptai*, "it is written") of v.20, though the context also suggests not exclusively by these predicates.

20 On the major blocks of OT material used within the early church as "the substructure of all Christian theology," see Dodd, *According to the Scriptures*, esp. pp. 61–108. Together with Ps 69, Dodd identifies principally Isa 42:1–44:5; 49:1–13; 50:4–11; 52:13–53:12; and Pss 22, 34, 118 as "Scriptures of the Servant of the Lord and the Righteous Sufferer" used christologically in the NT. For a further discussion of Jewish exegetical procedures and principles generally and of the NT's employment of the OT from a christocentric perspective and in accordance with standard Jewish exegetical practices in particular, cf. my *Biblical Exegesis*.

Τὴν ἐπισκοπὴν (*tēn episkopēn*) is used here, not in its later titular meaning of "bishop," but in the more functional sense of "overseership" or "leadership," being equivalent to τῆς διακονίας ταύτης (*tēs diakonias tautēs*, "this ministry") of vv.17, 25.

23 Joseph Barsabbas is to be distinguished from Judas Barsabbas of 15:22 and Jesus called Justus of Col 4:11; likewise from Joseph Barnabas of 4:36 (though D and some minor texts have

Βαρνάβαν, *Barnaban*, at 1:23). Having a Gentile name (Gr. or Rom.) along with a Heb. name and a Heb. nickname was quite common in the Jewish world (cf. 12:12; 13:9).

24 The expression προσευξάμενοι εἶπαν (*proseuxamenoi eipan*, "praying, they said") is like the LXX locution ἀποκριθεὶς εἶπεν (*apokritheis eipen*, "answering, he said"), which occurs thirty-eight times in the third Gospel and seven times in Acts; the aorist participle expresses action simultaneous with that of the main verb.

26 On the Day of Atonement, Aaron chose by lot a scapegoat to bear the sins of the people in the wilderness (cf. Lev 16:7–10, 21–22). After the conquest, Palestine was divided by casting lots (cf. Josh 14:2; 18:6; 1 Chron 6:54ff.); Jonathan's breaking of Saul's hasty vow was discovered by lot (1 Sam 14:41–42); and the service of the Jerusalem temple was regulated by the casting of lots (Neh 10:34ff.). Perhaps the Urim and the Thummim (Exod 28:30; Deut 33:8; Ezra 2:63) were at times used in this manner, the stones being placed upon the ephod of the high priest and the priest then picking up one or the other blindly in order to determine the divine will. In the NT we read of the soldiers at the cross casting lots for the clothing of Jesus (Matt 27:35) and, here in Acts, of using lots to determine the Lord's will about Judas's successor. While lots are not mentioned elsewhere in the NT, their use may have continued for a time.

E. *The Coming of the Holy Spirit* (2:1-41)

Luke's fourth constitutive factor that undergirds the expansion of the early Christian mission is the coming of the Holy Spirit upon the assembled believers at Pentecost. To this the other three factors have pointed. And now Luke gives us an extended account of it that includes the baptism of the Spirit on the Day of Pentecost and Peter's sermon to the multitude and welds these separate incidents into a unified whole.

Though all four Gospels include the preaching of John the Baptist, only Luke has preserved the Baptist's distinction between his baptism in water and the baptism to be conferred by the one to come, the "one more powerful" than he was (Luke 3:16). Also, Luke alone connects the Baptist's prophecy of a baptism "with the Holy Spirit and with fire" with the miracle at Pentecost (Acts 1:5; 11:16). So Luke brings John's baptism of Jesus in the Jordan and the Spirit's baptism of assembled believers at Pentecost into a parallel in which each event is seen as the final constitutive factor for all that follows in the ministry of Jesus (cf. Luke's Gospel) and the mission of the early church (cf. Acts).

1. *The miracle of Pentecost*

2:1-13

[1]When the day of Pentecost came, they were all together in one place. [2]Suddenly a sound like the blowing of a violent wind came from heaven and filled the whole house where they were sitting. [3]They saw what seemed to be tongues of fire that separated and came to rest on each of them. [4]All of them were filled with the Holy Spirit and began to speak in other tongues as the Spirit enabled them.

[5]Now there were staying in Jerusalem God-fearing Jews from every nation under heaven. [6]When they heard this sound, a crowd came together in bewilderment, because each one heard them speaking in his own language. [7]Utterly amazed, they asked: "Are not all these men who are speaking Galileans? [8]Then how is it that each of us hears them in his own native language? [9]Parthians, Medes and Elamites; residents of Mesopotamia, Judea, and Cappadocia, Pontus and Asia, [10]Phrygia and Pamphylia, Egypt and the parts of Libya near Cyrene; visitors from Rome [11](both Jews and converts to Judaism); Cretans and Arabs—we hear them declaring the wonders of God in our own tongues!" [12]Amazed and perplexed, they asked one another, "What does this mean?"

[13]Some, however, made fun of them and said, "They have had too much wine."

1 Luke describes the miracle of the coming of the Holy Spirit, with its accompanying signs, in four short verses, remarkable for their nuances. The miracle occurred on the festival known in Late Judaism as Pentecost (*hē pentēkostē*, "fiftieth"), which, according to Leviticus 23:15–16 (cf. Deut 16:9–12; Jos. Antiq. III, 252 [ix.6]; SBK, 2:597–602), was to be celebrated on the "day after the seventh Sabbath" and hence on the fiftieth day after Passover. It was originally the festival of the firstfruits of the grain harvest (Exod 23:16; Lev 23:17–22; Num 28:26–31); and it was called the Feast of Weeks because it came after a period of seven weeks of harvesting that began with the offering of the first barley sheaf during the Passover celebration and ended with the wheat harvest. By the time of the first Christian century, however, it was considered the anniversary of the giving of the law at Mount Sinai (as deduced from the chronological note at Exod 19:1) and as a time for the annual renewal of the Mosaic covenant (Jub 6:17; b *Peshaim* 68b; M *Tanchuma* 26c); and it was therefore looked upon as one of the three great pilgrim festivals of Judaism (along with Passover preceding it and Tabernacles some four months later).

Now no one who had been a companion of the apostle Paul (or, for that matter, even a distant admirer, should Lukan authorship of Acts be denied) could have failed to have been impressed by the fact that it was on the Jewish festival of Pentecost that the Spirit came so dramatically upon the early believers in Jerusalem. It is this significance that Luke emphasizes as he begins his Pentecost narrative; viz., that whereas Pentecost was for Judaism the day of the giving of the law, for Christians it is the day of the coming of the Holy Spirit. So for Luke the coming of the Spirit upon the early Christians at Pentecost is not only a parallel to the Spirit's coming upon Jesus at his baptism, it is also both in continuity with and in contrast to the law. To be sure, Luke does not draw out from this a portrayal of Jesus as either the giver of a new Torah or himself the embodiment of such a Torah (though if Matthew or John had written Acts, they might have done something like that). Rather, by paralleling Jesus' baptism with the experience of Jesus' early followers at Pentecost, Luke is showing that the mission of the Christian church, as was the ministry of Jesus, is dependent upon the coming of the Holy Spirit. And by his stress on Pentecost as the day when the miracle took place, he is also suggesting (1) that the Spirit's coming is in continuity with God's purposes in giving the law and yet (2) that the Spirit's coming signals the essential difference between the Jewish faith and commitment to Jesus, for whereas the former is Torah centered and Torah directed, the latter is Christ centered and Spirit directed—all of which sounds very much like Paul.

As to just where the believers were when they experienced the coming of the Spirit, Luke is somewhat vague. His emphasis is on the "when" and not at all on the "where" of the event. So all he tells us is that "they were all together in one place," which he refers to in the following verse as "the house" (*ton oikon*).

Many have taken this to be a reference to the Jerusalem temple because (1) *oikos* was at times used to refer to the temple (cf. Isa 6:4 LXX; Acts 7:47; Jos. Antiq. VIII, 65–75 [iii.1–3]); (2) Luke's Gospel closes with the statement that Jesus' disciples "stayed continually at the temple, praising God" (Luke 24:53); and (3) in the temple precincts they would have had the best opportunity of addressing a large crowd. Yet apart from this doubtful instance in Acts 2 and his report of Stephen's speech (ch. 7), Luke elsewhere always refers to the temple by *to hieron* (twenty-two times); and where *oikos* is occasionally used by others of the Jerusalem temple, it is always in a context that leaves no doubt of what is meant. Furthermore, the articular intensive pronoun *to auto* ("in one place," NIV) is best interpreted as referring to its antecedent in 1:12–26, "the upper room" (*to hyperōon*). Therefore it is likely that Luke meant us to picture that same upper room as the setting for the miracle of the Spirit's coming and the place from where the disciples first went out to proclaim the gospel.

2 There is, of course, nothing necessarily sensory about the Holy Spirit. Yet God in his providence often accompanies his Spirit's working by visible and audible signs—particularly at certain crises in redemptive history. This he does to assure his people of his presence, and usually within the appreciation—though not always the expectation—of his own. In vv.2-4 three signs of the Spirit's coming are reported to have appeared, each of them—wind, fire, inspired speech—being considered in Jewish tradition as a sign of God's presence.

Wind as a sign of God's Spirit is rooted linguistically in the fact that both the Hebrew word *rûaḥ* and the Greek word *pneuma* mean either wind or spirit, depending on the context, and this allows a rather free association of the two ideas (cf. John 3:8). Ezekiel had prophesied of the wind as the breath of God blowing over the dry bones in the valley of his vision and filling them with new life (Ezek 37:9-14), and it was this wind of God's Spirit that Judaism looked forward to as ushering in the final Messianic Age. Thus Luke tells us that as a sign of the Spirit's coming upon the early followers of Jesus, there was "a sound like the blowing of a violent wind." Just why he emphasized the "sound" (*ēchos*) of the blowing of the "wind" (*pnoē*) is difficult to say. Perhaps it was because he wanted to refer back later to "this sound" (*tēs phōnēs tautēs*, v.6). Perhaps, also, he wanted to retain the parallel with the Pentecost tradition of the giving of the law. In certain sectors of Judaism the events connected with the giving of the law were couched in terms of God's having caused a "sound" to arise on Mount Sinai. This "sound" then changed into a "fire," which all could perceive as a "language" (cf. Philo, *De Decalogo* 33). But whatever his exact rationale, Luke's main point is that this "sound like the blowing of a violent wind" that "came from heaven" and "filled the whole house" symbolized to all present—in a manner well within their appreciation—the presence of God's Spirit among them in a way more intimate, personal, and powerful than they had ever before experienced.

3 Fire as a symbol of the divine presence was well known among first-century Jews (cf. the burning bush [Exod 3:2-5], the pillar of fire that guided Israel by night through the wilderness [Exod 13:21], the consuming fire on Mount Sinai [Exod 24:17], and the fire that hovered over the wilderness tabernacle [Exod 40:38]). Also, 1 Enoch depicts God's heavenly court as "surrounded by tongues of fire" (14:8-25; cf. 71:5, though 1 Enoch 37-71 may be post-Christian). John the Baptist is reported as having explicitly linked the coming of the Spirit with fire (cf. his prophecy that the Messiah would baptize "with the Holy Spirit and with fire" [Matt 3:11; Luke 3:16]). The "tongues of fire" (*glōssai hōsei pyros*) here are probably not to be equated with the "other tongues" (*heterais glōssais*) of v.4 but should be taken as visible representations, given in the context of the appreciation of those there gathered, of the overshadowing presence of the Spirit of God.

Also significant is Luke's statement that these tokens of the Spirit's presence "separated and came to rest on each of them." This seems to suggest that, though under the old covenant the divine presence rested on Israel as a corporate entity and upon many of its leaders for special purposes, under the new covenant, as established by Jesus and inaugurated at Pentecost, the Spirit now rests upon each believer individually. In other words, though the corporate and individual aspects of redemption cannot actually be separated, the emphasis in the proclamation of redemption from Pentecost onward is on the personal relationship of God to the believer through the Spirit, with all corporate relationships resulting from this.

4 In OT times prophetic utterances were regularly associated with the Spirit's coming upon particular persons for special purposes (cf. Eldad and Medad [Num 11:26–29]; Saul [1 Sam 10:6–12]; et al.). In Judaism, however, the belief arose that with the passing of the last of the writing prophets in the early postexilic period the spirit of prophecy had ceased in Israel. Since then, therefore, God spoke to his people only through the Torah as interpreted by the teachers (cf. such passages as the Prologue to Sirach and ch. 1 of *Pirke Aboth*). But Judaism also expected that with the coming of the Messianic Age there would be a special outpouring of God's Spirit, in fulfillment of Ezekiel 37, and that prophecy would once again flourish. And this is exactly what Luke portrays as having taken place at Pentecost among the followers of Jesus: "All of them were filled with the Holy Spirit and began to speak in other tongues as the Spirit enabled them."

The "tongues" here are often identified with ecstatic utterances of the sort Paul discusses in 1 Corinthians 12–14. This identification is made largely because (1) in both instances (1 Cor 12–14; Acts 2) the expression "other tongues" (*heterais glōssais, heteroglōssois*) is used and (2) because the verb translated "enabled" or "gave utterance" (*apophthengomai*) is frequently used in other Greek literature in connection with ecstatics, whether of the givers of oracles (cf. Diodorus of Sicily *Historical Library* 16.27.1; Plutarch *Pythiae Oraculis* 23) or of the interpreters of oracles (cf. Mic 5:12; Zech 10:2). But the words spoken at Pentecost under the Spirit's direction were immediately recognized by those who heard them as being languages then current, while at Corinth no one could understand what was said till someone present received a gift of interpretation. And the verb *apophthengomai* used by Luke in Acts (its only three NT occurrences) appears in contexts that stress clarity of speech and understanding: here in 2:4; in 2:14 of Peter's address to the crowd at Pentecost; and in 26:25 of Paul's defense before Agrippa II, where it is explicitly contrasted with *mainomai*, which speaks of babblings stemming from madness over which the speaker has no control. Therefore, the tongues in 2:4 are best understood as "languages" and should be taken in accord with Philo's reference to understandable language as one of the three signs of God's presence in the giving of the law at Mount Sinai (*De Decalogo* 33).

The coming of the Holy Spirit at Pentecost was of utmost significance both theologically and practically for the early church. As for the question Was Pentecost the birthday of the Christian church? a great deal depends upon what one means by the term "church" (*ekklēsia*). Amid a variety of usages, the word appears in the NT for both "the body of Christ" (meaning the redeemed of all ages) and "an instrument of service" (distinguishable from the nation Israel) used by God for his redemptive purposes. Of the first, the church as the body of Christ, it can hardly be said that it had its beginning *only* at Pentecost. What can be said, however, and what Luke seems to be stressing in reporting that the tongues of fire separated and came to rest on each believer individually, is (1) that the relationship of the Spirit to the members of the body of Christ became much more intimate and personal at Pentecost, in fulfillment of Jesus' promise (later recorded in John 14:17) that the Spirit who "lives with you" (*par hymin menei*) "will be in you" (*en hymin estai*), and (2) that at Pentecost a new model of divine redemption was established as characteristic for life in the new covenant—one that, while incorporating both individual and corporate redemption, begins with the former in order to include the latter.

With regard to the church as an instrument of service, called by God to take up the mission formerly entrusted to Israel, Luke is certainly presenting the coming of the Spirit at Pentecost as the church's birthday. So he parallels the Spirit's coming on Jesus at his baptism with the Spirit's coming at Pentecost on the earliest followers, for neither Jesus' ministry nor the mission of the early church would have been possible apart from the

Spirit's empowering. So also Luke emphasizes Jesus' explicit command to the disciples to stay in Jerusalem till they were empowered from on high by the Spirit (Luke 24:49; Acts 1:4–5, 8).

5 Certain "God-fearing Jews" who were residing in Jerusalem from many parts of the Diaspora, together with a number of Jews and proselytes who had returned to Jerusalem as pilgrims for the Pentecost festival, were "in bewilderment," "utterly amazed," and "perplexed" by the miraculous coming of the Spirit (vv.6–7, 12). Others, however, mocked (v.13).

Aleph omits the word "Jews" (*Ioudaioi*), which some have considered to be a serious omission, particularly because of the importance of this MS as external evidence in establishing the text. But the word Luke uses for "God-fearing" (*eulabēs*) is used in the NT only of Jews (cf. Luke 2:25; Acts 8:2; 22:12). It never connotes elsewhere in the NT a Gentile convert to Judaism (*prosēlytos*, "proselyte"), a near convert or so-called Prose-lyte of the Gate (*sebomenos*, "worshiper"), or a devout Gentile (which is often implied by *phoboumenos*, "fearer," or *eusebēs*, "godly"). It is therefore highly unlikely that even if *Ioudaioi* were omitted from the text, that would be ground for arguing that in v.5 Luke had Gentiles in view. Furthermore, contrary to many who have assumed that the Jews mentioned here were pilgrims to Jerusalem coming for the Pentecost festival, it is more probable that they were residents of Jerusalem who had returned from Diaspora lands ("from every nation under heaven") at some earlier time to settle down in the homeland. That is how Luke uses *katoikountes* ("staying") here, a participial form of *katoikeō*, which he uses elsewhere in Acts (cf. 1:20; 7:2, 4, 48; 9:22; 11:29; 13:27; 17:24, 26; 22:12), in contrast to the verb *epidēmeō* used participially in v.10, in the sense of "being a stranger or visitor in town."

6 What drew the crowd and caused its bewilderment? Commentators differ as to whether it was the sound of the wind or the disciples' speaking in various languages. But if we break the sentence with some kind of punctuation after *to plēthos* ("a crowd") rather than (as is usually done) after *synechythē* ("bewilderment"), we have two coordinate sentences with two separate yet complementary ideas: "When they heard this sound, a crowd came together. And they were bewildered because each one heard them speaking in his own language." On this reading, *tēs phōnēs tautēs* ("this sound") refers back to *ēchos* ("sound") of v.2 and conjures up a picture of people rushing to the source of the noise to see what is going on. When they get there, they become bewildered on hearing Galileans speaking in their own native languages. The verb for "hear" (*ēkouon*) is in the imperfect tense, suggesting that their hearing took place over a period of time—perhaps first in the upper room itself, then in adjacent lanes and courtyards, and finally in the temple precincts.

7–8 Galileans had difficulty pronouncing gutturals and had the habit of swallowing syllables when speaking; so they were looked down upon by the people of Jerusalem as being provincial (cf. Mark 14:70). Therefore, since the disciples who were speaking were Galileans, it bewildered those who heard because the disciples could not by themselves have learned so many different languages.

9–11 Why these fifteen countries and no others are named here and why they are cited in this order are questions without ready solutions. In recent decades it has frequently been argued that Luke was probably drawing on some ancient astrological treatise that correlated the then-known nations of the world with the twelve signs of the zodiac, such as the fourth-century A.D. Egyptian Paulus Alexandrinus included in his *Rudiments of Astrology*. This, however, requires pruning Luke's list of fifteen down to twelve (deleting "Judea" as the fifth in the listing and "Cretans and Arabs" at the end, though all three are well attested in the MSS), stressing a few exact parallels, and making adjustments in order. Moreover, such astrological and historical listings of nations were common in the ancient world, and Luke may only be using a current literary convention to illustrate his more prosaic statement of v.5: "from every nation under heaven." As was probably customary, the list includes both ancient kingdoms and current political entities, moving generally from east to west and in its middle section naming first the northern and then the southern lands.

The appearance of "Judea" in the listing is, admittedly, strange because (1) it hardly ranks being sandwiched between Mesopotamia to the east and Cappadocia to the north; (2) as an adjective used as a noun, it is "corrupt" without an article when used substantively; and (3) it involves the curious anomaly of inhabitants of Judea being amazed to hear the apostles speak in their own language. Suggested solutions to this problem have been legion. Perhaps the most cogent one involves viewing "Judea" here in a wider prophetic sense, wherein the reference is to "the land of the Jews" that was held to stretch from the Euphrates to the Egyptian border. This would explain its sequence in the list, the omission of Syria from the list, and would allow for a variety of dialects different from the one that was native to Jerusalem. The inclusion of "Cretans and Arabs" probably refers to sea-faring peoples and to Nabatean Arabs, whose kingdom traditionally extended from the Euphrates to the Red Sea.

Each area and country named had a considerable Jewish population within its borders (cf. SBK, 2:606–14). Some of these had returned to Jerusalem to take up residence there (cf. comment on *katoikountes*, "staying," v.5). One group, however, is singled out as being religious pilgrims to the city (cf. the participle *hoi epidēmountes*, "visitors," of v.10). They are identified as being Jews and proselytes to Judaism from Rome. Undoubtedly there were other festival pilgrims in the crowd (just as there must have been other Diaspora Jews in attendance who were residents of Jerusalem), but Luke's interest in Acts is in the gospel reaching out even to Rome, the capital of the empire. So he singles out this pilgrim contingent for special mention. It may be that some of these "visitors" from Rome returned there and formed the nucleus of the church in that city. Ambrosiaster, a fourth-century Latin father, speaks of the church at Rome as having been founded "according to the Jewish rite, without seeing any sign of mighty works or any of the apostles" (cf. P.A. Ballerini, ed., *S. Ambrosii Opera* [Rome: Mediolani, 1877], 3:373–74).

12–13 The miraculous is not self-authenticating, nor does it inevitably and uniformly convince. There must also be the preparation of the heart and the proclamation of the message if miracles are to accomplish their full purpose. This was true even for the miracle of the Spirit's coming at Pentecost. The Greek of v.12 indicates that "all" of the "God-fearing Jews" (v.5), whose attention had been arrested by the signs at Pentecost and whose own religious heritage gave them at least some appreciation of them, were amazed and asked, "What does this mean?" Others, however, being spiritually insensitive only mocked, attributing such phenomena to drunkenness. All this prepares the reader for Peter's sermon, which is the initial proclamation of the gospel message to a prepared people.

Notes

1 Ἐν (en, "in"; NIV, "when") with the articular infinitive is a favorite Lukan construction, particularly to express the idea of time (cf. Acts 8:6; 11:15; 19:1). It occurs thirty-two times in Luke's Gospel (against three times in Matt and twice in Mark) and seven times in Acts. An exact parallel to the ἐν τῷ συμπληροῦσθαι (en tō symplērousthai; lit., "in the approaching of") of Acts 2:1 is to be found in Luke 9:51.

4 For rabbinic references to the cessation of prophecy in Israel in the early postexilic period and to its return in the Messianic Age, see P. Schäfer, *Die Vorstellung vom heiligen Geist in der rabbinischen Literatur* (München: Kösel, 1972), pp. 89–115, 143–46 (though on the continuance of the Spirit's activity, see also pp. 116–34, 147–49).

7 Ἐξίσταντο καὶ ἐθαύμαζον (existanto kai ethaumazon, "utterly amazed") is probably a hendiadys, as is also ἐξίσταντο καὶ διηπόρουν (existanto kai diēporoun, "amazed and perplexed") of v.12.

9 The first to postulate Luke's dependence on some ancient astrological treatise was S. Weinstock, "The Geographical Catalogue in Acts II, 9–11," *Journal of Roman Studies*, 38 (1948), 43–46, though he credits F.C. Burkitt's notes on an article by F. Cumont (1909) as his inspiration (and Metzger credits J. Halévy [1906] as the first to note the relationship here between Luke and Paulus Alexandrinus, though he explained it differently). For a balanced evaluation of the problem, see Bruce M. Metzger, "Ancient Astrological Geography and Acts 2:9–11," in Gasque and Martin, *Apostolic History*, pp. 123–33.

13 This is the only occurrence of γλεῦκος (gleukos, "sweet wine") in the NT. As there was no new wine by Pentecost, some think of this as wine sweetened with honey (SBK, 2:614) and others postulate a method for keeping wine from fermenting (BC, 4:20). This, however, has little relevance here because the apostles were accused of drunkenness.

2. Peter's sermon at Pentecost (2:14–41)

Peter's sermon at Pentecost consists of (1) an apologia for the occurrence of the phenomena (vv.14–21), (2) a kerygma ("proclamation") of the apostolic message in its most elemental form (vv.22–36), and (3) a call to repentance with a promise of blessing (vv.37–41). The sermon is headed by a brief introductory statement and followed by two summary sentences dealing with Peter's further preaching and the people's response. It was probably delivered in the outer court of the temple. And while the verb *apophthengomai* ("addressed") in v.14 is the same as in v.4, we should understand that Peter undoubtedly spoke in the local vernacular (whether some form of Aram. or koine Gr.) and not in a foreign language, for *apophthengomai* relates more to the inspired nature of the message than its mode.

a. Apologia section

2:14–21

> ¹⁴Then Peter stood up with the Eleven, raised his voice and addressed the crowd: "Fellow Jews and all of you who are in Jerusalem, let me explain this to you; listen carefully to what I say. ¹⁵These men are not drunk, as you suppose. It's only nine in the morning! ¹⁶No, this is what was spoken by the prophet Joel:
> ¹⁷" 'In the last days, God says,
> I will pour out my Spirit on all people.
> Your sons and daughters will prophesy,
> your young men will see visions,
> your old men will dream dreams.

¹⁸Even on my servants, both men and women,
I will pour out my Spirit in those days,
and they will prophesy.
¹⁹I will show wonders in the heaven above
and signs in the earth below,
blood and fire and billows of smoke.
²⁰The sun will be turned to darkness
and the moon to blood
before the coming of the great and glorious day
of the Lord.
²¹And everyone who calls
on the name of the Lord will be saved.'

14 The apologia section of Peter's sermon is addressed to the "fellow Jews" and "all . . . who are in Jerusalem." Later in the kerygma section these two groups are combined under the captions "Men of Israel" (v.22) and "Brothers" (v.29), for it is natural for them to be classed together. But here Peter apparently wanted to include particularly those who had been most bewildered by the multiplicity of the languages spoken. While undoubtedly many of the native-born Jews were awed by this, it was probably the Diaspora contingent there present that most appreciated the incongruity of the situation and called for an explanation.

15 Peter begins negatively by arguing that the apostles could not be drunk, for it was only "nine in the morning" ("the third hour of the day," lit. Gr.). Unfortunately, this argument was more telling in antiquity than today.

16–21 Positively, Peter explains the phenomena taking place among the early Christians at Pentecost as being the fulfillment of Joel 2:28–32 (MT = 3:1–5). His use of the Joel passage is in line with what since the discovery of the DSS we have learned to call a "pesher" (from Heb. *pēšer*, "interpretation"). It lays all emphasis on fulfillment without attempting to exegete the details of the biblical prophecy; it "interprets." So Peter introduces the passage with the typically pesher introductory formula "this is that" (*touto estin to;* NIV, "this is what"). The note of fulfillment is heightened by the alteration of the MT's and the LXX's simple "afterwards" (*'aḥᵃrê kēn, meta tauta*) to "in the last days" (*en tais eschatais hēmerais,* v.17) and by interrupting the quotation to highlight the restoration of prophecy by inserting the words "and they will prophesy" (v.18). The solemnity and importance of the words are emphasized by the addition of "God says" (v.18) at the beginning of the quotation.

The way Peter uses Joel 2:28–32 is of great significance (1) for an appreciation of early Christian exegetical practices and doctrinal commitments and (2) as a pattern for our own treatment of the OT. For Peter, we should note, what Joel said is what God says. And while what God says may have been somewhat enigmatic when first uttered, when seen from the perspective of eschatological fulfillment a great deal of what was unclear is clarified. Thus Peter can proclaim from the perspective of the Messiah's resurrection and living presence with his people (1) that "this" that he and the infant church were experiencing in the outpouring of God's Spirit "is that" prophesied by Joel, (2) that these are "the last days" of God's redemptive program, and (3) that the validation of all this is the fact of the return of prophesying. In other words, he is proclaiming that this is the time for the fulfillment of prophecy and that these are the long-awaited "last days" of the divine redemptive program; and he is also suggesting by his inclusion of the prophet's call for response that through the apostles' proclamation there will go out from Jerusalem a prophetic message of salvation and a call for repentance.

Debates arise between proponents of "realized eschatology" and "inaugurated eschatology," on the one hand, and between amillennialists (including here postmillennialists) and premillennialists (cf. "The Eschatology of the Bible," Robert L. Saucy, EBC, 1:103-26), on the other hand, about how Peter and the earliest followers of Jesus understood the more spectacular physical signs of Joel's prophecy (i.e., "blood and fire and billows of smoke," "the sun will be turned to darkness and the moon to blood"). Realized eschatologists and amillennialists usually take Peter's inclusion of such physical imagery in a spiritual way, finding in what happened at Pentecost the spiritual fulfillment of Joel's prophecy—a fulfillment not necessarily tied to any natural phenomena. This, they suggest, offers an interpretive key to the understanding of similar portrayals of natural phenomena and apocalyptic imagery in the OT. Moreover, some realized eschatologists and amillennialists, desiring to retain more than just the symbolic, suggest that these signs should be understood as having actually taken place in the natural world "during the early afternoon of the day of our Lord's crucifixion," when "the sun turned into darkness" and "the paschal full moon . . . appeared blood-red in the sky in consequence of that preternatural gloom" (Bruce, *Book of the Acts,* p. 69).

On the other hand, certain features in Peter's sermon show his reason for his emphatic citation of Joel's prophecy. These features are Peter's introductory formula "this is that," his alteration of "afterward" (Joel 2:28) to "in the last days," his addition of "God says" at the beginning of the quotation, and his interruption of the quotation to insert "and they will prophesy." He quotes the entire prophecy in Joel 2:28-32 because of its traditional messianic significance and because its final sentence ("And everyone who calls on the name of the Lord will be saved") leads logically to the kerygma section of his sermon. But Peter might not have known what to make of the more physical and spectacular elements of Joel's prophecy, though he probably expected them in some way to follow in the very near future. (Certainly he could not have foreseen a delay of many centuries before their fulfillment.) So his emphasis was on the inauguration of the Messianic Age ("the last days")—an emphasis we should see as being essential to his preaching and beyond which we are not compelled to go.

God has inaugurated, Peter proclaims, the long-awaited "last days" here and now, and we know this because of the reinstitution of prophecy. Other signs, to be sure, were part of Joel's vision, but Peter does not stress them. His emphasis is entirely on prophecy as the sign of the inauguration of the last days. Even though he might have had his own personal expectations, Peter leaves all else for God to work out in the Messianic Age that had been inaugurated.

Notes

14 The compound form Ἄνδρες Ἰουδαῖοι (*Andres Ioudaioi,* lit., "Men, Jews"; "Fellow Jews," NIV) is comparable to Luke's frequently employed Ἄνδρες ἀδελφοί (*Andres adelphoi;* lit., "Men, brothers"; "Brothers," NIV) of 1:16 (see discussion there). Cf. also Ἄνδρες Ἰσραηλῖται (*Andres Israēlitai;* lit., "Men, Israelites"; "Men of Israel," NIV) of 2:22.

16 On pesher interpretation at Qumran and in the NT, see my *Biblical Exegesis,* pp. 38-45, passim.

The name Joel is omitted in D, Irenaeus, Augustine (*Epistulae* 199. 23), and Hilarius, probably because subsequent introductory formulas to quotations from the Minor Prophets in Acts (7:42; 13:40; 15:15) omit the prophets' names.

17–20 The other textual variations from the MT and LXX are rather insignificant and probably without theological importance: (1) the rearrangement of clauses in v.17 so that "your young men will see visions" precedes "your old men will dream dreams" and (2) the addition in v.19 of the words "above," "signs," and "below."

---

b. *Kerygma section*

2:22–36

22"Men of Israel, listen to this: Jesus of Nazareth was a man accredited by God to you by miracles, wonders and signs, which God did among you through him, as you yourselves know. 23This man was handed over to you by God's set purpose and foreknowledge; and you, with the help of wicked men, put him to death by nailing him to the cross. 24But God raised him from the dead, freeing him from the agony of death, because it was impossible for death to keep its hold on him. 25David said about him:

" 'I saw the Lord always before me.
Because he is at my right hand,
I will not be shaken.
26Therefore my heart is glad and my tongue rejoices;
my body also will live in hope,
27because you will not abandon me to the grave,
nor will you let your Holy One see decay.
28You have made known to me the paths of life;
you will fill me with joy in your presence.'

29"Brothers, I can tell you confidently that the patriarch David died and was buried, and his tomb is here to this day. 30But he was a prophet and knew that God had promised him on oath that he would place one of his descendants on his throne. 31Seeing what was ahead, he spoke of the resurrection of the Christ, that he was not abandoned to the grave, nor did his body see decay. 32God has raised this Jesus to life, and we are all witnesses of the fact. 33Exalted to the right hand of God, he has received from the Father the promised Holy Spirit and has poured out what you now see and hear. 34For David did not ascend to heaven, and yet he said,

" 'The Lord said to my Lord:
"Sit at my right hand
35until I make your enemies
a footstool for your feet." '

36"Therefore let all Israel be assured of this: God has made this Jesus, whom you crucified, both Lord and Christ."

In his *Apostolic Preaching,* Dodd identifies six themes that appear repeatedly in Peter's sermons in Acts 2–4:

1. "The age of fulfillment has dawned."
2. "This has taken place through the ministry, death and resurrection of Jesus, of which a brief account is given, with proof from the Scriptures."
3. "By virtue of the resurrection, Jesus has been exalted at the right hand of God, as Messianic head of the new Israel."
4. "The Holy Spirit in the Church is the sign of Christ's present power and glory."
5. "The Messianic Age will shortly reach its consummation in the return of Christ."

6. "The *kerygma* always closes with an appeal for repentance, the offer of forgiveness and of the Holy Spirit, and the promise of 'salvation,' that is, of 'the life of the Age to Come,' to those who enter the elect community" (pp. 21-24).

With the exception of the return of Christ (which appears in these early sermons only at 3:20-21), all these themes come to the fore in Peter's Pentecost sermon: the note of fulfillment explicitly in the apologia section and inferentially throughout; the appeal for repentance and the promise of blessing at the close of the sermon; and the remaining themes in what we have designated the kerygma section proper, which focuses upon Jesus of Nazareth as mankind's Lord and Israel's promised Messiah.

Despite its denial by certain scholars, it yet remains true to say that Peter's sermons of Acts 2-4 "represent the *kerygma* of the Church at Jerusalem at an early period" (ibid., p. 21). They are not verbatim reports, and hardly anyone has so taken them. But though they have been styled and shaped by Luke in accordance with his own purposes, they are not simply reproductions of his own theology or that of his spiritual mentor, Paul. They rather exhibit Semitic features and primitive characteristics that show that they come from a period earlier than the writing of Acts and stem from the earliest Christian congregation at Jerusalem. Moreover, though many have thought otherwise, the early church *was* interested in the life and character of Jesus—not for mere biographical reasons, but to fill out the content of its preaching—since the focus of the apostolic proclamation was on Jesus of Nazareth, mankind's Lord and Israel's Messiah (cf. Stanton). Thus Peter in his Pentecost sermon includes a brief sketch of the ministry, death, and resurrection of Jesus.

The early preaching of the church regarding Jesus was characterized by (1) being principally functional in nature rather than philosophical and (2) stressing ultimate causality more than secondary causes or means. Indeed, one cannot speak of what has happened redemptively without dealing with questions of "who" and "how"—questions that are bound to arise in thinking about the "that" of divine redemption. Indispensable, therefore, to all purposive thinking, such as in Peter's preaching or later on in Paul's, are nuances relating to ontology (the nature of being) and speculation about why and how things happened. Yet in presenting the earliest preaching of the apostles at Jerusalem, it is significant that Luke did not attempt to put such nuances into their mouths. Instead, he presents Peter as proclaiming our Lord as "Jesus of Nazareth," "a man accredited," "handed over," put "to death," raised "from the dead." Peter also proclaimed God as the true author of Jesus' miracles, the ultimate agent in Jesus' death, and the only cause for Jesus' resurrection. There is, to be sure, some allusion to means in the statement "and you, with the help of wicked men, put him to death by nailing him to the cross" (v.23b). And there may be some ontological insight into who Jesus actually was in the statement "because it was impossible for death to keep its hold on him" (v.24b). Indeed, vv.25-35 explain this "impossibility" not only in terms of what Scripture has foretold, but also in terms of who this Holy One was. Yet the emphasis in Peter's preaching of Jesus—as also in his concluding declaration (v.36) and his call to repentance (v.38)—is strongly functional, apart from any definite philosophical speculation and with only a minimal attention to the way in which God's purpose in Christ was carried out.

22 Peter begins the kerygma or proclamation section of his sermon with an inclusive form of address: "Men of Israel," which he parallels with the synonymous vocative "Brothers" (v.29). (See note on v.14.) His topic concerns "Jesus of Nazareth"—a common title used of Jesus throughout Luke's writings (cf. Luke 18:37; Acts 3:6; 4:10; 6:14; 10:38;

22:8; 26:9) and one by which early Christians themselves were at times called (cf. 24:5).

The ministry of Jesus is characterized by "miracles, wonders and signs" that God did among the people through Jesus. The compound expression "wonders and signs" (*terata kai sēmeia*) appears quite often in various Greek writers, in the LXX, and in the NT itself (e.g., Acts 2:43; 4:30; 5:12; 6:8; 7:36; 14:3; 15:12; cf. 2:19); but the threefold "miracles, wonders and signs" is rare (cf. 2 Cor 12:12b, where the order is reversed).

23 The death of Jesus is presented as resulting from the interplay of divine necessity and human freedom. Nowhere in the NT is the paradox of a Christian understanding of history put more sharply than in this earliest proclamation of the death of Jesus the Messiah: God's purpose and foreknowledge stand as the necessary factors behind whatever happens; yet whatever happens occurs through the instrumentality of wicked men expressing their own human freedom. It is a paradox without ready solution. To deny it, however, is to go counter to the plain teaching of Scripture in both the OT and NT and to ignore the testimony of personal experience. "With the help of wicked men" points to the Roman authorities in Palestine, who carried out what had been instigated by the Jewish authorities. Gentiles are frequently referred to in Jewish literature as "wicked" (e.g., Jub 23:23–24) and "lawless" (e.g., Pss Sol 17:11, 18; cf. 1 Cor 9:21), either because of their actual sins or simply because they did not possess the Mosaic law.

24 Here the resurrection of Jesus is attributed directly to God, apart from any action of men or even Jesus himself—just as elsewhere in the NT it is so attributed in quotations from early Christian hymns and catechisms (e.g., 1 Cor 15:4; Phil 2:9). The imagery is of "death pangs" (*ōdinas tou thanatou*; NIV, "agony of death") and their awful clutches (cf. 2 Sam 22:6; Pss 18:4–6; 116:3), from which God is "freeing" Jesus "because it was impossible for death to keep its hold on him."

25–35 Here Peter quotes from Psalm 16:8–11 (LXX) and Psalm 110:1 in support of what he has just said about Jesus in v.24. The quotations are brought together according to the second of the midrashic exegetical rules (*middôt*) attributed by antiquity to Rabbi Hillel (viz., *gᵉzērâh šāwâh*, or "verbal analogy": where the same words appear in two separate passages, the same considerations apply to both). Both quotations have "at my right hand" and thus are deliberately treated together (cf. v.33). In addition, both quotations are used in pesher fashion (cf. comments on v.16), for it is a pesher understanding that evokes the introductory statement "David said about him" and that applies the quotations wholly to Jesus.

During the period of Late Judaism, both Psalm 16 and Psalm 110 were considered by Jewish interpreters to be somewhat enigmatic. Therefore they were variously understood. There was no problem with the confidence expressed in Psalm 16:8–9, 11. It was appropriate for the psalmist to whom God's love had been pledged and who had experienced God's covenant-keeping lovingkindness. (The word in v.27 for "Holy One," *hosios*, usually translates the Heb. word *hāsîd* in the LXX, which is related to *hesed*, the word for "pledged love," "faithfulness to the covenant," and "lovingkindness"; cf. DNTT, 2:237.) But how could the psalmist have expected God to keep him from the grave and from undergoing decay, as in v.10? And Psalm 110 was even more difficult, for who is this "my Lord" to whom "the Lord" has said, "Sit at my right hand until I make your enemies a footstool for your feet" (v.34)? Some early rabbis linked the psalm with Abraham, others with David, and some even with Hezekiah; but there is no clearly attested messianic understanding of Psalm 110 in rabbinic literature until about A.D. 260

(cf. SBK, 4:452–60; D.M. Hay, *Glory at the Right Hand: Psalm 110 in Early Christianity* [Nashville and New York: Abingdon, 1973], pp. 19–33).

Nevertheless, Jesus is reported in all three synoptic Gospels as having interpreted Psalm 110:1 as a messianic passage and as applying it to himself (Mark 12:35–37). And it was probably Jesus' own treatment of Psalm 110:1 that (1) furnished the exegetical key for the early church's understanding of their risen Lord, (2) served as the pattern for their interpretation of similar enigmatic OT passages (e.g., 2 Sam 7:6–16 with Ps 2:7 and Isa 55:3 with Ps 16:10 in Paul's Antioch address of Acts 13:16–41), and (3) anchored all other passages as could be brought together on a "verbal analogy" basis (e.g., the catena of passages in Heb 1:5–13).

Therefore working from Psalm 110:1 as an accepted messianic passage and viewing Psalm 16:8–11 as having a similar reference on the basis of the hermeneutical rule of *gᵉzērâh šāwâh* (verbal analogy), Peter proclaims that Psalm 16:10 ("You will not abandon me to the grave, nor will you let your Holy One see decay") refers to Israel's promised Messiah and no other. It is an argument based on the exegetical precedent set by Jesus, inspired by the church's postresurrection perspective, and worked out along the lines of commonly accepted midrashic principles of the day. Furthermore, Peter insists, David could not have been speaking about himself, for he did indeed die, was buried, and suffered decay—as the presence of his tomb in the city eloquently testifies (v.29). Nor did he ascend to heaven. Therefore, David must have been prophesying about the resurrection of the Messiah in Psalm 16:10 and about his exaltation in Psalm 110:1. And with God's raising of Jesus from the dead, these formerly enigmatic passages are clarified and the pouring out of the Spirit explained.

36 With the proclamation of Jesus as Lord and Messiah, Peter reaches the climax and conclusion of his sermon. The initial "therefore" shows that God's resurrection and exaltation of Jesus accredits him as mankind's Lord and Israel's Messiah. And Peter calls upon "all Israel" (lit., "all the house [*oikos*] of Israel") to know with certainty that "God has made this Jesus, whom you crucified, both Lord and Christ."

In certain quarters it has become commonplace to assert that the church did not proclaim Jesus as Lord and Christ till *after* the Resurrection—or, as many prefer to express it, till after the rise of "the Easter faith." The implication is that only later were such names as "Lord" and "Christ" attached to Jesus' memory since he himself did not think along these lines. And this verse is often cited in support of that view. But it is more in line with the evidence to say that Jesus was acknowledged and proclaimed Lord and Christ not just after his resurrection but *because of* his resurrection. In Jewish thought, no one has a right to the title Messiah till he has accomplished the work of the Messiah— in fact, in all of life accomplishment must precede acclamation. During his earthly ministry, as that ministry is portrayed in all the Gospels, Jesus was distinctly reluctant to accept titular acclaim, probably because his understanding of messiahship had to do with suffering and because his concept of lordship had to do with vindication and exaltation by God. But now that Jesus has accomplished his messianic mission in life and death and has been raised by God and exalted "at his right hand," the titles Lord and Christ are legitimately his. This theme of function and accomplishment as the basis for titular acclaim is a recurring note in the christological statements elsewhere in the NT (cf. Rom 1:4; Phil 2:9–11; Heb 2:14; 1 John 5:6).

The verb *epoiēsen*, translated "made," has sometimes been taken as implying an adoptionist Christology, as though Jesus became ontologically what he was not before. But in functional contexts, *epoiēsen* has the sense of "appointed" (cf. 1 Sam 12:6 LXX;

1 Kings 12:31 LXX; Mark 3:14; Heb 3:2), and it is in just such a context that Peter uses it here. He is proclaiming not an adoptionist Christology but a functional one with ontological overtones—viz., that the resurrection of Jesus from the dead is God's open avowal that the messianic work has been accomplished and that Jesus now has the full right to assume the messianic title; that the exaltation of Jesus is the proclamation of his lordship, which God calls all to acknowledge.

In the twelve instances in Acts where the word "Christ" appears singly (2:31, 36; 3:18; 4:26; 8:5; 9:22; 17:3a; 26:23; and in 3:20; 5:42; 18:5, 28, where "Christ" is in apposition to "Jesus" but still "used" singly), it is used as a title—usually articular in form (except here and at 3:20)—but not as a name. And in every instance where it appears as a title, it is in an address to a Jewish audience (only 8:5 and 26:23 are possible exceptions, though both the Samaritans and Agrippa II possessed something of a Jewish background and understanding). Even where the combination "Jesus Christ" or "Christ Jesus" appears, the original appellative idea is still reflected in the usage. Apparently, therefore, the messiahship of Jesus was the distinctive feature of the church's witness within Jewish circles, signifying, as it does, his fulfillment of Israel's hopes and his culmination of God's redemptive purposes.

The title "Lord" was also proclaimed christologically in Jewish circles, with evident intent to apply to Jesus all that was said of God in the OT (cf. the christological use of Isa 45:23 in Phil 2:10). But "Lord" came to have particular relevance to the church's witness to Gentiles just as "Messiah" was more relevant to the Jewish world. So in Acts Luke reports the proclamation of Jesus "the Christ" before Jewish audiences both in Palestine and among the Diaspora, whereas Paul in his letters to Gentile churches generally uses Christ as a proper name and proclaims Christ Jesus "the Lord."

Notes

---

22 On the critical issues involved in these early sermons, see Introduction: The Speeches in Acts. For a defense of the thesis that the early church was interested in the life and character of Jesus and that the primary (though not the only) *Sitz im Leben* of that interest was the missionary preaching of the church, see Stanton, passim.

Despite occasional assertions to the contrary, it is now widely accepted as linguistically and historically unimpeachable that the term Ναζωραῖος (*Nazōraios*) means "an inhabitant of Nazareth" (cf. G.F. Moore, "Nazarene and Nazareth," BC, 1 [1920], 426–32; W.F. Albright, "The Names 'Nazareth' and 'Nazoraean,'" JBL, 65 [1946], 397–401). There is no difference in intent between Ἰησοῦν τὸν ἀπὸ Ναζαρέθ (*Iēsoun ton apo Nazareth*, "Jesus from Nazareth") of 10:38 and Ἰησοῦν τὸν Ναζωραῖον (*Iēsoun ton Nazōraion*, "Jesus the Nazarene") here and elsewhere in Luke-Acts. And what is true here is also true, at least in part, for the much-disputed appearance of *Nazōraios* in Matt 2:23.

24 Such texts as D OL Vul. Pesh. and a number of Western fathers read or reflect the reading ὠδῖνας ἅδου (*ōdinas hadou*, "pangs of Hades") rather than ὠδῖνας θανάτου (*ōdinas thanatou*, "pangs of death"), probably to conform with the εἰς ἅδην (*eis hadēn*, "into Hades"; NIV, "grave") of 2:27, 31. But the expressions "pangs of death" and "pangs of Hades/hell" were employed interchangeably (cf. 2 Sam 22:6 and Ps 114:3 vs. Ps 17:6 LXX), and there is solid external support for the former.

25 It should be remembered that only Luke among the synoptists omitted the cry of dereliction from the cross: "My God, my God, why have you forsaken me?" (Matt 27:46; Mark 15:34); and only Luke has included the more filial, final word: "Father, into your hands I commit my spirit"

(Luke 23:46). Both the omission and the inclusion are in line with the quotation of Ps 16:8 here: "I saw the Lord always [διὰ παντός, *dia pantos*] before me. Because he is at my right hand, I will not be shaken."

25-28 The LXX of Ps 16:8-11 (15:8-11) has "I saw" (προωρώμην, *proōrōmēn*) for the MT's "I have set" (שׁוִּיתִי, *šiwwîtî*); "my tongue" (ἡ γλῶσσά μου, *hē glōssa mou*) for "my glory" (כְּבוֹדִי, *ke-bôdî*); "in hope" (ἐπ᾽ ἐλπίδι, *ep᾽ elpidi*) for "in safety" (לָבֶטַח, *lābeṭaḥ*); and "destruction/decay" (διαφθοράν, *diaphthoran*) for "pit" (שַׁחַת, *šaḥaṭ*).

34-35 On midrashic interpretation among the rabbis and in the NT, see my *Biblical Exegesis*, pp. 32–38. On Jesus' use of Ps 110:1 as setting a paradigm for continued study in the church, see same, pp. 73–78.

36 The expression πᾶς οἶκος Ἰσραήλ (*pas oikos Israēl*, "all the house of Israel"; NIV, "all Israel") occurs only here in the NT, though it is common in the liturgical prayers of Judaism, cf. also Ezek 37:11.

The adverb ἀσφαλῶς (*asphalōs*), meaning "beyond a doubt" or "assuredly," stands first in the sentence for emphasis.

On the christological title "Messiah" and its implications, see my *Christology*, pp. 63–119; on "Lord" and its attendant features, see same, pp. 120–47.

---

c. A call to repentance and a promise of blessing

2:37-41

37When the people heard this, they were cut to the heart and said to Peter and the other apostles, "Brothers, what shall we do?"

38Peter replied, "Repent and be baptized, every one of you, in the name of Jesus Christ so that your sins may be forgiven. And you will receive the gift of the Holy Spirit. 39The promise is for you and your children and for all who are far off—for all whom the Lord our God will call."

40With many other words he warned them; and he pleaded with them, "Save yourselves from this corrupt generation." 41Those who accepted his message were baptized, and about three thousand were added to their number that day.

37 Peter's preaching had been effective. The people were "cut to the heart" at the awful realization that in crucifying their long-awaited Messiah they had rejected their only hope of salvation. So with deep anguish they cried out, "Brothers, what shall we do?"

Luke uses the verb *katanyssomai* ("cut to the heart") to describe their feelings. The word may have been drawn from Psalm 109:16. It connotes a sharp pain associated with anxiety and remorse. In 1:20 Luke used Psalm 109:8 (108:8 LXX) not only to describe wicked men who oppose God's servant but also to describe *the* wicked man, Judas Iscariot. Now Luke apparently reaches back to that same psalm (v.16) to pick up the vivid phrase for those who stand with God's servant in opposing wicked men: "those who have been cut to the heart" (*katanenygmenōn tē kardia*)—or those who are "the humble of heart" because they realize their need and are open to God's working (in contrast to those Luke describes by the verb *diaprio* ["to be cut to the heart" in the sense of being "furious"] in Acts 5:33; 7:54). In fact, the way the men address the apostles, "Brothers" (lit., "men, brothers"), shows that their hearts had already been won over.

Codex D and some of its Western associates omit "others" (*loipous*) in "the other apostles," thus distinguishing Peter from the apostles. But Luke's stress is on the supremacy of the apostles in the church, not on the supremacy of Peter. While in both his Gospel and his Acts he portrays Peter as taking leadership among the apostles, nowhere does Luke suggest anything more than that Peter was the natural leader and spokesman of the Twelve.

38 Peter's answer to the people's anguished cry presents interpreters with a set of complex theological problems that are often looked upon only as grist for differing theological mills. But Peter's words came to his hearers as the best news they had ever heard—far better, indeed, than they deserved or could have hoped for. So today these words remain the best of good news and should be read as the proclamation of that news and not as just a set of theological problems.

Peter calls on his hearers to "repent" (*metanoēsate*). This word implies a complete change of heart and the confession of sin. With this he couples the call to "be baptized" (*baptisthētō*), thus linking both repentance and baptism with the forgiveness of sins. So far this sounds familiar, for John the Baptist proclaimed a "baptism of repentance for the forgiveness of sins" (Mark 1:4); and Jesus made repentance central in his preaching (cf. Matt 4:17; Mark 1:15) and also baptized (cf. John 3:22, 26; 4:1–2). Judaism also had repentance at the core of its message and emphasized baptism (at least for proselytes). But while there is much that appears traditional in Peter's exhortation, there is also much that is new and distinctive—particularly in three ways.

In the first place, Peter calls on "every one" of his audience to repent and be baptized. Jews thought corporately and generally viewed the rite of baptism as appropriate only for proselytes (though some sects within Judaism baptized Jews). But like John the Baptist (cf. Matt 3:9–10)—and probably Jesus, though in distinction to Judaism generally —Peter called for an individual response on the part of his hearers. So he set aside family and corporate relationships as having any final saving significance and stressed the response of the person himself—not, however, denying the necessity and value of corporate relationships, but placing them in a "new covenant" perspective.

Second, Peter identifies the repentance and baptism he is speaking of as being specifically Christian in that it is done "in the name of Jesus Christ" (*epi tō onomati Iēsou Christou*). The expression was probably not at this time a liturgical formula; and it appears in Acts with the prepositions *epi* ("on") as here, though there are variations in the textual tradition, *en* ("in," 10:48) and *eis* ("into," 8:16; 19:5). What it means, it seems, is that a person in repenting and being baptized calls upon the name of Jesus (cf. 22:16) and thereby avows his or her intention to be committed to and identified with Jesus.

A third feature in Peter's preaching at this point is the relation of the gift of the Holy Spirit to repentance and baptism. "The gift of the Holy Spirit" is another way of describing what the disciples had experienced in "the coming of the Holy Spirit," which Jesus called "the baptism of the Holy Spirit" (cf. 1:4–5, 8). All three expressions are connected with God's promise to his people and are used interchangeably in Acts 1 and 2.

We need, however, to distinguish between "the gift" of the Holy Spirit and what Paul called "the gifts" (*ta pneumatika*, 1 Cor 12:1; 14:1) of that self-same Spirit. "The gift" is the Spirit himself given to minister the saving benefits of Christ's redemption to the believer, while "the gifts" are those spiritual abilities the Spirit gives variously to believers "for the common good" and sovereignly, "just as he determines" (1 Cor 12:7, 11). Peter's promise of the "gift of the Holy Spirit" is a logical outcome of repentance and baptism. This primary gift includes a variety of spiritual gifts for the advancement of the gospel and the welfare of God's people. But first of all, it has to do with what God's Spirit does for every Christian in applying and working out the benefits of Christ's redemptive work.

In trying to deal with the various elements in this passage, some interpreters have stressed the command to be baptized so as to link the forgiveness of sins exclusively with baptism. But it runs contrary to all biblical religion to assume that outward rites have any value apart from true repentance and an inward change. The Jewish mind, indeed, could not divorce inward spirituality from its outward expression (though those of Gr. orientation often have done this). Wherever the gospel was proclaimed in a Jewish milieu, the rite of baptism was taken for granted as being inevitably involved (cf. 2:41; 8:12, 36–38; 9:18; 10:47–48; 18:8; 19:5; also Heb 10:22; 1 Peter 3:18–21). But Peter's sermon in Solomon's Colonnade (cf. 3:12–26) stresses only repentance and turning to God "so that your sins may be wiped out" (v.19) and makes no mention of baptism. This shows that for Luke at least, and probably also for Peter, while baptism with water was the expected symbol for conversion, it was not an indispensable criterion for salvation.

A few commentators have set Peter's words in v.38 in opposition to those of John the Baptist in Mark 1:8 (and par.) and those of Jesus in Acts 1:5, where the baptism of the Holy Spirit is distinguished from John's baptism and appears to supersede it. But neither the Baptist's prophecy nor Jesus' promise necessarily implies that the baptism of the Spirit would set aside water baptism. Certainly the early church did not take it that way. They continued to practice water baptism as the external symbol by which those who believed the gospel, repented of their sins, and acknowledged Jesus as their Lord publicly bore witness to their new life, which had been received through the baptism of the Holy Spirit. In line, then, with the Baptist's prophecy and Jesus' promise, baptism with the Holy Spirit is distinguished from baptism with water. But baptism with the Holy Spirit did not replace baptism with water; rather, the latter was given a richer significance because of the saving work of Christ and the coming of the Spirit.

Again, some have observed that there is no mention in this passage, either in the report of Peter's preaching (vv.38–40) or in the summary of the people's response (v.41), of any speaking in tongues, as at Pentecost, or of laying on of hands, as in Samaria (8:17). From this various implications have been drawn. In a Jewish context, however, it would not have been surprising if both occurred; in fact, one is probably justified in being surprised had they not occurred. Nevertheless, that they are not mentioned implies (as with the omission of baptism in 3:19) that speaking in tongues and laying on of hands were not considered prerequisites for receiving the Spirit.

A more difficult problem arises when we try to correlate Peter's words here with the accounts of the Spirit's baptism in 8:15–17 (at Samaria), 10:44–46 (in the house of Cornelius), and 19:6 (at Ephesus). In v.38 the baptism of the Spirit is the logical outcome of repentance and water baptism; but in 8:15–17; 10:44–46; and 19:6 it appears to be temporally separated from conversion and water baptism—either following them (as at Samaria and Ephesus) or preceding them (as with Cornelius). Catholic sacramentalists take this as a biblical basis for separating baptism and confirmation; and Charismatics of various kinds see it as justification for a doctrine of the baptism of the Spirit as a second work of grace after conversion. But lest too much be made of this difference theologically, we ought first to attempt to understand the historical situation of vv.37–41 and to explain matters more circumstantially. Assuming for the moment that Luke shared Paul's view of the indissoluble connection between conversion, water baptism, and the baptism of the Holy Spirit (cf. Rom 8:9; 1 Cor 6:11), the following question may be asked: What if the Pentecost experience, particularly in regard to the sequence and temporal relations of conversion, water baptism, and Holy Spirit baptism, had been fully present in each of these latter three instances?

Take the Samaritans (8:4–8, 14–17), for example, who were converted through the instrumentality of Philip, one of the Hellenists expelled from Jerusalem at the time of

Stephen's martyrdom. Samaritans had always been considered second-class citizens of Palestine by the Jerusalem Jews who kept them at arm's length. What if it had been the apostles residing at Jerusalem who had been the missioners to Samaria? Probably they would have been rebuffed, just as they were earlier when the Samaritans associated them with the city of Jerusalem (cf. Luke 9:51-56). But God providentially used Philip to bring them the gospel—Philip, who had also (though for different reasons) been rebuffed at Jerusalem. The Samaritans received him and believed his message. But what if the Spirit had come upon them at their baptism by Philip? Undoubtedly what feelings some of the Christians at Jerusalem had against Philip and the Hellenists would have rubbed off on the Samaritan believers and they would have been doubly under suspicion. But God providentially withheld the gift of the Holy Spirit till Peter and John laid their hands on the Samaritans—Peter and John, two leading Jerusalem apostles who at that time would have been accepted by the new converts of Samaria. So in this first advance of the gospel outside Jerusalem, God worked in ways conducive both to the reception of the Good News in Samaria and the acceptance of these new converts at Jerusalem—ways that promoted both the outreach of the gospel and the unity of the church.

Or take the conversion of Cornelius (10:34-48). What if, in Peter's ministry to this Gentile, the order of events Peter had set down after his sermon at Pentecost had occurred (2:38)—viz., repentance, baptism, forgiveness of sins, reception of the gift of the Holy Spirit? Some at Jerusalem might have accused Peter of manipulating the occasion for his own ends (as his lengthy defense before the Jerusalem congregation in 11:1-18 takes pains to deny). But God in his providence gave the gift of his Spirit, coupled with such signs as would convince both Peter and his possible critics at Jerusalem, even *before* Cornelius's baptism, so that all would attribute his conversion entirely to God rather than let their prejudices make Cornelius a second-class Christian.

As for the incident recorded in 19:1-4, this, along with the other two passages just mentioned, will be dealt with in loc. But enough has been said here to suggest that we should understand Peter's preaching at Pentecost as being theologically normative for the relation in Acts between conversion, water baptism, and the baptism of the Holy Spirit, with the situations having to do with the Samaritan converts, Cornelius, and the twelve whom Paul met at Ephesus (which is something of a case all to itself) to be more historically conditioned and circumstantially understood.

39 The "promise" of which Peter speaks includes both the forgiveness of sins and the gift of the Holy Spirit. Both are logically and indissolubly united in applying Christ's redemptive work to the believer, and they were only separated chronologically, it seems, for what could be called circumstantial reasons. The promise, Peter declares, is not only for his immediate hearers ("for you") but also for succeeding generations ("for your children") and for all in distant places ("for all who are far off"). It is a promise, Peter concludes, that is sure; for it has been given by God and rests upon the prophetic word of Joel 2:32: "And everyone who calls on the name of the Lord will be saved."

Some prefer to see in the expression "for all who are far off" (*pasin tois eis makran*) a temporal reference to future Jewish generations (cf. BAG, p. 488), paralleling the phrase "for your children" (*tois teknois hymōn*). But *makran* ("far off") is not used temporally in the LXX or anywhere else in the NT, and therefore it is probably better interpreted more spatially than temporally.

A spatial interpretation, however, raises the question of whether *makran* ("far off") refers exclusively to Diaspora Jews or also includes Gentiles. That two OT remnant passages are alluded to here (Isa 57:19 ["Peace, peace, to those far and near"] and Joel

2:32) has led some commentators to assume that *makran* refers to Diaspora Jews. On the other hand, the use of Luke's report of Paul's defense in Jerusalem (22:21; cf. Eph 2:13) has led other commentators to argue that *makran* ("far off") refers also to Gentiles.

Probably this is one of those situations where a narrator like Luke has read into what the speaker said more than was originally there and so implied that the speaker spoke better than he knew. It seems difficult to believe that Peter himself thought beyond the perspective of Jewish remnant theology. Just as he could hardly have visualized anything beyond the next generation, so he could hardly have conceived of anything spatially beyond God's call to a scattered but repentant Jewish remnant. But Luke's desire is to show how an originally Jewish gospel penetrated the Gentile world so extensively that it came to enter "without hindrance" (cf. 28:31) into the capital of the Roman Empire. Very likely, therefore, in recounting Peter's words here in Acts, Luke meant them to be read as having Gentiles in mind, whatever one might argue Peter was thinking of at the time. So we may conclude that he used *makran* in the same sense as in 22:21.

40–41 Two summary statements conclude Luke's report of Peter's Pentecost sermon. The first has to do with Peter's further words; the second indicates the extent of the people's response.

The earnestness of Peter's words is connoted by the prepositions in the verbs *diamartyromai* ("warned") and *parakaleō* ("pleaded"), which tend to strengthen the usual verbs for "witness" (*martyreō*) and "call" (*kaleō*). And his characterization of this age as a "corrupt generation" is paralleled by Jesus' words (cf. Matt 16:4; 17:17) and by those of Paul (cf. Phil 2:15). What we have here is the vision of an evangelist—a vision that is all too often lost as the gospel is acclimated to the world and the world to the church.

The Jews generally looked on baptism as a rite only for Gentile converts (i.e., proselytes), not for one born a Jew. It symbolized the break with one's Gentile past and the washing away of all defilement. So when Jews accepted baptism in the name of Jesus on hearing Peter's message, it was traumatic and significant for them in a way we in our mildly christianized culture have difficulty understanding. But as a result of Peter's preaching, "about" 3,000 took the revolutionary step of baptism. And thus, Luke tells us, the congregation of believers in Jesus came into being at Jerusalem—a congregation made up of the original 120 (1:15) and progressively augmented (as the imperfect form of the verb *prostithēmi* ["added to"] seems to suggest) by about 3,000 others.

Notes

37 On ἄνδρες, ἀδελφοί (*andres, adelphoi*, "men, brothers") as a fraternal Jewish form of address, see the comments on 1:16 and the note on 2:14.

In addition to the omission of λοιπούς (*loipous*, "others"), D has τί οὖν ποιήσομεν (*ti oun poiēsomen*, "what then will we do?") which adds a "then" and changes the subjunctive to an indicative); τῇ καρδίᾳ (*tē kardia*, "in the heart," as in the LXX at Ps 109:16 [MT=108:16], which changes the accusative to a dative); and adds ὑποδείξατε ἡμῖν (*hypodeixate hēmin*, "show us") after *andres, adelphoi.*

38 The prepositions ἐπί (*epi*, "on") and ἐν (*en*, "in") were frequently employed interchangeably (cf. 10:48), which probably accounts for the variations in the MS evidence from B and D. Likewise, εἰς (*eis*, "into") in 8:16 and 19:5 should probably be interpreted as being synonomous (cf. 7:4, 12; 19:22).

In Heb. thought, God's renewal of his people by his Spirit and a symbolic cleansing with water go hand in hand (cf. Ezek 36:25–27; 1QS 4.20–21).

41 On the use of μὲν οὖν (men oun) as a favorite Lukan connective, see the comments on 1:6. Elsewhere in Acts it appears in concluding statements at 5:41; 8:25; 9:31; and 16:5.

Haenchen objects to the numbers three thousand here and five thousand at 4:4, arguing that it would have been impossible to be heard by such crowds without a microphone and that Jerusalem had only between twenty-five thousand and thirty thousand inhabitants total at the time (*Acts of the Apostles*, pp. 188–89, 215). In agreement with Dibelius, he insists, "It is far more probable that the little flock of Christians led 'a quiet, even in the Jewish sense "devout" life in Jerusalem. It was a modest existence, and nothing but the triumphant conviction of the faithful betrayed that from this flock was to go forth a movement which would transform the world'" (ibid., p. 189, quoting Dibelius, *Studies in Acts*, p. 124). Recent acoustical tests in Palestine, however, have shown that such features as sound reflection and low ambient noise levels would have allowed biblical preachers to address large audiences, at least in certain locations (cf. B.C. Crisler, "The Acoustics and Crowd Capacity of Natural Theaters in Palestine," BA, 39 [1976], 128–41). More importantly, however, the imperfect verb προσετίθει (*prosetithei*, "added") suggests something of a process as a result of Peter's preaching, not necessarily a large crowd of three thousand who heard and responded en masse. And the five thousand of 4:4 should probably be understood as the total number (cf. 6:7; 16:5), not five thousand at another time in addition to the three thousand, with those additional two thousand converts also probably being added through a process inaugurated by the miracle and preaching recorded in ch. 3.

Estimates of the number of inhabitants in Jerusalem during the first Christian century are interesting but highly inferential (as the debate between J. Jeremias, E. Stauffer, and E. Bammel, based on the numbers that could get into the temple precincts during festival periods, shows). Ultimately, however, Dibelius, Haenchen, et al. are asking us to take their word for it as to how the church prospered in its earliest days over Luke's word, whereas it was Luke's version that was accepted by the church within a century of the time itself. All in all, the grounds for the objections of Dibelius, Haenchen, et al. are tenuous.

Part I. The Christian Mission to the Jewish World (2:42–12:24)

Luke gives us the theme of Acts in Jesus' words: "You will be my witnesses in Jerusalem, and in all Judea and Samaria, and to the ends of the earth" (1:8). Behind them stands Deuteronomy 19:15, with its requirement that every matter be established by two or three witnesses (cf. R. Morgenthaler, *Die Lukanische Geschichtsschreibung als Zeugnis*, 2 vols. [Zürich: Zwingli, 1949]; Trites, esp. pp. 128–53). In his Gospel Luke has frequently highlighted such matters as (1) the witness of the Scriptures coupled with the ministry of Jesus and the witness of the Spirit, (2) the pairings of the disciples in their journeys on behalf of Jesus (cf. 10:1), and (3) the two angels at the tomb (cf. 24:4, whereas Matt 28:2–5 and Mark 16:5 have only one). In his organization of the common tradition, he set up a number of parallels between our Lord's ministry in Galilee (4:14–9:50) and his ministry in the regions of Perea and Judea (9:51–19:27). So in Acts Luke continues his pairings of apostolic men in their ministries (e.g., Peter and John in 3:1, 3–4, 11; 4:13, 19; 8:14; Barnabas and Saul in 11:25–26; 12:25; 13:2; Paul and Barnabas in 13:43, 46, 50; 15:2, 12, 22, 35; Judas and Silas in 15:32; Barnabas and Mark in 15:39; Paul and Silas in 15:40; 16:19, 25; 17:4, 10; and Silas and Timothy in 17:14–15; 18:5). Luke also sets up a number of parallels between the ministry of Peter in the first half of his work and the ministry of Paul in the last half: both heal a lame man (3:2–8; 14:8–10); both do miracles at some distance (5:15; 19:12); both exorcise evil spirits (5:16; 16:18); both defeat sorcerers (8:18–24; 13:6–11); both raise the dead (9:36–43; 20:9–12); both defend themselves against Jewish authorities (4:8–12; 5:27–32; 22:3–21; 23:1–6; 28:25–28); both receive heavenly visions (10:9–16; 16:9); both are involved in bestowing the Holy Spirit on new converts (8:14–17; 19:1–7); and both are miraculously released from prison (5:19; 12:7–11; 16:25–27). More importantly, both proclaim the same message and even use to some extent the same set of proof texts (e.g., Ps 16:10; cf. 2:27; 13:35).

It is, then, from Jesus' declaration about the apostles' witness (1:8) that Luke derives the framework for his narrative of Acts. First he portrays the mission of the Jerusalem apostles and their colleagues within the Jewish world; next he portrays the mission of Paul and his companions within the Gentile world. Luke presents this material in six blocks or panels—three of them are given to the mission to the Jews, three to the mission to the Gentiles.

Panel 1—The Earliest Days of the Church at Jerusalem (2:42–6:7)

Acts 2:42–6:7 describes the earliest days of the church at Jerusalem and covers the first three to five years of the new messianic movement (i.e., from A.D. 30 to the mid-thirties). Luke deals with the events of this period by means of a thesis paragraph followed by a series of vignettes that illustrate that paragraph. In 1:1–2:41 Luke has dealt in some detail with the constitutive events of the Christian mission. Had he continued on at that rate, his second book would have been inordinately long. So he begins to use illustrative vignettes and portrayals of representative situations drawn from many experiences within the early church to present his material more succinctly. This he does in order to help his readers feel the nature of what God was doing by his Spirit through the witness of the apostles.

A. A Thesis Paragraph on the State of the Early Church

2:42–47

> ⁴²They devoted themselves to the apostles' teaching and to the fellowship, to the breaking of bread and to prayer. ⁴³Everyone was filled with awe, and many wonders and miraculous signs were done by the apostles. ⁴⁴All the believers were together and had everything in common. ⁴⁵Selling their possessions and goods, they gave to anyone as he had need. ⁴⁶Every day they continued to meet together in the temple courts. They broke bread in their homes and ate together with glad and sincere hearts, ⁴⁷praising God and enjoying the favor of all the people. And the Lord added to their number daily those who were being saved.

In addition to the six summary statements (6:7; 9:31; 12:24; 16:5; 19:20; 28:31) that respectively conclude the six panels or blocks of material, Acts also has in its first panel three short summary-like paragraphs (2:42–47; 4:32–35; and 5:12–16). Each of the latter two of these three paragraphs introduces the block of material that immediately follows it, with the specific details in that material directly related to the respective introductory paragraph. But the first of the three paragraphs (2:42–47) is longer than the others and introduces the entire first panel of material.

Rather than credit this paragraph to some supposed "Recension B" of a Jerusalem-Caesarean source (Harnack), or partly to some older body of material and partly to Luke's redaction (Jeremias, Cerfaux, and Benoit, though variously), we take vv.42–47 to be Luke's own thesis paragraph on the state of the church in its earliest days at Jerusalem.

Furthermore, we take the rest of the first panel to explicate by means of a series of vignettes the various points made in this first thesis paragraph.

42 Luke begins to describe the early church by telling us that the believers in it were distinguished by their devotion to the apostles' teaching, to fellowship with one another, to "breaking of bread," and "to prayer." The verb translated "devoted" (*proskartereō*) is a common one that connotes a steadfast and singleminded fidelity to a certain course of action. Luke uses it elsewhere in Acts to characterize the devotion of the 120 in the upper room to prayer (1:14) and the apostles' resolve in the matter of the Hellenistic widows to center their attention on prayer and the ministry of the word (6:4).

"The apostles' teaching" refers to a body of material considered authoritative because it was the message about Jesus of Nazareth proclaimed by accredited apostles. It undoubtedly included a compilation of the words of Jesus (cf. 20:35), some account of his earthly ministry, passion, and resurrection (cf. 2:22–24), and a declaration of what all this meant for man's redemption (cf. 1 Cor 15:3–5)—all of which was thought of in terms of a Christian "tradition" (*paradosis*) that could be passed on to others (cf. 1 Cor 11:2; 1 Thess 2:13; 2 Thess 2:15; 3:6). The number of references to teachers, teaching, and tradition within Acts and the letters to the churches (here, as well as in Rom 6:17; 12:7; 16:17; 1 Cor 11:2; 14:26; 2 Thess 2:15; 3:6; James 3:1), and the frequent linking of prophets and teachers in the NT (cf. Acts 13:1; 1 Cor 12:28; 14:6; Eph 4:11), suggest that—while not necessarily antithetical—the creative role of prophecy in the early church was balanced by the conserving role of teaching. Undoubtedly the early congregation at Jerusalem, amid differences of perspective and along with a lively eschatological expectation, had a general "sense of center" provided by the historical and doctrinal teaching of the apostles. And this, Luke tells us, was preeminently the *raison d'être* ("reason for being") and the focus of the early Christian community.

The definite article (*tē*) in "the fellowship" (*tē koinōnia*) implies that there was something distinctive in the gatherings of the early believers. With the influx of three thousand on the Day of Pentecost and with daily increases to their number after that (cf. 2:47), they must have had some externally recognizable identity. Perhaps in those early days others thought of them as a "Synagogue of Nazarenes" (cf. Tertullus's accusation in 24:5, which links them to "the Nazarene sect") and gave them a place among other such groups within the mosaic of Judaism. But the Christian community was not just a sect of Judaism, even though they continued to observe Jewish rites and customs and had no intention of breaking with the nation or its institutions. They held to the centrality of Jesus of Nazareth in the redemptive program of God and in their worship. Their proclamation of Jesus as Israel's promised Messiah and mankind's Lord set them apart in Jerusalem as a distinguishable entity.

Just what is meant by "the breaking of bread" in v.42 has been vigorously debated. Was it a type of Jewish fellowship meal (like the "Haburah" meals of the Pharisees), which showed the believers' mutual love and recalled their earlier association with Jesus but was devoid of any paschal significance as Paul later "illegitimately" saw in it (as H. Lietzmann charges)? Or was it in these early years a paschal commemoration of Christ's death, in line with Paul's later elaboration (cf. J. Jeremias)? Or was it at first an agape feast that emphasized the joy of communion with the risen Lord and of fellowship with one another, which Paul later quite "legitimately" saw to have also paschal import, in line with the intention of Jesus (cf. O. Cullmann)? The matter is somewhat difficult to determine, for while 2:42 and 20:7 may very well relate to the full Pauline understanding

(1 Cor 10:16; 11:24), and while Luke earlier referred to "the breaking of bread" in that way in his passion narrative (Luke 22:19), elsewhere he uses it for an ordinary meal (cf. Luke 24:30, 35; Acts 20:11; 27:35) and seems to mean just that even in 2:46.

Yet it is difficult to believe that Luke had in mind here only an ordinary meal, placing the expression, as he does, between two such religiously loaded terms as "the fellowship" and "prayer." Even an ordinary meal among Jews, of course, would have had something of a sacred flavor. In a Christian setting, where hearts were warmed by devotion, it would have been an occasion for joy, love, and praise connected inevitably with Jesus. Probably "the breaking of bread" should also be understood as subtly connoting the passion of Christ—though, of course, there may very well have been a deepening of understanding with regard to Christ's passion as the church's theology came more and more into focus, in accord with Paul's later elaboration of it.

References to "prayer" are frequent both in the summary statements and the narrative of Acts (in addition to 2:42, see 1:14, 24; 4:24-31; 6:4, 6; 9:40; 10:2, 4, 9, 31; 11:5; 12:5; 13:3; 14:23; 16:25; 22:17; 28:8). Just as Luke has set up in Luke-Acts the parallelism between the Spirit's work in relation to Jesus and the Spirit's work in the church, so he also sets up the parallelism between prayer in the life of Jesus and prayer in the life of the church. His use here of both the definite article and the plural in "the prayers" (*tais proseuchais*) suggest formal prayers, probably both Jewish and Christian. The earliest believers not only viewed the old forms as filled with new content, but also in their enthusiasm they fashioned new vehicles for their praise. In addition, it is not difficult to envision the earliest believers using extemporaneous prayers built on past models— such as Mary's *Magnificat* (Luke 1:46-55), Zechariah's Song of Praise (Luke 1:67-79), or Simeon's *Nunc Dimittis* (Luke 2:28-32).

43 Furthermore, Luke tells us that a lingering sense of awe rested on many who did not take their stand with the Christians and that miraculous things were done by the apostles. "Everyone" (*pasē psychē*), in contradistinction to "all the believers" (*pantes hoi pisteusantes*) of v.44, refers hyperbolically to nonbelievers in Jerusalem who knew of the events of Pentecost and were observing the life of the early congregation in the months that followed. In the expression "wonders and miraculous signs" (*terata kai sēmeia*), Luke picks up the phraseology of Joel's prophecy (cf. 2:19) and of Peter's characterization of Jesus' ministry (cf. 2:22). Luke probably used it to suggest that the miracles the apostles did should be taken as evidences of the presence of God with his people, just as throughout the ministry of Jesus the miracles he did showed that God was with him. The use of the verb *ginomai* ("to be") in the imperfect tense denotes that the awe "was" and the miracles "were" no momentary phenomena but continued to happen during those early days.

44-45 Within the Christian congregation at Jerusalem, the believers' sense of spiritual unity expressed itself in communal living and sharing with the needy members of their group. While Acts implies that overt persecution of Christians came somewhat later, in certain instances economic and social sanctions were undoubtedly imposed on the early believers. So the communal life described in vv.44-45 should be understood, at least in part, as a response to these pressures. Such treatment of minority groups is not uncommon, as both ancient and contemporary history show. In addition, the analogies that exist between the early Jewish Christians and the Qumran covenanters suggest that the Jewish Christians in stressing the primacy of spiritual community reflected a practice common to various Jewish sects (of which Qumran is a prominent example) of holding possessions in community. The repeated use of the imperfect tense in these two verses (five times) shows that this was their established practice, which involved both what we would call their real estate ("possessions," *ktēmata*) and their personal possessions ("goods," *hyparxeis*).

46 Here Luke shows that the early Jerusalem believers expressed their faith through daily adherence to the accustomed forms of their Jewish heritage. They not only ate together in their homes in a spirit of gladness and sincerity but also found a large measure of favor among the people. "Every day" (*kath' hēmeran*) applies to the whole sentence (which NIV breaks into two sentences) as far as the words "all the people" in the middle of v.47 and ties together a number of complementary ideas.

The favorite meeting place of the early believers was in the temple (cf. Luke 24:53), at the eastern edge of the outer court called Solomon's Colonnade (cf. 3:11; 5:12). There, in typically Semitic fashion, they carried on their discussions and offered praise to God. As Jews who were Christians and also Christians who were Jews, they not only considered Jerusalem to be their city but continued to regard the temple as their sanctuary and the Law as their law. Evidently they thought of themselves as the faithful remnant within Israel for whose sake all the institutions and customs of the nation existed. As such, their refocused eschatological hopes (cf. Mal 3:1) and all their desires to influence their own people were associated with the city of Jerusalem, the Jerusalem temple, and the Mosaic law. For both theological and practical reasons, therefore, as well as because of the inevitable tug of the traditional, the early Christians in Jerusalem sought to retain their hold on the religious forms they had inherited and to express their new faith through the categories of the old.

But while they met formally for discussion and worship in the temple precincts, they took their meals in their own homes (*kat' oikon*, lit. "by households"). The noun *trophē* ("food," "nourishment") in the phrase "they were sharing in the food" (*metelambanon tropēs*; NIV, "ate together") implies a substantial meal (cf. 9:19; 27:33-34), which it is said they ate with gladness and sincerity of heart.

47a In Luke's writings, "the people" (*ho laos*) usually refers to Israel as the elect nation to whom the message of redemption is initially directed and for whom (together with the Gentiles) it is ultimately intended (e.g., 3:9; 4:10; 5:13). Later in the narrative of Acts, the attitude of "the people" becomes more and more antagonistic to the Christian gospel and its missioners. But in this first panel we have a response of the people that is largely favorable toward the early Christians and their manner of life. This cannot be said for the attitude of the Sadducees as depicted in 4:1ff. and 5:17ff. (Later in the commentary, reasons will be given for the change of attitude on the part of the people that begins with Acts' second panel and worsens as the narrative develops.) What can be said here is that Luke shows, both in his emphasis on the early Christians' meeting in the temple courts and on the favor accorded them by the people, that early Christianity is the fulfillment of all that is truly Jewish and that it directed its mission first to the Jewish world. Luke continues to stress these themes throughout his second volume.

47b Luke's thesis paragraph on the state of the early church at Jerusalem concludes with the triumphant note that "the Lord added to their number daily those who were being saved"—a note that runs throughout this first panel but is not confined to it. It is the Lord himself who adds to his church, and thus the title *ho kyrios* ("the Lord") appears first in the sentence not only for grammatical reasons but also for emphasis. The force of the present participle *tous sōzomenous* ("those who were being saved") is iterative, suggesting that they were added *as* they were being saved. For a discussion of the expression "to their number" (*epi to auto*), see note on v.44.

Notes

44 One such analogy between the early Jewish Christians and the Qumran covenanters is the correspondence between the difficult phrase ἐπὶ τὸ αὐτό (*epi to auto;* NIV, "were together," cf. v.47) and the technical use of the term יחד (*yaḥad*, "the gathered fellowship") at Qumran.

45 The Western text reads καὶ ὅσοι κτήματα εἶχον ἢ ὑπάρξεις (*kai hosoi ktēmata eichon ē hyparxeis*, "and as many as had possessions and goods"), thereby qualifying the πάντες (*pantes*, "all") of v.44.

The word κτῆμα (*ktēma*) literally means a possession of any kind, but it came to be restricted to "landed property," "a field," or "a piece of ground." Its synonym ὕπαρξις (*hyparxis*) when used in tandem with *ktēma* likely signifies more what we would call personal possessions apart from real estate.

46 This is the only occurrence of ἀφελότης (*aphelotēs*, "sincere," NIV) in the NT, though it appears in the second-century writer Vettius Valens (153.30; 240.15) to mean something like "simplicity" or "generosity."

The Western text reads ὅλον τὸν κόσμον (*holon ton kosmon*, "all the world") for ὅλον τὸν λαόν (*holon ton laon*, "all the people"), thereby missing the point of Luke's emphasis.

47 The Western text reads ἐν τῇ ἐκκλησίᾳ (*en tē ekklēsia*, "in the church") for ἐπὶ τὸ αὐτό (*epi to auto*, "to their number"), thereby missing the point of the idiom, though rightly understanding the general thrust of the sentence.

B. *A Crippled Beggar Healed* (3:1–26)

In 2:42–47, Luke has spoken of the early Christians' continued attendance at the temple, the wonders and miracles the apostles did, the awe many of the Jews felt, and the apostles' teaching. Now he gives us a vignette illustrating these things. Much like the synoptic tradition that selected the healing of a leper as "Exhibit A" to represent the nature of Jesus' early ministry in Galilee (cf. Mark 1:40–45), or John's Gospel that uses the healing of a Capernaum official's son for the same purpose (cf. John 4:46–54), Luke now singles out this episode in the history of the early Jerusalem congregation to "bring the reader into the picture." No doubt the episode at the time was well known and frequently recounted in the early church long before Luke wrote of it.

1. *The healing*

3:1–10

¹One day Peter and John were going up to the temple at the time of prayer—at three in the afternoon. ²Now a man crippled from birth was being carried to the temple gate called Beautiful, where he was put every day to beg from those going into the temple courts. ³When he saw Peter and John about to enter, he asked them for money. ⁴Peter looked straight at him, as did John. Then Peter said, "Look at us!" ⁵So the man gave them his attention, expecting to get something from them.

⁶Then Peter said, "Silver or gold I do not have, but what I have I give you. In the name of Jesus Christ of Nazareth, walk." ⁷Taking him by the right hand, he helped him up, and instantly the man's feet and ankles became strong. ⁸He jumped to his feet and began to walk. Then he went with them into the temple courts, walking and jumping, and praising God. ⁹When all the people saw him

walking and praising God, [10]they recognized him as the same man who used to sit begging at the temple gate called Beautiful, and they were filled with wonder and amazement at what had happened to him.

1 The story of the healing of the crippled beggar begins with the straightforward statement that Peter and John went up to the temple at the time of prayer. In the Greek the pericope begins without a strong connective (though D apparently felt the need for a stronger connective and so begins with "in these days"; likewise, NIV has "one day"). This seems to suggest that the story originally circulated among Christians separately and for its own sake.

That the apostles were living in Jerusalem immediately after Jesus' ascension is in accord with his instructions to "stay in the city until you have been clothed with power from on high" (Luke 24:49), to "not leave Jerusalem, but wait for the gift my Father promised" (Acts 1:4), and to begin their mission there (Acts 1:8; cf. Luke 24:47). But what kept these Galilean disciples in Jerusalem after Pentecost? and why did Jewish Christianity become centered in Jerusalem rather than Galilee? Lohmeyer's thesis that there were really two centers of Christianity in Palestine from the earliest days, a Galilean and a Jerusalemite one, and that Acts has blurred the situation by locating the apostles from Galilee in Jerusalem is not convincing (Ernest Lohmeyer, *Galiläa und Jerusalem* [Gottingen: Vandenhoeck & Ruprecht, 1936]; cf. L.E. Elliott-Binns, *Galilean Christianity* [London: SCM, 1956]).

While there were Christians in Galilee who formed themselves into congregations there (cf. 9:31), the earliest extant Christian writings, the Pauline letters, take into account only the Jerusalem community and associate the Galilean apostles directly with that (cf. Gal 1:18–2:10; 1 Thess 2:14). It may be said with certainty, therefore, that the early Christians looked on Jerusalem as being of central importance. As God's righteous remnant within Israel and members of the Messiah's eschatological community, the apostles, even though originally from Galilee, centered their activities in Jerusalem. Along with that went their continued adherence to Israel's institutions and forms of worship. So Peter and John are presented as "going up to the temple at the time of prayer—at three in the afternoon" (lit., "at the ninth hour").

The stated times for prayer in Judaism were (1) early in the morning, in connection with the morning sacrifice; (2) at the ninth hour of the day, in connection with the evening sacrifice; and (3) at sunset (cf. SBK, 2:696–98). The imperfect verb *anebainon* ("they were going up") conveys a vivid visual impression of the apostles' movement toward Jerusalem. Going to the temple is always spoken of in terms of "going up"—principally out of reverential respect, though also because of location (Luke 18:10; John 7:14; Acts 11:2; cf. 15:2; 18:22).

2–3 The man is described as "crippled from birth" (*chōlos ek koilias mētros autou*, lit., "crippled from his mother's womb") and having to be carried daily "to the temple gate called Beautiful" to beg for his living. Since almsgiving was classed in Judaism as a meritorious act (cf. SBK, 1:387–88), he was placed at the gate so that those coming to the temple could gain merit by giving him a coin.

Just which gate is referred to as "Beautiful" is not easy to determine. Neither Josephus nor the Talmud refers to such a temple gate. And while Hellenistic Jews commonly called the entire temple complex "the temple" (*to hieron*) and reserved for the temple proper with its porch the name "Holy Place" and "Holy of Holies" (*ho naos*; cf. SBK, 1:150–51), Luke did not always maintain this distinction in Luke-Acts. We cannot, therefore, depend on his use of *to hieron* as a guide to whether "the gate called Beautiful" had to do with the outer court or one of the inner courts.

Since the fifth century A.D., the Eastern or Shushan Gate (so called because it portrays the palace of Shushan, or Susa), which is on the east side of the outer court and remained standing after the destruction of Jerusalem, has been identified by many as the Beautiful Gate. The weight of evidence from Josephus (Antiq. XV, 410–25 [xi.5–7]; War V, 190–221 [v.2–4]) and the Mishnah tractate *Middoth* (1:3–4; 2.3), however, favor identifying the Beautiful Gate with the Nicanor Gate (so named for a certain Nicanor, who in a perilous storm desired to be thrown overboard with the gate during its transport from Alexandria to Jerusalem and for whose sake a miracle occurred preserving both; cf. M *Yoma* 3:10). This gate led from the eastern part of the outer court (Court of the Gentiles) into the first of the inner courts (Court of the Women). Josephus describes it as having been overlaid with Corinthian bronze and says that it "far exceeded in value those plated with silver and set in gold" (War V, 201 [v.3]).

4–6 In response to the beggar's request for money, Peter fixed his eyes on him and said, "Look at us!" Thinking he had a benefactor, the beggar looked up expectantly. To his astonishment he heard the words: "In the name of Jesus Christ of Nazareth, walk." In Semitic thought, a name does not just identify or distinguish a person; it expresses the very nature of his being. Hence the power of the person is present and available in the name of the person. Peter, therefore, does not just ask the risen Jesus to heal but pronounces over the crippled beggar the name of Jesus, thereby releasing the power of Jesus (cf. 3:16; 4:10). And the power of the risen Jesus, coupled with the man's response of faith (cf. 3:16), effects the healing.

7–10 The healing is described as an instantaneous one, accomplishing in a moment what God in his providence through the normal healing processes usually takes months to do. The effect on the man was traumatic.

Some commentators have complained that structurally v.8 is overloaded in comparison with the rest of the narrative—what with all the walking about and jumping and praising God going on. But such a comment only reflects our jaded sensibilities in the presence of divine grace. Certainly it would have been hard to convince the man himself that his response was excessive. As for the people, they were "filled with wonder and amazement." What was taking place was but a token, to those who had eyes to see, of the presence of the Messianic Age, of which the prophet had long ago predicted: "Then will the lame leap like a deer" (Isa 35:6).

Notes

---

1 Even W. Marxsen, in *Mark the Evangelist*, tr. R.A. Harrisville (Nashville: Abingdon, 1969), acknowledges Lohmeyer to be in error here, though he goes on to try to salvage something of Lohmeyer's thesis by deducing from Mark's "eschatological-geographical" interest in Galilee the existence of a later Galilean Christianity that rivaled that in Jerusalem. But while there were undoubtedly Christians and a church in Galilee throughout the first Christian century, the full development of Marxsen's thesis is at best highly inferential.

The inclusion of John along with Peter has often been credited to Luke's redactional activity alone: (1) John seems to be somewhat tacked on in v.4; (2) Peter speaks in the singular in v.6; and

(3) John remains very much the silent partner throughout. But while Luke is obviously very interested in developing his two-witness motif wherever possible, it was not unusual for Peter to take the lead and overshadow his colleagues. Luke could not very well have had them address the crippled beggar in unison, particularly if the miracle occurred principally in response to Peter's invocation of Jesus' name.

2 Κοιλία (koilia) means both a "stomach" and a "womb" and appears in the NT with both meanings. Luke, however, always uses it in the latter sense (cf. Luke 1:15, 42; Acts 14:8).

6 The reading περιπάτει (peripatei, "walk") is better attested externally (א B D etc.), though ἔγειρε καὶ περιπάτει (egeire kai peripatei, "arise and walk") also appears widely in the textual sources (A C etc., and in many of the Fathers).

7 The expression παραχρῆμα (parachrēma, "instantly") is a favorite of Luke's, appearing in Luke 1:64; 4:39; 5:25; 8:44, 47, 55; 13:13; 18:43; 19:11; 22:60; Acts 3:7 (here); 5:10; 12:23; 13:11; 16:26, 33. Elsewhere in the NT it is used only in Matt 21:19-20 (also D has it at Acts 14:10).

9 On Luke's use of ὁ λαός (ho laos, "the people"), see comments on 2:47a.

---

2. Peter's sermon in Solomon's Colonnade

3:11-26

> [11]While the beggar held on to Peter and John, all the people were astonished and came running to them in the place called Solomon's Colonnade. [12]When Peter saw this, he said to them: "Men of Israel, why does this surprise you? Why do you stare at us as if by our own power or godliness we had made this man walk? [13]The God of Abraham, Isaac and Jacob, the God of our fathers, has glorified his servant Jesus. You handed him over to be killed, and you disowned him before Pilate, though he had decided to let him go. [14]You disowned the Holy and Righteous One and asked that a murderer be released to you. [15]You killed the author of life, but God raised him from the dead. We are witnesses of this. [16]By faith in the name of Jesus, this man whom you see and know was made strong. It is Jesus' name and the faith that comes through him that has given this complete healing to him, as you can all see.
>
> [17]"Now, brothers, I know that you acted in ignorance, as did your leaders. [18]But this is how God fulfilled what he had foretold through all the prophets, saying that his Christ would suffer. [19]Repent, then, and turn to God, so that your sins may be wiped out, that times of refreshing may come from the Lord, [20]and that he may send the Christ, who has been appointed for you—even Jesus. [21]He must remain in heaven until the time comes for God to restore everything, as he promised long ago through his holy prophets. [22]For Moses said, 'The Lord your God will raise up for you a prophet like me from among your own people; you must listen to everything he tells you. [23]Anyone who does not listen to him will be completely cut off from among his people.'
>
> [24]"Indeed, all the prophets from Samuel on, as many as have spoken, have foretold these days. [25]And you are heirs of the prophets and of the covenant God made with your fathers. He said to Abraham, 'Through your offspring all peoples on earth will be blessed.' [26]When God raised up his servant, he sent him first to you to bless you by turning each of you from your wicked ways."

Peter's sermon in Solomon's Colonnade is in many ways similar to his sermon at Pentecost (2:14-41). Structurally, both move from proclamation to a call for repentance. The Pentecost sermon, however, is finished and polished, whereas this one is comparatively roughhewn. Thematically, both focus on the denial and vindication of Jesus of Nazareth. But the Colonnade sermon expresses more of a remnant theology than the one at Pentecost. It shows a more generous attitude toward Israel, coupled with a greater stress on the nation's responsibility for the Messiah's death, than does the Pentecost sermon; and it makes explicit the necessity of receiving God's grace by faith. Christologically, Peter's sermon here (like his defense in 4:8–12) incorporates a number of archaic and primitive titles used of Jesus within early Jewish Christianity.

It seems strange, at first glance, that in his narrative Luke would place two such similar sermons of Peter so close together. But his putting the Pentecost sermon in the introductory section of Acts was evidently meant to be a kind of paradigm of early apostolic preaching—a paradigm Luke seems to have polished for greater literary effectiveness. As for the Colonnade sermon, Luke seems to have included it as an example of how the early congregation in Jerusalem proclaimed the message of Jesus to the people of Israel as a whole. Moreover, the material containing both the story of the miracle and Peter's sermon probably came to Luke as something of a self-contained unit, which he evidently was willing, for the most part, to leave in the form he found it.

11 We are not given many of the "stage directions" for Peter's Colonnade sermon. What we are told, however, is significant: (1) the healed cripple "held on to" (*kratountos*) Peter and John so as not to let them get away (*krateō* is also used to describe a police arrest, as in Matt 14:3; 21:46; 26:4, 48, 50, 55, 57); (2) "the people" came running to them in Solomon's Colonnade; and (3) they were "astonished" at what had happened. Solomon's Colonnade was a covered portico that ran the entire length of the eastern portion of the outer court of the temple precincts, along and just inside the eastern wall of the temple (cf. 5:12; John 10:23).

12–16 The proclamation section of the sermon is an exposition on "the name of Jesus" (twice repeated in v.16). Structurally and syntactically, v.16 is the most difficult verse in the chapter, probably because Luke chose to do less editorial polishing here since he saw that it contained the statement of Peter's theme.

The sermon begins by denying that it was through the apostles' "own power or godliness" that the cripple was healed. Rather, "the God of Abraham, Isaac and Jacob" brought about the healing that glorified Jesus. Just as Peter earlier spoke of God as the true author of Jesus' miracles (cf. 2:22), so here he attributes solely to God such wonders as occurred in the apostles' ministries. And just as Jesus' miracles were done by God to accredit him before the people (cf. again 2:22), so miracles continued to be done through the apostles in order for God to glorify Jesus.

The sermon focuses on God's Servant, Jesus, whom Israel disowned and killed but God raised from the dead. It is through his name and the faith that comes through him that the healing of the crippled beggar occurred. In speaking of Jesus, Peter uses a number of primitive and archaic christological titles. Their concentration in these few verses has rightly been considered highly significant by many.

The sermon begins and ends by ascribing to Jesus the title "God's Servant" (*ho pais autou*, vv.13, 26), which echoes the Servant theme of Isaiah 42–53—cf. "[he] has glorified his servant Jesus" (v.13) with "my servant . . . will be raised and lifted up and highly exalted" (Isa 52:13)—and the theme of Moses as prophet (Deut 18:15, 18–19; cf. the "raising up" motif of Acts 3:22, 26 with Deut 18:15, 18). It includes the titles "the Holy One" (*ho hagios*, v.14) and "the Righteous One" (*ho dikaios*, v.14), the ascription "the author of life" (*ho archēgos tēs zōēs*, v.15), and a reference to Jesus as "a prophet like me [Moses]" (*ho prophētēs hōs eme*, vv.22–23). And it stresses "the name of Jesus" as the powerful agent in the miracle—a significant fact since "the Name" (*to onoma*) was a pious Jewish surrogate for God and connoted his divine presence and power.

17–18 What strikes the reader immediately in the call-to-repentance section of Peter's sermon is its attitude toward Israel, which in its hopeful outlook is unmatched in the rest of the NT (except for certain features in Paul's discussion of Rom 9–11). In v.12 Peter addressed his audience as "Men of Israel" and in v.13 spoke of God as "the God of our [*hēmōn*] fathers." And though he had emphasized Israel's part in crucifying Jesus (vv.13–15), he now magnanimously says that they had acted "in ignorance" and, somewhat surprisingly, includes their leaders in this. Then he mitigates their guilt still further by saying that God himself had willed it in order to fulfill the words of the prophets.

19–21 Even more positively, Peter goes on to say that if his hearers repent, their repentance will have a part in ushering in the great events of the end time (cf. the idea of purpose expressed in the conjunction *hopōs*, "that," which starts v.20). Evidently Luke wants us to understand Peter's call to repentance here as being set within the context of a remnant theology and as being quite unlike Stephen's attitude (cf. ch. 7). Not only so, but he also wants us to view the earliest proclamation of the gospel in the Jewish world as a kind of intramural effort, with a self-conscious, righteous remnant issuing prophetic denunciations of Israel's part in the crucifixion of their Messiah and appealing to the people to turn to God in repentance for the remission of their sins.

The call to repentance itself is tersely stated. Then it is elaborated in words unique in the NT and reflective of Jewish remnant theology. "Repent, then, and turn to God," says Peter, "so that your sins may be wiped out"—and, further, so that there may be brought about the promised "times of refreshing" and that with the coming of God's appointed Messiah (*ton prokecheirismenon Christon*, lit., "the foreordained Christ"), he may "restore everything." The expressions "times of refreshing" (*kairoi anapsyxeōs*, v.20) and "to restore everything" (*chronoi apokatastaseōs pantōn*, v.21) are without parallel in the NT, though the verb *apokathistēmi* ("restore"), the verbal form of *apokatastasis* ("restoration"), is often used in the LXX of the eschatological restoration of Israel (cf. Jer 15:19; 16:15; 24:6; 50:19 [27:19 LXX]; Ezek 16:55; Hos 11:11).

Verses 20b and 21 present problems of interpretation because of their chronological ambiguity—viz., "that times of refreshing may come from the Lord and that he may send the Christ, who has been appointed for you—even Jesus. He must remain in heaven until the time comes for God to restore everything, as he promised long ago through his holy prophets." Robinson has suggested that here we probably have "the most primitive Christology of all" (J.A.T. Robinson, "The Most Primitive Christology of All?" JTS, 7 [1956], 177–89; cf. also his *Twelve New Testament Studies* [London: SCM, 1962], pp. 139–53). He says this because he takes the expression "the foreordained Christ" as an affirmation that messiahship was for Jesus a matter *for the future*. As Robinson views it (setting forth a Bultmannian position), Jesus was considered by the earliest believers to be "Messiah-designate" awaiting the future coming of the Son of Man (another than Jesus), who would then appoint Jesus to be Messiah in fact. Therefore, Robinson believes that in 3:19–21 we have an outcropping of that earliest stratum of christological speculation, which must have quickly faded away and which was later replaced by the Christology of Acts 2 and the remainder of Acts 3 and by the attribution of present messiahship to Jesus found throughout the rest of the NT. In fact, Robinson insists, Jesus was first considered only as Messiah-designate in the earliest congregation at Jerusalem, though later he was elevated in the thought of Christians to the actual rank of Messiah.

Robinson's view, however, entails two exegetical difficulties. First, he imposes on vv.20b–21 a rigid chronological structure unwarranted by the text itself. That Jesus is identified as "the foreordained Christ [Messiah]"—"the Christ who has been appointed for you" (NIV)—is clear. But the question as to when that messianic ordination was revealed or is to be revealed is not anywhere as clear as Robinson assumes. One could just as well read v.20 as "that he may send the foreordained Christ *again*" (understanding the Gr. *palin*, "again," to be in mind) as "that he may send the foreordained *and future* Christ" (as Robinson assumes).

Second, Robinson's interpretation makes Luke appear incredibly naive in placing two such distinct and differing Christologies (as Robinson would have it) side by side; for in v.18, which immediately precedes this passage, the Messiah of God (*ton Christon autou*, "his Christ") is identified as being the one who suffered. Yet Robinson would have us believe that in vv.19-21 Luke also inserts an affirmation that messiahship is only to be looked for in the future. To argue that Luke included vv.19-21 only to refute it by the preface of v.18, as Robinson speculates may have been the case, is absurd. Luke could better have refuted the supposedly earlier Christology of vv.19-21, should that have been his desire, simply by omitting it. And to say that Luke did not recognize the discrepancy, as Robinson thinks more likely, is to make him astonishingly obtuse. What has happened is that Robinson, having detached vv.19-21 from the context and played on the looseness of expression that results when they are read out of context, takes the liberty of imposing temporal strictures on the passage at the point where it is ambiguous when detached from its context. But Luke intended for it to be read *in context*. And when read in context, the passage sets up no contradictory messianology—though, admittedly, it may not be as chronologically precise as one might wish.

22-26 No group within Israel that considered itself to be God's righteous remnant in the inauguration of the final eschatological days could expect to win a hearing among Jews without attempting to define its position vis-à-vis Israel's great leaders of the past—particularly Abraham, Moses, and David. And that is exactly what Luke shows Peter doing as he concludes his call for repentance.

In vv.22-23 Peter does this with respect to Moses by quoting Deuteronomy 18:15, 18-19 ("The Lord your God will raise up for you a prophet like me . . ."). This was a widely accepted messianic proof text of the time, one that emphasized the command to "listen to him" by the addition of the phrase "in everything he tells you." Peter's argument here, though not stated, is implicitly twofold: (1) true belief in Moses will lead to a belief in Jesus, and (2) belief in Jesus places one in true continuity with Moses.

In v.24 Peter does this with respect to David by alluding to Samuel and all the prophets who followed him and by insisting that they too "foretold these days." Now it is certainly difficult to find any prophecy of Samuel that could be applied to Jesus as explicitly as the words of Moses just quoted. But Samuel was the prophet who anointed David to be king and spoke of the establishment of his kingdom (cf. 1 Sam 16:13; see also 13:14; 15:28; 28:17). Furthermore, Nathan's prophecy regarding the establishment of David's seed ("offspring," NIV) as recorded in 2 Samuel 7:12-16 was accepted in certain quarters within Late Judaism as having messianic relevance (cf. 4QFlor) and taken by Christians as having been most completely fulfilled in Jesus (cf. 13:22-23, 34; Heb 1:5).

In v. 25 Peter goes on to identify commitment to Jesus as Messiah with the promise God made to Abraham, quoting Genesis 22:18 and 26:4: "Through your offspring [lit., 'seed'] all nations on earth will be blessed." What exegetically ties this portion together with what has preceded it is, evidently, the word "offspring," which appears in 2 Samuel 7:12 in reference to David's descendants and in Genesis 22:18 and 26:4 in reference to the descendants of Abraham. And on the basis of the Hebrew exegetical principle

$g^e z\bar{e}r\hat{a}h\ \check{s}\bar{a}w\hat{a}h$ (i.e., verbal analogy: where the same words are applied to two separate cases it follows that the same considerations apply to both), Peter proclaims that the promise to Abraham also has its ultimate fulfillment in Christ.

Peter's call to repentance in this sermon is an expression of the remnant theology of the earliest Christian believers at Jerusalem. He addresses his hearers as "heirs of the prophets and of the covenant." He uses both a pesher approach (a "this is that" application) and midrashic exegesis (e.g., $g^e z\bar{e}r\hat{a}h\ \check{s}\bar{a}w\hat{a}h$) in his treatment of Scripture. And he concludes with an offer of blessing extended first to individuals of the nation Israel: "When God raised up his servant, he sent him first to you to bless you by turning each of you from your wicked ways" (v.26). In the Greek, *hymin prōton* ("first to you") comes first in the sentence and so occupies the emphatic position. Many have thought that this stress upon Israel "first" is merely a Pauline import by the hand of Luke (cf. 13:46; Rom 1:16; 2:9–10). But to assume this entails failure to see the remnant context of the sermon and the remnant perspective expressed throughout it. Luke, however, wants his readers to appreciate something of how the earliest Christian preaching began within a Jewish milieu. From this he will go on to tell how this preaching developed through the various representative sermons that he later includes.

Notes

---

11 The Western text reads: "And as Peter and John came out, he came with them while holding on to them. And others, being amazed, took up their position in the colonnade that is called Solomon's."

12 On the address Ἄνδρες Ἰσραηλῖται (*Andres Israēlitai*, "Men of Israel"), see comments at 1:16, 2:14, and 2:22.

13 The designation of God as "the God of Abraham, Isaac and Jacob" stems from God's self-identification in Exod 3:6. It was a common formula among Jews (cf. the opening words of the Shemoneh Esreh, or "Eighteen Benedictions": "Blessed art thou, O Lord our God and God of our fathers, God of Abraham, God of Isaac, and God of Jacob") and occurs frequently in various forms in the NT (cf. Mark 12:26; Acts 7:32). The Western text here and at 7:32 has the fuller form with the addition of θεὸς (*theos*, "God") before Isaac and Jacob as well.

13–26 On the Jewish history and Christian usage of the titles employed here, see my *Christology*, pp. 32–47, 53–58, 104–9.

15 The title ἀρχηγὸν τῆς ζωῆς (*archēgon tēs zoēs*, "author of life") is equivalent to ἡ σωτηρία (*hē sōtēria*, "God's salvation," "salvation") since both ζωή (*zoē*, "life") and σωτηρία (*sōtēria*, "salvation") are the Gr. translations of the one Hebrew word חיה (*ḥāyāh*, "be alive"; cf. 5:20).

16 Torrey (pp. 14–16) and Foakes-Jackson (BC, 2:42) declared the awkward syntax of this verse to be the result of Luke's mistranslation of his Aram. source. I prefer, however, to speak of its structural difficulties as the result of Luke's unwillingness to alter Peter's somewhat cumbersome thesis statement, principally because he could not rework the repetition of "the name of Jesus" without losing Peter's emphasis.

17 Peter's stress on the Jews' ignorance is reminiscent of Jesus' word from the cross, which is recorded only in Luke 23:34: "Father, forgive them, for they do not know what they are doing" (which is certainly a genuine logion, despite its omission in ℵ A C D). This appears also in Paul's preaching (cf. 13:27; 17:30; Rom 10:2; 1 Tim 1:13), but Stephen's attitude is quite different (cf. 7:51–53).

22–23 While Deut 18:15, 18–19 is quoted here, its text form is not according to either the MT or the LXX. Yet the Gr. of v.23 corresponds remarkably well to the Heb. text of Deut 18:18–19 in lines 5–8 of 4QTest, which suggests that "Luke draws here upon a Palestinian Jewish text tradition which is older than the composition of the speech" (de Waard, p.79; cf. also pp. 21–24).

25 On Paul's use of the promise-to-Abraham theme and the motif of Abraham's "seed" (NIV, "offspring"), see Gal 3:6–9, 14, 16–18, 29.

26 While in 3:15 the verb ἐγείρω (egeirō, "raise up") is used of the resurrection of Jesus, here ἀνίστημι (anistēmi, "raise up") is employed with evident reference to the same, in line with Luke's usual practice (cf. 2:24, 32; 7:37; 13:30, 34; 17:31; though with 9:41 and 13:33 as exceptions) and in parallel with the wording of Deut 18:15 and 18: "The Lord your God will raise up [ἀναστήσει, anastēsei] for you" and "I will raise up [ἀναστήσω, anastēsō] for them" —and perhaps with the wording of 2 Sam 7:12, which seems also to have been in Peter's mind: "I will raise up [anastēsō] your offspring to succeed you."

C. Peter and John Before the Sanhedrin (4:1-31)

As a direct outcome of the healing of the crippled beggar and as a further illustration of the thesis paragraph (2:42–47), Luke now presents a vignette concerning the arrest, trial, and witness of Peter and John. Source criticism, as noted earlier (cf. Introduction: The Question of Sources), has usually taken the two arrests and appearances of the apostles before the Sanhedrin (4:1ff.; 5:17ff.) as simply two versions of the same event, which were somehow brought together prior to Luke's writing to form one of his sources (perhaps "Recension A" of the Jerusalem-Caesarean source, cf. Harnack) and of which 4:1ff. was probably the original and 5:17ff. a legendary expansion.

Jeremias, however, has shown that far from being repetitious, and therefore artificial in their dual inclusion, the two accounts accurately reflect a significant point in Jewish jurisprudence and complement each other (Joachim Jeremias, "Untersuchungen zum Quellenproblem der Apostelgeschichte," ZNW, 36 [1937], 208–13). Jewish law, as Jeremias pointed out, held that a person must be aware of the consequences of his crime before being punished for it. This meant that in noncapital cases the common people—as distinguished from those with rabbinic training, who, presumably, would know the law—had to be given a legal admonition before witnesses and could only be punished for an offense when they relapsed into a crime after due warning. Acts 4:1ff., therefore, presents the Sanhedrin as judging that the apostles were "unschooled, ordinary men" (v.13) and tells how they were given a legal warning not to speak anymore in the name of Jesus (v.17). But Acts 5:17ff. tells how the Sanhedrin reminded the apostles of its first warning (v.28) and turned them over to be flogged because they had persisted in their "sectarian" ways (v.40). Jeremias's explanation has been rightly accepted by most commentators today.

This does not mean, however, that Luke himself clearly grasped the precise details of Jewish jurisprudence or that he was interested in detailing them for his readers. Probably he found these two accounts in his sources; and, while they reflect the legal procedures within Judaism of the day, they appealed to him and he used them because of the development of attitudes they show. Jeremias's explanation refers to the state of the tradition before the composition of Acts, not necessarily to Luke's handling of the material. But it shows that we should not take the historicity of the narratives in Acts lightly just because Luke has used sources for his own purposes.

1. *The arrest of Peter and John*

4:1-7

> [1]The priests and the captain of the temple guard and the Sadducees came up to Peter and John while they were speaking to the people. [2]They were greatly disturbed because the apostles were teaching the people and proclaiming in Jesus the resurrection of the dead. [3]They seized Peter and John, and because it was evening, they put them in jail until the next day. [4]But many who heard the message believed, and the number of men grew to about five thousand.
> [5]The next day the rulers, elders and teachers of the law met in Jerusalem. [6]Annas the high priest was there, and so were Caiaphas, John, Alexander and the other men of the high priest's family. [7]They had Peter and John brought before them and began to question them: "By what power or what name did you do this?"

1 Luke has so skillfully woven his sources together that vv.1–4 not only conclude the narrative of the crippled beggar's healing but also introduce the first appearance of Peter and John before the Sanhedrin. Linguistically, the adverbial participle *lalountōn* ("while they were speaking") joins vv.1–4 with what has gone before, and the statement "the next day" (v.5) is better taken as beginning a new unit of material. Yet, topically, vv.1–4 introduce what follows more than they conclude what has preceded.

The early opposition against preaching the gospel is shown by Luke as arising chiefly from priestly and Sadducean ranks—viz., "the priests and the captain of the temple guard and the Sadducees." "The captain of the temple guard" was the commanding officer of the temple police force. He was considered inferior in rank only to the high priest and had the responsibility of maintaining order in the temple precincts (cf. 5:24, 26; Jos. War II, 409–10 [xvii.1]; VI, 294 [v.3]; Antiq. XX, 131 [vi.1], 208 [ix.3]). The Sadducees were descendants of the Hasmoneans, who looked back to Mattathias, Judas, Jonathan, and Simon (168–134 B.C.) as having inaugurated the Messianic Age (cf. Jub 23:23–30; 31:9–20; 1 Macc 14:4–15, 41) and saw themselves as perpetuating what their fathers had begun. As priests from the tribe of Levi, they claimed to represent ancient orthodoxy and were uninterested in innovations. Thus they opposed any developments in biblical law (i.e., the "Oral Law"), speculations about angels or demons, and the doctrine of the resurrection (cf. 23:8; Mark 12:18–27; Jos. War II, 119 [viii.2], 164–65 [viii.14]; Antiq. XIII, 171–73 [v.9]; XVIII, 11 [i.1], 16–17 [i.4]). Likewise, they rejected what they considered to be vain hopes for God's heavenly intervention in the life of the nation and for a coming Messiah, since, as they believed, the age of God's promise had begun with the Maccabean heroes and was continuing on under their supervision. For them, the Messiah was an ideal, not a person, and the Messianic Age was a process, not a cataclysmic or even datable event. Furthermore, as political rulers and dominant landlords, to whom a grateful nation had turned over all political and economic powers during the time of the Maccabean supremacy, for entirely practical reasons they stressed cooperation with Rome and maintenance of the status quo. Most of the priests were of Sadducean persuasion; the temple police force was composed entirely of Levites; the captain of the temple guard was always a high-caste Sadducee, and so were each of the high priests.

2–3 The priests and Sadducees were "greatly disturbed" (*diaponoumenoi*, cf. 16:18) about two matters. First, the apostles were "teaching the people," an activity those of the Sadducean ranks saw as a threat to the status quo. Like their Master, Peter and John were rallying popular support and acting unofficially in a way as to disrupt established authority—an authority vested in Sadducean hands. Second, Peter and John were annoying the Sadducees because they were "proclaiming in Jesus the resurrection of the dead." This probably means they were attempting to prove from the fact of Jesus' resurrection (en tō Iēsou, which suggests "in the case of Jesus") the doctrine of the resurrection (cf. 17:31–32; 23:6–8), which the Sadducees denied.

So Peter and John were taken into custody by the temple guard and, since it was evening, put into prison till the Sanhedrin could be called together the next morning to judge their case.

4 Not everyone agreed with the Sadducees' view of the activities and message of the apostles. Later in Acts, Luke will speak of the general tolerance of the people, the moderation of the Pharisees, and the desire of Rome for peace in the land as each having a part in restraining the Sadducees from doing all they might have done to oppose the gospel and its early missioners. Here, however, he tells us that many who heard the message (ton logon, lit., "the word") believed, with the result that the Jerusalem congregation grew to a total of about five thousand.

5 Though the Sadducees had among them the nation's titular rulers, they were actually a minority party and could govern only through the Sanhedrin. Thus on the next day "the rulers" (hoi archontes, which is a frequent synonym for "the high priests"; cf. 23:5; Jos. War II, 333 [xv.6], 405 [xvii.1], 407 [xvii.1], 627–28 [xxi.7]), the "elders" (hoi presbyteroi), and the "teachers of the law" (hoi grammateis, usually translated "scribes") came together, with these three groups forming the Sanhedrin.

The Sanhedrin (synedrion, "council") was the senate and supreme court of the nation, which had jurisdiction in all noncapital cases—though it also advised the Roman governors in capital cases—and in one case, viz., that of Gentiles trespassing beyond the posted barriers into the inner courts of the temple, could on its own sentence even a Roman citizen to death (cf. 21:28–29; Jos. War VI, 124–28 [ii.4]). The Sanhedrin consisted of the high priest, who by virtue of his office was president, and seventy others, made up of members of the high priestly families, a few influential persons of various formal ideological allegiances or backgrounds within Judaism, and professional experts in the law drawn from both Sadducean and Pharisaic ranks. It was dominated by the Sadducees and probably came together mostly at their request. It met in a hall adjoining the southwest part of the temple area, probably at the eastern end of a bridge spanning the Tyropean Valley and next to an open-air meeting place called the Xystos (cf. Jos. War II, 344 [xvi.3]; V, 144 [iv.2]; VI, 354 [vi.2]).

6 In stressing that the early opposition to Christianity arose principally from among the Sadducees, Luke makes the point that the Sadducean element was especially well represented in this first trial of the apostles: "Annas the high priest was there, and so were Caiaphas, John, Alexander and the other men of the high priest's family." Annas was high priest for nine years (A.D. 6–15), though he continued to exercise great influence after that and is seen in the NT as the real power behind the throne (cf. Luke 3:2; John 18:13–24). Caiaphas, his son-in-law, was high priest for eighteen years (A.D. 18–36). Altogether, Annas arranged to have five of his sons, one son-in-law (Caiaphas), and one grandson appointed to the office of high priest. Just who John and Alexander were, we do not know, though the Western text suggests that the first was Annas's son Jonathan, who replaced Caiaphas in A.D. 36.

7 It was before such an assembly, which probably arranged itself in a semicircular fashion, that Peter and John were brought. The man who had been healed was also there (cf. v.14), though Luke does not say whether he had also been imprisoned or had been called in as a witness. The apostles were called on to account for their actions, and they used the occasion for an aggressive evangelistic witness.

Notes

1 While B and C read οἱ ἀρχιερεῖς (hoi archiereis, "the high priests"), probably in an attempt to correlate v.1 with v.6, the better textual evidence supports the reading οἱ ἱερεῖς (hoi hiereis, "the priests"), which evidently has in mind those priests serving in the temple at the time.

See L. Finkelstein, "The Pharisees: Their Origin and Their Philosophy," HTR, 22 (1929), 185–261; idem, The Pharisees, 2 vols. (Philadelphia: Jewish Publication Society of America, 1938), for a sociological understanding of the Pharisees, which treatment has importance here.

2 D reads ἀναγγέλειν τὸν Ἰησοῦν ἐν τῇ ἀναστάσει τῶν νεκρῶν (anangelein ton Iēsoun en tē anastasei tōn nekrōn, "proclaiming Jesus in the resurrection of the dead").

4 On the number five thousand, see note at 2:41. The noun ἀριθμός (arithmos, "number") probably means here the "total number," as in 6:7 and 16:5 (cf. Deut 26:5; 28:62 LXX).

5 The Jewish Sanhedrin (τὸ συνέδριον, to synedrion; cf. 4:15; Luke 22:66; John 11:47; Jos. Antiq. XIV, 167–81 [ix.3–5]) was also called "The Senate" (ἡ γερουσία, hē gerousia; cf. 5:21; Jos. Antiq. XII, 138 [iii.3]), "The Body of Elders" (τὸ πρεσβυτέριον, to presbyterion; cf. 22:5; Luke 22:66; Jos. Antiq. XIII, 428 [xvi.5]), "The Council" (ἡ βουλή, hē boulē; cf. Jos. War II, 331 [vii.34], 336 [vii.36]), "The Hall of Hewn Stone" (לשכה הגזית, liškāh haggāzît, which probably refers to the polished stones of the Xystos beside which it stood; cf. M Middoth 5.4), "The Great Sanhedrin" (סנהדרין גדלה, sanhēdrîn gᵉdōlāh), "The Great Law Court" (בית דין הגדל, bêt dîn haggādōl), and "The Sanhedrin of the Seventy One" (סנהדרין של שבעים ואחד, sanhēdrîn šel šib'îm wa'eḥād).

6 The Western text reads Ἰωναθάς (Iōnathas, "Jonathan") for Ἰωάννης (Iōannēs, "John").

2. Peter's defense and witness

4:8–12

> 8Then Peter, filled with the Holy Spirit, said to them: "Rulers and elders of the people! 9If we are being called to account today for an act of kindness shown to a cripple and are asked how he was healed, 10then know this, you and everyone else in Israel: It is by the name of Jesus Christ of Nazareth, whom you crucified but whom God raised from the dead, that this man stands before you completely healed. 11He is
> " 'the stone you builders rejected,
>   which has become the capstone.'
> 12Salvation is found in no one else, for there is no other name under heaven given to men by which we must be saved."

8 In a context of prophetic description of national calamities and cosmic turmoil, Luke has quoted Jesus as saying:

> But before all this, they will lay hands on you and persecute you. They will deliver you to synagogues and prisons, and you will be brought before kings and governors, and

all on account of my name. But make up your mind not to worry beforehand how you will defend yourselves. For I will give you words and wisdom that none of your adversaries will be able to resist or contradict (Luke 21:12–15).

Undoubtedly Luke was thinking of many incidents of opposition to the gospel message when he wrote down these words. Indeed, he records a number of such happenings in Acts. But certainly when he wrote about Peter's first defense before the Jewish Sanhedrin (and also about the apostles' second appearance before the Sanhedrin in 5:17ff.) these words were ringing in his ears. For almost every item of Jesus' oracle is exemplified in Luke's account of Peter's situation, attitude, and message here in Acts. The use of the aorist passive (*plēstheis*, "filled") in the expression "filled with the Holy Spirit" denotes a special moment of inspiration that complements and brings to a functional focus the presence in every believer's life of the person and ministry of God's Spirit.

9–10 Peter's defense focuses on the healing of the crippled man as being (1) "an act of kindness," which was (2) effected "by the name of Jesus Christ of Nazareth, whom you crucified but whom God raised from the dead." Luke uses the verb *anakrinomai* ("judge," "call to account"), which in classical Greek means a preliminary inquiry and suggests something about the nature of Jewish jurisprudence. Though Luke may very well have found this suggestion in his sources, his use of the same word in 12:19; 24:8; and 28:18 shows that he had no great desire to highlight it here. Peter's message is specifically addressed to the "rulers and elders of the people," though it also has "everyone else in Israel" in mind.

11–12 The double use of the verb *sōthēnai* ("to be saved") to mean both "restoration to health" physically and "preservation from eternal death" spiritually allows Peter to move easily from the healing of the cripple to the salvation of mankind and, therefore, from a defensive to an aggressive witness. And in his proclamation two quite early and primitive christological motifs are employed.

The first of these is that of "the rejected stone," which has become "the capstone" of the building. In Judaism there was a frequent word-play between the words for "stone" (*'eben*) and "son" (*bēn*)—rooted generally in the OT (cf. Exod 28:9; Josh 4:6–8, 20–21; 1 Kings 18:31; Isa 54:11–13; Lam 4:1–2; Zech 9:16)—which attained messianic expression in the combination of the stone and Son of Man imagery in Daniel 2:34–35 and 7:13–14 and continued to be used through the early rabbinic period (cf. Gen R 68.11; Exod R 29; Pseudo-Jonathan Targum on Exod 39:7). It was for this reason, evidently, that Jesus concluded his parable of the vineyard and the rejected son (Mark 12:1–12) with the quotation of Psalm 118:22–23: "The stone the builders rejected has become the capstone; the Lord has done this, and it is marvelous in our eyes." And it is this motif that Peter picks up here in his quotation of Psalm 118:22, building on the associations of "stone" and "son."

In the first-century A.D. Jewish *Testament of Solomon* 22.7–23.4, the expression "the stone at the head of the corner" (*ho lithos eis kephalēn gōnias*) unambiguously refers to the final copestone or capstone placed on the summit of the Jerusalem temple to complete the whole edifice. Peter quotes Psalm 118:22 in this connection. Yet there are also within Judaism instances of the "stone imagery" referring to a "foundation stone," a usage that employs Isaiah 28:16 for support (cf. 1QS 8.4; b *Yoma* 54a). Apparently the "stone imagery" was used variously in Late Judaism. And this same variety is reflected in the NT, for there the three christological stone passages (in addition to Mark 12:10–11;

Acts 4:11; cf. Luke 20:18; Rom 9:33; 1 Cor 3:11; 1 Peter 2:4–8) have varying nuances. Here, however, while elsewhere in the NT the ideas of a "foundation stone" and a "stumbling stone" based respectively on Isaiah 28:16 and 8:14 are dominant, the thought of Jesus as the rejected stone that becomes the capstone and completes the edifice is dominant (cf. Ps 118:22).

The second early christological motif in Peter's proclamation is "Salvation." In the longer Isaiah scroll of the DSS, "God's Salvation" and "Salvation" appear as Jewish designations of the expected Davidic Messiah (1QIsᵃ 51.4–5, as shown by the use of the third person masculine suffix and pronoun in connection with the expression "my Salvation"). Likewise, "Salvation" is used as a messianic title in other Qumran literature (cf. CD 9.43, 54; 1QH 7.18–19; 4QFlor on 2 Sam 7:14 and in connection with Amos 9:11), in various intertestamental writings (cf. Jub 31:19; also T Dan 5:10; T Naph 8:3; T Gad 8:1; T Jos 19:11, though the provenance of the Gr. Testaments of the Twelve Patriarchs is debated), and in the rabbinic materials (cf. b Berakoth 56b–57a).

Luke has already stressed this early christological motif in Zechariah's hymn of praise (Luke 1:69, "a horn of salvation"), in Simeon's prayer (Luke 2:30, "your salvation"), and in introducing the ministry of John the Baptist (Luke 3:6, "God's salvation"). Now in addressing the Sanhedrin, to whom such a messianic designation was doubtless well known, Peter proclaims, "Salvation is found in no one else [than in 'Jesus Christ of Nazareth, whom you crucified but whom God raised from the dead,' (v.10)], for there is no other name under heaven given to men by which we must be saved" (v.12). There was nothing of compromise or accommodation in Peter's preaching. As this magnificent declaration shows, he was wholly committed to the uniqueness of Jesus as the only Savior. Peter and the other apostles never watered down the fact that apart from Jesus there is no salvation for anyone.

Notes

11 On the word-play in Judaism between "stone" and "son," see M. Black, "The Christological Use of the Old Testament in the New Testament," NTS, 18 (1971), 11–14 (building upon the research of Klyne Snodgrass, then Black's research student). On the stone of Ps 118:22 as a "capstone," see Joachim Jeremias, "Κεφαλὴ γωνίας—Ἀκρογωνιαῖος," ZNW, 19 (1930), 264–80; idem, "Eckstein—Schlussstein," ZNW, 36 (1937), 154–57; idem, "γωνία, ἀκρογωνιαῖος, κεφαλὴ γωνίας," TDNT, 1:791–93; idem, "λίθος," TDNT, 4:271–80. See also my Christology, pp. 50–53.

12 On "Salvation" as a messianic ascription in Judaism, the NT, and postapostolic Christianity, see my Christology, pp. 99–103.

3. The apostles warned and released

4:13–22

¹³When they saw the courage of Peter and John and realized that they were unschooled, ordinary men, they were astonished and they took note that these men had been with Jesus. ¹⁴But since they could see the man who had been healed standing there with them, there was nothing they could say. ¹⁵So they ordered them to withdraw from the Sanhedrin and then conferred together. ¹⁶"What are we going to do with these men?" they asked. "Everybody living in

> Jerusalem knows they have done an outstanding miracle, and we cannot deny it.
> [17]But to stop this thing from spreading any further among the people, we must warn these men to speak no longer to anyone in this name."
>
> [18]Then they called them in again and commanded them not to speak or teach at all in the name of Jesus. [19]But Peter and John replied, "Judge for yourselves whether it is right in God's sight to obey you rather than God. [20]For we cannot help speaking about what we have seen and heard."
>
> [21]After further threats they let them go. They could not decide how to punish them, because all the people were praising God for what had happened. [22]For the man who was miraculously healed was over forty years old.

13-14 While literacy was high among Jews of the first century (cf. Jos. Contra Apion II, 178 [19]; Philo *Legatio ad Gaium* 210; M *Pirke Aboth* 5.21), theological disputations required rabbinic training. Since the so-called *'am hā'āres* ("people of the land") had not had such training, they were thought to be incapable of carrying on sustained theological discussion. But here were Peter and John, whom the council observed to be "unschooled, ordinary men," speaking fearlessly and confidently before the Jewish supreme court and senate. Their judges could not but wonder at such ordinary men having such a mastery of biblical argumentation (cf. Luke's précis of their words in 3:22-26; 4:11-12). So they had to fall back on the only possible explanation—"these men had been with Jesus," who, despite his lack of rabbinic training, taught "as one who had authority" (Mark 1:22). To this fact they directed their attention (cf. the use of the intensive verb *epeginōskon*, "took note," NIV) as an important piece of evidence in the case before them. Furthermore, just as Jesus' teaching was coupled with demonstrations of miraculous powers, which reinforced among the people the impression of authority (cf. Mark 1:23-28; 2:1-12; etc.), now Peter and John were beginning to do the same. There was no denying that the man *had* been healed. There he stood before them, physically regenerated at an age when regenerative cures do not occur of themselves (cf. v.22, "for the man . . . was over forty years old"). But even the miraculous is not self-authenticating apart from openness of heart and mind; and the Sadducees' preoccupation with protecting their vested interests shut them off from really seeing the miracle that occurred.

15-17 Just how Luke knew what went on among the members of the Sanhedrin in closed session has often been debated. Was Saul (Paul) a member of the council at that time and did he later tell Luke? Or had Paul heard the gist of the discussion from his teacher Gamaliel and then told it to Luke? Were there secret sympathizers of the apostles in the council who "leaked" to them what was said and from whom Luke picked it up? Or was the substance of the discussion inferred from what was said to Peter and John when they were brought back and so became embedded in Luke's source material? While the latter seems most probable, we are too far removed from the situation itself to be certain. What is certain about the council's response, however, is that (1) they would have denied the miracle if they could, (2) they had no disposition to be convinced either by what had happened or by the apostles' arguments, and (3) they felt the need of stopping the apostles' activity and teaching and therefore proposed to take the measures allowed them by Jewish law.

18-20 The decision of the council was to impose a ban on the apostles that would both warn them and provide a legal basis for further action should such be needed (cf. 5:28). So they called in the apostles and warned them "not to speak or teach at all in the name of Jesus" (*epi tō onomati tou Iēsou*). The prepositions *epi* ("on") and *en* ("in") are often used interchangeably in the NT, and therefore the phrase *epi tō onomati tou Iēsou* should probably be taken as synonymous with *en tō onomati tou Iēsou* ("in the name of Jesus," cf. 2:38; so also the preposition *eis* in 8:16; 19:5).

But the council had before it men whose lives had been transformed by association with Jesus, by God's having raised Jesus from the dead, and by the coming of the Holy Spirit. As with the prophets of old, God's word was in Peter's and John's hearts like a burning fire; and they could neither contain it nor be restrained from speaking it (cf. Jer 20:9). They had been witnesses of Jesus' earthly ministry and resurrection (cf. 10:39–41). They had been commanded by their risen Lord to proclaim his name to the people (cf. 1:8; 10:42). When faced with this ban, their response was never in doubt: "Judge for yourselves whether it is right in God's sight to obey you rather than God. For we cannot help speaking about what we have seen and heard." Established authority per se was not what the apostles found they must stand against, for Jewish Christianity in its earliest days often accommodated itself to the established forms and functions of Judaism as a baby to its cradle. But where that established authority stood in opposition to God's authority, thus becoming in effect demonic, the early believers knew where their priorities lay and judged all religious forms and functions from a christocentric perspective.

21–22 The Sanhedrin had given its warning. And after stressing its nature and what would happen if it went unheeded (cf. the participial form of the verb *prosapeileō*, "threaten further"), they let them go. The moderation of the people prevented them from doing more, for "all the people were praising God for what had happened." Yet a legal precedent had been set that would enable the council to take, if necessary, more drastic action in the future. Occasions for such action were soon to be multiplied, as Luke tells us in 5:12–16.

Notes

13 Ἀγράμματοι (*agrammatoi*) appears in the Gr. nonliterary papyri in the sense of "illiterate," though here it undoubtedly means "uneducated" or "unschooled" in rabbinic training. The word ἰδιῶται (*idiōtai*), while at times signifying "ignorant" (cf. 1 Cor 14:23–24), is here used in its ordinary Gr. sense of "commoner," "layman," or "ordinary person."

The preposition ἐπί (*epi*, "on") intensifies and gives directive force to the verb ἐπιγινώσκω (*epiginōskō*, "recognize," "take note"), thereby distinguishing it from γινώσκω (*ginōskō*, "know"). The council's explanation that the apostles "had been with Jesus" was, from Luke's perspective (as well as from a Christian perspective, generally), an instance of the council's speaking better than it knew.

15–17 Haenchen comments caustically, "The author reports the closed deliberations as if he had been present" (*Acts of the Apostles*, p. 218). His implication is that here Luke clearly reveals the fabricated nature of his work, inserting words on the lips of people when he had no possible knowledge of what was said. But while this may be one way to view what Luke is doing here, it is not the only way.

19 Peter and John had probably never heard of Socrates or read Plato's report of his response to those who offered him freedom if he would abandon the pursuit of truth: "I shall obey God rather than you" (*Apology* 29d). The parallel here is probably analogical, not genealogical—i.e., the sort of response any man of principle would give in such a situation.

4. The church's praise and petition

4:23–31

²³On their release, Peter and John went back to their own people and reported all that the chief priests and elders had said to them. ²⁴When they heard this, they raised their voices together in prayer to God. "Sovereign Lord," they said, "you made the heaven and the earth and the sea, and everything in them. ²⁵You spoke by the Holy Spirit through the mouth of your servant, our father David:

" 'Why do the nations rage
and the peoples plot in vain?
²⁶The kings of the earth take their stand
and the rulers gather together
against the Lord
and against his Anointed One.'

²⁷Indeed Herod and Pontius Pilate met together with the Gentiles and the people of Israel in this city to conspire against your holy servant Jesus, whom you anointed. ²⁸They did what your power and will had decided beforehand should happen. ²⁹Now, Lord, consider their threats and enable your servants to speak your word with great boldness. ³⁰Stretch out your hand to heal and perform miraculous signs and wonders through the name of your holy servant Jesus."

³¹After they prayed, the place where they were meeting was shaken. And they were all filled with the Holy Spirit and spoke the word of God boldly.

23–30 The church's response to the apostles' release was a spontaneous outburst of praise, psalmody, and petition. It begins (v.24) by addressing God as *Despota* ("Sovereign Lord"). This was a common title in the Greek world for rulers, and it appears occasionally in Jewish circles as a form of address to God (cf. 3 Macc 2:2; Luke 2:29; Rev 6:10). It is especially appropriate here in conjunction with the servant names used of David (v.25, *pais sou*, "your servant"), Jesus (vv.27, 30, *ho hagios pais sou*, "your holy servant"), and believers themselves (v.29, *hoi douloi sou*, "your servants"). Structurally, the church's response includes an ascription to God drawn from Hezekiah's prayer in Isaiah 37:16–20 (v.24b), a quotation of Psalm 2:1–2 (vv.25–26), the reference to Jesus' passion in terms of the psalm just cited (vv.27–28), and a petition for divine enablement in the Christians' present circumstances (vv.29–30).

In the prayer of the church two matters of theological interest stand out. First, there is a "pesher" treatment (cf. comments on 2:16) of Psalm 2 in which the groups enumerated in the psalm are equated with the various persons and groups involved in Jesus' crucifixion: "the kings of the earth" with King Herod; "the rulers" with the Roman governor Pontius Pilate; "the nations" with the Gentile authorities; and "the people" with "the people of Israel." The earliest extant suggestion that Psalm 2 had any messianic import in Jewish thinking is Psalms of Solomon 17:26, where "the Son of David," who is also spoken of as "the Lord's Anointed" (*ho Christos kyriou*, v.36), is presented as acting in terms of Psalm 2:9: "He shall destroy the pride of the sinners as a potter's vessel. With a rod of iron he shall break in pieces all their substance." Of late, and more explicitly, Psalm 2:1–2 has been found as a messianic testimonia portion in the DSS 4QFlorilegium, in connection with 2 Samuel 7:10–14 and Psalm 1:1. It seems, therefore, that sometime just prior to the Christian period, Psalm 2 was beginning to be used within Jewish nonconformist circles as a messianic psalm and that the early Jewish Christians knew of this usage and approved it—though, of course, in its application to Jesus of Nazareth (cf. also the use of Ps 2:7 in 13:33; Heb 1:5; 5:5; and Ps 2:9 in Rev 2:27; 12:5; 19:15).

Second, in the church's prayer the sufferings of Christian believers are related directly to the sufferings of Christ and inferentially to the sufferings of God's righteous servants in the OT. This theme of the union of the sufferings of Christ and those of his own is a theme that is developed in many ways throughout the NT (cf. esp. Mark 8–10; Rom 8:17; Col 1:24; 1 Peter 2:20–25; 3:14–4:2; 4:12–13). It reaches its loftiest expression in Paul's metaphor of the body of Christ.

Most significant is the fact that these early Christians were not praying for relief from oppression or judgment on their oppressors but for enablement "to speak your word with great boldness" amid oppressions and for God to act in mighty power "through the name of your holy servant Jesus" (v.30). Their concern was for God's word to go forth and for Christ's name to be glorified, leaving to God himself their own circumstances. With such prayer surely God is well pleased. Luke has evidently taken pains to give us this prayer so that it might serve as something of a pattern to be followed in our own praying.

31 As a sign of God's approval, Luke tells us that "the place where they were meeting was shaken" (cf. Exod 19:18; Isa 6:4) and "they were all filled with the Holy Spirit" (cf. comments on v.8). And with such motivation and divine enablement, their prayer was answered; and they "spoke the word of God boldly" (*parrēsias*, "with confidence," "forthrightly").

Notes

25 The Gr. of v.25a is well supported in the MS evidence but almost impossible to translate. Various minor textual sources and many modern commentators have attempted to delete either τοῦ πατρὸς ἡμῶν (*tou patros hēmōn*, "our father") or διὰ πνεύματος ἁγίου (*dia pneumatos hagiou*, "by the Holy Spirit") or both. It appears that we have a primitive error of syntax here that has been incorporated into the text, stemming either from the early Christians themselves or somehow worked into the source Luke employed.

D. *Christian Concern Expressed in Sharing*

(4:32–5:11)

Going back to one of the themes in his thesis paragraph of 2:42–47, Luke now illustrates the nature and extent of the early believers' commitment to one another in social concern. This he does by a summary statement, then by an example of genuine Christian concern, and finally by an example of disastrous deceit. The subject of Christian social concern, which appears in 2:42–47 quite naturally along with matters of fellowship and worship in the context of the believing community, also appears here by juxtaposition with the vignettes in 3:1–4:31 and the inclusion of v.33 in the context of the apostles' proclamation of Jesus' resurrection. For Luke as well as for the early Christians, being filled with the Holy Spirit not only concerned proclaiming the Word of God but also sharing possessions with the needy because of believers' oneness in Christ.

1. *Believers share their possessions*

4:32-35

> ³²All the believers were one in heart and mind. No one claimed that any of his possessions was his own, but they shared everything they had. ³³With great power the apostles continued to testify to the resurrection of the Lord Jesus, and much grace was upon them all. ³⁴There were no needy persons among them. For from time to time those who owned lands or houses sold them, brought the money from the sales ³⁵and put it at the apostles' feet, and it was distributed to anyone as he had need.

Source critical analyses of 4:32–35 have often concluded that the material is somewhat jumbled here, with either vv.32–33 representing one of Luke's sources and vv.34–35 being an editorial insertion, or vv.32, 34–35 stemming from an early source and v.33 being an editorial intruder. Underlying all such analyses is the assumption that v.32 and vv.34–35 speak of the same attitude toward property and, therefore, that either vv.34–35 must be a repetitious editorial comment or v.33 an editorial intrusion. In reality, however, v.32 and vv.34–35 express differing views of personal possessions and property; in the former these are retained and shared, whereas in the latter they are sold and the proceeds distributed to those in need. Likewise, there seems to be a difference between v.32 and vv.34–35 in the attitude of the believers to such practices; in the former they are presented as customary and continuous, whereas in the latter such action seems to be an extraordinary response to special needs.

In this prefatory statement (vv.32–35), Luke is, then, (1) emphasizing that both continuous and extraordinary acts of Christian social concern were occurring in the early church, and (2) tying these acts into the apostolic proclamation of the Resurrection. It was because of such acts and the recognition that they must always be an inextricable part of the Christian ministry that God's blessing rested upon the early church.

32 The designation *to plēthos tōn pisteusantōn* (lit., "the multitude of believers") means the whole congregation or, as in NIV, "all the believers" (cf. 6:2, 5; 15:12, 30), whose united allegiance to Jesus and one another is described by the common Hebraic idiom "one in heart and mind" (*kardia kai psychē mia*, lit., "one in heart and soul"; cf. Deut 6:5; 10:12; 11:13; 26:16; 30:2, 6, 10; passim). This sense of oneness extended to sharing their personal possessions with others in need (cf. 2:45).

Theologically, the early believers considered themselves the righteous remnant within Israel. So Deuteronomy 15:4 was undoubtedly in their mind: "There should be no poor among you, for in the land the Lord your God is giving you to possess as your inheritance, he will richly bless you." Other Jewish groups that thought of themselves in terms of a remnant theology expressed their spiritual oneness by sharing their goods, and the Jerusalem church seems to have done likewise. Practically, they had many occasions for such sharing. With the economic situation in Palestine steadily deteriorating because of famine and political unrest (cf. Jeremias, *Jerusalem*, pp. 121–22), employment was limited—not only for Galileans and others who had left their fishing and farming for living in the city, but also for the regular residents of Jerusalem who now faced economic and social sanctions because of their new messianic faith. Experientially, the spiritual oneness the believers found to be a living reality through their common allegiance to Jesus must, they realized, be expressed in caring for the physical needs of their Christian brothers and sisters. Indeed, their integrity as a community of faith depended on their doing this.

Here in v.32 we have, therefore, Luke's illustration of his thesis statement in 2:44–45 regarding the way the believers practiced communal living. They were not monastics, for the Jerusalem apostles and brothers of Jesus were married (cf. 1 Cor 9:5), and so were many of the other believers (e.g., Ananias and Sapphira, 5:1–11). Nor did the believers form a closed society like Qumran. They lived in their own homes (cf. 2:46; 12:12) and had their own possessions as any household would. In these ways the communal life of the early Christians differed from that of the Qumran covenanters. But though the Christians had personal possessions, they did not consider them private possessions (*idion einai*, "was his own," NIV) to be held exclusively for their own use and enjoyment. Rather, they shared what they had and so expressed their corporate life.

33 Because of its juxtaposition with v.32, we must understand the "great power" that accompanied the apostles' witness "to the resurrection of the Lord Jesus" not just as rhetorical, homiletical, or even miraculous power but as the power of a new life in the believing community—a new life manifest in sharing possessions to meet the needs of others. It was this kind of power Jesus had in mind when he said, "All men will know that you are my disciples if you love one another" (John 13:35). In view of such a combination of social concern and proclamation of the Word, it is no wonder that Luke goes on to say, "And much grace was upon them all" (cf. Luke 2:40).

34–35 "From time to time" brings out the iterative force of the imperfect verbs in these two verses. The acts Luke alludes to here were extraordinary and voluntary acts of Christian concern done in response to special needs among the believers, and they involved both sharing possessions and selling real estate. By separating these actions from those described in v.32 and by the way he treats them, Luke suggests that they were exceptional and were not meant to be normative for the church. The church at Jerusalem—even in its earliest days—was neither a monastic nor semimonastic community. Nevertheless, such acts were highly regarded as magnanimous expressions of a common social concern, though as with any noble deed they could be done either sincerely or hypocritically.

Notes

32 For πλῆθος (*plēthos*, "crowd," "assembly," "community") used of a Jewish group, cf. 2:6; 19:9; 23:7; 25:24; for its general sense of "multitude," cf. 14:1; 17:4.

34–35 Josephus says of the Essenes: "Riches they despise, and their community of goods [τὸ κοινωνικόν, *to koinōnikon*] is truly admirable; you will not find one among them distinguished by greater opulence than another. They have a law that new members on admission to the sect shall confiscate their property to the order, with the result that you will nowhere see either abject poverty or inordinate wealth; the individual's possessions join the common stock and all, like brothers, enjoy a single patrimony" (War II, 122 [viii.3]). And with this description, 1QS 1.11–13 seems initially to agree: "All who declare their willingness to serve God's truth must bring all of their mind, all of their strength, and all of their wealth into the community of God, so that their minds may be purified by the truth of God's precepts, their strength controlled by his perfect ways, and their wealth disposed of in accordance with his just design" (cf. Eusebius's version of Philo's statement in *Praeparatio Evangelica* VIII. 11).

Many commentators believe that such statements can only be read as referring to a complete sharing of possessions and property. Yet 1QS 7.5–8 assumes some retention of personal property when it speaks of the members paying fines within the community and carrying on business dealings with one another and with the community itself; and the Zad Frag suggest that only unjustified or ill-gotten possessions were forbidden and that only a portion of one's income (at least two working days per month) was to be donated to the fund for the poor (CD 6.15; 8.5; 19.17). It seems that what we are dealing with here has to do with two matters: (1) an idealized and rather sweeping characterization, with further explications that serve to clarify more precisely the situation (as with Josephus, Philo, and 1QS 1.11–13, as clarified by such passages as 1QS 7.5–7 and CD 6.15; 8.5; 19.17—and as I am suggesting to be the case in Acts 2:44–45 and 4:34–35); and (2) rules for the monastic community exclusively (as in 1QS) and rules more broadly applicable to life in both encampments and cities (as in CD). Indeed, the parallels between the communal sharing of the early Jerusalem Christians and that of the Qumran Essenes are close and may be legitimately spelled out. One must also, however, bear in mind (1) the variations that appear between the idealized characterizations and the explanations of the actual practice and (2) the differences that inevitably occurred between the communal life of monastic communities and the communal sharing of those living in nonmonastic situations.

---

2. The generosity of Barnabas

4:36–37

> [36]Joseph, a Levite from Cyprus, whom the apostles called Barnabas (which means Son of Encouragement), [37]sold a field he owned and brought the money and put it at the apostles' feet.

36 Luke uses the generosity of Barnabas as "Exhibit A" to illustrate the type of extraordinary social concern that was "from time to time" (v.34) expressed by believers at Jerusalem. Joseph was the Hebrew name used at home, in the synagogue, and among Jews generally. To this the apostles added the cognomen or descriptive nickname Barnabas, which means in Hebrew "Son of Encouragement," in order to distinguish him from others of the same name (cf. 1:23). His family came from Cyprus, and he may have had ancestral property there. John Mark was his cousin (cf. *ho anepsios,* "cousin," of Col 4:10), and the home of Mark's mother was in Jerusalem (cf. 12:12).

37 Barnabas is an important figure in Luke's account of the church's expansion from Jerusalem to Rome; he appears a number of times as a kind of hinge between the mission to the Jewish world and that to the Gentiles (cf. 9:27; 11:22–30; 13:1–14:28; 15:2–4, 12, 22, 36–41; see also 1 Cor 9:6). Here, however, he is introduced as one who sold a field (*hyparchontos autō agrou,* lit., "his possession of a field") and gave the money to the apostles for distribution among those in need. We are not told whether the property he sold was in Cyprus or Palestine. If his family was from Cyprus but had lived in Palestine, and if he continued to have connections with Cyprus while living in Palestine, he could have inherited or purchased property in Cyprus, Palestine, or both. Nor are we told how the biblical prohibition against Levites owning real estate applied in Barnabas's case (cf. Num 18:20; Deut 10:9)—though such a regulation seems not always to have been observed (cf. Jer 32:7–44; Jos. Life 76 [14]). What we are told, however, is that Barnabas gave a practical demonstration of Christian social concern, undoubtedly under no compulsion of either precedent or rule (cf. 5:4).

Notes

36 Jews in the Gr. and Rom. periods also had alternative Gr. names, but Luke does not give us Barnabas's Gr. name since he evidently viewed his ministry as being principally within a Jewish milieu (cf. comments on 13:9). Had he been a Rom. citizen, he would have also had three Rom. names, of which the third would probably have been identical with his Gr. name.

3. The deceit of Ananias and Sapphira

5:1-11

¹Now a man named Ananias, together with his wife Sapphira, also sold a piece of property. ²With his wife's full knowledge he kept back part of the money for himself, but brought the rest and put it at the apostles' feet.

³Then Peter said, "Ananias, how is it that Satan has so filled your heart that you have lied to the Holy Spirit and have kept for yourself some of the money you received for the land? ⁴Didn't it belong to you before it was sold? And after it was sold, wasn't the money at your disposal? What made you think of doing such a thing? You have not lied to men but to God."

⁵When Ananias heard this, he fell down and died. And great fear seized all who heard what had happened. ⁶Then the young men came forward, wrapped up his body, and carried him out and buried him.

⁷About three hours later his wife came in, not knowing what had happened. ⁸Peter asked her, "Tell me, is this the price you and Ananias got for the land?"

"Yes," she said, "that is the price."

⁹Peter said to her, "How could you agree to test the Spirit of the Lord? Look! The feet of the men who buried your husband are at the door, and they will carry you out also."

¹⁰At that moment she fell down at his feet and died. Then the young men came in and, finding her dead, carried her out and buried her beside her husband. ¹¹Great fear seized the whole church and all who heard about these events.

The case of Ananias and Sapphira is opposite that of Barnabas, though it was meant to look the same. No doubt the story circulated within the church as a warning of the awfulness of deceit, for at times of great enthusiasm such a warning is especially necessary. And though Luke has taken evident pleasure in reporting the progress of the gospel and the vitality of faith during these early days of the church in Jerusalem, he does not omit this most distressing event. It is a situation that must have lain heavily on the hearts of the early Christians, but it is also a message that needs to be constantly kept in mind by Christians today.

1-2 The details of the conspiracy are concisely stated. A certain man named Ananias (Heb., "God is gracious") and his wife, Sapphira (Aram., "beautiful"), both of whom were evidently Christians, wanted to enjoy the acclaim of the church, as Barnabas did, without making a genuine sacrifice. So they too sold a piece of real estate (*ktēma*, "property," NIV; cf. 2:45) and pretended to give the full price to the apostles for distribution to the needy, though they conspired to keep back part of the money for themselves. We could wish to know more about their purpose and expectations so that we might better understand what took place later. But not even the apostles knew all about these things, though Peter inferred the substance of what went on between them. Luke's use of the verb *nosphizō* ("kept back," "purloined," "put aside for oneself"), which in the LXX heads

313

the account in Joshua 7:1–26 of Achan's misappropriation of part of what had been dedicated to God, implies that Luke meant to draw a parallel between the sin of Achan as the Israelites began their conquest of Canaan and the sin of Ananias and Sapphira as the church began its mission—both incidents coming under the immediate and drastic judgment of God and teaching a sobering lesson. And this is very likely how the early church saw the incident as well.

3–4 Probably no account in Acts has provoked more wrath from critics than this one has. Commentators have complained about the difficulty of accepting the death of both husband and wife under such circumstances and have questioned Peter's ethics in not giving them an opportunity for repentance and in not telling Sapphira of her husband's death. Even more difficult for many is the way the story portrays Peter, who appears to be without the compassion or restraint of his Lord. Jesus' relations with even Judas, whose sin was a thousand times more odious, certainly were not on this level. Many have felt it impossible for a leader of the early church to have shown such harshness over a relatively "slight" offense and have doubted that the church would have wanted to preserve such an account. Many, therefore, have taken this to be a fictitious story that arose only within a certain part of the early Christian community, perhaps to explain why certain members of the community had died before the Parousia.

But Peter did not view the action of Ananias and Sapphira as merely incidental. He spoke of it as inspired by Satan and as a lie to both the Holy Spirit and God. It was a case of deceit and was an affront, not just on the community level, but primarily before God. Deceit is spiritually disastrous—a sin, whatever its supposed justification, that sours every personal relationship. Where there is even the suspicion of conscious misrepresentation and deception, trust is completely violated.

The Qumran community realized the seriousness of deceit and, in a situation somewhat similar to what we have here, ruled that "if there be found in the community a man who consciously lies in the matter of his wealth, he is to be regarded as outside the state of purity entailed by membership, and he is to be penalized one fourth of his food ration" (1QS 6.24–25). The penalty for this at Qumran was not nearly as severe as that in Acts 5. But neither were the situations exactly alike. Ananias and Sapphira were severely dealt with because of the voluntary nature of their act of pretended piety (cf. v.4) and because the greater freedom permitted in the church at Jerusalem made the individual Christian more responsible to be honest and more culpable when dishonest. In addition, the way Ananias and Sapphira attempted to reach their goals was so diametrically opposed to the whole thrust of the gospel that to allow it to go unchallenged would have set the entire mission of the church off course. Like the act of Achan, this episode was pivotal in the life and mission of God's people, for the whole enterprise was threatened at its start. And while we may be thankful that judgment upon deceit in the church is not now so swift and drastic, this incident stands as an indelible warning regarding the heinousness in God's sight of deception in spiritual and personal matters.

5 The psychological explanations of Ananias's sudden death attribute his fatal collapse to the shock and shame of being found out. The verb Luke uses for his death, however, is *ekpsychō* ("breathe one's last," "die")—the same one used in the LXX of Sisera's death (Judg 4:21). It appears in the NT only in contexts where someone is struck down by divine judgment (Acts 5:5, 10; 12:23). Psychological and physical factors may well have been secondary causes in Ananias's death, but Luke's emphasis is on the ultimate causation of God as the agent. This is the light in which he means his readers to understand his further comment: "And great fear seized all who heard what had happened."

6 The expression "the young men" (*hoi neōteroi*), particularly in parallel construction with its synonym in v.10 (*hoi neaniskoi*), should probably be understood as denoting age and referring to certain younger men in the Christian community, not as designating professional buriers. The verb *systellō* ("wrap up") was frequently used by ancient Greek physicians like Hippocrates, Galen, and Dioscorides to mean "to bandage a limb" or "to compress a wound by bandaging," though it was also used more widely in the sense of "cover up," "wrap up," "fold up," "take away," and "remove" (cf. BAG, p. 802). Whether the young men covered Ananias with a shroud and carried him away or wrapped him up in some manner and then carried him away or simply picked him up from the floor and took him off for burial is impossible to say. It is understandable that burial in hot climates takes place soon after death. But just why Ananias was buried so quickly and why his wife was not told seems strange, though we are not told enough about the circumstances to offer any explanation.

7-10 "About three hours later" the tragic episode was repeated with Sapphira. Just as man and wife were united in their conspiracy, so they were united in the judgment that came upon them. "All this is handled," as Haenchen says of Luke's account, "without pity, for we are in the presence of the divine punishment which should be witnessed in fear and trembling, but not with Aristotelian fear and pity" (p. 239).

11 It may seem redundant that Luke closes his account of Ananias and Sapphira's deception with the statement "Great fear seized the whole church and all who heard about these events." However, this is a vignette of warning; and in concluding it Luke wants to stress this note of reverent fear—as he expressly did in v.5 and implicitly did throughout his account.

This is the first time in Acts that the word "church" (*ekklēsia*) appears, though it is the regular word for both the church universal and local congregations elsewhere in the book (cf. 7:38; 8:1; 9:31; 11:22; 13:1; 14:23; 15:22, 41; 16:5; 19:32, 40; 20:28) and throughout the NT epistles (cf. Matt 16:18; 18:17).

Notes

3 The name "Satan" (Gr. ὁ Σατανᾶς, *ho Satanas*; Heb. הַשָּׂטָן, *ha śātān*) was originally a common noun meaning "adversary" (cf. 1 Kings 11:14; Ps 109:6), but it came to be a personal designation for the angel who accuses men before God (Job 1:6–12; 2:1–7) and tempts them to evil (1 Chron 21:1). In the NT period, Satan was considered the chief of the evil demons (cf. Jub 10:11, 23:29; 40:9; 50:5), who was also called Asmondeus (Tobit 3:8, 17; b *Gittim* 68b, *Pesahim* 110a), Semjaza (1 Enoch 6:3, 7; 8:3; 10:11), Azazel (1 Enoch 8:1; 10:4; 86:1; 88:1), Mastema (Jub 10:5–11; 17:16; 18:4, 12; 48:2), and Beliar or Belial (Jub 1:20; and as is common in Ascen Isa, T 12 Pat, and throughout the NT).

3–4 The parallel association of "the Holy Spirit" and "God" (see also "the Spirit of the Lord" in v.9) is suggestive for later doctrinal elaborations on the personality of the Spirit and the plurality of the Godhead.

5 D inserts the adverb παραχρῆμα (*parachrēma*, "immediately"), in parallel with v.10, before πεσών (*pesōn*, "falling down"), thereby heightening the dramatic effect.

11 The Western text also includes the word ἐκκλησία (*ekklēsia*, "church") at 2:47.

E. *The Apostles Again Before the Sanhedrin* (5:12-42)

Having apparently found both accounts of the apostles' arraignments before the Sanhedrin in his source materials, Luke now gives the second account. Whether he clearly grasped or fully appreciated the rationale in Jewish jurisprudence for two such appearances is debatable (cf. introductory comments on 4:1-31). Nevertheless, he takes the occasion in telling of the apostles' second appearance before the council to emphasize the development of attitudes in these earliest days of the Christian mission in Jerusalem; viz., the deepening jealousy and antagonism of the Sadducees, the moderation of the Pharisees, and the increasing joy and confidence of the Christians. In so doing, Luke continues the elaboration of his thesis paragraph (2:42-47).

1. *Miraculous signs and wonders*

5:12-16

> [12]The apostles performed many miraculous signs and wonders among the people. And all the believers used to meet together in Solomon's Colonnade. [13]No one else dared join them, even though they were highly regarded by the people. [14]Nevertheless, more and more men and women believed in the Lord and were added to their number. [15]As a result, people brought the sick into the streets and laid them on beds and mats so that at least Peter's shadow might fall on some of them as he passed by. [16]Crowds gathered also from the towns around Jerusalem, bringing their sick and those tormented by evil spirits, and all of them were healed.

This paragraph, like 2:42-47 and 4:32-35, is a Lukan summary introducing the material that follows. It includes some statements that reach back to what has been narrated before—principally vv.12a-14, which recall the Christians' practice of meeting in Solomon's Colonnade, the reverential fear aroused by the awful end of Ananias and Sapphira, and the increasing number of people who believed. In the main, however, the paragraph introduces the story of the apostles' second appearance before the Sanhedrin by giving a reason for the Sadducees' jealousy and for their second inquisition of the apostles, the reason being the continued success of the Christian mission at Jerusalem.

Source critics have been troubled by the facts that (1) there is no proper connection between vv.14 and 15 and that (2) v.15 links up quite nicely with v.12a apart from the intervening material. Some commentators, therefore, have taken vv.12-14 as a self-contained unit stemming from an earlier source with vv.15-16 as a rather awkward editorial addition; others have taken vv.12a and 15-16 as representative of Luke's source material and vv.12b-14 as an editorial intrusion. Luke, however, was probably faced in his source materials with the juxtaposition of the vignettes about the deceit of Ananias and Sapphira and the apostles' second appearance before the Jewish Sanhedrin and thus felt the need to provide his readers with a summary paragraph as a transition from the one to the other. We may fault him for crowding too much into his summary paragraph or for arranging it in a somewhat jumbled chronological sequence. But the course he plots in moving from reverential fear on the part of the church and the people (cf. 5:5, 11) to heightened jealousy on the part of the Sadducees (cf. 5:17-33) and increased rejoicing on the part of the apostles (cf. 5:41–42) is not too difficult to follow. And his purpose in constructing such a prefatory summary here—which, in fact, parallels in both motive and pattern what he has done at 4:32–35—is understandable.

12a The reason for the Sadducees' jealousy and the apostles' second appearance before the Jewish Sanhedrin is given quite concisely. In defiance of the council's orders, the apostles continued to carry on their ministry among the people, with "many miraculous signs and wonders" being performed. And as with his summary paragraph of 4:32–35, so Luke here puts his thesis statement at the very beginning of his treatment.

12b–14 Luke now speaks resumptively of three groups of people and their response to the Sanhedrin's warning and the fear engendered by Ananias and Sapphira's fate: (1) the Christians and their continued meeting together in Solomon's Colonnade; (2) the un-believing Jews (*hoi loipoi*, "the rest") and their reluctance to associate too closely with the Christians; and (3) the responsive Jews (*ho laos*, "the people") and their honoring the Christians—with, in fact, many men and women from this group coming to believe in the Lord and being added to the number of Christian believers. Thematically, the résumé serves to support the thesis statement of v.12a; structurally it relates to its paragraph much as 4:33 with its reference to the apostles' continued preaching relates to its own paragraph.

15–16 The material in these two verses is structurally much like that of 4:34–35, for in both cases there is a logical and linguistic connection with each thesis statement (cf. the *gar*, "for," in 4:34 and the *hōste kai*, "as a result," in 5:15). In both instances special and extraordinary expressions of the respective thesis statements are detailed. As healing virtue had flowed from Jesus just by touching in faith the edge of his cloak (cf. Mark 5:25–34), so Luke tells us of extraordinary situations where even Peter's shadow was used by God to effect a cure (cf. 19:11–12). Whereas, in fact, the healing of the crippled beggar had originally aroused the Sadducees' antagonism, now, Luke tells us, such a miracle was being repeated numerous times in the apostles' ministry. Thus crowds from the outlying districts around Jerusalem thronged the apostles. No wonder the Sadducees' jealousy erupted anew!

Notes

12 On the compound σημεῖα καὶ τέρατα (*sēmeia kai terata*, "signs and wonders"), see the comments on 2:22. Evidently when Luke is more controlled by his sources, he writes *terata kai sēmeia* (cf. 2:19, 22, 43; 6:8; 7:36); but when he writes more freely, he prefers the order *sēmeia kai terata* (cf. 5:12; 14:3; 15:12).

13 Various other suggestions for understanding the phrase οὐδεὶς ἐτόλμα κολλᾶσθαι αὐτοῖς (*oudeis etolma kollasthai autois*, "no one else dared join them," NIV) have been offered: (1) no one dared to join the believers on his own authority—i.e., apart from being received by them and baptized; (2) no one dared to meddle with (or contend with, antagonize) the believers; and (3) no one dared prevent the believers (from meeting in Solomon's Colonnade). Each of these, however, is a highly inferential reading, with the verb κολλάω (*kollaō*) best translated as "join," "associate with on intimate terms," "come in close contact with" (BAG, p. 442; cf. Luke 15:15). On the expression ὁ λαός (*ho laos*, "the people") in Luke's writings, see the discussion on 2:47a.

2. The arrest and trial of the apostles

5:17–33

[17]Then the high priest and all his associates, who were members of the party of the Sadducees, were filled with jealousy. [18]They arrested the apostles and put them in the public jail. [19]But during the night an angel of the Lord opened the doors of the jail and brought them out. [20]"Go, stand in the temple courts," he said, "and tell the people the full message of this new life."

[21]At daybreak they entered the temple courts, as they had been told, and began to teach the people.

When the high priest and his associates arrived, they called together the Sanhedrin—the full assembly of the elders of Israel—and sent to the jail for the apostles. [22]But on arriving at the jail, the officers did not find them there. So they went back and reported, [23]"We found the jail securely locked, with the guards standing at the doors; but when we opened them, we found no one inside." [24]On hearing this report, the captain of the temple guard and the chief priests were puzzled, wondering what would come of this.

[25]Then someone came and said, "Look! The men you put in jail are standing in the temple courts teaching the people." [26]At that, the captain went with his officers and brought the apostles. They did not use force, because they feared that the people would stone them.

[27]Having brought the apostles, they made them appear before the Sanhedrin to be questioned by the high priest. [28]"We gave you strict orders not to teach in this name," he said. "Yet you have filled Jerusalem with your teaching and are determined to make us guilty of this man's blood."

[29]Peter and the other apostles replied: "We must obey God rather than men! [30]The God of our fathers raised Jesus from the dead—whom you had killed by hanging him on a tree. [31]God exalted him to his own right hand as Prince and Savior that he might give repentance and forgiveness of sins to Israel. [32]We are witnesses of these things, and so is the Holy Spirit, whom God has given to those who obey him."

[33]When they heard this, they were furious and wanted to put them to death.

Luke's narrative of the apostles' second appearance before the Sanhedrin is divided into three sections, with a typically Lukan connective beginning each section: *anastas* ("rising up") at v.17, introducing the arrest and trial of the apostles (vv.17–33); *anastas* ("rising up"; "stood up," NIV) at v.34, introducing Gamaliel's wise counsel of moderation (vv.34–40); and *men oun* ("so," "then") at v.41, beginning the statements about the apostles' rejoicing and continued ministry (vv.41–42). NIV treats *anastas* in v.17 and *men oun* in v.41 as only stylistic connectives and, therefore, does not translate them.

17–18 Again, as in 4:1–31, Luke has the early opposition to Christianity arising principally from the Sadducees. Pharisees were undoubtedly present in the Sanhedrin (cf. comments on "the full assembly of the elders of Israel," v.21), but their presence in these earliest days of the church's existence (till, at least, the "apostasy" of Stephen and the Hellenists) is depicted as exerting a moderating influence on the antagonism of the Sadducees. Thus "the high priest and all his associates, who were members of the party [*hē ousa hairesis*] of the Sadducees," are presented as taking official action a second time against the apostles—arresting them and putting them "in the public jail" (*en tērēsei dēmosia*). The word *hairesis* ("party") is employed variously in the NT of Sadducees (here), of Pharisees (15:5; 26:5), of Christians (24:5, 14; 28:22), of divisions within the churches (1 Cor 11:19; Gal 5:20), and of heresies (2 Peter 2:1)—either with (in varying degrees) or without a pejorative nuance. The inclusion of the participle *ousa* ("being")

318

seems to be a Lukan mannerism drawn ultimately from Grecian jurisprudence and usually adds little to the sense (cf. 13:1; 14:13; 28:17). Here, however, it gives the sentence a somewhat official and menacing sound. The word *dēmosia* used as an adverb carries the meaning of "publicly" (cf. 16:37; 18:28; 20:20; 2 Macc 6:10; 3 Macc 2:27; 4:7; Jos. War II, 455 [xvii.10]), and therefore as an adjective with *tērēsis* ("prison") undoubtedly means "the public prison" or "the public jail." The word *dēmosion* as a substantive, in fact, in the form of the Hebrew *dêmôs*, passed into the language of the rabbis as the term for a "common jail" (cf. SBK, 2: 635).

19–21a In speaking of "The Door-Miracles of the New Testament," Jeremias has noted the widespread popularity within the ancient world of legends regarding prison doors that open of themselves under divine instigation (cf. TDNT, 3:175) and concludes the following:

> The threefold repetition of the motif of the miraculous opening of prison doors in Ac., its distribution between the apostles in Ac. 5:19, Peter in 12:6–11, and Paul in 16:26f., and the agreement with ancient parallels in many details, e.g., liberation by night, the role of the guards, the falling off of chains, the bursting open of the doors, the shining of bright light, earthquake, all suggest that in form at least Lk. is following an established *topos* (ibid., p. 176).

Undoubtedly the form of such stories must be judged to have influenced Luke to some extent in the composition of his narrative here, for literary conventions and forms, as well as ideas, were certainly "in the air." Yet, as Bruce observes, "In this as in all form-critical studies it must be remembered that the material is more important than the form; meat-pies and mud-pies may be made in pie-dishes of identical shape, but the identity of shape is the least important consideration in comparing the two kinds of pies" (*Book of the Acts*, p. 120,n).

The "angel of the Lord" (*angelos kyriou*) is the LXX term for the Hebrew "Angel of Yahweh" (*mal'ak YHWH*), which denotes God himself in his dealings with men (cf. Exod 3:2, 4, 7; passim). While the Greek *angelos*, like the Hebrew *mal'ak*, may simply mean "messenger," here it denotes the presence or agency of God himself (cf. 8:26; 12:7, 23 [probably also simply *angelos* in 7:30, 35, 38; 12:11; 27:23]; Matt 1:20, 24; 2:13, 19; 28:2; Luke 1:11; 2:9). By divine intervention, then, the apostles were released from the public jail and told: "Go, stand in the temple courts, and tell the people the full message of this new life" (v.20). The use of the aorist passive participle *stathentes* ("stand," or more appropriately, "hold your ground," "stand firm") with the present imperative *poreuesthe* ("go") suggests that dogged steadfastness on the apostles' part was required in face of the Sadducees' opposition. The apostles' message was to continue to be directed to the nation Israel (*ho laos*, "the people") and to continue to be proclaimed fully (*panta ta rhēmata*, lit., "all the words" or "things"), in spite of the Sanhedrin's attempt to silence it. The focus is on "this new life"—with "life" (*zōē*) and "salvation" (*sōtēria*) understood in the NT as being synonymous, since both are Greek translations of the Hebrew word *hayyāh*. And since the apostles had been miraculously released and divinely commissioned, that is exactly what they began to do.

21b–27 Having (as they thought) confined the apostles in the public jail for the night, in the morning "the high priest and his associates" called together the members of the

Sanhedrin in order to make some judgment and take some action about the disturbances the Christians caused. Luke adds "the full assembly of the elders of Israel" (*kai pasan tēn gerousian tōn huiōn Israēl*; lit., "even all the senate of the sons of Israel"), probably to make clear that the Pharisees were well represented in the council at this time, though they may not have been at the first trial but became vocal through Gamaliel at the second one (cf. vv.34–40). So the Sanhedrin sent to the jail for their prisoners—but did not find them. "The captain of the temple guard and the chief priests were puzzled," probably concluding that the escape was aided and abetted by members of the temple guard. But when they heard that the apostles were teaching the people in the temple courts, "the captain" took command of his temple police and brought the apostles in before the council to be interrogated (v.26a). In his narrative, Luke states that no violence was used in the arrest because the captain and his guard feared the reaction of the people (v.26b). This says something about the early Christians' response to Jesus' example of nonviolence and nonretaliation when he was arrested (cf. Mark 14:43–50), for they might have begun a riot and thus extricated themselves. It also continues the theme of "the favor of all the people" in 2:42–47.

28 As the apostles stood before the Sanhedrin, the high priest, as president of the council, began the interrogation by reminding the apostles of the council's order for them to be silent, which obviously had not been complied with. It is uncertain whether Luke had in mind Annas or Caiaphas as leading the interrogation; while the latter was officially the high priest at the time, the former is assumed in the NT to be the real power behind the throne and continues to be called the high priest (cf. Luke 3:2; John 18:13–24). Formally, the high priest's interrogation contains no question at all but only points up the apostles' refusal to obey the Sanhedrin's order (i.e., a charge of "contempt of court"). He also objects to their insistence on blaming the council for Jesus' death (cf. 4:10, "whom you crucified"). For the Sadducean leadership of the council, the uncontested charge of contempt of court was sufficient legal warrant for taking action against the apostles. With their vested interests, the Sadducees wanted only to preserve their own authority and put an end to the rising disturbance among the people. They evidently had no interest in determining the truth or falsity of the Christians' claims. Their hardened attitude is manifest in their refusal to mention the name of Jesus (cf. *epi tō onomati toutō*, "in this name," v.28; contra *epi tō onomati tou Iēsou*, "in the name of Jesus," 4:18) and in their spitting out the epithet "this man" when they had to refer directly to him.

29–32 By saying "Peter and the other apostles replied," Luke suggests Peter was the spokesman for the group of apostles on trial, with the others in some way indicating their agreement. Their response is hardly a reasoned defense but simply a reaffirmation of their position. As at the first trial (4:19), here they voice even more succinctly the noble principle "We must obey God rather than men." And also as at the first trial, the focus is on Jesus.

"By hanging him on a tree" (*kremasantes epi xylou*) is a locution for crucifixion and stems from Deuteronomy 21:22–23. While *xylon* was used in antiquity and in the LXX variously for "a tree," "wood" of any kind, "a pole," and various objects made of wood, including "a gallows," it is also used in the NT for the cross of Jesus (cf. 10:39; 13:29; Gal 3:13 [quoting Deut 21:23]; 1 Peter 2:24). The titles "Prince" and "Savior" are christological ascriptions rooted in the confessions of the early church and particularly associated with the NT themes of exaltation and Lordship.

33 As far as the Sadducees were concerned, the charge of contempt of court was not only uncontested but repeated. On hearing the apostles reaffirm what to them could only be considered intolerable obstinacy, the Sadducees were furious and wanted to destroy them. While the Sanhedrin did not have authority under Roman jurisdiction to inflict capital punishment, undoubtedly they would have found some pretext for handing these men over to the Romans for such action—as they did with Jesus himself—had it not been for the intervention of the Pharisees, as represented particularly by Gamaliel.

Notes

17 On the Sadducees, see comments on 4:1.

21 The verb ἐδίδασκον (edidaskon) should probably be understood as an inceptive imperfect (i.e., "they began to teach").

The epexegetical phrase καὶ πᾶσαν τὴν γερουσίαν τῶν υἱῶν Ἰσραήλ (kai pasan tēn gerousian tōn huiōn Israēl, "and all the senate of the sons of Israel"; NIV, "the full assembly of the elders of Israel") probably stems from the LXX wording of Exod 12:21. On the Sanhedrin, together with its other names, see comments and note on 4:5.

24-27 On "the captain of the temple guard" (ὁ στρατηγὸς τοῦ ἱεροῦ, ho stratēgos tou hierou) and his temple police force, see comments on 4:1.

26 D strangely omits the negative οὐ (ou, "not") in οὐ μετὰ βίας (ou meta bias, "not with force"), inserting it rather into the high priest's words at v.28.

27 On Annas and Caiaphas as high priests, see comments on 4:6.

28 D and some later MSS attempt to make the high priest's statement into a question by inserting the negative οὐ (ou) before παραγγελίᾳ (parangelia, "strict orders"). D heightens the caustic nature of the high priest's reference to Jesus by substituting the demonstrative pronoun ἐκεῖνος (ekeinos, "that") for τούτος (toutos, "this"). Perhaps, as Jocz suggests, the way in which Jesus is referred to here as "this man" is an early example of the reluctance of Judaism generally to pronounce the name of Jesus, particularly as seen in the Talmudic writings (Jakob Jocz, *The Jewish People and Jesus Christ* [London: SPCK, 1949], p. 111).

31 On the titles ἀρχηγός (archēgos, "Prince") and σωτήρ (sōtēr, "Savior") see my *Christology*, pp. 53-58, 99-103, 141-44.

3. Gamaliel's wise counsel of moderation

5:34-40

34But a Pharisee named Gamaliel, a teacher of the law, who was honored by all the people, stood up in the Sanhedrin and ordered that the men be put outside for a little while. 35Then he addressed them: "Men of Israel, consider carefully what you intend to do to these men. 36Some time ago Theudas appeared, claiming to be somebody, and about four hundred men rallied to him. He was killed, all his followers were dispersed, and it all came to nothing. 37After him, Judas the Galilean appeared in the days of the census and led a band of people in revolt. He too was killed, and all his followers were scattered. 38Therefore, in the present case I advise you: Leave these men alone! Let them go! For if their purpose or activity is of human origin, it will fail. 39But if it is from God, you will not be able to stop these men; you will only find yourselves fighting against God."

40His speech persuaded them. They called the apostles in and had them flogged. Then they ordered them not to speak in the name of Jesus, and let them go.

The portrayal of Gamaliel's counsel (vv.34-40) is the high point of Luke's account of the apostles' second appearance before the Sanhedrin and the main reason why he included the whole vignette. Structurally, the aorist participle *anastas* ("rising up") at v.17, used as a connective and introducing the heightened antagonism of the Sadducees to the Christians (vv.17-33), is balanced by the same connective *anastas* at v.34 to introduce the moderation of the Pharisees depicted in vv.34-40 (see introduction to vv.17-33). Apparently Luke's purpose here is to contrast the developed antagonism of the Sadducees with the moderation of Gamaliel as spokesman for the Pharisees.

34-35 The Pharisees represent the continuation of the ancient Hasidim, that group of "pious ones" in Israel who, during the Seleucid oppressions, joined the Hasmoneans (Maccabees) in the struggle for religious freedom but later opposed the Maccabean rulers in their political and territorial claims. They came from diverse family, occupational, and economic backgrounds and gave themselves to the study of the Law (Torah) in both its written and oral forms, to expounding the Law in terms of its contemporary relevance, and to preparing the people for the coming of the Messianic Age by means of education in Scripture and the oral tradition. The name "Pharisee" probably comes from the Aramaic verb meaning "to separate" (*pᵉraš*), which Pharisees themselves evidently understood in its plural participial form to mean "the separated ones," in the sense of "holy ones dedicated entirely to God." In the period before the Fall of Jerusalem in A.D. 70, they were in the minority in the Sanhedrin. But their support by the people was so great that all matters of life and ceremony were guided by their interpretations (cf. Jos. Antiq. XVIII, 15 [i.3]), and Sadducean magistrates had to profess adherence to their principles in order to hold the formal allegiance of the populace (ibid., XVIII, 17 [i.4]).

Theologically, the Pharisees looked for a Messianic Age and a personal Messiah; they accepted a doctrine of the resurrection of the dead (though they understood such a doctrine to mean either the immortality of the soul or the reanimation and resuscitation of the body); they believed in the presence and activity of angels and demons; they held in balance the tenets of God's eternal decrees and man's freedom of will; and they tried to live a life of simple piety apart from needless wealth and luxury (cf. Jos. War II, 162-63 [viii.14]; Antiq. XIII, 171-73 [v.9]; XVIII, 11-15 [i.2-3]).

The first-century Pharisee Gamaliel I, who was either the son or grandson of the famous Hillel, was himself so highly esteemed among his people that the Mishnah says of him: "Since Rabban Gamaliel the elder died there has been no more reverence for the law; and purity and abstinence died out at the same time" (*Sotah* 9.15). Here in Acts he is portrayed as having taken charge at a certain point in the council meeting and as having gained the acquiescence of those present—not through any vested authority but through personal forcefulness and respect for what he represented. And he addresses the council members with the traditional designation "Men of Israel" (cf. 2:22).

36-37 The most notorious historical blunder in Acts, as many see it, is Gamaliel's reference to the Jewish revolutionaries Theudas and Judas the Galilean in this speech. The major historical problems are two: (1) the conflict with Josephus as to the chronological order of these rebellions, for Josephus places that of Judas at about A.D. 6 (Antiq. XVIII, 4-10 [i.1]) with that of Theudas at about A.D. 44 (Antiq. XX, 97-98 [v.1]); and, more seriously, (2) that Gamaliel at about A.D. 34 refers to an uprising of Theudas that did not occur till a decade or so later. Nineteenth-century criticism usually explained this as a result of Luke's confused dependence on Josephus, arguing that Luke had misunderstood Josephus's later reminiscence in Antiquities XX, 102 (v.2) of Judas's revolt with the earlier actual revolt and had forgotten some sixty years or more after the event (if indeed he had ever known) that Gamaliel's speech preceded Theudas' rebellion by a decade or so. Many contemporary scholars continue to highlight this problem as being disastrous for any confidence in Luke's historical and chronological accuracy. Haenchen, for example, insists "that Luke should have been capable of transposing Theudas' march to the Jordan—which [on Haenchen's dating of Acts] took place perhaps forty years before the composition of Acts—to the time preceding the census of Quirinius, some *eighty* years distant from Acts, proves that the traditions reaching him had left him in utter confusion where chronology was concerned" (*Acts of the Apostles*, p. 257).

But the arguments for Luke's dependence on Josephus have been fairly well demolished by a number of comparative studies of the two writers; and Emil Schürer's dictum continues to hold true today: "Either Luke had not read Josephus, or he had forgotten all about what he had read" ("Lucas und Josephus," ZWT, 19 [1876], 582). And despite the usual caustic comment about "special pleading," it still remains true that the Theudas Gamaliel referred to may have been one of the many insurgent leaders who arose in Palestine at the time of Herod the Great's death in 4 B.C., and not the Theudas who led the Jewish uprising of A.D. 44, and that Gamaliel's examples of Jewish insurrectionists refer to a Theudas of about 4 B.C. and to Judas the Galilean of A.D. 6 whereas Josephus focused on the Judas of A.D. 6 and another Theudas of A.D. 44. Our problem with these verses, therefore, may result just as much from our own ignorance of the situation as from what we believe we know as based on Josephus.

38–39 It has frequently been claimed that the words of Gamaliel here are "an historical mistake," for they are not in character with what we know of Pharisaism (J. Weiss, *The History of Primitive Christianity*, 2 vols., tr., ed. F.C. Grant [London: Macmillan, 1937], 1:185). Yet in characterizing the respective attitudes of the Pharisees and the Sadducees, Josephus tells us: "The Pharisees are affectionate to each other and cultivate harmonious relations with the community. The Sadducees, on the contrary, are, even among themselves, rather boorish in their behavior, and in their relations with their compatriots are as rude as to aliens" (War II, 166 [viii.14]). And later he says that "the Pharisees are naturally lenient in the matter of punishments" (Antiq. XIII, 294 [x.6]). Likewise, Rabbi Johanan the sandal maker, a second-century disciple of Rabbi Akiba, is quoted in *Pirke Aboth* 4.11: "Any assembling together that is for the sake of Heaven shall in the end be established, but any that is not for the sake of Heaven shall not in the end be established" —a policy of waiting to see the end result of a matter that is exactly the attitude of Gamaliel as Luke reports it here.

Admittedly, both Josephus and Johanan had their own prejudices and purposes in saying what they did (this is also true of every writer and teacher, including commentators on Acts). Nevertheless, there is good reason to believe that such sentiments of tolerance and moderation, with history being viewed as the final judge of whether something is of God, characterized the better Pharisees of the day and that therefore Gamaliel's response to the proclamation and activity of the apostles was not out of line for such an Hillelian Pharisee as he.

Of course, later in Acts (cf. 8:1, 3; 9:1-2), Saul of Tarsus, who was trained under Gamaliel I (cf. 22:3), takes a very different attitude toward the Christians, joining with the Sadducees and obtaining the high priest's authorization to track them down and imprison them. But between Gamaliel's advice in Acts 5 and Saul's action in Acts 8 and 9, there arose from the depths of Christian conviction what the Pharisees as well as the Sadducees could only have considered to be a threat of Jewish apostasy. Before Gamaliel's counsel of moderation, Luke tells us that the central issues of the church's proclamation had been the messiahship, lordship, and saviorhood of Jesus of Nazareth—his heaven-ordained death, his victorious resurrection, and his present status as exalted Redeemer. "The stream of thought," as Manson observed in characterizing the church's early functional theology, "flowed in an intense but narrow channel; carrying in its flood much that for the time remained in solution in the subconscious rather than in the conscious region of the Christian mentality" (William Manson, *Jesus the Messiah* [London: Hodder & Stoughton, 1943], p. 52). To the Sadducees who instigated the early suppressions, such teaching not only upset orderly rule but, more importantly, impinged upon their authority. To the more noble of the Pharisees, however, the Jerusalem Christians were yet within the scope of Judaism and not to be treated as heretics.

The divine claims for Jesus as yet lay in the subconsciousness of the church, and those who were his followers showed no tendency to relax their observance of the Mosaic law because of their new beliefs. Other sects were tolerated within Judaism. Those whom the Pharisees considered to be deluded in their messianic commitment could be countenanced as well. As Nock said, "The Pharisees might wish all men to be even as they were; but that result could be attained only by persuasion" (A.D. Nock, *St. Paul* [New York: Harper, 1938], pp. 35–36).

Between Gamaliel's advice and Saul's action, however, there arose within Christian preaching something that could only be viewed within Jerusalem as a real threat of Jewish apostasy. In Acts 6–7 Stephen is portrayed as beginning to apply the doctrines of Jesus' messiahship and lordship to traditional Jewish views regarding the land, the law, and the temple. Moreover, he is seen as beginning to reach conclusions that related to the primacy of Jesus' messiahship and lordship and the secondary nature of Jewish views about the land, the law, and the temple. How Stephen got involved in such discussions and how he developed his argument will be dealt with in loc. For Stephen this was a dangerous path to tread, particularly in Jerusalem—a path even the apostles seemed unwilling to take at that time. Stephen's message was indeed Jewish apostasy! And had Rabbi Gamaliel the Elder faced this feature of Christian proclamation in the second Sanhedrin trial of the Jerusalem apostles, his attitude would undoubtedly have been different. With the whole basis of Judaism under attack in Stephen's preaching, as the Pharisees would have viewed it, Saul's persecution of the believers was probably undertaken later on with Gamaliel's full approval. As yet, however, that was not the situation; so Gamaliel here urges tolerance and moderation.

40 Gamaliel's wise counsel prevailed to some extent among his Sanhedrin colleagues and held back the worst of Sadducean intentions, though it did not entirely divert their wrath. Thus the apostles were flogged (probably with the severe beating of thirty-nine stripes detailed in *Makkoth* 3.10–15a), were warned that the ban against teaching in the name of Jesus was still in effect, and were then released.

Notes

34 On the Pharisees, see esp. L. Finkelstein, "The Pharisees: Their Origin and Their Philosophy," HTR, 22 (1929), 185–261; idem, *The Pharisees*, 2 vols. (Philadelphia: Jewish Publication Society of America, 1938). For the view that the name means "interpreters" (from the idea of "dividing" in the Aram. verb), see W.O.E. Oesterley, *The Jews and Judaism During the Greek Period* (London: SPCK, 1941), pp. 245ff.; and for the view that it originally meant "Persianizers"

because of their eschatology and angelology, see T.W. Manson, "Sadducee and Pharisee—the Origin and Significance of the Names," BJRL, 22 (1938), 153-59.

For the view that Hillel was Gamaliel's father, see HJP, 2.1:363, n.164; H.L. Strack, *Introduction to the Talmud and Midrash* (Philadelphia: Jewish Publication Society of America, 1931), p. 109. But probably Hillel as Gamaliel's grandfather is the more supportable position; cf. R.T. Herford, "Pirke Aboth," APOT, 2:694, and W. Bacher, "Gamaliel I," JE, 5:558-59. The title "Rabban" (lit., "our teacher") was an honorific one given to several successive teachers of the school of Hillel, which served to mark them off as more significant than those designated simply "rabbi" (lit., "my teacher").

38-39 On "The Piety of Hebraic Judaism," see my *Paul*, pp. 65-85. Possibly significant also in understanding Gamaliel's counsel of moderation are the statements in b *Sanhedrin* 98b and 99a, that "Hillel ... maintained that there will be no Messiah for Israel, since they have already enjoyed him during the reign of Hezekiah," and b *Sanhedrin* 99a: "May God forgive him [i.e., Hillel, for so saying]." J. Klausner (*The Messianic Idea in Israel*, tr. W.F. Stinespring [London: Allen & Unwin, 1956], p. 404) and G.F. Moore (*Judaism in the First Centuries of the Christian Era*, 3 vols. [Cambridge: Harvard University, 1927-30], 2:347, n.2) believe this to be a reference to another other than Hillel the Elder; but S. Mowinckel (*He That Cometh*, tr. G.W. Anderson [Oxford: Blackwell, 1956], p. 284, n.6, following H. Gressmann, *Der Messias*, pp. 449ff.) and M. Buttenwieser ("Messiah," JE, 8:508) insist that this is the great rabbi. If this be truly the Hillel of Herod the Great's day, then there was in Gamaliel's own family a tragedy of mistaken identity such as would urge upon Gamaliel a policy of moderation toward others who might in his opinion have had similarly mistaken views.

---

4. The apostles' rejoicing and continued ministry

5:41-42

> [41]The apostles left the Sanhedrin, rejoicing because they had been counted worthy of suffering disgrace for the Name. [42]Day after day, in the temple courts and from house to house, they never stopped teaching and proclaiming the good news that Jesus is the Christ.

Luke ends his account of the apostles' second appearance before the Sanhedrin with a brief summary that speaks of their rejoicing and continued ministry. It is a statement that has nuances of defiance, confidence, and victory; and in many ways it gathers together all Luke has set forth from 2:42 on. Dibelius prefers to think of these chapters as considerably exaggerated throughout and assumes the situation to have been more like the following:

> A band of people had been gathered together in a common belief in Jesus Christ and in the expectation of his coming again, and were leading a quiet, and in the Jewish sense, "pious" existence in Jerusalem. It was a modest existence, and nothing but the victorious conviction of the believers betrayed the fact that from this company a movement would go out which was to change the world, that this community was to become the centre of the Church (*Studies in Acts*, p. 124).

And Haenchen agrees, insisting that "in the quiet life of the primitive community there were no mass assemblies such as Luke places at the outset of the Christian mission, therefore no conflicts with the Sadducees arising from them," and that only with the rise of the Hellenists in the church sometime around A.D. 44 was "this secluded situation, in which the winning of souls for the Lord went on in the quiet personal encounter of man with man," brought to an end (*Acts of the Apostles*, p. 258).

Ultimately, of course, we are forced to take sides, either with Luke and his claim of having accurate source material that stems from reliable eyewitnesses or with Dibelius, Haenchen, et al. and their claim to "expert opinion." The latter would have us believe that it boils down to a choice between tradition and scholarship. In actual fact, however, it is a choice between two quite divergent historical traditions and two quite different philosophical perspectives, each of which has become "orthodox" in its own circle, and two fairly different ways of doing traditio-historical criticism. And while his material is selective in nature, styled, fragmentary, and incomplete, it is, as this commentary attempts to demonstrate, Luke's view and understanding of events that leads us much further along the path of truth than Dibelius or Haenchen do, despite their many acknowledged excellencies of insight and skill in handling details.

41 Luke connects his summary statement with his narrative by using one of his favorite connectives—*men oun* ("so," "then"). And he stresses the fact that just as the apostles performed miracles through the power of the name of Jesus (cf. 3:6) and proclaimed that name before the people and the council (cf. 3:16; 4:10, 12), so they rejoiced when "counted worthy of suffering disgrace for the Name."

42 Furthermore, Luke tells us that "they never stopped teaching and proclaiming the good news that Jesus is the Christ." In this somewhat formal statement, which comes close to concluding our author's whole first panel of material, there is both a correlation with the thesis paragraph of 2:42–47—explicitly in the phrases "in the temple courts and from house to house" (cf. 2:46), though also inferentially in the note of continuance that is sounded—and an anticipation of the final words of Luke's sixth panel at the very end of Acts: "boldly and without hindrance" (28:31).

Notes

41 On the connective μὲν οὖν (*men oun*, "so," "then") and its appearance elsewhere in Acts, see comments on 1:6.

The theme of being "counted worthy of suffering disgrace for the Name" is a major motif in the letter of 1 Peter (cf. esp. 2:21; 4:12–19).

F. The Hellenists' Presence and Problem in the Church

6:1–6

[1]In those days when the number of disciples was increasing, the Grecian Jews among them complained against those of the Aramaic-speaking community because their widows were being overlooked in the daily distribution of food. [2]So the Twelve gathered all the disciples together and said, "It would not be right for us to neglect the ministry of the word of God in order to wait on tables. [3]Brothers, choose seven men from among you who are known to be full of the Spirit and wisdom. We will turn this responsibility over to them [4]and will give our attention to prayer and the ministry of the word."

[5]This proposal pleased the whole group. They chose Stephen, a man full of faith and of the Holy Spirit; also Philip, Procorus, Nicanor, Timon, Parmenas, and Nicolas from Antioch, a convert to Judaism. [6]They presented these men to the apostles, who prayed and laid their hands on them.

The source or sources at Luke's disposal for his first panel of material on the earliest days of the church in Jerusalem seem to have been fairly well intact for chapters 2–5. Probably, as we have seen, Luke added 2:42–47, which serves as the thesis paragraph for the whole panel, and also inserted the two summary paragraphs 4:32–35 and 5:12–16, which provide the settings for their corresponding vignettes. Likewise, Luke's literary touch is everywhere apparent in the style and form of his presentation. In the main, it appears he had his sources fairly well in hand for most of this part of his narrative. Furthermore, his source material seems to have contained its own conclusion, which was probably very similar to what we have at 5:41–42.

But in moving on from this point, Luke seems to have been faced with a real procedural problem. In the first place, his second panel (6:8–9:31) focuses upon three individuals—Stephen, Philip, and Saul of Tarsus—whose ministries were essential for his developmental thesis but who have not as yet been mentioned. Lest they be thought of as isolated figures in the development of the early church, Luke must relate them to what has gone before. Also, since these three men were in some way related to the Hellenists (though Saul of Tarsus was not himself a Hellenist), and since thus far in the narrative there is, aside from 2:5–12, nothing regarding these Hellenistic Christians, Luke found it necessary to tell his readers something about this element in the church.

Luke might have started his second panel with discussing the presence of the Hellenistic Christians in Jerusalem, for that would have provided a good thematic introduction for the panel. To have done so, however, would have separated them from their roots in the early church and would have damaged his theme of continuity amid diversity and development. Instead, he chose to include the portrayal of the Hellenists in the Jerusalem congregation in his first panel and before the summary statement (6:7) that concludes that panel—even though the Jerusalem church itself, for reasons that will be recounted as we proceed, might not have provided him with source material on the Hellenists, and he had to ferret it out for himself.

1 Historically, this verse is not only one of the most important in Acts, it is also one of the most complicated and most discussed verses in the entire book. What one concludes regarding the identity of "the Grecian Jews" (*Hellēnistai*, lit., "Hellenists"), their relation to "the Aramaic-speaking community" (*Hebraioi*, lit., "Hebraists" or "Hebraic Jews"), and their circumstances within the church largely affects how one understands the material in Luke's second panel (6:8–9:31) and the whole course of events within the Jerusalem church as well. It is important, therefore, to understand as precisely as possible what Luke says *and* implies in describing this group within the early church (i.e., the Hellenists—NIV, "the Grecian Jews"), a group he introduces by the phrases "in those days" and "when the number of disciples was increasing."

As for differentiating the Hellenists from the believers of Hebrew background, most commentators from Chrysostom to the present have identified them by their language and geographical origin—i.e., as Greek-speaking Jews of the Diaspora who had settled in Jerusalem among the native-born and Aramaic-speaking populace (e.g., see BC, 5:59–74). But that such a definition lacks sufficient precision to be useful is pointed up by the fact that Paul classed himself among the *Hebraioi* ("Hebrews," 2 Cor 11:22) and a "Hebrew of the Hebrews" (Phil 3:5), though he was also fluent in Greek and came from a Diaspora city. Some interpreters, therefore, have understood Hellenists to mean Jewish proselytes (e.g., E.C. Blackman, "The Hellenists of Acts vi.1," ExpT, 48 [1937], 524–25), though the fact that only one of the seven men in v.5 is called a proselyte seems fatal to such a position (assuming that the seven chosen to supervise the daily distribution of food are identified with the Hellenists generally). A few have even argued that the term *Hellēnistēs* means no more than the noun *Hellēn* ("Greek") because of its derivation from the verb *hellēnizō*, which means "to live as a Greek" rather than just "to speak Greek"— and therefore have taken it to refer simply to Gentiles (e.g., H.J. Cadbury, BC, 3:106). But it is difficult to visualize Gentile believers, apart from those who first were Jewish proselytes, as accepted members within the Jerusalem church at any time during the first century, much less at such an early date as Acts 6 requires. The case of Cornelius is presented in 10:1–11:18 as quite exceptional, and this prohibits any easy assumption that such instances were common at an earlier time. Moreover, there is no indication that Cornelius actually joined the body of Jewish Christians at Jerusalem, though they accepted the fact of his conversion.

Of late, some have proposed that the Hellenists of Acts 6 were Jews who were related in some manner to the Essene movement in Palestine. Oscar Cullmann has urged that we view them as connected in some way with the Essenes (cf. esp. "The Significance of the Qumran Texts for Research into the Beginnings of Christianity," *The Scrolls and the New Testament*, ed. K. Stendahl [London: SCM, 1957], pp. 18–32) and has proposed that it was just such a group that formed "the Johannine circle" responsible for both the Johannine writings and the Letter to the Hebrews (*The Johannine Circle*, tr. J. Bowden [Philadelphia: Westminster, 1976], passim). Marcei Simon has spoken repeatedly of the Hellenists as a radical reforming "gentilistic" party within Essene sectarianism (passim); and Jean Daniélou raised the possibility that they were a Samaritan branch of Essenism (*The Theology of Jewish Christianity*, tr. J.A. Baker [Chicago: Regnery, 1964], p. 72).

To identify the Hellenists with the Essenes, however, is to presuppose a picture of Essene theology that goes much beyond the evidence now at hand and flies in the face of some of the data now available. It is difficult to see how Essene obsessions with ritual purity, strict observance of the law, and the eternal significance of the temple cultus— even though in opposition to the Jerusalem priesthood because of its secularization and impurity—can be correlated with what Acts 6 says about the Hellenists or with Stephen's message in Acts 7. And the anti-Samaritanism of the Qumran community, which comes to the fore in the various unfavorable allusions in the pesher commentaries to "the men of Ephraim and Manasseh" (cf. 4QpPs 37 on v.14; 4QpNah on 2:13; 3:1, 6), is hard to reconcile with the proclamation of the gospel in Samaria by those who were scattered throughout Judea and Samaria by the persecution that began with Stephen's martyrdom. If the Essenes are to be brought into the discussion of Acts 6 at all, it is much more likely (as we shall suggest later) that they are to be identified in some manner and to some degree with the "large number of priests" of 6:7 who "became obedient to the faith."

Nor is it likely that the Hellenists should be identified with the Samaritans, as Abram Spiro has argued on the basis of the linguistic and conceptual parallels he finds between Stephen's speech of Acts 7 and readings in the Samaritan Pentateuch and Samaritan views of history ("Stephen's Samaritan Background," Appendix V, in Munck, *Acts*, pp. 285–300). Variants of the Hebrew biblical text were more widespread than has been previously realized, as the DSS have taught us, and the parallels between Stephen and the Samaritans are more analogical than strictly genealogical. Furthermore, since Samaritan theology was so thoroughly dominated by sacerdotal interests, it is very hard to believe that anyone brought up in it could have given the kind of prophetic interpretation of the OT that is expressed in Stephen's discourse. In addition, it seems quite inconceivable that Luke would not have mentioned the Samaritan connection of either the Hellenists or Stephen and Philip, if there had been such. Elsewhere, he has not hesitated to speak approvingly of certain Samaritans (cf. Luke 10:33; 17:16), and in his account of the advance of the gospel into Samaria (8:4–25) it would have been to his advantage to have spoken of the connection of the Samaritans with the Hellenists. And if all this does not carry conviction, it seems even more inconceivable that Luke would have a Samaritan addressing the Jewish Sanhedrin as "brothers and fathers" (22:1).

C.F.D. Moule's suggestion that the Hellenists were "simply Jews (whether by birth or as proselytes) who spoke only Greek and no Semitic language, in contrast to *Hebraioi*, which would then mean the Jews who spoke a Semitic language in addition, of course, to Greek" ("Once More, Who Were the Hellenists?" ExpT, 70 [1959], 100) has much to commend it and seems to be an advance in the explicit meaning of the term. It hurdles the difficulty in the traditional interpretation as to how Paul could call himself an Hebraic Jew when he was from the Diaspora, it provides an explanation as to why Hellenistic synagogues were required in Jerusalem, and it offers an insight into the problem of why two of the seven men chosen in 6:5 (Stephen and Philip) appear almost immediately thereafter as evangelists within their own circle when they had actually been appointed to supervise more mundane concerns. Yet, as J.A. Fitzmyer remarks, "It should also be recalled that such a linguistic difference would also bring with it a difference in outlook and attitude" ("Jewish Christianity in Acts in Light of the Qumran Scrolls," Keck and Martyn, p. 238)—or, at least, would give rise within more Hebraic circles to suspicions and accusations of such a difference.

According to the Talmud, Pharisaism made little secret of its contempt for Hellenists and, unlike those from Syria or Babylonia (regions that are often considered extensions of the Holy Land in Talmudic discussions), they were frequently categorized by the native-born and assumedly more scrupulous populace of Jerusalem as second-class Israelites (cf. LTJM, 1:7–9). And to judge by the claim of some in the Corinthian church that they were true Hebraic Jews as opposed to being Hellenists (cf. 2 Cor 11:22a), and by the need for Paul to defend his Hebraic heritage so stoutly and so repeatedly (cf. 22:3; 2 Cor 11:22; Phil 3:5, probably in view of his Tarsian birth), it appears that this attitude of Hebraic superiority was rather widespread.

Probably, therefore, any definition of the *Hellēnistai* of Acts 6 based on linguistic or geographic considerations alone, while not entirely to be set aside, should be subsumed under a more primary understanding that stresses intellectual orientation (either actual or assumed). Also, we should very likely think of this element within the early church along the lines of "Hellenized Jewish Christians" or "Grecian Jewish believers"—that is, as Jews living in Jerusalem who had come from the Diaspora and were under some suspicion by reason of their place of birth, their speech, or both, of being more Grecian than Hebraic in their attitudes and outlook but who, since coming to Jerusalem, had become Christians. Many of them, no doubt, had originally returned to the homeland out of religious ardor and today would be called Zionists (cf. B. Reicke's identification of them as *"zionistischen Diasporajuden"* in "Der geschichtliche Hintergrund des Apostelkonzils und der Antioch-Episode," *Studia Paulina*, ed. W.C. van Unnik and G. Sevenster [Haarlem: Bohn, 1953], p. 178). Perhaps they tended to group together because of their similar backgrounds and common language, as the many Hellenistic synagogues in Jerusalem would seem to indicate (cf. E. Schürer, JE, 1:371–72, on the Diaspora synagogues in Jerusalem). But since attitudes and prejudices formed before conversion are often carried over into Christian life—too often the unworthy more than the worthy ones—some of the problems between the Hebraic Jews and the Hellenistic Jews in the church must be related to such earlier differences and prejudices.

In 6:1–6, Luke tells us that the Hellenists' "widows were being overlooked in the daily distribution of food" (v.1). Judaism had a system for the distribution of food and supplies to the poor, both to the wandering pauper and to those living in Jerusalem itself (cf. Jeremias, *Jerusalem*, pp. 126–34). There were also special religious communities (like the Pharisees and the Essenes) that had their own agents in every city to provide their members "a social service somewhere between the private and public services" (ibid., p. 130). The early Christian community at Jerusalem also expressed its spiritual unity in communal sharing of possessions and in charitable acts (cf. 2:44–45; 4:32–5:11). Apparently with the "increasing" number of believers and with the passing of time, the number of Hellenistic widows dependent on relief from the church became disproportionately large. Many pious Jews of the Diaspora had moved to Jerusalem in their later years in order to be buried near it, and their widows would have had no relatives near at hand to care for them as would the widows of the longtime residents. Nor as they became Christians would the "poor baskets" of the national system of relief be readily available to them. So the problem facing the church became acute.

The account of the dispute cannot have been invented by Luke because to do so would have been incompatible with the development of his conciliatory purpose. If anything, Luke's desire to emphasize harmonious relations within the early Christian community (cf. his three introductory summary statements—2:42–47; 4:32–35; 5:12–16) may have led him to downplay the details of the dispute, which is probably one reason why commentators have such a difficulty in interpreting the situation. Nor should we assume that the issue about the distribution of food was all that disrupted the fellowship. As Manson observed, "It is possible that the grievance in question was only the symptom of a larger tension between the two groups, arising from broad differences of outlook and sympathy" (William Manson, *The Epistle to the Hebrews* [London: Hodder & Stoughton, 1951], pp. 27–28). Earlier prejudices and resentments of this kind may have been reasserting themselves in the early Jerusalem church. And if the Hellenists spoke mostly in Greek, separate meetings within the Christian community may have been required for them—meetings which of themselves could have awakened old prejudices and resentments, both within the church and throughout the Jewish populace.

2–4 The apostles' response in this matter was to call the Christians together and suggest a solution. It is significant that the apostles were not prepared simply to ignore the problem; they seem to have realized that spiritual and material concerns are so intimately related in Christian experience that one always affects the other for better or worse. Similarly, there was no attempt either to assign blame or to act in any paternalistic fashion. Rather, their suggestion was that seven men "full of the Spirit and wisdom" be chosen from among the congregation (*ex hymōn*, "from among you," which may mean from among the Hellenists alone) who could take responsibility in the affair. The apostles sought to give their attention exclusively "to prayer and the ministry of the word."

The reference to the apostles as "the Twelve" occurs only here in Acts (cf. 1 Cor 15:5), though earlier Luke has spoken of "the Eleven" in such an absolute and corporate manner (cf. Luke 24:9, 33; Acts 2:14). Likewise, the references to Christians as "the disciples" (*hoi mathētai*) here and in v.1 are the first instances of this usage in Acts, though in the remainder of the book it occurs fairly often. However, the designation is not found in the Pauline Epistles or subapostolic literature. In using both these terms, Luke has gone back to the language of the earliest Christians and tried to make idiomatic use of it, though this may not have been natural for him. The words "full of the Spirit and wisdom" evidently refer to guidance by the Holy Spirit and skill in administration and business, which, singly and together, are so necessary in Christian service. While Christian ministers wish such qualities were more characteristic of their own boards and councils, it is only fair to say that boards and councils often wish their ministers were given more "to prayer and the ministry of the word"! A pattern is set here for both lay leaders and clergy, and God's work would move ahead more efficiently were it followed more carefully.

5-6 The apostles made a proposal, but the church, the community of God's Spirit, made the decision. The apostles therefore laid their hands on the Seven and appointed them to be responsible for the daily distribution of food. The laying on of hands recalls Moses' commissioning of Joshua in Numbers 27:18-23, where through this act some of Moses' authority was conferred on Joshua (cf. Lev 3:2; 16:21 for the symbolic transference of sin). That is evidently what the laying on of hands was meant to symbolize here, with the apostles delegating their authority to the seven selected by the church (cf. 8:17; 9:17; 13:3; 19:6 for other instances of this practice).

All seven men have Greek names; one of them is singled out as having been a Gentile convert to Judaism (that is, a "proselyte"). But it is impossible to be sure from the names themselves whether all seven were Hellenists, for at that time many Palestinian Jews also had Greek names. Nevertheless, the fact that Luke gives only Greek names suggests that all seven were in fact from the Hellenistic group within the church. Likewise, the text does not directly call these seven by the ecclesiastical title "deacon" (*diakonos*), even though it uses the cognate noun *diakonia* ("distribution") in v.1 and the verb *diakoneō* ("wait on") in v.2 for what they were to do (though it also uses the noun *diakonia*, "ministry," in v.4 for the apostles' proclamation). Yet the ministry to which the seven were appointed was functionally equivalent to what Paul covered in the title "deacon" (cf. 1 Tim 3:8-13)—which is but to affirm the maxim that in the NT "ministry was a function long before it became an office."

Acts 6:1-6 is particularly instructive as something of a pattern for church life today. In the first place, the early church took very seriously the combination of spiritual and material concerns in carrying out its God-given ministry. In doing so, it stressed prayer and the proclamation of the Word, but never to the exclusion of helping the poor and correcting injustices. And even when the church found it necessary to divide internal responsibilities and assign different functions, the early believers saw these as varying aspects of one total ministry.

Second, the early church seems to have been prepared to adjust its procedures, alter its organizational structure, and develop new posts of responsibility in response to existing needs and for the sake of the ongoing proclamation of the Word of God. Throughout the years various so-called restorationist movements in the church have attempted to reach back and recapture the explicit forms and practices of the earliest Christians and have tried to reproduce them as far as possible in their pristine forms, believing that in doing so they are more truly biblical than other church groups. But Luke's narrative here suggests that to be fully biblical is to be constantly engaged in adapting traditional methods and structures to meet existing situations, both for the sake of the welfare of the whole church and for the outreach of the gospel.

And, finally, Luke's account suggests certain restraining attitudes that could well be incorporated into contemporary churchmanship. Among these are (1) refusing to get involved in the practice of assigning blame where things have gone wrong, preferring rather to expend the energies of God's people on correcting injustices, prayer, and the proclamation of the Word, and (2) the refusal to become paternalistic in solving prob-

331

lems, which implies willingness to turn the necessary authority for working out solutions over to others—even, as was possibly the case here, to those who feel the problem most acutely and may therefore be best able to solve it.

Notes

1 NIV's translation of Ἑλληνίσται (Hellēnistai) as "Grecian Jews" is an endeavor to break away from the usual linguistic understanding of the term to a more cultural and ideological definition, and it succeeds admirably. But its translation of Ἑβραῖοι (Hebraioi) as "the Aramaic-speaking community" falls back into the old linguistic trap and raises a whole set of other problems. What is needed here is some such translation as "Grecian Jews" and "Hebraic Jews."

Luke has more references to widows and women than the other evangelists. Χήρα (chēra, "widow") occurs in Luke 2:37; 4:25–26; 7:12; 18:3, 5; 20:47–21:3 (=Mark 12:40–43); Acts 6:1; 9:39, 41; and in the rest of the NT 12 additional times; γυνή (gunē, "woman") occurs in Matt 29 times, in Mark 16 times, in Luke 41 times, in John 17 times, in Acts 19 times, and in the rest of the NT 87 times (209 times total).

2 F.M. Cross, Jr., has pointed out the linguistic and functional similarities between the use of רבים (rabbîm, "the many") in 1QS 6.8–13, which deals with the order of the public sessions at Qumran, and the use of τὸ πλῆθος (to plēthos, "the whole number," "entire") in Acts 6:2, 5 and 15:12, 30 (cf. *The Ancient Library of Qumran* [London: Duckworth, 1958], p. 174). While neither the Essene encampment at Qumran nor the Jerusalem church could be called in our modern sense a democratic assembly, it is clear that in both the congregation was involved in the deliberations of its leaders.

The expression ὁι μαθηταί (hoi mathētai, "the disciples") is also employed absolutely of Christians at 6:7; 9:1 (with τοῦ κυρίου, tou kyriou), 10, 19, 26, 38; 11:26, 29; 13:52; 14:20, 22, 28; 15:10; 16:1; 18:23, 27; 19:1, 9, 30; 20:1, 30; 21:4, 16. In 9:25 it is used of the followers of Paul.

The word τράπεζα (trapeza, "table") can mean a moneychanger's table as well as a table on which a meal is spread, but here the idea is not that of financial administration on behalf of the community but care for the poor.

5 Munck rightly cautions against a too-facile assumption on the basis of the Gr. names that all seven men chosen were Hellenists (which, of course, allows him, together with C.S. Mann, to view Stephen and Philip as Hebraic members of the Jewish Christian community). Rather conjecturally, however, Munck goes on to say: "Surely, to assume that the primitive church would choose a committee for social services in which only one of the feuding parties was represented would be to underestimate its efficiency in practical matters. Such procedure would probably have given rise to complaints from the Hebrews" (*Acts*, p. 57). Now Munck, of course, may be right. But perhaps the early church had a greater reliance on God's Spirit and a greater confidence in God's people than we have today and, therefore, was not interested in merely balancing the various concerns on the committee.

G. A Summary Statement

6:7

> [7]So the word of God spread. The number of disciples in Jerusalem increased rapidly, and a large number of priests became obedient to the faith.

7 Luke concludes his first panel of material on the earliest days of the church in Jerusalem with this summary statement, which is very much in line with his thesis paragraph (2:42–47) and his summary paragraphs (4:32–35; 5:12–16) that head their respective

units of material. His focus in this first panel has been on the advances of the gospel and the responses of the people. Therefore he concludes by saying that "the word of God spread" and "the number of disciples in Jerusalem increased rapidly."

Before he leaves his first panel of material, however, Luke—almost, it seems, as an afterthought—inserts the comment that "a large number of priests became obedient to the faith." At first glance this is, to say the least, somewhat perplexing because, in view of 4:1ff. and 5:17ff., it seems extremely difficult to believe that priests in any numbers would have become Christians. Nevertheless, as Jeremias has pointed out in detail, there were perhaps as many as eight thousand "ordinary" priests and ten thousand Levites, divided into twenty-four weekly courses, serving at the Jerusalem temple during the period of a year, whose social position was distinctly inferior to that of the high priestly families and whose piety in many cases could well have inclined them to an acceptance of the Christian message (cf. *Jerusalem*, pp. 198–213). In addition, the Qumran convenanters thought of themselves as the true sons of Zadok, as the so-called Zadokite Fragments from Caves 4 and 6 (which were formerly known as the Cairo Damascus Covenant) testify; and many of the common people in Israel undoubtedly respected— even if they could not support—the claim of these Essene covenanters to the priesthood.

Perhaps Luke himself was not aware of the distinctions in Palestine between high priestly families, ordinary priests, and Essene-type priests. What he evidently learned from his sources was that a great number of persons calling themselves priests became believers in Jesus and were numbered with the Christians in the Jerusalem church; and he seems to have just included that bit of information as something of an appendix to his portrayal of the church's earliest days in the city. He might also have found it a matter either difficult to believe or difficult to elaborate in view of what he had said earlier about the priests of Jerusalem. However, if he had known about the ordinary priests of the temple and the Essene-type priests at Qumran, the response of the priests might not have seemed so amazing and he may have said more.

Panel 2—Critical Events in the Lives of Three Pivotal Figures (6:8–9:31)

Luke now turns to three key events in the advance of the gospel beyond its strictly Jewish confines, that is, to the martyrdom of Stephen, the early ministries of Philip, and the conversion of Saul of Tarsus. Luke's presentation is largely biographical, with the initial word of each of the three accounts being the name of its central figure (cf. *Stephanos*, 6:8; *Philippos*, 8:5 [after an editorial introduction at 8:4, containing Luke's favorite connective *men oun*]; and *Saulos*, 9:1). This is the type of material that would have circulated widely among the dispossessed Hellenistic Christians, what with its heavy emphasis upon "who said what to whom" and its detailed account of Stephen's argument before the Sanhedrin. It is also the kind of material one picks up by talking with one or more of the participants. It is not too difficult, in fact, to imagine that in addition to such source materials as may have circulated within the Hellenistic Christian communities on Stephen's martyrdom, Philip's ministries, and Saul's conversion, Luke had also heard Philip and Paul speak together about these matters either during Paul's stay for "a number of days" at Philip's home in Caesarea (cf. 21:8–10a) or during Paul's imprisonment at Caesarea (cf. 25:27).

No doubt Stephen's martyrdom was indelibly imprinted on Philip's memory; and accounts of his defense, whether written or oral, had probably become the raison d'être for the Hellenists' continued ministry. Likewise, Philip must have made a lasting impression on Luke as an important figure in the advance of the Christian mission, just as he was an important person in the Christian community at Caesarea (cf. 8:40; 21:8–9). And certainly Paul was of such immense significance for Luke's narrative that an account of his conversion was inevitable—particularly because of its miraculous circumstances.

When the events of Luke's second panel took place depends largely on the dates for Paul's conversion and ministry. Since Stephen's death occurred before the conversion of Saul of Tarsus (cf. 7:58; 8:1), and since Luke presents Philip's ministries in Samaria and to the Ethiopian eunuch as following on the heels of the persecution that arose with Stephen's martyrdom, the accounts of these two Hellenistic spokesmen are historically tied to the conversion of Saul. For the chronological issues associated with Paul, see the comments on Acts 9:1–30 and other succeeding passages. As for this second panel, it is sufficient to say that the events Luke presents in it took place somewhere in the mid-thirties, possibly as early as A.D. 33 or as late as A.D. 37.

A. *The Martyrdom of Stephen* (6:8–8:3)

Interpreters have varied considerably regarding the significance of Stephen in the history of early Christianity. Most have attempted to understand him as in some manner the forerunner to Paul, proclaiming an elemental form of a law-free and universal gospel. Some, however, have taken him to be a proto-Marcionite (e.g., F.C. Baur), others as an early Ebionite (e.g., H.J. Schoeps), others as a nationalistic Zealot (e.g., S.G.F. Brandon), and a few as a thoroughly Jewish member of the Jerusalem church who represented the entire church's stance in opposition to Judaism (e.g., J. Munck). And between these various positions there is no want of variant opinion.

1. *Opposition to Stephen's ministry*

6:8–7:1

> 8Now Stephen, a man full of God's grace and power, did great wonders and miraculous signs among the people. 9Opposition arose, however, from members of the Synagogue of the Freedmen (as it was called)—Jews of Cyrene and Alexandria as well as the provinces of Cilicia and Asia. These men began to argue with Stephen, 10but they could not stand up against his wisdom or the Spirit by which he spoke.
>
> 11Then they secretly persuaded some men to say, "We have heard Stephen speak words of blasphemy against Moses and against God."
>
> 12So they stirred up the people and the elders and the teachers of the law. They seized Stephen and brought him before the Sanhedrin. 13They produced false witnesses, who testified, "This fellow never stops speaking against the holy place and against the law. 14For we have heard him say that this Jesus of Nazareth will destroy this place and change the customs Moses handed down to us."
>
> 15All who were sitting in the Sanhedrin looked intently at Stephen, and they saw that his face was like the face of an angel.
>
> 7:1Then the high priest asked him, "Are these charges true?"

8 Stephen has earlier been described as being "full of the Spirit and wisdom" (6:3) and "full of faith and of the Holy Spirit" (6:5). Now Luke says he was "full of God's grace and power." The three descriptions are complementary, though Luke may have drawn the precise wording from different sources. The word "grace" (*charis*) was previously used by Luke to characterize both Jesus (Luke 4:22) and the early church (Acts 4:33) and connotes "spiritual charm" or "winsomeness." "Power" (*dynamis*) has already appeared in Acts in conjunction with "wonders and signs" (2:22) and "grace" (4:33) and connotes divine power expressed in mighty works.

Like Jesus and the apostles (cf. 2:22, 43; 5:12), Stephen is portrayed as having done "great wonders and miraculous signs among the people." Just what these were, Luke does not say, though we are undoubtedly to think of them as being of the same nature as those done by Jesus and the apostles. Nor does Luke tell us just when these manifestations of divine power began in Stephen's ministry. Many have insisted that they were a direct result of the laying on of the apostles' hands (cf. 6:6), though it is possible that these acts characterized Stephen's ministry before that.

9–10 Stephen soon began preaching among his Hellenistic compatriots. Many commentators have found this to be a major problem in the narrative because Stephen was appointed to supervise relief for the poor, not to perform the apostolic function of preaching. Some, therefore, have viewed this as a Lukan discrepancy (e.g., Brandon), whereas others have claimed that Stephen was not really preaching at all but only uttering the name of Jesus and providing a Christian rationale for his divinely empowered acts (e.g., Zahn). Most commentators, however, are prepared to accept the fact of Stephen's preaching (just as Philip, another of the seven, also preached later on). Yet they are uneasy with Luke's portrayal because of its conflict with the division of labor spelled out in 6:3–4 (e.g., Haenchen).

But if we posit (1) the continuation, to some extent, of old tensions between Hebraic Jews and Hellenistic Jews in the Jerusalem church and (2) separate meetings, at least occasionally, for Aramaic-speaking and Greek-speaking believers (cf. comments on 6:1), several difficulties in the historical reconstruction of this period are partially explained. While not minimizing the importance of the apostles to the whole church, we may say that in some way Stephen, Philip, and perhaps others of the appointed seven may well have been to the Hellenistic believers what the apostles were to the native-born Christians. Philip seems to have performed such a function later on at Caesarea. And in the early church, where "ministry was a function long before it became an office," such preaching was evidently looked upon with approval.

Opposition to Stephen arose from certain members within the Hellenistic community. Opinion differs widely as to just how many Hellenistic synagogues are in view in v.9. Many have insisted that there are five: (1) those of the *Libertinoi* or Freedmen, (2) the Cyreneans, (3) the Alexandrians, (4) the Cilicians, and (5) the Asians (e.g., B. Weiss, H. Lietzmann, E. Schürer). Others have suggested that the twofold use of the article *tōn* ("the") groups these five into two: (1) those of the Freedmen synagogue, made up of Jews from Cyrene and Alexandria, and (2) another synagogue composed of Jews from Cilicia and Asia (e.g., H.H. Wendt, T. Zahn). And others, emphasizing the singular form of "synagogue" in the passage (*tēs synagōgēs*) and the epexegetical nature of the last four designations, posit only one synagogue as being in mind—viz., a synagogue of the Freedmen, made up of Jews from Cyrene, Alexandria, Cilicia, and Asia (e.g., J. Jeremias, F.F. Bruce, E. Haenchen). NIV takes the passage in this latter sense, and that is probably how it ought to be understood. The name *Libertinoi* in our text is a Latin loan word that probably refers to Jewish freedmen and the sons of such freedmen, with the adjective *legomenēs* ("so-called") perhaps included as an apology to Grecian sensibilities for the foreign word.

We have no account of the content of Stephen's preaching that so antagonized his Hellenistic compatriots. Luke labels the accusations against him (vv.11–14) as false—though, to judge by his response of chapter 7, they seem to have been false more in nuance and degree than in kind. From the accusations and from his defense, it is clear that Stephen had begun to apply his Christian convictions regarding the centrality of

Jesus of Nazareth in God's redemptive program to such issues as the significance of the land, the law, and the temple for Jewish Christians in view of the advent of the Messiah. This, however, was a dangerous path to tread, particularly for Hellenistic Jewish Christians! It was one that the apostles themselves seem to have been unwilling to explore. And it was a path that Jews who had lately returned to Jerusalem from the Diaspora would view with reticence.

Having originally immigrated to the homeland out of a desire to be more faithful Jews, and having come under some suspicion of an inbred liberalism by the native-born populace, the Hellenistic Jewish community in Jerusalem undoubtedly had a vested interest in keeping deviations among its members to a minimum, or else exposing them as outside its own commitments, lest its synagogues fall under further suspicion. Thus the Hellenistic members of the Synagogue of the Freedmen were probably quite eager to bait Stephen in order to root out such a threat from their midst—though it is evident from the record that Stephen welcomed the challenge. But as Luke tells us, "they could not stand up against his wisdom or the Spirit by which he spoke." This fulfills Jesus' promise of the gift of "words and wisdom" in the time of persecution (cf. Luke 21:15).

11–14 The subject "they" of the verbs of these sentences refers to those members of the synagogue of the Freedman represented in v.9 by the masculine plural indefinite pronoun *tines* ("some"; NIV, "members"). Four things are said about them: (1) "they secretly persuaded some men to say" that Stephen had spoken blasphemy; (2) "they stirred up the people and the elders and the teachers of the law" on their trumped-up charge against Stephen; (3) "they seized Stephen and brought him before the Sanhedrin"; and (4) "they produced false witnesses" at his trial.

The rumors had to do with Stephen's being "against Moses and against God"—"against Moses" because his arguments appeared to challenge the eternal validity of the Mosaic law, and "against God" because he appeared to be setting aside that which was taken to be the foundation and focus of national worship—the Jerusalem temple. In so doing, the rumors struck at the heart of both Pharisaic and Sadducean interests. Later rabbinic law held that "the blasphemer is not culpable [and therefore not subject to the penalty of death] unless he pronounces the Name itself " (M Sanhedrin 7.5, based on Lev 24:10–23). But in the first century of the Christian Era, the definition of blasphemy was more broadly interpreted along the lines of Numbers 15:30: "Anyone who sins defiantly, whether native-born or alien, blasphemes the Lord, and that person must be cut off from his people" (cf. G.H. Dalman, *The Words of Jesus,* tr. D.M. Kay [Edinburgh: T. & T. Clark, 1909], p. 314).

The testimony of witnesses who repeated what they had heard a defendant say was part of Jewish court procedure in a trial for blasphemy (cf. M Sanhedrin 7.5). But this testimony against Stephen, Luke tells us, was false. "We have heard him say," they claimed, "that this Jesus of Nazareth will destroy this place and change the customs Moses handed down to us" (v.14). Like the similar charge against Jesus (Matt 26:61; Mark 14:58; cf. John 2:19–22), its falseness lay not so much in its wholesale fabrication but in its subtle and deadly misrepresentation of what was intended. Undoubtedly Stephen spoke regarding a recasting of Jewish life in terms of the supremacy of Jesus the Messiah. Undoubtedly he expressed in his manner and message something of the subsidiary significance of the Jerusalem temple and the Mosaic law, as did Jesus before him (e.g., Mark 2:23–28; 3:1–6; 7:14–15; 10:5–9). But that is not the same as advocating the destruction of the temple or the changing of the law—though on these matters we must allow Stephen to speak for himself in Acts 7.

6:15–7:1 The members of the council "looked intently" at Stephen as he was brought before them and saw one whose appearance was "like the face of an angel." In Judaism very devout men were often spoken of as resembling angels. Luke here, however, probably wants us to understand that Stephen, being filled with the Holy Spirit (6:3, 5) and possessing a genuine spiritual winsomeness (6:8), radiated a presence marked by confidence, serenity, and courage. And with the question of the high priest—"Are these charges true?"—the stage is set for Stephen's defense.

Notes

Marcion was a Christian of Pontus, who came to Rome in A.D. 140 and was denounced as a heretic in 144. He accepted only Paul's letters (minus the Pastorals) and a purged version of Luke's Gospel, rejecting everything Jewish and Jewish Christian as opposed to the gospel.

Ebionism usually refers to Jewish Christians who thought of Jesus as Messiah but not as divine. It means literally "the poor" and connotes humility and piety before God.

8 On the compound σημεῖα καὶ τέρατα (sēmeia kai terata, "signs and wonders"), see comments on 2:22 and note at 5:12.

On Luke's use of the expression ὁ λαός (ho laos, "the people"), see comments on 2:47a.

10 The Western text expands this verse to read: "But they could not stand up against the wisdom which was in him and the Holy Spirit by whom he spoke, for they were confuted before him with all boldness of speech. Being unable, therefore, to face up to the truth. . . ."

14 The use of the demonstrative pronoun οὗτος (houtos, "this") in "this Jesus of Nazareth" probably carries a note of contempt.

15 Luke often employs the verb ἀτενίζω (atenizō, "look intently") to heighten the dramatic effect of a narrative (cf. Luke 4:20; 22:56; Acts 1:10; 3:4, 12; 7:55; 10:4; 11:6; 13:9; 14:9; 23:1). See comments on 1:10.

---

2. Stephen's defense before the Sanhedrin (7:2–53)

The defense of Stephen before the Sanhedrin is hardly a defense in the sense of an explanation or apology calculated to win an acquittal. Rather, it is a proclamation of the Christian message in terms of the popular Judaism of the day and an indictment of the Jewish leaders for their failure to recognize Jesus of Nazareth as their Messiah or to appreciate the salvation provided in him. Before the Fall of Jerusalem in A.D. 70, the three great pillars of popular Jewish piety were (1) the land, (2) the law, and (3) the temple. The Talmud shows that later on Rabbinic Judaism continued to exist apart from the Jerusalem temple and without any overriding stress on the land. And undoubtedly there were individual teachers even before the nation's calamities of A.D. 66–70 and 132–35 who thought in somewhat similar fashion. But before such a time, the land, the law, and the temple were the cardinal postulates in the religious faith of the vast majority of Jews. So it is this type of thought that Stephen confronts here, as the writer of Hebrews also did.

Dibelius has argued:

> The irrelevance of most of this [Stephen's] speech has for long been the real problem of exegesis. It is, indeed, impossible to find a connection between the account of the history of Israel to the time of Moses (7:2–19) and the accusation against Stephen; nor

is any accusation against the Jews, which would furnish the historical foundation for the attack at the end of the speech, found at all in this section. Even in that section of the speech which deals with Moses, the speaker does not defend himself; nor does he make any positive countercharge against his enemies, for the words *hoi de ou sunēkan* in 7:25 do not constitute such an attack any more than does the report of the gainsaying of Moses by a Jew in 7:27. It is not until 7:35 that we sense any polemic interest. From 7:2–34 the point of the speech is not obvious at all; we are simply given an account of the history of Israel (*Studies in Acts*, p. 167).

And Dibelius continues with such statements as the following: "The major part of the speech (7:2–34) shows no purpose whatever, but contains a unique, compressed reproduction of the story of the patriarchs and Moses" (ibid., p. 168); and "The most striking feature of this speech is the irrelevance of its main section" (ibid., p. 169). Just how wrong Dibelius was, however, will become evident as we proceed.

a. *On the land*

7:2–36

2To this he replied: "Brothers and fathers, listen to me! The God of glory appeared to our father Abraham while he was still in Mesopotamia, before he lived in Haran. 3'Leave your country and your people,' God said, 'and go to the land I will show you.'

4"So he left the land of the Chaldeans and settled in Haran. After the death of his father, God sent him to this land where you are now living. 5He gave him no inheritance here, not even a foot of ground. But God promised him that he and his descendants after him would possess the land, even though at that time Abraham had no child. 6God spoke to him in this way: 'Your descendants will be strangers in a country not their own, and they will be enslaved and mistreated four hundred years. 7But I will punish the nation they serve as slaves,' God said, 'and afterward they will come out of that country and worship me in this place.' 8Then he gave Abraham the covenant of circumcision. And Abraham became the father of Isaac and circumcised him eight days after his birth. Later Isaac became the father of Jacob, and Jacob became the father of the twelve patriarchs.

9"Because the patriarchs were jealous of Joseph, they sold him as a slave into Egypt. But God was with him 10and rescued him from all his troubles. He gave Joseph wisdom and enabled him to gain the goodwill of Pharaoh king of Egypt; so he made him ruler over Egypt and all his palace.

11"Then a famine struck all Egypt and Canaan, bringing great suffering, and our fathers could not find food. 12When Jacob heard that there was grain in Egypt, he sent our fathers on their first visit. 13On their second visit, Joseph told his brothers who he was, and Pharaoh learned about Joseph's family. 14After this, Joseph sent for his father Jacob and his whole family, seventy-five in all. 15Then Jacob went down to Egypt, where he and our fathers died. 16Their bodies were brought back to Shechem and placed in the tomb that Abraham had bought from the sons of Hamor at Shechem for a certain sum of money.

17"As the time drew near for God to fulfill his promise to Abraham, the number of our people in Egypt greatly increased. 18Then another king, who knew nothing about Joseph, became ruler of Egypt. 19He dealt treacherously with our people and oppressed our forefathers by forcing them to throw out their newborn babies so that they would die.

20"At that time Moses was born, and he was no ordinary child. For three months he was cared for in his father's house. 21When he was placed outside, Pharaoh's daughter took him and brought him up as her own son. 22Moses was educated in all the wisdom of the Egyptians and was powerful in speech and action.

23"When Moses was forty years old, he decided to visit his fellow Israelites. 24He saw one of them being mistreated by an Egyptian, so he went to his defense and avenged him by killing the Egyptian. 25Moses thought that his own people would realize that God was using him to rescue them, but they did not. [26]The next day Moses came upon two Israelites who were fighting. He tried to reconcile them by saying, 'Men, you are brothers; why do you want to hurt each other?'

[27]"But the man who was mistreating the other pushed Moses aside and said, 'Who made you ruler and judge over us? [28]Do you want to kill me as you killed the Egyptian yesterday?' [29]When Moses heard this, he fled to Midian, where he settled as a foreigner and had two sons.

[30]"After forty years had passed, an angel appeared to Moses in the flames of a burning bush in the desert near Mount Sinai. [31]When he saw this, he was amazed at the sight. As he went over to look more closely, he heard the Lord's voice: [32]'I am the God of your fathers, the God of Abraham, Isaac and Jacob.' Moses trembled with fear and did not dare to look.

[33]"Then the Lord said to him, 'Take off your sandals; the place where you are standing is holy ground. [34]I have indeed seen the oppression of my people in Egypt. I have heard their groaning and have come down to set them free. Now come, I will send you back to Egypt.'

[35]"This is the same Moses whom they had rejected with the words, 'Who made you ruler and judge?' He was sent to be their ruler and deliverer by God himself, through the angel who appeared to him in the bush. [36]He led them out of Egypt and did wonders and miraculous signs in Egypt, at the Red Sea and for forty years in the desert.

Declarations of faith within a Jewish milieu were often tied into a recital of God's intervention in the life of Israel, for God is the God who is known by his redemptive activity on behalf of his people in history. So by beginning his defense with a résumé of Israel's history, Stephen is speaking in accord with Jewish form. But while Jewish in form, in content his address runs counter to much of the popular piety of the day. He argues that God's significant activity has usually taken place outside the confines of Palestine, that wherever God meets his people can be called "holy ground," that God is the God who calls his own to move forward in their religious experience, and that therefore dwelling in the land of promise requires a pilgrim lifestyle in which the land may be appreciated but never venerated.

In the OT the important concepts of "rest" and "remnant" are frequently associated closely with the land. Deuteronomy 12:9-10, for example, reads: "You have not yet reached the resting place and the inheritance the Lord your God is giving you. But you will cross the Jordan and settle in the land the Lord your God is giving you as an inheritance, and he will give you rest from all your enemies around you so that you will live in safety" (cf. Deut 3:20; Josh 1:13; Joel 2:32b; Mic 4:6-7). And in the literature of Late Judaism the linking of God's righteous remnant with the Holy Land is common (cf. 2 Esdras 9:7-8; 12:31-34; 13:48; 2 Baruch 40:2). Facing much the same problem and with much the same purpose as the writer of Hebrews (cf. Heb 4:1-13; 11:8-16), though with a difference of method and structure in his argument, Stephen argues against a veneration of the Holy Land that would leave no room for God's further saving activity in Jesus of Nazareth, Israel's Messiah. Stephen is not renouncing Israel's possession of the land; he makes no attempt to deny or avoid mentioning God's promise that Abraham's descendants would inherit Palestine. He is rather delivering a polemic against a veneration of the land that misses God's further redemptive work. And while his message relates to his time and situation, it also has great relevance for us. For we Christians today are constantly tempted to assert that our nation and our possessions are God-given rather than to confess our dependence on a God who is not limited by anything he has bestowed and to affirm our readiness to move forward with him at all cost.

2–8 Stephen begins by addressing the council in a somewhat formal yet fraternal manner: "Men, brothers and fathers" (*Andres adelphoi kai pateres*; NIV, "Brothers and fathers," cf. 22:1). Then he launches into his message, taking up first the situation of Abraham. "The God of glory," Stephen says, "appeared to our father Abraham *while he was still in Mesopotamia, before he lived in Haran* [italics mine]." God's word to him was to move forward into the possession of a land that was promised to him and his descendants. But though he entered into his promised inheritance, he did not live in it as if living in it was the consummation of God's purposes for him. Rather, he cherished as most important the covenantal and personal relationship that God had established with him, whatever his place of residence—a relationship of which circumcision was the God-given sign.

There are a number of difficulties as to chronological sequence, historical numbers, and the use of biblical quotations in Stephen's address that have led to the most strenuous exercise of ingenuity on the part of commentators in their attempts to reconcile them. Four of these difficulties appear in vv.2–8. Verse 3 quotes the words of God to Abraham given in Genesis 12:1 and implies by its juxtaposition with v.2 that this message came to Abraham "while he was still in Mesopotamia, before he lived in Haran," whereas the context of Genesis 12:1 suggests that it came to him in Haran. Verse 4 says that he left Haran after the death of his father, whereas the chronological data of Genesis 11:26–12:4 suggests that Terah's death took place after Abraham's departure from Haran. Verse 5 uses the words of Deuteronomy 2:5 as a suitable description of Abraham's situation in Palestine, whereas their OT context relates to God's prohibition to Israel not to dwell in Mount Seir because it had been given to Esau. And v.6 speaks of 400 years of slavery in Egypt, whereas Exodus 12:40 says 430.

We need not, however, get so disturbed over such things as, on the one hand, to pounce on them to disprove a "high view" of biblical inspiration or, on the other hand, to attempt to harmonize them so as to support such a view. These matters relate to the conflations and inexactitude of popular Judaism, not necessarily to some then-existing scholastic tradition or to variant textual traditions. In large measure they can be paralleled in other popular writings of the day, whether overtly Hellenistic or simply more nonconformist in the broadest sense of that term. Philo, for example, also explained Abraham's departure from Ur of the Chaldees by reference to Genesis 12:1 (*De Abrahamo* 62–67), even though he knew that Genesis 12:1–5 is in the context of leaving Haran (cf. *De Migratione Abrahami* 176). Josephus spoke of Abraham's being seventy-five years old when he left Chaldea (contra Gen 12:4, which says he was seventy-five when he left Haran) and of leaving Chaldea because God bade him go to Canaan, with evident allusion to Genesis 12:1 (cf. Antiq. I, 154 [vii.1]). Likewise, Philo also placed the departure of Abraham from Haran after his father's death (*De Migratione Abrahami* 177). And undoubtedly the round figure of four hundred years for Israel's slavery in Egypt—a figure that stems from the statement credited to God in Genesis 15:13—was often used in popular expressions of religious piety in Late Judaism, as were also the transpositions of meaningful and usable phrases from one context to another.

There is a remarkable psychological or emotional truth in Luke's report of Stephen's address. Stephen, with his life at stake, was speaking under intense emotion and with God-given eloquence. With remarkable verisimilitude Luke shows him using commonly understood language as in vivid terms and with burning eloquence he refers to Israel's history. Stephen's speech was not a scholarly historical survey; it was a powerful portrayal of God's dealing with Israel and it mounted inexorably to a climax that unmasked the obstinancy and disobedience of Israel and of their leaders in Stephen's time. Church history knows of few, if any, greater displays of moral courage than Stephen showed in this speech. And to dissect it on precisionist grounds shows lack of understanding of its basic truth.

9–16 Stephen's address next turns to the sons of Jacob, or "the twelve patriarchs" as they were known more popularly (cf. 4 Macc 16:25 [together, of course, with Abraham, Isaac, and Jacob, as in 4 Macc 7:19] and the title to T 12 Pat). Here Stephen's point is that God was with Joseph and his brothers *in Egypt* (the name itself is repeated six times in vv. 9–16), even though the only portion of the Holy Land that they possessed was the family tomb in Palestine, to which their bones were brought back later for final burial.

Two further difficulties of the type noted in vv.2–6 that seem to appear somewhat regularly in Stephen's speech are (1) the number seventy-five in v.14 for the total number who originally went down to Egypt, whereas Genesis 46:27 (MT) sets the figure at seventy (i.e., sixty-six plus Jacob, Joseph, and the latter's two sons), and (2) the confusion in v.16 between Abraham's tomb at Hebron, in the cave of Machpelah, which Abraham bought from Ephron the Hittite (cf. Gen 23:3–20) and wherein Abraham, Isaac, and Jacob were buried (cf. Gen 49:29–33; 50:13), and the burial plot purchased by Jacob at Shechem from the sons of Hamor, wherein Joseph and his descendants were buried (cf. Josh 24:32). Again, these are but further examples of the conflations and inexactitudes of Jewish popular religion, which, it seems, Luke simply recorded from his sources in his attempt to be faithful to what Stephen actually said in his portrayal. And again, they can in large measure be paralleled elsewhere. Genesis 46:27 in the LXX, for example, does not include Jacob and Joseph but does include nine sons of Joseph in the reckoning, thereby arriving at "seventy-five souls" all together who went down to Egypt. And with this number both Exodus 1:5 (LXX) and 4QExod^a at 1:5 agree. Likewise, the telescoping of the two burial grounds in this verse can be compared to the similar phenomenon with regard to Abraham's two calls in vv.2–3. Interestingly, while the tradition in popular circles of Late Judaism was rather strong that the other eleven sons of Jacob were buried at Hebron (cf. Jub 46:8; Jos. Antiq. II, 199 [viii.2]; T 12 Pat, passim; SBK, 2:672–78), Josephus seems somewhat vague as to just where Joseph's bones were finally laid to rest apart from his rather general statement that "they conveyed them to Canaan" (Antiq. II, 200 [viii.2]).

17–36 Still on the subject of "the land," Stephen recounts the life of Moses. Incorporated into this section, largely by way of anticipation, is a Moses-rejection theme in vv.23–29 and 35, which will later be highlighted in vv.39–43 and then driven home in the scathing indictment of vv.51–53. But here Stephen's primary emphasis is on God's providential and redemptive action for his people apart from and outside of the land of Palestine, of which Stephen's hearers made so much: (1) God's raising up of the deliverer Moses *in Egypt* (vv.17–22); (2) his provision for the rejected Moses *in Midian* (v.29); (3) his commissioning of Moses *in the desert near Mount Sinai*—the place God himself identified as being "holy ground," for wherever God meets with his people is holy ground though it possesses no sanctity of its own (vv.30–34); and (4) Moses' resultant action in delivering God's people and doing "wonders and miraculous signs" for forty years *in Egypt, at the Red Sea, and in the desert.* This narration of events in Moses' life is not given just to introduce the Second Moses theme that follows in vv.37–43, though it certainly does that. Its primary purpose seems rather to be that of making the vital point, contrary to the popular piety of the day in its veneration of "the Holy Land," that no place on earth—even though given as an inheritance by God himself—can be claimed to possess such sanctity or be esteemed in such a way as to preempt God's further working on behalf of his people. By this method Stephen was attempting to clear the way for the proclamation of the centrality of Jesus in the nation's worship, life, and thought.

Notes

2 On the parallel form of address Ἄνδρες ἀδελφοί (Andres adelphoi, "Men, brothers"), see comments on 1:16.

12 Two peculiarities of koine Gr. usage may be noted here, which appear elsewhere in Acts: (1) the use of πρῶτος (prōtos, "first") for πρότερος (proteros, "former"), cf. 1:1; and (2) the use of εἰς (eis, "into") for ἐν (en, "in"), cf. 8:16; 19:5. D, following the LXX, reads en.

26 The Western text reads ἄνδρες ἀδελφοί (andres adelphoi, "men, brothers"), attempting thereby a harmony with the form of address at 1:16; 2:29, 37; 7:2; 13:15, 26, 38; 15:7, 13; 22:1; 23:1, 6; 28:17.

36 On the compound τέρατα καὶ σημεῖα (terata kai sēmeia, "wonders and signs"), see comments on 2:22 and note at 5:12.

b. On the law

7:37–43

37"This is that Moses who told the Israelites, 'God will send you a prophet like me from your own people.' 38He was in the assembly in the desert, with our fathers and with the angel who spoke to him on Mount Sinai; and he received living words to pass on to us.

39"But our fathers refused to obey him. Instead, they rejected him and in their hearts turned back to Egypt. 40They told Aaron, 'Make us gods who will go before us. As for this fellow Moses who led us out of Egypt—we don't know what has happened to him!' 41That was the time they made an idol in the form of a calf. They brought sacrifices to it and held a celebration in honor of what their hands had made. 42But God turned away and gave them over to the worship of the heavenly bodies. This agrees with what is written in the book of the prophets:

" 'Did you bring me sacrifices and offerings
forty years in the desert, O house of Israel?
43You have lifted up the shrine of Moloch
and the star of your god Rephan,
the idols you made to worship.
Therefore I will send you into exile' beyond Babylon.

Involved inevitably with the Jews' exaltation of the law were veneration of Moses the Law-giver and idealization of Israel's wilderness days. All parties within Judaism of the first century A.D.—whether Sadducees, Pharisees, Essenes, Zealots, Apocalypticists, Hellenists, Samaritans, or the so-called People of the Land—were united in this veneration and idealization. So in meeting the accusation that he was speaking blasphemous words "against Moses" (6:11) and "against the law" (6:13), Stephen argues two points clearly and a third inferentially: (1) Moses himself spoke of God's later raising up "a prophet like me" from among his people and for his people, which means therefore that Israel cannot limit the revelation and redemption of God to Moses' precepts (vv.37–38); (2) Moses had been rejected by his own people, even though he was God's appointed redeemer—which parallels the way Jesus of Nazareth was treated and explains why the majority within the nation refused him, even though he was God's promised Messiah (vv.39–40); and (3) even though Moses was with them and they had the living words of the law and the sacrificial system, the people fell into gross idolatry and actually opposed God (vv.41–43).

37–38 The twofold use of *houtos estin* ("this is that") with the articular adjectival participle in these verses is an intensification of the demonstrative pronouns *touton* and *houtos* in vv.35–36. This suggests a buildup of tension in Stephen's speech, starting from the rather placid historical narrative of vv.2–34, moving to the more strident conclusion in vv.35–36, and peaking with a passionate treatment of the Moses testimonium passage in Deuteronomy 18:15 and of the significance of Moses himself there. This probably reflects to some extent the type of pesher treatment of Scripture common to nonconformist Jews in general (cf. comments on 2:16) and is likely meant to point to the crux of Stephen's argument.

Stephen in no way disparages Moses. Indeed, when he referred to Moses as being "in the congregation in the wilderness, with our fathers and with the angel who spoke to him on Mount Sinai," he was speaking in a complimentary way. Likewise, in Stephen's statement that "he received living words to pass on to us," the expression "living words" (*logia zōnta*) implies the opposite of any disparagement of the Mosaic law. But Stephen's point is that in Deuteronomy 18:15 Moses pointed beyond himself and beyond the instruction that came through him to another whom God would raise up in the future and to whom Israel must give heed and that, therefore, Israel cannot limit divine revelation and redemption to the confines of the Mosaic law.

In the first century A.D., Judaism generally looked for a Messiah who would in some way be "like Moses." The inclusion of Deuteronomy 18:18–19 as the second testimonium passage in the five texts of 4QTest highlights this for us. And the degree to which a Mosaic understanding of messiahship was embedded in the first-century Jewish expectations is further illustrated by the many claimants to messiahship who attempted to validate their claims by reenacting the experiences of Moses (cf. Joachim Jeremias, "*Mōusēs*," TDNT, 4:862). The Samaritans talked about a Moses redivivus ("restored," "reborn") and, like the DS sectarians, used Deuteronomy 18:15–18 to support this notion. And though later rabbinic materials—in what appears to be a conscious reaction to Christian usage—use Deuteronomy 18:15–18 in a decidedly noneschatological and nonmessianic fashion (applied to Samuel in Mid Psalms 1.3; to Jeremiah in *Pesikta de Rab Kahana* 13.6; to the whole line of prophets in *Mekhilta de Rabbi Ishmael, Bah* 9.62–68 and in *Sifre Deuteronomium* 175–76), a number of Talmudic passages explicitly parallel Israel's first redeemer Moses with Israel's expected Messiah-Redeemer, who will be like Moses (cf. the "like the first redeemer, so the last Redeemer" theme of the Jerusalem Targum on Exod 12:42; Deut R 2.9; Song of Songs R 2.9; Ruth R 5.6; *Pesikta Rabbati* 15.10; *Pesikta de Rab Kahana* 5.8). Stephen's argument, therefore, as based on Moses' prophecy of Deuteronomy 18:15–18, was generally in accord with Jewish eschatological expectations. And he evidently used it, as Peter did before him (cf. 3:22–23), expecting it to be convincing.

39–40 But while Peter and Stephen agree in seeing christological significance in Deuteronomy 18:15–18 and in considering it a very important testimonium passage for a Jewish audience, their attitudes toward Israel are shown to be very different. For Peter, his hearers are the sons of the prophets who should hear the new Moses (cf. 3:22–26); whereas for Stephen, his hearers are the sons of those who rejected Moses and killed the prophets (cf. 7:35-40, 51-53). In vv.39-40 Stephen specifies his rejection-of-Moses theme by picking up the awful words of Numbers 14:3, "Their hearts turned back to Egypt" (v.39), and citing almost verbatim the people's defiance of Exodus 32:1: "Make us gods who will go before us. As for this fellow Moses who led us out of Egypt—we don't know what has happened to him" (v.40).

The Talmud also speaks of the people's rebellion in making the golden calf and generally views it as Israel's first, ultimate, and most heinous sin (e.g., b *Shabbath* 17a; b *Megillah* 25b; b *Abodah Zarah* 5a; b *Soferim* 35a; *Aboth de Rabbi Nathan* 18b,21b, 30a; *Exod R* 48.2; *Lev R* 2.15; 5.3; 9.49; 27.3; *Deut R* 3.10, 12). Some rabbis, however, tried to shift the blame onto the proselytes who came out of Egypt with the people (cf. *Exod R* 42.6; *Lev R* 27.8; *Pesiḳta de Rab Kahana* 9.8)—or even onto God himself because he blessed Israel with all the gold they constructed the idol with (cf. b *Sanhedrin* 102a). But while the rabbis have much to say about the awfulness of the incident in Israel's history, calling it by such euphemisms as "that unspeakable deed" (cf. *Pesiḳta Rabbati* 33.3; *Num R* 5.3) and forbidding a translation of the account into the vernacular in the synagogue services (cf. b *Megillah* 25b), there is a decided difference between the way they treat the people's rebellion and the way Stephen does. The rabbis do not take the golden calf episode as the people's rejection of Moses (though Korah's later rebellion was so considered), but the rabbis emphasize Moses' successful intercession for Israel (cf. esp. b *Sotah* 14a). Stephen, however, lays all his emphasis on Israel's rejection of their deliverer, implicitly drawing the parallel between their treatment of Moses and Israel's treatment of Jesus—a parallel he will broaden and drive home in his scathing indictment of vv.51-53.

41-43 "That was the time" (*en tais hēmerais ekeinais*, lit., "in those days"), says Stephen, "they made an idol in the form of a calf. They brought sacrifices to it and held a celebration in honor of what their hands had made." So detestable to God was this episode in Israel's wilderness experience that Stephen calls it a time when "God turned away and gave them over to the worship of the heavenly bodies" (cf. Rom 1:24, where the expression "God gave them over," *ho theos paredōken autous*, also occurs, though there the giving over was from idolatry to immorality). The inescapable inference from Stephen's words is that Israel's shameful behavior and God's drastic response to it find their counterparts in the nation's rejection of Jesus.

To support his assertion that Israel's idolatry caused God to give them over to the worship of heavenly bodies, Stephen quotes Amos 5:25-27. In the Greek this quotation is fairly close to the LXX, which understands "Sikkuth your king" (MT) to be "the shrine of Moloch" (deriving "shrine," *skēnē*, from vocalizing the Heb. *sikkût* to read *sukkoth*, "booths," and "Moloch" from a misreading of the Heb. *maleḵkem*, "your king"; cf. LXX at 4 Kings 23:10 [MT=2 Kings 23:10] and Jer 31:35 [MT=Jer 32:35]) and which transliterates the Hebrew name *Kiyyûn* as *Raiphan* (probably originally transliterated *Kaipan*). In context and application, however, Stephen's use of the Amos passage is very much like that found in CD 7.14-15: that rejection of God's activity in the eschatological day of salvation brings God's judgment, despite all the sacrifices and offerings that may be offered, just as Israel's idolatry of the golden calf eventuated in Israel's exile "beyond Babylon" (or as the LXX has it, "beyond Damascus").

Notes

---

38 In Deut 4:10; 9:10; and 18:16 (LXX), ἡ ἡμέρα τῆς ἐκκλησίας (hē hēmera tēs ekklēsias, lit., "the day of the assembly") means the day when the people gathered to receive the law. This may very well be what Stephen had principally in mind here—particularly in view of the immediately following juxtaposition and relationship of clauses in the Gr. text, which NIV rearranges. Probably we should read: "He was in the assembly in the desert [understood as 'the assembly' when the people gathered to receive the law] with the angel who spoke to him on Mount Sinai and with our fathers."

On the widely disseminated notion in Late Judaism that angels were instrumental in the giving of the law at Sinai, see Deut 33:2 (LXX); Jub 1:29; Philo *De Somniis* 1.141ff.; Jos. Antiq. XV, 136 [v.3]; T Dan 6:2; Acts 7:53; Gal 3:19; Heb 2:2.

The expression λόγια ζῶντα (*logia zōnta*, "living words") stems from αὕτη ἡ ζωὴ ὑμῶν (*hautē hē zōē hymōn*, "it is your life") in Deut 32:47. ℵ and B, together with P[74], read "to pass on to you [ὑμῖν, *hymin*]" rather than "to us [ἡμῖν, *hēmin*]"—which at first glance seems somewhat out of character with the rest of Stephen's speech, though not, of course, out of character with his indictment of vv.51–53 (note particularly his use of the second person plural pronouns and pronominal suffixes there).

43 On the relation between 7:43 and CD 7.14–15 in the use of Amos 5:26–27, see de Waard, pp. 41–47.

---

c. On the temple

7:44–50

44"Our forefathers had the tabernacle of Testimony with them in the desert. It had been made as God directed Moses, according to the pattern he had seen. 45Having received the tabernacle, our fathers under Joshua brought it with them when they took the land from the nations God drove out before them. It remained in the land until the time of David, 46who enjoyed God's favor and asked that he might provide a dwelling place for the God of Jacob. 47But it was Solomon who built the house for him.

48"However, the Most High does not live in houses made by men. As the prophet says:

49" 'Heaven is my throne,
and the earth is my footstool.
What kind of house will you build for me?

says the Lord.

Or where will my resting place be?
50Has not my hand made all these things?'

Stephen has met the accusation of blasphemy against the law by reassessing Moses' place in redemptive history and by countercharging his accusers with both rejecting the one Moses spoke of and turning to idolatry in their refusal of Jesus the Messiah. Stephen next proceeds to meet the charge of blasphemy against the temple in the same way. In form, this section of the address recalls the more placid manner of vv.2–34. In tone and content, however, it carries on the strident and passionate appeal of vv.35–43, which amounts to a vigorous denunciation of the Jerusalem temple and the type of mentality that would hold to it as the apex of revealed religion.

44–46 Stephen's assessment of Israel's worship experience lays all the emphasis on the tabernacle, which he eulogistically calls "the tabernacle of Testimony." It was with our forefathers, he says, during that period in the desert, which so many consider exemplary. It was made according to the exact pattern God gave Moses. It was central in the life of the nation during the conquest of Canaan under the leadership of Joshua. And it was the focus of national worship through the time of David, who found favor in God's sight. So significant was it in Israel's experience, in fact, that David asked to be allowed to provide a permanent type of "dwelling place" for God in Jerusalem. (Here Ps 132:5 is quoted and 2 Sam 6:17; 1 Chron 15:1 are alluded to.)

Like the covenanters at Qumran (cf. 1QS 8.7–8) and the writer to the Hebrews (cf. Heb 8:2, 5; 9:1–5, 11, 24), and probably like many other nonconformist Jews of his time, Stephen seems to have viewed the epitome of Jewish worship in terms of the tabernacle, not the temple. Very likely this was because he felt the mobility of the tabernacle was a restraint on the status quo mentality that had grown up around the temple. But unlike the Qumranites, who desired a restoration of that classical ideal, Stephen, as well as the writer to the Hebrews, was attempting to lift his compatriots' vision to something far superior to even the wilderness tabernacle—viz., to the dwelling of God with men in Jesus of Nazareth and as expressed through the new covenant.

47 "But it was Solomon," Stephen tersely says, "who built the house for him." This brevity shows something of Stephen's pejorative attitude toward the temple. And his contrast between the tabernacle (vv. 44–46) and the temple (v.47) expresses his disapproval. Probably Stephen had in mind 2 Samuel 7:5–16 (cf. 1 Chron 17:4–14). There God speaks through the prophet Nathan of his satisfaction with his "nomadic" situation and declines David's offer to build a house for his divine presence; but he goes on to announce that David's son would build such a house and promises to build a "house" (lineage) for David. Certainly 2 Samuel 7:5–16 was a foundational passage at Qumran (cf. 4QFlor on 7:10–14) and for much of early Christian thought (cf. Luke 1:32–33 alluding to 7:12–16; Acts 13:17–22 on 7:6–16; Heb 1:5b on 7:14; and, possibly, 2 Cor 6:18 on 7:14). But obviously Stephen did not consider Solomon's temple to be the final fulfillment of God's words to David in 2 Samuel 7. Probably he understood the announcement of a temple to be a concession on God's part and laid greater emphasis on the promise of the establishment of David's seed and kingdom (cf. 2 Sam 7:12–16).

48–50 Stephen reaches the climax of his antitemple polemic by insisting that "the Most High does not live in houses made by men"—a concept he supports by citing Isaiah 66:1–2a. Judaism never taught that God actually lived in the temple or was confined to its environs but spoke of his "Name" and presence as being there. In practice, however, this concept was often denied. This would especially appear so to Stephen, when further divine activity was refused out-of-hand by the people in their preference for God's past revelation and redemption as symbolized in the existence of the temple.

As a Hellenist, Stephen may have had a tendency to view things in a more "spiritual" manner (i.e., in more inward and nonmaterial terms)—a tendency with both good and bad features. As a Christian, he could have been aware of the contrast in the primitive catechesis (oral instruction of converts) between what is "made with hands" and what is "not made with hands" (cf. esp. Mark 14:58; Heb 8:2; 9:24). But whatever its source, Stephen's assertion is that neither the tabernacle nor the temple was meant to be such an institutionalized feature in Israel's religion as to prohibit God's further redemptive activity or to halt the advance of God's plan for his people. The response Stephen wants from his hearers was what God declared to be his desire for his people in the strophe that follows the Isaiah passage just cited:

This is the one I esteem:
he who is humble and contrite in spirit,
and trembles at my word (Isa 66:2b).

To those who desired to localize God's presence and confine his working, Stephen repeated the denunciation of Isaiah 66:1-2a and left this appeal in Isaiah 66:2b to be inferred.

Notes

---

46 א B D et al. read τῷ οἴκῳ Ἰακώβ (tō oikō Iakōb, "for the house of Jacob"), whereas A C and the TR read τῷ Θεῷ Ἰακώβ (tō theō Iakōb, "for the God of Jacob"). While the expression "the house of Jacob" was common among Jews, the parallel with Ps 132:5 and the contrast set up between David's desire in v.46 and Solomon's action in v.47 seem to require "the God of Jacob" here. Evidently there has arisen a primitive corruption in our usually better textual sources that A C and the TR have corrected.

49-50 Isa 66:1 is quoted in the Epistle of Barnabas 16:2 with reference to the destruction of the Jerusalem temple in A.D. 70 (and with the same variation in text from the LXX as here: ἢ τίς τόπος [ē tis topos, "or what place"; NIV, "or where"] for καὶ ποῖος τόπος [kai poios topos, "and what kind of place"]), and Isa 66:1-2 together with Amos 5:25-27 are quoted by Justin in *Dialogue* 22. This has raised the possibility that there existed in Christian circles a testimonia collection in which these two passages were brought together. But it is also possible that the writer of the Epistle of Barnabas and Justin Martyr were dependent on Acts.

---

d. The indictment

7:51-53

> 51"You stiff-necked people, with uncircumcised hearts and ears! You are just like your fathers: You always resist the Holy Spirit! 52Was there ever a prophet your fathers did not persecute? They even killed those who predicted the coming of the Righteous One. And now you have betrayed and murdered him— 53you who have received the law that was put into effect through angels but have not obeyed it."

The most striking feature of Stephen's speech and the one that sets it off most sharply from Peter's temple sermon of Acts 3 is its strong polemical stance toward Israel. As Stephen recounts the history of Israel, it is a litany of sin, rebellion, and rejection of God's purposes, emphasizing, as Marcel Simon rightly says, "the unworthiness and perpetual rebelliousness of the Jews who, in the long run, exhaust the immense riches of God's mercy" (p. 41).

Some have supposed that the suddenness and harshness of the indictment were occasioned by an angry outburst in the court, to which vv.51-53 are a kind of "knee-jerk" response. But there is little reason to assume that to be the case. Stephen's address has led naturally up to the invective; and after his quotation of Isaiah 66:1-2a, there was really nothing to add.

51 Stephen's description of his accusers is loaded with pejorative theological nuances. The phrase "stiff-necked" was fixed in Israel's memory as God's own characterization of the nation when it rebelled against Moses and worshiped the golden calf (cf. Exod 33:5; Deut 9:13). And the expression "with uncircumcised hearts and ears" recalls God's judgment on the apostates among his people as being "uncircumcised in heart" (cf. Lev 26:41; Deut 10:16; Jer 4:4; 9:26). And now, says Stephen, speaking like a prophet of old, God's indictment rests upon you just as it did on your idolatrous and apostate ancestors.

52 Israel's persecution and killing of her prophets is a recurrent theme in Judaic literature. The OT not only speaks of the sufferings of individual prophets but also has a number of general statements about how the nation had persecuted and killed the prophets of God (cf. 2 Chron 36:15–16; Neh 9:26; Jer 2:30). Various writings from the period of Late Judaism have elaborated on this theme, particularly as a result of the idealization of martyrdom that arose in Maccabean times (cf. Ecclus 49:7; Jub 1:12; 1 Enoch 89:51–53; Liv Proph, passim). In the Talmud, while there are scattered references to all the prophets being wealthy (cf. b *Nedarim* 38a) or living to a great age (cf. b *Pesahim* 87b), there are a great many statements about Israel's persecuting and killing her prophets (cf. b *Gittin* 57b; b *Sanhedrin* 96b; Lev R 10.2; Exod R 31.16; *Pesikta Rabbati* 26.1–2). All these, though, were for the council well-learned lessons from the past. Stephen's accusation, however, was that nothing had been learned from the past, since an even more horrendous crime had been committed in the present—the betrayal and murder of "the Righteous One"—by those who were so smug about Israel's past failures.

53 Stephen's address begins with the fraternal greeting "Men, brothers and fathers" (*Andres adelphoi kai pateres,* v.2). It affirms throughout his deep respect for such distinctly Jewish phenomena as the Abrahamic covenant (vv.3–8), circumcision (v.8), and the tabernacle (vv.44–46). Stephen repeatedly refers to "our father Abraham" and "our fathers" in such a way as to stress his ready acceptance of his Israelite heritage (vv.2, 11–12, 15, 19, 39, 44–45). Yet his repeated use of the second person plural pronoun in vv.51–53 shows his desire to disassociate himself from the nation in its recurrent refusal of God throughout its history. Therefore, taking the offensive, Stephen drives home his point: "*Your* fathers always resisted the Holy Spirit.... *Your* fathers persecuted the prophets.... *You* received the law put into effect through angels, but you have not obeyed it." Perhaps he jabbed with a finger at his accusers—though even a blind man would have felt his verbal blows.

Notes

52 On the christological title "the Righteous One," see commentary on 3:14.
53 On the law as mediated by angels, see the note at 7:38.

3. The stoning of Stephen

7:54–8:1a

54When they heard this, they were furious and gnashed their teeth at him. 55But Stephen, full of the Holy Spirit, looked up to heaven and saw the glory of God, and

Jesus standing at the right hand of God. [56]"Look," he said, "I see heaven open and the Son of Man standing at the right hand of God."

[57]At this they covered their ears and, yelling at the top of their voices, they all rushed at him, [58]dragged him out of the city and began to stone him. Meanwhile, the witnesses laid their clothes at the feet of a young man named Saul.

[59]While they were stoning him, Stephen prayed, "Lord Jesus, receive my spirit." [60]Then he fell on his knees and cried out, "Lord, do not hold this sin against them." When he had said this, he fell asleep.

[8:1]And Saul was there, giving approval to his death.

54 To interpret Stephen's address as an absolute renunciation of the land, the law, or the sacrificial system is an exaggeration. Indeed, like the Qumranites (though for different reasons), Stephen saw worship in terms of the tabernacle, not the temple, to be the ideal of Israel's worship. But that is not to say he rejected the worship of the temple, particularly as it continued the pattern of worship instituted by God in giving the tabernacle. Nor can it be said that Stephen was proclaiming a law-free and universal gospel or suggesting the futility of a Christian mission to Israel. Instead, his desire, it seems, was to raise a prophetic voice *within* Israel, pleading, as Filson summed up his message, for "a radical recasting of Jewish life to make Jesus, rather than these traditionally holy things, the center of Jewish faith, worship and thought" (p. 103). Certainly Stephen was more daring than the Jerusalem apostles, more ready to explore the logical consequences of commitment to Jesus than they were, and more ready to attribute Israel's rejection of its Messiah to a perpetual callousness of heart. Harnack, however, was probably right, at least in the main, to insist that "when Stephen was stoned, he died, like Huss, for a cause whose issues he probably did not foresee" (Adolf Harnack, *The Mission and Expansion of Christianity*, 2 vols., tr. J. Moffatt [London: Williams & Norgate, 1908], 1:50).

Nonetheless, Stephen's message was, for his hearers, flagrant apostasy—in both its content and its tone. While his purpose was to denounce the status quo mentality that had grown up around the land, the law, and the temple, thereby clearing a path for a positive response to Jesus as Israel's Messiah, this was undoubtedly taken as a frontal attack against the Jewish religion in its official and popular forms. And in the council's eyes, its assumed prophetic stance together with its obnoxious liberal spirit must have represented the worst of both Jewish Hellenism and the beginning Christian movement. So, Luke tells us, "they were furious and gnashed their teeth at him."

55–56 While the content and tone of his address infuriated the council, Stephen's solemn pronouncement raised again the specter of blasphemy and brought his hearers to a frenzied pitch: "Look, I see heaven open and the Son of Man standing at the right hand of God." Only a few years before, Jesus had stood before this same tribunal and had been condemned for answering affirmatively the high priest's question as to his being Israel's Messiah and for saying of himself: "And you will see the Son of Man sitting at the right hand of the Mighty One and coming on the clouds of heaven" (Mark 14:62). Now Stephen was saying, in effect, that his vision confirmed Jesus' claim and condemned the council for having rejected him. Unless the council members were prepared to repent and admit their awful error, they had no option but to find Stephen also guilty of blasphemy. Had he been judged only an impertinent apostate (cf. 5:40), the thirty-nine lashes of Jewish punishment would have been appropriate (cf. M *Makkoth* 3:10–15a). To be openly blasphemous before the council as well was a matter demanding death.

Luke's description of Stephen as "full of the Holy Spirit" is in line with his characterizations of him in 6:3, 5, 8, and 15. The identification of Jesus as "the Son of Man" is used outside the Gospels only here and at Revelation 1:13; 14:14 (also at Heb 2:6, though as a locution for man in line with Ps 8:4). In the Gospels Jesus alone used "Son of Man" in referring to himself (the apparent exceptions in Luke 24:7 and John 12:34 are in actuality echoes of Jesus' usage). Jesus used the expression both as a locution for the pronoun "I" and as a title reflecting the usage in Daniel 7:13–28 (esp. vv.13–14). As a title it carries the ideas of (1) identification with mankind and suffering and (2) vindication by God and glory. The title was generally not attributed to Jesus by the church between the time when his sufferings were completed and when he would assume his full glory. Here, however, an anticipation of Christ's full glory is set within a martyr context (as also at Rev 1:13; 14:14); and, therefore, "Son of Man" is used as being fully appropriate.

In Stephen's vision the juxtaposition of "the glory of God" and the name of Jesus—together with his saying that he sees "heaven open and the Son of Man standing at the right hand of God"—is christologically significant. Unlike the Greek understanding of *doxa* ("glory") as akin to "opinion," the Hebrew OT and the LXX viewed "the glory of God" (Heb. *kᵉḇôḏ YHWH*, Gr. *doxa theou*) as "the manifestation or revelation of the divine nature" and as even "the divine mode of being" itself (cf. TDNT, 2:233–47). The bringing together of "the glory of God" and the name of Jesus, therefore, suggests something about his person as the manifestation of the divine nature and the divine mode of being. Likewise, inasmuch as God dwells in the highest heaven, the open heaven with Christ at God's right hand suggests something about his work as providing access into the very presence of God.

Stephen's reference to Jesus "standing" at the right hand of God, which differs from the "sitting" of Psalm 110:1 (the passage alluded to here), has been variously understood. Dalman argued that it is merely "a verbal change," for both *estanai* ("to stand") and *kathēsthai* ("to sit") connote the idea "to be situated" (Heb. *ʾāmaḏ*), without any necessary implication for the configuration of posture (Gustaf Dalman, *The Words of Jesus*, tr. D.M. Kay [Edinburgh: T. & T. Clark, 1909], p. 311). The majority of commentators, however, have interpreted the "standing" to suggest Jesus' welcome of his martyred follower, who, like the repentant criminal of Luke 23:43, was received into heaven the moment he died (cf. BC, 4:84). Dispensational commentators have taken Stephen's reference to Jesus' "standing" as supporting their view that the distinctive redemptive message for this age was not proclaimed till the Pauline gospel (either at its inauguration, its close, or somewhere in between); and, therefore, in the transitional period between Israel and the church, Jesus is represented as not yet having taken his seat at God's right hand. Others speak of Jesus as "standing" in order to enter his messianic office on earth or depict him as "standing" in line with the common representation of angels standing in the presence of God.

Probably, however, Bruce is right in emphasizing the idea of "witness" as being connoted in Jesus' "standing":

> Stephen has been confessing Christ before men, and now he sees Christ confessing His servant before God. The proper posture for a witness is the standing posture. Stephen, condemned by an earthly court, appeals for vindication to a heavenly court, and his vindicator in that supreme court is Jesus, who stands at God's right hand as Stephen's advocate, his "paraclete" (*Book of the Acts*, p. 168).

Yet in accepting such an interpretation, it is well to keep Bruce's further comment in mind:

When we are faced with words so wealthy in association as these words of Stephen, it is unwise to suppose that any single interpretation exhausts their significance. All the meaning that had attached to Ps. 110:1 and Dan. 7:13f. is present here, including especially the meaning that springs from their combination on the lips of Jesus when He appeared before the Sanhedrin; but the replacement of "sitting" by "standing" probably makes its own contribution to the total meaning of the words in this context —a contribution distinctively appropriate to Stephen's present role as martyr-witness (ibid., pp. 168–69).

57–58 Haenchen has noted the progression in Luke's portrayals of the trial scenes of 4:1ff., 5:17ff., and here, with the first ending in threatenings (4:17, 21), the second with flogging (5:40), and the third with stoning (7:58–60). He concludes the following from the pattern: "It goes without saying that in the circumstances the moderating Gamaliel and the Pharisees who (according to Luke!) to some extent sympathized with the Christians do not make themselves heard—Luke possessed the happy gift of forgetting people when they might interfere with his literary designs" (*Acts of the Apostles*, p. 274). But while Haenchen rightly stresses Luke's developmental theme at this point, he fails to appreciate the historical interplay of divergent ideological factors that gave rise to Judaism's united stance against the Hellenists.

The message of Stephen, it seems, served as a kind of catalyst to unite Sadducees, Pharisees, and the common people against the early Christians. Had Gamaliel been confronted by this type of Christian preaching earlier, his attitude as reported in 5:34–39 would surely have been different. The Pharisees could tolerate Palestinian Jewish believers in Jesus because their messianic beliefs, though undoubtedly judged terribly misguided, effected no change in their practice of the Mosaic law: the Pharisaic and priestly devotees of the new movement continued their scrupulous observance of the law, and the Hebraic Christians continued to live in accordance with at least its minimal requirements. But the Hellenistic Christians, who had probably entered Palestine avowing their desire to become stricter in their religious practice, were now beginning to question the centrality of Israel's traditional forms of religious expression and to propagate within Jerusalem itself a type of religious liberalism that, from a Pharisaic perspective, would eventually undercut the basis for the Jewish religion itself. They might have been able to do little about such liberalism as it existed throughout the Diaspora and in certain quarters within Palestine. But they were determined to preserve the Holy City from further contamination by such outside elements and thus, as they saw it, best prepare the way for the coming of the Messianic Age.

It is not easy to determine whether the stoning of Stephen was only the result of mob action or whether it was carried out by the Sanhedrin in excess of its jurisdiction. Josephus recounts a somewhat parallel instance when the high priest Ananus killed James the Just during the procuratorial interregnum between Festus's death and Albinus's arrival in A.D. 61 (Antiq. XX, 200 [ix.1]). The reference to "the witnesses" in v.58, whose grisly duty it was to knock the offender down and throw the first stones, suggests an official execution. This hardly correlates, of course, with the stipulation in *Mishnah Sanhedrin* 4.1 that "in capital cases a verdict of acquittal may be reached on the same day [as the trial], but a verdict of conviction not until the following day." Nor is it in accord with the Roman regulation that death sentences in the provinces could not be carried out unless confirmed by the Roman governor. But if—as we believe—Stephen's martyrdom occurred sometime in the mid-thirties and during the final years of Pilate's governorship over Judea (A.D. 26–36), and if—as we have argued—the Pharisees were not prepared to come to his defense in the council, conditions may well have been at a stage where the Sanhedrin felt free to overstep its legal authority. Pontius Pilate normally resided at Caesarea, and the later years of his governorship were beset by increasing troubles that tended to divert his attention (e.g., the Samaritan affair where he killed a number of Samaritan fanatics, an action that ultimately resulted in his removal from office).

"The witnesses," Luke tells us, in preparing for their onerous work of knocking Stephen down and throwing the first stones, "laid their clothes at the feet of a young man named Saul." This suggests that Saul had some official part in the execution. "Young man" (*neanias*) is used in Greek writings of the day for those from about twenty-four to forty years old (cf. BAG, p. 536; see also 20:9; 23:17–18, 22). Some have argued from the action of the witnesses and from Saul's age that he was a member of the Jewish Sanhedrin at the time, though he may also have been exercising only delegated authority.

59–60 As Stephen was being stoned (note the imperfect verb *elithoboloun*, "they were stoning," which suggests a process), he cried out, "Lord Jesus, receive my spirit," and, "Lord, do not hold this sin against them." The cries are reminiscent of Jesus' words from the cross in Luke 23:34, 46, though the parallelism of sequence and wording is not exact. It is probably going too far to say that Luke meant Stephen's execution to be a reenactment of the first great martyrdom, that of Jesus, as many commentators have proposed (e.g., Charles H. Talbert, *Luke and the Gnostics* [Nashville: Abingdon, 1966], p. 76). Certainly, however, the parallelism here is not just inadvertent; and it was probably included to show that the same spirit of commitment and forgiveness that characterized Jesus' life and death was true of his earliest followers. The expression "fall asleep" (*koimaō*) is a common biblical way of referring to the death of God's own (cf. Gen 47:30 LXX; Deut 31:16 LXX; John 11:11; Acts 13:36; 1 Cor 7:39; 11:30; 15:6, 51; 2 Peter 3:4); and while the nuances of a doctrine of "soul sleep" are incompatible with the biblical message, the word "sleep" suggests something as to the nature of personal existence during that period of time theologians call "the intermediate state."

8:1a Again, as in 7:58, Luke makes the point that Saul was present at Stephen's death and approved of it. Because of the verb *syneudokeō* ("approve of," "consent to") and its parallel usage in 26:10, some have taken the reference here to be to Saul's official vote as a member of the Sanhedrin. But that is not necessarily implied. Nor is it possible to argue from v.1a that the seeds of Saul's later Christian teaching on the law were implanted either through the force of Stephen's preaching or the sublimity of his death. Paul himself credits his conversion and theology to other factors. All Luke wants to do here is provide a transition in the developing Christian mission.

Notes

---

56 P[74] reads τὸν υἱὸν τοῦ θεοῦ (*ton huion tou theou*, "Son of God") for τὸν υἱὸν τοῦ ἀνθρώπου (*ton huion tou anthrōpou*, "Son of Man"). On the christological title "Son of Man," see my *Christology*, pp. 82–93; idem, " 'Son of Man' Imagery: Some Implications for Theology and Discipleship," JETS, 18 (1975), 3–16.

Cullmann says of Stephen's death: "The Stoic departed this life dispassionately; the Christian martyr on the other hand died with spirited passion for the cause of Christ, because he knew that by doing so he stood within a powerful redemptive process. The first Christian martyr, Stephen, shows us (Acts 7:55) how very differently death is bested by him who dies in Christ than by the ancient philosopher: he sees, it is said, 'the heavens open and Christ standing at the right hand of God!' He sees Christ, the Conqueror of Death. With this faith that the death he must undergo is already conquered by Him who has Himself endured it, Stephen lets himself be stoned" (Oscar Cullmann, *Immortality of the Soul or Resurrection of the Dead?* [London: Epworth, 1958], p. 60).

58 CD 10.4–10 speaks of a complement of ten men to act as judges in its community, stipulating that "their minimum age shall be twenty-five and their maximum sixty," with no one over sixty eligible to hold a judicial office—an interesting parallel!

---

4. *The immediate aftermath*

8:1b–3

> On that day a great persecution broke out against the church at Jerusalem, and all except the apostles were scattered throughout Judea and Samaria. ²Godly men buried Stephen and mourned deeply for him. ³But Saul began to destroy the church. Going from house to house, he dragged off men and women and put them in prison.

1b Taken in the broader context of Luke's presentation, we should probably understand the persecution recorded here as directed primarily against the Hellenistic Christians of Jerusalem rather than chiefly against the whole church (as, e.g., Leitzmann, p. 90, and Filson, pp. 62–64; though roundly denied by G.W.H. Lampe, *St. Luke and the Church of Jerusalem* [London: Athlone, 1969], pp. 20–21). A certain stigma must also have fallen on the native-born and more scrupulous Jewish Christians, and they probably became as inconspicuous as possible in the countryside and towns around Jerusalem. The Hellenistic Jews of the city had been able to disassociate themselves from the Hellenistic Jewish Christians among them. Probably the Jewish leaders made a somewhat similar distinction between the Hellenistic and the more Hebraic Christians within the Jerusalem church, though not nearly so sharply. We are told by Luke in a somewhat sweeping statement that "all" (*pantes*) the Christians of Jerusalem "except the apostles were scattered throughout Judea and Samaria." Apparently, however, only the Hellenistic believers felt it inadvisable to return. So while we should not minimize God's protecting power or the apostle's courage, their remaining in Jerusalem in order to preserve the continuity of the community might not have been impossible.

As a result of the persecution that began with the martyrdom of Stephen, the gospel was carried beyond the confines of Jerusalem, in initial fulfillment of Jesus' directive in 1:8: "And you will be my witnesses in Jerusalem, and in all Judea and Samaria, and to the ends of the earth." From this time onward (till 135, when Hadrian banished all Jews from the city and refounded Jerusalem as the Roman colony Aelia Capitoline), the Jerusalem church seems to have been largely, if not entirely, devoid of Hellenistic believers. With the martyrdom of Stephen, the Christians of Jerusalem learned the bitter lesson that to espouse a changed relationship to the land, the law, and the temple was (1) to give up the peace of the church and (2) to abandon the Christian mission to Israel (cf. Walter Schmithals, *Paul and James*, tr. D.M. Barton [London: SCM, 1965], pp.

44-45). The issues and events connected with Stephen's death and the expulsion of those who shared his concerns would stand as a warning to the Jerusalem congregation throughout its brief and turbulent history and would exert mental pressure upon Christians in the city to be more circumspect in their future activities within Judea.

2 Luke has already used "godly men" (*andres eulabeis*) of the Jews at Pentecost who were receptive to the working of God's Spirit (cf. 2:5). He has also used the adjective *eulabēs* ("devout") of the aged Simeon in the temple (cf. Luke 2:25), and he will use it of Ananias of Damascus (cf. Acts 22:12). Therefore, when Luke says that "godly men buried Stephen," he apparently means that certain devout Jews who were open to the Christian message volunteered to ask for Stephen's body and bury him, much as Joseph of Arimathea did for Jesus (cf. Luke 23:50-53). The Mishnah speaks of "open lamentation" being inappropriate for one who has been stoned, burned, beheaded, or strangled under Sanhedrin judgment but allows "mourning, for mourning has place in the heart alone" (cf. *Sanhedrin* 6.6). And Luke tells us that those who buried Stephen "mourned deeply for him," which may well be Luke's way of suggesting their repentance toward God as well as their sorrow for Stephen.

3 Haenchen takes the occasion here to mock Luke's portrayal: "The transformation in the picture of Saul is breathtaking, to say the least. A moment ago he was a youth looking on with approval at the execution. Now he is the arch-persecutor, invading Christian homes to seize men and women and fling them into gaol" (*Acts of the Apostles*, p. 294). But, as we have noted, the Greek expression *neanias* in 7:58 signifies a man between the age of twenty-four and forty (hardly a youth in our modern sense); and the description of Saul's presence at the execution suggests some official capacity on his part, even though only that of a delegated authority. Saul, therefore, appears in 7:58 and 8:1 to have hardly been a casual onlooker. And while Luke reserves the fuller account of Saul's persecuting activities and his conversion for the narrative in 9:1-30 and the speeches in 22:1-21 and 26:2-23, here Luke introduces those accounts and ties them in with Stephen's martyrdom by using the inceptive imperfect verb *elymaineto* to tell us that at this time "Saul began to destroy the church."

Notes

1b On the use of πάντες (*pantes*, "all") in Luke's writings and the NT, see comments on 1.1.
    Barnabas of Cyprus (4:36) and Mnason of Cyprus (21:16), who is referred to as ἀρχαίῳ μαθητῇ (*archaiō mathētē*, "a disciple from the beginning"; NIV, "one of the early disciples") and to whose home Paul and his Gentile companions were brought on the occasion of the apostle's final visit to Jerusalem, may be seen as exceptions to the expulsion of the Hellenistic Christians from the city—though only if we define a Hellenist exclusively along geographic lines. Barnabas, however, is explicitly spoken of as a Levite in 4:36.

B. *The Early Ministries of Philip* (8:4-40)

The accounts of Philip's ministries in Samaria and to the Ethiopian minister of finance are placed in Acts between the Hellenists' expulsion from Jerusalem and the outreach

of the gospel to Gentiles—an outreach prepared for in Saul's conversion and first effected through the preaching of Peter to Cornelius. As such, Luke uses these accounts of
Philip's ministries as a kind of bridge in depicting the advance of the church. Each
account represents a further development in proclaiming the gospel within a Jewish
milieu: the first, an outreach to a dispossessed group within Palestine who were often
considered by Jerusalem Jews as "half-breeds," both racially and religiously; the second,
an outreach to a proselyte or near-proselyte from another land.

1. The evangelization of Samaria

8:4–25

⁴Those who had been scattered preached the word wherever they went. ⁵Philip
went down to a city in Samaria and proclaimed the Christ there. ⁶When the crowds
heard Philip and saw the miraculous signs he did, they all paid close attention to
what he said. ⁷With shrieks, evil spirits came out of many, and many paralytics and
cripples were healed. ⁸So there was great joy in that city.

⁹Now for some time a man named Simon had practiced sorcery in the city and
amazed all the people of Samaria. He boasted that he was someone great, ¹⁰and
all the people, both high and low, gave him their attention and exclaimed, "This
man is the divine power known as the Great Power." ¹¹They followed him because
he had amazed them for a long time with his magic. ¹²But when they believed Philip
as he preached the good news of the kingdom of God and the name of Jesus
Christ, they were baptized, both men and women. ¹³Simon himself believed and
was baptized. And he followed Philip everywhere, astonished by the great signs
and miracles he saw.

¹⁴When the apostles in Jerusalem heard that Samaria had accepted the word
of God, they sent Peter and John to them. ¹⁵When they arrived, they prayed for
them that they might receive the Holy Spirit, ¹⁶because the Holy Spirit had not yet
come upon any of them; they had simply been baptized into the name of the Lord
Jesus. ¹⁷Then Peter and John placed their hands on them, and they received the
Holy Spirit.

¹⁸When Simon saw that the Spirit was given at the laying on of the apostles'
hands, he offered them money and said, ¹⁹"Give me also this ability so that
everyone on whom I lay my hands may receive the Holy Spirit."

²⁰Peter answered: "May your money perish with you, because you thought you
could buy the gift of God with money! ²¹You have no part or share in this ministry,
because your heart is not right before God. ²²Repent of this wickedness and pray
to the Lord. Perhaps he will forgive you for having such a thought in your heart.
²³For I see that you are full of bitterness and captive to sin."

²⁴Then Simon answered, "Pray to the Lord for me so that nothing you have said
may happen to me."

²⁵When they had testified and proclaimed the word of the Lord, Peter and John
returned to Jerusalem, preaching the gospel in many Samaritan villages.

Historically, the movement of the gospel into Samaria following directly on the heels
of the persecution of Hellenistic Jewish Christians in Jerusalem makes a great deal of
sense. Doubtless a feeling of kinship was established between the formerly dispossessed
Samaritans and the recently dispossessed Christian Hellenists because of Stephen's
opposition to the mentality of mainstream Judaism and its veneration of the Jerusalem
temple—an opposition that would have facilitated a favorable response to Philip and his
message in Samaria. Redactionally, the thrust of the church into its mission after the
persecution of the Christian community in Jerusalem is parallel with Luke's portrayal in
his Gospel of the spread of Jesus' fame after the devil's assault in the wilderness.

The Tübingen school of "tendency criticism" focused upon this account of the Christian mission to Samaria as a prime example of Luke's tendentiousness in Acts, arguing that Luke's sources must originally have used Simon Magus as a cover figure for Paul who was bested by Peter (cf. the Pseudo-Clementine *Homilies* and *Recognitions*) and that Luke has recast Simon as an entirely different person with an entirely different history in an endeavor to protect his hero Paul. Modern "source criticism" tends to see two or three separate stories intertwined here, which Luke has somewhat confusedly worked together: that of Philip in Samaria, that of Peter and John in Samaria, and an account of the early "Christian" experience of the arch-Gnostic Simon Magus. Earlier source critics, however, following out the hypothesis of Harnack, viewed the intermeshing of these stories as the type of thing that results from an oral recounting of experiences on the part of an enthusiastic storyteller and suggested that Philip himself may have been the source of Luke's narrative here. We believe there is much in the narrative to support this suggestion, whether such a recounting was given him orally or came to him through some written form.

4 Luke connects his account of the evangelization of Samaria by his favorite connective *men oun* (Gr., "then," "so"; often untranslated in NIV), which he also uses in v.25 to conclude the narrative. Between the twofold use of this connective, he inserts the mission to Samaria as inaugurated by Philip and carried on by Peter and John as "Exhibit A" for his thesis that "those who had been scattered preached the word wherever they went." Luke does this because in the mission to Samaria he sees in retrospect a significant advance in the outreach of the gospel.

5 Philip, the second of the seven enumerated in 6:5 (cf. 21:8), and one of the Hellenistic believers expelled from Jerusalem in the persecution directed against Hellenistic Christians, traveled to the north and proclaimed "the Christ" (*ton Christon*) to Samaritans. The text is uncertain as to which city of Samaria Philip preached in, for every direction from Jerusalem is "down" (note the adverbial participle *katelthōn*). The MS evidence varies regarding the inclusion of the article *tēn* to read either "the city of Samaria" or "a city of Samaria." Some commentators, following the better-attested reading, insist that "the city of Samaria" can mean only the capital city of the province, which in OT times bore the name "Samaria." Herod the Great, however, rebuilt it as a Greek city and renamed it "Sebaste" in honor of Caesar Augustus (*Sebastos* is the Gr. equivalent to the Lat. *Augustus*). But Sebaste was a wholly pagan city in NT times, and it seems somewhat strange for it to be referred to here by its archaic name. Other commentators, accepting either the articular reading or preferring the less-well-attested one of "a city of Samaria" (RSV, NEB, NIV), believe that Shechem is the city in mind because during the Greek period it became the leading Samaritan city (cf. Jos. Antiq. XI, 340 [viii.6]) and was brought within the Jewish orbit of influence by the conquest of John Hyrcanus (ibid., XIII, 255 [ix.1]).

Others prefer to think of the Samaritan city of Gitta as in view here because Justin Martyr says that Simon Magus was a native of Gitta (*Apology* 1.26). Still others think of Sychar, for it was near Shechem (being even, at times, identified with Shechem) and is the Samaritan city in the gospel tradition (cf. John 4:5). But Luke, while he probably had some particular city in mind when he wrote, was evidently not interested in giving us a precise geographical identification (as his general reference to "many Samaritan villages" in v.25b also shows). So we shall have to leave it at that.

Animosity between Judeans and Samaritans stemmed from very early times and fed on a number of incidents in their respective histories. The cleavage began in the tenth century B.C. with the separation of the Ten Tribes from Jerusalem, Judah, and Benjamin in the disruption of the Hebrew monarchy after Solomon's death. It became racially fixed with Sargon's destruction of the city of Samaria in 722 B.C. and the Assyrians' policy of deportation and mixing of populations. It was intensified in Judean eyes by the Samaritans' opposition to the rebuilding of the Jerusalem temple in the fifth century (cf. Neh 2:10–6:14; 13:28; Jos. Antiq. XI, 84–103 [iv.3–6], 114 [iv.9], 174 [v.8]), by their erection of a schismatic temple on Mount Gerizim sometime around the time of Alexander the Great (cf. Jos Antiq. XI, 310–11 [viii.2], 322–24 [viii.4]; XIII, 255–56 [ix.1]), and by their identification of themselves as Sidonians and joining with the Seleucids against the Jews in the conflict of 167–164 B.C. (cf. ibid., XII, 257–64 [v.5]). It was sealed for the Samaritans by John Hyrcanus's destruction in 127 B.C. of the Gerizim temple (cf. ibid., XIII, 256 [ix.1]) and the city of Samaria (ibid., XIII, 275–77 [x.2]). The intensity of Samaritan feelings against Jerusalem is shown by the Samaritans' refusal of Herod's offer of 25 B.C. to rebuild their temple on Mount Gerizim when it was known that he also proposed to rebuild the Jerusalem temple—a rebuilding begun about 20–19 B.C. (ibid., XV, 280–425 [viii.3–xi.1]). The Judean antagonism to Samaria is evident as early as Ecclesiasticus 50:25–26, which lumps the Samaritans with the Idumeans and the Philistines as Israel's three detested nations and then goes on to disparage them further by the epithets "no nation" and "that foolish people that dwell in Shechem." Many such pejorative references to the Samaritans appear elsewhere in writings reflecting or reporting a Judean stance (e.g., 4QPs 37 on v.14; 4QpNah on 3:6; John 8:48). Nevertheless, while Jeremiah and Ezekiel treated the northern tribes as an integral part of Israel, there were always a few in Samaria who viewed Judean worship with respect (cf. 2 Chron 30:11; 34:9); and Samaritans accepted the Pentateuch as Holy Writ and looked for a coming messianic Restorer (the *ta'eb*) who would be Moses redivivus.

6–8 The equation of the Hellenists of Acts 6–7 with the Samaritans of Acts 8 is much too superficial (see comments on 6:1). Likewise, Cullmann's thesis of a "triangular relationship" between (1) his so-called Johannine Circle (which includes John, the Hellenists of Acts 6–7, and the writer of Hebrews), (2) the Samaritans, and (3) the Qumranites is much too specific for the data at our disposal (Oscar Cullmann, *The Johannine Circle*, tr. J. Bowden [Philadelphia: Westminster, 1976]). Nevertheless, it remains true that in the highly fluid and syncretistic atmosphere of first-century Palestine a number of analogical parallels of outlook and ideology existed between various nonconformist groups generally looked upon as being Jewish. Stephen, the covenanters of Qumran, and the Samaritans, for example, all had an antitemple polemic, which, at least superficially, could have drawn them together, though, in actuality, their positions were each based on quite different rationales. In addition, as the antagonism of Jerusalem Jews was focused upon the Hellenistic Christians, these lately dispossessed Jewish believers undoubtedly found something of a welcome among the Samaritans, who had felt themselves the objects of a similar animosity for so long.

Philip's preaching has been defined in v.5 as being a proclamation of "the Messiah" (*ton Christon*), with its content further specified in v.12 as being "the kingdom of God and the name of Jesus Christ." Undoubtedly he used Deuteronomy 18:15, 18–19 as a major testimonium passage in his preaching, as Peter and Stephen had done. With the Pentateuch as their Scriptures, and looking for the coming of a Mosaic Messiah, the Samaritans were open to Philip's message. Furthermore, God backed up his preaching by many "miraculous signs" (*ta sēmeia*), with many demoniacs, paralytics, and cripples healed. Thus Luke summarizes the response of these Samaritans to Philip's ministry by saying, "So there was great joy in that city."

9-13 Simon the sorcerer, or Simon Magus as he is called in postapostolic Christian writings, was a leading heretic in the early church. Justin Martyr (died c.165), who was himself a Samaritan, says that nearly all his countrymen revered Simon as the highest god (*Apology* 1.26; *Dialogue* 120). Irenaeus (c.180) speaks of him as the father of Gnosticism and identifies the sect of the Simonians as being derived from him (*Contra Haereses* 1.23). The second-century Acts of Peter has extensive descriptions of how Simon Magus corrupted Christians in Rome by his teachings and how he was repeatedly bested by Peter in displays of his magical powers. These themes were picked up by the Pseudo-Clementine *Homilies* and *Recognitions* of the third and fourth centuries, though in them Simon was used as a cover figure for Paul in a radically Ebionite manner. Hippolytus (died c.236) outlines Simon's system, which he avers was contained in a Gnostic tractate entitled *The Great Disclosure*, and tells how he allowed himself to be buried alive in Rome with the prediction that he would rise on the third day (*Refutation of All Heresies* 6. 2-15). And Justin Martyr (*Apology* 1.26), as followed by Tertullian (c. 197 in his Apology 13.9), tells of Simon's being honored with a statue in Rome on which was written "To Simon the Holy God"—probably a misreading either by Justin or the Simonians of an inscription beginning SEMONI SANCO DEO ("To the God Semo Sancus," an ancient Sabine deity), which either he or they read as SIMONI SANCTO DEO.

Just exactly how Simon of Acts 8 is related to Simon Magus of later legend is not clear. They may have been different men, though the church fathers regularly equated them. And Luke's statement about the Samaritans' veneration of Simon—that they said, "The man is the divine power known as the Great Power"—seems to support the Fathers' identification. Likewise, what exactly is meant by the title "the Great Power" (v.10) is uncertain. It may mean that Simon was acclaimed to be God Almighty (as Gustaf Dalman insisted, *The Words of Jesus*, tr. D.M. Kay [Edinburgh: T. & T. Clark, 1909], p. 200) or the Grand Vizier of God Almighty (as J. De Zwaan argued, BC, 2:58). At any rate, he claimed to be some exceedingly great person and supported his claim by many acts of magic.

Nevertheless, as the gospel advanced into Samaria, Simon believed and was baptized. His conversion must have greatly impressed the Samaritans, and their evangelist Philip must have long remembered it. But Simon himself, to judge by the narrative that follows, was more interested in the great acts of power accompanying Philip's preaching than God's reign in his life or the proclamation of Jesus' messiahship. Simon's belief in Jesus seems to have been like that spoken of in John 2:23-25—i.e., based only on miraculous signs and thus inferior to true commitment to Jesus.

14 For the early church the evangelization of Samaria was not just a matter of an evangelist's proclamation and people's response. It also involved the acceptance of these new converts by the mother church in Jerusalem. So Luke takes pains to point out here (see also his account of Cornelius's conversion in 10:1-11:18) that the Jerusalem church sought to satisfy itself as to the genuineness of Philip's converts and that they did this by sending Peter and John to Samaria. Along with his thesis about development and advance in the outreach of the gospel, Luke is also interested in establishing lines of continuity and highlighting aspects of essential unity within the church. Therefore, in his account of Philip's mission in Samaria, he tells also of the visit of Peter and John. Instead of minimizing Philip's success in Samaria, as some have proposed, it is more likely that Luke wants us to understand Peter and John's ministry in Samaria as confirming and extending Philip's ministry. Just as in Romans 15:26 and 2 Corinthians 9:2, where a whole province is regarded as acting in a Christian manner when represented by only

one or two congregations located there, so Luke here speaks sweepingly of the Jerusalem church hearing "that Samaria had accepted the word of God," even though in v.25 he refers to further evangelistic activity in other Samaritan villages.

15–17 When Peter and John arrived (lit., "went down," *katabantes*), they prayed for the Samaritan converts, laid their hands on them, and "they received the Holy Spirit." Before this, Luke tells us, "The Holy Spirit had not yet come upon any of them; they had simply been baptized into the name of the Lord Jesus." We are not told just how the coming of the Holy Spirit upon these new converts was expressed in their lives, but the context suggests that his presence was attended by such external signs as marked his coming on the earliest Christians at Pentecost—probably by some form of glossolalia.

The temporal separation of the baptism of the Spirit from commitment to Jesus and water baptism in this passage has been of paramount and perennial theological interest to many. Catholic sacramentalists take this as a biblical basis for the separation between baptism and confirmation. Charismatics of various denominational persuasions see in it a justification for their doctrine of the baptism of the Spirit as a second work of grace following conversion. But before making too much of this separation theologically, it is well, as we have noted earlier (cf. comments on 2:38), to look at the circumstances and ask what may seem an elementary question, yet one of immense importance: What if both the logical and the chronological relationships of conversion, water baptism, and the baptism of the Spirit as proclaimed in Peter's call to repentance at Pentecost (cf. 2:38; see also Rom 8:9; 1 Cor 6:11) had been fully expressed in this case?

The Jerusalem Jews considered the Samaritans to be second-class residents of Palestine and kept them at arm's length religiously. And on their part, the Samaritans returned the compliment. It is not too difficult to imagine what would have happened had the apostles at Jerusalem first been the missioners to Samaria. Probably they would have been rebuffed, just as they were rebuffed earlier in their travels with Jesus when the Samaritans associated them with the city of Jerusalem (cf. Luke 9:51–56). But God in his providence used as their evangelist the Hellenist Philip, who shared their fate (though for different reasons) of being rejected at Jerusalem; and the Samaritans received him and accepted his message. But what if the Spirit had come upon them at their baptism when administrated by Philip? Undoubtedly what feelings there were against Philip and the Hellenists would have carried over to them, and they would have been doubly under suspicion. But God in his providence withheld the gift of the Holy Spirit till Peter and John laid their hands on the Samaritans—Peter and John, two leading apostles who were highly thought of in the mother church at Jerusalem and who would have been accepted at that time as brothers in Christ by the new converts in Samaria. In effect, therefore, in this first advance of the gospel outside the confines of Jerusalem, God worked in ways that were conducive not only to the reception of the Good News in Samaria but also to the acceptance of these new converts by believers at Jerusalem.

The further question as to how far in practice this acceptance by the Jerusalem church would have gone had Samaritan Christians actually traveled to Jerusalem to meet and worship with the Jerusalem believers is left unanswered. Nor does Luke tell us anything about how these Samaritan believers expressed their commitment to Jesus in their Samaritan cultural and religious milieu. These are matters that would be of great interest to us today but which did not concern Luke. What he does tell us, however, is that in such a manner as this vignette shows, God was working in ways that promoted both the outreach of the gospel and the unity of the church. And rather than trying to extract from the account further theological nuances of a deeper kind, we would better expend our energies in trying to work out in theory and practice the implications of such a divine interest in outreach and unity for the church today.

18-24 Simon's response to the presence of God's Spirit and the evidences of God's power is one of those tragic stories that accompany every advance of the gospel. Whenever and wherever God is at work among people, there are not only genuine responses but also counterfeit ones. Simon "believed" and "was baptized," Luke has reported. Evidently Simon was included among those Peter and John laid their hands on. But the NT frequently reports incidents and events from a phenomenal perspective without always giving the divine or heavenly perspective. For this reason the verb "believe" (*pisteuō*) is used in the NT to cover a wide range of responses to God and to Christ (e.g., John 2:23; James 2:19). Neither baptism nor the laying on of hands conveys any status or power of itself, though Simon with his shallow spiritual perception thought they could.

Simon's offer to pay for the ability to confer the Holy Spirit through the laying on of hands evoked Peter's consignment of Simon and his money to hell. Simon regarded the bestowal of the Spirit as a specially effective bit of magic, and he had no idea of the spiritual issues at stake. Peter's analysis of the situation, however, is that Simon's heart was "not right before God" because it was still "full of bitterness and captive to sin." So Peter urges him, "Repent of this wickedness and pray to the Lord. Perhaps he will forgive you for having such a thought in your heart." But Simon, preoccupied with external consequences and physical effects, asks only and rather lamely, "Pray to the Lord for me so that nothing you have said may happen to me."

We would like to know more from this narrative. Did Simon later become the heretic Simon Magus of ecclesiastical legend? Or did he repent and genuinely respond to God, thereby becoming a true Christian? How did the Samaritan Christians respond to Simon's perverse request and to his possible later heretical activity? But beyond what Luke tells us, we can only speculate. Instead of such speculations, it is better to allow the sobering truth of what Luke does tell us to penetrate deeply into our consciousness: It is all too often possible to make a counterfeit response to the presence and activity of God's Spirit.

25 Luke closes his account of the evangelization of Samaria with a transitional sentence that uses the same connective he began with—*men oun* ("when," NIV). And here he tells us that on the apostles' return journey to Jerusalem, further evangelization of Samaria took place. The "they" of the third person pronominal suffix in the verb *hypestrephon* ("they returned") refers primarily to Peter and John, but it may also refer to Philip for part of the journey, as they evangelized together in the southern regions of Samaria.

Notes

4 On the use of μὲν οὖν (*men oun*, "so," "then") in Acts, see comments on 1:6.

5 For other references in Acts that speak of "going down" from Jerusalem, see κατέρχομαι (*katerchomai*) in 9:32; 11:27; 15:1, 30; 21:10; and καταβαίνω (*katabainō*) in 7:15; 8:26; 18:22; 24:1, 22; 25:6-7. On "going up" to Jerusalem, see ἀναβαίνω (*anabainō*) in 11:2; 21:12, 15; 24:11; 25:1, 9.

On the title ὁ Χριστός (*ho Christos*, "the Christ") in Acts, see comments on 2:36.

9–11 On Simon Magus, see R.P. Casey's article in BC, 5:151–63. Wilson identifies Simon in Acts 8 with the Simon Magus of later patristic reference but suggests that much of Simon's Gnosticism was probably attributed to him by later adherents (R. McL. Wilson, *Gnosis and the New Testament* [Philadelphia: Fortress, 1968], pp. 49, 141).

12 On the use of ἡ βασιλεία τοῦ θεοῦ (*hē basileia tou theou*, "the kingdom of God") in Acts, see comments on 1:3.

15 On the use of καταβαίνω (*katabainō*) in Acts in contexts of "going down" from Jerusalem, see note above at v.5.

16 On the use of εἰς (*eis*, "into") for ἐν (*en*, "in") in the expression "baptized in [or 'into'] the name of the Lord Jesus," see comments on and note at 2:38. The prepositions were frequently employed synonymously (cf. 7:4, 12) and probably should be taken in that way here and in 19:5.

17 For other instances in Acts of the practice of laying hands on someone, see 6:6; 9:17; 13:3; 19:6.

18 A C D E P⁴⁵P⁷⁴ read πνεῦμα τὸ ἅγιον (*pneuma to hagion*, "the Holy Spirit"), though both ℵ and B omit τὸ ἅγιον (*to hagion*, "holy") and are probably to be preferred.

24 D adds rather awkwardly at the end of the sentence ὃς πολλὰ κλαίων οὐ διελίμπανεν (*hos polla klaiōn ou dielimpanen*, "who never stopped weeping profusely"), evidently attempting to suggest some degree of repentance.

25 On the use of μὲν οὖν (*men oun*, "so," "then") in Acts, see above at v.4 and comments on 1:6.

---

2. An Ethiopian eunuch converted

8:26–40

> ²⁶Now an angel of the Lord said to Philip, "Go south to the road—the desert road—that goes down from Jerusalem to Gaza." ²⁷So he started out, and on his way he met an Ethiopian eunuch, an important official in charge of all the treasury of Candace, queen of the Ethiopians. This man had gone to Jerusalem to worship, ²⁸and on his way home was sitting in his chariot reading the book of Isaiah the prophet. ²⁹The Spirit told Philip, "Go to that chariot and stay near it."
>
> ³⁰Then Philip ran up to the chariot and heard the man reading Isaiah the prophet. "Do you understand what you are reading?" Philip asked.
>
> ³¹"How can I," he said, "unless someone explains it to me?" So he invited Philip to come up and sit with him.
>
> ³²The eunuch was reading this passage of Scripture:
>> "He was led like a sheep to the slaughter,
>> and as a lamb before the shearer is silent,
>> so he did not open his mouth.
>> ³³In his humiliation he was deprived of justice.
>> Who can speak of his descendants?
>> For his life was taken from the earth."
>
> ³⁴The eunuch asked Philip, "Tell me, please, who is the prophet talking about, himself or someone else?" ³⁵Then Philip began with that very passage of Scripture and told him the good news about Jesus.
>
> ³⁶As they traveled along the road, they came to some water and the eunuch said, "Look, here is water. Why shouldn't I be baptized?" ³⁸And he ordered the chariot to stop. Then both Philip and the eunuch went down into the water and Philip baptized him. ³⁹When they came up out of the water, the Spirit of the Lord suddenly took Philip away, and the eunuch did not see him again, but went on his way rejoicing. ⁴⁰Philip, however, appeared at Azotus and traveled about, preaching the gospel in all the towns until he reached Caesarea.

This account of Philip's ministry to a high-ranking Ethiopian government official represents a further step in the advance of the gospel from its strictly Jewish confines to a full-fledged Gentile mission. Though a Gentile, the official was probably a Jewish proselyte or near-proselyte (a so-called Proselyte of the Gate) and was therefore viewed by Luke as still within a Jewish religious milieu. He had been to Jerusalem to worship, was studying the prophecy of Isaiah, and was open to further instruction from a Jew. The "enthusiastic historiography" that many have detected in the narrative may well reflect Philip's enthusiasm in telling the story, which Luke may have captured either directly or from some written source. In any event, here was a notable instance of providential working that carried the development of the gospel proclamation even beyond Samaria.

26 We are not told just where Philip was when he received his divine directive to go south to the road from Jerusalem to Gaza. Most have assumed he was at the Samaritan city referred to in v.5, whether Sebaste, Samaria, Gitta, or Sychar. Some have seen him at Jerusalem because of the *eis Hierosolyma—apo Ierousalēm* ("into Jerusalem—from Jerusalem") couplet in vv.25–26, while others think of him as already at Caesarea. It is also possible that Philip was at the time in one of the Samaritan villages alluded to in v.25, if he is included in the pronominal suffix "they" of that verse. But Luke is not interested in the specifics of geography here, and it is idle to speculate further. What he is interested in is highlighting for his readers the fact that Philip's ministry to the Ethiopian eunuch was especially arranged by God and providentially worked out in all its details.

When Luke desires to stress the special presence and activity of God in his narrative, he frequently uses the expression "the angel of the Lord" (*angelos kyriou*) for the more normal reference to "the spirit of the Lord" (*pneuma kyriou*), as in Luke 1:11; 2:9; Acts 8:26; 12:7, 23 (cf. also *angelos tou theou* ["angel of God"] in 10:3 and simply *angelos* ["angel"] in 7:30, 35, 38; 10:7, 22; 11:13; 12:11; 27:23). Here Luke begins in just such a way and with such a purpose, telling us that "an angel of the Lord" began the action by giving instructions to Philip—and also sustained it throughout, though the more usual "the Spirit" and "the Spirit of the Lord" are used in vv.29, 39.

In the LXX the word *mesēmbria* usually means "midday" or "noon," and it is used that way in Acts 22:6. Here, however, as in Daniel 8:4, 9 LXX, *mesēmbria* probably means "south," with *kata mesēmbrian* meaning "southward." The clarifying phrase *hautē estin erēmos* ("this is desert") can refer grammatically either to "the road" (*tēn hodon*, as RSV, NEB, JB, NIV) or to the city of Gaza itself. This was the southernmost of the five chief Philistine cities in southwest Palestine and the last settlement before the desert waste stretching away to Egypt. The fifty-mile journey from Jerusalem to Gaza trailed off at its southwestern terminus into patches of desert, and most commentators believe that the expression "this is desert" has reference to that portion of the road. Sometime around 100–96 B.C., however, Gaza was destroyed by the Maccabean priest-king Alexander Jannaeus (cf. Jos. Antiq. XIII, 358–64 [xiii.3]), being literally laid waste, while about 57 B.C. a new city was built under Pompey's orders by Gabinius (ibid., XIV, 76 [iv.4], 88 [v.31]). Strabo and Diodorus of Sicily seem to refer to this new Gaza as located a bit to the south of the old site and to distinguish it from a "Desert Gaza" or "Old Gaza" (cf. HJP, 2.1:71). Therefore, some commentators understand the expression to specify the old city of Gaza ("Desert Gaza") rather than the new city.

27–28 It is difficult to determine from the text itself how Luke wanted his readers to understand the Ethiopian eunuch's relation to Judaism. Furthermore, it is uncertain how first-century Judaism would have viewed a eunuch coming to worship at Jerusalem. While Deuteronomy 23:1 explicitly stipulates that no emasculated male could be included within the Jewish religious community, Isaiah 56:3–5 speaks of eunuchs being accepted by the God of boundless lovingkindness. Likewise, it is not at all as clear as it might appear what was the Ethiopian official's physical condition, for the word eunuch (*eunouchos*) frequently appears in the LXX and in Greek vernacular writings "for high military and political officials; it does not have to imply emasculation" (TDNT, 2:766). Therefore, we are probably justified in taking "eunuch" to be a governmental title in an Oriental kingdom and in emphasizing two facts when considering the Ethiopian's relation to Judaism: (1) he had been on a religious pilgrimage to Jerusalem and (2) he was returning with a copy of the prophecy of Isaiah in his possession, which would have been difficult for a non-Jew to get.

Admittedly, Luke leaves us in some doubt when he might well have used some such expression as *prosēlytos* ("proselyte," "convert"; cf. 6:5; 13:43), *sebomenos ton theon* ("God-fearer," "Proselyte of the Gate," "near convert"; cf. 13:50; 16:14; 17:4, 17; 18:7), *phoboumenos ton theon* ("reverent," used in 13:16, 26, equivalent to *sebomenos ton theon*, though in 10:2, 22, 35 with no necessary relation to Judaism involved), or even *eusebēs* ("pious," with no relation to Judaism necessarily involved; cf. 10:2, 7), Nevertheless, judging by what Luke does tell us and by the placement of this vignette in his overall plan, we are probably to understand that this Ethiopian government official was a proselyte or near-proselyte to Judaism.

The ancient kingdom of Ethiopia lay between Aswan and Khartoum and corresponds to modern Nubia (not Abyssinia). It was ruled by a queen mother who had the dynastic title Candace and ruled on behalf of her son the king, since the king was regarded as the child of the sun and therefore too holy to become involved in the secular functions of the state (cf. Bion of Soli *Aethiopica* 1; Strabo *Geography* 17.1.54; Pliny the Elder *Natural History* 6.186; Dio Cassius *History of Rome* 54.5.4; Eusebius *Ecclesiastical History* 2.1.13). One of the ministers of the Ethiopian government—in fact, the minister of finance—having become either a full proselyte or a Proselyte of the Gate, had gone to Jerusalem to worship at one of the Jewish festivals and was now returning home reading Isaiah. It might even have been Isaiah 56:3–5 that first caught his attention and caused him to return to Isaiah again and again:

> Let no foreigner who has joined himself to the LORD say,
> "The Lord will surely exclude me from his people."
> And let not any eunuch complain,
> "I am only a dry tree."
> For this is what the LORD says:
> "To the eunuchs who keep my Sabbaths,
> who choose what pleases me
> and hold fast to my covenant—
> to them I will give within my temple and its walls
> a memorial and a name
> better than sons and daughters;
> I will give them an everlasting name
> that will not be cut off."

If he had begun reading here, he would doubtless have gone on to read what immediately follows (56:6–8):

> "And foreigners who bind themselves to the LORD
> to serve him,

> to love the name of the LORD,
>   and to worship him,
> all who keep the Sabbath without desecrating it
>   and who hold fast to my covenant—
> these I will bring to my holy mountain
>   and give them joy in my house of prayer.
> Their burnt offerings and sacrifices
>   will be accepted on my altar;
> for my house will be called
>   a house of prayer for all nations."
> The Sovereign LORD declares—
>   he who gathers the exiles of Israel:
> "I will gather still others to them
>   besides those already gathered."

But whatever got him into Isaiah's prophecy, the interpretation of the Servant passage of Isaiah 52:13-53:12 troubled him.

29-30 Having been directed to the desert road on the way to Gaza, Philip is again directed by the Spirit to the carriage the Ethiopian minister of finance is traveling in. As Philip approaches, he hears the minister reading from Isaiah, for reading aloud to oneself was "the universal practice in the ancient world" (Cadbury, *Book of Acts*, p. 18). So while running along beside the Ethiopian's carriage, Philip asks, "Do you understand what you are reading?" (*ginōskeis ha anaginōskeis*—a play on words).

31-34 The Ethiopian, being open to instruction from a Jew, invites Philip into his carriage to explain Isaiah 53:7-8 to him. His problem, it seems, concerns the suffering and humiliation references, and his question is "Who is the prophet talking about, himself or someone else?" Perhaps he had heard an official explanation of this passage at Jerusalem, but he still had questions about its meaning.

While in Late Judaism the concept of God's Servant carried messianic connotations in certain contexts and among certain groups, there is no evidence that anyone in pre-Christian Judaism ever thought of the Messiah in terms of a Suffering Servant. The Talmud, indeed, speaks of suffering sent by God as having atoning efficacy (cf. Davies, *Paul*, pp. 262-65); and there are many indications that "humility and self-humiliation, or acceptance of humiliation from God's hand, were expected of a pious man and thought to be highly praiseworthy" (E. Schweizer, *Lordship and Discipleship* [London: SCM, 1960], p. 23; cf. also pp. 23-31). But there is no explicit evidence that this general attitude toward suffering was ever consciously carried over to ideas regarding the Messiah, God's Servant par excellence. Klausner's dictum continues to hold true: "In the whole Jewish Messianic literature of the Tannaitic period there is no trace of the 'suffering Messiah'" (Joseph Klausner, *The Messianic Idea in Israel*, tr. W.F. Stinespring [New York: Macmillan, 1955], p. 405).

The Targum on the earlier and later prophets (so-called Pseudo-Jonathan), which stems from a Palestinian milieu, consistently applies all mention of suffering and humiliation in Isaiah 52:13-53:12 either to the nation Israel (at 52:14; 53:2, 4, 10) or to the wicked Gentile nations (at 53:3, 7-9, 11). Nor can it be said that the DSS have a suffering messianology. The Hymns of Thanksgiving, it is true, bring us somewhat closer to such a concept than anything extant from the world of Judaism, chiefly in their association of suffering and the Servant of God with ideas about the coming Messiah(s): (1) that the psalmist (the Teacher of Righteousness himself?) was conscious of being God's servant (cf. 1QH 13.18-19; 14.25; 17.26); (2) that persecution and suffering were the lot of both the Teacher and the community in following God's will (cf. 1QH 5.15-16; 8.26-27, 35-36); and (3) that the group at times expressed itself in language drawn from the Servant Songs of Isaiah (cf. 1QH 4.5-6, which is an expanded paraphrase of Isa 42:6). But that these ideas were ever brought together at Qumran to form a Suffering Servant messianology is at best quite uncertain. It may be that rabbinic Judaism later purged a Suffering Servant messianology based on the Isaian Servant Songs from its own traditions because of the use made of such a doctrine and these passages by Christians, as Joachim Jeremias has argued (cf. TDNT, 5:695-700). More likely, however, it seems that the lack of clarity regarding such a connection of concepts at Qumran—from whence we might reasonably expect greater precision on this point, had it existed in Late Judaism—points to the conclusion that, while the individual elements for a suffering conception of the Messiah may have been in process of being formed in certain quarters, a doctrine of a suffering Messiah was unheard of and considered unthinkable in first-century Jewish religious circles generally.

35 At a time when only what Christians call the OT was Scripture, what better book was there to use in proclaiming the nature of divine redemption than Isaiah, and what better passage could be found than Isaiah 52:13-53:12? Thus Philip began with the very passage the Ethiopian was reading and proclaimed to him "the good news about Jesus," explaining from Isaiah 53:7-8 and its context a suffering messianology. Of the evangelists, Matthew and John apply Isaiah 53 to Jesus' ministry of healing (cf. Matt 8:17 on 53:4; John 12:38 on 53:1; see also Matt 12:18-21 on 42:1-4). Luke, however, alone among the evangelists, portrays Jesus as quoting Isaiah 53 as being fulfilled in his passion (cf. Luke 22:37 on 53:12). In his volumes, therefore, Luke sets up a parallel between Jesus' use of Isaiah 53 and Philip's preaching based on Isaiah 53 and implies in that parallel that the latter was dependent upon the former (cf. also 1 Peter 2:22-25 on 53:4-6, 9, 12). But Philip, we are told, only began his preaching about Jesus with Isaiah 53. Probably he went on to include other passages from that early Christian block of testimonium material that has been dubbed "Scriptures of the Servant of the Lord and the Righteous Sufferer" that also included Isaiah 42:1-44:5; 49:1-13; 50:4-11; and Psalms 22, 34, 69, 118 (cf. C.H. Dodd, *According to the Scriptures* [London: Nisbet, 1952], pp. 61-108).

36-38 The eunuch responded to Philip by asking for baptism. As a Jewish proselyte or near-proselyte, the eunuch probably knew that water baptism was the expected external symbol for a Gentile's repentance and conversion to the religion of Israel. Therefore, it would have been quite natural for him to view baptism as the appropriate expression for his commitment to Jesus, whom he had come to accept as the fulfillment of Israel's hope and promised Messiah. Or perhaps Philip closed his exposition with an appeal similar to Peter's at Pentecost (cf. 2:38) and his own in Samaria (cf. 8:12). But however the subject of baptism arose, "both Philip and the eunuch went down into the water and Philip baptized him." Traditionally, Wadi el-Hesi that runs northeast of Gaza has been identified as the place of the eunuch's baptism. But Luke's interest here is not geography but the fact that in baptism the Ethiopian minister of finance proclaimed his commitment to Jesus. That is the climax Luke has been building up to.

39-40 The account of the Ethiopian's conversion ends as it began—with a stress on the special presence of God and his direct intervention. We are told that the Spirit of the

Lord "suddenly took" (*hērpasen*) Philip from the scene. The verb *harpazō* connotes both a forceful and sudden action by the Spirit and a lack of resistance from Philip.

With our Western interest in cause-and-effect relations and our modern understanding of historiography, we would like to know more about what exactly happened between the eunuch and Philip and more about their subsequent lives. Irenaeus writes that the eunuch became a missionary to the Ethiopians (*Contra Haereses* 3.12), though we do not know whether he only inferred that from this account or whether he had independent knowledge about it. All that Luke tells us about the eunuch is that his conversion was a significant episode in the advance of the gospel and that he "went on his way rejoicing."

Likewise, all Luke tells us about Philip is that his early ministries in Samaria and to the eunuch were important features in the development of the Christian mission from its strictly Jewish confines to its Gentile outreach. He refers to further evangelistic activity on the part of Philip in the maritime plain of Palestine and to a final ministry at Caesarea. Later he mentions Philip and his four prophetess daughters at Caesarea in connection with Paul's last visit to Jerusalem (cf. 21:8–9). Beyond these meager references, however, Luke tells us nothing because he is interested in the advances of the gospel proclamation and not in what happened after that.

Notes

28–29 The word τὸ ἄρμα (*to harma*) was commonly employed of a war chariot, though here undoubtedly it designates more a traveling chariot or a carriage (see also v.38).

34 The first messianic use in the Tal. of the suffering element in an Isaian Servant passage is in b *Sanhedrin* 98b, where the word נָגוּעַ (*nāgûa'*, "stricken") led some rabbis to speak of the Messiah as "the leprous one" or "the sick one." The attribution can be dated no earlier than A.D. 200.

37 Our better MSS omit v.37. D is lacking from 8:26–10:14, but E, a number of minor texts, and such church fathers as Irenaeus, Tertullian, Cyprian, Ambrosiaster, Ambrose, and Augustine add (with minor variations) the characteristically Western reading: "Philip said, 'If you believe with your whole heart, you may.' He answered and said, 'I believe that Jesus Christ is the Son of God.'" The Byzantine text also omits this reading, but Erasmus included it in his critical editions because he concluded that it had only inadvertently fallen out of the textual tradition he knew, and therefore it became embedded in the TR and the KJV. The construction τὸν Ἰησοῦν Χριστόν (*ton Iēsoun Christon*) and its use as a proper name, however, breaks a Lukan pattern in the first half of Acts (cf. comment on 2:36); and the verse adds nothing to the narrative except to make explicit what is already implied.

39 The Western text (though D lacking here) reads, "The Holy Spirit fell upon the eunuch, and the angel of the Lord suddenly took Philip away," thereby setting up a parallel of expression with the Spirit's coming upon believers at Pentecost and in Samaria, and also picking up the expression "the angel of the Lord" from v.26.

Luke's Gospel is aptly described as "the Gospel of Messianic Joy," with words for joy and exultation occurring with notable frequency: χαίρω (*chairō*, "rejoice," "be glad") twelve times (six times in Matt, twice in Mark); χαρά (*chara*, "joy") eight times (six times in Matt, once in Mark); ἀγαλλίασις (*agalliasis*, "exultation") twice (not at all in Matt or Mark); ἀγαλλιάω (*agalliaō*, "exult," "be glad") twice (once in Matt, not at all in Mark); σκιρτάω (*skirtaō*, "leap," "spring about" as a sign of joy) three times (not at all in Matt or Mark). And here in Acts that emphasis is continued.

C. The Conversion of Saul of Tarsus (9:1-30)

There are three accounts of Paul's conversion in Acts: the first here in chapter 9 and two more in Paul's defenses in chapters 22 and 26. Source criticism has had a field day with these accounts, often attributing the repetitions to a plurality of sources and the differences to divergent perspectives among the sources. Haenchen, however, rightly says, "Luke employs such repetitions only when he considers something to be extraordinarily important and wishes to impress it unforgettably on the reader. That is the case here" (*Acts of the Apostles*, p. 327).

The major charge against Paul was his willingness to carry the gospel directly to Gentiles, refusing to be confined to a mission to Israel. His defense before the people of Jerusalem in chapter 22 ends with him quoting his divinely given commission to go to the Gentiles and the people's fervent objection to it (cf. 22:21-22). Paul's defense before Agrippa II in chapter 26 also ends on this same note and is followed by Festus's comment that he was mad (cf. 26:23-24).

Paul would have had no great problem with either Judaism or Rome had he contented himself with a mission to Jews, and Christianity would have been spared the head-on collision with both Judaism and Rome. But Luke's point in chapter 9—one he makes twice more in chapters 22 and 26—is that Christ himself brought about this change in the strategy of divine redemption. It was not a strategy Paul thought up or a program given to him by another; it was a compelling call that came directly from Christ himself. Nor can it be explained psychologically or as an evolution of ideas whose time was ripe. Instead, it came to him by revelation and he had no choice but to obey. Luke, therefore, climaxes his portrayals of three pivotal figures in the advance of the gospel to the Gentile world by an account of the conversion of Saul of Tarsus that emphasizes the supernatural nature of the call and the miraculous circumstances of the conversion. With these emphases, though with inevitable variations in detail, Paul himself was in full agreement (cf. Gal 1:1-24).

1. The Christ encounter on the Damascus road

9:1-9

> [1]Meanwhile, Saul was still breathing out murderous threats against the Lord's disciples. He went to the high priest [2]and asked him for letters to the synagogues in Damascus, so that if he found any there who belonged to the Way, whether men or women, he might take them as prisoners to Jerusalem. [3]As he neared Damascus on his journey, suddenly a light from heaven flashed around him. [4]He fell to the ground and heard a voice say to him, "Saul, Saul, why do you persecute me?"
> [5]"Who are you, Lord?" Saul asked.
> "I am Jesus, whom you are persecuting," he replied. [6]"Now get up and go into the city, and you will be told what you must do."
> [7]The men traveling with Saul stood there speechless; they heard the sound but did not see anyone. [8]Saul got up from the ground, but when he opened his eyes he could see nothing. So they led him by the hand into Damascus. [9]For three days he was blind, and did not eat or drink anything.

1-2 The account of Saul's conversion opens with the picture of him "still breathing out murderous threats against the Lord's disciples." The adverb *eti* ("still") ties the narrative into what has gone before (cf. 8:3) and denotes that even after the death of Stephen and the expulsion of the Hellenistic Christians from Jerusalem, Saul saw it was necessary to

367

continue the persecution in places outside the Sanhedrin's immediate jurisdiction. The expression *apeilēs kai phonou*, which NIV (together with Ph and NEB) treats as a hendiadys and translates as "murderous threats," may very well have connoted in Luke's source material the dual ideas of a legal warning (*apeilē*) and a judicial punishment (*phonos*), as were inherent in Jewish jurisprudence (cf. Dupont, p. 44, n.43)—though Luke himself probably only took them as a hendiadys, without any desire to reflect the exact nuances of Jewish legal procedure.

The past generation of commentators, particularly those of the English-speaking world, often read into such passages as Romans 7:14–25, Galatians 1:13–14, Philippians 3:4–6 and the portrayals of Acts 9, 22, and 26 a mental and spiritual struggle on the part of Saul that was, either consciously or unconsciously, fighting fervently against the logic of the early Christians' preaching, the dynamic quality of their lives, and their fortitude under oppression. Therefore his "breathing out murderous threats" was taken as his attempt to slay externally the dragons of doubt he could not silence within his own heart and to repress "all humaner tendencies in the interests of his legal absolutism" (C.H. Dodd, *The Mind of Paul: Change and Development* [Manchester: John Rylands Library, 1934], p. 36; cf. also Dodd's companion lecture of the same year entitled *The Mind of Paul; A Psychological Approach*, esp. pp. 12–13). But the day of the psychological interpretation of Paul's conversion experience appears to be over, and deservedly so. Indeed, Luke connects historically the martyrdom of Stephen, the persecution of the Hellenistic Jewish Christians, and the conversion of Saul. But the argument for a logical connection is not as certain.

It is, of course, impossible today to speak with certainty about what was going on in Saul's subconscious mind at the time, for psychoanalysis two millennia or so later is hardly a fruitful exercise. His own references as a Christian to this earlier time in his life, however, do not require us to view him as struggling with uncertainty, doubt, and guilt before becoming a Christian. They rather suggest that humanly speaking he was immune to the Christian proclamation and immensely satisfied with his own ancestral faith (cf. my *Paul*, pp. 65–105). While he looked forward to the full realization of the hope of Israel, Paul seems from his reminiscences of those earlier days to have been thoroughly satisfied with the revelation of God that was given through Moses and to have counted it his chief delight to worship God through those revealed forms. Nor need we suppose that the logic of the early Christian preachers greatly affected Paul. His later references to "the offense of the cross" show that for him the cross was the great stumbling block to any acknowledgment of Jesus of Nazareth as Israel's Messiah—a stumbling block no amount of logic or verbal gymnastics could remove (cf. 1 Cor 1:23; Gal 5:11; note also Justin Martyr, *Dialogue* 32, 89).

It is probable that Saul took up his brutal task of persecution with full knowledge of the earnestness of his opponents, the stamina of the martyrs, and the agony he would necessarily cause. Fanaticism was not so foreign to Palestine in his day as to leave him unaware of these things, and it is quite possible that he was prepared for the emotional strain involved in persecuting those he believed to be dangerous schismatics within Israel.

More important, however, in days when the rabbis viewed the keeping of the Mosaic law as the vitally important prerequisite for the coming of the Messianic Age (cf. b *Sanhedrin* 97b–98a; b *Baba Bathra* 10a; b *Yoma* 86b), Paul could validate his actions against the Christians by reference to such godly precedents as (1) Moses' slaying of the immoral Israelites at Baal-peor (cf. Num 25:1–5); (2) Phinehas's slaying of the Israelite man and Midianite woman in the plains of Moab (cf. Num 25:6–15); and (3) the actions of Mattathias and the Hasidim in rooting out apostasy among the people (cf. 1 Macc 2:23–28, 42–48). Perhaps even the divine commendation of Phinehas's action in Numbers 25:11–13 rang in his ears:

> Phinehas son of Eleazar, the son of Aaron, the priest, has turned my anger away from the Israelites; for he was as jealous as I am for my honor among them, so that in my zeal I did not put an end to them. Therefore tell him I am making my covenant of peace with him. He and his descendants will have a covenant of a lasting priesthood, because he was zealous for the honor of his God and made atonement for the Israelites.

Second Maccabees 6:13 counsels that "it is a mark of great kindness when the impious are not let alone for a long time, but punished at once."

The DSS define a righteous man as one who "bears unremitting hatred toward all men of ill repute" (1QS 9.22). They speak of unswerving allegiance to God and his laws as alone providing a firm foundation for the Holy Spirit, truth, and the arrival of Israel's hope (cf. 1QS 9.3–4, 20–21) and call for volunteers who are blameless in spirit and body to root out apostasy in the final eschatological days (cf. 1QM 7.5; 10.2–5). The Qumran psalmist, in fact, directly associates commitment to God and his laws with zeal against apostates and perverters of the law when he says:

> The nearer I draw to you, the more am I filled with zeal against all that do wickedness and against all men of deceit. For they that draw near to you cannot see your commandments defiled, and they that have knowledge of you can brook no change of your words, seeing that you are the essence of right, and all your elect are the proof of your truth (1QH 14.13–15).

With such precedents and parallels, coupled with the rising tide of messianic expectation within Israel, Saul could very well have felt justified in mounting a further persecution against the Christians. Probably he felt that in light of Israel's rising messianic hopes the nation must be united and faithful in its obedience to the law and kept from schism or going astray. In his task, he doubtless expected to receive God's commendation.

According to 1 Maccabees, Judah, Jonathan, and Simeon (the three great Hasmonean rulers) established friendly relations with Rome (cf. 1 Macc 8:17–32; 12:1–4; 14:16–24), a reciprocal extradition clause being included in Rome's reply to Simeon (cf. 1 Macc 15:15–24). And the decrees of the Roman senate that Josephus records appear to indicate that the treaties of friendship between Rome and the Jewish people were renewed in the time of John Hyrcanus (cf. Antiq. XIII, 259–66 [ix.2]; XIV, 145–48 [viii.5]). While the Sadducean high priests of Jerusalem no longer exercised the civil authority of their predecessors, they were, it seems, recognized by Rome as the titular rulers of their people in most internal matters; and evidently they retained the right of extradition in strictly religious situations. Therefore Saul, seeking the return of Jewish Christians, "went to the high priest and asked him for letters to the synagogues in Damascus, so that if he found any there who belonged to the Way, whether men or women, he might take them as prisoners to Jerusalem" (cf. 22:5; 26:12).

Damascus was a large and thriving commercial center at the foot of the Anti-Lebanon mountain range. Since 64 B.C. it had been part of the Roman province of Syria and was granted certain civic rights by Rome as one of the ten cities of eastern Syria and the Transjordan called the Decapolis (cf. Mark 5:20; 7:31). It had a large Nabatean Arab population, and possibly was ruled by the Nabatean king Aretas IV (9 B.C.–A.D. 40) at some time during this period (cf. 2 Cor 11:32). It also had a large Jewish population, 10,500 of whom Josephus reports were killed by the people of Damascus at the outbreak of Jewish-Roman hostilities in A.D. 66 (cf. War II, 561 [xx.2]; though in War VII, 368 [viii.7] the figure is 18,000). It was to this city that Saul went with the authority of the Jewish Sanhedrin, seeking to return to Jerusalem those Christians who had fled the city—chiefly the Hellenistic Jewish Christians—in order to contain the spread of what he considered to be a pernicious and deadly contagion within Israel.

While we have spoken repeatedly of the early believers in Jesus as Christians, the term "Christian" (*Christianos*) was first coined at Antioch of Syria (cf. 11:26) and appears only three times in the entire NT (11:26; 26:28; 1 Peter 4:16). Before being named at Syrian Antioch and during the early existence of the church, those who accepted Jesus' messiahship and claimed him as their Lord called themselves those of "the Way" (*hē hodos*, as here and at 19:9, 23; 22:4; 24:14, 22; cf. also 16:17; 18:25–26), while their opponents spoke of them as members of "the sect of the Nazarenes" (*hē hairesis tōn Nazōraiōn*; cf. 24:5, 14; 28:22). The origin of the absolute use of "the Way" for Christians is uncertain, though it surely had something to do with the early believers' consciousness of walking in the true path of God's salvation and moving forward to accomplish his purposes. In the vignette of 9:1–30, it is synonymous with such self-designations as "the disciples of the Lord" (vv.2, 10, 19), "saints" (v.13), "all who call on your [Jesus'] name" (v.14), and "brothers" (vv.17, 30).

3–6 As he approached Damascus, Saul saw a light from heaven and heard a voice from heaven. In 9:3 the light is described as simply "a light from heaven," while in 22:6 it is "a bright light from heaven" and in 26:13 it is "a light from heaven, brighter than the sun." In 9:3 and 22:6 the light is spoken of as shining around Saul alone, whereas in 26:13 it includes his companions as well. But these are matters of small consequence in any threefold telling of an event. Haenchen notes, "It is open to a narrator [whether Paul himself or Luke] to counter the lulling effect of repetition by reinforcing the emphasis of salient features" (*Acts of the Apostles*, p. 321, n.3).

Likewise, in 9:4 it is reported that Saul heard the voice (*ēkousen phōnēn*) and in 9:7 that his companions also heard the voice (*akouontes men tēs phōnēs*), whereas in 22:9 it is said that his companions did not hear the voice (*tēn phōnēn ouk ēkousan*) and in 26:14 that only Saul heard the voice (*ēkousa phōnēn*). Some commentators have seen here a flagrant contradiction in Luke's source materials, which he unwittingly incorporated into his finished product. But since the Greek noun *phōnē* means both "sound" in the sense of any tone or voice and "articulated speech" in the sense of language, undoubtedly it was understood by all concerned (as the respective contexts suggest) to mean that while the whole group traveling to Damascus heard the sound from heaven, only Saul understood the spoken words.

As Saul fell to the ground, the voice from heaven intoned his name in solemn repetition: "Saul, Saul." It was common in antiquity for a person in a formal setting to be addressed by the repetition of his name (cf. Gen 22:11; 46:2; Exod 3:4; 1 Sam 3:10; Luke 10:41; 22:31; 2 Esd 14:1; 2 Baruch 22:2). The fact that here the transliterated form *Saoul* (from the Heb. and Aram. *šā'ûl*) was used in addressing Saul, rather than the Grecianized vocative *Saule*, suggests that the words came to him in either Hebrew or Aramaic (cf. 26:14). Of more significance is the fact that Saul understood the voice to be a message from God himself, for in rabbinism to hear a voice from heaven (a *baṭ qôl*, lit., "a daughter of the voice" of God) never meant either a lower deity in the pantheon of gods speaking, as in Greek speculations, or some psychological disturbance, as many would presume today. On the contrary, it always connoted a rebuke or a word of instruction from God. Therefore when the voice went on to ask the question "Why do you persecute me?" Saul was without doubt thoroughly confused. He was not persecuting God! Rather, he was defending God and his laws!

Some have translated Saul's reply in v.5 as "Who are you, sir?" since the Greek title *kyrios* was used in the ancient world not only as an ascription of worshipful acclaim but also as a form of polite address and since the context indicates that Saul did not know whom he was speaking to. But he did know that he had been struck down by a light from heaven and had been addressed by a voice from heaven, both of which signaled the divine presence. So his use of the term "Lord" was probably meant in a worshipful manner—even though he was thoroughly confused as to how he could be rebuked by God for doing the will and service of God. Unable even to articulate his confusion, though realizing the need for some response in the presence of the divine, he cries out in stumbling fashion, "Who are you, Lord?"

In what must have been for Saul almost total disbelief, he hears the following reply: "I am Jesus, whom you are persecuting." Then in a manner that throws him entirely upon the guidance of Jesus, apart from anything he could do or work out for himself, the voice continues: "Now get up and go into the city, and you will be told what you must do." Such a confrontation and such a rebuke must have been traumatic for Saul. Time would be needed to heal his emotions and work out the implications of his experience, and both Acts and his later Christian letters reveal something of the process of development throughout the rest of his life. But in this supreme revelational encounter, Saul received a new perspective on divine redemption, a new agenda for his life, and the embryonic elements of his new Christian theology.

Once Saul had been encountered by Christ on the Damascus road, a number of realizations must have begun to press in upon his consciousness—each of which was to receive further explication in his thought and life as time went on, though here in their elemental form they could not be evaded. First, Saul began to understand that despite his zeal and his sense of doing God's will, his previous life and activities in Judaism lay under God's rebuke. A voice from heaven had corrected him, and there was nothing more to be said.

Second, Saul could not escape the fact that the Jesus whose followers he had been persecuting was alive, exalted, and in some manner to be associated with God the Father, whom Israel worshiped. He, therefore, had to revise his whole estimate of the life, teaching, and death of the Nazarene because God had beyond any question vindicated him. Thus he came to agree with the Christians that Jesus' death on the cross, rather than discrediting him as an impostor, fulfilled prophecy and was really God's provision for man's sin and that Jesus' resurrection confirmed him as being the nation's Messiah and mankind's Lord.

Third, Saul came to appreciate that if Jesus is the nation's Messiah and the fulfillment of Israel's ancient hope, then traditional eschatology, rather than merely dwelling on the future, must be restructured to emphasize the realized and inaugurated factors associated with Jesus of Nazareth and focus on the personal and transcendent dimensions instead of just the historical.

Fourth, in the question "Why do you persecute me?" Saul came to realize something of the organic and indissoluble unity that exists between Christ and his own. For though he believed he was only persecuting the followers of Jesus, the heavenly interpretation of his action was that he was persecuting the risen Christ himself.

Fifth (though hardly "final"), Saul came to understand that he had a mission to carry out for Christ. Its details, to be sure, were first given in general terms by Ananias of Damascus (vv.15–16) and only later set forth more fully by various visions and providential circumstances (cf. comments on chs. 13–28). But though it was not till later that Saul understood that his mission involved the equality of both Jews and Gentiles before God and the legitimacy of a direct approach to the Gentile world, it was his constant habit to relate his Gentile commission firmly and directly to his encounter with Christ on the Damascus road.

7–9 The effect on Saul's traveling companions of his encounter with Christ was dramatic. Acts 26 says that they fell to the ground at the flash of heavenly light. Here we are told that after getting up they "stood there speechless." Evidently they were able to regain a semblance of composure and thus lead Saul into Damascus. For Saul, however, for whom the spoken message was even more traumatic than the light and the sound, the experience was overpowering. Physically, as his system reacted to the emotional shock, he became blind for three days, during which time he neither ate nor drank as he waited in Damascus for further instructions.

Notes

1 On the requirement in Jewish jurisprudence of first a warning and then the punishment, see Introduction: The Question of Sources and the introductory comments to 4:1–31.

2 Some have noted that in 9:1–2, 14, and 26:10, 12, it is the high priest (or "chief priests") from whom Saul received letters of authority, whereas in 22:5 he is shown as saying that he obtained letters from the whole council (i.e., "the high priest and all the council"). The difference, however, is merely verbal and hardly worth commenting on.

3–6 Though the apparition of 2 Macc 3 of the great horse, its frightful rider, and the two accompanying youths who attacked Heliodorus finds a parallel in Luke's portrayal here, the resemblances are superficial.

4 The locution of 26:14 "It is hard for you to kick against the goads" is added here by the Western text. But the best MSS do not include it here, though through Erasmus the phrase found its way into the TR.

2. Ananias's ministry to Saul

9:10–19a

10In Damascus there was a disciple named Ananias. The Lord called to him in a vision, "Ananias!"

"Yes, Lord," he answered.

11The Lord told him, "Go to the house of Judas on Straight Street and ask for a man from Tarsus named Saul, for he is praying. 12In a vision he has seen a man named Ananias come and place his hands on him to restore his sight."

13"Lord," Ananias answered, "I have heard many reports about this man and all the harm he has done to your saints in Jerusalem. 14And he has come here with authority from the chief priests to arrest all who call on your name."

15But the Lord said to Ananias, "Go! This man is my chosen instrument to carry my name before the Gentiles and their kings and before the people of Israel. 16I will show him how much he must suffer for my name."

17Then Ananias went to the house and entered it. Placing his hands on Saul, he said, "Brother Saul, the Lord—Jesus, who appeared to you on the road as you were coming here—has sent me so that you may see again and be filled with the Holy Spirit." [18]Immediately, something like scales fell from Saul's eyes, and he could see again. He got up and was baptized, [19]and after taking some food, he regained his strength.

10-16 Ananias was a Jew of Damascus and a believer in Jesus. Here (v.10) he is called a "disciple" and presented as one who immediately recognizes the Lord Christ, who speaks to him in a vision, while in 22:12 he is called "a devout observer of the law and highly respected by all the Jews." From Ananias's statement that he had heard reports about Saul's persecutions in Jerusalem (v.13), it may be inferred that he was not one of the Hellenistic Christians who had formerly lived in Jerusalem but that he lived in Damascus. We are not, however, told anything about how he became a Christian or about the Jewish Christian community of Damascus.

The Lord Jesus directed Ananias: "Go to the house of Judas on Straight Street and ask for a man from Tarsus named Saul, for he is praying." The street called Straight was an east-west street that is still one of the main thoroughfares of Damascus, the *Derb el-Mustaqîm*. It had colonnaded halls on either side and imposing gates at each end (cf. BC, 4:102) and presumably was as well known in antiquity as Regent Street in London or Michigan Avenue in Chicago today. The directions included not only the name of the street but also the house where Saul could be found.

More significantly, Jesus' words to Ananias identified Saul as one who was praying. For Luke, his hero Paul was a man of prayer (cf. 16:25; 20:36; 22:17), as was Jesus in his earthly ministry (cf. Luke 3:21; 6:12; 9:18, 28; 11:1; 22:41). Probably in the religious experience of Paul, as Stanley has suggested, "the most important link between his Christian life and Pharisaism was that devotion to prayer for which the Pharisees were rightly celebrated and held in esteem among their people" (David M. Stanley, *Boasting in the Lord: The Phenomenon of Prayer in Saint Paul* [New York: Paulist, 1973], p. 42). Stanley goes on to say, "If one may conjecture about Paul's preparation for the overpowering event which changed his life, surely the chief element was prayer" (ibid., p. 42).

It takes no great imaginative power to appreciate the reasons for Ananias's hesitation in going at once to meet Saul, and it is not at all difficult to sympathize with Ananias. Even the prophets of old had doubts about the appropriateness of what they understood to be God's will, particularly when it seemed so contrary to what might be expected. But Luke lays emphasis on Ananias's hesitancy, not just to humanize his narrative, but also to impress on his readers the magnitude of the change in Saul's life and to highlight the heaven-ordained nature of his later Christian mission: (1) that instead of a persecutor, he is Christ's "chosen instrument"; (2) that instead of a concern for Israel alone, his mission is "to carry my [Jesus'] name before the Gentiles and their kings and before the people of Israel"; and (3) that instead of prominence and glory, it is necessary for him "to suffer for my [Jesus'] name." In highlighting these features of being a "chosen instrument," sent to "the Gentiles," and to "suffer for my [Jesus'] name," Luke has, in effect, given a theological précis of all he will portray historically in chapters 13-28—a précis that also summarizes the self-consciousness of Paul himself as reflected in his own letters.

17-19a Ananias was obedient to his Lord and followed the directions given in the vision. He was undoubtedly comforted by knowing that Saul too had been given a vision about his coming (v.12), though he must have proceeded with some trepidation. Going to the house of Judas on Straight Street, he entered and laid his hands on Saul. Ananias greeted him, evidently in Hebrew or Aramaic (note the transliterated *Saoul;* cf. comments on v.4 above), with the fraternal greeting "brother"—believing, it seems, that whoever Jesus had accepted was his brother, whatever he might think about such a person himself, and that all further relationships between them must be built on that basis. He spoke about Jesus, who had appeared to Saul on the Damascus Road, and about the restoration of Saul's sight and his being filled with the Holy Spirit. And "immediately," Luke tells us, "something like scales fell from Saul's eyes, and he could see again. He got up and was baptized, and after taking some food, he regained his strength."

There is much more we would like to know about the persons and details of this event. What was the Jewish Christian community of Damascus like? What was Ananias's background, and whatever happened to him after this incident? When did Saul receive his vision regarding Ananias's coming and how? What was the "scaly substance" that fell from Saul's eyes? Where and how was Saul baptized? Were there any immediate evidences in Saul's life of his being filled with the Holy Spirit, such as appeared among believers at Jerusalem and in Samaria? On some of these matters (e.g., water baptism and the baptism of the Spirit), Luke probably means us to understand his presentation here in terms already given in his earlier portrayals and therefore feels no need to repeat himself. On other matters, though, he seems to have had no interest, and so we should not seek to squeeze anything more from the text.

What Luke does tell us, however, is significant. In the advance of the gospel to the Gentiles, the main missioner in that advance was converted to Christ and given his commission in a manner that fully showed the heaven-ordained nature of his conversion and call—a manner that did not make him dependent on the Jerusalem church for either his conversion or call, yet brought him into essential unity with all those who are Christ's and call themselves those of "the Way."

Notes

10 It is highly improbable that the sect of the Cairo Damascus Covenant (CD=4Q and 6QZad Frag) had any direct connection with the Jewish Christian community of Damascus, though certainly there must have been many analogical parallels between them.

17 On the laying on of hands, see comments on 6:6 and the other instances in Acts at 8:17; 13:3; 19:6.

   On being baptized and filled with the Holy Spirit, see comments on 2:38.

18 The term λεπίς (*lepis,* "scale," "scaly substance") is used in Tobit 3:17 and 11:13 for that which covered Tobit's eyes and blinded him.

19 On baptism and the gospel, cf. comments on 2:38.

3. *Saul's conversion evidenced in Damascus*

9:19b–25

Saul spent several days with the disciples in Damascus. [20]At once he began to preach in the synagogues that Jesus is the Son of God. [21]All those who heard him were astonished and asked, "Isn't he the man who raised havoc in Jerusalem among those who call on this name? And hasn't he come here to take them as prisoners to the chief priests?" ²²Yet Saul grew more and more powerful and baffled the Jews living in Damascus by proving that Jesus is the Christ.

²³After many days had gone by, the Jews conspired to kill him, ²⁴but Saul learned of their plan. Day and night they kept close watch on the city gates in order to kill him. ²⁵But his followers took him by night and lowered him in a basket through an opening in the wall.

It may seem strange, at first glance, for Luke to include in his account of Saul's conversion a sketchy report of his preaching Christ in Damascus and the unceremonious exit from the city it brought about. The material is so undeveloped that it raises more historical problems than it answers. Therefore, many source critics have viewed it as extraneous to the substance of vv.1–19a, and many commentators have treated it apart from the story of Saul's conversion. On closer inspection, however, we can discern a distinctly Lukan rationale for the inclusion of this material—viz., to emphasize the unprecedented nature of Saul's about face and the genuineness of his conversion. In clarifying his purpose, Luke (1) presents Saul as proclaiming Jesus as both "Son of God" and "Messiah," (2) depicts his hearers as being so astonished that they had to ask themselves if this was indeed the same man who had been persecuting Christians, and (3) highlights the fact that the persecution he once headed was now directed against him.

19b–22 Luke's references to Saul after his conversion—viz., his being "several days with the disciples in Damascus" (*meta tōn en Damaskō mathētōn hēmeras tinas*) and his beginning "at once" (*eutheōs*) to preach in the synagogues of the city—are, when compared with Paul's own account of his conversion and the immediately subsequent events, so general and ambiguous as to set up all sorts of historical problems for commentators today. No one familiar with Paul's precise delineation of chronology and personal relationships in Galatians 1:15–24 could have written the narrative here with such disregard for the emphases laid out there. Certainly no later admirer of Paul would have written it, disregarding, as it does, the most important autobiographical statement about Paul's conversion and commission and giving a portrayal that can be taken as ambiguous and contradictory. But if we are correct in holding to Luke's authorship of Acts and in understanding the "we" sections of the work as reflecting his times of personal association with Paul (see Introduction: The Question of Sources; also, Authorship), and, further, if we postulate an early date for the composition of the Letter to the Galatians (as we do) at a time before Luke himself became a Christian and joined Paul's missionary team, then it may very well have been the case that Luke was unfamiliar with the specific contents of Paul's earlier Galatian letter. If he knew of its existence, perhaps he believed that its essence appears in more finished form in Romans and therefore felt no need to interact with it.

Of more importance, however, is the fact that the purposes of Paul in Galatians 1:15–24 and Luke here are different, with these purposes affecting to a considerable extent the selection and shaping of each writer's presentation. Thus with his desire to assert the revelational nature of his Gentile ministry, Paul emphasized in Galatians that he was not dependent upon "any man" (cf. *sarki kai haimati*, lit., "flesh and blood," Gal 1:16) for his distinctive gospel, and particularly not upon the Jerusalem apostles. Luke, however, while also interested in depicting the heaven-ordained nature of Paul's conversion and commission, is concerned in 9:19b–25 to stress the genuineness of Saul's conversion and call. This he does by speaking of the new convert's distinctly Christian proclamation in the synagogues of Damascus and his being persecuted by the Jews of the city because of his preaching. Neither this preaching nor the persecution is necessarily ruled out by Galatians 1:15–24, though the intermeshing of historical details between the two accounts may be lacking. But such a failure of historical synchronization is fairly common between two narratives of the same set of circumstances where neither author seems to have read the other and where both have their own distinctive purposes.

It is not going beyond a reasonable historical reconstruction to suggest that the actual order of events was probably as follows: (1) Saul's conversion and commission (9:1–19a); (2) his preaching in the synagogues of Damascus for a time immediately following his conversion (9:19b–22); (3) his prolonged residence in Arabia (Gal 1:17); (4) his return to Damascus (9:23–25); and, as we must consider later, (5) his first visit to Jerusalem as a Christian some three years after his conversion, with his subsequent travel to Caesarea, Syria, and Cilicia (9:26–30; Gal 1:18–24).

The content of Saul's preaching in the Damascus synagogues focused on Jesus: "Jesus is the Son of God" (v.20) and "Jesus is the Christ" (v.22), i.e., the "Messiah." That Saul could preach such a message immediately after his conversion is not impossible because the certainty of Jesus' messiahship was deeply implanted in his soul by his experience on the Damascus road. And while he had much to understand and appreciate about the implications of commitment to Jesus as Israel's Messiah, he was certainly in a position to proclaim with conviction and enthusiasm the "thatness" of Jesus' messianic status.

Nor is it surprising that Saul also spoke of Jesus as "the Son of God," though this is the only occurrence in Acts of this christological title. In a number of NT passages the titles "Messiah" and "Son of God" are brought together (cf. Matt 16:16; 26:63; Luke 4:41; John 11:27; 20:31), for the Anointed One par excellence expressed uniquely that loving obedience inherent in the Hebraic understanding of sonship. That is how the concepts of Messiah and Son are used in 4QFlorilegium on 2 Samuel 7:14 and in 2 Esdras 7:28–29; 13:32, 37, 52; 14:9, and how Paul used the titles "Son" and "Son of God" some fifteen times later in his own letters (cf. Rom 1:3–4, 9; 5:10; 8:3, 29, 32; 1 Cor 1:9; 15:28; 2 Cor 1:19; Gal 1:16; 2:20; 4:4, 6; 1 Thess 1:10).

Those who heard Saul preach, Luke says, were "astonished" and "baffled." But with his interest in advance and growth (cf. Luke 2:52), Luke also says that "Saul grew more and more powerful," suggesting by that a growth in his understanding of the meaning of commitment to Jesus as Messiah and Son of God and also an increasing ability to demonstrate the validity of his proclamation.

23–25 Luke's expression "after many days had gone by" must be taken with Paul's statement in Galatians 1:18 that his first visit to Jerusalem as a Christian was three years after his conversion. Also, the description here of the plot against him and his escape from Damascus must be compared with Paul's words in 2 Corinthians 11:32–33: "In Damascus the governor under King Aretas had the city of the Damascenes guarded in order to arrest me. But I was lowered in a basket from a window in the wall and slipped through his hands." A number of details in the accounts, whether taken singly or conflated, are unclear to us. What is clear, however, is that Saul's preaching stirred such opposition that plans were laid to kill him; but rather ingeniously, though also somewhat ignominiously, he was able to elude his opponents' designs. What is also clear is that Luke recounts this episode in order to emphasize the genuineness of Saul's conversion, for now he too has become the object of persecution directed against believers in Jesus.

Luke credits the Jews of Damascus as being the perpetrators of the plot to kill Saul, whereas in 2 Corinthians 11:32 that honor is given to "the governor [*ho ethnarchēs*, lit., 'the ethnarch'] under King Aretas." The situation presupposed in the narrative is unclear chiefly because the status of the governor (or ethnarch) is uncertain. Did he have jurisdiction over the city of Damascus itself as the viceroy of the Nabatean king Aretas? This has often been argued on the ground that Damascus was at this time ruled by Aretas IV (9 B.C.–A.D. 40) and considered part of Nabatean Arabia (cf. HJP, 2.1:98). Or did the governor have jurisdiction to some extent over the Damascus suburbs where many Nabateans would have lived, serving as Aretas's representative to Arabs living under Roman rule (cf. BC, 5:193)? In either case, the city gates would have been strategic locations for an ambush of the Christian preacher and would have been closely watched. Also certain Jews and an Arab governor might have seen fit to join in common cause against Saul—particularly if Saul had also preached in Nabatean Arabia during this three-year period and stirred up opposition there as well, as some commentators have proposed. Luke just does not tell us enough of the situation to enable us to piece the story together historically. But then his purpose was not to enlighten us about the political and historical circumstances of the day but to support his portrayal of the genuineness of Saul's encounter with Christ on the Damascus Road.

Acts uses "disciple" (*mathētēs*) almost exclusively to denote the members of the Christian community (e.g., 6:1–2, 7; 9:19; 11:26, 29; 13:52; 15:10). The one exception to the normal usage in Acts is here in v.25, where it is used of followers of Saul and suggests that his proclamation of Jesus had a favorable response among at least some. One of these converts, it seems, had a home situated on the city wall (or, perhaps, was able to arrange for the use of such a home for a night), from whose window Saul was let down in a basket outside the wall and was thus able to elude his opponents. From there, evidently, he made his way directly to Jerusalem.

Notes

20 On the christological title "Son of God," see my *Christology*, pp. 93–99.

25 Luke employs the rather nondescript word σπυρίς (*spyris*, "basket," "hamper") for the means of conveyance in lowering Saul to the ground, whereas 2 Cor 11:33 uses the more specific term σαργάνη (*sarganē*), which connotes a braided rope basket or netting.

4. Saul's reception at Jerusalem

9:26–30

> 26When he came to Jerusalem, he tried to join the disciples, but they were all afraid of him, not believing that he really was a disciple. 27But Barnabas took him and brought him to the apostles. He told them how Saul on his journey had seen the Lord and that the Lord had spoken to him, and how in Damascus he had preached fearlessly in the name of Jesus. 28So Saul stayed with them and moved about freely in Jerusalem, speaking boldly in the name of the Lord. 29He talked and debated with the Grecian Jews, but they tried to kill him. 30When the brothers learned of this, they took him down to Caesarea and sent him off to Tarsus.

As in his narrative concerning the evangelization of Samaria (8:4–25), as well as in his later accounts of the conversion of Cornelius (10:1–11:18) and the founding of the church at Antioch of Syria (11:19–30)—in which he not only stresses features of advance and development but also shows continuity with the mother church at Jerusalem—Luke ends his account of the conversion of Saul of Tarsus by telling of his reception by the Christians at Jerusalem. As in Luke's depiction of Saul's preaching in Damascus (vv.19b–25), here the material, when compared with Paul's own account in Galatians 1:18–24 of his first visit to Jerusalem as a Christian, entails a number of problems relating to historical correlations—probably for much the same reasons as in vv.19b–25, though heightened here by Paul's purpose in Galatians to stress his lack of dependence upon the Jerusalem church whereas Luke's purpose is to trace out lines of continuity.

26–28 Saul's arrival at Jerusalem as a Christian, according to his own reckoning in Galatians 1:18, was three years after his conversion. Being persona non grata among his former associates and suspected by Christians, he probably stayed at his sister's home in the city (cf. 23:16). We can understand why his reception by his former colleagues might have been less than welcome. But that the apostles and other Christians in Jerusalem were leery of him does raise questions. Certainly they must have heard of his conversion and his preaching in Damascus. Yet, it seems, they never knew him personally, either as a persecutor or as a Christian; and stories about his motives and activities during a three-year period might well have become distorted. Many might, in fact, have asked why, if Saul had really become a Christian, he remained aloof from the Twelve and the Jerusalem congregation for such a long time. We may wish, and might even have expected, that there had been more openness toward Saul the convert on the part of the Jerusalem Christians. History, however, has shown that minority movements under persecution frequently become defensive and suspicious of news that sounds too good.

It was Barnabas, Luke says, who was willing to risk accepting Saul as a genuine believer and who built a bridge of trust between him and the Jerusalem apostles. Just why Barnabas alone showed such magnanimity, we are not told, though this is in character with what is said about him elsewhere in Acts (cf. 4:36–37; 11:22–30; 13:1–14:28; 15:2–4, 12, 22). In presenting Saul to the apostles, Barnabas told of what Saul had seen and heard on the Damascus Road and of his preaching "in the name of Jesus" in Damascus itself—thus summarizing Luke's account of Saul's conversion and explicitly using his activity in Damascus to support the genuineness of his conversion. So with Barnabas's help, Saul and the Jerusalem apostles were brought into fellowship.

In light of Paul's own insistence in Galatians 1:18–20 that he saw only Peter and James on this first Jerusalem visit, Luke's use of the term "apostles" must be considered a generalizing plural to be taken more broadly than "the Twelve." Likewise, in view of Paul's statement in Galatians 1:18 that he stayed with Peter for fifteen days, Luke's claim that he "stayed with them and moved about freely in Jerusalem" must be seen as somewhat overstated. Probably we are not far wrong in reconstructing the situation as follows: Saul resided with his sister's family on his first visit to Jerusalem as a Christian; through the aid of Barnabas he came to visit with Peter for fifteen days and to meet James as well; and, broadly speaking, his reception by the Christians he met was cordial, though there undoubtedly still existed some fears about him within the Christian congregation (which after the Hellenists' expulsion was made up entirely of native-born and more Hebraic types) and though his own activity within the city was largely within the Hellenistic Jewish synagogues.

29–30 At Jerusalem Saul took up a ministry to Jews in the Hellenistic synagogues there. It was a ministry that had been neglected, it appears, since Stephen's death and the expulsion of the Hellenistic Jewish Christians. But it was one Saul may have felt himself particularly suited to, coming as he did from Tarsus in Cilicia and having probably carried on such a ministry at Damascus (and, perhaps, in Nabatean Arabia). In so doing, however, he soon faced the same opposition Stephen had faced, and he seems to have gotten into the same difficulty Stephen did. The Jerusalem church apparently did not care to again go through the same kind of thing that followed Stephen's preaching. So when they realized what was taking place in Saul's newly begun ministry in Jerusalem, "they took him down to Caesarea and sent him off to Tarsus." Saul might have taken such a departure as a personal rebuff. But he took it as by divine approval, for in his defense in Acts 22 he speaks of having received a vision in the Jerusalem temple that not only confirmed his apostleship to the Gentiles but also warned him to flee Jerusalem (22:17–21).

Saul is not mentioned in the period between these experiences in Jerusalem and his ministry at Antioch (11:25–30), though from his words in Galatians 1:21–24 it seems fairly certain that he continued his witness to Diaspora Jews in Caesarea and his hometown of Tarsus. The cordiality of the Christians in Caesarea at the end of his third missionary journey may imply that Saul had an earlier association with Philip and the believers there. Many of the hardships and trials he enumerates in 2 Corinthians 11:23–27 may stem from situations in Caesarea and Tarsus during those days, for they find no place in the records of the later missionary journeys in Acts. Perhaps the ecstatic experience of 2 Corinthians 12:1–4 also comes from this period in his life.

D. *A Summary Statement*

9:31

> 31Then the church throughout Judea, Galilee and Samaria enjoyed a time of peace. It was strengthened; and encouraged by the Holy Spirit, it grew in numbers, living in the fear of the Lord.

31 Luke's second panel of material on the martyrdom of Stephen, the early ministries of Philip, and the conversion of Saul ends with a summary statement that speaks of the church throughout Judea, Galilee, and Samaria enjoying a time of peace after the turbulence resulting from what happened to Stephen, Philip, and Saul. Though in the first two panels there has been nothing about any advance of the Christian mission into Galilee, Luke's Gospel, in line with the synoptic tradition, has emphasized Galilee; and certainly there were believers in Jesus there. Here, however, Luke's reference to Judea, Galilee, and Samaria probably means all the Jewish homeland of Palestine. Here also he insists that the church in the homeland, instead of being torn apart by what God was doing in the advance of the gospel through these three pivotal figures, "was strengthened; and encouraged by the Holy Spirit, it grew in numbers, living in the fear of the Lord," despite a certain lack of discernment and openness.

Panel 3—Advances of the Gospel in Palestine-Syria (9:32–12:24)

In his portrayal of the gradual widening of the Christian mission from its strictly Jewish beginnings to its ultimate Gentile outreach, Luke presents in this third panel three episodes of the gospel's advance, then two vignettes giving a further glimpse of the Spirit's working on behalf of his people in Jerusalem, and finally a summary statement. The three episodes of advance concern (1) the ministry of Peter in the maritime plain of

Palestine (9:32–43), (2) the conversion of a Roman centurion and his friends at Caesarea (10:1–11:18), and (3) the founding of the church at Antioch of Syria (11:19–30). Two notes are sounded in these episodes of advance. The first has to do with geography and stresses the spread of the gospel into areas more distant from Jerusalem than before. The second, and undoubtedly the more important, has to do with the attitude of the converts and that of the missioners. Then, before moving on to speak of the distinctive advances of the gospel within the Gentile world through the ministry of his hero Paul, Luke again returns to an account of the circumstances at Jerusalem and God's continued working on behalf of his people there (12:1–23). In returning to Jerusalem at this stage in his overall picture, Luke seems to be trying to make the point that though his interest is in tracing the movement of the early Christian mission from Jerusalem to Rome, his readers are not to assume that God was finished with Jerusalem Christianity or that his divine activity within the Jewish world had come to an end—a point all-too-often ignored by Christians since then. Finally, in summation of all he has presented in this third panel of material, Luke appends the following statement: "But the word of God continued to increase and spread" (12:24).

A. The Ministry of Peter in the Maritime Plain of Palestine (9:32–43)

Luke's rationale for the inclusion of Peter's miracles at Lydda and Joppa has often been debated. Did Luke use the vignettes of the healing of Aeneas and the raising of Dorcas to shift the focus of his narrative from Jerusalem to the west country of Palestine, thereby setting the stage for the conversion of Cornelius at Caesarea? Or did he include them to suggest that with Peter's ministry in the maritime plain the evangelization of Palestine was completed and that it was therefore time to look farther afield? Or, since the maritime plain of Palestine was populated by both Jews and Gentiles, was Luke here depicting a further ideological widening of the range of the Christian mission—one having to do both with an outreach of the gospel to Jews living in a not entirely Jewish area and with the nonlegalistic attitude of Peter their Christian missioner? All three explanations can be supported from the text. But from the developing presentation in Acts, we should probably judge that geographical and ideological concerns were uppermost in Luke's mind here.

1. Aeneas healed at Lydda

9:32–35

> [32] As Peter traveled about the country, he went to visit the saints in Lydda. [33] There he found a man named Aeneas, a paralytic who had been bedridden for eight years. [34] "Aeneas," Peter said to him, "Jesus Christ heals you. Get up and take care of your mat." Immediately Aeneas got up. [35] All those who lived in Lydda and Sharon saw him and turned to the Lord.

32 Lydda (the OT Lod, cf. 1 Chron 8:12; Ezra 2:33; Neh 11:35) was located twenty-five miles northwest of Jerusalem, at the intersection of the highways from Egypt to Syria and from coastal Joppa to Jerusalem. Josephus calls it "a village that was in size not inferior to a city" (Antiq. XX, 130 [vi.2]). It had been restored to the Jews in the time of John Hyrcanus by Julius Caesar (cf. Antiq. XIV, 208 [x.6]), and later it became a center for both Pharisaic studies (prior to Jamnia) and Christian activity. Lydda was the legendary locale of Saint George's slaying of the dragon and of his later martyrdom in A.D. 303. In the fourth century, Lydda was the seat of episcopal authority for the Syrian church;

and in the fifth century the council that tried Pelagius for heresy met there (A.D. 415). It appears in the NT only here.

At this time Peter was engaged in an itinerant ministry in the western part of Palestine —a ministry somewhat like his earlier preaching in Samaria (cf. 8:25). In the course of his travels, he visited "the saints" in the important commercial center of Lydda. We are not told how they had become believers. Perhaps they received the gospel from some who were originally at Pentecost (cf. 2:5–41), or from some who were forced to flee Jerusalem during the persecution of the Hellenistic Christians (cf. 8:1, 4, 40). But however they came to commit themselves to Jesus as God's Messiah, Peter viewed them as within the sphere of his ministry—even though many of them were probably less scrupulous in keeping the Mosaic law than Jews of the capital city.

33 At Lydda Peter came upon Aeneas, a paralytic who had been bedridden for eight years. Luke does not say that Aeneas was a Jew nationally or a Christian by profession, though presumably, despite his thoroughly Greek name, he was both. It would hardly have been consistent with Luke's purpose to show Peter ministering to a Gentile before his encounter with Cornelius, and the "there" (*ekei*) of the sentence has as its antecedent the community of saints at Lydda and not just the city itself.

34 Peter's words, "Jesus Christ heals you. Get up and take care of your mat," are recorded in the present tense by Luke. They should be understood neither as a consummative perfect ("Jesus Christ has healed you") nor as a durative present ("Jesus Christ is engaged in healing you") but as an aoristic present ("this moment Jesus Christ heals you"). The expression *strōson seautō* ("prepare yourself"; NIV, "take care of your mat"), usually employed with the noun *klinē* ("bed," "sleeping mat," "cushion used at mealtimes"), may mean either "make up your bed [or mat]" or "prepare a meal for yourself" (cf. Mark 14:15). The latter would go well with the interest shown elsewhere by the evangelists in nourishment for convalescents (cf. Mark 5:43; Luke 8:55). But in the case of a paralytic for whom immobility not nourishment was the problem, getting up and taking care of his mat is probably in view.

35 News of Aeneas's healing spread throughout Lydda and into the Plain of Sharon to the north. Rather hyperbolically Luke says that "all those who lived in Lydda and Sharon saw him and turned to the Lord." The Plain of Sharon is the largest of the maritime plains of northern Palestine, stretching from Joppa to Mount Carmel and with Caesarea on the coast at its geographic center. So, Luke tells us, there was a further widening of the Christian mission within the Jewish nation, preparing the way geographically and ideologically for the accounts of Peter's ministry at Joppa in 9:36–43 and at Caesarea in 10:1–48.

Notes

33 Ἐξ ἐτῶν ὀκτώ (*ex etōn oktō*) could be translated "since he was eight years old," but "for eight years" is more probable.

34 Henry J. Cadbury has proposed "A Possible Perfect in Acts 9:34" (JTS, 49 [1948], 57–58) by accenting ἰᾶται (*iatai*, "heals") to read ἴαται (*iatai*, "has healed"), as in Mark 5:29.

2. *Dorcas raised at Joppa*

9:36–43

36In Joppa there was a disciple named Tabitha (which, when translated, is Dorcas), who was always doing good and helping the poor. 37About that time she became sick and died, and her body was washed and placed in an upstairs room. 38Lydda was near Joppa; so when the disciples heard that Peter was in Lydda, they sent two men to him and urged him, "Please come at once!"

39Peter went with them, and when he arrived he was taken upstairs to the room. All the widows stood around him, crying and showing him the robes and other clothing that Dorcas had made while she was still with them.

40Peter sent them all out of the room; then he got down on his knees and prayed. Turning toward the dead woman, he said, "Tabitha, get up." She opened her eyes, and seeing Peter she sat up. 41He took her by the hand and helped her to her feet. Then he called the believers and the widows and presented her to them alive. 42This became known all over Joppa, and many people believed in the Lord. 43Peter stayed in Joppa for some time with a tanner named Simon.

36–39 Joppa (modern Jaffa, also called *Yāpô* in Josh 19:46) was the ancient seaport for Jerusalem. Situated on the coast thirty-five miles northwest of the capital city and ten miles beyond Lydda, it possesses the only natural harbor on the Mediterranean between Egypt and Ptolemais (the OT city of Acco). Through Joppa Solomon brought cedar beams from Lebanon to build the temple (2 Chron 2:16); from it Jonah sailed for Tarshish (Jonah 1:3). Its rival in NT times was Caesarea, thirty miles to the north, which Herod the Great, because the people of Joppa hated him, built into a magnificent new port city and provincial capital.

At Joppa lived a woman called Tabitha (Heb.) or Dorcas (Gr.); both names mean "gazelle." She was a "disciple" (the only instance in the NT of *mathētria*, the feminine form of the word) and "was always doing good and helping the poor." Verse 39 indicates that her energies were devoted chiefly to helping destitute widows. When she died, the Christians at Joppa sent this message to Peter at Lydda: "Please come at once." Luke does not say what they expected from him or asked him to do. But since (1) Tabitha's body was washed but not anointed for burial (cf. M. *Shabbath* 23.5) and (2) her good deeds were told Peter when he arrived, they apparently wanted him to restore her to life. Having heard of Aeneas's healing, they seem to have thought it merely a slight extension of divine power to raise the dead.

40–42 Peter had been instrumental in a number of physical healings (cf. 3:1–10; 5:12–16; 9:32–35), and even pronounced the death sentence on Ananias and Sapphira (cf. 5:1–11). Yet raising people from the dead was hardly a common feature of his ministry. Nevertheless, knowing himself to be an apostle of Jesus empowered by the Holy Spirit— and probably remembering his Lord's raising of Jairus's daughter (cf. Mark 5:21–24, 35–43)—Peter responded to the urgent call. As he had seen Jesus do in the case of Jairus's daughter, he ordered the mourners out of the room and prayed. Then he spoke these words: "Tabitha, get up" (which in its Aram. form *Tabitha kûmî* would have differed in only one letter from Jesus' command *Talitha kûmî* ["Little girl, get up"] in Mark 5:41). When she opened her eyes and sat up, he took her by the hand, helped her to her feet, and presented her alive to the Christians who stood by. It was an exceptional exhibit of God's mercy and the Spirit's power, and "many people believed in the Lord."

43 This verse serves as a geographical and ideological hinge between the accounts of Peter's miracles in the maritime plain and the account of Cornelius's conversion at Caesarea. Instead of returning ten miles to Lydda, Peter remained at Joppa "for some time" (cf. 8:11), where the messengers from Cornelius later found him. Of greater significance, however, is the fact that Peter stayed there with a man called Simon, a tanner who was presumably working in his own home. The rabbis considered tanning an unclean trade (cf. SBK, 2:695), and Peter's lodging with such a man suggests that Peter himself was not overly scrupulous in observing Jewish ceremonial traditions (cf. Gal 2:14). This may not tell us anything more about Peter than can be easily inferred from the evangelists' representations of him in their Gospels. But Luke's stress on this feature of Peter's lifestyle provides a significant preface to 10:1–11:18.

Notes

---

38 Sending two messengers is a common feature of Luke's narrative (cf. 10:7; 11:30). The expression μὴ ὀκνήσῃς διελθεῖν ἕως ἡμῶν (mē oknēsēs dielthein heōs hēmōn; lit., "Do not hesitate to come over to us") is a formal and somewhat polite way of expressing an imperative command (cf. Num 22:16 LXX).

40 Perhaps it was the name Tabitha itself that triggered the memory of Jesus' raising of Jairus's daughter with the command Ταλιθα κουμ (Talitha koum, "Little girl, get up," Mark 5:41), though by his reproduction of Jesus' words in Luke 8:54 as ἡ παῖς, ἔγειρε (hē pais, egeire, "my child [fem.], get up"), it seems that Luke was not conscious of such a parallel.

B. The Conversion of Cornelius at Caesarea (10:1–11:18)

With the range of the Christian mission steadily broadening, the time had come for the gospel to cross the barrier that separated Jews from Gentiles and to be presented directly to Gentiles. Thus Luke next takes up the story of the conversion of Cornelius, the importance of which in his eyes can be judged in part by the space he devotes to it—sixty-six verses in all.

Four matters in the account of Cornelius's conversion receive special emphasis and in turn provide insight into Luke's purpose for presenting this material. The first has to do with the early church's resistance to the idea of Gentiles being either directly evangelized or accepted into the Christian fellowship apart from any relationship to Judaism (cf. 10:14, 28; 11:2–3, 8). The second is the demonstration that it was God himself who introduced the Gentiles into the church and miraculously showed his approval (cf. 10:3, 11–16, 19–20, 22b, 30–33, 44–46; 11:5–10, 13, 15–17). The third is that it was not Paul but Peter, the leader of the Jerusalem apostles, who was the human instrument in opening the door to the Gentiles (cf. 10:23, 34–43, 47–48; 11:15–17). The fourth has to do with the Jerusalem church's subsequent acceptance of a Gentile's conversion to Jesus the Messiah, apart from any allegiance to Judaism, for God had so obviously validated it (cf. 11:18).

Under the spell of the Tübingen school (cf. Introduction), many earlier commentators declared the Cornelius episode to be an unhistorical fabrication because it gives Peter the glory of the Gentile mission. But though Peter is presented as the first to go directly to a Gentile, he is not depicted in any way as an "Apostle to the Gentiles." "In fact," as Weiss has observed, "the story in no way settles the issue of whether the mission to the Gentiles is either lawful or obligatory, as it was considered to be a quite exceptional divine intervention that compelled Peter to preach the gospel to Cornelius" (Bernhard Weiss, *A Manual of Introduction to the New Testament*, tr. A.J.K. Davidson [London: Hodder & Stoughton, 1887], 1:169–70; 2:329).

Other commentators, influenced by Dibelius, treat the account of Peter's converting a "God-fearing Gentile" by the name of Cornelius as a pious "conversion legend" that must have sprung from some traditional story preserved in a Hellenistic Christian community but which by its use in 15:7–11, 14 is manifestly a Lukan creation in its present form (Dibelius, *Studies in Acts*, pp. 109–22). But this confuses the issues (related yet distinguishable) faced by the Jerusalem church in chapters 11 and 15 (cf. comments there). And as Williams observes, "Behind Dibelius' analysis there seems to lie a desire to reduce the supernatural element in Acts to nothing" (p. 134).

1. Cornelius's vision

10:1–8

> [1]At Caesarea there was a man named Cornelius, a centurion in what was known as the Italian Regiment. [2]He and all his family were devout and God-fearing; he gave generously to those in need and prayed to God regularly. [3]One day at about three in the afternoon he had a vision. He distinctly saw an angel of God, who came to him and said, "Cornelius!"
>
> [4]Cornelius stared at him in fear. "What is it, Lord?" he asked.
>
> The angel answered, "Your prayers and gifts to the poor have come up as a remembrance before God. [5]Now send men to Joppa to bring back a man named Simon who is called Peter. [6]He is staying with Simon the tanner, whose house is by the sea."
>
> [7]When the angel who spoke to him had gone, Cornelius called two of his servants and one of his soldiers who was a devout man. [8]He told them everything that had happened and sent them to Joppa.

1 Caesarea is in the center of the coastal Plain of Sharon in northern Palestine, on the shores of the Mediterranean, some sixty-five miles northwest of Jerusalem. It was named in honor of Augustus Caesar (Caius Octavianus, later called Augustus), the adopted heir of Julius Caesar. Formerly it was called Strato's Tower and was considered a second-class harbor because of its shallow entrance and openness to the strong southern winds. But in carrying out his pro-Roman policy, Herod the Great changed all that by making the harbor into a magnificent seaport and the village into a provincial capital. He deepened the harbor, built a breakwater against the southern gales, constructed an imposing city with an amphitheater and a temple in honor of Rome and Augustus, brought in fresh water through an aqueduct that ran over stately brick arches, and established a garrison of soldiers to protect not only the harbor and city but also the fresh water supply. The magnificence of the port dwarfed the splendor of the city, which is probably why a Neronian coin bears the inscription "Caesarea by Augustus's Harbor." Nevertheless, in the NT period the city was the Roman capital of the province of Judea. Here Rome had a safe haven for its administration of Palestine, though after Roman times the city fell into decay.

The name Cornelius was common in the Roman world from 82 B.C. onwards, when Cornelius Sulla liberated ten thousand slaves, all of whom took their patron's name as they established themselves in Roman society. Probably, therefore, Cornelius of Acts 10–11 was a descendant of one of the freedmen of Cornelius Sulla's day. He is identified as a centurion of the Italian cohort (NIV, "regiment"). A centurion was a noncommissioned officer who had worked his way up through the ranks to take command of a group of soldiers within a Roman legion, and would therefore be roughly equivalent to a captain today. A cohort was a tenth of a Roman legion and numbered anywhere from three hundred to six hundred men in size, being officially always the latter.

Commentators have frequently proposed that the Italian cohort mentioned here was probably the *Cohors II Miliaria Italica Civium Romanorum*. This consisted of archers who were freedmen originally from Italy, upon whom citizenship had been conferred. It was known to have been transferred to Syria sometime before A.D. 69 and remained in Palestine-Syria during the troublesome times associated with the two destructions of Jerusalem in A.D. 70 and 135 (cf. T.R.S. Broughton, "The Roman Army," BC, 5:427–45). On the basis of this identification, together with the suggestion that during the administration of Herod Agrippa I over Judea in A.D. 41–44 there would have been no need for a Roman occupying force in Palestine, Luke is frequently charged with error in speaking of a Roman cohort and its captain in Caesarea during the early or mid-forties. But surely the objection is unwarranted, for throughout Caesarea's history there was always the need for protection—particularly of its elegant but extremely vulnerable water supply, as well as of both the port and the city. While in times of nationalistic tumult a much larger garrison was required, that does not minimize the need for Rome's continual protection of Caesarea as its bridgehead of authority on alien soil.

2 Luke describes Cornelius as being "devout and God-fearing" (*eusebēs kai phoboumenos ton theon*). These characteristics are also attributed to all his household, which probably refers not only to his immediate family but also to his personal servants. Perhaps we are to understand by *phoboumenos ton theon* (lit., "one who fears God") that Cornelius was a near-proselyte to Judaism or a so-called Proselyte of the Gate (cf. comments on 8:27–28). And while *sebomenos ton theon* (lit., "one who worships God") is Luke's usual way of identifying this special class of Gentile followers in Acts (cf. 13:50; 16:14; 17:4, 17; 18:7), at times he also uses *phoboumenos* synonymously (cf. 13:16, 26).

Here in Acts 10, however, we should probably understand *phoboumenos ton theon* not as a technical term for this special class associated loosely with Judaism but more broadly as meaning something like "a religious man" (NEB, TEV) or "a deeply religious man" (Ph). The fact that Luke adds *eusebēs* ("devout," "pious") to his assessment of Cornelius here and *dikaios* ("righteous") in repeating his spiritual qualities in v.22 suggests that he meant *phoboumenos ton theon* to be taken not technically but generally. And from his report of Peter's use of this expression for Cornelius in v.35 ("men from every nation who fear him [God] and do what is right"), it seems that we must understand Cornelius to have been a Gentile who, having realized the bankruptcy of paganism, sought to worship a monotheistic God, practice a form of prayer, and lead a moral life, apart from any necessary association with Judaism. Probably we should view him as a pious and intensely religious man who might have known very little about the Jewish religion but in his own way "gave generously to those in need" (lit., "to the people," *tō laō*, which suggests "the Jewish people") and "prayed to God regularly."

In sum, Cornelius was a noble and spiritually sensitive Roman army officer, who seems to fit Virgil's picture of the Gentile world as one that "stretched out its hands in longing for the other shore" (*Aeneid* 6.314). It was, then, to such a spiritually minded Gentile, Luke tells us, that God first reached out his hand in the advance of the Christian mission.

3 "One day about three in the afternoon" (lit., "about the ninth hour of the day"), an angel of God appeared to Cornelius in a vision and called him by name. While the ninth hour was the second of the set times during the day for prayer in Judaism (see comments on 3:1), here the expression is used with *phanerōs* ("plainly," "distinctly") to emphasize that the vision happened in broad daylight.

4 Cornelius's response was that he "stared [participial form of *atenizō*] in fear" and could only blurt out the words "What is it, Lord?" (*Ti estin, kyrie?*). While the Greek title *kyrios* was used in antiquity for everything from polite address to worshipful acclamation, Cornelius undoubtedly meant it in some sense of worshipful acclaim—even though he might not have had any firm idea of whom he was addressing (cf. 9:5). He would hardly have been so blasé in the face of this heavenly vision as to have meant by the title only "Sir." In his consternation he heard the reassuring words that his prayers and alms had arisen as a memorial (*eis mnēmosynon*, or "remembrance") before God (cf. Lev 2:2; Tobit 12:12; Phil 4:18; Heb 13:15–16)—a biblical and traditional way of saying that he was commended before God and that God was attentive to his situation.

5–6 Cornelius was told to send to Joppa for Simon Peter. The surname Peter distinguishes the apostle from his host Simon the tanner, whose house was by the sea, probably in order to use the sea water in his trade. No indication is given as to why Peter was to be summoned. Instead, the emphasis is on the fact that Cornelius was prepared to respond to God.

7–8 Cornelius's response was immediate. Calling two of his household servants and one of his soldiers and telling them what had occurred and what he had been told to do, he sent them to Joppa to bring back Peter. The servants were probably two of those already mentioned in v.2 as part of Cornelius's household; and the soldier is identified as being also "pious" or "devout" (*eusebēs*), one to whom the full characterization of v.2 (also vv.22 and 35) also applied.

Notes

2 Because of their personal qualities, centurions were considered the salt of the Roman legions. Polybius describes their character thus: "Centurions are desired not to be bold and adventurous so much as good leaders, of steady and prudent mind, not prone to take the offensive or start fighting wantonly, but able when overwhelmed and hardpressed to stand fast and die at their post" (*History* 6. 24).

4 Ἀτενίζω (*atenizō*, "to stare") is a favorite expression with Luke, who uses it for twelve of its fourteen NT appearances (Luke 4:20; 22:56; Acts 1:10; 3:4, 12; 6:15; 7:55; 10:4 [here]; 11:6; 13:9; 14:9; 23:1).

2. *Peter's vision*

10:9–16

⁹About noon the following day as they were approaching the city, Peter went up on the roof to pray. ¹⁰He became hungry and wanted something to eat, and

while the meal was being prepared, he fell into a trance. [11]He saw heaven opened and something like a large sheet being let down to earth by its four corners. [12]It contained all kinds of four-footed animals, as well as reptiles of the earth and birds of the air. [13]Then a voice told him, "Get up, Peter. Kill and eat."

[14]"Surely not, Lord!" Peter replied. "I have never eaten anything impure or unclean."

[15]The voice spoke to him a second time, "Do not call anything impure that God has made clean."

[16]This happened three times, and immediately the sheet was taken back to heaven.

9–13 Though Peter was not by training or inclination an overly scrupulous Jew, and though as a Christian his inherited prejudices were gradually wearing thin, he was not prepared to go so far as to minister directly to Gentiles. A special revelation was necessary for that, and Luke now tells how God took the initiative in overcoming Peter's reluctance.

The revelation came to him on the day following Cornelius's vision (or, perhaps, the day after the messengers' start, if that was later), as the three from Caesarea were approaching Joppa. About noon Peter went to the roof of the tanner's house to pray, apparently looking not only for solitude but also for shade under an awning and a cooling breeze from the sea. Noon was not one of the stated times for prayer among the Jews, and some have viewed Peter as here engaging in a belated morning prayer or an early evening ("ninth hour," afternoon) prayer. Yet pious Jews on the basis of Psalm 55:17 (cf. Dan 6:10; *Didache* 8:3) often prayed at noon as well. Moreover, the stated hours for prayer, while prescriptive, were not restrictive.

While in prayer, Peter became very hungry and, it seems, somewhat drowsy. As he was waiting for food, he fell into a trance (*ekstasis*) and saw a vision (cf. *horama* in 10:17, 19; 11:5) of "something like [*skeuos ti hōs;* lit. 'a certain object like'] a large sheet being let down to earth by its four corners" on which were "all kinds of four-footed animals, as well as reptiles of the earth and birds of the air." Then he heard a voice say, "Get up, Peter. Kill and eat." Psychologically, the details of the vision may be explained in terms of (1) Peter's increasing perplexity about Jewish-Gentile relations within various Christian congregations of the maritime plain, (2) the flapping awning over him (or, perhaps, the full sail of a boat out on the sea), and (3) his gnawing hunger. God frequently reveals himself not only in but also by means of our human situations. And Peter took what the voice said as a message from God—a message in the form of an almost inscrutable riddle, but one soon to be clarified by both word and event.

14 Peter's shock and repugnance are expressed in his words: "Surely not, Lord." This response is in word and content like that of the prophet Ezekiel when called upon by God to eat unclean food among the Gentiles (Ezek 4:14). While not overly scrupulous, Peter nonetheless had always observed the basic dietary restrictions of Leviticus 11, which distinguished the clean quadrupeds (chewed the cud and had cloven hooves) that were fit for food from animals considered unclean. And while clean animals were represented in the sheet, Peter was scandalized by the unholy mixture of clean and unclean and by the fact that no distinctions were made in the command to "kill and eat." Indeed, it was a command given him by one he acclaimed as "Lord"—perhaps recognizable to him as the voice of Jesus (cf. Bruce, *Acts of the Apostles,* p. 220). But that did not leave him any less repelled by the idea.

15-16 The voice told Peter, "Do not call anything impure [*koinos*; lit., 'common,' a synecdoche for the dual expression *koinos kai akathartos*, 'impure or unclean,' of v.14] that God has made clean." The particular application had to do with nullifying Jewish dietary laws for Christians in accord with Jesus' remarks on the subject in Mark 7:17-23. But Peter was soon to learn that the range of the vision's message extended much more widely, touching directly on Jewish-Gentile relations as he had known them and on those relations in ways he could never have anticipated. Three times this interchange took place, with the message being three times indelibly impressed on Peter's subconscious. Luke then says, "The sheet [*skeuos*; lit., 'the object'] was taken back to heaven."

Notes

10 Πρόσπεινος (*prospeinos*, "very hungry") is a rare word used only here and by Demosthenes Ophthalmicus, a famous first-century eye doctor of Laodicea, as quoted by the sixth-century medical writer Aëtius (cf. F.W. Dillistone, ExpT, 46 [1934-35], 380). Peter's hunger is not explained, and he may not have been awaiting a noon meal. While Greeks and Romans usually had a noon meal, among the Jews breakfast was eaten in the forenoon and the main meal in the late afternoon (cf. SBK, 2:204-7).

Ἔκτασις (*ekstasis*, "trance") is a state where consciousness is wholly or partially suspended and the person feels himself to be outside himself. In the NT it is a state brought about by God (cf. 11:5; 12:11; 22:17).

11 Θεωρεῖ (*theōrei*, "he sees") here and εὑρίσκει (*heuriskei*, "he finds") of v.27 are among the few cases of a historic present in Luke-Acts (cf. BC, 4:115), perhaps reflecting the style of the author's source material more than his own.

3. *Messengers from Cornelius arrive at Joppa*

10:17-23a

> [17]While Peter was wondering about the meaning of the vision, the men sent by Cornelius found out where Simon's house was and stopped at the gate. [18]They called out, asking if Simon who was known as Peter was staying there.
> [19]While Peter was still thinking about the vision, the Spirit said to him, "Simon, three men are looking for you. [20]So get up and go downstairs. Do not hesitate to go with them, for I have sent them."
> [21]Peter went down and said to the men, "I'm the one you're looking for. Why have you come?"
> [22]The men replied, "We have come from Cornelius the centurion. He is a righteous and God-fearing man, who is respected by all the Jewish people. A holy angel told him to have you come to his house so that he could hear what you have to say." [23]Then Peter invited the men into the house to be his guests.

17-18 While Peter was recovering from the shock of the vision and its message, the men from Cornelius had found the tanner's house. It was nothing like a patrician's home, with a gatehouse and courtyard separating the living quarters from the street, but rather a craftsman's quarters, with immediate access from the street through a gateway or vestibule (*pylōn*). Thus at the gate the messengers shouted out their inquiry for anyone within earshot to hear: "Is Simon who is known as Peter staying here?"

19-20 But on the roof of the tanner's house, Peter was still so deep in thought about the vision that even their shouting and calling out his name failed to rouse him. Rather, the Spirit told him of the messengers' presence and then urged him to go with them, "For I have sent them," he said. A question naturally arises about the relation of the "angel of God" that appeared to Cornelius (10:3–6, 22, 30; 11:13), "the voice" that spoke to Peter (10:13–15; 11:7–9), and "the Spirit" who urges him to go with the messengers from Cornelius. But the question, though legitimate, is almost unanswerable because it is by the Holy Spirit that the ascended Christ manifests his presence to his own. Thus it is both exegetically and experientially difficult, if not impossible, to draw any sharp lines between "an angel of God," the Holy Spirit, and the ascended Christ. This is the same phenomenon that appeared in 8:26, 29, and 39 ("an angel of the Lord" and "the Spirit" directing Philip, with "the Spirit of the Lord" taking him away) and that will appear again in 16:6–7 ("the Holy Spirit" and "the spirit of Jesus" forbidding Paul). It crops out in even such closely reasoned didactic statements on the relation of Christ and the Spirit as Romans 8:9–11 and 2 Corinthians 3:17–18.

Whereas Codex Bezae (D) is lacking for Acts 8:26–10:14, here it adds its testimony to a number of the church fathers (e.g., Cyril, Ambrose, Chrysostom, Augustine) and various Western uncial and minuscule texts for the omission of any number (i.e., either "two" or "three") in v.19. Codices ℵ, A, C, E, together with P[74] and various other textual traditions, read that Peter was told by the Spirit: "Three [*treis*] men are looking for you." Yet Codex Vaticanus (B) speaks here of only "two [*duo*] men." The reading "three" is supported by the majority of the early MSS and conforms nicely with the description in 10:7 and Peter's words of 11:11. The reading "two," however, is supported by the very important fourth-century witness Codex B and is the "harder reading" and therefore on internal grounds probably to be preferred—evidently understanding 10:7 as speaking of the two servants as the messengers and the soldier as their guard. Either reading would allow Peter in 11:11 to refer later to three men coming from Caesarea for him. But the determination of the exact number is extremely difficult and probably beyond final resolution. It is not too difficult, however, to understand why Codex D and its Western associates decided to cut the Gordian knot by omitting any reference to a specific number in v.19 rather than trying to untie it.

21-23a In response to the Spirit's urging, and probably by means of an outside stairway, Peter went down to meet the messengers. After he identified himself and asked why they had come, they told him of their master, Cornelius, of the angel's visitation, and of their mission to bring Peter back so that he might tell their master what he had to say. In doing so they characterized Cornelius as not only "a righteous and God-fearing man" (cf. comments on 10:2) but also as one whose personal qualities are witnessed to "by all the Jewish people" (lit., "the whole nation of the Jews," *holou tou ethnous tōn Ioudaiōn*; here non-Jews refer to Jews by the term *ethnos*, "nation," rather than *laos*, "people"). Then Peter, in obedience to the command of the vision, received these Gentiles into the house as his guests, acting, no doubt with the tanner's permission, more as a host than a lodger.

4. Peter's reception by Cornelius

10:23b–33

> The next day Peter started out with them, and some of the brothers from Joppa went along. [24]The following day he arrived in Caesarea. Cornelius was expecting

them and had called together his relatives and close friends. [25]As Peter entered the house, Cornelius met him and fell at his feet in reverence. [26]But Peter made him get up. "Stand up," he said, "I am only a man myself."

[27]Talking with him, Peter went inside and found a large gathering of people. [28]He said to them: "You are well aware that it is against our law for a Jew to associate with a Gentile or visit him. But God has shown me that I should not call any man impure or unclean. [29]So when I was sent for, I came without raising any objection. May I ask why you sent for me?"

[30]Cornelius answered: "Four days ago I was in my house praying at this hour, at three in the afternoon. Suddenly a man in shining clothes stood before me [31]and said, 'Cornelius, God has heard your prayer and remembered your gifts to the poor. [32]Send to Joppa for Simon who is called Peter. He is a guest in the home of Simon the tanner, who lives by the sea.' [33]So I sent for you immediately, and it was good of you to come. Now we are all here in the presence of God to listen to everything the Lord has commanded you to tell us."

23b–24 The conversation in the tanner's house that evening must have been a lively one, with many of the Joppa believers joining in the discussion of the strange visions. Six of the Joppa believers accompanied Peter to Caesarea the next day (cf. 11:12)—a wise action in view of the questions that would later be raised at Jerusalem. So the party of ten set out for Caesarea. It apparently took them longer to cover the thirty miles than the messengers had taken earlier because they did not get to Caesarea till the following day. Cornelius was expecting them and had drawn together a group of relatives and close friends to hear Peter.

25–26 As Peter was brought into the centurion's home past the gatehouse and then into the courtyard, Cornelius came from his living quarters to meet him. Cornelius fell at Peter's feet and offered him "reverence" (*proskyneō*, a word used for homage offered to deity, to angels, and to men)—doubtless an expression of his belief that there was something supernatural about Peter. But Peter, not only unaccustomed to such honors but brought up to consider them blasphemous, ordered him to stand up and assured him: "I am only a man myself" (cf. 14:14–15; Rev 19:10; 22:8–9).

27–29 In Cornelius's living quarters Peter found a large group waiting to hear what he had to say. Perhaps self-consciously, he began by saying that Jewish law prohibited a Jew from associating with Gentiles. Admittedly, this was an ideal representation of the Jewish position (as so often happens in the Tal.), for Jewish ethical law contains a number of provisions for Jewish-Gentile business partnerships (e.g., b *Shabbath* 150a) and even for Jews' bathing with Gentiles (ibid., 151a). But such contacts made a Jew ceremonially unclean, as did entering Gentiles' buildings or touching their possessions (cf. M *Abodah Zarah*, passim). Above all, it was forbidden to accept the hospitality of Gentiles and eat with them, particularly because Gentiles did not tithe. Scrupulous Jews were not even permitted to be guests of a Jewish commoner (cf. M *Demai* 2.2–3), much less of a Gentile (ibid., 3.4). But God in a vision, Peter said, had taught him not to call anyone impure or unclean; so now he was associating with them without traditional scruples. Then he asked, "May I ask why you sent for me?"

30–33 Cornelius told all about his vision and described how he sent for Peter and invited him to relate "everything the Lord has commanded you to tell us." Few preachers have ever had a more receptive audience than Peter had on this occasion.

The reference to the "ninth hour" (or "three in the afternoon") is probably not meant to specify the time of evening prayer in Judaism (see comments on 10:3) but to express a circumstance of importance to Cornelius—viz., that the vision happened "at this very hour" (*mechri tautēs tēs hōras*). Also significant is that Luke's repetition of the details of Cornelius's vision and of the details of Peter's vision (11:4–10) serve an important function in the doublet structure of his whole presentation (cf. comments introducing Part I: The Christian Mission to the Jewish World).

Notes

24 א A C E P read εἰσῆλθον (*eisēlthon*, "they arrived"), though B and D read εἰσῆλθεν (*eisēlthen*, "he arrived").

D inserts καί (*kai*, "and") before the participial συγκαλεσάμενος (*synkalesamenos*) and adds περιέμεινεν (*periemeinen*, "waiting for them") at the end of the sentence.

25 D and its Western associates insert: "As Peter drew near to Caesarea, one of the servants ran ahead and reported that he had arrived. Cornelius sprang up and going to meet him, . . ." Whether this should be understood as a servant sent ahead to greet Peter, a servant stationed at the city gate to bring word of his approach, or one of the messengers in the party who ran ahead to tell his master of his soon arrival, the words appear to be a gloss.

30 D has ἀπὸ τῆς τρίτης ἡμέρας (*apo tēs tritēs hēmeras*, "three days ago"; lit., "from the third day"), which shortens the chronology.

D with its Western associates adds νηστεύων (*nēsteuōn*, "fasting") to Cornelius's activity: "I was in my house fasting and praying," which is a pietistic addition typical of this family of MSS.

32 The Western and Byzantine traditions (cf. KJV) add ὃς παραγενόμενος λαλήσει σοι (*hos paragenomenos lalēsei soi*, "who, when he arrives, will speak to you"), evidently seeking to parallel 11:14.

33 The Western text adds παρακαλῶν ἐλθεῖν πρὸς ἡμᾶς (*parakalōn elthein pros hēmas*, "requesting [you] to come to us") in the first clause and ἐν τάχει (*en tachei*, "so quickly") in the second.

P45 omits πάντες (*pantes*, "all") and ἐνώπιον τοῦ θεοῦ (*enōpion tou theou*, "in the presence of God").

5. Peter's sermon in Cornelius's house

10:34–43

[34]Then Peter began to speak: "I now realize how true it is that God does not show favoritism [35]but accepts men from every nation who fear him and do what is right. [36]This is the message God sent to the people of Israel, telling the good news of peace through Jesus Christ, who is Lord of all. [37]You know what has happened throughout Judea, beginning in Galilee after the baptism that John preached— [38]how God anointed Jesus of Nazareth with the Holy Spirit and power, and how he went around doing good and healing all who were under the power of the devil, because God was with him.

[39]"We are witnesses of everything he did in the country of the Jews and in Jerusalem. They killed him by hanging him on a tree, [40]but God raised him from the dead on the third day and caused him to be seen. [41]He was not seen by all the people, but by witnesses whom God had already chosen—by us who ate and drank with him after he rose from the dead. [42]He commanded us to preach to the people and to testify that he is the one whom God appointed as judge of the living and the dead. [43]All the prophets testify about him that everyone who believes in him receives forgiveness of sins through his name."

Peter's sermon in Cornelius's house is a précis of the apostolic kerygma. It is similar structurally and in content to his earlier sermons in 2:14-40 and 3:11-26, though it contains more information about Jesus' precrucifixion ministry than in those two sermons (cf. also 4:8-12; 5:29-32). Dibelius complains that "a speech which is so long, relatively speaking, cannot have had any place in a legend told among Christians about the conversion of a centurion" (*Studies in Acts*, p. 110). But surely a Gentile audience, even though knowing something about Jesus of Nazareth from living in Palestine, would require more details of Jesus' life and work than a Palestinian Jewish audience would. Peter's more lengthy account of Jesus' ministry here must therefore be considered particularly appropriate, considering his audience. Furthermore, the sermon is sprinkled with Semitisms, which show its rootage in history (cf. the discussion of Semitisms in the Introduction: The Question of Sources) and is comparable in both scope and emphasis to Mark's Gospel, which may very well reflect Peter's preaching (cf. Papias) in Rome (cf. C.H. Dodd, "The Framework of the Gospel Narrative," ExpT, 43 [1931-32], 396-400).

34-35 The sermon is prefaced by the words "opening his mouth, Peter said" (*anoixas de Petros to stoma eipen*). This was one way to introduce a weighty utterance (cf. Matt 5:2; 13:35 [quoting Ps 78:2]; Acts 8:35). And in Luke's eyes what Peter was about to say was indeed momentous in sweeping away centuries of racial prejudice. It begins by Peter's statement that God does not show racial "favoritism" (*prosōpolēmptēs*, which appears only here in the NT [a *hapax legomenon*], but whose synonym *prosōpolēmpsia* appears in Rom 2:11; Eph 6:9; Col 3:25; James 2:1; Peter 1:17) "but accepts men from every nation who fear him and do what is right." While some consciousness of this may be implicit in Israel's history and at times may have been expressed by her prophets (cf. Amos 9:7; Mic 6:8), it was only by means of a revelational clarification (a pesher) of what was earlier considered to be highly enigmatic (a "mystery"; cf. Eph 3:4-6) that Peter came to appreciate the racial challenge of the gospel.

36 Peter captions his sermon as "The message God sent to the people of Israel, telling the good news of peace through Jesus Christ, who is Lord of all." The Greek of vv.36-38 is syntactically awkward, suggesting either a translation from an earlier written Semitic source (C.C. Torrey), a Septuagintal "archaizing" on Luke's part (H.F.D. Sparks), or the reproduction of speech patterns of one who thought more in Semitic fashion even while speaking Greek. Interestingly and, I believe, significantly, Raymond A. Martin's study on *Syntactical Evidence of Semitic Sources in Greek Documents* (Missoula, Mont.: Scholars, 1974) does not credit the syntax of Peter's sermon here either to Lukan ingenuity or to written Semitic sources, though he includes Peter's defense of Cornelius's conversion in 11:1-18 among those portions that reflect an earlier written Semitic source. We may conclude, therefore, that the awkwardness of the syntax in the account of this sermon probably stems from Peter himself as he spoke before his Gentile audience in somewhat "broken" Greek. Had it been Luke's own composition, it would have been much clearer.

The caption of Peter's sermon contains three emphases that set the tone for what follows. First, there is the revelational emphasis. While the caption begins elliptically by omitting the understood subject and verb "this is" (*touto estin*), it nonetheless expresses in form and content a pesher type of revelational understanding so common in early apostolic Christianity (cf. *touto estin to* in 2:16). Second, there is the emphasis on the proclamation of the gospel "to the people of Israel," its immediate recipients. Joined with this is a third emphasis relating to bringing that gospel to the Gentile world in terms comprehensible to Gentiles—an emphasis characterized by the expression "Lord of all."

This was properly a pagan title for deity (cf. Cadbury, BC, 5:361–62), but it was rebaptized by the early Christians to become an appropriate christological title (cf. Col 1:15–20). So Peter's sermon in Cornelius's house concerns (1) a new revelational understanding of God's message of peace, (2) which is given the sons of Israel as its primary recipients, but (3) which also includes Gentiles under the rubric of Christ as "Lord of all," with "all" understood personally as connoting Christ's lordship over both Jews and Gentiles.

37–41 Peter begins his sermon with a résumé of Jesus' life and work during his earthly ministry. Though Peter assumes that his hearers already know something about this ministry through living in Palestine, he proceeds to summarize it in greater detail than anywhere else in his recorded preaching. In scope and emphasis, the account is much like the portrayal of Jesus' ministry in Mark's Gospel. It begins with John the Baptist, moves on to Jesus' anointing with the Holy Spirit, refers to Jesus' many acts of divine power in Galilee, alludes to his continued ministry throughout Palestine and in Jerusalem, stresses his crucifixion, and concludes with a declaration of his resurrection and its verification by his appearances to chosen followers.

As it stands before us, the sermon is only a summary of what Peter actually said at the time. Originally it may have contained a number of examples of Jesus' acts of kindness and healing, such as those recorded in the synoptic Gospels. In addition, as a précis of what Peter said, it shows the interests of Luke who put the sermon into its present form—viz., the influence of Isaiah 61:1 in v.38, an OT passage Luke highlighted in his theme paragraph of Luke 4:14–30 at the start of his two-volume writing (cf. Introduction: The Structure of Acts). Also, the importance of the apostolic witness in establishing the Christian tradition comes to the fore in vv.39–41, as it does elsewhere throughout Luke-Acts. Furthermore, Luke's interest in Jesus' postresurrection eating and drinking with his disciples is evident in v.41. Only Luke records this (Luke 24:41–43) as a convincing proof of Jesus' physical presence (since in Jewish thinking angels and apparitions are unable to eat or drink, being without digestive tracts).

42–43 Peter ends his sermon by stating that the risen Christ has commanded his apostles to preach "to the people" (*tō laō*) and to testify about his divine appointment as "judge of the living and the dead." By his use of *ho laos* ("the people"), Peter probably had in mind "the Jewish people." And till then the early church knew no other mission. But then Peter went on to speak of the OT prophets testifying about this risen Lord and saying that "everyone who believes in him receives forgiveness of sins through his name." It was this reference to "everyone who believes in him" that seems to have broken through the traditional barrier between Jews and Gentiles and to have encouraged Cornelius and those in his house to be bold enough to think that they together with Jews could receive the blessings promised to Israel.

Notes

34–36 On pesher interpretation at Qumran and in the NT, see my *Biblical Exegesis*, pp. 38–45, passim.

36–38 The Western text, evidently embarrassed by the awkward syntax of these verses, recasts them to read: "For you know the message that he sent to the sons of Israel, which was published throughout all Judea, when he preached the good news of peace through Jesus Christ (who is Lord of all). For beginning in Galilee, after the baptism that John preached, Jesus of Nazareth, whom God anointed with the Holy Spirit and power, went about doing good."

37 B reads κήρυγμα (kērygma, "proclamation") for βάπτισμα (baptisma, "baptism").

38 Ἰησοῦν τὸν ἀπὸ Ναζαρέθ (Iēsoun ton apo Nazareth, "Jesus of Nazareth") is grammatically the object of the verb ἔχρισεν (echrisen, "anointed"), but it appears at the beginning of its clause for emphasis and is caught up later in that clause by the pronoun αὐτόν (auton, "him").

40 D reads μετὰ τὴν τρίτην ἡμέραν (meta tēn tritēn hēmeran, "after the third day"), evidently attempting a harmony with Matt 27:63, et al.

41 The Western text adds "and conversed . . . forty days" to "ate and drank with him," evidently attempting a harmony with 1:3.

---

6. Gentiles receive the Holy Spirit

10:44-48

44While Peter was still speaking these words, the Holy Spirit came on all who heard the message. 45The circumcised believers who had come with Peter were astonished that the gift of the Holy Spirit had been poured out even on the Gentiles. 46For they heard them speaking in tongues and praising God.

Then Peter said, 47"Can anyone keep these people from being baptized with water? They have received the Holy Spirit just as we have." 48So he ordered that they be baptized in the name of Jesus Christ. Then they asked Peter to stay with them for a few days.

44 As Peter was "speaking these words, the Holy Spirit came on all who heard the message." "These words" (ta rhēmata tauta) may refer to the entire sermon just delivered, as epitomized in the expression "the message" (ton logon) in the predicate of this verse. Probably, however, "these words" have in mind the statement "everyone who believes in him receives forgiveness of sins through his name" (v.43)—particularly "everyone who believes in him" (panta ton pisteuonta eis auton), which appears at the end of v.43 in the Greek, probably for emphasis. If this is true, then Luke is saying that it was this phrase that struck like a thunderbolt into the consciousness of the assembled Gentiles, releasing their pent-up emotions and emboldening them to respond by faith. With the promise of forgiveness offered "through his name" and to "everyone who believes in him," they were given a reason for hoping beyond their fondest hopes. And with their reception of that inclusive message, the Holy Spirit came upon the Gentile congregation gathered there just as he had come upon the disciples at Pentecost. In fact, this was, as F.H. Chase called it, "the Pentecost of the Gentile world" (*The Credibility of the Acts of the Apostles* [London: Macmillan, 1902], p. 79).

45-46 The six Jewish believers (hoi ek peritomēs pistoi, "the circumcised believers") who were there with Peter were astonished at what they saw and heard. For in accepting these Gentiles and bestowing his Holy Spirit on them, God had providentially attested his action by the same sign of tongues as at Pentecost. The gift of tongues at Pentecost should probably be understood as distinguishable languages because they were immediately recognized as dialects then current (cf. comments on 2:4). Here, however, an outburst of foreign languages would have fallen on untuned ears and failed to be convincing. So we should probably view what was here expressed as being ecstatic utterances such as Paul later described in 1 Corinthians 12-14. Undoubtedly the sign of tongues was given primarily for the sake of the Jewish believers right there in Cornelius's house. But it was also given for Jerusalem believers, who would later hear of what happened, so that all would see the conversion of these Gentiles as being entirely of God and none would revert to their old prejudices and relegate these new converts to the role of second-class Christians.

47–48 Peter may not have been much of an abstract thinker. But to his great credit he was ready to follow the divine initiative, if only he could be sure that God was really at work. So, convinced by God and consistent with his conviction about the logical connections between Christian conversion, water baptism, and the baptism of the Holy Spirit (cf. comments on 2:38), Peter calls for the Gentiles who have received the baptism of the Spirit to be baptized with water "in the name of Jesus Christ." While Acts 2 and 8 indicate that water baptism does not take the place of the Spirit's baptism but that the two go hand-in-hand with conversion, so vv.47–48 speak of the baptism of the Holy Spirit not as supplanting baptism with water but rather as being the spiritual reality to which water baptism testifies. Thus the baptism of these Gentile converts pointed to a new spiritual reality in their lives. But it also had immense significance for Peter and his six companions. For in baptizing these Gentiles, Peter and those with him confessed that God in his sovereignty does bring Gentiles directly into relationship with Jesus Christ, apart from any prior relationship with Judaism. Peter may have remained uncertain as to just how Cornelius's new-found faith should be expressed in worship and service and how it would be related to the Roman social order and to Judaism. But now that God had broken down the traditional barriers between them, Peter was content to stay with them in Caesarea "for a few days."

Notes

46 The Western text adds ἑτέραις (heterais, "other") tongues, thus suggesting foreign languages rather than ecstatic utterances.

48 On the synonymous use of the prepositions ἐπί (epi, "on"), ἐν (en, "in"), and εἰς (eis, "into") with Christian baptism, see comments and note on 2:38.

The Western text adds τοῦ κυρίου (tou kyriou, "the Lord") before Ἰησοῦ Χριστοῦ (Iēsou Christou, "Jesus Christ"), as it also does in 2:38 in harmony with 8:16 and 19:5.

7. The response of the Jerusalem church

11:1–18

¹The apostles and the brothers throughout Judea heard that the Gentiles also had received the word of God. ²So when Peter went up to Jerusalem, the circumcised believers criticized him ³and said, "You went into the house of uncircumcised men and ate with them."

⁴Peter began and explained everything to them precisely as it had happened: ⁵"I was in the city of Joppa praying, and in a trance I saw a vision. I saw something like a large sheet being let down from heaven by its four corners, and it came down to where I was. ⁶I looked into it and saw four-footed animals of the earth, wild beasts, reptiles, and birds of the air. ⁷Then I heard a voice telling me, 'Get up, Peter. Kill and eat.'

⁸"I replied, 'Surely not, Lord! Nothing impure or unclean has ever entered my mouth.'

⁹"The voice spoke from heaven a second time, 'Do not call anything impure that God has made clean.' ¹⁰This happened three times, and then it was all pulled up to heaven again.

¹¹"Right then three men who had been sent to me from Caesarea stopped at the house where I was staying. ¹²The Spirit told me to have no hesitation about going with them. These six brothers also went with me, and we entered the man's house. ¹³He told us how he had seen an angel appear in his house and say, 'Send to Joppa for Simon who is called Peter. ¹⁴He will bring you a message through which you and all your household will be saved.'

¹⁵"As I began to speak, the Holy Spirit came on them as he had come on us at the beginning. ¹⁶Then I remembered what the Lord had said, 'John baptized with water, but you will be baptized with the Holy Spirit.' ¹⁷So if God gave them the same gift as he gave us, who believed in the Lord Jesus Christ, who was I to think that I could oppose God!"

¹⁸When they heard this, they had no further objections and praised God, saying, "So then, God has even granted the Gentiles repentance unto life."

The conversion of Cornelius was a landmark in the history of the gospel's advance from its strictly Jewish beginnings to its penetration of the Roman Empire. True, it did not settle any of the issues relating to Jewish-Gentile relations within the church, nor did Jewish believers take it as a precedent for a direct outreach to Gentiles. But it did show that the sovereign God was not confined to the traditional forms of Judaism and that he could bring a Gentile directly into relationship with himself through Jesus Christ and apart from any prior commitment to distinctive Jewish beliefs or lifestyle.

Cornelius's conversion is important to Luke not only because of the gospel's advance but also because of the response of the Christians in Jerusalem to it. Amid his thesis of development and advance, Luke is interested in emphasizing lines of continuity and areas of agreement within the early church. So he takes pains to point out here, as in his account of the conversion of the Samaritans (cf. 8:14–25), that—though there were objections—the leadership of the Jerusalem church accepted the validity of Cornelius's conversion apart from any prior affiliation with Judaism. And that acceptance was of as great importance in validating a later Gentile mission as the event itself.

1–3 News of Peter's activity at Caesarea reached Jerusalem and the believers there before Peter himself did. Codex D and its Western associates expand v.2 to read that he stayed in Caesarea "for a considerable time" and that "he did a great deal of preaching throughout the regions" around Caesarea after that. But however long it took to reach the apostles and brothers in Jerusalem, news of Peter's direct approach to Gentiles and his acceptance of them apart from the strictures of Judaism caused great alarm both within the church and among the Jewish populace generally. The Hellenistic believers had stirred up much antagonism by their liberal attitudes toward the tenets of Jewish popular piety (cf. 6:8–7:56). The immediate consequences were the martyrdom of Stephen and the expulsion of the believers from areas under Sanhedrin control (cf. 7:57–8:3). Now if it were really true that Peter, the leading member of the apostolic band, had gone further in disregarding the traditional laws of Judaism in favor of a direct association with Gentiles, what good will still remained toward believers in Jerusalem would be quickly dissipated. The practical implications for the existence and the mission of the Christian church in Jerusalem were grave, and such practical considerations undoubtedly led to principial questions.

Peter's return to Jerusalem, therefore, was hardly to a more comfortable situation after a strenuous journey. Instead, it was more like lighting a match in highly combustible air. "The circumcised believers" (*hoi ek peritomēs;* lit., "those of the circumcision," usually meaning only "the Jews," but in context certainly connoting "Jewish Christians" here) immediately confronted Peter and charged, "You went into the house of uncircumcised men and ate with them." This charge, while traditionally worded, was tantamount to saying that Peter had set aside Christianity's Jewish features and thereby seriously endangered its relation with the nation.

4–17 Peter defended his actions by recounting his experiences at Joppa and Caesarea, with an emphasis on (1) the divine initiative in all that transpired and (2) his inability to withstand God. Thus he recounts the details of the vision that came to him at Joppa (vv.5–10), of his reception by Cornelius (vv.11–14), and of the Spirit's coming upon the group gathered in Cornelius's house (vv.15–17). It was the Lord, insisted Peter, who gave him the vision and who explained its meaning. It was the Spirit who told him to have "no hesitation" (*mēden diakrinanta;* lit., "making no distinction") to go with the messengers to Caesarea and enter Cornelius's house. And it was God who took the initiative by baptizing Cornelius and his companions with the Holy Spirit. Therefore, concluded Peter, "Who was I to think that I could oppose God?"

Of interest in this account are the many Semitic features incorporated into its present Greek form—features that have led a number of scholars to postulate a written Aramaic source Luke drew on at this point. While Peter's sermon in Cornelius's house was probably delivered in "Semitized" Greek, his defense at Jerusalem may very well have been delivered in Aramaic and circulated at first among Jewish Christians in that form. Likewise of interest is the narrative's vividness here compared with the colorless third-person style in chapter 10. While in structure and content the two accounts are very similar, the retelling of Peter's experiences in chapter 11 has a freshness and vitality to it that make it more than a mere résumé of events related in chapter 10. This may only reflect the literary genius of Luke. But perhaps it points to a use of differing sources for chapters 10 and 11: the one of Caesarean origin narrating the events in Greek; the other of Jerusalem origin containing Peter's defense in Aramaic. With his stress on a twofold witness to truth (cf. comments introducing Part I: The Christian Mission to the Jewish World), Luke probably viewed them as together providing greater support for his presentation and therefore brought them together in the manner presently before us.

18 On hearing about Peter's experiences, the Christians at Jerusalem "remained silent" (*hēsychasan;* NIV, "had no further objections") and "praised God." This probably means that his critics, at least for the moment, were silenced, while those more receptive to God's working acknowledged that Peter was right and credited God rather than human ingenuity for what had happened. In view of what Peter reported, the Jerusalem church could come to no other conclusion than that "God has even granted the Gentiles repentance unto life."

This was a response of momentous importance by the church at Jerusalem, and Luke meant his readers to appreciate it as being as significant in validating a later Gentile mission as Cornelius's conversion itself. But while of vital significance for the acceptance of Gentiles, it said nothing about the many related questions that were bound to arise soon. For example, what lifestyle was appropriate for Gentiles coming to Christ directly out of paganism? How should they relate themselves as Christians to Jewish Christians and to Jews, who both followed a Jewish lifestyle? And how should the Jerusalem church relate itself in practice to these new Gentile believers it had in theory accepted? These are matters the Jerusalem church did not address itself to in chapter 11. Yet such matters were logically involved in its response and were to be taken up again later (cf. 15:1–35).

And just as there were ideological issues left unresolved in the response of the church in chapter 11, so there are also a number of historical matters about which Luke gives us no information, though we would like very much to know. For example, whatever happened to Cornelius and his fellow Gentile Christians after Peter left them? Did they troop en masse up to Jerusalem to worship with the Jewish believers there? For a number of reasons, this hardly seems likely. Or did they join with Philip and his converts in Caesarea (cf. 8:40) to form a worshiping community there? Or did they somehow inaugurate a distinctive form of Gentile Christian worship? Or, being doubtless all associated in one way or another with the Roman army and the Roman administration in Palestine, were these Gentile believers in Jesus transferred to other posts in the empire by Rome, either through due course or because of their recent alignment with a minority group within Palestine? Luke does not tell us.

Neither does Luke tell us how such a response affected the Jerusalem church itself. Did it lose some good will among its Jewish compatriots because it accepted Cornelius? Were there believers within its ranks who felt badly about this decision and who expressed their dissatisfaction—or would later express it—in ways disruptive for a further Gentile outreach? Was this one reason why the church soon found it appropriate to have as its leader the Pharisaically trained and legally scrupulous James the Just rather than one or more of the apostles (cf. comments on 12:2)? Again, Luke does not tell us, though some of these matters will come to the fore later in Acts.

Notes

2 On "going up to" and "down from" Jerusalem, see the comments and note at 8:5.

4–17 On the Semitisms of Peter's defense, see esp. Raymond A. Martin, *Syntactical Evidence of Semitic Sources in Greek Documents* (Missoula, Mont.: Scholars Press, 1974).

9 D reads ἐγένετο φωνὴ ἐκ τοῦ οὐρανοῦ πρός με (*egeneto phōnē ek tou ouranou pros me*, "there came a voice from heaven to me").

11 ℵ A B D, together with P[74], read ἦμεν (*ēmen*, "we were [staying]") whereas E P P[45], the Byzantine tradition, and all the versions support ἤμην (*ēmēn*, "I was [staying]"), which seems preferable in context.

12 The Western text omits μηδὲν διακρίναντα (*mēden diakrinanta*, "making no distinction"), which NIV translates as "to have no hesitation."

15 The use of the verb ἄρχω (*archō*, "begin") in the expression ἐν δὲ τῷ ἄρξασθαί με λαλεῖν (*en de tō arxasthai me lalein*, "as I began to speak") probably should be viewed as something of a redundant auxiliary (cf. 11:4; also 2:4; 18:26; 24:2; 27:35) and its temporal or chronological significance not pressed unduly.

C. *The Church at Antioch of Syria* (11:19–30)

Antioch of Syria was founded about 300 B.C. by Seleucus I Nicator, who named it after either his father or his son, both of whom bore the name Antiochus. It was situated on the Orontes River about three hundred miles north of Jerusalem and twenty miles east of the Mediterranean, at the joining of the Lebanon and Taurus mountain ranges where the Orontes breaks through and flows down to the sea. To distinguish it from some fifteen other Asiatic cities built by Seleucus and also named Antioch, it was frequently called "Antioch-on-the-Orontes," "Antioch-by-Daphne" (Daphne, the celebrated temple of Apollo, was nearby), "Antioch the Great," "Antioch the Beautiful," and "The Queen of the East." During the first Christian century, it was, after Rome and Alexandria, the third largest city in the empire, having a population of more than 500,000. In A.D. 540, Antioch was sacked by the Persians, a calamity it never recovered from. Today Antakiyeh (ancient Antioch) is a poor place of about 35,000 inhabitants.

First-century Antioch was a melting pot of Western and Eastern cultures, where Greek and Roman traditions mingled with Semitic, Arab, and Persian influences. The Jewish population is estimated to have been about one-seventh of the total population and had vested rights to follow its own laws within its three or more settlements in and around the city. During the reign of Caligula (A.D. 37–41), however, many Jews were killed; and during the tumultuous period of the middle and late 60's, Jewish acceptance and prosperity in Antioch came to an end. The city was not only known for its sophistication and culture but also for its vices. The beautiful pleasure park of Daphne was a center for moral depravity of every kind, and the expression *Daphnici mores* became a proverb for depraved living. The Roman satirist Juvenal (A.D. 60–140) aimed one of his sharpest gibes at his own decadent Rome when he said that the Orontes had flowed into the Tiber (*Satirae* 3. 62), flooding the imperial city with the superstition and immorality of the East.

In Christian history, apart from Jerusalem, no other city of the Roman Empire played as large a part in the early life and fortunes of the church as Antioch of Syria. It was the birthplace of foreign missions (13:2) and the home base for Paul's outreach to the eastern half of the empire. It was the place where those of "the way" (9:2) were first called "Christians" (11:26) and where the question as to the necessity for Gentile converts to submit to the rite of circumcision first arose (15:1–2; cf. Gal 2:11–21). It had among its teachers such illustrious persons as Barnabas, Paul, and Peter (cf. Gal 2:11–13) in the first century; Ignatius and Theophilus in the second; and Lucian, Theodore, Chrysostom, and Theodoret (as well as a host of others, including Nestorius) at the end of the third and throughout the fourth centuries.

In the light of its great importance for both the empire and the early church, it is somewhat surprising that Luke's account of the founding of the church at Syrian Antioch and of the progress of the gospel there is so compressed. Adolf Harnack proposed that 11:19–30 was part of a Jerusalem-Antiochean source that included 12:25–15:35 and was related to the source for 6:1–8:4 (see Introduction: The Sources of Acts). But the narrative here clearly differs in style from that which Luke has already used in his account of Stephen and the Hellenists or that which he will use in writing about Paul and his first missionary journey. Also, it is devoid of Semitisms, whereas 6:1–8:4 and 12:25–15:35 contain many (cf. Martin, *Semitic Sources*, passim); and it has a number of favorite Lukan expressions (e.g., *lalountes ton logon*, "speaking the word" [v.19]; *polys arithmos*, "a great number" [v.21]; *anēr agathos*, "a good man" [v.24a]; *prosetethē ochlos hikanos*, "a great crowd was added" [v.24b; cf. v.26]) as well as the repeated use of Luke's favorite christological title "Lord" (five times in vv. 20–24). Probably, therefore, we should view 11:19–30 as a free Lukan summary of certain items of information known to him—perhaps as the way Luke wrote when not having detailed, written source material at his disposal (such as seems to underlie much of the first half of Acts) and when not himself an eyewitness of the events (as seems to be the rationale for the "we" sections of the last half of Acts).

1. The founding of the church

11:19-26

> 19Now those who had been scattered by the persecution in connection with Stephen traveled as far as Phoenicia, Cyprus and Antioch, telling the message only to Jews. 20Some of them, however, men from Cyprus and Cyrene, went to Antioch and began to speak to Greeks also, telling them the good news about the Lord Jesus. 21The Lord's hand was with them, and a great number of people believed and turned to the Lord.
> 22News of this reached the ears of the church at Jerusalem, and they sent Barnabas to Antioch. 23When he arrived and saw the evidence of the grace of God, he was glad and encouraged them all to remain true to the Lord with all their hearts. 24He was a good man, full of the Holy Spirit and faith, and a great number of people were brought to the Lord.
> 25Then Barnabas went to Tarsus to look for Saul, 26and when he found him, he brought him to Antioch. So for a whole year Barnabas and Saul met with the church and taught great numbers of people. The disciples were first called Christians at Antioch.

19 Luke opens his account of the gospel's proclamation at Antioch of Syria with the same words with which he began the story of the mission to Samaria in 8:4—a fact that suggests he wanted to reach behind his accounts of Peter's ministries at Lydda, Joppa, and Caesarea and start a new strand of history beginning with the death of Stephen. From such an opening we should probably understand that the Hellenistic Christians' outreach to Phoenicia, Cyprus, and Antioch was (1) logically parallel to that in Samaria and not a continuation of Peter's outreach at Lydda, Joppa, and Caesarea and (2) chronologically parallel, at least in its early stages, to the accounts in 8:4–11:18. Phoenicia, Cyprus, and Antioch had large Jewish populations; and Syria, like Babylonia, was often considered an integral part of the Jewish homeland because of the many scrupulous Jews living there. Thus since this mission to the north was carried on within areas roughly considered to be Jewish terrain, was mounted by Hellenistic Jewish believers in Jesus, and was directed, at least at first, "only to Jews," Luke presents it here as still being part of the Christian witness to the Jewish world, even though the account speaks of a time when the categories "Jew" and "Gentile" were beginning to break down.

20-21 At Antioch, however, some of the Hellenistic Jewish Christians "began to speak to Greeks also." Some MSS read *Hellēnas* ("Greeks") while others read *Hellēnistas* (possibly "Grecian Jews"). The external evidence for the text is somewhat difficult to weigh at this point (see Notes). But while the textual evidence may be somewhat indeterminate, certainly the contrast drawn between the "Jews" of v.19 and those who receive the gospel here in v.20 makes it all but impossible to understand those referred to in v.20 as anything other than Gentiles. Thus it is necessary to read the text as meaning "Greeks" and as probably originally using the word *Hellēnas*.

Actually, the problem with reading "Greeks" here is more interpretative than textual. Did Luke have in mind Gentiles who had no affiliation whatever with Judaism, or did he have in mind Gentiles who had some kind of relationship with Judaism—perhaps "Proselytes of the Gate," or something like that? Usually Luke speaks of such near-proselytes as "God-fearers" (*sebomenoi ton theon*, cf. 13:50; 16:14; 17:4, 17; 18:7; see also *phoboumenoi ton theon* in 13:16, 26), which is not his expression here. Yet judging by his evident purpose in Acts to present Paul as the first to inaugurate a deliberate policy of a direct approach to Gentiles, it is extremely difficult to view these Greeks apart from the ministrations of Judaism. Peter's activity in Caesarea was indeed a direct approach to Gentiles, but it set no precedent and established no policy for such an outreach. If that is what Luke is saying happened at Antioch of Syria, he has nullified the point that he makes later in chapters 13–15.

On the other hand, by the way Luke treats these Greeks as being both a part of the mission to Jews and yet distinct from the Jews, probably we are to view them as having become Christians "through the door of the synagogue" (Ramsay, *St. Paul the Traveller*, p. 41) and thought of by the early church as an adjunct in its ministry to the Jewish nation. With the merging of cultures and blurring of distinctives that was taking place in Antioch generally, perhaps even Judaism faced some problems in drawing a sharp line between Gentiles who had some minimal relationship with the synagogue and those who were considered near-proselytes. But whatever their exact status, it seems fair to say that Luke did not look on the Greeks in v.20 as simply Gentiles unaffected by the influence of Judaism and that he did not view the Hellenistic Christians' approach to them as preempting the uniqueness of Paul's later Gentile policy.

All we are told about the identity of the Jewish-Christian missioners to Antioch is that they were from Cyprus and Cyrene. Perhaps Simeon Niger and Lucius of Cyrene were two of them (cf. 13:1), though Barnabas of Cyprus according to Luke's reckoning was not. But Luke does say that to the missioners' proclamation of "the good news about the Lord Jesus" there was a significant response so that "a great number of people believed and turned to the Lord." And since among that "great number" were both Jews and Gentiles, the Antioch church, though born within the synagogue, took on a decidedly different complexion from that of other early Christian congregations spoken of thus far. It was a mixed body of Jews and uncircumcised Gentiles meeting together for worship and fellowship in common allegiance to Jesus of Nazareth (cf. Gal 2:12).

22–24 News of the situation at Antioch was of definite concern to believers in Jerusalem. With the conversion of Samaritans, the conversion of some Gentiles in Caesarea, and now the report of a mixed congregation in Syrian Antioch, many in Jerusalem were doubtless fearful that the Christian mission was moving ahead so rapidly as to be out of control. The Jerusalem church, therefore, as in the case of the Samaritan conversions, decided to send a delegate to Antioch, probably in order to regularize whatever had gone awry and report back to the mother church. The man chosen for this task was Barnabas, a Jew from Cyprus who had gained an outstanding reputation for piety and generosity among the believers at Jerusalem (cf. 4:36–37). In all likelihood, it was the fact that Barnabas was both a Diaspora and "Zionistic" Jew coupled with his piety and generosity that qualified him in the eyes of the Jerusalem church for this mission to Antioch. In addition, the high esteem in which he was held made it certain that both his counsel and his report would be received with all seriousness.

The Jerusalem church could hardly have selected a better delegate, particularly from Luke's point of view. His generous spirit was gladdened by what he saw of the grace of God at work among the believers at Antioch, and, true to his nickname "Son of Encouragement" (Barnabas, or *huios paraklēseōs* [4:36]), he "encouraged them all to remain true to the Lord with all their hearts." Here was a crisis point in the history of the early church, for much depended on Barnabas's reaction, counsel, and report—not only at Antioch itself, but also at Jerusalem and in the later advance of the gospel through Paul's missions. With evident feeling, therefore, Luke says of him, "He was a good man, full of the Holy Spirit and faith." And as a result of his response, the work that was started at Antioch was enabled to go on, with many being brought to Christ.

25-26 Sometime after reaching Antioch, Barnabas went to Tarsus to find Saul to help him in the ministry back in Syria. We have no record of what Saul was doing between the time when he left Jerusalem (cf. 9:30) and when Barnabas found him in Tarsus. From Galatians 1:21-24 (cf. also Gal 2:2, 7), it is certain that in some way Saul continued preaching after leaving Jerusalem and that this was known back in Jerusalem. Perhaps the five lashings he received at the hands of the synagogue authorities (2 Cor 11:24), together with some of his other afflictions and hardships enumerated in 2 Corinthians 11:23-27, occurred during those days in Tarsus, for they find no place in the records of his later missionary endeavors. If so, this might indicate that in Tarsus and its environs he was trying to carry on a Gentile ministry within the Cilician synagogues and was getting into trouble for it. It also may have been during this period that he began to experience the loss of all things for Christ's sake (cf. Phil 3:8) through being disinherited by his family. Perhaps the ecstatic experience of 2 Corinthians 12:1-4 should also be associated with this period of his life as well.

It was Barnabas who had supported Saul when there was suspicion at Jerusalem about his conversion (cf. 9:27). And now, knowing of Saul's God-given commission to minister to the Gentiles, recalling his testimony at Jerusalem, and needing help for the work among the Gentiles, Barnabas involved Saul in the ministry at Antioch where they served together "for a whole year" and taught "a great crowd of people." Also, Barnabas may have heard of Saul's growing interest in the Gentiles and his effective work with them in Cilicia.

In joining Barnabas at Antioch, Saul may have thought he was carrying out the mandate received at his conversion to take the message of the risen Christ to Gentiles. Probably, however, the Antioch mission in those days was confined to the synagogue, the Antiochan Jews being more tolerant of Saul's activities than were those at Tarsus. It may also have been viewed as part of the ministry to Jews, without any thought of the propriety of appealing more widely and directly to Gentiles. All the early believers at Antioch, whether Jews or Gentiles, may well have been related in some way to the synagogue. Thus in the eyes of many Jewish Christians, the conversion of Gentiles who had some extent come under the ministry of Judaism before they believed in Jesus would not have been thought exceptional.

But others within the city—evidently nonbelievers who were more perceptive in this matter than the church itself—nicknamed this group of Jewish and Gentile believers "Christians" (*Christianoi*, i.e., "Christ followers," or "those of the household of Christ"). They saw that the ministry to Gentiles and the fellowship of Jews with Gentiles went beyond the bounds of what was usually permitted within Judaism. They also voiced an insight that the Christians themselves only saw clearly later on: Christianity is no mere variant of Judaism. The new name doubtless helped develop the self-consciousness of the early Christians, despite its having first been given in derision. Later the early Christians accepted it and used it of themselves (cf. 26:28; 1 Peter 4:16; Jos. Antiq. XVIII, 64 [iii.3]) along with their earlier self-designation of "the Way" (9:2; cf. 19:9, 23). But the use of the name "Christian" posed two great problems for the church. For one thing, Christians began to risk losing the protection Rome gave to a *religio licita* (i.e., a legal religion; cf. Introduction: Luke's Purposes in Writing Acts), which they had enjoyed when considered only a sect within Judaism. Furthermore, being now in some way differentiated from Judaism, Christians were faced with how to understand their continuity with the hope of Israel and the promises of the Jewish Scriptures. As we shall see, these problems were to loom large as the Christian mission moved onto Gentile soil.

Notes

19 On the use of μὲν οὖν (men oun, "now") in Acts, see comments and note at 1:6.

20 MS support for Ἕλληνας (Hellēnas, "Greeks") and Ἑλληνιστάς (Hellēnistas, "Grecian Jews") is inconclusive, though UBS 3d ed supports the latter. In one sense, Hellēnas could be considered the easier reading and Hellēnistas the more difficult, for the contrast with Ἰουδαίοις (Ioudaiois, "Jews") in v.19 clearly implies that these spoken of here were Gentiles, not Jews— which would make Hellēnistas the more difficult reading, indeed. On the other hand, if Hellēnas and Hellēnistas were understood as being roughly equivalent, as seems to have been the case within the ante-Nicene and post-Nicene church (cf. the versions), it is not too hard to imagine that an original Hellēnas was replaced by Hellēnistas in some texts to parallel the appearance of Hellēnistas in 6:1 and 9:29.

On the nature of the Ἑλληνίσται (Hellēnistai, "Grecian Jews") as distinguished from the Ἑβραῖοι (Hebraioi, "Hebraic Jews") and the Ἕλληνες (Hellēnes, "Greeks"), see commentary at 6:1 and 9:29.

2. The famine relief for Jerusalem

11:27–30

27During this time some prophets came down from Jerusalem to Antioch. 28One of them, named Agabus, stood up and through the Spirit predicted that a severe famine would spread over the entire Roman world. (This happened during the reign of Claudius.) 29The disciples, each according to his ability, decided to provide help for the brothers living in Judea. 30This they did, sending their gift to the elders by Barnabas and Saul.

27–28 Here Luke uses the connective "in those days" (en tautais de tais hēmerais; NIV, "during this time"), just as he does at 1:15 and 6:1, to link parts of his narrative. Now he tells of certain "prophets" who "came down from Jerusalem to Antioch." Among them was Agabus, with his dire prediction of impending famine in Jerusalem (cf. 21:10). The Jews believed that with the last of the writing prophets, the spirit of prophecy had ceased in Israel; but the coming Messianic Age would bring an outpouring of God's Spirit, and prophecy would again flourish. The early Christians, having experienced the inauguration of the Messianic Age, not only proclaimed Jesus to be the Mosaic eschatological prophet (cf. 3:22; 7:37) but also saw prophecy as a living phenomenon within the church (cf. also 13:1; 15:32; 21:9–10) and ranked it among God's gifts to his people next to that of being an apostle (cf. 1 Cor 12:28; Eph 4:11).

Agabus's prediction was of a "severe famine" affecting "the entire Roman world" (holēn tēn oikoumenēn), which took place, Luke notes, during the reign of the emperor Claudius (A.D. 41–54). The word oikoumenē (lit., "inhabited world") was commonly used in exaggerated fashion by Romans to refer to the empire (Lat., orbis terrarum) and probably has this meaning here. Although there is no record of a single famine that ravaged the whole empire in the time of Claudius, various Roman historians referred to a series of bad harvests and famine conditions during his reign (cf. Suetonius Vita

Claudius 18:2; Tacitus *Annales* 12.43; Dio Cassius *History of Rome* 60.11; Orosius *History* 7.6.17). Josephus tells of a particularly severe famine in Palestine about A.D. 45–47 (Antiq. XX, 51–53 [ii.5]; perhaps also idem, III, 320–21 [xv.3], if the mention of Claudius is not in error).

Josephus's reference to a famine is in his account of the conversion to Judaism of Helena and Izates, the queen mother and the king of Adiabene in northern Mesopotamia, who provided food and money for the people of Jerusalem. As Josephus tells it, Helena's coming to Jerusalem as a pilgrim sometime around A.D. 46

> was very advantageous for the people of Jerusalem, for at that time the city was hard pressed by famine and many were perishing from want of money to purchase what they needed. Queen Helena sent some of her attendants to Alexandria to buy grain for large sums and others to Cyprus to bring back a cargo of dried figs. Her attendants speedily returned with these provisions, which she thereupon distributed among the needy. She has thus left a very great name that will be famous forever among our whole people for her benefaction (Antiq. XX, 51–52 [ii.5]).

Josephus goes on to say, "When her son Izates learned of the famine, he likewise sent a great sum of money to the leaders of the Jerusalemites [*tois prōtois tōn Hierosolymitōn*]. The distribution of this fund to the needy delivered many from the extremely severe pressure of famine" (Antiq. XX, 53; [ii.5]; cf. b *Baba Bathra* 11a, which refers to Izates's successor Monobazus as also supplying such famine relief, probably also to Jerusalem, "in years of scarcity" later on).

29–30 Similarly, though doubtless not so extravagantly, the Christians (*hoi mathētai*; lit., "the disciples") at Antioch, in response to Agabus's prophecy, decided to provide help for their fellow believers at Jerusalem, whose plight as a minority group within the nation would be particularly difficult at such a time. Ramsay speculated that the arrangements for such a mission must have taken a good deal of time and the relief given only as the famine worsened, because "the manner of relief must, of course, have been by purchasing and distributing corn, for it would have shown criminal incapacity to send gold to a starving city; and the corn would not be given by any rational person until the famine was at its height" (*St. Paul the Traveller*, p. 50). But the text does not demand this reading, nor does the analogy of the action of Helena and Izates require it. We are not given any details as to how the relief was collected, how it was administered, or when it was delivered. All we know from the text is that it was an expression of Christian concern by the Antioch church "for the brothers (*adelphois*) living in Judea" and was taken by Barnabas and Saul "to the elders" (*pros tous presbyterous*) of the Jerusalem church. And while the term "elders" (*presbyteroi*) may indicate that at that time the Jerusalem church had a structured presbyterate, here we should probably understand it as somewhat parallel to Josephus's "leaders" (*prōtoi*) (in Antiq. XX, 53 [ii.5]) and in line with Luke's nontechnical usage of "disciples" (*mathētai*) in v.29.

The "famine visit" of Barnabas and Saul to Jerusalem of 11:27–30 should probably be dated about A.D. 46. That date, even though tentative and general, presents commentators with their first real date for working out a Pauline chronology (cf. comments on the reign of Herod Agrippa I at 12:1–23, the Edict of Claudius at 18:2, and Gallio's proconsulate at 18:12). But as to how we are to reconcile this date with what Paul tells us in his letters and how we are to fit it into an overall chronology depends largely on the answer to the conundrum of the relation of Paul's two Jersualem visits mentioned in Galatians to his three Jerusalem visits reported in Acts. While most accept the correlation of Galatians 1:18–20 with Acts 9:26–29 and count that as the first visit, many feel that Galatians 2:1–10 should be identified with the Jerusalem Council of Acts 15. But this makes Acts 11:27–30 either a fabrication on Luke's part or a doublet of the Acts 15 material placed here by Luke for his own purposes.

The issues are complex and have far-reaching consequences. (See comments on Acts 15 in the context of 12:25–16:5.) Here it is sufficient to say that the simplest solution that provides the most satisfactory and convincing reconstruction and leaves the fewest loose ends is that Galatians 2:1–10 corresponds to the famine visit of Acts 11:27–30. On such an understanding, and taking the temporal conjunctions "then" (*epeita*) of Galatians 1:18 and 2:1 as referring back to Saul's conversion (A.D. 33, allowing some flexibility in rounding off the years), his first visit to Jerusalem can be dated about 36, and his famine visit some fourteen years after his conversion, about 46. On such a basis, the reference in Galatians 2:2 to Saul's having gone to Jerusalem "in response to a revelation" (*kata apokalypsin*) should probably be related to Agabus's prophecy of 11:28.

Notes

27 On "going down from Jerusalem," see the comments and note at 8:5.

28 The Western text begins συνεστραμμένων δὲ ἡμῶν (*synestrammenōn de hēmōn*, "And while we were gathered together"), with the ἡμῶν (*hēmōn*, "we"; lit., "our") due either to the acceptance of the tradition that Luke was a native of Syrian Antioch (see Introduction: Authorship) or to an identification of our author with Lucius of Cyrene in 13:1.

On the cessation and revival of prophecy in Jewish thought, see the comments and note at 2:4.

C.C. Torrey (p. 21) conjectured that ὅλην τὴν οἰκουμένην (*holēn tēn oikoumenēn;* "the entire Roman world," NIV) mistakenly translates the Aram. כל אַרְעָא (*kol 'ar'ā'*, "all the land"), and therefore the famine should be understood to have been restricted to the land of Palestine. But 11:19–30, as we have noted, appears in other respects not to be based on a written, Semitic source.

The Byzantine text (TR, KJV) reads Κλαυδίου Καίσαρος (*Klaudiou Kaisaros,* "Claudius Caeser").

D. *Divine Intervention on Behalf of the Jerusalem Church* (12:1–23)

With its acceptance of the conversion of "half-Jews" in Samaria, a Gentile centurion and his friends at Caesarea, and Gentiles who were only loosely associated with the synagogue at Antioch of Syria, the Jerusalem church was straining the forms and commitments of Judaism almost to the breaking point. There was hardly any further room for expansion within the traditions of Judaism, and soon the Christian mission would break out of those limits to embrace a direct mission to the Gentile world. In fact, the preparations for this had begun with Saul's conversion and with his early attempts to carry on a Christian ministry, even though not till later would he formally espouse and explicitly carry out a direct mission to Gentiles.

But before Luke turns to his portrayal of the Christian mission to the Gentile world, he takes the opportunity of presenting two further glimpses of God's working on behalf of the believers at Jerusalem. Just as his mentor Paul, while arguing for the legitimacy of a direct outreach to Gentiles, continued to characterize Jewish Christianity as "the church of God" (Gal 1:13; cf. 1 Thess 2:14) and to respect God's ongoing activity within the Jewish world (cf. Rom. 9–11), so Luke seems desirous of making the point that, though he is about to portray the advances of the gospel within the Gentile world, it should not be assumed that God was finished with Jerusalem Christianity or that his activity within the Jewish world was finished. Luke has portrayed the Christian mission to the Jewish world that had its center at Jerusalem. Now he prepares to present the Christian mission to the Gentiles as a kind of ellipse emanating from that same center. Before doing so, however, Luke gives us two further vignettes relating to God's intervention on behalf of the Jerusalem church so that his readers might more fully appreciate the fact that while the Christian mission within the Jewish world and the Christian mission to the Gentiles differed, in many ways they possessed a common focus and also had many similarities. Or, like the analogy of a circle and ellipse that share a common center but extend to somewhat different areas, they should be seen as complementary and not contradictory. Divine activity on behalf of the Gentiles, Luke appears to be insisting, does not mean divine inactivity on behalf of Jewish Christians or unconcern for Jews—which is a heresy that has often afflicted Gentile Christians and resulted in horrendous calamities.

1. *The deliverance of Peter*

12:1–19a

¹It was about this time that King Herod arrested some who belonged to the church, intending to persecute them. ²He had James, the brother of John, put to death with the sword. ³When he saw that this pleased the Jews, he proceeded to seize Peter also. This happened during the Feast of Unleavened Bread. ⁴After arresting him, he put him in prison, handing him over to be guarded by four squads of four soldiers each. Herod intended to bring him out for public trial after the Passover.

⁵So Peter was kept in prison, but the church was earnestly praying to God for him.

⁶The night before Herod was to bring him to trial, Peter was sleeping between two soldiers, bound with two chains, and sentries stood guard at the entrance. ⁷Suddenly an angel of the Lord appeared and a light shone in the cell. He struck Peter on the side and woke him up. "Quick, get up!" he said, and the chains fell off Peter's wrists.

⁸Then the angel said to him, "Put on your clothes and sandals." And Peter did so. "Wrap your cloak around you and follow me," the angel told him. ⁹Peter followed him out of the prison, but he had no idea that what the angel was doing was really happening; he thought he was seeing a vision. ¹⁰They passed the first and second guards and came to the iron gate leading to the city. It opened for them by itself, and they went through it. When they had walked the length of one street, suddenly the angel left him.

¹¹Then Peter came to himself and said, "Now I know without a doubt that the Lord sent his angel and rescued me from Herod's clutches and from everything the Jewish people were anticipating."

¹²When this had dawned on him, he went to the house of Mary the mother of John, also called Mark, where many people had gathered and were praying. ¹³Peter knocked at the outer entrance, and a servant girl named Rhoda came to answer the door. ¹⁴When she recognized Peter's voice, she was so overjoyed she ran back without opening it and exclaimed, "Peter is at the door!"

¹⁵"You're out of your mind," they told her. When she kept insisting that it was so, they said, "It must be his angel."

¹⁶But Peter kept on knocking, and when they opened the door and saw him, they were astonished. ¹⁷Peter motioned with his hand for them to be quiet and de-

scribed how the Lord had brought him out of prison. "Tell James and the brothers about this," he said, and then he left for another place.

[18]In the morning, there was a great commotion among the soldiers. "What could have happened to Peter?" they asked. [19]After Herod had a thorough search made for him and did not find him, he cross-examined the guards and ordered that they be executed.

1–4 The narrative of Peter's miraculous deliverance from prison and death really begins at v.5, with Luke's favorite connecting phrase *men oun* signifying its start (see comments and note on 1:6). Probably Luke's source material for his narrative covered what we now have in vv.5–19, to which he has added an historical introduction in vv.1–4.

The narrative is introduced as having taken place "about this time," which probably refers to the events of the famine visit to Jerusalem of 11:27–30. But if the famine visit occurred about A.D. 46 and Herod Agrippa I died in A.D. 44 (as will be seen below), 11:27–30 and the material of 12:1–23 are chronologically reversed. Yet we must remember that ancient historians frequently grouped their materials *per species*, without always being concerned about chronology (see Introduction: Historical Writing in Antiquity). So Luke having begun his account of Christianity in Antioch by speaking of the founding of the church tied into that narrative a further vignette about the famine relief Antiochan believers sent to Jerusalem. As a result, his full account of the church at Antioch of Syria (11:19–30) reaches back behind Peter's ministries at Lydda, Joppa, and Caesarea at its start (cf. 11:19) and goes beyond the accounts of Peter's deliverance and Herod Agrippa I's death at its close. It is because he is working *per species* within a broad chronological framework that Luke begins the narrative of Peter's deliverance with just a general temporal statement. If we were to seek more chronological exactness, we might say that the events of chapter 12 occurred between those of 11:19–26 and 11:27–30. But Luke seems to have wanted to close his portrayals of the Christian mission within the Jewish world (2:42–12:24) with two vignettes having to do with God's continued activity on behalf of the Jerusalem church. Therefore he closes with chapter 12 and uses "about this time" to connect it with what has already been presented.

The Herod of Acts 12 is Agrippa I (born in 10 B.C.), the grandson of Herod the Great and the son of Aristobulus. After his father's execution in 7 B.C., he was sent with his mother Bernice to Rome, where he grew up on intimate terms with the imperial family. In his youth he was something of a playboy, and in A.D. 23 he went so heavily into debt that he had to flee to Idumea to escape his creditors. Later he received asylum at Tiberias and a pension from his uncle Herod Antipas, with whom, however, he eventually quarreled. In 36 he returned to Rome but offended the emperor Tiberius and was imprisoned. At the death of Tiberius in 37, he was released by the new emperor Caligula and received from him the northernmost Palestinian tetrarchies of Philip and Lysanias (cf. Luke 3:1) and the title of king. When Herod Antipas was banished in 39, Agrippa received his tetrarchy as well. And at the death of Caligula in 41, Claudius, who succeeded Caligula and was Agrippa's friend from youth, added Judea and Samaria to his territory, thus reconstituting for him the entire kingdom of his grandfather Herod the Great, over which he ruled till his death in 44.

Knowing how profoundly the masses hated his family, Herod Agrippa I took every opportunity during his administration in Palestine to win their affection. When in Rome, he was a cosmopolitan Roman. But when in Jerusalem, he acted the part of an observant Jew. So careful were both he and his wife Cypros regarding Jewish traditions that a Gemara says of them: "The King is guided by the Queen, and the Queen is guided by

Gamaliel" (b *Pesahim* 88b). In the pilgrim procession bearing firstfruits into the temple, the Mishnah records that "when they reached the Temple Mount even Agrippa the king would take his basket on his shoulder and enter in as far as the Temple Court" (M *Bikkurim* 3:4). And of the Festival of Tabernacles (*Sukkoth*) in A.D. 41, in accordance with the biblical prescription given in Deuteronomy 17:14–20 ("The Law of the Kingdom") that the king was to read in public, the Mishnah says,

> King Agrippa received it standing and read it standing [signs of respect, contrary to the practice of previous Roman rulers], and for this the Sages praised him. And when he reached "Thou mayest not put a foreigner over thee which is not thy brother" [Deut 17:15], his eyes flowed with tears [because of his Edomite ancestry]; but they called out to him, "Our brother art thou! Our brother art thou! Our brother art thou!" (M *Sotah* 7.8).

Such a Jewish show of affection for a Herodian may seem inconceivable. In reality, however, it was the response of a grateful nation for benefits received.

In A.D. 40 Agrippa had cajoled Caligula not to carry out his insane plan of erecting a statue to himself as a god in the Jerusalem temple and had intervened on behalf of the Jews in Alexandria for their more humane treatment. When Judea came under his jurisdiction, he moved the seat of government from Caesarea to Jerusalem. This established the holy city in Jewish eyes as the political capital of the country. He also began to rebuild the city's northern wall and fortifications, thus enhancing both its security and its prestige (cf. Jos. Antiq. XIX, 326–27 [vii.2]; War II, 218 [xi.6]; V, 151–62 [iv.2]). Many Jews viewed these days as the inauguration of a better era—perhaps even the Messianic Age—as their grief and prayers during Agrippa's fatal illness at Caesarea suggest (cf. Jos Antiq. XIX, 349 [viii.2]). Agrippa himself, however, seems to have been primarily interested in a successful reign through the cooperation of loyal subjects, and his expressions of concern for the people and their religion were probably more pragmatically based than sincere.

Agrippa's policy was the Pax Romana through the preservation of the status quo. He supported the majority within the land and ruthlessly suppressed minorities when they became disruptive. He viewed Jewish Christians as divisive and felt their activities could only disturb the people and inflame antagonisms. So he arrested some of the believers in Jesus and had James, one of Jesus' original disciples, beheaded by the sword. According to *Mishnah Sanhedrin* 9.1, murderers and apostates ("people of an apostate city") were to be beheaded—a form of execution probably ordered by Agrippa to show his Jewish subjects his evaluation of the embryonic Christian movement. Finding that this pleased the Jewish leaders, he then took Peter during Passover Week ("the Feast of Unleavened Bread") and imprisoned him till he could bring him out for public trial after the Jewish holy days. While in prison, the apostle was guarded by "four squads of four soldiers each," probably on shifts of three hours each (cf. Vegetius *De Re Mili* 3.8), with two soldiers chained to him on either side and two standing guard at the inner entrance to the prison (cf. v.6). Evidently Agrippa planned to make of Peter a spectacle and warning at a forthcoming show trial. And he did not want to be embarrassed by Peter's escape.

5 Most commentators speculate that the place of Peter's imprisonment was somewhere within the Fortress of Antonia, which overlooked the temple area to the north and had entrances to both the temple courts and the city (cf. BC, 4: 136). Of more importance to Luke, for whom prayer is the natural atmosphere of God's people and the normal context for divine activity (cf. 1:14, 24; 2:42; 4:24–31; 6:4, 6; 9:40; 10:2, 4, 9, 31; 11:5; 13:3; 14:23; 16:25; 22:17; 28:8), is the fact that "the church was earnestly praying to God for [Peter]."

6–9 On the night before Agrippa's show trial, "an angel of the Lord" appeared in the apostle's cell and began to take charge of affairs. The designation "angel of the Lord" (*angelos kyriou*) stems from the LXX and signifies God himself in his dealings with men (cf. Exod 3:2, 4, 7, passim; Matt 1:20, 24; 2:13, 19; 28:2; Luke 1:11; 2:9; Acts 5:19; 8:26; 12:23 [also *angelos* in 7:30, 35, 38; 12:11; 27:23]). The angel awoke Peter, and as he stirred, the chains by which he was bound fell from his wrists. Then the angel, like a parent with a child awakened from sound sleep, carefully instructed the groggy apostle to get dressed. Then he ordered Peter to follow him, and they left the cell. But Peter, too sleepy to grasp the reality of what was happening, thought he was dreaming.

Herod Agrippa I had planned to try Peter as the leader of the divisive minority in Palestine that identified itself with the crucified Jesus of Nazareth and then execute him as a warning to other followers of Jesus to stop their activities. Usually a prisoner was chained to only one guard (cf. Seneca *Epistulae* 5.7); but in view of Agrippa's intentions, the guard was doubled. The Christians in Jerusalem understood Agrippa's intentions because he had earlier imprisoned some of them and killed James the son of Zebedee. Neither Peter nor his fellow believers were in any doubt about what the king had in mind. It was a crisis of great magnitude for the life of the early Christian community at Jerusalem. But while God does not promise deliverance from persecution and death, at crucial times he often steps in to act for the honor of his name and the benefit of his people. In fact, Luke insists, this was what now happened: God acted directly in delivering Peter from Agrippa's designs. Peter's deliverance must be ascribed entirely to God, for it was in no way due to the apostle's own efforts or those of the Christian community —apart, of course, from their prayers.

10–11 Passing the two guards at the inner entrance to the prison, Peter and the angel came to the main iron gate, which opened automatically (*automatē*) as they approached. Then the angel left Peter a block away from the prison. Stories about prison doors opening of their own accord and of miraculous escapes from imprisonment were popular in the ancient world, and the form of such legends undoubtedly influenced to some extent Luke's narrative here (cf. comments on 5:19). But as C.S.C. Williams notes, "The 'form' of an escape story cannot of course decide the problem of its historicity" (p. 148). Some may prefer to believe, as did F.C. Burkitt, "that Peter's escape was contrived by human means"—"that some human sympathizer [unbeknown to Peter himself or the early church] was at work, who had drugged the guards and bribed the turnkey" (pp. 103–4). That the story is not told in much detail may lead to such a conjecture. God certainly has acted in history on behalf of his people through human agents. Yet for Peter, standing there alone in the street and brought to his senses by the cool night air, there was no doubt that "the Lord sent his angel and rescued [him] from Herod's clutches and from everything the Jewish people were anticipating." So quite apart from philosophical skepticism, there is no reason to doubt that his deliverance was miraculous and not arranged by human means.

12 Realizing where he was and the danger he faced if Herod's soldiers should find him there, Peter went to one of the meeting places of the early Jerusalem Christians, the home of Mary, John Mark's mother. A number of people were praying there. Luke's identification of Mary by her son implies that her son's name was better known to his readers than hers (cf. Mark 15:21, 40). It also suggests that the John Mark referred to here was the one who was with Paul and Barnabas on a portion of the first missionary journey (Acts 13:5, 13)—viz., a cousin of Barnabas (Col 4:10) who returned with him to Cyprus after the falling out with Paul (Acts 15:37–39), a later companion of both Paul (Col 4:10; Philem 24) and Peter (1 Peter 5:13), and the writer of the second Gospel.

13–16 Mary's house must have been of some size, with a vestibule opening onto the street, an intervening court, and rear living quarters. Not only were "many people gathered" there, but Luke says that Peter was knocking at the door of the vestibule (*tēn thyran tou pylōnos*; NIV, "the outer entrance") and Rhoda the servant girl was rushing back and forth for joy. The unfolding scene is one of confusion and joyful humor, which must have led to hilarity every time it was repeated among the early believers. There was Peter's knocking, becoming more and more urgent as he beat on the door; Rhoda's losing her wits for joy and forgetting to open the door; the Christians' refusal to believe it was Peter, even though they had just been praying for him; their belittling of Rhoda ("You are out of your mind" [*mainē*]) and of her saying she had heard Peter's voice at the door ("It must be his angel"); Rhoda's frantic persistence; and their utter astonishment when they finally opened the door and let him in.

17 On entering, Peter "motioned with his hand for them to be quiet." This was not the time for celebration—what with Herod's soldiers doubtless prowling about the streets and the city silent in sleep. Peter had to be moving on to escape being recaptured. So he gave them a quick summary of "how the Lord had brought him out of prison" and instructed them to tell James and the other brothers what had happened. And with that, Luke tells us, Peter left "for another place."

The James mentioned here is, of course, James the Lord's brother, not James the brother of John and son of Zebedee who was earlier beheaded by Herod Agrippa I (cf. v.2). Undoubtedly Peter was the leader of the first Christian community at Jerusalem, as the early chapters of Acts presuppose. But from the mid-thirties through the mid-forties James seems also to have exercised some form of administrative leadership along with Peter and the apostles (cf. Gal 1:19; 2:9), and he presided at the Jerusalem Council of A.D. 49 (cf. 15:13–21). Later still Luke refers to him as head of the Jerusalem church (cf. 21:18). In 62 he was martyred by the younger Ananus (cf. Jos. Antiq. XX, 200 [ix.1]). Luke does not state how or why the shift in leadership of the church from Peter to James came about, nor what qualified James for such a position. Apparently it had to do with (1) external pressures on the Jerusalem congregation to demonstrate its Jewishness and (2) the need within the church for someone who could lead the growing number of scrupulously minded converts drawn from Pharisaic and priestly backgrounds (perhaps Essene; cf. comments on 6:7).

After the expulsion of the Hellenists, both the Jews and the Jewish Christians in Jerusalem felt the need for the community of believers in Jesus to demonstrate more actively their continued respect for the traditions of Israel. Peter and his fellow apostles, all being 'am hā 'āreṣ (Jewish Christians; lit., "people of the land"), would hardly have been the best ones to head such an endeavor—in fact, Peter's association with the Samaritans and Cornelius may have made him particularly suspect in certain quarters. It is therefore not improbable that as the pressures mounted, the Jerusalem church found it advantageous to be represented in its leadership by one whose legal as well as spiritual qualifications were above reproach. Such a person, it seems, was James, the Lord's brother, whom Hegesippus (a second-century Christian of Aelia, the renamed Gentile Jerusalem) described as a Pharisee and ascetic so pious that his knees were like camel's knees from frequent praying in the temple on behalf of the people (cf. Epiphanius *Contra Haereses* 78.6–7; Eusebius *Ecclesiastical History* 2.1.23; 23.4–7) and who was not only physically related to Jesus but also had seen the risen Jesus (1 Cor 15:7).

Furthermore, the missionary activities of Peter and the apostles would require some kind of arrangement for the continuance of administrative authority at Jerusalem. That the apostles considered themselves to be something other than ecclesiastical functionaries has already been shown in Acts 6:2–6. And it is not too difficult to imagine that with the dispersion of the Hellenists and the Seven who were appointed to supervise the distribution of food within the community, the church turned to James for administrative leadership—not only, as has been suggested, to demonstrate its Jewishness, but also to free the apostles for their "ministry of the word." The writings of postapostolic Jewish Christianity speak of Peter and his fellow apostles remaining in Jerusalem for twelve (or seven) years and after that engaging in missionary activity throughout the Jewish Diaspora (cf. Clement of Alexandria *Stromata* 6.5.43, citing an earlier but now extinct work called *The Preaching of Peter; Acts of Peter* 5; *Clementine Recognitions* 1.43; 9.29; note also 1 Cor 9:5; 1 Clement 5; Justin *Apology* 1.50.12; *Dialogue* 53.5; 109.1; 110.2). Many of the details of this tradition are undoubtedly apocryphal. Yet the fact that the apostles carried on missionary activities away from Jerusalem and outside Palestine cannot be doubted. For these reasons administrative leadership within the Jerusalem church seems to have gradually shifted to James, the Lord's brother.

The mention of "another place" to which Peter went after his miraculous deliverance has led to all kinds of comment. Roman Catholicism has frequently asserted that this place was Rome, where, on the basis of the apocryphal Acts of Peter, the Clementine Recognitions, and the Clementine Homilies, it has been claimed that Peter arrived in A.D. 42 and remained for twenty-five years. This assertion, however, is improbable and has been abandoned by many Roman Catholic scholars today. If 12:1–19 precedes 9:32–11:18 chronologically, as some insist (see comments on 12:1), this other place may refer to the maritime plain of Palestine, with its cities of Lydda, Joppa, and Caesarea. But such a region, though geographically removed from Jerusalem, would hardly be separated from Herod Agrippa's jurisdiction. More likely Antioch of Syria is the place Luke had in mind—a place where Peter had fellowship with a mixed body of Jewish and Gentile believers till "certain men came from James," and where he suffered the rebuke of Saul of Tarsus (cf. Gal 2:11–21). Later on Peter appears at Jerusalem in connection with the Jerusalem Council (cf. 15:7–11, 14), though presumably only in transit.

18–19a In Roman law, a guard who allowed his prisoner to escape was subject to the same penalty the escaped prisoner would have suffered (cf. *Code of Justinian* 9.4.4). No wonder that in the morning when Peter's escape was discovered, "there was a great [*ouk oligos*; lit., 'not a little'] commotion among the soldiers." When Herod heard of Peter's escape, he instituted a search and cross-examined the guards. Frustrated by his lack of success, he ordered the guards "to be led away" (*apachthēnai*)—probably an idiom for being taken out to execution (as NIV; cf. Luke 23:26).

Notes

1 On Luke's use of μὲν οὖν (*men oun;* "so," "then"), see comments and note at 1:6.

3–4 Passover was celebrated on 14 Nisan, continuing on into the early hours of the fifteenth (cf. Jos. Antiq. III, 248–49 [x.5]). This was followed immediately by the Feast of Unleavened Bread on the fifteenth through the twenty-first. Popular usage merged the two festivals and treated them as one (τὸ πάσχα, *to pascha*), as, in fact, they were for practical purposes.

6 Commentators' statements to the effect that Peter slept "like a baby" or "calmly from a good conscience and with confidence in God" reflect pious imagination, not anything in the text. Nor does the text warrant speculation about the psychological state of the guards.

10 The Western text adds κατέβησαν τοὺς ἑπτὰ βαθμοὺς καί (*katebēsan tous hepta bathmous kai,* "went down the seven steps and") after the participle ἐξελθόντες (*exelthontes,* "went") and before the verb προῆλθον (*proēlthon,* "through"), which probably reflects a later tradition and not an original note of local color.

19a D clarifies the idiom ἀπαχθῆναι (*apachthēnai,* "to be led away") by substituting ἀποκταν-θῆναι (*apoktanthēnai,* "to be put to death").

---

2. *The death of Herod Agrippa I*

12:19b–23

> Then Herod went from Judea to Caesarea and stayed there a while. [20]He had been quarreling with the people of Tyre and Sidon; they now joined together and sought an audience with him. Having secured the support of Blastus, a trusted personal servant of the king, they asked for peace, because they depended on the king's country for their food supply.
> [21]On the appointed day Herod, wearing his royal robes, sat on his throne and delivered a public address to the people. [22]They shouted, "This is the voice of a god, not of a man." [23]Immediately, because Herod did not give praise to God, an angel of the Lord struck him down, and he was eaten by worms and died.

Peter had been miraculously delivered from prison and death, but the tyrant Herod Agrippa was still at large, continuing his oppression of the church. Therefore Luke gives us a second scene in his account of God's intervention on behalf of the Jerusalem church. Luke does this not only to show how far-reaching this intervention was but also to reinforce by a second witness the theme of God's continued interest in Jewish Christianity (cf. comments in introduction to Acts 2:42–12:24).

19b–20 The situation Luke describes in these verses is not entirely clear. Caesarea, with its excellent manmade harbor (see comments on 10:1), was still nominally the provincial capital of Palestine. Tyre and Sidon were important Phoenician seaport cities incorporated into the Roman Empire about 20 B.C. There is nothing in Josephus about any trouble between Caesarea and the seaports to the north at this time, though competition for trade between them was probably always fierce and the cities of the Phoenician seaboard were heavily dependent on Galilee for much of their food supply. Nevertheless, whatever the cause, Herod became enraged with the people of Tyre and Sidon; and they, in turn, sent a delegation to ask for peace, using in some way the good offices of Blastus, King Agrippa's personal servant, for their purposes. By his use of *kai* ("and";

NIV, "then") and the participle *katelthōn* ("he went down") in v.19b, Luke implies that Agrippa left Jerusalem for Caesarea shortly after the Jewish Passover, perhaps because of frustration over Peter's escape.

21-23 Luke's account of Agrippa's death is paralleled by Josephus:

> After the completion of the third year of his reign over the whole of Judaea, Agrippa came to the city of Caesarea, . . . [where] he celebrated spectacles in honour of Caesar. On the second day of the spectacles, clad in a garment woven completely of silver so that its texture was indeed wondrous, he entered the theatre at daybreak. There the silver, illumined by the touch of the first rays of the sun, was wondrously radiant and by its glitter inspired fear and awe in those who gazed intently upon it. Straightway his flatterers raised their voices from various directions—though hardly for his good—addressing him as a god. "May you be propitious to us," they added, "and if we have hitherto feared you as a man, yet henceforth we agree that you are more than mortal in your being." The king did not rebuke them nor did he reject their flattery as impious. But shortly thereafter he looked up and saw an owl perched on a rope over his head. At once, recognizing this as a harbinger of woes just as it had once been of good tidings [cf. Antiq. XVIII, 195, 200 (vi.7)], he felt a stab of pain in his heart. He was also gripped in his stomach by an ache that he felt everywhere at once and that was intense from the start. Leaping up he said to his friends: "I, a god in your eyes, am now bidden to lay down my life, for fate brings immediate refutation of the lying words lately addressed to me. I, who was called immortal by you, am now under sentence of death. But I must accept my lot as God wills it. In fact I have lived in no ordinary fashion but in the grand style that is hailed as true bliss." Even as he was speaking these words, he was overcome by more intense pain. They hastened, therefore, to convey him to the palace; and the word flashed about to everyone that he was on the very verge of death. . . . Exhausted after five straight days by the pain in abdomen, he departed this life in the fifty-fourth year of his life and the seventh of his reign (Antiq. XIX, 343–50 [viii.2]).

These two accounts of Herod Agrippa's death—that of Luke and that of Josephus—differ enough from one another that neither can be dependent on the other. Luke sets the scene by referring to a quarrel between the king and the people of Tyre and Sidon, whereas Josephus speaks of a festival in honor of Caesar—either the quinquennial games inaugurated by Herod the Great at the founding of Caesarea to honor Augustus (cf. War. I, 415 [xxi.8]) or a festival instituted by Agrippa to honor his patron Claudius. Josephus makes no mention of a delegation from Tyre and Sidon. Furthermore, Luke's account, though more concise, gives us the physical cause of Agrippa's death—his being "eaten by worms." On the other hand, the two accounts are so similar in outline that we may assume that we know in general how and when Herod Agrippa I died.

Agrippa I's death occurred in A.D. 44, "after the completion of the third year of his reign over the whole of Judea" (Jos. Antiq. XIX, 343 [viii.2]; War II, 219 [xi.6]) and in the fourth year of the emperor Claudius (Jos. Antiq. XIX, 351 [viii.2]). Luke's reference to worms suggests an infection by intestinal roundworms (*Ascaris lumbricoides*), which grow as long as ten to sixteen inches and feed on the nutrient fluids in the intestines. Bunches of roundworms can obstruct the intestines, causing severe pain, copious vomiting of worms, and death. But whatever its physical details, both Luke and Josephus attribute Agrippa's death to the king's impiety and God's judgment. Moreover, Luke sees it as part of God's activity on behalf of the Jerusalem church.

Notes

19b Caesarea, though the titular provincial capital, was distinguished from Judea, the territory of the Jews—as Jerusalem was distinguished from Judea by some Jews. One significant difference between the two, however, is that one goes "down" ($\kappa\alpha\tau\epsilon\lambda\theta\grave{\omega}\nu$, *katelthōn*) to Caesarea from Judea, whereas one always goes "up" to Jerusalem (cf. comments and note at 8:5).

21 If the festival Josephus refers to was the one established by Herod the Great to be celebrated every five years on the anniversary of the founding of Caesarea, it probably occurred on 5 March (cf. Eusebius *Martyrs of Palestine* 11.30), a month or two before the Jewish Passover. This would place Agrippa's death ten or eleven months after Peter's deliverance, which is possible but not the impression one receives from Acts by the juxtaposition of these two events. It may be, however, that the festival was specially instituted by Agrippa I to honor Claudius on his birthday on 5 August (cf. Suetonius *Vita Claudius* 2.1) or before.

E. *A Summary Statement*

12:24

24But the word of God continued to increase and spread.

24 Luke's third panel on the Christian mission within the Jewish world ends with a summary statement comparable to the summaries that conclude the two preceding panels (cf. 6:7; 9:31). In its context, v.24 contrasts the progress of the gospel to the awful end of the church's persecutor Herod Agrippa I. More broadly, it implies that though in the remainder of Acts Luke's attention will be focused on the advances of the gospel to Gentiles, within the Jewish world "the word of God continued to increase and spread." In other words, God was still at work on behalf of the Jerusalem church and its ministry and was still concerned for his ancient people Israel.

Part II. The Christian Mission to the Gentile World (12:25–28:31)

In the Nazareth pericope (Luke 4:14–30), Luke has set the main themes for all that follows in Luke-Acts (cf. Introduction: The Structure of Acts). And in his presentation of the themes, two features of particular relevance stand out.

First, Luke presents Jesus' reading of Isaiah 61 as ending in mid-sentence at Isaiah 61:2a, thereby emphasizing grace ("to proclaim the year of the Lord's favor") without sounding the note of judgment ("and the day of vengeance of our God"). The omission of the judgment theme underscores the fact that the period of the gospel is a time characterized by grace, when the offer of deliverance is freely extended. To such a message of salvation, as they understood it, the residents of Nazareth responded positively. They failed to see any other implication in a message of free grace than God's messianic blessings poured out on Israel. So they spoke well of Jesus and commented favorably about his "gracious words" (Luke 4:22).

Second, Luke shows Jesus as indicating that the blessings of the Messianic Age were not intended for Israel alone but were for Gentiles as well as Jews—with the blessings of God's grace extending even to a Phoenician widow and a Syrian leper. Here was a repudiation of the Jewish concept of exclusive election. At it Jesus' townsmen were furious, driving him out of the synagogue and trying to do away with him.

414

Jesus' own earthly ministry was, of course, limited almost entirely to Jews. Luke's Gospel depicts only one healing of a centurion's servant (7:1–10) and two very brief contacts with Samaritans (9:52–55; 17:11–19). Moreover, it even omits the pericope about the Syro-Phoenician woman of Mark 7:24–30 (cf. Matt 15:21–28), though it contains several intimations of a later inclusion of Gentiles (cf. Luke 2:30–32; 3:6; 11:31; 13:29; 14:16–24). Also, in the first half of Acts, Luke presents the Jerusalem church's ministry as focused primarily on the Jewish world, with such outreaches as at Samaria, Caesarea, and Syrian Antioch understood as being in some ways exceptional. In effect, then, Luke has reserved for Paul the mission to the Gentiles that Jesus saw as inherent in the Servant theology of Isaiah 61. And now as Luke turns to a portrayal of how the gospel advanced among the Gentiles through Paul, he is also concluding his two-volume work by explicating Jesus' promise of the universal extension of God's grace. This Luke does (1) by building on what Jesus accomplished in his earthly ministry, death, and resurrection, as presented in his Gospel, and (2) by paralleling in its Gentile advances many features of the extension of God's grace within the Jewish world, as presented in the first half of Acts.

Panel 4—The First Missionary Journey and the Jerusalem Council (12:25–16:5)

Luke's fourth panel, the first of his three on the Christian mission to the Gentile world, embodies both Paul's first missionary journey and the Jerusalem Council. It concludes by telling how believers in Syria, Cilicia, and Galatia received the decisions of the council. Luke presents his material more thematically than geographically. Therefore, before closing with the summary in 16:5, he draws together several matters: (1) a report of events on the first missionary journey that led up to the Jerusalem Council; (2) an account of the debate and decisions reached at the council; and (3) a précis of how those decisions were received in areas of Gentile outreach. Most commentators have tended to treat these topics as practically separate and distinguishable. But to judge by the way Luke groups his material thematically within his various panels, he evidently meant these topics to be taken together and understood as having some integral relation to one another.

Taken by themselves, chapters 13 and 14 are sometimes viewed as a "filler" inserted by Luke to get from the situation of the church under Agrippa I to the Jerusalem Council—or, worse yet, relegated to the status of either a Lukan invention or some misplaced aspect of the Pauline mission that probably occurred later (e.g., Haenchen, *Acts of the Apostles*, pp. 400–404, 438–39; idem, "The Book of Acts as Source Material for the History of Early Christianity," Keck and Martyn, p. 271). But to look on these chapters in that way is to miss Luke's point about an important advance in the Christian mission and to be left without an adequate rationale for the Jerusalem Council.

In reality, however, Paul's first missionary journey began a radically new policy for proclaiming the gospel and making converts: namely, the legitimacy of a direct approach to the Gentile world apart from any prior commitments to Judaism on the part of the converts or any Jewish stance on the part of the missioners, and the legitimacy of Gentile Christians expressing their faith in Jesus apart from a Jewish lifestyle and distinctive Jewish practices (cf. 14:27b; 15:3). For the early church with its Jewish roots such a policy was revolutionary. It had enormous significance and many implications for the Christian movement that, not having been foreseen, required a full discussion and decision at the Jerusalem Council.

A. The Missioners Sent Out

12:25–13:3

> 25When Barnabas and Saul had finished their mission, they returned from Jerusalem, taking with them John, also called Mark.
> 13:1In the church at Antioch there were prophets and teachers: Barnabas, Simeon called Niger, Lucius of Cyrene, Manaen (who had been brought up with Herod the tetrarch) and Saul. 2While they were worshiping the Lord and fasting, the Holy Spirit said, "Set apart for me Barnabas and Saul for the work to which I have called them." 3So after they had fasted and prayed, they placed their hands on them and sent them off.

25 For the important textual question relating to the reading "Barnabas and Saul from Jerusalem," see Notes. Verse 25 reaches back behind the events of chapter 12 to connect 13:1–3 with the account of the Antioch church (11:19–30). And, indeed, 12:25–13:3 exhibits the same terse and somewhat colorless style of 11:19–30, which suggests a topical as well as a literary connection. So Luke uses v.25 as a kind of bridge statement before turning to whatever source materials he has for the missionary journey itself (cf. the connective *men oun* of 13:4). Thus he shifts his readers' attention from Jerusalem to Antioch of Syria and tells of John Mark's return with his cousin Barnabas (Col 4:10) and with Saul from Jerusalem to Antioch.

13:1 At Antioch there were five "prophets and teachers" in the church. The Greek particle *te* (untranslatable) was used in antiquity to connect word pairs, coordinate clauses, and similar sentences, thereby often distinguishing one set of coordinates from another. Probably, therefore, we should understand Barnabas, Simeon, and Lucius, who are introduced by the first *te*, as the prophets, and Manaen and Saul, who are grouped by the second *te*, as the teachers—with prophecy here understood to include "forthtelling" as well as "foretelling" and teaching having to do with showing OT relationships and implications.

We know Barnabas as a Levite from Cyprus who resided in Jerusalem and became a leading figure in the Jerusalem church (4:36–37; 9:27; 11:22–30). He was, as Luke tells us, "a good man, full of the Holy Spirit and faith" (11:24) and undoubtedly served as a channel for the truth of the gospel direct from the Jerusalem congregation. As for Lucius and Manaen, however, we know nothing certain apart from this verse. Simeon Niger (a Lat. loan word meaning "black") may have been from Africa. He was possibly the Simon from Cyrene of Luke 23:26, whose sons Alexander and Rufus were later known to be among the Christians at Rome (cf. Mark 15:21; also possibly Rom 16:13). If he was made to carry Jesus' cross on the way to Golgotha, what a story he would have had to tell! Lucius of Cyrene was frequently identified in the postapostolic period with Luke the evangelist and author of Acts. But the Roman praenomen Lucius (Luke) was common in the empire. And if Luke has refrained from identifying himself with Paul's missionary journeys, except through the occasional use of the pronoun "we," it is hardly likely that he would point to himself by name. Nor should Luke be equated with the Lucius of Romans 16:21. Manaen (the Gr. form of the Heb. Menahem) is identified as a *syntrophos* (lit., a "foster brother" or "intimate friend") of Herod the Tetrarch. This suggests that he had been raised as an adopted brother or close companion of Herod Antipas. As for Saul, we know him from 7:58–8:3; 9:1–30; and 11:25–30.

2–3 While Barnabas and Saul were carrying out their activities at Antioch, the Holy Spirit directed that they should be set apart for a special ministry. Luke says, "After they had fasted and prayed, they placed their hands on them and sent them off " (apelysan; lit., "released them" from their duties at Antioch). Luke's literary style in these verses is somewhat clipped, and we could wish that he had given us more details. Luke does not tell us how the Spirit made his will known, though we may assume that it was through a revelation given to one of the believers. Neither does he tell us the nature of the special ministry the two were set apart for, though from what follows it is obvious that we are meant to understand that it was to be a mission to Gentiles. Nor do we have the antecedent of the third person verbal suffix "they" (apelysan), and so we do not have the precise identification of the sentence's subject. Still, we may infer from the parallel usage in 15:2 (etaxan, "they appointed," where the antecedent is relatively clear from the context) and from the descriptions of early church government in 6:2–6 and 15:4–30 (cf. note on to plēthos ["the whole number"; NIV, "all"] at 6:2) that the whole congregation, together with its leaders, was involved in attesting the validity of the revelation received, laid hands on the missioners, and sent them out. This is confirmed by the reference to the whole church in 14:27. For just as it was the whole church that sent them out, so it was the whole church the missioners reported to on returning to Antioch. Nevertheless, however we view the details of their call and commission, ultimately, Luke insists, Barnabas and Saul were "sent on their way by the Holy Spirit" (13:4).

Notes

12:25 The reading Βαρναβᾶς καὶ Σαῦλος ὑπέστρεψαν εἰς Ἰερουσαλὴμ (Barnabas kai Saulos hypestrepsan eis Ierousalēm, "Barnabas and Saul returned to Jerusalem") is supported by ℵ B P and is certainly the "harder reading." On this reading, however, the further references to having "finished their mission" and "taking with them John, also called Mark" are obscure, for presumably Barnabas and Saul returned to Antioch after accomplishing their mission at Jerusalem and, presumably, John Mark grew up in Jerusalem and was taken to Antioch of Syria. A and P^{74}, however, read ἐξ Ἰερουσαλήμ (ex Ierousalēm, "from Jerusalem"). D substantially agrees, though with a change in preposition from ἐξ (ex, "from") to ἀπὸ (apo, "from"). Other texts, evidently attempting to solve this problem, read εἰς Ἀντιόχειαν (eis Antiocheian, "to Antioch"), ἐξ or ἀπὸ Ἰερουσαλὴμ εἰς Ἀντιόχειαν (ex or apo Ierousalēm eis Antiocheian, "from Jerusalem to Antioch"), or even εἰς Ἰερουσαλὴμ εἰς Ἀντιόχειαν (eis Ierousalēm eis Antiocheian, "to Jerusalem unto Antioch"). But while eis Ierousalēm is slightly better attested externally, taking account of the problems it raises internally and judging by the fact that Luke begins his fourth panel of material with this verse (which panel deals with the outreach of the gospel from Syrian Antioch), it is probably better to assume that eis Ierousalēm crept into the text at an early date either through a slip of a copyist's pen or a marginal gloss and that ex Ierousalēm was the original reading.

13:3 D inserts the nominative πάντες (pantes, "all") after the participle προσευξάμενοι (proseuxamenoi, "praying"), thereby clarifying an ambiguity that was evidently not felt to be a problem until the rise of a more structured ecclesiastical hierarchy in postapostolic times.

B. *The Mission on Cyprus and John Mark's Departure*

13:4–13

> [4]The two of them, sent on their way by the Holy Spirit, went down to Seleucia and sailed from there to Cyprus. [5]When they arrived at Salamis, they proclaimed the word of God in the Jewish synagogues. John was with them as their helper.
> [6]They traveled through the whole island until they came to Paphos. There they met a Jewish sorcerer and false prophet named Bar-Jesus, [7]who was an attendant of the proconsul, Sergius Paulus. The proconsul, an intelligent man, sent for Barnabas and Saul because he wanted to hear the word of God. [8]But Elymas the sorcerer (for that is what his name means) opposed them and tried to turn the proconsul from the faith. [9]Then Saul, who was also called Paul, filled with the Holy Spirit, looked straight at Elymas and said, [10]"You are a child of the devil and an enemy of everything that is right! You are full of all kinds of deceit and trickery. Will you never stop perverting the right ways of the Lord? [11]Now the hand of the Lord is against you. You are going to be blind, and for a time you will be unable to see the light of the sun."
> Immediately mist and darkness came over him, and he groped about, seeking someone to lead him by the hand. [12]When the proconsul saw what had happened, he believed, for he was amazed at the teaching about the Lord.
> [13]From Paphos, Paul and his companions sailed to Perga in Pamphylia, where John left them to return to Jerusalem.

The first major outreach of the gospel from Antioch soon encountered the false prophet Bar-Jesus in Cyprus, just as the first major outreach from Jerusalem ran afoul of Simon the sorcerer in Samaria (cf. 8:9–24). By the manner in which he narrates both events, Luke apparently wanted his readers to see the parallel. Moreover, not only does Luke seem to have been interested in this parallel between these two episodes, he was also interested in showing how great a step forward the mission on Cyprus really was— with its revolutionary implications for the Christian mission to Gentiles and its radical effect on the missioners themselves.

4 Having brought his readers back to Syrian Antioch and shown how Barnabas and Saul were directed to undertake a mission to Gentiles, Luke now begins the account of the missioners' outreach to Cyprus, Pamphylia, and the southern portion of Galatia. That his descriptions of events on this first missionary journey are fuller and more detailed than the description of the church at Antioch (cf. 11:19–30; 12:25–13:3) suggests that here Luke was working from written source materials. And he links his portrayal of the first missionary journey to his summary introduction (12:25–13:3) by his favorite connective *men oun*. Furthermore, his use of the personal pronoun *autoi* ("they") at 13:4 and 14 seems to signal some distinction in his source materials concerning the ministry on Cyprus (13:4–12) and the ministry at Antioch of Pisidia (13:14–52).

While the church confirms in its own experience the divine will, identifies itself with God's purposes and those whom he has called for specific tasks, and releases them from their duties for wider service (cf. v.3), it is God who by his Spirit is in charge of events and sends out his missioners. Thus being "sent on their way by the Holy Spirit," they went down to Seleucia on the Mediterranean and sailed from there to the island of Cyprus. Just why they thought of going to Cyprus first in carrying out their mandate we don't know. But Barnabas was from Cyprus (4:36); and knowing generally the will of God, he and Saul were ready to move from the known to the unknown.

Seleucia was the port city of Antioch of Syria, some sixteen miles west of Antioch and four or five miles northeast of the mouth of the Orontes River. It was founded by

Seleucus I Nicator, the first king of the Seleucid dynasty, about 300 B.C. in conjunction with the founding of Antioch. Cyprus was an island of great importance from very early times, being situated on the shipping lanes between Syria, Asia Minor, and Greece. In 57 B.C. it was annexed by Rome from Egypt and in 55 B.C. incorporated into the province of Cilicia. In 27 B.C. it became a separate province governed on behalf of the emperor Augustus by an imperial legate. In 22 B.C. Augustus relinquished its control to the senate, and, like other senatorial provinces, it was administered by a proconsul.

5 Leaving the mainland of Syria, the missionary party sailed to Salamis on the eastern coast of Cyprus, about 130 miles from Seleucia. Salamis was the most important city of the island and the administrative center for its eastern half, though the provincial capital was 90 miles southwest at Paphos. The population of Cyprus was dominantly Greek, but many Jews lived there as well (cf. Philo *Legatio ad Gaium* 282; Jos. Antiq. XIII, 284, 287 [x.4]). Thus Barnabas and Saul began their mission in the synagogues of the city, and John Mark was with them as their helper (*hypēretēs*). Jewish grave inscriptions and various papyri use the word *hypēretēs* in the sense of a synagogue attendant, as does Luke also in his Gospel (4:20). This has caused many to view John Mark's responsibilities within the missionary party as related to caring for the scrolls (the Scriptures, together with a possible "Sayings of Jesus" collection) and serving as a catechist for new converts. Yet in Luke 1:2 and Acts 26:16 Luke also uses the term more broadly to mean a servant of Christ and in Acts 5:22, 26 to designate members of the temple guard. Here it probably should be understood in its broader sense.

6-11 From Salamis, Barnabas and Saul traveled throughout the island of Cyprus, continuing to preach within the Jewish synagogues to both Jews and "God-fearing" Gentiles. But when they reached Paphos—or, more exactly, New Paphos, the Roman provincial capital seven miles northwest of the old Phoenician city of Paphos—their ministry definitely changed. At Paphos the Roman proconsul Sergius Paulus asked them to present their message before him. This was probably meant to be an official inquiry into the nature of what the missioners were proclaiming in the synagogues so that the proconsul might know how to deal with charges already laid against these wandering Jewish evangelists and head off any further disruptions within the Jewish communities. Like a "command performance," the invitation could not have been refused. But neither the proconsul nor the missioners could have anticipated what actually happened at the inquiry.

Luke describes Sergius Paulus as a man of discernment (*anēr synetos*; lit., an "intelligent," "sagacious," or "understanding man"), which he proved to be in accepting the Christian message. Possibly he was the Lucius Sergius Paulus known to have been one of the curators of the Tiber during the reign of Claudius (cf. *Corpus Inscriptionum Latinarum* 6.4.2, No. 31545). If so, he probably went to Cyprus as proconsul after his curatorship in Rome (cf. BC, 5:458). Within his court at Paphos was a certain Jewish sorcerer and false prophet named Bar-Jesus (*Bariēsou*, which is Aram. for "Son of Jesus" and comes from a Semitic root meaning "to be worthy"). In assuming to be the Jewish spokesman in opposition to these Christian evangelists, this man probably wanted to enhance his own reputation. While sorcery and magic were officially banned in Judaism, there were still Jews who practiced it, both under the guise of Jewish orthodoxy and as renegades (cf. Luke 11:19; Acts 19:13-16). Bar-Jesus is also called Elymas ("sorcerer," "magician," "fortune-teller"), which cannot be a translation of the name Bar-Jesus. There is some evidence in the Western text for the spellings Etymas or Hetoimas, both of which mean something like "to be ready" and are therefore partly parallel to the root meaning of Bar-Jesus, which is "to be worthy." If either Etymas or Hetoimas was originally in his text, Luke may have been referring to a Jewish magician of Cyprus named Atomos, who, according to Josephus, was employed by Felix to procure Azizus's wife Drusilla for himself (cf. Antiq. XX, 142 [vii.2]).

In all of Saul's activities thus far, nothing had happened to suggest that he was anything but "a Hebrew born of Hebrew parents" (cf. Phil 3:5). He was interested in an outreach to Gentiles but made no special appeal to them directly. Nor did he approach them as being on an equal footing with Jews or apart from the synagogue. Though his preaching aroused strong feelings within certain Jewish communities, it engendered no more ill will than had been directed against the other apostles before him. Here in the hall of the proconsul, however, Saul was in new surroundings as he presented his message before a leading member of the Roman world, a world he himself was a member of. As a Jew, he proudly bore the name of Israel's first king, Saul. As a Roman citizen (cf. 16:37–38; 25:10–12), he undoubtedly had two Roman names, a praenomen and a nomen, though neither is used of him in the NT. But as a Jew of the Diaspora, who must necessarily rub shoulders with the Gentile world at large, he also bore the Greek name Paul (*Paulos*, meaning "little"), which became his cognomen in the empire and was used in Gentile contexts. So at this point in his narrative Luke speaks of "Saul, who was also called Paul," and hereafter refers to him only by this name.

As the gospel was being proclaimed to Sergius Paulus, Bar-Jesus tried to divert the proconsul from the faith. But Paul turned on the sorcerer and pronounced a curse upon him. In highly biblical language—which was what Paul used for solemn adjurations and curses—he denounced Bar-Jesus as "a child of the devil," "an enemy of every thing that is right," one "full of all kinds of deceit and trickery," always "perverting the right ways of the Lord," and pronounced a curse of temporary blindness upon him. "Immediately," Luke tells us, "mist and darkness came over him, and he groped about, seeking someone to lead him by the hand."

12 The nature of the proconsul's response has often been debated, chiefly because the text says nothing about his being baptized when he believed. Ramsay suggested that for Luke "belief" was only the first step in a process of conversion, with the second being "turning to the Lord," and therefore our author's reference to his believing (*episteusen*) should not be taken to mean that at this time he became a Christian (*Trustworthiness of the New Testament*, p. 165). Lake and Cadbury, on the other hand, proposed that the missioners "may have mistaken courtesy for conversion" and warned their readers not to take Luke's words in v.12 too seriously (cf. BC, 4:147). But the statement that Sergius Paulus believed can hardly be taken with any less significance than Luke's use of the same word in 14:1; 17:34; and 19:18, where baptism is also not mentioned yet where we might well assume it was performed.

The conversion of Sergius Paulus was, in fact, a turning point in Paul's whole ministry and inaugurated a new policy in the mission to Gentiles—viz., the legitimacy of a direct approach to and full acceptance of Gentiles apart from any distinctive Jewish stance. This is what Luke clearly sets forth as the great innovative development of this first missionary journey (14:27; 15:3). Earlier Cornelius had been converted apart from any prior commitment to Judaism, and the Jerusalem church had accepted his conversion to Christ. But the Jerusalem church never took Cornelius's conversion as a precedent for the Christian mission and apparently preferred not to dwell on its ramifications. However, Paul, whose mandate was to Gentiles, saw in the conversion of Sergius Paulus further aspects of what a mission to Gentiles involved and was prepared to take this conversion as a precedent fraught with far-reaching implications for his ministry. It is significant that from this point on Luke always calls the apostle by his Greek name Paul and, except for 14:14; 15:12; and 15:25 (situations where Barnabas was more prominent), always emphasizes his leadership by listing him first when naming the missioners. For after this, it was Paul's insight that set the tone for the church's outreach to the Gentile world.

13 Verse 13 has puzzled many commentators. Pamphylia was a geographically small and economically poor province on the southern coast of Asia Minor, with the mountains of Lycia to the west, the foothills of Pisidia to the north, and the Taurus range to the east. It contained a mixed population and seems to have been as open to the gospel as any other province. Yet Luke gives us no account of evangelization in Perga or its environs at this time, though he expressly states that the missioners "preached the word in Perga" on their return to Syrian Antioch (14:25). And it was at Perga that John Mark left the group to return to Jerusalem.

The usual explanation for the missioners' initially bypassing Perga and moving on to Antioch of Pisidia is that Paul may have been ill with a case of malaria and that this forced redirecting the mission to gain the higher ground to the north. As for John Mark's departure, it is usually explained as a combination of homesickness, the rigors of travel, dissatisfaction with Paul's assuming leadership over Mark's cousin Barnabas, and unhappiness at leaving Cyprus so soon. But discussion among the missioners after Paphos and during their stay at Perga may very well have focused on the implications of Sergius Paulus's conversion for their ministry. And it can plausibly be argued that (1) the lack of preaching in Perga at this time was due primarily to uncertainty within the missionary party itself about the validity of a direct approach to and full acceptance of Gentiles and that (2) John Mark's departure was because he disagreed with Paul. While this is only conjecture, Mark may have been concerned about the effect news of a direct Christian mission to Gentiles would have in Jerusalem and on the church there and may have wanted to have no part in it. It was his return to the Christian community in Jerusalem that may originally have stirred the "Judaizers" in the church to action. Other explanations for Mark's defection are at best only partial and at worst rather thin. They fail to account for Paul's strong opposition to Mark in 15:37–39, an opposition that suggests that Mark's departure on this first missionary journey may have been for reasons more than merely personal.

Notes

---

4 On Luke's use of μὲν οὖν (men oun, "so," "then"), see comments on 1:6. In this fourth panel of material, note the pattern that develops here (after four verses of introduction), at 14:3 (after a two-verse introduction), at 15:3 (after another two-verse introduction), and in summary at 15:30 and 16:5.

12 In his chapter on "Sergius Paulus and His Relation to Christian Faith" (*Trustworthiness of the NT*), Ramsay, while distinguishing between belief and turning to the Lord in conversion, argued from other literary sources that Sergia Paulla, the proconsul's daughter, was a Christian, as was her son Gaius Caristanius Fronto, the first citizen of Pisidian Antioch to enter the Roman senate.

C. *At Antioch of Pisidia* (13:14-52)

At Pisidian Antioch the typical pattern of the Pauline ministry was established: an initial proclamation in the synagogue to Jews and Gentile adherents and then, when refused an audience in the synagogue, a direct ministry to Gentiles. This pattern is reproduced in every city visited by Paul with a sizable Jewish population—except Athens. As he later declares in Romans, there is no difference between Jews and Gentiles in condemnation (Rom 2:1-3:20) or access to God (Rom 3:21-31); so his ministry at Pisidian Antioch began to express this equality. Historically, of course, Israel had been tremendously advantaged (Rom 3:1-2; 9:4-5). Paul himself had a great desire to see his nation respond positively to Christ (Rom 9:1-3; 10:1). But while the synagogues were appropriate for beginning his ministry in the various cities, offering as they did an audience of both Jews and Gentiles theologically prepared for his message, the synagogues were not the exclusive sphere of Paul's activity. Since Jews and Gentiles stood before God on an equal footing, they could be appealed to separately if need be.

This understanding of the validity of a direct approach to Gentiles and their full acceptance as Christians is what Paul speaks of as "my gospel" (Rom 16:25; cf. Gal 1:11-2:10). It was a gospel not different in content from the earliest gospel (1 Cor 15:1-11) but a gospel distinct in strategy and broader in scope. By revelation, the nature of Paul's Christian ministry had been given; by providential action at the beginning of his first missionary journey, its specifics were spelled out. This was, as Paul says later on, "the mystery made known to me by revelation, ... which was not made known to men in other generations as it has now been revealed by the Spirit to God's holy apostles and prophets. This mystery is that through the gospel the Gentiles are heirs together with Israel, members together of one body, and sharers together in the promise in Christ Jesus" (Eph 3:2-6).

1. *A welcome extended at Antioch*

13:14-15

> [14]From Perga they went on to Pisidian Antioch. On the Sabbath they entered the synagogue and sat down. [15]After the reading from the Law and the Prophets, the synagogue rulers sent word to them saying, "Brothers, if you have a message of encouragement for the people, please speak."

14a Pisidian Antioch was in reality not in Pisidia but in Phrygia near Pisidia (cf. Strabo *Geography* 12. 577). But to distinguish it from the other Antioch in Phrygia it was popularly called "Antioch of Pisidia." It was founded by Seleucus I Nicator about 281 B.C. as one of the sixteen cities he named in honor of either his father or his son, both of whom bore the name Antiochus. It was situated a hundred miles north of Perga on a lake-studded plateau some thirty-six hundred feet above sea level. The foothills between Perga and Pisidian Antioch largely ruled out any extensive east-west traffic till one reached the plateau area, but following the river valleys one could move northward from the Pamphylia area. On the plateau Antioch stood astride the Via Sebaste, the Roman road from Ephesus to the Euphrates. The city had been incorporated into the expanded Roman province of Galatia in 25 B.C. by Augustus, who at that time imported into it some three thousand army veterans and their families from Italy and gave it the title of Colonia Caesarea. Antioch was the most important city of southern Galatia and included within its population a rich amalgam of Greek, Roman, Oriental, and Phrygian traditions. Acts tells us that it also had a sizeable Jewish population.

14b–15 Arriving at Pisidian Antioch, Paul and Barnabas entered the synagogue on the Sabbath. A typical first-century synagogue service would have included the Shema, the Shemoneh Esreh (the liturgy of "The Eighteen Benedictions," "Blessings," or Prayers"), a reading from the Law, a reading from one of the prophets, a free address given by any competent Jew in attendance, and a closing blessing (cf. SBK, 4.1:153–249; also BC, 4:148). The leader of the synagogue (*archisynagōgos*—equivalent to the Heb. *rōʼš hakᵉnēseṭ*, "head of the synagogue") took charge of the building and made arrangements for the services (Luke 8:41, 49). He was usually one of the elders of the congregation. Generally there was only one leader in each synagogue (cf 18:8, 17), but at times two or more made up the synagogue chapter. The office was sometimes held for life and passed on within a family, and occasionally the title was given honorifically to women and children. Perhaps Paul's dress proclaimed him a Pharisee and thereby opened the way for an invitation to speak.

Notes

---

14 Though τῶν σαββάτων (*tōn sabbatōn*, "Sabbaths") is a neuter plural, its meaning was singular (cf. 16:13; see also Mark 16:2 par.; John 20:1, 19; Acts 20:7; 1 Cor 16:2). Discussions regarding the missioners' being asked to speak only on their second visit to the synagogue, therefore, are without warrant.
15 On the address Ἄνδρες ἀδελφοί (*Andres adelphoi*, "Men, brothers") as a type of formal address used within first-century synagogues and among congregated Jews, see comments on 1:16.

---

2. Paul's synagogue sermon at Antioch

13:16–41

> [16]Standing up, Paul motioned with his hand and said: "Men of Israel and you Gentiles who worship God, listen to me! [17]The God of the people of Israel chose our fathers and made the people prosper during their stay in Egypt. With mighty power he led them out of that country [18]and endured their conduct forty years in the desert. [19]He overthrew seven nations in Canaan and gave their land to his people as their inheritance. [20]All this took about 450 years.
>
> "After this, God gave them judges until the time of Samuel the prophet. [21]Then the people asked for a king, and he gave them Saul son of Kish, of the tribe of Benjamin, who ruled forty years. [22]After removing Saul, he made David their king. He testified concerning him: 'I have found David son of Jesse a man after my own heart; he will do everything I want him to do.'
>
> [23]"From this man's descendants God has brought to Israel the Savior Jesus, as he promised. [24]Before the coming of Jesus, John preached repentance and baptism to all the people of Israel. [25]As John was completing his work, he said: 'Who do you think I am? I am not that one. No, but he is coming after me, whose sandals I am not worthy to untie.'
>
> [26]"Brothers, children of Abraham, and you God-fearing Gentiles, it is to us that this message of salvation has been sent. [27]The people of Jerusalem and their rulers did not recognize Jesus, yet in condemning him they fulfilled the words of

the prophets that are read every Sabbath. [28]Though they found no proper ground for a death sentence, they asked Pilate to have him executed. [29]When they had carried out all that was written about him, they took him down from the tree and laid him in a tomb. [30]But God raised him from the dead, [31]and for many days he was seen by those who had traveled with him from Galilee to Jerusalem. They are now his witnesses to our people.

[32]"We tell you the good news: What God promised our fathers [33]he has fulfilled for us, their children, by raising up Jesus. As it is written in the second Psalm:

" 'You are my Son;
today I have become your Father.'

[34]The fact that God raised him from the dead, never to decay, is stated in these words:

" 'I will give you the holy and sure blessings promised
to David.'

[35]So it is stated elsewhere:

" 'You will not let your Holy One see decay.'

[36]"For when David had served God's purpose in his own generation, he fell asleep; he was buried with his fathers and his body decayed. [37]But the one whom God raised from the dead did not see decay.

[38]"Therefore, my brothers, I want you to know that through Jesus the forgiveness of sins is proclaimed to you. [39]Through him everyone who believes is justified from everything you could not be justified from by the law of Moses. [40]Take care that what the prophets have said does not happen to you:

[41]" 'Look, you scoffers,
wonder and perish,
for I am going to do something in your days
that you would never believe,
even if someone told you.' "

Three missionary sermons of Paul are presented in Acts: the first here in 13:16–41 before the synagogue at Antioch of Pisidia, the second in 14:15–17 to Lystrans assembled outside the city gates, and the third in 17:22–31 before the Council of Ares at Athens. Each sermon as we have it is only a précis of what was said, for the longest in its present form would take no more than three minutes to deliver and the shortest can be read in thirty seconds or less. But there is enough in each account to suggest that whereas Paul preached the same gospel wherever he went, he altered the form of his message according to the circumstances he encountered.

16 When Jesus addressed the congregation at Nazareth, he read the lesson standing and then sat down to speak (cf. Luke 4:16, 20). Luke, however, portrays Paul as "standing" (*anastas*) to address the synagogue worshipers at Pisidian Antioch. Indeed, Philo speaks of members of the synagogue as standing (*anastas*) to address the congregation (*De Specialibus Legibus* 2.62). Greek orators also stood to speak. But probably the difference here is best explained by postulating that Jesus' address at Nazareth was an exposition of Isaiah 61, whereas Paul's at Pisidian Antioch was an exhortation not arising from the passages read that day from the Law or the Prophets (cf. I. Abrahams, *Studies in Pharisaism and the Gospels*, 2 vols. [Cambridge: Cambridge University, 1917], 1:9). In Paul's audience were both Jews and "God-fearing" Gentiles. So he addressed them: "Men of Israel" (*Andres Israēlitai*) and "you who worship God" (*hoi phoboumenoi ton*

424

theon, see also v.26). With a gesture of his hand (typically Jewish, though some commentators prefer to see it only as a Greek affectation inserted by Luke) and with his words, he invites them to listen to him.

17-22 Paul's exhortation begins with a résumé of Israel's history that emphasizes the pattern of God's redemptive activity from Abraham to David. It is an approach in line with Jewish interests and practices and can be paralleled by Stephen's defense before the Sanhedrin, by the argument of the Letter to the Hebrews, and by the underlying structure of Matthew's Gospel.

Highlighted in this résumé is a four-point confessional summary that for Jews epitomized the essence of their faith: (1) God is the God of the people of Israel; (2) he chose the patriarchs for himself; (3) he redeemed his people from Egypt, leading them through the wilderness; and (4) he gave them the land of Palestine as an inheritance (cf. G.E. Wright, *God Who Acts* [London: SCM, 1952], p. 76). To such a confessional recital, Jews often added God's choice of David to be king and the promises made to him and his descendants (cf. Pss 78:67-72; 89:3-4, 19-37). Paul proclaims these great confessional truths of Israel's faith, which speak of God's redemptive concern for his people and undergird the Christian message.

Of importance also is the fact that underlying Paul's treatment of David is 2 Samuel 7:6-16 (cf. J.W. Doeve, *Jewish Hermeneutics in the Synoptic Gospels and Acts* [Assen: Van Gorcum, 1954], p. 172; E. Lövestam, *Son and Saviour: A Study of Acts 13, 32-37*, tr. M.J. Petry [Lund: Gleerup, 1961], pp. 6-15), the passage that speaks of David's descendant as God's "son" (cf. 2 Sam 7:14, "I will be his father, and he will be my son") and was understood in at least one Jewish community to have messianic significance (cf. 4QFlor on 2 Sam 7:10-14). By anchoring Israel's kerygma in the messianically relevant "son" passage of 2 Samuel 7, Paul has begun to build a textual bridge for the Christian kerygma—which kerygma he will root in the messianic "son" passage of Psalm 2:7. And by drawing these two passages together on a *gᵉzērâh šāwâh* (verbal analogy) basis, he will draw together Israel's confession and the church's confession, thereby demonstrating both continuity and fulfillment.

23 Paul's Christian proclamation begins by announcing that God has brought forth the messianic Deliverer from David's line in the person of Jesus. The promise Paul alludes to is in Isaiah 11:1-16, a messianic passage of special import for Judaism because it speaks of the Messiah's descent from David ("A shoot will come up from the stump of Jesse; from his roots a Branch will bear fruit"), of his righteous rule, of his victories, and of the establishment of his kingdom.

24-25 The announcement of Jesus as the Messiah is put in the usual form of the apostolic proclamation, beginning with John the Baptist and his ministry (cf. Mark 1:2-8). John's preaching and baptism of repentance paved the way for the public ministry of Jesus. John was the forerunner of the Messiah, as he himself confessed: "I am not that one. No, but he is coming after me, whose sandals I am not worthy to untie" (cf. Luke 3:15-18).

26-31 As Paul comes to the heart of his sermon, he appeals respectfully and urgently for a hearing. "Men, brothers [*Andres adelphoi*], children of Abraham [*huioi genous Abraam*], and you God-fearing Gentiles [*hoi en hymin phoboumenoi ton theon*]," he says, "it is to us [*hēmin*] that this message of salvation has been sent." Then he presents a four-point Christian confession like that in 1 Corinthians 15:3-5: (1) Jesus was crucified;

(2) they "laid him in a tomb"; (3) "God raised him from the dead"; and (4) "for many days he was seen by those who had traveled with him from Galilee to Jerusalem," who are "now his witnesses to our people." Also significant is the clear note of fulfillment explicitly sounded in v.27 ("in condemning him they fulfilled the words of the prophets that are read every Sabbath") and implied throughout the whole presentation.

32-37 To support this four-point confession, and to demonstrate the fulfillment of what God has promised, Paul cites three OT passages fraught with messianic meaning for Christians and also for some Jews. The first is Psalm 2:7 ("You are my Son; today I have become your Father"), which Paul uses to bind together Judaism's confession and Christianity's confession by juxtaposing it with 2 Samuel 7:6-16 underlying vv.17-22. Both 2 Samuel 7:14 and Psalm 2:7 portray God as speaking of his "son," and it was undoubtedly this that brought the two passages together. Linking passages on the basis of their verbal analogies was common in Judaism. Furthermore, the evidence from Qumran suggests that these two passages were also brought together by the Dead Sea covenanters before Christianity and understood to have messianic relevance at Qumran, for 4QFlorilegium is a pesher commentary on 2 Samuel 7:10-14; Psalm 1:1; and Psalm 2:1-2 (though with the remainder of the scroll unfortunately broken off); and Psalm 2:7 has been found in the material designated 3Q2 (though without an accompanying commentary). Knowledge of how Judaism viewed these two passages is not as full as one might desire, though their union and treatment at Qumran is suggestive. But whatever is concluded as to the pre-Christian union and usage of these two passages, this seems clear: (1) Paul is bringing these two "son" passages together as the substructure of his argument in the synagogue at Pisidian Antioch; (2) in so doing he is joining OT redemptive history and the history of Jesus, understanding both as having messianic significance; and (3) his approach and method were highly appropriate to his synagogue audience.

In addition to his use of 2 Samuel 7:6-16 and Psalm 2:7 as the textual substructure for his argument and to support Christ's resurrection, Paul quotes in tandem Isaiah 55:3 ("I will give you the holy blessings promised to David") and Psalm 16:10 ("You will not let your Holy One see decay"), joining his biblical testimonia passages again on the $g^e z\bar{e}r\hat{a}h$ $\check{s}\bar{a}w\hat{a}h$ (verbal analogy) principle of verbal similarities between *ta hosia* ("the holy blessings") and *ton hosion* ("the Holy One"). The messianic treatment of Psalm 16:10 stemmed from the earliest Christian preaching at Pentecost (cf. 2:27), if not also from pre-Christian Judaism.

38-41 Having begun his sermon by addressing his audience as "Men of Israel and you Gentiles who worship God" (v.16), and having focused it by his appeal "Men, brothers, children of Abraham, and you God-fearing Gentiles" (v.26), Paul now uses the simpler and broader appellation "Men, brothers" (*andres adelphoi*, v.38; NIV, "my brothers") in his application and call to repentance. Through Jesus, Paul declares, are "forgiveness of sins" and "justification" for "everyone who believes." The awkward sentence construction of v.38b-39 in the Greek has led some interpreters (e.g., B.W. Bacon, *The Story of St. Paul* [Boston: Houghton Mifflin Co., 1904], p. 103, echoing various German commentators of his day) to read Paul as saying here that the Mosaic law could set free from some sins while belief in Jesus would do so for the rest. This, however, is not only incompatible with Paul's teaching in Galatians and Romans, it would also be inconceivable for Luke—or any Pauline disciple drawing up a précis of his preaching—to put it on his lips. Haenchen is right to insist that "anyone who, like H.J. Holtzmann, Harnack, Preuschen, Vielhauer, makes the author here develop a doctrine that an incomplete justification through the law is completed by a justification through faith imputes to him a venture into problems which were foreign to him" (*Acts of the Apostles*, p. 412, n.4). What we have in the application of Paul's message (despite its cumbersome expression in its précis form) are his distinctive themes of "forgiveness of sins," "justification," and "faith," which resound in this first address ascribed to him in Acts just as they do throughout his extant letters.

The call to repentance is cast in terms of Habakkuk 1:5, a passage we now know was accepted at Qumran as having messianic significance (cf. 1QHab) and which may also have been so considered more widely in other circles of Late Judaism. In effect, then, Paul concludes by warning the congregation that Habakkuk's words apply to all who reject God's working in Jesus' ministry and who refuse Jesus as the divinely appointed Messiah: "Look, you scoffers, wonder and perish, for I am going to do something in your days that you would never believe, even if someone told you."

Notes

16 On the appellation ἄνδρες Ἰσραηλῖται (*andres Israēlitai*, "men of Israel") and its synonymous relation to ἄνδρες ἀδελφοί (*andres adelphoi*, "men, brothers") of vv.15, 26, and 38, see comments on 1:16 and the note at 2:14.

On οἱ φοβούμενοι τὸν θεόν (*hoi phoboumenoi ton theon*) as used both here and at v.26 (though not of Cornelius) as a synonym of οἱ σεβόμενοι τὸν θεόν (*hoi sebomenoi ton theon*) to mean "God-fearers" or "Proselytes of the Gate," see comments on 10:2.

18 א B D read ἐτροποφόρησεν (*etropophorēsen*, "he put up with," or "he endured their conduct"), whereas A C* with P[74] read ἐτροφοφόρησεν (*etrophophorēsen*, "he cared for," "carried," or "bore" them). The Heb. word נָשָׂא (*nāsā'*) may mean both "to endure" and "to care for" and could be represented by either Gr. word (as it is in the various LXX texts of Deut 1:31, to which Paul is here alluding).

20 The Western text reads "about 450 years" after "gave them judges," suggesting that the judges reigned for 450 years rather than that the 450 years was the time between the Exodus and the possession of the land (as is preferable from א A B C).

The Western and Byzantine texts omit μετὰ ταῦτα (*meta tauta*, "after this," "after these things").

23 א A B E P, together with P[74], read ἤγαγεν (*ēgagen*, "he has brought"), whereas C and D read ἤγειρε (*ēgeire*, "he has raised up") in line with ἀναστήσας Ἰησοῦν (*anastēsas Iēsoun*, "raised up Jesus") of v.33.

26 On the appellation Ἄνδρες ἀδελφοό (*Andres adelphoi*, "Men, brothers") and the designation οἱ φοβούμενοι τὸν θεόν (*hoi phoboumenoi ton theon*, "God-fearing Gentiles"), see v.16 above.

C E P P[45] read ὑμῖν (*hymin*, "to you") rather than ἡμῖν (*hēmin*, "to us"), as seems preferable in א A B D P[74].

33 א A B C* D P[74] read τοῖς τέκνοις ἡμῶν (*tois teknois hēmōn*, "to our children"), which produces an awkward sense. For internal reasons, D is probably to be preferred, which reads τοῖς τεκνοῖς ἡμῖν (*tois teknois hēmin*, "to us, their children").

The Western text reverentially expands the name to "the Lord Jesus Christ."

The Western text reads: "As it is written in the first psalm." Some church fathers seem to have known of a Heb. text for the Psalms that considered the first two psalms to be one. P[45] reads simply "in the psalms."

33–35 A difference exists between ἀναστήσας Ἰησοῦν (*anastēsas Iēsoun*, "raising up Jesus") of v.33 and ἀνέστησεν αὐτὸν ἐκ νεκρῶν (*anestēsen auton ek nekrōn*, "he raised him from the dead") of v.34. The first in context refers to Jesus' being "brought forth" for his people Israel and corresponds to ἤγαγεν (*ēgagen*, "brought") of v.23, while the second speaks of his being "raised from the dead."

On Hillel's seven exegetical rules and their development, see my *Biblical Exegesis*, pp. 33–38.

34–35 For a similar citing of Scripture in support of Jesus' resurrection, using similar exegetical methods, see 2:25–35.

38 On the appellation ἄνδρες ἀδελφοί (*andres adelphoi*, "men, brothers"), see vv.16 and 26 above.

41 J. de Waard (pp. 17–19, 78–80) points out that Hab 1:5 here shows affinity to the Dead Sea sectarians' text and usage in 1QpHab. See also 3:22–23 on Deut 18:15, 18–19; 7:43 on Amos 5:26–27; 15:16–17 on Amos 9:11–12.

---

3. Varying responses to the sermon

13:42–45

42As Paul and Barnabas were leaving the synagogue, the people invited them to speak further about these things on the next Sabbath. 43When the congregation was dismissed, many of the Jews and devout converts to Judaism followed Paul and Barnabas, who talked with them and urged them to continue in the grace of God.

44On the next Sabbath almost the whole city gathered to hear the word of the Lord. 45When the Jews saw the crowds, they were filled with jealousy and talked abusively against what Paul was saying.

42–43 The brevity of Luke's report of the responses to Paul's sermon has raised some questions in the minds of modern interpreters. Who are the "they" (*autōn*; NIV has "Paul and Barnabas" here) and the "them" of v.42? Where did the action take place, inside or outside the synagogue? How was it that the apostles were favorably received, yet rejected? And what does our author mean by the expression *hoi sebomenoi prosēlytoi* (NIV, "devout converts to Judaism") in v.43? Many commentators have expressed their perplexities over these things, often proposing various source-critical explanations or deleting what appear to be the more difficult statements. But if we take the account to be an abbreviated summary of what happened and allow for the generalizations that invariably appear in any such summary, Luke's comments about the varying responses to Paul's sermon are not too difficult to understand.

Evidently the pronouns in v.42 refer to Paul and Barnabas, who were requested by those who heard Paul's sermon "to speak further about these things on the next Sabbath." More than likely the synagogue authorities took a less favorable view of the sermon. But "many of the Jews and devout converts to Judaism" (*polloi tōn Ioudaiōn kai tōn sebomenōn prosēlytōn*) were interested and after the service followed the apostles to hear more. And "some" (*hoitines*, here used as a sweeping relative pronoun) of those who did this were "persuaded" (*epeithon*, "urged") by the apostles to continue "in the grace of God"—which, to judge by Paul's usual understanding of grace, must connote continuance in the Good News about salvation through Jesus.

44–45 "Almost the whole city," Luke says rather hyperbolically, gathered on the following Sabbath to hear "the word of the Lord" (*ton logon tou kyriou*)—an expression suggesting the christological content of Paul's preaching. But "when the Jews saw the crowds," their initial interest turned to antagonism. Not only was the synagogue being flooded by Gentiles as though it were a common theater or town hall, but, even more, it became clear that Paul and Barnabas were ready to speak directly to Gentiles without first relating them in some way to Judaism. The majority of the Jews, including undoubtedly the leaders of the Jewish community, were apparently unwilling to countenance a salvation as open to Gentiles as it was to Jews. So in their opposition they not only "talked abusively" (NIV) but "they were blaspheming" (*blasphēmountes*), because from Luke's perspective opposition to the gospel is directed not so much against the messengers as against the content of the message—Jesus himself (cf. 26:11).

Notes

43 The expression οἱ σεβόμενοι προσηλύτοι (*hoi sebomenoi prosēlytoi*) makes sense only if σεβόμενος (*sebomenos*) does not denote here a "God-fearing Gentile," as in 13:50; 16:14; 17:4, 17; and 18:7, but a "devout Gentile convert" to Judaism who had accepted circumcision and obligation to the entire Jewish law.

On the use of the verbs πείθω (*peithō*, "to persuade" or "urge"), διαλέγομαι (*dialegomai*, "to reason"), διανοίγω (*dianoigō*, "to explain"), and παρατίθημι (*paratithēmi*, "to prove") as characterizing Paul's manner of preaching and teaching, see the comments on 17:2-4, 17; 18:4, 19; 19:8-10; 20:9; 24:25; 26:28; 28:23.

45 D adds ἀντιλέγοντες καὶ βλασφημοῦντες (*antilegontes kai blasphēmountes*, "they were contradicting and blaspheming"), which is a tautological expansion of the obvious.

4. To the Jews first, but also to the Gentiles

13:46-52

46Then Paul and Barnabas answered them boldly: "We had to speak the word of God to you first. Since you reject it and do not consider yourselves worthy of eternal life, we now turn to the Gentiles. 47For this is what the Lord has commanded us:

" 'I have made you a light for the Gentiles,
that you may bring salvation to the ends of the earth.' "

48When the Gentiles heard this, they were glad and honored the word of the Lord; and all who were appointed for eternal life believed.
49The word of the Lord spread through the whole region. 50But the Jews incited the God-fearing women of high standing and the leading men of the city. They stirred up persecution against Paul and Barnabas, and expelled them from their region. 51So they shook the dust from their feet in protest against them and went to Iconium. 52And the disciples were filled with joy and with the Holy Spirit.

46-47 In response to the Jews' abuse and blasphemy, Paul and Barnabas asserted their new policy "To the Jews first, but also to the Gentiles" that began with the conversion of Sergius Paulus and had evidently been discussed by the missioners on the way from Paphos to Pisidian Antioch. It is significant that in his commentary on Isaiah (c. A.D. 403),

Jerome refers five times to an interpretation of Isaiah 9:1–2 (about the lands of Zebulun and Naphtali seeing a great light) that he found among the Nazoreans of Syria. This Nazorean interpretation, Jerome tells us, went beyond the use of Isaiah 9:1–2 in Matthew 4:13–16 in establishing the priority of the gospel outreach as being first to Jews and then to Gentiles. Since, according to Jerome, the Nazoreans as Jewish Christians had an uninterrupted tradition stretching back to the very beginning of the Christian church, we may fairly claim that the policy of preaching first to Jews and then to Gentiles, though initiated on Paul's first missionary journey and not in Jerusalem, was acknowledged very early even among certain Jewish Christians at Jerusalem.

As Paul and Barnabas saw it, the Jews of Pisidian Antioch in their exclusiveness had rejected the very thing they were looking for: "The Life of the Age to Come" (Heb., *hayyê ha'ôlām habbā'*)—i.e., "eternal life" (Gr., *hē aiōnios zōē*). Now, however, the gospel must be directed to the Gentiles, for included in its mandate is the promise of Isaiah 49:6, that God's servant will be "a light for the Gentiles" and a bringer of salvation "to the ends of the earth" (cf. Luke 2:28–32). It was, of course, Jesus of Nazareth who was uniquely God's Servant and who was at work through his Spirit in the church, completing what he had begun and also making the missioners God's servants and inheritors of the promise in Isaiah 49:6.

48–49 Many of the Gentiles responded with thanks for the apostles' ministry and with openness to their message (*ton logon tou kyriou*, "the word of the Lord"). "All who were appointed for eternal life believed" suggests that belief in Christ is not just a matter of one's faith but primarily involves divine appointment (cf. SBK, 2:726, on Jewish concepts of predestination). And through the conversion of many of the Gentiles, who brought the message of salvation to others, "the word of the Lord spread through the whole region." This spreading of the word, along with the apostles' own outreach to the cities named in chapters 13 and 14, probably led to the agitation of the so-called Judaizers that resulted in the problem Paul dealt with in Galatians.

50 Unable to confine the ministry of Paul and Barnabas to the synagogue, the Jews stirred up trouble against them and brought pressure on the city's magistrates (*tous prōtous tēs poleōs*; lit., "the leading men of the city") through their "God-fearing" wives (*tas sebomenas gynaikas tas euschēmonas*; lit., "the God-fearing women of high standing"). Since Luke speaks of the persecution as expulsion rather than mob action, it probably took the form of a charge that Christianity, being disowned by the local Jewish community, was not a *religio licita* in Rome's eyes and therefore must be considered a disturbance to the Pax Romana. Later in Acts, Luke will show how the agitation against the gospel usually arose from within the Jewish community, not from the Roman authorities, and that the charge was that Paul was preaching an illegal religion (cf. 16:20–21; 17:7; 18:13)—a charge Luke insists was unfounded. This is part of the fabric of his apologetic argument (see Introduction: Luke's Purposes in Writing Acts), and he probably meant to suggest it here as well.

51–52 Having been expelled from Pisidian Antioch, Paul and Barnabas "shook the dust from their feet in protest against them"—a Jewish gesture of scorn and disassociation, which was directed at the city's magistrates and the Jewish leaders. Then they went southeast on the Via Sebaste, heading for Iconium some eighty miles away. The new "disciples" left behind at Pisidian Antioch and environs, far from being discouraged at this turn of events, were "filled with joy and with the Holy Spirit."

Notes

48 D reads ἐδέξαντο (*edexanto*, "accepted") for ἐδόξαζον (*edoxazon*, "glorified").

50 The Western text reads θλίψιν μεγαλὴν καὶ διωγμόν (*thlipsin megalēn kai diōgmon*, "great tribulation and persecution"), a redundant expansion on διωγμόν (*diōgmon*, "persecution").

D. At Iconium, Lystra, and Derbe and the Return to Antioch (14:1–28)

The great Roman road from Ephesus to the Euphrates, which had been extended into the heart of the south Galatian plateau by Augustus's engineers in 6 B.C. and named Via Sebaste in his honor (Sebastos is the Gr. equivalent of Augustus), became two roads at Pisidian Antioch. One went north through mountainous terrain to the Roman colony of Comana about 122 miles away. The other moved southeast across rolling country, past the snow-capped peaks of Sultan Dag, to terminate at the important Greek city of Iconium, some 80 miles distant from Antioch. A few years later this road was extended another 24 miles southwest to reach the Roman colony of Lystra. As Paul and Barnabas left Pisidian Antioch, therefore, they were faced with a choice as to the future direction of their mission. Choosing the southeastern route, they headed off to what would become a ministry to people of three very different types of cities in the southern portion of the Roman province of Galatia.

1. The ministry at Iconium

14:1–7

> ¹At Iconium Paul and Barnabas went as usual into the Jewish synagogue. There they spoke so effectively that a great number of Jews and Gentiles believed. ²But the Jews who refused to believe stirred up the Gentiles and poisoned their minds against the brothers. ³So Paul and Barnabas spent considerable time there, speaking boldly for the Lord, who confirmed the message of his grace by enabling them to do miraculous signs and wonders. ⁴The people of the city were divided; some sided with the Jews, others with the apostles. ⁵There was a plot afoot among the Gentiles and Jews, together with their leaders, to mistreat them and stone them. ⁶But they found out about it and fled to the Lycaonian cities of Lystra and Derbe and to the surrounding country, ⁷where they continued to preach the good news.

1 Iconium, an ancient Phrygian town, had been transformed by the Greeks into a city-state. Situated in the heart of the high and healthy plateau of south-central Asia Minor, it was surrounded by fertile plains and verdant forests, with mountains to its north and east. With Augustus's reorganization of provinces in 25 B.C., Iconium became part of Galatia. But while Rome chose Antioch of Pisidia and Lystra as bastions of its authority in the area, Iconium remained largely Greek in temper and somewhat resistant to Roman influence, though Hadrian later made it a Roman colony. As a Greek city, it was governed by its assembly of citizens (the *Demos*) and held itself aloof from interference by the praetorian legate. Greek was the language of its public documents, and during the NT period it attempted to retain the ethos of the old city-state.

"Iconium" is probably a Phrygian name, but a myth was invented to give it a Greek meaning. According to the myth, Prometheus and Athena recreated mankind in the area after a devasting flood by making images of people from the mud and breathing life into them. The Greek for "image" is *eikōn* (*ikon* in modern Gr.), hence the name Iconium. Ramsay called Iconium the Damascus of Asia Minor, for like Damascus it was blessed with abundant water, a genial climate, rich vegetation, and great prosperity (*Cities of St. Paul*, pp. 317–19). It was a place of beauty and a natural center of activity, as its survival into modern times as the thriving town of Konya shows.

Entering Iconium, Paul and Barnabas went to the Jewish synagogue. The phrase *kata to auto* literally suggests that the apostles went into the synagogue "together" (so KJV, RSV). But since to say that they entered the synagogue together belabors the obvious, many commentators prefer to read it as "after the same manner" (i.e., as at Pisidian Antioch) and to translate it with some such expression as "similarly" (NEB), "as usual" (NIV), or "as they had at Antioch" (JB). At Iconium, therefore, as they proclaimed the same gospel in the same way as at Pisidian Antioch, a great number believed, both Jews and Gentiles.

2 Opposition to the gospel soon arose. The Western text recasts v.2 to read: "But the leaders of the synagogue and the rulers [of Iconium] brought persecution against the righteous and made the minds of the Gentiles hostile against the brothers, though the Lord soon gave peace." The Western text presupposes that the opposition against Christianity followed the normal pattern in Acts of Jewish agitation and local Roman action against a *religio illicita*, whereas Iconium was a Greek city governed by its assembly of citizens. And the Western revisers had trouble seeing how the apostles could continue an extensive ministry in the city, as v.3 presents, after such an official judgment; so they added the clause "though the Lord soon gave peace." But if we recognize that opposition to the gospel arose here within a city governed by Greek jurisprudence, and if we take the aorist verbs of v.2 to be ingressive, Luke's portrayal of Jews "stirring up" the Gentiles and "poisoning their minds" may be both appropriate and meaningful, without the addition of a qualifying clause (as D and its associates inserted) or reversing the order of vv.2 and 3 (as some commentators think necessary).

3 To judge by his use of the connective *men oun*, Luke is here returning to some written source for his account of the ministries of Paul and Barnabas in southern Galatia. He tells us that the apostles ministered for a "considerable time" in the city and preached boldly "for the Lord," with God confirming "the message of his grace" by "miraculous signs and wonders" (*sēmeia kai terata*). The mention of "the Lord" undoubtedly refers to Jesus the Lord, thus showing the Christocentric nature of the missioners' preaching. And the couplet "miraculous signs and wonders" places the ministry of Paul and Barnabas directly in line with that of Jesus (cf. 2:22) and the early church (cf. 2:43; 4:30; 5:12; 6:8; 7:36) in fulfillment of prophecy (cf. 2:19)—as it does also in 15:12. Later when writing his Galatian converts (assuming a "South Galatian" origin for the letter), Paul appeals to these mighty works performed by the Spirit as evidence that the gospel as he preached it and they received it was fully approved by God (cf. Gal 3:4–5).

In the latter half of the second century (perhaps as late as 185–95), a presbyter of Asia Minor (perhaps from Iconium) wrote a lengthy tract entitled *The Acts of Paul* that sought to fill in the details of Paul's ministries in the eastern part of the empire and for which, Tertullian tells us, he "was removed from his office after he had been convicted and had confessed that he did it out of love for Paul" (*De Baptismo* 17). The work has numerous legendary stories, only a few of which may be based on fact. But in the section of Paul's ministry at Iconium (the longest section of the work, often circulated separately as *The Acts of Paul and Thecla*), we have a picture of Paul that may rest on more-or-less accurate local tradition, for it does not read like a later idealization: "a man small of stature, with a bald head and crooked legs, in a good state of body, with eyebrows meeting and nose somewhat hooked, full of friendliness; for now he appeared like a man, and now he had the face of an angel."

4–5 Luke tells us that there was a division among "the people" (*to plēthos*, "the population," "assembly") of the city regarding the apostles and their message, with some siding with the Jews and others with the apostles. Interpreted broadly, *to plēthos* denotes no more than the populace of the city (so KJV, RSV, NEB, JB, NIV, et al.). On the other hand, the word was also used of a stated assembly (cf. 23:7) and may denote an assembly of prominent citizens that met to conduct the business of a Greek city-state. If this is its meaning here, then Luke is telling us that the official response to Paul and Barnabas in Iconium was mixed. While there may not have been any official action taken against them, there was a "plot" (*hormē*) brewing among some of the Gentiles and Jews to mistreat and stone them. The word *hormē* connotes impulsiveness and suggests an action not controlled by reason, which is exactly how Luke viewed the opposition at Iconium against the gospel and its missioners.

Also significant is Luke's calling Barnabas an apostle (cf. also v.14) and lumping him with Paul in the phrase *syn tois apostolois* ("with the apostles"). While Barnabas was neither one of the Twelve nor a claimant to any special revelation, he was probably one of the 120 (cf. 1:15) and may have been a witness of Jesus' resurrection. Yet as with most titles of the NT (e.g., "disciple," "prophet," "teacher," "elder"), Luke, like Paul himself (cf. 2 Cor 8:23; Gal 1:19; Phil 2:25), not only used "apostle" in the restricted sense of a small group of highly honored believers who had a special function within the church but also in the broader sense of messengers of the gospel.

6–7 The opposition to the ministry of Paul and Barnabas must have grown to sizable proportions, for they took it seriously enough to leave Iconium and travel to Lystra and Derbe. By referring to Lystra and Derbe as Lycaonian cities, Luke implies that Iconium belonged to a different region from Lystra and Derbe. All three, of course, were part of the Roman province of Galatia. But in the administration of so large a province, the Romans subdivided Galatia into various regions (*regiones* or *chōrai*), four of which have come down to us by name: Isauria, Pisidia, Phrygia, and Lycaonia. The fourth-century B.C. Greek general and writer Xenophon called Iconium "the last city of Phrygia" (*Anabasis* 1.2.19), though later Roman authors frequently referred to it as a Lycaonian city (e.g., Cicero *Ad Familiares* 15.4.2; Pliny *Natural History* 5.25). Ramsay, however, has shown that between A.D. 37 and 72—and at no other time under Roman rule— Iconium was on the Phrygian side of the regional border between Phrygia and Lycaonia, not only linguistically but also politically (*Trustworthiness of the NT*, pp. 39–114; idem, *St. Paul the Traveller*, pp. 110–12). In fleeing to Lystra and Derbe, therefore, Paul and Barnabas were leaving one political region to start afresh in another. Thus in that Lycaonian region they continued preaching the gospel, both in the cities of Lystra and Derbe and in the surrounding countryside, as Luke now tells us in a general way and as he will explain in the following verses.

Notes

---

3 On Luke's use of μὲν οὖν (men oun, "so," "then"), see comments on 1:6. In his fourth panel of material, note the pattern that develops at 13:4 (after four verses of introduction), here (after a two-verse introduction), at 15:3 (after another two-verse introduction), and in summary at 15:30 and 16:5.

4 The Western text adds "cleaving to them because of the word of God" after "with the apostles."

6 Luke's use of τὴν περίχωρον (tēn perichōron, "the surrounding country") probably has in mind the "large Lycaonian territory which contained no constitutionally organised city [as Lystra and Derbe], but only villages of the Anatolian type" (Ramsay, Cities of St. Paul, p. 409).

7 The Western text adds: "And the whole populace was moved at the teaching. And Paul and Barnabas spent some time at Lystra."

---

2. The ministry at Lystra

14:8–20

8In Lystra there sat a man crippled in his feet, who was lame from birth and had never walked. 9He listened to Paul as he was speaking. Paul looked directly at him, saw that he had faith to be healed 10and called out, "Stand up on your feet!" At that, the man jumped up and began to walk.

11When the crowd saw what Paul had done, they shouted in the Lycaonian language, "The gods have come down to us in human form!" 12Barnabas they called Zeus, and Paul they called Hermes because he was the chief speaker. 13The priest of Zeus, whose temple was just outside the city, brought bulls and wreaths to the city gates because he and the crowd wanted to offer sacrifices to them.

14But when the apostles Barnabas and Paul heard of this, they tore their clothes and rushed into the crowd, shouting: 15"Men, why are you doing this? We too are only men, human like you. We are bringing you good news, telling you to turn from these worthless things to the living God, who made heaven and earth and sea and everything in them. 16In the past, he let all nations go their own way. 17Yet he has not left himself without testimony: He has shown kindness by giving you rain from heaven and crops in their seasons; he provides you with plenty of food and fills your hearts with joy." 18Even with these words, they had difficulty keeping the crowd from sacrificing to them.

19Then some Jews came from Antioch and Iconium and won the crowd over. They stoned Paul and dragged him outside the city, thinking he was dead. 20But after the disciples had gathered around him, he got up and went back into the city. The next day he and Barnabas left for Derbe.

8–10 Lystra was an ancient Lycaonian village whose origins are unknown. Caesar Augustus turned it into a Roman colony in 6 B.C. and, by bringing army veterans and their families into it, made it the most eastern of the fortified cities of Galatia. Its population was mostly uneducated Lycaonians, who came from a small Anatolian tribe and spoke their own language. The ruling class was made up of Roman army veterans, while education and commerce were controlled by a few Greeks. Jews also lived there (16:1–3), but their influence seems to have been minimal. A secondary military road was built between Lystra and its more powerful sister colony Pisidian Antioch in 6 B.C., and a few years later an extension of the Via Sebaste also joined Lystra to Iconium.

That Paul began the ministry at Lystra by preaching to a crowd may imply that no synagogue was available for him to preach in. While he was speaking, Paul saw "a man crippled in his feet, who was lame from birth and had never walked" (the triple stress on his condition may reflect the pattern of a frequently told story) and who was listening to him attentively. Seeing "that he had faith to be healed," Paul commanded him to stand up, and the man jumped up and walked about. Luke undoubtedly wanted his readers to recognize the parallel between the healing of this crippled man and the healing of another one by Peter (cf. 3:1-8), for the expressions "lame from birth" (*ek koilias mētros autou;* lit. "from his mother's womb"), "looked directly at him" (*atenisas autō*), and "walking about" (*periepatei;* NIV, "began to walk") are common to both accounts. The Western text, in fact, heightens the parallel by inserting "I say to you in the name of the Lord Jesus" before Paul's command (cf. 3:6) and by adding "and immediately he leaped up and walked" after it (cf. 3:7-8). But the sequel to the healing of the crippled man here differs from that of Peter's miracle, and it is narrated by Luke with much local color.

11-13 The healing amazed and excited the crowd, and they shouted out in Lycaonian: "The gods have come down to us in human form!" (cf. 28:6). Barnabas they identified as Zeus, the chief of the Greek pantheon, probably because of his more dignified bearing. It was evidently because Luke wanted to reflect this esteem by the people that he lists him first in his pairing of the apostles here, as he does also in another context at 15:12, 25. Paul they identified as Hermes, Zeus's son by Maia and the spokesman for the gods, since "he was the chief speaker" (*ho hēgoumenos tou logou*—see Iamblichus's description of Hermes as "the god who leads in speaking" [*theos ho tōn logōn hēgemon*] in *On the Egyptian Mysteries* 1). Two inscriptions discovered at Sedasa, near Lystra, dating from the middle of the third century A.D., identify the Greek gods Zeus and Hermes as being worshiped in Lycaonian Galatia. On one inscription recording the dedication to Zeus of a statue of Hermes along with a sundial, the names of the dedicators are Lycaonian; the other inscription mentions "priests of Zeus" (cf. W.M. Calder, "Acts 14:12," ExpT, 37 [1926], 528). Also found near Lystra was a stone altar dedicated to "The Hearer of Prayer [presumably Zeus] and Hermes" (ibid.).

Approximately half a century before Paul's first missionary journey, Ovid (c. 43 B.C.– A.D. 17) in the *Metamorphoses* (8.626-724) retold an ancient legend that may have been well known in southern Galatia and may in good part explain the wildly emotional response of the people to Paul and Barnabas. According to the legend, Zeus and Hermes once came to "the Phrygian hill country" disguised as mortals seeking lodging. Though they asked at a thousand homes, none took them in. Finally, at a humble cottage of straw and reeds, an elderly couple, Philemon and Baucis, freely welcomed them with a banquet that strained their poor resources. In appreciation, the gods transformed the cottage into a temple with a golden roof and marble columns. Philemon and Baucis they appointed priest and priestess of the temple, who, instead of dying, became an oak and a linden tree. As for the inhospitable people, the gods destroyed their houses. Just where in "the Phrygian hill country" this was supposed to have taken place, Ovid does not say. But it appears that, seeing the healing of the crippled man and remembering the legend, the people of Lystra believed that Zeus and Hermes had returned and wanted to pay them homage lest they incur the gods' wrath.

That the people shouted in Lycaonian explains why the apostles were so slow to understand what was afoot till the preparations to honor them as gods were well advanced. But when the priest of Zeus—whether for principial or pragmatic reasons— joined the crowd and began to do them homage, Paul and Barnabas realized what was about to happen. Temples situated outside city gates were common in the ancient world, and therefore Luke's phrase "Zeus ... just outside the city" (*Dios ... pro tēs poleōs*) probably refers to the Temple of Zeus just outside the gates of Lystra. We can visualize the priest of Zeus bringing out sacrificial oxen (*taurous*, "bulls") draped in woolen "wreaths" (*stemmata*) and preparing to sacrifice at an altar that stood in front of the Temple of Zeus, hard by the city gates. And as the idolatrous worship proceeded, Paul and Barnabas began to see that they were the object of it.

14-18 When they finally realized what was going on, Paul and Barnabas tore their clothes in horror at such blasphemy and rushed out into the crowd—shouting their objections and trying to make the people understand them. There is no reason to think that the majority of the Lystrans knew anything of Jewish history or of the Jewish Scriptures, or that they were vitally affected by Athenian philosophies. Culturally, they were probably peasants living in the hinterland of Greco-Roman civilization, with all of the lack of advantages of people in their situation. Such is the context of Paul's second missionary sermon. By far the briefest of the three (cf. 13:16-41; 17:22-31), its brevity reflects its confused setting.

Negatively, Paul's sermon at Lystra has to do with the futility of idolatry; positively, it is a proclamation of the one true and living God. Its language, particularly in its denunciation of paganism, is biblical. Indeed, Paul knows no other (cf. 13:10). But its argument is suited to its hearers. And despite the brevity with which Luke reports it, two features stand out in the development of Paul's argument. First, his demonstration of the interest and goodness of God is drawn neither from Scripture (as at Pisidian Antioch) nor from philosophy (as later at Athens) but from nature: "He has shown kindness by giving you rain from heaven and crops in their seasons; he provides you with plenty of food and fills your hearts with joy." It is an approach to theism that peasants would understand. Here at Lystra Paul used it for all it was worth.

A second feature is the claim that "in the past, he [God] let all nations go their own way," which suggests that at Lystra Paul spoke of a progressive unfolding of divine redemption. While the sermon does not explicitly refer to salvation through Christ, it is hard to believe that it was not meant to point to Jesus Christ and his work as the divine climax of history. "We too are only men, human like you," Paul and Barnabas insisted. But we are men with a message from God, they went on to say, "bringing you good news"—the best news possible—of the unity and character of the one true God (for it would not have truly been good news in the Christian sense apart from this) and of redemption through the person and work of Jesus his Son. Yet for most of the Lystrans, the message fell on deaf ears and they tried to carry on the sacrifices in honor of the visitors.

19-20 Later on certain Jews from Pisidian Antioch and Iconium, disaffected with Paul and Barnabas, came to Lystra to spread their views. Complaining first among the Jewish residents of the city, they managed to gain a hearing with the people. The fickle Lystrans, thinking that if the apostles were not gods they were impostors, stoned Paul and dragged him outside the city for dead. But with the aid of those who had accepted the gospel, he revived; and, with great courage, that evening he returned to the city where he had almost been killed. The next day, Paul and Barnabas left for the border town of Derbe.

Some months later, when Paul wrote the believers in Galatia (again, we assume a "South Galatian" destination for the letter), he closed by saying, "Finally, let no one cause me trouble, for I bear on my body the marks [*ta stigmata*] of Jesus" (Gal 6:17). Apparently he interpreted these marks as showing that he belonged to Jesus and as protecting him from unjust accusations. Some of the marks may well have been scars caused by the stoning at Lystra. And when still later he wrote the Corinthians of his having been stoned (2 Cor 11:25), it was Lystra he had in mind (cf. also 2 Tim 3:11). Perhaps, as Chrysostom proposed, we should see in Paul's reference to his "thorn in the flesh" (2 Cor 12:7) an allusion to the persecutions he suffered and their lingering effects, of which those at Lystra were by no means least.

Notes

9 The Western text adds ὑπάρχων ἐν φόβῳ (hyparchōn en phobō, "being in fear") after the participle λαλοῦντος (lalountos, "speaking").

12-13 The names of the Gr. gods suggest that the Hellenization of the local Lycaonian gods had already taken place rather than that Luke interpreted Lycaonian gods in Gr. terms (cf. C.S.C. Williams, p. 170; contra, BC 4:164,n.).

13 The Western text reads "the priests of Zeus," since great temples usually had a college of priests in attendance. But the Lystran Temple of Zeus was probably more modest.

14 The Western text omits οἱ ἀπόστολοι (hoi apostoloi, "the apostles") here.

The Byzantine text reads εἰσεπήδησαν εἰς τὸν ὄχλον (eisepēdēsan eis ton ochlon, "rushed into the crowd"), which NIV appears to follow, rather than ἐξεπήδησαν εἰς τὸν ὄχλον (exepēdēsan eis ton ochlon, "rushed out into the crowd").

15 P[45] omits καί (kai, "also," "too").

18 C P[45] and a number of Western texts add to the end of the sentence "but that they should each go home," which was probably a rounding off of the section for lectionary purposes.

19 The Western text expands this verse to read: "And as they spent some time there and taught, there came certain Jews from Iconium and Antioch, and while they were discoursing with boldness they persuaded the people to revolt against them, saying, 'Nothing they say is true; it is all lies.' And having stirred up the people and having stoned Paul, they dragged him out of the city, thinking he was dead."

20 D and E, together with P[45], add αὐτοῦ (autou, "his"), thus reading "his disciples."

3. The ministry at Derbe and the return to Antioch

14:21–28

21They preached the good news in that city and won a large number of disciples. Then they returned to Lystra, Iconium and Antioch, 22strengthening the disciples and encouraging them to remain true to the faith. "We must go through many hardships to enter the kingdom of God," they said. 23Paul and Barnabas appointed elders for them in each church and, with prayer and fasting, committed them to the Lord in whom they had put their trust. 24After going through Pisidia, they came into Pamphylia, 25and when they had preached the word in Perga, they went down to Attalia.

26From Attalia they sailed back to Antioch, where they had been committed to the grace of God for the work they had now completed. 27On arriving there, they gathered the church together and reported all that God had done through them and how he had opened the door of faith to the Gentiles. 28And they stayed there a long time with the disciples.

21a Derbe was situated in the southeastern part of the Lycaonian region of Galatia, about sixty miles southeast of Lystra. According to the lexicographer Stephen of Byzantium, its name in the Lycaonian dialect meant "juniper tree." In 25 B.C. Augustus incorporated it into the province of Galatia, making it a provincial border town on the eastern edge of the southern Galatian plateau. During A.D. 41 through 72 it bore the prefix Claudia in recognition of its strategic position as a frontier town. For some time its exact location was disputed by archaeologists but has now been established as being at Kerti Hüyük (cf. M. Ballance, *The Site of Derbe: A New Inscription*, Anatolian Studies VII [London: British Institute of Archaeology at Ankora, 1957]).

Luke's account of the ministry at Derbe is very brief. All he says is that the apostles "preached the good news" there and "won a large number of disciples." Evidently Luke was more interested in the illustrious Phrygian cities of Antioch and Iconium than in the smaller Lycaonian towns of Lystra and Derbe. Probably the larger and more influential churches were in Antioch and Iconium as well, though the congregations in the smaller and more rural towns seem to have contributed more young men as candidates for the missionary endeavor (e.g., Timothy from Lystra [16:1-3; 20:4]; Gaius from Derbe [20:4]) —a pattern not altogether different from today, where the larger churches often capture the headlines and the smaller congregations provide much of the personnel.

21b-23 Having preached at Derbe, Paul and Barnabas returned to Lystra, Iconium, and Pisidian Antioch. Why they did not push further eastward through the passes of the Taurus range into Cilicia, Luke does not tell us. Perhaps Cilicia was considered already evangelized through Paul's earlier efforts (cf. comments on 9:30 and 11:25), which would also explain why the apostles began their missionary outreach on Cyprus and not in Cilicia (cf. 13:4). Undoubtedly their concern for the new converts in the Galatian cities led them to return by the same road. But this raises a question about how they could gain entrance into these cities after having so lately been forced to leave them. Here again Luke is silent. Ramsay suggests that "new magistrates had now come into office in all the cities whence they had been driven; and it was therefore possible to go back" (*St. Paul the Traveller*, p. 120). Yet in each of these cities the circumstances of their forced departure differed; and even with an annual change of administrators, it would have taken considerable courage to return. Probably in returning to Lystra, Iconium, and Pisidian Antioch, they confined their ministries to those already converted, and therefore did not stir up any further opposition (cf. 16:6; 18:23; 20:3-6).

While returning through the Galatian cities, Paul and Barnabas tried to strengthen their converts personally and corporately. They encouraged them to remain in the faith, telling them that many persecutions must necessarily (*dei*) be the lot of Christians in order to enter into the kingdom of God—that is, that the same pattern of suffering and glory exemplified in Jesus' life must be theirs as well if they are to know the full measure of the reign of God in their lives (cf. Mark 8:31-10:52; Rom 8:17; Phil 3:10-11; Col 1:24). And "they appointed [*cheirotonēsantes*] elders for them in each church," thus leaving them with suitable spiritual guides and an embryonic ecclesiastical administration. In the early Gentile churches (as also undoubtedly at Jerusalem), the terms "elders" (*presbyteroi*) and "bishops or overseers" (*episkopoi*) were used somewhat interchangeably and functionally rather than as titles. (See Acts 20, where Paul calls for the "elders" of the Ephesian church [v.17] and exhorts them: "Guard yourselves and all the flock of which the Holy Spirit has made you overseers" [v.28].) The elders were the "rulers" (*proistamenoi*) at Thessalonica (1 Thess 5:12) and at Rome (Rom 12:8). They were associated with the "deacons" as the constituted officials (Phil 1:1; 1 Tim 3:1–13; Titus 1:5–9).

24–25 Directly south of Phrygia was the region of Pisidia and south of that the province of Pamphylia. In Pamphylia the apostles preached at Perga, the chief city of the province, thus beginning the kind of witness in Perga they had been unable to begin on their first visit (cf. comments on 13:13). Of its results we know nothing, nor do we know the nature of their visit to the port of Attalia (modern Antalya), some eight miles further south on the Mediterranean coast at the mouth of the Cataractes (modern Ak Su) River. Ports in antiquity were often satellite towns of larger and more important cities situated some distance inland for protection from pirates. So Luke's mention of Attalia here probably has no more significance than his mention of Seleucia (13:4), the port of Syrian Antioch, and merely identifies the place of embarkation for the voyage back to Syria.

26–28 On returning to Antioch of Syria and to the congregation that had sent them out, Paul and Barnabas "reported all that God had done through them and how he had opened the door of faith to the Gentiles." They had gone out under divine ordination, and their report stressed the fact that God himself had brought about the new policy for evangelizing the Gentiles, which was inaugurated at Paphos and followed throughout the cities of southern Galatia—a claim that was called into question by some believers in Jerusalem and was soon to be tested at the Jerusalem Council. So having returned from a missionary journey that occupied the best part of a year, the apostles remained at Syrian Antioch ministering in the church there for approximately another year.

Notes

22 On the note of divine necessity implied in the word δεῖ (*dei*, "must"), see comments on 1:16.
    On the phrase ἡ βασιλεία τοῦ θεοῦ (*hē basileia tou theou*, "the kingdom of God") in Christian usage, see comments on 1:4.
23 The verb χειροτονέω (*cheirotoneō*) means "to choose" or "elect by raising hands" (cf. 2 Cor 8:19; also Ignatius *To the Philadelphians* 10.1; *To the Smyrneans* 11.2; *To Polycarp* 7.2; and *Didache* 15.1), but it can also mean "to appoint" or "install" directly (cf. Acts 10:41; also Philo *De Josepho* 248; *De Vita Mosis* 1. 198; Jos. Antiq. VI, 312 [xiii. 9]; XIII, 45 [ii. 2]). Here in the Galatian cities the initiative was taken by the apostles in the appointment of elders, but probably with the concurrence of the congregations (cf. 6:2–6; 13:2–3; 15:3–30).
25 The Western text adds εὐαγγελιζόμενοι αὐτούς (*euangelizomenoi autous*, "preaching the gospel to them") at Attalia, but without warrant.
27 The Western text reads μετὰ τῶν ψυχῶν αὐτῶν (*meta tōn psychōn autōn*, "with their souls") for μετ᾽ αὐτῶν (*met' autōn*, "with," "through them").

E. *The Jerusalem Council* (15:1–29)

The convening of the council of apostles and Christian leaders at Jerusalem in approximately A.D. 49 was an event of greatest importance for the early church. That Gentiles were to share in the promises to Israel is a recurring theme of the OT (cf. Gen 22:18; 26:4; 28:14; Isa 49:6; 55:5–7; Zeph 3:9–10; Zech 8:22). It was the underlying presupposition for Jewish proselytizing (cf. M *Pirke Aboth* 1.12; Matt 23:15) and was implicit in the sermons of Peter at Pentecost (2:39) and in the house of Cornelius (10:35). But the correlative conviction of Judaism was that Israel was God's appointed agent for the administration of these blessings—that only through the nation and its institutions could Gentiles have a part in God's redemption and share in his favor. And there seems to have been no expectation on the part of Christians at Jerusalem that this program would be materially altered, though they did insist that in these "last days" God was at work in and through Jewish Christians as the faithful remnant within the nation.

In the experience of the church, all Gentiles—with but one exception—who had come to acknowledge Jesus as Messiah had been either full proselytes or near proselytes ("God-fearers"). Only Cornelius's conversion did not fit into the pattern (cf. 10:1–11:18). But it was viewed as exceptional and not an occasion for changing policy. The practice of preaching directly to Gentiles begun by Paul in his mission on Cyprus and throughout southern Asia Minor, however, was a matter of far-reaching concern at Jerusalem, especially in view of the tensions that arose within Palestine after the death of Herod Agrippa I in A.D. 44.

As the faithful remnant, the Jerusalem church naturally expected the Christian mission to proceed along lines God laid down long ago. It could point to the fact that, with few exceptions, commitment to Jesus as Israel's Messiah did not make Jews less Jewish. Indeed, it sometimes brought Gentiles who were only loosely associated with the synagogues into greater conformity with Jewish ethics. The Christian movement had always insisted on its integral relation to the religion and nation of Israel, even though this relation contained some unresolved ambiguities and was defined in various ways within the movement. But Paul's new policy for reaching Gentiles, despite his claim of the authority of revelation and providence for it, seemed to many Jewish Christians to undercut the basis and thrust of the ministry of the Jerusalem church. It stirred serious questions within Jerusalem, for it seemed to give the lie to the stance of Jerusalem Christianity—particularly if condoned by believers of Jerusalem.

Excursus

Any discussion of Jerusalem's attitude toward the Pauline mission that seeks to go beyond generalities is immediately faced with the thorny question of the relation of Paul's "second visit" to Jerusalem (Gal 2:1–10) to the Jerusalem Council (Acts 15). The literary and historical issues are complex (cf. comments on 11:29–30). But one point drawn from the polemic in Galatians needs to be made here: Paul's silence in Galatians as to the decision of the Jerusalem Council forces the irreconcilable dilemma of saying either (1) that Luke's account in Acts 15 of a decision reached in Paul's favor at Jerusalem is pure fabrication or (2) that Galatians was written before the Jerusalem Council. That Paul felt obliged to explain his visits to Jerusalem shows that his adversaries had been using one or both of these visits in a manner detrimental to his position and authority. But that he should recount his contacts with the Jerusalem leaders and fail to mention the decision regarding his mission reached at the Jerusalem Council (accepting for the moment the veracity of Acts 15 and a late date for Gal) is entirely inconceivable. His lack of reference to the idolatry clause of the "decrees" in writing the Corinthians (cf. 1 Cor 8:1–11:1) may be explained on other grounds (cf. comments on 15:31). But in the context of the Judaizing problem at Galatia, the decision of the Jerusalem Council would have been the coup de grâce to the whole conflict.

Some commentators argue that Galatians 2:1–10 is the account of the Jerusalem Council from Paul's perspective. But if this is true, it is exceedingly strange that the decision of the council is so muted (if, indeed, "muted" is not too strong a word) in

Paul's account. One would have expected him to have driven the decision home more forcefully in his debate with the Judaizers had he known about the council's decision when writing Galatians. He certainly did not withhold his punches when speaking elsewhere in the letter.

Others suggest that since there is a possibility of the "decrees" being promulgated apart from Paul's knowledge (a possibility I consider highly improbable), there is a similar possibility of an early formulation of the council's primary decision without Paul's being aware of it—allowing Paul to write his Galatian converts at a later time without any mention of the Jerusalem decision, yet retaining the basic veracity of the account in Acts 15. But whatever is said of the decrees, the major decision of the Jerusalem Council was so overwhelmingly in Paul's favor that there is little likelihood of his not knowing about it and no reason for its having been kept from him. We cannot get out of the problem so easily. We are still faced with the dilemma that either Paul did not know of the council's decision when he wrote Galatians because he wrote before such a decision had been reached or that the decision in question has no basis in fact. And while others often assert this, I do not believe our only recourse is to discredit Luke's account in Acts.

Likewise, assuming that Paul's clash with Peter at Antioch took place after the Jerusalem Council, Paul's account of the clash between Peter and himself at the arrival of "certain men from James" (Gal 2:12) undercuts his whole argument and turns to the advantage of his Judaizing opponents. Indeed, it would reveal Paul's recognition of a chasm between himself and the Jerusalem apostles, which was only superficially bridged at the Jerusalem Council. Including the incident in his argument at a time *before* the council is understandable. But to use it in support of his polemic *after* the decision at Jerusalem, and without reference to that decision, casts doubt on Paul's logical powers. Of course, one might try to support Paul's rationality by reversing the order of events in Galatians 2, thus making Galatians 2:11–21 refer to a time before the Jerusalem Council and Galatians 2:1–10 reflect Paul's version of the council itself. But "the most natural interpretation of the biographical statements in Galatians i and ii," as many have insisted, "is that they were written before the 'Council' of Jerusalem" (Burkitt, p. 116). And while there are difficulties in an early dating of the Galatian letter, Carrington was right in asserting that "the arguments which perplexed the older theologians and still go on in the schools were due in no small degree to the fact that they accepted the late date of Galatians, which was traditional in their time" (Philip Carrington, *The Early Christian Church*, 2 vols. [Cambridge: Cambridge University, 1957], 1:91).

Accepting Galatians, then, as having been written before the Jerusalem Council, we have some idea from Paul himself concerning repercussions in Jerusalem in regard to his Gentile ministry, both as it was carried on in the synagogues at Antioch of Syria and as it was further developed in Cyprus and southern Asia Minor. On his second visit to Jerusalem after his conversion, which was evidently the "famine visit" of A.D. 46 (cf. 11:27–30 and comments on 11:29–30), the issue came to a head in the case of the uncircumcised Titus who accompanied Paul and Barnabas to Jerusalem. And Paul says that there were two responses to Titus's presence at Jerusalem: (1) that of "some false brothers" who "had infiltrated our ranks to spy on the freedom we have in Christ Jesus and to make us slaves" (Gal 2:4–5); and (2) that of James, Peter, and John, the so-called pillar apostles (cf. Gal 2:6–10).

It is somewhat difficult to say whether the "false brothers" were Jewish spies sent to see what treachery the Christians were next planning in conjunction with Gentiles or angry Jewish Christians who threatened to publish what was happening in the church unless Titus was circumcised. Nor can we tell whether Paul brought Titus to Jerusalem as a test case, or whether, having included him in the group from Antioch for some other reason, Paul underestimated the pressures a certain segment in the Jerusalem congregation would put on him. But the extremely important point here is that in spite of pressures and some uncertainty the Jerusalem apostles stood with Paul on the validity of a Gentile mission and the inappropriateness of making circumcision a requirement for Gentiles—though probably neither Paul nor they at that time saw that a direct ministry to Gentiles was in the offing.

From Galatians 2:1-10, therefore, we learn that as early as the mid-forties there was concern among Jerusalem Christians regarding the ministry to "God-fearing" Gentiles at Antioch of Syria and that there were pressures exerted by some to bring it more into line with strict Jewish practice.

Likewise, Paul's account of the Antioch episode in Galatians 2:11-21 clearly shows that the Gentile ministry was causing repercussions at Jerusalem and that pressures were being exerted on the Jerusalem congregation because of it. Just who "those who belonged to the circumcision group" were, who were feared by Peter, is difficult to say with any certainty. And just why Peter, together with the Antioch Jewish Christians and "even Barnabas," separated themselves from Gentile believers is difficult to determine precisely. It may be that they viewed such an action as a necessary, temporary expedient in order to avoid dangerous practical consequences for Jewish believers at Jerusalem and to quell rising demands for the circumcision of Gentile believers at Antioch, thus preserving both the Jewish mission of the church and Gentile freedom (cf. Dix, p. 44). However that may be, Galatians 2:11-21 points out that there were rising pressures at Jerusalem against an outreach to Gentiles and that these pressures were felt at Syrian Antioch. Furthermore, the passage suggests that the rationale for a separation of Jewish and Gentile believers was at times based on expediency rather than unmixed principle. And it was this issue of expediency versus theological principle that required clarification in the early church and lent urgency to the Jerusalem Council.

---

1. The delegation from Syrian Antioch

15:1-4

> [1]Some men came down from Judea to Antioch and were teaching the brothers: "Unless you are circumcised according to the custom taught by Moses, you cannot be saved." [2]This brought Paul and Barnabas into sharp dispute and debate with them. So Paul and Barnabas were appointed, along with some other believers, to go up to Jerusalem to see the apostles and elders about this question. [3]The church sent them on their way, and as they traveled through Phoenicia and Samaria, they told how the Gentiles had been converted. This news made all the brothers very glad. [4]When they came to Jerusalem, they were welcomed by the church and the apostles and elders, to whom they reported everything God had done through them.

1 The immediate occasion for the Jerusalem Council was the visit to Syrian Antioch of some Jewish Christians from Jerusalem and their teaching that circumcision was essential to salvation. These became known as "Judaizers," and their comrades were promoting similar teaching among Paul's converts in Galatia. They may have been incited by the return of John Mark and his unfavorable report (cf. comments in 13:13). That James and Peter stood behind these Judaizers is a fiction without factual support (contra Baur, et al.), though the other extreme—that the Jerusalem church was devoid of any Judaizing element—is just as erroneous (contra Munck). Both James and Peter were interested in minimizing conflicts between Judaism and Jewish Christianity. Yet neither was prepared to sacrifice the principles of the gospel to expediency when the implications of doing this became plain. The Judaizers, on the other hand, while probably first justifying their

legalism on practical grounds, were arguing as a matter of principle for the necessity of circumcision and a Jewish lifestyle. First Thessalonians 2:14–16 shows that Paul recognized nonbelieving Jews as the ultimate source of opposition to the mission among the Gentiles. Therefore, when he says in Galatians 6:13 that the Judaizers "want you to be circumcised that they may boast about your flesh," he probably means so that they could "point out to *non*-Christian Jews that conversion to Christianity does in fact *transfer Gentiles from the 'Greek' to the 'Jewish' cause*, in that wider conflict of the Two Cultures which is daily growing more intense [italics his]" (Dix, pp. 41–42). Undoubtedly the Judaizers thought of themselves as acting conscientiously and on sound theological principles (cf. comments on v.5 below). But as Paul saw it, they sought "a good impression outwardly . . . to avoid being persecuted for the cross of Christ" (Gal 6:12).

2 With the issues highlighted by the "sharp dispute and debate" that followed, Paul and Barnabas were appointed, along with certain others from the Antioch congregation, to go up to Jerusalem to meet with "the apostles and elders" about the matter. The antecedent of the third person plural verb *etaxan* ("they appointed") is not specified here. The Western text assumes the hierarchical authority of the mother church in its reading, "those who had come from Jerusalem charged Paul and Barnabas and certain others to go up to the apostles and elders at Jerusalem that they might be judged before them about this question." But that reflects a later ecclesiastical situation. Probably the reference in v.3 to being sent "by the church" (*hypo tēs ekklēsias*) gives the context for Luke's use of *etaxan*, so that we should understand "they" as signifying the involvement of the entire congregation at Antioch and its leaders in the appointment (cf. 13:3).

The church at Antioch was concerned with the Judaizers' challenge to the legitimacy of a direct ministry to Gentiles and to the validity of the conversion of Gentiles to Christ apart from any commitment to Judaism. The Jerusalem leaders had some practical concerns about Paul's new policy and were prepared to let some measure of expediency affect their relations with Israel. But the Judaizers had shifted these practical concerns over into the area of principle. Antioch Christians were therefore desirous for the relation between the Jerusalem church's policy of cautious expediency and the Judaizers' argument founded on theological principle to be clarified. Outside Judea there was growing confusion because of the Judaizers' equation of expediency with theological principle and their claim to be supported by the church's leaders at Jerusalem. The Jerusalem Christians, for their part, undoubtedly welcomed an opportunity to air their concerns—particularly the impasse created for them by Paul and Barnabas through their Gentile policy. For while there may have been general agreement on the validity of evangelizing Gentiles (cf. Gal 2:7–10), recent events opened that agreement for reconsideration.

3–4 The *men oun* ("so," RSV; untranslated in NIV) may mark off Luke's source material from his own introduction. As the delegation from Antioch journeyed to Jerusalem, they told the believers in Phoenicia and Samaria the news of "the conversion of the Gentiles" (*tēn epistrophēn tōn ethnōn*). This undoubtedly means that Gentiles were converted on a direct basis apart from any necessary commitment to Judaism, because the presence of proselytes and "God-fearing" Gentiles in the church was hardly newsworthy in A.D. 49. The Phoenician and Samaritan Christians, being themselves converts of the Hellenists' mission after Stephen's martyrdom (cf. 8:4–25; 11:19), probably took a broader view than that which prevailed at Jerusalem and rejoiced at the news. Believers at Jerusalem also were interested, but their interest by no means involved whole-hearted approval.

Notes

---

1 The Western text expands "some men" by adding "of the sect of the Pharisees who believed." It also reads "Unless you are circumcised and walk according to the custom taught by Moses," thereby clarifying the obvious.

2 On the expression "to go up [ἀναβαίνειν, anabainein] to Jerusalem," see comments at 3:1.

3 On Luke's use of μὲν οὖν (men oun), see comments and note at 1:6.

In his fourth panel of material, note the pattern that develops at 13:4, 14:3, and here, with summary usages at 15:30 and 16:5.

---

2. The nature and course of the debate

15:5–12

> 5Then some of the believers who belonged to the party of the Pharisees stood up and said, "The Gentiles must be circumcised and required to obey the law of Moses."
> 6The apostles and elders met to consider this question. 7After much discussion, Peter got up and addressed them: "Brothers, you know that some time ago God made a choice among you that the Gentiles might hear from my lips the message of the gospel and believe. 8God, who knows the heart, showed that he accepted them by giving the Holy Spirit to them, just as he did to us. 9He made no distinction between us and them, for he purified their hearts by faith. 10Now then, why do you try to test God by putting on the necks of the disciples a yoke that neither we nor our fathers have been able to bear? 11No! We believe it is through the grace of our Lord Jesus that we are saved, just as they are."
> 12The whole assembly became silent as they listened to Barnabas and Paul telling about the miraculous signs and wonders God had done among the Gentiles through them.

5 In the ensuing debate among believers in general and in the council itself, some Christian Pharisees, in support of the Judaizers, insisted that it was necessary for Gentile Christians to "be circumcised and required to obey the law of Moses." And by "necessary" (dei) they meant that these things were not only expedient but principally required by the revealed will of God. Indeed, the prophets spoke of the salvation of the Gentiles as an event of the last days (cf. Isa 2:2; 11:10; 25:8–9; Zech 8:23) through the witness of a restored Israel (cf. Isa 2:3; 60:2–3; Zech 8:23). Thus a believer could hardly oppose reaching Gentiles through the ministry of the church. But for these overscrupulous Christians in Jerusalem, the outreach to Gentiles was to come from within their group and to follow a proselyte model, not to come from outside their group and be apart from the law. In the last days, all nations are to flow to the house of the Lord at Jerusalem (cf. Isa 2:2–3; 25:6–8; 56:7; 60:3–22; Zech 8:21–23), not depart from it.

6 While Luke says only that the apostles and elders met to consider these questions, his mention of "the whole assembly" (pan to plēthos) in v.12 and "the whole church" (holē tē ekklēsia) in v.22 shows that other members of the congregation were also present. The discussion was undoubtedly heated, but Luke centers on its Pauline aspect.

7–11 Peter was no longer the chief figure of the Jerusalem church. James had at some time earlier assumed that role (cf. comments on 12:17). But Peter was dominant in the

Jewish Christian mission and responsible to the Jerusalem church. And it is as a missionary, not an administrator, that Peter spoke up and reminded the council that God had chosen to have the Gentiles hear the gospel from him and accept it. He argued that since God had established such a precedent within the Jewish Christian mission some ten years earlier—though it had not been recognized by the church as such—God has already indicated his approval of a direct Gentile outreach. Thus Paul's approach to the Gentiles could not be branded as a deviation from the divine will. Peter had evidently completely recovered from his temporary lapse at Syrian Antioch. Now he saw matters more clearly and was ready to agree with Paul's position that there is "no difference" between Jews and Gentiles and that the Mosaic law was a "yoke."

12 Luke's reference to the silence of the assembly after Peter spoke implies that the turning point had come. Though resisted at Jerusalem for almost a decade, the precedent of Cornelius's conversion had opened the way for Barnabas and Paul's report of God's validation of their missionary policy through "miraculous signs and wonders" (*sēmeia kai terata*). It was a report not of their successes but of how God had acted, and its implication was that by his acts God had revealed his will. As at Lystra, where Barnabas was taken to be the greater of the two (cf. 14:12, 14), so here Barnabas is mentioned first (cf. also v.25), probably because he enjoyed greater confidence at Jerusalem.

Notes

5 On δεῖ (*dei*) as connoting divine necessity, see comments on 1:16.

The Western text (except D) omits the reference to "some of the believers who belonged to the party of the Pharisees," which it inserted earlier at v.1, and reads (including D) "But those who charged them to go up to the elders stood up and said," in line with its treatment of v.2 above.

7 The Western text reads ἀνέστησεν ἐν πνεύματι (*anestēsen en pneumati*, "he rose up in spirit") for the simple ἀναστάς (*anastas*, "arising," "got up"). P[45] reads τοὺς ἀποστόλους (*tous apostolous*, "the apostles") for the simple αὐτούς (*autous*, "them").

12 The Western text starts the verse "And when the elders had consented to the words spoken by Peter" before going on to speak of the assembly keeping silent—thereby emphasizing Peter's authority, as is a common feature in the Western readings.

On the use of τὸ πλῆθος (*to plēthos*) to signal the involvement of the "whole assembly," see the note at 6:2.

On σημεῖα καὶ τέρατα (*sēmeia kai terata*, "miraculous signs and wonders") as characterizing the Pauline mission, thereby putting it in line with OT prophecy, the ministry of Jesus, and the ministry of the early church, see comments on 14:3 (also comments on 2:22).

3. *The summing up by James*

15:13–21

13When they finished, James spoke up: "Brothers, listen to me. 14Simon has described to us how God at first showed his concern by taking from the Gentiles a people for himself. 15The words of the prophets are in agreement with this, as it is written:

445

> 16" 'After this I will return
>   and rebuild David's fallen tent.
> Its ruins I will rebuild,
>   and I will restore it,
> 17that the remnant of men may seek the Lord,
>   and all the Gentiles who bear my name,
> says the Lord, who does these things'
> 18   that have been known for ages.

> 19"It is my judgment, therefore, that we should not make it difficult for the Gentiles who are turning to God. 20Instead we should write to them, telling them to abstain from food polluted by idols, from sexual immorality, from the meat of strangled animals and from blood. 21For Moses has been preached in every city from the earliest times and is read in the synagogues on every Sabbath."

13 James, the Lord's brother, presided at the Jerusalem Council. Known as "James the Just" because of his piety, he was ascetic and scrupulous in keeping the law. The Judaizers within the church looked to him for support, knowing his legal qualifications as well as his personal qualities (cf. comments on 12:17). But while rigorous and scrupulous in his personal practice of the faith, James was more broad-minded than many of his followers. After calling the council to order by using the formal mode of address "Men, brothers" (*Andres adelphoi*), he went on to sum up the emerging view of the council in a way that linked it to what had already been said.

14 If, as Luke's account implies, James in summing up made no reference to Paul and Barnabas's report, this was probably more for political reasons than any of principle. After all, it was the work of Paul and Barnabas that was on trial, and James wanted to win his entire audience to the position he believed to be right without causing needless offense. Therefore, he began by reminding the council of Peter's testimony, whom he called by his Hebrew name, "Simon" (cf. 2 Peter 1:1). And he showed how he felt about the question at issue by speaking of believing Gentiles as a "people" (*laos*) whom God has taken "for himself" (*tō onomati autou*; lit., "for his name")—thus (1) applying to Gentile Christians a designation formerly used of Israel alone and (2) agreeing with Peter that in the conversion of Cornelius God himself had taken the initiative for a direct Gentile ministry.

15–17 James's major contribution to the decision of the council was to shift the discussion of the conversion of Gentiles from a proselyte model to an eschatological one. Isaiah had expected Gentile converts to come to Jerusalem to learn God's ways so that they might walk in them. But Isaiah also spoke of the Gentiles' persistence as nations whose salvation did not destroy their national identities (cf. Isa 2:4; 25:6–7). Likewise, Amos spoke of "the remnant of men" (LXX, DSS) in the last days when "David's fallen tent" would be rebuilt as being "all the Gentiles who bear my name" and whose continuance as Gentiles was understood. In the end times, James is saying, God's people will consist of two concentric groups. At their core will be restored Israel (i.e., David's rebuilt tent); gathered around them will be a group of Gentiles (i.e., "the remnant of men") who will share in the messianic blessings but will persist as Gentiles without necessarily becoming Jewish proselytes. It is this understanding of Amos's message, James insisted, that Peter's testimony has affirmed, the result being that the conversion of Gentiles in the last days should be seen not as proselytizing but in an eschatological context.

James's quotation of Amos 9:11–12 is both textually and exegetically difficult. As given in Acts, the text of v.12 deviates from the MT and agrees with the LXX in reading "they will seek" (*ekzētēsōsin*) for "they will inherit" (*yîreŝû*), in reading "of men" (*tōn anthrō-pōn*) for "of Edom" (*'edôm*), and in treating "the remnant" (*hoi kataloipoi*) as the subject of the sentence rather than its object. It would have been impossible, in fact, for James to have derived his point from the text had he worked from the MT. On the other hand, the text of v.11 here differs from the LXX in reading "after this" (*meta tauta*) for "in that day" (*en tē hēmera ekeinē*), in reading "I will return and rebuild" (*anastrepsō kai anoikodomēsō*) for "I will raise up" (*anastēsō*), in reading "I will restore" (*anorthōsō*) for "I will raise up" (*anastēsō*), and in omitting the clause "and I will rebuild it as in the days of old" (*kai anoikodomēsō autēn kathōs hai hēmerai tou aiōnos*).

Focusing on the quotation's difference from the MT and essential agreement with the LXX, many commentators have complained that "the Jewish Christian James would not in Jerusalem have used a Septuagint text, differing from the Hebrew original, as scriptural proof," and have therefore concluded, "It is not James but Luke who is speaking here" (Haenchen, *Acts of the Apostles*, p. 448). But while the text of Amos 9:11–12 differs from the MT in meaning and the LXX in form, "it is exactly identical with that of 4QFlor," as de Waard has shown (pp. 24–26, 47, 78–79). And it is not too difficult to visualize James as using a Hebrew variant of Amos 9:11–12 then current, as incorporated in 4QFlorilegium 1.12, in arguing his point with the scrupulous Jewish Christians in the council—particularly if among those most concerned for Jewish legalities were some drawn from an Essene background (cf. comments on 6:7).

18 The interpretation of v.18 is notoriously difficult. Aleph, B, and C, together with the Coptic and Armenian versions, read "that have been known for ages" (*gnōsta ap aiōnos*). To accept this reading is to understand the clause as part of a conflated biblical citation that extends from v.16 through v.18 (as RSV, NEB, JB, TEV, NIV), probably alluding to Isaiah 45:21. But A and D, together with Bodmer P[74] and the major Latin and Syriac versions, read "known to the Lord from eternity is his work" (*gnōston ap aiōnos estin tō kyriō to ergon autou*); and E and P, together with the Byzantine text, read "known from eternity to God are all his works" (*gnōsta ap aiōnos esti tō theō panta ta erga autou*). To read the text in either of these latter two ways tends to separate the clause from the preceding biblical quotation, viewing it as a comment by James himself. It was not unusual in the Jewish world to express such a sentiment when the content of a passage seemed obvious but the logical connections were obscure. So it is perhaps best to interpret the words here as a comment by James to this effect: We cannot be in opposition to the express will of God, as evidenced by Peter's testimony and the prophets' words—but only God himself knows for certain how everything fits together and is to be fully understood!

19 On the basic issue that brought the members of the first ecumenical council together —that of the necessity of relating Gentiles to Judaism in the Christian mission—James refused to side with the Judaizers. He may not have been prepared to endorse openly all the details of Paul's Gentile policy. Certainly there is no indication that he expected the Jerusalem church to do that. But he could not be in opposition to the express will of God, and therefore his advice was that Jewish Christianity should not take any stance against the promotion of the Gentile mission. In so concluding, he swept aside the obstacles that had arisen to Paul's Gentile mission among believers at Jerusalem and left it free for further advances within the empire.

It is significant that while many insist that "what circumcision meant under the old dispensation, that and no less, is the meaning of baptism for those living in the new age" (W.F. Flemington, *The New Testament Doctrine of Baptism* [London: SPCK, 1948], p. 62), James made no mention at the council of baptism superseding circumcision—something that, had he advocated it, would have forever silenced the Jewish-Christian critics of Gentile salvation. Nor does Paul either in Galatians or Romans, where it might have been expected, make any such mention. Moreover, had Paul believed that baptism superseded circumcision, his circumcision of Timothy would have been nonsense (cf. 16:3).

20-21 On the practical question that troubled many Christians at Jerusalem and that originally gave rise to the Judaizers' assertion—viz., the question of fellowship between Jews and Gentiles in the church and of tolerance for the scruples of others—James's advice was that a letter be written to the Gentile Christians. This letter should request them to abstain "from food polluted by idols" (*tōn alisgēmatōn tōn eidōlōn*; lit., "from pollutions of idols"), "from sexual immorality" (*tēs porneias*, which probably means here "from marriage in prohibited degrees of relationship"; cf. SBK, 2:729), "from the meat of strangled animals" (*tou pniktou*; lit., "from things strangled"), and "from blood" (*tou haimatos*, i.e., "from eating blood").

These prohibitions have often been viewed as a compromise between two warring parties, which nullified the effect of James's earlier words and made the decision of the Jerusalem Council unacceptable to Paul. But in reality they should be viewed not as dealing with the principial issue of the council but as meeting certain practical concerns; not as being primarily theological but more sociological in nature; not as divine ordinances for acceptance before God but as concessions to the scruples of others for the sake of harmony within the church and the continuance of the Jewish Christian mission. Therefore James added the rationale of v.21: "For Moses has been preached in every city from the earliest times and is read in the synogogues on every Sabbath"—that is to say, since Jewish communities are to be found in every city, their scruples are to be respected by Gentile believers.

To sum up, we may say that two types of "necessary" questions were raised at the Jerusalem Council. The first had to do with the theological necessity of circumcision and the Jewish law for salvation, and that was rejected. The second had to do with the practical necessity of Gentile Christians abstaining from certain practices for the sake of Jewish-Gentile fellowship within the church and for the sake of the Jewish Christian mission throughout the Diaspora, and that was approved. The major work of the council had to do with the vindication of Gentile freedom, while a secondary matter was concerned with the expression of that freedom in regard to the scruples of others (cf. M. Luther, "On the Councils and the Churches," *Works of Martin Luther*, 6 vols., tr. C.M. Jacobs [Philadelphia: Holman, 1915–32], esp. 5:150–54, 188, 193–95).

Notes

---

13 On the address Ἄνδρες ἀδελφοί (*Andres adelphoi*, "Men, brothers"), see the comments on 1:16.

16-17 On other texts in Acts that show an affinity to the Dead Sea sectarians' text and usage, see 3:22–23 on Deut 18:15, 18–19; 7:43 on Amos 5:26–27; and 13:41 on Hab 1:5.

17 The καί (*kai*, "and") here is explicative and should probably be rendered "even all the Gentiles."

20 The Western text omits καὶ τοῦ πνικτοῦ (*kai tou pniktou*, "and from the meat of strangled animals") and adds the negative Golden Rule, thereby turning the four prohibitions into a set of three ethical axioms having to do with idolatry, immorality, and murder, with an appended injunction. And P[45], together with Origen (*Contra Celsum* 8.29) and the Ethiopic version, omits τῆς πορνείας (*tēs porneias*, "sexual immorality"). But the originality of the four prohibitions is well attested by ℵ A B C, together with P[74]. These four prohibitions, in fact, became widely known within Judaism as the Noachian precepts (cf. b *Sanhedrin* 56b, based on Lev 17:1–18:30) and were viewed by some rabbis as the essential requirements for Gentiles in the eschatological age (cf. Gen R 98.9).

For a fuller treatment of the Jerusalem decree and Paul's acceptance of it, see my *Paul*, pp. 254–60.

21 Some commentators see this verse as a justification for the exegesis of vv.16–17, while others see it as a justification for the judgment of v.19. But the γάρ (*gar*, "for") does not easily reach back to either.

---

4. The decision and letter of the Council

15:22–29

22Then the apostles and elders, with the whole church, decided to choose some of their own men and send them to Antioch with Paul and Barnabas. They chose Judas (called Barsabbas) and Silas, two men who were leaders among the brothers. 23With them they sent the following letter:

The apostles and elders, your brothers,

To the Gentile believers in Antioch, Syria and Cilicia:

Greetings.

24We have heard that some went out from us without our authorization and disturbed you, troubling your minds by what they said. 25So we all agreed to choose some men and send them to you with our dear friends Barnabas and Paul— 26men who have risked their lives for the name of our Lord Jesus Christ. 27Therefore we are sending Judas and Silas to confirm by word of mouth what we are writing. 28It seemed good to the Holy Spirit and to us not to burden you with anything beyond the following requirements: 29You are to abstain from food sacrificed to idols, from blood, from the meat of strangled animals and from sexual immorality. You will do well to avoid these things.

Farewell.

22 With James's judgment "the apostles and elders, with the whole church," agreed, deciding to send their decision back to Antioch of Syria not only by Paul and Barnabas but also by two leaders of the Jerusalem congregation, Judas Barsabbas and Silas, whose presence would assure reception of the decision and who could interpret the feelings of the council from a Jerusalem perspective. The reference to "the apostles" (*hoi apostoloi*), "the elders" (*hoi presbyteroi*), and "the whole church" (*holē hē ekklēsia*) is comparable to the Qumran structure of authority where executive action for religious matters was in the hands of the priests, other matters were in the hands of an "overseer" or "guardian," an advisory council of twelve to fifteen persons was apparently active, and all the mature members of the community (*hārabbîm*, "the many") gave their approval to the decisions of the priests, overseer, and council. Other models of organi-

zation were undoubtedly used among other groups within Palestine, and the lines of demarcation between officials were evidently quite flexible. But it seems clear that at Qumran and within the Jerusalem church, the congregation, while not equivalent to the Greek assembly (*dēmos*) in its governmental powers, was involved in the deliberations of its leaders.

When one considers the situation of the Jerusalem church in A.D. 49, the decision reached by the Jerusalem Christians must be considered one of the boldest and most magnanimous in the annals of church history. While still attempting to minister exclusively to the nation, the council refused to impede the progress of that other branch of the Christian mission whose every success meant further difficulty for them from within their own nation. Undoubtedly there was some uncertainty among the council's leaders about details of the decision. Certainly they reached it only after much agonizing. Likewise, there probably remained in the Jerusalem church a recalcitrant group that continued to predict ominous consequences. But the decision was made and the malcontents silenced—at least for a time.

The effects of the decision were far-reaching. In the first place, it freed the gospel from any necessary entanglement with Judaism and Israelite institutions, though without renouncing the legitimacy of continued Christian activity within them. Thus both Paul's mission to the Gentiles and the various Jewish Christian missions were enabled to progress side by side without conflict. Second, attitudes to Paul within Jewish Christianity were clarified. While some of the Jewish believers probably became even more opposed to Paul, others—e.g., John Mark (15:37-39)—seem to have become more reconciled to him. Also, as a result of the council, some felt happier in a Gentile ministry than at Jerusalem (Silas; cf. 15:40, passim). Third, the decision of the council had the effect of permanently antagonizing many Jews. From this time onward, the Christian mission within the nation—particularly in and around Jerusalem—faced very rough sledding (cf. Rom 11:28). And when coupled with the zealotism within the nation during the next two decades, this antagonism proved fatal to the life and ministry of the Jerusalem church.

23-29 With Judas, Silas, Paul, and Barnabas, who were going to Antioch, the Jerusalem church sent a letter. At the end of the second century, Clement of Alexandria spoke of this letter as "the Catholic epistle of all the Apostles" that was "conveyed to all the faithful by the hands of Paul himself" and was later incorporated into the Book of Acts (*Stromata* 4. 15). And by the appearance of such expressions as "the apostles and elders, brothers" (*hoi apostoloi kai hoi presbyteroi adelphoi*, v.23), "our beloved Barnabas and Paul" (*tois agapētois hēmōn Barnaba kai Paulō*, v.25), and "it seemed good to the Holy Spirit and to us" (*edoxen tō pneumati tō hagiō kai hēmin*)—all of them phrases more characteristic of Jerusalem than of Luke—it may be postulated that here "we are dealing with an original document copied by Luke more or less verbatim" (W.L. Knox, *Acts of the Apostles*, p. 50).

The placing of "brothers" in apposition to "the apostles and elders" (or, perhaps, to "the elders" alone) in the salutation is most unusual. Some commentators have attempted to read it as "the apostles and elders and brothers" (adding an "and") or as "the apostles and elders" (deleting "brothers") or as "the brothers" (deleting "apostles and elders"). But it should probably be understood as reflecting a form of expression used within the Jerusalem congregation, similar to "Men, brothers" (*Andres adelphoi*) of 1:16; 2:29, 37; 7:2; 13:15, 26, 38; 15:7, 13; 22:1; 23:1, 6; and 28:17—and almost as untranslatable. Likewise, the address "to the Gentile believers in Antioch, Syria and Cilicia" is surprising, for though Paul refers to spending some time in Syria and Cilicia, Luke has not spoken of any mission outside of Antioch in these areas. Yet 15:36, 41 assume that churches were established in these areas with Paul's assistance. And 16:4 shows that the content of the letter from the council was meant not only for congregations in the areas listed in 15:23 but that it applied to Gentile believers generally (cf. 15:19; 21:25).

The body of the letter encapsulates the problem confronted by the churches because of the Judaizers' claims and the Jerusalem Council's reaction to it, commending to the churches Barnabas and Paul (cf. comments on 14:14 and 15:12 for this order) and the Jerusalem emissaries Judas and Silas. On the fundamental matter of the theological necessity of circumcision and a Jewish lifestyle for Gentile Christians, the letter rebukes the Judaizers for going beyond their authority and assures the churches that there are no such requirements for salvation. On the practical issues of fellowship between Jewish and Gentile believers in the churches and of preventing needless offense to Jews throughout the empire, the letter asks Gentile Christians to abstain from "idolatry" (eidōlothytōn), "blood" (haimatos), "things strangled" (pniktōn), and "sexual immorality" (porneias)—which four prohibitions are given in a slightly different order and more abbreviated fashion than in v.20, but with the same sense. Then in closing there is the perfect passive imperative "Farewell" (errōsthe)—a typical way of ending a letter, as so many of the contemporary nonliterary papyri show.

Notes

22 Nothing further is known of Judas Barsabbas. He could be the brother of Joseph Barsabbas of 1:22, but the surname Barsabbas ("Son of the Sabbath," meaning "one born on the Sabbath") was common.

24 Many Western texts (though not D) add "you must be circumcised and keep the law" after "troubling your minds."

26 The Western text adds "in every trial" after "of our Lord Jesus Christ."

29 The Western text treats the prohibitions as a three-clause ethical maxim with appended negative Golden Rule, as it does at v.20. Likewise, P[45], Origen, and the Ethiopic version omit τῆς πορνείας (tēs porneias, "sexual immorality"), as at v.20.

The Western text adds φερόμενοι ἐν τῷ ἁγίῳ πνεύματι (pheromenoi en tō hagiō pneumati, "being carried along by the Holy Spirit") after the verb πράξετε (praxete, "you will do").

F. The Reception of the Council's Decision and of the Letter (15:30–16:4)

Luke describes the aftermath of the Jerusalem Council in three vignettes that all relate to the reception of the council's decision and letter in three localities of earlier Gentile outreach: Antioch of Syria (15:30–35), Syria and Cilicia (15:36–41), and the southern part of Galatia (16:1–4). Other items of information are also included, as Luke uses these final scenes of his fourth panel of material to prepare for the extensive outreach of the gospel through Paul's second and third missionary journeys.

1. At Antioch of Syria

15:30–35

[30] The men were sent off and went down to Antioch, where they gathered the church together and delivered the letter. [31] The people read it and were glad for

its encouraging message. ³²Judas and Silas, who themselves were prophets, said much to encourage and strengthen the brothers. ³³After spending some time there, they were sent off by the brothers with the blessing of peace to return to those who had sent them. ³⁵But Paul and Barnabas remained in Antioch, where they and many others taught and preached the word of the Lord.

30–32 The connective *men oun* (untranslated in NIV) opens this new section on the reception of the council's decision and letter. At Antioch of Syria the delegation on returning from Jerusalem "gathered the church [*to plēthos*] together and delivered the letter," with Judas and Silas saying "much to encourage and strengthen the brothers." And the believers, Luke tells us, "were glad."

Some commentators have complained that Luke's account here is pure idealization, for the fourfold decree of the supposed Jerusalem letter "was by no means an insignificant requirement" and cannot be seen as acceptable to Paul, who "undisturbedly ... pushed along the straight road of freedom from the law" (Leitzmann, p. 142). But if we view the Jerusalem Council's decision and letter as dealing with two matters—the first a matter of principle and the second a practical matter—it is not difficult to believe that, having gained a decided victory in the first matter, Paul and the existing Gentile churches were prepared to accept the so-called decrees as a modus operandi for reducing friction between two groups of people drawn from two different ways of life. Such an attitude is quite in accord with an apostle who could proclaim:

> Though I am free and belong to no man, I make myself a slave to everyone, to win as many as possible. To the Jews I became like a Jew, to win the Jews. To those under the law I became like one under the law (though I myself am not under the law), so as to win those under the law. To those not having the law I became like one not having the law (though I am not free from God's law but am under Christ's law), so as to win those not having the law. To the weak I became weak, to win the weak. I have become all things to all men so that by all possible means I might save some. I do all this for the sake of the gospel, that I may share in its blessings (1 Cor 9:19–23).

James's later reference to the decree (cf. 21:25) is not because it was then first promulgated but probably because James was reminding Paul of their agreed-on basis of fellowship and because Luke was reminding his readers of what they had already read. The fact that nothing is said of the decree in either Galatians or 1 and 2 Corinthians is no proof that Paul knew nothing about it or could not wholeheartedly accept it. If Galatians was written before the Jerusalem Council, reference to the Jerusalem decree in Galatians would have been miraculous. And while the reference to "food sacrificed to idols" (*eidōlothytōn*, v.29) exactly fits the problem at Corinth (cf. 1 Cor 8:1–11:1), Paul may not have been able to quote any type of ecclesiastical statement to his supraspiritual Gentile converts at Corinth if he desired to win them over to a truer understanding and expression of their Christian freedom. In fact, as many have suggested, it could just as well be argued that Paul's problems with the ultraspiritual segment of the Corinthian church arose, at least in part, because he had originally delivered the Jerusalem letter to them and thus in correcting them was forced to argue on different grounds, as that his silence regarding the decrees is incriminating.

33, 35 After some time, Judas and Silas returned to Jerusalem with the commendation of the Antioch believers. The Western and Byzantine texts add v.34, "But it seemed good to Silas to remain there" (*edoxe de tō Sila epimeinai autou*), no doubt to explain why Silas appears again at Antioch in v.40. But the addition contradicts the plain sense of v.33 and fails to take into account that Paul could have sent for Silas after the latter's return to Jerusalem. Paul and Barnabas, however, remained at Syrian Antioch and joined others in carrying on the ministry there.

Notes

30 On Luke's use of μὲν οὖν (*men oun*), see comments and note on 1:6. Note especially his use of this connective in his fourth panel at 13:4; 14:3; 15:3; and 16:5.

On going "down" (κατῆλθον, *katēlthon*) from Jerusalem to Antioch, see the comments on and note at 8:5.

On the term τὸ πλῆθος (*to plēthos*, "the assembly"), see the note at 6:2 (also v.12 above).

31 On Paul's manner of dealing with the issues at Corinth, a discussion relevant for understanding his acceptance of the Jerusalem decree, see my *Paul*, pp. 232–44.

32 D adds "full of the Holy Spirit" after "who were themselves prophets."

2. Disagreement and two missionary teams

15:36–41

36Some time later Paul said to Barnabas, "Let us go back and visit the brothers in all the towns where we preached the word of the Lord and see how they are doing." 37Barnabas wanted to take John, also called Mark, with them, 38but Paul did not think it wise to take him, because he had deserted them in Pamphylia and had not continued with them in the work. 39They had such a sharp disagreement that they parted company. Barnabas took Mark and sailed for Cyprus, 40but Paul chose Silas and left, commended by the brothers to the grace of the Lord. 41He went through Syria and Cilicia, strengthening the churches.

36 Beginning at this point in Acts, the preposition *meta* with a time designation (i.e., *meta tinas hēmeras*, "after some days"; *meta tauta*, "after these things"; or *meta tas hēmeras tauta*, "after these days"; see Notes for instances in the remainder of Acts) vies with the connective *men oun* (see Notes for instances in the remainder of Acts) to mark off the beginning of a new section and join it with what has gone before. So Luke now presents Paul as taking the initiative for another missionary journey. In Paul's mind, of course, it was no new outreach but only a revisiting of believers converted on the first missionary journey. Nevertheless, God was to bring the second missionary journey out of it. Actually, this section provides something of a bridge between the completion of the advances reported in panel 4 and the beginning of those reported in panel 5.

37–39 John Mark, Barnabas's cousin (cf. Col 4:10), probably became convinced of the appropriateness of Paul's Gentile policy by the action of the Jerusalem Council, despite earlier qualms about it (see comments on 13:13). Barnabas had evidently called him back to Syrian Antioch to minister in the church there. Barnabas's earlier involvement in the dispute at Antioch showed that his natural sympathies lay principally with Jewish Christians (cf. Gal 2:13), and it was also natural for him to want to take Mark with them in revisiting the churches. Paul, however, for what seem to have been reasons of principle rather than personal ones, did not want to have so unreliable a man with them day after day (note the present infinitive *symparalambanein*). The scar tissue of the wounds Paul suffered in establishing his missionary policy was still too tender for him to look favorably on Mark's being with them—particularly if, as we have assumed, Mark was in some way responsible for inciting the Judaizers to action.

The fact that Luke does not gloss over the quarrel between Paul and Barnabas shows his honesty. The Greek word for "disagreement" (*paroxysmos*) is so neutral as not to touch upon the question of responsibility, and it is idle for us to try to apportion blame. Yet far from letting the disagreement harm the outreach of the gospel, God providentially used it to double the missionary force, with Barnabas taking Mark and returning to Cyprus (cf. 13:4-12). Acts tells us nothing more about the mission to Cyprus or the missioners there, though Paul's letters refer in cordial terms to both Barnabas (cf. 1 Cor 9:6; perhaps also, as Luther and Calvin suggested, 2 Cor 8:18-19) and John Mark (cf. Col 4:10; 2 Tim 4:11; Philem 24).

40-41 Paul's selection of Silas (or "Silvanus," as he is referred to more formally by his Latinized name in 2 Cor 1:19; 1 Thess 1:1; 2 Thess 1:1; 1 Peter 5:12) to accompany him on his return visit to the churches was wise. He had evidently come to appreciate Silas in their contacts at Jerusalem and Syrian Antioch and concluded that he would make a congenial colleague. More than that, Silas was a leader in the Jerusalem congregation (15:22) and was explicitly identified in the Jerusalem letter as one who could speak with authority on the attitude of the Jerusalem church (15:27). He was also, it seems, a Roman citizen who could claim, if need be, the privileges of such citizenship along with Paul (16:37). This was not true of Barnabas. Likewise, Silas was a prophet (15:32), who appears to have been fluent in Greek (15:22, 32) and a helpful amanuensis (1 Thess 1:1; 2 Thess 1:1; 1 Peter 5:12). Thus Paul and Silas set out with the blessing of the Antioch congregation. The churches in Syria and Cilicia they revisited and strengthened were presumably founded through the efforts of Paul (15:23, 36). As such, they would be receptive to the decision and letter of the Jerusalem Council.

Notes

36 On μετὰ (*meta*, "after") with a time designation as a connective in Acts, see also 18:1; 21:15; 24:1, 24; 25:1; 28:11, 17. On μὲν οὖν (*men oun*, generally untranslated in NIV) in the remainder of Acts, see 16:5; 17:12, 17, 30; 19:32, 38; 23:18, 22, 31; 25:4, 11; 26:4, 9; 28:5.

3. *Paul adds Timothy to the team in Galatia*

16:1-4

> [1]He came to Derbe and then to Lystra, where a disciple named Timothy lived, whose mother was a Jewess and a believer, but whose father was a Greek. [2]The brothers at Lystra and Iconium spoke well of him. [3]Paul wanted to take him along on the journey, so he circumcised him because of the Jews who lived in that area, for they all knew that his father was a Greek. [4]As they traveled from town to town, they delivered the decisions reached by the apostles and elders in Jerusalem for the people to obey.

1-2 Pushing on through the Cilician Gates (modern Gülek Bogaz) in the Taurus mountains, Paul and Silas came to the Galatian border town of Derbe and then moved on to Lystra. At Lystra (note the use of *ekei*, "there") he found a young man who was highly spoken of by believers in both Lystra and the neighboring city of Iconium. The Jewish community at Lystra seems to have been small and without influence (cf. comments on 14:8-10). Probably for that reason Timothy's mother, a Jewess, was allowed to marry a Greek. Timothy, however, had never been circumcised. In Jewish law, a child takes the religion of its mother; so Timothy should have been circumcised and raised a Jew. But in Greek law the father dominates in the home. Apparently the Jewish community at Lystra was too weak or lax to interfere with Greek custom. Second Timothy 1:5 speaks of the sincere Jewish faith of Timothy's grandmother Lois and of his mother, Eunice, and 2 Timothy 3:15 speaks of Timothy's early instruction in the Hebrew Scriptures. Here Eunice is identified as a Jewess as well as a Christian believer, who had probably been converted during the first visit of Paul and Barnabas to Lystra. From the imperfect verb *hypērchen* ("he was") in v.3, it may be reasonably conjectured that her husband was now dead. Likewise, from Paul's reference to Timothy in 1 Corinthians 4:17 as his son, we may assume that Timothy's conversion to Christ also dates from the proclamation of the gospel on that first missionary journey.

3-4 Most scholars accept at face value the statements in vv.1-2 and the statement about Paul's desire to take Timothy along with him on his journey (v.3a). Many, however, question what is said about Paul's circumcizing Timothy and delivering the Jerusalem decisions to the Galatian Christians. The hand of a redactor has often been seen in vv.3-4 and Luke accused of perpetuating gross confusion—e.g., attributing to Paul's relations with Timothy an erroneous tradition concerning Titus (cf. BC, 4:184, citing Gal 2:3) or inadvertently taking over some slanderous rumor that Paul did on occasion circumcise his converts (cf. Haenchen, *Acts of the Apostles*, p. 482, citing Gal 5:11). But while Paul stoutly resisted any imposition of circumcision and the Jewish law upon his Gentile converts, he himself continued to live as an observant Jew and urged his converts to express their Christian faith through the cultural forms they had inherited (cf. 1 Cor 7:17-24). As for Timothy, because of his Jewish mother, he was a Jew in the eyes of the Jewish world. Therefore, it was both proper and expedient for Paul to circumcise him. As Paul saw it, being a good Christian did not mean being a bad Jew. Rather, it meant being a fulfilled Jew. Paul had no desire to flout Jewish scruples in his endeavor to bring both Jews and Gentiles to salvation in Christ. Similarly, there is no reason to think he would have refused to deliver the decision of the Jerusalem Council to his Galatian converts and every reason to believe he would—particularly if he had written Galatians to them earlier and was now able to say that the Jerusalem leaders supported his position, and if, as Luke shows, he thought of the Galatian Christians as within the scope of the mission from Syrian Antioch.

Notes

3 On Paul's own expression of his Christian faith through the forms of Judaism, see my *Paul*, esp. pp. 245-63.
4 The Western text recasts v.4 to read: "And going through the cities they preached with all boldness the Lord Jesus Christ, at the same time delivering the commandments of the apostles and elders at Jerusalem."

G. A Summary Statement

16:5

⁵So the churches were strengthened in the faith and grew daily in numbers.

5 This summary statement concludes what F.F. Bruce calls "perhaps the most crucial phase of Luke's narrative" (*Book of the Acts*, p. 324). It is comparable to the summary statements of 6:7; 9:31; and 12:24 that culminate their respective panels of material (cf. also 19:20 and 28:31 later). Introduced by Luke's favorite connective *men oun* (see comments on 1:6), it stresses the strengthening and growth of the churches as a result of Paul's missionary policy and the response of the Jerusalem church to it.

Panel 5—Wide Outreach Through Two Missionary Journeys (16:6–19:20)

Panel 5 presents the wide outreach of the Christian mission through two further missionary journeys of Paul in the eastern part of the empire. Having described the gradual extension of the gospel to new groups of people and through a new missionary policy, Luke now shows its entrance into new areas. Notable in this panel are Luke's emphases upon (1) God's direction in and supervision of the gospel's outreach, (2) Christianity's right to be considered a *religio licita*, and (3) Paul's circumstantial preaching in terms of proclamation and persuasion. Also of interest is the fact that the missionary outreach was confined to the major cities of the Aegean coastline connected by the main Roman roads, and that at the beginning of this panel we have our first "we" section (16:10–17) of the latter half of Acts (cf. 20:5–15; 21:1–18; 27:1–28:16). Temporal references in the panel are fairly general, even when datable—e.g., the Edict of Claudius (18:2) and Gallio's proconsulate (18:12) leave some margin for dispute. Generally, however, the material given here covers the years A.D. 49–56, with the first journey into Macedonia and Achaia taking place about 49–52 and the second centered in Ephesus during 53–56.

A. Providential Direction for the Mission

16:6–10

⁶Paul and his companions traveled throughout the region of Phrygia and Galatia, having been kept by the Holy Spirit from preaching the word in the province of Asia. ⁷When they came to the border of Mysia, they tried to enter Bithynia, but the Spirit of Jesus would not allow them to. ⁸So they passed by Mysia and went down to Troas. ⁹During the night Paul had a vision of a man of Macedonia standing and begging him, "Come over to Macedonia and help us." ¹⁰After Paul had seen the vision, we got ready at once to leave for Macedonia, concluding that God had called us to preach the gospel to them.

6 The missionary journeys of Paul reveal an extraordinary combination of strategic planning and sensitivity to the guidance of the Holy Spirit in working out the details of the main goals. This is especially noticeable here. Having revisited the churches at Derbe, Lystra, Iconium, and Pisidian Antioch, Paul evidently expected to follow the Via Sebaste westward to the important coastal city and capital of the Roman province of Asia, Ephesus. But he was "kept by the Holy Spirit" from entering Asia and so continued to travel throughout "the region of Phrygia and Galatia."

The heightening of terminology in vv.6–10 from "the Holy Spirit" to "the Spirit of Jesus" to "God" is not just stylistic but an unconscious expression of the early church's embryonic trinitarian faith. All three terms refer to God by his Spirit giving direction to the mission. But just how the Holy Spirit revealed his will we are not told. Perhaps in one or more instances Silas had a part, for he was a prophet (15:32).

Likewise, we are left somewhat uncertain as to what Luke meant by "the region of Phrygia and Galatia" (*tēn Phrygian kai Galatikēn chōran*). Many are of the opinion that the reference to *Galatikēn chōran* must be taken to mean that "Galatia" is "a second country named beside Phrygia" (Haenchen, *Acts of the Apostles*, p. 483, n.2), and that therefore Galatia cannot here be equated with Phrygia—thus ruling out a continued ministry around Iconium and "Pisidian" Antioch and suggesting a journey into northern Galatia (cf. also 18:23). But as E.D. Burton insisted: "The most obvious and, indeed, only natural explanation of the phrase *tēn Phrugian kai Galatikēn chōran* in v.6 is that *Phrugian* and *Galatikēn* are both adjectives and both limit *chōran*"; and, further, that "the joining of the words *Phrugian* and *Galatikēn* by *kai*, with the article before the first one only, implies that the region designated by *chōran* is one, Phrygian and Galatian" (*A Critical and Exegetical Commentary on the Epistle to the Galatians* [Edinburgh: T. & T. Clark, 1921], pp. xxxi–xxxii). There is no linguistic support here for a so-called North Galatian theory. We are rather left to explain this juxtaposition of adjectives either (1) politically, meaning not the entire province of Galatia but only the Phrygic region of Galatia, or, possibly, (2) ethnologically and popularly, meaning a district adjoining the region of Phrygia in the southern portion of the Roman province of Galatia where both Phrygian and Celtic (Galatic or Gaulish) dialects could be heard.

7–8 Mysia was a region in northwest Asia Minor that lacked precise boundries because it never was an independent political entity. It was generally considered to be bounded by the Aegean Sea on the west; the Hellespont (or Dardanelles), Propontis (or Sea of Marmara), and Bithynia along its northern extremities from west to east; Galatia on the east and southeast; Phrygia to the south; and the area of Lydia to the southwest. It included the historic Aegean seaport of Troas and the site of ancient Troy some ten miles inland.

As Paul's party moved northwest along the borders of Mysian territory, they decided to go on into the Thracian area of Bithynia in order to evangelize the strategic cities and important Black Sea ports there, all of which were interconnected by an elaborate Roman road system. But, Luke tells us, "the Spirit of Jesus would not allow them to" (v.7). Later, Christians in Bithynia were included in the salutation of 1 Peter (1:1). Also, Pliny the Younger, who was governor of Bithynia under Trajan in A.D. 110–12, spoke of Christians in the province who, though a minority, had to be taken into account (cf. Pliny *Letters* 10. 96–97). But Paul was not directed by God to evangelize in Bithynia. Instead, the missionary party turned westward again, traveling through Mysia till they reached Troas on the Aegean coast. The participle *parelthontes* literally means "they passed by" Mysia and at first glance seems somewhat out of place since one could not get to Troas without passing through Mysia. Probably, however, Luke used *parelthontes* instead of *dielthontes* ("they passed through") to indicate that they did not stay in Mysia to evangelize.

9–10 Troas became an important Greek port about 300 B.C. and was named Alexandria Troas. After the break-up of Alexander the Great's short-lived empire, Troas was ruled for a time by the Seleucids from Syrian Antioch, but it soon became an independent city-state. To the Greeks, mountains protected but separated people, whereas the sea, while frightening, united people. Therefore Troas, at the mouth of the Dardenelles, was the pivotal port between the land masses of Europe and Asia Minor and the great waterways of the Aegean and Black seas. When Rome annexed Anatolia, Julius Caesar seriously considered making Troas the governmental center of the entire area (cf. Suetonius *Divus Iulius* 79; Horace *Odes* 3.3).

At Troas Paul had a vision of a Macedonian asking for help. He took this as a divine call to evangelize Macedonia. Many commentators have suggested that Paul met Luke at Troas, perhaps initially for medical reasons, and that Luke impressed upon him during their conversations the need for the preaching of the gospel in Macedonia—an encounter God used in a vision to direct Paul and his colleagues to Macedonia. And perhaps that is how it happened. Luke gives us none of the psychological details, though it must be said that Paul's recognition of the man as being a Macedonian could as easily have been gained from his message as from any prior acquaintance or knowledge. But whatever secondary means God may have used to convey the vision, Paul and his party responded to it at once (*eutheōs*, "immediately") by making preparations to leave for Macedonia. Such preparations would have required finding passage on a ship sailing for Neapolis.

Authentic turning points in history are few. But surely among them that of the Macedonian vision ranks high. Because of Paul's obedience at this point, the gospel went westward; and ultimately Europe and the Western world were evangelized. Christian response to the call of God is never a trivial thing. Indeed, as in this instance, great issues and untold blessings may depend on it.

It is at Troas that the first of the "we" sections of Acts appears (16:10-17). Because (1) this "we" section stops at Philippi, (2) the second "we" section (20:5-15) begins when the missionaries revisit Philippi after the third missionary journey, and (3) the ministry at Philippi receives the greatest attention (thirty verses) in this fifth panel, we may reasonably suppose that the use of "we" points to a resident of Philippi who traveled from Troas to Philippi with Paul and Silas and that this person was Luke himself (cf. Introduction: The Sources of Acts).

Notes

8 The Western text reads διελθόντες (*dielthontes*, "passing through") for παρελθόντες (*parelthontes*, "passing by"), which is more geographically correct but ignores Luke's point. On further Pauline contacts with Troas, see Acts 20:1-12; 2 Cor 2:12-13; 2 Tim 4:13.

10 The Western text recasts v.10 to read: "Then awakening, he related the vision to us, and we recognized that the Lord had called us to evangelize those in Macedonia."

B. *At Philippi* (16:11-40)

Luke devotes more space to the mission in Philippi than he does to any other city on Paul's second and third missionary journeys—and he does this despite the brief stay there. Philippi is the only city Luke describes as a Roman colony. When he calls it "the leading city of the district of Macedonia" (see comments below on v.12), he seems to be reflecting local pride. To judge by the way the "we" sections in 16:10–17 and 20:5–15 focus on Paul's visits to Philippi, it may be that Luke had some part in the founding and growth of the church there.

1. Arrival in the city

16:11–12

11From Troas we put out to sea and sailed straight for Samothrace, and the next day on to Neapolis. 12From there we traveled to Philippi, a Roman colony and the leading city of that district of Macedonia. And we stayed there several days.

11 Samothrace is an island in the northeastern part of the Aegean Sea, lying between Troas and Philippi. The most conspicuous landmark in the North Aegean, it is mountainous and was also called Poseidon's Island because from the top of Mount Fengari (5,577 feet) Poseidon, the Greek god of the waters, earthquakes, and horses, was said to have surveyed the plains of ancient Troy (cf. Homer *Iliad* 13.12). It became a stopover for ships plying their trade in the North Aegean, as captains preferred to anchor there rather than face the hazards of the sea at night (cf. Pliny *Natural History* 4.23). Neapolis on the northern coast of the Aegean was the port for the commercial center of Philippi, which lay ten miles further inland. Neapolis was on the Via Egnatia, which ran east to Byzantium and west to Philippi, then to Thessalonica, and finally across the Balkan peninsula to Dyrrhachium and its port Egnatia (from which the road may have been named) on the Adriatic coast.

Since the narrator was on board, we have a port-by-port description of the voyage, with specific mention of the time it took—as we do also in the other "we" sections (cf. 20:5, 13–15; 21:1–8; 27:1–28:16). The wind at this crossing must have favored the travelers, for it took only two days to sail the 156 miles to Neapolis, though the trip in the other direction after the third missionary journey took five days (cf. 20:5).

12 Philippi was ten miles northwest of Neapolis, on a plain bounded by Mount Pangaeus to the north and northeast, with the rivers Strymon and Nestos on either side. Shielded from the sea by a very rocky ridge, it lay astride the Via Egnatia and near the Gangites River, a tributary of the Strymon. Its fame in earlier days came from its fertile plain and gold in the mountains to the north. Philip II of Macedon recognized the city's importance, and in 356 B.C. he established a large Greek colony there, changing its name from Krenides ("springs") to Philippi (cf. Diodorus *Historical Library* 7.6.7). With the subjugation of the Macedonians by Rome in 167 B.C., Philippi became part of the Roman Empire. In 146 B.C. it was included within the reorganized province of Macedonia, whose capital was at Thessalonica. Shortly thereafter it was connected to other important Roman cities by the Via Egnatia.

During Roman times, the fame of Philippi stemmed from its having been the site of the decisive battle of the second civil war in 42 B.C., when Mark Anthony and Octavian (later Augustus) defeated Brutus and Cassius. After the war many Roman army veterans were settled at Philippi and the city was designated a Roman colony. Its government was responsible directly to the emperor and not made subservient to the provincial administration. Philippi's importance during the NT period, therefore, resulted from its agriculture, its strategic commercial location on both sea and land routes, its still functioning gold mines, and its status as a Roman colony. In addition, it had a famous school of medicine with graduates throughout the then-known world.

Luke's reference to Philippi as "the leading [or 'first'] city of the district of Macedonia" (*prōtē tēs meridos Makedonias polis,* according to the majority reading of **א**, A, and C, together with P[74]—with B basically in agreement, though placing the article *tēs* before *Makedonias*) is somewhat confusing. Actually, Amphipolis, the early district capital between 167–146 B.C., and Thessalonica, the provincial capital after that, had a more valid claim to that title. Some Alexandrian MSS read *prōtēs* ("of the first") for *prōtē* ("the first"), thus suggesting that Philippi was "a city of the first district of Macedonia"—that is, a city of the first of the four administrative districts Macedonia was divided into by the Romans in 167 B.C., before the whole area was reorganized into the province of Macedonia in 146 B.C. Codex Bezae (D) reads *kephalē* ("the head" or "capital"), which wrongly asserts its status as the provincial capital.

Commentators have differed widely in interpreting the textual evidence here. We should probably, however, accept the majority reading of **א**, A, C, and P[74] and translate the ascription as "the leading city of the district of Macedonia"—understanding it as an expression of Luke's pride in his city, much as Pergamum, Smyrna, and Ephesus each claimed to be "the leading city of Asia" for other than merely governmental reasons. Yet it must be acknowledged that Codex Vaticanus (B) with its reading *prōtē meridos tēs Makedonias polis* could be understood more generally to mean "the leading city of that district of Macedonia" (as JB, NEB, NIV).

2. The conversion of Lydia

16:13-15

> [13]On the Sabbath we went outside the city gate to the river, where we expected to find a place of prayer. We sat down and began to speak to the women who had gathered there. [14]One of those listening was a woman named Lydia, a dealer in purple cloth from the city of Thyatira, who was a worshiper of God. The Lord opened her heart to respond to Paul's message. [15]When she and the members of her household were baptized, she invited us to her home. "If you consider me a believer in the Lord," she said, "come and stay at my house." And she persuaded us.

13 In Jewish law, a congregation was made up of ten men. Wherever there were ten male heads of households who could be in regular attendance, a synagogue was to be formed (cf. M *Sanhedrin* 1.6; M *Pirke Aboth* 3.6). Failing this, a place of prayer (*proseuchē*) under the open sky and near a river or the sea was to be arranged for (cf. Philo *In Flaccum* 14; Jos. Antiq. XIV, 258 [x.23], though rabbinic sources do not explicitly say it must be by water, cf. SBK, 2:742). But Philippi apparently did not have the quorum and so was without a synagogue. On the Sabbath, therefore, Paul and his companions walked outside the city in search of a Jewish place of prayer, probably heading toward the Gangites River about a mile and a half west of the city. There they found some women gathered to recite the Shema, to pray the Shemoneh Esreh, to read from the Law and the Prophets, to discuss what they had read, and, if possible, to hear from a traveling Jewish teacher an exposition or exhortation and receive a blessing (cf. comments on 13:15). Paul and his companions sat down with these women and began to speak to them.

14-15 One of the women was from Thyatira, a city of western Asia Minor. Formerly in the ancient kingdom of Lydia before its incorporation into the Roman province of Asia, Thyatira continued to be considered as in Lydia. Hence the woman was called Lydia (or, perhaps, "the Lydian lady"). Thyatira was famous for making purple dyes and for dyeing clothes—industries that were mostly carried on by women at home (cf. Homer *Iliad* 4. 141–42). As an artisan in purple dyes, Lydia had come to Philippi to carry on her trade. She is spoken of as a "God-fearer" (*sebomenē ton theon*), having doubtless received instruction at a synagogue in her native Thyatira before carrying her interest in Judaism with her to Philippi. We may surmise that she was either a widow or unmarried and that some of the women gathered for worship were relatives and servants living in her home. As she listened, God opened her heart to the Christian message and "she and the members of her household were baptized." Then she urged the missionary party to stay at her home, which they did.

From such small beginnings the church at Philippi began. To judge from his letter to the Philippians, it was one of Paul's most-loved congregations. Luke, as has been suggested, may have been involved in the establishment and growth of this church; probably Lydia was also prominent in it. Some commentators have suggested that the real name of this "Lydian lady" was either Euodia or Syntyche (Phil 4:2) and that the other was the wife of the converted jailer. Other commentators think that Paul had Lydia in mind when he referred to a "loyal yokefellow" (Phil 4:3), and a few even suppose that Paul married Lydia. But all this is mere conjecture. All we really know from the text is that Lydia, together with the members of her household, responded to the gospel and opened her house to Paul and his colleagues. Soon, it seems, her home became the center for Christian outreach and worship in Philippi (cf. 16:40).

Notes

13 The MS evidence for "we expected to find a place of prayer" is mixed and somewhat confusing. The Neutral text reads either ἐνομίζομεν προσευχήν (*enomizomen proseuchēn*), ἐνομίζομεν προσευχή (*enomizomen proseuchē*), or ἐνομίζαμεν προσευχήν (*enomizamen proseuchēn*), all of which, though somewhat different, are in basic agreement. The Byzantine text, however, reads ἐνομίζετο προσευχή (*enomizeto proseuchē*, "prayer was wont to be made," KJV), and the Western text reads ἐδόκει προσευχή (*edokei proseuchē*, "prayer was thought to be made").

Since προσευχή (*proseuchē*, "prayer") among Greek-speaking Jews was nearly always equivalent to συναγωγή (*synagōgē*), many have argued that an actual synagogue is here in view (cf. Schürer, HJP, 2. 4:499–500, 517–18). But probably "the place of prayer" of vv.13, 16 was not a synagogue, for only women are spoken of as being present and the word "synagogue" is used frequently elsewhere in Acts (e.g., 17:1, 10, 17).

15 For other instances of the conversion of members of a household with the head of the household, cf. 11:14 (also 10:2ff.); 16:31–34; 18:8; 1 Cor 16:15.

3. The demon-possessed girl

16:16–18

¹⁶Once when we were going to the place of prayer, we were met by a slave girl who had a spirit by which she predicted the future. She earned a great deal of money for her owners by fortune-telling. ¹⁷This girl followed Paul and the rest of us, shouting, "These men are servants of the Most High God, who are telling you

the way to be saved." 18She kept this up for many days. Finally Paul became so troubled that he turned around and said to the spirit, "In the name of Jesus Christ I command you to come out of her!" At that moment the spirit left her.

16 While on their way to the Jewish place of prayer (note the present participle *poreuomenōn*), the missionaries were met by a slave girl Luke describes as having a "Pythian spirit" (*pneuma pythōna*). The Python was a mythical serpent or dragon that guarded the temple and oracle of Apollo, located on the southern slope of Mount Parnassus to the north of the Gulf of Corinth. It was supposed to have lived at the foot of Mount Parnassus and to have eventually been killed by Apollo (cf. Strabo *Geography* 9.3.12). Later the word *python* came to mean a demon-possessed person through whom the Python spoke—even a ventriloquist was thought to have such a spirit living in his or her belly (cf. Plutarch *De Defectu Oraculorum* 9.414). Undoubtedly all who knew the girl regarded her as neither fraudulent nor insane but as demon possessed and able to foretell the future. By her fortunetelling, she earned her masters much money.

17–18 As the girl followed Paul and his companions around, she kept on screaming out (note the imperfect *ekrazen*): "These men are servants of the Most High God, who are telling you [*hymin*, pl.] the way to be saved." Her screaming recalls that of the demons during Jesus' ministry (Mark 1:24; 3:11; 5:7; Luke 4:34, 41; 8:28). In both instances there was a compulsive acknowledgment of the true character of those confronted. Here the acknowledgment is stated in terms acceptable to the Jewish world and readily understandable to Gentiles. The title "Most High God" (*ho theos ho hypsistos*), while originally a Phoenician ascription for deity (*'Ēl 'Elyôn*), was used by the Hebrews of Yahweh (cf. Num 24:16; Ps 78:35; Isa 14:14; Dan 3:26; 4:32; 5:18, 21; 1 Esd 2:3) and by the Greeks of Zeus (cf. C. Roberts, T.C. Skeat, and A.D. Nock, "The Guild of Zeus Hypsistos," HTR, 29 [1936], 39–88). And the announcement of "salvation" (*sōtēria*)—while for Paul and the Jews referring to deliverance from sin—would have connoted for Gentiles release from the powers governing the fate of man and of the material world. It was, therefore, cast in terms Gentiles could understand but Paul could build on.

But while the demon-inspired words provided some free publicity for the missionaries and helped gather an audience, when it continued for many days, it became a nuisance. The demon's words were getting more of a hearing than the proclamation of the gospel! So Paul commanded the evil spirit "in the name of Jesus Christ" to come out of the girl, and the demon left her. Presumably, having been delivered by the power of God, she became a Christian and—along with Lydia the businesswoman and members of her household, Luke the physician (notice that the "we" section stops at v.17), and an unnamed army veteran and jailer (vv.27–36)—a member of the embryonic church at Philippi.

Notes

17 P[45] omits δοῦλοι (*douloi*, "servants"). A C P, together with a number of minuscules and church fathers, read ἡμῖν (*hēmin*, "us") instead of ὑμῖν (*hymin*, "you"), as in ℵ B D E P[74] and the majority of versions.

4. Paul and Silas in prison

16:19-34

19When the owners of the slave girl realized that their hope of making money was gone, they seized Paul and Silas and dragged them into the marketplace to face the authorities. 20They brought them before the magistrates and said, "These men are Jews, and are throwing our city into an uproar 21by advocating customs unlawful for us Romans to accept or practice."

22The crowd joined in the attack against Paul and Silas, and the magistrates ordered them to be stripped and beaten. 23After they had been severely flogged, they were thrown into prison, and the jailer was commanded to guard them carefully. 24Upon receiving such orders, he put them in the inner cell and fastened their feet in the stocks.

25About midnight Paul and Silas were praying and singing hymns to God, and the other prisoners were listening to them. 26Suddenly there was such a violent earthquake that the foundations of the prison were shaken. At once all the prison doors flew open, and everybody's chains came loose. 27The jailer woke up, and when he saw the prison doors open, he drew his sword and was about to kill himself because he thought the prisoners had escaped. 28But Paul shouted, "Don't harm yourself! We are all here!"

29The jailer called for lights, rushed in and fell trembling before Paul and Silas. 30He then brought them out and asked, "Sirs, what must I do to be saved?"

31They replied, "Believe in the Lord Jesus, and you will be saved—you and your household." 32Then they spoke the word of the Lord to him and to all the others in his house. 33At that hour of the night the jailer took them and washed their wounds; then immediately he and all his family were baptized. 34The jailer brought them into his house and set a meal before them, and the whole family was filled with joy, because they had come to believe in God.

19-21 What Paul did for the slave girl was not appreciated by her masters. In exorcising the demon, he had exorcised their source of income. Because of interference with what they claimed as their property rights, and with callous disregard for the girl's welfare, they seized Paul and Silas and dragged them into the marketplace (*tēn agoran*, "the agora") to face the city's authorities. The charge laid was that Paul and Silas were advocating a *religio illicita* and thus disturbing the Pax Romana. But the charge, being couched in terms that appealed to the latent anti-Semitism of the people ("these men are Jews") and their racial pride ("us Romans"), ignited the flames of bigotry and prevented any dispassionate discussion of the issues.

Many have asked why only Paul and Silas were singled out for persecution, with Timothy and Luke left free. Of course, Paul and Silas were the leaders of the missionary party and therefore most open to attack. But we must also remember that Paul and Silas were Jews and probably looked very much like Jews (cf. comments on 14:3 on the tradition of Paul's appearance). Timothy and Luke, however, being respectively half-Jewish and fully Gentile (cf. Col 4:14, where Luke is grouped by Paul with his Gentile friends), probably looked Greek in both their features and their dress and therefore were left alone. Anti-Semitism lay very near the surface throughout the Roman Empire. Here it seems to have taken over not only in laying the charge but also in identifying the defendants.

22-24 As a Roman colony, Philippi had a form of government that was independent of the provincial administration headquartered in Thessalonica. There were two chief magistrates, called *duoviri* in most Roman colonies but in certain colonies referred to by the honorary title *praetores* (cf. Cicero *De Lege Agraria* 2.93), which translates into Greek as *stratēgoi* (vv.20, 22, 35–36, 38). At Philippi the magistrates were given this honorary title. Functioning under the magistrates were two *lictorae*, which translates into Greek as *rhabdouchoi* (vv.35, 38), who carried bundles of rods with axes attached (*fasces et secures*) as a sign of their judicial authority and whose job it was to carry out the orders of the magistrates. Jailers commonly were retired army veterans, who could be expected to follow orders and use their military skills as required.

Incited to anti-Semitic fury by the slave girl's owners, the crowd turned on Paul and Silas. The magistrates had them stripped and severely flogged as disturbers of the peace and then ordered them to be jailed. The jailer put them into the innermost cell (the comparative *esōtera* is used here as a superlative), fastening their feet in stocks. Though both Paul and Silas were Roman citizens and politically exempt from such treatment (cf. comments on v.37), the frenzy of the mob and the rough justice of the colonial magistrates overrode their protestations. Later when writing to the Christians at Corinth, Paul looked back on this experience as one of the afflictions he suffered as a servant of Christ and reminded the boasters among them that for the sake of the gospel he had "been in prison more frequently, been flogged more severely" than they had and had "been exposed to death again and again"—and had been "three times . . . beaten with rods" (2 Cor 11:23, 25).

25–28 One would expect that after such brutal treatment, Paul and Silas would be bemoaning their plight. Certainly they were suffering pain and shock from the flogging they had received. But about midnight, as Paul and Silas were "praying and singing hymns to God," an earthquake suddenly shook the prison, opened its doors, and loosened the chains of all the prisoners. When the awakened jailer saw the doors open, he surmised the worst. In Roman law a guard who allowed his prisoner to escape was liable to the same penalty the prisoner would have suffered (*Code of Justinian* 9.4.4). Thus the jailer drew his sword to kill himself, believing the prisoners had all escaped. But Paul saw him in the doorway and shouted out from within the prison, "Don't harm yourself! We are all here!"

Form criticism has pointed out (1) that stories regarding prison doors opening of their own accord and of miraculous escapes from confinement were popular in the ancient world (cf. Euripides *Bacchae* 443ff., 586ff., as early cited by Celsus [see Origen *Contra Celsum* 2.34]; Acts 5:19–24; 12:7–10; Acts of Thomas 154) and (2) that v.35 can be read immediately following v.24 without any noticeable break in the story. Various form critics have therefore concluded that vv.25–34 must be viewed as an "independent legend" inserted into some more original narrative by Luke. But the fact that a story resembles other accounts of a similar type provides very little basis for impugning its historicity. And to conclude that because one portion of a story follows nicely another portion separated from it by a block of material that this intervening material must be a later insertion is indeed a precarious critical procedure.

As a matter of fact, there is no escape from prison in vv.25–28. Therefore the appeal to parallels is vain. Not only Paul and Silas but all the other prisoners remained in their cells. The praying and singing, the earthquake, the opening of the doors, and the loosing of the chains all have special significance as vindicating God's servants Paul and Silas and preparing for the jailer's conversion. So while we may not be able to piece together each detail of the story according to strict logic, we cannot say that vv.25–34 constitute some independent miracle story Luke inserted into his narrative for effect. The account of the imprisonment of Paul and Silas has meaning only in the context of the whole presentation in vv.16–40.

29–30 Since it was midnight, the jailer called for torches to dispel the darkness of the prison. Rushing in, he fell trembling before Paul and Silas, doubtless taking them to be some kind of divine messengers. If he had not heard the demon-possessed slave girl shout, "These men are servants of the Most High God, who are telling you the way to be saved," he undoubtedly had heard from others what she was saying. And now what had happened confirmed her words about Paul and Silas. So he cried out, "Lords, [*kyrioi*, which certainly carries a note of adoration here], what must I do to be saved?" His question showed recognition of his spiritual need and opened the way for Paul and Silas to give him the Good News about Jesus Christ.

31–34 What Paul and Silas gave the Philippian jailer was the same Christ-centered gospel that had been proclaimed since Pentecost: "Believe in the Lord Jesus, and you will be saved—you and your household" (cf. 2:38–39; 3:19–26; 4:12; 8:12, 35; 10:43; 13:38–39). But since it was all new to the jailer, the missionaries took time to explain to him and the others of his household "the word of the Lord" (*ton logon tou kyriou*), setting the Good News of redemption in Jesus before them in terms they could understand. To judge by their actions, the jailer and his family believed in Christ and received the Holy Spirit. The jailer washed the wounds of Paul and Silas, probably at a well in the prison courtyard, and there too he and all his family were baptized. Then he brought the missionaries into his home and fed them. "And the whole family," Luke tells us, "was filled with joy, because they had come to believe in God."

Notes

22 The phrase περιρήξαντες αὐτῶν τὰ ἱμάτια (*perirēxantes autōn ta himatia*, lit., "tearing off their clothes") could be read to mean that the magistrates tore off their own clothes (cf. 14:14), but that is hardly likely.

26 B omits παραχρῆμα (*parachrēma*, "at once"), which is a favorite Lukan adverb (cf. Luke 1:64; 4:39; 5:25; 8:44, 47, 55; 13:13; 18:43; 19:11; 22:60; Acts 3:7; 5:10; 12:23; 13:11; 16:33), appearing elsewhere than in Luke's writings in the NT only at Matt 21:19–20.

30 The Western text adds "having secured the others" after "brought them out," an addition meant to satisfy the reader's curiosity about what happened to the other prisoners.

31 The Western and Byzantine texts characteristically add Χριστόν (*Christon*, "Christ"), thereby reading "the Lord Jesus Christ."

31–34 For other instances of the conversion of members of a household with the head of the household, cf. 11:14 (also 10:2ff.); 16:15; 18:8; 1 Cor 16:15.

5. Paul and Silas leave the city

16:35–40

35When it was daylight, the magistrates sent their officers to the jailer with the order: "Release those men." 36The jailer told Paul, "The magistrates have ordered that you and Silas be released. Now you can leave. Go in peace."

> [37]But Paul said to the officers: "They beat us publicly without a trial, even though we are Roman citizens, and threw us into prison. And now do they want to get rid of us quietly? No! Let them come themselves and escort us out."
>
> [38]The officers reported this to the magistrates, and when they heard that Paul and Silas were Roman citizens, they were alarmed. [39]They came to appease them and escorted them from the prison, requesting them to leave the city. [40]After Paul and Silas came out of the prison, they went to Lydia's house, where they met with the brothers and encouraged them. Then they left.

35-36 In the morning the magistrates sent the lictors to the prison with an order to release the two vagabond Jews. They make no mention of an earthquake during the night; apparently they did not relate it to the situation of Paul and Silas. They had probably only wanted to teach them a lesson about the peril of disturbing the peace in a Roman colony and felt that a public flogging and a night in the city's jail would be sufficient to do that. So they ordered the jailer to release Paul and Silas.

37 Paul, however, refused to be dealt with so summarily. Claiming the rights of Roman citizenship for himself and Silas, he demanded that they be shown the courtesy due a citizen and be escorted out of the prison by the magistrates themselves. According to the Valerian and Porcian laws, which were passed at various times between 509 B.C. (the time of the founding of the Roman Republic) and 195 B.C., a Roman citizen could travel anywhere within Roman territory under the protection of Rome. He was not subject to local legislation unless he consented (which was usually the case in business and personal relations), and he could appeal to be tried by Rome, not by local authorities, when in difficulty. As a citizen he owed allegiance directly to Rome, and Rome would protect him. Even Roman governors in the provinces were forbidden, as A.H.M. Jones points out, "to kill, scourge, torture, condemn or put in bonds a Roman citizen who appealed to the people, or to prevent a defendant from presenting himself in Rome within a certain time" (*Studies in Roman Government and Law* [New York: Praeger, 1960], p. 54)—with the situation being that "under the *principate,* appeal to the people was converted into appeal to Caesar, perhaps by the law of 30 B.C." (ibid.).

Evidence regarding the exercise of this right of appeal is scanty. Nor do we know how a citizen who made the claim "I am a Roman" (*ciuis Romanus sum*) supported his claim then and there. Cicero tells of a Roman citizen who was beaten in the marketplace of Messina in Sicily and speaks of it as a most disgraceful and illegal procedure (*Verrine Orations* 2.5.161-62). But other than that, most of our information on the Roman right of appeal is supplied from Acts itself (here, at 22:25-29; 25:9-12; 26:32; 27:1; and 28:16). Nevertheless, on the basis of the extant evidence, "it would seem that a Roman citizen was protected against arbitrary flogging without trial, and if accused could refuse to submit to trial by appealing to Caesar" (ibid., pp. 54-55).

Paul took pride in his Roman citizenship and valued it highly (22:25-28)—a feeling that was doubtless shared by Silas. Just why they didn't assert their rights earlier we can only conjecture. Perhaps the uproar of the mob and the hubbub of the beating kept their protestations from being heard. But now they claimed their rights as Roman citizens— probably not only for their own sakes but also to provide some measure of protection for the few believers meeting at Lydia's home.

38-39 To beat and imprison a Roman citizen without a trial was a serious offense. So when the magistrates heard that Paul and Silas were citizens, they came to apologize for their illegal actions and to escort them out of prison. Then in order to avoid any further embarrassment or opposition from the crowd, they asked Paul and Silas to leave Philippi. Here was a case where Roman officials took action against the gospel and its messengers. As such, it seems to run counter to Luke's apologetic purpose in Acts (cf. Introduction: Luke's Purposes in Writing Acts). But his point is that the magistrates initially acted in ignorance; and when they came to understand matters more fully, they apologized and did what they could to avoid repetition of the blunder.

40 After leaving the prison, Paul and Silas met with the small body of Christians (*hoi adelphoi*, "the brothers," used broadly for "believers"; cf. 18:18, 27) at the house of Lydia and encouraged them in their new faith. Then they left with Timothy to go westward toward Thessalonica. Apparently, however, Luke stayed at Philippi, for only later (20:5) does the second "we" section commence—again at Philippi. By that time the little congregation that had begun so modestly with Lydia and her household, Luke, the slave girl, and the jailer and his family had grown in size and spirituality; for in the letter Paul later wrote them, he speaks of their "overseers and deacons" (Phil 1:1), counsels them as believers growing in maturity, and commends them for their continuing concern for him (cf. Phil 2:25–30; 4:10–19).

Notes

35 The Western text expands this verse to read: "But when it was day, the magistrates came into the marketplace [the agora] and, calling to mind the earthquake that had taken place, they were afraid and they sent the lictors," attempting thereby to explain the magistrates' apparent change of attitude.

36 D and some Western texts omit ἐν εἰρήνῃ (*en eirēnē*, "in peace").

37 The Western text reads ἀναιτίους (*anaitious*, "without being guilty") instead of ἀκατακρίτους (*akatakritous*, "without a trial").

39 The Western text recasts this verse to read: "And arriving with many friends at the prison, they requested them to go out, saying: 'We did not know the truth about you, that you are righteous men.' And leading them out, they requested them, saying, 'Depart from this city, lest they come together again to us and and cry out against you.'"

40 The Western text adds "they related to them all that the Lord had done to them" before the final "then they left."

C. At Thessalonica

17:1–9

> ¹When they had passed through Amphipolis and Apollonia, they came to Thessalonica, where there was a Jewish synagogue. ²As his custom was, Paul went into the synagogue, and on three Sabbath days he reasoned with them from the Scriptures, ³explaining and proving that the Christ had to suffer and rise from the dead. "This Jesus I am proclaiming to you is the Christ," he said. ⁴Some of the Jews were persuaded and joined Paul and Silas, as did a large number of God-fearing Greeks and not a few prominent women.
> ⁵But the Jews were jealous; so they rounded up some bad characters from the marketplace, formed a mob and started a riot in the city. They rushed to Jason's house in search of Paul and Silas in order to bring them out to the crowd. ⁶But when they did not find them, they dragged Jason and some other brothers before the

city officials, shouting: "These men who have caused trouble all over the world have now come here, [7]and Jason has welcomed them into his house. They are all defying Caesar's decrees, saying that there is another king, one called Jesus." [8]When they heard this, the crowd and the city officials were thrown into turmoil. [9]Then they made Jason and the others post bond and let them go.

1 Thirty-three miles southwest of Philippi was Amphipolis, the capital of the northern district of Macedonia between 167–146 B.C. Situated on the east bank of the Strymon River, it straddled the Via Egnatia. But though it was larger and more important than Philippi, Paul and his companions "passed through" it. As they continued west-south-west on the Via Egnatia, they also passed through Apollonia some twenty-seven miles beyond Amphipolis. Their desire was to reach Thessalonica, the capital of the province of Macedonia and the largest and most prosperous city of all in Macedonia, which lay another forty miles southwest of Apollonia.

Thessalonica (modern Salonika) was strategically located on the Thermaic Gulf. It too straddled the Via Egnatia. It linked the rich agricultural plains of the Macedonian interior with the land and sea routes to the east. Cicero described it as "situated in the bosom of our domain" (*Pro Plancio* 41). It was probably founded by Cassander in 315 B.C. and named for his wife, the daughter of Philip II (cf. Strabo *Geography* 7.21), though other traditions trace its foundation to Philip himself and say it was named either for his daughter or in honor of his victory over the Thessalonians. When Rome conquered Macedonia in 167 B.C., Thessalonica became the capital of the second of the four administrative districts of the province. Then with the reorganization of Macedonia into one province in 142 B.C., Thessalonica became its capital. In the second civil war it sided with Mark Antony and Octavian (later Augustus) against Cassius and Brutus, and because of its loyalty it was declared a free city in 42 B.C. (cf. Plutarch *Brutus* 46).

As a large city of perhaps two hundred thousand, and one that dominated Macedonian government and commerce, Thessalonica naturally attracted diverse groups of people including a substantial Jewish contingent (1 Thess 2:14–16). Paul seems to have looked on it as the strategic center for the spread of the gospel throughout the Balkan peninsula (1 Thess 1:7–8). Therefore Paul and Silas—though doubtless in some pain from their recent beating and time in the stocks—pushed on resolutely the hundred miles from Philippi to Thessalonica.

2–3 In portraying the extension of the gospel to the main cities bordering the Aegean Sea, Luke lays special emphasis on the fact that Paul's preaching consisted of both proclamation and persuasion—interlocking elements of the one act of preaching. He had struck such a note earlier (cf. 13:43), and it will continue to be heard in 20:9; 24:25; 26:28; and 28:23. Here in Panel 5 it sounds with unmistakable clarity throughout the portrayals of the ministries at Thessalonica (17:2–4), Athens (17:17), Corinth (18:4), and Ephesus (18:19; 19:8–10).

At Thessalonica the missionaries, true to their policy of "To the Jews First, but Also to the Gentiles" (cf. comments on 13:46–52), sought out the local synagogue, sure of finding there a prepared audience of both Jews and "God-fearing" Gentiles. During the span of three Sabbath days Paul "reasoned [*dielexato*] with them from the Scriptures, explaining [*dianoigōn*] and proving [*paratithemenos*] that the Christ had to suffer and rise from the dead." "This Jesus I am proclaiming [*katangellō*] to you is the Christ," he said. And further, Luke tells us in v.4 that some "were persuaded [*epeisthēsan*] and joined Paul and Silas." The preaching of Paul in the Book of Acts generally and at

Thessalonica particularly took the form of a "proclaimed witness"—i.e., a witness to the facts that Jesus of Nazareth is the Christ, that his suffering and resurrection were in accord with the Scriptures, and that through his earthly ministry and living presence men and women can experience the reign of God in their lives. At times the proclamation was accompanied by miracles. But though miracles brought quick results, "reason," "prove," and "persuade"—words that describe Paul's method of preaching—imply his careful dealing with his hearers' questions and doubts.

4 "Some of the Jews were persuaded," but the greater number of those who responded positively to Paul's preaching in the Thessalonian synagogue were "God-fearing" Greeks (*hoi sebomenoi Hellēnōn*) and "prominent women" (*gynai tōn prōtōn*, which probably denotes women of high standing in the city who were the wives of the principal citizens). The Jason mentioned in v.5 as Paul's host was probably one of the Jewish converts; Aristarchus and Secundus, who are identified as Thessalonians in 20:4, may have also been converted at this time.

5-7 Just as at Antioch, Iconium, and Lystra, the Jews who did not believe the gospel were incensed at the Gentiles' response to Paul's preaching and with his direct approach to them. So they stirred up a riot. Their plan was to bring Paul and Silas before "the assembly of citizens" (*ton dēmon*) and "the politarchs" (*tous politarchas*) on a charge of disturbing the Pax Romana by preaching a *religio illicita* and by advocating another king in opposition to Caesar. But when they could not find the missionaries at Jason's house— evidently because Jason and some others who believed their message had hidden them away—they dragged Jason and some other Christian brothers before the politarchs. Jason (Gr. for Joshua) was probably a Diaspora Jew (see comment on v.4) who became one of Paul's first converts at Thessalonica. He need not be identified with Jason of Romans 16:21, for the name was fairly common.

As a free city, Thessalonica had its governing assembly of citizens, which is probably what Luke had in mind by the use of the term *dēmos* in v.5 (though v.8 speaks of the "crowd," *ochlos*, somewhat synonymously). The magistrates of Thessalonica were called "politarchs" (*politarchēs*), a title found in inscriptions ranging from the second century B.C. through the third century A.D. and applied almost exclusively to Macedonian cities. From five inscriptions referring to Thessalonica, it appears that a body of five politarchs ruled the city during the first century A.D.—a number expanded to a board of six in the second century (cf. E.D. Burton, "The Politarchs," AJT, 2 [1898], 598ff.).

Certainly the assembly of citizens and the politarchs at Thessalonica would have known of the troubles within the Jewish community at Rome in connection with Christianity and of Claudius's edict of A.D. 49–50 for all Jews to leave that city (see Suetonius *Vita Claudius* 25.4, who speaks of "constant riots at the instigation of *Chrestus*" and tells of the emperor's order of expulsion; cf. also 18:2). Probably the Jewish opponents of the missionaries played upon the fear that such a situation might be duplicated at Thessalonica, unless Paul and Silas were expelled. In addition, from their charge that the missionaries proclaimed "another king" (v.7), it may be inferred that they tried to use Paul's mention of "the kingdom of God" (cf. 14:22; 19:8; 20:25; 28:23, 31) to arouse suspicion that he was involved in anti-imperial sedition. Indeed, it may be for this reason that Paul avoided the use of "kingdom" and "king" in his letters to his converts, lest Gentile imperial authorities misconstrue them to connote opposition to the empire and emperor.

8-9 The charges against Paul and Silas and their companions naturally alarmed the Thessalonian politarchs. They certainly did not want riots like those at Rome in their city. But apparently they found the evidence for the charges scanty; after all, Paul and Silas against whom the charges were directed could not be found. Therefore, the politarchs took what they thought to be a moderate and reasonable course of action. They made Jason and those with him post a bond, assuring them that there would be no repetition of the trouble. This probably meant that Paul and Silas had to leave Thessalonica and that their friends promised they would not come back, at least during the term of office of the present politarchs.

When writing his Thessalonian converts a few months later, Paul speaks of many times desiring to visit them again but of being unable to because "Satan stopped us" (1 Thess 2:18). Likely Paul had in mind the fact that bond had been posted assuring his nonreturn, and therefore his hands were tied. But though he was unable to return, that did not stop either the spread of the gospel or the opposition of the Jews (cf. 1 Thess 1:2–10). Amid all their persecutions and difficulties, the Christians of Thessalonica maintained their faith and witness in a manner that filled Paul with joy when he heard of it (cf. 1 Thess 3:6–10).

Notes

4 The Western text reads, "And many of the God-fearers adhered to the teaching, and a large number of Greeks and not a few prominent women," thereby including pagan Greeks as well as "God-fearing" Gentiles.

D. *At Berea*

17:10–15

> ¹⁰As soon as it was night, the brothers sent Paul and Silas away to Berea. On arriving there, they went to the Jewish synagogue. ¹¹Now the Bereans were of more noble character than the Thessalonians, for they received the message with great eagerness and examined the Scriptures every day to see if what Paul said was true. ¹²Many of the Jews believed, as did also a number of prominent Greek women and many Greek men.
>
> ¹³When the Jews in Thessalonica learned that Paul was preaching the word of God at Berea, they went there too, agitating the crowds and stirring them up. ¹⁴The brothers immediately sent Paul to the coast, but Silas and Timothy stayed at Berea. ¹⁵The men who accompanied Paul brought him to Athens and then left with instructions for Silas and Timothy to join him as soon as possible.

10 The bail bond Jason and his friends posted would have been forfeited were Paul and Silas to be found in their homes. So the brothers sent them, together with Timothy, on to Berea (modern Verria), some fifty miles southwest of Thessalonica by way of Pella. A city in the foothills of the Olympian range south of the Macedonian plain, Berea was of little importance historically or politically, though it had a large population in NT times. It also was south of the Via Egnatia, but with access to the eastern coastal road that ran down to Achaia and Athens. In a fervent speech against Piso, Cicero (106–43 B.C.) had told how the Roman authorities in Thessalonica were so unpopular with the people that when he was on government business he found it wise to sneak into the provincial capital at night and at times withdraw from the storm of complaints to Berea

because it was "off the beaten track" (*In Pisonem* 36). On arriving at Berea, Paul and his companions went as usual to the synagogue to proclaim the Good News of salvation in Jesus the Christ.

11-12 Luke gave the Jews at Berea undying fame by characterizing them as being "more noble" (*eugenesteroi*) than the Thessalonian Jews because they tested the truth of Paul's message by the touchstone of Scripture rather than judging it by political and cultural considerations. So they examined the Scriptures daily (*kath hēmeran*) to see whether what Paul proclaimed was really true, and many believed. Among them was probably Sopater son of Pyrrhus, who is identified in 20:4 as from Berea (cf. Rom 16:21). Included among the Berean believers were not only "a number of prominent Greek women" but also "many Greek men" (*Hellēnidōn . . . andrōn ouk oligoi*)—that is, not just converts from among Gentile "God-fearers," but also converts who were pagan Gentiles.

13-15 The Thessalonian Jews, on hearing that "the word of God" was being preached at Berea, sent a delegation there to stir up the same opposition as at Thessalonica. Evidently the Berean Christians recognized that not only was Paul not safe at Thessalonica but he was not safe anywhere else in the region, because the Thessalonian Jews had the ear of the provincial authorities. So the Bereans acted immediately (*eutheōs*) as if they were taking Paul to a coastal town like Methone or Dium to sail for some other country. Having thrown their opponents off the track, the Bereans escorted Paul down to the province of Achaia and into Athens, apparently to stay there with some of their relatives. As for Silas and Timothy, they remained in Berea since they were not in such danger as Paul. But when the men who accompanied Paul to Athens returned to Berea, they brought with them a message from Paul for Silas and Timothy to join him as soon as possible—doubtless because he saw that Athens was another strategic center for proclaiming the gospel and wanted Silas and Timothy with him when he began.

The movements of Silas and Timothy after Paul left them at Berea are rather difficult to trace, because Luke was not always concerned with details of the minor characters in his narrative and because Paul's references to their activities are somewhat incidental and allusive. But in accord with Paul's instructions, Silas and Timothy rejoined Paul at Athens (1 Thess 3:1). Then Timothy was sent back to Thessalonica (1 Thess 3:2). Silas, however, seems to have gone back to Macedonia (cf. 18:5)—probably to Philippi, where he received from the young congregation there a gift of money for the support of the missioners (Phil 4:15). In the meantime, Paul had moved from Athens to Corinth (18:1) and was joined there by Silas and Timothy on their return from Macedonia (18:5; 1 Thess 3:6).

Notes

11 The Western text adds καθὼς Παῦλος ἀπαγγέλλει (*kathōs Paulos apangellei*, "as Paul proclaimed") at the end of the verse after οὕτως (*houtōs*, "so"), thus providing a logical clarification of ταῦτα (*tauta*, "these things").

12 On the use of μὲν οὖν (*men oun*), see comments and note at 1:6.

The Western text recasts the last half of the verse to read: "Also many of the Greeks and of the prominent men and women believed." The toning down of the prominence of women by the reversal of order is typical of the Western text (cf. notes at 17:34; 18:26).

13 The Western text adds οὐ διελίμπανον (*ou dielimpanon*, "they did not stop") after σαλεύοντες καὶ ταράσσοντες τοὺς ὄχλους (*saleuontes kai tarassontes tous ochlous*, "agitating the crowds and stirring them up"), while the Byzantine text and P[45] read only σαλεύοντες τοὺς ὄχλους (*saleuontes tous ochlous*, "agitating the crowds").

14 Whereas ℵ A B E, together with P[74], read ἕως ἐπὶ τὴν θάλασσαν (*eōs epi tēn thalassan*, "as far as the sea"), the Western text reads ἐπὶ τὴν θάλασσαν (*epi tēn thalassan*, "to the sea") and the Byzantine text reads ὡς ἐπὶ τὴν θάλασσαν (*hōs epi tēn thalassan*), "as [if] to the sea"). The Western text suggests a sea route to Athens, whereas the Byzantine text makes explicit the ruse that seems implied in the Neutral text.

15 The Western text recasts v.15 after "Athens" to read: "But he passed by Thessaly [τὴν Θεσσαλίαν, *tēn Thessalian*], for he was prevented from preaching the word to them. And having received a command from Paul to Silas and Timothy to come to him speedily, they departed."

E. *At Athens* (17:16–34)

Paul's coming to Athens appears to have been intended primarily to escape persecution in Macedonia. It seems to have been no part of his original plan to preach at Athens. When called to Macedonia, he had apparently planned to follow the Via Egnatia all the way to Dyrrhachium, then cross the Adriatic to Italy, and so to Rome. When writing the Christians at Rome some six or seven years later, Paul speaks of having often planned to visit them but being unable to do so (Rom 1:13; 15:22–23). Provincial action in Macedonia appears to have thwarted his plans for a continued mission in Macedonia, and news of Claudius's expulsion of the Jewish community in Rome (A.D. 49–50) would have caused him to change his plans.

Now Paul was in Athens, under circumstances not altogether what he would have planned. He was waiting for Silas and Timothy to come before beginning his mission in Athens. But the rampant idolatry he saw around him compelled him to present the claims of Christ to Jews and "God-fearing" Gentiles in the synagogue on the Sabbath and to whoever would listen in the agora (marketplace) on weekdays. As with Jeremiah (cf. Jer 20:9), "the word of God" burned within Paul like a fire in his bones, and he could not keep silent.

1. *Inauguration of a ministry*

17:16–21

> [16]While Paul was waiting for them in Athens, he was greatly distressed to see that the city was full of idols. [17]So he reasoned in the synagogue with the Jews and the God-fearing Greeks, as well as in the marketplace day by day with those who happened to be there. [18]A group of Epicurean and Stoic philosophers began to dispute with him. Some of them asked, "What is this babbler trying to say?" Others remarked, "He seems to be advocating foreign gods." They said this because Paul was preaching the good news about Jesus and the resurrection. [19]Then they took him and brought him to a meeting of the Areopagus, where they said to him, "May we know what this new teaching is that you are presenting? [20]You are bringing some strange ideas to our ears, and we want to know what they mean." [21](All the Athenians and the foreigners who lived there spent their time doing nothing but talking about and listening to the latest ideas.)

16 Athens is five miles inland from its port of Piraeus, which is on the Saronic Gulf, an arm of the Aegean Sea stretching fifty miles between Attica and the Peloponnesus. It is situated on a narrow plain between Mount Parnes to the north, Mount Pentelicus to the east, and Mount Hymettus to the southeast. Said to have been founded by Theseus, the hero of Attica who slew the Minotaur and conquered the Amazons, Athens was named in honor of the goddess Athena. When the Persians tried to conquer Greece in the fifth century B.C., Athens played a prominent part in resisting them. Though completely destroyed at that time, it quickly recovered and its fleet, which contributed decisively to the defeat of the Persians, became the basis of a maritime empire. Athens reached its zenith under Pericles (495–429 B.C.); and during the last fifteen years of his life, the Partheon, numerous temples, and other splendid buildings were built. Literature, philosophy, science, and rhetoric flourished; and Athens attracted intellectuals from all over the world. Politically it became a democracy.

But Athens had attained eminence at the expense of its allies in the Delian Confederacy. Many of them in dissatisfaction turned to its rival Sparta, and the Peloponnesian War (431–404 B.C.) put an end to the greatness of Athens. Culturally and intellectually, however, it remained supreme for centuries, with such figures as Socrates, Plato, Aristotle, Epicurus, and Zeno living there. In 338 B.C. Philip II of Macedonia conquered Athens, but the conquest only served to spread Athenian culture and learning into Asia and Egypt through his son, Alexander the Great. The Romans conquered Athens in 146 B.C. They were lovers of everything Greek, and under their rule Athens continued as the cultural and intellectual center of the world. Rome also left the city free politically to carry on her own institutions as a free city within the empire.

When Paul came to Athens, it had long since lost its empire and wealth. Its population probably numbered no more than ten thousand. Yet it had a glorious past on which it continued to live. Its temples and statuary were related to the worship of the Greek pantheon, and its culture was pagan. Therefore Paul, with his Jewish abhorrence of idolatry, could not but find the culture of Athens spiritually repulsive.

17 *Men oun* (NIV, "so") introduces a new scene, perhaps tying together Luke's introduction (v.16) with his source material (vv.17ff.). Though apparently not wanting to begin a mission in Athens till Silas and Timothy came from Macedonia, Paul could not keep from proclaiming the Good News about Jesus the Messiah when he attended the synagogue on the Sabbath. There he "reasoned" (*dielegeto*) with the Jews and God-fearing Gentiles. He also continued his presentation in the agora every day (*kata pasan hēmeran*) to all who would listen.

The agora lay west of the Acropolis. It was the forum and marketplace of the city and, therefore, the center of Athenian life. The commercial sections included the large Stoa of Attalus, stretching along the eastern side and flanked by a number of smaller colonnades on the northern and southern sides. The western side consisted of important public buildings: the circular Tholos, or office and dining room of the Prytaneum; the Bouleuterion, or senate house; the Metroon, or official archives, before which stood the temple of Ares and statues of the eponymous heroes of the city; the temple of Apollo Patroon; and the Stoa Basileios.

18 Athens was the home of the rival Epicurean and Stoic schools of philosophy. Epicurus (342–270 B.C.) held that pleasure was the chief goal of life, with the pleasure most worth enjoying being a life of tranquillity free from pain, disturbing passions, superstitious fears, and anxiety about death. He did not deny the existence of gods but argued in deistic fashion that they took no interest in the lives of men. The Cypriote Zeno (340–265 B.C.) was the founder of Stoicism, which took its name from the "painted Stoa" (colonnade or portico) where he habitually taught in the Athenian agora. His teaching centered on living harmoniously with nature and emphasized man's rational abilities and individual self-sufficiency. Theologically, he was essentially pantheistic and thought of God as "the World-soul."

Epicureanism and Stoicism represented the popular Gentile alternatives for dealing with the plight of humanity and for coming to terms with life apart from the biblical revelation and God's work in Jesus Christ. (Post-Christian paganism in our day has been unable to come up with anything better.) When the followers of Epicurus and Zeno heard Paul speaking in the agora, they began to dispute (*syneballon*; lit., "to converse," but also "to engage in argument") with him. Some in their pride declared him to be a *spermologos* ("babbler")—a word originally used of birds picking up grain, then of scrap collectors searching for junk, then extended to those who snapped up ideas of others and peddled them as their own without understanding them, and finally to any ne'er-do-well. Others, however, thought Paul was advocating foreign gods, probably mistaking *Anastasis* ("resurrection") for the goddess consort of a god named Jesus.

19–20 The Areopagus (*Areios Pagos;* lit., "Court" or "Council of Ares," the Gr. god of thunder and war) reaches back to legendary antiquity. Presumably it first met at Athens on the Hill of Ares (Lat. equivalent, "Mars Hill"), northwest of the Acropolis, for murder trials. Early descriptions of processions in ancient Greek city-states, however, depict the Areopagus of the cities as always heading the column of dignitaries, which suggests that the "Court" or "Council of Ares" was the senate or city council of a Greek city-state. At Athens, therefore, while the earlier powers of the Council of Ares were greatly reduced with the demise of the maritime empire, during Roman times it was still the chief judicial body of the city and exercised jurisdiction in such matters as religion and education. Today "Areopagus" survives as the title of the Greek Supreme Court. In Paul's time its membership consisted of all city administrators ("Archons") who after their term of office were free of official misconduct; it met since the fifth century B.C. in the Stoa Basileios ("The Royal Portico") at the northwest corner of the agora.

It was before this council that the followers of Epicurus and Zeno brought Paul—probably half in jest and half in derision, and certainly not seeking an impartial inquiry after truth. The city fathers, however, took their task seriously because the fame of Athens rested on its intellectual ferment and on the interplay of competing philosophies. So we should doubtless understand Paul's appearance before the Athenian Council of Ares as being for the purpose of explaining his message before those in control of affairs in the city so that he might either receive the freedom of the city to preach or be censored and silenced.

21 Luke's comment about the Athenians "doing nothing but talking about and listening to the latest ideas" is paralleled in the evaluation of his fellow Athenians by Cleon, a fifth-century B.C. politician and general: "You are the best people at being deceived by something new that is said" (Thucydides *History* 2.38.5). The Athenian orator Demosthenes (384–322 B.C.) also reproached his people for continually asking for new ideas in a day when Philip II of Macedon's rise to power presented the city with a threat calling for actions, not words (*Philip* 1.10). Evidently this characterization of the Athenians was widespread, particularly in Macedonia.

Notes

17 On the use of μὲν οὖν (*men oun*), see comments and note on 1:6; also vv.12 and 30 here.

On Luke's emphasis in Panel 5 on persuasion in Paul's preaching—here by the use of the verb διαλέγομαι (*dialegomai*, "to reason")—see comments on 17:2–3.

---

2. Paul's address before the Council of Ares

17:22–31

> 22Paul then stood up in the meeting of the Areopagus and said: "Men of Athens! I see that in every way you are very religious. 23For as I walked around and observed your objects of worship, I even found an altar with this inscription: TO AN UNKNOWN GOD. Now what you worship as something unknown I am going to proclaim to you.
>
> 24"The God who made the world and everything in it is the Lord of heaven and earth and does not live in temples built by hands. 25And he is not served by human hands, as if he needed anything, because he himself gives all men life and breath and everything else. 26From one man he made every nation of men, that they should inhabit the whole earth; and he determined the times set for them and the exact places where they should live. 27God did this so that men would seek him and perhaps reach out for him and find him, though he is not far from each one of us. 28'For in him we live and move and have our being.' As some of your own poets have said, 'We are his offspring.'
>
> 29"Therefore since we are God's offspring, we should not think that the divine being is like gold or silver or stone—an image made by man's design and skill. 30In the past God overlooked such ignorance, but now he commands all people everywhere to repent. 31For he has set a day when he will judge the world with justice by the man he has appointed. He has given proof of this to all men by raising him from the dead."

22–23 Paul does not begin his address by referring to Jewish history or by quoting the Jewish Scriptures, as he did in the synagogue of Pisidian Antioch (cf. 13:16–41). He knew it would be futile to refer to a history no one knew or argue from fulfillment of prophecy no one was interested in or quote from a book no one read or accepted as authoritative. Nor does he develop his argument from the God who gives rain and crops in their season and provides food for the stomach and joy for the heart, as he did at Lystra (cf. 14:15–17). Instead, he took for his point of contact with the council an altar he had seen in the city with the inscription *Agnōstō Theō* ("To an Unknown God"). Later the second-century geographer Pausanias (*Description of Greece* 1.1.4) and the third-century philosopher Philostratus (*Life of Apollonius Tyana* 6.3.5) were to speak of altars to unknown gods at Athens, by which they meant either altars to unknown deities generally or altars to individual unknown gods. But while there is insufficient evidence for us to know the number of such altars at Athens or what their dedicatory inscriptions were, it is not surprising that Paul came across such an altar in walking about the city. Paul used the words of the inscription to introduce his call to repentance.

Many critics have asserted that all the speeches in Acts—particularly that to the Areopagus—are Luke's free compositions, showing what he thought Paul would have said. Certainly, as with every précis, Luke edited the missionary sermons of Paul in Acts; he must also be credited with some genius for highlighting their suitability to their audiences (cf. Introduction: The Speeches in Acts). But for one who elsewhere said he was willing to be "all things to all men" for the sake of the gospel (1 Cor 9:20–22), Paul's approach to his Areopagus audience is by no means out of character. On the contrary, in his report of this address, Luke gives us another illustration of how Paul began on common ground with his hearers and sought to lead them from it to accept the work and person of Jesus as the apex of God's redemptive work for humanity.

24–28 The substance of the Athenian address concerns the nature of God and the responsibility of man to God. Contrary to all pantheistic and polytheistic notions, God is the one, Paul says, who has created the world and everything in it; he is the Lord of heaven and earth (cf. Gen 14:19, 22). He does not live in temples "made by hands" (*en cheiropoiētois*), nor is he dependent for his existence upon anything he has created. Rather, he is the source of life and breath and everything else humanity possesses. Earlier, Euripides (fifth century B.C.) asked, "What house built by craftsmen could enclose the form divine within enfolding walls?" (*Fragments* 968); and in the first century B.C., Cicero considered the image of Ceres worshiped in Sicily worthy of honor because it was not made with hands but had fallen from the sky (*In Verrem* 2.5.187). While Paul's argument can be paralleled at some points by the higher paganism of the day, its content is decidedly biblical (cf. 1 Kings 8:27; Isa 66:1–2) and its forms of expression Jewish as well as Greek (cf. LXX Isa 2:18; 19:1; 31:7; Sib Oracles 4.8–12; Acts 7:41, 48; Heb 8:2; 9:24 on the pejorative use of "made with hands" for idols and temples).

Contrary to the Athenians' boast that they had originated from the soil of their Attic homeland and therefore were not like other men, Paul affirms the oneness of mankind in their creation by the one God and their descent from a common ancestor. And contrary to the "deism" that permeated the philosophies of the day, he proclaimed that this God has determined specific times (*prostetagmenous kairous*) for men and "the exact places where they should live" (*tas orothesias tēs katoikias autōn;* lit., "the boundaries of their habitation") so that men would seek him and find him.

In support of this teaching about man, Paul quotes two maxims from Greek poets. The first comes from a quatrain attributed to the Cretan poet Epimenides (c. 600 B.C.), which appeared first in his poem *Cretica* and is put on the lips of Minos, Zeus's son, in honor of his father:

> They fashioned a tomb for thee, O holy and high one—
> The Cretans, always liars, evil beasts, idle bellies!
> But thou art not dead; thou livest and abidest for ever,
> *For in thee we live and move and have our being*
> (M.D. Gibson, ed., *Horae Semiticae X*
> [Cambridge: Cambridge University, 1913], p. 40, in Syriac; italics mine).

The second comes from the Cilician poet Aratus (c. 315–240 B.C.): "It is with Zeus that every one of us in every way has to do, *for we are also his offspring* [italics mine]" (*Phaenomena* 5); which is also found in Cleanthes's (331–233 B.C.) earlier *Hymn to Zeus*, line 4.

By such maxims, Paul is not suggesting that God is to be thought of in terms of the Zeus of Greek polytheism or Stoic pantheism. He is rather arguing that the poets his hearers recognized as authorities have to some extent corroborated his message. In his search for a measure of common ground with his hearers, he is, so to speak, disinfecting and rebaptizing the poets' words for his own purposes. Quoting Greek poets in support of his teaching sharpened his message. But despite its form, Paul's address was thoroughly biblical and Christian in its content. It is perhaps too strong to say that "the remarkable thing about this famous speech is that for all its wealth of pagan illustration its message is simply the Galilean gospel, 'The kingdom of God is at hand; repent and believe the tidings'" (Williams, p. 206). Nevertheless, there is nothing in it that really militates against Paul's having delivered it or that is in genuine opposition to his letters.

29-31 The climax of the address focuses on the progressive unfolding of divine redemption and the apex of that redemption in Jesus Christ. Being God's offspring—not in a pantheistic sense but in the biblical sense of being created by God in his image—we should not, Paul insists, think of deity in terms of gold, silver, or stone. All that idolatrous ignorance was overlooked by God in the past (cf. 14:16; Rom 3:25) because God has always been more interested in repentance than judgment (cf. Wisd Sol 11:23: "But you have mercy on all men, because you have power to do all things, and you overlook the sins of men to the end that they may repent"). Nevertheless, in the person and work of Jesus, God has acted in such a manner as to make idolatry particularly heinous. To reject Jesus, therefore, is to reject the personal and vicarious intervention of God on behalf of man and to open oneself up in the future to divine judgment meted out by the very one rejected in the present. And God himself has authenticated all this by raising Jesus from the dead.

Notes

26 The Western and Byzantine texts read ἐξ ἑνὸς αἵματος (ex henos haimatos, "from one blood") for ἐξ ἑνός (ex henos, "from one [man]").

27 The Western text reads ζητεῖν τὸ θεῖον (zētein to theion, "to seek the divine being") for ζητεῖν τὸν θεόν (zētein ton theon, "to seek God"), evidently in agreement with τὸ θεῖον (to theion, "the divine being") of v.29.

28 Clement of Alexandria attributed "the Cretans, always liars, evil beasts, idle bellies!" of Titus 1:12 to Epimenides (Stromata 1.14.59). The Syr. version of the quatrain comes to us from the Syr. church father Isho'dad of Mero (probably based on the work of Theodore of Mopsuestia), which J.R. Harris translated back into Gr. in Exp, 7 (1907), p. 336.

B and P[74] read ἡμᾶς ποιητῶν (hēmas poiētōn, "our poets"), perhaps taking into account that both Aratus and Paul were from Cilicia. The Western text omits ποιητῶν (poiētōn, "poets"), thereby suggesting "your own men."

30 On the use of μὲν οὖν (men oun), see comments and note at 1:6; also vv.12, 17 here.

3. The response to Paul's address

17:32-34

32When they heard about the resurrection of the dead, some of them sneered, but others said, "We want to hear you again on this subject." 33At that, Paul left the Council. 34A few men became followers of Paul and believed. Among them was Dionysius, a member of the Areopagus, also a woman named Damaris, and a number of others.

32 While the resurrection of Jesus from the dead was the convincing proof to the early Christians and Paul that "God was reconciling the world to himself in Christ" (2 Cor

5:19), to the majority of Athenians it was the height of folly. Five hundred years earlier the tragic poet Aeschylus (525–456 B.C.), when describing the institution of the Athenian Council of Ares, made the god Apollo say, "When the dust has soaked up a man's blood, once he is dead, there is no resurrection" (*Eumenides* 647–48). If Paul had talked about the immortality of the soul, he would have gained the assent of most of his audience except the Epicureans. But the idea of resurrection was absurd. Outright scorn was the response of some of his hearers. Others, probably with more politeness than curiosity or conviction, suggested that they would like to hear Paul on the subject at another time.

33–34 Paul obviously failed to convince the council of the truth of his message, and he evidently failed as well to gain the freedom of the city and the right to propagate his views. The council decided to hold the matter in abeyance for a time. But Paul could tell from this first meeting that sentiment was against him. Some, of course, did believe, for God always has his few in even the most difficult of situations. Among them were Dionysius, who was himself a member of the Council of Ares, and a woman named Damaris. But because no action had been taken to approve Paul's right to continue teaching in the city, his hands were legally tied. All he could do was wait in Athens till the council gave him the right to teach there or move on to some other place where his message would be more favorably received. And with a vast territory yet to be entered and a great number of people yet to be reached, Paul chose the latter. We hear of no church at Athens in the apostolic age; and when Paul speaks of "the first converts [*aparchē*; lit., 'first-fruits'] in Achaia," it is to "the household of Stephanas" that he refers (1 Cor 16:15).

Many have claimed that Paul's failure at Athens stemmed largely from a change in his preaching and that later on at Corinth he repudiated it (cf. 1 Cor 1:18–2:5). He spoke, they charge, about providence and being "in God" but forgot the message of grace and being "in Christ"; about creation and appealed to the Greek poets but did not refer to redemption or revelation; about world history but not salvation history; about resurrection but not the cross. We should remember, however, that going to Athens was not part of Paul's original missionary strategy, nor did he expect to begin work there till Silas and Timothy came from Macedonia. Moreover, there *were* some converts at Athens, and we should not minimize the working of God's Spirit or Paul's message because only a few responded or because we don't know what happened to them afterward. Still, the outreach of the gospel at Athens was cut off before it really began, and in overall terms the Christian mission in the city must be judged a failure. But the reason the gospel did not take root there probably lay more in the attitude of the Athenians themselves than in Paul's approach or in what he said.

Notes

34 Dionysius of Corinth (c. A.D. 171) is cited by Eusebius (*Ecclesiastical History* 3.4.11; 4.23.3) as saying that Dionysius the Areopagite was the first bishop of Athens, but that is probably only an inference drawn a century afterward from the text itself.

D omits any mention of Damaris as a convert, which is consistent with Bezae's attitude toward women (cf. 17:12; 18:26).

F. *At Corinth* (18:1–17)

Paul's coming to Corinth was "in weakness and fear, and with much trembling" (1 Cor 2:3). Though he was directed through a vision to minister in Macedonia (cf. 16:9–10), the mission had not gone at all as he had expected. Nor had his initial attempt in Achaia provided him with any reason to hope for a change in his fortunes. In fact, matters seemed to have gone from bad to worse at Athens, where he was dismissed with polite contempt rather than being violently driven out. So he must have traveled from Athens to Corinth in a dejected mood, wondering what worse could happen and why God had allowed matters to fall out so badly. Also, he was almost sick with anxiety over the state of the Thessalonian converts whom he had been forced to leave with the threat of persecution hanging over them (cf. 1 Thess 2:17–3:5).

This anxiety probably played a part in preventing Paul, while at Athens, from fully grasping the opportunities at hand (cf. 2 Cor 2:12–13, where he says that intense concern for the Corinthians prevented starting a mission at Troas). Consequently, anxiety continued to weigh upon him and drive him into depression. Paul was only human, and he found that his emotions affected his spiritual well-being and his work. Furthermore, he may have been ill during much of this period from the effects of the beating at Philippi—and this would have contributed further to his emotional depression. Perhaps it was at this time that he prayed repeatedly for deliverance from his "thorn in the flesh" (cf. 2 Cor 12:7–10) and God said to him, "My grace is sufficient for you, for my power is made perfect in weakness" (2 Cor 12:9).

As we read Luke's account of Paul's ministry at Corinth in the light of the Corinthian letters, we cannot help concluding that Luke has provided his readers with only a brief summary of what occurred. At Corinth more than anywhere else in the accounts of Paul's mission the exact situation is difficult to ascertain, simply because in his letters to the Corinthian church Paul provides so much allusive material about his relations with Christians there and Luke gives so little in Acts. Consequently, theories are rampant regarding historical, personal, and literary relationships between Paul and the church at Corinth. Furthermore, there are wide differences of purpose between Paul and Luke in their Corinthian materials because Paul's concern was pastoral and Luke's apologetic. Here in Acts 18 Luke is chiefly interested in the proceedings before Gallio (vv. 12–17). He presents them (1) to demonstrate that one of the wisest of the Roman proconsuls had declared Christianity to be a *religio licita* and (2) to warn that if Rome began to persecute the church, it would be acting contrary to Gallio, a ruler renowned for his urbanity and wit.

1. *Arrival at Corinth*

18:1–4

> ¹After this, Paul left Athens and went to Corinth. ²There he met a Jew named Aquila, a native of Pontus, who had recently come from Italy with his wife Priscilla, because Claudius had ordered all the Jews to leave Rome. Paul went to see them, ³and because he was a tentmaker as they were, he stayed and worked with them. ⁴Every Sabbath he reasoned in the synagogue, trying to persuade Jews and Greeks.

1 Corinth was on a plateau overlooking the isthmus connecting central Greece to the north with the Peloponnesus to the south. It was built on the north side of the Acrocorinth, an acropolis rising precipitously to 1,886 feet and providing an almost impregnable fortress for the city. To the east was the port of Cenchrea on the Saronic Gulf leading out to the Aegean Sea and to the west, the port of Lechaeum on the Gulf of Corinth opening to the Adriatic. Smaller ships were actually dragged over wooden rollers across the isthmus for the three and one-half miles between Cenchrea and Lechaeum in order to avoid the long and dangerous trip around Cape Malea at the southern tip of the Peloponnesus, while cargoes of larger ships were carried overland from port to port.

Because of its strategic land and sea location, Corinth became a prosperous city-state in the eighth century B.C. During the seventh and sixth centuries B.C., it reached the zenith of its prestige and power, with a population numbering approximately two hundred thousand free men and five hundred thousand slaves. In the fifth century B.C., it declined in importance and size due to the imperialism of Athens—though the Peloponnesian War of 431–404 B.C. won by Sparta and her associates was disastrous for both. In 338 B.C. the city was captured by Philip II of Macedon, who made it the center of his Hellenic League; and from the death of Alexander the Great to the rise of Roman influence in Greece, it became a leading member of the Achaian League of Greek city-states—for a time even the chief city of that league. In 196 B.C. Corinth was captured by the Romans and declared a free city. In 146 B.C., however, it was leveled to the ground and its population sold into slavery by the general Lucius Mummius as retribution for the leading part it played in the revolt of the Achaian League against Rome. For one hundred years the city lay in ruins, until Julius Caesar decreed in 46 B.C. that it should be rebuilt. It was refounded as a Roman colony in 44 B.C., and in 27 B.C. it became the capital of the Roman province of Achaia.

The population of Corinth in NT times was probably over two hundred thousand (at least twenty times that of Athens), and was made up of local Greeks, freedmen from Italy, Roman army veterans, businessmen and governmental officials, and Orientals from the Levant—including a large number of Jews. Thanks to its commercial advantages at the convergence of land and sea trade routes, the city greatly prospered. But along with its wealth and luxury, there was immorality of every kind. Beginning with the fifth century B.C., the verb "to Corinthianize" (*korinthiazesthai*) meant to be sexually immoral, a reputation that continued to be well-deserved in Paul's day.

Corinth was the center for the worship of the goddess Aphrodite, whose temple with its thousand sacred prostitutes crowned the Acrocorinth. At the foot of the Acrocorinth stood the temple of Melicertes (the Gr. form of Melkart, the principal god of Tyre), the god of sailors. Temples to Apollo and to Asclepius, the god of healing, have also been found in the ruins of the first-century city, and there were undoubtedly many more such pagan shrines there. The city became a favorite of the Roman emperors. Every two years the pan-Hellenic Isthmian Games were held in the city, presided over by its administrators.

2–3 Entering this large and thriving city, Paul may have asked a passerby where he could find a master tentmaker or leather worker (*skēnopoios*) to seek a job from so that he could support himself by his trade. Jewish law directed that young theological students be taught a trade (cf. M *Pirke Aboth* 2.2; see SBK, 2:745–46), and on his missionary journeys Paul earned his living as a tentmaker and leather worker (cf. 20:34; 1 Cor 9:1–18; 2 Cor 11:7–12; 1 Thess 2:9; 2 Thess 3:7–10). So he came in contact with the

Jewish Christian couple Aquila and Priscilla, with whom he lived and worked, presumably alongside other journeymen in their shop.

Aquila was a native of Pontus, a region in northern Asia Minor on the south shore of the Black Sea. Priscilla is the diminutive of the more formal name Prisca. Luke's habit is to use the colloquial, diminutive form of names (e.g., Silas, Sopatros, Priscilla, Apollos), whereas Paul usually refers to his friends by their more formal names (e.g., Silvanus, Sosipatros, Prisca, Epaphroditus)—though in certain situations he also speaks of some more popularly (e.g., Apollos, Epaphras). Since Priscilla is often listed before her husband (18.18-19, 26; Rom 16:3; 2 Tim 4:19), we may conclude that she came from a higher social class than her husband or was in some way considered more important. Perhaps Aquila was a former Jewish slave who became a freedman in Rome and married a Jewess connected with the Roman family Prisca (*gens Prisca*), which possessed citizenship rights. Together, perhaps through Aquila's craftsmanship and Priscilla's money and contacts, they owned a tentmaking and leather-working firm, with branches of the business at Rome, Corinth, and Ephesus (cf. 18:2, 18-19, 26; Rom 16:3; 1 Cor 16:19; 2 Tim 4:19).

Lately Aquila and Priscilla had been forced to leave Rome because of the Edict of Claudius, an expulsion order proclaimed during the ninth year of Emperor Claudius's reign (i.e., 25 January A.D. 49 to 24 January 50) and directed against the Jews in Rome to put down the riots arising within the Jewish community there (cf. Suetonius *Vita Claudius* 25.4: "As the Jews were indulging in constant riots at the instigation of *Chrestus*, he banished them from Rome"). The "Chrestus" Suetonius speaks of may have been an otherwise unknown agitator who was active in Jewish circles within Rome in the forties (the Gr. *Chrēstos* means "useful" or "kindly" and was a common name for slaves in the Greco-Roman world). Probably, however, Suetonius, writing seventy years after the event, had no clear understanding of who this Chrestus really was and assumed him to be a local troublemaker, whereas the dispute in the Jewish community was over Jesus Christ and between those who favored his messiahship and those who rejected it.

We do not know whether Aquila and Priscilla had any part in the riots—either as agitators or victims. They are not classed as Paul's converts either in Acts or in Paul's letters. Probably they had been converted to Christianity at Rome. If Priscilla was from a family with Roman citizenship, she might not have been included under Claudius's expulsion order; but her husband, if a former Jewish slave and now a freedman, would, and she would have cast her lot in with him. However, Luke's hero is Paul, and he treats minor characters only as they come into contact with Paul. As for Paul, he calls Priscilla and Aquila his "fellow workers in Christ Jesus," speaks of their having "risked their lives for me" (probably at Ephesus, cf. 19:23-41), and says of them, "Not only I but all the churches of the Gentiles are grateful to them" (Rom 16:3-4)—all of which suggests that he considered them close and loyal friends and that their services to the Christian cause far exceeded their assistance to him.

4 While working with Aquila and Priscilla, Paul attended the local synagogue every Sabbath. There, Luke tells us, "he reasoned" (*dielegeto*) with those gathered, "trying to persuade" (*epeithen*) both Jews and Gentiles. But his ministry during those weeks seems to have been relatively unobtrusive, probably conforming to the kind of witness Aquila and Priscilla were already carrying on among their Jewish compatriots. As was his intention at Athens, though he was unable to hold to it there, Paul may have wanted to refrain from a more aggressive ministry in Corinth till Silas and Timothy could join him.

Notes

1 On μετὰ ταῦτα (*meta tauta*, "after these things," or "after this," NIV) as vying with the connective μὲν οὖν (*men oun*, see comments and note at 1:6) in the latter half of Acts to mark off the beginning of a new section and connect it with what has gone before, see comments on 15:36.

A E P, together with a number of versions and minuscule MSS, add ὁ Παῦλος (*ho Paulos*, "Paul") to the text to clarify the subject of the verb in this new section, as does NIV.

3 On σκηνοποιός (*skēnopoios*) as a term covering both "tentmaker" (etymology) and "leather worker" (usage), see J. Jeremias, "Zöllner und Sünder," ZNW, 30 (1931), 299.

4 On Luke's emphasis in Panel 5 on persuasion in Paul's preaching—here by the use of the verbs διαλέγομαι (*dialegomai*, "to reason") and πείθω (*peithō*, "to persuade")—see comments on 17:2–3.

The Western text adds "and he inserted the name of the Lord Jesus" after "he reasoned," thereby expanding on Paul's method by suggesting that as the OT Scriptures were read he inserted the name of Jesus where appropriate. It further heightens Paul's early ministry to Gentiles at Corinth by reading "and he persuaded not only Jews but also Greeks."

2. *An eighteen-month ministry*

18:5–11

⁵When Silas and Timothy came from Macedonia, Paul devoted himself exclusively to preaching, testifying to the Jews that Jesus was the Christ. ⁶But when the Jews opposed Paul and became abusive, he shook out his clothes in protest and said to them, "Your blood be on your own heads! I am clear of my responsibility. From now on I will go to the Gentiles."

⁷Then Paul left the synagogue and went next door to the house of Titius Justus, a worshiper of God. ⁸Crispus, the synagogue ruler, and his entire household believed in the Lord; and many of the Corinthians who heard him believed and were baptized.

⁹One night the Lord spoke to Paul in a vision: "Do not be afraid; keep on speaking, do not be silent. ¹⁰For I am with you, and no one is going to attack and harm you, because I have many people in this city." ¹¹So Paul stayed for a year and a half, teaching them the word of God.

5 The coming of Silas and Timothy to Corinth altered the situation for Paul. They brought good news about the Christians at Thessalonica (cf. 1 Thess 3:6) and a gift of money from the congregation at Philippi (cf. 2 Cor 11:9; Phil 4:14–15). The news from Thessalonica was better than Paul dared expect, and it greatly comforted and encouraged him (cf. 1 Thess 3:7–10)—though it also told of a slanderous campaign started against him outside the congregation (1 Thess 2:3–6) and of some perplexity within it concerning the return of Christ (1 Thess 4:13–5:11). The money from Philippi was especially welcome at this time. Therefore with his spirits lifted by the report of his Thessalonian converts' spiritual well-being and the gift from Philippi providing him freedom from earning a living, "Paul devoted himself exclusively to preaching" (*syneicheto tō logō ho Paulos*; lit., "Paul held himself to the word"). The verb *syneicheto* is reflexive (middle voice), durative (imperfect tense), and inchoative (a function of the imperfect), suggesting that with the coming of Silas and Timothy, Paul began to devote himself exclusively to the ministry of the word and continued to do so throughout his

stay in Corinth. His initial purpose was to proclaim the Good News to the Jews of the
synagogue, and his message to them was that Jesus is "the Christ" (*ton Christon;* lit., "the
Messiah").

It was in response to the report from Thessalonica that Paul wrote 1 Thessalonians,
in which are interwoven (1) commendation for growth, zeal, and fidelity; (2) encouragement in the face of local persecution; (3) defense of his motives against hostile attack;
(4) instruction regarding holiness of life; (5) instruction about the coming of the Lord;
and (6) exhortation to steadfastness and patience. Some weeks later, on learning of
continued confusion at Thessalonica regarding the return of Christ and the believer's
relation to it, he wrote 2 Thessalonians. In that second letter, while acknowledging that
the church lives in eager expectation of the Lord's return, Paul insists that imminency
must not be construed to mean immediacy but is rather the basis for dogged persistence
in doing right.

6–7 The ministry at Corinth followed the pattern set at Pisidian Antioch (cf. 13:46–52)
of initial proclamation in the synagogue, rejection by the majority of Jews, and then a
direct outreach to Gentiles. In solemn biblical style (cf. Neh 5:13), Paul "shook out his
clothes"—an act symbolizing repudiation of the Jews' opposition, exemption from further responsibility for them (cf. 13:51), and protest against what he considered the Jews'
"blasphemy" (*blasphēmountōn;* NIV, "became abusive"; cf. 13:45; 26:11). So leaving the
synagogue (*metabas ekeithen;* lit., "leaving from there"), he went next door to the house
of Titius Justus, a "God-fearing" Gentile who was receiving instruction at the synagogue
(a *sebomenos ton theon;* cf. 13:50; 16:14; 17:4, 17). He invited Paul to make his home
the headquarters for his work in Corinth, presumably because he believed Paul's message. The house of Titius Justus therefore became the first meeting place of the Corinthian church.

Though MSS vary as to the form of the name of Paul's host, we should probably read
it as "Titius Justus." With two names, he was doubtless a Roman citizen and may have
been from a family brought in by Julius Caesar to colonize Corinth. Many have plausibly
argued that while his Roman nomen was Titius and his cognomen Justus, his praenomen
was Gaius and he should be identified with the Gaius of Romans 16:23, of whom Paul
says, "whose hospitality I and the whole church here [at Corinth] enjoy" (cf. W.M.
Ramsay, *Pictures of the Apostolic Church* [London: Hodder & Stoughton, 1910], p. 205,
n. 2; E.J. Goodspeed, "Gaius Titius Justus," JBL, 69 [1950], 382–83). In 1 Corinthians
1:14 Paul speaks of a Gaius he personally baptized at the inauguration of the Christian
ministry in Corinth. Presumably he was referring to this man who hosted the Christian
mission when it needed a center, after being expelled from the synagogue.

8 One of the first to accept Paul's message at Corinth was Crispus, the leader or ruler
of the synagogue (*ho archisynagōgos*), who, together with his whole household, "believed in the Lord." He was not the first believer at Corinth (Stephanas and his family
were; cf. 1 Cor 16:15). But he was certainly one of the most prominent believers, and
his conversion must have made a great impression and led to other conversions. Paul lists
him first in 1 Corinthians 1:14–16 among the few that he had personally baptized.

9–10 Paul had come to Corinth in a dejected mood, burdened by the problems in
Macedonia and his dismissal at Athens. Of course, he had been encouraged by the
reports and the gift brought by Silas and Timothy, and he was beginning to witness a
significant response to his ministry. But a pattern had developed in his Galatian and

Macedonian journeys of a promising start followed by opposition strong enough to force him to leave. Undoubtedly he was beginning to wonder whether this pattern would be repeated at Corinth. So one night God graciously gave Paul a vision in which "the Lord" (ho kyrios—evidently Jesus, as in 23:11) encouraged him not to be afraid but to keep on, assured him of his presence and of suffering no harm, and told him that many "people" (laos) in the city were to be Christ's own. Here was one of those critical periods in Paul's life when he received a vision strengthening him for what lay ahead (cf. 23:11; 27:23–24). In this case, it was confirmed by the Gallio incident that followed it.

11 With such a promising start and encouraged by the vision, Paul continued to minister at Corinth for eighteen months. (The figure should be understood to indicate the entire length of his stay.) This period probably stretched from the fall of 50 to the spring of 52, as can be determined from the pericope about Gallio (vv.12–17). So Luke summarizes the whole of Paul's mission at Corinth by telling us that for eighteen months he taught in the city "the word of God" (ton logon tou theou)—i.e., the message about Jesus, belief in whom brings forgiveness of sins, salvation, and reconciliation with God.

Notes

5 The Western text characteristically reads κύριον Ἰησοῦν (kyrion Iēsoun, "the Lord Jesus") for Ἰησοῦν (Iēsoun, "Jesus") and then adds at the end of the verse: "But when much discussion took place and the Scriptures were interpreted."

7 The Western text reads ἀπὸ Ἀκύλα (apo Akyla, "from Aquila") for ἐκεῖθεν (ekeithen, "from there"), suggesting that Paul moved his personal lodgings as well as the headquarters for his mission to the home of Titius Justus. Probably, however, all Luke means is the latter, and we should visualize Paul (and his colleagues) still residing with Aquila and Priscilla.

B and P⁷⁴ read Τιτίου Ἰούστου (Titiou Ioustou, "Titius Justus"); א and E read Τίτου Ἰούστου (Titou Ioustou, "Titus Justus"); A and D read only Ἰούστου (Ioustou, "Justus"); and various Lat., Syr., and Coptic versions read only Τίτου (Titou, "Titus"). The argument that "Titius" arose by dittography from the last two letters of ὀνόματι (onomati, "by name") before "Titus" is weakened by the fact that onomati does not appear in A, the chief support for the omission of both Titius and Titus. It is more probable to suppose that later scribes changed Titius to the easier Titus (א E) or omitted it altogether (A D).

8 On the office and function of ὁ ἀρχισυνάγωγος (ho archisynagōgos, "the ruler of the synagogue") see comments on 13:15 (cf. Luke 8:41, 49; Acts 18:17).

For other instances of the conversion of members of a household with the head of the household, cf. 11:14 (also 10:2ff.); 16:15, 31–34; 1 Cor 16:15.

10 On λαός (laos, "people") in Luke-Acts as usually referring to Israel as the elect nation, to whom the message of redemption is initially directed and for whom it is ultimately intended, see 2:47; 3:9; 4:10; 5:13. Here, however, as in 15:14, it is used of the new people of God that includes Gentiles (cf. Titus 2:14; 1 Peter 2:9–10).

3. Before the proconsul Gallio

18:12–17

12While Gallio was proconsul of Achaia, the Jews made a united attack on Paul and brought him into court. 13"This man," they charged, "is persuading the people to worship God in ways contrary to the law."

> [14]Just as Paul was about to speak, Gallio said to the Jews, "If you Jews were making a complaint about some misdemeanor or serious crime, it would be reasonable for me to listen to you. [15]But since it involves questions about words and names and your own law—settle the matter yourselves. I will not be a judge of such things." [16]So he had them ejected from the court. [17]Then they all turned on Sosthenes the synagogue ruler and beat him in front of the court. But Gallio showed no concern whatever.

12–13 The promise given Paul in the vision was that he would be protected from harm at Corinth, not that he would be free from difficulties or attack (the wording *oudeis epithēsetai soi tou kakōsai se* of v.10 is best understood as "You will not be harmed by anyone's attacks" [NEB mg.] or "No one will be able to harm you" [TEV]). As more and more people responded to Paul's preaching, his Jewish opponents attacked him and laid a charge against him. This occurred, Luke says, "while Gallio was proconsul of Achaia" (see Notes).

That Luke distinguishes correctly between senatorial and imperial provinces and has the former governed by a proconsul on behalf of the senate and the latter governed by a propraetor representing the emperor says much for his accuracy, for the status of provinces changed with the times. Achaia was a senatorial province from 27 B.C. to A.D. 15 and then again from A.D. 44 onwards (as were Cyprus from 22 B.C. and Asia from 84 B.C.; cf. comments on 13:4 and 19:1). It was therefore governed by a proconsul (as were also Cyprus and Asia during this time; cf. comments on 13:7 and 19:38). Macedonia, however, was an imperial province, and therefore Luke rightly called the magistrates at Philippi praetors (*praetores* or *stratēgoi;* cf. comments on 16:12, 22–24) while he called those at Thessalonica by the special designation of politarchs (cf. comments on 17:6).

Gallio was the son of Marcus Annaeus Seneca, the distinguished Spanish rhetorician (50 B.C.–A.D. 40), and a younger brother of Lucius Annaeus Seneca, the Stoic philosopher, politician, and dramatist (4 B.C.–A.D. 65). He was born in Cordova at the beginning of the Christian Era and named Marcus Annaeus Novatus. On coming to Rome with his father during the reign of Claudius (A.D. 41–54), he was adopted by the Roman rhetorician Lucius Junius Gallio, and thereafter bore the name of his adoptive father. He was renowned for his personal charm. His brother Seneca said of him, "No mortal is so pleasant to any person as Gallio is to everyone" (*Naturales Quaestiones* 4a, Preface 11); and Dio Cassius spoke of his wit (*History of Rome* 61. 35). An inscription at Delphi recording a reply from the emperor Claudius to the people of Delphi mentions Gallio as being proconsul of Achaia during the period of Claudius's twenty-sixth acclamation as imperator—a period known from other inscriptions to have covered the first seven months of A.D. 52. Proconsuls entered office in the senatorial provinces on 1 July, and therefore it is reasonable to assume that Gallio became proconsul of Achaia on 1 July 51. Gallio was not proconsul of Achaia very long. Seneca tells us that soon after becoming proconsul, Gallio went on a cruise to rid himself of a recurring fever (*Epistulae Morales* 104. 1); and Pliny the Elder speaks of him as later (55 or 56) taking another cruise from Rome to Egypt to relieve his asthma (*Natural History* 31. 33). In 65, along with his brother Mela (the father of the poet Lucan)—and after the enforced suicide of his other brother Seneca—he became a victim of Nero's suspicions and was killed (Dio Cassius *History of Rome* 62. 25.3).

Paul seems to have been preaching in Corinth for eight or nine months before Gallio came to Achaia as proconsul (i.e., from the fall of 50 to 1 July 51). When Gallio took office, the Jews decided to try out the new proconsul. They brought Paul before Gallio on a charge that he was preaching a *religio illicita* and therefore acting contrary to Roman law. The Greek text says that they brought Paul *epi to bēma*, which is variously translated "to the judgment seat" (KJV), "before the tribunal" (RSV, JB), and "into court" (NEB, TEV, NIV)—all of which are attempts to translate the expression into a form suitable to modern ears. The "Bema" at Corinth, however, was a large, raised platform that stood in the agora (marketplace) in front of the residence of the proconsul and served as a forum where he tried cases.

14–16 The word "law" (*nomos*) in v.13 is somewhat ambiguous. Undoubtedly when it was first used by Paul's antagonists in their synagogue, it referred to God's law against which they were convinced Paul was speaking. But at the proconsul's forum, they meant "law" to be understood as Roman law, which they charged Paul was breaking. Gallio, however, after hearing their charges, was not at all convinced that this was true. For him the squabble was an intramural one about "a word [NIV, 'words'] and names and their own law" (*peri logou kai onomatōn, kai nomou tou kath hymas*)—which doubtless means a squabble concerning "a message" (*logos*), not some disruptive action, "names" having to do with an expected Messiah (*onomata*), and particular interpretations of the Jewish law. Gallio's responsibility, as he saw it, was to judge civil and criminal cases, not to become an arbitrator of intramural religious disputes. What Paul was preaching, in his view, was simply a variety of Judaism that did not happen to suit the leaders of the Jewish community at Corinth but which was not for that reason to be declared *religio illicita*. Thus he did not need to hear Paul's defense but ejected the plaintiffs from the forum as not having a case worth being heard by a proconsul.

The importance of Gallio's decision was profound. Luke highlights it in his account of Paul's ministry at Corinth and makes it the apex from an apologetic perspective of all that took place on Paul's second missionary journey. There had been no vindication from Roman authorities of Christianity's claim to share in the *religio licita* status of Judaism in Macedonia, and the issue had been left entirely unresolved at Athens. If Gallio had accepted the Jewish charge and found Paul guilty of the alleged offense, provincial governors everywhere would have had a precedent, and Paul's ministry would have been severely restricted. As it was, Gallio's refusal to act in the matter was tantamount to the recognition of Christianity as a *religio licita*; and the decision of so eminent a Roman proconsul would carry weight wherever the issue arose again and give pause to those who might want to oppose the Christian movement. Later, in the sixties, Rome's policy toward both Judaism and Christianity would be reversed. But for the coming decade or so, the Christian message could be proclaimed in the provinces of the empire without fear of coming into conflict with Roman law, thanks largely to Gallio's decision.

17 Taking their cue from the snub Gallio gave the leaders of the Jewish community, the crowd at the forum (*to bēma*)—in an outbreak of the anti-Semitism always near the surface in the Greco-Roman world—took Sosthenes, the synagogue ruler, and beat him in the marketplace before the forum. Gallio, however, turned a blind eye to what was going on, evidently because he wanted to teach those who would waste his time with such trivialities a lesson. Larger Jewish synagogues sometimes had more than one leader or ruler (cf. comments on 13:15), and Sosthenes may have served jointly with Crispus (before his conversion) in the local synagogue chapter at Corinth. Or perhaps he took Crispus's place after the latter's conversion. Perhaps he became a Christian and is the

Sosthenes of 1 Corinthians 1:1, who served as Paul's amanuensis in writing the Corinthian believers from Ephesus, though that is only conjecture.

Notes

12 The Western text (though not D) reads ἤγαγον αὐτὸν πρὸς τὸν ἀνθύπατον (*ēgagon auton pros ton anthypaton*, "brought him to the proconsul"), evidently unable to understand what τὸ βῆμα (*to bēma*, "the Bema") was.

13 The Western text typically expands λέγοντες (*legontes*, "saying"; NIV, "they charged") to καταβοῶντες καὶ λέγοντες (*kataboōntes kai legontes*, "shouting and saying").

14 The Western text expands the vocative ὦ Ἰουδαῖοι (*ō Ioudaioi*, "O Jews" or "Jews") to ὦ ἄνδρες Ἰουδαῖοι (*ō andres Ioudaioi*, "O men, Jews").

17 The Western and Byzantine texts read πάντες οἱ Ἕλληνες (*pantes hoi Hellēnes*, "all the Greeks"), thereby making explicit the text. The tenth and eleventh century minuscules 307 and 431 read πάντες οἱ Ἰουδαῖοι (*pantes hoi Ioudaioi*, "all the Jews"), which is surely an error of interpretation.

The Western text (D wanting) reads the last sentence of v.17 as "Then Gallio pretended not to see."

G. *An Interlude* (18:18–28)

The ministry at Corinth proceeded without any legal hindrance and with considerable success for some nine months after Gallio's decision. In the spring of 52, however, Paul left Corinth to return to Jerusalem and then to Syrian Antioch—principally to complete a vow at Jerusalem he had taken earlier, probably while at Corinth. In vv.18–23 Luke briefly summarizes Paul's route. And in vv.24–28 he uses this interlude in his portrayal of the advance of the Good News to the Gentile world to introduce Apollos (cf. 1 Cor 3:5–9; 4:6–7; 16:12).

1. *Paul's return to Palestine-Syria*

18:18–23

> [18]Paul stayed on in Corinth for some time. Then he left the brothers and sailed for Syria, accompanied by Priscilla and Aquila. Before he sailed, he had his hair cut off at Cenchrea because of a vow he had taken. [19]They arrived at Ephesus, where Paul left Priscilla and Aquila. He himself went into the synagogue and reasoned with the Jews. [20]When they asked him to spend more time with them, he declined. [21]But as he left, he promised, "I will come back if it is God's will." Then he set sail from Ephesus. [22]When he landed at Caesarea, he went up and greeted the church and then went down to Antioch.
> [23]After spending some time in Antioch, Paul set out from there and traveled from place to place throughout the region of Galatia and Phrygia, strengthening all the disciples.

18 Luke's brevity in this part of Acts has left open in many minds the reason for Paul's leaving Corinth and sailing for Jerusalem and then going on to Syrian Antioch. The

reading of the Western and Byzantine texts at v.21—"I must by all means keep the coming festival at Jerusalem"—assumes that he wanted to be in Jerusalem for either the Passover or Pentecost. Knox, on the other hand, supposes that Paul returned to Jerusalem at this time to attend the Jerusalem Council (which he dates at A.D. 51 and finds depicted in Gal 2:1–10) and that Luke plays down that purpose here because he had mistakenly presented the Jerusalem Council in 15:1–29, refusing to acknowledge that the issue of Gentile freedom was settled so late in Paul's ministry (John Knox, pp. 68–69; see also J.C. Hurd, Jr., "Pauline Chronology and Pauline Theology," in *Christian History and Interpretation: Studies Presented to John Knox,* edd. W.R. Farmer, C.F.D. Moule, and R.R. Niebuhr [Cambridge: Cambridge University, 1967], pp. 225–48). Luke himself, however, may well suggest the reason in telling his readers that Paul "had his hair cut off at Cenchrea because of a vow he had taken"—though as a Gentile writing to Gentiles, Luke doubtless felt no need to expand on such a distinctly Jewish practice.

Nevertheless, that Paul cut his hair at Cenchrea shows that he had earlier taken a Nazirite vow for a particular period of time that had now ended. Such a vow had to be fulfilled at Jerusalem, where the hair would be presented to God and sacrifices offered (cf. Num 6:1–21; M *Nazir* 1.1–9.5; Jos. War II, 313 [xv.1]). Some have proposed that Paul cut off his hair at the beginning of his vow. But there is no evidence for this, and much in the literature about Nazirite vows speaks directly against it. Others have called this a "Nazirite-like" vow, feeling somewhat uneasy that Paul at any time in his Christian ministry took a Jewish vow. But for one who thought of himself as a Jewish Christian (2 Cor 11:22; cf. Rom 9–11) and who at the conclusion of three missionary journeys to the Gentile world could still insist that he was "a Pharisee, the son of a Pharisee" (Acts 23:6; cf. 26:5), such an action should not be thought strange.

Evidently at some time during his residence at Corinth—perhaps at its beginning when he was depressed—Paul had taken a Nazirite vow to God as he asked for his intervention. And now having seen God's hand at work in Corinth and a thriving church established there, Paul was determined to return to Jerusalem to fulfill his vow by presenting his hair as a burnt offering and offering sacrifices in the temple (cf. 21:26). The vow could only be fulfilled after a thirty-day period of purification in the Holy City (cf. M *Nazir* 3.6, according to the more lenient ruling of the School of Shammai).

19 Boarding a ship at Cenchrea, Paul crossed to Ephesus, the major commercial center and capital of the Roman province of Asia. With him were Aquila and Priscilla, his hosts at Corinth, who were either transferring their business from Corinth to Ephesus or leaving their Corinthian operation in charge of a manager (as possibly they did earlier at Rome) in order to open a new branch at Ephesus. Perhaps Aquila and Priscilla, who seem to have been fairly well-to-do, paid Paul's passage as they joined him on board the ship for Ephesus—and perhaps also paid his passage on to Jerusalem. Being themselves Jewish Christians, they would have appreciated Paul's desire to fulfill his vow at Jerusalem.

What happened to Silas and Timothy during this time, we do not know. They may have remained at Corinth to carry on the ministry there. Or perhaps they went with Paul to Jerusalem, then to Antioch in Syria, and back to Ephesus. Less likely it would seem is the suggestion that they sailed to Ephesus with Paul and then stayed with Aquila and Priscilla awaiting his return.

On arriving at Ephesus, Aquila and Priscilla set about their business in the city. There they were to remain for four or five years, hosting a congregation of believers in their home and sending their greetings back to their Corinthian friends in one of Paul's letters (cf. 1 Cor 16:19). They were probably there during Demetrius's riot (cf. 19:23–41), even risking their lives to protect Paul (cf. Rom 16:4). Sometime after Claudius's death in A.D. 54 (perhaps 56), they probably returned to Rome (cf. Rom 16:3). Paul, however, having wanted earlier to minister at Ephesus (cf. 16:6), went to the synagogue and "reasoned" (*dielexato*) with the Jews gathered there. Though it was not the Sabbath, he knew he could find an audience in the synagogue and probably desired to "test the waters" in anticipation of his later return.

20–21 In the synagogue at Ephesus, Paul found a receptive audience. But though they encouraged him to stay, he seems to have felt that fulfilling his vow at Jerusalem took priority over everything else. Nevertheless, he promised to return, if it were in the will of God. And with a heart lightened by the prospect of a future ministry at Ephesus, he sailed for Jerusalem.

22 Some have suggested that the ship Paul sailed on was really trying to make harbor at Seleucia, the port of Syrian Antioch, but under a heavy north-northeastern spring gale found it easier to land at Caesarea, some 250 miles further south. But that assumes Paul wanted only to return to Syrian Antioch, and it discredits the capability of ancient navigation for the sake of a theory. Paul, however, probably booked passage for Caesarea, the port city of Jerusalem since the time of Herod the Great (cf. comments on 10:1), and that is where he finally disembarked.

From Caesarea, Paul "went up" to Jerusalem, some sixty-five miles southeast. That the name "Jerusalem" does not appear in the text has led some to suppose Luke meant only that Paul went up from the harbor at Caesarea into the city to greet the congregation there. But Jerusalem is certainly implied by the expressions "went up" (*anabas*) and "went down" (*katebē*), and also by the absolute use of the term "the church" (*hē ekklēsia*). At Jerusalem, then, he met with the mother church, from which the gospel had spread to both the Diaspora and the Gentile worlds. In addition, and in accord with fulfilling his aim in coming, he entered into a thirty-day program of purification (cf. M *Nazir* 3.6), after which he presented his shorn hair to God in thanksgiving and offered sacrifices. Then he "went down" to Antioch of Syria, some three hundred miles north, reporting to and ministering within the church that originally commissioned him to reach the Gentiles.

23 Paul remained at Syrian Antioch, Luke tells us, for "some time," probably from the summer of 52 through the spring of 53. Then, on what was to be his third missionary journey, he set out for Ephesus some fifteen hundred miles to the west, revisiting the churches throughout "the region of Galatia and Phrygia" and "strengthening all the disciples." The readings "the region of Phrygia and Galatia" (16:6) and "the region of Galatia and Phrygia" (here) seem to be only stylistic variations for the same locality (cf. BC, 5:239). Here, as in 16:6, the expression probably means the Phrygian region of Galatia or some district in southern Galatia where both Phrygian and Celtic (Galatic or Gaulish) dialects could be heard (cf. comments on 16:6). There is no warrant here for supposing that Paul entered the country around Ancyra, Pessinus, or Tavium. "Strengthening all the disciples" most naturally refers to converts made at and in the areas surrounding Pisidian Antioch, Iconium, Lystra, and Derbe.

Notes

---

18 The Lat. Cod. h has Aquila cutting off his hair because he had a vow, while the Vul. reads "Priscilla and Aquila, who had shorn their heads in Cenchrea, for they had a vow." But while the Gr. word order may allow for either Aquila alone or Priscilla and Aquila together to be the subject(s), Luke usually does not provide such details regarding a secondary figure in his portrayals. The more natural interpretation is Paul himself.

19 The Western text inserts τῷ ἐπιόντι σαββάτῳ (tō epionti sabbatō, "on the following Sabbath") between the καί (kai) and the pronoun ἐκείνους (ekeinous) of the conflated κἀκείνους (kakeinous, "and they," referring to Priscilla and Aquila), but Paul did not visit synagogues only on Sabbaths.

On Luke's emphasis in Panel 5 on persuasion in Paul's preaching—here by the use of the verb διαλέγομαι (dialegomai, "to reason")—see comments on 17:2–3.

22 On the reverential use of the verbs ἀναβαίνω (anabainō, "to go up") and καταβαίνω (katabainō, "to go down") in connection with Jerusalem, see comments on 3:1 and 8:5 (also note); cf. also 11:27.

---

2. Apollos at Ephesus and Corinth

18:24–28

24Meanwhile a Jew named Apollos, a native of Alexandria, came to Ephesus. He was a learned man, with a thorough knowledge of the Scriptures. 25He had been instructed in the way of the Lord, and he spoke with great fervor and taught about Jesus accurately, though he knew only the baptism of John. 26He began to speak boldly in the synagogue. When Priscilla and Aquila heard him, they invited him to their home and explained to him the way of God more adequately.

27When Apollos wanted to go to Achaia, the brothers encouraged him and wrote to the disciples there to welcome him. On arriving, he was a great help to those who by grace had believed. 28For he vigorously refuted the Jews in public debate, proving from the Scriptures that Jesus was the Christ.

24–26 Between the time of Paul's stopover at Ephesus (18:19–21) and his return to the city on his third missionary journey (19:1ff.), Apollos came to Ephesus. A native of Alexandria, he was an educated man (*anēr logios*, which came also to connote "an eloquent man") and possessed a thorough knowledge of the Jewish Scriptures. Somewhere and somehow he had received instruction about Jesus, and up to a point he knew the gospel "accurately" (*akribōs*). What he knew he accepted. "He spoke with great fervor" (*zeōn tō pneumati elalei*, taking *tō pneumati*, "in the spirit," to refer to Apollos's own spirit) concerning Jesus. When Priscilla and Aquila heard Apollos in the synagogue, they recognized some deficiencies in his understanding of the Christian message. So they invited him to their home and explained "the way of God" (*tēn hodon tou theou*) to him "more accurately" (the comparative *akribesteron*).

Apollos's knowledge of Jesus seems to have come through disciples of John the Baptist ("he knew only the baptism of John"), either when he was in Alexandria or somewhere else in the empire (perhaps even at Ephesus). Presumably he knew that Jesus of Nazareth was the Messiah and something of Jesus' earthly ministry, but he may have known nothing more. When instructed further by Priscilla and Aquila, Apollos readily accepted all God had done in the death and resurrection of Jesus and in sending the Holy Spirit at Pentecost. There is no suggestion that he was baptized then. As with some of Jesus' disciples, probably Apollos's earlier "baptism of repentance" was considered Christian baptism when viewed as pointing to Jesus and was therefore not to be redone every time there was a growth in understanding. Nothing is said about his having received the Holy Spirit, though the nature of his later ministry leads to that assumption.

27-28 A number of people who identified themselves in some way with the gospel were at Ephesus before Paul began to minister there—people like Priscilla and Aquila who understood clearly, like Apollos whose understanding was growing, or like those mentioned in 19:1-7, 13-16, whose faith was to some extent deviant. So when Apollos desired to visit Achaia, apparently on behalf of the gospel, the Christians of Ephesus (*hoi adelphoi*, "the brothers"; cf. 16:40; 18:18) encouraged him and sent a letter of commendation, probably written by Priscilla and Aquila, to the believers at Corinth. There he vigorously debated with the Jews and showed from the OT that Jesus was the Messiah (*ton Christon*). First Corinthians 1-4 indicates how highly Apollos was thought of in the Corinthian church and also how highly he was respected by Paul. Perhaps, as Martin Luther first suggested (cf. *Luther's Works*, 55 vols., edd. J. Pelikan and H.T. Lehman [Saint Louis: Concordia, 1958-67], 29:109-241), the Letter to the Hebrews is an example of his biblical argumentation to a group of Jewish Christians in danger of lapsing back to their former Judaistic commitments.

Notes

---

24 ℵ calls him Ἀρελλῆς (*Apellēs*, "Apelles"). D uses the more formal Ἀπολλώνιος (*Apollōnios*, "Apollonius"). Vul. has Apollo.

25 The Western text adds ἐν τῇ πατρίδι (*en tē patridi*, "in his native land") after κατηχημένος (*katēchēmenos*, "he had been instructed"), thereby specifying his conversion through the agency of disciples of John the Baptist as having taken place at Alexandria.

26 The Western text reverses the names Priscilla and Aquila to read "Aquila and Priscilla," in line with its attitude toward women as in 17:12, 34.

27 The Western text recasts this verse to read: "And certain Corinthians who were residing at Ephesus heard him [Apollos] and requested him to cross over with them to their native land. And when he consented, the Ephesians wrote to the disciples at Corinth to receive the man. And when he took up residence in Achaia, he was of great help in the churches." Such recasting was apparently felt necessary to clarify a number of ambiguities in Luke's more concise statement of the matter.

28 The Western text characteristically expands ἐπιδεικνύς (*epideiknys*, "proving") to διαλεγόμενος καὶ ἐπιδεικνύς (*dialegomenos kai epideiknys*, "reasoning and proving").

H. *At Ephesus* (19:1-19)

The third missionary journey of Paul was chiefly devoted to an extended ministry at Ephesus, the city he apparently hoped to reach at the start of his second journey. On his brief visit there less than a year before, it had shown a real response to the gospel. Luke's account of the ministry at Ephesus is much abbreviated, with a very short summary of only five verses (vv.8-12) sandwiched between two striking vignettes of a deviant kind of faith (vv.1-7, 13-19). In all, Paul's Ephesian ministry lasted about three years, from approximately 53 through 56.

1. *Twelve men without the Spirit*

19:1–7

> [1]While Apollos was at Corinth, Paul took the road through the interior and arrived at Ephesus. There he found some disciples [2]and asked them, "Did you receive the Holy Spirit when you believed?"
>
> They answered, "No, we have not even heard that there is a Holy Spirit."
> [3]So Paul asked, "Then what baptism did you receive?"
> "John's baptism," they replied.
> Paul said, "John's baptism was a baptism of repentance. He told the people to believe in the one coming after him, that is, in Jesus." [5]On hearing this, they were baptized into the name of the Lord Jesus. [6]When Paul placed his hands on them, the Holy Spirit came on them, and they spoke in tongues and prophesied. [7]There were about twelve men in all.

1 Ephesus was on the western coast of Asia Minor, at the mouth of the Cayster (or Little Meander) River and between the Koressos mountain range and the Aegean Sea. It was founded in the twelfth or eleventh century B.C. by Ionian colonists from Athens as a gateway to the vast resources of the Asian steppes. In its early days it was a secondary port to Miletus, thirty miles south at the mouth of the Meander River. But when Miletus's harbor became clogged with silt and Miletus itself destroyed by the Persians, commerce and power shifted to Ephesus. In 334 B.C. Alexander the Great captured it at the start of his "drive to the East." From Alexander's death to 133 B.C. it was ruled by the Pergamum kings, the most dynamic and powerful of the lesser rulers of Alexander's divided empire. With the inevitability of a Roman takeover, Attalus III, the last of the kings of Pergamum, willed the city to Rome at his death; and Ephesus was made the capital of the newly formed Roman province of Asia.

Ephesus relied upon two important assets for its wealth and vitality. The first was its position as a center of trade, linking the Greco-Roman world with the rich hinterland of western Asia Minor. But because of excessive lumbering, charcoal burning, and over-grazing the land, topsoils slipped into streams, streams were turned into marshes, and storm waters raced to the sea laden with silt that choked the river's mouth. The Pergamum kings promoted the maintenance of the harbor facilities at Ephesus, and Rome followed suit. But it was a losing battle against the unchecked erosion of the hinterland. In Paul's day, the zenith of Ephesus's commercial power was long since past. Deepening economic decline had cast a shadow over the city. Efforts were repeatedly made to improve the harbor (in A.D. 65 a large-scale attempt was undertaken), but they either failed or provided only temporary relief. Domitian at the end of the first century A.D. was the last ruler to attempt to repair the harbor's facilities and enlarge its dwindling capacities. Today the mouth of the Cayster River is so choked with silt that the ancient harbor works of Ephesus sit back behind a swamp, some seven miles from the sea.

The second factor the life of Ephesus depended on was the worship of Artemis (the Lat. Diana), the multibreasted goddess of fertility whose temple was one of the Seven Wonders of the ancient world. The relation of Artemis of Ephesus to the Greek goddess Artemis is very vague. Though in their distinctive characteristics they were quite different, in the popular mind they were often equated. King Croesus of nearby Lydia (reigned 564–546 B.C.) built the first temple to Artemis one and a half miles northeast of Ephesus. It was rebuilt on the same site in the fourth century B.C. after having been set on fire in 356 B.C. This temple was almost four times the size of the Parthenon at Athens and stood till the Goths sacked Ephesus in A.D. 263. With the decline of its commerce, the prosperity of Ephesus became more and more dependent on the tourist and pilgrim trade associated with the temple and cult of Artemis. At the time of Paul's arrival, the people of Ephesus, while surrounded by signs of past wealth and still enjoying many of its fruits, were becoming conscious of the precariousness of their position as a commercial and political center of Asia and were turning more toward the temple of Artemis in support of their economy.

After revisiting the churches of Galatia (cf. 18:23), Paul "took the road through the interior" (*dielthonta ta anōterika merē*; lit., "going through the interior districts") and came to Ephesus. He arrived after Apollos had left for Corinth, entering the city probably in the summer of 53. There he found "about twelve men" (v.7) who professed to be Christian "disciples" (*mathētai*), but in whom Paul discerned something amiss.

2-3 The question Paul put to the twelve, "Did you receive the Holy Spirit when you believed," suggests two things: (1) that he assumed they were truly Christians, since they professed to believe; and (2) that he held that true belief and the reception of the Holy Spirit always went together, being unable to be separated either logically or chronologically. These two assumptions caused Paul some difficulty when he met these twelve men, for something in their life indicated that one or the other assumption was wrong. When they answered his question by saying, "We have not even heard that there is a Holy Spirit," he knew the second assumption was not in error. So he asked further about the first one and found that they claimed to have been baptized only with "John's baptism."

The account is extremely difficult to interpret, principally because it is so brief. Probably we should assume that these twelve men, while considering themselves Jewish Christian "disciples" in some sense, thought of John the Baptist as the height of God's revelation—perhaps even as the Messiah himself. John 1:19–34 and 2:22–36 are directed against anyone thinking of the Baptist as superior to Jesus. Together with the emphasis upon "one Lord, one faith, one baptism" in Ephesians 4:5, they suggest that a John-the-Baptist sect existed within Jewish Christian circles in Asia in the first century (assuming, of course, the Ephesian connections of the fourth Gospel and the Letter to the Ephesians). As in any such group—particularly before issues become defined and positions solidified—some would have appreciated John the Baptist and ﹞•t looked forward to the greater fulfillment of which he spoke, whereas others would have gone no further in their devotion than the Baptist himself—perhaps honoring him as an equal with Jesus or even elevating him higher than Jesus.

Apollos seems to have been in the first category for, though from a John-the-Baptist group, he had been taught "accurately" and needed only that Priscilla and Aquila teach him "more adequately" (18:24–26). "Though," as Luke says, "he knew only the baptism of John," he considered it a prolegomenon to the reception of God's Messiah; and when taught about further events and implications, he readily accepted them.

The twelve men Paul met, however, apparently made the Baptist the focus of their devotion. Luke calls them "disciples," just as he speaks of Simon of Samaria as having "believed" (cf. 8:13), of the Judiazers as "believers" (cf. 15:5), of the seven sons of Sceva as exorcising demons "in the name of Jesus," and of Sceva their father as "a Jewish chief priest" (cf. 19:13–14). Luke's practice is to portray the spiritual condition of his characters by their actions without always evaluating it. Here it seems, both from their own statements and from how Paul deals with them, that we should consider these men as sectarians with no real commitment to Jesus at all.

4-7 Despite their being known as disciples, Paul preached Jesus to the men as he would to any of the Jews. "John's baptism," he said, "was a baptism of repentance" that pointed beyond itself and the Baptist to "the one coming after him"—that is, to Jesus. So on their acceptance of Jesus as the focus of Christian faith, they were baptized "into the name of the Lord Jesus" (*eis to onoma tou kyriou Iēsou*). Then Paul laid his hands on them and they received the Holy Spirit, evidencing the same signs of the Spirit's presence as the first Jewish believers did at Pentecost—viz., tongues and prophecy. Doubtless in Paul's mind they were not rebaptized but baptized into Christ once and for all. When baptism by John the Baptist was seen as pointing beyond itself to Jesus (as with Apollos), it was apparently taken as Christian baptism and was not repeated on learning and experiencing more of the faith. But when John's baptism was understood as rivaling commitment to Jesus, then on profession of faith in him, Christian baptism "into the name of the Lord Jesus" was administered.

Notes

1 The Western text recasts the opening of this verse to read: "But when Paul, according to his own plan, wanted to go to Jersualem, the Spirit told him to return to Asia," deleting the first clause, which NIV translates as "while Apollos was at Corinth." Evidently the Western reviser took "the church" of 18:22 to be the Caesarean church and recast 19:1 to explain why Paul did not carry out his plans (as per the Western reading) of 18:21 (cf. 16:6–7).

5 On the synonymous use of the prepositions ἐπί (*epi*, "on"), ἐν (*en*, "in"), and εἰς (*eis*, "into") with Christian baptism, see the note at 2:38.

The Western text reads Ἰησοῦν Χριστόν (*Iēsoun Christon*, "Jesus Christ") and then continues εἰς ἄφεσιν ἁμαρτιῶν (*eis aphesin hamartiōn*, "so that sins may be forgiven"), thereby paralleling the wording of 2:38.

6 For other instances of the laying on of hands in a variety of circumstances, see 6:6; 8:17; 9:17; 13:3.

On tongues and prophecy as signs of the Spirit's presence at Pentecost, see 2:3–4.

2. A summary of the apostle's ministry

19:8–12

> [8]Paul entered the synagogue and spoke boldly there for three months, arguing persuasively about the kingdom of God. [9]But some of them became obstinate; they refused to believe and publicly maligned the Way. So Paul left them. He took the disciples with him and had discussions daily in the lecture hall of Tyrannus. [10]This went on for two years, so that all the Jews and Greeks who lived in the province of Asia heard the word of the Lord.
> [11]God did extraordinary miracles through Paul. [12]Handkerchiefs and aprons that had touched him were taken to the sick, and their illnesses were cured and the evil spirits left them.

8–10 The ministry of Paul at Ephesus lasted approximately three years (cf. 20:31). It is remarkable how concisely Luke summarizes this extensive period—though perhaps not so remarkable if we may assume from the absence of the pronoun "we" that Luke was not himself an eyewitness of the events here narrated. The conciseness of the passage is particularly notable when compared with Luke's expansive, anecdotal treatments of the ministry at Philippi (cf. 16:10ff.) and the return journey to Jerusalem (cf. 20:5ff.), where, to judge by the presence of the "we," he was an eyewitness. Yet though we would like to know much more than Luke gives us here, we cannot for that reason fault what we have.

In the synagogue at Ephesus, Paul was "arguing persuasively [*dialegomenos kai peithōn;* lit., 'arguing and persuading,' a hendiadys construction] about the kingdom of God." He was speaking to those who had earlier received him favorably (cf. 18:19-21), and the three-month hearing they gave him was one of the longest he had in any synagogue. When opposition to "the Way" (*hē hodos*) arose within the synagogue, he withdrew and continued to minister for two more years at the lecture hall of Tyrannus. This was probably the hall of a local philosopher named Tyrannus ("Tyrant") or one rented out to traveling philosophers by a landlord of that name. Since it is difficult (except in certain bleak moments of parenthood) to think of any parent naming his or her child "Tyrant," the name must have been a nickname given by the man's students or tenants.

As for the rent for the hall, perhaps Priscilla and Aquila shared it or the growing congregation underwrote it. Following the Western text, we might picture Paul as using the hall between the hours of 11 A.M. and 4 P.M.—the time of the usual midday rest and after Tyrannus had dismissed his students and Paul had completed his morning's work (cf. 20:34). But that is merely conjecture. All we really know is that for two years Paul "reasoned daily" (*kath hēmeran dialegomenos;* or "had discussions daily," NIV) about the claims of Christ and that during this time the gospel radiated out from Ephesus through Paul's converts so that "all the Jews and Greeks who lived in the province of Asia heard the word of the Lord," with the result that many churches in the outlying cities and villages were founded (cf. Col 1:7; 2:1; 4:16; Rev 2-3; Ignatius *To the Ephesians; To the Magnesians; To the Trallians; To the Philadelphians; To the Smyrneans*). Then after sending Timothy and Erastus as his envoys to Macedonia and Achaia, Paul stayed for a while longer at Ephesus (cf. 19:21-22).

While there, Paul wrote the Corinthian church a letter on the subject of separation from the ungodly (cf. 1 Cor 5:9-10)—a letter either not now extant or partially preserved (as often suggested) in 2 Corinthians 6:14-7:1. In reply he received a letter from certain members of the Corinthian church (cf. 1 Cor 7:1) seeking his advice on matters concerning marital problems at Corinth, food previously dedicated to idols, the decorum of women in worship, the observance of the Lord's Supper, spiritual gifts, and (possibly) the nature and significance of the Resurrection. At about the same time he had some visitors from Corinth, whom he identifies as "Chloe's household" (1 Cor 1:11), who told of deep and bitter divisions within the church. And from rumors widely circulating (cf. 1 Cor 5:1), he knew that among the Corinthian believers there existed blatant immorality and also litigations in the public lawcourts. To deal with all these matters, the apostle wrote a second pastoral letter—1 Corinthians.

The problems at Corinth seem to have taken the course of opposition to Paul's authority and criticism of his doctrine, and he was forced to make a "painful visit" to the city in an attempt to settle matters within the church (cf. 2 Cor 2:1; 12:14; 13:1). This visit to Corinth from Ephesus is extremely difficult to place historically because Luke's summary of events during this time is so brief and Paul's references so allusive. It may even have been conducted on his behalf by Timothy and Erastus (cf. 19:22) or by Titus (cf. 2 Cor 12:17-18; see also 2:13; 7:6, 13-14; 8:6, 16, 23). Nevertheless, the fact that Paul speaks of it as a "painful visit" and that he found it necessary to continue to rebuke his Corinthian converts suggests that it was not entirely successful. His opponents even taunted him, it seems, with being humble in their presence but bold when away (cf. 2 Cor 10:1). (For a fuller discussion of the problems at Corinth, see the Introductions to 1 and 2 Corinthians—esp. the latter—in EBC, 10:175–82; 302–15.)

11–12 From his Corinthian correspondence we learn that Paul, while at Ephesus, had his difficulties, which arose chiefly from conditions at Corinth. But Luke does not speak of them or mention any further difficulties at Ephesus beyond his general reference to Jewish opposition (v.9) and the Demetrius incident (vv.23–41). Instead, he rounds off his summary of Paul's Ephesian ministry by speaking of "extraordinary miracles" (*dynameis ou tas tychousas*; lit., "miracles not of the ordinary kind"—a somewhat strange way to talk about the miraculous) taking place directly through Paul and through his handkerchiefs and aprons being taken to the sick and demon possessed.

The particle *te* and the adverbial use of *kai* in the Greek sentence indicate that Luke had in mind two types of "extraordinary miracles": (1) direct healings through the laying on of Paul's hands (note the phrase *dia tōn cheirōn Paulou*, "through the hands of Paul," which NIV does not pick up), and (2) indirect healings through the application of Paul's handkerchiefs and aprons. The Greek word *soudarion* (a Lat. loan word from *sudarium*) means a face-cloth used for wiping perspiration, corresponding somewhat to our handkerchief—though, of course, the garments of antiquity had no pockets—and the word *simikinthion* (another Lat. loan word from *semicinctium*) means a workman's apron. So prominent was the divine presence in Paul's ministry at Ephesus, Luke tells his readers, that even such personal garments as Paul's sweat-cloths and work-aprons used in his trade of tentmaking and leather working were taken out to the sick and demon possessed, and through their application there were cures.

It is certainly strange to read of healings occurring through sweat-cloths and work-aprons. Most commentators are uneasy with the account here and either explain it away as a pious legend or downplay it as verging on the bizzare. Even when the account is accepted as factual, some would prefer to take it as having been done apart from Paul's knowledge and approval. But Ephesus was the home of all sorts of magic and superstition, and the phrase "Ephesian writings" (*Ephesia grammata*) was common in antiquity for documents containing spells and magical formulae (cf. Athenaeus *Deipnosophistae* 12.548; Clement of Alexandria *Stromata* 5. 242). So it need not be thought unnatural that just as Paul met his audiences at a point of common ground ideologically in order to lead them on to the Good News of salvation in Christ, so at Ephesus he acted in the way here depicted. The virtue, of course, lay not in the materials themselves but in the power of God and the faith of the recipients.

Luke's interest throughout this chapter is in emphasizing the supernatural power of the gospel. Therefore he has highlighted these "extraordinary miracles." Also, he doubtless included reference to miracles done through sweat-cloths and work-aprons in order to set up a further parallel with the ministries of Jesus and Peter, where healings took place by touching Jesus' cloak (Luke 8:44) and through Peter's shadow (Acts 5:15).

Notes

8 The Western text adds ἐν δυνάμει μεγάλη (*en dynamei megalē*, "with great power") before the verb ἐπαρρησιάζετο (*eparrēsiazeto*, "spoke boldly").

On Luke's emphasis in Panel 5 on persuasion in Paul's preaching—here by the use of διαλεγόμενος καὶ πείθων (*dialegomenos kai peithōn*, "arguing persuasively") and in v.9 by the verb διαλέγομαι (*dialegomai*, "to reason" or "discuss")—see comments on 17:2–3.

On ἡ βασιλεία τοῦ θεοῦ (*hē basileia tou theou*, "the kingdom of God") in Acts (cf. 1:3; 8:12; 20:25; 28:23, 31), see comments on 1:3.

9 On the self-designation of Christians as those of "the Way" (ἡ ὁδός, *hē hodos*; cf. 9:2; 19:23; 22:4; 24:14, 22; also 16:17; 18:25–26; 2 Peter 2:2), see comments on 9:2.

The Western text adds ἀπὸ ὥρας ε ἕως δεκάτης (*apo hōras e heōs dekatēs*, "from the fifth to the tenth hour") after the name Tyrannus, which translates to "from 11 A.M. to 4 P.M." in our reckoning.

---

3. The seven sons of Sceva

19:13–19

> ¹³Some Jews who went around driving out evil spirits tried to invoke the name of the Lord Jesus over those who were demon-possessed. They would say, "In the name of Jesus, whom Paul preaches, I command you to come out." ¹⁴Seven sons of Sceva, a Jewish chief priest, were doing this. ¹⁵The evil spirit answered them, "Jesus I know and Paul I know about, but who are you?" ¹⁶Then the man who had the evil spirit jumped on them and overpowered them all. He gave them such a beating that they ran out of the house naked and bleeding.
>
> ¹⁷When this became known to the Jews and Greeks living in Ephesus, they were all seized with fear, and the name of the Lord Jesus was held in high honor. ¹⁸Many of those who believed now came and openly confessed their evil deeds. ¹⁹A number who had practiced sorcery brought their scrolls together and burned them publicly. When they calculated the value of the scrolls, the total came to fifty thousand drachmas.

13–16 Most commentators are convinced at this point that Luke has completely set aside his sources for some popular Oriental legend, which he then attempted to recast into an edifying Christian story. Even so staunch a defender of the historical reliability of Acts as Ramsay, after squirming through an account of rebaptism (as he interpreted it) in vv.1–7 and of healings by means of sweat-cloths and work-aprons in vv.11–12, found this section to be the proverbial "last straw" and declared: "In this Ephesian description one feels the character, not of weighed and reasoned history, but of popular fancy; and I cannot explain it on the level of most of the narrative" (*St. Paul the Traveller*, p. 273).

The use of magical names in incantations to exorcise evil spirits was common in the ancient world, and it seems to have been especially prominent at Ephesus. In addition, Jewish practitioners of magic were highly esteemed in antiquity, for they were believed to have command of particularly effective spells. The great reluctance of the Jews to pronounce the divine name was known among the ancients and often misinterpreted according to magical principles. Moreover, those connected with the Jewish priesthood would have enjoyed great prestige in magical circles since they were the most likely ones to know the true pronunciation of the Ineffable Name and therefore most able to release its power (cf. Bruce M. Metzger, "St. Paul and the Magicians," *Princeton Seminary Bulletin*, 38 [1944], 27–30).

Some Jewish exorcists, on coming into contact with Paul and his preaching about Jesus, attempted to make magical use of this new name they had heard. Luke identifies them as "seven sons of Sceva, a Jewish chief priest" (*Skeua Ioudaiou archiereōs hepta huioi*). Perhaps they did belong to one of the high priestly families of Jerusalem (even the best families have their deviants), though undoubtedly the title "Jewish chief priest" was a self-designation manufactured to impress their clients and is reported by Luke without evaluation. Perhaps they even professed to accept Paul's message and to be committed to Jesus personally themselves, much as Simon of Samaria did (cf. 8:9–24). But if they thought of themselves as in some sense Jewish Christians, it was primarily for the benefits they could derive for their magical arts from the power of the name of Jesus, and so they simply continued in their old ways with a new twist.

When, however, they tried to use this more powerful name in their exorcisms, Sceva's sons found they were dealing with realities far beyond their ability to cope. The demon they were trying to exorcise turned violently on them, and they fled from the house naked and bleeding. The name of Jesus, like an unfamiliar weapon misused, exploded in their hands; and they were taught a lesson about the danger of using the name of Jesus in their dabbling in the supernatural.

17–19 News of what happened spread quickly throughout Ephesus. All who heard were overcome by reverential fear (*phobos*) and held the name of Jesus in high honor. Negatively, they learned not to misuse the name of Jesus or treat it lightly, for it is a powerful name. Positively, many Christians renounced their secret acts of magic and several magicians were converted. Openly demonstrating the change in their lives, they brought their magical scrolls together and burned them in the presence of the gathered congregation (*enōpion pantōn*, or "publicly"). The value of the papyrus scrolls, Luke adds, was estimated at fifty thousand pieces of silver (*argyriou myriadas pente*; NIV, "fifty thousand drachmas").

Notes

13 A parallel use of the name of Jesus in exorcism appears in the Paris magical papyrus No. 574, lines 3018–19: "I adjure you by Jesus the god of the Hebrews" (cf. K. Preisendanz, *Papyri Graecae Magicae*, 2 vols. [Leipzig: Teubner, 1928, 1931] 1: plate IV). Rabbinic writings denounce the invoking of the name of Jesus in healings (cf. Tos *Hulin* 2.22–23; j. *Shabbath* 14.4.14d; j *Abodah Zarah* 2.2.40d–41a; b *Abodah Zarah* 27b), which suggests that some Jewish exorcists and healers were doing just that.

14 The Western text recasts this verse to read: "Among whom also the sons of Sceva, a priest, desired to do the same (it was their practice to exorcise such people); and coming before the demon-possessed man, they began to invoke the Name, saying: 'We command you by Jesus, whom Paul proclaims, to come out.'" The Western text thereby tones down Sceva's priestly title and omits reference to the sons as being "seven" (ἐπτά, *hepta*) in number. The Lat. cod. Gigas (thirteenth century) reads "two [δύο, *duo*] sons."

15 Two verbs for "to know" are used in this verse: γινώσκω (*ginōskō*) of the demon's knowledge of Jesus and ἐπίσταμαι (*epistamai*) of his knowledge of Paul. But it is doubtful that they should be understood here as denoting differing types or degrees of knowledge (as NIV suggests). Certainly it cannot be said that the demon knew Jesus in some intimate fashion but had only heard about Paul.

16 Ἀμφότεροι (*amphoteroi*) means "both" but was also used more loosely to mean "all" (so NIV; cf. 23:8). The Western reviser evidently read it as "both" and therefore omitted "seven" in v.14, as did the Lat. Gigas, and corrected the number to "two."

19 For a collection of such magical texts now brought together at London, Paris, and Leiden, see K. Preisendanz, *Papyri Graecae Magicae*, 2 vols. (Leipzig, 1928–31).

I. A Summary Statement

19:20

20In this way the word of the Lord spread widely and grew in power.

20 The advances of the gospel into Macedonia, Achaia, and Asia did not come about without great difficulty and repeated discouragements. At times, in fact, matters looked very bleak. Viewed externally, one might even be tempted to agree with W.L. Knox that Paul's "journey into Macedonia had been the height of unwisdom and its results negligible" (*St. Paul and the Church of the Gentiles*, p. 85). Perhaps Paul felt that way himself when forced to leave the province. But such a view forgets that at Philippi, Thessalonica, and Berea a flame had been lit that was to spread throughout the area and that, to judge by Paul's extant letters, the churches founded in these cities (certainly at Philippi and Thessalonica, and probably also at Berea) were among his best and most loyal ones.

At Athens Paul faced the snobbery and polite refusal of self-satisfied people; and their lack of response, on top of his difficulties in Macedonia, almost drove him to despair. But at Corinth, in spite of his own feelings of "weakness," "fear," and "much trembling" (1 Cor 2:3), God worked remarkably, giving Paul an open door and a successful ministry. With success also came problems, though this time from within the congregation. Nevertheless, Paul had much to thank God for, and he evidently went to Jerusalem to fulfill his Nazirite vow with much joy. And at Ephesus, after revisiting his Galatian converts, his ministry continued in ways that showed God's presence and power.

Paul's second and third missionary journeys read like a slice of life. Having shown in his earlier panels the gradual widening of the gospel to new groups of people and the establishment of a new missionary policy to the Gentiles, Luke in Panel 5 has presented for his readers a graphic account of the gospel's entrance into new regions. It is the story of the church's dedicated service under the guidance and power of the Holy Spirit in proclaiming the Good News to those who desperately needed to hear it. It is a story not without elements of opposition and not without times of depression and heart searching. But it is also one of divine blessing, times of elation, and periods of confidence. Through it all God was at work. In looking back on those days, Luke simply says, "In this way the word of the Lord spread widely and grew in power."

Panel 6—To Jerusalem and Thence to Rome (19:21–28:31)

The last panel in Acts presents Paul's somewhat circuitous journey to Jerusalem, his arrest and defenses in Jerusalem, his imprisonment and defenses in Caesarea, his voyage to Rome, and his entrance into and ministry at Rome. The panel is introduced by the programmatic statement of 19:21–22 and concludes with the summary statement of 28:31. Three features immediately strike the reader in this sixth panel: (1) the disproportionate length of the panel, including one-third of the total material of Acts; (2) the prominence given the speeches of Paul in his defense; and (3) the dominance of the "we" sections in the narrative portions (cf. 20:5–15; 21:1–18; 27:1–28:16). It cannot be said that the length is related to the theological significance of the material presented. It seems rather to be related to the apologetic purpose of Luke, particularly in the five defenses, and to the eyewitness character of the narrative with its inevitable elaboration of details (cf. the Philippian anecdotes of 16:11–40). The events narrated here span the time from approximately 56 through 62.

A. A Programmatic Statement

19:21–22

> [21]After all this had happened, Paul decided to go to Jerusalem, passing through Macedonia and Achaia. "After I have been there," he said, "I must visit Rome also." [22]He sent two of his helpers, Timothy and Erastus, to Macedonia, while he stayed in the province of Asia a little longer.

21 "After all this had happened" (*hōs de eplērōthē tauta*; lit., "when these things were fulfilled") refers to the events bracketed by the participle *plērōsantes* ("having fulfilled," or "when they finished," NIV) of 12:25 and the verb *eplērōthē* ("were fulfilled," or "happened," NIV) of 19:21—viz., the events of the first, second, and third missionary journeys of Paul, as recorded in Panels 4 and 5 (12:25–19:20). Some have conjectured that "after all this had happened" has reference only to the two-year ministry of v.10. But for Luke the fulfillment of the Gentile mission came (1) in the inauguration of the new missionary policy for reaching Gentiles that was established on the first missionary journey and confirmed at the Jerusalem Council (i.e., Panel 4) and (2) in the extensive outreach to the Gentile world that took place during the second and third missionary journeys (i.e., Panel 5). All that took place earlier (i.e., Panels 1–3) was for Luke a preparation for the Gentile mission; and all that happened afterwards (i.e., Panel 6), its aftermath and extension into Rome.

With the eastern part of the empire evangelized (cf. Rom 15:23, "now there is no more place for me to work in these regions"), Paul decided to return to Jerusalem and then go on to Rome. On the way he would revisit the churches of Macedonia and Achaia, ministering to them and gathering from them a collection for the Jewish Christians of Jerusalem (cf. 1 Cor 16:1–4). After Jerusalem and Rome, he planned to take up a Gentile mission in the western part of the empire, using the Roman congregation as the base for that western outreach just as the church at Syrian Antioch had been his base for evangelizing the eastern part of the empire (cf. Rom 15:24–29). Now, however, he must return to Jerusalem, knowing full well that serious difficulties could befall him there (cf. Rom 15:30–32).

Luke says that Paul's decision to go to Jerusalem and thence to Rome was *en tō pneumati*, which may mean "by his human spirit" and is thus included in the translation "decided" or "resolved" (so NEB, JB, TEV, NIV), or it may refer to direction "by the Holy Spirit" (so RSV). This same expression is used in 18:25 to refer to Apollos's own spirit ("with great fervor," NIV). But in 20:22 *tō pneumati* probably has reference to the Holy Spirit and in 21:4 *dia tou pneumatos* certainly does, and both references relate to Paul's travel plans. So we should probably understand *etheto ho Paulos en tō pneumati* here as meaning that "Paul decided by the direction of the Spirit" to go to Jerusalem and then on to Rome. This seems to be supported by the use of the impersonal verb *dei* ("must"), which in Luke's writings usually connotes the divine will. By the combination of *en tō pneumati* and *dei*, Luke appears to be making the point in this programmatic statement that the aftermath of the Gentile mission and its extension into Rome were likewise under the Spirit's direction, just as the Gentile mission itself had been.

22 Before going to Jerusalem, Paul sent Timothy and Erastus into Macedonia while he remained "in Asia" (*eis tēn Asian;* "in the province of Asia," NIV) somewhat longer— which probably means that he stayed on at Ephesus a while, not that he went on a further mission throughout the province of Asia. Luke has not mentioned Timothy since his

return from Macedonia to rejoin Paul at Corinth (cf. 18:5). But he was with Paul at Ephesus and served at some time during Paul's Ephesian ministry as his emissary to Corinth (cf. 1 Cor 4:17; 16:10–11). This is the first time we hear of Erastus, though in 2 Timothy 4:20 he is spoken of as a well-known companion of Paul's who had a special interest in the church at Corinth. That he was the treasurer of Corinth referred to in Romans 16:23, however, is not at all likely. Nor can he be identified with the Erastus mentioned in a Latin inscription found at Corinth in 1929, which reads, "Erastus, commissioner of public works [*aedile*], laid this pavement at his own expense" (H.J. Cadbury, "Erastus of Corinth," JBL, 50 [1931], 42–58). Erastus was a common Greek name, and it is unlikely that Luke would mention so casually such a significant figure as the treasurer or commissioner of public works of Corinth.

As for Silas, though Luke speaks of him repeatedly in describing the second missionary journey (nine times in 15:40–18:5), he makes no reference to him in the rest of Acts. But while Luke's interest in the last chapters of Acts is focused solely on his hero Paul, that is no reason for us to assume that others were no longer with Paul. For example, Titus is not mentioned at all by Luke, but Paul refers to him as having been extensively involved at various times during the Gentile mission (cf. 2 Cor 2:13; 7:6, 13–14; 8:6, 16, 23; 12:18; Gal 2:1, 3; 2 Tim 4:10; Titus 1:4).

Notes

21 On the use of δεῖ (*dei*) in Luke-Acts, see comments on 1:16.
22 On the synonymous use of the prepositions εἰς (*eis*, "into") and ἐν (*en*, "in"), see comments and note on 2:38 (cf. 7:4, 12 [also note]; 8:16 [note]; 19:5 [note]).

B. *The Journey to Jerusalem* (19:23–21:16)

1. *The riot at Ephesus*

19:23–41

23About that time there arose a great disturbance about the Way. 24A silversmith named Demetrius, who made silver shrines of Artemis, brought in no little business for the craftsmen. 25He called them together, along with the workmen in related trades, and said: "Men, you know we receive a good income from this business. 26And you see and hear how this fellow Paul has convinced and led astray large numbers of people here in Ephesus and in practically the whole province of Asia. He says that man-made gods are no gods at all. 27There is danger not only that our trade will lose its good name, but also that the temple of the great goddess Artemis will be discredited, and the goddess herself, who is worshiped throughout the province of Asia and the world, will be robbed of her divine majesty."

28When they heard this, they were furious and began shouting: "Great is Artemis of the Ephesians!" 29Soon the whole city was in an uproar. The people seized Gaius and Aristarchus, Paul's traveling companions from Macedonia, and rushed as one man into the theater. 30Paul wanted to appear before the crowd, but the disciples would not let him. 31Even some of the officials of the province, friends of Paul, sent him a message begging him not to venture into the theater.

32The assembly was in confusion: Some were shouting one thing, some another. Most of the people did not even know why they were there. 33The Jews pushed Alexander to the front, and some of the crowd shouted instructions to him. He motioned for silence in order to make a defense before the people. [34]But when they realized he was a Jew, they all shouted in unison for about two hours: "Great is Artemis of the Ephesians!"

[35]The city clerk quieted the crowd and said: "Men of Ephesus, doesn't all the world know that the city of Ephesus is the guardian of the temple of the great Artemis and of her image, which fell from heaven? [36]Therefore, since these facts are undeniable, you ought to be quiet and not do anything rash. [37]You have brought these men here, though they have neither robbed temples nor blasphemed our goddess. [38]If, then, Demetrius and his fellow craftsmen have a grievance against anybody, the courts are open and there are proconsuls. They can press charges. [39]If there is anything further you want to bring up, it must be settled in a legal assembly. [40]As it is, we are in danger of being charged with rioting because of today's events. In that case we would not be able to account for this commotion, since there is no reason for it." [41]After he had said this, he dismissed the assembly.

Before Paul left Ephesus, a riot threatened his life and could have put an end to the outreach of the gospel in Asia. The situation was undoubtedly more dangerous than Luke's account taken alone suggests. For in what may well be allusions to this riot, Paul said later that he had "fought wild beasts in Ephesus" (1 Cor 15:32), had "despaired even of life" in the face of "a deadly peril" in Asia (2 Cor 1:8–11), and that Priscilla and Aquila had "risked their lives" for him (Rom 16:4). Luke's purpose in presenting this vignette is clearly apologetic, in line with his argument for the *religio licita* status of Christianity (cf. Panel 5 [16:6–19:20]) and in anticipation of the themes stressed in Paul's speeches of defense (Panel 6, esp. chs. 22–26). Politically, Luke's report of the friendliness of the Asiarchs ("officials of the province," NIV) toward Paul and of the city clerk's intervention on his behalf is the best defense imaginable against the charge that Paul and Christianity threatened the official life of the empire. Religiously, Luke's description of the Ephesian riot makes the point that "in the final analysis the only thing heathenism can do against Paul is to shout itself hoarse" (Haenchen, *Acts of the Apostles*, p. 578).

23 The temporal notation "about that time" (*kata ton kairon ekeinon*) is indefinite (cf. 12:1). By itself, it does not necessarily place the riot at the end of Paul's Ephesian ministry. Nevertheless, by the separation of this pericope from the account of Paul's mission in Ephesus (19:1–19) that closes the fifth panel, and by the temporal reference in 20:1 ("when the uproar had ended"), Luke certainly wanted his readers to understand that the riot set off by Demetrius took place at the close of Paul's ministry there. Also, by the absolute use of "the Way" (*hē hodos*, cf. v.9), he wanted them to understand that what happened was not simply against Paul personally but that it was primarily a threat to the continued outreach of the gospel.

24–27 Artemis of Ephesus was not the fair and chaste huntress of Greek mythology but a Near-Eastern mother-goddess of fertility. Her image at Ephesus, believed to have been fashioned in heaven and to have fallen from the sky (cf. v.35), depicted her as a grotesque, multibreasted woman. Probably the Ephesian Artemis was originally a meteorite that resembled a multibreasted woman and became the object of worship, just as other meteorites at Troy, Pessinus, Enna, and Emesa became sacred cult objects. Her worship incorporated the traditional features of nature worship. Her high priest was a eunuch with the Persian title Megabyzos, and under him other eunuch priests and three classes of priestesses served (cf. L.R. Taylor, "Artemis of Ephesus," BC, 5:251–56).

With the silting up of the harbor, the Temple of Artemis became the primary basis for Ephesus's wealth and continued prosperity (cf. comments on 19:1). Situated one and one-half miles northeast of the city, it measured about four hundred by two hundred feet in size and stood as one of the Seven Wonders of the ancient world. Thousands of pilgrims and tourists came to it from far and near; around it swarmed all sorts of trades-men and hucksters who made their living by supplying visitors with food and lodging, dedicatory offerings, and souvenirs. The Temple of Artemis was also a major treasury and bank of the ancient world, where merchants, kings, and even cities made deposits, and where their money could be kept safe under the protection of deity.

Paul's preaching had turned many away from the idolatry of the Artemis cult, with the result that the economy of Ephesus was being affected. One profitable business was the making of "silver shrines of Artemis" (*naous argyrous Artemidos*), which probably does not mean "miniature silver replicas of the Artemis temple" but "silver statuettes of Artemis" herself to be used as souvenirs, votive offerings, and amulets. When the gospel began to touch their income, the silversmiths, led by their guild master Demetrius, instigated a disturbance they hoped would turn the people against the missionaries and stir up greater devotion for the goddess Artemis—a greater devotion that would result in greater profits for them.

28–29 The silversmiths began shouting out the ceremonial chant: "Great is Artemis of the Ephesians!" (cf. *Bel and the Dragon* 18, "Great is Bel," and 41, "Great art thou, O Lord, thou God of Daniel"), hoping thereby to stir up the city on a pretext of religious devotion. The Western text inserts "and running into the street" after the reference to their being "furious," and thus adds a note of local color that may well fit the situation. A magnificent boulevard (the so-called Arcadian Way) ran through the heart of Ephesus from its harbor to its great theater at the foot of Mount Pion. Lined with fine buildings and columned porticoes, it was the main artery of Ephesian life. Into this boulevard Demetrius and his fellow craftsmen poured, sweeping along with them in noisy proces-sion all the residents and visitors within earshot. Their destination was the large open-air theater on the eastern side of the city—a theater whose ruins show it could hold some twenty-four thousand people. In it the city assembly probably met. On their way, the crowd laid hold of Gaius and Aristarchus, two traveling companions of Paul from Derbe and Thessalonica respectively (cf. 20:4; 27:2; the genitive *Makedonas* probably orig-inally referred only to Aristarchus, contra NIV), and dragged them along into the theater. There, much to the delight of Demetrius and his fellow silversmiths, the procession became a fanatical mob.

30–31 While there is no evidence that Paul was ever tried by a kangaroo court or imprisoned at Ephesus, as some have maintained, the riot faced him with an extremely serious situation. He wanted to appear before "the assembly" (*ho dēmos*; "the crowd," NIV), doubtless believing that because of his Roman citizenship and his earlier successful appearances before government officials, he could quiet the mob, free his companions, and turn the whole affair to the advantage of the gospel. But his Ephesian converts would not let him enter the theater, and even some of "the Asiarchs" (*hoi Asiarchoi*; "the officials of the province," NIV) who were his friends sent an urgent message for him not to go there.

The Asiarchs were members of the noblest and wealthiest families of the province of Asia and were bound together in a league for promoting the cult of the emperor and

Rome. Their headquarters were at Pergamum, where their chief temple was erected about 29 B.C.; other temples were erected in honor of the ruling Caesar at Smyrna and Ephesus. Every year an Asiarch was elected for the entire province, and additional Asiarchs were elected for each city that had a temple honoring the emperor. The title was probably borne for life by officers in the league; so in Paul's day there could have been a number of Asiarchs at Ephesus. Like similar leagues in the other provinces (e.g., the Lyciarch of Lycia, the Galatarch of Galatia), the Asiarch was a quasi-religious organization with certain political functions. While it did not have political authority, it served Rome's interests by securing loyalty to Roman rule (cf. L.R. Taylor, "The Asiarchs," BC, 5:256–62). That some of these men were friendly to Paul and gave him advice in such an explosive situation suggests that imperial policy at this time was not hostile to Christianity. Luke had an apologetic purpose in stressing their action, for, as Haenchen says, "A sect whose leader had Asiarchs for friends cannot be dangerous to the state" (*Acts of the Apostles*, p. 578).

32 The crowd had been worked up into a frenzy. "Some," Luke says, "were shouting one thing, some another. Most of the people did not even know why they were there"—a remark that reveals Luke's Greek sense of ironical humor. What united them was a common resentment against those who paid no honor to the goddess Artemis. Yet, it seems, there was widespread confusion among the people as to the focus of their resentment.

33–34 The Jewish community at Ephesus was large and enjoyed a number of special exemptions granted by past provincial proconsuls (cf. Jos. Antiq. XIV, 227 [x.12], 263–64 [x.25]). Yet it also suffered from the latent anti-Semitism that lay beneath the surface of Greco-Roman society. In an endeavor to disassociate themselves from the Christians in such an explosive situation, the Jews sent one of their number, Alexander, to the podium. This may be the same Alexander of 1 Timothy 1:19–20 or 2 Timothy 4:14, but that is difficult to prove because the name Alexander was common among both Gentiles and Jews (cf. Jos. Antiq. XIV, 226 [x.12]). To the idolatrous mob, however, Jews were as insufferable as Christians on the point at issue in the riot because both worshiped an invisible deity and rejected all idols. So Alexander was shouted down with the chant "Great is Artemis of the Ephesians." This shouting kept on for about two hours.

35–40 The "city clerk" (*ho grammateus*) of Ephesus was the scribe of "the assembly" and its chief executive officer. He came to his position from within the assembly and was not appointed by Rome. As the most important native official of the city, he was held responsible for disturbances within it. He argued with the crowd that a riot would hardly enhance the prestige of the city in the eyes of Rome, and therefore any complaint raised by Demetrius and his guild of silversmiths should be brought before the legally constituted authorities. Gaius and Aristarchus who stood before them were neither robbers of temples nor blasphemers of other gods, which were common accusations made by Gentiles against Jews generally (including Jewish Christians) in antiquity (cf. Jos. Antiq. IV, 207 [viii.10]; Contra Apion II, 237 [33]).

"The courts [*agoraioi*] are open and there are proconsuls [*anthypatoi*]," the city clerk insisted. "Courts" and "proconsuls" are probably generic references and should not be taken to mean that Ephesus had two agora courts (cf. comments on 18:12) or two provincial proconsuls (as some argue occurred in late A.D. 54, when two assassins of the proconsul Junius Silanus usurped power in Asia; cf. Tacitus *Annals* 13.1). The clerk continued by saying that anything further that could not be brought before the courts and the proconsuls could be presented "in the regular assembly" (*en tē ennomō ekklēsia;* "in a legal assembly," NIV), which, according to Chrysostom (*Homilies* 42:2), met three times a month. Otherwise, he concluded, the city would risk being called to account by Rome and losing its favorable status because of a riot for which there was no reason.

41 So the city clerk dismissed the crowd. His arguments (stated above) are highlighted because they are important elements in Luke's apologetic motif in Acts, which he emphasizes further in the accounts of Paul's five speeches in his own defense.

Notes

24 B omits ἀργυροῦς (*argyrous,* "silver"), reading only "shrines of Artemis."

25 The Western text expands the vocative Ἄνδρες (*Andres,* "Men") to Ἄνδρες Συντεχνῖται (*Andres Syntechnitai,* "Men, Fellow Craftsmen"); cf. 17:22; 19:35.

26 D inserts ἕως (*heōs,* "as far as") before "Ephesus."

The Western text adds τίς ποτε (*tis pote,* "whoever he may be") after ὁ Παῦλος οὗτος (*ho Paulos houtos,* "this fellow Paul"), thereby heightening the pejorative nature of the identification.

28 The Western text turns the ceremonial chant Μεγάλη Ἄρτεμις Ἐφεσίων (*Megalē Artemis Ephesiōn,* "Great Artemis of the Ephesians!") into an invocation (also at v.34).

29 Probably the final sigma of Μακεδόνας (*Makedonas,* "Macedonia") came about through a scribal dittography with the following word συνεκδήμους (*synekdēmous,* "traveling companions").

32 On the use of μὲν οὖν (*men oun*) in Acts, see comments on 1:6 (also at v.38).

32, 39-40 Ἡ ἐκκλησία (*hē ekklēsia,* "the assembly") is used in these verses in its purely secular sense of a duly summoned gathering of people. Its use here is more specific than σύλλογος (*syllogos,* "a gathering"), being synonymous with ὁ δῆμος (*ho dēmos,* "the assembly") of v.33 (cf. 12:22). Elsewhere in Acts the word is used in its distinctive biblical sense of "the people of God," "the church," both universally and locally (e.g., 5:11; 7:38; 8:1, 3; 9:31; 11:22, 26; 12:1, 5; 14:23, 27; 15:3-4, 22, 41; 16:5; 18:22; 20:17, 28).

33 The Western text reads κατεβίβασαν (*katebibasan,* "they pulled him down") for συνεβίβασαν (*synebibasan,* "they instructed him"; "they shouted instructions to him," NIV), thereby presenting a picture of the crowd pulling him down from the podium when the Jews put him up.

35 On the address Ἄνδρες Ἐφέσιοι (*Andres Ephesioi,* "Men, Ephesians"; "Men of Ephesus," NIV), cf. 1:16; 2:14, 22; 17:22.

37 The Byzantine and a number of Western (though not D) texts read "your [ὑμῶν, *hymōn*] goddess" for "our [ἡμῶν, *hēmōn*] goddess."

40 D E P[74] omit οὐ (*ou,* "not") in "we would not be able to account for this commotion."

2. *A return visit to Macedonia and Achaia*

20:1-6

[1]When the uproar had ended, Paul sent for the disciples and, after encouraging them, said good-by and set out for Macedonia. [2]He traveled through that area, speaking many words of encouragement to the people, and finally arrived in Greece, [3]where he stayed three months. Because the Jews made a plot against him just as he was about to sail for Syria, he decided to go back through Mace-

donia. ⁴He was accompanied by Sopater son of Pyrrhus from Berea, Aristarchus and Secundus from Thessalonica, Gaius from Derbe, Timothy also, and from the province of Asia Tychicus and Trophimus. ⁵These men went on ahead and waited for us at Troas. ⁶But we sailed from Philippi after the Feast of Unleavened Bread, and five days later joined the others at Troas, where we stayed seven days.

This report of Paul's return visit to Macedonia and Achaia is the briefest account of an extended ministry in all of Acts—even more so than the summary of the ministry at Ephesus (cf. 19:8–12). Nevertheless, it can be filled out to some extent by certain personal references and historical allusions in 2 Corinthians and Romans, which were written during this time.

1 Leaving Ephesus, Paul moved north to Troas—probably following the Roman coastal road that connected Ephesus with the Hellespont or perhaps going by ship. At Troas he hoped to find Titus, whom he had earlier sent to Corinth to deal with and report on the situation in the church there. Not finding him and being disturbed about conditions at Corinth, he went on to Macedonia without any further preaching in either Troas itself or the surrounding region (cf. 2 Cor 2:12–13). As at Athens and Corinth when his concern for the Christians at Thessalonica prevented him from giving full attention to an evangelistic outreach (cf. introductory comments on 18:1–17), so at Troas Paul seems to have been consumed with concern about the Christians at Corinth and unable to launch out into any new missionary venture.

2 In Macedonia (probably at Philippi) Paul met Titus, who brought him reassuring news about the church at Corinth (cf. 2 Cor 7:5–16). In response to the triumphs and continuing problems that Titus told him about, Paul sent back to the church the letter known as 2 Corinthians. Many have proposed that 2 Corinthians 10–13, the "Severe Letter," preceded the writing of 2 Corinthians 1–9 (with or without 6:14–7:1), the "Conciliatory Letter." That is possible, though there is nothing to require it.

Just how long Paul stayed in Macedonia we do not know. Luke's words seem to suggest a fairly prolonged period. It was probably during this time that the gospel entered the province of Illyricum in the northwest corner of the Balkan peninsula (Rom 15:19; cf. also 2 Tim 4:10, where Titus is mentioned as returning to Dalmatia, the southern district of the province of Illyricum). Perhaps Paul himself traveled across the Balkan peninsula on the Via Egnatia to the city of Dyrrhachium, from which the southern district of Illyricum (i.e., Dalmatia) would have been readily accessible. Or perhaps one or more of his traveling companions (e.g., Titus) were the missionaries to this area. But however we visualize the movements of Paul and his colleagues during this time, we are doubtless not far wrong in concluding that this ministry in Macedonia lasted for a year or more, probably from the summer of 56 through the latter part of 57.

One activity that especially concerned Paul at this time was collecting money for the relief of impoverished believers at Jerusalem. He instructed the churches in Galatia, Asia, Macedonia, and Achaia about this (cf. Rom 15:25–32; 1 Cor 16:1–4; 2 Cor 8–9). The collection was an act of love like that undertaken by the church at Syrian Antioch earlier (cf. 11:27–30). More than that, Paul viewed it as a symbol of unity that would help his Gentile converts realize their debt to the mother church in Jerusalem and give Jewish Christians an appreciation of the vitality of faith in the Gentile churches.

3 After spending some time in Macedonia, Paul went to Corinth, where he stayed for

three months, probably during the winter of 57–58. While there, and before his final trip to Jerusalem, Paul wrote his letter to the church at Rome (cf. Rom 15:17–33). The Greek world in the eastern part of the empire had been evangelized (cf. Rom 15:19, 23)—the flame had been kindled, the fire was spreading—and he desired to transfer his ministry to the Latin world, as far west as Spain (cf. Rom 15:24). He evidently expected to use the Roman church as his base of operations, much as he had previously used the church at Antioch in Syria. Earlier he had hoped to go directly to Rome from Macedonia and later to go from Achaia. But now he needed to go to Jerusalem if the collection from the Gentile Christians was to have the meaning he wanted it to have (cf. Rom 15:25–32). So, in place of a visit at this time and in preparation for his future coming to them—and also to expound the righteousness of God—Paul sent a formal letter to the Christians at Rome.

The Letter to the Romans is the longest and most systematic of Paul's writings and more a comprehensive exposition of the gospel than a letter as such. Some have suggested that the body of the work was composed earlier in Paul's ministry and circulated among his Gentile churches as a kind of missionary tractate giving a résumé of his message and, when directed to Rome, was supplemented by an epistolary introduction (Rom 1:1–17) and the personal elements of chapters 15 and 16 (esp. Rom 15:14–16:24, with the doxology of 16:25–27 part of the original tractate). This view would do much to explain the uncertainties within the early church regarding the relation of the final two chapters to the rest of the writing, the absence of "in Rome" at 1:7 and 15 in some minor MSS, and the presence of two doxologies at 15:33 and 16:25–27.

At the end of three months in Corinth, Paul sought to sail for Palestine-Syria, doubtless intending to reach Jerusalem in time for the great pilgrim festival of Passover (held in conjunction with the Feast of Unleavened Bread) and probably on a Jewish pilgrim ship. But a plot to kill him at sea was uncovered, and he decided to travel overland through Macedonia. Brigandage was endemic on the ancient roads, and inns were not always safe. With Paul carrying a substantial amount of money collected from the Gentile churches, he undoubtedly wanted to get to Jerusalem as quickly and safely as possible. Nevertheless, he felt it best to spend time on the longer land route, preferring its possible dangers to the known perils of the sea voyage; so he began to retrace his steps through Macedonia.

4 Gathered at Corinth for the return journey to Jerusalem with Paul were representatives from the churches: Sopater of Berea, Aristarchus and Secundus of Thessalonica, Gaius of Derbe, Timothy of Lystra, and Tychicus and Trophimus from Asia. With the change in travel plans, they then accompanied him (together with Silas and perhaps others) into Macedonia. Almost all the main centers of the Gentile mission were represented, with the notable exception of Corinth. Perhaps Paul himself had been delegated by the Corinthian church to represent it. On the other hand, the lack of mention of Corinth may suggest continued strained relations within the church there. Luke, who appears to have joined the group at Philippi (cf. v.5), may have done so as representing Philippi.

5–6 Having been unable to get to Jerusalem for Passover, Paul remained at Philippi to celebrate it and the week-long Feast of Unleavened Bread (cf. Jos. Antiq. XIV, 21 [ii.1]; War VI, 421–27 [ix.3], for the conjunction of the two festivals in the first century). He sent his Gentile companions on to Troas and stayed on at Philippi, apparently with Silas and Timothy. Then after the Feast of Unleavened Bread, the missionaries—accompanied by Luke (note the "we" section of vv.5–15; cf. also 16:10–17; 21:1–18; 27:1–28:16)—went down to Neapolis, the port city of Philippi, and crossed the Aegean to Troas. It was evidently a difficult crossing because it took five days instead of two days as earlier (16:11).

Notes

2 Ἑλλάδα (*Hellada*, "Greece") is the popular title for the Rom. province of Achaia (cf. 18:12). Luke prefers the popular territorial names; Paul prefers the Rom. provincial names (cf. Rom 15:26; 1 Cor 16:15; 2 Cor 1:1; 9:2).

3 On "Syria" as a broad designation for "Palestine-Syria," cf. 18:18.

The Western text recasts the last clause of this verse to read "the Spirit told him to return through Macedonia," as it does also at 19:1 (see note).

4 The Byzantine text reads "They accompanied him as far as Asia," whereas D reads "When he was about to go, they accompanied him to Asia."

The Byzantine text omits Πύρρου (*Pyrrou*, "son of Pyrrhus").

The Western text calls Gaius Δουβήριος (*Doubērios*, a "Doberian"), thereby making him a native of Doberus in Macedonia (twenty-six miles from Philippi), in agreement with the plural genitive Μακεδόνας (*Makedonas*, which probably resulted from dittography) of 19:29.

The Western text explicitly calls Tychicus and Trophimus Ἐφέσιοι (*Ephesioi*, "Ephesians"), not Ἀσιανοί (*Asianoi*, "Asians").

D has Εὔτυχος (*Eutychos*, "Eutychus") instead of Τυχικός (*Tychikos*, "Tychicus") by confusion with v.9.

5 ℵ B E P have οὗτοι δὲ προσελθόντες (*houtoi de proselthontes*, "these men had come"), but the reading of B* D P74, οὗτοι δὲ προελθόντες (*houtoi de proelthontes*, "these men went on ahead"), fits the context better.

3. *The raising of Eutychus*

20:7–12

> 7On the first day of the week we came together to break bread. Paul spoke to the people and, because he intended to leave the next day, kept on talking until midnight. 8There were many lamps in the upstairs room where we were meeting. 9Seated in a window was a young man named Eutychus, who was sinking into a deep sleep as Paul talked on and on. When he was sound asleep, he fell to the ground from the third story and was picked up dead. 10Paul went down, threw himself on the young man and put his arms around him. "Don't be alarmed," he said. "He's alive!" 11Then he went upstairs again and broke bread and ate. After talking until daylight, he left. 12The people took the young man home alive and were greatly comforted.

From 20:5 through the end of Acts (28:31), Luke's narrative gives considerable attention to ports of call, stopovers, and time spent on Paul's travels and includes various anecdotes. It contains the kind of details found in a travel journal, and the use of "we" in 20:5–15; 21:1–18; and 28:16 shows its eyewitness character.

7 Though Paul himself had not undertaken a mission at Troas (cf. 2 Cor 2:12–13), the gospel had radiated out from many centers of influence in Galatia, Asia, Macedonia, and

Achaia to penetrate the Gentile world of the eastern part of the Roman Empire. Thus at Troas Paul and his colleagues found a group of believers and met with them "to break bread" and to give instruction regarding the Christian life. The mention of their meeting "on the first day of the week" (*en de tē mia tōn sabbatōn*) is the earliest unambiguous evidence we have for Christians gathering together for worship on that day (cf. John 20:19, 26; 1 Cor 16:2; Rev 1:10). The Christians met in the evening, which was probably the most convenient time because of the necessity of working during the day. They met, Luke tells us, "to break bread" (*klasai arton*), which after Paul's teaching in 1 Corinthians 10:16-17 and 11:17-34 must surely mean "to celebrate the Lord's Supper" (cf. comments on 2:42). At this time Paul "spoke to" (*dielegeto;* lit., "reasoned" or "discussed with") the believers till midnight.

8-9 "As Paul talked on and on" (*dialegomenou tou Paulou;* lit., "during the course of the discussion by Paul"), Eutychus went to sleep and fell to his death. He may simply have been bored by Paul's long discussion. Luke's reference to "many lamps [*lampades hikani;* lit., "many torches"] in the upstairs room" suggests that lack of oxygen and the hypnotic effect of flickering flames caused Eutychus's drowsiness—thereby clearing his hero Paul of any blame. But whatever its cause, Eutychus's fall brought the meeting to a sudden and shocking halt. They dashed down and found him dead.

10-11 Of course, Paul also ran down. In an action reminiscent of Elijah and Elisha (cf. 1 Kings 17:21; 2 Kings 4:34-35), he "threw himself on the young man and put his arms around him." Eutychus was restored to life. Then they returned to their third-story room, where they had a midnight snack (here the compound "broke bread and ate," *klasas ton arton kai geusamenos,* signifies an ordinary meal, not the Lord's Supper) and Paul talked on till dawn.

12 There is no hint that Paul took the incident as a rebuke for long-windedness. Nor were the people troubled by the meeting's length. They were eager to learn and only had Paul with them a short time. It was an evening of great significance for the church at Troas: Paul had taught them, they had had fellowship in the Lord's Supper, and they had witnessed a dramatic sign of God's presence and power. No wonder Luke says that they "were greatly comforted" (*pareklēthēsan ou metriōs;* lit., "they were comforted not a little").

Notes

7 On Luke's emphasis on persuasion in Paul's preaching—here by the use of the verb διαλέγομαι (*dialegomai,* "speak," "discuss") and in v.9 by the adverbial participle διαλεγόμενος (*dialegomenos*)—cf. comments on 17:2-3.

8 D reads ὑπολαμπάδες (*hypolampades,* "windows") for λαμπάδες (*lampades,* "lamps," "torches"), though the Lat. version of D has *faculae* ("little torches").

12 The Western text reads "and as they were saying goodby, he brought" for "they took" or "brought," thereby having Paul bring Eutychus to the people.

4. From Troas to Miletus

20:13–16

> ¹³We went on ahead to the ship and sailed for Assos, where we were going to take Paul aboard. He had made this arrangement because he was going there on foot. ¹⁴When he met us at Assos, we took him aboard and went on to Mitylene. ¹⁵The next day we set sail from there and arrived off Kios. The day after that we crossed over to Samos, and on the following day arrived at Miletus. ¹⁶Paul had decided to sail past Ephesus to avoid spending time in the province of Asia, for he was in a hurry to reach Jerusalem, if possible, by the day of Pentecost.

13 Leaving Troas, Paul's companions took passage on a coastal vessel that was to stop at various ports along the western coast of Asia Minor. Paul, however, waited a while longer at Troas, perhaps to make sure Eutychus was all right; and then, while the boat went around Cape Lectum, he took the direct route to Assos on the Roman coastal road and got there in time to join his colleagues on board. He may have wanted to avoid the northeastern winds that blew around Cape Lectum or may just have wanted to be alone with God on the walk to Assos.

14–15 Assos (modern Bahram Koi) was twenty miles south of Troas, on the Gulf of Adramyttium. It was on the Roman coastal road and faced south toward the island of Lesbos. The boat went on to Mitylene, a splendid port on the southeast coast of Lesbos and the chief city of this largest of the islands of western Asia Minor. From there they went to Kios, the major city of the island of Kios and an early free port (until Vespasian suspended its rights and brought it under Roman authority); then they passed through (*parebalomen*; "we crossed over," NIV) the channel separating Kios from the mainland of Asia Minor to come to Samos, an island directly west of Ephesus. So the boat arrived at Miletus, the ancient port at the mouth of the Meander River, some thirty miles south of Ephesus (cf. comments on 19:1).

16 Paul had to miss the Passover at Jerusalem (cf. comments on vv.3, 5–6). But he wanted, if at all possible, to get to Jerusalem for Pentecost on the fiftieth day after Passover (cf. comments on 2:1). This was the second of the great pilgrim festivals of Judaism. (Sukkoth or Tabernacles, some four months after Pentecost, was the third.) Paul had previously decided not to take a boat that stopped at Ephesus, for he evidently preferred to forego the emotional strain of another parting with the entire Ephesian church and to avoid (possibly) some local danger. The Aegean crossing had taken five days, Paul and his companions had remained at Troas seven days, the trip along the western coast of Asia Minor would have taken at least another ten days, and they had yet to sail across the Mediterranean and then travel by land from Caesarea up to Jerusalem. So Paul was content to sail past Ephesus.

Notes

---

13 The OS version (preserved in an Armenian translation of Ephrem the Syrian's commentary on Acts) seems to have read ἐγὼ δὲ Λουκᾶς καὶ οἱ μετ᾽ ἐμοῦ (*egō de Loukas kai hoi met emou,*

"And I, Luke, and those with me") instead of ἡμεῖς (hēmeis, "we"). The reading may stem from a Western text.

A B E P read προσελθόντες ἐπὶ τὸ πλοῖον (proselthontes epi to ploion, "had come to the ship") and D reads κατελθόντες ἐπὶ τὸ πλοῖον (katelthontes epi to ploion, "went down to the ship"), but the reading of ℵ B* C P⁷⁴, προελθόντες ἐπὶ τὸ πλοῖον (proelthontes epi to ploion, "went on ahead to the ship") fits the context better (cf. v.5).

Some Byzantine texts and P⁴¹ read Θάσον (Thason, "Thasos") for Ἄσσον (Asson, "Assos")

15 B reads τῇ ἑσπέρᾳ (tē hespera, "in the evening") for τῇ ἑτέρᾳ (tē hetera, "on the following day"), which is probably a scribal error.

The Western and Byzantine texts insert καὶ μείναντες ἐν Τρωγυλλίᾳ [-ίῳ] (kai meinantes en Trōgyllia [-iō], "having remained at Trogyllia" or "Trogyllium") after Σάμον (Samon, "Samos").

---

5. Paul's farewell address to the Ephesian elders

20:17–38

17From Miletus, Paul sent to Ephesus for the elders of the church. 18When they arrived, he said to them: "You know how I lived the whole time I was with you, from the first day I came into the province of Asia. 19I served the Lord with great humility and with tears, although I was severely tested by the plots of the Jews. 20You know that I have not hesitated to preach anything that would be helpful to you but have taught you publicly and from house to house. 21I have declared to both Jews and Greeks that they must turn to God in repentance and have faith in our Lord Jesus.

22"And now, compelled by the Spirit, I am going to Jerusalem, not knowing what will happen to me there. 23I only know that in every city the Holy Spirit warns me that prison and hardships are facing me. 24However, I consider my life worth nothing to me, if only I may finish the race and complete the task the Lord Jesus has given me—the task of testifying to the gospel of God's grace.

25"Now I know that none of you among whom I have gone about preaching the kingdom will ever see me again. 26Therefore, I declare to you today that I am innocent of the blood of all men. 27For I have not hesitated to proclaim to you the whole will of God. 28Keep watch over yourselves and all the flock of which the Holy Spirit has made you overseers. Be shepherds of the church of God, which he bought with his own blood. 29I know that after I leave, savage wolves will come in among you and will not spare the flock. 30Even from your own number men will arise and distort the truth in order to draw away disciples after them. 31So be on your guard! Remember that for three years I never stopped warning each of you night and day with tears.

32"Now I commit you to God and to the word of his grace, which can build you up and give you an inheritance among all those who are sanctified. 33I have not coveted anyone's silver or gold or clothing. 34You yourselves know that these hands of mine have supplied my own needs and the needs of my companions. 35In everything I did, I showed you that by this kind of hard work we must help the weak, remembering the words the Lord Jesus himself said: 'It is more blessed to give than to receive.'"

36When he had said this, he knelt down with all of them and prayed. 37They all wept as they embraced him and kissed him. 38What grieved them most was his statement that they would never see his face again. Then they accompanied him to the ship.

Paul's farewell address to the Ephesian elders is the nearest approximation to the Pauline letters in Acts. Its general content recalls how in his letters Paul encouraged, warned, and exhorted his converts. Moreover, its theological themes and vocabulary are distinctly Pauline. In his three missionary sermons (13:16–41; 14:15–17; 17:22–31) and five defenses (chs. 22–26), Paul addressed non-Christian audiences. But he was speaking to Christians here. It is significant that, in a situation similar to those he faced in many of his letters, this farewell to the Ephesian elders reads like a miniature letter of his. This becomes all the more significant when we recall that nowhere else in Acts is there any evidence for a close knowledge of Paul's letters.

The address is constructed in a way familiar to all readers of Paul's letters. The body of it has three parts, which deal with (1) Paul's past ministry at Ephesus (vv.18–21), (2) Paul's present plans in going to Jerusalem (vv.22–24), and (3) the future of Paul himself and of the church at Ephesus (vv.25–31). It concludes with a blessing (v.32) and then adds further words of exhortation that point the hearers to Paul's example and the teachings of Jesus (vv.33–35). Heading each section is an introductory formula: "you know" (*hymeis epistasthe*) at v.18; "and now behold" (*kai nyn idou*) at v.22; "and now behold I know" (*kai nyn idou egō oida*) at v.25; and "and now" (*kai ta nyn*) at v.32.

17 At Miletus the coastal boat docked for a number of days to load and unload cargo. So Paul took the opportunity of sending for the elders of the Ephesian church to join him at Miletus. The road back to Ephesus around the gulf was considerably longer than the thirty miles directly between Ephesus and Miletus. It would have taken some time to engage a messenger and summon the elders, who could hardly have made the return trip as quickly as a single runner. Doubtless, therefore, we should think of the elders as getting to Miletus, at the earliest, on the third day of Paul's stay there.

18–21 Paul's address to the Ephesian elders begins with an apologia that closely parallels 1 Thessalonians 2:1–12. As at Thessalonica, evidently Paul's Ephesian opponents had been prejudicing his converts against him in his absence; he therefore found it necessary to defend his conduct and teaching by appealing to his hearers' knowledge of him. The opposition at Ephesus, like that at Thessalonica, seems to have been chiefly Jewish and to have insisted that full acceptance with God could come only through a fully developed Judaism. Therefore Paul had to declare, "I have not hesitated to preach anything that would be helpful to you." His preaching to both Jews and Gentiles focused on "repentance to God" (*tēn eis theon metanoian;* "that they must turn to God," NIV) and "faith in the Lord Jesus" (*pistin eis ton kyrion Iēsoun;* "faith in our Lord Jesus," NIV)—a content wholly sufficient for salvation (cf. Rom 10:9–10; 2 Cor 5:20–6:2; also Acts 26:20–23).

22–24 The second section of Paul's address concerns his plans to go to Jerusalem. Many have claimed a discrepancy between his being "compelled by the Spirit" to go to Jerusalem (20:22–24) and his being warned by the Spirit not to go to Jerusalem in 21:4, 10–14, and have questioned Luke's reporting here in light of their understanding of the situations at Tyre and Caesarea. But Luke opened Panel 6 of Acts with the statement that Paul's decision to go to Jerusalem was "by the Spirit" (cf. comments on 19:21), and nothing here is incompatible with that programmatic statement. Both compulsion and warning were evidently involved in the Spirit's direction, with both being impressed upon Paul by the Spirit at various times as he journeyed—probably through Christian prophets he met along the way. So he considered it necessary to complete his ministry of testifying to the grace of God throughout the eastern part of the empire by taking to the Jerusalem believers the money sent by Gentile believers in Galatia, Macedonia, Achaia, and Asia—a contribution he looked on as a tangible symbol of the faith of these Gentiles and the unity of Jews and Gentiles in Christ.

25-27 In the third section of his address, Paul began by speaking of his own future expectations after visiting Jerusalem. He told the Ephesian elders that neither they nor any of those he had ministered to in the eastern part of the empire would ever see him again and that he felt free from any further responsibility in the East because he had done all that he could in proclaiming "the whole will of God." Harnack, who accepted the hypothesis of two Roman imprisonments, concluded from 2 Timothy 4 that Paul did in fact return later to Asia after being released from his imprisonment at Rome and that therefore for Luke to record the premonition in v.25 (which was falsified by later events) meant that he wrote before Paul's release and further ministry (*Date of Acts*, p. 103). On the other hand, Dibelius, who denied such an early date for the writing of Acts, used this passage to dismiss a two-imprisonment theory, for, as Haenchen (Dibelius's closest disciple) says, "Anyone who writes thus knows nothing of Paul's deliverance and return to the East, but rather of his death in Rome" (*Acts of the Apostles*, p. 592).

However, in accord with our acceptance of an early date for the writing of Acts (cf. Introduction: Date of Composition) and our belief that two Roman imprisonments can be inferred from the data, we judge Harnack's view to be closer to the truth. Romans 15:23-29 clearly indicates that Paul at this time intended to leave his ministry in the East and, after visiting Jerusalem, move on to the western part of the empire with Rome as his base. But it is not impossible that later his plans changed (as they did at various times throughout his eastern campaign) and that Luke wrote at a time when the remembrance of Paul's purpose not to return to the East was still fresh and his modification of it still future.

28-31 The third section of Paul's address continues with an exhortation to the Ephesian elders in light of what Paul sees will soon take place in the church. He warns regarding persecution from outside and apostasy within (cf. 1 Tim 1:19-20; 4:1-5; 2 Tim 1:15; 2:17-18; 3:1-9, which tell of a later widespread revolt against Paul's teaching in Asia, and Rev 2:1-7, which says that the Ephesian church abandoned its first love). So he gives the elders the solemn imperative of v.28.

Theologically, much in Luke's précis of Paul's address reflects Paul's thought and expression at this stage in his life, as these are revealed in the letters he wrote at Ephesus (1 Cor), in Macedonia (2 Cor), and at Corinth (Rom) right before this time. Paul's use of the word "church" (*ekklēsia*) is an interesting case in point. While in the salutations of his Galatian and Thessalonian letters he used "church" in a local sense (cf. Gal 1:2, "to the churches in Galatia"; 1 Thess 1:1 and 2 Thess 1:1, "to the church of the Thessalonians"), in addressing his converts at Corinth he used the word more universalistically: "To the church of God in Corinth" (1 Cor 1:2; 2 Cor 1:1). And thereafter in his writings "church" appears always in a universal sense (cf. esp. Eph, Col). Likewise, his easy association of "God" with the one who obtained the church for himself "with his own blood" (i.e., Jesus) corresponds most closely in expression to the doxology of Romans 9:5 that speaks of "Christ, who is God over all, forever praised." In addition, reference to the blood of Jesus (i.e., *hē haima tou idiou*, "his own blood") as being instrumental in man's redemption appears first in Paul's writings at Romans 3:25 and 5:9 (thereafter Eph 1:7; 2:13; Col 1:20).

32 Paul concluded his address with a blessing, committing them "to God and to the word of his grace." Though Paul must leave them, God was with them and so was his word—the word of grace that was able to build them up, give them an inheritance, and sanctify them. Again, the expressions used in Luke's précis of Paul's blessing comprise a catena of Pauline terms: "grace" (which appears in almost all his salutations and benedictions, as well as at the heart of his expositions); "build up" (cf. 1 Cor 8:1; 10:23; 14:4, 17; 1 Thess 5:11); "inheritance" (cf. Rom 8:17; Gal 3:18; Eph 1:14; 5:5; Col 3:24); and "sanctified" (cf. Rom 15:16; 1 Cor 1:2; 6:11; 7:14; Eph 5:26; 1 Thess 5:23).

33–35 Following his blessing, Paul adds a few words of exhortation (as in his letters), urging the elders of the Ephesian church to care for the needs of God's people without thought of material reward. He asks them to follow his example (cf. Phil 3:17) and calls on them to remember the words of Jesus applicable here: "It is more blessed to give than to receive." Paul often related his ethical exhortations to the teachings of Jesus (cf. Rom 12–14; 1 Thess 4:1–12) and the personal example of Jesus (cf. Phil 2:5–11). So he does that here. The words themselves do not appear in any of the Gospels. But they can be approximately paralleled by Luke 6:38, and the spirit they express certainly permeates the portrayals of Jesus in all four Gospels. While some believe the words to be a post-ascension revelatory oracle by a Christian prophet that was attributed to Jesus, it is probably truer to ascribe them to the original Jesus tradition that circulated among the churches in a collection of Jesus' "Sayings" (the "Logia," or "Q"), whether written or oral.

36–38 When Paul had finished speaking, he knelt down with the Ephesian elders and prayed with them. On the basis of the parallels between this farewell address and Paul's letters, the substance of what he prayed for can be found in such places as Ephesians 1:15–23; Philippians 1:3–11; Colossians 1:3–14; and 1 Thessalonians 1:2–3; 3:11–13; 5:23–24. After a deeply affectionate and sorrowful farewell with tears on both sides, Paul and his traveling companions boarded the ship.

Notes

21 ℵ A C E P[74] read εἰς τὸν κύριον ἡμῶν Ἰησοῦν Χριστόν (eis ton kyrion hēmōn Iēsoun Christon, "in our Lord Jesus Christ"), though E omits hēmōn, while D reads διὰ τοῦ κυρίου ἡμῶν Ἰησοῦν Χριστόν (dia tou kyriou hēmōn Iesou Christou, "through our Lord Jesus Christ").

24 The Western text expands this verse to read ἀλλ᾽ οὐδένος λόγον ἔχω μοι οὐδὲ ποιοῦμαι τὴν ψυχήν μοι τιμίαν ἐμαυτοῦ (all oudenos logon echō moi oude poioumai tēn psychēn moi timian emautou, "but I take no account regarding myself nor do I value my own life as being precious to me"); while the Byzantine text has the same expansion but reverses the verbs echō and poioumai.

The Byzantine text adds μετὰ χαρᾶς (meta charas, "with joy") after τὸν δρόμον μου (ton dromon mou, "the race"; lit., "my race").

D adds τοῦ λόγου (tou logou, "of the word") after τὴν διακονίαν (tēn diakonian, "the ministry"; "the task," NIV).

D adds Ἰουδαίοις καὶ Ἕλλησιν (Ioudaiois kai Hellēsin, "to Jews and Greeks") after διαμαρτύρασθαι (diamartyrasthai, "testifying"), paralleling v.21.

25 The Western text adds τοῦ Ἰησοῦ (tou Iēsou, "of Jesus") after τὴν βασιλείαν (tēn basileian, "the kingdom") while the Byzantine text adds τοῦ θεοῦ (tou theou, "of God").

28 A C E P[74] and the Western text read τοῦ κυρίου (tou kyriou, "of the Lord") for τοῦ θεοῦ (tou theou, "of God"), while other texts read variously τοῦ κυρίου καὶ θεοῦ (tou kyriou kai theou, "of the Lord and of God"); τοῦ κυρίου τοῦ θεοῦ (tou kyriou tou theou, "of the Lord the God"); and τοῦ κυρίου Ἰησοῦ (tou kyriou Iēsou, "of the Lord Jesus"). But tou theou is supported by the combined witness of ℵ and B, together with several other authorities.

On the christological title "God" in Rom 9:5, see my *Christology*, pp. 138–39.

32 B reads τῷ κυρίῳ (*tō kyriō*, "to the Lord") for τῷ θεῷ (*tō theō*, "to God"), as do also some minuscules, the Lat. Gigas, and the Coptic versions.

The Western text (though D is corrupt) seem to add at the end of this verse "To him be the glory for ever and ever. Amen," thus filling out the doxological character of the blessing.

---

6. *On to Jerusalem*

21:1–16

¹After we had torn ourselves away from them, we put out to sea and sailed straight to Cos. The next day we went to Rhodes and from there to Patara. ²We found a ship crossing over to Phoenicia, went on board and set sail. ³After sighting Cyprus and passing to the south of it, we sailed on to Syria. We landed at Tyre, where our ship was to unload its cargo. ⁴Finding the disciples there, we stayed with them seven days. Through the Spirit they urged Paul not to go on to Jerusalem. ⁵But when our time was up, we left and continued on our way. All the disciples and their wives and children accompanied us out of the city, and there on the beach we knelt to pray. ⁶After saying good-by to each other, we went aboard the ship, and they returned home.

⁷We continued our voyage from Tyre and landed at Ptolemais, where we greeted the brothers and stayed with them for a day. ⁸Leaving the next day, we reached Caesarea and stayed at the house of Philip the evangelist, one of the Seven. ⁹He had four unmarried daughters who had the gift of prophecy.

¹⁰After we had been there a number of days, a prophet named Agabus came down from Judea. ¹¹Coming over to us, he took Paul's belt, tied his own hands and feet with it and said, "The Holy Spirit says, 'In this way the Jews of Jerusalem will bind the owner of this belt and will hand him over to the Gentiles.'"

¹²When we heard this, we and the people pleaded with Paul not to go up to Jerusalem. ¹³Then Paul answered, "Why are you weeping and breaking my heart? I am ready not only to be bound, but also to die in Jerusalem for the name of the Lord Jesus." ¹⁴When he would not be dissuaded, we gave up and said, "The Lord's will be done."

¹⁵After this, we got ready and went up to Jerusalem. ¹⁶Some of the disciples from Caesarea accompanied us and brought us to the home of Mnason, where we were to stay. He was a man from Cyprus and one of the early disciples.

The narrative of Paul's journey to Jerusalem is of literary and historical significance because it comprises the third of Luke's four "we" sections (21:1–18; cf. 16:10–17; 20:5–15; 27:1–28:16). The material in this section seems to be based on a travel journal of one of Paul's companions (cf. Introduction: The Sources of Acts) and includes various details about the trip, along with some anecdotes. This section is also theologically significant because Luke appears to be describing Paul's trip to Jerusalem in terms of Jesus' going up to Jerusalem to die. Luke knows, of course, that Paul did not die at Jerusalem. Yet he seems to sketch out Paul's journey to Jerusalem in terms that roughly parallel that of Jesus: (1) a similar plot by the Jews; (2) a handing over to the Gentiles (cf. v.11); (3) a triple prediction on the way of coming suffering (cf. 20:22–24; 21:4, 10–11; see also Luke 9:22, 44; 18:31–34); (4) a steadfast resolution (cf. v.13); and (5) a holy resignation to God's will (cf. v.14). As Luke has reserved for Paul the mission to the Gentiles, which Jesus saw as inherent in the Servant theology of Isaiah 61 (cf. Luke 4:16–21; see comments at introduction to Part II: The Christian Mission to the Gentile World), so he describes Paul's journey to Jerusalem in terms reminiscent of the Suffering Servant.

1-2 "After we had torn ourselves away" (the passive participle *apospasthentas* suggesting emotional violence in the parting), Luke says "we" (i.e., Paul and his party) continued by boat to Cos. This small island was one of the Dodecanese group and a free state within the province of Asia in NT times. The next day they sailed to Rhodes, the capital of the large Dodecanese island of Rhodes just twelve miles off the mainland of Asia Minor. In the Greek period, Rhodes had been a rich and powerful city-state. But in Paul's day it was little more than a beautiful port with an aura of past glory that still lingers in the Rhodes of today. The next stop was Patara, a Lycian city on the southwest coast of Asia Minor. Patara, a large commercial city with a fine harbor, served as a favorite port of call for large ships traveling between the eastern Mediterranean ports of Syria, Palestine, and Egypt and the Aegean ports in Asia, Macedonia, and Achaia. There Paul and his party boarded a large merchant ship bound nonstop for Tyre, for they desired to travel quickly.

3 Sailing the four hundred miles from Patara to Tyre, the famous Phoenician seaport of Syria, they passed by Cyprus to the south. John Chrysostom of Syrian Antioch said that the voyage took five days (*Homilies* 45.2), which is as intelligent an approximation as any.

4 A church had been established at Tyre through the witness of the Christian Hellenists forced to leave Jerusalem at the time of Stephen's martyrdom (cf. 11:19). Paul had fellowship with the believers there while the ship was unloading. Their trying to dissuade him "through the Spirit" (*dia tou pneumatos*) from going on to Jerusalem may mean that the Spirit was ordering Paul not to continue with his plans. In that case his determination to proceed was disobedience to the Spirit. Or it may be that Paul doubted the inspiration of these Tyrian believers (so K. Lake, BC, 4:266). Probably, however, we should understand the preposition *dia* ("through") as meaning that the Spirit's message was the occasion for the believers' concern rather than that their trying to dissuade Paul was directly inspired by the Spirit. So in line with 19:21 and 20:22-24, we should treat this not as Paul's rejection of a prophetic oracle but as another case of the Spirit's revelation to Christian prophets of what lay in store for Paul at Jerusalem and of his new friends' natural desire to dissuade him (cf. vv.10-15).

5-6 After a scene reminiscent of the parting with the Ephesian elders (cf. 20:36-37), Paul and his companions sailed from Tyre.

7 The ship went on to Ptolemais (Acco, or modern Acre on the north cove of Haifa bay), another ancient Phoenician seaport some twenty-five miles south of Tyre. There it made harbor for a a day, undoubtedly again to unload cargo. Once more Paul met with the believers of the city. Probably Christianity at Ptolemais also stemmed from the witness of the Hellenistic Christians (cf. 11:19).

8-9 Paul and his party came to Caesarea, the magnificent harbor and city built by Herod the Great as the port of Jerusalem and the Roman provincial capital of Judea (cf. comments on 10:1). Caesarea is thirty-two miles south of Ptolemais. Luke does not say so, but Paul and his companions probably reached it by the ship they had crossed the Mediterranean on instead of disembarking at Ptolemais and walking to Caesarea.

There they stayed with Philip the evangelist (not the apostle Philip)—one of the seven who had been appointed in the early days of the Jerusalem church to take care of the daily distribution of food (cf. 6:1-6). He had evangelized in Samaria and the maritime plain of Palestine (cf. 8:4-40), after which he apparently settled at Caesarea for some twenty years. Paul stayed at Philip's home for "a number of days" (*hēmeras pleious*, v.10). The timing of Paul's stopovers from Troas to Caesarea had been largely dependent on the shipping schedules. But having disembarked at Caesarea, he could arrange his own schedule. For a man in a hurry to get to Jerusalem, this delay of several days (perhaps up to two weeks) seems strange and leads us to ask why Paul broke his journey here. He might have wanted to rest after his strenuous trip from Corinth to Philippi by land and from Philippi to Caesarea by sea. Certainly he would have been warmly welcomed by the Caesarean believers. More to the point, however, is the fact that he wanted to be in Jerusalem on the Day of Pentecost (cf. 20:16)—not just to get there as early as possible, but to arrive at what he believed was the strategic moment. So Paul's stay in Caesarea was probably a deliberate matter of timing.

Luke speaks of Philip's four unmarried daughters as prophetesses (*prophēteuousai*), yet says nothing about what they prophesied. Had he been in the habit of making up speeches for the characters in Acts, this would have been a prime opportunity for doing so. Perhaps these prophesying maidens and their father gave Luke source material for his two volumes, possibly on women for his Gospel or on the mission in Samaria and the Ethiopian eunuch for Acts. He could have received this matter from them during this visit and during the two-year period of Paul's imprisonment in the city (cf. Harnack, *Luke*, pp. 155-57). Eusebius tells us that Philip and his daughters eventually moved to Hierapolis in the province of Asia (probably fleeing the Roman antagonism toward the Jews in Palestine from the mid-sixties on), and that his daughters provided information on the early days of the Jerusalem church for Papias, the author of five books (not extant) on "Our Lord's Sayings" (cf. *Ecclesiastical History* 3.39).

10-14 While Paul was at Caesarea, the Jerusalemite prophet Agabus (cf. 11:27-28) came there. With the belt that held Paul's outer cloak together, he tied his own feet and hands in an act of prophetic symbolism (cf. 1 Kings 11:29-39; Isa 20:2-6; Ezek 4:1-5:17) and announced, "In this way the Jews of Jerusalem will bind the owner of this belt and will hand him over to the Gentiles." In response to this dramatic prophecy, the Caesarean believers—together with Paul's own traveling companions (note the "we" of v.12)—begged him not to go. But Paul's determination to go to Jerusalem came from an inward spiritual constraint that could not be set aside. It had come to Paul by the Spirit's direction (cf. 19:21; 20:22) in response to a growing conviction that he must present the gift from the churches personally for it to be understood as the symbol of unity he intended it to be (cf. 1 Cor 16:4 with Rom 15:31). Paul well knew that his reception at Jerusalem might be less than cordial (cf. Rom 15:30-32). And when they learned of the dangers ahead of him, his friends naturally tried to dissuade him.

15-16 Paul and his colleagues, accompanied by some Caesarean Christians, took the road up to Jerusalem, some sixty-five miles away to the southeast. There they brought him to the home of Mnason, a Cypriot and "an early disciple" (*archaiō mathētē*—viz., a disciple of Jesus from the beginning of the Jerusalem church). Not everyone in the Jerusalem church would have been prepared to have Paul and his company of Gentile converts as house guests during Pentecost. But the Caesarean Christians knew their man.

Notes

1 The Western text reads εἰς Πάταρα καὶ Μύρα (*eis Patara kai Myra*, "to Patara and Myra") and P⁴¹ (eighth century) apparently reads only εἰς Μύρα (*eis Myra*, "to Myra"). Myra was a Lycian port further east of Patara on the south coast of Asia Minor. Probably it was added here under the influence of 27:5.

12 On "going up" (ἀναβαίνω, *anabainō*) to Jerusalem, see 11:2; 24:11; 25:1, 9. On the reverential use of the expressions "to go down" and "to go up," see comments on 3:1 and 8:5 (cf. also v.15).

15 On the preposition μετά (*meta*) with a temporal designation (here μετὰ τὰς ἡμέρας ταύτας, *meta tas hēmeras tautas*, "the next day") as vying with μὲν οὖν (*men oun*) as a Lukan connective in the latter half of Acts, see comments on 15:36.

The participle ἐπισκευασάμενοι (*episkeuasamenoi;* "we got ready," NIV) is without parallel in the middle voice. Its general meaning seems to be "having furnished ourselves for the journey," but it may suggest anything from "packed our baggage" (NEB, JB)—a refinement on "took up our baggage" (RSV, ASV), which was in turn a modernization of "took up our carriages" (KJV)—to "saddled horses" (cf. W.M. Ramsay, HDB, 5:398).

16 The Western text recasts the last half of this verse to read: "And these brought us to those with whom we were to lodge. And when we arrived at a certain village, we put up with a certain Mnason of Cyprus, an early disciple." On such a reading, Paul and his companions stayed with Mnason in a village outside Jerusalem. But that is highly conjectural and wholly unnecessary to postulate.

C. *Various Events and Paul's Defenses at Jerusalem* (21:17–23:22)

1. *Arrival at Jerusalem*

21:17–26

17When we arrived at Jerusalem, the brothers received us warmly. 18The next day Paul and the rest of us went to see James, and all the elders were present. 19Paul greeted them and reported in detail what God had done among the Gentiles through his ministry.

20When they heard this, they praised God. Then they said to Paul: "You see, brother, how many thousands of Jews have believed, and all of them are zealous for the law. 21They have been informed that you teach all the Jews who live among the Gentiles to turn away from Moses, telling them not to circumcise their children or live according to our customs. 22What shall we do? They will certainly hear that you have come, 23so do what we tell you. There are four men with us who have made a vow. 24Take these men, join in their purification rites and pay their expenses, so that they can have their heads shaved. Then everybody will know there is no truth in these reports about you, but that you yourself are living in obedience to the law. 25As for the Gentile believers, we have written to them our decision that they should abstain from food sacrificed to idols, from blood, from the meat of strangled animals and from sexual immorality."

26The next day Paul took the men and purified himself along with them. Then he went to the temple to give notice of the date when the days of purification would end and the offering would be made for each of them.

17–18 With these two verses, the third "we" section of Acts concludes (cf. 16:10–17; 20:5–15; 21:1–18; 27:1–28:16). But it is likely that the "we" is dropped in 21:19–26:32 for purely literary reasons and that we should assume Luke's presence in Palestine for a longer time than vv.17–18 themselves imply. Where Paul is the focus of the narrative—

particularly in his discussion with the leaders of the Jerusalem church, his arrest in the temple precincts, and his five speeches of defense at Jerusalem and Caesarea—Luke speaks only of him.

It was probably at Mnason's house that the believers gathered to receive Paul and his party "warmly." Then on the next day, as Luke says, "Paul and the rest of us" called on James. Perhaps Peter, John, and others of the Jerusalem apostles had been in the city fifty days earlier for Passover. But from Luke's not mentioning them here we may assume that they were away from Jerusalem at the time. James was the resident leader of the Jerusalem church (cf. comments on 12:17 and 15:13). Sharing with him in the administration of the church was a body of elders (*hoi presbyteroi*—perhaps a band of seventy, patterned, as many have surmised, on the Sanhedrin)—who were also there to meet Paul and his colleagues.

19 On this occasion Paul "reported in detail what God had done among the Gentiles through his ministry." Undoubtedly he also presented the collection from the Gentile churches to James and the elders. Nowhere in Acts (except later at 24:17, in reporting Paul's speech before Felix) has Luke mentioned this collection for the Christians of Jerusalem, probably because he did not know how to explain to his Gentile readers (1) its significance as being much more than a way of currying favor and (2) Paul's fears that the Jerusalem Christians might not accept it. But the presentation of this collection was the chief motive of Paul's going to Jerusalem (cf. 1 Cor 16:1–4; Rom 15:25–27). And he felt it absolutely necessary to present it personally to the Jerusalem church so that it be viewed as a true symbol of faith and unity and not as a bribe—though he feared both opposition from the Jews and rejection by the Jewish Christians of the city (cf. Rom 15:30–31).

To understand Paul's fears, we must realize that the Jerusalem church was increasingly being caught between its allegiance to the nation and its fraternal relation to Paul's Gentile mission. To accept the contribution from the Gentile churches was to be identified further with that mission and to drive another wedge between themselves and their compatriots. True, they had accepted such a contribution earlier (cf. 11:27–30) and had declared their fraternity with Paul in previous meetings (cf. Gal 2:6–10; Acts 15:13–29). But with the rising tide of Jewish nationalism and a growing body of scrupulous believers in the Jerusalem church (perhaps as a result of a large number of Essenes being converted), Jewish Christian solidarity with the Gentile mission was becoming more and more difficult to affirm if the Jerusalem church's relations with the nation were to be maintained and opportunities for an outreach to Israel kept open. Undoubtedly Paul recognized the increased tensions at Jerusalem. No wonder he feared that James and the elders, for the sake of their Jewish relations and mission, might feel themselves constrained to reject the contribution, thus severing, in effect, the connection between the Pauline churches and the Jerusalem church—which would have been a disaster in many ways. Luke, however, seems to have found all this exceedingly difficult to explain to his Gentile readers and so excluded any mention of the collection here and earlier in his account. (Such a rationale as this for Luke's handling of the collection Paul brought to Jerusalem in no way impugns the fact of biblical inspiration. Like all the biblical writers, Luke shows his humanness in his writing. His reticences, as in this instance, are not incompatible with inspiration.)

20–24 James and the elders responded to Paul's report and the gift from the churches by praising God. Yet they also urged Paul to join with four Jewish Christians who were fulfilling their Nazirite vows and to pay for their required offerings. In effect, they were saying to Paul, "We can accept this gift from the churches and so identify ourselves openly with your Gentile mission, if you will join with these men and identify yourself openly with the nation." Thus they were protecting themselves against Jewish recriminations while at the same time affirming their connection with Paul and his mission. And, as they saw it, they were providing Paul with a way of protecting himself against a slanderous accusation floating about that he was teaching Jews to apostatize from Judaism. In view of his having come earlier to Jerusalem in more placid circumstances to fulfill a Nazirite vow of his own (cf. 18:18–19:22), Paul would not have viewed such a suggestion as particularly onerous. It doubtless seemed to all concerned a particularly happy solution to the vexing problems both Paul and the Jerusalem church were facing.

25 Many commentators have argued that the fourfold Jerusalem decree (cf. 15:20, 29) has no relevance to this situation but was only brought in to inform Paul for the first time of something drawn up behind his back at Jerusalem after the Jerusalem Council. Yet the reference to the decree here is closely connected with what has gone before and should be viewed as a reminder of the early Christians' agreed-on basis for fellowship between Jewish and Gentile believers. Having urged Paul to follow their proposed course of action, the leaders of the Jerusalem church go on to assure him that this in no way rescinds their earlier decision to impose nothing further on Gentile converts than these four injunctions given for the sake of harmony within the church and in order not to impede the progress of the Jewish Christian mission.

26 Coming from abroad, Paul would have had to regain ceremonial purity by a seven-day ritual of purification before he could be present at the absolution ceremony of the four Jewish Christians in the Jerusalem temple. This ritual included reporting to one of the priests and being sprinkled with water of atonement on the third and seventh days. To imagine that Paul was here taking upon himself a seven-day Nazirite vow conflicts with Jewish law because thirty days were considered the shortest period for such a vow (cf. M *Nazir* 3.6). What Paul did was to report to the priest at the start of his seven days of purification, inform him that he was providing the funds for the offerings of the four impoverished men who had taken Nazirite vows, and return to the temple at regular intervals during the week for the appropriate rites. He would have also informed the priest of the date when the Nazirite vows of the four would be completed (or, perhaps, they were already completed, awaiting only the offerings and presentation of the hair) and when he planned to be with them (either with all of them together or with each one individually) for the absolution ceremony. To pay the charges for Nazirite offerings was considered an act of piety and a symbol of identification with the Jewish people (cf. Jos. Antiq. XIX, 294 [vi.1], on Herod Agrippa I's underwriting the expenses for a number of poor Nazirites).

Notes

17 The Western text reads "And when we departed thence [i.e., from the village outside Jerusalem where it assumes Mnason lived, cf. note at v.16], we came to Jerusalem" for "When we arrived at Jerusalem."

21 A D E omit πάντας (*pantas*, "all"), as do also the Lat. Vul. and the Coptic Bohairic versions.

23 For εὐχή (euchē, "oath" or "vow") as meaning a Nazirite vow, see TDNT, 2:777 (cf. 18:18).

24 The Greek verb ξυράω (xyraō, "to shave") is the equivalent of the Heb. גלה (gillah), which appears several times in M Nazir 2.5–6 to mean "to bring the offerings of a Nazarite" (i.e., a male lamb, a female lamb, a ram, and their associated meal and drink offerings, as given in Num 6:14–15).

25 The Western text treats the Jerusalem decree as a three-clause ethical maxim, as it does at 15:20 and 29 (though here without the appended negative Golden Rule).

---

2. Arrest in the temple

21:27–36

27When the seven days were nearly over, some Jews from the province of Asia saw Paul at the temple. They stirred up the whole crowd and seized him, 28shouting, "Men of Israel, help us! This is the man who teaches all men everywhere against our people and our law and this place. And besides, he has brought Greeks into the temple area and defiled this holy place." 29(They had previously seen Trophimus the Ephesian in the city with Paul and assumed that Paul had brought him into the temple area.)

30The whole city was aroused, and the people came running from all directions. Seizing Paul, they dragged him from the temple, and immediately the gates were shut. 31While they were trying to kill him, news reached the commander of the Roman troops that the whole city of Jerusalem was in an uproar. 32He at once took some officers and soldiers and ran down to the crowd. When the rioters saw the commander and his soldiers, they stopped beating Paul.

33The commander came up and arrested him and ordered him to be bound with two chains. Then he asked who he was and what he had done. 34Some in the crowd shouted one thing and some another, and since the commander could not get at the truth because of the uproar, he ordered that Paul be taken into the barracks. 35When Paul reached the steps, the violence of the mob was so great he had to be carried by the soldiers. 36The crowd that followed kept shouting, "Away with him!"

27–29 The strategy of Paul's taking a vow and paying for the Nazirite offerings hardly proved successful—probably nothing could have conciliated those whose minds were already prejudiced against Paul. Jews from Asia who had come to Jerusalem for Pentecost determined to take more effective action against him than they had at Ephesus. So toward the end of Paul's seven-day purification (possibly when he came to receive the water of atonement on the seventh day), they instigated a riot under the pretense that he had brought Trophimus, the Gentile representative from Ephesus, beyond the barrier (the *Soreg*) that separated the Court of the Gentiles from the temple courts reserved for Jews alone.

Josephus described the wall separating the Court of the Gentiles from the Holy Place, or inner courts reserved for Jews alone, as "a stone balustrade, three cubits high [c.4½ feet high; though M *Middoth* 2.3 says it was 'ten hand-breadths high,' c.2½ feet high] and of excellent workmanship" (Jos. War V, 193 [v.2]). "In this at regular intervals," he said, "stood slabs giving warning, some in Greek, others in Latin characters, of the law of purification, to wit that no foreigner was permitted to enter the Holy Place, for so the second enclosure of the temple was called" (ibid., V, 194 [v.2]; cf. VI, 124–26 [ii.4]; Antiq. XV, 417 [xi.5]). One of these Greek notices was found by C.S. Clermont-Gannau in 1871 and two Greek fragments of another were found in 1935. The complete notice reads: "No foreigner is to enter within the balustrade and embankment around the sanctuary. Whoever is caught will have himself to blame for his death which follows" (cf. "New Discoveries," PEQ, 3 [1871], 132). Roman authorities were so conciliatory of Jewish scruples about this matter that they ratified the death penalty for any Gentile—even a Roman citizen—caught going beyond the balustrade (Soreg) (cf. Jos. War VI, 126 [ii.4]).

The charge against Paul resulted from the fact that he and Trophimus were seen together in the city, which led to the assumption that they went together into the Holy Place in the temple. But as Bruce observes, "It is absurd to think that Paul, who on this very occasion was going out of his way to appease Jewish susceptibilities, should have thus wantonly flouted Jewish law and run his own head into danger" (Book of the Acts, p. 434, n.46).

30 "The whole city [hē polis holē]," Luke tells us in natural hyperbole, "was aroused." The crime Paul was alleged to have committed (cf. comments on v.29) was a capital one and could easily ignite the fanatical zeal of the many pilgrims in Jerusalem. So they seized Paul in one of the inner courts of the temple and dragged him out to the Court of the Gentiles. Then the temple police who patrolled the area and stood guard at the gates leading into the inner courts closed the gates in order to prevent the inner courts from being defiled by the tumult and possible bloodshed (cf. Jeremias, Jerusalem, pp. 209–10).

31–32 Word of the riot came to "the commander of the cohort" (tō chiliarchō tēs speirēs; "the commander of the Roman troops," NIV) garrisoned in the Fortress of Antonia, to the north of the temple precincts, who, with soldiers (stratiōtēs) and some centurions (hekatontarchēs), rushed into the mob and prevented the people from beating Paul further. While the temple police were drawn from the ranks of the Levites (cf. comments on 4:1), the commander of the fortress was a Roman military officer whose responsibility it was to keep peace in the city. The Fortress of Antonia was built by Herod the Great to overlook the temple area to the south and the city to the north and west, with exits to both the Court of the Gentiles and the city proper (cf. BC, 4:136). The commander was not a chief priest (contra SBK, 2:631; 4:644) and had nothing to do with the priests and officials of the temple (contra HJP, 2.1:267). Rather, he represented Rome's interests and was commissioned to intervene in the affairs of the people on behalf of those interests (cf. Jeremias, Jerusalem, pp. 211–12).

33–36 The commander formally arrested Paul and ordered him bound with two chains. Undoubtedly he thought him to be a criminal and was prepared to treat him as one. But when he asked the mob about his crime, he got no clear answer. Therefore he ordered him to be taken into the fortress where he could be questioned directly and where a confession could be extracted from him. But the mob still pressed hard after their quarry, so hard that the soldiers had to carry Paul up the steps to the fortress (though probably, they dragged him more than carried him). All the while the mob was crying out, "Away with him!" (Aire auton)—a cry that on the basis of its other occurrences in Luke's writings certainly means "Kill him!" (cf. Luke 23:18; Acts 22:22; see also John 19:15; Martydom of Polycarp 3.2; 9.2).

3. Paul's defense before the people

21:37–22:22

> ³⁷As the soldiers were about to take Paul into the barracks, he asked the commander, "May I say something to you?"

"Do you speak Greek?" he replied. [38]"Aren't you the Egyptian who started a revolt and led four thousand terrorists out into the desert some time ago?"

[39]Paul answered, "I am a Jew, from Tarsus in Cilicia, a citizen of no ordinary city. Please let me speak to the people."

[40]Having received the commander's permission, Paul stood on the steps and motioned to the crowd. When they were all silent, he said to them in Aramaic: [22:1]"Brothers and fathers, listen now to my defense."

[2]When they heard him speak to them in Aramaic, they became very quiet.

Then Paul said: [3]"I am a Jew, born in Tarsus of Cilicia, but brought up in this city. Under Gamaliel I was thoroughly trained in the law of our fathers and was just as zealous for God as any of you are today. [4]I persecuted the followers of this Way to their death, arresting both men and women and throwing them into prison, [5]as also the high priest and all the council can testify. I even obtained letters from them to their brothers in Damascus, and went there to bring these people as prisoners to Jerusalem to be punished.

[6]"About noon as I came near Damascus, suddenly a bright light from heaven flashed around me. [7]I fell to the ground and heard a voice say to me, 'Saul! Saul! Why do you persecute me?'

[8]" 'Who are you, Lord?' I asked.

" 'I am Jesus of Nazareth, whom you are persecuting,' he replied. [9]My companions saw the light, but they did not understand the voice of him who was speaking to me.

[10]" 'What shall I do, Lord?' I asked.

" 'Get up,' the Lord said, 'and go into Damascus. There you will be told all that you have been assigned to do.' [11]My companions led me by the hand into Damascus, because the brilliance of the light had blinded me.

[12]"A man named Ananias came to see me. He was a devout observer of the law and highly respected by all the Jews living there. [13]He stood beside me and said, 'Brother Saul, receive your sight!' And at that very moment I was able to see him.

[14]"Then he said: 'The God of our fathers has chosen you to know his will and to see the Righteous One and to hear words from his mouth. [15]You will be his witness to all men of what you have seen and heard. [16]And now what are you waiting for? Get up, be baptized and wash your sins away, calling on his name.'

[17]"When I returned to Jerusalem and was praying at the temple, I fell into a trance [18]and saw the Lord speaking. 'Quick!' he said to me. 'Leave Jerusalem immediately, because they will not accept your testimony about me.'

[19]" 'Lord,' I replied, 'these men know that I went from one synagogue to another to imprison and beat those who believe in you. [20]And when the blood of your martyr Stephen was shed, I stood there giving my approval and guarding the clothes of those who were killing him.'

[21]"Then the Lord said to me, 'Go; I will send you far away to the Gentiles.' "

[22]The crowd listened to Paul until he said this. Then they raised their voices and shouted, "Rid the earth of him! He's not fit to live!"

The account of Paul's defense before the people consists of three parts: (1) Paul's request to address the people (21:37–40), (2) his speech in defense (22:1–21), and (3) the people's response (22:22). In this first of Paul's five defenses, Luke's apologetic interests come to the fore in highlighting the nonpolitical character of Christianity (contrary to other messianic movements of the day, cf. 21:38) and in presenting Paul's mandate to the Gentiles as being the major reason for Jewish opposition to the gospel (cf. 22:10–22).

37–38 At the head of the stone stairway leading into the Fortress of Antonia, Paul asked for permission to say something to Claudius Lysias the commander (cf. 23:26). The commander was startled to hear his charge speaking in fluent Greek and surmised that perhaps the prisoner was the Egyptian Jew (note the inferential particle *ara* in the commander's question) who three years earlier had appeared in Jerusalem claiming to be a prophet and had led a large band of followers into the wilderness and then to the Mount of Olives in preparation for the messianic overthrow of Jerusalem (cf. Jos. War II, 261–63 [xiii.1]; Antiq. XX, 169–72 [viii.1]). Most people considered him a charlatan. Felix and his soldiers drove him off.

39–40 But Paul assured the commander that he was not the Egyptian revolutionary. The epithet "no ordinary city" (*ouk asēmou poleōs*), by which Paul referred to Tarsus, had been used by various cities to publicize their greatness (cf. Euripides' reference some five hundred years earlier to Athens as "no ordinary city of the Greeks" [*ouk asēmos Hellenōn polis*] in *Ion* 8). Paul's use of it here reflects his pride in the city of his birth. Jerome records a tradition that Paul's parents originally came from Gischala in Galilee and migrated to Tarsus after the Roman devastation of northern Palestine in the first century B.C. (cf. *On Illustrious Men* 5; *Commentary on Philemon* 23).

Paul spoke to the crowd in Aramaic (lit. "in the Hebrew dialect," which throughout the NT means "in Aramaic," except at Rev 9:11 and 16:16). Haenchen says that the record here is clearly unhistorical for three reasons: (1) Paul would have been physically unable to make such a speech after having been mauled by the mob, (2) the commander would not have allowed him to speak just because he asked to, and (3) the crowd would not have honored Paul's request for silence (*Acts of the Apostles*, pp. 620–21). But these objections are pedantic. We need not think that the rioters had beaten Paul into insensibility. The Roman commander may well have been impressed by Paul's courteous composure under such trying circumstances. He may also have thought that by letting him speak, he might gain some insight into the cause of the riot. As for the crowd, they may also have been momentarily impressed by Paul's composure and their attentiveness encouraged by gestures of the commander and his soldiers for them to be quiet. Moreover, Paul's use of Aramaic (the lingua franca of Palestine)—though probably frustrating for the commander—would have been appreciated by the crowd and elicited for him a temporary measure of good will.

22:1–2 Paul opens his defense (apologia) with the formal Jewish address "Men, brothers" (*Andres adelphoi*), to which he adds "and fathers" (*kai pateres*) as Stephen did before the Sanhedrin (cf. 7:2). Some have thought that this form of address implies that members of the Sanhedrin were in the crowd. But that need not follow either from the parallel with Stephen's defense or from the way Paul addressed the Sanhedrin later on (cf. 23:1). Many commentators have objected that this defense does not fit the occasion, for it makes no mention of the people's charge that Paul had defiled the temple by taking Trophimus, a Gentile, into its inner courts (cf. 21:28b–29). In reality, however, this speech from the steps of the Fortress of Antonia deals eloquently with the major charge against him—that of being a Jewish apostate (cf. 21:28a). It does this by setting all that had happened in his Christian life in a Jewish context and by insisting that what others might consider apostasy really came to him as a revelation from heaven. Indeed, the speech parallels much of what Luke has already given us about Paul's conversion in 9:1–19 and what he will give us again in 26:2–23. He repeats in this way to impress something of exceptional importance indelibly on his readers' minds (cf. comments introducing 9:1–30). Yet it is remarkable how Luke fits the variations in each of these three accounts so closely to their respective contexts and purposes.

3 The triad of "birth" (*gennēsis*), "upbringing" (*trophē*, lit. "nourishment"), and "training" (*paideia*) was a conventional way in antiquity of describing a man's youth (cf. W.C. van Unnik, *Tarsus or Jerusalem: The City of Paul's Youth*, tr. G. Ogg [London: Epworth, 1962], pp. 9, 28). Alternative ways of punctuating this verse leave open the question as to whether Paul's early childhood was spent in Jerusalem (as van Unnik proposes) or whether his coming to Jerusalem was related to his studying under Gamaliel I some time in his teens (as I have argued in *Paul*, pp. 25–27). If each participle of this triad is taken as heading its respective clause (so KJV, RSV, TEV; contra JB, NEB, NIV), Paul is here saying, "I am a Jew, 'born' [*gegennēmenos*] in Tarsus of Cilicia, 'brought up' [*anatethrammenos*] in this city at the feet of Gamaliel, and 'instructed' [*pepaideumenos*] in the strict manner of the law of our fathers." From this he argues that his Jewishness cannot be disputed and insists that with such a background he was as zealous for all that Judaism stands for as any of those in the crowd before him (cf. Gal 1:14).

Needless to say, not all have accepted these biographical claims. Many used to take Paul's birth in Tarsus as ground for consigning him to the ranks of Hellenistic Judaism. Also, various of Paul's attitudes, actions, teachings, and turns of phrase have been cited as negating any real knowledge on his part of Judaism as it existed in the orthodox circles of Jerusalem. Theologically, the assertion has often been made that Paul's doctrine of the law is so gross a caricature of Pharisaic teaching and his understanding of repentance so deficient as to prohibit his having had any real association with the famed rabbi Gamaliel I (cf. BC, 4:279). Methodologically, the claim has sometimes been made that Paul's exegetical procedures do not correspond to rabbinic practices (cf. Haenchen, *Acts of the Apostles*, p. 625). But these assertions and claims must be judged from the evidence to be very wide of the mark (cf. my *Paul*, pp. 21–64, on Paul's biographical claims, and my *Biblical Exegesis*, pp. 28–50, 104–32, on rabbinic and Pauline exegetical procedures). Paul himself claims to be "a Hebrew of Hebrews" (2 Cor 11:22; Phil 3:5), and the evidence is almost overwhelming in support of his claims in his letters and in the presentation of his claims as Luke states them here in Acts.

4–5 As evidence of his zeal for God and the Jewish religion, Paul cites his earlier persecution of Christians (cf. comments on 9:1–2). The ascription "the Way" (*hē hodos*) picks up what was the earliest self-designation of the first believers in Jesus at Jerusalem —viz., "those of the Way" (cf. comments on 9:2; also 19:9, 23; 24:14, 22).

6–9 This description of Christ's encounter with Paul on the road to Damascus, except for stylistic differences, closely parallels the one in 9:3–6 (cf. comments on 9:3–6). As in Acts 9, here both Paul and Luke describe the encounter from the viewpoint that Paul's conversion to Jesus as God's Messiah was the result of a heavenly confrontation and that it was not something Paul originated subjectively or others imposed on him. It was, indeed, "Jesus of Nazareth" who confronted him, and this places his messianology in the matrix of the Jewish homeland. But it was the risen and ascended Jesus of Nazareth, the heavenly Christ, who rebuked him and turned him about spiritually; and this alone explains his new understanding of life and his new outlook on all things Jewish.

10–11 In response to the heavenly confrontation, and as a good Jew who thought first in terms of how he should act in obedience to divine revelation, Paul's question was "What shall I do, Lord?" He was told to go into Damascus, where the divine will would be revealed to him. So in his blindness he was led into Damascus by his companions to await instructions as to God's purposes for him.

12–16 At Damascus Paul was visited by Ananias, God's messenger to bring about renewal of Paul's sight and to announce God's purpose for him as a witness "to all men" (*pros pantas anthrōpous*). The Jewish matrix of Paul's commission is highlighted by the description of Ananias as "a devout observer of the law and highly respected by all the Jews living there" (v.12); and the Jewish flavor of the episode is strengthened by the expression "the God of our fathers" and the messianic title "the Righteous One" (v.14; cf. 3:14). The words "Brother Saul, receive your sight" (v.13) are a summary of the fuller statement reported in 9:17. What was important in the present circumstance was not to reproduce the exact words of Ananias but to emphasize that the commission Paul received from the risen Christ was communicated by a pious Jew who spoke in distinctly Jewish terms. Later on, when Paul defended himself before Agrippa II (ch. 26), there was no need for this particular emphasis; and therefore the substance of what Ananias said in the name of the Lord Jesus is there included in the words spoken by the heavenly voice on the Damascus Road (cf. 26:16–18). Having thus delivered the Lord's message, Ananias called on Paul to respond: "Get up, be baptized and wash your sins away, calling on his name" (v.16)—an exhortation reminiscent of Peter's at Pentecost (cf. 2:38).

17–21 Paul's commission at Damascus to be God's witness "to all men" was reaffirmed and amplified in a vision he received as he was praying in the temple. Most likely the visit to the temple and the vision referred to here occurred on Paul's return to Jerusalem three years after his conversion (cf. 9:26–29; Gal 1:18–19). At that time, Luke tells us, Paul faced opposition from the Hellenistic Jews of the city, who viewed him as a renegade and sought to kill him (cf. 9:29). It was evidently at that time—at a period in his life when he most needed divine direction and support—that the same heavenly personage he met on the road to Damascus, the risen and exalted Jesus, directed him to "leave Jerusalem immediately, because they will not accept your testimony about me" (v.18). More importantly, it was at that time that the same exalted Jesus also ordered him: "Go, I will send you far away to the Gentiles" (v.21). Jerusalem, therefore, Paul says, was his intended place of witness and the temple God's place of revelation. Nevertheless, his testimony was refused in the city, and by revelation his commission "to all men" was to have explicit reference to Gentiles who are "far away" (*makran,* lit., "far off"; cf. comments on 2:39).

22 During most of Paul's defense, the crowd listened with a certain respect, for he had spoken mostly of Israel's messianic hope and had done so in a thoroughly Jewish context. Even his identification of Jesus with his people's messianology and with the Revealer from heaven, while straining the credibility of many in the crowd, could have been tolerated by a people given more to orthopraxis (authorized practice) than orthodoxy (correct thought). When, however, Paul spoke of being directed by divine revelation to leave Jerusalem and go far away to Gentiles who had no relation to Judaism, that was "the last straw." In effect, Paul was saying that Gentiles can be approached directly with God's message of salvation without first being related to the nation and its institutions. This was tantamount to placing Jews and Gentiles on an equal footing before God and for Judaism was the height of apostasy indeed! With this Paul was shouted down, the crowd calling for his death: "Rid the earth of him! He's not fit to live!" And in reporting this, Luke stresses as the major reason for the Jewish opposition to Paul his universal outlook that was willing to include Gentiles in God's redemptive plan on the same basis as Jews.

Notes

38 The number thirty thousand in War II, 261 [xiii.5] for the followers of the Egyptian self-styled prophet possibly derives from a misreading by Josephus or his secretary of the Gr. capital letter Δ (D), which equals four thousand (as Luke has it here), for Λ (L), which equals thirty thousand (cf. BC, 4:277).

22:1 On the address Ἄνδρες ἀδελφοί (Andres adelphoi, "Men, brothers"), see comments on 1:16.

3 The Vul. reads "zealous for the law" (legis); the Harclean Syr. version reads "zealous for the traditions of my ancestors" (cf. Gal 1:14).

5 Some minor Western texts add "Ananias," reading "the high priest Ananias."

7 Some Western texts (E and various Lat., Syr., and Georgian versions) add "it is hard for you to kick against the goads," picking up the Greek locution for being in opposition to deity of 26:14 (cf. note at 9:4).

9 The Western and Byzantine texts add "and were afraid," reading "My companions saw the light and were afraid."

11 The Western text adds as a prefix to the verse "And rising up I could not see."

B reads οὐδὲν ἔβλεπον (ouden eblepon, "saw nothing") for οὐκ ἐνέβλεπον (ouk eneblepon, "could not see"; NIV, "had blinded").

4. Paul claims his Roman citizenship

22:23-29

23As they were shouting and throwing off their cloaks and flinging dust into the air, 24the commander ordered Paul to be taken into the barracks. He directed that he be flogged and questioned in order to find out why the people were shouting at him like this. 25As they stretched him out to flog him, Paul said to the centurion standing there, "Is it legal for you to flog a Roman citizen who hasn't even been found guilty?"

26When the centurion heard this, he went to the commander and reported it. "What are you going to do?" he asked. "This man is a Roman citizen."

27The commander went to Paul and asked, "Tell me, are you a Roman citizen?"

"Yes, I am," he answered.

28Then the commander said, "I had to pay a big price for my citizenship."

"But I was born a citizen," Paul replied.

29Those who were about to question him withdrew immediately. The commander himself was alarmed when he realized that he had put Paul, a Roman citizen, in chains.

23-24 The garrison commander, at a loss to ascertain from the people why they were rioting and probably unable to understand Paul's speaking in Aramaic, decided to find out the truth of the matter by torturing Paul. His earlier friendliness toward Paul soured, and the brutal part of his nature and job came to the fore.

The scourge (Lat. flagellum), an instrument of Roman inquisition and punishment, consisted of leather thongs studded with pieces of metal or bone and fastened to a wooden handle. Its use often crippled for life and sometimes killed. Earlier in his ministry, Paul had five times received thirty-nine lashes at the hands of Jewish authorities and had three times been beaten with rods by the order of Roman magistrates (cf. 2 Cor 11:24-25 and comments on 9:30; 11:25; 16:22-24). But being flogged with the flagellum was a far more brutal penalty than these. Here Paul was at the brink of the kind of unjust punishment Christ endured when Pilate, in a travesty of justice, had him flogged after declaring him innocent (John 18:38–19:1).

25 Roman citizens were exempt from examination under torture. The Valerian and Porcian laws, confirmed and amplified by the Edicts of Augustus, prescribed that in trials of Roman citizens there must first be a formulation of charges and penalties, then a formal accusation laid, and then a hearing before a Roman magistrate and his advisory cabinet. Therefore as the soldiers "stretched him [Paul] out to flog him"— on the stone floor or at a pillar or post, or perhaps by suspension from the ceiling or a hook—he said to the centurion in charge, "Is it legal for you to flog a Roman citizen who hasn't even been found guilty?"

26–28 At this time, Roman citizenship was a highly prized right conferred only on those of high social or governmental standing, those who had done some exceptional service for Rome, or those able to bribe some imperial or provincial administrator to have their names included on a list of candidates for enfranchisement. In the second and third centuries A.D., the use of bribery became increasingly common, but earlier it accounted for only a small minority of citizens. New citizens received a *diploma civitatis Romanae* or *instrumentum,* and their names were recorded on one of the thirty-five tribal lists at Rome and also on their local municipal register. Succeeding generations of a citizen's family possessed a *professio* or registration of birth recording their Roman status and were registered as citizens on the taxation tables of their respective cities.

No article of apparel distinguished a Roman citizen from the rest of the people except the toga, which only Roman citizens could wear. But even at Rome the toga was unpopular because of its cumbersomeness and was worn only on state occasions. Papers validating citizenship were kept in family archives and not usually carried on one's person. The verbal claim to Roman citizenship was accepted at face value; penalties for falsifying documents and making false claims of citizenship were exceedingly stiff—Epictetus speaks of death for such acts (*Dissertations* 3.24, 41; cf. Suetonius *Vita Claudius 25*).

We do not know how and when Paul's family acquired Roman citizenship. Ramsay argued that it stemmed from 171 B.C., when Tarsus received its constitution as a Greek city and many of the socially elite in Tarsus and Cilicia were made citizens (*Cities of St. Paul,* p. 185). Cadbury proposed that Pompey, in settling the eastern provinces during the 60's B.C., transferred a number of Jewish prisoners to Tarsus, set them free, and bestowed Roman citizenship upon them (*Book of Acts,* pp. 73–74). But Roman citizenship was not a corollary of citizenship in a Greek city-state, nor were former prisoners or slaves considered fit subjects for enfranchisement. Most likely one of Paul's ancestors received Roman citizenship for valuable services rendered to a Roman administrator or general (perhaps Pompey) in either the Gischala region of northern Palestine or at Tarsus.

Therefore, when Paul claimed his Roman citizenship, the centurion immediately stopped the proceedings and reported to the commander: "This man is a Roman citizen" (v.26). This brought the commander posthaste to question Paul, who convinced him that he was indeed a Roman citizen (v.27). His own citizenship, the commander said, was purchased by a large sum of money—probably, since his name was Claudius Lysias (23:26), during the reign of Claudius through paying one of the members of Claudius's court. Paul's response, "But I was born a citizen" (v.28), implies his high estimate of his citizenship.

29 That Paul was a citizen put the situation in a different light (cf. 16:37–39). Examination under torture, while suitable for ordinary men in the empire, had to be abandoned, and some other way of determining the nature of the charge had to be found. Undoubtedly the commander shuddered as he realized how close he had come to perpetrating a serious offense against a Roman citizen.

Notes

27 D reads εἶπεν εἰμί (*eipen eimi*, " 'I am,' he said") for ἔφη ναί (*ephē nai*, " 'Yes,' he answered"), which NIV appears to incorporate in its colloquial treatment of the Neutral text here.

28 The Western text reads "I know for how large a sum I acquired this citizenship," which is probably to be understood as a sarcastic comment meaning "It cost me a huge sum, but it seems to have become cheap nowadays when even a disreputable person like you can obtain it."

5. *Paul's defense before the Sanhedrin*

22:30–23:11

> ³⁰The next day, since the commander wanted to find out exactly why Paul was being accused by the Jews, he released him and ordered the chief priests and all the Sanhedrin to assemble. Then he brought Paul and had him stand before them.
> ²³:¹Paul looked straight at the Sanhedrin and said, "My brothers, I have fulfilled my duty to God in all good conscience to this day." ²At this the high priest Ananias ordered those standing near Paul to strike him on the mouth. ³Then Paul said to him, "God will strike you, you whitewashed wall! You sit there to judge me according to the law, yet you yourself violate the law by commanding that I be struck!"
> ⁴Those who were standing near Paul said, "You dare to insult God's high priest?"
> ⁵Paul replied, "Brothers, I did not realize that he was the high priest; for it is written: 'Do not speak evil about the ruler of your people.' "
> ⁶Then Paul, knowing that some of them were Sadducees and the others Pharisees, called out in the Sanhedrin, "My brothers, I am a Pharisee, the son of a Pharisee. I stand on trial because of my hope in the resurrection of the dead." ⁷When he said this, a dispute broke out between the Pharisees and the Sadducees, and the assembly was divided. ⁸(The Sadducees say that there is no resurrection, and that there are neither angels nor spirits, but the Pharisees acknowledge them all.)
> ⁹There was a great uproar, and some of the teachers of the law who were Pharisees stood up and argued vigorously. "We find nothing wrong with this man," they said. "What if a spirit or an angel has spoken to him?" ¹⁰The dispute became so violent that the commander was afraid Paul would be torn to pieces by them. He ordered the troops to go down and take him away from them by force and bring him into the barracks.
> ¹¹The following night the Lord stood near Paul and said, "Take courage! As you have testified about me in Jerusalem, so you must also testify in Rome."

The irregular structure of Luke's account of Paul's defense before the Sanhedrin evidently reflects the tumultuous character of the session itself. Three matters pertaining to Luke's apologetic purpose come to the fore: (1) Christianity is rooted in the Jewish doctrine of the resurrection of the dead (cf. 23:6); (2) the debate Paul was engaged in regarding Christianity's claims must be viewed as first of all a Jewish intramural affair (cf. 23:7–10); and (3) the ongoing proclamation of the gospel in the Gentile world stems from a divine mandate (cf. 23:11).

30 Still unsuccessful in ascertaining why the people were so angry at Paul, the commander ordered the Jewish Sanhedrin (cf. comments on 4:5) to come together to interrogate his captive. As a Roman citizen, Paul had a right to know the nature of the charges against him and the penalties involved before formal accusations were laid. The commander also needed to know these things in order to decide what else should be done. Perhaps he had talked with Paul after releasing him from his chains (cf. 21:33). Since this was a religious matter, he decided to have it clarified before the highest judicial body of Judaism. As a Roman military commander, he had no right to participate in the Sanhedrin's deliberations. But as the Roman official charged with keeping peace in Jerusalem, he could order the Sanhedrin to meet to determine the cause of the riot.

23:1 Paul began his defense by addressing the members of the Sanhedrin as "Men, brothers" (*Andres adelphoi*, NIV, "My brothers"), the common formal address used among assembled Jews. Then he asserted, "I have fulfilled my duty to God in all good conscience to this day"—a bold claim but not without parallel on Paul's part in other situations (cf. 20:18–21, 26–27; 24:16; Rom 15:19b, 23; Phil 3:6b; 2 Tim 4:7).

2 This so enraged the high priest that, in violation of the law, he ordered those near Paul to strike him on the mouth. Ananias the son of Nedebaeus reigned as high priest from A.D. 48 to 58 or 59 and was known for his avarice and liberal use of violence. Josephus says he confiscated for himself the tithes given the ordinary priests and gave lavish bribes to Romans and also Jews (cf. Antiq. XX, 205–7 [ix.2], 213 [ix.4]). In a parody on Psalm 24:7, the Talmud lampoons Ananias's plundering and greed: "The temple court cried out, 'Lift up your heads, O you gates, and let Yohanan [mixing the letters in the Heb. name Hananiah, which is Ananias in Gr.], the son of Narbai [a textual corruption that confuses the similarly formed Heb. letters 'r' and 'd' and reads Narbai for Nadbai, a title meaning 'generous one' and used ironically] and disciple of Pinqai [a satirical word-play on the Heb. verb *pānaq*, 'to pamper'], enter and fill his stomach with the divine sacrifices" (b *Pesahim* 57a). He was a brutal and scheming man, hated by Jewish nationalists for his pro-Roman policies. When the war with Rome began in A.D. 66, the nationalists burned his house (cf. Jos. War II, 426 [xvii.6]) and he was forced to flee to the palace of Herod the Great in the northern part of Jerusalem (ibid., 429 [xvii.6]). Ananias was finally trapped while hiding in an aqueduct on the palace grounds and was killed along with his brother Hezekiah (ibid., 441–42 [xvii.9]).

3 Indignant at the affront, Paul lashed out at Ananias and accused him of breaking the Jewish law, which safeguarded the rights of defendants and presumed them innocent until proved guilty. Paul had not even been charged with a crime, let alone tried and found guilty. Anyone who behaved as Ananias did, Paul knew, was bound to come under God's judgment. Paul's words, however, were more prophetic than he realized. Ananias's final days—despite all his scheming and bribes—were lived as a hunted animal and ended at the hands of his own people.

Ananias's order to strike the defendant was in character. But Paul's retort seems quite out of character for a follower of the one who "when they hurled their insults at him, he did not retaliate; when he suffered, he made no threats" (1 Peter 2:23). Paul, it seems, momentarily lost his composure—as evidently Ananias hoped he would—and put himself at a disadvantage before the council. We cannot excuse this sudden burst of anger, though we must not view it self-righteously. We are made of the same stuff as Paul, and his provocation was greater than most of us will ever face. Yet his quickness in acknowledging his wrong (v.5) was more than many of us are willing to do.

4–5 In his apology, Paul cited Exodus 22:28. Zahn supposed that, in disclaiming knowledge of Ananias's being the high priest, Paul was speaking ironically (Theodore Zahn, *Die Urausgabe der Apostelgeschichte des Lucas* [Leipzig: Deichert, 1916], p. 763). But the tone of the statement (cf. "brothers") and the reference to Exodus 22:28 suggest that the words were meant quite seriously. Ramsay proposed that a meeting convened by a Roman officer would have been run like a Roman assembly, with Paul on one side, the Sanhedrin (including the high priest) on the other, and the commander himself presiding (*Trustworthiness of the NT*, pp. 90ff.). But while Rome's chief administrative officer in the city could order the Sanhedrin to meet, he was not a part of the council, nor would he have so offended Jewish sensibilities as to have taken any part in the meeting.

It is frequently claimed that Paul's failure to recognize the high priest shows that he had an eye condition that obscured his vision. But this is an illegitimate inference drawn from the juxtaposition of Paul's mention of an illness in Galatians 4:13–14 and his colloquial idiom of concern ("you would have torn out your eyes and given them to me") in Galatians 4:15. Luke was not averse to excusing his hero from blame wherever possible (cf. comments on 20:8); so we may well assume that he would have mentioned Paul's failing eyesight if it were relevant here.

At regular meetings of the Sanhedrin, the high priest presided and would have been identifiable for that reason. But this was not a regular meeting, and the high priest may not have occupied his usual place or worn his robes of office. Also, since Paul had visited Jerusalem only sporadically during the past twenty years, and since the high priest's office had passed from one to another within certain priestly families (cf. comments on 4:6), Paul might very well not have known who the high priest in A.D. 58 was—Ananias who reigned since A.D. 48 or Ishmael ben Phabi who took the office in A.D. 58–59 (cf. comments on 25:2). Nor, in fact, would he have known any of the current high priestly claimants by sight. All he could do when told he was speaking to the high priest was apologize—though more to the office than to the man—and acknowledge by citing Scripture that, while he did not accept the view that laws provided the supreme direction for life (cf. 1 Cor 2:15; 9:20–21), he had no intention in being guided by Christ and his Spirit to act contrary to the law or do less than the law commanded.

6 Ananias's interruption changed the entire course of the meeting, but not as he had expected. Instead of being cowed into submission, Paul began again (note the resumptive use of the formal address "Men, brothers" [*Andres adelphoi*; NIV, "My brothers"]). This time he took the offensive. "I am a Pharisee, the son of a Pharisee," he declared; "I stand on trial because of my hope in the resurrection of the dead" (cf. 24:21; 26:6–8; 28:20b).

Many have agreed with Weiss that "we must be on our guard against spoiling the portrait of Paul by the impressions we receive from the speeches of the Apostle which have been interpolated, especially the speeches in the defence during his trial" (J. Weiss, *The History of Primitive Christianity*, 2 vols., tr., ed. F.C. Grant [London: Macmillan, 1937], 1:148). Therefore adjectives such as "improbable," "incomprehensible," and "unhistorical" have been frequently used of the narrative here. Even when Luke's account is accepted, Paul is often interpreted as having played the *enfant terrible* before rather unworthy opponents and engaged in an adroit maneuver that was not really sincere. But Pharisaism in Paul's day was not as stereotyped as it later became under rabbinic development. He could still have been considered a Pharisee because of his personal observance of the law and his belief in the Resurrection, even though he did not separate himself from Gentiles.

And as for saying he was tried "because of my hope in the resurrection of the dead," we must realize, as Harnack pointed out, that "whenever the Resurrection was spoken of, our Lord, as a matter of course, formed for St Paul, for St Luke, and for the listeners the efficient cause" (*Date of Acts*, p. 87). The phrase "the resurrection of the dead" seems to have been used by Paul and by Luke to refer to the whole doctrine of resurrection as that doctrine was validated and amplified by the resurrection of Jesus (cf. 17:32 in the context of 17:31)—even before members of the Jewish Sanhedrin. We need not, therefore, attribute deceit to Paul in this matter. Luke may have been condensing Paul's speech by leaving out the obvious, as seems to have been done in 17:32. But as Harnack argued,

> We may even believe that St Paul, at the beginning of his discourse, said roundly, "Touching the Resurrection of the dead I stand here called in question"; for Luther also declared a hundred times that he was called in question touching the merits and honour of Jesus Christ, while his opponents asserted that these things did not come at all into the question (ibid., p. 87).

7–10 Paul's declaration served to divide the council, with Sadducees on the one side (cf. comments on 4:1) and Pharisees on the other (cf. comments on 5:34). Some of the Pharisees saw in the inquisition of Paul an attempt by the Sadducees to discredit Pharisaism theologically (viz., to make Paul and his message the *reductio ad absurdum* of a Pharisaic position) and rose to his defense. The Sadducees, however, kept pressing their objections, and the debate soon got out of hand. So violent, in fact, did it become that the commander had to bring in soldiers and rescue Paul. Once more the commander was frustrated in his effort to learn exactly why the Jews were so adamantly opposed to his prisoner.

11 Paul had feared such a reception at Jerusalem (cf. 20:22–23; 21:13; Rom 15:31), and now his worst fears were being realized. He had planned to go to Rome and minister throughout the western part of the empire after his visit to Jerusalem (cf. Rom 15:24–29). But developments at Jerusalem were building up to a point where it appeared his life could come to an end in the city through any number of circumstances beyond his control. Undoubtedly he was despondent as he awaited the next turn of events in his cell in the fortress. But "the following night" (*tē epiousē nykti;* lit., "the night of the next day") the risen and exalted Jesus appeared to Paul—as he has done at other critical moments in his ministry (cf. 18:9–10; 22:17–21)—and encouraged him by his presence. So now the Lord said, "Take courage!" And he assured Paul that he would yet testify in Rome as he had done in Jerusalem. Certainly, as Bruce observes, "this assurance meant much to Paul during the delays and anxieties of the next two years, and goes far to account for the calm and dignified bearing which seemed to mark him out as a master of events rather than their victim" (*Book of the Acts*, p. 455).

Notes

1 On the address Ἄνδρες ἀδελφοί (*Andres adelphoi*, "Men, brothers"), cf. comments on 1:16.
Some have had difficulty in squaring Paul's claim to a good conscience here with their interpretation of his words in Rom 7:7-25. On Rom 7:7-25, however, as a preconversion autobiographical statement, a postconversion autobiographical statement, or a gnomic (timeless) statement expressing a more general truth, see my *Paul*, pp. 86-127.

6 On the address "Men, brothers," see note on v.1 above.

6. A plot to kill Paul

23:12-22

> [12]The next morning the Jews formed a conspiracy and bound themselves with an oath not to eat or drink until they had killed Paul. [13]More than forty men were involved in this plot. [14]They went to the chief priests and elders and said, "We have taken a solemn oath not to eat anything until we have killed Paul. [15]Now then, you and the Sanhedrin petition the commander to bring him before you on the pretext of wanting more accurate information about his case. We are ready to kill him before he gets here."
>
> [16]But when the son of Paul's sister heard of this plot, he went into the barracks and told Paul.
>
> [17]Then Paul called one of the centurions and said, "Take this young man to the commander; he has something to tell him." [18]So he took him to the commander.
>
> The centurion said, "Paul, the prisoner, sent for me and asked me to bring this young man to you because he has something to tell you."
>
> [19]The commander took the young man by the hand, drew him aside and asked, "What is it you want to tell me?"
>
> [20]He said: "The Jews have agreed to ask you to bring Paul before the Sanhedrin tomorrow on the pretext of wanting more accurate information about him. [21]Don't give in to them, because more than forty of them are waiting in ambush for him. They have taken an oath not to eat or drink until they have killed him. They are ready now, waiting for your consent to their request."
>
> [22]The commander dismissed the young man and cautioned him, "Don't tell anyone that you have reported this to me."

12-15 Failing in their earlier plot to kill Paul in the temple precincts, more than forty fanatical Jews (probably many of them Asian Jews who had instigated the earlier plot, cf. 21:27-29) resolved to do away with him by ambushing him in the narrow streets of Jerusalem. For this they needed a pretext to lure him out of the fortress. So they arranged with "the chief priest and elders" (evidently Ananias, together with some of his Sadducean cohorts) to ask for Paul's return before the Sanhedrin for further questioning. They pledged that they would kill him as he was brought from the Fortress of Antonia north of the temple to the hall of the Sanhedrin southwest of the temple area (cf. comments on 4:5). To show their determination, they vowed not to eat or drink till they had accomplished their purpose. That did not mean, however, that they would necessarily have to starve if they failed. The rabbis allowed four types of vows to be broken: "vows of incitement, vows of exaggeration, vows made in error, and vows that cannot be fulfilled by reason of constraint" (M *Nedarim* 3.1-3)—exclusions allowing for almost any contingency. The conspirators' plan, though violating both the letter and the spirit of

Jewish law pertaining to the Sanhedrin (cf. b *Sanhedrin* 82a), was in keeping with the character of the high priest Ananias (cf. comments on 23:2).

16–17 We have no knowledge about Paul's sister and his nephew, or of how the young man learned of the plot. In his letters Paul says nothing of his immediate family, and this is Luke's only reference to any of Paul's relatives. Perhaps Paul had stayed with his sister and her family when he studied under Gamaliel I at Jerusalem (cf. 22:3) and when he returned from Damascus as a Christian (cf. 9:26–28)—though he probably did not stay with her on later visits to the city, and certainly not on his last visit (cf. 21:16). From Philippians 3:8, where Paul speaks of having "lost all things" for the sake of Christ, many have supposed that he was disinherited by his family for accepting and proclaiming Jesus as the Messiah. Such a supposition seems likely. Yet family ties are not easily broken; so when his uncle was in mortal danger, Paul's nephew could not stand by without warning him. After all, in Judaism the saving and preservation of life takes precedence over everything else.

As a Roman citizen under protective custody, Paul could receive visitors—among them his nephew. So when Paul heard his warning, he asked one of the centurions to take his nephew to the commander.

18–22 This pericope is set off as almost a separate unit by Luke's favorite connecting phrase *men oun* ("so," "then") both at its beginning and at its end. Luke may have inferred from the commander's action what was said between him and Paul's nephew, though the use of *men oun* suggests a separate source for his information—that is, the nephew himself. The seriousness with which the commander took the warning about the plot shows that he knew Ananias was the kind of man to fall in with it and realized that Jewish feeling against Paul was strong enough to nurture such a plot.

Notes

12 The Western and Byzantine texts read τινὲς τῶν Ἰουδαίων (*tines tōn Ioudaiōn*, "some of the Jews") for οἱ Ἰουδαῖοι (*hoi Ioudaioi*, "the Jews"), but v.13 sufficiently explains the general statement.
15 The Western text expands the first part of this verse to read as follows: "Now therefore we ask you to grant us this: Gather the Sanhedrin together and notify the commander in order that he might bring him down to you." It ends the verse with the addition "even if we must die for it."
18 On Luke's use of μὲν οὖν (*men oun*), see comments on 1:6.
20 The Byzantine text (probably also the original Western text) reads μέλλοντες (*mellontes*, "as though they would"; NIV, "on the pretext of "), with the plural of the masculine nominative participle referring to "the Jews" (as KJV, RSV, JB). A B E P[74] read μέλλων (*mellōn*, "as though he would"), with the singular of the masculine nominative participle evidently referring to the high priest. ℵ, however, reads μέλλον (*mellon*, "as though it would"), with the singular of the neuter accusative participle agreeing with its immediate antecedent τὸ συνέδριον (*to synedrion*, "the Sanhedrin")—which, though not as well supported externally, is probably to be preferred for internal reasons (as UBS, TEV).
22 On μὲν οὖν (*men oun*), see v.18 above.

D. Imprisonment and Defenses at Caesarea (23:23–26:32)

1. Imprisonment at Caesarea

23:23–35

23Then he called two of his centurions and ordered them, "Get ready a detachment of two hundred soldiers, seventy horsemen and two hundred spearmen to go to Caesarea at nine tonight. 24Provide mounts for Paul so that he may be taken safely to Governor Felix."
25He wrote a letter as follows:

26Claudius Lysias,

To His Excellency, Governor Felix:

Greetings.

27This man was seized by the Jews and they were about to kill him, but I came with my troops and rescued him, for I had learned that he is a Roman citizen. 28I wanted to know why they were accusing him, so I brought him to their Sanhedrin. 29I found that the accusation had to do with questions about their law, but there was no charge against him that deserved death or imprisonment. 30When I was informed of a plot to be carried out against the man, I sent him to you at once. I also ordered his accusers to present to you their case against him.

31So the soldiers, carrying out their orders, took Paul with them during the night and brought him as far as Antipatris. 32The next day they let the cavalry go on with him, while they returned to the barracks. 33When the cavalry arrived in Caesarea, they delivered the letter to the governor and handed Paul over to him. 34The governor read the letter and asked what province he was from. Learning that he was from Cilicia, 35he said, "I will hear your case when your accusers get here." Then he ordered that Paul be kept under guard in Herod's palace.

23–24 Since the commander could not risk having a Roman citizen assassinated while in his custody, he took steps to transfer Paul to the jurisdiction of Felix, the governor (*ho hēgemōn*, "the procurator") of the province of Judea. He wanted to get Paul to Caesarea, the provincial capital (cf. comments on 10:1), as quickly as possible and before the conspirators got wind of it. So the commander ordered two centurions to ready two hundred infantry and seventy cavalry, together with two hundred "spearmen" (*dexiolaboi*) for escort duty, leaving for Caesarea at nine that evening (lit., "the third hour of the night"). In addition, he ordered that "mounts" (*ktēnē*) be provided for Paul, which probably means, since *ktēnē* means both "riding animals" and "pack animals," not only a horse for Paul but also another one for either riding or carrying his baggage, or both.

The word *dexiolaboi* appears only here in the NT and nowhere else in extant Greek literature until the sixth century A.D. All that can be said for certain is that it is a Greek term translating some Latin title used in the Roman army. Most translators have guessed that it means "spearmen" since *dexios* means "right handed" and spears were usually thrown with the right hand (cf. KJV, ASV, RSV, TEV, NIV). Others prefer not to infer its meaning from its etymology and translate it as either "light-armed troops" (NEB) or "auxiliaries" (JB). Perhaps, however, the *dexiolaboi* were not another kind of soldiers but "led horses" included within the cavalry contingent as additional mounts and pack animals (cf. BC, 4:293).

The purpose of the detachment was security and speed. So we should probably visualize the first being provided by the two hundred infantry and the second by the seventy cavalry with their two hundred extra mounts and pack animals, many of which may also have been used to carry infantry during the night. Luke has repeatedly called the commander a *chiliarchos* (cf. 21:31–33, 37; 22:24, 26–29; 23:10, 15, 17–19, 22)—literally, "commander of a thousand," but usually involving command of about six hundred soldiers. If, therefore, we surmise that the garrison at Jerusalem consisted of about six hundred men in all and that *dexiolaboi* refers not to infantry but to additional mounts and pack animals, then the commander had considered the plot against Paul serious enough to commit almost half the garrison at the Fortress of Antonia to escort Paul, with most of them due to return in a day or two (cf. v.32).

In saying that the commander wrote a letter "of this type" (*echousan ton typon touton*, lit., "having this pattern"; NIV, "as follows"), Luke acknowledged that what follows is only the general purport of the letter. He would hardly have been in a position to read the correspondence between a Roman commander and a Roman provincial governor. What he knew of the letter probably came from Paul, who himself would only have known about its contents as the governor used it in the initial questioning of his prisoner.

26 To have begun the letter with a salutation that (1) named the sender, (2) named the recipient, and (3) sent greetings would not have taxed Luke's ingenuity. That is standard form for a letter of antiquity and is common to every letter of the NT, except Hebrews and 1 John.

For the first time in Acts, the commander's name is given. He was evidently a freeborn Greek who had worked his way up through the ranks of the Roman army and at some time paid an official of Claudius's government to receive Roman citizenship (cf. comments on 22:28). At that time his Greek name Lysias became his Roman cognomen, and he then took the nomen Claudius in honor of the emperor. Felix was the governor of the Roman province of Judea from A.D. 52–59 (on Felix, cf. comments on 24:1). The title "Excellency" (*kratistos*) originally denoted a member of the Roman equestrian order (Lat. *egregius*), like that of knights in Britain. Later it became an honorific title for highly placed officials in the Roman government (as here, 24:3; 26:25), but it was also used as a form of polite address (cf. 1:1).

27–30 The body of the letter summarizes the events from the riot in the temple precincts to the commander's discovery of a plot against Paul's life. Paul may very well have smiled to himself when he heard how Lysias stretched the truth to his own benefit in claiming to have rescued Paul from the mob because "I had learned that he is a Roman citizen" and had omitted any reference to the proposed flogging. But the most important part of the letter, that concerning Lysias's evaluation of the Jewish opposition to Paul, was clear: "I found that the accusation had to do with questions about their law, but there was no charge against him that deserved death or imprisonment" (v.29). And that was of great significance not only for Paul's fortunes but also for Luke's apologetic purpose.

31–32 "So" (*men oun*), Luke says, completing his account of the transfer of Paul from Jerusalem to Caesarea with a note of evident relief, the soldiers carried out their orders and brought Paul during the night to Antipatris, a town built by Herod the Great in honor of his father Antipater. (The exact location of Antipatris is unknown. Most have identified it with modern Kulat Ras el Ain some thirty-five miles northwest of Jerusalem, at the foot of the Judean hills.) Having left Jerusalem at nine in the evening (cf. v.23), the detachment would have lost no time in covering the distance by morning. If the cavalry contingent included two hundred extra mounts and pack horses (cf. comments on v.23), perhaps the infantry were allowed to ride and jog alternately. At any rate, the purpose of the mission was both safety and speed. And when the conspirators were left far behind and ambush was less likely, the infantry turned back to Jerusalem and the cavalry took Paul to Caesarea, some forty miles distant.

33–35 At Caesarea, the prisoner and Lysias's letter were turned over to Felix, the governor. On reading the letter, he questioned Paul on the basis of its contents. Had Paul been from one of the client kingdoms in Syria or Asia Minor, Felix would probably have wanted to consult the ruler of the kingdom. But on learning that Paul was from the Roman province of Cilicia, he felt competent as a provincial governor to hear the case himself, when Paul's accusers arrived from Jerusalem. In the meantime, Paul was kept under guard in the palace Herod the Great built for himself at Caesarea. It now served as the governor's headquarters and also had cells for prisoners.

Notes

23 A reads δεξιοβόλους (*dexiobolous*, "slingers," "javelin-throwers"; lit., "throwing with the right hand") for δεξιολάβους (*dexiolabous*; NIV, "spearmen").

The Western text recasts this verse and the next to read as follows: " 'Get ready soldiers under arms to go to Caesarea, a hundred horsemen and two hundred spearmen [δεξιολάβους, *dexiolabous*].' And they said, 'They are ready.' And he ordered the centurions also to provide mounts that they might set Paul on them and bring him safely by night to Caesarea to Felix the governor. For he was afraid that the Jews might seize and kill him and that he himself should be blamed meanwhile for having taken bribes."

25 The Western text has περιέχουσαν τάδε (*periechousan tade*, "containing these things") for ἔχουσαν τὸν τύπον τοῦτον (*echousan ton typon touton*; lit., "having this pattern"). For other uses of τύπος (*typos*) in this fashion, see 1 Macc 11:29; 2 Macc 1:24; 3 Macc 3:30.

29 The Western text adds Μωσέως καὶ Ἰησοῦ τινος (*Mōseōs kai Iēsou tinos*, "of Moses and a certain Jesus"), reading "questions about their law of Moses and a certain Jesus." It then concludes the verse with the addition "I brought him out with difficulty, by force"—in harmony with its addition at 24:7.

30 On a classical model, the Gr. of the first part of this verse is confused, with a genitive absolute passing into an indirect statement.

א A E with the Lat. and Armenian versions have ἐξ αὐτῶν (*ex autōn*, "from among them") for ἐξαυτῆς (*exautēs*, "at once"), reading "When I was informed of a plot to be carried out against the man from among them, I sent to you."

א and the Byzantine text add a final "Farewell" (either ἔρρωσο, *errōso*, or ἔρρωσθε, *errōsthe*), in agreement with the usual close of a letter as witnessed in numerous nonliterary papyri.

32 On Luke's use of μὲν οὖν (*men oun*), cf. comments on 1:6.

2. Paul's defense before Felix

24:1–27

¹Five days later the high priest Ananias went down to Caesarea with some of the elders and a lawyer named Tertullus, and they brought their charges against Paul before the governor. ²When Paul was called in, Tertullus presented his case before Felix: "We have enjoyed a long period of peace under you, and your

foresight has brought about reforms in this nation. ³Everywhere and in every way, most excellent Felix, we acknowledge this with profound gratitude. ⁴But in order not to weary you further, I would request that you be kind enough to hear us briefly.

⁵"We have found this man to be a troublemaker, stirring up riots among the Jews all over the world. He is a ringleader of the Nazarene sect ⁶and even tried to desecrate the temple; so we seized him. ⁸By examining him yourself you will be able to learn the truth about all these charges we are bringing against him."

⁹The Jews joined in the accusation, asserting that these things were true.

¹⁰When the governor motioned for him to speak, Paul replied: "I know that for a number of years you have been a judge over this nation; so I gladly make my defense. ¹¹You can easily verify that no more than twelve days ago I went up to Jerusalem to worship. ¹²My accusers did not find me arguing with anyone at the temple, or stirring up a crowd in the synagogues or anywhere else in the city. ¹³And they cannot prove to you the charges they are now making against me. ¹⁴However, I admit that I worship the God of our fathers, as a follower of the Way, which they call a sect. I believe everything that agrees with the Law and that is written in the Prophets, ¹⁵and I have the same hope in God as these men, that there will be a resurrection of both the righteous and the wicked. ¹⁶So I strive always to keep my conscience clear before God and man.

¹⁷"After an absence of several years, I came to Jerusalem to bring my people gifts for the poor and to present offerings. ¹⁸I was ceremonially clean when they found me in the temple courts doing this. There was no crowd with me, nor was I involved in any disturbance. ¹⁹But there are some Jews from the province of Asia, who ought to be here before you and bring charges if they have anything against me. ²⁰Or these who are here should state what crime they found in me when I stood before the Sanhedrin—²¹unless it was this one thing I shouted as I stood in their presence: 'It is concerning the resurrection of the dead that I am on trial before you today.'"

²²Then Felix, who was well acquainted with the Way, adjourned the proceedings. "When Lysias the commander comes," he said, "I will decide your case." ²³He ordered the centurion to keep Paul under guard but to give him some freedom and permit his friends to take care of his needs.

²⁴Several days later Felix came with his wife Drusilla, who was a Jewess. He sent for Paul and listened to him as he spoke about faith in Christ Jesus. ²⁵As Paul discoursed on righteousness, self-control and the judgment to come, Felix was afraid and said, "That's enough for now! You may leave. When I find it convenient, I will send for you." ²⁶At the same time he was hoping that Paul would offer him a bribe, so he sent for him frequently and talked with him.

²⁷When two years had passed, Felix was succeeded by Porcius Festus, but because Felix wanted to grant a favor to the Jews, he left Paul in prison.

In his account of Paul's defense before Felix, Luke gives almost equal space to (1) the Jewish charges against Paul (vv.1–9), (2) Paul's reply to these charges (vv.10–21), and (3) Felix's response (vv.22–27). He does this, it seems, because he wants to show that despite the devious skill of the Jewish charges and the notorious cruelty and corruptibility of Felix, no other conclusions can be drawn from Paul's appearance before him than that (1) Christianity had nothing to do with political sedition and (2) Jewish opposition to Christianity sprang from the Christian claim to legitimate fulfillment of the hopes of Judaism.

1 There are a number of time notations in the narrative covering the period from Paul's arrival at Jerusalem to his being brought to Caesarea (cf. 21:17–18, 26–27; 22:30; 23:11–12, 23, 32). Yet helpful as they are, it is difficult to correlate Luke's temporal connective here ("five days later," *meta pente hēmeras*) with any of them. One would naturally suppose "five days later" to mean five days after Paul's arrival at Caesarea. But in view

of his quoting Paul's remark that "no more than twelve days ago I went up to Jerusalem to worship" (v.11), Luke evidently meant the five days to be reckoned from Paul's arrest in the temple—whether that occurred on the last day of the seven-day purification period (cf. comments on 21:26) or a day or two before its end (cf. "when the seven days were nearly over," 21:27).

With the notations of time ("five days later") and of place ("Caesarea"), the names of Paul's adversaries ("the high priest Ananias . . . with some of the elders and a lawyer named Tertullus"), and the identification of the judge ("the governor" Felix), the stage is set for Paul's defense. It was characteristic of Ananias to prosecute Paul as quickly as possible (cf. comments on 23:2); so to present his trumped-up charges as effectively as possible he employed a lawyer named Tertullus. Tertullus was a common Greek name in the Roman world, and all we know of the man comes from this passage. Probably he was a Hellenistic Jew chosen by Ananias because of his expertise in affairs of the empire and his allegiance to Judaism. Perhaps Ananias also felt confident that in Felix he had a governor he could manipulate for his own purposes.

Antonius Felix was born a slave and freed by Antonia, the mother of the emperor Claudius. He was a brother of Pallas, who was also a freedman of Antonia and became a good friend of the young prince Claudius in the imperial household. Through the influence of Pallas, in A.D. 48 Felix was appointed to a subordinate government post in Samaria under the provincial governor Ventidius Cumanus. In A.D. 52 Claudius appointed him governor of Judea when Cumanus was deposed—an office usually reserved for freemen of the Roman equestrian order but which he obtained through intrigue and the support of the governor of Syria, Quadratus (cf. Tacitus *Annales* 12.54; Jos. War II, 247 [xii.1]; Antiq. XX, 137 [vii.1]). During his governorship, insurrections and anarchy increased throughout Palestine. Try as he would to put down the uprisings and regain control, his brutal methods only alienated the Jewish population more and led to further disturbances (cf. Jos. War II, 253–70 [xiii.2–7]; Antiq. XX, 160–81 [viii.5–8]). Tacitus described him as "a master of cruelty and lust who exercised the powers of a king with the spirit of a slave" (*Historiae* 5.9).

Despite his low birth, Felix had a succession of three wives, each in her own right a princess (cf. Suetonius *Vita Claudius* 28). The first was the granddaughter of Antony and Cleopatra, making Felix the grandson-in-law (Claudius being a grandson) of Antony. The third was Drusilla, the youngest daughter of Agrippa I, who was unhappy as the wife of Azizus, king of Emesa, and whom Felix desired because of her beauty and who was persuaded through the intervention of a Cyprian magician named Atomus (cf. comments on 13:6–8) to leave her husband for him (cf. Jos. Antiq. XX, 141–44 [vii.2]). Nero recalled Felix to Rome sometime during A.D. 59. Nothing is known of his subsequent fate.

2–4 Tertullus began the case for the prosecution with the customary flattery for the judge in words chosen for his purpose. Many Jews would have been shocked to hear the high priest's mouthpiece attributing "a long period of peace" and "reforms" to Felix's administration; and few would have joined in any expression of "profound gratitude" for the governor's frequent displays of ferocity, cruelty, and greed. But Tertullus knew how to appeal to Felix's vanity. It was also customary to promise brevity (cf. Lucian *Bis Accusatus* 26: "But in order not to make a long speech, since much time has elapsed already, I will begin with the accusation"), though such is human nature that the promise was rarely kept.

5–9 The three charges laid against Paul (v.5) are probably only a précis of the entire case, which Tertullus had gone on to elaborate. But this précis makes it clear that Tertullus intended to create the impression of political sedition against Rome in his first two charges (disturbing the peace among the Jews; being a ringleader of the Nazarenes) and to argue the right for Judaism to impose the death penalty in his third charge (attempting to desecrate the temple; cf. comments on 21:28–29). During his reign over Judea, Felix had repeatedly crucified the leaders of various uprisings and had killed many of their followers for disturbing the Pax Romana (cf. Jos. War II, 253–63 [xiii.2–5]). Tertullus's endeavor, as supported by the high priest and the Jewish elders with him, was to put Paul on the same level as these brigands, with the hope that in his insensitivity to the issues, Felix would act in his usual manner simply on the basis of their testimony. As in Jesus' trial before Pilate, their accusations were framed principally in terms of political sedition (cf. Luke 23:2, 5), though all along their main grievance was religious.

10 Invited to respond, Paul also began with a complimentary statement—but a briefer and truer one. Felix had been in contact with the Jewish nation in Palestine for over a decade, first in Samaria and then as governor over the entire province of Judea. Therefore Paul was pleased to make his defense before one who was in a position to know the situation as it was and to understand his words in their context.

11–13 In refuting the charges against him, Paul dealt with each in turn. First, it was "no more than twelve days ago" that he came to Jerusalem, not for political agitation but for worship. In such a short time, he implied, there would hardly have been sufficient opportunity to foment a revolt. Second, his accusers could hardly charge him with being a ringleader of any sedition, for he was alone when they arrested him in the temple; and they could not cite any time when he was stirring up a crowd anywhere in the city (v.12). Third, their claim that he desecrated the temple was unproved because it was entirely without foundation (v.13).

14–16 The real reason Ananias and the Jewish elders opposed him, Paul insisted, was religious: "I worship the God of our fathers, as a follower of the Way, which they call a sect—though I believe [understanding *pisteuōn* as a concessive adverbial participle] everything that agrees with the Law and that is written in the Prophets, and I have the same hope in God as these men, that there will be a resurrection of both the righteous and the wicked" (vv.14–15). And while he differed from Ananias and the elders in his acceptance of "the Way," his conscience in the matter was "clear before God and man" (cf. 23:1) since his position was in agreement with the Law and the Prophets.

Paul's statements about having "the same hope in God as these men" and accepting "a resurrection of both the righteous and the wicked" have led to much comment since Ananias himself would not have accepted the doctrine of a resurrection (cf. comments on 4:1 regarding Saducean beliefs) and Paul in his letters speaks only of a resurrection of the righteous (cf. 1 Cor 15:12–58; 1 Thess 4:13–5:11; 2 Thess 2:1–12). But evidently there were some Pharisees among the elders who came down to Caesarea with Ananias (cf. v.1). And though Sadducees did not share with Pharisees the hope of a resurrection, Paul as a Pharisee was probably sufficiently self-confident to believe that it was the Pharisaic hope that characterized—or, at least, should characterize—all true representations of the Jewish faith. Furthermore, while Paul in his letters speaks only of a resurrection of the righteous (as also our Lord in Luke 14:14; 20:35–36), this is probably because the treatment is pastoral in nature and deals only with the righteous. But we should not assume from this that neither Pharisaic Judaism nor Paul ever spoke of a twofold resurrection (as in Dan 12:2; John 5:28–29; Rev 20:12–15).

17 Reconstructing for Felix what happened in Jerusalem, Paul spoke of coming to Jerusalem "to bring my people [*eis to ethnos mou;* lit. 'for my nation'] gifts for the poor and to present offerings" (cf. "to worship," v.11). This is the only time Luke mentions the collection for the poor at Jerusalem, which was so dear to Paul's own heart (cf. Rom 15:25–27, 31; 1 Cor 16:1–4). Some have complained that for Paul to say that the gift was "for my nation" adds a note of insincerity that should be discounted, for certainly Paul's efforts were directed toward relieving the plight of poor believers in the Jerusalem church and not of Jews in general. Yet it need not be thought strange for the man who said in Romans 15:31 that the collection he was taking for Jewish Christians was "my service that is *for Jerusalem*" (*eis Ierousalēm;* NIV, "in Jerusalem") to also say that "I came to Jerusalem to bring *for my nation* (*eis to ethnos mou*) gifts for the poor." What he did, he did not only for the relief of Christians and as a symbol of unity between believers but also, as Harnack insisted, "for *all* Israel; he had ever before his eyes the nation *in its entirety.* . . . The conversion of the whole nation was the ultimate aim of all his exertions [italics his]" (*Date of Acts,* p. 74). By aiding that branch of the church whose mission it was to call the nation to its Messiah, he was indirectly engaged in a mission to his own nation (cf. Rom 11:13b–14).

18–21 Continuing the summary of what took place at Jerusalem, Paul spoke of his arrest in the temple (v.18) and his arraignment before the Sanhedrin (v.20). But, he insisted, there was no crowd to incite nor any attempt on his part to create a disturbance; rather, he was taken by the crowd while worshiping in a ceremonially clean condition. If the Asian Jews who instigated the riot had any serious charge against him, they should have been present to accuse him before the governor. Roman law imposed heavy penalties upon accusers who abandoned their charges (*destitutio*), and the disappearance of accusers often meant the withdrawal of a charge. Their absence, therefore, suggested that they had nothing against him that would stand up in a Roman court of law. Nor did the Sanhedrin, Paul went on, find any crime in him—except that he believed in the resurrection of the dead. Therefore, Paul declared, he was on trial because of his belief in "the resurrection of the dead" (v.21).

22–23 Felix seems to have summed up the situation accurately. After a decade in Palestine (cf. comments on v.1), he was, in his own way, "well acquainted with the Way" (v.22). While certainly not a Christian, he could see that the Jewish charges against Paul were entirely religious in nature—even though presented in the guise of political sedition. He therefore sought to preserve the Pax Romana within his jurisdiction simply by removing the possibility of confrontation between the disputants and by delays in judicial procedure. So Paul was placed under protective custody in the palace of Herod the Great, and Ananias was given the deceptive promise of a decision being reached when the commander Lysias came down to Caesarea and presented his testimony (which he had already given in his letter, cf. 23:25–30). As a Roman citizen, Paul was allowed some freedom and permitted visits from friends to care for his needs. But both he and Ananias seem to have realized that Felix had no intention of bringing the case to a decision in the near future; and they evidently, each for his own reasons, decided to await the appointment of a new provincial governor before pressing for a resolution—an appointment, given the recent course of Felix's reign, they expected soon.

24–26 Added to the description of Felix's response is this vignette about the interaction between the Roman governor, his Jewish wife, and the Christian apostle, which elaborates further the nature of Felix's response and highlights one aspect of Paul's continued, though restricted, ministry while under protective custody at Caesarea. The vignette is joined to the rest of the narrative by a favorite Lukan connective—viz., the preposition *meta* with a time designation (*meta hēmeras tinas,* "after certain days"; or "several days later," NIV). While it may be tempting to see in the expression a chronological note of significance, Luke's earlier use of *meta hēmeras tinas* (cf. comments on 9:19b) prohibits this.

Drusilla, Felix's third wife and the youngest daughter of Herod Agrippa I, had broken off her marriage to Azizus, the king of Emesa, because of Felix (cf. comments on v.1). Emesa was a small kingdom in Syria (modern Homs), and Azizus had agreed to become a convert to Judaism in order to marry her. But the teenage Drusilla was unhappy with Azizus; and, as captivated by Felix's ruthlessness and power as he was with her beauty, she accepted his offer of marriage. Neither his birth as a slave, his Roman paganism, nor her Jewish scruples deterred her from what she considered a higher station in life. The relationship between Felix and his young wife seems to have been based upon greed, lust, and expectations of grandeur. Yet they apparently still had some qualms of conscience and therefore took the opportunity to send for Paul and hear his message.

Paul spoke to Felix and his wife about the necessity of "faith in Christ Jesus" (v.24). He also made it plain that this involved an ethical life, for he spoke of "righteousness, self-control and the judgment to come" (v.25)—three subjects Felix and Drusilla particularly needed to learn about! His preaching touched the quick of their kind of living and Felix ordered him to stop. Apparently Drusilla was offended by what she considered Paul's moralistic ranting, for Luke makes no mention of her having listened to him again. Felix also seems to have been unhappy at the shift in the discussion from divergent religious views to personal morality and responsibility. He was, Luke tells us, "afraid" (*emphobos;* lit., with the preposition strengthening the noun, "terrified") in the presence of such preaching. Yet his cupidity and corruption led him to call Paul often before him in hope of getting a bribe for his release. Felix must have believed that Paul had access to some money—either from an inheritance from his parents, as Ramsay postulated, or through Christian friends who visited him (cf. 24:23; 27:3)—and he hoped to get his hands on some of it.

27 After two years Festus replaced Felix as governor of Judea. Felix's downfall came through an outbreak of hostilities between Jews and Greeks at Caesarea, with both claiming dominant civil rights in the city—the Jews because of their greater numbers and wealth and because Herod the Great, a Jew, had rebuilt the city; the Greeks because they had the support of the military and because they claimed the city was always meant to be a Gentile city (cf. Jos. War II, 266–70 [xiii.7]; Antiq. XX, 173–78 [viii.7]). Using the Syrian troops under his command, Felix's intervention took the form of military retaliation upon the Jews. Many were killed, taken prisoner, or plundered of their wealth; and a delegation of Jews went to Rome to complain. Felix was recalled to Rome and would have suffered severe punishment had not his brother Pallas interceded for him before Nero (cf. Jos. Antiq. XX, 182 [viii.9]). Felix was replaced by Festus in A.D. 60.

During this time, Paul remained in Herod's palace at Caesarea—with Felix undoubtedly rationalizing his imprisonment as a protection for Paul and a favor to the Jews, though in reality it was an expression of Felix's cupidity. It must have been an extremely tedious time for Paul. Luke, however, seems to have made full use of the two years to investigate "everything from the beginning" about Christianity (cf. Luke 1:3). And while we cannot say whether he at this time produced either a preliminary draft of his Gospel ("Proto-Luke") or any portion of Acts, it is probable that during this time he became quite familiar with (1) the traditions comprising Mark's Gospel (whenever that Gospel was written), (2) other materials having to do with the story of Jesus that he would also incorporate into his Gospel (so-called Q and L material), (3) accounts circulating in Palestine of events in the early church that he would include in the first half of Acts, and (4) recollections and interpretations of Paul as to his activities before Luke joined him. Undoubtedly as well, he had begun to sketch out during this time the structure and scope of his two-volume work we know as Luke-Acts.

Notes

1 On μετά (meta, "after," or "later," NIV) with a time designation (here "five days") in the latter half of Acts as a Lukan connective, see comments on 15:36.

On the verb καταβαίνω (katabainō, "to go down"), see note at 8:5 (also comments on 3:1 and 11:27).

3 On the title κράτιστε (kratiste, "most excellent"), cf. comments on 23:26.

6b-8a The Western text (taken over into the TR) adds: "and wanted to judge him according to our law. 7But the commander, Lysias, came and with the use of much force snatched him from our hands 8and ordered his accusers to come before you." The Western editor evidently felt it unlikely that παρ᾽ οὗ (par hou, "from whom") of v.8 referred to Paul, thinking that Felix would hardly have gotten the whole story only "by examining him." Therefore he inserted vv.6b-8a and brought the commander Lysias into the account as the antecedent of the relative pronoun. While vv.6b-8a are in Luke's style, the account is quite straightforward and understandable without them.

14 On the self-designation of Christians as those of "the Way" (ἡ ὁδός, hē hodos), cf. comments on 9:2. See also 19:9, 23; 22:4; and v.22 below (also 16:17; 18:25-26; 2 Peter 2:2).

15 The Byzantine text (E P), together with some Lat. and Syr. versions, adds νεκρῶν (nekrōn, "of the dead"), reading, "There will be a resurrection of the dead of both the righteous and the wicked."

17 Six years had passed since Paul's brief visit to Jerusalem in fulfillment of his Nazirite vow (cf. 18:22), and nine since his coming to the city for the Jerusalem Council (cf. 15:1-29).

20 ℵ A B P74 omit ἐν ἐμοί (en emoi, "in me"), reading only "what crime they found when I stood before the Sanhedrin." The omission is probably to be preferred (contra NIV).

22 On the self-designation "the Way," see note on v.14 above.

24 A and the Byzantine text read Χριστόν (Christon, "Christ") for "Christ Jesus."

On μετά (meta, "after," or "later," NIV) with a time designation as a Lukan connective, see note on v.1 above.

3. Paul's defense before Festus

25:1-12

25:1Three days after arriving in the province, Festus went up from Caesarea to Jerusalem, 2where the chief priests and Jewish leaders appeared before him and presented the charges against Paul. 3They urgently requested Festus, as a favor to them, to have Paul transferred to Jerusalem, for they were preparing an ambush to kill him along the way. 4Festus answered, "Paul is being held at Caesarea, and I myself am going there soon. 5Let some of your leaders come with me and press charges against the man there, if he has done anything wrong."

⁶After spending eight or ten days with them, he went down to Caesarea, and the next day he convened the court and ordered that Paul be brought before him. ⁷When Paul appeared, the Jews who had come down from Jerusalem stood around him, bringing many serious charges against him, which they could not prove.

⁸Then Paul made his defense: "I have done nothing wrong against the law of the Jews or against the temple or against Caesar."

⁹Festus, wishing to do the Jews a favor, said to Paul, "Are you willing to go up to Jerusalem and stand trial before me there on these charges?"

¹⁰Paul answered: "I am now standing before Caesar's court, where I ought to be tried. I have not done any wrong to the Jews, as you yourself know very well. ¹¹If, however, I am guilty of doing anything deserving death, I do not refuse to die. But if the charges brought against me by these Jews are not true, no one has the right to hand me over to them. I appeal to Caesar!"

¹²After Festus had conferred with his council, he declared: "You have appealed to Caesar. To Caesar you will go!"

The account of Paul's defense before Festus is the briefest of his five defenses. Most of it parallels in summary fashion the account of Paul's appearance before Felix. The new element is Paul's appeal to Caesar, which sets the stage for his journey to Rome. In this pericope, Luke's apologetic purpose is to show that only when Roman administrators were largely ignorant of the facts of the case were concessions made to Jewish opposition that could prove disastrous for the Christian movement.

1 For the Jewish population of Palestine, Porcius Festus was a welcome successor to Felix (cf. Jos. War II, 271 [xiv.1]; Antiq. XX, 185–88 [viii.10])—immeasurably better than the villanous Lucceius Albinus (A.D. 62–64) and the totally corrupt Gessius Florus (A.D. 64–66) who succeeded him in office (cf. Jos. War II, 272–83 [xiv.1–3]). Nothing is known of Festus before he assumed the governorship of Judea. Nor can the time of his nomination for the post or his arrival in Palestine be precisely fixed. Probably Festus began to rule in Judea in 60. He inherited all the troubles and tensions that were mounting during Felix's maladministration, which culminated in the disaster of 66–70 (cf. Jos. War II, 271 [xiv.1]; Antiq. XX, 185–96 [viii.10–11]). His term of office was cut short by his death in 62.

The situation in Palestine demanded immediate action to bring together opposing factions within the Jewish nation. Therefore on arriving in Palestine, Festus took only three days to settle in at Caesarea before going up to Jerusalem to meet with the leaders of the nation.

2 The high priest at Jerusalem when Festus took office was Ishmael, the son of Phabi, whom Herod Agrippa II appointed to succeed Ananias during the final days of Felix's governorship (cf. Jos. Antiq. XX, 179 [viii.8], 194 [viii.11], 196 [viii.11]). The Talmud says that he served as high priest for ten years (b *Yoma* 9a), though Josephus reports that he was replaced by Agrippa II with Joseph, the son of Simeon, during Festus's rule because of a dispute over a wall erected to block the king's view of the temple and while Ishmael was detained at Rome (cf. Jos. Antiq. XX, 189–96 [viii.11]). Ananias, however, continued to exercise a dominant role in Jerusalem affairs right up to his death in 66 at the hands of Jewish nationalists (cf. Jos. Antiq. XX, 205 [ix.2], 209 [ix.3]). It is probably for this reason that Luke speaks of "the chief priests" (*hoi archiereis*) and not just the high priest Ishmael as appearing before him with the elders when Festus came to Jerusalem (cf. 4:23; 9:14; 22:30; 23:14; 25:15).

3 Counting on the new governor's inexperience, the Jewish authorities urged Festus to transfer Paul's case to Jerusalem for trial. Luke says they did this in order to ambush and murder him on the way (cf. 23:12–15). Perhaps also they hoped that with such a change of venue, should their plans for an ambush again be frustrated, they could arrange to have Paul tried before the Sanhedrin on the single charge of profaning the temple—for which they had the right to impose the death penalty (cf. comments on 21:27–29)—without having to sustain the charade of claiming political sedition as was required for the death penalty in a Roman court.

4–5 Unwittingly, Festus overturned their plans by inviting the Jewish leaders to return with him to Caesarea and press charges against Paul there. Evidently he desired to carry out only such business as was absolutely necessary on his first visit to Jerusalem and preferred to preside over any extended trial back at Caesarea—particularly since the prisoner was already there.

6–8 Festus convened court and ordered Paul brought before him, thus reopening the whole case against Paul, and the Jewish accusers restated their charges against him (cf. 24:5–6). But again they produced no witnesses, nor could they prove their charges. As for Paul, he stoutly continued to insist on his innocence (v.8). So the impasse remained.

9 Festus was at a loss to know what to make of the Jewish charges and Paul's denials (cf. vv.18–20a). Yet the Sanhedrin plainly wanted the case transferred to Jerusalem for trial; and as the new governor of Judea, Festus saw no reason why he could not concede the Jews this. Festus seems not to have fully appreciated what lay behind their request and apparently thought it would be politic to gain their good will by a change of venue.

10–11 Paul understood that to return to Jerusalem was to place himself in serious jeopardy. It would be tantamount to being turned over to the Sanhedrin; for once he was in Jerusalem, the Jewish authorities would exert every pressure on Festus to have Paul turned over to them for trial on the charge of profaning the temple. "I am now standing before Caesar's court, where I ought to be tried," he asserted. But being unsure as to just what action Festus might take in the matter if left at that, Paul went on to claim one final right he had as a Roman citizen: "I appeal to Caesar!"

Roman law in the Julio-Claudian period (the *lex Iulia*) protected Roman citizens who invoked the right of *provocatio ad Caesarem* (appeal to the emperor) from violent coercion and capital trials by provincial administrators. By the beginning of the second century A.D., Roman citizens were automatically sent off to Rome by provincial governors for trial for a variety of offenses (cf. Pliny the Younger *Epistolae* 6.31.3; 10.96.4; Tacitus *Annales* 16.10.2); in the third century, when everyone except a slave was considered a citizen, the right of *appellatio ad Caesarem* (appeal to the emperor) in two or three days after a civil or criminal conviction was universally allowed. But in the Julio-Claudian period when Roman citizenship was not widely diffused, a citizen of Rome living outside Italy could appeal to Caesar for trial by an imperial court at Rome only in cases that went beyond the normal civil and criminal jurisdiction (i.e., beyond the *ordo* to the *extra ordinem*) of a governor—particularly where the threat of violent coercion or capital punishment was present.

As many have noted, the texts that tell of Paul's appeal to Caesar (25:11–12, 21, 25–26; 26:32; 28:19) do not connect it explicitly to the fact of his Roman citizenship. "But there was no necessity," as Sherwin-White points out, "to reassert what had been established very circumstantially at the beginning of the inquiry" (p.66). Likewise, it may seem somewhat strange that Paul should have preferred to appeal to the emperor Nero (A.D. 54–68), the persecutor of Christians at Rome, rather than continue to entrust his case to Festus, whether at Caesarea or Jerusalem. But the early years of Nero's rule (54–62), under the influence of the Stoic philosopher Seneca and the prefect of the praetorian guard Afranius Burrus, were looked upon as something of a Golden Age. There was little in the year 60 that would have warned regarding Nero's later character and relations with Christianity during the last five years of his life.

12 Festus's discussion with his advisors was probably not whether a *provocatio ad Caesarem* should be allowed. The *lex Iulia* required that such an appeal by a Roman citizen be honored if the charges against him were judged to be *extra ordinem*. What Festus had to determine was (1) whether the charges against his prisoner fell into the category of normal provincial jurisdiction (the *ordo*) or went beyond that jurisdiction (the *extra ordinem*), and (2) whether it was either just or feasible to acquit the prisoner so as to make such an appeal unnecessary. Since the charges against Paul concerned political sedition, which in Roman law could be punished by death, and profanation of the Jerusalem temple, which in Jewish law called for death, Festus had no choice but to acknowledge the *extra ordinem* character of the charge and accept Paul's appeal. But Festus still could pronounce an acquittal after the act of appeal. Legally he had the right. Yet politically no newly arrived governor would have dreamt of antagonizing the leaders of the people he sought to govern by acquitting one against whom they were so vehemently opposed. It was more a political than legal decision Festus had to make, and he was probably only too glad to have this way out of a very sticky situation. So he agreed to the appeal, happy to rid himself of the prisoner and the problem.

Notes

1 On μετά (*meta*, "after") with a time designation (here "three days") in the latter half of Acts as a Lukan connective, cf. comments on 15:36 (though here its connective force is less obvious in Gr.).

On "going up" to Jerusalem (ἀναβαίνω, *anabainō*), cf. note at 8:5.

4 On μὲν οὖν (*men oun*) as a favorite Lukan connective, cf. comments on 1:6. Also see v.11.

6 On "going down" to Caesarea (καταβαίνω, *katabainō*), cf. note at 8:5.

7 On "going down" from Jerusalem (καταβαίνω, *katabainō*), cf. note at 8:5.

10 B adds a second ἑστώς (*hestōs*, "standing"), reading, "Standing before Caesar's court, I am standing where I ought to be tried"—an attractive reading, whose flavor seems to be captured in NIV's "now."

11 On μὲν οὖν (*men oun*) as a favorite Lukan connective, see note on v.4 above.

4. *Festus consults with Herod Agrippa II*

25:13–22

13A few days later King Agrippa and Bernice arrived at Caesarea to pay their respects to Festus. 14Since they were spending many days there, Festus discussed Paul's case with the king. He said: "There is a man here whom Felix left as a prisoner. [15]When I went to Jerusalem, the chief priests and elders of the Jews brought charges against him and asked that he be condemned.

[16]"I told them that it is not the Roman custom to hand over any man before he has faced his accusers and has had an opportunity to defend himself against their charges. [17]When they came here with me, I did not delay the case, but convened the court the next day and ordered the man to be brought in. [18]When his accusers got up to speak, they did not charge him with any of the crimes I had expected. [19]Instead, they had some points of dispute with him about their own religion and about a dead man named Jesus who Paul claimed was alive. [20]I was at a loss how to investigate such matters; so I asked if he would be willing to go to Jerusalem and stand trial there on these charges. [21]When Paul made his appeal to be held over for the Emperor's decision, I ordered him held until I could send him to Caesar."

[22]Then Agrippa said to Festus, "I would like to hear this man myself."
He replied, "Tomorrow you will hear him."

Though ridding himself of one problem, Festus now took on another—though a more minor one than the first: What would he write in his report to the imperial court at Rome about the charges against Paul and the issues in the case? Undoubtedly, Luke had no direct knowledge of what was said in private between a Roman governor and the king of a neighboring principality. But the gist of what was discussed would certainly have been evident from their resultant actions, and Luke here fleshes out the details of that conversation in order to prepare the way for Paul's last great defense before Herod Agrippa II.

13 Marcus Julius Agrippa II (A.D. 27-100) was the son of Agrippa I, the grandson of Aristobulus, and the great-grandson of Herod the Great. He was brought up at Rome in the court of Claudius and, like his father, was a favorite of the emperor. At his father's death in 44, he was only seventeen years old—too young to rule over his father's domains (cf. comments on 12:1). Therefore Palestine became a Roman province to be administered by a provincial governor. In 50, however, following the death of his uncle in 48, Claudius appointed Agrippa II king of Chalcis, a petty kingdom to the northeast of Judea. In 53 Claudius gave him the tetrarchy of Philip, Abilene (or Abila), Trachonitis, and Acra (the tetrarchy of Varus) in exchange for the kingdom of Chalcis. And in 56 Nero added to his kingdom the Galilean cities of Tarichea and Tiberias with their surrounding lands and the Perean city of Julias (or Betharamphtha) with fourteen villages belonging to it (cf. Jos. War II, 220-23 [xi.6-xii.1], 247 [xii.8], 252 [xiii.2]; Antiq. XX, 104 [v.2], 138 [vii.1], 159 [viii.4]). As ruler of the adjoining kingdom to the north, Herod Agrippa II came to pay his respects to Festus, the new governor of Judea.

Later Agrippa tried to prevent the Jews from revolting against Rome (cf. Jos. War II, 343-404 [xvi.3-5]), but his efforts were in vain (ibid., 405-7 [xvii.1]). During the war of 66-70 he was firmly on the side of Rome, and after the war Vespasian confirmed him as king in the territory he previously governed and added new areas to his domain. The Talmud implies that he had two wives (cf. b Sukkah 27a). But Josephus gives no indication of his being married or having children, and his death marked the end of the Herodian dynasty.

With Agrippa II was Bernice (properly Berenice or Pherenika—Veronica in Lat.), his sister one year younger than himself. She had been engaged to Marcus, a nephew of the philosopher Philo. Then she was married to her uncle Herod, king of Chalcis, but at his death in A.D. 48, she came to live with her brother Agrippa. Rumors of their incestuous relationship flourished in both Rome and Palestine (cf. Juvenal *Satirae* 6. 156–60; Jos. Antiq. XX, 145–47 [vii.3]), and in an effort to silence them she married King Polemo of Cilicia in 63. In 66, however, she returned to live with her brother. She became Titus's mistress at the close of the Roman war in Palestine, and in 75 went to Rome to live with him. Her relationship with Titus became a public scandal, and he was forced to send her away (cf. Tacitus *Historiae* 2.2). When Titus became emperor in 79, Bernice returned once more to Rome; but he was obliged to have nothing to do with her, and she returned to Palestine (cf. Dio Cassius *History of Rome* 56.18).

14 Though Agrippa II did not rule over Judea, he had been appointed by Claudius—like his uncle Herod, king of Chalcis, before him (Jos. Antiq. XX, 103 [v.2])—to be "the curator of the temple" (*hē epimeleia tou hierou*), with power to depose and appoint the high priest and the responsibility of preserving the temple's treasury and priestly vestments (Jos. Antiq. XX, 213 [ix.4], 222 [ix.7]). The Talmud reports that his mother Cypros took a profound interest in the Jewish religion (cf. comments on 12:1, citing b *Pesahim* 88b), and some of this interest may have rubbed off on him. Agrippa II, in fact, was looked upon by Rome as an authority on the Jewish religion. And it was for this reason that Festus broached the subject of Paul's case when Agrippa visited him.

15–21 Festus told Agrippa how the Jewish leaders confronted him with Paul's case when he first went to Jerusalem and that they had asked for Paul's death (v.15), but he acted in accordance with Roman law in demanding that charges be properly laid and the defendant allowed his day in court (v.16). Furthermore, he insisted, he acted with due dispatch, for on the day after he and the Jewish leaders returned to Caesarea, he convened court in order to try the case (v.17). To his surprise he found that the charges did not concern real offenses punishable under Roman law but theological differences of a Jewish intramural nature (vv.18–19a) and a debate "about a dead man named Jesus who Paul claimed was alive" (v.19b). Such matters were plainly incomprehensible and pointless to a Roman administrator. With a shrug of his shoulders, Festus confessed his total inadequacy to deal with them (v.20a). In an endeavor to resolve the impasse, Festus told Agrippa he was prepared to accede to the Sanhedrin's request for a change of venue to Jerusalem (v.20b). But Paul objected to this and appealed to Caesar, an appeal Festus had granted (v.21). Now then, what in the world was he to write in sending Paul on to the imperial court regarding the charges against the prisoner and the issues of the case?

22 This stirred Agrippa's interest so that instead of merely giving his advice, he asked to hear Paul himself. The Greek expression *kai autos* ("also myself"; "myself," NIV) makes the "I" emphatic, laying stress on Agrippa's real desire to meet Paul. Festus was only too happy to arrange a meeting for the very next day.

Paul's meeting with Herod Agrippa II has often been paralleled with that of Jesus before Herod Antipas in Luke 23:6–12. Not only was each arraigned before a Roman governor, but each was brought before a Jewish king who wanted very much to meet him (Luke 23:8). Paul's time with Agrippa II, however, turned out far more harmoniously than that of Jesus before Antipas. While Luke may have had the parallels in mind (only Luke includes the pericope of Jesus' appearance before Antipas), the differences of purpose and detail are too great to class the accounts of the two meetings as doublets.

Notes

13 The Byzantine text has the future participle ἀσπασόμενοι (aspasomenoi, "to greet," "to pay respects") for the aorist participle ἀσπασάμενοι (aspasamenoi, "to greet," "to pay respects"), evidently believing it better expresses intent. But the aorist participle functions in this manner as well.

18 ℵ A C P⁷⁴ read either πονηράν (ponēran) or πονηρά (ponēra) (i.e., "evil") for πονηρῶν (ponērōn, "wickedness"; NIV, "crimes"), thereby agreeing linguistically with ζήτησιν (zētēsin, "charges") of v.20.

5. Paul's defense before Herod Agrippa II

25:23–26:32

²³The next day Agrippa and Bernice came with great pomp and entered the audience room with the high ranking officers and the leading men of the city. At the command of Festus, Paul was brought in. ²⁴Festus said: "King Agrippa, and all who are present with us, you see this man! The whole Jewish community has petitioned me about him in Jerusalem and here in Caesarea, shouting that he ought not to live any longer. ²⁵I found he had done nothing deserving of death, but because he made his appeal to the Emperor I decided to send him to Rome. ²⁶But I have nothing definite to write to His Majesty about him. Therefore I have brought him before all of you, and especially before you, King Agrippa, so that as a result of this investigation I may have something to write. ²⁷For I think it is unreasonable to send on a prisoner without specifying the charges against him."

²⁶:¹Then Agrippa said to Paul, "You have permission to speak for yourself." So Paul motioned with his hand and began his defense: ²"King Agrippa, I consider myself fortunate to stand before you today as I make my defense against all the accusations of the Jews, ³and especially so because you are well acquainted with all the Jewish customs and controversies. Therefore, I beg you to listen to me patiently.

⁴"The Jews all know the way I have lived ever since I was a child, from the beginning of my life in my own country, and also in Jerusalem. ⁵They have known me for a long time and can testify, if they are willing, that according to the strictest sect of our religion, I lived as a Pharisee. ⁶And now it is because of my hope in what God has promised our fathers that I am on trial today. ⁷This is the promise our twelve tribes are hoping to see fulfilled as they earnestly serve God day and night. O king, it is because of this hope that the Jews are accusing me. ⁸Why should any of you consider it incredible that God raises the dead?

⁹"I too was convinced that I ought to do all that was possible to oppose the name of Jesus of Nazareth. ¹⁰And that is just what I did in Jerusalem. On the authority of the chief priests I put many of the saints in prison, and when they were put to death, I cast my vote against them. ¹¹Many a time I went from one synagogue to another to have them punished, and I tried to force them to blaspheme. In my obsession against them, I even went to foreign cities to persecute them.

¹²"On one of these journeys I was going to Damascus with the authority and commission of the chief priests. ¹³About noon, O king, as I was on the road, I saw a light from heaven, brighter than the sun, blazing around me and my companions. ¹⁴We all fell to the ground, and I heard a voice saying to me in Aramaic, 'Saul, Saul, why do you persecute me? It is hard for you to kick against the goads.'

¹⁵"Then I asked, 'Who are you, Lord?'

" 'I am Jesus, whom you are persecuting,' the Lord replied. ¹⁶'Now get up and stand on your feet. I have appeared to you to appoint you as a servant and as a witness of what you have seen of me and what I will show you. ¹⁷I will rescue you from your own people and from the Gentiles. I am sending you ¹⁸to open their eyes and turn them from darkness to light, and from the power of Satan to God, so that they may receive forgiveness of sins and a place among those who are sanctified by faith in me.'

19"So then, King Agrippa, I was not disobedient to the vision from heaven. 20First to those in Damascus, then to those in Jerusalem and in all Judea, and to the Gentiles also, I preached that they should repent and turn to God and prove their repentance by their deeds. 21That is why the Jews seized me in the temple courts and tried to kill me. 22But I have had God's help to this very day, and so I stand here and testify to small and great alike. I am saying nothing beyond what the prophets and Moses said would happen— 23that the Christ would suffer and, as the first to rise from the dead, would proclaim light to his own people and to the Gentiles."

24At this point Festus interrupted Paul's defense. "You are out of your mind, Paul!" he shouted. "Your great learning is driving you insane."

25"I am not insane, most excellent Festus," Paul replied. "What I am saying is true and reasonable. 26The king is familiar with these things, and I can speak freely to him. I am convinced that none of this has escaped his notice, because it was not done in a corner. 27King Agrippa, do you believe the prophets? I know you do."

28Then Agrippa said to Paul, "Do you think that in such a short time you can persuade me to be a Christian?"

29Paul replied, "Short time or long—I pray God that not only you but all who are listening to me today may become what I am, except for these chains."

30The king rose, and with him the governor and Bernice and those sitting with them. 31They left the room, and while talking with one another, they said, "This man is not doing anything that deserves death or imprisonment."

32Agrippa said to Festus, "This man could have been set free, if he had not appealed to Caesar."

Paul's defense before Herod Agrippa II was evidently for Luke the most important of the five defenses. It is the longest and most carefully constructed of the five—factors that of themselves give notice as to something of its importance in Luke's eyes. Perhaps Luke was in the audience chamber through the courtesy of an officer of the guard, or perhaps he heard Paul's account of the event and what was said at some time later. But however he got the information, he chose to conclude his reports of Paul's five defenses with this speech, which has quite properly been called the apostle's *Apologia Pro Vita Sua* (cf. Bruce, *Book of the Acts,* p. 488).

All the attention in the account is focused on Paul himself and the gospel, not on the charges brought forward by the Jews, and certainly not on any rumored incest between Agrippa and Bernice. Inherent in Luke's account are at least three apologetic themes: (1) Paul's relations with the Roman provincial government in Judea did not end in dissonance but with an acknowledgment of his innocence (cf. 25:25; 26:31); (2) even though the Jewish high priests and Sanhedrin opposed Paul, the Jewish king who in Rome's eyes outranked them agreed with a verdict of innocence (cf. 26:32); and (3) Paul's innocence was demonstrated not only before Roman and Jewish rulers but also publicly before "the high ranking officers and the leading men of the city" (25:23).

Yet Paul's speech before Agrippa II is not just an apologia in the narrow sense of the word. It is also a positive presentation of the gospel with an evangelistic appeal: Christ would suffer, rise from the dead, and proclaim light to both Jews and Gentiles (26:23); what God did in and through Jesus the Christ was done openly, "not done in a corner" (v.26); all the prophets pointed forward to redemption in Christ, and believing them leads one on to accepting Christ (v.27); and Paul's prayer for all who hear is that they "may become what I am, except for these chains" (v.29). It is with such a kerygmatic purpose that Luke penned his two volumes (cf. Introduction: Luke's Purposes in Writing Acts), and this account of Paul's final defense is a fitting climax to that purpose. All that remains is to sketch out the apostle's journey to Rome and his ministry there, thus completing the geographical framework of Luke's presentation and concluding it on a note of triumph (cf. 28:31).

23 Luke describes Agrippa and Bernice as entering the audience chamber of Herod the Great's Caesarean palace "with great pomp" (*meta pollēs phantasias*), accompanied by a procession of "high ranking officers" (*chiliarchoi*; lit., "commanders of a thousand men") and "the leading men of the city." The Romans always knew how to process well. The sight of Agrippa's royal robes, Bernice's finery, and the military and civil dignitaries decked out in their official attire doubtless overwhelmed those unaccustomed to such displays—which was the effect the whole affair was calculated to produce. After the procession, Paul the prisoner was brought in. But though the situation was contrived to assert the importance of Roman officialdom and the inferiority of the man who stood before it, Luke's divinely inspired insight penetrated the trappings and saw that the situation was really reversed. And his evaluation has prevailed in history.

24–27 Festus opened the proceedings by turning the dignitaries' attention to Paul with the words "You see this man!" (*theōreite touton*). After saying that he could not substantiate the charges against Paul, he told them how Paul had appealed to Caesar. Then, asking for help with what he would have to write in sending Paul to the imperial court at Rome, Festus turned the conduct of the inquiry over to King Agrippa.

A number of subtle touches in these verses are particularly appropriate for the situation. The title *Sebastos* ("Emperor," v.25), found only here and in v.21 in the NT, is the Greek equivalent of Augustus. It was first conferred on Octavian, the adopted heir of Julius Caesar, by the Senate in 27 B.C. to denote "one who is augmented" or lifted above other mortals and was restricted to the reigning emperor (and, at times, his wife). The addition of *Kyrios* ("Lord" or "His Majesty") to the imperial title began in the time of Nero (A.D. 54–68), and its usage steadily increased till it became common during the reign of Trajan (98–117). Despite its associations with deity in the eastern realms of the empire, the growth of the imperial cult, and the pretensions to divinity of such emperors as Nero and Domitian, the title *Kyrios* did not by itself signal to Romans the idea of deity but rather connoted that of majesty (cf. TDNT, 3: 1054–58). Likewise, Festus's statement (v.27) that he thought it "unreasonable" (*alogos*) to send on a prisoner with unspecified charges against him is typical of the face-saving language used among officials when what is really meant is that the failure to specify charges would be a dereliction of duty.

26:1 At Agrippa's invitation to speak for himself, Paul, though manacled by chains (v.29), motioned with his hand for attention (cf. 21:40) and began speaking. While we have only a précis of what was said, it is the longest précis of Paul's five defenses and undoubtedly reflects the relative length of the address itself. Agrippa was considered something of an authority on the Jewish religion (at least by the Romans); therefore he might have been expected to listen closely to Paul's lengthy explanation of the relation of his message and ministry to the hope of Israel.

2–3 This was just the kind of situation Paul had longed for during two bleak years in prison—viz., a knowledgeable judge and a not inherently antagonistic audience before whom he could not only make his defense but also proclaim his message. Therefore he began with unusual fervor, expressing appreciation for the opportunity of speaking, complimenting the judge, and asking for patience in hearing him out. Since Festus had already said that Paul had not committed a capital crime (cf. 25:25), Paul chose to defend himself only against the charge that he had transgressed against Judaism.

4–8 It was not in spite of his Jewish heritage but because of it, Paul insisted, that he believed and proclaimed what he did. So he began the body of his address (note the connective *men oun* at the start of v.4) by drawing together his Pharisaic background and his Christian commitment, arguing that the Jewish hope and the Christian message are inseparably related. His life had been spent among his people in his own country and in Jerusalem (v.4; cf. 22:3). He had lived as a Pharisee, "the strictest sect" (*tēn akribestatēn hairesin*) of the Jewish religion (v.5; cf. Phil 3:5–6). It was because of the Jewish hope in the resurrection of the dead that he was being tried (v.6). And the ironic thing was that the charges against him were brought, of all people, by the Jews themselves (note that *hypo Ioudaiōn*, "by the Jews," is in the place of emphasis at the end of v.7). Yet why should any of his audience (note the pl. *hymin*, "you") think it "incredible that God raises the dead" (v.8), particularly when God had validated the truth of the resurrection by raising Jesus from the dead (cf. comments on 23:6)?

9–11 Speaking retrospectively, Paul went on (note the resumptive use of *men oun*) to acknowledge that he too once thought that Christian preaching about the resurrection of Jesus was incredible. Pharisee though he was, he too had denounced belief in the resurrection of Jesus and had persecuted those who claimed to have seen Jesus alive after his crucifixion. He put Christians in prison, agreed with the death penalty for their "heresy" (cf. 8:1, taking "I cast my vote against them" as a metaphor for *syneudokeō*, "I give approval"), and went through the synagogues seeking to punish them for apostasy (cf. M *Makkoth* 3.10–15a on synagogue whippings) and to get them to recant. This he did not only in Jerusalem but also in cities outside Judea (*kai eis tas exō poleis*, lit., "also to the outside cities"; "even to foreign cities," NIV).

12–14 While Paul was trying to stamp out nascent Christianity, the encounter that changed his life took place. That Paul's account of his Damascus Road conversion appears three times in Acts (chs. 9,22,26) undoubtedly shows how important this event was not only for Paul but also for Luke (cf. introductory comments on 9:1–30). And it is in this third account that Luke's kerygmatic purpose (i.e., to proclaim the gospel of Christ) in Luke-Acts reaches its climax. Yet the threefold repetition of what happened is more than a simple retelling of the same details. Each account fits its own special context in Paul's life and in Luke's purpose. Here there is an intensification and explication of the details that is not found in the earlier accounts: (1) the heavenly light was "brighter than the sun" (cf 9:3; 22:6); (2) it blazed around both "me and my companions" (cf 9:3; 22:6); (3) "we all fell to the ground" (cf. 9:4; 22:7); and (4) the voice from heaven spoke "in Aramaic" (lit., "in the Hebrew dialect"). None of these is necessarily in contradiction to the other two accounts, but each was intended to clarify for Paul's hearers and Luke's readers the significance of the events.

Likewise in v.14b we have the only place (i.e., if we reject the Western addition at 22:7, incorporated into the TR by Erasmus) in the three accounts where "It is hard for you to kick against the goads" (*sklēron soi pros kentra laktizein*) is included. In the Greek world this was a well-known expression for opposition to deity (cf. Euripides *Bacchanals* 794–95; Aeschylus *Prometheus Bound* 324–25; *Agamemnon* 1624; Pindar *Pythia* 2.94–95; Terence *Phormio* 1.2.27). Paul may have picked it up in Tarsus or during his missionary journeys. He used it here to show his Greek-oriented audience the implications of the question "Saul, Saul, why do you persecute me?" Lest he be misunderstood as proclaiming only a Galilean prophet he had formerly opposed, he pointed out to his hearers what was obvious to any Jew: correction by a voice from heaven meant opposition to God himself. So he used a current expression familiar to Agrippa and the others (cf. my *Paul*, pp. 98–101).

15–18 On the other hand, this third account leaves out certain features we might have come to expect from the other two: (1) the heavenly speaker identifies himself only as Jesus (cf. 22:8); (2) there is no mention of Ananias (cf. 9:10–19; 22:12–16); (3) there is no mention of Paul's blindness and subsequent healing (cf. 9:8–9; 18–19; 22:11, 13). There was, however, no need to refer to Nazareth (particularly having mentioned it in v.9) or to refer to the devout Jew Ananias, as when addressing the crowd in the temple (cf. comments on 22:8, 12). Nor was it necessary for Paul to refer to his blindness and healing, which might have been confusing to a pagan audience. Rather, in his address before Agrippa and the others, Paul merged the words of Christ as spoken on the road to Damascus (cf. 9:5–6; 22:8, 10), as given through Ananias of Damascus (cf. 22:14–15), and as received in a vision at Jerusalem (cf. 22:18–21). The result was that Paul did not emphasize details of time or human aid in this third account of his conversion. What Paul did emphasize was the lordship of Christ and the divine commission Christ gave him.

The words of the risen Jesus calling Paul to his mission (vv.16–17) recall the commissioning of the prophets Ezekiel and Jeremiah: "Stand up on your feet and I will speak to you. . . . I am sending you . . . to a rebellious nation that has rebelled against me" (Ezek 2:1, 3); "You must go to everyone I send you to and say whatever I command you. Do not be afraid of them, for I am with you and will rescue you" (Jer 1:7–8). The commission itself (v.18) echoes that of the Servant of the Lord in Isaiah 42:6b–7: "I . . . will make you . . . a light for the Gentiles, to open eyes that are blind, to free captives from prison and to release from the dungeon those who sit in darkness." Indeed, Paul's mission was a prophetic one that perpetuated the commission originally given to God's Righteous Servant, Jesus Christ. And Christians today, as God's servants and prophets, are called to the same kind of ministry.

19–21 Having been confronted by the risen and glorified Jesus, Paul henceforth knew but one Master and found it impossible to resist his commands. So he told Agrippa how he began preaching about Jesus in Damascus and continued to do so in Jerusalem (cf. 9:20–30). The words "and in all Judea" (*pasan te tēn chōran tēs Ioudaias*; lit., "all the region of Judea") are grammatically strange (i.e., an accusative construction in the midst of datives, without the necessary preposition *eis*) and conflict with the evidence of Acts 9:20–30 and Galatians 1:18–24 that Paul did *not* preach the gospel throughout "all the region of Judea." Perhaps the preposition *eis* was accidentally omitted by an early scribe after *Ierosolymois* (as such diverse scholars as Blass, Ramsay, and Dibelius have postulated). More likely "and in all Judea" was an early gloss that entered the text through a false reading of Romans 15:19. Not only in Damascus and Jerusalem, however, but also to the Gentiles did Paul preach a message of repentance and conversion. And it was because of his preaching to Gentiles, he insisted, that the Jews were so aggressively opposed to him.

22–23 Nevertheless, in fulfillment of Christ's promise (v.17), God had stood by Paul, protecting him and enabling him to proclaim "to small and great alike" a message thoroughly in accord with Israel's faith and in harmony with all that the prophets and

Moses said would happen: "that [*ei* here equaling *hoti*, "that"; cf. v.8] the Christ would suffer and, as the first to rise from the dead, would proclaim light to his own people and to the Gentiles." Despite occasional claims to the contrary, there is no evidence that pre-Christian Judaism ever thought of the Messiah in terms of suffering. Certainly many of the building blocks for a later doctrine of a suffering Messiah were present in the Jewish consciousness during the period of Late Judaism, and there is some indication that these elements were later brought together at times into either an inchoate (cf. 4 Ezra 7:29–30) or distorted (cf. the medieval Sabbati Svi sect) suffering Messiah doctrine. But the proclamation of both a suffering Messiah and the resurrection of Jesus were distinctive to early Christianity. To these foundation tenets of the early faith, Paul, by revelation (cf. Gal 1:11–12; Eph 3:1–6), added the legitimacy of a direct outreach to Gentiles. Indeed, such features of the Christian message went beyond the explicit beliefs and expectations of Judaism. But Paul's claim was that they were developments brought about by God himself to show the true intent of Israelite religion and in continuity with all that the prophets and Moses said would happen.

24 At this point Festus broke into Paul's address, unable to endure it any longer. Festus may not have been speaking for the Jews, to whom a suffering Messiah and a direct ministry to Gentiles were outrageous. But no sensible Roman could believe in the resurrection of a man from the dead—and even if he did privately accept such a strange view, he would not allow it to interfere with his practical living or bring him into danger of death. Paul, Festus concluded, was so learned in his Jewish traditions that he had become utterly impractical. Such talk was the height of insanity. Down through the ages Festus's response has been echoed by men and women too trapped by the natural to be open to the supernatural, too confined by the "practical" to care about life everlasting.

25–27 But what Festus declared to be madness Paul insisted was "true and reasonable" (*alētheias kai sōphrosynēs rhēmata*; lit., "of true and reasonable words"). Then he turned to Agrippa for support. The ministry of Jesus was widely known in Palestine, and Agrippa would have heard of it. Jesus' death and resurrection were amply attested, and the Christian gospel had now been proclaimed for three decades. Certainly the king knew of these things, "because it was not done in a corner" (*ou gar estin en gōnia pepragmenon touto*)—another (cf. v.14b) Greek idiom of the day (cf. Plato *Gorgias* 485D; Epictetus *Dissertations* 2.12.17; Terence *Adelphi* 5.2.10). And certainly the king believed the prophets—a belief, as Paul saw it, that inevitably brought one to Christ. So the prisoner became the questioner, as Paul boldly said, "King Agrippa, do you believe the prophets?"

28 Paul's direct question embarrassed Agrippa. He had his reputation to maintain before Festus and the other dignitaries. Whatever he may have thought about Paul's message personally, he was too worldly-wise to commit himself in public to what others thought was madness. So he parried Paul's question with his own clever, though rather inane, one: "Do you think that in such a short time you can persuade me to be a Christian?" The adjective *oligos* often has reference to quantity and here could mean "with such few words" or "with such a brief argument." But it is also used with the preposition *en* ("in") to denote duration (cf. BAG, p. 566b). And this is how NIV rightly translates it here—"in such a short time" (so also RSV and TEV). KJV's translation of Agrippa's reply to Paul, "Almost thou persuadest me to be a Christian," has become one of the famous quotations in history. Countless sermons have been preached on it and a gospel hymn inspired by it. Nevertheless, it is not what Agrippa said, nor is KJV's translation of v.29 what Paul said.

29 Addressing the king with extreme politeness (note the use of the optative *euxaimēn an*, "I could wish," "I pray," which in Paul's day had become rare) and taking up Agrippa's own word *oligos* ("short time"), Paul replied, "Short time or long—I pray God that not only you but all who are listening to me today may become what I am." Undoubtedly he spoke with evangelistic fervor, directing his appeal not only to the king but also to the other dignitaries. Then in a lighter vein, recognizing the apparent incongruity of appealing for their acceptance of spiritual freedom while he himself stood chained before them, he raised his hands and added, "except for these chains."

30–32 Paul had had the last word, and his light touch at the end of his response evidently broke up the meeting. With it Agrippa dismissed the proceedings and with Festus and Bernice strode out of the audience chamber. We need not visualize them gathering in an adjoining room to render an official judgment. In appealing to Caesar, Paul had removed the case from their jurisdiction. Yet Agrippa had presumably heard enough to instruct Festus what he should write in his report to Rome. Their conclusion was that Paul had done nothing that in Rome's eyes merited death or imprisonment, and Agrippa was heard to comment, "This man could have been set free, if he had not appealed to Caesar."

Agrippa's comment should not be taken to mean that a provincial governor could not free a prisoner after an appeal to Caesar. In this situation, however, Paul's status was not a question of law only but also of politics (cf. comments on 25:12). Luke has picked up these words of Agrippa and uses them to conclude his accounts of Paul's defenses before Roman as well as Jewish judges. In fact, they conclude Luke's apologetic motif in Acts and vindicate both Paul and Christianity from any suspicion of sedition.

Notes

24 The Western text adds at the end of this verse: "and that I should hand him over to them for punishment without any defense. But I could not hand him over, because of the commands that we have from the emperor. But if anyone was going to accuse him, I said he should follow me to Caesarea, where he was in custody. And when they came, they insisted that he should be put to death."

26:1 A Western addition (a marginal reading in the Harclean Syr. version) reads "So Paul, being confident and encouraged by the Holy Spirit, motioned . . . ."

4 On Luke's use of μὲν οὖν (*men oun*), cf. comments on 1:6.

8 One Western text (P[29]) omits τί ἄπιστον κρίνεται παρ᾽ ὑμῖν (*ti apiston krinetai par hymin*, "Why should any of you consider it incredible").

9 On μὲν οὖν (*men oun*), see note on v.4 above.

14 The Western text adds διὰ τὸν φόβον (*dia ton phobon*, "because of fear") and μόνος (*monos*, "alone"), reading, "We all fell to the ground because of fear, and I alone heard a voice saying to me."

15 The Western text adds ὁ Ναζωραῖος (*ho Nazōraios*, "of Nazareth" or "the Nazarene"), thereby harmonizing with 22:8.

16 B omits καὶ στῆθι (kai stēthi, "and stand"), probably inadvertently.

‫ א‬A C E P P⁷⁴ omit με (me, "of me"), reading "what you have seen and what I will show you."

20 The addition of the preposition εἰς (eis, "in") in the Byzantine codd. EHLP (sixth and ninth century MSS) is a later correction and conjecture.

24 One OL MS (h) has "You are out of your mind, Paul; you are out of your mind" (insanisti, Paule; insanisti).

25 The Western and Byzantine texts omit Παῦλος (Paulos, "Paul").

On the title κράτιστε (kratiste, "most excellent"), cf. comments on 23:26.

26 B omits καὶ (kai, "also"), as does NIV. Including the "also," the verse would read "And I can also speak freely to him."

28 A has πείθῃ (peithē, "you trust") for πείθεις (peitheis, "persuade"), reading "You trust you can make me a Christian." The Byzantine text has γενέσθαι (genesthai, "to be") for ποιῆσαι (poiēsai, "to make"), which NIV has evidently accepted here.

On the designation Χριστιανός (Christianos, "Christian"), used only three times in the NT (11:26; 26:28; 1 Peter 4:16), cf. comments on 11:26.

30 The Western and Byzantine texts begin the verse καὶ ταῦτα εἰπόντος αὐτοῦ (kai tauta eipontos autou, "And when he said these things").

E. The Journey to Rome (27:1–28:15)

There are many things one would like to know about Paul's two-year imprisonment at Caesarea. For instance, how was the apostle supported during this time? Felix thought he was a man who had access to some money (cf. 24:26), but on what basis did he suppose this? How cordial were Paul's relations with the Jerusalem Christians and their leaders during his imprisonment? How cordial were his contacts with the Caesarean believers or with other groups of Christians in the vicinity? What happened to Silas, who was originally a member of the Jerusalem congregation (cf. 15:22)? What were Timothy and Luke doing during these two years? What happened to the rest of those who represented the Gentile churches at the time of Paul's last visit to Jerusalem (cf. 20:4)? Aristarchus is mentioned in 27:2 as embarking with Paul for Rome, and this implies that he remained in the area during Paul's imprisonment. But what did he and the others do during that time? Other questions arise as well. Such matters, however, were evidently not of interest to Luke or to Paul in his letters. In an endeavor to fill these gaps in Luke's account of Paul's stay in Caesarea, some have proposed that several of Paul's letters (notably Eph, Col, Philem) were written while he was in prison in Caesarea. But internal evidence points to their composition during his subsequent Roman imprisonment.

Luke's account of Paul's voyage to Rome stands out as one of the most vivid pieces of descriptive writing in the whole Bible. Its details regarding first-century seamanship are so precise and its portrayal of conditions on the eastern Mediterranean so accurate (cf. James Smith, The Voyage and Shipwreck of St. Paul, 4th ed. [London: Longman, Brown, Green & Longmans, 1880]) that even the most skeptical have conceded that it probably rests on a journal of some such voyage as Luke describes. Critical discussion, therefore, has focused not so much on the trip itself as on Luke's portrayal of Paul on the trip—viz., on Paul (1) as a prisoner receiving special favors (cf. 27:3, 43; 28:7); (2) as a speaker giving advice (cf. 27:10, 21–26, 33–34); and (3) as a miracle worker honored by all (cf. 28:3–6, 8–10). Haenchen speaks for many when he says of the author:

> He certainly possessed a journal of this voyage. Yet Paul was no noble traveller with special authority, but a prisoner accused of inciting to riot. He therefore had no say in any of the decisions. Just those edifying supplements which extol Paul are additions

by the author to a journal of reminiscences which could not report anything special about Paul, but only described the voyage, the danger and the rescue (*Acts of the Apostles*, p. 709).

But such a judgment is far too extreme. Clearly Luke viewed Paul as his hero and thus may be suspected of having minimized Paul's own fears during the voyage and of having cast him into a more heroic mold than was justified. Nevertheless, Paul was a Roman citizen who still retained rights until proven guilty. In addition, he was a man of powerful personality, who commanded respect in various situations. Most of all, he was an apostle of Jesus Christ, who had been promised divine protection and assured that he would reach Rome (cf. 23:11) and through whom God by his Spirit worked in an extraordinary fashion (cf. 19:11–12; 20:10–12). Historians may criticize Luke for his preoccupation with Paul and for his enthusiastic portrayal of his hero's nobility under great difficulties. But such criticisms as those of Haenchen reflect theological skepticism rather than perceptive scholarship and philosophical naturalism rather than Christian testimony to God's supernatural activity.

1. From Palestine to Crete

27:1–12

¹When it was decided that we would sail for Italy, Paul and some other prisoners were handed over to a centurion named Julius, who belonged to the Imperial Regiment. ²We boarded a ship from Adramyttium about to sail for ports along the coast of the province of Asia, and we put out to sea. Aristarchus, a Macedonian from Thessalonica, was with us.

³The next day we landed at Sidon; and Julius, in kindness to Paul, allowed him to go to his friends so they might provide for his needs. ⁴From there we put out to sea again and passed to the lee of Cyprus because the winds were against us. ⁵When we had sailed across the open sea off the coast of Cilicia and Pamphylia, we landed at Myra in Lycia. ⁶There the centurion found an Alexandrian ship sailing for Italy and put us on board. ⁷We made slow headway for many days and had difficulty arriving off Cnidus. When the wind did not allow us to hold our course, we sailed to the lee of Crete, opposite Salmone. ⁸We moved along the coast with difficulty and came to a place called Fair Havens, near the town of Lasea.

⁹Much time had been lost, and sailing had already become dangerous because by now it was after the Fast. So Paul warned them, ¹⁰"Men, I can see that our voyage is going to be disastrous and bring great loss to ship and cargo, and to our own lives also." ¹¹But the centurion, instead of listening to what Paul said, followed the advice of the pilot and of the owner of the ship. ¹²Since the harbor was unsuitable to winter in, the majority decided that we should sail on, hoping to reach Phoenix and winter there. This was a harbor in Crete, facing both southwest and northwest.

1 The account of Paul's journey to Rome is the longest of Luke's four "we" sections (27:1–28:16; cf. 16:10–17; 20:5–15; 21:1–18). And the vividness and precision of the narrative confirm what the use of "we" implies—that it is an eyewitness report.

Luke says that the centurion Julius, who was to take Paul to Rome, was a member of "the Imperial Regiment" (*speirēs Sebastēs*; lit., "the Augustan Cohort"). Many commentators (following Mommsen and Ramsay) see this as a reference to a group of imperial officials called the *frumentarii*, who not only organized the transportation of grain to Rome but also had police duties and performed escort services on their travels throughout the empire. But Aurelius Victor (cf. *Liber de Caesaribus* 13.5–6) seems to attribute the organization of the *frumentarii* to the emperor Trajan (A.D. 98–117), and there is nothing to indicate that even if there were *frumentarii* earlier that they had police or escort responsibilities. The soldiers who performed these services in Paul's day were the *speculatores*, a special body of imperial guards who were particularly prominent in times of military intrigue (cf. Tacitus *Historiae* 1.24–25; 2.73). These *speculatores* belonged to no particular division of a Roman army legion (though there was a Cohors Augusta I in Syria during the reign of Augustus, and there is evidence of a Cohors Augusta III at Rome). Instead, they formed a special unit of their own, assigned to various police and judicial functions.

2 While it is not stated explicitly, the port of embarkation was undoubtedly Caesarea. If it had been any other, Luke, in accord with his usual practice, would have mentioned it. The boat they boarded was a coastal vessel from the city of Adramyttium, a seaport of Mysia on the northwest coast of Asia Minor, opposite the island of Lesbos. Embarking with Paul were Luke (cf. "we") and Aristarchus, who were possibly entered on the passenger list as Paul's personal doctor and servant, respectively. As a Roman citizen who had appealed to the emperor, Paul would naturally have had a more favored position than the other prisoners; and the centurion would have recognized his superiority as a gentleman with attendants. That Aristarchus is included in Colossians 4:10 and Philemon 24 as sending greetings from Rome (assuming a Roman origin for these letters) suggests that he traveled with Paul all the way to Rome and remained with him during his imprisonment there, rather than returning to his home at Thessalonica.

3 At Sidon, the ancient Phoenician port some seventy miles north of Caesarea and twenty-five miles north of Tyre, the boat took on cargo. Here Paul was permitted to visit the Christians of the city, who, like those at Tyre (cf. comments on 21:4), had probably become believers through the witness of Christian Hellenists forced to leave Jerusalem at the time of Stephen's martyrdom (cf. 11:19). The centurion Julius had probably been advised by Festus to be lenient with Paul, and doubtless Paul had already made a good impression on Julius. Yet a soldier would have been always with him during his visit with the believers of Sidon.

4-5 From Sidon, the boat sailed northwest toward Cyprus, staying close to the long east coast of the island ("the lee of Cyprus") because of the westerly winds that blow from spring through fall on the eastern Mediterranean. Two and one half years earlier Paul and his companions had sailed with that westerly wind from Patara to Tyre and had passed Cyprus on the south, perhaps making the entire voyage in only five days (cf. comments on 21:3). Now, however, their voyage from Sidon to Myra was considerably slower as their boat had to run against the winds and tried to stay in the lee of sheltering land masses. Crossing the open sea between Cyprus and Cilicia to the north, the vessel worked its way westward to Myra in Lycia, on the southwest coast of Asia Minor, helped along by local land breezes and a westward current that runs along that coast.

6 Myra was two and one-half miles inland to the north of its port Andriaca. In Paul's day it was the most illustrious city in Lycia, with distinguished public buildings, a very large theater, and many evidences of wealth (Strabo *Geography* 14.3.7). Its port became the natural port of call for grain ships bound for Rome from Egypt, and in commercial importance it overshadowed its rival Patara to the west (cf. comments on 21:1). At Myra Julius arranged with the owner of a larger Alexandrian grain ship to take the soldiers and prisoners on board for the longer voyage to Italy.

7-8 Leaving Myra, the grain ship moved slowly along the peninsula that thrusts seaward between the islands of Cos and Rhodes to the port of Cnidus, at the southwestern tip of Asia Minor. Cnidus was a free city in the province of Asia and the last port of call before sailing west across the Aegean for the Greek mainland. But the northern winds that blow down the length of the Aegean at this time of year pushed the ship off course and forced the pilot to seek protection along the southern coast ("the lee") of Crete, the 160-mile-long island southeast of Greece. Passing Cape Salmone on the eastern tip of Crete, the ship entered the small bay of Fair Havens (modern Limeonas Kalous) near the town of Lasea and about 5 miles east of Cape Matala.

9-10 Navigation in this part of the Mediterranean was always dangerous after 14 September and was considered impossible after 11 November (cf. Vegetius *De Re Militari* 4.39). The ship had lost valuable time since leaving Myra, and it was obvious that there was no hope of reaching Italy before winter. Yom Kippur ("Day of Atonement"), the chief festival of Judaism celebrated on the 10th of the lunar month Tishri (between the latter part of September and the first part of October in a solar calendar), was already past. So Paul warned that disaster would befall them if they tried to go further.

11-12 But the pilot and the ship's owner preferred not to winter in the small, open bay of Fair Havens, being reluctant to seek quarters for themselves and their passengers in the small town of Lasea. They hoped to winter at the larger and safer port of Phoenix (modern Phineka) some forty miles west of Fair Havens. Between Fair Havens and Phoenix, however, west of Cape Matala, the south coast of Crete turns suddenly to the north and exposes a ship to the northern gales before it regains the protection of the coast just before Phoenix. Nevertheless, the centurion agreed with the pilot and the ship's owner that it would, if at all possible, be best to winter at Phoenix, with its harbor looking toward the southwest and northwest (*bleponta kata liba kai kata chōron;* "facing both southwest and northwest," NIV).

Notes

1 The Western text expands this verse to read as follows: "So, then the governor decided to send him to Caesar. And the next day he called a centurion named Julius, who belonged to the Imperial Regiment, and handed Paul over to him along with other prisoners."
2 The Western text adds Secundus, in harmony with 20:4.
5 The Western text adds δι᾽ ἡμερῶν δεκάπεντε (*di hēmerōn dekapente,* "for fifteen days"), reading "When we had sailed across the open sea for fifteen days."

2. Storm and shipwreck

27:13-44

¹³When a gentle south wind began to blow, they thought they had obtained what they wanted; so they weighed anchor and sailed along the shore of Crete. ¹⁴Before very long, a wind of hurricane force, called the "Northeaster," swept down from the island. ¹⁵The ship was caught by the storm and could not head into the wind; so we gave way to it and were driven along. ¹⁶As we passed to the lee of a small island called Cauda, we were hardly able to make the lifeboat secure. ¹⁷When the

men had hoisted it aboard, they passed ropes under the ship itself to hold it together. Fearing that they would run aground on the sandbars of Syrtis, they lowered the sea anchor and let the ship be driven along. [18]We took such a violent battering from the storm that the next day they began to throw the cargo overboard. [19]On the third day, they threw the ship's tackle overboard with their own hands. [20]When neither sun nor stars appeared for many days and the storm continued raging, we finally gave up all hope of being saved.

[21]After the men had gone a long time without food, Paul stood up before them and said: "Men, you should have taken my advice not to sail from Crete; then you would have spared yourselves this damage and loss. [22]But now I urge you to keep up your courage, because not one of you will be lost; only the ship will be destroyed. [23]Last night an angel of the God whose I am and whom I serve stood beside me [24]and said, 'Do not be afraid, Paul. You must stand trial before Caesar; and God has graciously given you the lives of all who sail with you.' [25]So keep up your courage, men, for I have faith in God that it will happen just as he told me. [26]Nevertheless, we must run aground on some island."

[27]On the fourteenth night we were still being driven across the Adriatic Sea, when about midnight the sailors sensed they were approaching land. [28]They took soundings and found that the water was a hundred and twenty feet deep. A short time later they took soundings again and found it was ninety feet deep. [29]Fearing that we would be dashed against the rocks, they dropped four anchors from the stern and prayed for daylight. [30]In an attempt to escape from the ship, the sailors let the lifeboat down into the sea, pretending they were going to lower some anchors from the bow. [31]Then Paul said to the centurion and the soldiers, "Unless these men stay with the ship, you cannot be saved." [32]So the soldiers cut the ropes that held the lifeboat and let it fall away.

[33]Just before dawn Paul urged them all to eat. "For the last fourteen days," he said, "you have been in constant suspense and have gone without food—you haven't eaten anything. [34]Now I urge you to take some food. You need it to survive. Not one of you will lose a single hair from his head." [35]After he said this, he took some bread and gave thanks to God in front of them all. Then he broke it and began to eat. [36]They were all encouraged and ate some food themselves. [37]Altogether there were 276 of us on board. [38]When they had eaten as much as they wanted, they lightened the ship by throwing the grain into the sea.

[39]When daylight came, they did not recognize the land, but they saw a bay with a sandy beach, where they decided to run the ship aground if they could. [40]Cutting loose the anchors, they left them in the sea and at the same time untied the ropes that held the rudders. Then they hoisted the foresail to the wind and made for the beach. [41]But the ship struck a sandbar and ran aground. The bow stuck fast and would not move, and the stern was broken to pieces by the pounding of the surf.

[42]The soldiers planned to kill the prisoners to prevent any of them from swimming away and escaping. [43]But the centurion wanted to spare Paul's life and kept them from carrying out their plan. He ordered those who could swim to jump overboard first and get to land. [44]The rest were to get there on planks or on pieces of the ship. In this way everyone reached land in safety.

13–15 Shortly after the decision to winter at Phoenix was made, a gentle southern breeze began to blow; and it appeared that they would have no trouble in crossing the Gulf of Messara that began west of Cape Matala on the southern coast of Crete. But no sooner had they rounded the cape and entered the gulf than they were caught in a hurricane coming from Mount Ida to the north. Sailors called this wind the Euroquilo (Gr. *Eurakylōn*)—a hybrid word from the Greek *euros* meaning "east wind" and the Latin *aquilo* meaning "north wind"—so "Northeaster" (NIV). Before it they were helpless.

16–17 Driven southwest some twenty-three miles to the small island of Cauda (modern Gavdos or Gozzo), the ship managed to gain the lee of the island. The sailors pulled in the dinghy, which was full of water, reinforced the ship with ropes to keep it from breaking up, and put out the sea anchor to keep the ship from running onto the sandbars of Syrtis, off the African coast west of Cyrene.

The statement *echrōnto hypozōnnyntes to ploion* ("they passed ropes under the ship," NIV) is difficult to translate precisely because *hypozōnnymi* is an ancient nautical term that could have signified any one of a number of procedures: (1) passing ropes under a ship and securing them above deck in order to reinforce the hull in a heavy sea (so KJV, RSV, NEB, NIV); (2) tying ropes around a ship's hull above water for the same purpose (so JB, TEV); or (3) frapping or hogging a vessel by tying the stem and stern tightly together with ropes above the deck in order to keep it from breaking its back in a heavy sea (cf. Cadbury's argument in BC, 5:345–54, and *Book of Acts*, p. 10, based on an Egyptian drawing of boats in Queen Hatseput's expedition some eighteen and a half centuries before Luke).

18–20 For fourteen days and nights (cf. v.27), the ship was in the grip of the Northeaster. The crew tried to lighten the ship by throwing overboard all the deck cargo (v.18), then by disposing of the ship's tackle (v.19). In the darkness of the storm they could not take their bearings from the sun or stars. All hope of being saved had vanished.

21–26 Undoubtedly Paul shared the general pessimism on board ship (cf. the inclusive use of "we" in v.20). But one night toward the close of the fourteen-day storm, "an angel of God" stood by Paul and reassured him (v.24) with a message of comfort for this time of crisis (cf. 23:11). The next morning when Paul shared it with his companions on shipboard, he was human enough to (in effect) say "I told you so" to those who had not taken his advice at Fair Havens. Moreover, ever one to give advice, he added that in his opinion they would not be saved without running aground on some island.

27–29 During the fourteenth night after leaving Crete, it was clear—probably from the running swell and the roar of surf—that they were off shore. Soundings indicated shallower water. To keep the ship from being wrecked against the rocks of an unknown coast in the darkness, they dropped four anchors and waited for dawn. Luke tells us that they were in the Adrian Sea (*en tō Adria*), which many (including NIV and JB, though not KJV, RSV, NEB, and TEV) have confused with the Adriatic Sea (though cf. footnote in JB). Strabo, however, in A.D. 19, said that "the Ionian Sea is part of what is now called the Sea of Hadria" (*Geography* 2.5.20). And Josephus reports that in A.D. 63 he suffered shipwreck together with six hundred others bound for Rome in the central Mediterranean "in the midst of the sea of Adria" (*kata meson ton Adrian*), with only eighty being plucked from the waters to continue their journey (cf. Life 15 [3]). This suggests that the name Adrian or Hadrian was used for all that part of the Mediterranean between Greece, Italy, and Africa.

30–32 Contrary to the best tradition of the sea, the sailors schemed to save themselves by lowering the dinghy (cf. vv.16–17) under cover of lowering some more anchors from the bow. But Paul saw through the ruse, doubtless realizing that no sailor would drop anchors from the bow under such conditions. He knew to try to make shore in the morning without a full crew would be disastrous. So Paul warned Julius that all would be lost if the sailors deserted the ship. Though he had not listened to Paul earlier (cf. vv.11–12), Julius took his advice here and ordered his men to cut the lines holding the dinghy and let it fall away.

33-38 The storm had been so fierce that preparing food had been impossible. In this time of crisis, Paul's great qualities of leadership came to the fore. Urging all on board to eat, he took some bread, gave thanks to God, and ate it. The others on board also ate. Then, strengthened by the food, they threw the cargo of grain overboard to give the ship a shallower draft as they beached her.

Only at v.37 does Luke tell us how many were on board. Probably it became necessary when distributing the food to know the exact number, and Luke himself may have had a part in supervising the distribution. Though there is some MS evidence for reading 76, there is nothing improbable in the larger and better-attested number 276. Josephus tells of making a Mediterranean crossing to Rome in A.D. 63 in a ship that had 600 on board and which was also wrecked (cf. Life 15 [3]).

39-41 Here Luke tells with a profusion of nautical detail that makes this chapter unique how the ship was beached amid the pounding surf on a sandbar (*eis topon dithalasson*; lit., "on a place of two seas" with deep water on either side) some distance from land, and began to break apart. From then on it was every man for himself.

42-44 Roman military law decreed that a guard who allowed his prisoner to escape was subject to the same penalty the escaped prisoner would have suffered (cf. comments on 12:18-19a; 16:25-28). Thus the soldiers wanted to kill the prisoners, lest they escape while getting to land. Julius, however, determined to protect Paul, prevented this. He ordered all to get to land either by swimming or by holding on to pieces of the wreckage. So God in his providence brought them all safely to shore, as he had promised Paul he would (cf. v.24). Many, like Luke, undoubtedly saw the relation between the promise and their safety and in their own ways praised the God Paul served.

Notes

14 The Byzantine text calls the wind Εὐροκλύδων (*Euroklydōn*, thus "Euroclydon" of KJV), though P of the Byzantine tradition omits "the one called" and any name.

15 The Western text expands the last portion of this verse to read: "We gave way to the wind that was blowing and shortened the sail and, as happens in such cases, were driven before it."

16 ℵ and the Byzantine text have Κλαῦδα (*Klauda*, "Clauda") for Καῦδα (*Kauda*, "Cauda").

19 The Byzantine text reads ἐρρίψαμεν (*erripsamen*, "we threw out") for ἔριψαν (*eripsan*, "they threw out"; NIV, "they threw overboard"). The Western text adds εἰς τὴν θάλασσαν (*eis tēn thalassan*, "into the sea").

27 B has the idea of their sensing "the resounding surf" (προσαχεῖν, *prosachein*) for "the approaching land" (προσάγειν, *prosagein*), which is carried on in the *resonare* of the Lat. MSS g and s (ninth and sixth century MSS respectively).

34 A and P, supported by the Harclean Syr. version, read ἡμετέρας (*hēmeteras*, "we need it"; lit., "incumbent upon us") for ὑμετέρας (*hymeteras*, "you need it").

35 The Western text adds at the end of the verse ἐπιδιδοὺς καὶ ἡμῖν (*epididous kai hēmin*, "giving also to us").

37 B, supported by the Sahidic Coptic and Ethiopic versions, reads ὡς ἑβδομήκοντα ἕξ (*hōs hebdomēkonta hex*, "about 76"), though Luke's usual use of ὡς (*hōs*, "about"; cf. note at 1:15) seems somewhat out of place with so exact a number (which is probably why Epiphanius has ὡς ἑβδομήκοντα [*hōs hebdomēkonta*, "about 70"], thereby bringing it into line with Lukan practice). A reads διακόσιαι ἑβδομήκοντα πέντε (*diakosiai hebdomēkonta pente*, "275").

39 B and C, supported by the Coptic and Armenian versions, read ἐκσῶσαι τὸ πλοῖον (eksōsai to ploion, "to bring the ship safe to shore") for ἐξῶσαι τὸ πλοῖον (exōsai to ploion, "to run the ship aground"), which is a more prosaic way to express good nautical language.

41 This is the only instance of ναῦς (naus, "ship") in the NT and possibly reflects Homeric usage.

ℵ A B omit τῶν κυμάτων (tōn kymatōn, "of the surf"), reading only "by the pounding" or "violence."

---

3. Ashore at Malta

28:1-10

> [1]Once safely on shore, we found out that the island was called Malta. [2]The islanders showed us unusual kindness. They built a fire and welcomed us all because it was raining and cold. [3]Paul gathered a pile of brushwood and, as he put it on the fire, a viper, driven out by the heat, fastened itself on his hand. [4]When the islanders saw the snake hanging from his hand, they said to each other, "This man must be a murderer; for though he escaped from the sea, Justice has not allowed him to live." [5]But Paul shook the snake off into the fire and suffered no ill effects. [6]The people expected him to swell up or suddenly fall over dead, but after waiting a long time and seeing nothing unusual happen to him, they changed their minds and said he was a god.
>
> [7]There was an estate nearby that belonged to Publius, the chief official of the island. He welcomed us to his home and for three days entertained us hospitably. [8]His father was sick in bed, suffering from fever and dysentery. Paul went in to see him and, after prayer, placed his hands on him and healed him. [9]When this had happened, the rest of the sick on the island came and were cured. [10]They honored us in many ways and when we were ready to sail, they furnished us with the supplies we needed.

1 Malta (Melitē), on which the ship was wrecked, is an island about 18 miles long and 8 miles wide. It lies 58 miles south of Sicily and 180 miles north and east of the African coast. It had been colonized about 1000 B.C. by Phoenicians, and the vernacular language in Paul's day was a Punic (Carthaginian) dialect. But in 218 B.C. it was captured by Rome at the start of the Second Punic War waged against Carthage and granted the status of a municipium, which allowed a large measure of local autonomy. Augustus established a Roman governor on the island, who bore the title municipi Melitesium primus omnium ("the chief man over all in the municipality of Malta," Corpus Inscriptionum Latinarum 10.7495; cf. Corpus Inscriptionum Graecarum 5754—or, as at v.7, ho prōtos tēs nēsou, "the first man of the island"). He also settled a number of army veterans and their families there. In Paul's day the island was known for its prosperity and residential architecture, and its native population must have spoken not only Phoenician but also some Latin and Greek.

Melitē has at times been identified with Meleda or Mljet off the Dalmatian coast (modern Yugoslavia) in the northeastern part of the Adriatic Sea, far to the northeast of Malta. But that is linked to the confusion of "Adrian" with "Adriatic" (cf. comments on 27:27). In all likelihood the ship was blown west from Crete to the east coast of Malta, rather than northwest into the Adriatic. So the traditional location of Saint Paul's Bay on Malta should continue to be considered the most probable site for Paul's landing. The island was first named by Phoenicians, in whose language melita meant "a place of refuge"—a function that naturally fits it.

2 Luke calls the natives who welcomed them *hoi barbaroi* ("barbarians," cf. also v.4), which NIV well translates unpejoratively as "islanders." *Barbaroi* is an onomatopoetic word; to the Greeks and Romans strange languages sounded like "bar-bar-bar," hence the word "barbarian" (Lat., *barbarus*). Today "barbarian" connotes a savage or primitive person, or a crude, uneducated one. But that was not always what the Greeks and Romans meant by it. As for the Maltese, though their language sounded strange, they were hardly savages. They built a fire, Luke says, to welcome "us all" (*pantas hēmas*— viz., all 276 survivors), which was just what was needed in the cold and rain.

3-4 When Paul was bitten by the viper, the islanders concluded he was a murderer whom Justice (*hē dikē*) had at last caught up with since he hadn't died at sea. The Greek goddess Dike, or her Phoenician counterpart, was apparently venerated by the Maltese. Had he died, they might have written an epitaph like the one Statyllius Flaccus wrote for a shipwrecked sailor who was killed by snakebite:

> O, he escaped the storm and the raging of the murderous sea. But as he lay stranded in the libyan sand, not far from the beach and heavy with sleep, at last, naked and destitute, weary as he was from the terrible shipwreck, the viper struck him dead. Why did he struggle against the waves? He did not escape the lot which was destined for him on land (*Palatine Anthology* 7.290).

Today Malta has no venomous snakes. But, as Ramsay noted, "Such changes [in animal life] are natural and probable in a small island, populous and long civilised" (*St. Paul the Traveller*, p. 343).

5-6 Seeing that Paul was unaffected by the snakebite, the islanders decided that he must be a god—or, perhaps, a favorite of the gods (cf. BC, 4:342, which quotes Plutarch's statement that Cleomenes, who was miraculously protected by a snake, was a *theophilēs*, "a favorite of the gods"). Nothing is said about Paul's rebuking the islanders as he had rebuked the people at Lystra (cf. 14:15-18), for evidently there was no attempt at Malta to offer Paul any worship.

Luke gives us such a vividly detailed account of the incident because he wants his readers to appreciate that Paul was not only a heaven-directed man with a God-given message but also a heaven-protected man. The powerful account of the storm and shipwreck has shown this, and now this vignette stresses it once more.

7 Though Paul spent three months (cf. v.11) on Malta, Luke gives us only one more incident from his stay there—the healing of Publius's father. It is an account much like that of Peter and the crippled beggar (cf. 3:1ff.) in purpose, though not in length. Luke seems to have included it to illustrate the continuing power of Paul's ministry despite his being in Malta as a prisoner destined for a hearing before Caesar. No matter what the circumstances are, the true servant of Christ is, like Paul, never off duty for his Lord.

As the Roman governor of Malta, Publius had the title "the first man of the island" (cf. *Corpus Inscriptionum Latinarum* 10. 7495; *Corpus Inscriptionum Graecarum* 5754). As an act of official courtesy, he brought the survivors of the wreck to his estate and entertained them for three days while their respective situations were sorted out and arrangements made for their lodgings over the winter elsewhere on the island. Luke's reference to the governor only by his praenomen, though remarkable, was not exceptional in the ancient world. Perhaps the islanders regularly spoke of the governor simply by his first name, and Luke, who had no great sympathy for Roman nomenclature, simply reported the name he heard in common use. Or perhaps this use of the first name reflects the friendly relationship that had developed between Publius, Paul, and Luke during those three months.

8–9 The malady the father of Publius was suffering from may have been Malta fever, which was long common in Malta, Gibraltar, and other Mediterranean locales. In 1887 its cause, the microorganism *Micrococcus melitensis*, was discovered and traced to the milk of Maltese goats. A vaccine for its treatment has been developed. Cases of Malta fever are long-lasting—an average of four months, but in some cases lasting two or three years. Luke uses the plural *pyretois* ("fevers") in his description, probably with reference to the way it affects its victims with intermittent attacks.

After Paul had healed Publius's father-in-law through prayer and laying on of hands, "the rest of the sick on the island" came to him and were healed. Luke's use of "the rest" (*hoi loipoi*), implying that all the island's sick flocked to Paul and that he healed them all, is doubtless somewhat hyperbolical. What Luke is telling us is that Paul's ministry to those he met consisted in both proclaiming the Good News of Christ Jesus and healing them physically. Luke's inclusion of this vignette prepares for the climax of his book—Paul's entrance into Rome and the triumphant note "without hindrance" (*akōlytōs*) on which his two volumes end (cf. v.31).

10 As a result of Paul's ministry during his months on Malta, the islanders honored him and his party in many ways (*pollais timais etimēsan hēmas*; lit., "they honored us with many honors"). Paul was no god, as they had soon learned. But he was a messenger of the one true God, with good news of life and wholeness in Jesus Christ. In carrying out his God-given commission, Paul gave of himself unstintingly on behalf of people. That they appreciated his ministry is evidenced by their giving him and his colleagues supplies for the rest of their journey.

From what Luke tells us it seems that Paul may have looked on his stay in Malta as a high point in his ministry—a time of blessing when God worked in marvelous ways, despite the shipwreck and his being still a prisoner. God seems, through the experiences at Malta, to have been refreshing Paul's spirit after the two relatively bleak years at Caesarea and the disastrous time at sea and preparing him for his witness in Rome.

Notes

1 B has Μελιτήνη (*Melitēnē*) for Μελίτη (*Melitē*), and a few minuscule MSS support B or read Μελιτίνη (*Melitinē*) or Μελητήνη (*Melētēnē*)—forms that appear in the OL and Vul. MSS as *Militinae, Militenae,* or *Militene.* Probably such readings originated through a dittography in writing Μελίτη ἡ νῆσος (*Melitē hē nēsos,* "the island was called Malta").

5 On Luke's use of μὲν οὖν (*men oun*), cf. comments on 1:6. Here the connective is used to join two parts of one account (as is more common in the second half of Acts) rather than to tie together source material, editorial introductions, and conclusions (as in the first half of Acts).

4. Arrival at Rome

28:11–16

> [11]After three months we put out to sea in a ship that had wintered in the island. It was an Alexandrian ship with the figurehead of the twin gods Castor and Pollux. [12]We put in at Syracuse and stayed there three days. [13]From there we set sail and arrived at Rhegium. The next day the south wind came up, and on the following day we reached Puteoli. [14]There we found some brothers who invited us to spend a week with them. And so we went to Rome. [15]The brothers there had heard that we were coming, and they traveled as far as the Forum of Appius and the Three Taverns to meet us. At the sight of these men, Paul thanked God and was encouraged. [16]When we got to Rome, Paul was allowed to live by himself, with a soldier to guard him.

11 "After three months" (*meta treis mēnas*), the centurion Julius arranged for another ship to take his contingent of prisoners and soldiers on to Italy. According to Pliny the Elder, navigation on the Mediterranean began each spring on 8 February, when the westerly winds started to blow (*Natural History* 2.122)—though Vegetius says that the seas were closed until 10 March (cf. *De Re Militari* 4.39), by which, however, he probably had reference to travel on the high seas and not coastal shipping. Therefore sometime in early or mid-February 61, Paul and his colleagues boarded ship again for the last leg of their voyage to Italy after their shipwreck on Malta, perhaps in late October (cf. comments on 27:9). The ship was another Alexandrian vessel, probably another grain ship (cf. comments on v.13) from Egypt that had been able to make harbor at Malta before winter set in and the disastrous Northeaster struck. Ships, like inns, took their names from their figureheads; and this one, Luke tells us, "was distinguished by the Dioscuroi" (*parasēmō Dioskourois*)—i.e., the painted carving at its prow of Castor and Pollux, the sons of Leda, queen of Sparta, who in Greek mythology were transformed by Zeus into twin gods represented by the constellation Gemini. The cult of the Dioscuroi (lit., "sons of Zeus") was especially widespread in Egypt and the Gemini were considered by sailors a sign of good fortune in a storm. For an Alexandrian ship, the figurehead was an appropriate one.

12 Sailing north-northeast, the ship reached the harbor of Syracuse, on the east coast of Sicily. There at the most important city of Sicily, it remained for three days, probably awaiting better wind conditions and loading and unloading cargo.

13 From Syracuse the ship "set sail" (*perielontes*, lit., "weighed anchor") for Rhegium (modern Reggio di Calabria), an important harbor at the toe of Italy and on the Italian side of the Strait of Messina. There it docked to await a more favorable breeze. On the next day, however, a southerly wind began to blow, and they were able to make the 180 miles up the coast of Italy to Puteoli (modern Pozzuoli) in only two days. Puteoli was a resort city on the Bay of Naples, the port city of Neapolis (modern Naples), and the principal port of southern Italy. It vied with Ostia, the port of Rome at the mouth of the Tiber, as a terminus for the grain ships from Egypt. There Paul and his party, as members of Julius's contingent, disembarked.

14 There are two rather surprising statements in this verse. At Puteoli Paul and his companions "found some brothers who invited us to spend a week with them." It was not, of course, unusual for Christians to be found in such an important city as Puteoli.

There was a Jewish colony there (cf. Jos. War II, 104 [vii.1]; Antiq. XVII, 328 [xii.1]), from which some may have become Christians on their travels or through the witness of believers who visited Puteoli. What is surprising, however, is that Paul a prisoner was at liberty to seek out the Christians of the city and accept their invitation to spend seven days in fellowship with them. Nevertheless, it is possible that for some reason Julius found it necessary to stop at Puteoli for a week after disembarking and that during that time he allowed Paul the freedom (though undoubtedly accompanied by a guard) to seek out his fellow believers and enjoy their hospitality, as he did at Sidon when the journey to Rome began (cf. 27:3). As Luke presses toward the end of his story, his account becomes more and more concise—so much so that the reader feels some measure of surprise.

A second surprising feature of v.14 is its forthright conclusion: "And so we came to Rome" (*kai houtōs eis tēn Rōmēn ēlthamen;* which NIV, following the KJV and BDF [par. 327], tones down to "went to Rome" by treating the verb as an imperfect rather than as an aorist). It is not surprising that they came to Rome; that had for some time been the goal of Paul's journey and Luke's narrative. But that the mention of their arrival appears here before v.15 and not as the opening statement of v.16—where it would seem to have been more appropriate—is indeed surprising. Ramsay argued that this double mention of Rome was probably due to "the double sense that every name of a city-state bears in Greek"—that is, the whole administrative district of Rome (the *ager Romanus*) and the actual city itself (*St. Paul the Traveller*, pp. 346–47). But the adverb *kakeithen* ("and from there"; "there," NIV) that begins v.15 shows that the actual city of Rome is in view, not just an administrative district (cf. BC, 4:345). The problem, therefore, is not so easy to explain away, either by treating the verb as an imperfect (so KJV, BDF, NIV) or by understanding the direct object as an administrative district (so Ramsay).

All things considered, the best explanation for the appearance of "and so we came to Rome" in v.14 is that it reflects Luke's eagerness to get to the climax of his story and that this eagerness led him to anticipate their arrival at Rome—even though he had to go back in v.15 and include another detail of the last stage of the journey before finally bringing Paul and his colleagues to Rome (vv.16ff). So the solution lies along psychological rather than linguistic or administrative lines.

15 Taking the Via Domitiana from Puteoli to Neapolis, Paul would have passed the tomb of the poet Virgil (Publius Vergilius Maro, 70–19 B.C.). In the Mass of Saint Paul that was celebrated at Mantua, Virgil's birthplace, till the fifteenth century, this Latin poem about Paul at Virgil's tomb was included:

> Virgil's tomb the saint stood viewing,
> And his aged cheek bedewing,
> Fell the sympathetic tear;
> "Ah, had I but found thee living,
> What new music wert thou giving,
> Best of poets and most dear"
> (T.R. Glover's free translation).

Imaginary though this is, it points to the link between Virgil's vibrant humanity and intense longing for a savior and Paul's dynamic gospel with its answer to this longing.

At Neapolis, Julius and his contingent turned northwest to travel to Rome on the Via

Appia—that oldest, straightest, and most perfectly made of all the Roman roads, named after the censor Appius Claudius who started its construction in 312 B.C. During the seven-day stopover at Puteoli, news of Paul's arrival in Italy reached Rome. So a number of Christians there set out to meet him and escort him back to Rome. Some of them got as far as the Forum of Appius (*Forum Appii*), one of the "halting stations" built every ten to fifteen miles along the entire length of the Roman road system. It was forty-three miles from Rome in the Pontine marshland, and a market-town had grown up around it. Others only got as far as the Three Taverns (*Tres Tabernae*) Inn, another halting station about thirty-three miles from Rome. Paul's gratitude to God for the delegation that met him must have been unusually fervent, because Luke pauses to make special mention of it. In his letters, Paul often urges his readers to be thankful, and here he illustrated his advice.

16 At Rome, Paul was allowed to live in private quarters, though a soldier guarded him at all times. The chain he wore (v.20) was probably attached to his wrists. Yet in Luke's eyes Paul entered Rome in triumph. Through his coming the gospel penetrated official circles in the capital of the empire, and God used his detention there for two years to spread the proclamation of the kingdom of God and the Lord Jesus Christ throughout the city (cf. vv.30–31).

With this verse, the last "we" section in Acts closes. To judge by the greetings in Colossians 4:10–14 and Philemon 23–24 (assuming a Roman origin for these letters), Luke and Aristarchus must have remained with Paul through most—if not all—of his detention at Rome, being joined from time to time by such friends as Epaphras, John Mark, Demas, and Jesus, who was surnamed Justus.

Notes

11 On μετά (*meta*, "after") with a time designation (here "three months") in the latter half of Acts as a Lukan connective, cf. comments on 15:36 (see also v.17 below).

13 The Byzantine text, together with a corrected ℵ and P⁷⁴, read περιελθόντες (*perielthontes*, "sailed around," "made a circuit"; "fetched a compass," KJV). But that seems to be an unwarranted correction since their voyage followed almost a straight line.

14 RSV, JB, and TEV treat ἤλθαμεν (*ēlthamen*) as an aorist and translate it "And so we came to Rome." NEB tries to sidestep the issue with its "and so to Rome" but ends up in agreement with KJV and NIV in wrongly understanding the verb as an imperfect.

Contra Ramsay, since the Forum of Appius and the Three Taverns (cf. v.15) were both within the *ager Romanus*, Luke would hardly have distinguished them from the *ager Romanus* by the use of the adverb κἀκεῖθεν (*kakeithen*, "and from there"), for one would not go "from there" (i.e., according to Ramsay's view, from the administrative district governed by the city of Rome) to these halting stations if they lay within that same district.

16 The Western text, followed in part by the Byzantine, expands this verse to read: "When we got to Rome, the centurion turned over his prisoners to the stratopedarch [τῷ στρατοπεδάρχῳ, tō stratopedarchō], but Paul was allowed. . . ." What the Western and Byzantine editors had in mind by the term "stratopedarch" has been surmised to be either the commander of the *castra peregrinorum* on the Caelian Hill (i.e., the headquarters of legionary officers on furlough in Rome) or the prefect of the praetorian guard (who was the noble Afranius Burrus during A.D. 51–62).

The Western text also adds ἔξω τῆς παρεμβολῆς (*exō tēs parembolēs*, "outside the barracks") after ἑαυτὸν (*heauton*, "himself").

F. *Rome at Last* (28:17-30)

At last, Paul's great desire to visit the capital of the empire (cf. Rom 15:22–24, 28–29) was fulfilled. Despite his manacles, guard, and house arrest, he was free to receive visitors. Among them, Luke tells us, were (1) the leading Jews of the city, whom he asked to visit him when he first arrived (vv.17–28) and (2) others, evidently both Jews and Gentiles, who came to his quarters at various times during his two-year detention (v.30).

1. *Meetings with the Jewish leaders*

28:17-28

> 17Three days later he called together the leaders of the Jews. When they had assembled, Paul said to them: "My brothers, although I have done nothing against our people or against the customs of our ancestors, I was arrested in Jerusalem and handed over to the Romans. 18They examined me and wanted to release me, because I was not guilty of any crime deserving death. 19But when the Jews objected, I was compelled to appeal to Caesar—not that I had any charge to bring against my own people. 20For this reason I have asked to see you and talk with you. It is because of the hope of Israel that I am bound with this chain."
>
> 21They replied, "We have not received any letters from Judea concerning you, and none of the brothers who has come from there has reported or said anything bad about you. 22But we want to hear what your views are, for we know that people everywhere are talking against this sect."
>
> 23They arranged to meet Paul on a certain day, and came in even larger numbers to the place where he was staying. From morning till evening he explained and declared to them the kingdom of God and tried to convince them about Jesus from the Law of Moses and from the Prophets. 24Some were convinced by what he said, but others would not believe. 25They disagreed among themselves and began to leave after Paul had made this final statement: "The Holy Spirit spoke the truth to your forefathers when he said through Isaiah the prophet:
>
> > 26" 'Go to this people and say,
> > "You will be ever hearing but never understanding;
> > you will be ever seeing but never perceiving."
> > 27For this people's heart has become calloused;
> > they hardly hear with their ears,
> > and they have closed their eyes.
> > Otherwise they might see with their eyes,
> > hear with their ears,
> > understand with their hearts
> > and turn and I would heal them.'
>
> 28"Therefore I want you to know that God's salvation has been sent to the Gentiles, and they will listen!"

17-20 Three days after (*meta hēmeras treis*) arriving at Rome, Paul invited the leaders of the Jewish community to meet with him in his own quarters. He wanted to learn what they had heard from Jerusalem about him and to find out their attitude toward him. Through their contacts in the imperial court and with their money, they could, if they desired, support the charges against him. Since they undoubtedly knew something about his case, he wanted to defend himself before them. Also, he hoped the occasion would be an opportunity for proclaiming the message about Jesus the Messiah and that some would respond to it.

Paul began with the formal salutation used at Jewish gatherings: "Men, brothers" (*andres adelphoi*; "My brothers," NIV). The first word of his address "I" (*egō*)—which in his précis Luke places before the salutation—clearly shows that Paul was about to

569

deliver a personal apologia. He had done nothing, he insisted, against the Jewish people or against the customs of the fathers (v.17). The Roman authorities had judged that he had not committed any capital crime and were willing to release him (vv.17b–18). But objections from Jerusalem forced him to appeal to Caesar—not to accuse his own people but to save his life (v.19). The point of contention between him and his accusers at Jerusalem had to do with the messianic hope of Israel, which Paul believed was fulfilled in Jesus of Nazareth and they did not. Therefore he concluded: "It is because of the hope of Israel that I am bound with this chain" (v.20; cf. 23:6; 24:21; 26:6–8).

21–22 The immediate response of the Roman Jewish leaders to Paul's address is surprising. Apparently they did not want to get involved. They disclaimed having gotten any letters about him from the authorities at Jerusalem and said they had heard nothing, officially or unofficially, against him from any Jew who had come to them from Judea (v.21). Yet Christianity had been known within the Jewish community at Rome for some time (cf. comments on 2:10). In fact, in the late forties Jews at Rome had been so sharply divided about Christianity that the emperor Claudius banished them all from the city to stop the riots there (cf. comments on 18:2). Certainly the Jewish leaders at Rome knew a great deal about Christianity generally and at least something about Paul, and their claim to know only "that people everywhere are talking against this sect" (v.22) seems much too "diplomatic" in light of their knowledge.

It is, however, in the light of their recent experience that we should judge the Jewish leaders' response to Paul's words. Having been expelled from Rome in 49 or 50 because of riots about Christianity in their community, and having only recently returned to their city after Claudius's death in 54, they were simply not prepared in 61 to become involved in Paul's case one way or another. They doubtless had their own opinions about it. But (1) the Jerusalem authorities had not requested them to get involved; (2) Paul was a Roman citizen who had had essentially favorable hearings before Felix, Festus, and Agrippa II; and (3) his case was now to be tried before Caesar himself. So they wanted to have as little as possible to do with Paul and Christianity. But they did say that they were willing at some future time to hear his views on "this sect" (*hairesis*, from which the word "heresy" is derived).

23–24 So they arranged this second meeting, and an even larger delegation came to Paul's quarters. Luke tells us only that it lasted "from morning till evening" and that Paul proclaimed "the kingdom of God" (cf. comments on 1:3) focusing on Jesus, to whom the Law and the Prophets bore witness (v.23; cf. v.31). For the content of what he said, we should probably think of his sermon in the synagogue at Pisidian Antioch (13:17–41) and the letter sent to the Romans. As for his method, he "tried to convince them" (*peithōn autous*), which implies that Paul combined proclamation with persuasion (cf. comments on 17:2–4) and that there was a good deal of impassioned debate. The day-long session proved profitable, for "some were convinced by what he said"—though, sadly, "others would not believe" (v.24).

25–28 The points at which many of the Jewish leaders disagreed with Paul and left the session, Luke says, were two: (1) Paul's attempt to prove the obduracy of Israel from Scripture on the ground that Isaiah had foretold the Jews' rejection of Jesus as Messiah, and (2) his insistence that because of Israel's hardened attitude the message of "God's salvation" has been sent directly to Gentiles where it would find a positive response. He documented the first point by quoting Isaiah 6:9–10. The LXX had already turned the imperatives of vv.9b–10a into finite verbs, with the result that the entire blame for Israel's estrangement from God is placed on the stubbornness of the people themselves. That is how Jesus also is reported as having used the passage in the "Logia" collection (cf. Matt 13:13–15; Luke 8:10; see also the use of the passage in Mark 4:12 and John 12:40, though not with quite the same thrust) and how Paul explained Israel's predicament in Romans 9–11. But Paul quotes prophecy here not just to explain Israel's stubbornness but to set the stage for his second point: In the providence of God, redemption was now being offered directly to Gentiles and they were responding.

A revolutionary new policy for proclaiming the gospel and making converts had been providentially worked out during Paul's first missionary journey and at the Jerusalem Council (cf. 12:25–16:5 and comments in loc.). That policy was then carried out through two more missionary journeys extending into Macedonia, Achaia, and Asia (cf. 16:6–19:20). It was a policy that advocated the proclamation of the gospel "first for the Jew, then for the Gentile" (Rom 1:16; cf. Acts 13:46–52). Luke has taken pains to show how everything that happened in the ministry of the early Jerusalem church essentially looked forward to the inauguration of this policy and how this policy lay at the heart of Paul's missionary purpose. Now having traced the story of the advance of the gospel to Rome, Luke reports how that same pattern was followed at Rome. And his account of the gospel's advance from Jerusalem to Rome in terms of the distinctive policy of first the Jew, then the Gentile comes to a fitting conclusion with the quotation of Isaiah 6:9–10—one of the oldest Christian testimonia portions from the OT.

Notes

17 On μετά (meta, "after"; NIV, "later") with a time designation (here "three days"), see note on v.11 above.
On the address Ἄνδρες ἀδελφοί (Andres adelphoi, "Men, brothers"), cf. comments on 1:16.
18 The Western text adds πολλά (polla, "much"), reading "they examined me much" (in line with its expansion at 24:6b–8a).
19 The Western text adds καὶ ἐπικραζόντων, Αἶρε τὸν ἐχθρὸν ἡμῶν (kai epikrazontōn, Aire ton echthron hēmōn, "and cried out, 'Away with our enemy'"), reading: "But when the Jews objected and cried out, 'Away with our enemy.'" It also adds to the end of the verse "but in order that I might deliver my soul from death."
25 The Byzantine text has ἡμῶν (hēmōn, "our") for ὑμῶν (hymōn, "your"), reading "our forefathers."
29 The Western and Byzantine texts add v.29: "And when he said these things, the Jews departed, and they had a great deal of controversy among themselves."

2. Continued ministry for two years

28:30

30For two whole years Paul stayed there in his own rented house and welcomed all who came to see him.

30 Luke has accomplished his purpose in showing how the gospel Paul proclaimed entered Rome and in depicting the initial response in the city. Now he gives us this terse reference to Paul's two years of house arrest.

Luke does not give us details about Paul's two years in Rome because he is not writing Paul's biography. Some argue that Paul was executed at the end of his two-year detention and that Luke did not speak of his execution because to do so would have ruined his portrayal of the triumphant advance of the gospel. Others argue that (1) Paul's case never came to trial because the prosecutors failed to appear within the statutory eighteen-month period, and that (2) Luke expected his readers to understand that since a two-year period of detainment went beyond the statutory period for prosecution, Paul was released. But during the storm at sea, the angel of the Lord had assured Paul that he would stand trial before Caesar (cf. 27:24). Therefore, it seems proper to assume that Luke intended his readers to infer that Paul's case, whatever its outcome, did come before the imperial court.

Cadbury speaks of "the extraordinary darkness which comes over us as students of history when rather abruptly this guide leaves us with Paul a prisoner in Rome" (*Book of Acts*, p. 3). Indeed, we are forced to look elsewhere for information about Paul's Roman imprisonment and its aftermath. Accepting the Prison Epistles as having been written during his Roman imprisonment, we may surmise that Paul fully expected to stand before Caesar's court and that, while he could not be certain about the outcome, he also expected to be released (cf. Phil 1:19–26; Philem 22). There is little reason to doubt his intuition. Therefore we may date such a release somewhere around 63. Accepting the Pastoral Epistles as genuine, we may believe that after Paul's release from this Roman imprisonment he continued his evangelistic work in the eastern portion of the empire (at least in lands surrounding the Aegean Sea)—perhaps even fulfilling his long-cherished desire to visit Spain (Rom 15:23–24; cf. 1 Clement 5). And since 2 Timothy 4:6–18 speaks of an approaching second trial in a tone of resignation, we may conclude that Paul was rearrested about 67 and, according to tradition, beheaded at Rome by order of the emperor Nero.

Notes

---

30 For a discussion of the major stylistic issues pertaining to the authorship of the Prison and Pastoral epistles, see my "Ancient Amanuenses and the Pauline Epistles," *New Dimensions in New Testament Study*, edd. R.N. Longenecker and M.C. Tenney (Grand Rapids: Zondervan, 1974), pp. 281–97.

G. A Summary Statement

28:31

³¹Boldly and without hindrance he preached the kingdom of God and taught about the Lord Jesus Christ.

31 This summary statement has often been viewed as only an amplification of v.30, indicating the nature of Paul's ministry during his two years of detention at Rome. But to judge by Luke's practice in the other five summary statements in Acts (6:7; 9:31; 12:24; 16:5; 19:20), we are evidently meant to take it as the summary statement for the whole of Panel 6 (19:21–28:31). In all of his prison experiences at Jerusalem, Caesarea,

and Rome, Luke is saying, Paul "boldly" (*meta pasēs parrēsias*; lit., "with all boldness," which connotes publicly, candidly, and forcefully) "preached the kingdom of God and taught about the Lord Jesus Christ." And he did this, Luke goes on to insist, "without hindrance" (*akōlytōs*). This shows the tolerance of Rome at that time toward Christianity and the gospel proclamation—a tolerance Luke passionately desired would continue and hoped to promote through these last chapters. Furthermore, since the last word of Acts is the crisp adverb *akōlytōs*, we may say with reasonable confidence that it was Luke's desire to close his two-volume work on this victorious note: the apostolic proclamation of the kingdom of God and of the Lord Jesus Christ, despite all difficulties and misunderstandings, had moved forward throughout the Jewish homeland and into the Roman Empire "without hindrance."

The Western text adds the following words to the end of this verse: "Because this is the Messiah, Jesus the Son of God, by whom the whole world is to be judged." But while the addition was intended to round off Luke's apparent abruptness, it only weakens his point and spoils his unique ending. Luke's instinct in closing his great work as he did was completely right. In seeming to leave his book unfinished, he was implying that the apostolic proclamation of the gospel in the first century began a story that will continue until the consummation of the kingdom in Christ (Acts 1:11).